CARSWELL

THE 2016 ANNOTATED ONTARIO HIGHWAY TRAFFIC ACT

Murray D. Segal
B.A., B.C.L., LL.B.

Formerly Deputy Attorney General
Province of Ontario
Counsel, Murray D. Segal, Professional Corporation
Toronto

STATUTES OF ONTARIO ANNOTATED

THOMSON REUTERS

D1218416

A cataloguing record for this publication is available from Library and Archives Canada.

ISSN 1202-5135

ISBN 978-0-7798-7129-2 (2016 edition)

Printed in the United States by Thomson Reuters

TELL US HOW WE'RE DOING
Scan the QR code to the right with your smartphone to send your comments regarding our products and services. Free QR Code Readers are available from your mobile device app store. You can also email us at carswell.feedback@thomsonreuters.com

THOMSON REUTERS

THOMSON REUTERS CANADA, A DIVISION OF THOMSON REUTERS CANADA LIMITED

One Corporate Plaza
2075 Kennedy Road
Toronto, Ontario
M1T 3V4

Customer Relations
Toronto 1-416-609-3800
Elsewhere in Canada/U.S. 1-800-387-5164
Fax 1-416-298-5082
www.carswell.com
Contact www.carswell.com/email

To my Mother

PREFACE TO THE 2016 EDITION

This edition of the 2016 Ontario *Highway Traffic Act* incorporated the revised statutes and regulations as amended to the Ontario Gazette Volume 149:19 (May 7, 2016) and to Votes and Proceedings No. 171 (May 10, 2016). It updates all relevant *Highway Traffic Act* cases, all legislation which has been passed but not proclaimed, and all regulatory activity.

Some important case highlights in the past year include:

- *Moore v. Getahun.* It is permitted that counsel assist an expert in the preparation of a report.
- *Westerhof v. Gee Estate.* Rule 53.03 of the *Civil Rules* does not apply to participant experts and non-party experts.
- *R. v. Vander Griendt.* Section 48.1 regarding alcohol stops, does not apply to a parking lot.
- *R. v. Michaud.* Section 68.1 regarding speed regulators, is constitutional.
- *Goodwin v. British Columbia*; *R. v. Wilson.* The Province of British Columbia's automatic pre-criminal charge driving prohibition scheme is constitutional.

Important amendments to the *Highway Traffic Act* include:

- S. 191.2(2) in force July 1, 2015 defining a "valid toll device" for purposes of toll highways.
- 2014, c. 9, Sched. 2 amendments as listed below will now come into force January 1, 2017:
    - "commercial motor vehicle" definition
    - "compensation" definition
    - "CVOR certificate" definition
    - "goods" definition
    - "safety record" definition
- Section 1(10) providing that the definition of "commercial motor vehicle" can change depending on what part of the *Act* is being referenced
- Section 1(1)(a) amending ability to impose administrative monetary penalties for suspended drivers; s. 1(1)(b) regarding exemptions; s. 5.1(2) regarding interest

S.O. 2014, c. 9 Sched. 2 provisions in force include:

- Section 17.0.2 refusal to issue a CVOR certificate for non-payment of fees, fines and penalties
- Section 21(1) increasing fines for commercial vehicle infractions
- Section 47(2.2) providing for the immediate suspension of a CVOR certificate
- Section 103(1) requiring commercial vehicles to have a sign on both sides of their vehicle
- Section 171(3.1) adding a prohibition for tow truck drivers breaching regulations

S.O. 2015, c. 14

- The following are in force:
  - Section 133 "bicycle traffic control signal" and "traffic control sign"
  - Section 140 changes to the duties of a driver at a pedestrian crossover
  - Section 148 added protections for cyclists
  - Section 159 regarding emergency vehicles
  - Section 165 regarding opening doors on vehicles
  - Section 175 regarding service of *Provincial Offence Act* notices outside Ontario
  - Section 205.25 permitting service of offence notices for red light camera offences.
  - Section 210.1 regarding out-of-province evidence regarding vehicle ownership.

Some provisions of S.O. 2015, c. 27 are now in force. They include:

- Changes to ss. 5.3 and 17.1, 47.1 regarding how the Registrar may give notice to drivers regarding changes of status.

The following are new regulations:

- O. Reg. 419/15 defining a commercial motor vehicle to include a tow truck.
- O. Reg. 402/15 providing for pedestrian crossover signs.
- O. Reg. 306/15 providing for a pilot project for automated vehicles.

The following are important amending regulations:

- O. Reg. 256/15 amending O. Reg. 199/07 regarding Commercial Motor Vehicle Inspections and, in particular, motor coaches and inter-city buses performance standards under s. 107(3) of the *Act*
- O. Reg. 226/15 amending O. Reg. 339/94 regarding the demerit point system including additions for driving with a display screen visible to the driver, driving while holding or using a hand-held device and protections for bicycles
- O. Reg. 144/15 amending O. Reg. 341/94 regarding driver licence examinations for drivers of vehicles with air brakes
- O. Reg. 185/15 amending O. Reg 340/94 regarding drivers' licences for members or former members of the armed forces; O. Reg. 227/15 also amending O. Reg. 340/94 regarding novice drivers using devices
- O. Reg. 255/15 amending Reg. 601 R.R.O. 1990 regarding Motor Vehicle Inspection Stations
- O. Reg. 254/15 amending Reg. 611 of R.R. O. 1990 regarding Safety Inspections regarding light duty vehicles
- Fee increases to licences and permits
- O. Reg. 335/15 amending Reg. 615 of R.R.O. 1990 regarding various signs
- O. Reg. 408/15 amending Reg. 626 of R.R.O. 1990 regarding Traffic Control Systems
- O. Reg. 328/15 amending Reg. 628 of R.R.O. 1990 regarding Vehicle Permits

- O. Reg. 8/16 amending O. Reg. 413/05 regarding Vehicle Weights and Dimensions
- Several amended regulations dealing with changes to the definition of commercial motor vehicles

Murray D. Segal

July, 2016

PREFACE TO THE FIRST EDITION

In preparing the *Annotated Ontario Highway Traffic Act, 1993*, I have set out to produce a book suitable to a wide range of users. Driving offences constitute the single largest type of case litigated in Ontario and Canadian courts. The *Manual of Motor Vehicle Law* (3d ed.) is a substantial text, in three volumes, however, it is ideally suited to comprehensive library research. There was no text that could serve the diverse needs of those who require a portable yet topical reference source. The annotated series by Carswell provided such an opportunity.

This text has been designed to provide a number of groups with helpful information. For busy practitioners, it is a companion to the *Manual of Motor Vehicle Law*. For those involved in the investigation, regulation, prosecution, defence, civil litigation or adjudication of motor vehicle matters, it is hoped that the organization of the text will prove useful. It has been designed to assist police officers, regulators, provincial prosecutors, paralegals, prosecutors and defence counsel and the judiciary, while at the same time being easily accessible to members of the public and students.

The organization of the text is uncomplicated. It follows the section numbers of the text. Sections of the *Highway Traffic Act* are set out in bold. Where appropriate, Commentary respecting the section is provided. Commentary is directed at summarizing the key features of the section and, where helpful, its legislative history or the intent behind the section. Case law follows, segregating quasi-criminal and civil decisions, broken down by topic into easy to use subheadings. As well, sections of the Act have a feature entitled "Related Provisions" noting other relevant sections of the Act, regulations and related statutes.

For easy reference, the key regulations are found at the back of the text, complete with an Index. The Index, along with the Table of Cases, will help the reader.

Because of the legislative changes which an area such as highway traffic undergoes from time to time, the subject is one that should be ideally suited for regular publication.

Murray D. Segal

November 1, 1992

TABLE OF CONTENTS

Table of Contents

Table of Contents

PART IV — LICENCES
Driver, Driving Instructor

Table of Contents

Table of Contents

Table of Contents

Table of Contents

Table of Contents

Table of Contents

ONT. REG. 424/97 — COMMERCIAL MOTOR VEHICLE OPERATORS' INFORMATION

PART I — CVOR CERTIFICATES

Table of Contents

ONT. REG. 287/08 — CONDUCT REVIEW PROGRAMS

Suspension and Frame

SCHEDULE 1

SCHEDULE 2

ONT. REG. 393/02 — DEFINITIONS AND REQUIREMENTS UNDER SECTION 142.1 OF THE ACT (YIELDING RIGHT OF WAY TO BUSES)

ONT. REG. 419/15 — DEFINITIONS OF COMMERCIAL MOTOR VEHICLE AND TOW TRUCK

[PROPOSED] COMMERCIAL MOTOR VEHICLE

COMMENCEMENT

ONT. REG. 339/94 — DEMERIT POINT SYSTEM

INTERPRETATION

GENERAL

DEMERIT POINTS: FULLY LICENSED DRIVERS

DEMERIT POINTS: NOVICE DRIVERS

Table of Contents

TABLE

ONT. REG. 618/05 — DESIGNATION OF BUS BY-PASS SHOULDERS ON KING'S HIGHWAY

SCHEDULE 1 — HIGHWAY NO. 403

SCHEDULE 2 — HIGHWAY NO. 417

SCHEDULE 3 — HIGHWAY NO. 8

ONT. REG. 579 — DESIGNATION OF HIGHWAYS

ONT. REG. 366/09 — DISPLAY SCREENS AND HAND-HELD DEVICES

DEFINITIONS

DISPLAY SCREENS

HAND-HELD DEVICES

COMMENCEMENT

Table of Contents

ONT. REG. 341/94 — DRIVER LICENCE EXAMINATIONS

ONT. REG. 340/94 — DRIVERS' LICENCES

NOVICE LICENCE CONDITIONS

LICENCES: GENERAL

FEE ADJUSTMENT — CONSUMER PRICE INDEX

Table of Contents

Table of Contents

SCHEDULE 1

ONT. REG. 588 — EXEMPTION FROM SECTION 7 OF THE ACT — AMERICAN STATES [REVOKED]

ONT. REG. 589 — EXEMPTION FROM SECTIONS 7 AND 11 OF THE ACT — STATES OF THE UNITED STATES OF AMERICA [REVOKED]

ONT. REG. 590 — EXEMPTION FROM SECTIONS 7 AND 11 OF THE ACT — STATE OF ILLINOIS [REVOKED]

ONT. REG. 591 — EXEMPTION FROM SECTIONS 7 AND 11 OF THE ACT — STATE OF MICHIGAN [REVOKED]

ONT. REG. 592 — EXEMPTION FROM SECTIONS 7 AND 11 OF THE ACT — STATE OF SOUTH DAKOTA [REVOKED]

ONT. REG. 595 — GARAGE LICENCES

ONT. REG. 596 — GENERAL
Headlamps

Table of Contents

ONT. REG. 555/06 — HOURS OF SERVICE

ONT. REG. 251/02 — IGNITION INTERLOCK DEVICES

Table of Contents

Table of Contents

PART III — DRIVING SCHOOL LICENCES
Classes of Instruction

Issuance and Renewal of Licences

Refusal to Renew and Revocation of a Licence

Obligations of Licensees

PART IV — RIGHT TO BE HEARD

PART V — GENERAL

PART VI — REVOCATIONS AND COMMENCEMENT

ONT. REG. 8/03 — LOCAL MUNICIPALITIES WHERE 80 KILOMETRES PER HOUR SPEED LIMIT APPLIES

Table of Contents

TABLE

Table of Contents

ONT. REG. 316/03 — OPERATION OF OFF-ROAD VEHICLES ON HIGHWAYS

Table of Contents

Table of Contents

Table of Contents

Table of Contents

ONT. REG. 609 — RESTRICTED USE OF THE KING'S HIGHWAY AND TOLL HIGHWAYS

SCHEDULE 1

ONT. REG. 610 — SAFETY HELMETS

ONT. REG. 611 — SAFETY INSPECTIONS

DEFINITIONS

APPLICATION OF NSC STANDARD 11B

APPLICATION

SAFETY STANDARDS CERTIFICATE

STRUCTURAL INSPECTION CERTIFICATE

Table of Contents

ONT. REG. 363/04 — SECURITY OF LOADS

PART 1 — GENERAL

PART 2 — COMMERCIAL MOTOR VEHICLES OF 4,500 KILOGRAMS OR LESS

PART 3 — COMMERCIAL MOTOR VEHICLES OVER 4,500 KILOGRAMS

PART 4 — REVOCATION, COMMENCEMENT

ONT. REG. 415/10 — SHORT-TERM VEHICLE IMPOUNDMENT UNDER SECTION 55.2 OF THE ACT

ONT. REG. 615 — SIGNS

SPEED LIMIT SIGNS

Table of Contents

Table of Contents

Table of Contents

ONT. REG. 623 — STOP SIGNS AT INTERSECTIONS

ONT. REG. 624 — STOP SIGNS IN TERRITORY WITHOUT MUNICIPAL ORGANIZATION

ONT. REG. 622 — STOPPING OF VEHICLES ON PARTS OF THE KING'S HIGHWAY

ONT. REG. 381/02 — TESTING, REPAIR AND COMPLIANCE REQUIREMENTS FOR UNSAFE VEHICLES UNDER SECTION 82 OF THE ACT

ONT. REG. 625 — TIRE STANDARDS AND SPECIFICATIONS

ONT. REG. 147/97 — TOLL DEVICES

Table of Contents

ONT. REG. 413/05 — VEHICLE WEIGHTS AND DIMENSIONS — FOR SAFE, PRODUCTIVE AND INFRASTRUCTURE-FRIENDLY VEHICLES

Table of Contents

Table of Contents

ONT. REG. 630 — VEHICLES ON CONTROLLED-ACCESS HIGHWAYS

ONT. REG. 631 — YIELD RIGHT-OF-WAY SIGNS IN TERRITORY WITHOUT MUNICIPAL ORGANIZATION

COMPULSORY AUTOMOBILE INSURANCE ACT

Table of Contents

ONT. REG. 409/12 — ADMINISTRATIVE PENALTIES

GENERAL ADMINISTRATIVE PENALTIES IMPOSED UNDER SECTION 14.4 OF THE ACT

SUMMARY ADMINISTRATIVE PENALTIES IMPOSED UNDER SECTION 14.5 OF THE ACT

COMMENCEMENT

SCHEDULE 1 — GENERAL ADMINISTRATIVE PENALTIES IMPOSED UNDER SECTION 14.4 OF THE ACT — LESSER MAXIMUM PENALTIES PRESCRIBED

SCHEDULE 2 — SUMMARY ADMINISTRATIVE PENALTIES IMPOSED UNDER SECTION 14.5 OF THE ACT — PRESCRIBED PENALTY

ONT. REG. 239/10 — AUTOMOBILE INSURANCE REPORTING INFORMATION

ONT. REG. 95 — EXEMPTIONS

CIVIL REMEDIES ACT, 2001

PHOTO CARD ACT, 2008

Table of Contents

ONT. REG. 176/09 — GENERAL

INTERPRETATION

TABLE OF CONCORDANCE

R.S.O. 1980	R.S.O. 1990	R.S.O. 1980	R.S.O. 1990
1	1	17d	29, repealed
2	2	17e	30
3	3	17f	31
4	4	18	32
—	4.0.1	—	32.1–32.2
5	5	19	33
—	5.1–5.3	20	34
6	6	21	35
7	7	22	36
—	7.1–7.17	23	37
8	8	24	38
9	9	25	39
9a	10	—	39.1
10	11	25a	40
repealed	—	26	41
—	11.1	—	41.1–41.4
12	12	27	42
13	13	27a	43
14	14	27b	44
15	15	—	44.1
15a	16	28	45
15b	17	29	46
—	17.1	30	47
15c	18	—	47.1–47.2
15d	19	30a	48
15e	20	—	48.1–48.4
15f	21	31	49
15g	22	32	50
—	23	—	50.1–50.3
—	23.1	33	51
16	24, repealed	34	52
17	25, repealed	35	53
17a	26	36	54
17b	27	37	55
17c	28	—	55.1–55.2

Table of Concordance

R.S.O. 1980	R.S.O. 1990	R.S.O. 1980	R.S.O. 1990
38	56	71	88
39	57, repealed	72	89
—	57.1–57.2	repealed	—
—	57.1.1	74	90
40	58	75	91
—	58.2	76	92
41	59	77	93
42	60	78	94
43	61	79	95
44	62	80	96
45	63	81	97
46	64	82	98
47	65	83	99
48	66	84	100
49	67	85	101
50	68	86	102
—	68.1	87	103
51	69	88	104
52	70	—	104.1
53	71	89	105
—	71.1	90	106
54	72	90a	107
55	73	91	108
56	74	92	109
57	75	93	110
58	76	—	110.1–110.4
59	77	94	111
60	78	95	112
—	78.1	96	113
61	79	97	114
—	79.1	98	115
62	80	99	116
63	—	100	117
64	81	101	118
65	82	102	119
—	82.1	103	120
66	83	104	121
67	84	104a	122
—	84.1	104b	123
68	85	105	124
69	86	106	125
70	87	107	126

Table of Concordance

R.S.O. 1980	R.S.O. 1990	R.S.O. 1980	R.S.O. 1990
108	127	140	162
109	128	141	163
—	128.1	142	164
110	129	143	165
111	130	144	166
112	131	145	167
113	132	146	168
113a	133	146a	169
114	134	147	170
—	134.1	147a	171
115	135	148	172
116	136	149	173
117	137	150	174
118	138	151	175
119	139	152	176
120	140	153	177
121	141	154	178
122	142	155	179
—	142.1	156	180
123	143	157	181
124	144	158	182
124a	145	159	183
125	146	160	184
—	146.1	161	185
126	147	162	186
127	148	163	187
128	149	164	188
129	150	165	189
130	151	165a	190
131	152	165b	191
132	153	—	191.0.1–191.8
133	154	—	191.9
—	154.1	166	192
—	154.2	167	193
134	155	168	194
135	156	169	195
135a	157	170	196
136	158	171	197, repealed
137	159	172	198
—	159.1	—	198.1–198.5
138	160	173	199
139	161	—	199.1

Table of Concordance

R.S.O. 1980	R.S.O. 1990	R.S.O. 1980	R.S.O. 1990
174	200	—	214.1
175	201	189	215
176	202	189a	216
177	203	—	216.1
178	204	190	217
179	205	190a	218
—	205.0.1	191	219
—	205.1–205.25	192	220
180	206, repealed	192a	221
181	207	193	222
182	208	194	223
183	209	194a	224
184	210	194b	225
185	211	194c	226
186	212	—	227
187	213	—	228
188	214		

TABLE OF CASES

All references are to sections of the Highway Traffic Act.

Table of Cases

Table of Cases

Table of Cases

Table of Cases

Table of Cases

Table of Cases

Table of Cases

Table of Cases

Table of Cases

Table of Cases

Table of Cases

Table of Cases

Table of Cases

INTRODUCTION

Selected Cases

Purpose of the Act

Harris v. Yellow Cab Ltd., 59 O.L.R. 8, [1926] 3 D.L.R. 254 (C.A.) — The Highway Traffic Act is a collection of duties and obligations imposed on motor vehicle drivers and others, based on the operation of motor vehicles upon public highways, for which owners of cars are made responsible. It is not intended to be exhaustive as to all liabilities which arise at common law.

Swyrd v. Tulloch, [1954] S.C.R. 199, *see also Johnston Nat. Storage Ltd. v. Mathieson*, [1953] 2 D.L.R. 604 (S.C.C.) — Generally speaking, the statutory provisions will be in addition to but not in lieu of the common law obligation to exercise due care; they will be regarded as no more than a minimum requirement. Compliance will not excuse the driver from the observance of his or her common law duty.

R. v. Hajivasilis (2013), 41 M.V.R. (6th) 175, 2013 ONCA 27, 2013 CarswellOnt 508, 114 O.R. (3d) 337, 302 O.A.C. 65, [2013] O.J. No. 253 (Ont. C.A.) — The name of the statute, including the equally authoritative French, suggest that the Act is not limited to "highways".

Constitutional Validity

Prov. Sec. of P.E.I. v. Egan, [1941] S.C.R. 396, [1941] 3 D.L.R. 305 — The regulation and control of traffic on a highway, as well as the regulation and control of motor vehicles operating in the province, come under the heading in the British North America Act, 1867 [now the Constitution Act, 1867 (U.K.), 30 & 31 Vict., c. 3] of Property and Civil Rights, in respect of which the province has exclusive jurisdiction. The fact that a violation of the Act is punishable by fine or imprisonment does not make it criminal law and thus outside the jurisdiction of the province.

O'Grady v. Sparling, [1960] S.C.R. 804, *see also Stephens v. R.*, [1960] S.C.R. 823 — So long as there is not complete repugnancy between the provincial and federal legislation, some degree of overlapping is permissible if the provisions can live together and operate concurrently. Clearly certain conduct may contain the elements of an offence both under the Criminal Code and under provincial legislation. Thus, a police officer will have certain discretion determining the charge to be laid.

Gonzalez v. Alberta (Driver Control Board) (2003), [2003] 11 W.W.R. 631, 327 A.R. 308, 296 W.A.C. 308, (sub nom. *Thomson v. Alberta (Transportation & Safety Board)*) 2003 ABCA 112, 2003 CarswellAlta 487, 19 Alta. L.R. (4th) 229, (sub nom. *Thomson v. Alberta (Transportation & Safety Board)*) 36 M.V.R. (4th) 37 (Alta. C.A.) — Driving is not a Charter right protected by s. 7.

R. v. Cooper, 2005 CarswellBC 1032, 18 M.V.R. (5th) 1, 197 C.C.C. (3d) 391, 212 B.C.A.C. 165, 350 W.A.C. 165, 2005 BCCA 256, 130 C.R.R. (2d) 307 (C.A.); leave to appeal refused (2005), 2005 CarswellBC 2680, 2005 CarswellBC 2681, 134 C.R.R. (2d)

375 (note), [2005] S.C.C.A. No. 321, 349 N.R. 193 (note), 373 W.A.C. 320 (note), 226 B.C.A.C. 320 (note) — Having a police officer prosecute traffic violation tickets is a violation of s. 11(d) of the *Charter* but is justifiable under s. 1.

Lévis (Ville) c. Tétreault, 2006 CarswellQue 2911, 2006 CarswellQue 2912, [2006] S.C.J. No. 12, 36 C.R. (6th) 215, 2006 SCC 12, 31 M.V.R. (5th) 1, 346 N.R. 331, 207 C.C.C. (3d) 1, [2006] 1 S.C.R. 420, 266 D.L.R. (4th) 165.

The analytical framework set out in *R. v. Sault Ste. Marie (City)*, 1978 CarswellOnt 24, 1978 CarswellOnt 594, [1978] S.C.J. No. 59, [1978] 2 S.C.R. 1299, 85 D.L.R. (3d) 161, 21 N.R. 295, (sub nom. *Regina ex rel. caswell v. Sault Ste. Marie)* 7 C.E.L.R. 53, 3 C.R. (3d) 30, 40 C.C.C. (2d) 353 (S.C.C.) was confirmed and the defence of officially induced error was accepted in Canadian Law.

Hartling v. Nova Scotia (Attorney General), 2009 CarswellNS 10, 70 C.C.L.I. (4th) 25, 78 M.V.R. (5th) 170, 2009 NSSC 2, [2009] I.L.R. I-4795, 278 N.S.R. (2d) 112, 886 A.P.R. 112; additional reasons at 2009 CarswellNS 68, 70 C.C.L.I. (4th) 105, 78 M.V.R. (5th) 250, 279 N.S.R. (2d) 44, 887 A.P.R. 44, 2009 NSSC 38, 186 C.R.R. (2d) 306; affirmed (2009), 2009 NSCA 130, 2009 CarswellNS 685, 286 N.S.R. (2d) 219, [2010] I.L.R. I-4950, 314 D.L.R. (4th) 114, 79 C.C.L.I. (4th) 46, 87 M.V.R. (5th) 161, 909 A.P.R. 219; leave to appeal refused 2010 CarswellNS 328, 2010 CarswellNS 329, 307 N.S.R. (2d) 399 (note), 975 A.P.R. 399 (note), 409 N.R. 383 (note) (S.C.C.) — The cap on soft tissue injury of $2,500 does not contravene s. 15(1) of the *Charter of Rights*, and, in any event, was justified under s. 1.

R. v. Nedelcu, 2012 SCC 59, 2012 CarswellOnt 13663, 2012 CarswellOnt 13664, [2012] 3 S.C.R. 311, 290 C.C.C. (3d) 153, 30 C.P.C. (7th) 14, 96 C.R. (6th) 391, 353 D.L.R. (4th) 199, 35 M.V.R. (6th) 1, 270 C.R.R. (2d) 177, 436 N.R. 1, 297 O.A.C. 93, [2012] S.C.J. No. 59 (S.C.C.); reversing 2011 ONCA 143, 2011 CarswellOnt 1090, 269 C.C.C. (3d) 1, 5 C.P.C. (7th) 16, 83 C.R. (6th) 41, 7 M.V.R. (6th) 10, 227 C.R.R. (2d) 364, 276 O.A.C. 76, [2011] O.J. No. 795 (Ont. C.A.) — The use of the accused's non-incriminating civil discovery evidence for impeachment purposes and nothing else could not and did not trigger the application of s. 13 of the Charter at his subsequent criminal trial.

R. v. Aucoin, 2012 SCC 66, 2012 CarswellNS 847, 2012 CarswellNS 848, [2012] 3 S.C.R. 408, 324 N.S.R. (2d) 1, 290 C.C.C. (3d) 448, 97 C.R. (6th) 294, 353 D.L.R. (4th) 417, 36 M.V.R. (6th) 1, 1029 A.P.R. 1, 273 C.R.R. (2d) 213, 437 N.R. 1, [2012] S.C.J. No. 66 (S.C.C.) — The court explored the necessity of putting the defendant in a cruiser and of performing a pat down for routine motor vehicle stops.

R. v. Jamieson, 304 C.C.C. (3d) 64, 2013 CarswellOnt 17714, 118 O.R. (3d) 327, 53 M.V.R. (6th) 1, 297 C.R.R. (2d) 58, 297 C.R.R. (2d) 243, 313 O.A.C. 313, [2013] O.J. No. 5836, 2013 ONCA 760 (Ont. C.A.); leave to appeal refused 2014 CarswellOnt 14802, 2014 CarswellOnt 14803 (S.C.C.) — The *Provincial Offences Act* scheme which warns a defendant that he will be tried and convicted *in absentia* does not contravene s. 11(d) of the *Charter*.

Re: Moore, 369 D.L.R. (4th) 385, 2013 CarswellOnt 17670, 53 M.V.R. (6th) 169, (sub nom. *Canada (Superintendent of Bankruptcy) v. 407 ETR Concession Company Ltd.)* 118 O.R. (3d) 161, 7 C.B.R. (6th) 167, (sub nom. *Moore (Bankrupt), Re)* 314 O.A.C. 152, 2013 ONCA 769 (Ont. C.A.); affirmed 2015 CSC 52, 2015 SCC 52, 2015 CarswellOnt 17183, 2015 CarswellOnt 17184, [2015] 3 S.C.R. 397, 30 C.B.R. (6th) 207, 391 D.L.R. (4th) 248, 85 M.V.R. (6th) 1, (sub nom. *Moore, Re)* 477 N.R. 1, 340 O.A.C. 1 — A discharge from bankruptcy permitted bankrupt persons to obtain a fresh start unencumbered by debts incurred prior to bankruptcy. The collection and enforcement of unpaid toll charges resulting in a licence suspension was not operative.

R. v. Ul-Rashid (2014), 2014 CarswellOnt 18386, 70 M.V.R. (6th) 181, 2014 ONCA 896 (Ont. C.A.) — The City conceded that as a self-represented litigant the driver was not adequately informed of his right to disclosure and that significant evidence had been lost. The city agreed that the appeal should be allowed for failure to obey a traffic sign or traffic light.

407 ETR Concession Co. v. Canada (Superintendent of Bankruptcy), 2015 CSC 52, 2015 SCC 52, 2015 CarswellOnt 17183, 2015 CarswellOnt 17184, [2015] 3 S.C.R. 397, 30 C.B.R. (6th) 207, 391 D.L.R. (4th) 248, 85 M.V.R. (6th) 1, *(sub nom. Moore, Re)* 477 N.R. 1, 340 O.A.C. 1; affirming 2013 ONCA 769, 2013 CarswellOnt 17670, *(sub nom. Canada (Superintendent of Bankruptcy) v. 407 ETR Concession Company Ltd.)* 118 O.R. (3d) 161, 7 C.B.R. (6th) 167, 369 D.L.R. (4th) 385, 53 M.V.R. (6th) 169, *(sub nom. Moore (Bankrupt), Re)* 314 O.A.C. 152 — The debt collection mechanism of the provincial toll highway was in conflict with the federal *Bankruptcy and Insolvency Act*.

Application of Act

General

R. v. Greening (1992), 43 M.V.R. (2d) 53 (Ont. Prov. Ct.); affirmed (1993), 47 M.V.R. (2d) 167 (Ont. Prov. Div.) — The intention of the Legislature was to bind all users of the highway to a uniform code of driving behaviour. Canada Post Corporation does not have immunity from prosecution.

Halushka v. Canada (Attorney General) (2003), 43 M.V.R. (4th) 149, 23 Alta. L.R. (4th) 8, [2003] A.J. No. 1135, [2004] 3 W.W.R. 466, 2003 ABCA 262, 2003 CarswellAlta 1302 (C.A.) — It was arguable whether the six-month limitation period in s. 269 of the National Defence Act applied to ordinary driving on public highways in the absence of apprehended war or insurrection.

Bartley v. Ontario, 2007 CarswellOnt 1779, 45 M.V.R. (5th) 1, 154 C.R.R. (2d) 373, 47 C.C.L.I. (4th) 9 (C.A.) — The province's policy of seeking compensation for fire services fees from persons involved in motor vehicle accidents does not violate s. 7 of the *Charter*.

Emergency Vehicles

Under the Highway Traffic Act, originally there was no exception made for the operation of motor vehicles operated by the police in the course of their duties; the provisions of the Act were applicable to the police as well as to other members of the public making use of the highways. Over a number of years, the operation of emergency vehicles such as police, fire, ambulance and road clearing has been exempted from certain requirements of the Act. See ss. 128, 136, 144, 147(2)(c) and 148(3) of the Act.

Aboriginals

Francis v. R., [1988] 1 S.C.R. 1025 — The Act is one of general application, and is applicable to Aboriginals and Indian Reservations.

Effect of Finding of Guilt on Civil Proceedings

English v. Richmond, [1956] S.C.R. 383, 3 D.L.R. (2d) 385 — On the basis of the general admissibility of admissions made by a party at any time, evidence may be given in a civil action of a plea of guilty to a criminal charge or an infraction of the Highway Traffic Act in order to show inconsistency in the position adopted by the party at trial that he or she was not at fault.

Campbell v. Pickard (1961), 30 D.L.R. (2d) 152, 36 W.W.R. 222 (Man. C.A.), *see also Cohen v. Bates* (1962), 32 D.L.R. (2d) 763 (Man. C.A.); *Ferris v. Monahan* (1956), 4 D.L.R. (2d) 539 (N.B. C.A.) — The weight to be given to the admission is a matter for the appreciation of the court in the light of the circumstances surrounding its making.

Hollington v. Hewthorn & Co., [1943] K.B. 587 (C.A.) — Although a plea of guilty may be admissible, different considerations apply to a conviction entered on a charge for an offence arising out of the circumstances of the accident involved in the civil action. The result of the criminal proceedings is inadmissible even as *prima facie* proof. It is only proof that another court considered that the party was guilty of, for example, careless driving.

R. v. Soni (2014), 2014 CarswellAlta 1934, 598 A.R. 158, 8 Alta. L.R. (6th) 1, 71 M.V.R. (6th) 39, 2014 ABQB 649, [2014] A.J. No. 1174 (Alta. Q.B.) — A Statement of Claim was found not to be reliable and the prejudicial effect significant in a criminal case.

Wotherspoon v. Hameluck (2014), 2014 CarswellNS 965, 354 N.S.R. (2d) 101, 71 M.V.R. (6th) 271, 2014 NSSC 442, 1120 A.P.R. 101 (B.C.S.C.) — A conviction for disobeying a "don't walk" sign or walking against a red light meant that the plaintiff could not sue and attempt to relitigate whether the defendant driver crossed against a red.

Effect of Non-Compliance with Act

Breach as Evidence of Negligence

Baldwin v. Bell, [1933] S.C.R. 1, *see also Gauthier & Co. v. R.*, [1945] S.C.R. 143, [1945] 2 D.L.R. 48 — The non-observance by a driver of the precautions prescribed or the duties imposed by the Legislature may be *prima facie* evidence of negligence.

Bruce v. McIntyre, [1954] O.R. 265 (C.A.); affirmed [1955] S.C.R. 251 — It must be shown that the breach of statute was a proximate cause of the injury complained of and whether such breach is negligence causing or contributing to an accident is a question of fact, depending on the circumstances in each case.

Morin v. Blais, [1977] 1 S.C.R. 570, 10 N.R. 489 — Many traffic provisions lay down elementary standards of care and make them binding regulations as well. Breach of such regulations constitutes civil fault and, where such fault is immediately followed by an accident which the standard is expressly designed to prevent, it is reasonable to presume that there is a causal link between the fault and the accident in the absence of evidence to the contrary.

Gauthier & Co. v. R., *supra* — If on the facts a breach of statute is proved, and also a connection between that breach and the accident, the onus will fall on the offending driver to explain how the accident might have occurred without negligence on his or her part.

United Motors v. Hutson, [1937] S.C.R. 294 — Broadly speaking, where the defendant produces an explanation equally consistent with negligence and no negligence, the burden of establishing negligence will still remain with the plaintiff.

Ryan v. Victoria (City), [1999] 1 S.C.R. 201, 40 M.V.R. (3d) 1, 1999 CarswellBC 79, 50 M.P.L.R. (2d) 1, 168 D.L.R. (4th) 513, 44 C.C.L.T. (2d) 1, 59 B.C.L.R. (3d) 81, [1999] 6 W.W.R. 61 — Legislative standards are relevant to the common law standard of care, but the two are not necessarily co-extensive. The fact that a statute prescribes or prohibits certain activities may constitute evidence of reasonable conduct in a given situation, but it does not extinguish the underlying obligation of reasonableness. Thus, a statutory breach does not automatically give rise to civil liability; it is merely some evidence of negligence. Mere compliance does not of itself preclude liability. Statutory standards can be highly relevant to the assessment of reasonable conduct in a particular case, and may render reasonable an act or omission which would otherwise appear to be negligent.

Handjiev v. Aviscar Inc. (2003), 45 M.V.R. (4th) 75, 2003 ABPC 170, 2003 CarswellAlta 1323 (Prov. Ct.) — A breach of licensing compliance such as where the plaintiff found out shortly after purchase that the defendant had notified the Motor Vehicle Branch that the vehicle was written off for vehicle registration purposes did not give rise to an actionable claim for breach of contract or misrepresentation.

Evidence

Moore v. Getahun, 2015 ONCA 55, 2015 CarswellOnt 911, 124 O.R. (3d) 321, 65 C.P.C. (7th) 1, 381 D.L.R. (4th) 471, 73 M.V.R. (6th) 169, 329 O.A.C. 363, [2015] O.J. No. 398; additional reasons 2015 ONCA 443, 2015 CarswellOnt 12512; leave to appeal refused 2015 CarswellOnt 14066, 2015 CarswellOnt 14067 (S.C.C.) — It is permitted that counsel assist an expert in preparation of a report.

Westerhof v. Gee Estate, 2015 ONCA 206, 2015 CarswellOnt 3977, 124 O.R. (3d) 721, 47 C.C.L.I. (5th) 246, 384 D.L.R. (4th) 343, 77 M.V.R. (6th) 181, 331 O.A.C. 129, [2015] O.J. No. 1472; additional reasons 2015 ONCA 456, 2015 CarswellOnt 9294; leave to appeal refused 2015 CarswellOnt 16499, 2015 CarswellOnt 16500 (S.C.C.); leave to appeal refused 2015 CarswellOnt 16501, 2015 CarswellOnt 16502 (S.C.C.) — Rule 53.03 of the civil rules does not apply to participant experts and non-party experts giving opinion evidence.

Breach as Bar to Action

Vancouver v. Burchill, [1932] S.C.R. 620, *see also Fuller v. Nickel*, [1949] S.C.R. 601; *Downey v. Hyslop*, 65 O.L.R. 548, [1930] 4 D.L.R. 578 (C.A.) — Generally speaking, the effect of a breach of the provisions of the Act is only to incur the penalties prescribed by the Act for such breach, and does not preclude a party from recovering damages caused to him or her by the fault of another party or parties.

Fuller v. Nickel, supra, see also Roy Swail Ltd. v. Reeves (1956), 2 D.L.R. (2d) 326 (S.C.C.); *Horne v. Fortalsky*, [1952] O.W.N. 121 (H.C.) — It was not the intention of the Act to deal in any way with the liability for actionable negligence. Infractions are important in fixing the responsibility for a collision in an action between parties only if they constitute a direct cause of that collision. Moreover, since the enactment of the Contributory Negligence Acts, even if the infraction does constitute such direct cause, the offender will not necessarily be wholly barred from recovering, but may be relieved in proportion to the degree in which the opposing party or parties were at fault.

Introduction

Korody v. Bell (2008), [2008] O.J. No. 5392, 2008 CarswellOnt 8062, 79 M.V.R. (5th) 101, 73 C.C.L.I. (4th) 145 (S.C.J.) — A motion by the plaintiff seeking an order that the agreed upon facts in the criminal proceeding constituted conclusive evidence that the accused was operating another's vehicle with consent was rejected. The criminal proceeding involving a guilty plea to impaired causing bodily harm while unlicensed and uninsured did not preclude the accused from testifying on the question of consent.

HIGHWAY TRAFFIC ACT

R.S.O. 1990, c. H.8 [s. 144(2), (3) not in force at date of publication. Repealed 2006, c. 21, Sched. F, s. 10.1.], as am. S.O. 1992, c. 20, s. 2; 1993, c. 8; 1993, c. 13, s. 1; 1993, c. 18, s. 1; 1993, c. 27, s. 3 (Sched.); 1993, c. 31, s. 2; 1993, c. 34; 1993, c. 40; 1994, c. 27, s. 138; 1994, c. 28; 1994, c. 29; 1994, c. 35; 1996, c. 1, Sched. E, s. 2; 1996, c. 9, s. 26; 1996, c. 20 [ss. 6, 11, 12, 22, 31 not in force at date of publication.] [ss. 12, 22 cannot be applied.] [ss. 6, 11 repealed 2006, c. 21, Sched. F, s. 10.1.] [s. 31 repealed 2009, c. 5, s. 58.]; 1996, c. 31, ss. 68–71 [s. 71 not in force at date of publication. Repealed 2006, c. 21, Sched. F, s. 10.1.]; 1996, c. 32, s. 71; 1996, c. 33, ss. 1–17; 1997, c. 4, s. 81; 1997, c. 12; 1997, c. 26, s. 137 (Sched.); 1997, c. 41, s. 120; 1998, c. 5, ss. 25–27; 1998, c. 6; 1998, c. 18, Sched. G, s. 56; 1998, c. 28, s. 67; 1998, c. 35, s. 103; 1998, c. 38 [s. 7 amended 2002, c. 15.] [s. 7(1), (2) repealed 1998, c. 38, s. 7(3).]; 1999, c. 8, s. 7; 1999, c. 12, Sched. B, s. 9, Sched. G, s. 24, Sched. R, ss. 1–19 [Sched. R, ss. 1(1), (4), 2(2), (4), (6), 4, 5(2), 6(2), 7–11, 15, 16, 18 not in force at date of publication.] [Sched. R, ss. 1(1), (4), 2(2), (4), 4, 5(2), 6(2), 9–11, 15(1), (3), 18 repealed 2006, c. 21, Sched. F, s. 10.1.] [Sched. R, s. 2(6) repealed 2002, c. 22, s. 101; ss. 7, 15(2), 16 repealed 2009, c. 5, s. 57(1), (3).] [Sched. R, s. 8 cannot be applied.] [Sched. R, ss. 10(1), (2), 11, 15(1) repealed 2009, c. 5, s. 57(2). Cannot be applied.]; 1999, c. 13, s. 1; 2000, c. 15; 2000, c. 26, Sched. O, ss. 1–15; 2000, c. 29; 2000, c. 30, s. 10; 2000, c. 35; 2001, c. 4, s. 4; 2001, c. 9, Sched. O, ss. 1–6; 2001, c. 13, s. 18; 2001, c. 32, s. 26; 2002, c. 4, s. 64; 2002, c. 5, s. 32 [Not in force at date of publication. Repealed 2006, c. 21, Sched. F, s. 10.1.]; 2002, c. 17, Sched. C, s. 15, Sched. F, s. 1; 2002, c. 18, Sched. P, ss. 1–28, 29(1)–(4), (5) (Fr.), 30–39 [ss. 2, 16, 20, 25(5), 31 not in force at date of publication. Repealed 2006, c. 21, Sched. F, s. 10.1.]; 2002, c. 21; 2002, c. 22, ss. 95–100 [s. 96 not in force at date of publication. Repealed 2006, c. 21, Sched. F, s. 10.1.]; 2002, c. 24, Sched. B, s. 25, item 11; 2002, c. 30, Sched. E, s. 7; 2004, c. 22, ss. 1–6; 2004, c. 31, Sched. 18; 2005, c. 14; 2005, c. 26, Sched. A [ss. 17(6), 18 not in force at date of publication. Repealed 2006, c. 21, Sched. F, s. 10.1.]; 2005, c. 31, Sched. 10; 2005, c. 32, s. 2; 2006, c. 11, Sched. B, s. 6(2), (4), (5); 2006, c. 19, Sched. D, s. 9, Sched. T, ss. 4–7 [Sched. D, s. 9(4) cannot be applied.]; 2006, c. 20; 2006, c. 21, Sched. F, ss. 10.1(1), 115, 136(1), Table 1, 139 [s. 139(4) conditions not yet satisfied. Repealed 2006, c. 21, Sched. F, s. 10.1.]; 2006, c. 25; 2006, c. 32, Sched. C, s. 24(1)–(4), (6), (7), Sched. D, s. 4; 2006, c. 33, Sched. M; 2007, c. 13, ss. 1–24; 2008, c. 8; 2008, c. 17, ss. 28–48; 2009, c. 4, ss. 1, 2; 2009, c. 5, ss. 1(1), (2), (3) (Fr.), (4)–(8), 2, 3–5 (Fr.), 6–14, 15(1)–(4) (Fr.), (5)–(14), 16(1) (Fr.), (2)–(13), 17–29, 30 (Fr.), 31–37, 38 (Fr.), 39 (Fr.), 40–52, 53 (Fr.), 54–56 [ss. 15(5), (7), (10), (12), 16(2), (6), (12), 17(1), 43 not in force at date of publication.] [ss. 15(5), (7), (10), (12), 16(2), (6), 17(1), 57(2) cannot be applied.]; 2009, c. 19, s. 68; 2009, c. 33, Sched. 4, s. 3, Sched. 26, s. 3(1) (Fr.), (2)–(7), (8) (Fr.) (9)–(14); 2010, c. 16, Sched. 12, s. 2; 2011, c. 9, Sched. 41, s. 3; 2012, c. 8, Sched. 22, s. 20; 2014, c. 9, Sched. 2 [ss. 1–8, 10, 11(2), 12–44, 45(1), 46

7

to come into force January 1, 2017; ss. 9, 11(1), 45(2) not in force at date of publication.] [s. 13 repealed 2015, c. 14, s. 61(4) conditions not yet satisfied.]; 2015, c. 14, ss. 4–59, 61(3) [ss. 4–20, 24–35, 54, 55, 58, 59 not in force at date of publication; ss. 38, 40(1), (3) to come into force January 1, 2017; s. 61(3) conditions not yet satisfied.]; 2015, c. 27, Sched. 7, ss. 1(1), (2) (Fr.), (3), 2, 3 (Fr.), 4 (Fr.), 5–11, 12 (Fr.), 13 (Fr.), 14–16, 17 (Fr.), 18 (Fr.), 19, 20 (Fr.), 21, 22, 23 (Fr.), 24 (Fr.), 25, 26 (Fr.), 27 [ss. 1(3), 5, 6, 7(2), 9, 10(2), (4)–(6), 11, 25, 27 not in force at date of publication.]; 2016, c. 5, Sched. 12 [ss. 1, 2, 4–10 not in force at date of publication.].

1. (1) Definitions — In this Act,

"ambulance" includes,

(a) an ambulance as defined in the *Ambulance Act*,

(b) a cardiac arrest emergency vehicle operated by or under the authority of a hospital, and

(c) an emergency response vehicle, other than an ambulance as defined in the *Ambulance Act*, operated by an ambulance service that is used to provide emergency response services, and that has been assigned an emergency response vehicle number by the Ministry of Health and Long-Term Care;

"bicycle" includes a tricycle, a unicycle and a power-assisted bicycle but does not include a motor-assisted bicycle;

"Board" [Repealed 1999, c. 12, Sched. G, s. 24(1).]

"built-up area" means a territory contiguous to a highway not within a local municipality, other than a local municipality that had the status of a township on December 31, 2002 and, but for the enactment of the *Municipal Act, 2001*, would have had the status of a township on January 1, 2003, where,

(a) not less than 50 per cent of the frontage upon one side of the highway for a distance of not less than 200 metres is occupied by dwellings, buildings used for business purposes, schools or churches,

(b) not less than 50 per cent of the frontage upon both sides of the highway for a distance of not less than 100 metres is occupied by dwellings, buildings used for business purposes, schools or churches, or

(c) not more than 200 metres of the highway separates any territory described in clause (a) or (b) from any other territory described in clause (a) or (b),

and signs are displayed as required by the regulations;

"bus" means a motor vehicle designed for carrying ten or more passengers and used for the transportation of persons;

"chauffeur" means a person who operates a motor vehicle and receives compensation therefor;

"commercial motor vehicle" means a motor vehicle having permanently attached thereto a truck or delivery body and includes ambulances, hearses, casket wagons, fire apparatus, buses and tractors used for hauling purposes on the highways;

Proposed Amendment — 1(1) "commercial motor vehicle"

"commercial motor vehicle", unless otherwise defined by regulation, means a motor vehicle having attached to it a truck or delivery body and includes an ambulance, a hearse, a casket wagon, a fire apparatus, a bus and a tractor used for hauling purposes on a highway;

> 2014, c. 9, Sched. 2, s. 1(1) [To come into force January 1, 2017.]

Proposed Addition — 1(1) "compensation"

"compensation" includes any rate, remuneration, reimbursement or reward of any kind paid, payable, promised, received or demanded, directly or indirectly;

> 2014, c. 9, Sched. 2, s. 1(2) [To come into force January 1, 2017.]

"conversion unit" means a mechanical device consisting of a single axle designed to convert a two-axle vehicle into a three-axle vehicle;

"conviction" includes a disposition made under the *Young Offenders Act* (Canada) or a sentence imposed under the *Youth Criminal Justice Act* (Canada);

"crosswalk" means,

> (a) that part of a highway at an intersection that is included within the connections of the lateral lines of the sidewalks on opposite sides of the highway measured from the curbs or, in the absence of curbs, from the edges of the roadway, or
>
> (b) any portion of a roadway at an intersection or elsewhere distinctly indicated for pedestrian crossing by signs or by lines or other markings on the surface;

Proposed Addition — 1(1) "CVOR certificate"

"CVOR certificate" means a Commercial Vehicle Operator's Registration Certificate issued under section 17;

> 2014, c. 9, Sched. 2, s. 1(2) [To come into force January 1, 2017.]

"Deputy Minister" means the Deputy Minister of Transportation;

"driver" means a person who drives a vehicle on a highway;

"driver's licence" means a licence issued under section 32 to drive a motor vehicle on a highway;

"farm tractor" means a self-propelled vehicle designed and used primarily as a farm implement for drawing ploughs, mowing-machines and other implements of husbandry and not designed or used for carrying a load;

"fire department vehicle" includes an emergency crash extrication vehicle owned and operated by a rescue organization approved by the Minister in writing for the purposes of this Act and a vehicle designated in writing by the Fire Marshal of Ontario as a fire department vehicle;

"garage" means every place or premises where motor vehicles are received for housing, storage or repairs for compensation;

Proposed Addition — 1(1) "goods"

"goods" includes all classes of materials, wares and merchandise and livestock;
2014, c. 9, Sched. 2, s. 1(2) [To come into force January 1, 2017.]

"gross weight" means the combined weight of vehicle and load;

"highway" includes a common and public highway, street, avenue, parkway, driveway, square, place, bridge, viaduct or trestle, any part of which is intended for or used by the general public for the passage of vehicles and includes the area between the lateral property lines thereof;

"intersection" means the area embraced within the prolongation or connection of the lateral curb lines or, if none, then of the lateral boundary lines of two or more highways that join one another at an angle, whether or not one highway crosses the other;

"King's Highway" includes the secondary highways and tertiary roads designated under the *Public Transportation and Highway Improvement Act*;

"median strip" means the portion of a highway so constructed as to separate traffic travelling in one direction from traffic travelling in the opposite direction by a physical barrier or a raised or depressed paved or unpaved separation area that is not intended to allow crossing vehicular movement;

"Minister" means the Minister of Transportation;

"Ministry" means the Ministry of Transportation;

"mobile home" means a vehicle, other than a motor vehicle, that is designed and used as a residence or working accommodation unit and exceeds 2.6 metres in width or eleven metres in length;

"motor assisted bicycle" means a bicycle,

    (a) that is fitted with pedals that are operable at all times to propel the bicycle,

    (b) that weighs not more than fifty-five kilograms,

    (c) that has no hand or foot operated clutch or gearbox driven by the motor and transferring power to the driven wheel,

    (d) that has an attached motor driven by electricity or having a piston displacement of not more than fifty cubic centimetres, and

    (e) that does not have sufficient power to enable the bicycle to attain a speed greater than 50 kilometres per hour on level ground within a distance of 2 kilometres from a standing start;

"motor vehicle" includes an automobile, a motorcycle, a motor-assisted bicycle unless otherwise indicated in this Act, and any other vehicle propelled or driven otherwise than by muscular power, but does not include a street car or other motor vehicle running only upon rails, a power-assisted bicycle, a motorized snow vehicle, a traction engine, a farm tractor, a self-propelled implement of husbandry or a road-building machine;

"motorcycle" means a self-propelled vehicle having a seat or saddle for the use of the driver and designed to travel on not more than three wheels in contact with the ground, and includes a motor-scooter, but does not include a motor assisted bicycle;

"motorized snow vehicle" has the same meaning as in the *Motorized Snow Vehicles Act*;

"official sign" means a sign approved by the Ministry;

"park" or "parking", when prohibited, means the standing of a vehicle, whether occupied or not, except when standing temporarily for the purpose of and while actually engaged in loading or unloading merchandise or passengers;

"peace officer" includes a mayor, warden, reeve, sheriff, deputy sheriff, sheriff's officer, justice of the peace, jailer or keeper of a prison, and a police officer, bailiff, or other person employed for the preservation and maintenance of the public peace, or for the service or execution of civil process, or any officer appointed for enforcing or carrying out the provisions of this Act;

"pedestrian crossover" means any portion of a roadway distinctly indicated for pedestrian crossing by signs on the highway and lines or other markings on the surface of the roadway as prescribed by the regulations;

"power-assisted bicycle" means a bicycle that,

(a) is a power-assisted bicycle as defined in subsection 2(1) of the *Motor Vehicle Safety Regulations* made under the *Motor Vehicle Safety Act* (Canada),

(b) bears a label affixed by the manufacturer in compliance with the definition referred to in clause (a),

(c) has affixed to it pedals that are operable, and

(d) is capable of being propelled solely by muscular power;

"public vehicle" has the same meaning as in the *Public Vehicles Act*;

"Registrar" means the Registrar of Motor Vehicles appointed under this Act;

"regulations" means the regulations made under this Act;

"road-building machine" means a self-propelled vehicle of a design commonly used in the construction or maintenance of highways, including but not limited to,

(a) asphalt spreaders, concrete paving or finishing machines, motor graders, rollers, tractor-dozers and motor scrapers,

(b) tracked and wheeled tractors of all kinds while equipped with mowers, post-hole diggers, compactors, weed spraying equipment, snow blowers and snow plows, front-end loaders, back-hoes or rock drills, and

(c) power shovels on tracks and drag lines on tracks,

but not including a commercial motor vehicle;

Proposed Amendment — 1(1) "road-building machine"

"road-building machine" means a self-propelled vehicle of a design commonly used in the construction or maintenance of highways that,

(a) belongs to a class of vehicle prescribed in the regulations,

(b) has the features or equipment prescribed in the regulations, or

(c) is being used as prescribed in the regulations;

2016, c. 5, Sched. 12, s. 1(1) [Not in force at date of publication.]

"road service vehicle" means a vehicle while it is being used for highway maintenance purposes by or on behalf of a municipality or other authority with jurisdiction and control of the highway;

"roadway" means the part of the highway that is improved, designed or ordinarily used for vehicular traffic, but does not include the shoulder, and, where a highway includes two or more separate roadways, the term "roadway" refers to any one roadway separately and not to all of the roadways collectively;

"safety glass" means any product that is composed of glass and so manufactured, fabricated or treated as substantially to prevent the shattering and flying of the glass when struck or broken and that is approved by the Ministry, or such other or similar product that is approved by the Ministry;

Proposed Addition — 1(1) "safety record"

"safety record" means the safety record of an operator, as defined in subsection 16(1), determined in accordance with the regulations made under section 22;

2014, c. 9, Sched. 2, s. 1(2) [To come into force January 1, 2017.]

"self-propelled implement of husbandry" means a self-propelled vehicle manufactured, designed, redesigned, converted or reconstructed for a specific use in farming;

"stand" or "standing", when prohibited, means the halting of a vehicle, whether occupied or not, except for the purpose of and while actually engaged in receiving or discharging passengers;

"state of the United States of America" includes the District of Columbia;

"stop" or "stopping", when prohibited, means the halting of a vehicle, even momentarily, whether occupied or not, except when necessary to avoid conflict with other traffic or in compliance with the directions of a police officer or of a traffic control sign or signal;

"street car" includes a car of an electric or steam railway;

"through highway" means a highway or part of a highway designated as such by the Minister or by by-law of a municipality, and every such highway shall be marked by a stop sign or yield right-of-way sign in compliance with the regulations of the Ministry;

"trailer" means a vehicle that is at any time drawn upon a highway by a motor vehicle, except an implement of husbandry, a mobile home, another motor vehicle or any device or apparatus not designed to transport persons or property, temporarily drawn, propelled or moved upon such highway, and except a side car attached to a motorcycle, and shall be considered a separate vehicle and not part of the motor vehicle by which it is drawn;

"trailer converter dolly" means a device consisting of one or more axles, a fifth wheel lower-half and a tow bar;

"Tribunal" means the Licence Appeal Tribunal.

"vehicle" includes a motor vehicle, trailer, traction engine, farm tractor, road-building machine, bicycle and any vehicle drawn, propelled or driven by any kind of power, including muscular power, but does not include a motorized snow vehicle or a street car;

"wheelchair" means a chair mounted on wheels driven by muscular or any other kind of power that is designed for and used by a person whose mobility is limited by one or more conditions or functional impairments.

(2) Suspension or cancellation of licence or permit — Where in this Act the Minister, a provincial judge, a justice of the peace or other official is authorized or directed to suspend or cancel the licence or permit of any person, and the person is the holder of both a licence and a permit issued under this Act, every such authority extends to both licence and permit and every such direction may in the discretion of the Minister, provincial judge, justice of the peace or other official be made to apply to both licence and permit.

(3) Overpass and underpass — For the purposes of Part IX and any regulations or municipal by-laws made thereunder, every overpass and underpass shall be deemed to form part of the highway that it connects.

(4) References to *Criminal Code* — Any reference in this Act to the *Criminal Code* (Canada) or any provision thereof shall be deemed to be a reference to the *Criminal Code* (Canada) as amended or re-enacted from time to time.

(5) Idem — Any reference in this Act or the regulations to a conviction or discharge for an offence under the *Criminal Code* (Canada) includes a conviction or discharge for the corresponding offence under the *National Defence Act* (Canada).

(6) Pardons — This Act and the regulations apply to a person who has been granted a pardon under the *Criminal Records Act* (Canada) in the same manner as if the person had not been granted the pardon.

(7) Transition, police villages — This Act, as it read on December 31, 2002, continues to apply to police villages continued under subsection 456(1) of the *Municipal Act, 2001*.

(8) Calculation of days — Where a suspension or impoundment is imposed under section 41.4, 48, 48.1, 48.2.1, 48.4, 55.2 or 172, the period of the suspension or impoundment shall be determined by counting 24 hours for each day.

Proposed Amendment — 1(8)

(8) Calculation of days — Where a suspension or impoundment is imposed under section 41.4, 48, 48.0.1, 48.1, 48.2.1, 48.4, 55.2 or 172, the period of the suspension or impoundment shall be determined by counting 24 hours for each day.

2015, c. 27, Sched. 7, s. 1(3) [Not in force at date of publication.]

(9) Definition of resident of Ontario — The Lieutenant Governor in Council may make regulations prescribing who is a resident of Ontario for any purpose of this Act.

Proposed Addition — 1(10)

(10) Definition of "commercial motor vehicle" — The Lieutenant Governor in Council may make regulations defining "commercial motor vehicle" differently from its definition in subsection (1) for the purposes of any Part or provision of this Act, and those regulations may include or exclude any vehicle or class of vehicles for the purposes of that definition, including the inclusion or exclusion of vehicles or classes of vehicles based on a use or uses to which a vehicle may be put.

2014, c. 9, Sched. 2, s. 1(3) [To come into force January 1, 2017.]

Proposed Addition — 1(11)

(11) Definition of "road-building machine" — The Lieutenant Governor in Council may make regulations for the purpose of the definition of "road-building machine" in subsection (1),

(a) prescribing classes of vehicles that are or are not road-building machines;

(b) prescribing features and equipment that a vehicle must have or must not have to be a road-building machine;

(c) prescribing uses to which a vehicle must be put or must not be put to be a road-building machine.

2016, c. 5, Sched. 12, s. 1(2) [Not in force at date of publication.]

1994, c. 27, s. 138(1); 1999, c. 12, Sched. G, s. 24(1), (2); 2001, c. 9, Sched. O, s. 1; 2002, c. 17, Sched. F, s. 1; 2006, c. 19, Sched. D, s. 9(1); 2007, c. 13, s. 1; 2008, c. 17, s. 28; 2009, c. 5, s. 1(1), (2), (4)–(8); 2009, c. 33, Sched. 26, s. 3(2); 2015, c. 27, Sched. 7, s. 1(1)

Commentary and Related Provisions

"Bicycle"

See R.R.O. 1990, Reg. 630 — Vehicles on Controlled-Access Highways.

"Board"

Under s. 47, the Registrar has a broad discretion to suspend a permit or licence for any misconduct or contravention of the Act or any regulation thereunder. The Minister has the right under s. 32(5)(b) to impose conditions depending on the results of examinations. A person aggrieved by such a decision may appeal to the Board. A further appeal lies to the Ontario Court (General Division). See R.R.O. 1990, Reg. 574 — Appeals concerning the Board.

"Built-Up Area"

The relevance of the definition of a built-up area is in relation to proof of speeding under s. 144 and the requirement to post signs depending on the nature of the highway.

"Bus"

See ss. 174 and 175 respecting the duties incumbent on bus and school bus drivers. See also R.R.O. 1990, Regs. 611 and 612 as am. respecting safety standards for buses. The Public Vehicles Act, R.S.O. 1990, c. P.54, governs the licensing of buses.

"Chauffeur"

The provisions of R.S.O. 1970, c. 202, s. 16, providing for a separate form of chauffeur's licence, were repealed in 1973 and such licences are now in the category of ordinary licence under s. 32. The definition is still applicable to other sections of the Act, the most important being s. 192 respecting the liability of an owner of a motor vehicle. That section imposes on the owner absolute liability for loss or damage resulting from negligence in the operation of a motor vehicle by the owner's chauffeur even if the chauffeur was driving at the relevant time without the owner's consent or contrary to express wishes.

"Commercial Motor Vehicle"

See R.R.O. 1990, Reg. 575 — Commercial Motor Vehicle Inspections; R.R.O. 1990, Reg. 576 — Commercial Vehicle Operator's Registration Certificates; and O. Reg. 4/93 — Hours of Work. The Truck Transportation Act, R.S.O. 1990, c. T.22, and the Public Vehicles Act, R.S.O. 1990, c. P.54, also regulate commercial motor vehicles.

"Driver"

R. v. Atchison, 2006 CarswellAlta 1568, 274 D.L.R. (4th) 188, 39 M.V.R. (5th) 165, 2006 ABCA 258, 67 Alta. L.R. (4th) 221, 391 W.A.C. 198, 401 A.R. 198 (C.A.) — A person on a skateboard is a pedestrian.

"Driver's Licence"

Section 1(2) of the Act provides that wherever a licence or permit may be suspended or cancelled, both may be suspended or cancelled. See O. Regs. 341/94 and 340/94 regarding, respectively, Driver's Licence Examinations, and Driver's Licences.

"Garage"

See R.R.O. 1990, Reg. 595 — Garage Licences. The Motor Vehicle Repair Act, R.S.O. 1990, c. M.43, regulates garages where repairs are carried out.

"Highway"

See the definition of "highway" in s. 2 of the Criminal Code; s. 1 of the Ontario Public Transportation and Highway Improvement Act, R.S.O. 1990, c. P.50; and s. 63 of the Public Lands Act, R.S.O. 1990, c. P.43.

With respect to the duty to repair, the common law has largely been superseded by ss. 284 and 285 of the Municipal Act, R.S.O. 1990, c. M.45, and s. 33 of the Public Transportation and Highway Improvement Act, R.S.O. 1990, c. P.50, which cast on municipalities and the province, respectively, the duty to keep in repair highways and imposing liability for breach of that duty. Timely notice must be given in writing within seven days in the case of an urban municipality and within 10 days in the case of other municipalities or the province.

See s. 1(3) of the Act which deems overpasses and underpasses to be part of the highway with which they connect for purposes of Part IX of the Act, Rate of Speed, and any regulations or municipal by-laws thereunder.

See the following Regulations relating to highways:

      R.R.O. 1990, Reg. 579 as am. — Designation of Highways;

      R.R.O. 1990, Reg. 580 — Designation of Paved Shoulders on the King's Highways;

      R.R.O. 1990, Reg. 599 — Highway Closings;

      R.R.O. 1990, Reg. 604 — Parking;

      R.R.O. 1990, Reg. 609 — Restricted Use of the King's Highways;

      R.R.O. 1990, Reg. 622 — Stopping of Vehicles on Parts of the King's Highways;

      R.R.O. 1990, Reg. 627 — Use of Controlled-Access Highways by Pedestrians;

      R.R.O. 1990, Reg. 630 — Vehicles on Controlled-Access Highways.

"Intersection"

See ss. 135–139 of the Act as to the right of way at an intersection.

"King's Highway"

See "highway", *supra*.

"Motor Vehicle"

See also the definition of "vehicle". The definition in the Act may be contrasted with the definition in s. 2 of the Criminal Code which provides that a motor vehicle is "a vehicle that is drawn, propelled or driven by any means other than by muscular power, but does not include a vehicle of a railway that operates. . . ."

See also the Motorized Snow Vehicles Act, R.S.O. 1990, c. M.44, and the Off-Road Vehicles Act, R.S.O. 1990, c. O.4.

"Official Sign"

See the following sections of the Act: s. 137 — Stop Signs; s. 138 — Yield Signs; s. 182 — Signs. See also R.R.O. 1990, Reg. 615 — Signs; R.R.O. 1990, Reg. 616 — Slow Moving Vehicle Sign.

"Park" or "Parking"

For provisions as to parking, see s. 170 of the Act. See R.R.O. 1990, Regs. 604 and 605 regarding, respectively, Parking and Parking of Vehicles in Territory without Municipal Organization. See s. 140 of the Act as to the duties of a driver at a pedestrian crossover. See also R.R.O. 1990, Reg. 615 — Signs. Part II of the Provincial Offences Act, R.S.O. 1990, c. P.33 deals with enforcement of parking tickets.

"Safety Glass"

See s. 72 of the Act.

"Stop"

See R.R.O. 1990, Reg. 622 — Stopping of Vehicles on Parts of the King's Highway.

"Through Highway"

Section 136 of the Act governs the obligation to stop at a stop sign.

"Trailer"

See R.R.O. 1990, Reg. 618 — Specifications and Standards for Trailer Couplings.

"Vehicle"

See the definition of "motor vehicle".

Case Law

"Driver"

R. v. Miller, [1944] O.W.N. 617, 82 C.C.C. 314 (Co. Ct.) — The accused was steering a tank which was being towed by a truck. The tank crossed the centre line of the roadway and collided with a car going in the opposite direction. The accused was convicted of dangerous driving.

Wallace v. Major, [1946] 2 All E.R. 87, [1946] K.B. 473 (D.C.) — A person who is merely steering a vehicle which is being drawn by another vehicle is not driving.

R. v. MacDonagh, [1974] Q.B. 448, 59 Cr. App. R. 55, [1974] 2 All E.R. 257 (C.A.) — The Court disapproved of *Wallace v. Major, supra*, approving the test in *Ames v. Mac-Leod*, [1969] S.C. 1 (Scot.) as to whether the accused was "in a substantial sense controlling the movement and direction of the car" but being careful to indicate that the test is not exhaustive and must be subject to determining whether the activity in question can fall within the ordinary meaning of the word "driving".

R. v. Belanger, [1970] S.C.R. 567, [1970] 2 C.C.C. 206, 10 C.R.N.S. 373 — The accused, a passenger in a police cruiser, was being driven home when he grabbed the steering wheel, causing a head-on collision with an oncoming car. This was found to be evidence of dangerous driving.

Saycell v. Bool, [1948] 2 All E.R. 83 (D.C.) — A truck was standing at the head of an incline. There was no gas in the tank. The respondent released the brake and set the truck in motion by pushing it. He got into the driver's seat and let the truck go down the hill so as to get to his garage. He was found to be the driver.

R. v. Kitson (1955), 39 Cr. App. R. 66 (C.C.A.) — The accused was found to be driving where, after being asleep in the passenger seat of a motionless car, he awoke to find it in motion, reacted by grabbing the steering wheel, moving to the driver's seat and controlling it while it continued to roll down a hill.

Tyler v. Whatmore, [1976] Crim. L.R. 315 (Div. Ct.) — The person in the driver's seat was controlling the propulsion but not the braking. The accused passenger was controlling the steering and was in a position to control the braking. The accused passenger was properly convicted notwithstanding the fact that the person in the driver's seat had been convicted as a driver in a separate trial.

R. v. Martin, 2009 ONCJ 673, 2009 CarswellOnt 7335, 90 M.V.R. (5th) 317 — A driver includes someone steering and braking a towed vehicle with its engine removed.

"Highway"

Consumers Gas Co. v. Toronto, [1941] O.R. 175, [1940] 4 D.L.R. 670 (C.A.) — Unless its meaning is affected by context or association or definition, "highway" means, in its common uses, a public road or way open equally to everyone for travel.

Hughes v. J.H. Watkins & Co., 61 O.L.R. 587, [1928] 2 D.L.R. 176 (C.A.) — "Highway" means not only that part of the highway which is designed for motor traffic, but may include the curb or sidewalk. But see *R. v. Wall* (1968), 11 Cr. L. Q. 223 (Ont.), where it was held that a sidewalk was not within the definition of "highway" and that a charge of careless driving could not be based on the act of driving on the sidewalk.

Bell Telephone Co. v. Kan Yan Gan Co., [1940] O.R. 510, [1941] 1 D.L.R. 223 (C.A.) — "Highway" has been held to include not only the surface of a bridge, but also the road allowance underneath the bridge.

R. v. Red Line Ltd. (1930), 66 O.L.R. 53 (C.A.) — It was considered that the roadways of the Federal District Commission would probably be highways within the meaning of the Act, otherwise what rules of the road would apply not only in these, but other public grounds like those of the University of Toronto?

R. v. Taggart, [1966] 1 O.R. 764, [1966] 1 C.C.C. 137 (C.A.) — The National Capital Commission was held to have power to enact a regulation prohibiting the operation of commercial vehicles on a driveway within the property of the Commission without the Commission's consent.

Woodworth v. Farmer (1963), 39 D.L.R. (2d) 179 (N.S. T.D.) — The Act may in certain circumstances have application to privately owned roads to which the public has unrestricted right of access.

R. v. Fox (1979), 20 A.R. 451 (C.A.); *Galligos v. Louis* (1984), 33 M.V.R. 102, 15 D.L.R. (4th) 458 (B.C. S.C.); appeal dismissed (1987), 46 M.V.R. 288 (B.C. C.A.); *R. v. Ear* (1987), 1 M.V.R. (2d) 253, 82 A.R. 148 (Prov. Ct.) — A road on an Indian Reserve for the use of which non-residents must obtain a permit is not a highway.

R. v. Carr (1976), 16 N.B.R. (2d) 638 (Co. Ct.) — The accused was charged with driving a vehicle with metal tires on a highway contrary to the New Brunswick Act. The vehicle in question ran on two tracks or belts. The section of highway involved was closed off with signs which read "road closed to through traffic" and "pass at your own risk." The accused was convicted by a provincial court judge. On appeal to the County Court it was held that the appeal should be allowed. The metal tracks were not metal tires within the meaning of the Act. On the other hand, the section of highway on which the accused was driving constituted a highway within the meaning of the Act notwithstanding that it was closed to through traffic.

Cirillo v. R. (1981), 11 M.V.R. 16 (Ont. Co. Ct.) — The appellant, whose licence had been suspended, was employed as a backhoe operator removing debris from a demolition site. The portion of the street on which he was operating the backhoe had been blocked off to traffic. The appellant was convicted of driving while suspended. The issue on appeal was whether the street retained its characteristics as a "highway" for the purposes of the Highway Traffic Act notwithstanding that it had been blocked off to traffic. In allowing the appeal and setting aside the conviction it was held that during the period of time the defendant was operating the backhoe the general public did not have the privilege of passage on the area of the street which was blocked off. On a strict interpretation of "highway", it could not be said that the portion of the street in question was a "highway" during this period of time.

Gill v. Elwood, [1969] 2 O.R. 49, 4 D.L.R. (3d) 322 (Co. Ct.); affirmed [1970] 2 O.R. 59, 9 D.L.R. (3d) 681 (C.A.) — The definition of highway still requires that the area in question be open as a matter of right to all members of the public and before any such right can arise, there has to be a dedication of the land by the owner to the public and an acceptance by the public. Accordingly, a shopping centre plaza, being used only with the leave or licence of the owner, is not a highway within the meaning of the Act and the statutory rules of the road do not apply thereto.

R. v. Mansour, [1979] 2 S.C.R. 916 — A parking lot adjacent to an apartment building is not a "highway".

Woodbridge v. Bragg (1956), 5 D.L.R. (2d) 413 (B.C. S.C.); *Lawson v. Watts* (1957), 7 D.L.R. (2d) 758 (B.C. S.C.) — A service station area, although in a sense a public place, is not a highway since it is not designed or intended for, or used by, the general public for the passage of vehicles.

R. v. Cheadle (1972), 9 C.C.C. (2d) 111 (Alta. S.C.) — A parking lot of a university, access to which was limited to vehicles with windshield stickers, was held to be a highway.

R. v. Carlberg (1971), 3 C.C.C. (2d) 396 (Sask. Q.B.) — A privately owned right of way used by the public for parking and turning around upon occasion did not constitute a highway.

R. v. S. (No. 2), [1975] W.W.D. 57 (Man. Prov. Ct.) — The premises of an automatic car wash were held not to be a highway.

Laroque v. Lutz, 29 B.C.L.R. 300, [1981] 5 W.W.R. 1 (C.A.); varying 16 B.C.L.R. 348, [1980] 2 W.W.R. 97 (C.A.) — An accident that occurred on a logging road that was only open to the public on weekends was considered to have occurred on a "highway" as it happened during the time when the public could use the road.

Parrill v. Genge (1994), 8 M.V.R. (3d) 228, 125 Nfld. & P.E.I.R. 27, 389 A.P.R. 27 (Nfld. T.D.) — A highway includes a shoulder and road reservation. The Highway Traffic Act imposes liability on an owner of a snowmobile driven on a highway. A special degree of caution is required of snowmobile operators when operating them on a highway and in proximity of motor vehicles.

R. v. Douglas (1997), 35 O.R. (3d) 197, 29 M.V.R. (3d) 161 (Ont. Prov. Ct.) — The definition does not include private property such as a parking lot adjacent to an apartment building established primarily for the provision for its inhabitants and to which the public has access. A public road is one to which members of the public have access, not one constructed by and for a social group such as the residents of an apartment building.

R. v. Wong (1997), 29 M.V.R. (3d) 194 (B.C. S.C.) — The British Columbia Act is interpreted to include a ferry.

Becamon v. Wawanesa Mutual Insurance Co., 2009 ONCA 113, 2009 CarswellOnt 624, [2009] O.J. No. 478, (sub nom. *Shah v. Becamon*) 94 O.R. (3d) 297, 72 M.V.R. (5th) 51, 308 D.L.R. (4th) 80, 81 C.C.L.I. (4th) 1, 246 O.A.C. 24 — Although the parking lot was used by some drivers as a shortcut, both the intended use and the actual use were overwhelmingly as a parking area for customers. The strip mall's paramount use was not that of a highway.

R. v. Maddess, 2008 BCSC 1329, 2008 CarswellBC 2092, 74 M.V.R. (5th) 161 (S.C.) — The relationship between "roadway" and "shoulder" was reviewed under British Columbia's highway traffic regime.

R. v. Mills, 2011 CarswellOnt 2145, 14 M.V.R. (6th) 109, [2011] O.J. No. 1574 (C.J.) — A roadway when completely closed to the travelling public may lose its character as a highway. Where local traffic is permitted, it is a public roadway.

R. v. R. (M. D.), 2012 BCPC 3, 2012 CarswellBC 124, 27 M.V.R. (6th) 336 (B.C. P.C.) — A campground roadway was not a "highway" as defined in the British Columbia Act.

R. v. Lux (2012), 41 M.V.R. (6th) 22, 2012 SKCA 129, 2012 CarswellSask 849, 295 C.C.C. (3d) 236, [2013] 5 W.W.R. 732, 405 Sask. R. 214, 563 W.A.C. 214, [2012] S.J. No. 796 (Sask. C.A.) — Ontario courts have consistently held the definition of a "highway" does not include a shopping centre parking area or other private parking areas.

R. v. Hajivasilis (2013), 41 M.V.R. (6th) 175, 2013 ONCA 27, 2013 CarswellOnt 508, 114 O.R. (3d) 337, 302 O.A.C. 65, [2013] O.J. No. 253 (Ont. C.A.) — The *obiter* in *Becamon* [72 M.V.R. (5th) 51, 2009 CarswellOnt 624, 2009 ONCA 113] limiting the operation of the "entire HTA" to "highways" is wrong and should not be followed.

Right to Use

Big Point Club v. Lozon, [1943] O.R. 491, [1943] 4 D.L.R. 136 (H.C.) — Ownership of highways is held by municipalities in trust for all persons who have occasion to make use of them for purposes of communication or for other lawful purposes, or in order to gain access to or egress from adjacent lands. But, in the absence of express statutory authority, a municipality would appear to have no right to use or to permit the use of a highway for any purpose which would substantially interfere with or obstruct its primary use for such purposes.

Toleff v. Pember, [1944] O.W.N. 604 (H.C.) — While the primary purpose of the highway is for public travel and passage, there are many other modes of use which are recognized as permissible and legitimate, so long as public convenience is not interfered with. Accordingly, a peanut vendor has as much right on the highway as a motorist.

Ricketts v. Markdale (1900), 31 O.R. 610 (H.C.) — Children may play on the highways when there is no local prohibitory law and where their presence is not prejudicial to the ordinary user of the street for traffic and passage.

Jacob v. Tilbury, [1940] O.W.N. 530, [1941] 1 D.L.R. 456 at 458 (C.A.) — Generally speaking, and subject to any restrictions imposed by law, pedestrians may use the highways for the purpose of travel to and fro as the occasion may warrant, even where there are sidewalks. However, "the growth of motor traffic ... [has] caused a great falling off in this general use of the roadway, but that arises from the exercise of discretion on the part of pedestrians and not from any alteration of their right."

Groves v. Wentworth, [1939] O.R. 138 (C.A.) — It is not just the roadway that must be kept in repair — walls and other constructions erected upon the highway for the purpose of its use as a highway may be part of the highway that must be kept in repair.

Vancouver v. Burchill, [1932] S.C.R. 620, [1932] 4 D.L.R. 200 — At common law and as a member of the public, any individual has the right to the use of the highway under the protection of the law; the liability of the municipality exists towards every member of the public so using the highway.

May v. R., [1948] O.W.N. 669 (H.C.) — The standard of repair that a municipality is obliged to maintain is relative only. The municipality is not to be regarded as an insurer and therefore answerable in all circumstances for damages due to disrepair.

Foley v. East Flamborough (1897), 29 O.R. 139 (H.C.) — If the particular road is kept in such a reasonable state of repair that those requiring to use the road may, using ordinary care, pass to and fro upon it in safety, the requirement of the law is satisfied.

Sandlos v. Brant (1921), 49 O.L.R. 142, 58 D.L.R. 673 (C.A.) — "Repair" is a more comprehensive word than "maintain". To keep in repair necessarily includes maintenance; it involves original construction and putting in repair in the first instance and reconstruction when necessary.

Dubois v. City of Sault Ste. Marie, [1971] 1 O.R. 462, 15 D.L.R. (3d) 564 (C.A.); *Houser v. Township of West Lincoln* (1983), 29 M.P.L.R. 55 (Ont. C.A.); leave to appeal to S.C.C. refused (1983), 1 O.A.C. 400, 52 N.R. 239n; *R. v. Jennings*, [1966] S.C.R. 532, 57 D.L.R. (2d) 644; *Cook v. Bergevin* (1977), 16 O.R. (2d) 418, 2 M.P.L.R. 273 (H.C.); *Greatrex v. Ennismore* (1984), 33 M.V.R. 287 (Ont. H.C.) — There is a duty to erect signs to warn of a particular danger or hazard.

Barratt v. Dist. of North Vancouver, 8 M.V.R. 294, [1980] 2 S.C.R. 418 — The municipality exercises a power. It is under no statutory duty to do so. Its method of exercising its power is a matter of policy to be determined by the municipality itself. If in the implementation of its policy its servants acted negligently, causing damage, liability could arise, but the municipality could not be held negligent because it formulated one policy of operation rather than another.

Just v. B.C., [1989] 2 S.C.R. 1228 — Once a policy to inspect is established, it must be open to a litigant to attack the system as not having been adopted in a *bona fide* exercise of discretion, and to demonstrate that in all circumstances, including budgetary restraints, it is appropriate for a court to make a finding on the issue.

Bland v. R., [1941] O.R. 273, [1941] 4 D.L.R. 414 (C.A.) — The obligation to keep the entire highway in repair does not mean that all of it must be kept in the same condition of repair. Regard is always to be had to the use that is reasonable to expect will be made of the several parts of the highway, and they are to be kept in repair accordingly.

Millette v. Cote, [1971] 2 O.R. 155, 17 D.L.R. (3d) 247 (H.C.); affirmed [1972] 3 O.R. 224, 27 D.L.R. (3d) 676 (C.A.); varied on other grounds *R. v. Cote*, [1976] 1 S.C.R. 595, (sub nom. *Millette v. Kalogeropoulos*) — Liability may attach where a small portion of the highway is dangerous while generally the highway is in good condition.

Fuller v. Niagara Falls (1920), 48 O.L.R. 332, 56 D.L.R. 13 (C.A.) — Repair is not *per se* an admission or evidence of previous negligent non-repair, nor does it imply that the site was previously in a dangerous condition.

Terminal Warehouse Ltd. v. R., [1943] O.R. 133, [1943] 1 D.L.R. 556 (H.C.) — The duty of repair exists even while work is in progress, and extends to taking such care, by notice, of lighting, etc., as may be reasonably necessary for the protection of the public during the period of such temporary repairs.

Trueman v. R., [1932] O.R. 703 at 709, [1932] 4 D.L.R. 676 (C.A.) — A municipality will not be liable unless it has had notice of the condition of disrepair, and that "[on] the occurrence of a want of repair, the municipality is not liable unless, after such occurrence, [it] has had an opportunity to repair the defect, either by notice or knowledge, or by the lapse of such time as should have enabled it to have discovered the defect."

May v. R., [1948] O.W.N. 669 (H.C.) — Although notice of need of repair may be a controlling factor in the question whether that duty has been performed, it is not an ingredient of the duty to repair. There is no justification for the idea that the municipality is entitled to allow its roads to fall into disrepair and then escape liability on the ground that it had no notice or knowledge of the situation.

Trueman v. R., *supra*; *Trachsler v. Halton*, [1955] O.W.N. 909 (C.A.) — The duty is reasonably performed if the repair is made within a reasonable time after the municipality is informed, knows or should have acquired knowledge of the need of repair.

Gardam v. R., [1948] O.R. 61 (H.C.); affirmed [1948] O.R. 641, [1948] 4 D.L.R. 175 (C.A.); *Gilbert v. Georgetown*, [1950] O.W.N. 455 (H.C.); *Jamieson v. Edmonton* (1917), 54 S.C.R. 443 — Where a dangerous condition exists and the municipality could by due diligence have knowledge of the danger and thus take steps to avert it and warn persons using the highway, the failure to make an adequate inspection is a breach of the municipality's duty.

McCready v. Brant, [1939] S.C.R. 278, [1939] 3 D.L.R. 358; *Edgeworth v. R.*, [1937] O.R. 721, [1937] 4 D.L.R. 136 (C.A.); *Longo v. R.*, [1938] O.W.N. 475 (H.C.) — Ice and snow ruts on the highway in winter will not generally amount to non-repair. A municipality is not under a duty to remove snow and ice from the highway after every storm creating the conditions common to the winter climate in Ontario.

Newell v. Morrison, [1954] O.R. 656, [1954] 3 D.L.R. 574 (C.A.) — The failure to sand of itself will not impose liability even though icy conditions might make travel unsafe on grades or hills.

Caswell v. St. Mary's etc. Road Co. (1869), 28 U.C.Q.B. 247 (H.C.); *Hogg v. Brooke* (1904), 7 O.L.R. 273 — If a small area is in very dangerous condition, exceptionally and particularly dangerous as distinct from the rest of the road, and it can be put in a safe state at a reasonable expense, then a duty lies to make the place fit and safe for travel.

McCready v. Brant, *supra* — The question is whether there is a trap to the knowledge, actual or implied, of the municipality such as to cast a duty on it either to repair or to prevent the use of the road at such point.

Curlis v. Bolton, [1939] O.R. 201 (H.C.) — The obligation of the municipality to keep the highway in repair does not extend to keeping all parts of a sidewalk accurately level. Slight inequalities of the surface which might lead to an exceptional slip or fall are not to be considered as a condition of disrepair. Whether the differences in the level of slabs in the pavement amount to non-repair will depend on the particular circumstances.

Gregson v. Vancouver, [1940] 2 W.W.R. 85, [1940] 3 D.L.R. 105 (B.C. C.A.) — The reasonable repair of sidewalks must take into consideration the reasonable use of them by pedestrians. The fact that they wear low or dangerously high heels, or no heels at all, or have crutches, is among the circumstances that have to be considered in determining reasonable repair and also reasonable use.

Belling v. Hamilton (1902), 3 O.L.R. 318 (Div. Ct) — If a pedestrian chooses to walk on the road and not on the sidewalk he or she must take the road as he or she finds it. The pedestrian has a right to expect to find it reasonably safe for vehicles, but has no right to expect any higher degree of repair.

Paul v. Dauphin, [1941] 1 W.W.R. 43, [1941] 1 D.L.R. 775 (Man. K.B.); affirmed [1941] 2 W.W.R. 224, [1941] 3 D.L.R. 756 (Man. C.A.) — The requirement of proving gross negligence means that the duty of preventing accidents due to "snow or ice upon the sidewalks" is shifted largely from the municipality to the pedestrian, the municipality's duty being thereby greatly decreased and that of the pedestrian being correspondingly increased.

Humenick v. Toronto, [1949] O.R. 362, [1949] 3 D.L.R. 104 (H.C.) — A plaintiff suing for injury from ice or snow must show very great neglect by the municipality in the performance of its duty.

Domanski v. Hamilton, [1959] O.R. 262, 18 D.L.R. (2d) 765 (C.A.); *Hancock v. Gillespie* (1956), 20 W.W.R. 657, 7 D.L.R. (2d) 632 (Man. Q.B.); *Reynolds v. Vancouver*, [1937] 3 W.W.R. 46 (B.C. S.C.) — There is no special duty with regard to sections of the roadway where bus stops are located; the municipality need only show reasonable repair.

Kingston v. Drennan (1897), 27 S.C.R. 46 — The object of requiring notice under the Municipal Act is to enable a defendant to investigate and to be prepared to meet the plaintiff's case by getting at the facts while the evidence is available and fresh in the minds of the witnesses.

McGregor v. R., 35 O.W.N. 166, [1929] 1 D.L.R. 181 (H.C.) — The notice will be sufficient if it states that the plaintiff met with an accident at a definite place, the date of the accident, and the cause thereof.

Killeleagh v. Brantford (1916), 38 O.L.R. 35, 32 D.L.R. 457 (C.A.); *McInnes v. Egremont* (1903), 5 O.L.R. 713 (Div. Ct.) — However, even if the place and time are not properly or accurately set out, and even if the wrong date was given, the action will not be barred if the defendant knew the relevant facts and was not prejudiced.

Filip v. Waterloo (City) (1992), 41 M.V.R. (2d) 190, 12 M.P.L.R. (2d) 113, 12 C.R.R. (2d) 113, 60 O.A.C. 298, 98 D.L.R. (4th) 534, 12 C.R.R. (2d) 113 (C.A.) — Overruling *Colangelo v. Mississauga (City)*; *Morencie v. Windsor (City)* (1988), 66 O.R. (2d) 29, 12 M.V.R. (2d) 1, 39 M.P.L.R. 209, 46 C.C.L.T. 188, 30 C.P.C. (2d) 92, 30 O.A.C. 26, 41 C.R.R. 85, 53 D.L.R. (4th) 283 (C.A.), the provisions in the Municipal Act respecting the snow and ice exception do not infringe s. 15 of the Charter of Rights.

Mero v. Waterloo (Regional Municipality) (1992), 37 M.V.R. (2d) 56 (Ont. C.A.) — The law in Ontario has developed on the assumption that there is no common law liability upon a municipality respecting maintenance of highways except for nuisance and, as the natural evolution of what might have been termed a very restrictive statutory cause of action in s. 284(1) of the Municipal Act has progressed, the courts have been increasingly liberal in the interpretation of what constitutes non-repair of a highway. The scope of s. 284 is now so broad as to encompass "something wrong with the highway." As the opportunity for plaintiffs to base a cause of action upon s. 284(1) has expanded, so has the ambit of the limitation period in s. 284(2). All factual situations which fit within the ambit of what the jurisprudence has determined to be non-repair of the highway or nuisance should be accorded benefit of presumed liability provided in s. 284 for claims for non-repair and should be embraced by the limitation period in s. 284(2) and s. 285.

Osborne (Litigation Guardian of) v. Bruce (County) (1999), 39 M.V.R. (3d) 159 (Ont. Gen. Div.) — The county was partly responsible for an accident because a stop sign was obstructed by a hill and tree branches and was not visible until motorists were close to the sign. There was no stop-ahead sign.

Ryan v. Victoria (City) (1999), 40 M.V.R. (3d) 1, 50 M.P.L.R. (2d) 1, 234 N.R. 201, 168 D.L.R. (4th) 513, [1999] 6 W.W.R. 61 (S.C.C.) — A railway was negligent with respect to the width of flangeways and subject to the ordinary principles of negligence.

Lewis (Guardian ad litem of) v. British Columbia (1997), 31 M.V.R. (3d) 149, 220 N.R. 81, 153 D.L.R. (4th) 594, [1997] 3 S.C.R. 1145, 43 B.C.L.R. (3d) 154, [1998] 5 W.W.R. 732 (S.C.C.); *Mochinski v. Trendline Industries Ltd.* (1997), 31 M.V.R. (3d) 193, 220 N.R. 148, 154 D.L.R. (4th) 212, [1997] 3 S.C.R. 1176, 43 B.C.L.R. (3d) 149, [1998] 5 W.W.R. 756 (S.C.C.) — The applicable statutes clearly, indicated that the Ministry had the paramount authority and direction for repairs and maintenance of the highways. The imposition of personal liability on the Ministry for its contractor's failure to discharge the duty to take care ancillary to the Ministry's statutory authority may give rise to a non-delegable duty to use reasonable care. Policy factors, such as the vulnerability of the travelling public, supported the finding that the Ministry should be responsible for the negligence of its independent contractors.

Richard v. New Brunswick, 2009 CarswellNB 268, 2009 CarswellNB 447, 2009 NBCA 40, 84 M.V.R. (5th) 181, 889 A.P.R. 209, 345 N.B.R. (2d) 209 (C.A.) — The award against the province for faulty design of a 90-degree turn and a lack of signage on a new highway was upheld where the single vehicle tractor trailer rolled over killing the experienced driver.

Deering v. Scugog (Township), 2010 ONSC 5502, 2010 CarswellOnt 7526, [2010] O.J. No. 4229, 76 M.P.L.R. (4th) 178, 3 M.V.R. (6th) 33, 77 C.C.L.T. (3d) 167 (S.C.J.); affirmed 2012 ONCA 386, 2012 CarswellOnt 7056, 93 C.C.L.T. (3d) 198, 97 M.P.L.R. (4th) 49, 33 M.V.R. (6th) 1, [2012] O.J. No. 2546; leave to appeal refused 2012 CarswellOnt 15883, 2012 CarswellOnt 15884, 447 N.R. 385 (note), 309 O.A.C. 398 (note), [2012] S.C.C.A. No. 351 (S.C.C.) — The municipalities failed in their duties to maintain the road in reasonable repair. The municipalities had "rehabilitated" the road and opened it without any markings, signage, or any assessment of the potential hazard.

Meghji v. Lee, 2011 BCSC 1108, 2011 CarswellBC 2126, 19 M.V.R. (6th) 200 (B.C. S.C.); additional reasons 2012 BCSC 379, 2012 CarswellBC 696, 31 B.C.L.R. (5th) 410, 25 C.P.C. (7th) 29, 30 M.V.R. (6th) 317; reversed in part 2014 BCCA 105, 2014 CarswellBC 726, 60 B.C.L.R. (5th) 121, 50 C.P.C. (7th) 315, 65 M.V.R. (6th) 1, [2014] 6 W.W.R. 489, 353 B.C.A.C. 7, 603 W.A.C. 7; additional reasons (2014), 2014 BCCA 345, 2014 CarswellBC 2649, 60 B.C.L.R. (5th) 167, 56 C.P.C. (7th) 127, 65 M.V.R. (6th) 47, [2015] 5 W.W.R. 203, 360 B.C.A.C. 309, 617 W.A.C. 309; reversed in part 2014 BCCA 105, 2014 CarswellBC 726, 60 B.C.L.R. (5th) 121, 50 C.P.C. (7th) 315, 65 M.V.R. (6th) 1, [2014] 6 W.W.R. 489, 353 B.C.A.C. 7, 603 W.A.C. 7 — Liability was apportioned at 10% for a poor design of the road which put power lines in conflict with overhead lighting, making visibility more difficult.

Fordham v. Dutton-Dunwich (Municipality) (2014), 2014 CarswellOnt 17325, 17 C.C.L.T. (4th) 1, 70 M.V.R. (6th) 1, 2014 ONCA 891, 31 M.P.L.R. (5th) 269, 327 O.A.C. 302 (Ont. C.A.) — A municipality's duty of repair is limited to ensuring that its roads could be driven safely by ordinary drivers who exercised reasonable care. The duty of reasonable repair did not extend to making roads safe for negligent drivers.

"Motor Vehicle"

R. v. Swarychewski (1957), 22 W.W.R. 91, 118 C.C.C. 126, 26 C.R. 176 (Man. C.A.); *R. v. MacKenzie*, [1961] O.W.N. 344 (Dist. Ct.) — Since a farm tractor is excluded from the definition, a provincial prohibition from driving does not prevent a person from driving a farm tractor or make him or her guilty thereby of an offence under the Criminal Code of driving while disqualified, notwithstanding that a farm tractor is a motor vehicle within the meaning of the Criminal Code.

Fortin v. Laplante (2000), 47 O.R. (3d) 443, 129 O.A.C. 317, 1 M.V.R. (4th) 72, 19 C.C.L.I. (3d) 161 (C.A.); affirming (1999), 8 M.V.R. (4th) 108 (Ont. S.C.J.); leave to appeal refused (November 9, 2000), Doc. 27885 (S.C.C.) — Although a snowmobile is required to have insurance, it is neither a motor vehicle nor an automobile under the Insurance Act.

Grummett v. Federation Insurance Co. of Canada (1999), 46 O.R. (3d) 340, 1 M.V.R. (4th) 75 (S.C.J.) — In attempting to determine if a vehicle is an automobile for insurance purposes, it is appropriate to consider the function and purpose of the vehicle. A race car is not an automobile.

Adams v. Pineland Amusements Ltd., 2007 CarswellOnt 7800, [2008] I.L.R. I-4660, 88 O.R. (3d) 321, 231 O.A.C. 177, 2007 ONCA 844, 55 C.C.L.I. (4th) 1, 54 M.V.R. (5th) 25, 289 D.L.R. (4th) 744 (C.A.); reversing 2006 CarswellOnt 8322, 42 M.V.R. (5th) 198, 46 C.C.L.I. (4th) 47, 85 O.R. (3d) 147, [2007] I.L.R. I-4570 (Ont. S.C.J.) — The motions judge erred in basing his conclusion that the go-kart was an automobile for purposes of the *Insurance Act* because it could be driven on a highway. The proper question was whether the go-kart required insurance at the time and circumstances of the accident in the case at bar. The go-kart here did not require motor vehicle insurance as it was operated on a separate track.

R. v. Joncas, 2007 CarswellNB 208, 2007 CarswellNB 209, 49 M.V.R. (5th) 100, 2007 NBCA 28, 313 N.B.R. (2d) 353, 809 A.P.R. 353, [2007] N.B.J. No. 152 (N.B. C.A.); affirming 2006 CarswellNB 803, 800 A.P.R. 100, 310 N.B.R. (2d) 100, 49 M.V.R. (5th) 91, 316 N.B.R. (2d) 1, 816 A.P.R. 1, 2006 NBQB 306 (N.B. Q.B.) — Convictions were entered for operating, on a highway, a vehicle whose registration and safety inspection certificate was expired arising out of the use of a modified truck which had a flatbed, and was hauling an open trailer with bales of hay on a highway.

Walsh v. Marwood Ltd., 2009 CarswellNS 123, 2009 NSSC 15, 275 N.S.R. (2d) 92, 877 A.P.R. 92, 83 M.V.R. (5th) 168 — A forklift is not a vehicle which requires registration in Nova Scotia.

R. v. Martin, 2009 ONCJ 673, 2009 CarswellOnt 7335, 90 M.V.R. (5th) 317 — A driver includes someone steering and braking a towed vehicle with its engine removed.

R. v. Vanberlo, 2010 ONCA 242, 2010 CarswellOnt 1929, (sub nom. *R. v. Van Berlo*) 260 O.A.C. 291, 94 M.V.R. (5th) 11 — To be "converted for a specific use in farming", the vehicle must be changed significantly enough that, viewed objectively, its essential character or function has been transformed for that specific use, although it may retain some limited capacity for other functions.

Wormall v. Insurance Corp. of British Columbia, 2011 BCCA 166, 2011 CarswellBC 791, 16 B.C.L.R. (5th) 282, 95 C.C.L.I. (4th) 243, 11 M.V.R. (6th) 11, 303 B.C.A.C. 177, 512 W.A.C. 177 — An attached crane on a truck was used to adjust the truck's load following inspection at a government weigh scale.

"Stop"

R. v. MacAdam (1976), 22 N.S.R. (2d) 204, 31 A.P.R. 204 (Co. Ct.) — On a charge of failing to stop, a stop means a full stop where all forward motion ceases.

"Through Highway"

R. v. Snelling, [1952] O.W.N. 214 (H.C.) — Judicial notice cannot be taken of the passing of a municipal by-law designating a through highway. Such a by-law and its terms must be proved.

R. v. Lavelle (1958), 29 C.R. 156, 122 C.C.C. 111 (Ont. S.C.); *R. v. Clark* (1974), 3 O.R. (2d) 716, 18 C.C.C. (2d) 52 (C.A.); reversing (1973), 1 O.R. (2d) 210, 24 C.R.N.S. 65, 14 C.C.C. (2d) 73 (H.C.); *R. v. McLaren* (1981), 10 M.V.R. 42 (Ont. C.A.); *R. v. Margetis* (1988), 9 M.V.R. (2d) 19 (Ont. H.C.) — It is not necessary that proof be given that the sign complies with the regulations; a *prima facie* case is established by evidence that a stop sign has been erected in a particular location and by production of a certified copy of the by-law establishing the through highway with a form of approval typed on it.

1.1 Application of Act to places other than highways — **The Lieutenant Governor in Council may make regulations providing that this Act or any provision of this Act or of a regulation applies to a specified place or class of place that is not a highway.**

2007, c. 13, s. 2

Case Law

R. v. Hajivasilis (2013), 41 M.V.R. (6th) 175, 2013 ONCA 27, 2013 CarswellOnt 508, 114 O.R. (3d) 337, 302 O.A.C. 65, [2013] O.J. No. 253 (Ont. C.A.) — The section contemplates the extension of the entire Act or parts of it to places other than a highway.

Proposed Addition — 1.2

1.2 Modification of application of Act or regulations — **The Lieutenant Governor in Council may make regulations,**

    (a) providing that any Part or provision of this Act, or any regulation or provision of a regulation, applies to a specified class of vehicles or to drivers, operators, owners or lessees of a specified class of vehicles in addition to the vehicles, drivers, operators, owners or lessees that the Part, provision or regulation otherwise applies to, prescribing modifications to that Part, provision or regulation for any such application and prescribing conditions and circumstances for any such application;

    (b) exempting a specified class of vehicles, or drivers, operators, owners or lessees of a specified class of vehicles, from any Part or provision of this Act, or any regulation or provision of a regulation, and prescribing conditions and circumstances for any such exemption;

    (c) defining "operator" and "owner" for the purposes of regulations made under clause (a) or (b).

2016, c. 5, Sched. 12, s. 2 [Not in force at date of publication.]

PART I — ADMINISTRATION

2. Powers and duties of Ministry — Where by this Act powers are conferred or duties are imposed upon the Ministry, the powers may be exercised and the duties discharged by the Minister.

3. (1) Registrar of Motor Vehicles — There shall be a Registrar of Motor Vehicles appointed by the Lieutenant Governor in Council.

(2) Duties — The Registrar shall act under the instructions of the Minister and Deputy Minister and has general supervision over all matters relating to highway traffic within Ontario, and shall perform the duties that are assigned to him or her by this Act, by the Lieutenant Governor in Council, or by the Minister or Deputy Minister.

(3) Delegation of powers, etc., to Deputy Minister and Registrar — The Minister may authorize the Deputy Minister and the Registrar or either of them to exercise and discharge in his or her place any of the powers conferred or the duties imposed upon him or her under this Act or the regulations and, where both the Deputy Minister and the Registrar are so authorized, either of them may exercise and discharge any of the powers and duties.

(4) Delegation of powers of Registrar — The Deputy Minister, with the consent of the Minister, may authorize any public servant or servants in the Ministry to exercise any or all of the powers and duties of the Registrar.

1996, c. 20, s. 1

Commentary

The Act is administered by the Ministry of Transportation and Communications. The administrator of the Act is the Registrar of Motor Vehicles. See s. 205 of the Act regarding the general duties of the Registrar.

4. Deputy Registrar — There shall be a Deputy Registrar appointed by the Lieutenant Governor in Council who shall have all the powers and may perform all the duties of the Registrar.

4.0.1 Forms — The Minister may require that forms approved by the Minister be used for any purpose under this Act.

2008, c. 17, s. 29

4.1 (1) Power to do things electronically — Anything that the Minister, the Ministry or the Registrar is required or authorized to do or to provide under this Act may be done or provided by electronic means or in an electronic format.

(2) Same — Anything that any person is required or authorized to do or to provide to the Minister, the Ministry or the Registrar under this Act may be done or provided by electronic means or in an electronic format, in the circumstances and in the manner specified by the Ministry.

2007, c. 13, s. 3

5. (1) Regulations re fees — The Lieutenant Governor in Council may make regulations,

(a) providing for the payment of fees for the issue, renewal, replacement or transfer of permits, licences and number plates under this Act and prescribing the amount of the fees;

(b) providing for the payment of fees for copies of or access to any writing, paper or document filed in the Ministry pursuant to this Act or any statement containing information from the records of the Ministry and prescribing the amount of the fees;

(c) providing for the payment of fees upon application to the Ministry for any approval required under this Act in respect of any equipment to be used on a vehicle and prescribing the amount of the fees;

(d) providing for and governing the imposition and payment of administrative fees for the reinstatement of suspended licences;

(d.1) providing for exemptions from payment of the administrative fees prescribed under clause (d) and prescribing conditions and circumstances for any such exemption;

(e) providing for the payment of administrative fees for handling dishonoured payments tendered for the issue, renewal, replacement, transfer, validation or reinstatement of permits, licences and number plates;

(f) prescribing a rate of interest for purposes of subsection (2), when interest starts to run and the method of calculating the interest;

(g) prescribing penalties for the purposes of subsections (2) and 5.1(2) and the method of determining the amount of any penalty;

(h) prescribing fees for anything done or provided by or on behalf of the Minister, the Ministry or the Registrar under this Act;

(i) prescribing consequences in regard to a licence, permit or number plate where a fee or penalty required or imposed under this Act is not paid or its payment is dishonoured.

(2) Interest and penalties when payment dishonoured — Where payment for any fee or tax is dishonoured, interest at a prescribed rate may be charged on the amount of the payment and a penalty may be imposed.

(3) Fees may include cost recovery portion — A fee prescribed or set under this Act for the issuance or renewal of any permit or licence or for the validation of any permit may include a portion that is for the recovery of costs related to public highway infrastructure.

1994, c. 27, s. 138(2), (3); 1996, c. 20, s. 2; 2006, c. 33, Sched. M, s. 1; 2007, c. 13, s. 4

Related Provisions: See O. Reg. 340/94, Driver's Licences; R.R.O. 1990, Reg. 628, Vehicle Permits.

5.1 (1) Administrative monetary penalties — The Lieutenant Governor in Council may make regulations,

(a) providing for and governing the imposition and payment of administrative monetary penalties payable by persons whose driver's licence has been suspended, including prescribing different penalties based on the number of times the licence has previously been suspended and on the grounds for suspension;

Proposed Amendment — 5.1(1)(a)

(a) providing for and governing the imposition and payment of administrative penalties payable by persons whose driver's licence has been suspended, including prescribing different penalties based on the number of times the licence has previously been suspended and on the grounds for suspension;
2014, c. 9, Sched. 2, s. 2(1) [To come into force January 1, 2017.]

(b) providing for exemptions from payment of an administrative monetary penalty and prescribing conditions and circumstances for any such exemption.

Proposed Amendment — 5.1(1)(b)

(b) providing for exemptions from payment of an administrative penalty and prescribing conditions and circumstances for any such exemption.
2014, c. 9, Sched. 2, s. 2(2) [To come into force January 1, 2017.]

(2) Interest and penalties when payment dishonoured — Where payment for an administrative monetary penalty is dishonoured, interest at a prescribed rate may be charged on the amount of the payment and a further penalty may be imposed.

Proposed Amendment — 5.1(2)

(2) Interest and penalties when payment dishonoured — Where payment for an administrative penalty is dishonoured, interest at a prescribed rate may be charged on the amount of the payment and a further penalty may be imposed.
2014, c. 9, Sched. 2, s. 2(3) [To come into force January 1, 2017.]

2007, c. 13, s. 5

Related Provisions: See O. Reg. 273/07, Administrative Monetary Penalties.

5.2 (1) Cancellation of permit, licence where false information is provided — If the Minister is satisfied that any information provided by the holder of a vehicle permit or driver's licence to the Ministry or the Ministry's delegate is false, the Minister may, without prior notice to the holder, do either or both of the following:

1. Cancel the vehicle permit or driver's licence.

2. Correct and amend the Ministry's records.

(2) Benefits obtained under false information nullified — The holder of a vehicle permit or driver's licence cancelled under subsection (1) is subject to the requirements of this Act without the benefit of anything done under this Act in reliance on the false information.

2008, c. 17, s. 30

5.3 (1) **Cancellation of permit, licence where information on permit, licence is incorrect** — The Minister may cancel a vehicle permit or driver's licence if the Minister is satisfied that any information appearing on the vehicle permit or driver's licence is incorrect.

(2) **Notice to holder** — Before taking any action under subsection (1), the Minister shall cause notice to be given to the holder of the vehicle permit or driver's licence of his or her intention to cancel the permit or licence and the notice shall state that the holder has 60 days from the date of the notice to provide the Minister with the correct information.

(2.1) **Same** — Notice under subsection (2) is sufficiently given to the holder of the vehicle permit or driver's licence if delivered personally or mailed to the latest address or any previous address of the holder on the records of the Ministry or to another address at which there is reason to believe the holder may be found.

(3) **Holder to provide correct information** — The Minister shall not take the proposed action under subsection (1) if the holder of the vehicle permit or driver's licence provides the Minister with revised information in the form and manner required by the Minister within 60 days after the date of the notice under subsection (2) and the Minister is satisfied that the revised information is correct.

(4) **Holder fails to provide correct information** — If the holder fails to provide the correct information as required under subsection (3), the Minister may take the action proposed under subsection (1), but not earlier than 60 days after the date of the notice, and the Minister shall mail notice of the action taken to the holder at the latest address of the holder on the records of the Ministry.

2008, c. 17, s. 30; 2015, c. 27, Sched. 7, s. 2

5.4 (1) **Protection from personal liability** — No action or other proceeding for damages shall be instituted against the Minister, the Registrar of Motor Vehicles, a public servant, a delegate or agent of the Minister for anything done in good faith in the execution or intended execution of a power or duty under section 5.2 or 5.3.

(2) **Crown not relieved of liability** — Despite subsections 5(2) and (4) of the *Proceedings Against the Crown Act*, subsection (1) does not relieve the Crown of liability in respect of a tort committed by a person mentioned in subsection (1) to which it would otherwise be subject.

2008, c. 17, s. 30

PART II — PERMITS

6. (1) **Definitions** — In this Part,

"CAVR cab card" means a permit issued by the Ministry pursuant to the Canadian Agreement on Vehicle Registration;

"holder", when used in relation to a permit, means the person in whose name the plate portion of a permit is issued;

"IRP cab card" means a permit issued by the Ministry or another jurisdiction pursuant to the International Registration Plan.

"IRP inspector" means a person appointed as an IRP inspector under subsection 7.3(1);

"lessee" means a person who has leased a vehicle for a period of not less than one year;

"number", when used in relation to a permit or plate means a number, a series of letters or a combination of letters and numbers, and **"numbered"**, when so used, has a corresponding meaning;

"permit" means a permit issued under subsection 7(7) consisting, except when the permit is a CAVR cab card or an IRP cab card, of a vehicle portion and a plate portion.

"police officer" includes an officer appointed for carrying out the provisions of this Act;

"prescribed" means prescribed by the regulations;

"validate" means render in force for the prescribed period of time and **"validation"** and **"validated"** have corresponding meanings.

(2) Person authorized by Minister — Where, in this Part, it is specified that an act may be done by the Ministry, it may be done by a person authorized by the Minister to do the act.

1999, c. 12, Sched. R, s. 1(2), (3); 2002, c. 22, s. 95

Commentary

Effective December 1, 1982, the system of registering vehicles and assigning number plates to vehicles was revised. All drivers, except in the case of self-propelled implements of husbandry, must have a valid permit and their vehicles and trailers must bear valid licence plates. In lieu of a permit, a driver may have a CAVR cab card issued by the Ministry pursuant to the Canadian Agreement on Vehicle Registration.

A permit is issued consisting of a vehicle portion that links number plates to a vehicle and a plate portion that will link the same number plates to a person. Upon the vehicle being sold or otherwise transferred, the transferor removes the plates from the vehicle and retains the plate portion of the permit. The vehicle portion of the permit is turned over to the transferee. The transferee either affixes his or her plates to the vehicle or obtains plates from the Ministry. In either case, the transferee surrenders the vehicle portion of the permit and receives a new permit linking those plates to the vehicle and to him or her. Provision is made to allow a transferee six days to obtain a new permit. Number plates, therefore, are never to be transferred, although any person may have several different number plates.

Permits, except for trailers, continue to require periodic validation.

Provision is made for the issuing of various types of permits, such as an unfit vehicle permit or a permit that is not validated, which provide evidence of registration of the vehicle in the name of the owner but do not permit the operation of the vehicle on the highway.

Provision is made for exemptions, by regulation, which deal with matters such as estate transfers and transfers by car dealers.

Provision is also made in respect of vehicles that are leased for a year or more.

The Ministry has authority to refuse to validate a permit where the applicant is in default of payment of parking fines or is indebted for vehicle-related fees or taxes.

Drivers are required to carry the vehicle permit or a copy thereof and to surrender it to the police, on demand, for inspection.

The Red Tape Reduction Act, 1999, S.O. 1999, c. 12, Sched. R. (ss. 1(2), 1(3), 2(1), 2(3), 2(5), 5(1), and 6(1) in force January 1, 2001) would amend ss. 6, 7, 12 and 14 of the Highway Traffic Act to facilitate Ontario's participation in the International Registration Plan, which contains reciprocal provisions in respect of commercial motor vehicles that travel across provincial or international borders. The Plan provides for the issuance of IRP cab cards as permits for these vehicles and for the appointment of registration and licence fees in each member jurisdiction on the basis of the distances travelled in each jurisdiction. Persons residing or based in other jurisdictions that are members of the Plan are exempt from the requirements of and fees prescribed under Part II of the Highway Traffic Act.

Related Provisions: Section 1(2) of the Act provides that whenever a permit or licence may be suspended or revoked, both may be suspended or revoked; O. Reg. 424/97, Commercial Motor Vehicle Operators' Information; O. Reg. 11/04, International Registration Plan; R.R.O. 1990, Reg. 628, Vehicle Permits.

7. (1) Permit, etc., required — No person shall drive a motor vehicle on a highway unless,

> **(a) there exists a currently validated permit for the vehicle;**

> **(b) there are displayed on the vehicle, in the prescribed manner,**

>> **(i) number plates issued in accordance with the regulations showing the number of the permit issued for the vehicle, or**

>> **(ii) number plates described in subsection (7.2) if the vehicle is an historic vehicle and the Ministry has issued a currently validated permit for it; and**

> **(c) evidence of the current validation of the permit is affixed, in the prescribed manner, to,**

>> **(i) one of the number plates mentioned in subclause (b)(i) displayed on the vehicle, or**

>> **(ii) to a mini-plate attached to the number plate exposed on the rear of the vehicle, if number plates described in subsection (7.2) are displayed on the vehicle.**

(1.1) Historic vehicle — In this section,

"historic vehicle" means a motor vehicle that,

> **(a) is at least 30 years old, and**

> **(b) is substantially unchanged or unmodified from the original manufacturer's product.**

(2) **Self-propelled implement of husbandry** — Subsection (1) applies to a self-propelled implement of husbandry that is operated on a highway other than when travelling from farm to farm in relation to the specific use for which it was manufactured, designed, redesigned, converted or reconstructed or in travelling to or from such places as may be necessary for the maintenance or repair of the vehicle.

(3) **Exemptions for cls. (1)(b, c)** — Clauses (1)(b) and (c) do not apply in respect of a motor vehicle for which the permit is a CAVR cab card or an IRP cab card.

(4) **Permit for trailer** — No person shall draw a trailer on a highway unless,

(a) there exists a permit for the trailer; and

(b) there is displayed on the trailer, in the prescribed manner, a number plate showing the number of the permit issued for the trailer.

(5) **Permit to be carried** — Subject to subsection (6), every driver of a motor vehicle on a highway shall carry,

(a) the permit for it or a true copy thereof; and

(b) where the motor vehicle is drawing a trailer, the permit for the trailer or a true copy thereof,

and shall surrender the permits or copies for inspection upon the demand of a police officer.

(6) **Same** — Where a permit is a CAVR cab card or an IRP cab card, the requirements of subsection (5) apply to the original permit and not to a copy and to the permit from the jurisdiction that issued the number plates for the vehicle.

(7) **Issuance of permits and number plates** — The Ministry may issue a permit of any prescribed class, number plates and evidence of validation to any person who meets the requirements of this Act and the regulations.

(7.1) **Permit for historic vehicle** — If the Ministry issues a permit to an applicant for an historic vehicle and the applicant is in possession of number plates described in subsection (7.2), the number of the permit shall be the same as the number shown on those number plates.

(7.2) **Number plates for historic vehicle** — Subsection (7.1) applies to number plates that,

(a) are Ontario number plates that were issued during the year of manufacture of the motor vehicle;

(b) are in a condition satisfactory to the Ministry; and

(c) show no numbers that duplicate the number of any other existing permit.

(8) **Use of plates** — The Ministry may authorize number plates in an applicant's possession for use on a vehicle.

(9) **Refusal to validate** — Validation of a permit may be refused where the permit holder is indebted to the Minister of Finance in respect of a vehicle-related fee or tax or in respect of a penalty imposed under this Act.

(10) No permit validation when fines unpaid — Where a permit holder is in default of payment of a fine imposed for a parking infraction or of a fine imposed upon conviction of an offence under subsection 39.1(2), an order or direction may be made under section 69 of the *Provincial Offences Act* directing that validation of that person's permit and issuance of a new permit to that person shall be refused until the fine is paid.

Proposed Amendment — 7(10)

(10) No permit when fines unpaid re specified offences — If the payment of a fine imposed on conviction for an offence described in subsection (11) is in default, an order or direction may be made under section 69 of the *Provincial Offences Act* directing that,

(a) a permit held by the convicted person not be validated until the fine is paid; and

(b) no permit be issued to the convicted person until the fine is paid.

2015, c. 14, s. 4(1) [Not in force at date of publication.]

(11) No permit issued when fines unpaid — Where a person who is not a permit holder is in default of payment of a fine imposed for a parking infraction or of a fine imposed upon conviction of an offence under subsection 39.1(2), an order or direction may be made under section 69 of the *Provincial Offences Act* directing that the issuance of a permit shall be refused to that person until the fine is paid.

Proposed Amendment — 7(11)

(11) Same, specified offences — The following are the offences referred to in subsection (10):

1. A parking infraction.

2. An offence under subsection 39.1(2).

3. An offence where the conviction is based on evidence obtained through the use of a photo-radar system.

4. An offence where the conviction is based on evidence obtained through the use of a red light camera system.

5. An offence under subsection 175(19) or (20).

2015, c. 14, s. 4(1) [Not in force at date of publication.]

(11.1) No permit when photo-radar fine unpaid — If an owner of a vehicle is in default of payment of a fine imposed for a conviction based on evidence obtained through the use of a photo-radar system, an order or direction may be made under section 69 of the *Provincial Offences Act* directing that,

(a) if the owner holds a permit, validation of that owner's permit be refused until the fine is paid; or

(b) if the owner does not hold a permit, the issuance of a permit be refused until the fine is paid.

Proposed Repeal — 7(11.1)

(11.1) [Repealed 2015, c. 14, s. 4(1). Not in force at date of publication.]

(11.2) No permit when red light camera fine unpaid — If an owner of a vehicle is in default of payment of a fine imposed for a conviction based on evidence obtained through the use of a red light camera system, an order or direction may be made under section 69 of the *Provincial Offences Act* directing that,

(a) if the owner holds a permit, validation of that owner's permit be refused until the fine is paid; or

(b) if the owner does not hold a permit, the issuance of a permit be refused until the fine is paid.

Proposed Repeal — 7(11.2)

(11.2) [Repealed 2015, c. 14, s. 4(1). Not in force at date of publication.]

(11.3) No permit when owner's fine for passing school bus unpaid — If an owner of a vehicle is in default of payment of a fine imposed for a conviction of an offence under subsection 175(19) or (20), an order or direction may be made under section 69 of the *Provincial Offences Act* directing that,

(a) if the owner holds a permit, validation of that owner's permit be refused until the fine is paid; or

(b) if the owner does not hold a permit, the issuance of a permit be refused until the fine is paid.

Proposed Repeal — 7(11.3)

(11.3) [Repealed 2015, c. 14, s. 4(1). Not in force at date of publication.]

(12) Exception to permit denials — If a person holds more than one permit and an order or direction in respect of that person is made under section 69 of the *Provincial Offences Act* pursuant to this section, the order or direction shall not apply so as to prevent validation of any permit in respect of which the numbered plate evidencing current validation of the permit had not been displayed on the vehicle involved in the infraction.

Proposed Amendment — 7(12)

(12) Same, validation of more than one permit — For the purposes of clause (10)(a), if a person holds more than one permit, the order or direction may apply, at any given time, to prevent validation of only one of the permits.

2015, c. 14, s. 4(1) [Not in force at date of publication.]

Proposed Addition — 7(12.0.1)

(12.0.1) No permit when fines unpaid re s. 46(1) offences — If the payment of a fine imposed on conviction for an offence described in subsection 46(1) (other than an offence described in subsection (11)) is in default, an order or direction may be made under section 69 of the *Provincial Offences Act* directing that,

(a) no permit held by the convicted person be validated until the fine is paid; and

(b) no permit be issued to the convicted person until the fine is paid.

2015, c. 14, s. 4(1) [Not in force at date of publication.]

(12.1) Firefighters — On application by a person who meets the requirements of this Act and the regulations and who is a firefighter under the *Fire Protection and Prevention Act, 1997*, the Ministry or a person authorized by the Ministry may issue to the applicant a sticker, that indicates that the vehicle is registered to or leased by a firefighter, to be attached to the lower left hand corner of the front number plate of any motor vehicle of which the person is the registered owner or lessee.

(12.2) [Repealed 2009, c. 5, s. 2.]

(12.3) Same — A person to whom a sticker has been issued under subsection (12.1) shall not display the sticker upon ceasing to be a firefighter under the *Fire Protection and Prevention Act, 1997* or upon ceasing to meet the requirements prescribed by the regulations.

(12.4) Regulations — The Lieutenant Governor in Council may make regulations respecting the issuance, replacement and cancellation of a sticker referred to in subsection (12.1).

(13) Records — The Ministry shall maintain,

    (a) a numerical index record of all permits issued and in force under this section; and

    (b) an alphabetical index record of the names and addresses of all persons to whom permits that are in force have been issued.

(14) Effective term of permit — A permit that is issued or validated is in force during the period of time prescribed by the regulations.

(15) One permit only — No person shall apply for, secure or retain in the person's possession more than one permit bearing the same plate number or describing the same vehicle.

(16) Minister may refuse to issue or validate or may cancel permit — The Minister may, in his or her discretion, refuse to issue or validate or may cancel any permit issued for any motor vehicle or trailer that is to be used or is used as a public vehicle within the meaning of the *Public Vehicles Act*, unless the owner of such motor vehicle or trailer is in possession of an operating licence as required by that Act.

(17) [Repealed 2002, c. 22, s. 97(1).]

(18) [Repealed 2002, c. 22, s. 97(2).]

(19) [Repealed 2002, c. 22, s. 97(2).]

(20) [Repealed 2002, c. 22, s. 97(2).]

(21) Retaining portion of fee — Despite section 2 of the *Financial Administration Act*, any person who issues permits or provides any other service in relation to permits on behalf of the Minister, pursuant to an agreement with the Minister, may retain, from the fee paid, the amount that is approved by the Minister from time to time.

(22) Permit documentation — Before the issuance or validation of a permit under this section, the Minister may require production of the documentation that the Minister considers necessary to enable him or her to determine whether a permit may be issued or validated and that documentation may be different for different vehicles or classes of vehicles or in respect of the same vehicles or classes of vehicles used for different purposes.

(23) Administration of declarations and affidavits — Declarations or affidavits in connection with the issuance of permits and licences under this Act or required by the Ministry in that regard may be taken before any person having authority to administer oaths or before any person specially authorized for that purpose by the Lieutenant Governor in Council, but any person so specially authorized shall not charge any fee therefor.

(24) Regulations re permits and number plates — The Lieutenant Governor in Council may make regulations respecting any matter ancillary to the provisions of this Part with respect to permits and number plates and in particular,

(a) prescribing forms for the purposes of this section and requiring their use;

(b) respecting the issuance and validation of permits and the issuance of number plates;

(c) prescribing the period of time or the method of determining the period of time during which permits shall be in force that are issued or validated for motor vehicles or trailers or any class or type of either of them;

(d) prescribing fees for the issuance, validation and replacement of permits and number plates and of evidence of validation of permits;

(e) governing the manner of displaying number plates on motor vehicles and trailers or any class or type of either of them;

(f) governing the method of validating permits and the form of and manner of affixing, displaying or showing evidence of the validation of permits on motor vehicles;

(g) respecting permits and number plates for use, on a temporary basis, on motor vehicles or trailers owned by or in the possession of,

(i) vehicle manufacturers, or

(ii) vehicle dealers,

where the vehicles are kept for sale only and prescribing conditions under which the vehicles may be operated on the highway;

(h) respecting permits and number plates for use, on a temporary basis, on motor vehicles or trailers owned by or in the possession of persons in the business of repairing, road testing, customizing, modifying or transporting vehicles where the vehicles are not kept for private use or for hire and prescribing conditions under which the vehicles may be operated on the highway;

(i) prescribing when a permit becomes valid;

(j) classifying persons and vehicles and exempting any class of person or any class of vehicle from any requirement in this Part or any regulation made under this Part and prescribing conditions for any such exemptions;

(k) requiring the surrender of number plates;

(l) classifying permits, providing for the issuing or validating of any class of permit and the requirements therefor and for the issuing of number plates and evidence of validation and the requirements therefor;

(m) prescribing requirements for the purposes of subsections 11(3) and (4);

(n) prescribing conditions precedent or subsequent for the issuing or validating of any class of permit or number plate or the issuing of any evidence of validation;

Proposed Addition — 7(24)(n.1)

(n.1) providing for exemptions from the application of orders or directions made under section 69 of the *Provincial Offences Act* pursuant to subsection (12.0.1), including exemptions from all or part of an order or direction and providing for conditions or limitations on exemptions;

2015, c. 14, s. 4(2) [Not in force at date of publication.]

(o) prescribing the criteria for the issuance, retention and return of a number plate bearing a requested number.

Proposed Addition — 7(25)

(25) Application of subss. (10) and (12.0.1) — Subject to any exemptions in the regulations, subsections (10) and (12.0.1) apply with respect to an offence even if the offence, conviction, imposition of the fine or default of payment of the fine occurred before those subsections, as enacted by subsection 4(1) of the *Transportation Statute Law Amendment Act (Making Ontario's Roads Safer), 2015*, come into force.

2015, c. 14, s. 4(3) [Not in force at date of publication.]

[Editor's Note: The International Registration Plan is a plan that allows for the distribution of registration fees for commercial motor vehicles travelling interjurisdictionally through member states and provinces. Ontario implementation is April 1, 2001. All carriers travelling outside Ontario with vehicles having a gross weight in excess of 11, 793 kg. should register in IRP. Otherwise, these carriers will have to purchase trip permits to travel outside Ontario. All U.S. states and B.C., Alta. and Sask. are already members. New Brunswick and Quebec also had an April 1, 2001 implementation date.]

1992, c. 20, s. 2; 1993, c. 8, s. 1; 1993, c. 31, s. 2; 1994, c. 27, s. 138(4), (5); 1998, c. 38, s. 1; 1999, c. 12, Sched. R, s. 2(1), (3), (5); 2000, c. 29, s. 1; 2002, c. 18, Sched. P, s. 1; 2002, c. 22, s. 97; 2004, c. 22, s. 1; 2005, c. 26, Sched. A, s. 1; 2006, c. 19, Sched. T, s. 4; 2006, c. 33, Sched. M, s. 2; 2009, c. 5, s. 2

Commentary

No one may drive a motor vehicle on a highway unless there is a currently validated permit, number plates and evidence of current validation (subs. (1)).

Number plates and evidence of validation are not necessary if the motor vehicle has a CAVR (Canadian Agreement on Vehicle Registration) cab card (subs. (4)).

Drivers must carry the original or a true copy of the permit (subs. (5)) or the CAVR cab card (subs. (6)).

Permit validation may be refused where the holder is indebted to the province for a vehicle-related fee or tax (subs. (9)). Validation or a new permit may be refused where a fine imposed for a parking infraction is owing (subss. (10)–(12)). Similar powers exist relating to permits under the Public Vehicles Act, R.S.O. 1990, c. P.54, and the Truck Transportation Act, R.S.O. 1990, c. T.22 (subs. (16)), or in relation to CAVR cab cards (subss. (17)–(20)).

Commercial motor vehicles from reciprocating jurisdictions in Canada and the United States are exempt from compliance. See s. 45 of the Act and regulations.

The "owner", on whom rests the obligation to register a motor vehicle before operating it, is not defined in the Ontario Act. Clearly, different considerations arise under s. 192 where the liability imposed on an "owner" may attach to either the registered or the true owner depending on the circumstance.

The permit must be shown to a police officer upon demand.

The Red Light Camera Pilot Projects Act, 1998, S.O. 1998, c. 38 (in force November 20, 2000) permits evidence obtained from red light cameras to be used in areas designated by regulation for the purpose of enforcing subsection 144(18) of the Highway Traffic Act (failing to stop at a red light or proceeding before the light turns green). O. Reg. 277/99 dealing with the admissibility and use of Red Light Camera System evidence in proceedings under the Act, was brought into force contemporaneously with the Act.

The Red Tape Reduction Act, 1999, S.O. 1999, c. 12, Sched. R. (ss. 1(2), 1(3), 2(1), 2(3), 2(5), 5(1), and 6(1) in force January 1, 2001) would amend ss. 6, 7, 12 and 14 of the Highway Traffic Act to facilitate Ontario's participation in the International Registration Plan, which contains reciprocal provisions in respect of commercial motor vehicles that travel across provincial or international borders. The Plan provides for the issuance of IRP cab cards as permits for these vehicles and for the appointment of registration and licence fees in each member jurisdiction on the basis of the distances travelled in each jurisdiction. Persons residing or based in other jurisdictions that are members of the Plan are exempt from the requirements of and fees prescribed under Part II of the Highway Traffic Act.

The Highway Traffic Act Amendment Act (Historic Vehicles), 2000, S.O. 2000, c. 29 (in force December 21, 2000) amends the Highway Traffic Act to allow number plates to be used on historic vehicles if they are Ontario number plates that were issued during the year of manufacture of the vehicle, are in a condition satisfactory to the Ministry and show no numbers that duplicate the number of any other existing permit.

The International Registration Plan is a plan that allows for the distribution of registration fees for commercial motor vehicles travelling interjurisdictionally through member states and provinces. Ontario implementation was April 1, 2001. All carriers travelling outside Ontario with vehicles having a gross weight in excess of 11,793 kg. should register in IRP. Otherwise, these carriers will have to purchase trip permits to travel outside Ontario. All U.S. states except Alaska and all Canadian jurisdictions except the territories are already members. Questions and answers about the IRP can be found at http://www.mto. gov.on.ca/english/trucks/irp/index.html#faq.

Case Law

Sleigh v. Stevenson, [1943] O.W.N. 465 (C.A.) — No person other than the owner may register under the Act; "registered owner" in an application for insurance is to be read as the person entitled to register. Where a son had purchased a vehicle and transferred it to his mother some months before an application for insurance, a statement by the mother in the application for insurance that she was the "registered owner" was a false representation vitiating the contract of insurance.

Flood v. Waterloo Motors Ltd., 3 M.P.R. 318, [1931] 1 D.L.R. 762 (N.B. C.A.) — In view of the fact that there may be a separation of the legal and beneficial interests in a motor vehicle, no strict definition can be given of the person obliged to register. Likewise, registration will not be conclusive for all purposes and it will be possible to go behind the record to establish the true interest of a person other than the registered owner. Thus, the registering, for purposes of convenience, of a motor car in the name of another has been held not to take away from the real owner his or her title and ownership so as to deprive him or her of an insurable interest in the car.

Cairns v. Worthy, 1 M.P.R. 108, [1929] 3 D.L.R. 123 (P.E.I. S.C.) — On the other hand, a person who registered or caused to be registered a motor vehicle in the name of another was estopped from claiming that he was the real owner in derogation of the rights of an execution creditor.

Ritchie v. Rayner (1933), 5 M.P.R. 568 (P.E.I. C.A.); affirmed [1933] 4 D.L.R. 808 (S.C.C.) — It is a matter of prime importance that the law respecting the registration of motor vehicles be strictly observed. The number on a registration plate of a car proclaims to the world its ownership, and is the first essential step towards the enforcement of laws controlling the operation of motor vehicles on the public highways.

Godfrey v. Cooper (1920), 46 O.L.R. 565, 51 D.L.R. 455 (C.A.) — The absence of registration has no effect on the duty of the motorist to comply with other provisions of the Act. The rules of the road are applicable to all vehicles on the highway.

R. v. Halldorson, 1999 NWTTC 2, 48 M.V.R. (3d) 188 (N.W.T. Terr. Ct.) — Registering, licensing and operation of motor vehicles is one of the most common and basic of activities to the vast majority of citizens. The accused's defence that he lost documents was not accepted.

R. v. Newton (2003), 41 M.V.R. (4th) 184, 107 C.R.R. (2d) 269, 2003 CarswellOnt 2031, [2003] O.J. No. 2189 (Ont. S.C.J.) — A police officer stopped an accused driver because he believed him to be a teenager and wanted to check for compliance with the requirements of a G1 or G2 class licence that the driver have no alcohol in his system. The officer then observed the indicia of impairment. Comparisons between race and age profiling were inappropriate.

R. v. Seguin (2003), 2003 CarswellOnt 4628, 46 M.V.R. (4th) 252 (Ont. C.J.) — A motorcycle's plate must be attached on a conspicuous place at the rear. The rear refers to a 180 degree plane from the point of view of a person following the vehicle and viewing it from that position.

R. v. Edwards, 60 M.V.R. (5th) 59, 56 C.R. (6th) 192, 2007 ONCJ 581, 2007 CarswellOnt 7845 (C.J.) — S. 13.1(1)(a) of the *Compulsory Automobile Insurance Act* creates a full *mens rea* offence so that knowledge or willful blindness about false or the invalid nature of an insurance card must be proved.

R. v. Hajivasilis (2013), 41 M.V.R. (6th) 175, 2013 ONCA 27, 2013 CarswellOnt 508, 114 O.R. (3d) 337, 302 O.A.C. 65, [2013] O.J. No. 253 (Ont. C.A.) — The requirements are not restricted to "highways".

R. v. Westover (2013), 49 M.V.R. (6th) 336, 2013 ONCJ 472, 2013 CarswellOnt 11933, [2013] O.J. No. 3904 (Ont. C.J.) — Freedom of religion did not justify a belief that the accused should not abide by the rules and regulations related to motor vehicles and highways.

Related Provisions: See R.R.O. 1990, Reg. 628, Vehicle Permits; O. Reg. 424/97, Commercial Motor Vehicle Operators' Information; O. Reg. 555/06, Hours of Service; O. Reg. 11/04, International Registration Plan and O. Reg. 381/98, Special Permits.

7.1 (1) International Registration Plan — The Minister may apply to have Ontario made a member of the reciprocal agreement known as the International Registration Plan.

(2) Effect of membership in Plan — If Ontario is a member of the Plan, the provisions of this Part and the regulations made under this Part are subject to the provisions of the Plan with respect to,

(a) the issuance of permits for commercial motor vehicles engaged in inter-provincial or international travel; and

(b) the registration and licence fees for such vehicles, which shall be apportioned, as provided in the Plan, on the basis of the distance travelled by the vehicles within each jurisdiction that is a member of the Plan.

(3) Exemptions — If Ontario is a member of the Plan, persons who reside in or are based in another jurisdiction that is a member of the Plan are exempt, if so provided in the Plan, from the requirements of this Part and from the fees prescribed under this Part with respect to commercial motor vehicles owned or leased by such persons.

(4) Same — A person is not entitled to an exemption under subsection (3) unless the person is in compliance with the motor vehicle laws of the jurisdiction where the commercial motor vehicle owned or leased by the person is registered.

(5) Interpretation — For the purpose of subsection (3), where a person resides or is based shall be determined in accordance with the terms of the Plan.

1999, c. 12, Sched. R, s. 3

Commentary

The Red Tape Reduction Act, 1999, S.O. 1999, c. 12, Sched. R. (ss. 1(2), 1(3), 2(1), 2(3), 2(5), 5(1), and 6(1) in force January 1, 2001) would amend ss. 6, 7, 12 and 14 of the Highway Traffic Act to facilitate Ontario's participation in the International Registration Plan, which contains reciprocal provisions in respect of commercial motor vehicles that travel across provincial or international borders. The Plan provides for the issuance of IRP cab cards as permits for these vehicles and for the appointment of registration and licence fees in each member jurisdiction on the basis of the distances travelled in each jurisdiction. Persons residing or based in other jurisdictions that are members of the Plan are exempt from the requirements of and fees prescribed under Part II of the Highway Traffic Act.

Related Provisions: See O. Reg. 11/04, International Registration Plan.

7.2 (1) Record-keeping by IRP permit holders — Every holder of an IRP cab card issued under subsection 7(7) shall maintain and preserve the prescribed records for five years after the registration year for which the IRP cab card was issued.

(2) Offence — Every person who fails to comply with subsection (1) is guilty of an offence and on conviction is liable to a fine of not less than $250 and not more than $20,000.

2002, c. 22, s. 98; 2004, c. 31, Sched. 18, s. 1

Related Provisions: See O. Reg. 11/04, International Registration Plan.

7.3 (1) Examination and inspection — The Minister may appoint one or more employees of the Government of Ontario as IRP inspectors.

(2) Identification — An IRP inspector conducting an examination and inspection shall produce, on request, evidence of his or her appointment.

(3) Powers — For any purpose related to the administration or enforcement of the International Registration Plan, an IRP inspector may, at any reasonable time, enter any place where activities related to an IRP cab card holder's operation of commercial motor vehicles are carried on or where anything is kept or done in connection with such operation or any records are kept under this Part.

(4) Same — An IRP inspector may conduct an examination and inspection at the place entered under subsection (3) and for such purpose may,

    (a) examine and inspect a record or other thing that may be relevant to the examination and inspection;

    (b) require the production of a record or other thing that the IRP inspector thinks may be relevant to the examination and inspection;

    (c) remove for examination, inspection or copying any record or other thing that the IRP inspector thinks may be relevant to the examination and inspection;

    (d) in order to produce a record in readable form, use data storage, information processing or retrieval devices or systems that are normally used in carrying on business in the place and require any person, including the IRP cab card holder, any partner, director, officer, agent, representative or employee of the holder, any driver engaged by the holder or any person at the place, to give the IRP inspector all reasonable assistance in using them;

    (e) require any person, including the IRP cab card holder, any partner, director, officer, agent, representative or employee of the holder, any driver engaged by the holder or any person at the place, to give the IRP inspector all reasonable assistance in the examination and inspection;

    (f) question any person, including the IRP cab card holder, any partner, director, officer, agent, representative or employee of the holder, any driver engaged by the holder or any person at the place, on matters that the IRP inspector thinks may be relevant to the examination and inspection and require answers to be made orally or in writing;

    (g) require any person, including the IRP cab card holder, any partner, director, officer, agent, representative or employee of the holder or any driver engaged by the holder, to attend at the place with the IRP inspector for the purpose of clause (d), (e) or (f).

(5) **Written demand for records** — An IRP inspector may at any time, for any purpose related to the administration or enforcement of the International Registration Plan, deliver a demand personally on an IRP cab card holder, any partner, director, officer, agent, representative or employee of the holder or any driver engaged by the holder, or mail a demand to such person at the latest address of the person appearing on the records of the Ministry, requiring that the person deliver to the IRP inspector, within the time specified in the demand, any record or other thing the production of which could be required under clause (4)(b).

(6) **Same** — A demand sent by mail shall be deemed to have been received on the fifth day after it was mailed, unless the person to whom the demand was mailed establishes that the person did not, acting in good faith, through absence, accident, illness or other cause beyond the person's control, receive the demand.

(7) **Obligation to produce and assist** — If an IRP inspector requires that a record or other thing be produced under clause (4)(b) or delivered to him or her under subsection (5), the person upon whom the demand is made shall produce or deliver it and, in the case of a record, shall on request provide any assistance that is reasonably necessary to interpret the record or to produce it in a readable form.

(8) **Records and things removed** — An IRP inspector who removes a record or other thing under clause (4)(c) or to whom a record or other thing is delivered pursuant to a demand made under subsection (5) shall give a receipt for the record or thing and return the record or thing to the person who produced or delivered it within a reasonable time.

(9) **Powers to assist other IRP jurisdictions** — An IRP inspector, accompanied by an official from another jurisdiction that is a member of the International Registration Plan, may exercise his or her powers under this section for any purpose related to the administration or enforcement of the International Registration Plan by the other jurisdiction and subsections (2) and (3), clause (12)(c) and subsection (13) apply, with necessary modifications, to and in respect of an official from another jurisdiction accompanying an IRP inspector who is conducting an examination and inspection under this section.

(10) **Copies admissible in evidence** — A copy of a record that purports to be certified to be a true copy by the IRP inspector or other employee of the Government of Ontario who made the copy is admissible in evidence in any proceeding or prosecution as proof, in the absence of evidence to the contrary, of the original record and its contents.

(11) **Same** — A copy made from an electronic record that purports to be certified by the IRP inspector or other employee of the Government of Ontario who made the copy to be a paper copy of the electronic record and to be a true and accurate representation of the electronic record or the information contained in the electronic record, is admissible in evidence in any proceeding or prosecution as proof, in the absence of evidence to the contrary, of the original record and its contents.

(12) Offence — No person shall,

(a) fail to comply with a direction or requirement of an IRP inspector conducting an examination and inspection;

(b) give an IRP inspector conducting an examination and inspection information that the person knows to be false, deceptive or misleading; or

(c) obstruct or interfere with an IRP inspector in the performance of his or her duties under this section.

(13) Penalty — A person who contravenes subsection (12) is guilty of an offence and on conviction is liable to a fine of not less than $250 and not more than $20,000 or to imprisonment for a term of not more than six months, or to both.

2002, c. 22, s. 98

7.4 Sharing examination, inspection findings with other IRP jurisdictions — The Minister shall, in accordance with the terms of the International Registration Plan, provide the findings from every examination and inspection conducted under section 7.3,

(a) to such other member jurisdictions of the Plan, or their delegates, that have an interest in the findings; and

(b) to the governing body of the Plan or its delegate.

2002, c. 22, s. 98

7.5 IRP inspector's costs — Where an IRP inspector travels outside of Ontario to conduct an examination and inspection under section 7.3 respecting a holder of an IRP cab card issued under subsection 7(7), the holder shall pay to the Minister the IRP inspector's travel expenses and a daily fee for the IRP inspector's work.

2002, c. 22, s. 98

7.6 (1) Assessment and reassessment of fees, etc. — The Minister may assess or reassess the amount of fees owed by a holder of an IRP cab card issued under subsection 7(7) pursuant to the International Registration Plan to the Minister and to every other member jurisdiction of the Plan and the amount of taxes owed by a holder of an IRP cab card issued under subsection 7(7) to every other member jurisdiction of the Plan that Ontario is required to collect pursuant to the Plan at any time or times within three years after the registration year for which the fees and taxes were owed.

(2) Same — Despite subsection (1), where the Minister establishes that the holder has made any misrepresentation that is attributable to neglect, carelessness or wilful default, or has committed any fraud, in supplying any information under this Part in respect of the Plan or in omitting to disclose any information, then the Minister may assess or reassess the fees and taxes described in subsection (1) at any time the Minister considers reasonable.

(3) Same — The Minister may, under subsection (1) or (2), assess or reassess the amount of fees and taxes using whatever method the Minister considers appropriate where, as a result of an examination and inspection under section 7.3, the IRP inspector determines that,

(a) the information filed by the holder with the Ministry is not substantiated by the records examined and inspected;

(b) the holder failed to maintain and preserve the records required by section 7.2; or

(c) a record or other thing was not produced or delivered or information disclosed as required by section 7.3.

(4) Same — The assessment or reassessment shall be based on all relevant information available to the Minister, including information about comparable permit holders.

(5) Penalty — Where the Minister assesses or reassesses an IRP cab card holder, he or she may assess a penalty equal to 10 per cent of the assessment or reassessment.

(6) Refund to holder — Where, as a result of an examination and inspection under section 7.3, it is determined that an IRP cab card holder paid fees or taxes in excess of what the holder owed pursuant to the International Registration Plan, the Minister shall assess or reassess the amount of the fees and taxes owed accordingly and the Minister may refund the excess to the holder.

(7) Notice — The Minister shall deliver a notice of assessment or reassessment personally on the IRP cab card holder or shall mail it to the holder at the latest address for the holder appearing on the records of the Ministry.

(8) Same — A notice of assessment or reassessment sent by mail shall be deemed to have been received on the fifth day after it was mailed unless the holder establishes that the holder did not, acting in good faith, through absence, accident, illness or other cause beyond the holder's control, receive it.

(9) Payment — Every person assessed or reassessed under this section shall pay to the Minister the amount assessed or reassessed within 30 days after receiving the notice of assessment or reassessment, whether or not an objection to the assessment or reassessment is outstanding.

(10) Included in assessment, reassessment — For the purposes of this section, an assessment or reassessment of fees and taxes includes travel costs and fees owed under section 7.5, penalties assessed under this section and interest owed under section 7.7.

2002, c. 22, s. 98

7.7 Interest — **(1) Application** — This section applies with respect to registration years that end on or after December 9, 2002.

(2) Interest payable on unpaid fees and penalties — Interest is payable to the Minister on the amount of any unpaid fees and penalties owed to the Minister and on the amount of any unpaid fees and taxes owed to another member of the International Registration Plan and collected by Ontario pursuant to the Plan.

(3) **Same** — Interest is payable for the period commencing on the day after the last day of the registration year for which the unpaid amount is owed until the date on which the unpaid amount, including interest, is paid.

(4) **Interest rate** — Interest is to be calculated at the rate or rates determined in accordance with the regulations.

(5) **Waiver of interest** — Despite subsection (2), the Minister may exempt a person from payment of part or all of the interest owing in respect of a registration year if the Minister is of the opinion that owing to special circumstances it is inequitable to charge and collect the whole amount of the interest.

(6) **Decision final** — The Minister's decision under subsection (5) about whether to exempt a person from the payment of interest and the amount of the exemption, if any, is final and not subject to review.

(7) **Transition** — Interest in respect of a period before the date on which the *Budget Measures Act (Fall), 2004* receives Royal Assent is to be determined in accordance with this section as it reads on and after that date, and not in accordance with this section as it read before that date.

2002, c. 22, s. 98; 2004, c. 31, Sched. 18, s. 2

Related Provisions: See O. Reg. 11/04, International Registration Plan.

7.8 (1) Objections — An IRP cab card holder who objects to an assessment, reassessment or penalty may, within 30 days after receiving the notice of assessment or reassessment, serve on the Minister a written objection in the form approved by the Minister.

(2) **Decision** — The Minister shall consider the written submissions and shall confirm, vary or set aside the assessment, reassessment or penalty objected to.

(3) **Extension of time** — The Minister may extend the time for objecting if the person seeking to object proves to the satisfaction of the Minister that the objection could not have been served on time.

2002, c. 22, s. 98

Related Provisions: See O. Reg. 11/04, International Registration Plan.

7.9 (1) Appeal or review from Minister's decision — No further appeal or other review shall be available from a decision under subsection 7.8(2) except as provided in the International Registration Plan.

(2) **Appeal or review under IRP binding** — Where an appeal or review is provided for and conducted under the terms of the International Registration Plan, the Minister and the IRP cab card holder who was a party to the appeal or review are bound by the decision made on that appeal or review.

2002, c. 22, s. 98

7.10 (1) False statements on IRP documents — Every person is guilty of an offence who has made, or participated in, assented to or acquiesced in the making of, false or deceptive statements in an application or other documentation filed with the Ministry with respect to an IRP cab card.

(2) Penalty — A person convicted of an offence under subsection (1) is liable to one or both of the following penalties in addition to any assessment, penalty or interest under section 7.6 or 7.7:

    1. A fine that is,

        i. not less than $1,000 or 50 per cent of the amount of the fees and taxes that was evaded, whichever is greater, and

        ii. not more than double the amount of the fees and taxes that was evaded, if the maximum so calculated is greater than the amount determined under subparagraph i.

    2. Imprisonment for a term of not more than six months.

2002, c. 22, s. 98

7.11 (1) Permit refusal or cancellation — The Minister may, in his or her discretion, cancel or refuse to issue an IRP cab card where the owner or lessee of the vehicle for which an IRP cab card has been issued under subsection 7(7) or applied for,

    (a) has been convicted of an offence under section 7.2, 7.3 or 7.10;

    (b) has not paid all of the amounts owed by the person under this Part with respect to the IRP cab card; or

    (c) has not paid all of the amounts owed by the person under section 3 of the *Retail Sales Tax Act*.

(2) Same — The Minister may, in his or her discretion, cancel or refuse to issue an IRP cab card where the owner or lessee of the vehicle for which an IRP cab card has been issued under subsection 7(7) or applied for is related to,

    (a) a person who has been convicted of an offence under section 7.2, 7.3 or 7.10;

    (b) a person who has not paid all of the amounts owed by the person under this Part with respect to the IRP cab card; or

    (c) a person who has not paid all of the amounts owed by the person under section 3 of the *Retail Sales Tax Act*.

(3) Interpretation — An owner or lessee of a vehicle is related to a person for the purpose of subsection (2) if,

    (a) the owner or lessee and the person are related individuals;

    (b) either the owner or lessee or the person is a partner of the other or was a partner of the other or they have or have had partners in common;

    (c) either the owner or lessee or the person, directly or indirectly, controls or controlled or manages or managed the other; or

    (d) the owner or lessee and the person have or have had common officers or directors or they are or have been controlled, directly or indirectly, by the same shareholders.

(4) Modification of permit — The Minister may, at the request of another member jurisdiction of the International Registration Plan and in accordance with the terms of the Plan, remove that jurisdiction from an IRP cab card issued under subsection 7(7).

(5) Notice — The Minister shall give notice of the cancellation or modification of or refusal to issue an IRP cab card by delivering the notice personally on the IRP cab card holder or applicant or by mailing the notice to the person at the latest address of the person appearing on the records of the Ministry.

(6) Same — Notice sent by mail shall be deemed to have been received on the fifth day after it was mailed unless the person to whom the notice was mailed establishes that the person did not, acting in good faith, through absence, accident, illness or other cause beyond the person's control, receive the notice.

(7) Objection — A person who has received notice that the Minister has cancelled an IRP cab card or refused to issue an IRP cab card may, within 30 days after receiving the notice, serve on the Minister a written objection in the form approved by the Minister.

(8) Decision — The Minister shall consider the written submissions and shall confirm, vary or set aside the decision objected to.

(9) Decision final — The Minister's decision under subsection (8) is final and no further appeal or other review shall be available from it.

(10) Extension of time — The Minister may extend the time for objecting if the person seeking to object proves to the satisfaction of the Minister that the objection could not have been served on time.

2002, c. 22, s. 98

Related Provisions: See O. Reg. 11/04, International Registration Plan.

7.12 (1) Collection and disclosure of information — The Minister may, for any purpose related to the administration or enforcement of the International Registration Plan, collect information, directly or indirectly, and retain and use such information, including,

   (a) information collected and disclosed to the Minister by another minister, another member jurisdiction of the Plan or its delegate or the governing body of the Plan or its delegate; and

   (b) information about the employees and agents of an IRP cab card holder or an applicant for an IRP cab card.

(2) Same — Every other minister of the Crown shall disclose to the Minister information collected by the other minister that may assist the Minister in carrying out his or her duties in the administration or enforcement of the International Registration Plan.

2002, c. 22, s. 98

7.13 Assignment to another minister — If any power or duty of the Minister under this Part, as it relates to the International Registration Plan or an IRP cab card holder, is assigned to another minister of the Crown under the *Executive Council Act*, section 7.12 both applies to the other minister of the Crown as if he or she were the Minister and continues to apply to the Minister.

2002, c. 22, s. 98

7.14 Disclosure to Minister of Finance re taxing statutes — The Minister shall disclose any information collected by the Minister with respect to the International Registration Plan or an IRP cab card holder to the Minister of Finance, or to any employee of the Ministry of Finance, that may assist the Minister of Finance or the employee in carrying out his or her duties in the administration or enforcement of the *Fuel Tax Act, Gasoline Tax Act* or *Retail Sales Tax Act*.

2002, c. 22, s. 98

7.15 (1) Regulations — The Lieutenant Governor in Council may make regulations,

(a) prescribing information to be included in an application for an IRP cab card;

(b) prescribing the records to be maintained and preserved under section 7.2;

(c) prescribing information and reports to be filed with the Ministry with respect to an IRP cab card;

(d) governing the calculation of interest for the purposes of section 7.7;

(e) prescribing the manner of serving objections under subsections 7.8(1) and 7.11(7).

(2) Same — A regulation may establish classes of IRP cab card holders and may contain different provisions and requirements for different classes.

(3) Retroactive — A regulation made under clause (1)(d) is, if it so provides, effective with reference to a period before it was filed but not earlier than December 9, 2002.

2002, c. 22, s. 98; 2004, c. 31, Sched. 18, s. 3

7.16 Fees — The Minister may set a daily fee for work by IRP inspectors outside of Ontario for the purpose of section 7.5.

2002, c. 22, s. 98

7.17 [Repealed 2008, c. 17, s. 31.]

8. (1) Permit limitations — Where the fee prescribed by the regulations for a permit or validated permit for a motor vehicle is calculated with regard to specific limitations or restrictions on the use of a vehicle, the owner of the vehicle shall not drive or cause or permit the vehicle to be driven on a highway except in accordance with the limitations or restrictions.

(2) Penalty — Every person who contravenes subsection (1) is guilty of an offence and on conviction is liable to a fine of not less than $100 and not more than $500.

9. (1) Penalty for false statement, inaccurate information — Every person who submits a false or inaccurate document, makes a false statement or includes inaccurate information in or with a written or electronic application, declaration, affidavit or other document required by the Ministry or under this Act is guilty of an offence and on conviction, in addition to any other penalty or punishment to which the person may be liable, is liable to a fine of not less than $400 and not more than $5,000 or to imprisonment for a term of not more than 30 days, or to both, and in addition the person's driver's licence or vehicle permit may be suspended for a period of not more than six months.

(1.1) Defence — A person is not guilty of an offence under subsection (1) if the person exercised all reasonable care to avoid making a false statement or including inaccurate information.

(2) Change of name or address — Where an owner of a motor vehicle or a plate holder changes the name or address of the owner as set out in the owner's application for a permit or validation of a permit or in a previous notice filed under this subsection, the owner shall within six days file with the Ministry notice of the new name or address.

(3) Idem — Where the name or address of a lessee is on a permit and the lessee changes the name or address of the lessee from the name or address shown on the permit or from that filed under this subsection, the lessee shall within six days file with the Ministry notice of the new name or address.

(4) Filing — A notice may be filed under subsection (2) or (3) by forwarding it to the Ministry by registered mail.

(5) Where vehicle identification number obliterated — No permit shall be issued for a motor vehicle or a trailer that has a gross weight exceeding 1,360 kilograms where the manufacturer's vehicle identification number or similar identifying mark has been obliterated or defaced until the owner has filed with the Ministry satisfactory proof of the ownership of the vehicle or trailer, and, if known, the reason for the obliteration or defacement, and, if satisfied as to the statements made, the Minister may grant permission to cut, impress, emboss or attach permanently to the vehicle or trailer a special identification number or mark, which thereafter shall be deemed sufficient for the purpose of the issuance, validation or transfer of a permit for the vehicle or trailer.

(6) Limitation — No proceeding for an offence under subsection (1) shall be instituted more than six years after the facts on which the proceeding is based are alleged to have occurred.

2005, c. 26, Sched. A, s. 2; 2008, c. 17, s. 32

Commentary

It is an offence to make a false statement to the Ministry in connection with any application. In addition to a fine and/or imprisonment, the licence or permit may be suspended up to six months. A vehicle owner has six days to notify the Ministry of a change in ownership.

10. (1) Manufacturer's vehicle identification number to be affixed — No owner of a motor vehicle shall drive or permit his, hers or its motor vehicle to be driven on a highway unless the motor vehicle has the manufacturer's vehicle identification number permanently affixed.

(2) Idem — No owner of,

    (a) a trailer that has a manufacturer's gross vehicle weight rating exceeding 1,360 kilograms;

    (b) a conversion unit; or

    (c) a trailer converter dolly,

shall draw or permit the trailer, conversion unit or trailer converter dolly to be drawn on a highway unless the trailer, conversion unit or trailer converter dolly, as the case may be, has an identification number permanently affixed.

Commentary

Every motor vehicle has a unique serial number called a "manufacturer's vehicle identification" number, or "VIN". The VIN must be affixed to the vehicle. Most vehicles have the VIN on at least two or three areas.

11. (1) Where transfer of ownership or end of lease — Upon the holder of a permit ceasing to be the owner or lessee of the motor vehicle or trailer referred to in the permit, he, she or it shall,

    (a) remove his, her or its number plates from the vehicle;

    (b) retain the plate portion of the permit; and

    (c) on delivery of the vehicle,

        (i) to the new owner, complete and sign the transfer application of the vehicle portion of the permit including the date of the delivery and give that portion of the permit to the new owner, or

        (ii) to a lessor, give the vehicle portion of the permit to the lessor.

(2) Re-issue of permit — Every person shall, within six days after becoming the owner of a motor vehicle or trailer for which a permit has been issued, apply to the Ministry, on the form provided therefor, for a new permit for the vehicle.

(3) Temporary use of plates — Despite section 12, a person to whom number plates have been issued under subsection 7(7) for a vehicle the person no longer owns or leases may affix the number plates to a similar class of vehicle that the person owns or leases where it is done in accordance with the prescribed requirements.

(4) Idem — Despite section 7 and clauses 12(1)(d) and (e), a person may drive a motor vehicle or draw a trailer on a highway within six days after becoming the owner of the motor vehicle or trailer where the person complies with the prescribed requirements.

Commentary

The Red Tape Reduction Act, 1999, S.O. 1999, c. 12, Sched. R. (ss. 1(2), 1(3), 2(1), 2(3), 2(5), 5(1), and 6(1) in force January 1, 2001) would amend ss. 6, 7, 12 and 14 of the Highway Traffic Act to facilitate Ontario's participation in the International Registration Plan, which contains reciprocal provisions in respect of commercial motor vehicles that travel across provincial or international borders. The Plan provides for the issuance of IRP cab cards as permits for these vehicles and for the appointment of registration and licence fees in each member jurisdiction on the basis of the distances travelled in each jurisdiction. Persons residing or based in other jurisdictions that are members of the Plan are exempt from the requirements of and fees prescribed under Part II of the Highway Traffic Act.

11.1 (1) Used vehicle information package — Every person who sells, offers for sale or transfers a used motor vehicle shall provide a valid used vehicle information package in respect of the vehicle for inspection by proposed purchasers or transferees and shall deliver the package to the purchaser or transferee at the time of sale or transfer of the vehicle.

(2) Issuance of package — The Ministry shall issue a used vehicle information package in respect of any used motor vehicle to any person who applies therefor and pays the prescribed fee.

(3) Permit for vehicle — The purchaser or transferee of the used motor vehicle shall deliver the used vehicle information package mentioned in subsection (1) to the Ministry before obtaining from the Ministry a new permit for the vehicle.

(4) Regulations — For the purposes of subsection (1), the Lieutenant Governor in Council may make regulations,

    (a) defining "used motor vehicle" and "used vehicle information package";

    (b) prescribing the period of time during which a used vehicle information package is valid after it is issued;

    (c) prescribing and providing for the payment of fees for the issuance of used vehicle information packages;

    (d) exempting any class of sellers or transferors from the application of subsection (1) or any class of purchasers or transferees from the application of subsection (3).

(5) Offence — Every person who fails to comply with subsection (1) is guilty of an offence and on conviction is liable to a fine of not less than $100 and not more than $500 on a first conviction and not less than $200 and not more than $1,000 on each subsequent conviction.

1993, c. 13, s. 1

Commentary

When a holder of a permit ceases to be the owner or lessee, he or she removes the plates, signs over the transfer portion of the permit and retains the plate portion of the permit. The new owner must apply for a new permit within six days of the transfer.

Related Provisions: See under s. 7 of the Act certain regulations exempting reciprocating American States from compliance. See also O. Reg. 601/93, Used Vehicle Information Package.

12. (1) Violations as to number plates — Every person who,

(a) defaces or alters any number plate, evidence of validation or permit;

(b) uses or permits the use of a defaced or altered number plate, evidence of validation or permit;

(c) without the authority of the permit holder, removes a number plate from a motor vehicle or trailer;

(d) uses or permits the use of a number plate upon a vehicle other than a number plate authorized for use on that vehicle;

(e) uses or permits the use of evidence of validation upon a number plate displayed on a motor vehicle other than evidence of validation furnished by the Ministry in respect of that motor vehicle; or

(f) uses or permits the use of a number plate or evidence of validation other than in accordance with this Act and the regulations,

is guilty of an offence and on conviction is liable to a fine of not less than $100 and not more than $1000 or to imprisonment for not more than thirty days, or to both, and in addition the person's licence or permit may be suspended for not more than six months.

(2) Property of the Crown — Every number plate is the property of the Crown and shall be returned to the Ministry when required by the Ministry.

(3) Same — For the purpose of subsection (2),

"number plate" includes,

(a) a number plate bearing a requested number,

(b) evidence of validation,

(c) a permit,

(d) a CAVR cab card, and

(e) an IRP cab card issued by the Ministry.

1994, c. 27, s. 138(6); 1999, c. 12, Sched. R, s. 5(1)

Commentary

It is an offence to alter a number plate, remove plates unless transferring, or display without validation.

The Red Tape Reduction Act, 1999, S.O. 1999, c. 12, Sched. R. (ss. 1(2), 1(3), 2(1), 2(3), 2(5), 5(1), and 6(1) in force January 1, 2001) would amend ss. 6, 7, 12 and 14 of the Highway Traffic Act to facilitate Ontario's participation in the International Registration Plan, which contains reciprocal provisions in respect of commercial motor vehicles that travel across provincial or international borders. The Plan provides for the issuance of IRP cab cards as permits for these vehicles and for the appointment of registration and licence fees in each member jurisdiction on the basis of the distances travelled in each jurisdiction. Persons residing or based in other jurisdictions that are members of the Plan are exempt from the requirements of and fees prescribed under Part II of the Highway Traffic Act.

Case Law

R. v. Blackburn (1980), 9 M.V.R. 146 (B.C. C.A.) — The offence of driving without proper plates is one of strict liability.

R. v. Queensway Motors (1986), 47 M.V.R. 144 (Ont. Prov. Ct.) — The accused was a dealer in used motor vehicles. It sold a motor vehicle to X, who had to return the vehicle for repairs. The accused lent X first one, then another vehicle while X's vehicle was under repair. The second vehicle which the accused lent did not have plates, so the accused transferred to it the plates from another vehicle owned by it. The accused was convicted under s. 12(1)(d) of the Highway Traffic Act for permitting the use of a number plate upon a vehicle other than a number plate authorized for use on that vehicle. It appealed. The appeal was dismissed. The vehicle to which the plates were attached was not a vehicle which had been sold by the accused to X. The accused simply transferred the plates from one vehicle owned by the company to another vehicle owned by the company. The accused still owned the vehicle from which the plates were removed. Consequently, the provisions of s. 10 of the Highway Traffic Act were not applicable and the accused was properly convicted.

R. v. David (2014), 2014 CarswellOnt 17261, 123 O.R. (3d) 598, 70 M.V.R. (6th) 351 (Ont. Prov. Ct.) — The use of a dealer plate is not restricted to a family member of the dealer or for the purposes of demonstration for sale. The section in O. Reg. 628 as amended by O. Reg. 244/13 permits private use in Ontario *or* for purposes related to the sale of the motor vehicle. The Regulation does not preclude the private use in Ontario by a dealer's employee of a number plate on a motor vehicle owned by the dealer.

13. (1) No other numbers to be exposed — **No number other than that upon the number plate furnished by the Ministry shall be exposed on any part of a motor vehicle or trailer in such a position or manner as to confuse the identity of the number plate.**

(2) Number plate to be kept clean — **Every number plate shall be kept free from dirt and obstruction and shall be affixed so that the entire plate, including the numbers, is plainly visible at all times, and the view of the number plate shall not be obscured or obstructed by spare tires, bumper bars, any part of the vehicle, any attachments to the vehicle or the load carried.**

(3) Obstruction prohibited — **The number plates shall not be obstructed by any device that prevents the entire number plates including the numbers from being accurately photographed using a photo-radar system.**

(3.0.1) Same — **The number plates shall not be obstructed by any device that prevents the entire number plates including the numbers from being accurately photographed using a red light camera system.**

(3.1) Same — **The number plates shall not be obstructed by any device or material that prevents the entire number plates including the numbers from being identified by an electronic toll system.**

(4) Offence — **Every person who contravenes subsection (2), (3), (3.0.1) or (3.1) is guilty of an offence.**

1993, c. 31, s. 2(5); 1994, c. 27, s. 138(7); 1996, c. 1, Sched. E, s. 2(1), (2); 1998, c. 38, s. 2

Commentary

The Red Light Camera Pilot Projects Act, 1998, S.O. 1998, c. 38 (in force November 20, 2000) permits evidence obtained from red light cameras to be used in areas designated by regulation for the purpose of enforcing subsection 144(18) of the Highway Traffic Act (failing to stop at a red light or proceeding before the light turns green). O. Reg. 277/99 dealing with the admissibility and use of Red Light Camera System evidence in proceedings under the Act, was brought into force contemporaneously with the Act.

Case Law

Lowry v. Thompson (1913), 29 O.L.R. 478, 15 D.L.R. 463 (C.A.); *Cillis v. Oakley* (1914), 31 O.L.R. 603, 20 D.L.R. 550 (C.A.) — Evidence of car numbers may well establish *prima facie* identity of a car involved in a collision. Since it would be a crime for any other car to bear the same numbers, a jury would be entitled, with the ordinary presumption against crime, to find that the car involved was that of the defendant.

14. (1) Improper number plate — **Where a police officer or an officer appointed under this Act has reason to believe that,**

　　(a) a number plate attached to a motor vehicle or trailer,

　　　　(i) has not been authorized under this Act for use on that vehicle,

　　　　(ii) was obtained by false pretences, or

　　　　(iii) has been defaced or altered;

　　(b) evidence of validation of a permit displayed on a motor vehicle,

　　　　(i) was not furnished under this Act in respect of that motor vehicle,

　　　　(ii) was obtained by false pretences, or

　　　　(iii) has been defaced or altered; or

　　(c) a permit carried by a driver of a motor vehicle,

　　　　(i) was not authorized under this Act in respect of that motor vehicle,

　　　　(ii) was obtained by false pretences, or

　　　　(iii) has been defaced or altered,

the officer may take possession of the number plate, evidence of validation or permit and retain it until the facts have been determined.

(2) Invalid cab card — **Where a police officer or an officer appointed under this Act has reason to believe that a CAVR cab card or an IRP cab card produced by a driver as being the permit for the vehicle,**

　　(a) was not furnished in accordance with this Act for that motor vehicle;

　　(b) has been canceled; or

　　(c) has been defaced or altered,

the officer may take possession of the CAVR cab card or the IRP cab card, as the case may be, and retain it until the facts have been determined.

1999, c. 12, Sched. R, s. 6(1)

Commentary

The Red Tape Reduction Act, 1999, S.O. 1999, c. 12, Sched. R. (ss. 1(2), 1(3), 2(1), 2(3), 2(5), 5(1), and 6(1) in force January 1, 2001) would amend ss. 6, 7, 12 and 14 of the Highway Traffic Act to facilitate Ontario's participation in the International Registration Plan, which contains reciprocal provisions in respect of commercial motor vehicles that travel across provincial or international borders. The Plan provides for the issuance of IRP cab cards as permits for these vehicles and for the appointment of registration and licence fees in each member jurisdiction on the basis of the distances travelled in each jurisdiction. Persons residing or based in other jurisdictions that are members of the Plan are exempt from the requirements of and fees prescribed under Part II of the Highway Traffic Act.

Case Law

R. v. Jutras (1954), 18 C.R. 229, 109 C.C.C. 190 (B.C. Pol. Mag. Ct.) — Special statutory powers in connection with seizure of number plates wrongly used must be strictly construed.

15. (1) Exceptions as to residents of other provinces — Section 7 and subsection 13(1) do not apply to a motor vehicle owned by a person who does not reside or carry on business in Ontario for more than six consecutive months in each year if the owner thereof is a resident of some other province of Canada and has complied with the provisions of the law of the province in which the person resides as to registration of a motor vehicle and the display of the registration number thereon, and provided the province of residence grants similar exemptions and privileges with respect to motor vehicles owned by residents of Ontario for which permits are issued and in force under this Act and the regulations.

(2) Exemption from s. 7 for thirty days — Upon the owner of a motor vehicle becoming a resident of Ontario, the owner is exempt from the provisions of section 7 for the thirty days immediately following provided the owner has complied with the provisions of the law of the jurisdiction in which the owner resided immediately prior to taking up residence in Ontario as to the registration of the motor vehicle and the displays of the registration number thereon, and continues to display the registration number in accordance with that law.

(3) Exceptions as to residents of foreign countries — Section 7 and subsection 13(1) do not apply to a motor vehicle owned by a person who does not reside or carry on business in Ontario for more than three months in any one year if the owner thereof is a resident of a country or state that grants similar exemptions and privileges with respect to motor vehicles owned by residents of Ontario for which permits are issued and in force under this Act and the regulations and has complied with the provisions of the law of the country or state in which the person resides as to registration of a motor vehicle and the display of registration plates thereon, but this subsection does not apply to commercial motor vehicles.

(4) Registration of vehicles of certain non-residents — Despite subsections (1) and (3), section 7 and subsection 13(1) apply to a motor vehicle owned by a person who does not reside in Ontario that displays registration plates of a jurisdiction other than Ontario and that is,

(a) based and operated in Ontario by the person; or

(b) operated by a resident of Ontario for more than a thirty-day period in any calendar year.

(5) Regulations — The Lieutenant Governor in Council may make regulations providing for the temporary exemption of vehicles or any class thereof from section 7 or any provision thereof.

Commentary

Exemptions from the Ontario Act apply to those ordinarily resident in other provinces. Upon becoming a resident of Ontario, such a person has 30 days to register in Ontario. Similar provisions apply, with modifications, to foreign owners.

Case Law

R. v. Macaulay (1958), 120 C.C.C. 372 (N.B. Co. Ct.) — The finding of a resident driving a car registered out of the province creates a *prima facie* case, requiring the driver to bring himself or herself within the exception.

Related Provisions: See Vehicle Permits; R.R.O. 1990, Reg. 628.

16. (1) Definitions — In this section and in sections 17 to 23.1,

Proposed Amendment — 16(1) opening words

(1) Definitions — In this section and in sections 17 to 22,
2015, c. 27, Sched. 7, s. 5(1) [Not in force at date of publication.]

"commercial motor vehicle" does not include,

(a) a commercial motor vehicle, other than a bus, having a gross weight or registered gross weight of not more than 4,500 kilograms, an ambulance, a fire apparatus, a hearse, a casket wagon, a mobile crane, a motor home or a vehicle commonly known as a tow truck,

(b) a commercial motor vehicle leased for no longer than thirty days by an individual for the transportation of goods kept for that individual's personal use or the gratuitous carriage of passengers,

(c) a commercial motor vehicle operated under a permit and number plates issued under a regulation made under clause 7(24)(g) or (h) that is not transporting passengers or goods,

(d) a commercial motor vehicle operated under the authority of an In-Transit permit, and

(e) a bus that is used for personal purposes without compensation;

Proposed Repeal — 16(1) "commercial motor vehicle"

"commercial motor vehicle" [Repealed 2014, c. 9, Sched. 2, s. 3(1). To come into force January 1, 2017.]

"compensation" includes any rate, remuneration, reimbursement or reward of any kind paid, payable or promised, or received or demanded, directly or indirectly;

Proposed Repeal — 16(1) "compensation"

"compensation" [Repealed 2014, c. 9, Sched. 2, s. 3(1). To come into force January 1, 2017.]

"CVOR certificate" means a Commercial Vehicle Operator's Registration Certificate issued under this Act;

Proposed Repeal — 16(1) "CVOR certificate"

"CVOR certificate" [Repealed 2014, c. 9, Sched. 2, s. 3(1). To come into force January 1, 2017.]

"goods" includes all classes of materials, wares and merchandise and livestock;

Proposed Repeal — 16(1) "goods"

"goods" [Repealed 2014, c. 9, Sched. 2, s. 3(1). To come into force January 1, 2017.]

"operator" means the person directly or indirectly responsible for the operation of a commercial motor vehicle including the conduct of the driver of, and the carriage of goods or passengers, if any, in the vehicle or combination of vehicles;

"owner-driver authority" [Repealed 2002, c. 18, Sched. P, s. 3(3).]

"safety record" means the safety record of an operator determined in accordance with the regulations;

Proposed Repeal — 16(1) "safety record"

"safety record" [Repealed 2014, c. 9, Sched. 2, s. 3(1). To come into force January 1, 2017.]

"single-source authority" [Repealed 2002, c. 18, Sched. P, s. 3(3).]

(2) **CVOR certificate required** — No person shall drive or operate a commercial motor vehicle on a highway unless the operator is the holder of a valid CVOR certificate.

Proposed Addition — 16(2.1)

(2.1) **Same** — No person shall hold themselves out to be the holder of a CVOR certificate unless the person is the holder of a CVOR certificate.

2015, c. 27, Sched. 7, s. 5(2) [Not in force at date of publication.]

(3) Documents to be carried — Every driver of a commercial motor vehicle shall carry the original or a copy of,

    (a) the CVOR certificate issued to the operator of the vehicle; or

    (b) the lease of the vehicle meeting the requirements of subsection (5) if it is a leased vehicle;

    (c) [Repealed 2002, c. 18, Sched. P, s. 3(5).]

and where the operator has been issued fleet limitation certificates, a fleet limitation certificate.

Proposed Amendment — 16(3)

(3) Documents to be carried — Every driver of a commercial motor vehicle shall carry,

    (a) the original or a copy of the CVOR certificate issued to the operator of the vehicle or, if it is a leased vehicle, the original or a copy of the lease that meets the requirements of subsection (5);

    (b) if the operator has been issued fleet limitation certificates, an original fleet limitation certificate; and

    (c) any other prescribed document, in its original form or as a copy, as prescribed.

                   2014, c. 9, Sched. 2, s. 3(2) [To come into force January 1, 2017.]

---

(4) Documents to be surrendered — Every driver of a commercial motor vehicle shall, upon the demand of a police officer, surrender for inspection the documents that are required under subsection (3) to be carried.

(5) Requirements for lease — Every lease carried under subsection (3) shall clearly identify the vehicle involved, the parties to the lease and their addresses, the operator of the vehicle and the operator's CVOR certificate.

(6) [Repealed 2002, c. 18, Sched. P, s. 3(6).]

(7) [Repealed 2002, c. 18, Sched. P, s. 3(6).]

              1994, c. 27, s. 138(8); 1996, c. 33, s. 1; 2002, c. 18, Sched. P, s. 3

Commentary

Drivers and operators of commercial motor vehicles are issued a "Commercial Vehicle Operator's Registration Certificate", or "CVOR" certificate, in lieu of a permit and must carry it in the vehicle along with a lease, contract or notice of contract. Such documents must be produced for inspection.

Related Provisions: See O. Reg. 424/97, Commercial Motor Vehicle Operators' Information, and R.R.O. 1990, Reg. 628, Vehicle Permits.

17. (1) CVOR certificates issued, renewed by Registrar — The Registrar shall issue a CVOR certificate to and renew a CVOR certificate of every person who applies for the certificate or renewal in the form approved by the Minister and meets the requirements of this Act and the regulations.

(1.1) Terms and conditions — The Registrar may issue a CVOR certificate subject to any terms and conditions that the Registrar considers appropriate.

(2) Refusal to issue — The Registrar may refuse to issue a CVOR certificate to an applicant if the Registrar has reason to believe, having regard to the applicant's safety record and any other information that the Registrar considers relevant, that the applicant will not operate a commercial motor vehicle safely or in accordance with this Act, the regulations and other laws relating to highway safety.

(3) Same — The Registrar may refuse to issue a CVOR certificate to an applicant if the applicant is related to,

(a) a person whose CVOR certificate has been cancelled, is or has been under suspension or is or has been subject to a fleet limitation;

(b) a person whose CVOR certificate suspension, cancellation or fleet limitation is under appeal; or

(c) a person who the Registrar has reason to believe, having regard to the person's safety record and any other information that the Registrar considers relevant, will not operate a commercial motor vehicle safely or in accordance with this Act, the regulations and other laws relating to highway safety.

(3.1) Same — The Registrar may refuse to issue, replace or renew a CVOR certificate if the applicant is indebted to the Minister of Finance in respect of,

(a) an outstanding fee, or an outstanding penalty or interest in respect of a fee, due under this Act or the *Public Vehicles Act*; or

(b) an outstanding public vehicle-related fee, or an outstanding penalty or interest in respect of such fee, under the *Motor Vehicle Transport Act, 1987* (Canada).

Proposed Repeal — 17(3.1)

(3.1) [Repealed 2014, c. 9, Sched. 2, s. 4. To come into force January 1, 2017.]

(3.2) Same — The Registrar shall refuse to renew a CVOR certificate,

(a) that was issued subject to terms or conditions; or

(b) that has been invalid for more than 12 months before the application for renewal is received by the Registrar.

Proposed Repeal — 17(3.2)

(3.2) [Repealed 2014, c. 9, Sched. 2, s. 4. To come into force January 1, 2017.]

(4) Interpretation — An applicant is related to a person for the purpose of subsection (3) if,

(a) the applicant and the person are related individuals;

(b) either the applicant or the person is a partner of the other or was a partner of the other or they have or have had partners in common;

(c) either the applicant or the person, directly or indirectly, controls or controlled or manages or managed the other; or

(d) the applicant and the person have or have had common officers or directors or they are or have been controlled, directly or indirectly, by the same shareholders.

(5) **Expiry** — A CVOR certificate issued or renewed on or after the day subsection 4(3) of Schedule P to the *Government Efficiency Act, 2002* comes into force expires as provided in the regulations.

Proposed Amendment — 17(5)

(5) **Expiry** — A CVOR certificate expires as provided in the regulations.
> 2015, c. 27, Sched. 7, s. 6 [Not in force at date of publication.]

(5.1) **Expiry date assigned to existing CVOR certificates** — The Registrar may at any time assign an expiry date to a CVOR certificate that was issued before the day subsection 4(3) of Schedule P to the *Government Efficiency Act, 2002* comes into force.

Proposed Repeal — 17(5.1)

(5.1) [Repealed 2015, c. 27, Sched. 7, s. 6. Not in force at date of publication.]

(5.2) **Notice** — The Registrar shall give the holder of a CVOR certificate notice, in the prescribed manner, of the assignment of an expiry date under subsection (5.1).

Proposed Repeal — 17(5.2)

(5.2) [Repealed 2015, c. 27, Sched. 7, s. 6. Not in force at date of publication.]

(6) **One certificate only** — No person, alone or in partnership, is entitled to hold more than one CVOR certificate.

(7) **Not transferable** — A CVOR certificate is not transferable.
> 1996, c. 33, s. 2; 2002, c. 18, Sched. P, s. 4

Related Provisions: See O. Reg. 424/97, Commercial Motor Vehicle Operators' Information.

17.0.1 (1) Revocation of CVOR certificate for dishonoured payments —
The Registrar may revoke a CVOR certificate if the payment of the issuance, renewal or replacement fee in respect of the certificate has been dishonoured.

(2) **Notice** — The Registrar shall give the holder of the CVOR certificate notice, in the prescribed manner, of the proposed revocation under subsection (1) and, subject to subsection (3), the revocation shall take effect on the 30th day after the day the notice was given.

(3) **Payment honoured** — If the amount of the dishonoured payment, and any related fees, interest and penalties, are paid to the Registrar before the 30th day after the day the notice was given, the revocation shall not take effect.
> 2002, c. 18, Sched. P, s. 5

Proposed Addition — 17.0.2

17.0.2 Refusal to issue, replace or renew CVOR certificates — (1) Non-payment of fees, fines, penalties — The Registrar may refuse to issue, replace or renew a CVOR certificate if the applicant owes an outstanding fee, fine or administrative penalty, or any interest or penalty that is in respect of such a fee, fine or penalty, under this Act, the *Provincial Offences Act*, the *Public Vehicles Act* or the *Motor Vehicle Transport Act, 1987* (Canada).

(2) Subject to terms or conditions or invalid for more than 12 months — The Registrar shall refuse to renew a CVOR certificate,

(a) that was issued subject to any terms or conditions pursuant to subsection 17(1.1); or

(b) that has been invalid for more than 12 months before the application for renewal is received by the Registrar.

(3) Prescribed reason — The Registrar may refuse to issue, replace or renew CVOR certificate for any other reason that may be prescribed.

2014, c. 9, Sched. 2, s. 5 [To come into force January 1, 2017.]

17.1 (1) Safety ratings — The Registrar shall assign a safety rating to every operator in accordance with the regulations.

(2) Notice of rating to operator — Where the Registrar proposes to assign a safety rating to an operator for the first time or to change an operator's safety rating, he or she shall notify the operator of the proposed rating.

(3) Methods for giving notice — Notice under subsection (2) is sufficiently given if,

(a) it is delivered personally to the operator;

(b) it is delivered by courier to the operator;

(c) it is sent by mail to the operator at the latest address provided by the operator to the Ministry;

(d) it is sent by fax to the operator at the latest fax number provided by the operator to the Ministry; or

(e) it is sent by another electronic means of transmission prescribed by regulation in accordance with the regulations.

(4) Operator may dispute first or changed rating — An operator may, within 30 days after being notified under subsection (2), submit to the Registrar documents, records and written submissions that may show cause why the Registrar should not assign the proposed safety rating to the operator.

(5) Registrar to confirm or change safety rating — Upon the expiration of the 30-day period referred to in subsection (4) and consideration of any documents, records and submissions submitted under that subsection, the Registrar shall assign to the operator the proposed safety rating or a different rating.

(6) **Written hearing** — Despite the *Statutory Powers Procedure Act*, the Registrar shall consider the matter under subsection (5) by means of a written hearing unless the Registrar agrees to an oral or electronic hearing.

(7) **Parties, privacy** — The Registrar and the operator whose safety rating is under dispute are the only parties to the hearing and, unless they otherwise agree, the hearing shall be closed to the public.

(8) **No appeal** — The safety rating assigned by the Registrar is final and binding and there is no appeal therefrom.

(9) **Available to the public** — The Registrar shall make the safety ratings of operators available to the public in the manner that the Registrar considers appropriate.

Proposed Amendment — 17.1(9)

(9) **Available to the public** — The Registrar shall make the safety ratings of operators, and any other information respecting operators that he or she thinks should be publicly known, available to the public in the manner that the Registrar considers appropriate.

2015, c. 27, Sched. 7, s. 7(2) [Not in force at date of publication.]

(10) **Protection from personal liability** — No action or other proceeding for damages shall be instituted against the Registrar or any employee of the Ministry for any act done in good faith in the execution or intended execution of a duty under this section or for any alleged neglect or default in the execution in good faith of a duty under this section.

(11) **Crown not relieved of liability** — Despite subsections 5(2) and (4) of the *Proceedings Against the Crown Act*, subsection (10) does not relieve the Crown of liability in respect of a tort committed by a person mentioned in subsection (10) to which it would otherwise be subject.

(12) **Regulations** — The Lieutenant Governor in Council may make regulations,

(a) prescribing other electronic means of transmission for giving notice;

(b) governing the giving of notice by mail, fax or a means of transmission prescribed under clause (a), including prescribing rules governing when notice is deemed to have been received.

1996, c. 33, s. 3; 2015, c. 27, Sched. 7, s. 7(1), (3)

Related Provisions: See O. Reg. 424/97, Commercial Motor Vehicle Operators' Information.

18. (1) **Holder to report changes** — Every holder of a CVOR certificate shall notify the Registrar in writing within 15 days after any change in the holder's name, address, fax number or address or number used for another electronic means of transmission or, where applicable, the persons constituting the officers, directors or partners of the holder, of the change made.

(2) **Same** — Every holder of a CVOR certificate shall notify the Registrar of any change in the holder's commercial motor vehicle fleet size or in the total distance

travelled by the commercial motor vehicle fleet in a specified period, in accordance with the regulations.

Proposed Repeal — 18

18. [Repealed 2014, c. 9, Sched. 2, s. 6. To come into force January 1, 2017.]

1996, c. 33, s. 4; 2015, c. 27, Sched. 7, s. 8

Related Provisions: See O. Reg. 424/97, Commercial Motor Vehicle Operators' Information.

19. Person deemed to be operator — In the absence of evidence to the contrary, where no CVOR certificate or lease applicable to a commercial motor vehicle is produced, the holder of the plate portion of the permit for the vehicle shall be deemed to be the operator for the purposes of sections 18 and 20.

Proposed Amendment — 19

19. Person deemed to be operator — In the absence of evidence to the contrary, where no CVOR certificate or lease applicable to a commercial motor vehicle is produced, the holder of the plate portion of the permit for the vehicle shall be deemed to be the operator for the purposes of section 20.

2014, c. 9, Sched. 2, s. 7 [To come into force January 1, 2017.]

2002, c. 18, Sched. P, s. 6

20. (1) Retaining lease — Every person who gives up possession of a commercial motor vehicle under a lease shall retain a copy of the lease in the person's place of business for a period of one year after the termination of the lease.

(2) Where contravention of subs. 16(2) or 47(8) — A police officer who has reason to believe that a commercial motor vehicle is being operated in contravention of subsection 16(2) or 47(8) may,

(a) detain the vehicle at any location that is reasonable in the circumstances; and

(b) seize the permits and number plates for the vehicle,

until the vehicle can be moved without a contravention of this Act occurring.

(3) Permit suspended — Every permit seized under subsection (2) shall be deemed to be under suspension for the purposes of section 51 while it is in the custody of the officer seizing it.

(4) Lien — The costs incurred in detaining a vehicle under subsection (2) are a lien on the vehicle, which may be enforced in the manner provided under Part III of the *Repair and Storage Liens Act*.

(5) Court application — The person entitled to possession of a vehicle that is detained or the permits or plates of which are seized under subsection (2) may apply to the Superior Court of Justice for an order that the vehicle be released or the permits and plates returned, as the case may be.

(6) Security — On an application being made under subsection (5), the Court may make the order applied for on condition that a security, for the payment of any fine imposed, in the amount that is determined by the Court but not exceeding $5,000 be deposited with the Court.

(7) Return of security — Every security deposited under subsection (6) shall be returned,

(a) upon a final acquittal under all charges arising in connection with the seizure or detention;

(b) where a charge is not laid within six months after the seizure or detention, on the expiration of the six-month period; or

(c) upon a conviction arising in connection with the seizure or detention, after withholding the amount of the fine.

2002, c. 18, Sched. P, s. 7; 2009, c. 5, s. 6

Commentary

The Red Tape Reduction Act, 1999, S.O. 1999, c. 12, Sched. R. (ss. 1(2), 1(3), 2(1), 2(3), 2(5), 5(1), and 6(1) in force January 1, 2001) would amend ss. 6, 7, 12 and 14 of the Highway Traffic Act to facilitate Ontario's participation in the International Registration Plan, which contains reciprocal provisions in respect of commercial motor vehicles that travel across provincial or international borders. The Plan provides for the issuance of IRP cab cards as permits for these vehicles and for the appointment of registration and licence fees in each member jurisdiction on the basis of the distances travelled in each jurisdiction. Persons residing or based in other jurisdictions that are members of the Plan are exempt from the requirements of and fees prescribed under Part II of the Highway Traffic Act.

21. (1) Offence — Every person who contravenes subsection 16(3) or (4), section 18 or 20 or a regulation made under section 22 is guilty of an offence and on conviction is liable to a fine of not more than $500.

Proposed Amendment — 21(1)

(1) Offences, commercial motor vehicles — Every person who contravenes subsection 16(3) or (4) or section 20 or a regulation made under subsection 22(1) is guilty of an offence and on conviction is liable to a fine of not more than $1,000.

2014, c. 9, Sched. 2, s. 8 [To come into force January 1, 2017.]

(2) Idem — Every person who contravenes subsection 16(2) is guilty of an offence and on conviction is liable to a fine of not more than $2,000 or to imprisonment for a term of not more than six months, or to both.

Proposed Addition — 21(2.1)

(2.1) Same — Every person who contravenes subsection 16(2.1) is guilty of an offence and on conviction is liable to a fine of not more than $2,000.

2015, c. 27, Sched. 7, s. 9 [Not in force at date of publication.]

(3) Same — Every person who contravenes or fails to comply with a term or condition of a CVOR certificate issued to the person is guilty of an offence and on conviction is liable to a fine of not more than $2,000 or to imprisonment for a term of not more than six months, or to both.

(4) **Same** — Every person who provides, uses or permits the use of a fictitious, altered or fraudulently obtained CVOR certificate, or improperly uses a CVOR certificate, is guilty of an offence and on conviction is liable to a fine of not less than $400 and not more than $5,000 or to imprisonment for a term of not more than six months, or to both.

1996, c. 33, s. 5; 2002, c. 18, Sched. P, s. 8

Proposed Addition — 21.1

21.1 Administrative penalties — (1) **Purpose** — An administrative penalty may be imposed under this section in order to promote compliance with this Act and the regulations.

(2) **Order imposing administrative penalties** — If a prescribed authorized person is satisfied that a person is contravening or not complying with or has contravened or failed to comply with a prescribed provision of this Act or of the regulations, the prescribed authorized person may, by order, impose an administrative penalty on the person in accordance with this section and the regulations.

(3) **May only be imposed on prescribed persons** — An administrative penalty may only be imposed on a person who belongs to a prescribed class.

(4) **May be imposed with other measures** — An administrative penalty may be imposed alone or in conjunction with any other regulatory measure provided by this or any other Act; however, an administrative penalty may not be imposed if the person is charged with an offence under this Act in respect of the same contravention or failure to comply.

(5) **Limitation** — An administrative penalty may only be imposed within the prescribed time period.

(6) **No right to be heard** — There is no right to be heard before an order imposing an administrative penalty is made.

(7) **Appeal** — A person who is subject to an order imposing an administrative penalty may, in accordance with the regulations, appeal the order to a person prescribed for the purpose of this subsection and the prescribed person may confirm, vary or set aside the order.

(8) **Same** — An appeal commenced under subsection (7) operates as a stay of the order until the matter is finally disposed of.

(9) **Parties to judicial review** — The parties to any judicial review brought in respect of this section are the Registrar and the person subject to the order imposing an administrative penalty.

(10) **Maximum administrative penalty** — An administrative penalty shall not exceed $20,000 or such lesser amount as may be prescribed.

(11) Enforcement — If a person fails to pay an administrative penalty in accordance with the terms of the order imposing the penalty, the Minister may file the order with the Superior Court of Justice and the order may be enforced as if it were an order of the court.

(12) Same — For the purposes of section 129 of the *Courts of Justice Act*, the date on which the order is filed with the court is deemed to be the date of the order.

(13) Same — An administrative penalty that is not paid in accordance with the terms of the order imposing the penalty is a debt due to the Crown and is also enforceable as such.

(14) Regulations — The Lieutenant Governor in Council may make regulations governing the administrative penalties that may be imposed under this section and, without limiting the generality of the foregoing, may make regulations,

(a) prescribing authorized persons for the purpose of subsection (2);

(b) prescribing provisions of this Act and of the regulations for the purpose of subsection (2);

(c) prescribing classes of persons who may be subject to an order under subsection (2);

(d) prescribing persons for the purpose of subsection (7);

(e) prescribing the amount of a penalty, or method for calculating the amount of a penalty, and prescribing different penalties or ranges of penalties for different types of contraventions or failures to comply and different penalties or ranges of penalties depending on specified criteria;

(f) authorizing a person prescribed under clause (a) to determine the amount of a penalty, if the amount of the penalty or method for calculating the amount of the penalty is not prescribed, and prescribing criteria that may or must be considered when making an order under subsection (2), including prescribing that the criteria may include aggravating or mitigating factors;

(g) authorizing that a penalty may be imposed for each day or part of a day on which a contravention or failure to comply continues;

(h) authorizing higher penalties (not to exceed the maximum penalty established under subsection (10) or prescribed under clause (k)) for a second or subsequent contravention or failure to comply;

(i) governing the payment of penalties, including requiring that a penalty be paid before a specified deadline, and authorizing the Registrar to approve a plan of periodic payments that extends beyond the deadline;

(j) authorizing the imposition of late payment fees respecting penalties that are not paid before the specified deadline, including graduated late payment fees, and providing that such fees are included as part of the penalty for enforcement purposes;

(k) prescribing a lesser maximum penalty and the provisions of this Act or of the regulations to which the lesser maximum penalty applies for the purpose of subsection (10);

(l) prescribing and governing procedures for making and serving an order under this section, including prescribing rules for service, prescribing the day on which an order is deemed to have been received and providing for service on persons outside Ontario;

(m) governing the appeal of an order under subsection (7), including,

(i) establishing procedures for commencing and conducting an appeal,

(ii) establishing time limits for the stages of an appeal and authorizing the person prescribed under clause (d) to extend any time limit,

(iii) prescribing that the appeal must or may be conducted orally, electronically or in writing or authorizing the person prescribed under clause (d) to make that determination,

(iv) prescribing fees to be paid to commence an appeal, and

(v) establishing criteria to be considered and criteria not to be considered by the person prescribed under clause (d) when determining whether to confirm, vary or set aside an order.

2014, c. 9, Sched. 2, s. 9 [Not in force at date of publication.]

22. (1) Regulations — The Lieutenant Governor in Council may make regulations,

(a) [Repealed 2002, c. 18, Sched. P, s. 9(1).]

Proposed Amendment — 22(1)(a)

(a) prescribing standards and specifications for the use, operation and maintenance of commercial motor vehicles, or any class of them;

2014, c. 9, Sched. 2, s. 10(1) [To come into force January 1, 2017.]

(b) prescribing methods of issuing CVOR certificates, including by electronic transmission, and governing the issue of CVOR certificates by such methods;

(c) classifying persons and vehicles and exempting any class of person or vehicle from section 16 and prescribing conditions for any such exemption;

(d) prescribing the requirements to obtain, renew and hold CVOR certificates and authorizing the Registrar to waive any requirements that are specified in the regulations under the circumstances prescribed therein;

Proposed Amendment — 22(1)(d)

(d) prescribing requirements, qualifications and standards for owners, operators and drivers of commercial motor vehicles, or any class of them, including requirements, qualifications and standards to obtain, renew and hold a CVOR certificate, and authorizing the Registrar to waive any requirements, qualifications or standards that are specified in the regulations under the circumstances specified in the regulations;

2014, c. 9, Sched. 2, s. 10(2) [To come into force January 1, 2017.]

Proposed Amendment — 22(1)(d)

(d) prescribing requirements, qualifications and standards for owners, operators and drivers of commercial motor vehicles or any class of them, or for any other person or class of persons, including requirements, qualifications and standards to obtain, renew and hold a CVOR certificate;

2015, c. 27, Sched. 7, s. 10(2) [Not in force at date of publication.]

Proposed Addition — 22(1)(d.0.1)–(d.0.3)

(d.0.1) prescribing standards and specifications for commercial motor vehicles, or any class of them, requiring the use of any equipment or other thing in commercial motor vehicles, or any class of them, and governing that use;

(d.0.2) governing the operation of commercial motor vehicles, or any class of them, including prescribing requirements, qualifications and standards for their operation and prescribing the duties of owners, operators, drivers and other persons, or any class of them, with respect to their operation;

(d.0.3) requiring owners and operators of commercial motor vehicles, or any class of them, to carry insurance and governing that insurance, including prescribing the form, amount, nature, class, provisions and conditions of the insurance and requirements respecting the evidence of such insurance;

2015, c. 27, Sched. 7, s. 10(2) [Not in force at date of publication.]

(d.1) [Repealed 2002, c. 18, Sched. P, s. 9(3).]

Proposed Amendment — 22(1)(d.1)

(d.1) prescribing reasons to refuse to issue, replace or renew a CVOR certificate for the purpose of subsection 17.0.2 (3);

2014, c. 9, Sched. 2, s. 10(2) [To come into force January 1; 2017.]

(e) governing the suspension or cancellation of CVOR certificates under subsection 47(1) or the imposition of a limitation on the fleet size operated under a CVOR certificate under subsection 47(2).

(f) respecting documents and information to be filed with or supplied to the Ministry prior to the issuance or renewal of CVOR certificates or as a condition of retention thereof by the holders of CVOR certificates;

Proposed Amendment — 22(1)(f)

(f) respecting documents and information to be filed with or supplied to the Ministry by owners, operators and drivers of commercial motor vehicles, prescribing the time or times or circumstances when such information is to be provided, governing the form and manner in which such information must be provided and, with respect to owners who are applicants for a CVOR certificate and operators, requiring the information prior to the issuance or renewal of CVOR certificates or as a condition of retention of CVOR certificates;

2014, c. 9, Sched. 2, s. 10(3) [To come into force January 1, 2017.]

Proposed Addition — 22(1)(f.1)

(f.1) prescribing and governing documents and records to be kept by owners, operators and drivers of commercial motor vehicles, or any class of them, and governing the retention of such documents and records;

2014, c. 9, Sched. 2, s. 10(3) [To come into force January 1, 2017.]

(g) defining "fleet size" for the purpose of subsection 18(2), and exempting any class or classes of CVOR certificate holders from all or part of the requirements of subsection 18(2);

Proposed Amendment — 22(1)(g)

(g) prescribing documents for the purpose of clause 16(3)(c) and prescribing whether each prescribed document may or must be carried in its original form or as a copy;

2014, c. 9, Sched. 2, s. 10(3) [To come into force January 1, 2017.]

(h) prescribing the method for determining an operator's safety record;

(i) prescribing the method for assigning safety ratings to operators;

Proposed Addition — 22(1)(i.1)

(i.1) requiring specified classes of owners and operators to install or to carry in their commercial motor vehicles, or in some of their commercial motor vehicles, as specified in the regulation, a device that is capable of recording and transmitting data about the operation of the vehicle and the conduct of the driver, prescribing standards and specifications for the device and requiring and governing its use;

2014, c. 9, Sched. 2, s. 10(4) [To come into force January 1, 2017.]

(j) providing for the reciprocal recognition of safety ratings, safety records and similar records of territories, other provinces and states of the United States of America;

(k) governing the expiry of CVOR certificates, including establishing classes of CVOR certificate holders and providing different expiry dates, or different methods of determining expiry dates, for CVOR certificates held by different classes of holders;

(l) prescribing methods of giving notice and governing the giving of notice by those methods, including prescribing rules governing when notice is deemed to have been received;

Proposed Addition — 22(1)(l.1)

(l.1) authorizing the Registrar, in specified circumstances, to waive any requirement, qualification, standard or specification in the regulations made under clause (d), (d.0.1) or (d.0.2);

2015, c. 27, Sched. 7, s. 10(4) [Not in force at date of publication.]

Proposed Addition — 22(1)(m)

(m) exempting any class of owners, operators, drivers or vehicles from any requirement of sections 16 to 23 or of a regulation made under this subsection, and prescribing circumstances and conditions for any such exemption.

Proposed Amendment — 22(1)(m)

(m) exempting any class of owners, operators, drivers or vehicles from any requirement of sections 16 to 22 or of a regulation made under this subsection, and prescribing circumstances and conditions for any such exemption.

2015, c. 27, Sched. 7, s. 10(5) [Not in force at date of publication.]
2014, c. 9, Sched. 2, s. 10(4) [To come into force January 1, 2017.]

> **Proposed Addition — 22(1)(n)**
>
> **(n) prescribing and governing transition rules to address the transportation services governed by Part X.2 before its repeal, including exemptions from any provision of this Act or of a regulation made under this section for a specified period of time or until a specified event occurs.**
>
> 2015, c. 27, Sched. 7, s. 10(6) [Not in force at date of publication.]

(2) Fees — The Registrar may set fees, subject to the approval of the Minister, for the application for and for the renewal and replacement of CVOR certificates.

(3) Same — Subject to the approval of the Minister, the Registrar may exempt any class of persons from the requirement to pay a fee set under subsection (2).

> 1996, c. 33, s. 6; 2002, c. 18, Sched. P, s. 9; 2015, c. 27, Sched. 7, s. 10(1), (3), (7)

Related Provisions: See O. Reg. 424/97, Commercial Motor Vehicle Operators' Information.

23. (1) Liability insurance for commercial motor vehicles — No operator or owner of a commercial motor vehicle shall operate the vehicle or cause or permit the vehicle to be operated on a highway unless, in addition to the minimum liability insurance required under the *Compulsory Automobile Insurance Act*, motor vehicle liability insurance in the amount prescribed by the regulations is carried for the vehicle with an insurer licensed under the *Insurance Act*.

(2) Non-residents — If an operator or owner of a commercial motor vehicle is not a resident of Ontario, the insurance required by subsection (1) may be carried with an insurer who is authorized to transact the insurance in the state or province in which the owner or operator resides.

(3) Driver to carry evidence of insurance — Every driver of a commercial motor vehicle shall carry evidence of a type prescribed by the regulations that the vehicle is insured as required by this section and shall surrender the evidence for reasonable inspection upon the demand of a police officer.

(4) Offence — An operator or owner who contravenes subsection (1) is guilty of an offence and on conviction is liable to a fine of not less than $500 and not more than $2,500.

(5) Idem — A driver who contravenes subsection (3) is guilty of an offence and on conviction is liable to a fine of not less than $100 and not more than $500.

(6) Regulations — The Lieutenant Governor in Council may make regulations,

    (a) prescribing the amount of motor vehicle liability insurance to be carried for a commercial motor vehicle;

    (b) prescribing documents that may be accepted as evidence that a commercial motor vehicle is insured as required by this section.

    (c) prescribing the form, amount, nature, class, provisions and conditions of the insurance required by section 23.1 and the nature of the evidence of that insurance that is to be carried in the vehicle.

Proposed Repeal — 23

23. [Repealed 2015, c. 27, Sched. 7, s. 11. Not in force at date of publication.]

2002, c. 18, Sched. P, s. 10

Commentary

Drivers must maintain insurance and demonstrate proof of same upon being requested to do so by a police officer.

Related Provisions: Compulsory Automobile Insurance Act, R.S.O. 1990, c. C.25, Insurance Act, R.S.O. 1990, c. I.8.

23.1 Insurance — Every person carrying goods for any other person for compensation shall obtain and carry the insurance that is required by the regulations and shall ensure that the evidence of the insurance is carried in every commercial motor vehicle of the operator that is being used to transport goods for compensation.

Proposed Repeal — 23.1

23.1 [Repealed 2015, c. 27, Sched. 7, s. 11. Not in force at date of publication.]

2002, c. 18, Sched. P, s. 11

24. [Repealed 2002, c. 22, s. 99.]

25. [Repealed 2002, c. 22, s. 99.]

PART III — PARKING PERMITS

26. (1) Accessible parking permits — The Minister shall issue an accessible parking permit to every person or organization that applies for it and meets the requirements of the regulations.

(2) Term — An accessible parking permit is in force during the period of time shown on the permit.

(3) Cancellation of permit — The Minister may cancel an accessible parking permit or may refuse to issue a replacement permit if the permit has been used in contravention of this Part or the regulations or of a municipal by-law passed under section 9, 10, 11 or 102 of the *Municipal Act, 2001* or under section 7, 8 or 80 of the *City of Toronto Act, 2006*, as the case may be, for establishing a system of accessible parking.

(4) Refusal to issue new permit — If the Minister cancels an accessible parking permit, the Minister may refuse to issue a new permit to the holder of the cancelled permit.

2002, c. 17, Sched. F, s. 1; 2006, c. 32, Sched. C, s. 24(1); 2009, c. 33, Sched. 26, s. 3(3)

Case Law

1747114 Ontario Inc. v. Mississauga (City) (2013), 58 M.V.R. (6th) 281, 2013 ONCJ 623, 2013 CarswellOnt 15942, 17 M.P.L.R. (5th) 296, [2013] O.J. No. 5344 — A municipal by-law under which a courier company vehicle was caught parking in an accessible space was consistent with ss. 195 and s. 26(3) of the *Act*.

Related Provisions: See R.R.O. 1990, Reg. 581, Accessible Parking for Persons with Disabilities.

27. (1) Offence, accessible parking permit — No person shall,

(a) **have in his or her possession an accessible parking permit that is fictitious, altered or fraudulently obtained;**

(b) **display an accessible parking permit otherwise than in accordance with the regulations;**

(c) **fail or refuse to surrender an accessible parking permit in accordance with this Part or the regulations;**

(d) **use an accessible parking permit on land owned and occupied by the Crown otherwise than in accordance with the regulations;**

(e) **give, lend, sell or offer for sale an accessible parking permit or permit the use of it by another person otherwise than in accordance with the regulations; or**

(f) **make, permit the making of, give, lend, sell or offer for sale a fictitious or altered accessible parking permit.**

(2) Penalty — **A person who contravenes clause (1)(a), (b), (c), (d), (e) or (f) is guilty of an offence and on conviction is liable to a fine of not less than $300 and not more than $5,000.**

2001, c. 32, s. 26; 2009, c. 33, Sched. 26, s. 3(4)

Case Law

R. v. Ferranti (2013), 50 M.V.R. (6th) 23, 2013 CarswellOnt 14072 (Ont. C.A.) — The word "display" is capable of different meanings. As the intention of the statute was to prevent persons other than persons issued permits from using permits, interpreting the statute to require an officer to actually see the violator place the permit in the window would defeat this intention.

Related Provisions: See R.R.O. 1990, Reg. 581, Accessible Parking for Persons with Disabilities.

28. (1) Inspection, accessible parking permit — Every person having possession of an accessible parking permit shall, on the demand of a police officer, police cadet, municipal law enforcement officer or an officer appointed for carrying out the provisions of this Act, surrender the permit for reasonable inspection to ensure that the provisions of this Part and the regulations and any municipal by-law passed under section 9, 10, 11 or 102 of the *Municipal Act, 2001* or under section 7, 8 or 80 of the *City of Toronto Act, 2006*, as the case may be, for establishing a system of accessible parking are being complied with.

(2) Officer may take possession of the permit — An officer or cadet to whom an accessible parking permit has been surrendered may retain it until disposition of the case if the officer or cadet has reasonable ground to believe that the permit,

(a) was not issued under this Part;

(b) was obtained under false pretences;

(c) has been defaced or altered;

(d) has expired or been cancelled; or

(e) is being or has been used in contravention of the regulations or of a by-law passed under section 9, 10, 11 or 102 of the *Municipal Act, 2001* or under section 7, 8 or 80 of the *City of Toronto Act, 2006*, as the case may be, for establishing a system of accessible parking.

2002, c. 17, Sched. F, s. 1; 2006, c. 32, Sched. C, s. 24(2), (3); 2009, c. 33, Sched. 26, s. 3(5), (6)

Related Provisions: See R.R.O. 1990, Reg. 581, Accessible Parking for Persons with Disabilities.

29. [Repealed 2002, c. 17, Sched. F, s. 1.]

30. Regulations, accessible parking permits — The Lieutenant Governor in Council may make regulations,

(a) prescribing any form for the purposes of this Part and requiring its use;

(b) respecting the issuance, renewal, cancellation, replacement and disposal of accessible parking permits;

(c) prescribing the requirements for obtaining an accessible parking permit;

(d) prescribing the period of time or the method of determining the period of time during which accessible parking permits shall be in force;

(e) governing the manner of displaying accessible parking permits on or in vehicles;

(f) requiring the erection of signs and the placing of markings to identify designated parking spaces for the use of vehicles displaying an accessible parking permit, and prescribing the types, content and location of the signs and markings;

(g) prescribing the conditions of use of an accessible parking permit on land owned and occupied by the Crown;

(h) requiring and governing the surrender of accessible parking permits;

(i) providing for and governing the recognition of permits, number plates and other markers and devices issued by other jurisdictions as being equivalent to accessible parking permits issued under this Part.

2009, c. 33, Sched. 26, s. 3(7)

Commentary

The Ministry is responsible for issuing Disabled Person Parking Permits. The scheme works in conjunction with municipalities which are responsible for passing and enforcing by-laws. The by-laws are to create spaces.

Case Law

Dice v. Ontario, [2004] O.J. No. 4646, 2004 CarswellOnt 5147, 12 M.V.R. (5th) 41 (S.C.J.) — The onus is placed squarely on the driving public to satisfy the government that they are likely to handle a car safely, otherwise no driver's licences will be issued to them.

Related Provisions: R.R.O. 1990, Reg. 581, Accessible Parking for Persons with Disabilities; sections 49, 102 and 425 of the Municipal Act, 2001, S.O. 2001, c. 25 give municipalities the power to regulate parking for disabled persons, including the power to require owners and operators of parking lots and other parking facilities to which the public has access to provide designated spaces.

PART IV — LICENCES

Driver, Driving Instructor

31. Driving a privilege — **The purpose of this Part is to protect the public by ensuring that,**

    (a) the privilege of driving on a highway is granted to, and retained by, only those persons who demonstrate that they are likely to drive safely; and

    (b) full driving privileges are granted to novice and probationary drivers only after they acquire experience and develop or improve safe driving skills in controlled conditions.

1993, c. 40, s. 1

32. (1) Driver's licence — **No person shall drive a motor vehicle on a highway unless the motor vehicle is within a class of motor vehicles in respect of which the person holds a driver's licence issued to him or her under this Act.**

(2) Idem — **No person shall drive a street car on a highway unless he or she holds a driver's licence.**

(3) Endorsement required — **No person shall drive on a highway a type of motor vehicle or combination of vehicles for which the regulations require a driver's licence endorsement or in circumstances for which the regulations require a driver's licence endorsement unless the person's driver's licence permits him or her to drive that class of motor vehicle or combination of vehicles and is endorsed to permit him or her to drive that type of motor vehicle or combination of vehicles or to drive in those circumstances, as the case may be.**

(4) [Repealed 2002, c. 18, Sched. P, s. 12(1).]

(5) Issuance of driver's licence, endorsements — The Minister may require an applicant for a driver's licence or an endorsement or a person who holds a driver's licence to submit to the examinations that are authorized by the regulations at the times and places required by the Minister and to meet other prescribed requirements, and the Minister may,

> (a) in the case of an applicant for a driver's licence,
>
> > (i) issue the driver's licence of the class and subject to the conditions authorized by the regulations that, in the opinion of the Minister, are justified by the results of the examinations and other prescribed requirements, or
> >
> > (ii) where the applicant fails to submit to or to successfully complete the examinations or fails to meet the other prescribed requirements, refuse to issue a driver's licence to the applicant;
>
> (b) in the case of a person who holds a driver's licence,
>
> > (i) impose the conditions authorized by the regulations, remove any conditions or endorsements or change the class or classes of driver's licence held by the person, in accordance with the results of the examinations and other prescribed requirements, or
> >
> > (ii) where the person fails to submit to or to successfully complete the examinations or fails to meet the other prescribed requirements, impose the conditions authorized by the regulations, remove any endorsements, suspend or cancel the driver's licence held by the person or change the class or classes of driver's licence held by the person;
>
> (c) in the case of a person who holds a driver's licence and who is an applicant for an endorsement,
>
> > (i) grant the endorsements authorized by the regulations that, in the opinion of the Minister, are justified by the results of the examinations and other prescribed requirements, or
> >
> > (ii) where the person fails to submit to or to successfully complete the examinations or fails to meet the other prescribed requirements, refuse to grant the endorsements applied for.

(6) Retaining portion of fee — Despite section 2 of the *Financial Administration Act*, any person who issues licences or provides any other service in relation to licences on behalf of the Minister, pursuant to an agreement with the Minister, may retain, from the fee paid, the amount that is approved by the Minister from time to time.

(7) Contingent validity — Where a driver's licence issued under subsection (5) has been suspended, it is not valid for purposes of subsection (1) until the prescribed administrative fee for its reinstatement has been paid.

(8) [Repealed 2002, c. 18, Sched. P, s. 12(2).]

(9) Driving in breach of condition prohibited — No person shall drive a motor vehicle on a highway while contravening a condition contained in his or her driver's licence or imposed by the regulations.

(10) Responsibility of owner — No person who is the owner or is in possession or control of a motor vehicle or combination of vehicles shall permit any person to drive the motor vehicle or combination of vehicles on a highway unless that person holds a driver's licence for the class of motor vehicles or combination of vehicles to which the motor vehicle or combination of vehicles belongs.

(10.1) Same — No person who is the owner or is in possession or control of a motor vehicle or combination of vehicles shall permit any person to drive the motor vehicle or combination of vehicles on a highway where to do so would contravene a condition on the person's driver's licence.

(11) Same — No person who is the owner or is in possession or control of a motor vehicle or combination of vehicles shall permit any person to drive the motor vehicle or combination of vehicles on a highway unless that person holds a driver's licence containing endorsements that are required to drive that motor vehicle or combination of vehicles under the circumstances in which the person will be driving.

(11.1) Same, novice drivers — No person who is the owner or is in possession or control of a motor vehicle or combination of vehicles shall permit a novice driver, as defined under section 57.1, to drive the motor vehicle or combination of vehicles on a highway while contravening a condition or restriction imposed upon the novice driver by this Act or the regulations.

(12) [Repealed 2002, c. 18, Sched. P, s. 12(5).]

(13) Applicant for driver's licence may be photographed — The Minister may require as a condition for issuing a driver's licence that the applicant therefor submit to being photographed by equipment provided by the Ministry.

(14) Regulations — The Lieutenant Governor in Council may make regulations relating to this section,

(a) prescribing classes of motor vehicles;

(b) prescribing the term of validity of drivers' licences;

(c) prescribing conditions that may be imposed on a driver's licence or on a class or classes of drivers' licences;

(d) prescribing classes of drivers' licences;

(e) respecting practical and written driving examinations, mental examinations and physical examinations, including ophthalmic and auditory examinations, for applicants for and holders of drivers' licences and endorsements;

(f) prescribing the qualifications of applicants for and holders of drivers' licences or any class or classes of drivers' licences and authorizing the Minister to waive the qualifications that are specified in the regulations under the circumstances prescribed therein;

(g) prescribing the requirements to be met by an applicant for a driver's licence;

(h) prescribing types of motor vehicles or of combinations of vehicles for which endorsements are required and prescribing the endorsements;

(i) prescribing the circumstances for which endorsements are required and prescribing the endorsements;

(j) prescribing the requirements to be met by a person applying for an endorsement;

(k) prescribing the requirements to be met by a person for a condition to be removed from his or her driver's licence;

(l) prescribing the qualifications of applicants for and holders of endorsements and authorizing the Minister to waive the qualifications that are specified in the regulations under the circumstances prescribed in the regulations;

(m) respecting documents required to be filed with the Ministry prior to the issuance of a driver's licence or any class or classes of drivers' licences or prior to granting an endorsement or as a requirement for retaining a driver's licence or endorsement by the holder of a driver's licence;

Proposed Addition — 32(14)(m.1)

(m.1) providing that a driver's licence or an endorsement cannot be issued or renewed if the applicant or holder of the licence or endorsement has not paid an administrative penalty imposed under section 21.1;

2014, c. 9, Sched. 2, s. 11(1) [Not in force at date of publication.]

(n) prescribing the kinds of decisions under subsection (5) which an applicant or person who holds a driver's licence may appeal under section 50;

(o) respecting any matter that the Lieutenant Governor in Council considers necessary or advisable to carry out the intent and purpose of this section.

(15) **Documents privileged** — Documents filed with the Ministry relating to mental and physical, including opthalmic and auditory, examinations pursuant to this section are privileged for the information of the Ministry only and shall not be open for public inspection.

(16) **Penalty** — Every person who contravenes subsection (1), (2), (3), (10), (10.1), (11) or (11.1) is guilty of an offence and on conviction is liable to a fine of not less than $200 and not more than $1,000.

(17) **Penalty — commercial motor vehicle** — Despite subsection (16), every person who contravenes subsection (1), (3), (9), (10), (10.1), (11) or (11.1) is guilty of an offence and, if the offence was committed by means of a commercial motor vehicle within the meaning of subsection 16(1), on conviction is liable to a fine of not less than $200 and not more than $20,000.

Proposed Amendment — 32(17)

(17) **Penalty — commercial motor vehicle** — Despite subsection (16), every person who contravenes subsection (1), (3), (9), (10), (10.1), (11) or (11.1) is guilty of an offence and, if the offence was committed by means of a commercial motor vehicle, on conviction is liable to a fine of not less than $200 and not more than $20,000.

2014, c. 9, Sched. 2, s. 11(2) [To come into force January 1, 2017.]

(18) **Limitation on driver's licence** — For greater certainty, a person who holds a driver's licence to drive a class of motor vehicle may nevertheless be re-

stricted to driving a type of motor vehicle or combination of vehicles within that class of motor vehicle,

(a) by a condition prescribed under clause (14)(c) that is imposed on the person's licence; or

(b) by the absence of an endorsement prescribed under clause (14)(h) or (i) on the person's licence.

1993, c. 40, s. 2; 1996, c. 20, s. 3; 2002, c. 18, Sched. P, s. 12; 2009, c. 5, s. 7

Commentary

All drivers must be licensed. The licence must relate to the class of vehicle being driven. The Minister may impose restrictions. Owners shall ensure that drivers have a valid licence. To obtain a licence, a driver must pass an examination. Licences have two parts, one of which contains a photograph. Offences in relation to licences attract a minimum fine of $200 and a maximum of $1,000.

Note: As of the time of this writing, a proclamation date had not yet been announced for subss. 32(7), (8).

Case Law

R. v. Lumiala, [1957] O.W.N. 417, 25 C.R. 361 (H.C.) — The requirement that a driver holding only a temporary permit be accompanied by a licensed driver does not of itself impose duties on the accompanying person so that he or she might be deemed to be in charge or control of the vehicle in the absence of proof of that fact.

R. v. Fuchs, [1972] 4 W.W.R. 627, 7 C.C.C. (2d) 366 (B.C. S.C.) — A person does not cease to be the "holder" of a driver's licence merely because he or she has not signed the licence as required by the Act.

Feener v. McKenzie (1973), 5 N.S.R. (2d) 660 (C.A.) — The failure to be accompanied by a licensed driver is not *per se* negligence creating a cause of action.

Vancouver v. Burchill, [1932] S.C.R. 620 — An unlicensed driver is not prevented from recovering judgment for damages occasioned to him or her by the negligence of another person in the use of the highway.

R. v. Minister of Highways (1959), 28 W.W.R. (N.S.) 36 (Alta. T.D.) — While the requirement of technical competence in the operation of motor vehicles may, for the public safety, require a person prove that competence as a condition of the issue of a licence to drive — and the consequent right to drive — that requirement does not reduce a "right" to a "privilege". Accordingly, any power given to suspend or revoke a licence must be exercised only according to law and in strict compliance with the conditions governing the exercise of such power. (See also s. 31 of the Highway Traffic Act (Ont.).)

Field v. Supertest Petroleum Corp., [1943] O.W.N. 482 (H.C.); *Jenner v. Pelland* (1953), 9 W.W.R. (N.S.) 417 (Man. Q.B.) — A licence is not a certificate of the fitness to drive or skill of the holder, and not having a licence is not a material fact upon which a plaintiff may rely in a negligence action. A pleading to that effect will be struck out.

Lewis v. B.C. Supt. of Motor Vehicles (1979), 108 D.L.R. (3d) 525 (B.C. S.C.) — In considering the fitness and ability of an applicant to drive and operate a vehicle of a particular category, the superintendent must consider not only the standard and assessment criteria, but also all available evidence relating to the applicant's driving ability, including his or her driving and medical history, the results of written examinations and driving tests, and the fact that the applicant has held a similar class of licence in another jurisdiction.

Flint (Litigation Guardianship of) v. Beaton (1997), 28 M.V.R. (3d) 52, 101 O.A.C. 54 (Ont. C.A.) — An intoxicated licensee accompanied a driver with a learner's permit. The licensee was in breach of a duty to provide driving instruction and exercise some degree of care over the operation of the vehicle. The licensee was 50% responsible for the accident which killed the driver.

R. v. Parkinson (2003), 45 M.V.R. (4th) 275, 2003 CarswellBC 2114, 2003 BCPC 299 (B.C. Prov. Ct.) — The purpose of the sections relating to truck drivers is to limit on-duty hours on consecutive days and compel drivers to take time off in order to be sufficiently rested.

Griffin v. Ontario (Minister of Transportation) (2004), 2004 CarswellOnt 45, 1 M.V.R. (5th) 51, [2004] O.J. No. 54 (Ont. S.C.J.) — In order to drive safely, persons require a field of vision that includes an area of observation that extends both above and below a particular object on which vision is fixated.

Shepherd v. Ontario (Ministry of Transportation) (2004), 5 M.V.R. (5th) 114, 2004 CarswellOnt 1582 (Ont. Div. Ct.) — The Ministry has no discretion to issue a licence to a person whose field of vision is greatly reduced.

Campbell v. Ontario (Ministry of Transportation) (2004), 5 M.V.R. (5th) 204, 2004 CarswellOnt 699 (Ont. Div. Ct.) — Sections 14 and 15 of Ontario Reg. 340/94 authorize the Registrar to request that the applicant submit to a medical examination once a letter from the doctor is received under s. 203 of the Act.

Bothwell v. Ontario (Minister of Transportation) (2005), 2005 CarswellOnt 193, 193 O.A.C. 383, 13 M.V.R. (5th) 13, 24 Admin. L.R. (4th) 288 (Div. Ct.) — An application by a driver for judicial review of a decision denying him a permanent photo exemption based on religious freedom was dismissed.

R. v. Caine, 2006 CarswellOnt 3465, 2006 ONCJ 206, 33 M.V.R. (5th) 284 (C.J.) — Convictions for contravening zero alcohol for probationary drivers and Criminal Code drinking and driving offences away may both stand arising out of the same transaction.

Hutterian Brethren of Wilson Colony v. Alberta, 2009 CarswellAlta 1094, 2009 CarswellAlta 1095, [2009] S.C.J. No. 37, 2009 SCC 37, 310 D.L.R. (4th) 193, 9 Alta. L.R. (5th) 1, 81 M.V.R. (5th) 1, 390 N.R. 202, [2009] 9 W.W.R. 189, (sub nom. *Alberta v. Hutterian Brethren of Wilson County*) [2009] 2 S.C.R. 567, 460 A.R. 1, 194 C.R.R. (2d) 12, 462 W.A.C. 1; reversing [2007] A.J. No. 518, 2007 CarswellAlta 622, [2007] 9 W.W.R. 459, 49 M.V.R. (5th) 45, 283 D.L.R. (4th) 136, 77 Alta. L.R. (4th) 281, 417 A.R. 68, 410 W.A.C. 68, 2007 ABCA 160, (sub nom. *R. v. Hutterian Brethren of Wilson Colony)* 156 C.R.R. (2d) 234; affirming 2006 CarswellAlta 576, 33 M.V.R. (5th) 16, 57 Alta. L.R. (4th) 300, 141 C.R.R. (2d) 227, 2006 ABQB 338, [2006] 8 W.W.R. 190, 269 D.L.R. (4th) 757, 398 A.R. 5 — The universal photo requirement for licences infringed s. 2(a) of the *Charter of Rights* but was justified under s. 1.

Ontario (Ministry of Transportation) v. 457784 Ontario Ltd., 2009 CarswellOnt 1793, 2009 ONCJ 141, 83 M.V.R. (5th) 280 — A car rental agency was liable under s. 32(10) for permitting a person who was improperly licenced to operate a commercial motor vehicle. Under s. 47(3) of the *Provincial Offences Act* (Ontario), the burden fell on the defendant. To come under the exception of s. 16(1)(e) of the *Highway Traffic Act* by which a commercial motor vehicle does not include a bus used for personal purposes without compensation.

R. v. Maharaj, 2010 CarswellOnt 4414, 98 M.V.R. (5th) 316 (C.J.) — Operating a motor vehicle with blood alcohol exceeding zero milligrams is an offence of absolute liability.

Borton v. Ontario, 2013 CarswellOnt 14272, 53 M.V.R. (6th) 41, 2013 ONSC 6418 (Ont. S.C.J.) — The applicant's withdrawal from a rehabilitation program followed by silence provided ample justification for the decision to suspend the applicant's driver's license.

Becamon v. Wawanesa Mutual Insurance Co., 2009 ONCA 113, *(sub nom. Shah v. Becamon)* 2009 CarswellOnt 624, 94 O.R. (3d) 297, *(sub nom. Shah v. Becamon)* 81 C.C.L.I. (4th) 1, 308 D.L.R. (4th) 80, *(sub nom. Shah v. Becamon)* 72 M.V.R. (5th) 51, 246 O.A.C. 24, [2009] O.J. No. 478 (Ont. C.A.) — The graduated licence scheme set out in the Act applied only to the operation of a motor vehicle on a "highway".

R. v. Westover (2013), 49 M.V.R. (6th) 336, 2013 ONCJ 472, 2013 CarswellOnt 11933, [2013] O.J. No. 3904 (Ont. C.J.) — Freedom of religion did not justify a belief that the accused should not abide by the rules and regulations related to motor vehicles and highways.

MacLennan v. Ontario (Minister of Transportation) (2014), 66 M.V.R. (6th) 122, 2014 ONSC 2946, 2014 CarswellOnt 8189, 121 O.R. (3d) 134, 313 C.R.R. (2d) 57, 323 O.A.C. 27 (Div. Ct.) — The older driver renewal process for drivers over eighty under s. 32(14) and O. Reg. 340/94 of the *Act* does not violate s. 15 of the *Charter of Rights*.

Related Provisions: O. Regs. 341/94 and 340/94, Driving Examinations and Driver's Licences, respectively; O. Reg. 287/08; Conduct Review Programs.

32.1 (1) Combined photo card in lieu of driver's licence card — The driver's licence card issued under this Act may be replaced with a combined photo card issued under the *Photo Card Act, 2008*, but the provisions of this or any other Act imposing a duty on the holders of drivers' licences, including a requirement to carry, present or surrender a driver's licence, apply to the combined photo card and the holder of a combined photo card as if the combined photo card were a driver's licence.

(2) Combined photo card is also driver's licence — A combined photo card issued under the *Photo Card Act, 2008* is also the holder's driver's licence for all purposes and the one combined photo card constitutes his or her enhanced photo card under that Act and his or her driver's licence.

(3) Driver's licence remains valid if photo card ceases to be valid — If a combined photo card holder's photo card ceases to be valid under the *Photo Card Act, 2008* for any reason, the holder's driver's licence remains valid unless this Act requires otherwise, and the holder may be issued a replacement driver's licence card.

2008, c. 17, s. 33

Commentary

On March 6, 2009, the *Photo Card Act, 2008*, S.O. 2008, c. 17, came into force. The Act authorizes the issuance of photo cards to individuals by the Minister of Transportation. There are three kinds of photo cards: basic, enhanced and combined. A basic card contains the holder's name and photograph and other prescribed information about the holder. An enhanced photo card contains as well, a notation that the holder is a Canadian citizen. It has security features that may allow it to be used for travel. A combined photo card contains an enhanced card and a driver's licence. A basic photo card may be issued to an individual who is resident in Ontario and does not hold a valid driver's licence. There is no obligation to get a photo card. Combined cards were to be made available first with the rest to be phased in. There are offences for improper acquisition or use and other offences. The Act makes amendments to the *Highway Traffic Act*. See s. 32.1 and 32.2 of the *Highway Traffic Act* regarding the responsibilities of holders and security enhancements. Section 35(4.0.1) of the Act states that a person who holds a basic or enhanced photo card may apply for a driver's licence if the photo card is retained. Section 1(9) authorizes a regulation. See O. Reg. 176/09 made under the *Photo Card Act, 2008*. Starting May 19, 2009 applicants were permitted to apply for a card. On May 26, cards were made available.

32.2 (1) Photo-comparison technology — The Minister may use photo-comparison technology to compare the photographs taken of any applicants for or holders of a driver's licence or photo card.

(2) Not admissible — The photo-comparison technology used by the Minister, the methodology used to compare photographs and the measurements and results used for comparison are not admissible in evidence for any purpose and cannot be required for production in a civil proceeding before a court or tribunal.

(3) Definitions — In this section,

"photo card" has the same meaning as in the *Photo Card Act, 2008*;

"photo-comparison technology" means a software application that measures the characteristics of a person's face in a photograph and compares the results of that measurement with those of other photographs.

2008, c. 17, s. 34

33. (1) As to carrying licences and surrender on demand — Every driver of a motor vehicle or street car shall carry his or her licence with him or her at all times while he or she is in charge of a motor vehicle or street car and shall surrender the licence for reasonable inspection upon the demand of a police officer or officer appointed for carrying out the provisions of this Act.

(2) Same, re novice driver rules — Every accompanying driver, as defined under section 57.1, shall carry his or her licence and shall surrender the licence for reasonable inspection upon the demand of a police officer or officer appointed for carrying out the provisions of this Act.

(3) Identification on failure to surrender licence — Every person who is unable or refuses to surrender his or her licence in accordance with subsection (1) or (2) shall, when requested by a police officer or officer appointed for carrying out the provisions of this Act, give reasonable identification of himself or herself and, for the purposes of this subsection, the correct name and address of the person shall be deemed to be reasonable identification.

1993, c. 40, s. 3

Commentary

A driver, including a novice driver, must carry the licence with him or her and surrender it for reasonable inspection to a police office or officer appointed under the Act. In the event a person is unable or refuses to show the licence to a police officer, that person must give his or her correct name and address.

Case Law

R. v. Dedman, [1985] 2 S.C.R. 2, 34 M.V.R. 1 — Random stops under a "R.I.D.E." ("Reduce Impaired Driving Everywhere") were permitted at common law. The same result obtained when considering the Charter of Rights: *R. v. Hufsky*, [1988] 1 S.C.R. 621, 4 M.V.R. (2d) 170, 84 N.R. 365.

R. v. Tricker (1995), 8 M.V.R. (3d) 47, 21 O.R. (3d) 575 (C.A.); leave to appeal to the S.C.C. refused (March 3, 1995), Doc. 24592 (S.C.C.) — A peace officer may enter private property to speak to the suspected driver under s. 33(2). The driver may withdraw permission from the officer to enter the property.

R. v. Rubb (1997), 30 M.V.R. (3d) 193 (Ont. Prov. Ct.) — The word "driver" should be attributed some degree of past signification to avoid an absurd result.

R. v. Richards (1999), 42 M.V.R. (3d) 70 (Ont. C.A.) — An accused is "in charge" of a motor vehicle in circumstances where custody of the vehicle is relinquished on a temporary basis for a limited purpose.

R. v. Blake (2003), 2003 CarswellOnt 715, 35 M.V.R. (4th) 151 (S.C.J.) — Section 33(3) contemplates a two-stage process. First the police officer must make a demand for the driver's licence and if the driver of the vehicle who has been asked refuses, the officer then must make a request for reasonable identification of the driver. It is not an offence to refuse to produce insurance and ownership on demand. It is an offence to fail to give reasonable identification, where such identification is required under the circumstances.

R. v. Walker (2005), 2005 CarswellOnt 6938, 28 M.V.R. (5th) 306 (S.C.J.) — An Ontario health card is reasonable identification and satisfies the driver's obligation under s. 33(3).

R. v. Plummer (2006), 38 M.V.R. (5th) 187, [2006] O.J. No. 4530, 214 C.C.C. (3d) 84, 83 O.R. (3d) 528, 2006 CarswellOnt 7056, 217 O.A.C. 201, 45 C.R. (6th) 3 (C.A.) — There is no power to arrest without a warrant until the officer has made a request for alternative identification. The officer must make a specific request for identification other than the driver's licence; and until the request has been made and the person has refused to comply, there has not been any intervention. A request for ownership and insurance did not constitute a request for alternative identification.

34. (1) Exemption as to non-residents — **Section 32 and any regulation made thereunder do not apply to any person who is,**

    (a) a resident of any other province of Canada, who is at least sixteen years of age and has complied with the law of the province in which he or she resides as to the drivers of motor vehicles; or

    (b) a resident of any other country or state,

        (i) who is at least sixteen years of age and is the holder of a valid International Driver's Permit, or

(ii) who is at least sixteen years of age and has not resided in Ontario for more than three months in any one year and has complied with the law of the country or state in which he or she resides as to the licensing of drivers of motor vehicles.

(2) Exemption of new residents — Section 32 and any regulation made thereunder do not apply to a person for sixty days after he or she has become a resident of Ontario if during such period he or she holds a subsisting driver's licence in accordance with the laws of the province, country or state of which he or she was a resident immediately before becoming a resident of Ontario.

Commentary

Non-residents are exempt from the requirements of the Act regarding licences provided they are otherwise properly licensed.

35. (1) Displaying licence that has been suspended, altered, etc. — No person shall,

(a) display or cause or permit to be displayed or have in his or her possession a fictitious, imitation, altered or fraudulently obtained driver's licence;

(b) display or cause or permit to be displayed or have in his or her possession a cancelled or suspended driver's licence or a driver's licence that has been changed in respect of its class, other than a licence card that has been marked by the Ministry as valid only to show the driver's photograph;

(c) lend his or her driver's licence or any portion thereof or permit the use of it by another person;

(d) display or represent as his or her own a driver's licence not issued to him or her;

(e) apply for, secure or retain in his or her possession more than one driver's licence;

(e.1) secure or retain in his or her possession a driver's licence if he or she holds a photo card issued under the *Photo Card Act, 2008*; or

(f) fail to surrender to the Ministry upon its demand a driver's licence that has been suspended, cancelled or changed in respect of its class.

(2) Idem — In subsection (1), "licence" includes any portion thereof.

(3) Seizing licence — Any police officer who has reason to believe that any person has in his or her possession a driver's licence referred to in subsection (1) may take possession of the licence and, where the officer does so, shall forward it to the Registrar upon disposition of the case.

Proposed Addition — 35(3.1)

(3.1) Display, possession of suspended licence permitted — Despite clause (1)(b), a person may display or cause or permit to be displayed or have in his or her possession a driver's licence that has been suspended under a provision or for a reason under this Act that is prescribed by regulation made under subsection 211(5).

2015, c. 14, s. 5 [Not in force at date of publication.]

(4) Second driver's licence permitted — Despite clause (1)(e), a person may hold a second driver's licence if the second licence is,

(a) issued solely to permit the licensee to obtain experience in the driving of a motorcycle for the purpose of qualifying for a driver's licence that authorizes him or her to drive a motorcycle; or

(b) required by any other province or territory of Canada or any state of the United States of America and has been issued in compliance with the law of that province, territory or state.

(4.0.1) Application for driver's licence by photo card holder — A person who holds a basic photo card or enhanced photo card issued under the *Photo Card Act, 2008* may apply for a driver's licence if he or she surrenders the photo card at the time of the application.

(4.1) Offence — Every person who contravenes clause (1)(a) is guilty of an offence and on conviction is liable to a fine of not less than $400 and not more than $50,000.

(5) Definition — For the purposes of this section, "driver's licence" includes a licence issued by any other province or territory of Canada or by any state of the United States of America.

1996, c. 20, s. 4; 2005, c. 26, Sched. A, s. 3; 2008, c. 17, s. 35

Commentary

It is an offence to have a licence which is fictitious, altered or fraudulently obtained, cancelled, revoked or suspended.

36. Driving prohibited while licence suspended — A person whose driver's licence or privilege to drive a motor vehicle in Ontario has been suspended shall not drive a motor vehicle or street car in Ontario under a driver's licence or permit issued by any other jurisdiction during the suspension.

Commentary

If a person's licence is suspended by Ontario, he or she cannot use an out-of-province licence.

Case Law

R. v. Gour (1986), 40 M.V.R. 139 (Ont. C.A.) — A Quebec resident had been convicted in Ontario of the Criminal Code drinking and driving offence of "over 80". It was held that his licence was suspended by virtue of the Quebec Highway Code. As such, the respondent was one who could not drive by virtue of ss. 27, 29 and 31 of the Highway Traffic Act (Ont.). In order to protect Ontario roads it was necessary to take the licence in Ontario and remit it to Quebec.

R. v. Cail, 2009 ABPC 235, 2009 CarswellAlta 1244, 88 M.V.R. (5th) 97 — A conviction for driving while unauthorized under the *Traffic Safety Act* (Alta.) precludes a conviction under s. 259 for driving while disqualified under the *Criminal Code*.

37. (1) **Drivers under 16 prohibited** — No person under the age of sixteen years shall drive or operate a motor vehicle, street car, road-building machine, self-propelled implement of husbandry or farm tractor on a highway.

(2) **Employment of drivers under 16 prohibited** — No person shall employ or permit anyone under the age of sixteen years to drive or operate a motor vehicle, street car, road-building machine, self-propelled implement of husbandry or farm tractor on a highway.

(3) **Exception** — Subsections (1) and (2) do not apply in respect of the driving or operating of a self-propelled implement of husbandry or farm tractor directly across a highway.

38. (1) **Minimum age to drive motor-assisted, power-assisted bicycle** — No person under the age of 16 years shall drive or operate a motor-assisted bicycle or power-assisted bicycle on a highway.

(2) **Same** — No person who is the owner or is in possession or control of a motor-assisted bicycle or power-assisted bicycle shall permit a person who is under the age of 16 years to ride on, drive or operate the motor-assisted bicycle or power-assisted bicycle on a highway.

2009, c. 5, s. 8

39. (1) **Prohibition as to letting or hiring** — No person shall hire or let for hire a motor vehicle unless the person by whom the motor vehicle is to be driven is a person licensed to drive a motor vehicle as required by this Act.

(2) **Non-resident's licence** — Subsection (1) does not apply to a resident of any other province of Canada who does not reside or carry on business in Ontario for more than six consecutive months in any one year or to a resident of a country or state that grants similar exemptions and privileges to residents of Ontario, who does not reside in Ontario for more than three consecutive months in any one year, provided the person is the holder of a driver's licence issued by the province, country or state in which he or she resides.

(3) **Production of licence when hiring motor vehicle** — Every person, whether a resident of Ontario or not, hiring a motor vehicle shall produce his or her driver's licence for the inspection of the person from whom the vehicle is being hired.

39.1 (1) **Picking up passenger for compensation prohibited without licence, etc.** — A driver of a motor vehicle other than a bus shall not pick up a passenger for the purpose of transporting him or her for compensation where a licence, permit or authorization is required to do so by,

(a) the *Public Vehicles Act*;

(b) a municipal by-law passed under Part IV of the *Municipal Act, 2001*;

(c) a regulation made under the *Department of Transport Act* (Canada); or

(d) an airport or airport authority,

except under the authority of such licence, permit or authorization.

(2) **Same** — The owner of a motor vehicle other than a bus shall not permit the motor vehicle to be driven by a person who the owner knows or has reason to believe intends to contravene subsection (1).

(3) **Same** — No person shall arrange or offer to arrange for a passenger to be picked up in a motor vehicle other than a bus for the purpose of being transported for compensation except under the licence, permit or authorization that is required to do so, as described in subsection (1).

(4) **Documents to be carried and surrendered** — Every driver of a motor vehicle other than a bus who picks up a passenger for the purpose of transporting him or her for compensation where a licence, permit or authorization is required to do so, as described in subsection (1), shall,

(a) carry the original or a copy of the required licence, permit or authorization; and

(b) upon the demand of a police officer or officer appointed for carrying out the provisions of this Act, surrender the original or copy of the required licence, permit or authorization for reasonable inspection.

(5) **Officer may require identification** — A police officer or officer appointed for carrying out the provisions of this Act who has reasonable and probable grounds to believe that a person has contravened subsection (3) may require that person to provide identification of himself or herself.

(6) **Same** — Every person who is required to provide identification under subsection (5) shall identify himself or herself to the officer and, for that purpose, giving his or her correct name, date of birth and address is sufficient identification.

(7) **Same** — A police officer may arrest without warrant any person who does not comply with subsection (6).

(8) **Offence** — Every person who contravenes subsection (1), (2), (3), (4) or (6) is guilty of an offence and on conviction is liable to a fine of not less than $300 and not more than $20,000.

(9) **Consent to prosecutions** — No prosecution shall be instituted under this section without the consent of a police officer or officer appointed for carrying out the provisions of this Act.

(10) **Regulations** — The Minister may make regulations,

(a) exempting any area of Ontario from this section;

(b) exempting any person or class of persons from this section and prescribing conditions for such exemption;

(c) exempting any motor vehicle or class or type of motor vehicles from this section and prescribing conditions for such exemption;

(d) prescribing circumstances under which any person or class of persons or any motor vehicle or class or type of motor vehicles is exempt from this section.

(11) Definitions — In this section,

"compensation" includes any rate, remuneration, reimbursement or reward of any kind paid, payable, promised, received or demanded, directly or indirectly;

"owner" means, in the absence of evidence to the contrary, the holder of the permit or the plate portion of the permit for the vehicle.

Proposed Amendment — 39.1(11)

(11) Definition — In this section,

"owner" means, in the absence of evidence to the contrary, the holder of the permit or the plate portion of the permit for the vehicle.

2014, c. 9, Sched. 2, s. 12 [To come into force January 1, 2017.]

2005, c. 26, Sched. A, s. 4

Case Law

R. v. Alrifai, 64 M.V.R. (5th) 159, [2008] O.J. No. 2870, 242 O.A.C. 88, 2008 ONCA 564, *(sub nom. Alrifai v. Ontario)* 235 C.C.C. (3d) 374, 2008 CarswellOnt 4338 (C.A.); affirming (2007), 48 M.V.R. (5th) 144, 2007 CarswellOnt 2913 (S.C.J.) — Absent the consent of a police office to the laying of an information, the justice of the peace was not required to receive an information under s. 23(1) of the *Provincial Offences Act* in relation to s. 39.1(9) of the Act. There was no discrimination under s. 15 of the *Charter* in that requirement.

R. v. Hajivasilis (2013), 41 M.V.R. (6th) 175, 2013 ONCA 27, 2013 CarswellOnt 508, 114 O.R. (3d) 337, 302 O.A.C. 65, [2013] O.J. No. 253 (Ont. C.A.) — The requirements are not restricted to "highways".

40. (1) Agreements with other jurisdictions — The Minister may enter into a reciprocal agreement with the government of any province or territory of Canada or of any state of the United States of America providing for,

(a) the sanctioning by the licensing jurisdiction of drivers from that jurisdiction who commit offences in the other jurisdiction; and

(b) on a driver's change of residence, the issuance of a driver's licence by one jurisdiction in exchange for a driver's licence issued by the other jurisdiction.

(2) Effect of agreement — The provisions of this Act and the regulations with respect to the licensing of drivers are subject to any agreement made under this section.

2009, c. 5, s. 9

Commentary

The same applies and is in effect respecting provinces and territories.

Related Provisions: See R.R.O. 1990, Reg. 607, Reciprocal Suspension of Licences.

41. (1) Suspension on conviction for certain offences — Subject to subsections 41.1(1), (2) and (3), the driver's licence of a person who is convicted of an offence,

Proposed Amendment — 41(1) opening words

(1) Suspension on conviction for certain offences — The driver's licence of a person who is convicted of an offence,

2015, c. 14, s. 6(1)(a) [Not in force at date of publication.]

(a) under section 220, 221 or 236 of the *Criminal Code* (Canada) committed by means of a motor vehicle or a street car within the meaning of this Act or a motorized snow vehicle;

(b) under section 249, 249.1, 249.2, 249.3, 249.4 or 252 of the *Criminal Code* (Canada) committed while driving or having the care, charge or control of a motor vehicle or street car within the meaning of this Act or a motorized snow vehicle;

(b.1) under section 253 or 255 of the *Criminal Code* (Canada) committed while,

(i) driving or having the care, charge or control of a motor vehicle or street car within the meaning of this Act or a motorized snow vehicle, or

(ii) operating or having the care or control of a vessel within the meaning of section 48;

(c) under section 254 of the *Criminal Code* (Canada) committed in relation to,

(i) driving or having the care, charge or control of a motor vehicle or street car within the meaning of this Act or a motorized snow vehicle, or

(ii) operating or having the care or control of a vessel within the meaning of section 48;

(d) under a provision that is enacted by another jurisdiction, including by a municipality in another jurisdiction, and is designated in a reciprocal agreement entered into under section 40; or

(e) referred to in a predecessor to this subsection,

is thereupon suspended,

Proposed Amendment — 41(1) preceding (f)

is thereupon suspended, subject to any continuation under subsection (4.1) or early reinstatement under section 57

2015, c. 14, s. 6(1)(b) [Not in force at date of publication.]

(f) upon the first conviction, for one year;

(g) upon the first subsequent conviction, for three years; and

(h) upon the second subsequent conviction or an additional subsequent conviction, indefinitely.

(2) Determining subsequent conviction — In determining whether a conviction is a subsequent conviction or an additional subsequent conviction, as the case may be, for the purpose of clauses (1)(g) and (h), the only question to be considered is the sequence of convictions and no consideration shall be given to the sequence of commission of offences or whether any offence occurred before or after any conviction.

(3) **Ten-year limitation** — Clauses (1)(g) and (h) do not apply when the subsequent conviction is more than 10 years after the previous conviction.

(3.01) **Exception** — Despite subsection (3), when the subsequent conviction is within 10 years after the previous conviction, all previous convictions that were not followed by a 10-year period without a conviction shall be taken into account for the purpose of clauses (1)(g) and (h).

(3.02) **Transition** — Despite subsections (3) and (3.01), a conviction that was more than five years before the date on which this subsection comes into force shall not be taken into account for the purpose of clauses (1)(g) and (h).

(3.1) **Suspension concurrent with s. 48.3 suspension** — The licence suspension under this section runs concurrently with the remaining portion, if any, of a suspension under section 48.3.

(4) **Order extending suspension** — Where the court or judge, as the case may be, making the conviction referred to in subsection (1) considers it to be desirable for the protection of the public using the highways, the court or judge may make an order extending the suspension of the licence,

> (a) for any period in addition to the period specified in subsection (1) that the court or judge considers proper, if the person is liable to imprisonment for life in respect of the offence; or

> (b) for any period in addition to the period specified in subsection (1) that the court or judge considers proper but not exceeding three years, if the person is not liable to imprisonment for life in respect of the offence.

(4.1) **Reduced suspension with ignition interlock condition** — A person whose driver's licence is suspended under subsection (1) for an offence listed in clause (1)(b.1) or (c) may apply to the Registrar for the reinstatement of his or her licence before the end of the licence suspension period, and the Registrar may reinstate the person's licence before the end of the licence suspension period, if the person has been notified under section 57 that he or she is required to participate in a conduct review program under that section that consists of or includes an ignition interlock program.

Proposed Amendment — 41(4.1)

(4.1) **Suspension continued until conduct review program completed** — The suspension of a person's driver's licence under clause (1)(f) or (g) continues beyond the one-year or three-year period of suspension imposed under those clauses until the person has successfully completed any conduct review program under section 57 that he or she has been required to participate in.

2015, c. 14, s. 6(2) [Not in force at date of publication.]

Proposed Addition — 41(4.2), (4.3)

(4.2) **Same, transition** — Despite the repeal of section 41.1 under section 7 of the *Transportation Statute Law Amendment Act (Making Ontario's Roads Safer), 2015,* the suspension of a driver's licence that was imposed under subsection 41.1(3) before its repeal and that was in effect on the day of its repeal is deemed to continue until the holder of the driver's licence successfully completes any remedial program that he or she was required to participate in under section 41.1 or any conduct review program that he or she was required to participate in under section 57, as the case may be.

(4.3) Transition, ignition interlock condition — Despite the repeal of section 41.2 under section 7 of the *Transportation Statute Law Amendment Act (Making Ontario's Roads Safer), 2015*, a condition that was imposed on a driver's licence under subsection 41.2(1), (5) or (9) before its repeal and that was in effect on the day of its repeal is deemed to continue until the condition is removed or replaced under a conduct review program under section 57.

2015, c. 14, s. 6(2) [Not in force at date of publication.]

(5) Order for discharge — This section applies in the same manner as if a person were convicted of an offence if the person pleads guilty to or is found guilty of an offence referred to in subsection (1) and,

(a) an order directing that the accused be discharged is made under section 730 of the *Criminal Code* (Canada) or under a provision that is enacted by a state of the United States of America and that is designated by the regulations; or

(b) a disposition is made under section 20 or sections 28 to 32 of the *Young Offenders Act* (Canada) or a youth sentence is imposed under section 42, 59, 94, 95 or 96 of the *Youth Criminal Justice Act* (Canada) or an adult sentence is imposed under the *Youth Criminal Justice Act* (Canada), including a confirmation or variation of the disposition or sentence.

(6) Appeal — An appeal may be taken from an order for additional suspension made under subsection (4) and the provisions of the *Criminal Code* (Canada) applying to an appeal from the conviction referred to in subsection (1) apply in respect of an appeal from an order made under subsection (4).

(7) Stay of order on appeal — Where an appeal is taken under subsection (6), the court being appealed to may direct that the order being appealed from shall be stayed pending the final disposition of the appeal or until otherwise ordered by that court.

(8) No cause of action — No person whose licence is or was suspended under subsection (1) or a predecessor thereof has a cause of action against the Registrar of Motor Vehicles or Her Majesty the Queen in right of Ontario for any misapplication of, or misadvice about, the suspension period under subsection (1) or predecessor thereof.

1996, c. 20, s. 5; 1997, c. 12, s. 1; 2000, c. 26, Sched. O, s. 1; 2001, c. 9, Sched. O, s. 2; 2006, c. 19, Sched. D, s. 9(2); 2006, c. 20, s. 1; 2007, c. 13, s. 6; 2009, c. 5, s. 10

Commentary

The Criminal Code provides for a schedule of increasing minimum suspensions following a Criminal Code drinking and driving conviction for the lesser offences of impaired, "over 80" and failing or refusing to provide a breath or blood sample. More serious offences, while not attracting minimum suspensions, also attract suspensions. However, the Highway Traffic Act provides for its own suspensions following a Criminal Code driving conviction. The Act's minimums are more severe than those found in the Code.

As the result of the Road Safety Act, 1997, the suspensions are for one year, three years, and indefinitely for a first offence, first subsequent offence and second subsequent offence, respectively. The judge may extend the minimum periods. The minimum periods attach to a conviction or discharge under the Criminal Code. The minimum periods may only be challenged by appealing conviction. An appeal against a discretionary additional suspension alone would be taken to the same court that one would go to if appealing conviction. Transitional provisions for calculating the length of the mandatory suspensions are provided for. New section 41.1 provides a regime for a subsequent offender to complete prescribed assessments and remedial programs before the licence is reinstated. An indefinite suspension may be reduced to 10 years if the Registrar's requirements are satisfied.

It appears that the Crown has no right of appeal from the quantum of a trial judge's additional suspension or from a refusal to impose any additional suspension.

If appealing conviction, filing a copy of the notice of appeal with the Ministry's head office automatically stays the suspension (subs. (5)). If the appeal is solely taken against an order of additional suspension under the Act, the accused must obtain a stay from the court in which the appeal is filed. By contrast, all Criminal Code suspensions require that a stay be sought.

If an Ontario driver commits an offence in another province or a territory, the suspension will also take effect in Ontario.

Note: Regarding the provisions in subsections 41(1) and (3) of the Act, the *Comprehensive Road Safety Act*, 1997, c. 12, s. 1, allows, respectively, the following:

> (3) The periods of suspension provided for in subsection 41(1) of the Act, as it read immediately before its re-enactment by subsection 1(1) of this Act, continue to apply with respect to convictions for offences committed before subsection 1(1) of this Act comes into force.

> (4) The five-year limitation provided for in subsection 41(3) of the Act, as it read immediately before its re-enactment by subsection 1(2) of this Act, continues to apply with respect to convictions for offences committed before subsection 1(2) of this Act comes into force.

The Red Tape Reduction Act, 1999, S.O. 1999, c. 12, Sched. R. (ss. 1(2), 1(3), 2(1), 2(3), 2(5), 5(1), and 6(1) in force January 1, 2001) would amend ss. 6, 7, 12 and 14 of the Highway Traffic Act to facilitate Ontario's participation in the International Registration Plan, which contains reciprocal provisions in respect of commercial motor vehicles that travel across provincial or international borders. The Plan provides for the issuance of IRP cab cards as permits for these vehicles and for the appointment of registration and licence fees in each member jurisdiction on the basis of the distances travelled in each jurisdiction. Persons residing or based in other jurisdictions that are members of the Plan are exempt from the requirements of and fees prescribed under Part II of the Highway Traffic Act.

The Red Tape Reduction Act, 2000, S.O. 2000, c. 26, Sched. O. (ss. 1-4, 5(1) and (2) and 14 in force December 6, 2000; ss. 6-13 in force January 1, 2001) would re-enact s. 52 of the Highway Traffic Act to allow for notice to be given by regular mail for suspensions unrelated to Criminal Code (Canada) offences, and to allow for other prescribed methods of service; amend s. 55.1 to provide that the impoundment history of leased vehicles is linked to the holder of the plate portion of the registration certificate, to extend vehicle impound provisions to persons who are found driving while their licence is under suspension as a result of a court order and to clarify who is responsible for paying storage charges related to impoundment; amend existing provisions dealing with vehicle weights and dimensions to establish a framework for the implementation of an agreement between Ontario and Quebec; and amends s. 175(6)(c) of the Act to clarify when overhead red signal lights and stop arms on school buses must be used.

Case Law

Constitutional

Prov. Sec. of P.E.I. v. Egan, [1941] S.C.R. 396, [1941] 3 D.L.R. 305; *Ross v. Ont. (Reg. of Motor Vehicles)*, [1975] 1 S.C.R. 5; *Bell v. A.G. P.E.I.* (1973), 24 C.R.N.S. 232, 42 D.L.R. (3d) 82 (S.C.C.) — A provision such as s. 41 for automatic suspension on conviction is valid provincial legislation since it deals with control of roads and regulation of traffic. It is not in conflict with s. 259 of the Criminal Code; it is not an attempt to impose an additional penalty for a violation of the criminal law, but provides for a civil disability arising out of a conviction for a criminal offence.

Carroll v. R. (1981), 35 O.R. (2d) 532, 14 M.V.R. 175 (Co. Ct.) — The same conclusion was reached regarding the discretionary additional suspension a judge may impose under this section.

Paganelli v. Ontario (Reg. of Motor Vehicles) (1987), 6 M.V.R. (2d) 252 (Ont. Div. Ct.) — Section 41(1) of the Highway Traffic Act imposes a civil consequence of a criminal act when invoked as a result of conviction under s. 253 of the Criminal Code. Accordingly, it is valid provincial legislation. Furthermore, s. 259(1) of the Code does not create an actual conflict sufficient to invoke the doctrine of paramountcy. Therefore the provincial statutory provision is not rendered inoperative by the federal provision. Finally, there is no contravention of ss. 6, 7, 11 and 15 of the Charter by the operation of s. 41(1).

Perry v. Prince Edward Island (Reg. of Motor Vehicles) (1987), 7 M.V.R. (2d) 16, 70 Nfld. & P.E.I.R. 32, 215 A.P.R. 32 (P.E.I. S.C.) — P was convicted of dangerous driving contrary to the Criminal Code. She applied for an order in the nature of prohibition in relation to the subsequent suspension of her driver's licence pursuant to the Highway Traffic Act. Her contention was that the provincial statutory provision violated s. 11(h) of the Charter. The application was dismissed. The suspension of a driver's licence is not a criminal or penal matter. Accordingly, the Charter provision is not applicable. Moreover, the suspension affected what was merely a privilege and not a right as contemplated by the Charter.

R. v. Janes (1983), 21 M.V.R. 316 (B.C. Prov. Ct.) — The applicant received a six-month automatic licence suspension for a Criminal Code driving offence. He sought a remedy pursuant to s. 24(1) of the Charter of Rights, alleging that the suspension violated ss. 7, 11(d), (h) and 12 of the Charter. It was held that s. 7 was fulfilled when the applicant was tried for the Criminal Code offence. The trial was held in accordance with ss. 11(d) and (h). The suspension was not cruel or unusual as it arose out of the applicant's own actions.

R. v. Ross (1985), 32 M.V.R. 261 (B.C. S.C.) — The minimum three-year driving prohibition that is mandatory upon conviction under s. 92.1(3) of the Motor Vehicle Act (B.C.) is not cruel and unusual punishment within the meaning of s. 12 of the Canadian Charter of Rights and Freedoms even when the accused's occupation is that of a truck driver.

Rowland v. R. (1984), 28 M.V.R. 239, 10 D.L.R. (4th) 724 (Alta. Q.B.); *Zukowski v. R.* (1986), 38 M.V.R. 293 (B.C. S.C.); *Rennie v. Supt. of Motor Vehicles* (1986), 45 M.V.R. 205 (B.C. S.C.); *Johnston v. Supt. of Motor Vehicles* (1987), 46 M.V.R. 59 (B.C. S.C.); *R. v. McGee* (1989), 19 M.V.R. (2d) 81 (P.E.I. T.D.) — The same result was reached regarding s. 7 and an automatic six-month suspension.

Roenspies v. Saskatchewan Government Insurance (1992), 36 M.V.R. (2d) 129, 71 C.C.C. (3d) 220, 100 Sask. R. 147, 18 W.A.C. 147 (C.A.) — A mandatory five-year suspension following a fourth Criminal Code conviction does not infringe s. 12 of the Charter.

Yehia v. Alberta (Solicitor General) (1992), 40 M.V.R. (2d) 57, 10 C.R.R. (2d) 191 (Alta. C.A.) — An automatic five-year suspension consequent upon a conviction for dangerous driving causing bodily harm does not infringe s. 7 of the Charter.

R. v. Brady (1992), 42 M.V.R. (2d) 131, 78 C.C.C. (3d) 134, 21 B.C.A.C. 120, 37 W.A.C. 120 (C.A.) — It is inappropriate to look to provincial legislation to impose a greater sentence than that provided by the Criminal Code.

Cardo v. Ontario (Registrar of Motor Vehicles) (1999), 43 M.V.R. (3d) 107 ((Ont. Div. Ct.) — An automatic ten year suspension does not violate ss. 7, 11(b) and 12 of the Charter of Rights.

Westendorp v. Westendorp (2000), 8 R.F.L. (5th) 225, 3 M.V.R. (4th) 287, 74 C.R.R. (2d) 280 (Ont. S.C.J.); additional reasons at (2000), 9 R.F.L. (5th) 228 (Ont. S.C.J.) — A suspension of a driver's licence by the Director of the Family Responsibility Office for non-payment of spousal support under the Family Responsibility and Support Arrears Enforcement Act is constitutional.

R. v. Sull (2003), 183 B.C.A.C. 223, 301 W.A.C. 223, 43 M.V.R. (4th) 20, 2003 BCCA 321, 2003 CarswellBC 1304, 176 C.C.C. (3d) 46 (B.C. C.A.) — A civil disability such as a 10-year provincial prohibition is not an "order by which punishment is imposed" under the Criminal Code.

R. v. McNab, 2007 CarswellSask 426, 2007 SKPC 79, 54 M.V.R. (5th) 30, 305 Sask. R. 12 (Prov. Ct.) — The continuing suspension of a driver's licence under Provincial law until he completed addictions screening and prescribed education and a recovery program which he failed to do was an extension of his original suspension for *Criminal Code* drinking and driving and therefore a proper foundation for the *Criminal Code* offence of driving while prohibited.

R. v. Rezek (2008), 67 M.V.R. (5th) 236, 2008 CarswellOnt 553 (C.J.) — There is no jurisdiction to reduce the minimum suspension period under s. 41, or under the *Criminal Code*, despite the accused having been under a two year ban from driving because of bail on other charges later dropped.

Calculation

Ficko v. Ontario (Reg. of Motor Vehicles) (1989), 13 M.V.R. (2d) 30, 33 O.A.C. 120 (C.A.) — It was clear from the transcript that the sequence of the convictions was such that one conviction followed the other. Section 41(2) was clearly designed to exclude Lord Coke's rule and has achieved that purpose.

Breen v. Ontario (Registrar of Motor Vehicles) (1992), 42 M.V.R. (2d) 172 (Ont. C.A.); reversing (1990), 23 M.V.R. (2d) 108 (H.C.); leave to appeal to S.C.C. refused *Breen v. Registrar of Motor Vehicles (Ont.)* (1993), 47 M.V.R. (2d) 124n, 68 O.A.C. 159n, 164 N.R. 160n (S.C.C.) — It is not open to the Registrar or the reviewing court to go behind a conviction to determine the admissibility of evidence adduced to prove that the accused's refusal to provide breath samples related to her driving or care or control of a motor vehicle.

R. v. Brady (1992), 42 M.V.R. (2d) 131, 78 C.C.C. (3d) 134, 21 B.C.A.C. 120, 37 W.A.C. 120 (C.A.) — A trial judge does not have the power to impose a provincial licence suspension to make up for an inadequacy in the Criminal Code prohibition powers.

White v. Nova Scotia (Registrar of Motor Vehicles) (1996), 147 N.S.R. (2d) 259, 426 A.P.R. 259 (S.C.) — Section 15 of the Charter is not applicable to the initial suspension since it was not penal in nature. Whether fair trial interests were violated at trial was a matter for the initial trial judge. The rights to silence and against self-incrimination were not violated by bringing a review or by having to disclose potential witnesses or defences for purposes of the review.

Appeals

R. v. Joslin (1981), 10 M.V.R. 29 (Ont. C.A.) — The appellant was sentenced to 30 days in jail and was given an additional discretionary suspension of six months in addition to the mandatory suspension for dangerous driving. He appealed to the County Court. His notice of appeal requested a reduction of the sentence to time served and made no mention of the suspension. The County Court reduced the sentence but increased the discretionary suspension. An appeal was brought to the Court of Appeal. In allowing the appeal it was held that the suspension is not an additional penalty imposed for a violation of the criminal law but a civil disability arising out of a conviction for a criminal offence. No appeal was taken from the order imposing the additional suspension. Accordingly, all the County Court could deal with was the sentence, and the additional suspension imposed by the County Court must be quashed.

Fingland v. Ontario (Ministry of Transportation), 70 M.V.R. (5th) 15, 2008 CarswellOnt 7179, 2008 ONCA 812, 243 O.A.C. 37, 93 O.R. (3d) 268 (C.A.); affirming (2007), 56 M.V.R. (5th) 143, 230 O.A.C. 78, 2007 CarswellOnt 6513 (Div. Ct.) — Mandamus issued directing the Ministry to issue a valid driver's licence. In the unusual circumstances of the case, the applicant had been misled regarding his entitlement after serving a suspension.

Related Provisions: See sections 42 to 44 and 55 of the Act; see O. Reg. 287/08; Conduct Review Programs; O. Reg. 340/94, Drivers' Licences; O. Reg. 251/02, Ignition Interlock Devices; O. Reg. 37/93, Reciprocal Suspension of Drivers' Licences, see also sections 259 and 260 of the Criminal Code.

41.1 (1) Reinstatement of suspended licence — Where the Registrar is satisfied that a person whose driver's licence is suspended under clause 41(1)(f) or (g) has completed the prescribed assessments and remedial programs that are applicable to the person, if any, and meets the prescribed requirements that are applicable

to the person, if any, the Registrar shall reinstate the driver's licence upon the expiry of the suspension, subject to any other suspension under this Act.

(2) Reduction of indefinite suspension and reinstatement of licence — Where the Registrar is satisfied that a person whose driver's licence is suspended under clause 41(1)(h) for a second subsequent conviction has completed the prescribed assessments and remedial programs that are applicable to the person, if any, and meets the prescribed requirements that are applicable to the person, if any, the Registrar shall reduce the period of the suspension to 10 years and shall reinstate the driver's licence upon the expiry of the reduced suspension, subject to any other suspension under this Act.

(3) Further suspension — If, upon the expiry of a suspension under subsection 41(1), the person whose driver's licence is suspended has not satisfied the Registrar that he or she has completed the prescribed assessments and remedial programs that are applicable to the person, if any, and meets the prescribed requirements that are applicable to the person, if any, the Registrar shall suspend the person's driver's licence until such time as the Registrar is so satisfied.

(4) Effective date of further suspension — A suspension under subsection (3) takes effect from the time notice of the suspension is given, in accordance with section 52, to the person whose driver's licence is suspended.

(5) Parties to judicial review — The parties to any judicial review brought in respect of this section are the Registrar and the person whose driver's licence is suspended.

(6) Documents privileged — Documents filed with the Ministry for the purposes of this section are privileged for the information of the Ministry only and shall not be open for public inspection.

(6.1) Persons authorized to provide programs — The Minister may authorize or require any person or class of persons to provide or conduct assessments and programs for the purposes of this section and may require them to prepare, keep and submit reports to the Ministry as specified by the Ministry.

(7) Protection from personal liability — No action or other proceeding for damages shall be instituted against a person authorized or required to conduct an assessment or program or submit a report for the purposes of this section, unless the person was negligent in the conduct of the assessment or program or in the preparation or submission of the report.

(8) Same — No action or other proceeding for damages shall be instituted against the Registrar or any employee of the Ministry for the suspension or reinstatement of a driver's licence in good faith in the execution or intended execution of a duty under this section.

(9) Crown not relieved of liability — Despite subsections 5(2) and (4) of the *Proceedings Against the Crown Act*, subsections (7) and (8) do not relieve the Crown of liability in respect of a tort committed by a person mentioned in subsection (7) or (8) to which it would otherwise be subject.

(10) Regulations — The Lieutenant Governor in Council may make regulations,

(a) governing the assessments and remedial programs required under this section and prescribing what constitutes their completion;

(b) prescribing fees for assessments and remedial programs;

(c) [Repealed 2007, c. 13, s. 7(3).]

(d) respecting documents required to be filed with the Registrar to satisfy him or her with respect to the completion of assessments and remedial programs;

(e) prescribing the requirements to be met by a person in order to have his or her suspension reduced or his or her driver's licence reinstated under this section;

(f) prescribing conditions that the Minister may impose on a driver's licence reinstated under this section;

(g) prescribing the length of time that conditions imposed on a driver's licence reinstated under this section will apply, or a method for determining it;

(h) requiring a person whose licence is suspended under subsection 41(1) or whose licence is reinstated under this section to attend an interview with an official of the Ministry and prescribing the circumstances where the interview will be required and the purposes of the interview;

(i) defining classes of persons, based on the nature of the offence or offences for which a driver's licence may be suspended under section 41 and on the number of convictions a person has for offences described in subsection 41(1);

(j) providing that this section, or any part of it, applies to a class or classes of persons or exempting any class or classes of persons from this section or any part of it, prescribing conditions for any such applications or exemptions and prescribing circumstances in which any such applications or exemptions apply.

(11) Same — A regulation made under subsection (10) may provide differently for different classes of persons and in different parts of Ontario.

Proposed Repeal — 41.1

41.1 [Repealed 2015, c. 14, s. 7. Not in force at date of publication.]

1997, c. 12, s. 2; 2007, c. 13, s. 7

Commentary

A person whose driver's licence is suspended under s. 41(1) will have to complete prescribed assessments and remedial programs and meet prescribed conditions before his or her licence will be reinstated on the expiry of the suspension. A person convicted for a second subsequent conviction may get an indefinite suspension reduced to 10 years.

Case Law

Fontana v. Ontario (Registrar of Motor Vehicles) (2002), 30 M.V.R. (4th) 52, 2002 CarswellOnt 3192 (Ont. Div. Ct.) — A "remedial program" as found in s. 32.4(1)(b), (k) of O. Reg 340/94 *Drivers' Licenses* can and does include the three components of the Ontario

Remedial Measures Program, being the assessment component, the education or treatment course component and the six-month follow-up interview.

R. v. Wilson, 2011 ONSC 89, 2011 CarswellOnt 103, [2011] O.J. No. 40, 225 C.R.R. (2d) 234, 270 C.C.C. (3d) 110, 7 M.V.R. (6th) 24 (S.C.J.) — The accused charged with impaired driving unsuccessfully advanced s. 11(i) of the *Charter of Rights* to argue he could obtain the benefit of ignition interlock provisions in unproclaimed legislation.

Related Provisions: Section 41 of the Act, see also O. Reg. 287/08; Conduct Review Programs; O. Reg. 340/94; Drivers' Licences.

41.2 (1) Reinstated licence subject to condition: first conviction — If a person's driver's licence is suspended under section 41 as a result of a first conviction for an offence under section 253, 254 or 255 of the *Criminal Code* (Canada) and his or her driver's licence is reinstated under section 41.1 and not under subsection 41(4.1), it is a condition of the person's driver's licence that he or she is prohibited from driving any motor vehicle that is not equipped with an approved ignition interlock device.

(2) Application to remove condition — A person mentioned in subsection (1) may apply to the Registrar to remove the condition prohibiting him or her from driving any motor vehicle that is not equipped with an approved ignition interlock device.

(3) Time limit — An application under subsection (2) may not be made earlier than one year from the day the person's driver's licence was reinstated under section 41.1.

(4) Prescribed criteria must be met — On receiving an application made in accordance with subsections (2) and (3), the Registrar shall remove the condition, if the person meets the criteria prescribed for the purpose of this subsection.

(5) Reinstated licence subject to condition: second conviction — If a person's driver's licence is suspended under section 41 as a result of a second conviction for an offence under section 253, 254 or 255 of the *Criminal Code* (Canada) and his or her driver's licence is reinstated under section 41.1, it is a condition of the person's driver's licence that he or she is prohibited from driving any motor vehicle that is not equipped with an approved ignition interlock device.

(6) Application to remove condition — A person mentioned in subsection (5) may apply to the Registrar to remove the condition prohibiting him or her from driving any motor vehicle that is not equipped with an approved ignition interlock device.

(7) Time limit — An application under subsection (6) may not be made earlier than three years from the day the person's driver's licence was reinstated under section 41.1.

(8) Prescribed criteria must be met — On receiving an application made in accordance with subsections (6) and (7), the Registrar shall remove the condition, if the person meets the criteria prescribed for the purpose of this subsection.

(9) Reinstated licence subject to permanent condition — If, in accordance with subsection 41.1(2), the Registrar reduces an indefinite licence suspension that was imposed for a second subsequent conviction or an additional subsequent conviction of an offence under section 253, 254 or 255 of the *Criminal Code* (Canada), and reinstates a person's driver's licence, it is a permanent condition of the person's driver's licence that he or she is prohibited from driving any motor vehicle that is not equipped with an approved ignition interlock device.

(10) Responsibility of owner of motor vehicle — No person who is the owner or is in possession or control of a motor vehicle that is not equipped with an approved ignition interlock device shall knowingly permit a person to drive the vehicle, if that person is prohibited from driving any motor vehicle that is not equipped with such a device.

(11) No tampering with devices — Except in accordance with an authorization under subsection (14), no person shall tamper with an approved ignition interlock device.

(12) Inspections — If, under the authority of this Act, a police officer stops a motor vehicle, inspects a person's driver's licence and determines that the person is prohibited from driving any motor vehicle that is not equipped with an approved ignition interlock device, the police officer may, without warrant or court order, inspect the vehicle to the extent that is reasonably necessary to determine,

    (a) whether the vehicle is equipped with such a device; and

    (b) if the vehicle has the device, whether the device has been tampered with in any manner.

(13) Penalty — Every person who drives a motor vehicle that is not equipped with an approved ignition interlock device while prohibited from doing so or who contravenes subsection (10) or (11) is guilty of an offence and on conviction is liable,

    (a) in the case involving a commercial motor vehicle within the meaning of subsection 16(1), to a fine of not less than $200 and not more than $20,000;

> **Proposed Amendment — 41.2(13)(a)**
>
> (a) in the case involving a commercial motor vehicle, to a fine of not less than $200 and not more than $20,000;
>
> 2014, c. 9, Sched. 2, s. 13 [To come into force January 1, 2017. Repealed 2015, c. 14, s. 61(4). Conditions not yet satisfied.]

    (b) in every other case, to a fine of not less than $200 and not more than $1,000.

(14) Authorization to install devices — The Minister may in writing authorize any person to install, maintain and remove approved ignition interlock devices.

(15) Authorization to charge fees — Where, under subsection (14), the Minister has authorized a person to install, maintain and remove approved ignition interlock devices, the Minister may in writing authorize that person to charge a fee for the installation, maintenance and removal of such devices.

(16) Regulations — The Lieutenant Governor in Council may make regulations,

    (a) approving ignition interlock devices for the purpose of this section;

(b) respecting the standards governing the installation, operation and maintenance of approved ignition interlock devices for the purposes of this section and Part III.1 of the *Civil Remedies Act, 2001* and requiring persons authorized under subsection (14) to comply with those standards;   .

(c) providing for the purposes of this section that "motor vehicle" includes a streetcar or a motorized snow vehicle;

(d) prescribing exemptions from subsection (1), (5) or (9) and providing that an exemption is subject to restrictions or conditions specified in the regulations and providing that any such restriction or condition shall be deemed to be a condition contained on a person's driver's licence;

(e) prescribing criteria for the purpose of subsections (4) and (8);

(f) requiring a driver who is prohibited from driving any motor vehicle that is not equipped with an approved ignition interlock device to attend upon a person authorized under subsection (14) for the purpose of enabling that person to gather information from the device;

(g) governing reports that shall be made to the Ministry by persons authorized under subsection (14) in respect of information gathered under clause (f);

(h) respecting programs of supervision for persons prohibited from driving a motor vehicle that is not equipped with an approved ignition interlock device;

(i) respecting any other matter necessary for the administration of this section.

(17) **Same** — A regulation made under subsection (16) may be general or particular in its application.

(18) **Adoption of codes in regulations** — A regulation under clause (16)(b) may adopt by reference, in whole or in part, with such changes as the Lieutenant Governor in Council considers necessary, any code, standard, protocol, procedure or policy, and may require compliance with any code, standard, protocol, procedure or policy.

(19) **Amendments to codes** — The power to adopt by reference and require compliance with a code, standard, protocol, procedure or policy in subsection (18) includes the power to adopt a code, standard, protocol, procedure or policy as it may be amended from time to time.

(20) **Definitions** — In this section and in section 41.3,

"approved" means approved under clause (16)(a);

"driver's licence" includes a driver's licence issued by any other jurisdiction;

"ignition interlock device" means a device designed to ascertain the presence of alcohol in the driver's body and to prevent a motor vehicle from being started if the concentration of alcohol in the driver's body exceeds the prescribed limit.

Proposed Repeal — 41.2

41.2 [Repealed 2015, c. 14, s. 7. Not in force at date of publication.]

2000, c. 35, s. 1; 2002, c. 18, Sched. P, s. 13; 2007, c. 13, s. 8

Commentary

The Highway Traffic Amendment Act (Ignition Interlock Device), 2000, S.O. 2000, c. 35 amends the Highway Traffic Act to provide for the implementation of an ignition interlock program in Ontario for persons who violate laws related to drinking and driving. Where a first-time offender's licence is reinstated following the required suspension period under the Act, the person's driver's licence is subject to the condition prohibiting him or her from driving any motor vehicle that is not equipped with an ignition interlock device. One year following reinstatement, a first-time offender may apply to the Registrar to remove the condition and the Registrar is required to do so if the person meets the criteria prescribed in the regulations. When a second-time offender's driver's licence is reinstated under the Act, his or her licence is also subject to the same condition. A second-time offender is permitted to make an application for the removal of the condition three years following his or her licence reinstatement. If a third-time offender's licence is reinstated by the Registrar under the Act, then the condition on his or her licence is permanent. Owners of motor vehicles that are not equipped with ignition interlock devices are prohibited from knowingly permitting a person to drive the vehicle, if that person's licence prohibits him or her from doing so. A person is also not allowed to tamper with an ignition interlock device. The Minister may in writing authorize any person to install, maintain and remove ignition interlock devices, and to charge fees for such services. The Act also empowers the Lieutenant Governor in Council to make regulations concerning: the approval of ignition interlock devices; the standards for the installation, operation and maintenance of the devices; and requirements for drivers to attend upon authorized service providers for the purpose of allowing them to gather information from the device.

Related Provisions: See O. Reg. 287/08; Conduct Review Programs; O. Reg. 251/02, Ignition Interlock Devices.

41.3 (1) Parties to judicial review — **The parties to any judicial review brought in respect of section 41.2 are the Registrar and the person whose driver's licence is subject to the condition prohibiting him or her from driving any motor vehicle that is not equipped with an approved ignition interlock device.**

(2) Documents privileged — **Documents filed with the Ministry for the purposes of section 41.2 are privileged for the information of the Ministry only and shall not be open for public inspection.**

(3) Protection from personal liability — **No action or other proceeding for damages shall be instituted against a person authorized under subsection 41.2(14) to install or maintain an approved ignition interlock device, unless the person was negligent in the performance of his or her duties and responsibilities under section 41.2.**

(4) Same — **No action or other proceeding for damages shall be instituted against the Registrar or any employee of the Ministry for the removal of a condition prohibiting a person from driving a motor vehicle that is not equipped with an approved ignition interlock device or for the failure to remove the condition, if the Registrar or employee acted in good faith in the execution or intended execution of his or her duties under section 41.2.**

(5) Crown not relieved of liability — **Despite subsections 5(2) and (4) of the** *Proceedings Against the Crown Act*, **subsections (3) and (4) do not relieve the Crown**

101

of liability in respect of a tort committed by a person mentioned in subsection (3) and (4) to which it would otherwise be subject.

Proposed Repeal — 41.3

41.3 [Repealed 2015, c. 14, s. 7. Not in force at date of publication.]

2000, c. 35, s. 1

Commentary

The Highway Traffic Amendment Act (Ignition Interlock Device), 2000, S.O. 2000, c. 35 amends the Highway Traffic Act to provide for the implementation of an ignition interlock program in Ontario for persons who violate laws related to drinking and driving. Where a first-time offender's licence is reinstated following the required suspension period under the Act, the person's driver's licence is subject to the condition prohibiting him or her from driving any motor vehicle that is not equipped with an ignition interlock device. One year following reinstatement, a first-time offender may apply to the Registrar to remove the condition and the Registrar is required to do so if the person meets the criteria prescribed in the regulations. When a second-time offender's driver's licence is reinstated under the Act, his or her licence is also subject to the same condition. A second-time offender is permitted to make an application for the removal of the condition three years following his or her licence reinstatement. If a third-time offender's licence is reinstated by the Registrar under the Act, then the condition on his or her licence is permanent. Owners of motor vehicles that are not equipped with ignition interlock devices are prohibited from knowingly permitting a person to drive the vehicle, if that person's licence prohibits him or her from doing so. A person is also not allowed to tamper with an ignition interlock device. The Minister may in writing authorize any person to install, maintain and remove ignition interlock devices, and to charge fees for such services. The Act also empowers the Lieutenant Governor in Council to make regulations concerning: the approval of ignition interlock devices; the standards for the installation, operation and maintenance of the devices; and requirements for drivers to attend upon authorized service providers for the purpose of allowing them to gather information from the device.

41.4 (1) Administrative vehicle impoundment for contravening ignition interlock condition — Where a police officer is satisfied that a person was driving a motor vehicle in contravention of a condition that was imposed on the person's driver's licence under section 41.2 or pursuant to a conduct review program under section 57 that prohibits him or her from driving a motor vehicle that is not equipped with an approved ignition interlock device, the officer shall detain the motor vehicle that was being driven by the person and the vehicle shall, at the cost and risk of its owner,

Proposed Amendment — 41.4(1) opening words

(1) Administrative vehicle impoundment for contravening ignition interlock condition — Where a police officer is satisfied that a person was driving a motor vehicle in contravention of a condition imposed on the person's driver's licence under a conduct review program under section 57 that prohibits him or her from driving a motor vehicle that is not equipped with an ignition interlock device, the officer shall detain the motor vehicle that was being driven by the person and the vehicle shall, at the cost and risk of its owner,

2015, c. 14, s. 8 [Not in force at date of publication.]

(a) be removed to an impound facility as directed by a police officer; and

(b) be impounded for seven days from the time it was detained.

(2) **Release of vehicle** — Subject to subsection (14), the motor vehicle shall be released to its owner from the impound facility upon the expiry of the period of impoundment.

(3) **Early release of vehicle** — Despite the detention or impoundment of a motor vehicle under this section, a police officer may release the motor vehicle to its owner before it is impounded or, subject to subsection (14), may direct the operator of the impound facility where the motor vehicle is impounded to release the motor vehicle to its owner before the expiry of the seven days if the officer is satisfied that the motor vehicle was stolen at the time that it was driven as described in subsection (1).

(4) **Duty of officer re impoundment** — Every officer who detains a motor vehicle under this section shall, as soon as practicable,

(a) prepare a notice identifying the motor vehicle that is to be impounded, the name and address of the driver, the date and time of the impoundment, the period of time for which the motor vehicle is impounded and the place where the vehicle may be recovered; and

(b) serve the driver with a copy of the notice.

(5) **Service on driver is deemed service on owner and operator** — Service of a copy of a notice under subsection (4) on the driver of the motor vehicle is deemed to be service on and sufficient notice to the owner of the vehicle and the operator of the vehicle, if there is an operator.

(6) **Further notice to owner** — In addition to serving the owner of the motor vehicle through service on the driver under subsection (4), a police officer shall provide a copy of the notice prepared under subsection (4) to the owner of the motor vehicle by delivering it personally or by mail to the address of the owner shown on the permit for the motor vehicle or to the latest address for the owner appearing on the records of the Ministry.

(7) **Surrender of documents, information re trip and goods carried** — If the motor vehicle that is to be impounded contains goods, the police officer may require the driver and any other person present who is in charge of the motor vehicle to surrender all documents in his or her possession or in the vehicle that relate to the operation of the vehicle or to the carriage of the goods and to furnish all information within that person's knowledge relating to the details of the current trip and the ownership of the goods.

(8) **Operator, owner to remove load** — Upon being served with notice of the impoundment through service on the driver under subsection (4), the operator of the motor vehicle or, if there is no operator, the owner shall forthwith remove any vehicle drawn by the motor vehicle and any load from the motor vehicle.

(9) Application of _Dangerous Goods Transportation Act_ — If the goods are dangerous goods, within the meaning of the _Dangerous Goods Transportation Act_, the operator or, if there is no operator, the owner shall remove them in accordance with that Act.

(10) Officer may remove load, trailer at operator's cost, risk — If, in the opinion of a police officer, the operator or owner fails to remove a drawn vehicle or load as required by subsection (8) within a reasonable time after being served with notice of the impoundment, the officer may cause the drawn vehicle or load to be removed and stored or disposed of at the cost and risk of the operator or, if there is no operator, the owner.

(11) Same — If a police officer is of the opinion that the operator or owner has not made appropriate arrangements for the removal of a drawn vehicle or load, having regard to the nature of the goods, including the fact that they are or appear to be dangerous goods within the meaning of the _Dangerous Goods Transportation Act_ or are perishable, the officer may cause the drawn vehicle or load to be removed, stored or otherwise disposed of at the cost and risk of the operator or, if there is no operator, the owner.

(12) Personal property in vehicle available to owner — Any personal property that is left in the impounded motor vehicle and that is not attached to or used in connection with its operation shall, upon request and proof of ownership, be made available, at reasonable times, to the owner of the property.

(13) No appeal or right to be heard — There is no appeal from, or right to be heard before, a vehicle detention or impoundment under subsection (1).

(14) Impound costs to be paid before release of vehicle — The person who operates the impound facility where a motor vehicle is impounded under this section is not required to release the motor vehicle until the removal and impound costs for the vehicle have been paid.

(15) Lien for impound costs — The costs incurred by the person who operates the impound facility where a motor vehicle is impounded under this section are a lien on the motor vehicle that may be enforced under the _Repair and Storage Liens Act_.

(16) Impound costs a recoverable debt — The costs incurred by the person who operates the impound facility where a motor vehicle is impounded under this section are a debt due by the owner and the driver of the motor vehicle at the time the vehicle was detained, for which the owner and the driver are jointly and severally liable, and the debt may be recovered in any court of competent jurisdiction.

(17) Owner may recover losses from driver — The owner of a motor vehicle that is impounded under this section may bring an action against the driver of the motor vehicle at the time the vehicle was detained under subsection (1) to recover any costs or other losses incurred by the owner in connection with the impoundment.

(18) Debt due to police or Crown — The costs incurred by a police force or the Crown in removing, storing or disposing of a drawn vehicle or load from a motor vehicle under subsection (10) or (11) are a debt due to the police force or Crown, as the case may be, and may be recovered by the police force or Crown in any court of competent jurisdiction.

(19) Offence — Every person who obstructs or interferes with a police officer in the performance of his or her duties under this section is guilty of an offence and on conviction is liable to a fine of not less than $200 and not more than $5,000 or to imprisonment for a term of not more than six months, or to both.

(20) Intent of impoundment — The impoundment of a motor vehicle under this section is intended to promote compliance with this Act and to thereby safeguard the public and does not constitute an alternative to any proceeding or penalty arising from the same circumstances or around the same time.

(21) Impoundment concurrent with other administrative impoundments — The impoundment of a motor vehicle under this section runs concurrently with an impoundment, if any, of the same motor vehicle under section 48.4, 55.1, 55.2, 82.1 or 172.

(22) Forms — The Minister may require that forms approved by the Minister be used for any purpose of this section.

(23) Regulations — The Minister may make regulations,

(a) requiring police officers to keep records with respect to vehicle impoundments under this section for a specified period of time and to report specified information with respect to vehicle impoundments to the Registrar and governing such records and reports;

(b) exempting any class of persons or class or type of vehicles from any provision or requirement of this section or of any regulation made under this section and prescribing conditions and circumstances for any such exemption;

(c) exempting commercial motor vehicles, or any class or type of commercial motor vehicles, or drivers, owners or operators of commercial motor vehicles or any class of them, from any provision or requirement of this section or of any regulation made under this section, prescribing a different scheme of consequences and requirements from those set out in this section if a police officer is satisfied that a person was driving a commercial motor vehicle, or a specified class or type of commercial motor vehicle, as described in subsection (1), including prescribing different penalties, and prescribing conditions and circumstances for any such exemption or for a different scheme to apply;

(d) designating provisions of legislation enacted by another province, a territory of Canada or a state of the United States of America that are comparable to the provisions referred to in subsection (1) and providing that this section applies to a person who is driving a motor vehicle in contravention of a condition or requirement imposed under such provisions.

(24) Contravention of different scheme — Every person who contravenes or fails to comply with a regulation made under clause (23)(c) that prescribes a different scheme of consequences and requirements from those set out in this section is guilty of an offence and on conviction is liable to a fine of not less than $400 and not more than $20,000.

(25) Definition — In this section,

"operator" means,

    (a) the person directly or indirectly responsible for the operation of a commercial motor vehicle, including the conduct of the driver of, and the carriage of goods or passengers, if any, in, the commercial motor vehicle or combination of vehicles, and

    (b) in the absence of evidence to the contrary, where no CVOR certificate, as defined in subsection 16(1), or lease applicable to a commercial motor vehicle, is produced, the holder of the plate portion of the permit for the commercial motor vehicle.

> **Proposed Amendment — 41.4(25) "operator" (b)**
>
> **(b)** in the absence of evidence to the contrary, where no CVOR certificate, or lease applicable to a commercial motor vehicle, is produced, the holder of the plate portion of the permit for the commercial motor vehicle.
>
> 2014, c. 9, Sched. 2, s. 14 [To come into force January 1, 2017.]

2009, c. 5, s. 11; 2010, c. 16, Sched. 12, s. 2(1)

Commentary

A seven-day administrative impoundment is provided if a driver is not driving with a required ignition interlock.

42. (1) Suspension for driving while disqualified — The driver's licence of a person who is convicted of an offence under subsection 259(4) of the *Criminal Code* (Canada) or under a provision that is enacted by another jurisdiction, including by a municipality in another jurisdiction, and is designated in a reciprocal agreement entered into under section 40 is thereupon suspended for a period of,

    (a) upon the first conviction, one year; and

    (b) upon a subsequent conviction, two years,

in addition to any other period for which the licence is suspended and consecutively thereto.

(2) Determining subsequent conviction — In determining whether a conviction is a subsequent conviction for the purposes of subsection (1), the only question to be considered is the sequence of convictions and no consideration shall be given to the sequence of commission of offences or whether any offence occurred before or after any conviction.

(3) Five-year limitation — Clause (1)(b) does not apply when the subsequent conviction is more than five years after the previous conviction.

(4) Order for discharge — This section applies in the same manner as if a person were convicted of an offence if the person pleads guilty to or is found guilty of an offence referred to in subsection (1) and,

    (a) an order directing that the accused be discharged is made under section 730 of the *Criminal Code* (Canada) or under a provision that is enacted by a state of the United States of America and that is designated by the regulations; or

(b) a disposition is made under section 20 or sections 28 to 32 of the *Young Offenders Act* (Canada) or a youth sentence is imposed under section 42, 59, 94, 95 or 96 of the *Youth Criminal Justice Act* (Canada) or an adult sentence is imposed under the *Youth Criminal Justice Act* (Canada), including a confirmation or variation of the disposition or sentence.

(5) [Repealed 2009, c. 5, s. 12(2).]

1993, c. 27, s. 3 (Sched.); 2000, c. 26, Sched. O, s. 2; 2006, c. 19, Sched. D, s. 9(3); 2009, c. 5, s. 12

Commentary

If a driver is convicted of driving while prohibited under the Criminal Code or in a reciprocating American state, the driver will receive an automatic additional minimum suspension.

The Red Tape Reduction Act, 2000, S.O. 2000, c. 26, Sched. O. (ss. 1-4, 5(1) and (2) and 14 in force December 6, 2000; ss. 6-13 in force January 1, 2001) re-enacts s. 52 of the Highway Traffic Act to allow for notice to be given by regular mail for suspensions unrelated to Criminal Code (Canada) offences, and to allow for other prescribed methods of service; amends s. 55.1 to provide that the impoundment history of leased vehicles is linked to the holder of the plate portion of the registration certificate, to extend vehicle impound provisions to persons who are found driving while their licence is under suspension as a result of a court order and to clarify who is responsible for paying storage charges related to impoundment; amends existing provisions dealing with vehicle weights and dimensions to establish a framework for the implementation of an agreement between Ontario and Quebec; and amends s. 175(6)(c) of the Act to clarify when overhead red signal lights and stop arms on school buses must be used.

Related Provisions: See O. Reg 287/08; Conduct Review Programs, 25(1)(b)(v); O. Reg. 37/93; Reciprocal Suspension of Driver's Licence.

43. (1) Suspension while prohibited from driving — Where the licence of a person who is subject to an order made under section 259 of the *Criminal Code* (Canada), if the order is the result of an offence committed while operating a motor vehicle or street car within the meaning of this Act, a vessel within the meaning of section 48 or a motorized snow vehicle, is suspended under subsection 41(1) or under subsection 42(1), the licence shall remain suspended during the period of prohibition set out in the order despite the expiration of any other period of suspension.

(2) Expanded meaning of order — For the purposes of subsection (1), "an order made under section 259 of the *Criminal Code* (Canada)" includes an order made under subsection 238(1) of the *Criminal Code* (Canada) before the 26th day of April, 1976.

2006, c. 20, s. 2; 2009, c. 5, s. 13

Commentary

This section confirms that if the Criminal Code prohibition is longer than that provided under the Act, the licence remains suspended.

44. (1) Increased suspension time — Where an order is made under section 259 of the *Criminal Code* (Canada) or under subsection 41(4) of this Act and the court or judge, when sentencing the offender or making the conviction, orders the imprisonment of the offender and that the period of prohibition or suspension, as the case may be, shall start to run on the termination of the imprisonment, the suspension imposed by subsection 41(1) of this Act is thereupon increased by the period of imprisonment.

(2) Modification to increased suspension — Where the period of imprisonment referred to in subsection (1) is less than that ordered by the court or judge, the length of the increased suspension imposed by subsection (1) shall, upon the application of the offender, be reduced by a period equal to that by which the period of imprisonment was reduced.

Commentary

This section indicates that provincial suspensions only take effect on the termination of imprisonment.

44.1 Condition on licence that blood alcohol concentration level be zero — (1) Novice drivers — It is a condition of the driver's licence of every novice driver that his or her blood alcohol concentration level be zero while he or she is driving a motor vehicle on a highway.

(2) Young drivers — It is a condition of the driver's licence of every young driver that his or her blood alcohol concentration level be zero while he or she is driving a motor vehicle on a highway.

(3) Penalty, novice drivers — Every novice driver who contravenes the condition of his or her driver's licence imposed under subsection (1) is guilty of an offence and on conviction is liable to a fine of not less than $60 and not more than $500.

(4) Same — If a novice driver is convicted of an offence under subsection (3), the Registrar may suspend, cancel or change his or her driver's licence in accordance with the regulations.

(5) Same, young drivers — Every young driver who contravenes the condition of his or her driver's licence imposed under subsection (2) is guilty of an offence and on conviction is liable to a fine of not less than $60 and not more than $500 and his or her driver's licence is thereupon suspended for 30 days.

(6) Intent of suspension — The suspension of a licence under this section is intended to ensure that novice drivers and young drivers acquire experience and develop or improve safe driving skills in controlled conditions and to safeguard the licensee and the public and does not constitute an alternative to any proceeding or penalty arising from the same circumstances or around the same time.

(7) Regulations — The Lieutenant Governor in Council may make regulations governing the suspension or cancellation of drivers' licences of novice drivers or the change in respect of their class for the purpose of subsection (4).

(8) Definitions — In this section,

"driver" includes a person who has care or control of a motor vehicle;

"driver's licence" includes a motorized snow vehicle operator's licence and a driver's licence issued by any other jurisdiction;

"motor vehicle" includes a motorized snow vehicle;

"novice driver" has the meaning prescribed by the regulations made under section 57.1;

"young driver" means a driver who is under 22 years old.

2009, c. 5, s. 14

Commentary

A condition is imposed on the drivers' licences of novice drivers and young drivers (drivers under 22 years old) that their blood alcohol concentration be zero when driving. It is an offence to contravene this condition. In addition, a novice driver's licence may be suspended, cancelled or changed in respect of its class and a young drivers' licence suspended for 30 days.

Related Provisions: See O. Reg. 340/94, Drivers' Licences, ss. 1, 9, 29.

45. When driver may be disqualified — A provincial judge or justice of the peace by whom a person is convicted of a contravention of this Act, if the person convicted is required to hold a driver's licence and does not hold the licence, may declare him or her disqualified to hold the licence for the time that the provincial judge or justice of the peace thinks fit and shall so report with the certificate of the conviction to the Minister.

Commentary

If the suspended driver does not have a licence, his or her right to obtain one is suspended. See also s. 1(2) of the Act which provides that if a licence or permit may be suspended or revoked, both may be suspended or revoked.

46. (1) Defaulted fine — This section applies if a fine is imposed on conviction for an offence and the offence is an offence,

    (a) under this Act or the regulations;

    (b) under any other Act listed in the Schedule to this section or under the regulations made under such an Act;

    (c) under clause 17(1)(a) or subsection 24(1) of the *Fish and Wildlife Conservation Act, 1997*;

    (d) under subsection 32(1) of the *Liquor Licence Act*; or

    (e) that was committed with a motor vehicle under section 249, 249.1, 249.2, 249.3, 249.4, 252, 253, 254, 255 or 259 of the *Criminal Code* (Canada).

(2) Order or direction — If the payment of a fine imposed on conviction for an offence is in default, an order or direction may be made under section 69 of the

Provincial Offences Act directing that the convicted person's driver's licence be suspended and that no driver's licence be issued to him or her until the fine is paid.

(3) Suspension by Registrar — On being informed of an outstanding order or direction referred to in subsection (2), the Registrar shall suspend the person's driver's licence if it has not already been suspended under another order or direction referred to in subsection (2).

(4) Reinstatement — On being informed that the fine and any applicable administrative fee for reinstatement of the person's driver's licence have been paid, the Registrar shall reinstate the licence, unless he or she has also been informed that,

(a) another order or direction referred to in subsection (2) is outstanding;

(b) the licence is suspended under any other order or direction or under another statute;

(c) interest charged or a penalty imposed under subsection 5(2) has not been paid; or

(d) an applicable prescribed administrative fee for handling a dishonoured cheque has not been paid.

(5) Regulations — The Lieutenant Governor in Council may make regulations prescribing forms and procedures and respecting any matter considered necessary or advisable to carry out effectively the intent and purpose of this section.

SCHEDULE
(Section 46)

Compulsory Automobile Insurance Act

Dangerous Goods Transportation Act

Motorized Snow Vehicles Act

Off-Road Vehicles Act

Public Vehicles Act

1993, c. 27, s. 3 (Sched.); 1993, c. 31, s. 2(6); 1997, c. 41, s. 120; 2001, c. 9, Sched. O, s. 3; 2002, c. 18, Sched. P, s. 14; 2007, c. 13, s. 9

Case Law

R. v. Giagnocavo (1975), 32 C.R.N.S. 27 (Ont. H.C.); affirmed (1977), 38 C.C.C. (2d) 463 (Ont. Div. Ct.) — The justice is not required to grant a hearing before issuing an order pursuant to s. 46(2) as the act to be performed is administrative as opposed to judicial or quasi-judicial.

R. v. Middlebrook; *R. v. Miller*; *R. v. Laporta* (1988), 5 M.V.R. (2d) 236 (Ont. C.A.); affirming *Miller v. R.* (1986), 55 O.R. (2d) 417, 41 M.V.R. 141, 27 C.C.C. (3d) 30 (H.C.) — Section 46(1) of the Act is constitutionally valid and not in violation of s. 7 of the Charter of Rights.

R. v. Wall, 2010 BCPC 316, 2010 CarswellBC 3398, 6 M.V.R. (6th) 228 — Any reasonable person having signed for a registered letter would have gone one step further and satisfied him or herself of the contents.

Related Provisions: See sections 196 to 198.5 of the Act, see also R.R.O. 1990, Reg. 607; Reciprocal Suspension of Licences.

47. (1) Suspension and cancellation of licence, etc., general — Subject to section 47.1, the Registrar may suspend or cancel,

Proposed Amendment — 47(1) opening words

(1) Suspension and cancellation of licence, etc., general — Subject to section 47.1, the Registrar may, by order, suspend or cancel,

2014, c. 9, Sched. 2, s. 15(1) [To come into force January 1, 2017.]

(a) the plate portion of a permit as defined in Part II;

(b) a driver's licence; or

(c) a CVOR certificate,

on the grounds of,

(d) misconduct for which the holder is responsible, directly or indirectly, related to the operation or driving of a motor vehicle;

(e) conviction of the holder for an offence referred to in subsection 210(1) or (2);

(f) the Registrar having reason to believe, having regard to the safety record of the holder or of a person related to the holder, and any other information that the Registrar considers relevant, that the holder will not operate a commercial motor vehicle safely or in accordance with this Act, the regulations and other laws relating to highway safety; or

(g) any other sufficient reasons not referred to in clause (d), (e) or (f).

(2) Restriction — As an alternative to a suspension or cancellation under subsection (1), the Registrar may, subject to section 47.1, restrict the number of commercial motor vehicles that may be operated by a holder of a CVOR certificate during the period that the Registrar stipulates.

(2.1) Interpretation — Subsection 17(4) applies, with necessary modifications, for the purpose of determining who are related persons under clause (1)(f).

Proposed Addition — 47(2.2), (2.3)

(2.2) Immediate suspension or cancellation of CVOR certificate — The Registrar may by order provide that a suspension or cancellation of a CVOR certificate or of a plate portion of a permit under subsection (1) is of immediate effect if the Registrar has reason to believe that,

(a) the CVOR certificate holder's or plate holder's safety record or failure to comply with this or any other Act demonstrates a significant risk to road safety or to road users; and

(b) it is in the public interest that the operator immediately cease operating all commercial motor vehicles.

(2.3) Same — A CVOR certificate holder who is subject to an order described in subsection (2.2) shall immediately, in accordance with the order and any regulations, cease to operate any commercial motor vehicle.

2014, c. 9, Sched. 2, s. 15(2) [To come into force January 1, 2017.]

(3) New permit not to be issued — A person whose permit is under suspension or is cancelled under this section is not entitled to be issued a plate portion of a permit while the permit is under suspension or is cancelled.

(3.1) New licence not to be issued — A person whose licence is under suspension or is cancelled under this section is not entitled to be issued a licence while the licence is under suspension or is cancelled.

(3.2) New CVOR certificate not to be issued — A person whose CVOR certificate is under suspension under this section or is revoked under section 17.0.1 is not entitled to be issued a CVOR certificate while the CVOR certificate is under suspension or is revoked.

(3.3) Same — A person whose CVOR certificate has been cancelled under this section is never entitled to be issued a CVOR certificate.

(4) Fleet limitation certificates — Where a restriction is imposed under subsection (2), the Registrar shall issue to the holder of the CVOR certificate fleet limitation certificates in a number equal to the number of vehicles permitted to be operated.

(5) Offence — Every person whose permit for a motor vehicle is suspended or cancelled and who, while prohibited from having such a motor vehicle registered in their name, applies for or procures the issue or has possession of the plate portion of a permit for a motor vehicle issued to them is guilty of an offence and on conviction is liable,

(a) to a fine of not less than $60 and not more than $500 where the vehicle is not a commercial motor vehicle; or

(b) to a fine of not less than $200 and not more than $2,000 where the vehicle is a commercial motor vehicle,

or to imprisonment for a term of not more than thirty days, or to both a fine and imprisonment.

(6) Same — Every person whose licence is suspended or cancelled and who, while prohibited from driving a motor vehicle, applies for or procures the issue of or has possession of any portion of a licence issued to him or her, other than a licence card that has been marked by the Ministry as valid only to show the driver's photograph, is guilty of an offence and on conviction is liable to a fine of not less than $60 and not more than $500 and to imprisonment for a term of not more than 30 days.

(7) Idem — Every person whose CVOR certificate is suspended or cancelled who applies for or procures the issue of a CVOR certificate to themself is guilty of an offence and on conviction is liable to a fine of not less than $200 and not more than $2,000 or to imprisonment for a term of not more than thirty days, or to both.

(8) Idem — Every person,

(a) in respect of whom a restriction is imposed under subsection (2) who operates a commercial motor vehicle in which a valid fleet limitation certificate is not carried; or

(b) who operates a commercial motor vehicle without a permit or certificate or when their permit or certificate is under suspension,

Proposed Amendment — 47(8)(b)

(b) who operates a commercial motor vehicle without a permit or certificate or when their permit or certificate is under suspension or cancelled,

2014, c. 9, Sched. 2, s. 15(3) [To come into force January 1, 2017.]

is guilty of an offence and on conviction is liable to a fine of not more than $5,000 or to imprisonment for a term of not more than six months, or to both.

(8.1) Power to seize number plates — If the plate portion of a permit is suspended or cancelled under clause (1)(a), the Registrar may order that the plate portion of the permit or the number plates issued in connection with the plate portion of the permit be seized and any police officer or officer appointed for carrying out this Act may seize the plate portion of the permit and the number plates and deliver them to the Ministry.

(9) Definitions — For the purposes of this section and section 47.1,

"commercial motor vehicle", "operator" and "safety record" have the same meanings as in subsection 16(1).

Proposed Amendment — 47(9)

(9) Definition — For the purposes of this section and section 47.1,

"operator" has the same meaning as in subsection 16(1).

2014, c. 9, Sched. 2, s. 15(4) [To come into force January 1, 2017.]

(10) Power to seize out-of-province permits and plates — The Registrar may, at any time, for misconduct or contravention of this Act or the *Public Vehicles Act* or of any regulation thereunder by an owner or lessee of one or more motor vehicles or trailers for which permits have been issued by a jurisdiction or jurisdictions other than the Province of Ontario, order that the permit and number plates issued for the vehicle or vehicles be seized.

(11) Same — Any police officer or officer appointed for carrying out this Act or for the enforcement of the *Public Vehicles Act* may seize the permit and number plates pursuant to an order under subsection (10) and deliver them to the Ministry, which shall return them to the authority that issued them.

Proposed Addition — 47(12)

(12) Regulations — The Lieutenant Governor in Council may make regulations governing the ceasing of operations by CVOR certificate holders who are subject to an order described in subsection (2.2).

2014, c. 9, Sched. 2, s. 15(5) [To come into force January 1, 2017.]

1996, c. 33, s. 7; 2001, c. 9, Sched. O, s. 4; 2002, c. 18, Sched. P, s. 15; 2008, c. 17, s. 36

Commentary

The Registrar has broad discretionary powers to suspend or cancel permits, licences and CVOR certificates for misconduct. It is a serious offence to drive while under suspension by the Registrar. The Registrar has entered into reciprocal arrangements with other provinces and territories which ensure that Ontario drivers convicted of serious offences will be suspended or have demerit points registered in Ontario.

Effective April 1, 1989, Ontario and Quebec entered into a reciprocal agreement covering licence suspensions following Criminal Code convictions for Quebec drivers committed in Ontario and vice-versa. The Agreement also applies to serious highway traffic offences and failure to pay fines relating thereto. Infractions committed under the Traffic Act of the neighbouring province will result in demerit points being registered on the driver's record just as if those infractions were committed in the home province.

On June 1, 1991, the Canadian Driver Licence Compact between the provinces and territories came into effect. It serves the same purpose as the Ontario-Quebec Agreement.

Case Law

Acker v. N.B. (Registrar of Motor Vehicles) (1991), 34 M.V.R. (2d) 101, 119 N.B.R. (2d) 77, 300 A.P.R. 77, 84 D.L.R. (4th) 555 (C.A.) — After receiving a report from the R.C.M.P. referring to a near accident allegedly caused by A and expressing doubts as to A's ability to operate a motor vehicle safely, the Registrar of Motor Vehicles, acting under s. 309 of the Motor Vehicle Act (N.B.), wrote to A asking him to file a medical certificate stating that his health was such that he was capable of operating a motor vehicle safely, and to take a driver's test. No reasons were given to A as to why his driving competence had been called into question, other than the reference to his health. A filed the required medical certificate and passed the written examination. He failed the practical part of the driving test because of his inability to parallel park. The Registrar revoked his licence to operate a motor vehicle and indefinitely suspended his driving privileges. A judge of the Court of Queen's Bench refused to set aside the suspension. A appealed. The appeal was allowed. The information that the Registrar possessed gave him good cause to question A's ability to drive on the basis of his health. The question was answered by the medical certificate and the matter should have ended there. The Registrar did not have good cause to require a complete driver's test.

Garrity v. British Columbia (1997), 30 M.V.R. (3d) 106, 38 B.C.L.R. (3d) 207, 1 Admin. L.R. (3d) 194 (B.C. S.C.) — The petitioner's record of alcohol-related offences justified the ordering of a medical examination.

British Columbia (Superintendent of Motor Vehicles) v. British Columbia (Council of Human Rights) (1999), 47 M.V.R. (3d) 167 (S.C.C.) — A claimant's peripheral vision was impaired by an opthalmic condition. The claimant's driver's licence was cancelled on the ground that his vision did not meet the standard minimum field of vision. The standard constituted prima facie discrimination. It had not been shown that the standard was a bona fide occupational requirement or that it had a bona fide reasonable justification. The claimant was entitled to an individual assessment to prove safe driving ability.

Devlin v. Ontario (Registrar of Motor Vehicles) (2003), 40 M.V.R. (4th) 68, [2003] O.J. No. 2012, 2003 CarswellOnt 1948 (Ont. S.C.J.) — The standard of review is correctness.

Dice v. Ontario, [2004] O.J. No. 4646, 2004 CarswellOnt 5147, 12 M.V.R. (5th) 41 (S.C.J.) — The exercise of authority under s. 47 of the Act and s. 14 of the Regulation is an operational decision in which government policy is implemented and a duty of care owed.

Boechler v. British Columbia (Superintendent of Motor Vehicles), 2006 CarswellBC 2893, 41 M.V.R. (5th) 80, 2006 BCSC 1631 (B.C. S.C. [In Chambers]) — The B.C. Superintendent erred in taking into account a transcript relating to the other aggressive driver in a two car incident.

Lee Trans. Corp. v. Ontario (Registrar of Motor Vehicles), 2011 ONSC 6003, 2011 CarswellOnt 13367, 24 M.V.R. (6th) 200, [2011] O.J. No. 4820 (Div. Ct.) — Where the Registrar had cancelled and seized licences under s. 47(1)(f) which was confirmed by the Licence Appeal Tribunal, an appeal was dismissed. The Tribunal's findings of mixed fact and law were entitled to deference. Assuming without deciding that the proposed fresh evidence was admissible, there was no evidence of real steps taken to improve the safety record.

47.1 (1) Notice of proposed action — Before taking any action under clause 47(1)(a) or (c) or subsection 47(2), the Registrar shall notify the person whose plate portion of a permit or CVOR certificate is to be affected of his or her proposed action.

(1.1) Notice of safety record concerns — The Registrar may also notify an operator at any time if the Registrar has reason to believe that the operator may not operate a commercial motor vehicle safely or in accordance with this Act, the regulations or other laws relating to highway safety.

(2) Methods for giving notice — Notice under subsection (1) or (1.1) is sufficiently given if,

    (a) it is delivered personally to the person;

    (b) it is delivered by courier to the person;

    (c) it is delivered by mail to the person at the latest address provided by the person to the Ministry;

    (d) it is sent by fax to the person at the latest fax number provided by the person to the Ministry; or

    (e) it is sent by another electronic means of transmission prescribed by regulation in accordance with the regulations.

(3) [Repealed 2015, c. 27, Sched. 7, s. 14(1).]

(4) Restrictions on vehicle transfers — If a notice under subsection (1) or (1.1) is issued to an operator, no person shall, without the consent of the Registrar, transfer or lease any commercial motor vehicle or trailer for which the operator's name is on the vehicle or plate portion of the permit or do anything that will result in a change of name on the vehicle or plate portion of the permit for any such vehicle or trailer.

(4.1) Duration of restrictions — Subsection (4) is effective in respect of a notice under subsection (1) from the earlier of the date the notice is actually received by the operator and the date the notice is deemed by a regulation made under subsection (7) to have been received by the operator,

(a) in the case of a proposed suspension or fleet limitation, until the end of the suspension or fleet limitation;

(b) in the case of a proposed cancellation, forever.

(4.2) Same — Despite subsection (4.1), subsection (4) ceases to apply in respect of a notice under subsection (1),

(a) if the Registrar withdraws the proposal to suspend or cancel the plate portion of the permit or the CVOR certificate or to impose a fleet limitation; or

(b) if the suspension, cancellation or limitation is set aside on appeal.

(5) Same — Subsection (4) is effective in respect of a notice under subsection (1.1) from the earlier of the date the notice is actually received by the operator and the date the notice is deemed by subsection (3) to have been received by the operator,

(a) if a notice under subsection (1) is issued to the operator on or before the first anniversary of the date the notice under subsection (1.1) was issued, until the earlier of the date the notice under subsection (1) is actually received by the operator and the date the notice under subsection (1) is deemed by a regulation made under subsection (7) to have been received by the operator;

(b) if a notice under subsection (1) is not issued to the operator on or before the first anniversary of the date the notice under subsection (1.1) was issued, until the earlier of the date the Registrar withdraws the notice under subsection (1.1) or the first anniversary of the date the notice under subsection (1.1) was issued.

(6) Registrar not to withhold consent without reason — The Registrar shall not withhold consent under subsection (4) if the operator satisfies him or her that the transfer, lease or other action is not being made for the purpose of avoiding an action under clause 47(1)(a) or (c) or subsection 47(2).

(7) Regulations — The Lieutenant Governor in Council may make regulations,

(a) prescribing other electronic means of transmission for giving notice;

(b) governing the giving of notice by mail, fax or a means of transmission prescribed under clause (a), including prescribing rules governing when notice is deemed to have been received.

1996, c. 33, s. 8; 2001, c. 9, Sched. O, s. 5; 2015, c. 27, Sched. 7, s. 14

48. Administrative licence suspension for blood alcohol concentration above .05 — (1) **Determining whether to make a demand** — A police officer, readily identifiable as such, may require the driver of a motor vehicle to stop for the purpose of determining whether or not there is evidence to justify making a demand under section 254 of the *Criminal Code* (Canada).

(2) Screening device breath test — Where, upon demand of a police officer made under section 254 of the *Criminal Code* (Canada), the driver of a motor vehicle or the operator of a vessel provides a sample of breath which, on analysis by an approved screening device as defined in that section, registers "Warn" or "Alert" or otherwise indicates that the concentration of alcohol in the person's blood is 50 milligrams or more of alcohol in 100 millilitres of blood, the police officer may request that the person surrender his or her driver's licence.

(3) Approved instrument test — Where, upon demand of a police officer made under section 254 of the *Criminal Code* (Canada), the driver of a motor vehicle or the operator of a vessel provides a sample of breath which, on analysis by an instrument approved as suitable for the purpose of section 254 of the *Criminal Code* (Canada), indicates that the concentration of alcohol in his or her blood is 50 milligrams or more of alcohol in 100 millilitres of blood, a police officer may request that the person surrender his or her driver's licence.

(4) Licence suspension — Upon a request being made under subsection (2) or (3), the person to whom the request is made shall forthwith surrender his or her driver's licence to the police officer and, whether or not the person is unable or fails to surrender the licence to the police officer, his or her driver's licence is suspended from the time the request is made for the period of time determined under subsection (14).

(5) Suspension concurrent with administrative suspensions — The licence suspension under this section runs concurrently with a suspension, if any, under section 48.1, 48.2.1 or 48.3.

> **Proposed Amendment — 48(5)**
>
> **(5) Suspension concurrent with administrative suspensions** — The licence suspension under this section runs concurrently with a suspension, if any, under section 48.0.1, 48.1, 48.2.1, 48.3 or 48.3.1.
>
> 2015, c. 14, s. 9(1) [Not in force at date of publication.]

(5.1) [Repealed 2007, c. 13, s. 10.]

(6) Opportunity for second analysis — Where an analysis of the breath of a person is made under subsection (2) and registers "Warn" or "Alert" or otherwise indicates that the concentration of alcohol in the person's blood is 50 milligrams or more of alcohol in 100 millilitres of blood, the person may require that a second analysis be performed if the person requests the second analysis immediately after the police officer requests the surrender of his or her licence under subsection (2).

(6.1) Screening device, instrument used for second analysis — The second analysis must be performed with a different approved screening device than was used in the analysis under subsection (2) or, if the police officer thinks it is preferable, with an instrument approved as suitable for the purpose of section 254 of the *Criminal Code* (Canada).

(6.2) Second analysis governs — Where a person provides a sample of breath for the second analysis requested under subsection (6) immediately upon being requested to do so by the police officer, the result of the second analysis governs and any suspension resulting from the analysis under subsection (2) continues or terminates accordingly.

(7) Calibration of screening device — For the purposes of subsection (2), the approved screening device shall not be calibrated to register "Warn" or "Alert" or to otherwise indicate that the concentration of alcohol in the person's blood is 50 milligrams or more of alcohol in 100 millilitres of blood if the concentration of alcohol in the blood of the person whose breath is being analyzed is less than 50 milligrams of alcohol in 100 millilitres of blood.

(8) Same — It shall be presumed, in the absence of proof to the contrary, that any approved screening device used for the purposes of subsection (2) has been calibrated as required under subsection (7).

(9) No appeal or hearing — There is no appeal from, or right to be heard before, the suspension of a driver's licence under this section.

(10) Intent of suspension — The suspension of a licence under this section is intended to safeguard the licensee and the public and does not constitute an alternative to any proceeding or penalty arising from the same circumstances or around the same time.

(11) Duties of officer — Every officer who asks for the surrender of a licence under this section shall,

> (a) notify the Registrar of that fact, or cause the Registrar to be so notified, in the form and manner and within the time prescribed by the regulations;

> (b) keep a record of the licence received with the name and address of the person and the date and time of the suspension; and

> (c) as soon as practicable after receiving the licence, provide the licensee with a notice of suspension showing the time from which the suspension takes effect and the period of time for which the licence is suspended.

Proposed Amendment — 48(11)

(11) Duties of officer — Every police officer who asks for the surrender of a licence under this section shall,

> (a) notify the Registrar of that fact, or cause the Registrar to be so notified, in the form and manner and within the time required by the Registrar;

> (b) keep a record of the licence received with the name and address of the person and the date and time of the suspension;

> (c) provide the licensee with a written statement of the time from which the suspension takes effect, the period of time for which the licence is suspended and the place where the licence may be recovered; and

> (d) forward to the Registrar such other material or information as may be prescribed by the regulations.

2015, c. 14, s. 9(2) [Not in force at date of publication.]

(12) Removal of vehicle — If the motor vehicle of a person whose licence is suspended under this section is at a location from which, in the opinion of a police officer, it should be removed and there is no person available who may lawfully remove the vehicle, the officer may remove and store the vehicle or cause it to be removed and stored, in which case the officer shall notify the person of the location of the storage.

(13) Cost of removal — Where a police officer obtains assistance for the removal and storage of a motor vehicle under this section, the costs incurred in moving and storing the vehicle are a lien on the vehicle that may be enforced under the *Repair and Storage Liens Act* by the person who moved or stored the vehicle at the request of the officer.

(14) Period of suspension — A driver's licence suspended under subsection (4) shall be suspended for,

    (a) three days, in the case of a first suspension under this section;

    (b) seven days, in the case of a second suspension under this section;

    (c) 30 days, in the case of a third or subsequent suspension under this section.

(15) Same — The following previous suspensions shall not be taken into account in determining whether the current suspension is a first, second or subsequent suspension for the purpose of subsection (14):

    1. A previous suspension that took effect more than five years before the current suspension takes effect.

    2. A previous suspension that took effect before section 10 of the *afer Roads for a Safer Ontario Act, 2007* comes into force.

(16) Police officer's other powers unchanged — Subsection (1) shall not be construed so as to prevent a police officer from requiring a driver stopped under that subsection to surrender any licence, permit, card or other document that the officer is otherwise authorized to demand under this Act or the *Compulsory Automobile Insurance Act* or from requiring a driver to submit a vehicle to examinations and tests under subsection 82(2) of this Act.

(17) Regulations — The Lieutenant Governor in Council may make regulations,

    (a) respecting the form, manner and time within which the Registrar must be notified under subsection (11);

    (b) prescribing other material or information to be forwarded to the Registrar under subsection (11).

Proposed Amendment — 48(17)

(17) Regulations — The Lieutenant Governor in Council may make regulations prescribing other material or information to be forwarded to the Registrar under clause (11)(d).

2015, c. 14, s. 9(3) [Not in force at date of publication.]

(18) Definitions — In this section,

"driver" includes a person who has care or control of a motor vehicle;

"driver's licence" includes a motorized snow vehicle operator's licence and a driver's licence issued by any other jurisdiction;

"motor vehicle" includes a motorized snow vehicle;

Proposed Amendment — 48(18) "motor vehicle"

"motor vehicle" includes a street car and a motorized snow vehicle;

2015, c. 14, s. 9(4) [Not in force at date of publication.]

"vessel" means a vessel within the meaning of section 214 of the *Criminal Code* (Canada).

(19) Meaning of suspension for out-of-province licences — With respect to a driver's licence issued by another jurisdiction, instead of suspending the person's driver's licence, the Registrar shall suspend the person's privilege to drive a motor vehicle in Ontario for the applicable period determined under subsection (14).

Proposed Amendment — 48(19)

(19) Meaning of suspension for out-of-province licences — With respect to a driver's licence issued by another jurisdiction, instead of the person's driver's licence being suspended, the person's privilege to drive a motor vehicle in Ontario is suspended for the applicable period determined under subsection (14), and this section and section 53 apply to the suspension of that privilege with necessary modifications.

2015, c. 14, s. 9(5) [Not in force at date of publication.]

1993, c. 40, s. 4; 1996, c. 20, s. 7; 2006, c. 20, s. 3; 2007, c. 13, s. 10; 2008, c. 17, s. 37; 2009, c. 5, s. 15(6), (8), (9), (11), (13)

Case Law

Bro v. British Columbia (Superintendent of Motor Vehicles) (2014), 2014 CarswellBC 2635, 72 B.C.L.R. (5th) 90, 70 M.V.R. (6th) 89, 2014 BCSC 1682, [2014] 12 W.W.R. 736, 318 C.R.R. (2d) 331, [2014] B.C.J. No. 2261 (B.C.S.C.) — Drivers have a reduced expectation of privacy in breath samples provided in response to roadside breath demands.

Related Provisions: See O. Reg. 287/08; Conduct Review Programs; O. Reg. 407/08, Reporting to the Registrar: Administrative Suspension of Drivers' Licences.

Proposed Addition — 48.0.1

48.0.1 Short-term administrative licence suspension for drug or drug and alcohol impairment — (1) **Licence surrendered** — Where a police officer is satisfied that a person driving or having the care, charge or control of a motor vehicle or operating or having the care or control of a vessel meets the criteria set out in subsection (2), and where the officer reasonably believes, taking into account all of the circumstances, including the criteria set out in subsection (2), that the person's ability to operate a motor vehicle or vessel is impaired by a drug or by a combination of a drug and alcohol, the officer shall request that the person surrender his or her driver's licence.

(2) **Criteria** — The criteria for the purpose of subsection (1) are the following:

　　1. The person has performed physical co-ordination tests under paragraph 254(2)(a) of the *Criminal Code* (Canada) in connection with the driving or the

care, charge or control of a motor vehicle or with the operating or the care or control of a vessel.

2. The person has performed or submitted to tests or examinations prescribed by regulation for the purpose of this section, if any, in connection with the driving or the care, charge or control of a motor vehicle or with the operating or the care or control of a vessel.

(3) **Licence suspension** — Upon a request being made under subsection (1), the person to whom the request is made shall forthwith surrender his or her driver's licence to the police officer and, whether or not the person is unable or fails to surrender the licence to the police officer, his or her driver's licence is suspended for,

(a) three days, in the case of a first suspension under this section;

(b) seven days, in the case of a second suspension under this section;

(c) 30 days, in the case of a third or subsequent suspension under this section.

(4) **Same** — A previous suspension that took effect more than five years before the current suspension takes effect shall not be taken into account in determining whether the current suspension is a first, second or subsequent suspension for the purpose of subsection (3).

(5) **Suspension concurrent with other administrative suspensions** — The licence suspension under this section runs concurrently with a suspension, if any, under section 48, 48.1, 48.2.1, 48.3 or 48.3.1.

(6) **No right to be heard** — A person has no right to be heard before the suspension of a driver's licence under this section.

(7) **Application of s. 48** — Subsections 48(10) to (13) and (17) to (19) apply to this section with necessary modifications.

(8) **Regulations** — The Lieutenant Governor in Council may make regulations for the purpose of paragraph 2 of subsection (2) prescribing and governing tests and examinations described in or under the *Criminal Code* (Canada).

2015, c. 14, s. 10 [Not in force at date of publication.]

48.1 (1) **Application of subss. (2), (3) and (4)** — Subsections (2) and (3) apply and subsection (4) does not apply if the police officer who stops a novice driver uses one screening device for the purposes of section 48 and another screening device for the purposes of this section, and subsection (4) applies and subsections (2) and (3) do not apply if the police officer uses one screening device for the purposes of both section 48 and this section.

(2) **Screening device test, novice drivers** — Where a novice driver has been brought to a stop by a police officer under the authority of this Act and has provided a sample of breath under section 48 which, on analysis registers "Pass" or otherwise indicates that the novice driver has no alcohol in his or her body, but the police officer reasonably suspects that the novice driver has alcohol in his or her body, the police officer may, for the purposes of determining compliance with the regulations respecting novice drivers, demand that the novice driver provide within a reasonable time such a sample of breath as, in the opinion of the police officer, is

necessary to enable a proper analysis of the breath to be made by means of a provincially approved screening device and, where necessary, to accompany the police officer for the purpose of enabling such a sample of breath to be taken.

(3) Surrender of licence — Where, upon demand of a police officer made under subsection (2), a novice driver fails or refuses to provide a sample of breath or provides a sample of breath which, on analysis by a provincially approved screening device, registers "Presence of Alcohol" or otherwise indicates that the novice driver has alcohol in his or her body, the police officer may request the novice driver to surrender his or her driver's licence.

(4) Same — Where a novice driver has been brought to a stop by a police officer under the authority of this Act and has provided a sample of breath under section 48 which, on analysis registers "Warn", "Alert" or "Presence of Alcohol" or otherwise indicates that the novice driver has alcohol in his or her body, or, upon demand of a police officer made under section 254 of the *Criminal Code* (Canada), fails or refuses to provide a sample of breath, the police officer may request the novice driver to surrender his or her licence.

(5) Suspension of licence — Upon a request being made under subsection (3), the novice driver to whom the request is made shall forthwith surrender his or her driver's licence to the police officer and, whether or not the novice driver is unable or fails to surrender the licence to the police officer, his or her licence is suspended for a period of 24 hours from the time of the request.

(5.1) Same — Upon a request being made under subsection (4), the novice driver to whom the request is made shall forthwith surrender his or her driver's licence to the police officer and, whether or not the novice driver is unable or fails to surrender the licence to the police officer, his or her licence is suspended,

> (a) if the novice driver provides a sample of breath that on analysis registers "Presence of Alcohol" or otherwise indicates that the novice driver has alcohol in his or her body, for 24 hours from the time the request is made;

> (b) if the novice driver provides a sample of breath that on analysis registers "Warn" or "Alert" or otherwise indicates that the concentration of alcohol in the novice driver's blood is 50 milligrams or more of alcohol in 100 millilitres of blood, for the period determined under subsection 48(14).

(5.2) Same — A suspension under clause (5.1)(b) is deemed to be a suspension under section 48.

(5.3) Suspension concurrent with other administrative suspensions — The licence suspension under this section runs concurrently with a suspension, if any, under section 48, 48.2.1 or 48.3.

Proposed Amendment — 48.1(5.3)

(5.3) Suspension concurrent with other administrative suspensions — The licence suspension under this section runs concurrently with a suspension, if any, under section 48, 48.0.1, 48.2.1, 48.3 or 48.3.1.

2015, c. 14, s. 11(1) [Not in force at date of publication.]

(6) **Opportunity for second analysis** — Where an analysis of the breath of the novice driver is made under subsection (3) or (4) and registers "Warn", "Alert" or "Presence of Alcohol" or otherwise indicates that the novice driver has alcohol in his or her body, the novice driver may require that a second analysis be performed if the novice driver requests the second analysis immediately after the police officer requests the surrender of his or her licence under subsection (3) or (4).

(6.1) **Screening device, instrument used for second analysis** — The second analysis must be performed with a different approved screening device than was used in the analysis under subsection (3) or (4), as the case may be, or, if the police officer thinks it is preferable, with an instrument approved as suitable for the purpose of section 254 of the *Criminal Code* (Canada).

(6.2) **Second analysis governs** — Where a novice driver provides a sample of breath for the second analysis requested under subsection (6) immediately upon being requested to do so by the police officer, the result of the second analysis governs and any suspension resulting from the analysis under subsection (3) or (4) continues or terminates accordingly.

(7) **Calibration of screening device** — The provincially approved screening device shall not be calibrated to register "Presence of Alcohol" if the concentration of alcohol in the blood of the person whose breath is being analyzed is less than 10 milligrams of alcohol in 100 millilitres of blood, and despite anything in this section, the reading shown on a provincially approved screening device for "Presence of Alcohol" may be another term or symbol that conveys the same meaning.

(8) **Same** — It shall be presumed, in the absence of proof to the contrary, that any provincially approved screening device used for the purposes of this section has been calibrated as required by subsection (7).

(8.1) **No appeal or right to be heard** — There is no appeal from, or right to be heard before, the suspension of a driver's licence under this section.

(9) **Intent of suspension** — The suspension of a licence under this section is intended to ensure that novice drivers acquire experience and develop or improve safe driving skills in controlled conditions and to safeguard the licensee and the public and does not constitute an alternative to any proceeding or penalty arising from the same circumstances or around the same time.

(10) **Duty of officer** — Every officer who asks for the surrender of a licence under this section shall keep a written record of the licence received with the name and address of the person and the date and time of the suspension and, at the time of receiving the licence, shall provide the licensee with a written statement of the time from which the suspension takes effect, the length of the period during which the licence is suspended and the place where the licence may be recovered.

Proposed Amendment — 48.1(10)

(10) **Duties of officer** — Every police officer who asks for the surrender of a licence under this section shall,

    (a) notify the Registrar of that fact, or cause the Registrar to be so notified, in the form and manner and within the time required by the Registrar;

(b) keep a record of the licence received with the name and address of the person and the date and time of the suspension;

(c) provide the licensee with a written statement of the time from which the suspension takes effect, the period of time for which the licence is suspended and the place where the licence may be recovered; and

(d) forward to the Registrar such other material or information as may be prescribed by the regulations.

2015, c. 14, s. 11(2) [Not in force at date of publication.]

(11) Removal of vehicle — If the motor vehicle of a person whose licence is suspended under this section is at a location from which, in the opinion of a police officer, it should be removed and there is no person available who may lawfully remove the vehicle, the officer may remove and store the vehicle or cause it to be removed and stored, in which case, the officer shall notify the person of the location of the storage.

(12) Cost of removal — Where a police officer obtains assistance for the removal and storage of a motor vehicle under this section, the costs incurred in moving and storing the vehicle are a lien on the vehicle that may be enforced under the *Repair and Storage Liens Act* by the person who moved or stored the vehicle at the request of the officer.

(13) Offence — Every person commits an offence who, without reasonable excuse, fails or refuses to comply with a demand made to him or her by a police officer under this section.

Proposed Addition — 48.1(13.1)

(13.1) Regulations — The Lieutenant Governor in Council may make regulations prescribing other material or information to be forwarded to the Registrar under clause (10)(d).

2015, c. 14, s. 11(3) [Not in force at date of publication.]

(14) Definitions — In this section,

"driver" includes a person who has care or control of a motor vehicle;

"driver's licence" includes a motorized snow vehicle operator's licence and a driver's licence issued by any other jurisdiction;

"motor vehicle" includes a motorized snow vehicle;

"novice driver" has the meaning prescribed by the regulations made under section 57.1;

"provincially approved screening device" means,

(a) an approved screening device as defined in the *Criminal Code* (Canada), or

(b) a screening device that meets the standards of the Alcohol Test Committee of the Canadian Society of Forensic Sciences.

(15) Meaning of suspension for out-of-province licences — With respect to a driver's licence issued by another jurisdiction, instead of suspending the person's driver's licence, the Registrar shall suspend the person's privilege to drive a motor vehicle in Ontario for the applicable period specified in subsection (5) or determined under subsection (5.1).

Proposed Amendment — 48.1(15)

(15) Meaning of suspension for out-of-province licences — With respect to a driver's licence issued by another jurisdiction, instead of the person's driver's licence being suspended, the person's privilege to drive a motor vehicle in Ontario is suspended for the applicable period specified in subsection (5) or determined under subsection (5.1), and this section and section 53 apply to the suspension of that privilege with necessary modifications.

2015, c. 14, s. 11(4) [Not in force at date of publication.]

1993, c. 40, s. 5; 2007, c. 13, s. 11; 2008, c. 17, s. 38; 2009, c. 5, s. 16(3)–(5), (7)–(11)

Case Law

R. v. Vander Griendt, 2015 ONSC 6644, 2015 CarswellOnt 16612, 331 C.C.C. (3d) 135, 25 C.R. (7th) 206, 88 M.V.R. (6th) 45, [2015] O.J. No. 5675 (S.C.J.); *R. v. Nield*, 2015 ONSC 5730, 2015 CarswellOnt 14092, 88 M.V.R. (6th) 274, [2015] O.J. No. 4810 (S.C.J.) — Section 48 only applies to a highway and could not be a basis for stopping a vehicle on a private parking lot.

Related Provisions: See sections 48, 48.2.1 and 48.3 of the Act.

48.2 (1) Screening device test, accompanying driver — Where a police officer has brought a novice driver to a stop under the authority of this Act, and the police officer reasonably suspects that the accompanying driver has alcohol in his or her body, the police officer may, for the purposes of determining whether the novice driver is in compliance with the conditions and restrictions imposed upon novice drivers by this Act and the regulations, demand that the accompanying driver provide forthwith a sample of breath into an approved screening device as defined in section 254 of the *Criminal Code* (Canada) as if he or she was the person operating the motor vehicle.

(2) Direction to novice driver — Where, upon demand of a police officer made under subsection (1), an accompanying driver fails or refuses to provide a sample of breath or provides a sample of breath which, on analysis by an approved screening device, as defined in section 254 of the *Criminal Code* (Canada), registers "Warn", "Alert" or "Fail" or otherwise indicates that the concentration of alcohol in the accompanying driver's blood is 50 milligrams or more of alcohol in 100 millilitres of blood, the police officer may direct the novice driver not to drive a motor vehicle on a highway except in compliance with the regulations respecting novice drivers.

(3) Opportunity for second analysis — Where an analysis of the breath of an accompanying driver is made under subsection (2) and registers "Warn", "Alert" or "Fail" or otherwise indicates that the concentration of alcohol in the accompanying driver's blood is 50 milligrams or more of alcohol in 100 millilitres of blood, the accompanying driver may require that a second analysis be performed if the accompanying driver requests the second analysis immediately after the police officer gives a direction to the novice driver under subsection (2).

(3.1) Screening device, instrument used for second analysis — The second analysis must be performed with a different approved screening device than was used in the analysis under subsection (2) or, if the police officer thinks it is preferable, with an instrument approved as suitable for the purpose of section 254 of the *Criminal Code* (Canada).

(3.2) Second analysis governs — Where an accompanying driver provides a sample of breath for the second analysis requested under subsection (3) immediately upon being requested to do so by the police officer, the result of the second analysis governs and any direction given by the police officer under subsection (2) continues or terminates accordingly.

(4) Calibration of screening device — For the purposes of subsection (2), the approved screening device referred to in that subsection shall not be calibrated to register "Warn" or "Alert" if the concentration of alcohol in the blood of the person whose breath is being analyzed is less than 50 milligrams of alcohol in 100 millilitres of blood.

(5) Same — It shall be presumed, in the absence of proof to the contrary, that any approved screening device used for the purposes of subsection (2) has been calibrated as required under subsection (4).

(6) Intent of direction — The direction under this section to a novice driver not to drive a motor vehicle on a highway is intended to ensure that novice drivers acquire experience and develop or improve safe driving skills in controlled conditions and to safeguard the licensee and the public and does not constitute an alternative to any proceeding or penalty arising from the same circumstances or around the same time.

(7) Removal of vehicle — If the motor vehicle of a person who is directed not to drive under this section is at a location from which, in the opinion of a police officer, it should be removed and there is no person available who may lawfully remove the vehicle, the officer may remove and store the vehicle or cause it to be removed and stored, in which case, the officer shall notify the person of the location of the storage.

(8) Cost of Removal — Where a police officer obtains assistance for the removal and storage of a motor vehicle under this section, the costs incurred in moving and storing the vehicle are a lien on the vehicle that may be enforced under the *Repair and Storage Liens Act* by the person who moved or stored the vehicle at the request of the officer.

(9) Offence — Every person commits an offence who, without reasonable excuse, fails or refuses to comply with a demand made to him or her by a police officer under this section.

(10) Definitions — In this section, "accompanying driver" and "novice driver" have the meanings prescribed by the regulations made under section 57.1.

1993, c. 40, s. 5; 2007, c. 13, s. 12; 2009, c. 5, s. 17(2); 2015, c. 27, Sched. 7, s. 15

48.2.1 Breath testing, young drivers — (1) **Application of subss. (2), (3), (4) and (5)** — Subsections (2) and (3) apply and subsections (4) and (5) do not apply if the police officer who stops a young driver uses one screening device for the purposes of section 48 and another screening device for the purposes of this section, and subsections (4) and (5) apply and subsections (2) and (3) do not apply if the police officer uses one screening device for the purposes of both section 48 and this section.

(2) Test registers "Pass", second test requested for presence of alcohol — Where a young driver has been brought to a stop by a police officer under the authority of this Act and has provided a sample of breath under section 48 which, on analysis registers "Pass" or otherwise indicates that the young driver has no alcohol in his or her body, but the police officer reasonably suspects that the young driver has alcohol in his or her body, the police officer may, for the purposes of determining the concentration of alcohol in the young driver's blood, demand that the young driver provide within a reasonable time such a sample of breath as, in the opinion of the police officer, is necessary to enable a proper analysis of the breath to be made by means of a provincially approved screening device and, where necessary, to accompany the police officer for the purpose of enabling such a sample of breath to be taken.

(3) Test registers "Presence of Alcohol", surrender of licence — Where, upon demand of a police officer made under subsection (2), a young driver fails or refuses to provide a sample of breath or provides a sample of breath which, on analysis by a provincially approved screening device, registers "Presence of Alcohol" or otherwise indicates that the young driver has alcohol in his or her body, the police officer may request that the young driver surrender his or her driver's licence.

(4) Test registers "Warn" or "Alert", surrender of licence — Where a young driver has been brought to a stop by a police officer under the authority of this Act and fails or refuses to provide a sample of breath or provides a sample of breath under section 48 which, on analysis registers "Warn", "Alert" or "Presence of Alcohol" or otherwise indicates that the young driver has alcohol in his or her body, the police officer may request that the young driver surrender his or her licence.

(5) Test registers "Warn" or "Alert", surrender of licence — Where, upon demand of a police officer made under section 254 of the *Criminal Code* (Canada), a young driver fails or refuses to provide a sample of breath or provides a sample of breath which, on analysis by an approved screening device as defined in that section, registers "Warn" or "Alert" or otherwise indicates that the young driver has alcohol in his or her body, the police officer may request that the young driver surrender his or her driver's licence.

(6) Test indicates presence of alcohol, surrender of licence — Where, upon demand of a police officer made under section 254 of the *Criminal Code* (Canada), a young driver fails or refuses to provide a sample of breath or provides a sample of breath which, on analysis by an instrument approved as suitable for the purpose of that section, indicates the presence of alcohol in the young driver's body, the police officer may request that the young driver surrender his or her driver's licence.

(7) Opportunity for second analysis — Where an analysis of the breath of the young driver is made under subsection (3), (4) or (5) and registers "Warn", "Alert" or "Presence of Alcohol" or otherwise indicates that the young driver has alcohol in his or her body, the young driver may require that a second analysis be performed if the young driver requests the second analysis immediately after the police officer requests the surrender of his or her licence under any of those subsections.

(8) Screening device, instrument used for second analysis — The second analysis must be performed with a different approved screening device than was used in the analysis under subsection (3), (4) or (5), as the case may be, or, if the police officer thinks it is preferable, with an instrument approved as suitable for the purpose of section 254 of the *Criminal Code* (Canada).

(9) Second analysis governs — Where a young driver provides a sample of breath for the second analysis requested under subsection (7) immediately upon being requested to do so by the police officer, the result of the second analysis governs and any suspension resulting from the analysis under subsection (3), (4) or (5) continues or terminates accordingly.

(10) Licence suspension — Upon a request being made under subsection (3), the young driver to whom the request is made shall forthwith surrender his or her driver's licence to the police officer and, whether or not the young driver is unable or fails to surrender the licence to the police officer, his or her driver's licence is suspended for 24 hours from the time the request is made.

(11) Same — Upon a request being made under subsection (4), (5) or (6), the young driver to whom the request is made shall forthwith surrender his or her driver's licence to the police officer and, whether or not the young driver is unable or fails to surrender the licence to the police officer, his or her driver's licence is suspended,

    (a) if the young driver provides a sample of breath that on analysis registers "Presence of Alcohol" or otherwise indicates that the young driver has alcohol in his or her body, for 24 hours from the time the request is made;

    (b) if the young driver provides a sample of breath that on analysis registers "Warn" or "Alert" or otherwise indicates that the concentration of alcohol in the young driver's blood is 50 milligrams or more of alcohol in 100 millilitres of blood, for the period determined under subsection 48(14).

(12) Same — A suspension under clause (11)(b) is deemed to be a suspension under section 48.

(13) Suspension concurrent with other administrative suspensions — The licence suspension under this section runs concurrently with a suspension, if any, under section 48, 48.1 or 48.3.

> **Proposed Amendment — 48.2.1(13)**
>
> **(13) Suspension concurrent with other administrative suspensions** — The licence suspension under this section runs concurrently with a suspension, if any, under section 48, 48.0.1, 48.1, 48.3 or 48.3.1.
>
> 2015, c. 14, s. 12(1) [Not in force at date of publication.]

(14) Calibration of screening device — The provincially approved screening device shall not be calibrated to register "Presence of Alcohol" if the concentration of alcohol in the blood of the person whose breath is being analyzed is less than 10 milligrams of alcohol in 100 millilitres of blood, and despite anything in this section, the reading shown on a provincially approved screening device for "Presence of Alcohol" may be another term or symbol that conveys the same meaning.

(15) Same — It shall be presumed, in the absence of proof to the contrary, that any provincially approved screening device used for the purposes of this section has been calibrated as required by subsection (14).

(16) No appeal or right to be heard — There is no appeal from, or right to be heard before, the suspension of a driver's licence under this section.

(17) Intent of suspension — The suspension of a licence under this section is intended to ensure that young drivers acquire experience and develop or improve safe driving skills in controlled conditions and to safeguard the licensee and the public and does not constitute an alternative to any proceeding or penalty arising from the same circumstances or around the same time.

(18) Duty of officer — Every police officer who asks for the surrender of a licence under this section shall keep a written record of the licence received with the name and address of the person and the date and time of the suspension and, at the time of receiving the licence, provide the licensee with a written statement of the time from which the suspension takes effect, the length of the period during which the licence is suspended and the place where the licence may be recovered.

Proposed Amendment — 48.2.1(18)

(18) Duties of officer — Every police officer who asks for the surrender of a licence under this section shall,

(a) notify the Registrar of that fact, or cause the Registrar to be so notified, in the form and manner and within the time required by the Registrar;

(b) keep a record of the licence received with the name and address of the person and the date and time of the suspension;

(c) provide the licensee with a written statement of the time from which the suspension takes effect, the period of time for which the licence is suspended and the place where the licence may be recovered; and

(d) forward to the Registrar such other material or information as may be prescribed by the regulations.

2015, c. 14, s. 12(2) [Not in force at date of publication.]

(19) Removal of vehicle — If the motor vehicle of a young driver whose licence is suspended under this section is at a location from which, in the opinion of a police officer, it should be removed and there is no person available who may lawfully remove the vehicle, the officer may remove and store the vehicle or cause it to be removed and stored, in which case the officer shall notify the person of the location of the storage.

(20) Cost of removal — Where a police officer obtains assistance for the removal and storage of a motor vehicle under this section, the costs incurred in moving and storing the vehicle are a lien on the vehicle that may be enforced under the *Repair and Storage Liens Act* by the person who moved or stored the vehicle at the request of the officer.

(21) Offence — Every person commits an offence who, without reasonable excuse, fails or refuses to comply with a demand made to him or her by a police officer under this section.

Proposed Addition — 48.2.1(21.1)

(21.1) Regulations — The Lieutenant Governor in Council may make regulations prescribing other material or information to be forwarded to the Registrar under clause (18)(d).

2015, c. 14, s. 12(3) [Not in force at date of publication.]

(22) Definitions — In this section,

"driver" includes a person who has care or control of a motor vehicle;

"driver's licence" includes a motorized snow vehicle operator's licence and a driver's licence issued by any other jurisdiction;

"motor vehicle" includes a motorized snow vehicle;

Proposed Amendment — 48.2.1(22) "motor vehicle"

"motor vehicle" includes a street car and a motorized snow vehicle;

2015, c. 14, s. 12(4) [Not in force at date of publication.]

"provincially approved screening device" means,

    (a) an approved screening device as defined in the *Criminal Code* (Canada), or

    (b) a screening device that meets the standards of the Alcohol Test Committee of the Canadian Society of Forensic Sciences;

"young driver" means a driver who is under 22 years old.

(23) Meaning of suspension for out-of-province licences — With respect to a driver's licence issued by another jurisdiction, instead of suspending the person's driver's licence, the Registrar shall suspend the person's privilege to drive a motor vehicle in Ontario for the applicable period specified in subsection (10) or determined under subsection (11).

Proposed Amendment — 48.2.1(23)

(23) Meaning of suspension for out-of-province licences — With respect to a driver's licence issued by another jurisdiction, instead of the person's driver's licence being suspended, the person's privilege to drive a motor vehicle in Ontario is suspended for the applicable period specified in subsection (10) or determined under subsection (11), and this section and section 53 apply to the suspension of that privilege with necessary modifications.

2015, c. 14, s. 12(5) [Not in force at date of publication.]

2009, c. 5, s. 18

Related Provisions: See sections 48, 48.1 and 48.3 of the Act.

48.3 Administrative suspension of licence for blood alcohol concentration above .08, failing or refusing to provide breath sample — (1) Licence surrendered — Where a police officer is satisfied that a person driving or having the care, charge or control of a motor vehicle or operating or having the care or control of a vessel meets one of the criteria set out in subsection (3), the officer shall request that the person surrender his or her driver's licence.

(2) 90-day licence suspension — Upon a request being made under subsection (1), the person to whom the request is made shall forthwith surrender his or her driver's licence to the police officer and, whether or not the person is unable or fails to surrender the licence to the police officer, his or her driver's licence is suspended for 90 days from the time the request is made.

(2.1) [Repealed 2009, c. 5, s. 19(1).]

(3) Criteria — The criteria for the purpose of subsection (1) are:

1. The person is shown, by an analysis of breath or blood taken pursuant to a demand made under subsection 254(3) of the *Criminal Code* (Canada) or pursuant to section 256 of the *Criminal Code* (Canada), to have a concentration of alcohol in his or her blood in excess of 80 milligrams in 100 millilitres of blood.

2. The person failed or refused, in response to a demand made under section 254 of the *Criminal Code* (Canada),

    i. to provide a sample of breath, blood, oral fluid or urine,

    ii. to perform physical co-ordination tests, or

    iii. to submit to an evaluation.

(3.1) No right to be heard — A person has no right to be heard before surrendering his or her licence under subsection (2).

Proposed Amendment — 48.3(3.1)

(3.1) No right to be heard — A person has no right to be heard before the suspension of a driver's licence under this section.

2015, c. 14, s. 13(1) [Not in force at date of publication.]

(4) Duty of officer — Every officer who asks for the surrender of a person's driver's licence under this section shall keep a record of the licence received with the name and address of the person and the date and time of the suspension and shall, as soon as practicable after receiving the licence,

(a) provide the person with a notice of suspension showing the time from which the suspension takes effect and the period of time for which the licence is suspended; and

(b) forward a copy of the notice to the Registrar.

Proposed Amendment — 48.3(4)

(4) Duties of officer — Every police officer who asks for the surrender of a licence under this section shall,

(a) notify the Registrar of that fact, or cause the Registrar to be so notified, in the form and manner and within the time required by the Registrar;

(b) keep a record of the licence received with the name and address of the person and the date and time of the suspension;

(c) provide the licensee with a written statement of the time from which the suspension takes effect, the period of time for which the licence is suspended and the place where the licence may be recovered; and

(d) forward to the Registrar such other material or information as may be prescribed by the regulations.

2015, c. 14, s. 13(2) [Not in force at date of publication.]

(5) Notice by Registrar — The Registrar may provide a notice of suspension, containing the information included on the notice of suspension required by subsection (4), to the person whose licence is suspended by mailing it to the address of the person shown on his or her driver's licence or to the latest address for the person appearing on the records of the Ministry.

(6) Same — Where the officer is unable to request that a person surrender his or her driver's licence under subsection (1), the officer shall notify the Registrar of that fact and the Registrar shall mail a notice of suspension, containing the information included on the notice of suspension required by subsection (4), to the person whose licence is suspended by mailing it to the address of the person shown on his or her driver's licence or to the latest address for the person appearing on the records of the Ministry.

(7) Effective date of suspension — Despite subsection (2), the driver's licence of a person who is notified of the suspension under subsection (6) is suspended from the date set out in the notice.

(7.1) Suspension concurrent with other administrative suspensions — The licence suspension under this section runs concurrently with a suspension, if any, under section 48, 48.1 or 48.2.1.

Proposed Amendment — 48.3(7.1)

(7.1) Suspension concurrent with other administrative suspensions — The licence suspension under this section runs concurrently with a suspension, if any, under section 48, 48.0.1, 48.1, 48.2.1 or 48.3.1.

2015, c. 14, s. 13(3) [Not in force at date of publication.]

(8) [Repealed 2008, c. 17, s. 39(2).]

(9) Licence delivered to Registrar — A police officer who has notified the Registrar under subsection (1) or a police officer who has personally delivered notice of the suspension to the person shall, as soon as practicable, forward to the Registrar,

(a) the person's driver's licence, if the licence was surrendered to the police officer; and

(b) such other material or information as may be prescribed by the regulations.

Proposed Repeal — 48.3(9)

(9) [Repealed 2015, c. 14, s. 13(4). Not in force at date of publication.]

(10) **Intent of suspension** — The suspension of a driver's licence under this section is intended to safeguard the public and does not constitute an alternative to any proceeding or penalty arising from the same circumstances or around the same time.

(11) **Removal of vehicle** — If the motor vehicle of a person whose licence is suspended under this section is at a location from which, in the opinion of a police officer, it should be removed and there is no person available who may lawfully remove the vehicle, the officer may remove and store the vehicle or cause it to be removed and stored, in which case the officer shall notify the person of the location of the storage.

(12) **Cost of removal** — Where a police officer obtains assistance for the removal and storage of a motor vehicle under this section, the costs incurred in moving and storing the vehicle are a lien on the vehicle that may be enforced under the *Repair and Storage Liens Act* by the person who moved or stored the vehicle at the request of the officer.

(13) **Protection from personal liability** — No action or other proceeding for damages shall be instituted against the Registrar or any employee of the Ministry for the suspension of a licence in good faith in the execution or intended execution of a duty under this section.

Proposed Repeal — 48.3(13)

(13) [Repealed 2015, c. 14, s. 13(4). Not in force at date of publication.]

(14) **Crown not relieved of liability** — Despite subsections 5(2) and (4) of the *Proceedings Against the Crown Act*, subsection (13) does not relieve the Crown of liability in respect of a tort committed by a person mentioned in subsection (13) to which it would otherwise be subject.

Proposed Repeal — 48.3(14)

(14) [Repealed 2015, c. 14, s. 13(4). Not in force at date of publication.]

(15) **Regulations** — The Lieutenant Governor in Council may make regulations,

(a) [Repealed 2009, c. 5, s. 19(2).]

(b) respecting the information to be provided to persons whose licences are suspended under this section;

(c) prescribing other material or information to be forwarded to the Registrar under subsection (9).

Proposed Amendment — 48.3(15)

(15) Regulations — The Lieutenant Governor in Council may make regulations prescribing other material or information to be forwarded to the Registrar under clause (4)(d).

2015, c. 14, s. 13(5) [Not in force at date of publication.]

(16) Definitions — In this section and in section 50.1,

"driver's licence" includes a motorized snow vehicle operator's licence and a driver's licence issued by any other jurisdiction;

"motor vehicle" includes a street car and a motorized snow vehicle.

"vessel" means a vessel within the meaning of section 214 of the *Criminal Code* (Canada).

(17) Meaning of suspension for out-of-province licences — With respect to a driver's licence issued by another jurisdiction, instead of suspending the person's driver's licence, the Registrar shall suspend the person's privilege to drive a motor vehicle in Ontario for a period of ninety days, and this section and section 50.1 apply to the suspension of that privilege with necessary modifications.

Proposed Amendment — 48.3(17)

(17) Meaning of suspension for out-of-province licences — With respect to a driver's licence issued by another jurisdiction, instead of the person's driver's licence being suspended, the person's privilege to drive a motor vehicle in Ontario is suspended for a period of 90 days, and this section and section 53 apply to the suspension of that privilege with necessary modifications.

2015, c. 14, s. 13(6) [Not in force at date of publication.]

1996, c. 20, s. 8; 1997, c. 12, s. 3; 2006, c. 20, s. 4; 2007, c. 13, s. 13; 2008, c. 17, s. 39; 2009, c. 5, s. 19

Commentary

Section 48 regarding spot checks and the power of a police officer under the Act to investigate for drinking and driving was first introduced in 1981 while the legality of spot checks in *R. v. Dedman, infra*, was working its way up through the appeal courts. Over the years the powers of a police officer under the Act in respect of alcohol impairment have been enhanced as have the consequences when alcohol is detected.

As of May 1, 2009, the consequences were seriously altered by raising a suspension for a first time offender from 12 hours to three days and providing for suspensions of seven days for a second suspension and 30 days for a third or subsequent suspension.

The overall outline of the provisions is that a police officer, under the Act, may require a driver to stop to determine whether or not there is evidence to justify to make a breath demand under the Criminal Code. Where a driver registers a "warn" on an approved roadside screening device, between 50 milligrams and 100 milligrams, in 100 millilitres of blood, or refuses to supply a breath sample, a suspension for three days will occur.

Under s. 48.1, a police officer is empowered to obtain a roadside sample from a "novice driver" as defined under s. 57.1. Even where the novice driver passes the approved screening device, but the officer continues to suspect alcohol in the novice driver's system, a breath sample may be taken. An officer has the power to cause the novice driver to surrender his or her licence. Under s. 48.2, an officer has the power to demand a sample from an "accompanying driver" as defined under s. 57.1 of the Act.

If a young driver provides a breath sample indicating the presence of alcohol in the body or fails or refuses to provide a sample, a suspension for 24 hours may follow. If over 50 milligrams, a three-day suspension for a first offender, seven days for a second and 30 days for a subsequent suspension follows. The suspension runs concurrently with a suspension under ss. 48, 48.1 or 48.3.

Section 48.3 provides for an immediate 90-day administrative suspension where a person's blood alcohol level exceeds 80 milligrams or there is a refusal of breath or blood as the result of Criminal Code enforcement.

Provisions exist for the above suspensions applying concurrently and for the impoundment of vehicles in related, appropriate circumstances.

Case Law

R. v. Dedman, [1985] 2 S.C.R. 2, 34 M.V.R. 1 — The Supreme Court of Canada upheld the propriety of random spot checks prior to the introduction of ss. 48 and 216 of the Highway Traffic Act of Ontario.

R. v. Hufsky, [1988] 1 S.C.R. 621, 4 M.V.R. (2d) 170, 84 N.R. 365 — The Supreme Court of Canada came to the same conclusion as *Dedman*, *supra*, when considering the Charter of Rights. The Court relied on s. 216 of the Act as a reasonable justification under s. 1 of the Charter for the arbitrary detention inherent in random stopping.

R. v. Becker (1988), 9 M.V.R. 144 (Ont. Dist. Ct.) — Stops based on suspicion not conducted pursuant to an organized programme are justifiable.

R. v. Huber (1985), 36 M.V.R. 10 (Ont. C.A.) — A 12-hour licence suspension is not the equivalent of a conviction for, or charging of, an offence. Consequently, neither a plea of *autrefois convict* nor s. 11(h) of the Charter is applicable in a subsequent proceeding under the Criminal Code.

R. v. Wolff (1979), 1 M.V.R. 261, 9 B.C.L.R. 390, 6 C.R. (3d) 346, 46 C.C.C. (2d) 467 (C.A.) — The validity of British Columbia's 24-hour licence suspension scheme was held to be within the powers of the Legislature. Under that scheme, the suspension comes into effect immediately upon the officer's demand for surrender of the licence. It is not incumbent upon the officer to advise the driver of how the licence may be returned, nor does the validity of the suspension depend on the driver moving his or her car to the nearest place off the travelled portion of the highway.

R. v. Fraser (1984), 28 M.V.R. 209 (Ont. Co. Ct.); affirmed (April 16, 1985), Doc. CA 764/84 (Ont. C.A.); *R. v. Sandmoen* (1986), 43 M.V.R. 255 (Ont. Dist. Ct.) — Section 48 of the Highway Traffic Act of Ontario is not inconsistent with ss. 7, 8 and 9 of the Charter of Rights.

R. v. Saunders (1988), 4 M.V.R. (2d) 199, 63 C.R. (3d) 37, 27 O.A.C. 184 (C.A.) — Section 48 permits co-ordination tests to ascertain sobriety at the roadside without the necessity of a prior caution under s. 10(b) of the Charter of Rights.

R. v. Mellenthin, [1992] 3 S.C.R. 615, 40 M.V.R. (2d) 204, 16 C.R. (4th) 273, [1993] 1 W.W.R. 193, 5 Alta. L.R. (3d) 232, 76 C.C.C. (3d) 481, 144 N.R. 50, 12 C.R.R. (2d) 65, 135 A.R. 1, 33 W.A.C. 1 — A check stop does not constitute a general search warrant for searching every vehicle, driver and passenger. Unless there are reasonable and probable grounds for conducting the search, or drugs or weapons in plain view in the interior of the vehicle, the evidence flowing from such a search should not be admitted.

R. v. McNeil (1992), 41 M.V.R. (2d) 1, 19 B.C.A.C. 292, 34 W.A.C. 292 (C.A.) — A demand for a sobriety test made after the accused had asserted a right to counsel violated the accused's s. 10(b) Charter rights.

R. v. Smith (1996), 46 C.R. (4th) 229, 105 C.C.C. (3d) 58, 88 O.A.C. 374 (C.A.) — The section authorizes an officer who has stopped a vehicle to take reasonable steps to determine whether there is evidence to justify a Criminal Code breathalyzer demand. Roadside questioning regarding alcohol consumption is such a step, which is justified under s. 1 of the Charter as a reasonable limit on the s. 10(b) right to counsel, and it does not violate the s. 7 right to silence. In roadside screening of sobriety, police are entitled to employ a combination of investigative techniques.

R. v. Milne (1996), 18 M.V.R. (3d) 161 (Ont. C.A.) — The taking of sobriety tests is justified under s. 1 of the Charter only when used as an investigative tool. The use of the tests to help establish impairment produces an unfair trial because the motorist is being compelled to create self-incriminating evidence. The result may be different if the motorist is given s. 10(b) rights at the roadside.

R. v. Lauzon (1996), 21 M.V.R. (3d) 308, 37 C.R.R. (2d) 168 (Ont. Gen. Div.)"Readily identifiable" relates to the police officer not the unmarked car. Where the officer is in an unmarked car, regard should be had to the officer's apparel and signage worn or carried or displayed.

Buhlers v. British Columbia (Superintendent of Motor Vehicles) (1999), 132 C.C.C. (3d) 478, 170 D.L.R. (4th) 344, 23 C.R. (5th) 1 (B.C. C.A.) — Provincial 90-day suspensions where the officer has reasonable grounds to believe the driver is over the Criminal Code limit or refuses a breath or blood Criminal Code demand does not violate s. 7 of the Charter.

Horsefield v. Ontario (Registrar of Motor Vehicles) (1999), 118 O.A.C. 291, 134 C.C.C. (3d) 161, 172 D.L.R. (4th) 43 (Ont. C.A.); varied on reconsideration (May 14, 1999), Doc. CA C29157 (Ont. C.A.) — Secion 48.3 providing for a 90-day administrative licence suspension upon the Registrar receiving notice that a peace officer is satisfied that a person driving or having the care, charge or control of a motor vehicle was "over 80" as revealed by a Criminal Code breath or blood demand, or a refusal to give same, does not contravene s. 7 of the Charter of Rights. The right to drive does not engage the liberty interest. No liberty interest is indirectly engaged by penalizing driving without a licence because of ADLS with the threat of imprisonment. Principles of fundamental justice do not mandate a right of review from an administrative act. The fact that other provincial schemes provide for more elaborate review does not impact on the ability of the legislature override common law administrative principles. The legislation is within the jurisdiction of the province. There is no conflict, actual or by implication, between the ADLS Program and the Criminal Code.

Gonzalez v. Alberta (Driver Control Board) (2003), 41 M.V.R. (4th) 290, (sub nom. *Thomson v. Alberta (Transportation & Safety Board)*) [2003] A.J. No. 1115, 4 Admin. L.R. (4th) 261, (sub nom. *Thomson v. Alberta (Transportation & Safety Board)*) 178

C.C.C. (3d) 508, 232 D.L.R. (4th) 237, 330 A.R. 262, 299 W.A.C. 262, [2004] 4 W.W.R. 535, 19 Alta. L.R. (4th) 236, 2003 ABCA 256, 2003 CarswellAlta 1276 (Alta. C.A.); leave to appeal refused (2004), 2004 CarswellAlta 501, 2004 CarswellAlta 502, [2003] S.C.C.A. No. 510, 330 N.R. 196 (note), 363 A.R. 398 (note), 343 W.A.C. 398 (note) (S.C.C.) — An administrative licence suspension before a drinking and driving conviction is appropriate provincial legislation. It does not violate s. 11(d) of the Charter as there is no offence but merely the withdrawal of a privilege. Section 13 is not violated because the driver is not compelled to testify before the Board and can raise the issue during subsequent criminal proceedings. While the ALS does not authorize Charter breaches, evidence obtained in breach of the Charter is admissible governed by the tribunal's duty of fairness. Driving is not a liberty interest protected by the Charter.

Sigurdson v. British Columbia, 2003 BCCA 535, 2003 CarswellBC 2643, 42 M.V.R. (4th) 296, (sub nom. *Sigurdson v. British Columbia (Superintendent of Motor Vehicles)*) 178 C.C.C. (3d) 500, 232 D.L.R. (4th) 228, 187 B.C.A.C. 312, 307 W.A.C. 312 (C.A.); affirming (2002), 31 M.V.R. (4th) 85, 2002 BCSC 945, 2002 CarswellBC 1496 (S.C.) — The provisions that empower the Superintendent to enquire into the fitness of an individual to safely operate a motor vehicle on the highway do not attract Charter scrutiny.

R. v. Houben (2006), [2007] 2 W.W.R. 195, 39 M.V.R. (5th) 84, 2006 CarswellSask 746, 2006 SKCA 129, 214 C.C.C. (3d) 519, 382 W.A.C. 118, 149 C.R.R. (2d) 244, 44 C.R. (6th) 338, 289 Sask. R. 118, [2006] S.J. No. 715 (C.A.) — Under Saskatchewan's legislation the officers must have "highway traffic safety reasons" in mind when they stop the accused. Checking someone in the interests of "preventative policing" did not meet the test.

R. v. Doell, 2007 CarswellSask 287, 2007 SKCA 61, [2007] 9 W.W.R. 51, 158 C.R.R. (2d) 365, 50 M.V.R. (5th) 9, 397 W.A.C. 262, 293 Sask. R. 262, 221 C.C.C. (3d) 336, [2007] S.J. No. 264 (C.A.); reversing 2006 CarswellSask 337, 2006 SKQB 260, 282 Sask. R. 78, 34 M.V.R. (5th) 240 (Q.B.) — The courts have accepted the validity of limiting the rights of drivers in the interests of promoting highway safety. Vehicle stops which are random or arbitrary have been found to be justifiable under s. 1 of the *Charter* so long as they are conducted for a purpose which relates to driving a car such as checking the driver's licence and insurance, the sobriety of the driver, the mechanical fitness of the vehicle and to check seat belt use.

Goodwin v. British Columbia (Superintendent of Motor Vehicles), 2015 CSC 46, 2015 SCC 46, 2015 CarswellBC 2938, 2015 CarswellBC 2939, [2015] 3 S.C.R. 250, 75 B.C.L.R. (5th) 213, 329 C.C.C. (3d) 545, 23 C.R. (7th) 1, 391 D.L.R. (4th) 1, 84 M.V.R. (6th) 40, [2015] 11 W.W.R. 1, (sub nom. *Silvia v. Superintendent of Motor Vehicles (B.C.)*) 378 B.C.A.C. 1, 476 N.R. 3, 650 W.A.C. 1, [2015] A.C.S. No. 46, [2015] S.C.J. No. 46; affirming 2014 BCCA 79, 2014 CarswellBC 488, 55 B.C.L.R. (5th) 1, 307 C.C.C. (3d) 77, 370 D.L.R. (4th) 609, 64 M.V.R. (6th) 7, [2014] 6 W.W.R. 1, 352 B.C.A.C. 86, 302 C.R.R. (2d) 1, 601 W.A.C. 86, [2014] B.C.J. No. 346; affirming 2011 BCSC 1783, 2011 CarswellBC 3493, 27 B.C.L.R. (5th) 326, 23 M.V.R. (6th) 282, [2012] 4 W.W.R. 506, 249 C.R.R. (2d) 368 (In Chambers); *Wilson v. British Columbia (Superintendent of Motor Vehicles)*, 2015 CSC 47, 2015 SCC 47, 2015 CarswellBC 2940, 2015 CarswellBC 2941, [2015] 3 S.C.R. 300, 76 B.C.L.R. (5th) 1, 329 C.C.C. (3d) 527, 23 C.R. (7th) 44, 391 D.L.R. (4th) 43, 84 M.V.R. (6th) 1, [2015] 11 W.W.R. 429, 378 B.C.A.C. 58, 476 N.R. 60, 650 W.A.C. 58, [2015] A.C.S. No. 47, [2015] S.C.J. No. 47; affirming 2014 BCCA 202, 2014 CarswellBC 1453, 60 B.C.L.R. (5th) 371, 311 C.C.C. (3d) 369, 66 M.V.R. (6th) 99, [2015] 4 W.W.R. 579, 356 B.C.A.C. 133, 610

W.A.C. 133, [2014] B.C.J. No. 1055 — The Province of British Columbia's automatic pre-criminal charge driving prohibition scheme is constitutional.

Related Provisions: See O. Reg. 273/07, Adminstrative Monetary Penalties, O. Reg. 407/08, Reporting to the Registrar: Adminstrative Suspension of Drivers' Licences.

Proposed Addition — 48.3.1

48.3.1 Long-term administrative licence suspension for drug or drug and alcohol impairment — (1) **Licence surrendered** — Where a police officer is satisfied that a person driving or having the care, charge or control of a motor vehicle or operating or having the care or control of a vessel meets the criteria set out in subsection (2), and where the officer reasonably believes, taking into account all of the circumstances, including the criteria set out in subsection (2), that the person's ability to operate a motor vehicle or vessel is or, at the time the person was driving or having the care, charge or control of the motor vehicle or operating or having the care or control of the vessel, was impaired by a drug or by a combination of a drug and alcohol, the officer shall request that the person surrender his or her driver's licence.

(2) **Criteria** — The criteria for the purpose of subsection (1) are the following:

    1. The person has been evaluated by an evaluating officer under subsection 254(3.1) of the *Criminal Code* (Canada) in connection with the driving or the care, charge or control of a motor vehicle or with the operating or the care or control of a vessel.

    2. The person has performed or submitted to tests or examinations prescribed by regulation for the purpose of this section, if any, in connection with the driving or the care, charge or control of a motor vehicle or with the operating or the care or control of a vessel.

(3) **90-day licence suspension** — Upon a request being made under subsection (1), the person to whom the request is made shall forthwith surrender his or her driver's licence to the police officer and, whether or not the person is unable or fails to surrender the licence to the police officer, his or her driver's licence is suspended for 90 days from the time the request is made.

(4) **Suspension concurrent with other administrative suspensions** — The licence suspension under this section runs concurrently with a suspension, if any, under section 48, 48.0.1, 48.1, 48.2.1 or 48.3.

(5) **No right to be heard** — A person has no right to be heard before the suspension of a driver's licence under this section.

(6) **Continuation or termination of short-term suspension based on evaluation** — If an evaluating officer conducts an evaluation of a person under subsection 254(3.1) of the *Criminal Code* (Canada), the evaluating officer's determination as to whether the person's ability to operate a motor vehicle or vessel is or, at the time the person was driving or having the care, charge or control of the motor vehicle or operating or having the care or control of the vessel for which the evaluation was conducted, was impaired by a drug or by a combination of a drug and alcohol, governs, and any suspension that was imposed under section 48.0.1 arising

out of the same circumstances for which the evaluation was conducted is continued or terminates accordingly.

(7) Application of s. 48.3 — Subsections 48.3(4) to (7), (10) to (12), (15) and (17) apply to this section with necessary modifications.

(8) Regulations — The Lieutenant Governor in Council may make regulations for the purpose of paragraph 2 of subsection (2) prescribing and governing tests and examinations described in or under the *Criminal Code* (Canada).

(9) Definitions — In this section,

"driver's licence" includes a motorized snow vehicle operator's licence and a driver's licence issued by any other jurisdiction;

"evaluating officer" has the same meaning as in subsection 254(1) of the *Criminal Code* (Canada);

"motor vehicle" includes a street car and a motorized snow vehicle;

"vessel" means a vessel within the meaning of section 214 of the *Criminal Code* (Canada).

2015, c. 14, s. 14 [Not in force at date of publication.]

48.4 (1) Administrative vehicle impoundment for blood alcohol concentration above .08, failing or refusing to provide breath sample — Where a police officer is satisfied that a person driving or having the care, charge or control of a motor vehicle meets one of the criteria set out in subsection 48.3(3), the officer shall detain the motor vehicle that was being driven by the person and the vehicle shall, at the cost and risk of its owner,

Proposed Amendment — 48.4(1) opening words

(1) Administrative vehicle impoundment for drug or drug and alcohol impairment, blood alcohol concentration above .08, failing to provide sample or submit to tests — Where a police officer is satisfied that he or she is required by subsection 48.3(1) or 48.3.1(1) to request that a person surrender his or her driver's licence, the officer shall detain the motor vehicle that was being driven by the person and the vehicle shall, at the cost and risk of its owner,

2015, c. 14, s. 15 [Not in force at date of publication.]

(a) be removed to an impound facility as directed by a police officer; and

(b) be impounded for seven days from the time it was detained.

(2) Release of vehicle — Subject to subsection (14), the motor vehicle shall be released to its owner from the impound facility upon the expiry of the period of impoundment.

(3) Early release of vehicle — Despite the detention or impoundment of a motor vehicle under this section, a police officer may release the motor vehicle to its owner before it is impounded or, subject to subsection (14), may direct the operator of the impound facility where the motor vehicle is impounded to release the motor vehicle to its owner before the expiry of the seven days if the officer is satisfied that the motor vehicle was stolen at the time that it was driven as described in subsection (1).

(4) Duty of officer re impoundment — Every officer who detains a motor vehicle under this section shall, as soon as practicable,

(a) prepare a notice identifying the motor vehicle that is to be impounded, the name and address of the driver, the date and time of the impoundment, the period of time for which the motor vehicle is impounded and the place where the vehicle may be recovered; and

(b) serve the driver with a copy of the notice.

(5) Service on driver is deemed service on owner and operator — Service of a copy of a notice under subsection (4) on the driver of the motor vehicle is deemed to be service on and sufficient notice to the owner of the vehicle and the operator of the vehicle, if there is an operator.

(6) Further notice to owner — In addition to serving the owner of the motor vehicle through service on the driver under subsection (4), a police officer shall provide a copy of the notice prepared under subsection (4) to the owner of the motor vehicle by delivering it personally or by mail to the address of the owner shown on the permit for the motor vehicle or to the latest address for the owner appearing on the records of the Ministry.

(7) Surrender of documents, information re trip and goods carried — If the motor vehicle that is to be impounded contains goods, the police officer may require the driver and any other person present who is in charge of the motor vehicle to surrender all documents in his or her possession or in the vehicle that relate to the operation of the vehicle or to the carriage of the goods and to furnish all information within that person's knowledge relating to the details of the current trip and the ownership of the goods.

(8) Operator, owner to remove load — Upon being served with notice of the impoundment through service on the driver under subsection (4), the operator of the motor vehicle or, if there is no operator, the owner shall forthwith remove any vehicle drawn by the motor vehicle and any load from the motor vehicle.

(9) Application of *Dangerous Goods Transportation Act* — If the goods are dangerous goods, within the meaning of the *Dangerous Goods Transportation Act*, the operator or, if there is no operator, the owner shall remove them in accordance with that Act.

(10) Officer may remove load, trailer at operator's cost, risk — If, in the opinion of a police officer, the operator or owner fails to remove a drawn vehicle or load as required by subsection (8) within a reasonable time after being served with notice of the impoundment, the officer may cause the drawn vehicle or load to be removed and stored or disposed of at the cost and risk of the operator or, if there is no operator, the owner.

(11) Same — If a police officer is of the opinion that the operator or owner has not made appropriate arrangements for the removal of a drawn vehicle or load, having regard to the nature of the goods, including the fact that they are or appear to be dangerous goods within the meaning of the *Dangerous Goods Transportation Act* or are perishable, the officer may cause the drawn vehicle or load to be removed, stored or otherwise disposed of at the cost and risk of the operator or, if there is no operator, the owner.

(12) Personal property in vehicle available to owner — Any personal property that is left in the impounded motor vehicle and that is not attached to or used in connection with its operation shall, upon request and proof of ownership, be made available, at reasonable times, to the owner of the property.

(13) No appeal or right to be heard — There is no appeal from, or right to be heard before, a vehicle detention or impoundment under subsection (1).

(14) Impound costs to be paid before release of vehicle — The person who operates the impound facility where a motor vehicle is impounded under this section is not required to release the motor vehicle until the removal and impound costs for the vehicle have been paid.

(15) Lien for impound costs — The costs incurred by the person who operates the impound facility where a motor vehicle is impounded under this section are a lien on the motor vehicle that may be enforced under the *Repair and Storage Liens Act*.

(16) Impound costs a recoverable debt — The costs incurred by the person who operates the impound facility where a motor vehicle is impounded under this section are a debt due by the owner and the driver of the motor vehicle at the time the vehicle was detained, for which the owner and the driver are jointly and severally liable, and the debt may be recovered in any court of competent jurisdiction.

(17) Owner may recover losses from driver — The owner of a motor vehicle that is impounded under this section may bring an action against the driver of the motor vehicle at the time the vehicle was detained under subsection (1) to recover any costs or other losses incurred by the owner in connection with the impoundment.

(18) Debt due to police or Crown — The costs incurred by a police force or the Crown in removing, storing or disposing of a drawn vehicle or load from a motor vehicle under subsection (10) or (11) are a debt due to the police force or Crown, as the case may be, and may be recovered by the police force or Crown in any court of competent jurisdiction.

(19) Offence — Every person who obstructs or interferes with a police officer in the performance of his or her duties under this section is guilty of an offence and on conviction is liable to a fine of not less than $200 and not more than $5,000 or to imprisonment for a term of not more than six months, or to both.

(20) Intent of impoundment — The impoundment of a motor vehicle under this section is intended to promote compliance with this Act and to thereby safeguard the public and does not constitute an alternative to any proceeding or penalty arising from the same circumstances or around the same time.

(21) Impoundment concurrent with other administrative impoundments — The impoundment of a motor vehicle under this section runs concurrently with an impoundment, if any, of the same motor vehicle under section 41.4, 55.1, 55.2, 82.1 or 172.

(22) Forms — The Minister may require that forms approved by the Minister be used for any purpose of this section.

(23) Regulations — The Minister may make regulations,

(a) requiring police officers to keep records with respect to vehicle impoundments under this section for a specified period of time and to report specified information with respect to vehicle impoundments to the Registrar and governing such records and reports;

(b) exempting any class of persons or class or type of vehicles from any provision or requirement of this section or of any regulation made under this section and prescribing conditions and circumstances for any such exemption;

(c) exempting commercial motor vehicles, or any class or type of commercial motor vehicles, or drivers, owners or operators of commercial motor vehicles or any class of them, from any provision or requirement of this section or of any regulation made under this section, prescribing a different scheme of consequences and requirements from those set out in this section if a police officer is satisfied that a person driving or having the care, charge or control of a commercial motor vehicle, or a specified class or type of commercial motor vehicle, meets one of the criteria set out in subsection 48.3(3), including prescribing different penalties, and prescribing conditions and circumstances for any such exemption or for a different scheme to apply.

(24) Contravention of different scheme — Every person who contravenes or fails to comply with a regulation made under clause (23)(c) that prescribes a different scheme of consequences and requirements from those set out in this section is guilty of an offence and on conviction is liable to a fine of not less than $400 and not more than $20,000.

(25) Definitions — In this section,

"driver's licence" includes a driver's licence issued by another jurisdiction;

"operator" means,

(a) the person directly or indirectly responsible for the operation of a commercial motor vehicle, including the conduct of the driver of, and the carriage of goods or passengers, if any, in, the commercial motor vehicle or combination of vehicles, and

(b) in the absence of evidence to the contrary, where no CVOR certificate, as defined in subsection 16(1), or lease applicable to a commercial motor vehicle, is produced, the holder of the plate portion of the permit for the commercial motor vehicle.

Proposed Amendment — 48.4(25) "operator" (b)

(b) in the absence of evidence to the contrary, where no CVOR certificate, or lease applicable to a commercial motor vehicle, is produced, the holder of the plate portion of the permit for the commercial motor vehicle.

2014, c. 9, Sched. 2, s. 16 [To come into force January 1, 2017.]

2009, c. 5, s. 20

Commentary

A seven-day administrative impoundment follows if the criteria set out in S. 48.3(3) is met.

49. Proceedings before Tribunal — **Subsections 210(7), (8), (11) and (13) apply with necessary modifications to proceedings before the Tribunal with respect to appeals to the Tribunal under this Act.**

[Editor's Note: The Licence Appeal Tribunal Act, 1999, S.O. 1999, c. 12, Sch. G, established the Licence Appeal Tribunal, which assumed the functions previously performed by the Licence Suspension Appeals Board. Section 24(3) of the Act amended s. 49 by effectively repealing subsections (1)-(5), which had dealt with the establishment and composition of the Board, the remuneration of its members, certain aspects of Board procedure, and regulation making power with respect to the Board. Equivalent provisions applicable to the Tribunal are contained in the new Act. Pursuant to s. 24(4) of S.O. 1999, c. 12, Sch. G, in spite of the amendments to s. 49 by s. 24(3), members of the Licence Suspension Appeal Board immediately before s. 24(3) came into force on April 1, 2000, were deemed to be members of the Licence Appeal Tribunal for the purpose of performing the duties of the Tribunal with respect to proceedings before the Board that were commenced before that date.]

1996, c. 20, s. 9; 1999, c. 12, Sched. G, s. 24(3)

50. (1) Appeal — **Every person aggrieved by a decision of the Minister made under subsection 32(5) for which there is a right of appeal pursuant to a regulation made under clause 32(14)(n) or a decision of the Registrar under section 17 or 47 may appeal the decision to the Tribunal.**

Proposed Amendment — 50(1)

(1) Appeal — **Every person aggrieved by a decision of the Minister made under subsection 32(5) for which there is a right of appeal pursuant to a regulation made under clause 32(14)(n) or a decision or order of the Registrar under section 17 or 47 may appeal the decision to the Tribunal.**

2014, c. 9, Sched. 2, s. 17(1) [To come into force January 1, 2017.]

Proposed Addition — 50(1.1)

(1.1) Immediate suspension, cancellation of CVOR certificate not stayed — **Despite the *Statutory Powers Procedure Act*, the filing of an appeal under subsection (1) in respect of an order immediately suspending or cancelling a CVOR**

certificate pursuant to subsection 47(2.2) does not stay the order, unless the Tribunal orders otherwise.

2014, c. 9, Sched. 2, s. 17(2) [To come into force January 1, 2017.]

(2) Powers of Tribunal — The Tribunal may confirm, modify or set aside the decision of the Minister or Registrar.

Proposed Amendment — 50(2)

(2) Powers of Tribunal — The Tribunal may confirm, modify or set aside the decision or order of the Minister or Registrar.

2014, c. 9, Sched. 2, s. 17(3) [To come into force January 1, 2017.]

(3) Appeal to judge — Every person aggrieved by a decision of the Tribunal with respect to a decision of the Minister under subsection 32(5) for which there is a right of appeal pursuant to a regulation made under clause 32(14)(n) or a decision of the Registrar under clause 47(1)(b) may, within 30 days after a notice of the decision is sent to the person's latest address as recorded with the Tribunal, appeal the decision of the Tribunal to a judge of the Superior Court of Justice.

Proposed Amendment — 50(3)

(3) Appeal to judge — Every person aggrieved by a decision of the Tribunal with respect to a decision of the Minister under subsection 32(5) for which there is a right of appeal pursuant to a regulation made under clause 32(14)(n) or an order of the Registrar under clause 47(1)(b) may, within 30 days after a notice of the decision is sent to the person's latest address as recorded with the Tribunal, appeal the decision of the Tribunal to a judge of the Superior Court of Justice.

2014, c. 9, Sched. 2, s. 17(4) [To come into force January 1, 2017.]

(3.1) Appeal to Divisional Court — Every person aggrieved by a decision of the Tribunal with respect to a decision of the Registrar under section 17 or 47, other than a decision under clause 47(1)(b), may, within 30 days after a notice of the decision is sent to the person's latest address as recorded with the Tribunal, appeal the decision of the Tribunal to the Divisional Court.

Proposed Amendment — 50(3.1)

(3.1) Appeal to Divisional Court — Every person aggrieved by a decision of the Tribunal with respect to a decision or order of the Registrar under section 17 or 47, other than an order under clause 47(1)(b), may, within 30 days after a notice of the decision is sent to the person's latest address as recorded with the Tribunal, appeal the decision of the Tribunal to the Divisional Court.

2014, c. 9, Sched. 2, s. 17(5) [To come into force January 1, 2017.]

(3.2) Decision not stayed — Despite the *Statutory Powers Procedure Act*, the filing of an appeal under subsection (3.1) does not stay the decision of the Tribunal being appealed, unless the Divisional Court orders a stay.

(3.3) Extension of time to appeal — The time to appeal a decision under subsection (3) or (3.1) may be extended by a judge of the Superior Court of Justice or the Divisional Court, as the case may be, before or after the expiration of the time limit set out in those subsections.

(4) Powers of judge — The judge may confirm, modify or set aside the decision of the Tribunal.

(5) Application of s. 55 — Section 55 does not apply to the suspension or cancellation of a licence or permit under section 47.

1993, c. 27, s. 3 (Sched.); 1996, c. 33, s. 9; 1999, c. 12, Sched. G, s. 24(5)–(8), item 1; 2001, c. 9, Sched. O, s. 6; 2002, c. 18, Sched. P, s. 17; 2016, c. 5, Sched. 12, s. 3

Commentary

The Red Tape Reduction Act, 1999, S.O. 1999, c. 12, Sched. R. (ss. 1(2), 1(3), 2(1), 2(3), 2(5), 5(1), and 6(1) in force January 1, 2001) amends ss. 6, 7, 12 and 14 of the Highway Traffic Act to facilitate Ontario's participation in the International Registration Plan, which contains reciprocal provisions in respect of commercial motor vehicles that travel across provincial or international borders. The Plan provides for the issuance of IRP cab cards as permits for these vehicles and for the appointment of registration and licence fees in each member jurisdiction on the basis of the distances travelled in each jurisdiction. Persons residing or based in other jurisdictions that are members of the Plan are exempt from the requirements of and fees prescribed under Part II of the Highway Traffic Act.

Case Law

Re Williams and Registrar of Motor Vehicles (1973), 2 O.R. (2d) 473 (Co. Ct.); *Grexton v. Ontario (Licence Suspension Appeal Board)* (1994), 3 M.V.R. (3d) 185 (Ont. Gen. Div.) — Section 50(4) enables a judge to decide a case on its merits as a hearing *de novo*. The burden of proof is on the Registrar to show on a balance of probabilities that the licence to which the driver is *prima facie* entitled should be suspended or revoked. But as a result of *Johnson*, below, proceedings before the Board are apparently on the record.

Johnson v. Reg. of Motor Vehicles (1985), 34 M.V.R. 80 (Ont. Dist. Ct.); *Johnston v. Ontario* (1987), 48 M.V.R. 57 (Ont. Dist. Ct.); reversed (December 7, 1987), Doc. C.A. 226/87 (Ont. C.A.) — Restricted or revoked licences based on health reasons were reinstated.

White v. Nova Scotia (Registrar of Motor Vehicles) (1996), 147 N.S.R. (2d) 259, 426 A.P.R. 259 (S.C.) — Section 15 of the Charter is not applicable to the initial suspension since it was not penal in nature. Whether fair trial interests were violated at trial was a matter for the initial trial judge. The rights to silence and against self-incrimination were not violated by bringing a review or by having to disclose potential witnesses or defences for purposes of the review.

Gough v. Ontario (Ministry of Transportation) (2003), 2003 CarswellOnt 4538, 46 M.V.R. (4th) 138 (Ont. S.C.J.) — The licence tribunal ought to be accorded deference on findings of fact but a test of correctness ought to apply to other issues.

Mortillaro v. Ontario (Ministry of Transportation) (2004), 2004 CarswellOnt 4264, 191 O.A.C. 70, 13 M.V.R. (5th) 152 (Div. Ct.) — Under s. 50 if the Registrar has suspended a licence under s. 32(12)(b)(ii), no appeal lies to the Licence Appeal Tribunal. In order to suspend under s. 32(12)(b)(ii), the Registrar may do so pursuant to s. 3(3) of the Act, which allows for the delegation of power from the Ministry to the Registrar. In order to decline jurisdiction, the tribunal was required to be satisfied that the order had been made under s. 32(12)(b)(ii) or, that there had been a valid delegation.

50.1 (1) Appeal of ninety day suspension — A person whose driver's licence is suspended under section 48.3 may appeal the suspension of the Tribunal.

Proposed Amendment — 50.1(1)

(1) Appeal of ninety day suspension — A person whose driver's licence is suspended under section 48.3 or 48.3.1 may appeal the suspension of the Tribunal.
2015, c. 14, s. 16(1) [Not in force at date of publication.]

(2) Grounds for appeal — The only grounds on which a person may appeal a suspension under section 48.3 and the only grounds on which the Tribunal may order that the suspension be set aside are,

    (a) that the person whose licence was suspended is not the same individual to whom a demand was made, or from whom a sample was taken, or who performed physical co-ordination tests or submitted to an evaluation, as the case may be, under section 254 or 256 of the *Criminal Code* (Canada); or

    (b) that the person failed or refused to comply with a demand made under section 254 of the *Criminal Code* (Canada) because he or she was unable to do so for a medical reason.

Proposed Amendment — 50.1(2)

(2) Grounds for appeal — The only grounds on which a person may appeal a suspension under section 48.3 or 48.3.1 and the only grounds on which the Tribunal may order that the suspension be set aside are,

    (a) in the case of a suspension under section 48.3,

        (i) that the person whose licence was suspended is not the same individual to whom a demand was made under section 254 or 256 of the *Criminal Code* (Canada), or

        (ii) that the person failed or refused to comply with a demand made under section 254 of the *Criminal Code* (Canada) because he or she was unable to do so for a medical reason;

    (b) in the case of a suspension under section 48.3.1,

        (i) that the person whose licence was suspended is not the same individual who submitted to an evaluation under section 254 of the *Criminal Code* (Canada), or

        (ii) that the person's ability to operate a motor vehicle or vessel was not impaired by a drug or by a combination of a drug and alcohol, and the person had a medical condition, at the time of the activity for which the suspension was imposed, that impaired his or her performance of the evaluation that was conducted under section 254 of the *Criminal Code* (Canada).
2015, c. 14, s. 16(2) [Not in force at date of publication.]

(3) Supporting material — A person who appeals to the Tribunal under subsection (1) shall file such written material in support of the appeal as may be required by the Tribunal, together with such other material as the person may wish to submit, and the Tribunal shall not hold a hearing until all the supporting material is filed.

Proposed Amendment — 50.1(3)

(3) Supporting material — A person who appeals to the Tribunal under subsection (1) shall file written material in support of the appeal, and the Tribunal shall not hold a hearing until all the supporting material is filed.

2015, c. 14, s. 16(3) [Not in force at date of publication.]

(4) Powers of Tribunal — The Tribunal may confirm the suspension or may order that the suspension be set aside.

(5) Licence reinstated — If the Tribunal orders that the suspension be set aside, it shall give written notice of the order to the appellant and the Registrar and, upon receipt of such notice, the Registrar shall reinstate the appellant's driver's licence, subject to any other suspension under this Act.

(6) Decision final — The decision of the Tribunal under this section is final and binding.

(7) Suspension not stayed — The suspension under section 48.3 continues to apply despite the filing of an appeal under this section unless the Registrar reinstates the licence pursuant to the Tribunal's order that the suspension be set aside, and this subsection prevails over the *Statutory Powers Procedure Act*.

Proposed Amendment — 50.1(7)

(7) Suspension not stayed — The suspension under section 48.3 or 48.3.1 continues to apply despite the filing of an appeal under this section unless the Registrar reinstates the licence pursuant to the Tribunal's order that the suspension be set aside, and this subsection prevails over the *Statutory Powers Procedure Act*.

2015, c. 14, s. 16(4) [Not in force at date of publication.]

(8) When oral hearing required — The Tribunal is not required to hold an oral hearing under this section unless the appellant requests an oral hearing at the time of filing the appeal and bases the appeal on one of the grounds set out in subsection (2).

(9) Exception — Despite a request by the appellant for an oral hearing, the Tribunal may order that the suspension be set aside on the basis of the material filed with the Tribunal without holding an oral hearing.

(10) [Repealed 1999, c. 12, Sched. G, s. 24(11).]

1996, c. 20, s. 10; 1997, c. 12, s. 4; 1999, c. 12, Sched. G, s. 24(8), items 2–4, (11); 2009, c. 5, s. 21; 2015, c. 27, Sched. 7, s. 16

50.2 (1) Appeal of a long-term vehicle impoundment for driving while suspended — The owner of a motor vehicle that is impounded under section 55.1

may, upon paying the fee established by the Tribunal, appeal the impoundment to the Tribunal.

(2) Parties — The owner and the Registrar are the parties to an appeal under this section.

(3) Grounds for appeal — The only grounds on which an owner may appeal under subsection (1) and the only grounds on which the Tribunal may order the Registrar to release the motor vehicle are,

> (a) that the motor vehicle that is impounded was stolen at the time it was detained in order to be impounded;

> (b) that the driver's licence of the driver of the motor vehicle at the time it was detained in order to be impounded was not then under suspension;

Proposed Addition — 50.2(3)(b.1)

(b.1) that the driver's licence of the driver of the motor vehicle at the time it was detained in order to be impounded was not then subject to the condition described in paragraph 2 of subsection 55.1(1);

2015, c. 14, s. 17(1) [Not in force at date of publication.]

> (c) that the owner of the motor vehicle exercised due diligence in attempting to determine that the driver's licence of the driver of the motor vehicle at the time it was detained in order to be impounded was not then under suspension; or

Proposed Amendment — 50.2(3)(c)

(c) that the owner of the motor vehicle exercised due diligence in attempting to determine that the driver's licence of the driver of the motor vehicle at the time it was detained in order to be impounded was not then under suspension or subject to the condition described in paragraph 2 of subsection 55.1(1); or

2015, c. 14, s. 17(2) [Not in force at date of publication.]

> (d) that the impoundment will result in exceptional hardship.

(4) Exception — Clause (3)(d) does not apply if there was a previous impoundment under section 55.1 with respect to any motor vehicle then owned by the same owner.

(5) Powers of Tribunal — The Tribunal may confirm the impoundment or order the Registrar to release the motor vehicle.

(6) Notice of decision — The Tribunal shall give written notice of its decision to the owner and the Registrar.

(7) Registrar's actions if Tribunal orders release of vehicle — If the Tribunal orders the Registrar to release the motor vehicle, the Registrar shall, upon receipt of the notice,

> (a) issue an order to release the vehicle;

> (b) pay on behalf of the owner the amount incurred by the owner, as a result of the impoundment, for removing and impounding the vehicle, not including any amount for economic losses; and

(c) pay the operator or the owner the amount incurred by the operator or owner, as a result of the impoundment, for removing the load or drawn vehicle from the motor vehicle, not including any amount for economic losses.

(8) Decision final — The decision of the Tribunal under this section is final and binding.

(9) Impoundment not stayed — Despite the *Statutory Powers Procedure Act*, the filing of an appeal under this section does not suspend or terminate the impoundment under section 55.1.

(10) *Civil Remedies Act, 2001* prevails — Subsection (7) does not apply if the vehicle is subject to an order under Part III.1 of the *Civil Remedies Act, 2001*.

(11) Definitions — In this section,

"operator" has the same meaning as in section 55.1;

"owner" means each person whose name appears on the certificate of registration for the vehicle but in subsection (4) "owner" means the person whose name appears on the plate portion of a permit in cases where the certificate of registration consists of a vehicle portion and a plate portion and different persons are named on each portion.

1997, c. 12, s. 5; 1999, c. 12, Sched. G, s. 24(12), (13); 2000, c. 26, Sched. O, s. 3; 2007, c. 13, s. 14; 2009, c. 5, s. 22

Commentary

The Red Tape Reduction Act, 2000, S.O. 2000, c. 26, Sched. O. (ss. 1-4, 5(1) and (2) and 14 in force December 6, 2000; ss. 6-13 in force January 1, 2001) re-enacts s. 52 of the Highway Traffic Act to allow for notice to be given by regular mail for suspensions unrelated to Criminal Code (Canada) offences, and to allow for other prescribed methods of service; amends s. 55.1 to provide that the impoundment history of leased vehicles is linked to the holder of the plate portion of the registration certificate, to extend vehicle impound provisions to persons who are found driving while their licence is under suspension as a result of a court order and to clarify who is responsible for paying storage charges related to impoundment; amends existing provisions dealing with vehicle weights and dimensions to establish a framework for the implementation of an agreement between Ontario and Quebec; and amends s. 175(6)(c) of the Act to clarify when overhead red signal lights and stop arms on school buses must be used.

Related Provisions: Section 55.1 of the Act, See also O. Reg. 631/98, Long-Term Vehicle Impoundment Under Section 55.1 of the Act.

50.3 (1) Appeal of impoundment, commercial motor vehicles — The owner of a commercial motor vehicle or trailer that is impounded under section 82.1 may, upon paying the fee established by the Tribunal, appeal the impoundment to the Tribunal.

(2) Parties — The owner and the Registrar are the parties to an appeal under this section.

(3) Grounds for appeal — The only grounds on which an owner may appeal under subsection (1) and the only grounds on which the Tribunal may order the Registrar to release the vehicle are,

    (a) that the commercial motor vehicle or trailer that is impounded was stolen at the time the vehicle was detained under section 82.1; or

    (b) that the commercial motor vehicle or trailer had no critical defects at the time of the inspection under section 82.1.

(4) Effect of withdrawal of appeal — If the owner withdraws the appeal after the Registrar has ordered the release of the vehicle pursuant to an order by the Superior Court of Justice under section 82.1, the Registrar shall order the owner of the commercial motor vehicle or trailer to return it, without any load, to an impound facility at a location and within the time specified in the Registrar's order, failing which the security deposited in the Superior Court of Justice under section 82.1 shall be forfeited to the Crown.

(5) Powers of Tribunal — The Tribunal may confirm the impoundment or order the Registrar to release the vehicle.

(6) Notice of decision — The Tribunal shall give written notice of its decision in the owner and the Registrar.

(7) Owner must return vehicle to impound facility if order confirmed — If the Tribunal confirms the impoundment, the Registrar shall order the owner of the commercial motor vehicle or trailer, if the vehicle had been previously released from the impound facility, to return it, without any load, to an impound facility at a location and within the time specified in the Registrar's order and for the period set out in subsection 82.1(8) less the number of days the vehicle was impounded prior to its release under subsection 82.1(24), failing which the security deposited in the Superior Court of Justice under section 82.1 shall be forfeited to the Crown.

(8) Registrar's actions if ordered to release vehicle — If the Tribunal orders the Registrar to release the vehicle, the Registrar shall, upon receipt of the notice,

    (a) issue an order to release the vehicle;

    (b) reinstate the vehicle portion of the permit that was suspended under subsection 82.1(12);

    (c) pay on behalf of the owner the amount incurred by the owner, as a result of the impoundment, for removing and impounding the vehicle, not including any amount for economic losses; and

    (d) pay the operator of the vehicle the amount incurred by the operator, as a result of the impoundment, for removing the load from the vehicle, not including any amount for economic losses.

(9) Vehicle cannot be operated until made safe — Despite the fact that the Registrar is ordered to release the vehicle, the order to suspend the vehicle portion of the vehicle's permit is set aside and the vehicle portion of the permit is reinstated, no person shall drive or operate on a highway the vehicle that was the subject of the order until it has been placed in a safe condition.

(10) Decision final — The decision of the Tribunal under this section is final and binding.

(11) Impoundment not stayed — Despite the *Statutory Powers Procedure Act*, the filing of an appeal under this section does not suspend or terminate the impoundment or order to suspend under section 82.1.

(12) [Repealed 1999, c. 12, Sched. G, s. 24(15).]

(13) Definitions — In this section,

"commercial motor vehicle", "operator", "owner" and "permit" have the same meanings as in section 82.1.

> ### Proposed Amendment — 50.3(13)
>
> **(13) Definitions** — In this section,
>
> "operator", "owner" and "permit" have the same meanings as in section 82.1.
>
> 2014, c. 9, Sched. 2, s. 18 [To come into force January 1, 2017.]

1997, c. 12, s. 6; 1999, c. 12, Sched. G, s. 24(14), (15); 2009, c. 5, s. 23

Commentary

The Red Tape Reduction Act, 1999, S.O. 1999, c. 12, Sched. R. (ss. 1(2), 1(3), 2(1), 2(3), 2(5), 5(1), and 6(1) in force January 1, 2001) amends ss. 6, 7, 12 and 14 of the Highway Traffic Act to facilitate Ontario's participation in the International Registration Plan, which contains reciprocal provisions in respect of commercial motor vehicles that travel across provincial or international borders. The Plan provides for the issuance of IRP cab cards as permits for these vehicles and for the appointment of registration and licence fees in each member jurisdiction on the basis of the distances travelled in each jurisdiction. Persons residing or based in other jurisdictions that are members of the Plan are exempt from the requirements of and fees prescribed under Part II of the Highway Traffic Act.

Related Provisions: See O. Reg. 512/97, Critical Defects of Commercial Motor Vehicles, s. 4(10).

51. Penalty for operating motor vehicle when permit suspended or cancelled — Every person who drives a motor vehicle the permit for which is under suspension or has been cancelled is guilty of an offence and on conviction is liable to a fine of not less than $200 and not more than $1000 or to imprisonment for a term of not more than six months, or to both.

52. (1) Service of notice of licence suspension — Where a person's driver's licence is suspended, notice of the suspension is sufficiently given if delivered personally or,

(a) in the case of a suspension under section 41 or 42, sent by registered mail addressed to the person to whom the licence was issued at the latest current address of the person appearing on the records of the Ministry;

(b) in the case of all other suspensions, sent by mail addressed to the person to whom the licence was issued at the latest current address of the person appearing on the records of the Ministry.

(2) Deemed date of service — Notice sent by registered mail under clause (1)(a) or by mail under clause (1)(b) shall be deemed to have been given on the seventh day after the mailing unless the person to whom the notice is sent establishes that he or she did not, acting in good faith, through absence, accident, illness or other cause beyond his or her control, receive the notice.

(3) Regulations — The Lieutenant Governor in Council may make regulations,

(a) prescribing other methods of service that may be used in the case of a suspension described in clause (1)(a) or a suspension described in clause (1)(b) and prescribing the day on which the notice sent or delivered by such other means shall be deemed to have been given;

(b) prescribing means of proving that a notice was given by a method permitted by subsection (1) or by a method permitted by regulation.

2000, c. 26, Sched. O, s. 4

Commentary

The Red Tape Reduction Act, 2000, S.O. 2000, c. 26, Sched. O. (ss. 1-4, 5(1) and (2) and 14 in force December 6, 2000; ss. 6-13 in force January 1, 2001) re-enacts s. 52 of the Highway Traffic Act to allow for notice to be given by regular mail for suspensions unrelated to Criminal Code (Canada) offences, and to allow for other prescribed methods of service; amends s. 55.1 to provide that the impoundment history of leased vehicles is linked to the holder of the plate portion of the registration certificate, to extend vehicle impound provisions to persons who are found driving while their licence is under suspension as a result of a court order and to clarify who is responsible for paying storage charges related to impoundment; amends existing provisions dealing with vehicle weights and dimensions to establish a framework for the implementation of an agreement between Ontario and Quebec; and amends s. 175(6)(c) of the Act to clarify when overhead red signal lights and stop arms on school buses must be used.

53. (1) Driving while driver's licence suspended — Every person who drives a motor vehicle or street car on a highway while his or her driver's licence is suspended under an Act of the Legislature or a regulation made thereunder is guilty of an offence and on conviction is liable,

(a) for a first offence, to a fine of not less than $1,000 and not more than $5,000; and

(b) for each subsequent offence, to a fine of not less than $2,000 and not more than $5,000.

or to imprisonment for a term of not more than six months, or to both.

(1.1) Same — Despite subsection (1), every person who drives a motor vehicle or street car on a highway while his or her driver's licence is suspended under section 41 or 42, even if it is under suspension at the same time for any other reason, is guilty of an offence and on conviction is liable,

(a) for a first offence, to a fine of not less than $5,000 and not more than $25,000; and

(b) for each subsequent offence, to a fine of not less than $10,000 and not more than $50,000,

or to imprisonment for a term of not more than six months, or to both.

(2) Subsequent offence — Where a person who has previously been convicted of an offence under subsection (1) is convicted of the same offence within five years after the date of the previous conviction, the offence for which he or she is last convicted shall be deemed to be a subsequent offence for the purpose of clause (1)(b).

(2.1) Same — Where a person who has previously been convicted of an offence under subsection (1.1) is convicted of the same offence within five years after the date of the previous conviction, the offence for which he or she is last convicted shall be deemed to be a subsequent offence for the purpose of clause (1.1) (b).

(3) Licence suspended — The driver's licence of a person who is convicted of an offence under subsection (1) or (1.1) is thereupon suspended for a period of six months in addition to any other period for which the licence is suspended, and consecutively thereto.

1997, c. 12, s. 7; 1998, c. 5, s. 25

Case Law

R. v. MacDougall, [1982] 2 S.C.R. 605, 18 M.V.R. 180, 142 D.L.R. (3d) 216 — Driving while suspended is a strict liability offence.

R. v. Robertson (1984), 30 M.V.R. 248, 49 C.R. (3d) 39 (Ont. Prov. Ct.) — The accused had mistakenly sent a cheque toward payment for fines for two minor traffic violations to the Ministry of Transport instead of the Provincial Offences Court. On inquiring with the Ministry upon receiving a notice of suspension of her licence for not paying the fines, the accused had been told to wait a few days before driving again. The accused was involved in a minor accident a few months later and charged under the Provincial Offences Act, for driving while her licence was suspended. She appealed her conviction. The appeal was dismissed, but the sentence was varied. The accused was operating under a mistake of law, and ignorance of the law was no excuse. The officially induced error might have been applicable in jurisdictions like Nova Scotia where the common law principle (that ignorance of the law was no excuse) had not been codified, but it was inapplicable to Ontario where sections of the Provincial Offences Act had codified that principle (R.S.O. 1980, c. 400, s. 81 [now R.S.O. 1990, c. P.33, s. 81]). The circumstances relevant to such a defence were, however, relevant in mitigation of sentence.

R. v. West (1981), 35 O.R. (2d) 179, 13 M.V.R. 70, 64 C.C.C. (2d) 417 (H.C.) — The Provincial Court had quashed an information as being a nullity which charged the respondent that he "did unlawfully operate a motor vehicle on a highway ... when his driver's licence was suspended by operation of the *Highway Traffic Act*, contrary to the *Highway*

Traffic Act, section 30b." Section 30(b) only provided for driving while one's licence was suspended. The Crown brought an application for *mandamus*. The application was granted. It was held that the reference to the section number incorporated the essential element of driving. Although it would have been preferable for the information to be in the words of the section, it did in fact comply with the requirements of an information as set out in s. 26 of the Provincial Offences Act (Ont.).

R. v. Zembal (1987), 1 M.V.R. (2d) 335 (Ont. Prov. Ct.) — The accused was charged under s. 53 of the Act. His licence was suspended for non-payment of fines. He had paid the outstanding fines before being stopped by the police. The charge was dismissed. It was found that the *actus reus* of the crime was not proven. The licence was pending reinstatement as opposed to under suspension.

R. v. Azzoli (1983), 24 M.V.R. 205 (Ont. Prov. Ct.) — The accused was acquitted where the notice of suspension was ambiguous and he acted with due diligence in trying to arrange payment of the fine shown on the notice.

R. v. Moody (1985), 33 M.V.R. 198 (B.C. Co. Ct.) — A conviction for driving without a licence does not preclude a conviction for driving while suspended based on the same facts.

R. v. Middlebrook; *R. v. Miller*; *R. v. Laporta* (1988), 5 M.V.R. (2d) 236 (Ont. C.A.); affirming *Miller v. R.* (1986), 55 O.R. (2d) 417, 41 M.V.R. 141, 27 C.C.C. (3d) 30 (H.C.) — Section 52 of the Act was not in violation of either s. 7 or s. 11(d) of the Charter of Rights and s. 53(3) of the Act was not in violation of either s. 7 or s. 12 of the Charter of Rights.

R. v. Goltz, [1991] 3 S.C.R. 485, 31 M.V.R. (2d) 137, 131 N.R. 1 — The mandatory minimum sentence of seven days' imprisonment and a $300 fine for a first conviction of driving while prohibited does not infringe s. 12 of the Charter when the prohibition is made pursuant to s. 86(1)(a)(ii) of the Motor Vehicle Act (B.C.). Section 86(1)(a)(ii) is aimed at drivers with unsatisfactory driving records and the prohibition must be in the publc interest.

R. v. Pontes, [1995] 3 S.C.R. 44, 41 C.R. (4th) 201, 100 C.C.C. (3d) 353, 13 M.V.R. (3d) 145; affirming (1994), 1 M.V.R. (3d) 87, 89 B.C.L.R. (2d) 271 (C.A.); which affirmed (1992), 37 M.V.R. (2d) 162 (S.C.) — As the result of committing an underlying offence, the accused was subject to an automatic driving prohibition without notice. While prohibited, he drove and was charged with driving while prohibited. While the offence was one of absolute liability, there was no contravention of s. 7 of the Charter because he was not liable to imprisonment upon conviction or upon failure to pay a fine.

R. v. Bellomo (1995), 14 M.V.R. (3d) 63 (Ont. Prov. Ct.) — The Act's requirement that a person has to prove on a balance of probabilities that he was unaware of the license suspension contravenes ss. 7 and 11(d) of the Charter and is not justified under s. 1. The defendant need only raise a reasonable doubt regarding knowledge.

R. v. Alexis (1999), 48 M.V.R. (3d) 1, 181 D.L.R. (4th) 719, 132 B.C.A.C. 270, 215 W.A.C. 270 (C.A.) — A certificate of disqualification is inadmissible as unreliable where the certificate is so flawed as to deprive the trier of fact of conclusive proof of the accused's knowledge of the certificate. The certificate will stand as prima facie proof of knowledge where the identity of the accused, period of suspension and the fact of prohibition are clear on the face. A typographical error, being a dual imperfection in the form of a document, does not render the information the document contains ambiguous. The test is whether the accused may be misled and prejudiced or, are the phrases containing the error, or the whole certificate, capable of more than one meaning.

R. v. Muys, 2006 CarswellBC 2469, 2006 BCSC 1483, 37 M.V.R. (5th) 173 (S.C.) — Convictions for the provincial and criminal code offences for driving while prohibited cannot stand together and the lesser offence was stayed conditionally on appeal.

R. v. Reid, 2012 ONCJ 305, 2012 CarswellOnt 6779, 34 M.V.R. (6th) 307, [2012] O.J. No. 2540 — Where the trial court always imposed a seven day sentence, it was a de facto minimum sentence which breached s. 7 of the Charter.

54. Where person whose permit or licence suspended does not hold permit or licence — Where by or under the provisions of an Act of the Legislature or a regulation made thereunder a permit or licence is suspended and the person to whom the suspension applies is not the holder of a permit or licence, as the case may be, the person shall be deemed for all the purposes of this Act or the regulations to be a person whose permit or licence, as the case may be, has been suspended.

Commentary

The Motorized Snow Vehicles Amendment Act, 2000, S.O. 2000, c. 30 (in force May 31, 2001) amends section 54 of the Highway Traffic Act (dealing with the effect of suspension provisions if a person holds no permit or licence) to reflect the fact that a person's driver's licence may now also be suspended under the Motorized Snow Vehicles Act.

55. Suspension on appeal — If a person whose licence has been suspended enters an appeal against his or her conviction and serves notice of the appeal on the Registrar, the suspension is stayed from the time notice is serviced on the Registrar unless the conviction is sustained on appeal.

1996, c. 33, s. 10

Related Provisions: This section may be contrasted with s. 41(5) of the Act which provides that if the appeal is only against the additional suspension, leave must be granted by the court being appealed from to stay the suspension.

55.1 Long-term vehicle impoundment for driving while suspended —
(1) Detention — Where a police officer or officer appointed for carrying out the provisions of this Act is satisfied that a person was driving a motor vehicle on a highway while his or her driver's licence is under suspension under section 41, 42 or 43 even if it is under suspension at the same time for any other reason, the officer shall detain the motor vehicle that was being driven by the person whose driver's licence is under suspension.

Proposed Amendment — 55.1(1)

(1) Detention — Where a police officer or officer appointed for carrying out the provisions of this Act is satisfied that a person was driving a motor vehicle on a highway in one of the following circumstances, the officer shall detain the motor vehicle that was being driven by the person:

1. While his or her driver's licence is under suspension under section 41, 42 or 43, even if it is under suspension at the same time for any other reason.

2. In contravention of a condition, imposed for a prescribed reason on his or her driver's licence under a conduct review program under section 57, that prohibits him or her from driving a motor vehicle that is not equipped with an ignition interlock device.

3. While his or her driver's licence is under suspension for a prescribed reason under a conduct review program under section 57, even if it is under suspension at the same time for any other reason.

2015, c. 14, s. 18(1) [Not in force at date of publication.]

(2) Impoundment — Once the drawn vehicle and load, if any, have been removed as may be required by subsection (10), (11), (12) or (13), the detained vehicle shall, at the cost and risk of the owner,

(a) be removed to an impound facility as directed by a police officer or officer appointed for carrying out the provisions of this Act; and

(b) be impounded from the time it was detained for the period described in subsection (3) or until ordered to be released by the Registrar under subsection (14) or under section 50.2.

(3) Impound period — A motor vehicle detained under subsection (1) shall be impounded as follows:

1. For 45 days, if there has not been any previous impoundment under this section, within a prescribed period, with respect to any motor vehicle then owned by the owner of the vehicle currently being impounded.

2. For 90 days, if there has been one previous impoundment under this section, within a prescribed period, with respect to any motor vehicle then owned by the owner of the vehicle currently being impounded.

3. For 180 days, if there have been two or more previous impoundments under this section, within a prescribed period, with respect to any motor vehicle then owned by the owner of the vehicle currently being impounded.

(4) Release of vehicle — Subject to subsection (20), the motor vehicle shall be released to its owner from the impound facility upon the expiry of the period of the impoundment or upon being ordered to be released by the Registrar under subsection (14) or under section 50.2.

(5) Duty of officer re impoundment — Every officer who detains a motor vehicle under this section shall, as soon as practicable,

(a) prepare a notice identifying the motor vehicle that is to be impounded, the name and address of the driver, the date and time of the impoundment, the period of time for which the motor vehicle is impounded and the place where the vehicle may be recovered;

(b) serve the driver with a copy of the notice; and

(c) forward a copy of the notice to the Registrar.

(6) Service on driver is deemed service on owner and operator — Service of the notice of the impoundment on the driver of the motor vehicle under clause (5)(b) is deemed to be service on and sufficient notice to the owner of the vehicle and the operator of the vehicle, if there is an operator.

(7) Notice by Registrar — The Registrar may provide notice of the impoundment to the owner and operator of the motor vehicle by mailing it to them at the latest address for them appearing on the records of the Ministry.

(8) No hearing before impoundment — There is no right to be heard before a vehicle detention or impoundment under this section.

(9) Surrender of documents, information re trip and goods carried — If the motor vehicle that is to be impounded contains goods, the police officer or officer appointed for carrying out the provisions of this Act may require the driver and any other person present who is in charge of the motor vehicle to surrender all documents in his or her possession or in the vehicle that relate to the operation of the vehicle or to the carriage of the goods and to furnish all information within that person's knowledge relating to the details of the current trip and the ownership of the goods.

(10) Operator, owner to remove load — Upon being served with notice of the impoundment through service on the driver under subsection (5), the operator of the motor vehicle or, if there is no operator, the owner shall forthwith remove any vehicle drawn by the motor vehicle and any load from the motor vehicle.

(11) Application of *Dangerous Goods Transportation Act* — If the goods are dangerous goods, within the meaning of the *Dangerous Goods Transportation Act*, the operator or, if there is no operator, the owner shall remove them in accordance with that Act.

(12) Officer may remove load, trailer at operator's cost, risk — If, in the opinion of a police officer or officer appointed for carrying out the provisions of this Act, the operator or owner fails to remove a drawn vehicle or load as required by subsection (10) within a reasonable time after being served with notice of the impoundment, the officer may cause the drawn vehicle or load to be removed and stored or disposed of at the cost and risk of the operator or, if there is no operator, the owner.

(13) Same — If a police officer or officer appointed for carrying out the provisions of this Act is of the opinion that the operator or owner has not made appropriate arrangements for the removal of a drawn vehicle or load, having regard to the nature of the goods, including the fact that they are or appear to be dangerous goods within the meaning of the *Dangerous Goods Transportation Act* or are perishable, the officer may cause the drawn vehicle or load to be removed, stored or otherwise disposed of at the cost and risk of the operator or, if there is no operator, the owner.

(14) Release of vehicle before end of impound period — The Registrar may, on application by a person belonging to a class of persons prescribed by regulation, order the release of an impounded motor vehicle of a prescribed class prior to the end of the impound period on such conditions as he or she considers just.

(14.1) [Repealed 2009, c. 5, s. 24.]

(14.2) [Repealed 2009, c. 5, s. 24.]

(15) Consequence of order to release — Where an order to release is made under subsection (14), the impoundment shall not be considered a previous impoundment for the purposes of subsection (3) or subsection 50.2(4).

(16) Personal property in vehicle available to owner — Any personal property that is left in the impounded motor vehicle and that is not attached to or used in connection with its operation shall, upon request and proof of ownership, be made available, at reasonable times, to the owner of the property.

(16.1) [Repealed 2009, c. 5, s. 24.]

(16.2) [Repealed 2009, c. 5, s. 24.]

(16.3) [Repealed 2009, c. 5, s. 24.]

(17) Vehicle released from impound facility — Upon the expiry of the period of impoundment, the Registrar shall order that the motor vehicle be released to its owner from the impound facility.

(18) Release to holder of vehicle portion — Despite subsection (17), the holder of the vehicle portion of a certificate of registration may apply to the Registrar for the motor vehicle to be released to that holder upon the expiry of the period of impoundment, rather than to the holder of the plate portion, and the Registrar may order the motor vehicle released to the applicant on such conditions as he or she considers appropriate.

(18.1) [Repealed 2009, c. 5, s. 24.]

(18.2) [Repealed 2009, c. 5, s. 24.]

(19) Obligations of holder of vehicle portion — An order under subsection (18) has the effect of making the applicant liable for meeting the owner's obligations under subsection (22).

(19.1) [Repealed 2009, c. 5, s. 24.]

(20) Costs to be paid before release — Despite subsection (15) and despite being served with an order under subsection (14) or (18), the person who operates the impound facility is not required to release the motor vehicle until the removal and impound costs for the motor vehicle have been paid.

(21) Lien on vehicle for removal, impound costs — The costs incurred by the person who operates the impound facility in respect of an impoundment under this section are a lien on the motor vehicle, which may be enforced in the manner provided under Part III of the *Repair and Storage Liens Act*.

(21.1) [Repealed 2009, c. 5, s. 24.]

(22) Impound costs — The costs incurred by the person who operates the impound facility in respect of an impoundment under this section are a debt due by the owner and the driver of the motor vehicle at the time the vehicle was detained under this section, for which the owner and the driver are jointly and severally liable, and the debt may be recovered in any court of competent jurisdiction.

(23) **Defence** — It is a defence to an action referred to in subsection (22) that the owner sold or transferred the motor vehicle to another person before the vehicle was detained.

(24) **Debt due to police, Crown** — The costs incurred by a police force or the Crown in removing, storing or disposing of a drawn vehicle or load from a motor vehicle under subsection (12) or (13) are a debt due to the police force or Crown, as the case may be, and may be recovered by the police force or Crown in any court of competent jurisdiction.

(25) *Civil Remedies Act, 2001* **prevails** — Despite subsections (14), (17) and (18), a vehicle that is subject to an order under Part III.1 of the *Civil Remedies Act, 2001* shall not be released from detention or the impound facility except in accordance with the terms of that order, or another order, made under that Act.

(26) **Impound, removal service providers are independent contractors** — Persons who provide removal services or load removal services or who operate impound facilities, and their subcontractors, are independent contractors and not agents of the Ministry for the purposes of this section; such persons shall not charge more for their services in connection with this section than is permitted by regulation.

(27) **Owner may recover losses from driver** — The owner of a motor vehicle that is impounded under this section may bring an action against the driver of the motor vehicle at the time the motor vehicle was detained under this section to recover any costs or other losses incurred by the owner in connection with the impoundment.

(27.1) [Repealed 2009, c. 5, s. 24.]

(28) **Holder of vehicle portion may recover costs** — The holder of the plate portion of the permit and the driver of the motor vehicle at the time of the impoundment are jointly and severally liable to the holder of the vehicle portion of the permit who obtains an order under subsection (18) for any costs or losses incurred in connection with the impoundment, and the costs and losses may be recovered in any court of competent jurisdiction.

(29) **Protection from personal liability** — No action or other proceeding for damages shall be instituted against the Registrar or any employee of the Ministry for any act done in good faith in the execution or intended execution of his or her duty under this section or for any alleged neglect or default in the execution in good faith of that duty.

(30) **Crown not relieved of liability** — Despite subsections 5(2) and (4) of the *Proceedings Against the Crown Act*, subsection (29) does not relieve the Crown of liability in respect of a tort committed by a person mentioned in that subsection to which it would otherwise be subject.

(31) Offence — Every person who fails to comply with subsection (10) or with a requirement of a police officer or officer appointed for carrying out the provisions of this Act under subsection (9) is guilty of an offence and on conviction is liable to a fine of not less than $200 and not more than $20,000.

(32) Same — Every person who drives or operates or removes a motor vehicle that is impounded under this section and every person who causes or permits such a motor vehicle to be driven, operated or removed is guilty of an offence and on conviction is liable to a fine of not less than $200 and not more than $20,000.

(33) Same — Every person who provides removal services or who operates an impound facility and who charges fees for services provided in connection with this section in excess of those permitted by regulation is guilty of an offence and on conviction is liable to a fine of not less than $100 and not more than $1,000.

(34) Same — Every person who obstructs or interferes with a police officer or officer appointed for carrying out the provisions of this Act in the performance of his or her duties under this section is guilty of an offence and on conviction is liable to a fine of not less than $200 and not more than $20,000 or to imprisonment for a term of not more than six months, or to both.

(35) Decision without hearing is final — The Registrar shall assess applications made under subsections (14) and (18) without a hearing and the Registrar's decision is final.

(36) Intent of impoundment — The impoundment of a motor vehicle under this section is intended to promote compliance with this Act and to thereby safeguard the public and does not constitute an alternative to any proceeding or penalty arising from the same circumstances or around the same time.

(37) Impoundment concurrent with other administrative impoundments — The impoundment of a motor vehicle under this section runs concurrently with an impoundment, if any, of the same motor vehicle under section 41.4, 48.4, 55.2, 82.1 or 172.

(38) Regulations — The Lieutenant Governor in Council may make regulations,

(a) requiring police officers and officers appointed for carrying out the provisions of this Act to keep records with respect to vehicle impoundments under this section for a specified period of time and to report specified information with respect to vehicle impoundments to the Registrar and governing such records and reports;

(b) prescribing the period for the purpose of subsection (3);

(c) prescribing a schedule of fees that may be charged by independent contractors for services in connection with this section;

(d) prescribing the manner in which notices of impoundments under this section may be given under this section;

(e) prescribing methods for and rules of service for any notices required to be given under this section;

(f) classifying persons and motor vehicles and exempting any class of person or any class of motor vehicle from any provision of this section or any regulation made under this section and prescribing conditions for any such exemptions;

Proposed Addition — 55.1(38)(f.1)

(f.1) prescribing reasons for the purpose of paragraphs 2 and 3 of subsection (1);

2015, c. 14, s. 18(2) [Not in force at date of publication.]

(g) prescribing a period of time during which all persons and motor vehicles are exempt from paragraphs 2 and 3 of subsection (3) and providing that an order to impound for 45 days under paragraph 1 of subsection (3) shall be made during that period where paragraph 2 or 3 of subsection (3) would otherwise apply;

(h) classifying persons and motor vehicles and exempting any class of person or motor vehicle from paragraphs 2 and 3 of subsection (3) and providing that an order to impound for 45 days under paragraph 1 of subsection (3) shall be made with respect to that class of person or motor vehicle where paragraph 2 or 3 of subsection (3) would otherwise apply, and prescribing conditions for any such exemption;

(i) prescribing classes of persons and motor vehicles for the purposes of subsection (14) and specifying eligibility criteria;

(j) prescribing fees for the administration of this section;

(k) prescribing the time within which an appeal may be brought under section 50.2 with respect to an impoundment under this section, and governing any other time requirements in the appeal process;

(l) prescribing criteria to be considered, and criteria not to be considered, by the Tribunal in determining in an appeal under section 50.2 whether exceptional hardship will result from an impoundment under this section;

(m) prescribing rules, time periods and procedures with respect to applications under subsection (14).

(39) **Forms** — The Minister may require that forms approved by the Minister be used for any purpose of this section.

Proposed Addition — 55.1(39.1)

(39.1) **Transition** — For the purposes of paragraph 1 of subsection (1), a driver's licence suspension that was imposed under section 41.1 before its repeal under section 7 of the *Transportation Statute Law Amendment Act (Making Ontario's Roads Safer), 2015* and that was in effect on the day of its repeal is deemed to be a suspension under section 41.

2015, c. 14, s. 18(3) [Not in force at date of publication.]

(40) **Definitions** — In this section,

"operator" means,

(a) the person directly or indirectly responsible for the operation of a commercial motor vehicle, including the conduct of the driver of, and the carriage of goods or passengers, if any, in, the commercial motor vehicle or combination of vehicles, and

(b) in the absence of evidence to the contrary, where no CVOR certificate, as defined in subsection 16(1), or lease applicable to a commercial motor vehicle, is produced, the holder of the plate portion of the permit for the commercial motor vehicle;

Proposed Amendment — 55.1(40) "operator" (b)

(b) in the absence of evidence to the contrary, where no CVOR certificate, or lease applicable to a commercial motor vehicle, is produced, the holder of the plate portion of the permit for the commercial motor vehicle;

2014, c. 9, Sched. 2, s. 19 [To come into force January 1, 2017.]

"owner" means the person whose name appears on the certificate of registration for the vehicle, and, where the certificate of registration for the vehicle consists of a vehicle portion and a plate portion and different persons are named on each portion, means,

(a) in subsections (2), (6) and (7), the person whose name appears on the vehicle portion, and

(b) in subsections (2), (3), (4), (6), (7), (10), (11), (12), (13), (17), (19), (22), (23) and (27), the person whose name appears on the plate portion.

1997, c. 12, s. 8; 1999, c. 12, Sched. G, s. 24(16), item 1; 2000, c. 26, Sched. O, s. 5; 2002, c. 18, Sched. P, s. 18; 2007, c. 13, s. 15; 2008, c. 17, s. 40; 2009, c. 5, s. 24

Commentary

The Registrar may, without any hearing, immediately order that a motor vehicle that is being driven by a person whose driver's licence is under suspension for certain driving-related criminal offences be seized and impounded. The motor vehicle will be impounded as follows: for 45 days if owner had never, in a prescribed period, owned a vehicle impounded under the same section; for 90 days for the second time in a prescribed period; for 180 days for the third or subsequent time in a prescribed period. An appeal is possible under s. 50.2 of the Act on the grounds that the vehicle was stolen, or driven by a person who was not suspended, or that the owner exercised due diligence in trying to determine that the driver's licence was not suspended, or that the order will result in exceptional hardship. In the case of a subsequent impoundment, hardship is not available.

The *Red Tape Reduction Act*, 1999, S.O. 1999, c. 12, Sched. R. (ss. 1(2), 1(3), 2(1), 2(3), 2(5), 5(1), and 6(1) in force January 1, 2001) amends ss. 6, 7, 12 and 14 of the *Highway Traffic Act* to facilitate Ontario's participation in the International Registration Plan, which contains reciprocal provisions in respect of commercial motor vehicles that travel across provincial or international borders. The Plan provides for the issuance of IRP cab cards as permits for these vehicles and for the appointment of registration and licence fees in each member jurisdiction on the basis of the distances travelled in each jurisdiction. Persons residing or based in other jurisdictions that are members of the Plan are exempt from the requirements of and fees prescribed under Part II of the *Highway Traffic Act*.

The *Red Tape Reduction Act*, 2000, S.O. 2000, c. 26, Sched. O. (ss. 1-4, 5(1) and (2) and 14 in force December 6, 2000; ss. 6-13 in force January 1, 2001) re-enacts s. 52 of the

Highway Traffic Act to allow for notice to be given by regular mail for suspensions unrelated to *Criminal Code* (Canada) offences, and to allow for other prescribed methods of service; amends s. 55.1 to provide that the impoundment history of leased vehicles is linked to the holder of the plate portion of the registration certificate, to extend vehicle impound provisions to persons who are found driving while their licence is under suspension as a result of a court order and to clarify who is responsible for paying storage charges related to impoundment; amends existing provisions dealing with vehicle weights and dimensions to establish a framework for the implementation of an agreement between Ontario and Quebec; and amends s. 175(6)(c) of the Act to clarify when overhead red signal lights and stop arms on school buses must be used.

The progressive periods of impoundment are now operative upon a police officer's action and no longer require the Registrar to act. A shorter impoundment period may apply under s. 55.2.

Related Provisions: Section 50.2 of the Act, see also O. Reg. 631/98, Long-Term Vehicle Impoundment Under Section 55.1 of the Act.

55.2 (1) Short-term vehicle impoundment for driving while suspended — Where a police officer is satisfied that a person was driving a motor vehicle on a highway while his or her driver's licence is under suspension other than under section 32, 41, 42, 43, 46 or 47, the officer shall detain the motor vehicle that was being driven by the person and the vehicle shall, at the cost and risk of the owner,

---

Proposed Amendment — 55.2(1) opening words

(1) Short-term vehicle impoundment for driving while suspended — Where a police officer is satisfied that a person was driving a motor vehicle on a highway while his or her driver's licence is under suspension (other than under section 32, 41, 42, 43, 46 or 47 or for a reason prescribed under clause 55.1(38)(f.1)), the officer shall detain the motor vehicle that was being driven by the person and the vehicle shall, at the cost and risk of its owner,

2015, c. 14, s. 19 [Not in force at date of publication.]

(a) be removed to an impound facility as directed by a police officer; and

(b) be impounded for seven days from the time it was detained.

(2) Release of vehicle — Subject to subsection (14), the motor vehicle shall be released to its owner from the impound facility upon the expiry of the period of impoundment.

(3) Early release of vehicle — Despite the detention or impoundment of a motor vehicle under this section, a police officer may release the motor vehicle to its owner before it is impounded or, subject to subsection (14), may direct the operator of the impound facility where the motor vehicle is impounded to release the motor vehicle to its owner before the expiry of the seven days if the officer is satisfied that the motor vehicle was stolen at the time that it was driven as described in subsection (1).

(4) Duty of officer re impoundment — Every officer who detains a motor vehicle under this section shall, as soon as practicable,

    (a) prepare a notice identifying the motor vehicle that is to be impounded, the name and address of the driver, the date and time of the impoundment, the period of time for which the motor vehicle is impounded and the place where the vehicle may be recovered; and

    (b) serve the driver with a copy of the notice.

(5) Service on driver is deemed service on owner and operator — Service of a copy of a notice under subsection (4) on the driver of the motor vehicle is deemed to be service on and sufficient notice to the owner of the vehicle and the operator of the vehicle, if there is an operator.

(6) Further notice to owner — In addition to serving the owner of the motor vehicle through service on the driver under subsection (4), a police officer shall provide a copy of the notice prepared under subsection (4) to the owner of the motor vehicle by delivering it personally or by mail to the address of the owner shown on the permit for the motor vehicle or to the latest address for the owner appearing on the records of the Ministry.

(7) Surrender of documents, information re trip and goods carried — If the motor vehicle that is to be impounded contains goods, the police officer may require the driver and any other person present who is in charge of the motor vehicle to surrender all documents in his or her possession or in the vehicle that relate to the operation of the vehicle or to the carriage of the goods and to furnish all information within that person's knowledge relating to the details of the current trip and the ownership of the goods.

(8) Operator, owner to remove load — Upon being served with notice of the impoundment through service on the driver under subsection (4), the operator of the motor vehicle or, if there is no operator, the owner shall forthwith remove any vehicle drawn by the motor vehicle and any load from the motor vehicle.

(9) Application of *Dangerous Goods Transportation Act* — If the goods are dangerous goods, within the meaning of the *Dangerous Goods Transportation Act*, the operator or, if there is no operator, the owner shall remove them in accordance with that Act.

(10) Officer may remove load, trailer at operator's cost, risk — If, in the opinion of a police officer, the operator or owner fails to remove a drawn vehicle or load as required by subsection (8) within a reasonable time after being served with notice of the impoundment, the officer may cause the drawn vehicle or load to be removed and stored or disposed of at the cost and risk of the operator or, if there is no operator, the owner.

(11) Same — If a police officer is of the opinion that the operator or owner has not made appropriate arrangements for the removal of a drawn vehicle or load, having regard to the nature of the goods, including the fact that they are or appear to be dangerous goods within the meaning of the *Dangerous Goods Transportation Act* or are perishable, the officer may cause the drawn vehicle or load to be removed, stored or otherwise disposed of at the cost and risk of the operator or, if there is no operator, the owner.

(12) Personal property in vehicle available to owner — Any personal property that is left in the impounded motor vehicle and that is not attached to or used in connection with its operation shall, upon request and proof of ownership, be made available, at reasonable times, to the owner of the property.

(13) No appeal or right to be heard — There is no appeal from, or right to be heard before, a vehicle detention or impoundment under subsection (1).

(14) Impound costs to be paid before release of vehicle — The person who operates the impound facility where a motor vehicle is impounded under this section is not required to release the motor vehicle until the removal and impound costs for the vehicle have been paid.

(15) Lien for impound costs — The costs incurred by the person who operates the impound facility where a motor vehicle is impounded under this section are a lien on the motor vehicle that may be enforced under the *Repair and Storage Liens Act*.

(16) Impound costs a recoverable debt — The costs incurred by the person who operates the impound facility where a motor vehicle is impounded under this section are a debt due by the owner and the driver of the motor vehicle at the time the vehicle was detained, for which the owner and the driver are jointly and severally liable, and the debt may be recovered in any court of competent jurisdiction.

(17) Owner may recover losses from driver — The owner of a motor vehicle that is impounded under this section may bring an action against the driver of the motor vehicle at the time the vehicle was detained under subsection (1) to recover any costs or other losses incurred by the owner in connection with the impoundment.

(18) Debt due to police or Crown — The costs incurred by a police force or the Crown in removing, storing or disposing of a drawn vehicle or load from a motor vehicle under subsection (10) or (11) are a debt due to the police force or Crown, as the case may be, and may be recovered by the police force or Crown in any court of competent jurisdiction.

(19) Offence — Every person who obstructs or interferes with a police officer in the performance of his or her duties under this section is guilty of an offence and on conviction is liable to a fine of not less than $200 and not more than $5,000 or to imprisonment for a term of not more than six months, or to both.

(20) Intent of impoundment — The impoundment of a motor vehicle under this section is intended to promote compliance with this Act and to thereby safeguard the public and does not constitute an alternative to any proceeding or penalty arising from the same circumstances or around the same time.

(21) Impoundment concurrent with other administrative impoundments — The impoundment of a motor vehicle under this section runs concurrently with an impoundment, if any, of the same motor vehicle under section 41.4, 48.4, 55.1, 82.1 or 172.

(22) Forms — The Minister may require that forms approved by the Minister be used for any purpose of this section.

(23) Regulations — The Minister may make regulations,

(a) requiring police officers to keep records with respect to vehicle impoundments under this section for a specified period of time and to report specified information with respect to vehicle impoundments to the Registrar and governing such records and reports;

(b) exempting any class of persons or class or type of vehicles from any provision or requirement of this section or of any regulation made under this section and prescribing conditions and circumstances for any such exemptions;

(c) exempting commercial motor vehicles, or any class or type of commercial motor vehicles, or drivers, owners or operators of commercial motor vehicles or any class of them, from any provision or requirement of this section or of any regulation made under this section, prescribing a different scheme of consequences and requirements from those set out in this section if a police officer is satisfied that a person was driving a commercial motor vehicle, or a specified class or type of commercial motor vehicle, as described in subsection (1), including prescribing different penalties, and prescribing conditions and circumstances for any such exemption or for a different scheme to apply.

(d) designating provisions of legislation enacted by another province, a territory of Canada or a state of the United States of America that are comparable to the provisions under which a person's driver's licence is suspended under this Act and for which his or her motor vehicle may be impounded under this section and providing that this section applies to a person whose driver's licence is suspended under such provisions.

(24) Contravention of different scheme — Every person who contravenes or fails to comply with a regulation made under clause (23)(c) that prescribes a different scheme of consequences and requirements from those set out in this section is guilty of an offence and on conviction is liable to a fine of not less than $400 and not more than $20,000.

(25) Definition — In this section,

"operator" means,

(a) the person directly or indirectly responsible for the operation of a commercial motor vehicle, including the conduct of the driver of, and the carriage of goods or passengers, if any, in, the commercial motor vehicle or combination of vehicles, and

(b) in the absence of evidence to the contrary, where no CVOR certificate, as defined in subsection 16(1), or lease applicable to a commercial motor vehicle, is produced, the holder of the plate portion of the permit for the commercial motor vehicle.

Proposed Amendment — 55.2(25) "operator" (b)

(b) in the absence of evidence to the contrary, where no CVOR certificate, or lease applicable to a commercial motor vehicle, is produced, the holder of the plate portion of the permit for the commercial motor vehicle.

2014, c. 9, Sched. 2, s. 20 [To come into force January 1, 2017.]

2009, c. 5, s. 25

Related Provisions: See O. Reg. 415/10, Short-term Vehicle Impoundment under Section 55.2 of the Act.

56. (1) Demerit point system — The Lieutenant Governor in Council may make regulations providing for a demerit point system for drivers of motor vehicles or of street cars.

(2) Same — The demerit point system may provide for the cancellation and suspension of licences and may require that a driver, in order to show cause why his or her licence should not be cancelled or suspended, attend an interview or group session with an official of the Ministry or provide written information to the Ministry or both attend an interview or group session and provide written information.

(3) Format for interviews, group sessions — An interview or group session required under the demerit point system may be held in person or by telephone or other electronic means, as specified by the Ministry.

(4) Fees — The Minister may require the payment of fees for the attendance at an interview or group session or for providing written information under the demerit point system.

(5) Same — The Minister may set the amount of the fees required under subsection (4) and may set different fees for different classes of persons and for different circumstances.

2005, c. 26, Sched. A, s. 5

Commentary

Demerit points stay with the driver for two years. The relevant date for purposes of calculation is the date of the offence, not of conviction.

If a driver is convicted of more than one offence arising out of the same set of circumstances, demerit points are only assigned for the most serious of the offences.

If a suspension is imposed as part of a sentence relating to one or more offences, no demerit points are recorded.

See the Ontario-Quebec Agreement and the Canadian Driver Licence Compact which provide that Ontario drivers who commit serious highway traffic offences in other provinces or the territories will have the appropriate number of demerit points assigned in Ontario.

When a driver's points within a two-year period total at least six but below nine, the Registrar will send a written caution out.

If the driver accumulates nine to 14, the Registrar may ask the driver to come in to be interviewed, provide information and explain why the licence should not be suspended.

The Registrar has the power to suspend a driver for up to two years.

If 15 or more points are reached, the Registrar will suspend for 30 days. If 15 points are reached within two years of the first suspension, a six-month suspension will be ordered.

Probationary drivers are subject to greater restrictions. Probationary drivers are new drivers holding an Ontario licence for three years, or a licence issued elsewhere in Canada or the United States for two of the preceding three years. Probationary drivers will be suspended for six points and do not graduate as full-fledged drivers unless they have survived suspension-free.

Where a defendant appeals conviction, the Registrar should be served with a notice of appeal which has the effect of staying the recording of demerit points.

Case Law

Bogdane v. R. (1962), 39 W.W.R. 641 (Sask. Dist. Ct.) — Under the Saskatchewan Act, where an order is made by a magistrate directing demerit points be entered in the record of the accused, there is no jurisdiction on an appeal against sentence to consider the order as to demerit points.

R. v. Harper (1985), 35 M.V.R. 134, 45 C.R. (3d) 186, 17 C.R.R. 113 (B.C. Co. Ct.); affirmed (1986), 44 M.V.R. 313, 53 C.R. (3d) 185 (B.C. C.A.) — British Columbia's demerit point system was upheld in the face of an attack under s. 7 of the Charter of Rights and Freedoms.

R. v. Sentell (1981), 16 M.V.R. 292 (B.C. Co. Ct.) — Even though fines and imprisonment are unavailable under a demerit point system, a *voir dire* must still be held regarding the voluntariness of any admission made to a person in authority.

Related Provisions: See s. 57.1 of the Act regarding novice drivers; see O. Reg. 339/94, Demerit Point System; see the Ontario-Quebec Agreement and the Canadian Driver Licence Compact.

57. (1) Conduct review programs — **The Lieutenant Governor in Council may make regulations establishing conduct review programs for persons who are applicants for or holders of a licence, permit or certificate under this Act.**

(2) Different programs — **Different** conduct review programs may be established for,

    (a) persons whose driver's licence has been suspended under this Act;

    (b) persons involved in more than one motor vehicle accident;

    (c) persons convicted of an offence under this Act or the regulations; or

    (d) any other prescribed class of persons.

(3) Program features — **A conduct review program may consist of or include interviews, assessments, remedial programs, courses, individual or group education sessions, examinations, the required installation and use of a device in a motor vehicle, such as an ignition interlock device, and any other feature that, in the opinion of the Lieutenant Governor in Council, may serve to improve road safety, including by improving individuals' driving skills and by assisting individuals in changing their past conduct.**

(4) Same — A regulation made under subsection (1) may,

(a) establish criteria and conditions to determine who may be required to participate in a conduct review program;

(b) prescribe classes of persons for the purpose of clause (2)(d);

(c) establish the features of a conduct review program, including features that may only apply to a person based on the results of an interview, assessment or examination;

(d) establish and govern ignition interlock programs, including an ignition interlock program for the purposes of subsection 259(1.1) of the *Criminal Code* (Canada) and govern the required installation and use of other devices in a motor vehicle;

Proposed Amendment — 57(4)(d)

(d) establish and govern ignition interlock programs, including an ignition interlock program for the purposes of subsection 259(1.1) of the *Criminal Code* (Canada), and programs that require the installation and use of other devices in motor vehicles that may affect the operation of the vehicle and may record and transmit data from the vehicle;

2015, c. 14, s. 20(1) [Not in force at date of publication.]

(e) prescribe what constitutes the successful completion of a conduct review program or of any feature or stage of a conduct review program;

(f) prescribe the circumstances in which a participant in a conduct review program will be required to leave the program;

(g) govern the requirements, conditions and circumstances for a person who does not successfully complete a conduct review program to participate in a conduct review program again, including prescribing the period of time that a person must wait before recommencing a program, or any feature or stage of it, or before commencing another conduct review program;

(h) provide for and govern the suspension, cancellation or change of class of a licence, permit or certificate in specified circumstances, including for failure to successfully complete a conduct review program or a feature or stage of a conduct review program;

Proposed Amendment — 57(4)(h)

(h) provide for and govern the suspension, cancellation, reinstatement or change of class of a licence, permit or certificate, and the imposition and removal of any condition, restriction, limitation or endorsement on a licence, permit or certificate, in specified circumstances including for failure to successfully complete a conduct review program or any feature or stage of a conduct review program or as part of an ignition interlock program referred to in subsection 259(1.1) of the *Criminal Code* (Canada);

2015, c. 14, s. 20(2) [Not in force at date of publication.]

(i) provide for and govern the imposition of a specified condition, restriction or limitation on a licence, permit or certificate in specified circumstances, including for failure to successfully complete a conduct review program or a feature or stage of a conduct review program;

Proposed Amendment — 57(4)(i)

(i) require or prohibit the doing of any thing by persons participating in a conduct review program;

2015, c. 14, s. 20(2) [Not in force at date of publication.]

(j) govern the reinstatement of a licence, permit or certificate that is suspended or cancelled under a conduct review program, the reinstatement of a class of licence, permit or certificate that is changed under a conduct review program and the removal of a condition, restriction or limitation that is imposed on a licence, permit or certificate under a conduct review program;

Proposed Repeal — 57(4)(j)

(j) [Repealed 2015, c. 14, s. 20(2). Not in force at date of publication.]

(k) require that participants in a conduct review program prepare or obtain and keep specified records and submit them as specified in the regulation to the Ministry during the program and at its conclusion.

Proposed Addition — 57(4.1), (4.2)

(4.1) Same — A regulation made under clause (4)(h) may not provide for the reinstatement of a driver's licence suspended by court order, except for a court order made under subsection 259(1) of the *Criminal Code* (Canada).

(4.2) Same — A regulation made under clause (4)(h) may not provide for the reinstatement of a suspended drivers licence, except in one of the following circumstances:

1. Where the licence is suspended under a conduct review program.

2. Where the licence is suspended under subsection 41(1) for an offence listed in clause 41(1)(b.1) or (c) and the reinstatement is for the purpose of requiring the holder of the licence to participate in an ignition interlock program.

3. Where the licence is suspended for a second subsequent suspension under clause 41(1)(h) and the suspension has been in effect for at least 10 years before the reinstatement takes effect.

2015, c. 14, s. 20(3) [Not in force at date of publication.]

(5) Same — A regulation made under this section may provide differently for different classes of persons and in different parts of Ontario.

(6) Persons authorized to provide programs — The Minister may authorize or require any person or class of persons to provide or conduct a conduct review program, or any feature or stage of a conduct review program and may require them to prepare, keep and submit to the Ministry records and reports as specified by the Ministry.

(7) Records, reports privileged — Records and reports filed with the Ministry for the purposes of this section are privileged for the information of the Ministry only and shall not be open for public inspection.

(8) Format for courses, sessions, etc. — Participation in any course, individual or group session or other feature or stage of a conduct review program may be in person or by telephone or other electronic means, as specified by the Ministry.

(9) Fees — The Minister,

(a) may require a participant in a conduct review program to pay fees to the Minister or to the person who is providing or conducting a conduct review program or any feature or stage of a conduct review program or to both the Minister and the person; and

(b) may require different fees for different classes of persons and for different circumstances.

(10) Same — The Minister may require that any fees be paid, in whole or in part,

(a) prior to participating in a conduct review program;

(b) in instalments based on the completion of different features or stages of a conduct review program;

(c) together with the submission of any required records during or on the completion of a conduct review program; or

(d) in any combination of clauses (a), (b) and (c).

(11) Notification — The Registrar may notify a person who meets the prescribed criteria and conditions that he or she is required to participate in a conduct review program, but not every person who meets the prescribed criteria and conditions will be notified by the Registrar, and the decision whether to notify a person or not is in the discretion of the Registrar.

(12) Same — The notification shall be delivered personally or mailed to the person at his or her latest address appearing on the records of the Ministry.

(13) Required to attend — A person who receives a notification to participate in a conduct review program shall do so as specified by the Ministry, and a person who does not receive a notification to participate in a conduct review program is not permitted to do so.

(14) Registrar's discretion in requiring persons to participate — In exercising his or her discretion under subsection (11), the Registrar shall take into account the interests of road safety, the driving record and past conduct of any person who meets the prescribed criteria and conditions and the capacity of any conduct review program to accommodate all of the persons who meet the prescribed criteria and conditions.

(15) Parties to judicial review — The parties to any judicial review brought in respect of this section are the Registrar and the person whose licence, permit or certificate is affected.

(16) Protection from personal liability — No action or other proceeding for damages shall be instituted against a person authorized or required by this section to provide or conduct a conduct review program, or any feature or stage of a conduct review program, or to submit a record or report for the purposes of this section, unless the person was negligent in the conduct of the program or feature or stage of the program or in the preparation or submission of the record or report.

(17) **Same** — No action or other proceeding for damages shall be instituted against the Minister, the Registrar or any employee of the Ministry for any action taken or not taken, in respect of a licence, permit or certificate or in respect of a person's participation in a conduct review program, in good faith in the execution or exercise or intended execution or exercise of a duty or power under this section, including the Registrar's decision to notify or not notify a person that he or she is required to participate in a conduct review program.

(18) **Crown not relieved of liability** — Despite subsections 5(2) and (4) of the *Proceedings Against the Crown Act*, subsections (16) and (17) do not relieve the Crown of liability in respect of a tort committed by a person mentioned in subsection (16) or (17) to which it would otherwise be subject.

Proposed Addition — 57(19), (20)

(19) **Penalty** — Every person who contravenes this section, a regulation made under this section or a condition imposed on a driver's licence under a conduct review program established under this section is guilty of an offence and on conviction is liable to a fine of not less than $200 and not more than $1,000.

(20) **Penalty — commercial motor vehicle** — Despite subsection (19), every person who contravenes this section, a regulation made under this section or a condition imposed on a driver's licence under a conduct review program established under this section is guilty of an offence and, if the offence was committed by means of a commercial motor vehicle within the meaning of subsection 16(1), on conviction is liable to a fine of not less than $200 and not more than $20,000.

Proposed Amendment — Conditional Amendment — 57(20)

On the coming into force of both S.O. 2015, c. 14, s. 20(4) [Not in force at date of publication.] and S.O. 2014, c. 9, Sched. 2, s. 3(1) [To come into force January 1, 2017.], s. 57(20) is amended as follows:

> (20) **Penalty — commercial motor vehicle** — Despite subsection (19), every person who contravenes this section, a regulation made under this section or a condition imposed on a driver's licence under a conduct review program established under this section is guilty of an offence and, if the offence was committed by means of a commercial motor vehicle, on conviction is liable to a fine of not less than $200 and not more than $20,000.

> 2015, c. 14, s. 61(3) [Conditions not yet satisfied.]
> 2015, c. 14, s. 20(4) [Not in force at date of publication.]

1993, c. 40, s. 6; 2005, c. 26, Sched. A, s. 6; 2007, c. 13, s. 16

Related Provisions: See. O. Reg. 287/08, Conduct Review Programs.

57.1 (1) Regulations — The Lieutenant Governor in Council may make regulations in respect of novice drivers,

(a) defining novice driver and accompanying driver;

(b) prescribing drivers' licences of different classes and levels for novice drivers;

(b.1) prescribing the qualifications of applicants for and holders of any class or level of driver's licence for novice drivers;

(c) prescribing the qualifications and requirements, including a maximum blood alcohol concentration level, for accompanying drivers;

(d) requiring novice drivers with drivers' licences of any class or level to be accompanied, while driving, by an accompanying driver;

(e) respecting practical and written driving examinations and mental and physical, including ophthalmic and auditory, examinations for applicants for drivers' licences for novice drivers of any class or level;

(f) prescribing the length of time or the method of determining the length of time during which a person shall be a novice driver or shall be restricted to any level of driver's licence for novice drivers;

(g) prescribing circumstances under which the driver's licence of a novice driver shall be cancelled or suspended and the length of the suspension or suspensions;

(h) prescribing circumstances under which a novice driver may be required to attend before an official of the Ministry for an interview and the examination or examinations that may be required;

(i) prescribing circumstances under which a novice driver may be required to produce evidence with regard to successful completion of a Ministry-approved driver education or improvement course;

(j) [Repealed 2005, c. 26, Sched. A, s. 7(1).]

(k) prescribing modifications to the demerit point system prescribed under section 56 in so far as it applies to novice drivers and exempting novice drivers or any class or level of driver's licence for novice drivers from any of the provisions of the demerit point system;

(l) prescribing conditions and restrictions that shall apply to any class or level of driver's licence for novice drivers;

(l.1) prescribing circumstances under which the driver's licence of a novice driver may be changed in respect of its class as a consequence of a conviction for any offence under this Act or for a contravention of any condition on his or her driver's licence;

(m) prescribing markers or identifying devices to be displayed on or in motor vehicles driven by novice drivers or novice drivers with drivers' licences of any class or level and governing the conditions of their use and the manner of displaying them;

(n) exempting novice drivers or novice drivers with a driver's licence of any class or level from any requirement under this Part or any regulation made under this Part and prescribing conditions for the exemption;

(o) [Repealed 2009, c. 5, s. 26(2).]

(2) **Classes** — A regulation under subsection (1) may apply in respect of any class of driver's licence for novice drivers.

(3) Approved courses — The Minister may approve driver education and improvement courses for the purpose of clause (1)(i).

> 1993, c. 40, s. 7; 2004, c. 22, s. 2; 2005, c. 26, Sched. A, s. 7; 2009, c. 5, s. 26

Related Provisions: See O. Reg. 341/94, Driver Licence Examinations; O. Reg. 340/94, Drivers' Licences.

57.1.1 (1) Police request for novice driver's passenger's identification — A police officer or officer appointed for carrying out the provisions of this Act may request that a passenger in a motor vehicle driven by a novice driver identify himself or herself if the officer suspects that the novice driver is contravening a regulation made under section 57.1 and the passenger of whom the request is made shall give the officer his or her correct name and address.

(2) Additional information — The officer may also request additional prescribed information from a passenger of whom he or she requests identification under subsection (1) and the passenger of whom the request is made shall give the officer the requested information.

(3) Regulations — The Lieutenant Governor in Council may make regulations prescribing additional information that a police officer or officer appointed for carrying out the provisions of this Act may request and that a passenger is required to give under subsection (2).

> 2004, c. 22, s. 3

Related Provisions: See O. Reg. 340/94, Drivers' Licences.

57.2 (1) Offence — Every novice driver who contravenes a condition or restriction prescribed by a regulation made under section 57.1 is guilty of an offence.

(2) Defence to accompanying driver charge — It is a defence to a charge under subsection (1) relating to the qualifications or requirements of the accompanying driver if the accused novice driver establishes that he or she took all reasonable measures to comply with the regulations.

> 1993, c. 40, s. 7

Commentary

A broad power to make regulations for "novice drivers" replacing the scheme of "probationary drivers" is created. A novice driver who contravenes the regulations is guilty of an offence.

Related Provisions: See s. 56 of the Act; see O. Reg. 339/94, Demerit Point System; O. Reg. 340/94, Driver's Licences.

58. (1) Driving instructors — An individual shall not provide a prescribed class of driving instruction for compensation except under the authority of a driving instructor licence issued under this section that authorizes the individual to provide that class of driving instruction.

(2) Issuance of driving instructor licence — The Minister may issue a driving instructor licence to an individual authorizing the individual to provide a prescribed class or classes of driving instruction if the individual applies for the licence and meets the requirements of this section and the regulations made under it.

(3) **Conditions** — The Minister may issue a driving instructor licence subject to such conditions as the Minister considers appropriate.

(4) **Licensee's authority and duty** — A licensed driving instructor may provide driving instruction for compensation in the prescribed class or classes of driving instruction authorized by his or her licence and shall provide such instruction in accordance with this Act and the regulations made under this section.

(5) **Licence not transferable** — A driving instructor licence is not transferable.

(6) **Holding out** — No person shall hold themself out as being qualified to provide driving instruction for compensation in a prescribed class of driving instruction unless the person is licensed to do so under this section.

(7) **Fees** — It is a condition of a driving instructor licence that the licensee pay all prescribed fees in the manner and at the times prescribed.

(8) **Co-operation with inspector** — It is a condition of a driving instructor licence that the licensee co-operate with an inspector carrying out his or her duties under section 58.2.

(9) **Regulations** — The Minister may make regulations,

(a) prescribing classes of driving instruction for which a driving instructor licence is required in order to provide such instruction for compensation and prescribing classes of driving instructor licences;

(b) prescribing the qualifications and requirements for the issue of driving instructor licences or any class of them;

(c) governing the issuing and renewal of driving instructor licences;

(d) prescribing standards for driving instruction or for any prescribed class of driving instruction;

(e) governing the safety and maintenance of motor vehicles and other equipment used by licensed driving instructors or any class of them;

(f) prescribing qualifications and requirements for holders of driving instructor licences or any class of them;

(g) governing the suspension and revocation of driving instructor licences or any class of them;

(h) governing appeals from a refusal to issue or renew a driving instructor licence or from a suspension or revocation of a driving instructor licence and a right to be heard in respect of a proposal to refuse to issue or renew or to suspend or revoke a driving instructor licence, including prescribing circumstances in which there is no right to an appeal or to be heard;

(i) prescribing books and records to be maintained by licensed driving instructors and requiring and governing the submission of reports and returns to the Ministry by licensees;

(j) prescribing fees to be paid for applications and for the issue and renewal of licences;

(k) establishing a system of fees to be paid by licensees in respect of the driving instruction they provide;

(l) governing the manner and times of payment of any prescribed fees;

(m) exempting driving instructors holding any class of licence from any provision of this section or of a regulation made under this section and prescribing conditions and circumstances for such exemption.

(10) Classes — A regulation made under subsection (9) may apply in respect of any class of persons, driving instruction or licences.

(11) Conflict between regulations and by-law — Where there is a conflict between a regulation made under subsection (9) and a by-law of a municipal council or police services board regulating or governing driving instructors or driving instruction, the regulation prevails.

(12) Definition — In this section,

"compensation" includes any rate, remuneration, reimbursement or reward of any kind paid, payable, promised, received or demanded, directly or indirectly.

Proposed Repeal — 58(12)

(12) [Repealed 2014, c. 9, Sched. 2, s. 21. To come into force January 1, 2017.]

(13) Interpretation — For the purposes of this section,

(a) a person who provides driving instruction as part of his or her employment or contractual duties is providing driving instruction for compensation;

(b) a person who provides driving instruction as an employee or contractor of a licensed driving school or otherwise under the auspices of a licensed driving school is providing driving instruction for compensation even if the compensation for the driving instruction is paid to the driving school.

2005, c. 26, Sched. A, s. 8

Related Provisions: See O. Reg. 473/07, Licences for Driving Instructors and Driving Schools.

58.1 Driving schools — **(1) Definitions** — In this section and in section 58.2,

"driving school" means a business of providing driving instruction;

"licensed driving school" means a driving school operated by one or more persons who hold a driving school licence.

(2) Licence required — No person shall operate a driving school that offers or provides a Ministry-approved course in a prescribed class of driving instruction except under the authority of a driving school licence issued under this section that authorizes that class of driving instruction.

(3) Issuance of driving school licence — The Minister may issue a driving school licence to a person or persons authorizing the person or persons to provide a Ministry-approved course or courses in a prescribed class or classes of driving instruction if the person or persons apply for the licence and meet the requirements of this section and the regulations made under it.

(4) Conditions — The Minister may issue a driving school licence subject to such conditions as the Minister considers appropriate.

(5) Licensee's authority and duty — A licensed driving school may offer or provide Ministry-approved courses in the prescribed class or classes of driving instruction authorized by its licence and shall provide such instruction in accordance with this Act and the regulations made under this section.

(6) Driver education certificate — No person shall issue a driver education certificate prescribed under a regulation made under this section unless the person is licensed as a driving school under this section and issues the certificate in accordance with the regulations.

(7) Licence not transferable — A driving school licence is not transferable.

(8) Notice of change — A corporation that holds a driving school licence and persons that hold a driving school licence as a partnership shall, within 15 days of any change in officers, directors or partners, as the case may be, notify the Minister in writing of the change and of any other prescribed information, in accordance with the regulations.

(9) Fees — It is a condition of a driving school licence that the licensee pay all prescribed fees in the manner and at the times prescribed.

(10) Co-operation with inspector — It is a condition of a driving school licence that the licensee and the officers, directors, employees and contractors of the licensee co-operate with an inspector carrying out his or her duties under section 58.2.

(11) Holding out — No person shall hold themself out as being a licensed driving school or as being qualified to offer or provide a Ministry-approved course in a prescribed class of driving instruction unless the person is licensed to do so under this section.

(12) Regulations — The Minister may make regulations,

(a) prescribing classes of driving instruction for which a driving school licence is required in order to provide instruction in Ministry-approved driving courses;

(b) prescribing the qualifications and requirements for the issue of driving school licences or any class of them;

(c) governing the issuing and renewal of driving school licences;

(d) prescribing standards for driving instruction or any class of driving instruction to be met by licensed driving schools or any class of them;

(e) governing the safety and maintenance of the premises, motor vehicles and other equipment used by licensed driving schools or any class of them;

(f) prescribing qualifications and requirements for holders of driving school licences or any class of them;

(g) governing the suspension and revocation of driving school licences or any class of them;

(h) governing appeals from a refusal to issue or renew a driving school licence or from a suspension or revocation of a driving school licence and a right to be heard in respect of a proposal to refuse to issue or renew or to suspend or revoke a driving school licence, including prescribing circumstances in which there is no right to an appeal or to be heard;

(i) prescribing information for the purpose of subsection (8) and governing the notification required under that subsection;

(j) prescribing books and records to be maintained by licensed driving schools and requiring and governing the submission of reports and returns to the Ministry by licensees;

(k) prescribing fees to be paid for applications and for the issue and renewal of licences;

(l) establishing a system of fees to be paid by licensees in respect of the driving instruction they provide;

(m) requiring applicants for a licence to pay a fee determined in accordance with the regulation in respect of the driving education provided, between November 6, 2004 and the date the licence is issued, by the applicant or, if the applicant is two or more persons or a corporation, by one of the persons or shareholders;

(n) governing the manner and times of payment of any prescribed fees;

(o) governing the issuing of driver education certificates by licensed driving schools and governing the provision of driver education certificate forms by the Ministry to licensed driving schools, including prescribing fees to be paid by licensed driving schools for the certificate forms and governing the return of unused certificate forms to the Ministry and the payment of refunds for their return;

(p) exempting any class of persons, driving instruction or driving schools from any provision of this section or of a regulation made under this section and prescribing conditions and circumstances for such exemption.

(13) **Classes** — A regulation made under subsection (12) may apply in respect of any class of persons, driving instruction, driving schools or driving school licences.

(14) **Conflict between regulations and by-law** — Where there is a conflict between a regulation made under subsection (12) and a by-law of a municipal council or police services board regulating or governing driving instructors, driving schools or driving instruction, the regulation prevails.

(15) **Approved courses** — The Minister may approve courses in classes of driving instruction for the purposes of this section.

2005, c. 26, Sched. A, s. 9

Related Provisions: See O. Reg. 473/07, Licences for Driving Instructors and Driving Schools.

58.2 (1) Inspectors — The Minister may appoint one or more persons as inspectors for the purposes of this section.

(2) Certificate of appointment — The Minister shall issue to every inspector appointed under subsection (1) a certificate of appointment and every inspector, in the execution of his or her duties under this section, shall produce his or her certificate of appointment upon request.

(3) Powers of inspectors — For the purpose of ensuring compliance with sections 58 and 58.1 and the regulations made under them, an inspector may, without a warrant,

(a) enter any premises of a licensed driving school;

(b) enter any premises where the records of a licensed driving instructor or licensed driving school or the motor vehicles, equipment and other things used by a licensed driving instructor or licensed driving school in providing driver education are kept;

(c) examine a record, motor vehicle, equipment or other thing that is relevant to the inspection;

(d) demand the production for inspection of a motor vehicle, equipment, record or other thing that is relevant to the inspection;

(e) remove for examination or testing a motor vehicle or any equipment or thing that is relevant to the inspection;

(f) remove for review and copying a record or other thing that is relevant to the inspection;

(g) in order to produce a record in readable form, use data storage, information processing or retrieval devices or systems that are normally used in carrying on business in the place;

(h) carry out any examination, test, audit or investigation procedure that is relevant to the inspection; and

(i) question a person on matters relevant to the inspection.

(4) Dwellings — The power to enter and inspect a place shall not be exercised to enter and inspect a part of the place that is used as a dwelling without the consent of the occupier.

(5) Time of entry — The power to enter and inspect a place shall be exercised during the regular business hours of the place or, if it does not have regular business hours, at any time the place is open for business.

(6) Written demand — A demand that a motor vehicle, equipment, record or other thing be produced for inspection must be in writing and must include a statement of the nature of the motor vehicle, equipment, record or thing required.

(7) Obligation to produce and assist — If an inspector demands that a motor vehicle, equipment, record or other thing be produced for inspection, the person who has custody of the motor vehicle, equipment, record or thing shall produce it immediately and, in the case of a record, shall on request provide any assistance that is reasonably necessary to interpret the record or to produce it in a readable form.

(8) Things removed — An inspector who removes a motor vehicle, equipment, record or other thing under clause (3)(e) or (f) or to whom a motor vehicle, equipment, record or other thing is delivered pursuant to a demand made under clause (3)(d) shall give a receipt for the motor vehicle, equipment, record or thing and return it to the person who produced or delivered it within a reasonable time.

(9) Copy admissible in evidence — A copy of a record that purports to be certified by an inspector as being a true copy of the original is admissible in evidence to the same extent as the original, and has the same evidentiary value.

(10) Obstruction — No person shall hinder, obstruct or interfere with an inspector conducting an inspection, refuse to answer questions on matters relevant to the inspection or provide the inspector with information, on matters relevant to the inspection, that the person knows to be false or misleading.

(11) Regulations re costs of inspection — The Minister may make regulations requiring licensees to pay to the Ministry the costs of any inspection conducted under this section.

(12) Definition — In this section,

"inspection" includes an examination, test, audit, inquiry and investigation.

2005, c. 26, Sched. A, s. 10

Related Provisions: See O. Reg. 473/07, Licences for Driving Instructors and Driving Schools.

PART V — GARAGE AND STORAGE LICENCES

59. (1) Licence respecting dealing in motor vehicles, etc. — No person shall deal in motor vehicles or trailers, operate a used car lot or engage in the business of wrecking or dismantling of vehicles without having been licensed so to do by the Ministry in respect of each separate premises used by the person for the purpose of the business.

(2) Exception — Subsection (1) does not apply to a person who is registered as a motor vehicle dealer in accordance with the *Motor Vehicle Dealers Act, 2002*.

(3) Fee — The fee for the licence shall be such as may be fixed from time to time by the Lieutenant Governor in Council on the recommendation of the Minister.

(4) Penalty — Every person who deals in motor vehicles or trailers or operates a used car lot or engages in the wrecking or dismantling of vehicles in contravention of subsection (1) is guilty of an offence and on conviction is liable to a fine of not more than $1000.

(5) Right of entry and inspection — Any police officer or any officer appointed for carrying out the provisions of this Part may enter into any place where motor vehicles, trailers or bicycles are stored or dealt in, or into any garage, repair shop, used car lot or premises used for the wrecking or dismantling of vehicles, and make the investigation and inspection that he or she thinks proper for the purposes of this Part.

(6) **Penalty for interference with police officer** — Every person who obstructs, molests or interferes with any police officer or officer in the performance of his or her duties under subsection (5) is guilty of an offence and on conviction is liable to a fine of not less than $100 and not more than $500 or to imprisonment for a term of not more than six months, or to both.

(7) **Suspension or cancellation of licence by Minister** — The Minister may suspend or cancel the licence issued for dealing in motor vehicles or trailers, operating a used car lot, or for wrecking or dismantling vehicles, for misconduct or for non-compliance with or infraction of any of this Act or the regulations by the holder of the licence or by any of the licence holder's employees or for any other reason appearing to him or her to be sufficient.

(8) **Regulations** — The Lieutenant Governor in Council may make regulations controlling and governing the business of dealing in motor vehicles or trailers, operating a garage, repair shop or used car lot, or the wrecking or dismantling of vehicles.

(9) **Definition** — In this section, "motor vehicle" does not include a motor assisted bicycle.

2002, c. 30, Sched. E, s. 7

Case Law

R. v. Hajivasilis (2013), 41 M.V.R. (6th) 175, 2013 ONCA 27, 2013 CarswellOnt 508, 114 O.R. (3d) 337, 302 O.A.C. 65, [2013] O.J. No. 253 (Ont. C.A.) — The requirements are not restricted to "highways".

Related Provisions: Motor Vehicle Dealers Act, R.S.O. 1990, c. M.42; Motor Vehicle Dealers Act, 2002, S.O. 2002, c. 30, Sched. B, Motor Vehicle Repair Act, R.S.O. 1990, c. M.43, see also R.R.O. 1990, Reg. 595, Garage Licences.

60. (1) **Record of second-hand vehicles bought, sold, etc.** — Every person who buys, sells, wrecks or otherwise deals in second-hand motor vehicles, trailers or bicycles shall keep a complete record of all motor vehicles, trailers and bicycles bought, sold or wrecked and of the information that will enable the motor vehicles, trailers and bicycles to be readily identified, and shall transmit to the Ministry, within six days after the event, on forms furnished by the Ministry, a statement of each motor vehicle or trailer bought, sold or wrecked by the person and the information with reference thereto that may be required by the Ministry.

(2) **Prohibition as to buying where number obliterated** — No person shall buy, sell, wreck or otherwise deal with any motor vehicle or bicycle or a trailer that has a gross weight exceeding 1,360 kilograms where the manufacturer's vehicle identification number or similar identifying mark has been obliterated or defaced or is not readily recognizable.

(3) **Defacing vehicle identification** — No person shall deface or remove the manufacturer's vehicle identification number or identifying mark from a motor vehicle or from the engine thereof or from a bicycle or from a trailer that has a gross weight exceeding 1,360 kilograms.

(4) Report as to cars stored or parked — If a motor vehicle is placed in the possession of a person who repairs, buys, sells, wrecks or stores motor vehicles or operates a garage business, parking station, parking lot or used car lot and the vehicle remains in the person's possession for more than two weeks without good reason, the person shall forthwith, upon the expiration of the two-week period, make a report to the nearest police officer in accordance with subsection (6).

(5) Report as to damaged or bullet-marked cars — If a motor vehicle that shows evidence of having been involved in a serious accident or having been struck by a bullet is brought into a garage, parking station, parking lot, used car lot or repair shop, the person in charge of the garage, parking station, parking lot, used car lot or repair shop shall forthwith make a report to the nearest police officer in accordance with subsection (6).

(6) Information to be reported — A person making a report under subsection (4) or (5) shall give a description of the vehicle and, if known, the vehicle identification number, the permit number, and the name and address of the owner or operator.

(7) Offence — Every person who contravenes,

    (a) subsection (1) is guilty of an offence and on conviction is liable to a fine of not less than $50 and not more than $100;

    (b) subsection (2) or (3) is guilty of an offence and on conviction is liable to a fine of not less than $500 and not more than $1,000;

    (c) subsection (4) is guilty of an offence and on conviction is liable to a fine of not less than $20 and not more than $100;

    (d) subsection (5) is guilty of an offence and on conviction is liable to a fine of not less than $100 and not more than $500.

Case Law

R. v. Hajivasilis (2013), 41 M.V.R. (6th) 175, 2013 ONCA 27, 2013 CarswellOnt 508, 114 O.R. (3d) 337, 302 O.A.C. 65, [2013] O.J. No. 253 (Ont. C.A.) — The requirements are not restricted to "highways".

PART VI — EQUIPMENT

61. Definitions — In this Part,

"ambulance" [Repealed 2009, c. 5, s. 27.]

"fire department vehicle" [Repealed 2009, c. 5, s. 27.]

"motor vehicle" does not include a motor assisted bicycle;

"vehicle", in addition to the meaning set out in subsection 1(1), includes a conversion unit and a trailer converter dolly.

2009, c. 5, s. 27

62. (1) Lamps required on all motor vehicles except motorcycles —
When on a highway at any time from one-half hour before sunset to one-half hour
after sunrise and at any other time when, due to insufficient light or unfavourable
atmospheric conditions, persons and vehicles on the highway are not clearly discernible at a distance of 150 metres or less, every motor vehicle other than a motorcycle
shall carry three lighted lamps in a conspicuous position, one on each side of the
front of the vehicle which shall display a white or amber light only, and one on the
rear of the vehicle which shall display a red light only.

(2) Lamps required on motorcycles — Subject to subsection (3), when on a
highway at any time every motorcycle shall carry two lighted lamps in a conspicuous position, one on the front of the vehicle which shall display a white light only,
and one on the rear of the vehicle which shall display a red light only.

(3) Idem — When on a highway at any time every motorcycle with a side car shall
carry a lighted lamp in a conspicuous position on each side of the front of the vehicle
which lamps shall display a white or amber light only and a lighted lamp on the rear
of the vehicle which shall display a red light only.

(4) Light requirement — Any lamp required under subsection (1), (2) or (3)
shall, when lighted, be clearly visible at a distance of at least 150 metres from the
front or rear, as the case may be.

(5) Exception — Despite subsections (2) and (3), where a motorcycle that was
manufactured prior to the 1st day of January, 1970 is operated on a highway, the
lighted lamps required under subsections (2) and (3) shall be required only during
the period from one-half hour before sunset to one-half hour after sunrise, or at any
other time when, due to insufficient light or unfavourable atmospheric conditions,
persons and vehicles on the highway are not clearly discernible at a distance of 150
metres or less.

(6) Strength of lamps — Lamps on the front of a motor vehicle shall be so constructed, located, arranged and adjusted that when lighted as required by subsections (1), (2) and (3) they produce under normal atmospheric conditions and on a
level road a driving light sufficient to render clearly discernible to the operator of
the motor vehicle any person or vehicle on the highway within a distance of 110
metres ahead of the motor vehicle.

(7) Attachment that affects lamps prohibited — No person shall drive upon
a highway a motor vehicle if either or both of the lamps that are required on the
front of the vehicle by subsections (1), (2) and (3),

(a) are coated or covered with a coloured material; or

(b) have been modified by the attachment to the lamps or the motor vehicle of
any device that reduces the effective area of the lenses or the intensity of the
beam of the lamps.

(7.1) Exception — Clause (7)(a) does not apply if the lamps are of the prescribed
type or meet the prescribed standards.

(8) Lighted streets — Subsection (6) does not apply to a motor vehicle parked on
a highway and subsections (1), (2), (3), (10), (11), (13), (23), (24), (26) and (27) do not

apply to a vehicle parked on a highway upon which the speed limit is not greater than 50 kilometres per hour and which is so lighted by the means of any system of street or highway lighting that the vehicle is clearly discernible within a distance of sixty metres.

(9) Strength of front lamps — No motor vehicle shall carry on the front thereof more than four lighted lamps that project a beam having an intensity of over 300 candela.

(10) Clearance lamps required on wide vehicles — When on a highway at any time from one-half hour before sunset to one-half hour after sunrise and at any other time when, due to insufficient light or unfavourable atmospheric conditions, persons and vehicles on the highway are not clearly discernible at a distance of 150 metres or less,

> (a) every commercial motor vehicle and trailer having a width at any part in excess of 2.05 metres, other than a truck tractor, shall carry, in addition to the lamps required by subsection (1), two lighted clearance lamps, one on each side of the front of the vehicle, which shall display an amber light, and two lighted clearance lamps, one on each side of the rear of the vehicle, which shall display a red light; or

> (b) every truck tractor having a width at any part in excess of 2.05 metres shall carry, in addition to the lamps required by subsection (1), two lighted clearance lamps, one on each side of the front of the vehicle, which shall display an amber light, and one lighted clearance lamp on the left side of the rear of the vehicle, which shall display a red light,

and the Ministry may by regulation permit a reflector, approved by the Ministry, to be displayed in lieu of clearance lamps on the rear of the vehicle, and all the lamps shall be affixed so as to indicate the overall width of the vehicle.

(11) Identification lamps — When on a highway at any time from one-half hour before sunset to one-half hour after sunrise and at any other time when, due to insufficient light or unfavourable atmospheric conditions, persons and vehicles on the highway are not clearly discernible at a distance of 150 metres or less, every commercial motor vehicle or combination of a commercial motor vehicle and a trailer having a length in excess of 9.2 metres or a width in excess of 2.05 metres shall carry three lighted lamps displaying green or amber lights at the front, except in the case of a public vehicle which shall display amber lights at the front, and three lighted lamps displaying red lights at the rear, and the lights of each colour shall be evenly placed not less than 150 millimetres nor more than 310 millimetres apart along a horizontal line as near the top of the commercial motor vehicle or combination of a commercial motor vehicle and a trailer as the permanent structure permits, and shall be visible for distances of 150 metres from the front and rear respectively of the commercial motor vehicle or combination of a commercial motor vehicle and a trailer.

(12) Rear identification lamps on tractor without trailer — Notwithstanding subsection (11), a truck tractor driver on a highway without a trailer or semi-trailer is not required to carry the three red lamps displaying red lights to the rear.

(13) Side marker lamps — When on a highway at any time from one-half hour before sunset to one-half hour after sunrise and at any other time when, due to insufficient light or unfavourable atmospheric conditions, persons and vehicles on the highway are not clearly discernible at a distance of 150 metres or less, every motor vehicle or combination of vehicles having a length in excess of 6.1 metres shall carry not fewer than four lighted side marker lamps, one of which shall be located on each side of the vehicle or combination of vehicles near the front and shall display a green or amber light and one of which shall be located on each side of the vehicle or combination of vehicles near the rear and shall display a red light and each of which lights shall be visible for a distance of 150 metres from the side of the vehicle or combination of vehicles upon which it is located; provided that a vehicle or combination of vehicles may carry four reflectors approved by the Ministry instead of the side marker lamps required by this section; and provided further that, if the clearance lamps upon the left side of any vehicle or combination of vehicles display lights visible for a distance of 150 metres from the left side of the vehicle or combination of vehicles, it is not necessary to carry side marker lamps as required by this subsection on the left side of the vehicle.

(14) Intermittent red light restricted — Subject to subsections (14.1), (15) and (17.1), no person shall use a lamp, other than the vehicular hazard warning signal lamps commonly known as four way flashers, that produces intermittent flashes of red light.

(14.1) Red and blue lights to the front restricted — In addition to the lighting requirements in this Part, a police department vehicle may carry lamps that cast red and blue lights, but no other motor vehicle shall carry any lamp that casts red and blue lights to the front.

(15) Red light in front — In addition to the lighting requirements in this Part, a vehicle described in subsection (15.1) may carry lamps that cast a red light only or such other colour of light that may, with the approval of the ministry, be designated by a by-law of the municipality in which the vehicle is operated, but no other motor vehicle shall carry any lamp that casts a red light to the front.

(15.1) Same — The following are vehicles to which subsection (15) applies:

1. An ambulance, fire department vehicle, police department vehicle, public utility emergency vehicle or school bus.

2. A ministry vehicle operated by an officer appointed for carrying out the provisions of this Act or the *Public Vehicles Act*, while the officer is in the course of his or her employment.

3. A vehicle while operated by a conservation officer, fishery officer, provincial park officer or mine rescue training officer, while the officer is in the course of his or her employment.

4. A vehicle while operated by a provincial officer designated under the *Environmental Protection Act*, the *Nutrient Management Act, 2002*, the *Ontario Water Resources Act*, the *Pesticides Act*, the *Safe Drinking Water Act, 2002* or the *Toxics Reduction Act, 2009*, while the officer is in the course of his or her employment.

5. A prescribed class or type of vehicle, driven by a prescribed class of persons or engaged in a prescribed activity or in prescribed conditions or circumstances.

(16) Green flashing light restricted — The following persons may carry on or in his or her vehicle and operate a lamp that produces intermittent flashes of green light:

1. A firefighter, within the meaning of subsection 1(1) of the *Fire Protection and Prevention Act, 1997*, while proceeding to a fire or other emergency.

2. A prescribed class of volunteer medical responder, while driving a prescribed class or type of vehicle or engaging in a prescribed activity or in prescribed conditions or circumstances.

(16.1) Same — No person other than a person described in subsection (16) shall operate a lamp that produces intermittent flashes of green light.

(17) Lights and reflectors on bicycles, etc. — When on a highway at any time from one-half hour before sunset to one-half hour after sunrise and at any other time when, due to insufficient light or unfavourable atmospheric conditions, persons and vehicles on the highway are not clearly discernible at a distance of 150 metres or less, every motor-assisted bicycle and bicycle (other than a unicycle) shall carry a lighted lamp displaying a white or amber light on its front and a lighted lamp displaying a red light or a reflector on its rear, and in addition white reflective material shall be placed on its front forks, and red reflective material covering a surface of not less than 250 millimetres in length and 25 millimetres in width shall be placed on its rear.

(17.1) Same — A bicycle may carry a lighted lamp on its rear that produces intermittent flashes of red light at any time, and may carry such a lamp at the times described in subsection (17) instead of or in addition to the lighted lamp displaying a red light or reflector required by that subsection.

(18) [Repealed 2015, c. 14, s. 21(3).]

(19) Rear lamps to illuminate number plate — The lamp on the rear of a motor vehicle or trailer shall be of at least three candela and shall be so placed that it will, at any time from one-half hour before sunset to one-half hour after sunrise and at any other time when, due to insufficient light or unfavourable atmospheric conditions, persons and vehicles on the highway are not clearly discernible at a distance of 150 metres or less, illuminate the numbers on the number plate, or, if provision is made on the number plate or on any attachment furnished or required by the Ministry for affixing the lamp, it shall be affixed in the position or space provided, and the lamp shall face to the rear and reflect on the number plate a white light only.

(20) Parking lights — A motor vehicle, other than a commercial motor vehicle, while standing upon a highway at the times that lights are required by this section for the vehicle may, in lieu of the lighting equipment specified in this section, show one light carried on the left side of the vehicle in such a manner as to be clearly visible to the front and rear for a distance of at least sixty metres and to show white to the front and red to the rear of the vehicle; provided that the light shall not be displayed while the motor vehicle is in motion.

(21) Regulations as to lights on vehicles — The Lieutenant Governor in Council may make regulations,

(a) prescribing the type and maximum strength of lights that shall be carried by vehicles, and regulating the location, direction, focus and use of the lights;

(b) regulating or prohibiting the use of lights on vehicles that automatically produce intermittent flashes of light;

(c) prescribing types of, or standards for, lamps coated or covered with a coloured material that may be used for the purpose of subsection (7.1);

(d) prescribing classes or types of vehicles, classes of drivers, activities, conditions and circumstances for the purpose of paragraph 5 of subsection (15.1);

(e) prescribing classes of volunteer medical responders, classes or types of vehicles, activities, conditions and circumstances for the purpose of paragraph 2 of subsection (16);

(f) governing the training, qualifications and certification of persons prescribed under clause (d) or (e) or who may drive vehicles prescribed under those clauses.

(21.1) Same — A regulation made under clause (21)(c) may prescribe different types of lamps and different standards for different classes of motor vehicles.

(21.2) Same — A regulation made under subsection (21) may provide differently for different classes of persons, different types or classes of vehicles or for different activities, conditions or circumstances.

(22) Spotlamps — No motor vehicle, other than a public utility emergency vehicle, shall be equipped with more than one spotlamp and every lighted spotlamp shall be so directed, upon approaching or upon the approach of another vehicle, that no part of the high intensity portion of the beam from the lamp will be directed to the left of the prolongation of the extreme left side, nor more than thirty metres ahead, of the vehicle to which it is attached.

(23) Lamps to be carried on engine — Every traction engine shall, at any time from one-half hour before sunset to one-half hour after sunrise and at any other time when, due to insufficient light or unfavourable atmospheric conditions, persons and vehicles on the highway are not clearly discernible at a distance of 150 metres or less, carry a lighted lamp in a conspicuous place in front, which shall display a white or green light only, and one on the rear of the engine or of any vehicle that may be attached to it, which shall display a red light only.

(24) Lamps required on rear of trailer, etc. — When on a highway at any time from one-half hour before sunset to one-half hour after sunrise and at any other time when, due to insufficient light or unfavourable atmospheric conditions, persons and vehicles on the highway are not clearly discernible at a distance of 150 metres or less, every trailer and every object or contrivance drawn by a vehicle shall carry on the rear thereof one lighted lamp, which shall display a red light only.

(25) **Lights on vehicles, objects and contrivances over 2.6 metres in width** — When on a highway at any time from one-half hour before sunset to one-half hour after sunrise and at any other time when, due to insufficient light or unfavourable atmospheric conditions, persons and vehicles on the highway are not clearly discernible at a distance of 150 metres or less, every vehicle, and every object or contrivance drawn by a vehicle, having a width at any part in excess of 2.6 metres, shall carry at the rear two lighted lamps displaying red lights or two red reflectors, one of which shall be affixed as nearly as possible to the extreme left side and one as nearly as possible to the extreme right side of the vehicle, and such lamps or reflectors shall be clearly visible at a distance of at least 150 metres from the rear of the vehicle.

(26) **Lamps on all vehicles, except motor vehicles, etc.** — Subject to subsection (28), every vehicle, other than a motor vehicle, motor-assisted bicycle, bicycle (except a unicycle) or a vehicle referred to in subsection (24), (25) or (27), when on a highway at any time from one-half hour before sunset to one-half hour after sunrise and at any other time when, due to insufficient light or unfavourable atmospheric conditions, persons and vehicles on the highway are not clearly discernible at a distance of 150 metres or less, shall carry in a conspicuous position on the left side a lighted lamp which shall display a white light to the front and a red light to the rear or a lighted lamp which shall display a white light to the front and a lighted lamp which shall display a red light to the rear, and any lamp so used shall be clearly visible at a distance of at least 150 metres from the front and the rear of the vehicle, as the case may be.

(27) **Lights on farm tractors** — Every farm tractor and every self-propelled unit of farm equipment or implement of husbandry equipped with an electric lighting system, when on a highway at any time from one-half hour before sunset to one-half hour after sunrise and at any other time when, due to insufficient light or unfavourable atmospheric conditions, persons and vehicles on the highway are not clearly discernible at a distance of 150 metres or less, shall carry the lighted lamps required for motor vehicles under subsection (1).

(28) **Reflectors in certain cases** — The Ministry may by regulation permit a reflector approved by the Ministry to be displayed instead of a lighted lamp on vehicles commonly used for conveying flammable materials or vehicles that are structurally unsuitable for carrying lighted lamps.

(29) **Signalling devices required on trucks, buses, etc.** — Every motor vehicle or combination of motor vehicle and trailer having a width at any part in excess of 2.05 metres or having a length in excess of 6.1 metres shall be equipped with mechanical or electrical signalling devices that comply with subsections 142(6) and (8).

(30) **Visibility of lights** — Where any light is required by any provision of this Act to be visible for a specified distance, the requirement shall be deemed to apply during the times indicated in the provision upon level ground and under normal atmospheric conditions.

(31) **Flashing blue light on snow-removal equipment** — No person shall, while operating a road service vehicle on a highway, plow, salt or de-ice the highway

or apply chemicals or abrasives to the highway for snow or ice control unless the road service vehicle is equipped with a lamp producing intermittent flashes of blue light visible for a distance of 150 metres from all directions.

(32) Restriction on use of flashing blue light — No person shall operate a lamp that produces intermittent flashes of blue light on a highway except,

    (a) a person operating a road service vehicle in the circumstances described in subsection (31); or

    (b) a person operating a police department vehicle, together with a lamp that produces intermittent flashes of red light, as permitted by subsection (14.1).

(33) Penalty — commercial motor vehicle — Every person who contravenes subsection (1), (6), (7), (9), (10), (11), (13), (14), (14.1), (15), (16.1), (22), (24), (25), (26), (29), (31) or (32) or who contravenes a regulation made under subsection (21) is guilty of an offence and, if the offence was committed by means of a commercial motor vehicle within the meaning of subsection 16(1), on conviction is liable to a fine of not less than $200 and not more than $20,000.

> **Proposed Amendment — 62(33)**
>
> **(33) Penalty — commercial motor vehicle** — Every person who contravenes subsection (1), (6), (7), (9), (10), (11), (13), (14), (14.1), (15), (16.1), (22), (24), (25), (26), (29), (31) or (32) or who contravenes a regulation made under subsection (21) is guilty of an offence and, if the offence was committed by means of a commercial motor vehicle, on conviction is liable to a fine of not less than $200 and not more than $20,000.
>
> 2014, c. 9, Sched. 2, s. 22 [To come into force January 1, 2017.]

1994, c. 35, s. 1; 1996, c. 20, s. 13; 1996, c. 33, s. 11; 1997, c. 4, s. 81; 1998, c. 35, s. 103; 2002, c. 4, s. 64; 2002, c. 18, Sched. P, s. 19; 2007, c. 13, s. 17; 2009, c. 5, s. 28; 2009, c. 19, s. 68(1); 2015, c. 14, s. 21

Commentary

This comprehensive section requires that all vehicles (subs. (1)) and motorcycles (subs. (2)) have front and rear lights which shall be on one-half hour before sunset to one-half hour after sunrise. Lights shall be visible for 150 metres (subss. (4) and (30)). The strength of lamps shall permit the driver to see in front 110 metres (subs. (6)). Covering or coating is prohibited (subs. (7)), as are excessively bright lights (subss. (9) and (14)).

Commercial motor vehicles and combinations of vehicles have their own requirements (subss. (10)–(13)). Emergency and like vehicles must comply with subss. (15) and (16). Bicycles and like vehicles must comply with subs. (17) or the driver is liable under subs. (18).

Number plates must be illuminated (subs. (19)) and parking lights are required (subs. (20)).

The use of spotlamps is restricted (subs. (22)). Tractor engines must have lamps (subs. (23)).

The rear of trailers and objects which are towed are subject to subss. (24) and (25). The section regulates lights on farm tractors (subs. (27)) and any other vehicle on a highway (subs. (26)).

189

Certain vehicles may require reflectors (subs. (28)).

Wide vehicles require special signalling devices (subs. (29)).

Limitations on the use of flashing blue lights are set out in subss. (31) and (32).

Regulations may be made regarding lights pursuant to subs. (21).

The adequacy of lights on vehicles for various purposes has been a frequent subject of litigation, the question almost invariably being related to the more comprehensive duty resting on a driver to keep a proper lookout. A breach of the provisions in this section, and also inadequate lighting in other respects, have in many instances been held to constitute negligence, but in the great majority of the cases such negligence has been found to be no more than contributory or to have not been causative of the accident at all.

Case Law

General

Brooks v. Ward, [1956] S.C.R. 683; *McCallum v. Tetroe and Polenski* (1958), 25 W.W.R. 49 (Man. C.A.); *Holgate v. Can. Tumbler Co.* (1931), 40 O.W.N. 565 (C.A.); *Billings v. Mooers & McGuire*, [1937] 4 D.L.R. 518, 11 M.P.R. 553 (N.B. C.A.); *Dugas v. Le Clair* (1962), 32 D.L.R. (2d) 459; *Bruce v. McIntyre*, [1955] S.C.R. 251; *Ritchie v. Ptaff*, [1954] O.W.N. 865 (C.A.) — The fact that a vehicle may be improperly lit will be immaterial if a clear line of demarcation can be drawn between this and the negligence of the other party that actually caused the accident.

Bedard v. Fortier, [1964] Que. S.C. 474 (S.C.) — Even where there is no statutory requirement for lights, as, *e.g.*, for horse-drawn carts, the common law may require that lights or reflectors be used during periods of darkness or poor visibility.

R. v. Rodrigues (2013), 62 M.V.R. (6th) 331, 2013 ONCJ 719, 2013 CarswellOnt 18477, [2013] O.J. No. 6041 — Under s. 62(29), a set fine for a non-commercial vehicle was $85 and $200 for a commercial vehicle. The certificate was irregular as the fine was set at $85 and the certificate indicated that the vehicle was commercial. Notwithstanding that the error favoured the defendant the certificate was not regular and could not support a conviction.

Headlights

R. v. Lightheart, [1952] Ex. C.R. 12 — The fact that a motorist drives his or her car on the highway in the dark without lights constitutes negligence.

Maxwell v. Callbeck, [1939] S.C.R. 440, [1939] 3 D.L.R. 580 — Even in the absence of any statutory provision, a driver will not be excused for failing to have on the front of the vehicle a light not only sufficient for his or her driving purposes, but ample to properly warn others of his or her approach. Anything less would constitute negligence on the driver's part.

Wilkins v. Weyer, [1946] 3 W.W.R. 418 (Sask. C.A.); *Currie v. Nilson* (1954), 13 W.W.R. 497 (Man. Q.B.) — Driving with only one headlight burning was held to be actionable negligence. However, there will be no liability if the driver did not know, and could not reasonably have known, that the headlamp had failed, as might be the case just after sundown and before full darkness.

Elder v. Lockridge, [1952] O.W.N. 210, [1952] 3 D.L.R. 418 (C.A.); *Western Can. Greyhound Lines Ltd. v. Trans-Can. Auto Tpt.* (1952), 6 W.W.R. 695 (Alta. T.D.);

Carlson v. Chochinov, [1947] 1 W.W.R. 755, [1947] 2 D.L.R. 641 (Man. K.B.) — Driving with dimmed headlights, and therefore not seeing the other vehicle or object on the highway as soon as the driver should have, was held to be contributory negligence.

Casselman v. Sawyer, [1954] O.W.N. 50 (C.A.) — It was negligence not to turn the headlights back to high beam as soon as reasonably possible after passing the car for which they had been dipped.

Dazzling Lights

Ward v. R., [1954] Ex. C.R. 185; reversed on other grounds *Brooks v. Ward and R.*, [1956] S.C.R. 683; *Tinker v. Gobel*, [1931] 2 W.W.R. 413 (Sask. C.A.); *Bennett v. Gardewine*, [1948] 2 W.W.R. 474 (Man. K.B.); *Rubin v. Steeves* (1951), 28 M.P.R. 421 (N.B.C.A.) — The failure to dim headlights, and therefore cause unnecessary dazzle to an approaching driver, may, in some circumstances, be negligence.

Brockie v. McKay, [1934] 1 W.W.R. 725, [1934] 2 D.L.R. 690 (Man. C.A.) — Interference with a driver's vision by the lights of an approaching car was accepted as an excuse, under the circumstances, for his colliding with a car parked without a tail-light.

Forrest v. Davidson and Melnyk (1951), 4 W.W.R. (N.S.) 273 (Sask. C.A.) — Recognition was given to the fact that a motorist, after passing an oncoming car carrying the lights required by law, cannot see well during the short time it takes his or her eyes to become accustomed again to the comparative darkness.

Voth v. Friesen, 15 W.W.R. 625, [1955] 4 D.L.R. 509 (Man. C.A.); *Le Blanc v. Ouellet*, [1948] Que. S.C. 127 (S.C.); *Pelrine v. MacDonald* (1957), 39 M.P.R. 300 (N.S. T.D.) — The duty of a driver dazzled by approaching lights cannot be clearly stated. There is some authority for the proposition that a driver so "blinded" should stop or reduce speed so as to be able to stop instantly if danger arises. A driver is under a duty to be able to see a reasonable distance ahead or proceed with more than usual caution.

Northern Elec. Co. v. Kelly, [1931] 3 W.W.R. 527 (Sask. C.A.) — However, there can be no general rule in this regard. If it is the duty of one driver to stop, it would also often be the duty of the other driver to stop, since he or she would in all probability be affected in the same way, and the result on a well-travelled highway might well be an almost complete stoppage of traffic.

Armand v. Carr, [1926] S.C.R. 575; *Northern Elec. Co. v. Kelly, supra; Smith v. McConnell Bros.* (1954), 11 W.W.R. 600 (Man. Q.B.) — In a particular case, knowledge, *e.g.*, that the roadway was often used by pedestrians, might call for much greater care, but the surrounding circumstances in each case can alone determine the conduct of the "dazzled" driver.

Driving Within Range of Lights

Tart v. G.W. Chitty & Co., [1933] 2 K.B. 453 (D.C.); *Baker v. Longhurst & Sons Ltd.*, [1933] 2 K.B. 461 (C.A.); *Ristow v. Wetstein*, [1934] S.C.R. 128, [1934] 1 D.L.R. 787 — Generally speaking, a driver who runs into a stationary vehicle or other object on the highway will not have an easy task in establishing that he or she was not negligent and was keeping a proper lookout, although it is open for him or her to do so if possible. It would seem to be that a person driving at night must drive at such a speed that he or she can pull up within the limits of vision and, on colliding with anything, is faced with the dilemma that either he or she was driving at an undue speed, or was not keeping a proper lookout, unless there was some other factor causative of the collision.

Brockie v. McKay, [1934] 1 W.W.R. 725, [1934] 2 D.L.R. 690 (Man. C.A.) — The mere occurrence of the collision is not, in itself, conclusive evidence of excessive speed or improper lookout.

Irvine v. Metro. Tpt. Co., [1933] O.R. 823, [1933] 4 D.L.R. 682 (C.A.); *Ritchie v. Ptaff*, [1954] O.W.N. 865 (C.A.); *Engele v. Poss* (1958), 16 D.L.R. (2d) 430 (Sask. C.A.) — There certainly is no rule of law that a motor vehicle must in all cases, without exception or qualification, be limited mathematically to such a rate that the vehicle can be brought to a standstill without collision after the driver (keeping a reasonable lookout) observes a stationary object confronting him or her.

Bruce v. McIntyre, [1955] S.C.R. 251 — Persons driving on the highway at night are entitled to proceed on the assumption that the drivers of other vehicles will comply with the provisions of the Act as to lighting, flares and other warning devices.

Stewart v. Hancock, [1940] 2 All E.R. 427, [1941] 1 W.W.R. 161 (P.C.); *Burnett v. Christie Brown & Co.*, [1946] O.W.N. 30 (C.A.); *Western Can. Greyhound Lines Ltd. v. Lord*, [1953] 2 D.L.R. 694 (S.C.C.); *Elder v. Lockridge*, [1952] O.W.N. 210, [1952] 3 D.L.R. 418 (C.A.); *Smyrski v. Smirnos* (1958), 66 Man. R. 105 (C.A.) — It can be safely said that there is no rule of law that a careful driver is bound under all circumstances to see an unlighted object in time to avoid it; each case must depend on its own facts.

Rear Lights and Clearance Lights

Sterling Trusts Corp. v. Postma, [1965] S.C.R. 324, 48 D.L.R. (2d) 423; *Falsetto v. Brown*, [1933] O.R. 645, [1933] 3 D.L.R. 545 (C.A.) — The mere fact that the rear light was not burning did not, of itself, impose liability on the owner or driver; it had to be shown that that state resulted from negligence.

Grubbe v. Grubbe, [1953] O.W.N. 626 (C.A.) — Where the accident occurred seconds after the defendant's vehicle had stalled, and there was no evidence and no suggestion that the rear light was out before the vehicle stopped, it was said that it would be quite unreasonable and improper to hold him liable solely on the ground that the rear light was out.

Connell v. Olsen, [1933] 1 W.W.R. 654 (Man. C.A.); *Schmidt v. McLaughlan* (1971), 4 N.B.R. (2d) 385 (Q.B.); *Rawding v. Crouse* (1970), 1 N.S.R. (2d) 562 (T.D.) — The complete absence of any rear lamp at all was held to be negligence.

Eastern Metals Corp. v. Proteau, [1960] S.C.R. 96; *Wolman v. Wood* (1959), 43 M.P.R. 1 (N.S. T.D.) — Liability stemmed from inadequate lighting on a truck transporting rails or pipes which protruded beyond the end of the vehicle.

Ritchie v. Ptaff, [1954] O.W.N. 865 (C.A.) — The absence of lighted lamps on the back of a tractor at a time when other vehicles had lighted theirs has been held to be concurrent negligence contributing to the accident. If the lights had been lighted, it is common experience that a motorist, unless totally oblivious to all that is about him or her, naturally sees the red lights ahead and is put on guard.

Tinling v. Bauch (1951), 59 Man. R. 310 (K.B.); *Antoine v. Larocque*, [1954] O.W.N. 641 (H.C.) — Full compliance with all the requirements of the Act as to rear lights may not be necessary if, in fact, reasonable warning of the presence of the vehicle on the highway has been given. Thus, two red clearance lights of the same power and range of visibility as required of a tail light by the Act were held to give an adequate warning to overtaking vehicles, and it could not be said that the failure to have an operative tail light was a contributing cause to the collision.

Jordan v. Fitzgerald & Coakley, [1949] O.W.N. 730 (H.C.) — Having only a reflector, and no red lamp, on the rear of a motorcycle was held under the circumstances to be an inadequate warning, and to be negligence contributing to the accident.

Fralick v. G.T.R. Co. (1910), 43 S.C.R. 494 — Since specific types of rear lights are required by the statute as a warning, a person substitutes means other than those prescribed entirely at his or her own peril. To discharge him or herself from liability, the person must see that the protection thus provided proves efficacious. That person takes the risk of all injuries which observance of the statute would probably have prevented.

Carroll v. Cudney and Bennett, [1963] 1 O.R. 551, 38 D.L.R. (2d) 113 (H.C.) — A driver operating a tractor on the highway after dark without either the prescribed, or suitable alternative, rear lights was held solely responsible for the collision and the other driver approaching from the rear was excused from seeing the unlighted tractor by reason of the glare of other headlights.

Kuhnle v. Ottawa Elec. Ry., [1946] 3 D.L.R. 681 (Ont. C.A.) — The plaintiff's car was struck from the rear by the defendant's motor bus at night when there was a dense fog making the visibility poor. The defendant contended that the car did not have the requisite lamps alight. It was held that: (i) the onus that the tail light was burning at the time of the accident rested on the plaintiff, and (ii) the requirements as to visibility of the rear lights did not apply under the abnormal atmospheric conditions prevailing.

Sterling Trusts Corp. v. Postma, supra — Where the alleged negligence is that the tail light of the vehicle was not lighted, the onus rests on the party to prove his or her allegation.

Equilease Co. v. Daley (1978), 27 N.B.R. (2d) 539, 60 A.P.R. 539, [1989] I.L.R. 88-165 (Q.B.) — The defendant's trailer was not equipped with rear lights, contrary to the Act. A rear-end collision occurred on a well-lighted urban street at dusk. The plaintiff's claim was dismissed because the accident was not due to an absence of trailer lights but to the plaintiff's inattention and to the fact that he was following too closely.

Hingtgen v. Everett (1988), 53 Man. R. (2d) 157 (Q.B.) — A pedestrian suddenly appeared in the roadway. The driver swerved, lost control of his vehicle, and landed in a ditch, and so injured his wife, a passenger. The accident occurred at night on a road where no other vehicles were approaching. The driver was found 25% liable for not making use of his highbeams at the time.

Thring Estate v. Vecchioli (1987), 62 Sask. R. 83 (Q.B.); affirmed (1990), 83 Sask. R. 137 (C.A.) — The plaintiff and her husband were riding on a motorcycle. The plaintiff was injured and her husband was killed when the motorcycle collided with a car operated by the defendant. The rear lights were not working at the time of the accident, and the back of the vehicle was in darkness. The defendant was found 80% liable.

R. v. Zanoski (2004), 5 M.V.R. (5th) 101, 2004 ONCJ 19, 2004 CarswellOnt 1552 (Ont. C.J.) — Where the accused had a proper rear light and an additional ten-inch neon blue ultraviolet tube light installed on the top of his rear window, a charge of driving without a proper rear light did not lie.

Related Provisions: See ss. 142(6) and (8) of the Act regarding signalling devices for wide vehicles and buses; see R.R.O. 1990, Reg. 587, Equipment; R.R.O. 1990, Reg.

596, General; R.R.O. 1990, Reg. 611, Safety Inspections; O. Reg. 484/07, Lamps — Use of Flashing Red or Green Lights; O. Reg. 316/03, Operation of Off-Road Vehicles on Highways; O. Reg. 455/07, Races, Contests and Stunts, Safety Inspections; see also the Motor Vehicle Safety Act, S.C. 1993, c. 16.

63. Vehicles with right hand drive — Every vehicle that is equipped with a right hand drive shall, unless it is equipped with a mechanical or electrical signal device as described in subsection 142(6), have prominently displayed on the rear thereof, in bold face letters of not less than 50 millimetres in height and of a colour which is in contrast to that of the vehicle, the words,

"RIGHT HAND DRIVE VEHICLE".

Case Law

R. v. Anderson, [1946] S.C.R. 129 — The existence of a sign on the rear of a vehicle indicating a right hand drive vehicle was not such a warning as to call for greater care to guard against possible turns or to free the driver of such vehicle from clearly indicating his intention to make a turn.

64. (1) Brakes, two systems required — Every motor vehicle, other than a motorcycle, when driven on a highway shall be equipped with at least two braking systems, each with a separate means of application and effective on at least two wheels, one of which shall be adequate to stop the vehicle as required by regulations made by the Ministry and the other of which shall be adequate to hold the vehicle stationary.

(2) Motorcycles, etc. — Every motorcycle, motor-assisted bicycle or power-assisted bicycle when being driven on a highway shall be equipped with at least two braking systems, each with a separate means of application, with one effective on the front wheel and one effective on the rear wheel.

(3) Brakes on bicycle — No person shall ride a bicycle on a highway unless it is equipped with at least one brake system acting on the rear wheel that will enable the rider to make the braked wheel skid on dry, level and clean pavement.

(4) Meaning of bicycle — In subsection (3),

"bicycle" does not include a unicycle, tricycle or power-assisted bicycle.

(5) Trailer or semi-trailer — Every trailer or semi-trailer having a gross weight of 1,360 kilograms or more shall be equipped with brakes adequate to stop and to hold the vehicle.

(6) Additional brakes — The Lieutenant Governor in Council may make regulations,

　　(a) requiring vehicles or any type or class thereof to be equipped with brakes or braking systems in addition to the brakes required by subsection (1), (2), (3) or (5);

(b) prescribing the standards and specifications of brakes and braking systems or any class or type thereof that are required by this section or regulations made under clause (a); and

(c) exempting any person or class of persons or any class of bicycles from subsection (3) and prescribing conditions for any such exemption.

(7) Condition of brakes — All such brakes and braking systems shall be maintained in good working order and shall conform to the regulations made under this section.

(8) [Repealed 1999, c. 12, Sched. R, s. 12.]

(9) Penalty — Every person who contravenes subsection (1), (5) or (7) or a regulation made under subsection (6) is guilty of an offence and, if the offence was committed by means of a commercial motor vehicle within the meaning of subsection 16(1) or any trailer within the meaning of subsection (5) that is drawn by a commercial motor vehicle within the meaning of subsection 16(1), on conviction is liable to a fine of not less than $400 and not more than $20,000.

Proposed Amendment — 64(9)

(9) Penalty — Every person who contravenes subsection (1), (5) or (7) or a regulation made under subsection (6) is guilty of an offence and, if the offence was committed by means of a commercial motor vehicle or any trailer within the meaning of subsection (5) that is drawn by a commercial motor vehicle, on conviction is liable to a fine of not less than $400 and not more than $20,000.

2014, c. 9, Sched. 2, s. 23 [To come into force January 1, 2017.]

1996, c. 20, s. 14; 1999, c. 12, Sched. R, s. 12; 2009, c. 5, s. 29

Commentary

Every motor vehicle shall have wheel brakes and a parking brake (subs. (1)). Motorcycles or motor assisted bicycles (subs. (2)) and bicycles (subss. (3) and (4)) require brakes. Trailers and semi-trailers are required to have brakes that are adequate to stop and hold their weight (subs. (5)). All brakes shall be maintained in good working order and shall conform to regulations (subs. (7)). Regulations may be passed pursuant to subs. (6). A police officer or officer appointed under the Act may inspect the brakes and cause them to be repaired.

The Red Tape Reduction Act, 1999, S.O. 1999, c. 12, Sched. R. (ss. 1(2), 1(3), 2(1), 2(3), 2(5), 5(1), and 6(1) in force January 1, 2001) amends ss. 6, 7, 12 and 14 of the Highway Traffic Act to facilitate Ontario's participation in the International Registration Plan, which contains reciprocal provisions in respect of commercial motor vehicles that travel across provincial or international borders. The Plan provides for the issuance of IRP cab cards as permits for these vehicles and for the appointment of registration and licence fees in each member jurisdiction on the basis of the distances travelled in each jurisdiction. Persons residing or based in other jurisdictions that are members of the Plan are exempt from the requirements of and fees prescribed under Part II of the Highway Traffic Act.

Case Law

Rintoul v. X-Ray and Radium Indust. Ltd., [1956] S.C.R. 674 — There is such a strong presumption that a motorist, with proper brakes and keeping a proper lookout, should be able to avoid colliding with other objects on the highway that it has been said that, generally speaking, when a car, in broad daylight, runs into the rear of another which is stationary on the highway and which has not come to a sudden stop, the fault is in the driving of the moving car. The driver of such car must, in order to escape liability, satisfy the court that the collision did not occur as a result of his or her negligence.

Loach v. B.C. Elec. Ry., [1916] 1 A.C. 719, 8 W.W.R. 1263, 23 D.L.R. 4 (P.C.); *Brooks v. Lee* (1914), 7 O.W.N. 219 (H.C.); *Thorne v. Cadman* (1955), 37 M.P.R. 25 (N.B. C.A.); *Paul v. Dines*, [1929] 3 W.W.R. 287, [1929] 3 D.L.R. 617 (B.C. C.A.); *Grise v. Rankin*, [1951] O.W.N. 21 (C.A.) — Liability will attach to a motorist who operates a vehicle on the highway with inadequate or defective brakes which prevent the driver from being able to stop in time to avoid an accident.

Parker v. Miller (1926), 42 T.L.R. 408 (C.A.) — The brakes on an automobile must be of sufficient strength to hold it upon a hill. If it runs down the hill when left unattended, this is, in itself, sufficient evidence of negligence against its owner.

Johnson v. Sorochuk, [1941] 1 W.W.R. 445 (Alta. T.D.); *Scott v. Calgary*, [1927] 1 W.W.R. 524, [1927] 2 D.L.R. 263 (Alta. C.A.); *Payne v. Lane*, [1949] O.W.N. 284 (H.C.) — There will be no liability where it is shown that, although the brakes are defective, it would not have been possible to avoid the accident even if the brakes had been perfect since, in such a case, the defect was not the real cause.

Winnipeg Elec. Co. v. Geel, [1931] S.C.R. 443, [1931] 3 D.L.R. 737; affirmed [1932] A.C. 690, [1932] 3 W.W.R. 49, [1932] 4 D.L.R. 51 (P.C.) — Liability may result even where there has been a sudden failure of the brakes if negligence can be imputed to the defendant in not adequately maintaining or inspecting the vehicle.

Simoneau v. R. (1952), 102 C.C.C. 282 (Ont. Dist. Ct.); *Elliot v. Toronto Transit Comm.* (1926), 59 O.L.R. 609 (C.A.) — Public carriers, in particular, are bound to inspect minutely the braking equipment. However, a mere want of inspection should not be considered negligence unless it is shown that an inspection would have revealed the dangerous condition.

Rintoul v. X-Ray and Radium Indust. Ltd., *supra* — To escape liability, the defendant must establish that: (i) the alleged failure of the brakes could not have been prevented by the exercise of reasonable care, and (ii) assuming that such failure occurred without negligence, the defendant could not, by the exercise of reasonable care, have avoided the collision which he or she claimed was the effect of such failure.

Ross v. Grenier, [1956] O.W.N. 901 (C.A.); *Marschler v. Masser's Garage*, [1956] O.R. 328, 2 D.L.R. (2d) 484 (C.A.) — Where the defective condition of the brakes is due to faulty repair in a garage, the garagekeeper will be liable to persons injured by reason of the failure of the brakes.

Modern Motor Sales Ltd. v. Masoud, [1953] 1 S.C.R. 149 — A second-hand car dealer selling a car with defective brakes may be liable.

Clelland v. Berryman; *Clelland v. Lester*, [1975] 1 W.W.R. 147, 56 D.L.R. (3d) 395 (B.C. S.C.) — The failure of the brakes resulted from the negligent reassembly of the master cylinder and the defendant was entitled to recover 75% of the judgment awarded against him from the repairer.

Lacosse v. Nygard (1989), 20 M.V.R. (2d) 179 (Ont. H.C.) — The plaintiffs sued the defendant following a motor vehicle accident. The defendant's vehicle had struck the plaintiffs while they were walking on the roadway. The plaintiffs contended that the brakes on the vehicle were defective, and brought a motion for an order to inspect and test the braking mechanism on the vehicle. They also sought to reconstruct the events by way of simulation as part of the order. The motion was allowed in part. The plaintiff's allegation of defective brakes was not a bald assertion and there was some evidence at the scene to support their contention. The issue of defective brakes was crucial and the plaintiffs were entitled to full disclosure. A brake inspection was therefore appropriate. However, a reconstruction of the accident was not warranted. An inspection, when coupled with the discovery process and the use of available direct and circumstantial evidence, was sufficient.

Joubert v. Rosetown (Town) (1987), 60 Sask. R. 200 (C.A.); reversing (1986), 50 Sask. R. 41 (Q.B.) — The appeal was allowed in part because the motorcyclist should have applied both front and rear brakes.

Related Provisions: See Motor Vehicle Safety Act, S.C. 1993, c. 16; R.R.O. 1990, Reg. 575, Commercial Motor Vehicle Inspections; R.R.O. 1990, Reg. 587, Power-Assisted Bicycles; O. Reg. 369/09, Equipment; R.R.O. 1990, Reg. 611, Safety Inspections.

65. (1) Hydraulic brake and system fluid — No person shall sell, offer for sale or install,

    (a) hydraulic brake fluid; or

    (b) hydraulic system mineral oil,

for use in vehicles upon a highway that does not comply with the standards and specifications prescribed by the regulations or in containers not marked in compliance with the regulations.

(2) Regulations — The Lieutenant Governor in Council may make regulations,

    (a) prescribing the standards and specifications of hydraulic brake fluid or hydraulic system mineral oil or any type or class thereof for use in vehicles;

    (b) providing for the identification and labelling of containers used for hydraulic brake fluid or hydraulic system mineral oil or any type or class thereof.

(3) Adoption of codes by reference — Any regulation may adopt by reference, in whole or in part with the changes that the Lieutenant Governor in Council considers necessary, any code of standards or specifications of hydraulic brake fluid or hydraulic system mineral oil.

(4) Penalty — Every person who contravenes this section or any regulation made under this section is guilty of an offence and on conviction is liable to a fine of not less than $200 and not more than $1000.

Case Law

Shallow v. Fort Nelson (Town) (1995), 11 M.V.R. (3d) 248 (B.C. S.C.) — An owner of a car has a duty not to permit persons to drive a car which he knows or ought to know is defective in a way that is likely to cause an accident. An owner does not fail to meet the standard of care where the loss of brake fluid is gradual and there is no warning of impending brake failure.

Related Provisions: See R.R.O. 1990, Reg. 596, General (which includes brake fluid specifications).

66. (1) Windshield wiper, mirror — Every motor vehicle other than a motorcycle shall be equipped with,

(a) a device for cleaning rain, snow and other moisture from the windshield so constructed as to be controlled or operated by the driver;

(b) a mirror or mirrors securely attached to the vehicle and placed in such a position as to afford the driver a clearly reflected view of the roadway in the rear, or of any vehicle approaching from the rear.

(2) Exception — Clause (1)(b) applies to all motorcycles except those manufactured in or imported into Canada before the 1st day of January, 1971.

(3) Mudguards — Every motor vehicle and every trailer shall be equipped with mudguards or fenders or other device adequate to reduce effectively the wheel spray or splash of water from the roadway to the rear thereof, unless adequate protection is afforded by the body of the motor vehicle or trailer or by a trailer drawn by the motor vehicle.

(4) Exception — Subsection (3) does not apply to motor vehicles or trailers in an unfinished condition while proceeding to a works for completion.

(5) Odometers — Every motor vehicle other than a motorcycle shall be equipped with an odometer in good working order.

(6) Penalty — Every person who contravenes this section is guilty of an offence and, if the offence was committed by means of a commercial motor vehicle within the meaning of subsection 16(1) or a trailer that is drawn by a commercial motor vehicle within the meaning of subsection 16(1), on conviction is liable to a fine of not less than $200 and not more than $20,000.

Proposed Amendment — 66(6)

(6) Penalty — Every person who contravenes this section is guilty of an offence and, if the offence was committed by means of a commercial motor vehicle or a trailer that is drawn by a commercial motor vehicle, on conviction is liable to a fine of not less than $200 and not more than $20,000.

2014, c. 9, Sched. 2, s. 24 [To come into force January 1, 2017.]

1996, c. 20, s. 15

Case Law

Windshield Wipers

Foster v. Kerr, [1939] 3 W.W.R. 428 (Alta. T.D.); affirmed [1940] 1 W.W.R. 385, [1940] 2 D.L.R. 47 (Alta. C.A.) — Driving with a dirty windshield after passing through a puddle was held to be contributory negligence.

Johnson v. Desharnais (1952), 6 W.W.R. (N.S.) 261 (Alta. C.A.); affirmed [1953] 1 S.C.R. 324 — A windshield covered with hoarfrost so that a driver cannot see through it may attract liability.

O'Brien v. Devries (1970), 3 N.S.R. (2d) 231 (T.D.) — A windshield obscured due to frozen windshield washer will attract liability.

Duguay v. Mallet (1971), 4 N.B.R. (2d) 281 (Q.B.) — Using a defective windshield wiper in rain will attract liability.

Rines v. Chambers (1949), 25 M.P.R. 33 (N.S. T.D.); *Turner v. Cantone*, [1929] 3 W.W.R. 413, [1929] 4 D.L.R. 724 (B.C. C.A.) — Driving at excessive speed where heavy rain causes the windshield to become obscurbed may result in a finding of negligence.

Rear View Mirror

Nicol v. Bowman, [1953] O.R. 624 (C.A.) — A rear view mirror which was ineffective to the extent that the driver was unable by looking in it to see a vehicle behind him unless it was some distance back, did not comply with the section.

Gemmell v. Grain, [1935] 2 W.W.R. 447 (Man. K.B.); *Gill v. St. John's* (1950), 32 M.P.R. 372 (Nfld. T.D.); *Ottawa Brick Co. v. Marsh*, [1940] S.C.R. 392, [1940] 2 D.L.R. 417; *Forbes v. Coca Cola*, [1941] 3 W.W.R. 909, [1942] 1 D.L.R. 184 (Sask. C.A.); affirmed [1942] S.C.R. 366, [1942] 3 D.L.R. 194 — If the surrounding circumstances of an accident are such that it could have been avoided but for the absence of a rear view mirror, the failure to have such installed is an act of negligence contributing directly to the accident.

Martin v. Gray (1986), 67 N.B.R. (2d) 196, 172 A.P.R. 196 (Q.B.) — The plaintiff army jeep driver signalled to turn left from the southbound lane of a two-lane highway into a side road. The jeep had an exterior but not an interior rear view mirror. The driver checked the mirror for following traffic appreciably back from the intersection. A van struck the vehicle while attempting to overtake it at an appreciable rate of speed. The plaintiff driver was held to be 40% contributorily negligent. The lack of an interior mirror required special caution. The plaintiff driver failed to check adequately for any overtaking vehicle before turning.

67. Extended mirrors — No person shall drive upon a highway a motor vehicle, other than a commercial motor vehicle, that has attached thereto any mirror or mirrors that extend more than 305 millimetres from the side of the vehicle, except when the motor vehicle is towing another vehicle.

68. Speedometers required in buses — Every bus when driven on a highway shall be equipped with a speedometer which shall be maintained in good working order.

68.1 Speed-limiting systems — (1) **Required use by commercial motor vehicles** — No person shall drive, or permit the operation of, a commercial motor vehicle on a highway unless the vehicle is equipped with a speed-limiting system that is activated and functioning in accordance with the regulations.

(2) **Same** — Except as authorized by the regulations, no person shall,

(a) deactivate, or permit a person to deactivate, a commercial motor vehicle's speed-limiting system; or

(b) modify, or permit a person to modify, a commercial motor vehicle's speed-limiting system such that it ceases to function in accordance with the regulations.

(3) **Tampering device prohibited** — No person shall drive, or permit the operation of, a commercial motor vehicle on a highway if the vehicle is equipped with, has attached to it or carries,

(a) a prescribed device or prescribed equipment; or

(b) another device or equipment that is designed to disguise the fact that the vehicle is not equipped with a speed-limiting system that is activated and functioning in accordance with the regulations.

(4) **Verifying compliance** — A police officer or officer appointed for carrying out the provisions of this Act, in exercising his or her powers under section 82 or 216.1, may require that the driver or other person in charge of a commercial motor vehicle,

(a) provide the officer with access to the vehicle's computer system in order to retrieve and read any information relevant to the activation and functioning of the vehicle's speed-limiting system;

(b) surrender to the officer any device or equipment carried in the vehicle that operates as part of the vehicle's speed-limiting system; and

(c) surrender to the officer any records that the driver is required by the regulations to carry with him or her while driving the vehicle.

(5) **Same** — A driver or other person in charge of a commercial motor vehicle shall comply with any requirement made under subsection (4) by a police officer or officer appointed for carrying out the provisions of this Act.

(6) **Seizure of tampering device** — If a police officer or officer appointed for carrying out the provisions of this Act finds a device or equipment prohibited by subsection (3) in the course of any inspection of a commercial motor vehicle, he or she may detach, if necessary, and seize any such device or equipment.

(7) **Sale of tampering devices prohibited** — No person shall sell, offer or advertise for sale a device or equipment prohibited by subsection (3).

(8) **Offence** — Every person who contravenes or fails to comply with subsection (1), (2), (3), (5) or (7), or a regulation made under this section, is guilty of an offence and on conviction is liable to a fine of not less than $250 and not more than $20,000.

(9) **Evidentiary presumption** — In any proceeding under this section and in the absence of evidence to the contrary, proof that a commercial motor vehicle was driven on a highway at a speed equal to or greater than the speed prescribed for the purpose of this subsection is proof that the vehicle was not equipped with a speed-limiting system that was activated and functioning as required by subsection (1).

(10) Forfeiture of tampering device — Where a person is convicted of an offence under subsection (3), any device or equipment seized under subsection (6) by means of which the offence was committed is forfeited to the Crown.

(11) Regulations — The Lieutenant Governor in Council may make regulations,

    (a) defining "commercial motor vehicle" for the purposes of this section;

Proposed Repeal — 68.1(11)(a)

    (a) [Repealed 2014, c. 9, Sched. 2, s. 25. To come into force January 1, 2017.]

    (b) prescribing standards for speed-limiting systems;

    (c) governing the activation and functioning of speed-limiting systems, including prescribing and governing the speed at which speed-limiting systems must be set and prescribing different speed settings for different circumstances;

    (d) prescribing devices and equipment for the purpose of clause (3)(a);

    (e) governing methods to verify compliance with this section and the regulations, including prescribing devices and software to be used to retrieve and read information in computer systems;

    (f) prescribing the speed for the purpose of subsection (9);

    (g) requiring and governing the inspection and maintenance of speed-limiting systems;

    (h) governing records to be kept and submitted in relation to the inspection, maintenance, activation and functioning of speed-limiting systems;

    (i) governing records to be kept and carried by drivers in relation to the activation and functioning of speed-limiting systems;

    (j) exempting any person or class of persons or any commercial motor vehicle or class of commercial motor vehicles from any requirement or provision of this section or of a regulation made under this section and prescribing conditions and circumstances for any such exemption.

2008, c. 8, s. 1

Case Law

Ontario (Ministry of Transportation) v. Don's Triple F Transport Inc., 2012 ONCA 536, 2012 CarswellOnt 9883, 38 M.V.R. (6th) 8, 291 C.C.C. (3d) 530, 295 O.A.C. 114, [2012] O.J. No. 3754 (Ont. C.A.) — Where the charge was permitting the operation of a commercial motor vehicle not equipped with a working speed-limiting system contrary to s. 68(1) but the evidence disclosed that there was a device but that is was set to 10 miles per hour higher than the proper limit, the wrong charge was laid.

R. v. Michaud, 2015 ONCA 585, 2015 CarswellOnt 13209, 127 O.R. (3d) 81, 328 C.C.C. (3d) 228, 22 C.R. (7th) 246, 82 M.V.R. (6th) 171, 339 O.A.C. 41, [2015] O.J. No. 4540; affirming 2014 ONCJ 243, 2014 CarswellOnt 6753, 66 M.V.R. (6th) 149, 311 C.R.R. (2d) 170, [2014] O.J. No. 2443 — Section 68.1 is constitutional.

69. (1) Requirements as to tires — All self-propelled vehicles other than traction engines, and all trailers having a gross weight in excess of 1,820 kilograms, shall be equipped with rubber tires or tires of some composition equally resilient, and a vehicle shall not be operated on any highway with a tire that is broken or defective in such a manner as to cause additional impact or pounding on or cutting of the highway, and in the case of motor vehicles and trailers equipped with solid rubber tires there shall be at least 31.5 millimetres of rubber between the wheel rim and the roadway.

(2) **Flanges and clamps** — No vehicle shall be operated or object moved over or upon any highway with any flange, rib, clamp or other device attached to its wheels, or made a part thereof, which will injure the highway.

(3) **Lock-shoes** — No person driving a vehicle drawn by a horse or other animal and used for carrying articles of burden, goods, wares or merchandise shall when descending a grade on a highway lock any wheel of such vehicle except with the device commonly known as a lock-shoe.

Commentary

All vehicles shall be outfitted with suitable tires (s. 69(1)). Items which may injure the highway are prohibited (s. 69(2)). Lock-shoes may be used by animal-drawn vehicles (s. 69(3)). Regulations may be made (ss. 70(1) and (2)) and failure to have tires in conformity with the regulations is an offence (s. 70(3)) punishable by a fine of up to $1,000 (s. 70(4)). A police officer or officer appointed under the Act may inspect tires and cause them to be replaced (ss. 70(5) and (6)). Rebuilt tires are regulated pursuant to s. 71.

Case Law

Fraser v. Children's Aid Society, [1935] 1 W.W.R. 667 (Man. K.B.) — Where a tire was, to the knowledge of the driver and the owner, so worn and damaged as to be unsafe, the driver was held to be negligent in driving the vehicle in that condition, and the owner was negligent in not exercising reasonable care in maintaining the tires.

Wing v. Banks, [1947] O.W.N. 897 (C.A.); *Peterson v. Crump* (1955), 16 W.W.R. 247 (Alta. Dist. Ct.) — Where the defendant knew that his tires were in a poor condition of repair, he could not avoid liability on a plea of inevitable accident when one of the tires disintegrated while the car was being operated at an excessive speed.

Barkway v. South Wales Tpt. Co., [1950] 1 All E.R. 392 (H.L.) — A tire-burst was caused by an impact fracture due to one or more heavy blows on the outside of the tire leading to disintegration of the inner parts. Although it was not possible to affirm that the fracture would have been discovered by the exercise of due diligence, it was held that the defendants had not taken all the steps they should have taken to protect passengers because they had not instructed their drivers to report heavy blows to tires likely to cause impact fractures.

Greenlund v. Drysdale (1958), 12 D.L.R. (2d) 765 (N.S. T.D.) — Evidence that a car had left the highway because of a blow-out was sufficient answer to an allegation of gross negligence.

Duchaine v. Armstrong and Legault, [1957] O.W.N. 251 (C.A.) — Where a car left the highway while rounding a curve at high speed, and a blow-out was pleaded as the cause of the accident, it was held to be more probable that the damage to the tire occurred when the car came into contact with rock or some other hard object after leaving the road.

Moreover, even if the tire had blown out, the defendant was driving at such an excessive speed that he had incapacitated himself from controlling the car in those circumstances.

Murphy v. D. & B. Holdings Ltd. (1978), 28 N.S.R. (2d) 316, 43 A.P.R. 316 (T.D.); affirmed (1979), 31 N.S.R. (2d) 380, 52 A.P.R. 380, (sub nom. *Goodwear Treaders Ltd. v. D. & B. Holdings Ltd.)* 8 C.C.L.T. 87 (C.A.) — The plaintiffs were involved in a head-on collision with a gravel truck when a retread tire on the front of the truck failed. The manufacturer advised the truck owner not to use a retread tire on the front. The plaintiffs sued the truck owner and manufacturer. Liability was apportioned 80% to the truck owner and 20% to the manufacturer. The truck owner was negligent for overloading and underinflating the tire and for installation of a tube too large for the tire cavity. The manufacturer was liable because it sold the tire to the owner knowing it was to be used on the front contrary to warning.

Romaniuk v. Gosling (1983), 48 A.R. 85 (Q.B.) — Driving with mismatched summer and winter tires, combined with other factors, was held to constitute gross negligence.

Ashabi v. Lemaire (2003), 2003 BCCA 527, 2003 CarswellBC 2628, 43 M.V.R. (4th) 30, 187 B.C.A.C. 276, 307 W.A.C. 276 (C.A.) — A failure to use a torque wrench was found to breach the standard of care.

Related Provisions: See R.R.O. 1990, Reg. 575, Commercial Motor Vehicle Inspection; R.R.O. 1990, Reg. 596, General; R.R.O. 1990, Reg. 611, Safety Inspection; R.R.O. 1990, Reg. 612, School Buses; R.R.O. 1990, Reg. 625, Tire Standards and Specifications; see also Motor Vehicle Safety Act, S.C. 1993, c. 16.

70. (1) Regulations — The Lieutenant Governor in Council may make regulations,

    (a) prescribing the standards and specifications of tires or any class or classes thereof in use on vehicles or any class or classes thereof;

    (b) prescribing classes of tires;

    (c) prescribing the standards and specifications of used or retreaded tires offered for sale and prohibiting the sale of such tires or any type thereof that do not comply with the standards and specifications therefor prescribed by the regulations or that are not marked in accordance with the regulations;

    (d) providing for and requiring the identification and marking of used or retreaded tires;

    (e) prohibiting the use of any type of tire on a highway at any time or during any period of the year and designating the period;

    (e.1) exempting any vehicle or person or class or type of vehicles or class of persons from a prohibition under clause (e) and regulating the use of a type of tire that is otherwise prohibited under clause (e) for the purpose of such exemption, including prescribing the period of the year during which and geographic areas where the exemption applies and other conditions and circumstances that must exist for the exemption to apply;

    (f) prescribing procedures for examining tires for the purpose of determining whether the prescribed standards and specifications have been met;

    (g) regulating installation and placement of tires to be used on vehicles or any class or classes thereof;

(h) regulating combinations of tires installed on vehicles or any class or classes thereof;

(i) [Repealed 2006, c. 19, Sched. T, s. 5.]

(2) **Codes** — Any regulation may adopt by reference, in whole or in part, with the changes that the Lieutenant Governor in Council considers necessary, any code, and may require compliance with any code that is so adopted.

(3) **Offence** — No person shall operate or permit to be operated upon a highway a vehicle that is,

(a) fitted with a tire that does not conform with the standards and specifications prescribed in the regulations; or

(b) fitted with tires that are installed in a manner, in a place or in a combination that does not conform with the specifications prescribed in the regulations.

(4) **Penalty** — Every person who contravenes this section or any regulation made under this section is guilty of an offence and on conviction is liable to a fine or not more than $1000.

(4.1) **Same — commercial motor vehicle** — Despite subsection (4), every person who contravenes this section or any regulation made under this section is guilty of an offence and, if the offence was committed by means of a commercial motor vehicle within the meaning of subsection 16(1), on conviction is liable to a fine of not less than $200 and not more than $20,000.

Proposed Amendment — 70(4.1)

(4.1) **Same — commercial motor vehicle** — Despite subsection (4), every person who contravenes this section or any regulation made under this section is guilty of an offence and, if the offence was committed by means of a commercial motor vehicle, on conviction is liable to a fine of not less than $200 and not more than $20,000.

2014, c. 9, Sched. 2, s. 26 [To come into force January 1, 2017.]

(5) [Repealed 1999, c. 12, Sched. R, s. 13.]

(6) [Repealed 1999, c. 12, Sched. R, s. 13.]

1996, c. 20, s. 16; 1999, c. 12, Sched. R, s. 13; 2005, c. 26, Sched. A, s. 11; 2006, c. 19, Sched. T, s. 5

Commentary

The Red Tape Reduction Act, 1999, S.O. 1999, c. 12, Sched. R. (ss. 1(2), 1(3), 2(1), 2(3), 2(5), 5(1), and 6(1) in force January 1, 2001) amends ss. 6, 7, 12 and 14 of the Highway Traffic Act to facilitate Ontario's participation in the International Registration Plan, which contains reciprocal provisions in respect of commercial motor vehicles that travel across provincial or international borders. The Plan provides for the issuance of IRP cab cards as permits for these vehicles and for the appointment of registration and licence fees in each member jurisdiction on the basis of the distances travelled in each jurisdiction. Persons residing or based in other jurisdictions that are members of the Plan are exempt from the requirements of and fees prescribed under Part II of the Highway Traffic Act.

Related Provisions: See R.R.O. 1990, Reg. 625, Tire Standards and Specifications.

71. (1) Rebuilt tires, definition — In this section, "rebuild" means to make or impose a new tread or new surface or to otherwise alter the surface of a used tire so that it will resemble a new tire, by cutting into or adding rubber to the surface thereof, or by a combination of both.

(2) Rebuilt tires, to be marked — No person shall rebuild any tire designed for use upon a motor vehicle unless the person causes it to be indicated in letters of not less than six millimetres in height, clearly embossed upon or imposed or cut into the outside surface of each wall of the tire, that it has been rebuilt.

(3) Idem — No person shall sell, offer or expose for sale, or have in the person's possession with intent to sell, any tire designed for use upon a motor vehicle that has been rebuilt unless it is indicated in letters of not less than six millimetres in height, clearly embossed upon or imposed or cut into the outside surface of each wall of the tire, that it has been rebuilt.

(4) Penalty — Every person who contravenes subsection (2) or (3) is guilty of an offence and on conviction is liable to a fine of not less than $200 and not more than $20,000.

1996, c. 20, s. 17

Related Provisions: See O. Reg. 199/07, Commercial Motor Vehicle Suspensions; R.R.O. 1990, Reg. 611, Safety Inspections; R.R.O. 1990, Reg. 612, School Buses.

Case Law

Hutton v. General Motors of Canada Ltd. (2010), 2010 ABQB 606, 2010 CarswellAlta 1879, 501 A.R. 90, [2011] 4 W.W.R. 284, 76 B.L.R. (4th) 225, 33 Alta. L.R. (5th) 340, 2 M.V.R. (6th) 120 — The court dealt with a claim for a defective air bag holding that the company failed in its duty respecting a recall and the description of the risk.

R. v. Hajivasilis (2013), 41 M.V.R. (6th) 175, 2013 ONCA 27, 2013 CarswellOnt 508, 114 O.R. (3d) 337, 302 O.A.C. 65, [2013] O.J. No. 253 (Ont. C.A.) — The requirements are not restricted to "highways".

72. (1) Safety glass, interpretation — In this section, "motor vehicle" includes any apparatus or device that is permanently or temporarily attached to a motor vehicle, other than for the purpose of towing it, and in which a person can ride.

(2) Motor vehicles to be equipped with safety glass — No person shall sell any new motor vehicle nor shall any new motor vehicle be registered with the Ministry unless the vehicle is equipped with safety glass wherever glass is used in doors, windows and windshields.

(3) Installation of safety glass — No person shall install glass other than safety glass in the door, window or windshield of any motor vehicle.

(4) Regulations as to safety glass in vehicles — The Lieutenant Governor in Council may make regulations,

(a) prescribing standards and specifications for safety glass used or intended to be used in a door, window or windshield of any motor vehicle;

(b) providing for and requiring the marking and identification of safety glass used or intended to be used in a door, window or windshield of any motor vehicle.

(5) Adoption of code by reference — Any regulation made under subsection (4) may adopt by reference, in whole or in part with the changes that the Lieutenant Governor in Council considers necessary, any code or standard and may require compliance with any code or standard that is so adopted.

(6) Penalty — Every person who contravenes this section or a regulation made under this section is guilty of an offence and on conviction is liable to a fine of not less than $200 and not more than $1,000.

Related Provisions: See R.R.O. 1990, Reg. 575, Commercial Motor Vehicle Inspection; R.R.O. 1990, Reg. 611, Safety Inspections; R.R.O. 1990, Reg. 612, School Buses.

73. (1) Signs, objects, etc., obstructing view prohibited — No person shall drive a motor vehicle upon a highway,

(a) with any sign, poster or other non-transparent material or object placed on the windshield or on any window of such motor vehicle; or

(b) with any object placed in, hung on or attached to the motor vehicle,

in a manner that will obstruct the driver's view of the highway or any intersecting highway.

(2) Colour coating obstructing view prohibited — No person shall drive a motor vehicle upon a highway where the surface of the windshield or of any window of the vehicle has been coated with any colour spray or other colour coating in such a manner as to obstruct the driver's view of the highway or any intersecting highway.

(3) Colour coating obscuring interior — No person shall drive on a highway a motor vehicle on which the surface of the windshield or of any window to the direct left or right of the driver's seat has been coated with any coloured spray or other coloured or reflective material that substantially obscures the interior of the motor vehicle when viewed from outside the motor vehicle.

(4) Signs, etc., required by Act or regulations — This section does not prevent the use of signs, markers or equipment required under this Act or the regulations.

Case Law

R. v. Lovett (1986), 43 M.V.R. 282 (N.B. Q.B.) — The accused was convicted under s. 238(1)(a) of the Motor Vehicle Act (N.B.) with driving a motor vehicle with non-transparent material on his vehicle windows which obstructed or was likely to obstruct his clear view of the highway. The windows of the accused's vehicle, except for his windshield, had been tinted. The Crown led expert evidence that assuming the tint on the windows was of a certain type, the accused's visibility would be hampered not at all during daylight hours, significantly at twilight, and would be practically nil at night. The accused had been arrested at 8 a.m. The amount of visibility of the accused at the time the vehicle was operated was relevant to sustaining the charge. If a motor vehicle was constructed in such a way that there would be an obstruction to view only at night, it was no offence to drive the vehicle during the day. The Crown's expert evidence concerning the vehicle indicated no obstruction during the day. No Crown witnesses had gone inside the vehicle so as to be able to testify first hand as to the visibility for a driver within the vehicle at the time in question.

R. v. Belair, 2005 CarswellOnt 3328, 2005 ONCJ 345, 23 M.V.R. (5th) 192 (C.J.) — The offence is one of strict liability. The section is not impermissibly vague.

74. (1) Windows to afford clear view — **No person shall drive a motor vehicle upon a highway,**

> **(a) unless the windshield and the windows on either side of the compartment containing the steering wheel are in such a condition as to afford the driver a clear view to the front and side of the motor vehicle; and**

> **(b) unless the rear window is in such a condition as to afford the driver a clear view to the rear of the motor vehicle.**

(2) Application of cl. (1)(b) — **Clause (1)(b) does not apply to a motor vehicle that is equipped with a mirror or mirrors securely attached to the motor vehicle and placed in such a position and maintained in such a condition as to afford the driver, otherwise than through the rear window, a clearly-reflected view of the roadway in the rear or of any vehicle approaching from the rear.**

Case Law

Schwartzenberger v. Lawrence (1988), 87 A.R. 1 (Q.B.) — The defendant was found solely negligent for a collision at traffic lights because, in part, his windshield was very dirty.

R. v. McQuaig (1998), 36 M.V.R. (3d) 223, 221 A.R. 185 (Alta. Prov. Ct.) — On a charge of having tinting or glazing on the side windows, the offence is strict liability. A prima facie case is established once the Crown has adduced credible evidence of the coating. The defendant has the onus of establishing an exception.

R. v. Arnand (1998), 45 M.V.R. (3d) 212 (N.B. Prov. Ct.) — Where the accused relied on approval at a qualified inspections station the charge was dismissed.

R. v. Bennett (2013), 42 M.V.R. (6th) 343, 2013 CarswellNfld 96, 335 Nfld. & P.E.I.R. 171, 1040 A.P.R. 171, [2013] N.J. No. 101 (N.L. Prov. Ct.) — No steps were cited to demonstrate due diligence regarding tinted windows contrary to the regulations.

Related Provisions: See s. 66 of the Act regarding windshield wipers.

75. (1) Muffler — **Every motor vehicle or motor assisted bicycle shall be equipped with a muffler in good working order and in constant operation to prevent excessive or unusual noise and excessive smoke, and no person shall use a muffler cut-out,**

straight exhaust, gutted muffler, hollywood muffler, by-pass or similar device upon a motor vehicle or motor assisted bicycle.

(2) **Same** — Subsection (1) does not apply to,

    (a) a motor-assisted bicycle with an attached motor that is driven entirely by electricity; or

    (b) a motor vehicle that is driven entirely by electricity.

(3) **Fumes from engine** — The engine and power mechanism of every motor vehicle shall be so equipped and adjusted as to prevent the escape of excessive fumes or smoke.

(4) **Unnecessary noise** — A person having the control or charge of a motor vehicle shall not sound any bell, horn or other signalling device so as to make an unreasonable noise, and a driver of any motor vehicle shall not permit any unreasonable amount of smoke to escape from the motor vehicle, nor shall such driver at any time cause the motor vehicle to make any unnecessary noise, but this subsection does not apply to a motor vehicle of a municipal fire department while proceeding to a fire or answering a fire alarm call.

(5) **Alarm bell to be sounded** — Every motor vehicle, motor assisted bicycle and bicycle shall be equipped with an alarm bell, gong or horn, which shall be kept in good working order and sounded whenever it is reasonably necessary to notify pedestrians or others of its approach.

(6) **Prohibition as to use of siren horn** — No vehicle other than an ambulance, fire or police department vehicle, public utility emergency vehicle or vehicle operated by the Ministry shall be equipped with a siren horn or a device producing a sound which so nearly resembles that produced by a siren horn as to deceive or confuse.

2009, c. 5, s. 31

Commentary

This section seeks to avoid excessive noise or smoke coming from mufflers or other parts of a car (subs. (1)). Certain types of show mufflers are prohibited (subs. (1)). Fumes from any part of a motor vehicle are banned (subs. (3)). Excessive noise, such as from a horn, is proscribed (subs. (4)). However, where necessary, horns and bells must be sounded (subs. (5)). Only emergency vehicles may use sirens (subs. (6)).

Case Law

Unnecessary Noise

R. v. Martin, [1960] O.W.N. 60, 126 C.C.C. 329 (H.C.) — The mere production of unnecessary noise does not constitute an offence under s. 75(4). There has to be some positive act on the part of the operator which produced the noise complained of. This does not mean, however, that in no case could a deliberate omission to prevent the production of excessive noise be an offence.

R. v. Sawicki (1960), 32 W.W.R. 380 (Sask. Q.B.) — The requirement of the Alberta Act that a vehicle should be equipped with a proper muffler was held to be an absolute one, and an owner was under a duty to see that his vehicle was properly equipped before being put on the road.

R. v. Samograd (1963), 45 W.W.R. 636 (Alta. Dist. Ct.) — The requirement under s. 55 [now R.S.A. 1980, c. H-7, s. 46] of the Alberta Act that a motor vehicle be equipped with a muffler of such kind and description as will prevent any unreasonable noise is not fulfilled if the muffler on the vehicle is, by reason of a break in the connecting pipe, not connected to the engine.

Sounding Horn

Marshall v. Gowans (1911), 24 O.L.R. 522 (C.A.) — The object of sounding the horn is to give warning to pedestrians and others of the approach of the motor car. There is no absolute requirement that it shall be sounded, or that it should be sounded at any particular distance. If a reasonable warning is otherwise given, the mere failure to sound the horn would not be negligence.

Harris v. Smith (1932), 5 M.P.R. 378 (N.B. K.B.); *Jowett v. Morrow*, [1950] 1 W.W.R. 35 (Man. K.B.); affirmed [1950] 2 W.W.R. 1056 (Man. C.A.) — Such "other" warning might, for example, be amply given by the lights of the car at night.

Bliss v. Malmberg, [1929] 3 W.W.R. 641, [1930] 1 D.L.R. 361 (Alta. C.A.); reversed [1931] S.C.R. 710, [1931] 4 D.L.R. 264 — The occasion for the sounding of the horn or the giving of a warning is a matter of discretion on the part of the driver to be determined by the particular circumstances and conditions as they arise.

Nadeau v. Morgan (1926), 30 O.W.N. 15 (H.C.); *Williams v. Fedoryshin*, [1959] S.C.R. 248, 17 D.L.R. (2d) 225 — Where there are pedestrians on the highway or in near proximity thereto who may not be aware of the approach of a vehicle, it will generally be reasonably necessary to sound the horn.

Briand v. Dunphy (1926), 59 N.S.R. 120 (C.A.) — A sufficient warning had not been given to a pedestrian where the motorist sounded the horn when only 25 feet away.

Gooley v. Clark, [1968] 1 O.R. 411 (H.C.) — A motorist who failed to sound his horn before passing two cyclists to warn of his approach was held solely responsible for the accident that ensued.

Cyr v. Landry (1980), 30 N.B.R. (2d) 588, 70 A.P.R. 588 (Q.B.) — An oncoming driver has a duty to sound his horn upon seeing a pedestrian emerging from a parked car to cross the highway.

Wilson v. Rebotoy, 64 O.L.R. 458, [1930] 1 D.L.R. 273 (C.A.) — A motorist is not expected to foresee every possible contingency. Thus, if a pedestrian is out of the way of traffic and there is nothing to indicate that he might move into it, it may well be not reasonably necessary to sound the horn.

Brownlee v. Zinn (1924), 27 O.W.N. 148 (H.C.); *Stanley v. Nat. Fruit Co.*, [1931] S.C.R. 60, [1931] 1 D.L.R. 306; *Robertson v. Antoniuk*, [1934] 2 W.W.R. 293, [1934] 4 D.L.R. 46 (Man. C.A.) — Where the pedestrian is obviously aware of the approach of the vehicle, there can be no necessity to sound the horn since the purpose of sounding it has already been achieved.

Wood v. Powell, [1932] 3 W.W.R. 100 (B.C. S.C.); *Malawski v. Walton*, [1932] 3 W.W.R. 330 (Alta. T.D.); *Nakasnay v. Bater*, [1948] 1 W.W.R. 61 (Sask. C.A.) — The sounding of the horn may not necessarily discharge the entire obligation of the motorist to take care under the circumstances, but may be merely an extra precaution that must be observed. If he sees that a pedestrian is not heeding his horn and is apparently unaware of his approach, he should take additional care to be able to guard against an accident if the pedestrian suddenly moves into his path.

Hulme v. Creelman, 66 O.L.R. 360, [1931] 1 D.L.R. 682 (C.A.) — There is no obligation on a driver to sound his horn at every intersection, whether or not there is any indication of jeopardy or peril to anyone, and he might even be guilty of an offence in making unreasonable noise if he does so.

Ottawa Brick Co. v. Marsh, [1940] S.C.R. 392; *Beaumont v. Ruddy*, [1932] O.R. 441, [1932] 3 D.L.R. 75 (C.A.) — A motorist was held contributorily negligent where he failed to sound his horn soon enough before endeavouring to overtake another vehicle which turned across his path. The onus in fact rests heavily on the driver of the following car to show than an accident with a vehicle ahead was not due to his negligence, and this may well be more difficult if he has not sounded his horn.

R. v. Anderson, [1946] S.C.R. 129 — The following driver was held not bound to antici-pate that the vehicle ahead would turn in the absence of any indication that such was its driver's intention, and there was accordingly no obligation to sound the horn.

Ottawa Brick Co. v. Marsh, *supra*; *Low v. Prentice & Bateman*, [1949] O.W.N. 602 (C.A.) — The position and actions of the car ahead should have increased the alertness of the following driver and obliged him not to pass unless proper warning was given and he could do so safely.

Penney's Transport Ltd. v. O'Brien (1988), 72 Nfld. & P.E.I.R. 80, 223 A.P.R. 80 (Nfld. T.D.) — The plaintiff automobile driver passed the defendant's tractor trailer and turned back into the defendant's lane while slowing down. The defendant claimed that he was unable to slow as much as the plaintiff and so veered to the left to pass the plaintiff, but without sounding his horn. The plaintiff moved back into the defendant's lane and a colli-sion occurred. The plaintiff was largely responsible, but the defendant was 20% responsi-ble for not sounding his horn.

76. (1) Slow moving vehicle sign — **No person shall operate a slow moving vehicle on a highway unless a slow moving sign is attached, in accordance with the regulations,**

> **(a) to the rear of the slow moving vehicle, if no trailer, implement of husbandry or other device is being towed;**

> **(b) to the rear of the rearmost trailer, implement of husbandry or other device that is being towed by the slow moving vehicle, if one or more trailers, imple-ments or other devices are being towed.**

(2) Slow moving vehicles — The following are slow moving vehicles:

1. Farm tractors and self-propelled implements of husbandry.

2. Vehicles (other than bicycles, motor assisted bicycles and disabled motor ve-hicles in tow) that are not capable of attaining and sustaining a speed greater than 40 kilometres per hour on level ground when operated on a highway.

3. Motor vehicles towing an implement of husbandry.

Proposed Addition — 76(2), para. 4

4. Road-building machines.

2016, c. 5, Sched. 12, s. 4 [Not in force at date of publication.]

(3) Exception — The slow moving vehicle sign is not required if the slow moving vehicle is operated on a highway only to cross it directly.

(4) Prohibition — No person shall place a slow moving vehicle sign on or near a fixed object where it is readily visible from a highway.

(5) Exceptions — Subsection (4) does not apply to a facsimile of a slow moving vehicle sign that is displayed for the information of highway users.

(6) Prohibition — No person shall operate on a highway a vehicle, other than a slow moving vehicle, with a slow moving vehicle sign attached to it or to a trailer, implement of husbandry or other device being towed by it.

(6.1) Same — No person shall operate on a highway a slow moving vehicle with a slow moving vehicle sign attached to it or to a trailer, implement of husbandry or other device being towed by it, at a speed greater than 40 kilometres per hour.

(7) Regulations — The Lieutenant Governor in Council may make regulations,

(a) prescribing the type and specifications of the slow moving vehicle sign and its location on the vehicle;

(b) providing that subsection (1) does not apply to a horse-drawn vehicle when driven by a person whose religious convictions or beliefs prohibit the display of devices such as the slow moving vehicle sign;

(c) prescribing the type and specifications of a marker or device, requiring that it be displayed, instead of the slow moving vehicle sign, on a horse-drawn vehicle when driven by a person described in clause (b), and prescribing the location of the marker or device on the vehicle;

(d) respecting any matter considered necessary or advisable to carry out the intent and purpose of this section.

1994, c. 28, s. 1; 2002, c. 18, Sched. P, s. 21; 2009, c. 5, s. 32

Case Law

Nova Scotia (A.G.) v. Richard (1986), 39 M.V.R. 262, 72 N.S.R. (2d) 301, 173 A.P.R. 301 (S.C.) — The employee of the plaintiff was operating the plaintiff's power broom truck at night in heavy fog on a damp highway. The power broom was not equipped with a rear view mirror. The defendant was operating a tractor-trailer on the same highway at a speed of approximately 50 to 55 m.p.h. The defendant stated that he saw a yellow blur, swerved to the left and struck the power broom, which had also swerved to the left. The plaintiff commenced an action for damages for negligence and the defendant counterclaimed for damages to his vehicle. The plaintiff and defendant were each found 50% at fault. The defendant was travelling too fast given the weight of his vehicle and the conditions existing at the time of the collision. The plaintiff's vehicle did not have a rear view mirror, which was in violation of the Act. Because it was a slow-moving vehicle and because of the foggy conditions and the fact that it did not have a rear view mirror, it was incumbent on the plaintiff's employee to have removed the vehicle from the highway.

Related Provisions: See O. Reg. 316/03, Operation of Off-Road Vehicles on Highways; R.R.O. 1990, Reg. 603, Over-Dimensional Farm Vehicles; R.R.O. 1990, Reg. 616, Slow-Moving Vehicles Sign.

77. (1) Sleigh bells — Every person travelling on a highway with a sleigh or sled drawn by a horse or other animal shall have at least two bells attached to the harness or to the sleigh or sled in such a manner as to give ample warning sound.

(2) Penalty — Every person who contravenes subsection (1) is guilty of an offence and on conviction is liable to a fine of not more than $5.

78. (1) Display screen visible to driver prohibited — No person shall drive a motor vehicle on a highway if the display screen of a television, computer or other device in the motor vehicle is visible to the driver.

(2) Exceptions — Subsection (1) does not apply in respect of the display screen of,

    (a) a global positioning system navigation device while being used to provide navigation information;

    (b) a hand-held wireless communication device or a device that is prescribed for the purpose of subsection 78.1(1);

    (c) a logistical transportation tracking system device used for commercial purposes to track vehicle location, driver status or the delivery of packages or other goods;

    (d) a collision avoidance system device that has no other function than to deliver a collision avoidance system; or

    (e) an instrument, gauge or system that is used to provide information to the driver regarding the status of various systems of the motor vehicle.

(3) Same — Subsection (1) does not apply to the driver of an ambulance, fire department vehicle or police department vehicle.

(4) Exemption by regulation — The Minister may make regulations exempting any class of persons or vehicles or any device from this section and prescribing conditions and circumstances for any such exemption.

(5) Penalty — Every person who contravenes this section is guilty of an offence and on conviction is liable to a fine of not less than $300 and not more than $1,000.
2009, c. 4, s. 1; 2015, c. 14, s. 22

Related Provisions: See O. Reg. 366/09, Display Screens and Hand-Held Devices; R.R.O. 1990, Reg. 587, Equipment.

78.1 Hand-held devices prohibited — **(1) Wireless communication devices** — No person shall drive a motor vehicle on a highway while holding or using a hand-held wireless communication device or other prescribed device that is capable of receiving or transmitting telephone communications, electronic data, mail or text messages.

(2) Entertainment devices — No person shall drive a motor vehicle on a highway while holding or using a hand-held electronic entertainment device or other prescribed device the primary use of which is unrelated to the safe operation of the motor vehicle.

(3) **Hands-free mode allowed** — Despite subsections (1) and (2), a person may drive a motor vehicle on a highway while using a device described in those subsections in hands-free mode.

(4) **Exceptions** — Subsection (1) does not apply to,

(a) the driver of an ambulance, fire department vehicle or police department vehicle;

(b) any other prescribed person or class of persons;

(c) a person holding or using a device prescribed for the purpose of this subsection; or

(d) a person engaged in a prescribed activity or in prescribed conditions or circumstances.

(5) **Same** — Subsection (1) does not apply in respect of the use of a device to contact ambulance, police or fire department emergency services.

(6) **Same** — Subsections (1) and (2) do not apply if all of the following conditions are met:

1. The motor vehicle is off the roadway or is lawfully parked on the roadway.

2. The motor vehicle is not in motion.

3. The motor vehicle is not impeding traffic.

(6.1) **Penalty** — Every person who contravenes this section is guilty of an offence and on conviction is liable to a fine of not less than $300 and not more than $1,000.

(7) **Regulations** — The Minister may make regulations,

(a) prescribing devices for the purpose of subsections (1) and (2);

(b) prescribing persons, classes of persons, devices, activities, conditions and circumstances for the purpose of subsection (4).

(8) **Definition** — In this section,

"motor vehicle" includes a street car, motorized snow vehicle, farm tractor, self-propelled implement of husbandry and road-building machine.

2009, c. 4, s. 2; 2015, c. 14, s. 23

Case Law

R. v. Chadwick, 2011 ONCJ 402, 2011 CarswellOnt 8302, 25 M.V.R. (6th) 324, [2011] O.J. No. 3748 — The offence is one of absolute liability. There are two separate offences, one holding a hand-held communication device, and the other using such a device. The legislation is clear that there should be no distraction in hands of drivers while operating a motor vehicle, whether the hand-held wireless communication is working or not.

R. v. Gill, 2012 ONCJ 326, 2012 CarswellOnt 6936, 34 M.V.R. (6th) 340, [2012] O.J. No. 2511 — The very notorious nature of a cell phone made it unnecessary for the Justice of the Peace to state how she found it was a wireless communication device. The Justice could take judicial notice of what cell phones did.

R. v. Kazemi, 2012 ONCJ 383, 2012 CarswellOnt 7870, 35 M.V.R. (6th) 322, [2012] O.J. No. 2826; reversed 2013 ONCA 585, 2013 CarswellOnt 13276, 117 O.R. (3d) 300, 307 C.C.C. (3d) 307, 49 M.V.R. (6th) 179, 311 O.A.C. 76, [2013] O.J. No. 4300 — Moving the phone from the floor to the passenger seat while at a stop light when it was safe to do so resulted in a momentary handling which did not fall within the meaning of "holding".

R. v. Kazemi (2013), 49 M.V.R. (6th) 179, 2013 ONCA 585, 2013 CarswellOnt 13276, 117 O.R. (3d) 300, 307 C.C.C. (3d) 307, 311 O.A.C. 76, [2013] O.J. No. 4300 (Ont. C.A.) — The ordinary meaning of "holding" does not require sustained contact. The Legislature's purpose of promoting road safety is best served by a complete prohibition of holding cell phones.

R. v. Schull (2013), 44 M.V.R. (6th) 338, 2013 BCPC 132, 2013 CarswellBC 1687 (B.C. Prov. Ct.) — The notorious nature of a cell phone in such common usage today coupled with the officer's observations that it was being held with the left hand up to the side of his head while talking supported the common sense inference that the device had telephone capabilities.

R. v. Ferguson (2013), 46 M.V.R. (6th) 114, 2013 NSSC 191, 2013 CarswellNS 469, 331 N.S.R. (2d) 196, 1051 A.P.R. 196 (N.S. S.C.) — Although the accused had a Bluetooth in her ear when using Google Map Quest, she had a cellular telephone in her hand and was properly convicted.

R. v. Pizzurro, 50 M.V.R. (6th) 1, 2013 ONCA 584, 2013 CarswellOnt 13475, 117 O.R. (3d) 779, 117 O.R. (3d) 782, 311 O.A.C. 74, [2013] O.J. No. 4299 (Ont. C.A.) — It was not necessary that the Crown prove that a cell phone was capable of receiving or transmitting telephone communications, electronic data, mail or text messages in order to convict. The requirement that the device be capable in those respects applied to prescribed devices but not to cell phones. Cell phones were well known as a kind of device that was capable of receiving or transmitting. To impose a requirement that a cell phone held by a driver while driving was capable of receiving or transmitting would be unreasonable both for enforcement and for prosecution.

R. v. Farden (2014), 2014 CarswellSask 697, 71 M.V.R. (6th) 58, 2014 SKQB 340, 459 Sask. R. 248 (Sask. Q.B.) — Listening to an earlier dictated message was a prohibited use.

R. v. MacDonald (2014), 2014 CarswellNS 965, 354 N.S.R. (2d) 101, 71 M.V.R. (6th) 246, 2014 NSSC 442, 1120 A.P.R. 101 (N.S.S.C.) — Holding and looking at one's cellphone while driving is inconsistent with preventing distracted driving.

R. v. Whalen (2014), 67 M.V.R. (6th) 340, 2014 ONCJ 233, 2014 CarswellOnt 5880, [2014] O.J. No. 2386 — Where the accused's head was tilted significantly to the right and there was a cell phone between her right ear and her shoulder, she was "holding" the device and not using a "hands-free" device.

R. v. Pumphrey, 2015 YKTC 2, 2015 CarswellYukon 4, 73 M.V.R. (6th) 160; reversed 2015 YKSC 19, 2015 CarswellYukon 34, 76 M.V.R. (6th) 304, [2015] Y.J. No. 34 — "Holding" a phone between the shoulder and ear was caught by legislation.

R. v. Ikede, 2015 NSSC 264, 2015 CarswellNS 879, 366 N.S.R. (2d) 230, 25 C.R. (7th) 171, 86 M.V.R. (6th) 284, 1154 A.P.R. 230, [2015] N.S.J. No. 459.

Using SIRI, the voice-activated navigation system for directions, did not breach the Nova Scotia legislation.

Related Provisions: See O. Reg. 366/09, Display Screens and Hand-Held Devices.

79. (1) Definition — In this section, "speed measuring warning device" means any device or equipment designed or intended for use in a motor vehicle to warn the driver of the presence of speed measuring equipment in the vicinity and includes any device or equipment designed or intended for use in a motor vehicle to interfere with the effective operation of speed measuring equipment.

(2) Speed measuring warning device prohibited — No person shall drive on a highway a motor vehicle that is equipped with or that carries or contains a speed measuring warning device.

(3) Powers of police officer — A police officer may at any time, without a warrant, stop, enter and search a motor vehicle that he or she has reasonable grounds to believe is equipped with or carries or contains a speed measuring warning device contrary to subsection (2) and may seize and take away any speed measuring warning device found in or upon the motor vehicle.

(4) Forfeiture of device — Where a person is convicted of an offence under this section, any device seized under subsection (3) by means of which the offence was committed is forfeited to the Crown.

(5) Penalty — Every person who contravenes subsection (2) is guilty of an offence and on conviction is liable to a fine of not less than $100 and not more than $1000.

(6) Exception — Subsection (2) does not apply to a person who is transporting speed measuring warning devices in sealed packages in a motor vehicle from a manufacturer to a consignee.

(7) Sale of speed measuring warning devices prohibited — No person shall sell, offer or advertise for sale a speed measuring warning device by retail.

(8) Penalty — Every person who contravenes subsection (7) is guilty of an offence and on conviction is liable,

    (a) for a first offence, to a fine of not more than $1,000; and

    (b) for each subsequent offence, to a fine of not more than $5,000.

1996, c. 33, s. 12

Case Law

R. v. Boivin (1978), 42 C.C.C. 363 (Ont. Prov. Ct.); affirmed (1979), 1 M.V.R. 44, 44 C.C.C. (2d) 348, 93 D.L.R. (3d) 557 (Ont. H.C.); appeal to Ont. Div. Ct. dismissed and leave to appeal to Ont. C.A. refused (1979), 2 M.V.R. xliv (Ont. C.A.); *R. v. Crosstown Motors Ltd.*, [1975] W.W.D. 52, 22 C.C.C. (2d) 404 (Alta. Prov. Ct.); *R. v. Olin* (1978), 6 Alta. L.R. (2d) 229, 12 A.R. 93, 41 C.C.C. (2d) 241, 87 D.L.R. (3d) 152 (Q.B.); *R. v. Grusko*, 11 M.V.R. 239, [1981] 6 W.W.R. 479, 13 Man. R. (2d) 318, 127 D.L.R. (3d) 751 (C.A.); leave to appeal to S.C.C. refused (1981), 13 Man. R. (2d) 360n, 41 N.R. 446; *R. v. Van Dermark* (1994), 5 M.V.R. (3d) 274, 120 Nfld. & P.E.I.R. 271 (Nfld. S.C.) — Section 79 of the Ontario Highway Traffic Act is not unconstitutional, but *intra vires* of the province, being legislation in relation to highways and highway safety.

R. v. Henuset, 20 M.V.R. 1, [1983] 4 W.W.R. 267, 20 Man. R. (2d) 330 (Co. Ct.) — This case presents a consideration of how the police should gather evidence in support of the charge and how the device should be tested under the Manitoba Act.

R. v. Shuler (1983), 21 M.V.R. 189, 26 Alta. L.R. (2d) 270, 46 A.R. 96 (C.A.) — The respondent was acquitted at trial of driving a vehicle equipped with a radar warning device. An appeal to the Court of Queen's Bench was dismissed. The issue was whether the driver of a vehicle equipped with a radar detector from which a fuse was missing was guilty of having a device "capable of detecting" radar. The device could be rendered operative by "popping in a fuse". It was held, allowing the Crown appeal, that effect must be given to the intent of the Legislature, and that it would be absurd to conclude that the device was not capable of detecting radar merely because of the absence of a component that could be added within an extremely short period of time.

R. v. Fehr (1983), 25 M.V.R. 302 (Man. Prov. Ct.); reversed (1984), 29 M.V.R. 63 (Man. Q.B.) — The accused was charged with the offence of having in his possession a radar detecting device contrary to the Highway Traffic Act of Manitoba. The defence moved to have excluded from evidence the testimony of the officer relating to the search and seizure of the radar detecting device from the glove compartment of the accused's vehicle based on ss. 8 and 24(2) of the Charter of Rights. The officer was making routine inspections of vehicles on the highway when he signalled the accused to pull over. He observed the accused lean forward in the driver's seat in a manner which indicated to the officer that the accused might be placing something into his glove compartment. The accused's speed was normal, and aside from such routine check, the accused would have aroused no suspicion of any breach of law. The officer asked the accused if he had a radar detecting device in his vehicle but in the stand was not able to recall what, if any, answer was given. The officer then reached over and opened the glove compartment and took out what he believed to be a radar detecting device. There was no evidence that the accused was asked whether he consented to a search, nor was there any indication that the accused, in fact, did consent. At all times the accused was polite and cooperative. The application was allowed by the trial Judge. The trial Judge held that the administration of justice would be brought into disrepute. On appeal by the Crown it was held that the evidence should not have been excluded. The invasion was minor in the face of no objections during the search. The officer was acting in good faith.

R. v. Munn (1990), 23 M.V.R. (2d) 118, 54 C.C.C. (3d) 397, 82 Nfld. & P.E.I.R. 296, 257 A.P.R. 296 (Nfld. T.D.) — The accused was convicted of operating a motor vehicle containing a radar detector. He subsequently applied to court for the return of the detector which had been seized by the police. The Provincial Court Judge ruled that s. 198A(3) of the Act, which provided that the device was "forfeited to the Crown", was unconstitutional on the basis that it infringed s. 8 of the Canadian Charter of Rights and Freedoms. He ordered that the detector be returned to the accused. The Crown appealed. The appeal was allowed. The weight of authority concerning the application of s. 8 was that seizure was defined by its plain meaning. Accordingly, the retention or use of things could not be challenged under s. 8 of the Charter. There was no merit in the accused's submissions based on s. 11(d) of the Charter. The forfeiture of the device did not shift the burden of proof to the accused and the Crown was still required to prove every element of the offence, including the nature of the device seized, to obtain a conviction.

Lavin c. Québec (Procureur géneral), 42 M.V.R. (2d) 320, 16 C.R. (4th) 112, 76 C.C.C. (3d) 279, [1992] R.J.Q. 1843 (C.A.) — A refusal to hand over a radar detector in the absence of a legal obligation to hand it over does not constitute a criminal obstruction.

R. v. Shannon (1992), 42 M.V.R. (2d) 128, 64 O.A.C. 61 (C.A.) — The accused was charged with driving a motor vehicle with a radar warning device. She was granted an order prohibiting the holding of the trial until disclosure was made by the Crown to the defence of a copy of either the operator's handbook or the service manual for the VG2 interceptor. The Crown appealed. The appeal was allowed. The motions court judge erred in compelling pre-trial disclosure. The matter should have been left to the trial judge. If the Crown were to rely on the interception made by the VG2 to prove that the device seized in the accused's car was a radar detector, the defence would be entitled to challenge the capacity, functioning and accuracy of the VG2. The defence would therefore be entitled to disclosure of the manual. If the Crown did not rely on the VG2 to prove its case at trial, its technical specifications would be irrelevant to the conduct of the defence. The functioning of the VG2 could also be relevant to a defence motion for exclusion of evidence on the basis that the seizure of the device found in the accused's car was made without reasonable and probable grounds. No such motion had been made to date.

R. v. Stone, 2006 CarswellOnt 3421, 2006 ONCJ 201, 35 M.V.R. (5th) 86 (C.J.) — The provisions do not contravene ss. 7 or 8.

R. v. Gurung (2007), 59 M.V.R. (5th) 153, 164 C.R.R. (2d) 110, 2007 CarswellOnt 6994 (S.C.J.) — Under s. 79(3) of the *Act*, a warrantless search for a radar device is permitted.

R. v. Moskalenko, 2009 CarswellOnt 5052, [2009] O.J. No. 3659, 88 M.V.R. (5th) 159 (C.J.) — A new trial was afforded to the Crown where the trier's finding that there was no evidence of a speed detecting device was in error. The officer's machine detected a device and there was a Velcro fastener on the dash.

79.1 (1) Pre-empting traffic control signal devices prohibited — **No person shall drive on a highway a motor vehicle that is equipped with, carries, contains or has attached to it a pre-empting traffic control signal device.**

(2) [Repealed 2005, c. 26, Sched. A, s. 12(1).]

(3) Powers of police officer — **A police officer may at any time, without a warrant, stop, enter and search a motor vehicle that he or she has reasonable grounds to believe is equipped with, carries, contains or has attached to it a pre-empting traffic control signal device contrary to subsection (1) and may detach, if required, seize and take away any such device found in or upon the motor vehicle.**

(4) Forfeiture of device — Where a person is convicted of an offence under this section, any device seized under subsection (3) is forfeited to the Crown.

(5) Penalty — Every person who contravenes subsection (1) is guilty of an offence and on conviction is liable to a fine of not less than $100 and not more than $1,000.

(5.1) Regulations — The Lieutenant Governor in Council may make regulations exempting any class of persons or any class or type of vehicles from subsection (1) and prescribing conditions for such exemptions.

(6) Definition — In this section,

"pre-empting traffic control signal device" means any device or equipment that may temporarily suppress or extend an indication on a traffic control signal from its current setting.

(7) Same — In subsection (6),

"indication" and "traffic control signal" have the same meanings as in section 133.

2002, c. 18, Sched. P, s. 22; 2005, c. 26, Sched. A, s. 12

Related Provisions: See O. Reg. 34/06, Pre-Empting Traffic Control Signal Devices.

Proposed Addition — 79.2

79.2 Powers of police officer re ignition interlock — If a police officer determines that the driver's licence of the driver of a motor vehicle is subject to a condition that prohibits him or her from driving any motor vehicle that is not equipped with an ignition interlock device, the police officer may, without a warrant, stop, enter and inspect the vehicle to determine,

(a) whether the vehicle is equipped with such a device; and

(b) if the vehicle has the device, whether the device has been tampered with in any manner.

2015, c. 14, s. 24 [Not in force at date of publication.]

---

80. (1) Attachments required when vehicle drawn on highway — No motor vehicle, other than a motor vehicle in which there is a person licensed to drive a motor vehicle on a highway, trailer or other object or device shall be drawn by a motor vehicle or farm tractor on a highway unless there are two separate means of attachment so constructed and attached that the failure of one such means will not permit the motor vehicle, trailer, object or device being drawn to become detached; but this section does not apply to a trailer, object or device attached or coupled to the towing vehicle by means of a fifth wheel attachment or to a trailer or other object or device when drawn directly across a highway by a farm tractor.

(2) Penalty — Every person who contravenes this section is guilty of an offence and, if the offence was committed by means of a commercial motor vehicle within the meaning of subsection 16(1), on conviction is liable to a fine of not less than $200 and not more than $20,000.

Proposed Amendment — 80(2)

(2) Penalty — Every person who contravenes this section is guilty of an offence and, if the offence was committed by means of a commercial motor vehicle, on conviction is liable to a fine of not less than $200 and not more than $20,000.

2014, c. 9, Sched. 2, s. 27 [To come into force January 1, 2017.]

1996, c. 20, s. 18

Case Law

Maki v. Corcoran, [1953] O.W.N. 843 — A disabled vehicle being towed by another vehicle is a "trailer" and there should therefore be two separate means of attachment, but no liability will flow from the failure to have two such means if the failure was not an effective cause of the accident.

Langan v. Moore, [1951] O.W.N. 632 (H.C.); appeal dismissed [1951] O.W.N. 927 (C.A.) — The failure to investigate the swaying of a trailer was held to be an act of negligence, quite apart from any question of compliance with this section as to fastenings.

Related Provisions: See the definition of "trailer" in s. 1(1); see R.R.O. 1990, Reg. 618, Specifications and Standards for Trailer Couplings.

81. Regulations re bumpers — **The Lieutenant Governor in Council may make regulations requiring any type or class of commercial motor vehicle or trailer to be equipped with rear bumpers and prescribing the location and means of attachment of the bumpers and prescribing the specifications for the bumpers.**

82. (1) Definitions — In this section,

"commercial motor vehicle" has the same meaning as in subsection 16(1);

Proposed Repeal — 82(1) "commercial motor vehicle"

"commercial motor vehicle" [Repealed 2014, c. 9, Sched. 2, s. 28(1). To come into force January 1, 2017.]

"operator" means,

    (a) the person directly or indirectly responsible for the operation of a commercial motor vehicle, including the conduct of the driver of, and the carriage of goods or passengers, if any, in, the commercial motor vehicle or combination of vehicles, and

    (b) in the absence of evidence to the contrary, where no CVOR certificate, as defined in subsection 16(1), or lease applicable to the commercial motor vehicle, is produced, the holder of the plate portion of the permit for the commercial motor vehicle.

Proposed Amendment — 82(1) "operator" (b)

(b) in the absence of evidence to the contrary, where no CVOR certificate, or lease applicable to the commercial motor vehicle, is produced, the holder of the plate portion of the permit for the commercial motor vehicle.

2014, c. 9, Sched. 2, s. 28(2) [To come into force January 1, 2017.]

(2) Examination of vehicle — Every police officer and every officer appointed for the purpose of carrying out the provisions of this Act may require the driver of any motor vehicle or motor assisted bicycle to stop, move the vehicle to a safe location as directed by the police officer or officer and submit the vehicle, together with its equipment and any vehicle drawn by it, to the examinations and tests that the police officer or officer may consider expedient.

Proposed Amendment — 82(2)

(2) Examination of vehicle — Every police officer and every officer appointed for the purpose of carrying out the provisions of this Act may require the driver of any vehicle, other than a bicycle to stop, move the vehicle to a safe location as directed by the police officer or officer and submit the vehicle, together with its equipment and any vehicle drawn by it, to the examinations and tests that the police officer or officer may consider expedient.

2016, c. 5, Sched. 12, s. 5(1) [Not in force at date of publication.]

(3) **Same** — Every police officer and every officer appointed for the purpose of carrying out the provisions of this Act may require the owner of a motor vehicle, motor assisted bicycle or vehicle drawn by a motor vehicle and the operator of a commercial motor vehicle to submit the vehicle, together with its equipment and, in the case of a commercial motor vehicle, any vehicle drawn by it, to the examinations and tests that the police officer or officer may consider expedient.

Proposed Amendment — 82(3)

(3) **Same** — Every police officer and every officer appointed for the purpose of carrying out the provisions of this Act may require the owner of a vehicle, other than a bicycle and the operator of a commercial motor vehicle to submit the vehicle, together with its equipment and, in the case of a commercial motor vehicle, any vehicle drawn by it, to the examinations and tests that the police officer or officer may consider expedient.

2016, c. 5, Sched. 12, s. 5(2) [Not in force at date of publication.]

(4) **Requirement to bring vehicle into compliance** — Where any vehicle examined or tested under subsection (2) or (3), or any of its equipment, is found not to be in compliance with the requirements of this Act or the regulations, the police officer or officer making the examinations or tests may require the owner or operator of the vehicle to have the vehicle or its equipment repaired and to,

(a) submit the vehicle for further examinations and tests to satisfy a police officer or officer appointed for the purpose of carrying out the provisions of this Act that the vehicle and its equipment comply with the requirements of this Act and the regulations; or

(b) submit evidence to the person or office specified by the police officer or officer that the vehicle and its equipment comply with the requirements of this Act and the regulations.

(5) **Same** — Where any vehicle examined or tested under clause (4)(a), or any of its equipment, is found still not to be in compliance with the requirements of this Act or the regulations, the police officer or officer making the examinations or tests may require the owner or operator of the vehicle to have the vehicle or its equipment repaired and to submit evidence to the person or office specified by the police officer or officer that the vehicle and its equipment comply with the requirements of this Act and the regulations.

(6) **Notice required** — A police officer or officer appointed for the purpose of carrying out the provisions of this Act shall serve written notice in an approved form of a requirement under subsection (3), (4) or (5).

(7) **Deemed service** — Service of a notice under subsection (6) to the driver of the vehicle shall be deemed to be service on the owner and operator, if any, of the vehicle.

(8) **Requirement to assist** — The driver of a vehicle submitted for examinations and tests as required under subsection (2), (3) or (4) and any other person in charge of the vehicle who is present shall, if directed by a police officer or officer appointed for the purposes of carrying out the provisions of this Act, assist with the examinations and tests of the vehicle and of its equipment.

(9) **Offence** — Every person is guilty of an offence and on conviction is liable to a fine of not more than $1,000 who,

(a) refuses or fails to comply with a requirement made under subsection (2), (3), (4), (5), (8) or (12); or

(b) contravenes an order or prohibition made under subsection (12).

(10) **Same, commercial motor vehicle** — Despite subsection (9), every person is guilty of an offence and on conviction is liable to a fine of not less than $400 and not more than $20,000 who, in respect of a commercial motor vehicle or a vehicle drawn by a commercial motor vehicle,

(a) refuses or fails to comply with a requirement made under subsection (2), (3), (4), (5), (8) or (12); or

(b) contravenes an order or prohibition made under subsection (12).

(11) **Defence if notice not received** — Despite subsections (9) and (10), a person is not guilty of an offence for refusing or failing to comply with a requirement under subsection (3), (4) or (5) unless the police officer or officer appointed for the purpose of carrying out the provisions of this Act gave the person a written notice as required by subsection (6).

(12) **Use of vehicle prohibited** — Where any vehicle examined or tested under subsection (2), (3) or (4), or any of its equipment, is found to have a prescribed defect or to be in a dangerous or unsafe condition, with or without a prescribed defect, the police officer or officer appointed for carrying out the provisions of this Act making the examination or tests may,

(a) require the driver, owner or operator of the vehicle to have the prescribed defect repaired and the vehicle and its equipment placed in a safe condition;

(b) order the vehicle to be removed from the highway; and

(c) prohibit the operation of the vehicle on the highway until the prescribed defect has been repaired and the vehicle and its equipment are in a safe condition.

(13) **Seizure of plates, vehicle inspection sticker** — Where the operation of a vehicle has been prohibited under subsection (12), the police officer or officer may,

(a) seize the number plates of the vehicle; and

(b) remove the vehicle inspection sticker, or comparable device issued by another jurisdiction, from the vehicle.

Proposed Amendment — 82(13)(b)

(b) remove the vehicle inspection sticker or stickers or other type of proof of inspection prescribed by the regulations, or comparable evidence issued by a reciprocating province or territory of Canada or any state of the United States designated by the regulations.

2015, c. 14, s. 25 [Not in force at date of publication.]

(14) [Repealed 2008, c. 17, s. 41.]

(15) Regulations — The Lieutenant Governor in Council may make regulations,

(a) prescribing the forms and kinds of evidence that may be required under clause (4)(b) and subsection (5) and prescribing rules for submitting the evidence to the person or office specified;

(b) prescribing the methods and rules for service of notices required to be served under this section;

(c) prescribing types of defects for the purposes of subsection (12);

(d) classifying persons and vehicles, exempting any class of person or class of vehicle from any requirement or provision of this section or of any regulation made under this section and prescribing conditions for any such exemption and prescribing different requirements for different classes of persons or vehicles.

1997, c. 12, s. 9; 1999, c. 12, Sched. R, s. 14; 2008, c. 17, s. 41

Commentary

Sections 82–100 (inclusive) form a unit of the Act relating to a scheme of vehicle inspection.

A police officer or officer appointed under the Act may require a vehicle to be examined and tested (s. 82(1)). The officer accomplishes this by means of written notice (s. 82(4)). Failure to comply with such notice is punishable by a fine of up to $1,000 (s. 82(3)). The Regulations govern the form of notice (s. 82(6)).

Where a vehicle is found to be in a dangerous or unsafe condition, the officer may require the driver or owner to have the vehicle placed in a safe condition and may prohibit the vehicle to be removed from the highway (s. 82(2)). The officer may seize the plates and inspection sticker of such a vehicle (s. 82(5)).

The Red Tape Reduction Act, 1999, S.O. 1999, c. 12, Sched. R. (ss. 1(2), 1(3), 2(1), 2(3), 2(5), 5(1), and 6(1) in force January 1, 2001) amends ss. 6, 7, 12 and 14 of the Highway Traffic Act to facilitate Ontario's participation in the International Registration Plan, which contains reciprocal provisions in respect of commercial motor vehicles that travel across provincial or international borders. The Plan provides for the issuance of IRP cab cards as permits for these vehicles and for the appointment of registration and licence fees in each member jurisdiction on the basis of the distances travelled in each jurisdiction. Persons residing or based in other jurisdictions that are members of the Plan are exempt from the requirements of and fees prescribed under Part II of the Highway Traffic Act.

Impoundment no longer depends on the Registrar but issues by the action of a police officer.

Related Provisions: Section 82.1 of the Act. See O. Reg. 381/02, Testing, Repair and Compliance Requirements for Unsafe Vehicles under Section 82 of the Act.

82.1 (1) Definitions — In this section,

"commercial motor vehicle" has the same meaning as in subsection 16(1);

Proposed Repeal — 82.1(1) "commercial motor vehicle"

"commercial motor vehicle" [Repealed 2014, c. 9, Sched. 2, s. 29(1). To come into force January 1, 2017.]

"designated inspection station" means any location designated by the Registrar for the purpose of inspecting commercial motor vehicles;

"operator" means,

(a) the person directly or indirectly responsible for the operation of a commercial motor vehicle, including the conduct of the driver of, and the carriage of goods or passengers, if any, in, the commercial motor vehicle or combination of vehicles, and

(b) in the absence of evidence to the contrary, where no CVOR certificate, as defined in subsection 16(1), or lease applicable to a commercial motor vehicle, is produced, the holder of the plate portion of the permit for the commercial motor vehicle;

Proposed Amendment — 82.1(1) "operator" (b)

(b) in the absence of evidence to the contrary, where no CVOR certificate, or lease applicable to a commercial motor vehicle, is produced, the holder of the plate portion of the permit for the commercial motor vehicle;

2014, c. 9, Sched. 2, s. 29(2) [To come into force January 1, 2017.]

"owner" means the person whose name appears on the certificate of registration for the vehicle, and, where the certificate of registration for the vehicle consists of a vehicle portion and plate portion, means the person whose name appears on the vehicle portion;

"permit" means the permit issued under subsection 7(7).

(2) Commercial motor vehicles ordered to stop for inspection — In exercising his or her powers under section 82, a police officer or officer appointed for carrying out the provisions of this Act may, at any time, require the driver of a commercial motor vehicle being driven on a highway to stop for inspection and the driver of the vehicle, when signalled or requested to stop by the officer, who is readily identifiable as such, shall immediately come to a safe stop.

(3) Direction to move vehicle to another location — A police officer or officer appointed for carrying out the provisions of this Act may, at any time before, during or after inspecting a commercial motor vehicle or trailer, direct the driver of the commercial motor vehicle to drive it and to draw the attached trailer, if any, to another location where the inspection will be carried out or continued or the vehicle's load will be removed, or any of them.

(4) Inspection — The police officer of officer appointed for carrying out the provisions of this Act may, at the location where the commercial motor vehicle was first stopped or at the location to which it was directed, inspect the commercial motor vehicle and its trailer for critical defects.

(5) **Driver, person in charge to assist inspector** — The driver and any other person in charge of the commercial motor vehicle who is present shall assist the police officer or officer appointed for carrying out the provisions of this Act in his or her inspection of the commercial motor vehicle and its trailer.

(6) **If critical defect found** — If the police officer or officer appointed for carrying out the provisions of this Act inspects the commercial motor vehicle and its trailer at a designated inspection station and finds that the commercial motor vehicle or trailer has one or more critical defects, the vehicle shall be deemed to have been found to be in dangerous or unsafe condition under section 82, but instead of exercising the powers set out in section 82, the police officer or officer appointed for carrying out the provisions of this Act shall forthwith,

> (a) seize the number plates of the vehicle that has the critical defect or defects and remove its vehicle inspection sticker or comparable device issued by another jurisdiction; and

Proposed Amendment — 82.1(6)(a)

(a) seize the number plates of the vehicle that has the critical defect or defects and remove its vehicle inspection sticker or stickers or other type of proof of inspection prescribed by the regulations, or comparable evidence issued by a reciprocating province or territory of Canada or any state of the United States designated by the regulations; and

2015, c. 14, s. 26 [Not in force at date of publication.]

> (b) detain the vehicle that has the critical defect or defects.

> (c) [Repealed 2009, c. 5, s. 33(2).]

(7) **Impoundment** — Once the load, if any, has been removed as may be required by subsection (15), (16), (17) or (18), the detained vehicle shall, at the cost and risk of the owner,

> (a) be removed to an impound facility as directed by a police officer or officer appointed for carrying out the provisions of this Act; and

> (b) be impounded from the time it was detained for the period described in subsection (8) or until ordered to be released by the Registrar under subsection (23) or (24) or under section 50.3.

(8) **Impound period** — A vehicle detained under subsection (6) shall be impounded as follows:

> 1. For 15 days, if the vehicle has not previously been impounded under this section within a prescribed period.

> 2. For 30 days, if the vehicle has previously been impounded once under this section within a prescribed period.

> 3. For 60 days, if the vehicle has previously been impounded two or more times under this section within a prescribed period.

(9) Release of vehicle — Subject to subsection (20), the vehicle shall be released to its owner from the impound facility upon the expiry of the period of the impoundment or upon being ordered to be released by the Registrar under subsection (23) or (24) or under section 50.3.

(10) Duty of officer re impoundment — Every officer who detains a vehicle under this section shall, as soon as practicable,

(a) prepare a notice identifying the vehicle that is to be impounded, the name and address of the driver, the date and time of the impoundment, the period of time for which the vehicle is impounded and the place where the vehicle may be recovered;

(b) serve the driver with a copy of the notice; and

(c) forward a copy of the notice to the Registrar.

(11) Service on driver is deemed service on owner and operator — Service of a copy of a notice of the impoundment on the driver of the vehicle under clause (10)(b) is deemed to be service on and sufficient notice to the owner and operator of the vehicle.

(12) Permit suspended — Upon being notified under clause (10)(c), the Registrar may issue an order to suspend the vehicle portion of the permit for the impounded vehicle by mailing it to the owner and operator of the commercial motor vehicle at the most recent address for them appearing in the records of the Ministry, and upon issuing such an order, the Registrar shall suspend the vehicle portion of the permit of the vehicle, and the suspension shall be effective when the order is issued.

(13) Notice by Registrar — The Registrar may provide notice of the impoundment to the owner and operator of the vehicle by mailing it to them at the latest address for them appearing in the records of the Ministry.

(14) Surrender of documents, information re trip and goods carried — If the commercial motor vehicle or trailer that is to be impounded contains goods, the police officer or officer appointed for carrying out the provisions of this Act may require the driver and any other person present who is in charge of the vehicle to surrender all documents in his or her possession or in the vehicle that relate to the operation of the vehicle or to the carriage of the goods and to furnish all information within that person's knowledge relating to the details of the current trip and the ownership of the goods.

(15) Operator to remove load — Upon being served with notice of the impoundment through service on the driver under subsection (10), the operator of the vehicle shall forthwith remove the load from the commercial motor vehicle or trailer, or both, and from the inspection site.

(16) Application of _Dangerous Goods Transportation Act_ — If the goods are dangerous goods, within the meaning of the _Dangerous Goods Transportation Act_, the operator shall remove them in accordance with that Act.

(17) Officer may remove load at operator's cost, risk — If, in the opinion of a police officer or officer appointed for carrying out the provisions of this Act, the operator fails to remove the load as required by subsection (15) within a reasonable time after being served with notice of the impoundment, the officer may cause the load to be removed and stored or disposed of at the cost and risk of the operator.

(18) **Same** — If the police officer or officer appointed for carrying out the provisions of this Act is of the opinion that the operator has not made appropriate arrangements for the removal of the load, having regard to the nature of the goods, including the fact that they are or appear to be dangerous goods, within the meaning of the *Dangerous Goods Transportation Act*, or are perishable, the officer may cause the load to be removed, stored or otherwise disposed of at the cost and risk of the operator.

(19) [Repealed 2009, c. 5, s. 33(4).]

(20) **Personal property in vehicle available to owner** — Any personal property that is left in the impounded commercial motor vehicle or trailer and that is not attached to or used in connection with its operation shall, upon request and proof of ownership, be make available, at reasonable times, to the owner of the property.

(21) **Court application for interim release of vehicle** — The owner of a vehicle impounded under this action may, on notice to the Registrar, apply to the Superior Court of Justice for an order directing the Registrar to release the vehicle and reinstate the vehicle portion of its permit.

(22) **Registrar may request to be a party** — The Registrar may, on his or her request, be made a party to an application under subsection (21).

(23) **Court order to release vehicle, security required** — On an application being made under subsection (21), the court may make the order applied for,

(a) if the owner has also commenced as appeal under section 50.3; and

(b) on condition that the owner deposit with the court security in the prescribed form and in the amount determined by the court, which shall not be less than $5,000 or more than $10,000.

(24) **Vehicle released from impound facility** — If the court makes the order requested, the Registrar, on being served with a copy of the order by the owner of the vehicle, shall,

(a) order that the vehicle be released to its owner from the impound facility; and

(b) reinstate the vehicle portion of the permit.

(25) **Same** — If an order is made under subsection (24) but the Registrar later orders the vehicle returned to the impound facility under section 50.3, the Registrar shall, upon the expiry of the remainder of the period of impoundment,

(a) order that the vehicle be released to its owner from the impound facility; and

(b) reinstate the vehicle portion of the permit.

(26) Owner must pay removal costs — Despite being served with an order under subsection (24) or (25) by the owner of the vehicle, the person who operates the impound facility is not required to release the vehicle to the owner until the owner pays the removal and impound costs related to the Registrar's order to impound and suspend.

(27) Vehicle cannot be operated until made safe — Despite the release of the vehicle and the reinstatement of the vehicle portion of the permit, no person shall drive or operate the vehicle on a highway until it has been placed in a safe condition.

(28) Lien on vehicle for removal, impound costs — The costs incurred by the person who operates the impound facility in respect of an order to impound and suspend under this section are a lien on the vehicle, which may be enforced in the manner provided under Part III of the *Repair and Storage Liens Act*.

(29) Debt due to police, Crown — The costs incurred by a police force or the Crown in removing, storing or disposing of a load from a commercial motor vehicle or trailer under subsection (17) or (18) are a debt due to the police force or Crown, as the case may be, and may be recovered by the police force or Crown in any court of competent jurisdiction.

(30) Impound, removal service providers are independent contractors — Persons who provide removal services or load removal services or who operate impound facilities, and their subcontractors, are independent contractors and not agents of the Ministry for the purposes of this section; such persons shall not charge more for their services in connection with this section than is permitted by regulation.

(31) Protection from personal liability — No action or other proceeding for damages shall be instituted against the Registrar or any employee of the Ministry for any act done in good faith in the execution or intended execution of his or her duty under this section or for any alleged neglect or default in the execution in good faith of that duty.

(32) Crown not relieved of liability — Despite subsections 5(2) and (4) of the *Proceedings Against the Crown Act*, subsection (31) does not relieve the Crown of liability in respect of a tort committed by a person mentioned in that subsection to which it would otherwise be subject.

(33) Offence — Every person who fails to comply with subsection (2), (5) or (15), or with a requirement or direction of a police officer or officer appointed for carrying out the provisions of this Act under subsection (3) or (14), is guilty of an offence and on conviction is liable to a fine of not less than $200 and not more than $20,000 and in addition the person's driver's licence may be suspended for a period of not more than six months.

(34) Same — Every person who drives or operates or removes a commercial motor vehicle or trailer that is impounded under this section and every person who causes or permits such a commercial motor vehicle or trailer to be driven, operated or removed is guilty of an offence and on conviction is liable to a fine of not less than $200 and not more than $20,000.

(35) Same — Every person who provides removal services or who operates an impound facility and who charges fees for services provided in connection with this section in excess of those permitted by regulation is guilty of an offence and on conviction is liable to a fine of not less than $100 and not more than $1,000.

(36) Same — Every person who obstructs or interferes with a police officer or officer appointed for carrying out the provisions of this Act in the performance of his or her duties under this section is guilty of an offence and on conviction is liable to a fine of not less than $200 and not more than $20,000 or to imprisonment for a term of not more than six months, or to both.

(36.1) Intent of impoundment and suspension — The impoundment and suspension under this section are intended to promote compliance with the safety standards set out in and under this Act and to thereby safeguard the public and do not constitute an alternative to any proceeding or penalty arising from the same circumstances or around the same time.

(36.2) Impoundment concurrent with other administrative impoundments — The impoundment of a commercial motor vehicle under this section runs concurrently with an impoundment, if any, of the same motor vehicle under section 41.4, 48.4, 55.1, 55.2 or 172.

(37) Regulations — The Lieutenant Governor in Council may make regulations,

(a) prescribing what constitutes a critical defect;

(b) governing the training and certification of police officers and officers appointed for carrying out the provisions of this Act to carry out an inspection under this section;

(c) prescribing inspection procedures, inspection requirements and equipment and performance standards for carrying out inspections under this section;

(c.1) requiring police officers to keep records with respect to vehicle impoundments under this section for a specified period of time and to report specified information with respect to vehicle impoundments to the Registrar and governing such records and reports;

(d) prescribing the period for the purpose of subsection (8);

(e) prescribing a schedule of fees that may be charged by independent contractors for services in connection with this section;

(f) prescribing the form of security that may be deposited pursuant to an order made under subsection (23) and governing the forfeiture and return of the security;

(g) prescribing the manner in which orders may be issued and notification of them given under this section;

(h) prescribing methods for and rules of service for any notices or orders required to be served under this section;

(i) classifying commercial motor vehicles and trailers and exempting any class of commercial motor vehicle or trailer from any provision of this section or from any regulation made under this section and prescribing conditions for any such exemption.

(38) [Repealed 2008, c. 17, s. 42.]
    1997, c. 12, s. 10; 2002, c. 18, Sched. P, s. 23; 2008, c. 17, s. 42; 2009, c. 5, s. 33

Commentary

The Act is amended to provide that if a "critical defect" which will be defined in regulations, is found in a commercial motor vehicle or trailer in the course of a roadside inspection, the Registrar of Motor Vehicles may, without any hearing, immediately order that the commercial motor vehicle or trailer be impounded and its vehicle permit suspended. The period of impoundment and suspension is as follows: 15 days for a vehicle that hasn't been previously, in a prescribed period, impounded under the same section: 30 days for a vehicle that has been impounded once, in a prescribed period, under the same section; 60 days for a vehicle that has been impounded more than once, in a prescribed period, under the same section.

The owner of the impounded commercial motor vehicle or trailer may appeal the order to impound and suspend to the Licence Suspension Appeal Board. The only grounds for appealing the orders are that the vehicle was stolen when the critical defect was found or that it had no critical defect at the time of the inspection.

The owner of the impounded commercial motor vehicle or trailer may obtain an interim release of the vehicle from the Ontario Court (General Division), pending final decision of the Licence Suspension Appeal Board, on posting security of $5,000 to $10,000 with the court. If the owner fails to return the vehicle to the impound facility when ordered to by the Registrar, the security is forfeited to the Crown.

The Red Tape Reduction Act, 1999, S.O. 1999, c. 12, Sched. R. (ss. 1(2), 1(3), 2(1), 2(3), 2(5), 5(1), and 6(1) in force January 1, 2001) amends ss. 6, 7, 12 and 14 of the Highway Traffic Act to facilitate Ontario's participation in the International Registration Plan, which contains reciprocal provisions in respect of commercial motor vehicles that travel across provincial or international borders. The Plan provides for the issuance of IRP cab cards as permits for these vehicles and for the appointment of registration and licence fees in each member jurisdiction on the basis of the distances travelled in each jurisdiction. Persons residing or based in other jurisdictions that are members of the Plan are exempt from the requirements of and fees prescribed under Part II of the Highway Traffic Act.

Case Law

R. v. Nolet, 2009 CarswellSask 39, 2009 SKCA 8, 74 M.V.R. (5th) 1, 444 W.A.C. 179, 320 Sask. R. 179, [2009] 4 W.W.R. 604, 245 C.C.C. (3d) 419, 183 C.R.R. (2d) 138; affirmed 2010 SCC 24, 2010 CarswellSask 368, 2010 CarswellSask 369, EYB 2010-175730, [2010] S.C.J. No. 24, [2010] A.C.S. No. 24, [2010] 1 S.C.R. 851, 256 C.C.C. (3d) 1, 320 D.L.R. (4th) 1, 213 C.R.R. (2d) 52, 403 N.R. 1, 76 C.R. (6th) 1, 350 Sask. R. 51, 487 W.A.C. 51, [2010] 8 W.W.R. 1, 95 M.V.R. (5th) 1 — The authority to stop and search a commercial motor vehicle was canvassed.

Related Provisions: Sections 50.3, 82 of the Act; O. Reg. 512/97, Critical Defects of Commercial Motor Vehicles.

83. Regulations re inspection of certain motor vehicles — The Lieutenant Governor in Council may make regulations,

(a) requiring the owners of commercial motor vehicles, or any type or class thereof, uninsured motor vehicles or motor assisted bicycles, and motor vehicles or motor assisted bicycles that have been involved in accidents that are reportable under section 199 to submit them to inspection;

(b) prescribing the inspection procedures, inspection requirements and performance standards required for the motor vehicles and motor assisted bicycles;

(c) prohibiting the operation on a highway of motor vehicles and motor assisted bicycles that do not comply with the requirements and standards, and providing for the seizure of the number plates of the motor vehicles and for holding them until the motor vehicle is made to comply with the requirements and standards.

Related Provisions: See R.R.O. 1990, Reg. 629, Accessible Vehicles; O. Reg. 199/07, Commercial Motor Vehicle Inspections; R.R.O. 1990, Reg. 587, Equipment; R.R.O. 1990, Reg. 596, General; R.R.O. 1990, Reg. 611, Safety Inspections; R.R.O. 1990, Reg. 612, School Buses; R.R.O. 1990, Reg. 613, Seat Belt Assemblies; R.R.O. 1990, Reg. 618, Specifications and Standards for Trailer Couplings; R.R.O. 1990, Reg. 625, Tire Standards and Specifications.

84. (1) Penalty for driving unsafe vehicle — No person shall drive or operate or permit the driving or operation upon a highway of a vehicle, a street car or vehicles that in combination are in a dangerous or unsafe condition.

(1.1) Vehicle with critical defect deemed unsafe — If a commercial motor vehicle or trailer has one or more critical defect, as prescribed by regulation, it shall be deemed to be in a dangerous or unsafe condition.

(2) Penalty — Every person who contravenes this section is guilty of an offence and, if the offence was committed by means of a commercial motor vehicle within the meaning of subsection 16(1), on conviction is liable to a fine of not less than $400 and not more than $20,000.

Proposed Amendment — 84(2)

(2) Penalty — Every person who contravenes this section is guilty of an offence and, if the offence was committed by means of a commercial motor vehicle, on conviction is liable to a fine of not less than $400 and not more than $20,000.

2014, c. 9, Sched. 2, s. 30 [To come into force January 1, 2017.]

1996, c. 20, s. 19; 1997, c. 12, s. 11; 2009, c. 33, Sched. 26, s. 3(9), (10)

Case Law

Morton v. Sykes, [1951] O.W.N. 687 (H.C.) — The owner and driver of a motor vehicle cannot be expected to be an insurer of its mechanical perfection at all times. It is sufficient if he uses reasonable care and skill to ensure that it operates safely on the highway.

Phillips v. Britannia Hygienic Laundry Co., [1923] 1 K.B. 539; affirmed [1923] 2 K.B. 832 (C.A.) — The duty is not to have the vehicle reasonably fit for the road, but to take reasonable care that it is fit for the road. The duty is discharged by the owner if he puts the vehicle into the hands of a competent repairer to do what is necessary to put it, and maintain it, in a fit state for the road.

Gascon v. Belhumeur, [1942] Que. S.C. 89 (S.C.); *Winter v. B.C. Elec. Ry.* (1910), 15 B.C.R. 81, 13 W.L.R. 352 (C.A.) — Failure to apply the latest improvements and devices is not, *per se*, to be regarded as negligence.

Morrison v. Leyenhorst, [1968] 2 O.R. 741, 70 D.L.R. (2d) 469 (Co. Ct.) — A breach of s. 84 provides *prima facie* evidence of negligence provided it is the proximate cause of the accident.

Rintoul v. X-Ray and Radium Indust. Ltd., [1956] S.C.R. 674; *Grise v. Rankin*, [1951] O.W.N. 21 (C.A.) — Driving with defective apparatus is a negligent act if the defect might reasonably have been discovered and it will be a question of fact in each case whether adequate care was taken in inspection and maintenance.

Warren v. Gray Goose Stage Ltd., [1938] S.C.R. 52, [1938] 1 D.L.R. 104; *Barkway v. South Wales Tpt. Co.*, [1950] 1 All E.R. 392 (H.L.) — Common carriers, in particular, are required to exercise a high degree of care in the inspection of their vehicles.

Phillips v. Ford Motor Co., [1970] 2 O.R. 714 (H.C.) — The distributor, vendor and re-pairer were held liable for damages sustained by the owner in an accident caused by failure of the brake system.

Fearon v. Toljander; Hillier v. Hagell (1984), 28 M.V.R. 140 (B.C. S.C.) — The defendant was held 25% liable where the brakes, steering and wheel alignment were faulty. The severity of the accident could have been reduced.

R v. Paul Tokiwa Cartage Ltd. (2002), 31 M.V.R. (4th) 315, 2002 CarswellOnt 2262 (C.J.) — The fact that s. 84 also makes the owner of an unsafe trailer liable for permitting a trailer to be operated on a highway in an unsafe condition does not relieve the owner of the tractor unit pulling an unsafe trailer from liability.

R. v. Quality Carriers Inc., 2009 CarswellOnt 3718, 2009 ONCA 523, 254 O.A.C. 5, 83 M.V.R. (5th) 102 — There is nothing in the language of s. 84(1.1) to suggest that the intention of the legislature was to have what was prescribed by regulation as a critical defect for s. 82.1 to also be a critical defect for s. 84(1.1).

R. v. Tsapoitis (2013), 42 M.V.R. (6th) 168, 2013 ONCJ 41, 2013 CarswellOnt 1221 (Ont. C.J.) — A wood chipper was considered a vehicle.

84.1 (1) Offence if wheel detaches from commercial motor vehicle —
Where a wheel becomes detached from a commercial motor vehicle, or from a vehicle being drawn by a commercial motor vehicle, while the commercial motor vehicle is on a highway, the operator of the commercial motor vehicle and the owner of the vehicle from which the wheel became detached are guilty of an offence.

(2) Exception — **If a wheel is detached for the purpose of carrying out a roadside repair, subsection (1) does not apply while the wheel is so detached.**

(3) Penalty — **Upon conviction of an offence under subsection (1), the person is liable to a fine of not less than $2,000 and not more than $50,000.**

(4) No imprisonment or probation — **A person convicted of an offence under subsection (1) is not liable to imprisonment or to a probation order under subsection**

72(1) of the *Provincial Offences Act* as a result of the conviction or as a result of default in payment of the fine resulting from the conviction.

(5) Absolute liability offence — It is not a defence to a charge under subsection (1) that the person exercised due diligence to avoid or prevent the detaching of the wheel.

(6) Deemed owner — For the purpose of this section, the holder of the permit or of the plate portion of the permit shall be deemed to be the owner of the vehicle, if the number plate displayed on the vehicle at the time the offence was committed corresponds to the permit, unless the permit holder proves that the number plate was displayed on the vehicle without the permit holder's consent.

(7) Definitions — In this section,

"operator" means,

(a) the person directly or indirectly responsible for the operation of a commercial motor vehicle, including the conduct of the driver of, and the carriage of goods or passengers, if any, in, the commercial motor vehicle or combination of vehicles, and

(b) in the absence of evidence to the contrary, where no CVOR certificate, as defined in subsection 16(1), or lease applicable to a commercial motor vehicle, is produced, the holder of the plate portion of the permit for the commercial motor vehicle;

Proposed Amendment — 84.1(7) "operator" (b)

(b) in the absence of evidence to the contrary, where no CVOR certificate, or lease applicable to a commercial motor vehicle, is produced, the holder of the plate portion of the permit for the commercial motor vehicle;

2014, c. 9, Sched. 2, s. 31 [To come into force January 1, 2017.]

"wheel" includes a major component of a wheel, such as a wheel rim or wheel assembly, and a large piece of a wheel or of a major component of a wheel, but does not include a tire or large piece of a tire.

(8) Same — In this section and in sections 84.2 and 84.3,

"commercial motor vehicle" does not include a commercial motor vehicle, other than a bus, having a gross vehicle weight, as defined in subsection 114(1), or manufacturer's gross vehicle weight rating, or gross vehicle weight for the purpose of determining the permit fee under subsection 121(1) of 4,500 kilograms or less;

"permit" means a permit issued under subsection 7(7) or a vehicle permit issued by another province or state.

1997, c. 12, s. 12; 2002, c. 18, Sched. P, s. 24; 2005, c. 26, Sched. A, s. 13

Commentary

The owner and operator of a commercial vehicle are guilty of an absolute liability offence if a wheel or part of a wheel becomes detached from the vehicle while it is on a highway.

Case Law

Ontario (Minister of Transportation) v. Ryder Truck Rental Canada Ltd. (2000), *(sub nom. Ontario (Minister of Transport) v. Ryder Truck Rental Canada Ltd.)* 47 O.R. (3d) 171, *(sub nom. R. v. Ryder Truck Rental Canada Ltd.)* 129 O.A.C. 80, 1 M.V.R. (4th) 10 (C.A.) — Section 84.1 was enacted because of a concern over the threat to the public from flying truck wheels resulting from faulty wheel fastening mechanisms. Under the section a wheel becomes detached only when the wheel itself separates from the vehicle and not when an assembly of which the wheel is a part separates from the vehicle. The latter situation could be caught by s. 84.

R. v. 1260448 Ontario Inc. (2003), 2003 CarswellOnt 4617, *(sub nom. R. v. Transport Robert (1973) ltée)* 178 O.A.C. 361, 16 C.R. (6th) 136, 46 M.V.R. (4th) 24, 180 C.C.C. (3d) 254, 68 O.R. (3d) 51, 234 D.L.R. (4th) 546 (Ont. C.A.); leave to appeal refused (2004), 2004 CarswellOnt 1624, 2004 CarswellOnt 1625, [2004] S.C.C.A. No. 8, *(sub nom. R. v. Transport Robert (1973) Ltée)* 330 N.R. 197 (note), *(sub nom. R. v. Transport Robert (1973) Ltée)* 196 O.A.C. 398 (note), 236 D.L.R. (4th) viii, 182 C.C.C. (3d) vi, *(sub nom. R. v. Transport Robert (1973) Ltée)* 114 C.R.R. (2d) 188 (note) (S.C.C.) — The offence does not violate the Charter. The legislature did not place an unconstitutional burden of proof of the elements of the offence on the defence. The only constitutional issue was whether s. 7 mandates that the accused be permitted to raise the defence of due diligence. A prosecution does not engage the kind of exceptional state-induced psychological stress that would trigger a security of the person guarantee in s. 7. The regulatory offence focuses on the unintended but harmful consequences of the commercial trucking industry rather than on moral turpitude. The diminished stigma is not sufficient to trigger the security interest in s. 7, even with the possibility of a significant fine.

84.2 (1) Offence if parts, etc., detach — Where any part of a vehicle or anything affixed to a vehicle becomes detached from the vehicle while it is on a highway, the driver of the vehicle is guilty of an offence.

(2) Exception — If a part or thing is detached from a vehicle for the purpose of carrying out a roadside repair, subsection (1) does not apply while the part or thing is so detached.

(3) Penalty — Upon conviction of an offence under subsection (1), the driver of the vehicle is liable to a fine of not less than $100 and not more than $2,000.

(4) Same — Where the vehicle from which the part or thing becomes detached is a commercial motor vehicle, a vehicle drawn by a commercial motor vehicle, a mobile crane or a road-building machine, the driver of the vehicle is liable on conviction to a fine of not less than $400 and not more than $20,000, and not as provided in subsection (3).

(5) Licence suspension — In addition to the penalty under subsection (3) or (4), as the case may be, the court may suspend the person's driver's licence for a period of not more than 60 days.

2005, c. 26, Sched. A, s. 14

84.3 (1) Offence of causing parts to detach — Every person who performs work to repair or maintain a vehicle or a vehicle part and who does anything that causes a part of the vehicle or anything affixed to the vehicle to become detached from the vehicle while it is on a highway is guilty of an offence.

(2) **Same** — Every person who carries on a business of repairing or maintaining vehicles or vehicle parts and who does anything or permits another person to do anything that causes a part of a vehicle or anything affixed to a vehicle to become detached from the vehicle while it is on a highway is guilty of an offence.

(3) **Exception** — If a part or thing is detached from a vehicle for the purpose of carrying out a roadside repair, subsections (1) and (2) do not apply while the part or thing is so detached.

(4) **Penalty** — Upon conviction of an offence under subsection (1) or (2), a person is liable to a fine of not less than $100 and not more than $2,000.

(5) **Same, commercial motor vehicle** — Where the vehicle from which the part or thing becomes detached is a commercial motor vehicle, a vehicle drawn by a commercial motor vehicle, a mobile crane or a road-building machine, the person who is guilty of an offence under subsection (1) or (2) is liable on conviction to a fine of not less than $400 and not more than $20,000, and not as provided in subsection (4).

2005, c. 26, Sched. A, s. 15

85. (1) Prohibition where evidence of inspection required — No person shall operate or permit to be operated on a highway a vehicle of a type or class prescribed by the regulations made under clause 87(a) unless the vehicle displays, affixed in the place and manner prescribed in the regulations, a device issued by the Ministry as evidence that the inspection requirements and performance standards prescribed by the regulations have been complied with.

Proposed Amendment — 85(1)

(1) **Prohibition where evidence of inspection required** — No person shall operate or permit to be operated on a highway a vehicle of a type or class prescribed by the regulations made under clause 87(a) unless,

> (a) the vehicle displays, affixed in the place and manner prescribed by the regulations, an annual inspection sticker and, if prescribed, a semi-annual inspection sticker; or

> (b) where permitted by the regulations and in a form prescribed by the regulations, the vehicle has attached to it or is associated with another type of proof of inspection issued by a vehicle inspection centre.

2015, c. 14, s. 27 [Not in force at date of publication.]

(2) **Where subs. (1) does not apply** — Subsection (1) does not apply to an operator of a vehicle of a class or type prescribed by the regulations who produces evidence that the vehicle has met the inspection requirements and performance standards of a reciprocating province or state designated by the regulations.

Proposed Amendment — 85(2)

(2) Exception, proof from reciprocating Canadian jurisdiction or state — Subsection (1) does not apply to a vehicle where its driver produces evidence that the vehicle was inspected in accordance with the inspection procedures and met the equipment and performance standards of a reciprocating province or territory of Canada or any state of the United States designated by the regulations, subject to any conditions or limitations set out in the regulations.

2015, c. 14, s. 27 [Not in force at date of publication.]

(3) Removal of plates by officer — Where the device required by subsection (1) is not displayed as prescribed by the regulations, a police officer or officer appointed for the purpose of carrying out the provisions of this Act may seize the number plates of the vehicle.

Proposed Amendment — 85(3)

(3) Removal of plates by officer — Where, as required by subsection (1), the sticker or stickers or other type of proof of inspection are not displayed as prescribed by the regulations, a police officer or officer appointed for the purposes of carrying out the provisions of this Act may seize the sticker or stickers or other type of proof of inspection and the number plates of the vehicle.

2015, c. 14, s. 27 [Not in force at date of publication.]

(4) Penalty — Every person who contravenes this section is guilty of an offence and on conviction is liable to a fine of not less than $200 and not more than $20,000.

1996, c. 20, s. 20

Case Law

Ontario (Ministry of Transportation) v. Underground Services (1983) Ltd. (2006), 41 M.V.R. (5th) 252, 2006 CarswellOnt 6930 (C.J.) — Under a provision under s. 85(1), a proper reading of the regulations requires that actual weight be added to actual weight, and registered gross weight to registered gross weight.

Related Provisions: See R.R.O. 1990, Reg. 575, Commercial Motor Vehicle Inspections; R.R.O. 1990, Reg. 601, Motor Vehicle Inspection Stations; R.R.O. 1990, Reg. 611, Safety Inspections.

86. Certificates and stickers provided by Ministry — No person shall issue a safety standards certificate or affix a vehicle inspection sticker except a certificate or sticker provided by the Ministry.

Proposed Repeal — 86

86. [Repealed 2015, c. 14, s. 28. Not in force at date of publication.]

Related Provisions: See s. 85 of the Act.

87. Regulations re inspection of vehicles — **The Lieutenant Governor in Council may make regulations,**

    (a) prescribing the types or classes of vehicles requiring the device mentioned in section 85;

Proposed Amendment — 87(a)

(a) governing, for the purposes of section 85, annual inspection stickers and semi-annual inspection stickers and other types of proof of inspection;

> 2015, c. 14, s. 29 [Not in force at date of publication.]

    (b) designating reciprocating provinces and states and prescribing types and classes of vehicles for the purposes of subsection 85(2);

Proposed Amendment — 87(b)

(b) prescribing the types or classes of vehicles requiring annual inspection stickers or semi-annual inspection stickers or other types of proof of inspection mentioned in section 85;

> 2015, c. 14, s. 29 [Not in force at date of publication.]

    (c) prescribing the methods and procedures relating to the use or issue of a device as evidence that the prescribed inspection procedures, inspection requirements and performance standards have been complied with;

Proposed Amendment — 87(c)

(c) governing alternative methods of complying with section 85 by employing other types of proof of inspection, including requiring or permitting a method other than displaying annual and semi-annual inspection stickers;

> 2015, c. 14, s. 29 [Not in force at date of publication.]

    (d) prescribing the period of time for which the device referred to in clause (c) shall be valid and the manner of affixing and displaying the device;

Proposed Amendment — 87(d)

(d) designating reciprocating provinces or territories of Canada or states of the United States for the purposes of subsection 85(2) and setting conditions or limitations on the recognition of evidence of inspection results;

> 2015, c. 14, s. 29 [Not in force at date of publication.]

    (e) prescribing the times that vehicles shall be submitted to inspection; and

Proposed Amendment — 87(e)

(e) prescribing the period of time for which the stickers or other types of proof of inspection referred to in section 85 shall be valid and any conditions for their validity;

> 2015, c. 14, s. 29 [Not in force at date of publication.]

    (f) defining for purposes of the regulations any word or expression used in the Act or regulations.

Related Provisions: See ss. 85 and 86 of the Act.

88. Definitions — In this section and in sections 89 to 100,

"Director" means the Director of Vehicle Inspection Standards appointed under section 89;

"licensee" means a person who is the holder of a motor vehicle inspection station licence issued under section 91;

"motor vehicle inspection mechanic" means a person who certifies by means of a safety standards certificate that a motor vehicle complies with the equipment and performance standards prescribed by the regulations;

"motor vehicle inspection station" means any premises maintained or operated for the inspection of motor vehicles and the issuance of safety standards certificates or vehicle inspection stickers in respect of the motor vehicles;

"registrant" means a person who is registered as a motor vehicle inspection station mechanic under section 92;

"vehicle inspection record" means a form required to be completed in accordance with the regulations prior to the issue of a vehicle inspection sticker;

"vehicle inspection sticker" means the device issued as evidence that the inspection requirements and performance standards referred to in section 85 have been complied with.

Proposed Repeal — 88

88. [Repealed 2015, c. 14, s. 30. Not in force at date of publication.]

Commentary

Sections 88–100 provide for a scheme of inspection. There shall be a Director of Vehicle Inspection Standards (s. 88) who shall certify "motor vehicle inspection stations". Upon examination by a "motor vehicle inspection mechanic", a vehicle may receive a "safety standards certificate" or "vehicle inspection sticker" which is certification that the vehicle has passed inspection requirements and performance standards.

Related Provisions: See R.R.O. 1990, Reg. 601, Motor Vehicle Inspection Stations; R.R.O. 1990, Reg. 611, Safety Inspections.

89. Director — The Minister shall appoint an officer of the Ministry to be the Director of Vehicle Inspection Standards for purposes of sections 88 to 100.

Proposed Repeal — 89

89. [Repealed 2015, c. 14, s. 30. Not in force at date of publication.]

90. (1) Issue of safety standards certificate — No person other than a licensee or a person authorized in writing by the licensee shall issue a safety standards certificate.

(2) Affixing vehicle inspection sticker — No person other than a licensee, a motor vehicle inspection mechanic or a person authorized in writing by the licensee shall affix a vehicle inspection sticker to a vehicle.

(3) Prerequisite for issue of safety standards certificate or affixing vehicle inspection sticker — A safety standards certificate in respect of a motor vehicle shall not be issued or a vehicle inspection sticker affixed to a vehicle unless,

    (a) the vehicle has been inspected by a motor vehicle inspection mechanic in the motor vehicle inspection station and the vehicle complies with the inspection requirements and performance standards prescribed by the regulations; and

    (b) the safety standards certificate or a vehicle inspection record,

        (i) is made by the motor vehicle inspection mechanic who inspected the vehicle, and

        (ii) is countersigned by the licensee or a person authorized in writing by the licensee.

Proposed Repeal — 90

90. [Repealed 2015, c. 14, s. 30. Not in force at date of publication.]

Case Law

Purpose of Certificate

Cohen v. Mullin, [1960] O.W.N. 115, 23 D.L.R. (2d) 293 (C.A.); *Henzel v. Brussels Motors Ltd.*, [1973] 1 O.R. 339, 31 D.L.R. (3d) 131 (Co. Ct.) — The issuance of a certificate constituted an express warranty that the vehicle had been inspected pursuant to the regulations.

R. v. Biluk (1981), 14 M.V.R. 53 (Ont. Prov. Ct.) — The section was framed so as to encompass two situations: it was intended to prohibit unlicensed persons or unlicensed stations from issuing certificates; it was also intended to prevent licensed stations from issuing certificates without first ascertaining that the inspected vehicle met the requirements of the regulations. Assuming that the former purpose was not intended by the Legislature, which was not conceded, and there was a need to prove the existence of the enabling licence, it need not be produced in evidence. That evidence was found in the safety standards certificate itself in which the respondent held himself out to be properly licensed and that the station in question was a motor vehicle inspection station, both pursuant to former s. 58 of the Act. A new trial was ordered.

R. v. Servacar Ltd. (1983), 25 M.V.R. 83, 1 O.A.C. 95 (C.A.) — The statutory requirement of the licensee for the purposes of this appeal was first to see to it that the vehicle had been inspected by a motor vehicle inspection mechanic. The licensee also must have been satisfied that the mechanic found the vehicle to comply with the inspection requirements and performance standards. Both of these requirements had been satisfied in this case. If liability is to be imposed on someone for the acts or omissions of others, then it is important that the statute clearly manifest such an intention. The statute here did not clearly impose such a liability.

Ali v. 301077 Ontario Ltd. (1984), 27 M.V.R. 95 (Ont. Prov. Ct.) — The issuing of a certificate under the Highway Traffic Act is to protect the public interest. A vendor obtains such a certificate in order to sell an automobile. The issuer of the certificate is not only fulfilling his or her statutory duty but is performing a service which he or she knows or reasonably ought to know will be relied upon by a prospective purchaser. Therefore, in the context of a purchase and sale there arises a duty of care owned by the issuer of the certificate to the prospective purchaser. The certificate is not issued in a vacuum, but in the context of an anticipated sale.

Liability will arise where there is carelessness, reliance, financial and economic disadvantage and a relationship of proximity between the plaintiff and the defendant. The plaintiff would not have bought the car but for the representations contained in the certificate. The Court concluded that the plaintiff relied on the expertise of the defendant, on the certificate and the statements contained therein to reach his decision to buy the automobile. The plaintiff suffered economic loss as a result of that reliance. The Court concluded that the defendant was responsible to the plaintiff on the basis of negligent misrepresentation. Judgment for the plaintiff was awarded for a reasonable amount of repairs, costs and counsel fee.

Gervais v. Johnson (1990), 22 M.V.R. (2d) 143 (Ont. Dist. Ct.) — There was no duty owing to the defendant respecting economic loss since the certificate indicated that there was no warranty on the general condition of the vehicle. Moreover, there was no negligent misrepresentation made with respect to the condition of the brakelines. The relevant regulation indicated that there was to be no leakage or heavy corrosion scaling and MA Ltd.'s inspection had complied with this requirement, notwithstanding the existence of pitting and rust. There may have been an innocent misrepresentation, but such misrepresentation was not actionable in tort.

R. v. Springdale Ultramar Ltd. (1990), 27 M.V.R. (2d) 47, *(sub nom. R. v. Springdale Ultramar Ltd. (No. 2))* 86 Nfld. & P.E.I.R. 230, 268 A.P.R. 230 (Nfld. Prov. Ct.) — The accused was a garage that did repairs and inspections. A mechanic working for the accused issued an inspection certificate for a vehicle which he did not inspect and which did not meet the standards. The accused was charged with contravening the Highway Traffic (Official Inspection Station) Regulations (Nfld.). The accused was convicted. The offence, involving as it did a breach of a public welfare statute, was one of strict liability. The defence of due diligence was available, but the accused failed to establish on the balance of probabilities that it took all reasonable care to avoid the event. Lack of knowledge alone is not sufficient to establish the defence. The garage owner had the necessary influence over his employee if he wished to exercise it. The regulations make the official inspection station responsible for the issuance of inspection certificates, not the employee. Thus, the station was responsible for ensuring compliance with the regulations and was liable for non-compliance.

R. v. Atkinson (2003), 2003 CarswellNfld 258, [2003] N.J. No. 292, 45 M.V.R. (4th) 110 (N.L. Prov. Ct.) — The elements of issuing an improper vehicle inspection certificate were canvassed.

R. v. Khan (2003), 5 M.V.R. (5th) 295, [2003] O.J. No. 4137, 2003 CarswellOnt 6095 (Ont. C.J.) — A conviction for a false certificate was set aside where the trier had relied on hearsay written reports confirming the defects the inspector testified about.

R. v. Richardson, 2008 CarswellNB 410, 72 M.V.R. (5th) 261, 866 A.P.R. 1, 338 N.B.R. (2d) 1, 2008 NBPC 27 (Prov. Ct.) — The requirement to display a valid certificate of inspection was not clear regarding a mobile office trailer.

Sale of Vehicle

R. v. W.T. Boychuk Motors Ltd., [1970] 3 O.R. 162 (H.C.) — The predecessor section imposed an absolute liability on a vendor of a used car to physically deliver a certificate of mechanical fitness to a purchaser before entering into the contract; delivery after completion of the sale was not compliance with the provision.

Carvalho v. Baldwin, [1962] O.R. 545, 33 D.L.R. (2d) 21 (C.A.) — Failing to request a certificate when purchasing a car may affect the question of taking reasonable care to assure that the car is in a safe condition.

Schmidt v. Internat. Harvester Co. (1962), 38 W.W.R. 180 (Man. Q.B.) — Section 19 of the Manitoba Act, which contains a prohibition against sale of a vehicle unless such vehicle and its equipment comply with the Act, is concerned only with the roadworthiness of motor vehicles from the point of view of traffic on the highway and was not intended to affect contracts for sale of goods or the freedom to contract.

R. v. Bermuda Holdings Ltd., 8 C.R.N.S. 328, 70 W.W.R. 754, [1970] 3 C.C.C. 374, 9 D.L.R. (3d) 595 (B.C. S.C.) — Under the British Columbia Act, the presence of vehicles on a used car lot did not constitute an offering for sale within the meaning of a provision against offering vehicles for sale that are not equipped as required by the Act.

Related Provisions: See s. 107 of the Act regarding commercial motor vehicle inspections. See also R.R.O. 1990, Reg. 611, Safety Inspections.

91. (1) Motor vehicle inspection station licence — **No person shall establish, operate or maintain a motor vehicle inspection station except under the authority of a licence issued by the Director under this Act and the Director may issue a licence for a motor vehicle inspection station subject to the conditions that the Director may specify in the licence.**

(2) Issuance of licence — **Subject to subsection (3), any person who applies in accordance with this Act and the regulations for a licence to establish, operate or maintain a motor vehicle inspection station and who meets the requirements of this Act and the regulations and who pays the prescribed fee is entitled to be issued the licence.**

(3) Grounds for refusal — **Subject to section 95, the Director may refuse to issue a motor vehicle inspection station licence where, in his or her opinion,**

    (a) the past conduct of the applicant or, where the applicant is a corporation, of its officers or directors affords reasonable grounds for belief that the motor vehicle inspection station will not be operated in accordance with the law and with honesty and integrity;

(b) the proposed motor vehicle inspection station or its operation would contravene this Act or the regulations or any other Act or regulation or any municipal by-law respecting its establishment or location;

(c) the applicant is not competent to operate a motor vehicle inspection station in accordance with this Act and the regulations; or

(d) the equipment and premises are not suitable for the performance of the inspections for which the licence is sought.

(4) **Expiration and renewal of motor vehicle inspection station licence** — A motor vehicle inspection station licence expires with the 31st day of December in the year in which it is issued and a renewal shall be issued where the applicant is not disqualified under subsection (8).

(5) **Not transferable** — A motor vehicle inspection station licence is not transferable.

(6) **Operator named in licence** — It is a condition of a motor vehicle inspection station licence that the operation of the motor vehicle inspection station be under the charge and control of the licensee.

(7) **Notice of change** — Where the licensee is a corporation, the corporation shall notify the Director in writing within fifteen days of any change in the officers or directors of the corporation.

(8) **Revocation of licence** — The Director may revoke or refuse to renew a motor vehicle inspection station licence where,

(a) any person has made a false statement in the application for the licence or a renewal thereof or in any safety standards certificate signed by the licensee or a person authorized in writing by the licensee or in any report, document or other information required to be furnished by this Act or the regulations or any other Act or regulation that applies to the motor vehicle inspection station;

(b) any inspection authorized by the licence is incompetently performed;

(c) the licensee or any motor vehicle inspection mechanic employed in the motor vehicle inspection station has misrepresented the condition of a vehicle with respect to the standards of equipment and performance prescribed by the regulations upon an inspection of the vehicle in the station for the purpose of determining whether or not to issue a safety standards certificate, sign a vehicle inspection record or affix a vehicle inspection sticker;

(d) there is a breach of a condition of the licence;

(e) the licensee does not comply with this Act or the regulations;

(f) the inspections that can be performed by the motor vehicle inspection station are misrepresented; or

(g) a change in the officers or directors of any corporation that is a licensee would afford grounds for refusing to issue a motor vehicle inspection station licence under clause (3)(a).

Proposed Repeal — 91

91. [Repealed 2015, c. 14, s. 30. Not in force at date of publication.]

Related Provisions: R.R.O. 1990, Reg. 601, Motor Vehicle Inspection Stations.

92. (1) Motor vehicle inspection mechanic — No person shall sign a vehicle inspection record as mechanic or certify in a safety standards certificate that a vehicle complies with the standards of equipment and performance prescribed by the regulations unless the person is registered by the Director as a motor vehicle inspection mechanic in a motor vehicle inspection station and the Director may so register any person for whom application is made under subsection (2).

(2) Registration — Where a licensee or an applicant for a motor vehicle inspection station licence applies for the registration as a motor vehicle inspection mechanic in the motor vehicle inspection station of the licensee or in the proposed motor vehicle inspection station of the applicant for a licence, as the case may be, of any person who meets the requirements of this Act and the regulations, the person is entitled to be registered as a motor vehicle inspection mechanic in the motor vehicle inspection station.

(3) Expiration of registration — The registration of a motor vehicle inspection mechanic expires with the licence of the motor vehicle inspection station to which the mechanic is registered.

(4) Grounds for refusal — Subject to section 95, the Director may refuse to register a motor vehicle inspection mechanic where, in his or her opinion,

    (a) the past conduct of the mechanic affords reasonable grounds for belief that the mechanic will not act as a motor vehicle inspection mechanic in accordance with the law and with honesty and integrity; or

    (b) the mechanic is not competent to act as a motor vehicle inspection mechanic.

Proposed Repeal — 92

92. [Repealed 2015, c. 14, s. 30. Not in force at date of publication.]

Related Provisions: See R.R.O. 1990, Reg. 601, Motor Vehicle Inspection Stations.

93. Revocation of registration — The Director may revoke the registration of a motor vehicle inspection mechanic where,

    (a) the registrant or the licensee has made a false statement in the application for registration of the registrant or in a safety standards certificate or in any report, document or other information required to be furnished by this Act or the regulations or any other Act or regulation that applies to the registrant;

    (b) any inspection performed under the authority of the mechanic's registration is incompetently performed by the registrant; or

    (c) the registrant does not comply with this Act or the regulations.

Proposed Repeal — 93

93. [Repealed 2015, c. 14, s. 30. Not in force at date of publication.]

94. (1) **Hearing re terms of licence** — Where the Director issues a licence under this Act and the licensee is dissatisfied with the conditions thereof prescribed by the Director, he or she may by written notice given to the Director and the Tribunal require a hearing by the Tribunal, and the Tribunal shall appoint a time for and hold a hearing.

(2) **Decision of Tribunal** — After a hearing under subsection (1), the Tribunal may affirm the conditions prescribed for the licence by the Director or may cancel the conditions or may prescribe the other conditions for the licence in the place of those prescribed by the Director that it considers proper and the conditions shall be conditions of the licence.

Proposed Repeal — 94

94. [Repealed 2015, c. 14, s. 30. Not in force at date of publication.]

1999, c. 12, Sched. G, s. 24(16), item 2

95. (1) **Proposal to refuse to issue or revoke** — Where the Director proposes,

> (a) to refuse to issue or renew a licence;
>
> (b) to refuse to make a registration; or
>
> (c) to revoke a licence or registration,

the Director shall serve notice of his or her proposal, together with written reasons therefor,

> (d) in the case of a proposal to refuse to issue a licence, upon the applicant;
>
> (e) in the case of a proposal to revoke or to refuse to renew a licence, upon the licensee;
>
> (f) in the case of a proposal to refuse to make a registration, upon the applicant or licensee and upon the proposed registrant; and
>
> (g) in the case of a proposal to revoke a registration, upon the registrant and the licensee of the motor vehicle inspection station in which the registrant is employed.

(2) **Notice** — A notice under subsection (1) shall inform the person who is the applicant, licensee, registrant or proposed registrant, as the case may be, that the person is entitled to a hearing by the Tribunal if the person mails or delivers, within fifteen days after receiving service of the notice under subsection (1), notice in writing to the Director and the Tribunal requiring a hearing by the Tribunal and the person may so require the hearing.

(3) **Powers of Director where no hearing** — Where the applicant, licensee, registrant or proposed registrant does not require a hearing by the Tribunal in ac-

cordance with subsection (2), the Director may carry out the proposal stated in the notice under subsection (1).

(4) Power of Tribunal where hearing — Where the applicant, licensee, registrant or proposed registrant requires a hearing by the Tribunal in accordance with subsection (2), the Tribunal shall appoint a time for and shall hold the hearing and may by order direct the Director to carry out his or her proposal or refrain from carrying out his or her proposal and to take the action that the Tribunal considers the Director ought to take in accordance with this Act and the regulations, and for such purposes the Tribunal may substitute its opinion for that of the Director.

(5) Extension of time for requiring hearing — The Tribunal may extend the time for the giving of notice requiring a hearing by the applicant, licensee, registrant or proposed registrant, under this section either before or after the expiration of the time where it is satisfied that there are apparent grounds for granting relief to the applicant, licensee, registrant or proposed registrant, pursuant to a hearing and that there are reasonable grounds for applying for the extension, and the Tribunal may give the directions that it considers proper consequent upon the extension.

(6) Continuation of licence pending renewal — Where, within the time prescribed therefor or, if no time is prescribed, before the expiry of the licence, the licensee has applied for renewal of the licence and paid the prescribed fee, the licence shall be deemed to continue,

(a) until the renewal is granted; or

(b) where the licensee is served with notice that the Director proposes to refuse to grant the renewal, until the time for giving notice requiring a hearing by the Tribunal has expired and, where a hearing is required, until the Tribunal has made its decision.

Proposed Repeal — 95

95. [Repealed 2015, c. 14, s. 30. Not in force at date of publication.]

1999, c. 12, Sched. G, s. 24(16), items 3, 4

96. (1) Parties — The Director, the applicant, licensee, registrant or proposed registrant who has required the hearing and the other persons that the Tribunal may specify are parties to proceedings before the Tribunal under this Act.

(2) Notice of hearing — Notice of a hearing under section 94 or 95 shall afford the applicant, licensee, registrant or proposed registrant a reasonable opportunity to show or to achieve compliance before the hearing with all lawful requirements for the issue or retention of the licence or for the registration or continuation of the registration, as the case may be.

(3) Examination of documentary evidence — Any party to proceedings under section 94 or 95 shall be afforded an opportunity to examine before the hearing any written or documentary evidence that will be produced or any report the contents of which will be given in evidence at the hearing.

(4) Members holding hearing not to have taken part in investigation, etc. — Members of the Tribunal holding a hearing shall not have taken part before the hearing in any investigation or consideration of the subject-matter of the hearing and shall not communicate directly or indirectly in relation to the subject-matter of the hearing with any person or with any party or the party's representative except upon notice to and opportunity for all parties to participate, but the Tribunal may seek legal advice from an adviser independent from the parties and in that case the nature of the advice should be made known to the parties in order that they may make submissions as to the law.

(5) Recording of evidence — The oral evidence taken before the Tribunal at a hearing shall be recorded and, if so required, copies of a transcript thereof shall be furnished upon the same terms as in the Superior Court of Justice.

(6) Findings of fact — The findings of fact of the Tribunal pursuant to a hearing shall be based exclusively on evidence admissible or matters that may be noticed under sections 15 and 16 of the *Statutory Powers Procedure Act*.

(7) Only members at hearing to participate in decision — No member of the Tribunal shall participate in a decision of the Tribunal pursuant to a hearing unless the member was present throughout the hearing and heard the evidence and argument of the parties and, except with the consent of the parties, no decision of the Tribunal shall be given unless all members so present participate in the decision.

(8) Release of documentary evidence — Documents and things put in evidence at a hearing shall, upon the request of the person who produced them, be released to the person by the Tribunal within a reasonable time after the matter in issue has been finally determined.

(9) Appeal to court — Any party to the proceedings before the Tribunal may appeal from its decision or order to the Divisional Court in accordance with the rules of court.

(10) [Repealed 2009, c. 5, s. 34(2).]

(11) Minister entitled to be heard — The Minister is entitled to be heard, by counsel or otherwise, upon the argument of an appeal under this section.

(12) Powers of court on appeal — An appeal under this section may be made on questions of law or fact or both and the court may affirm or may rescind the decision of the Tribunal and may exercise all powers of the Tribunal to direct the Director to take any action which the Tribunal may direct him or her to take and as the court considers proper and for such purposes the court may substitute its opinion for that of the Director or of the Tribunal, or the court may refer the matter back to the Tribunal for rehearing, in whole or in part, in accordance with the directions that the court considers proper.

Proposed Repeal — 96

96. [Repealed 2015, c. 14, s. 30. Not in force at date of publication.]

1999, c. 12, Sched. G, s. 24(16), item 5, (17), (18); 2009, c. 5, s. 34

Commentary

The Red Tape Reduction Act, 1999, S.O. 1999, c. 12, Sched. R. (ss. 1(2), 1(3), 2(1), 2(3), 2(5), 5(1), and 6(1) in force January 1, 2001) amends ss. 6, 7, 12 and 14 of the Highway Traffic Act to facilitate Ontario's participation in the International Registration Plan, which contains reciprocal provisions in respect of commercial motor vehicles that travel across provincial or international borders. The Plan provides for the issuance of IRP cab cards as permits for these vehicles and for the appointment of registration and licence fees in each member jurisdiction on the basis of the distances travelled in each jurisdiction. Persons residing or based in other jurisdictions that are members of the Plan are exempt from the requirements of and fees prescribed under Part II of the Highway Traffic Act.

97. Service of notice — Except where otherwise provided, any notice required by sections 88 to 96 or the regulations to be served may be served personally or by registered mail addressed to the person to whom notice is to be given at the person's latest known address and, where notice is served by registered mail, the service shall be deemed to have been made on the fifth day after the day of mailing unless the person to whom notice is given establishes that the person did not, acting in good faith, through absence, accident, illness or other cause beyond the person's control receive the notice until a later date.

Proposed Repeal — 97

97. [Repealed 2015, c. 14, s. 30. Not in force at date of publication.]

98. (1) **Appointment of inspectors** — The Minister may appoint one or more persons as inspectors for the purposes of sections 88 to 99 and the regulations and the appointments shall be in writing.

(2) **Certificate of appointment** — The Minister shall issue every inspector appointed under subsection (1) a certificate of appointment and every inspector, in the execution of his or her duties under this section and the regulations, shall produce his or her certificate of appointment upon request.

(3) **Powers of inspectors** — An inspector may at all reasonable times inspect the premises, operations and all records of all motor vehicle inspection stations to ensure that sections 88 to 92 and the regulations are complied with.

(4) **Idem** — Upon an inspection under this section, the inspector may upon giving a receipt therefor remove any material referred to in subsection (3) that relates to the purpose of the inspection for the purpose of making a copy thereof, provided that the copying is carried out with reasonable dispatch and the material in question is promptly thereafter returned to the licensee of the motor vehicle inspection station.

(5) **Admissibility of copies** — Any copy made as provided in subsection (4) and purporting to be certified by an inspector is admissible in evidence in any proceeding or prosecution as proof, in the absence of evidence to the contrary, of the original.

(6) Obstruction — No person shall obstruct the inspector or withhold or destroy, conceal or refuse to furnish any information or thing required by the inspector for the purposes of the inspection.

Proposed Repeal — 98

98. [Repealed 2015, c. 14, s. 30. Not in force at date of publication.]

99. (1) Penalty — Subject to subsection (1.1), any person who contravenes sections 88 to 98 or the regulations made under section 100 is guilty of an offence and on conviction is liable to a fine of not less than $200 and not more than $20,000.

(1.1) Idem — Any person who contravenes subsection 90(3), 91(1), 92(1) or 98(6) is guilty of an offence and on conviction is liable to a fine of not less than $400 and not more than $20,000.

(2) Same — Any person who makes a false statement in a safety standards certificate is guilty of an offence and on conviction is liable to a fine of not less than $400 and not more than $20,000.

(3) Report on conviction to Director — A provincial judge or justice of the peace who makes a conviction for an offence under sections 88 to 98 or any regulation made under section 100, or the clerk of the court in which the conviction is made, shall forthwith certify the conviction to the Director setting out the name, address and description of the person convicted and the provision of this Act contravened.

Proposed Repeal — 99

99. [Repealed 2015, c. 14, s. 30. Not in force at date of publication.]

1996, c. 20, s. 21

100. (1) Regulations — The Lieutenant Governor in Council may make regulations,

(a) prescribing the form and content of safety standards certificates;

(b) prescribing inspection procedures, inspection requirements and equipment and performance standards of those items to be inspected for a safety standards certificate, a structural inspection certificate or a vehicle inspection sticker;

(c) governing the safety, equipment, premises, maintenance and operation of motor vehicle inspection stations;

(d) prescribing forms for the purposes of sections 88 to 98 and this section and providing for their use;

(e) prescribing conditions that shall attach to motor vehicle inspection station licences or the registrations of motor vehicle inspection mechanics or any class of either of them;

(f) classifying vehicles, motor vehicle inspection stations and motor vehicle inspection mechanics for the purposes of sections 88 to 92;

(g) prescribing fees that shall be paid upon applications for motor vehicle inspection station licences and upon the issuance of the licences or renewals thereof and upon applications for and the registration of motor vehicle inspection mechanics;

(h) prescribing the amount that shall be paid to the Ministry for forms of safety standards certificates and vehicle inspection stickers;

(i) prescribing the books, records and accounts that shall be kept by licensees;

(j) governing the reports and returns that shall be made to the Director by licensees and registrants;

(k) prescribing the qualifications of motor vehicle inspection mechanics;

(l) prescribing other duties of inspectors;

(m) prescribing the form, size and content of signs that identify motor vehicle inspection stations and governing the use of such signs;

(n) requiring and governing the return to the Ministry of unused forms of safety standards certificates, vehicle inspection records and vehicle inspection stickers and providing for refunds of amounts paid for such forms of certificates and stickers;

(o) requiring and governing the return to the Ministry of signs provided by the Ministry to identify motor vehicle inspection stations.

(2) **Adoption by reference** — Any regulation made under clause (1) (b) may adopt by reference any code, in whole or in part, with the changes that the Lieutenant Governor in Council considers necessary and may require compliance with any code that is adopted.

(3) **Exemptions** — A regulation made under clause (1)(b) may provide that a structural inspection certificate is not required for such classes of vehicles or in such circumstances as are described in the regulation.

Proposed Repeal — 100

100. [Repealed 2015, c. 14, s. 30. Not in force at date of publication.]

2000, c. 15, s. 1

Related Provisions: See R.R.O. 1990, Reg. 601, Motor Vehicle Inspection Stations; R.R.O. 1990, Reg. 611, Safety Inspections.

Proposed Addition — 100.1

100.1 **Transition** — (1) **Regulations** — The Minister may make regulations,

(a) governing the transition from the motor vehicle inspection station system, as set out in sections 88 to 100, to the vehicle inspection centre system, as set out in sections 100.2 to 100.8;

(b) governing, for purposes of transition, the application or the partial application of portions of the vehicle inspection centre system to the motor vehicle inspection station system.

(2) Regulation prevails — Where there is a conflict between a regulation made under subsection (1) and this Act, the regulation prevails.

(3) Notice — The Ministry may give notice to any person holding a motor vehicle inspection station licence,

(a) requiring that the person return to the Ministry any forms or materials received from the Ministry;

(b) setting out the time within which the person must return the forms or materials; and

(c) requiring the person to retain the records specified in the notice for the period of time specified in the notice.

(4) Same — The notice may be served by a method prescribed by a regulation made under subsection (1) and the notice is deemed to be served within the time period prescribed by a regulation made under subsection (1).

(5) Deemed service — Where the notice is deemed to be served within the time period prescribed by regulation, it shall be deemed to have been served within that time in the absence of evidence to the contrary.

(6) Compliance — A person to whom a notice is given shall comply with the provisions of the notice.

Proposed Repeal — 100.1

100.1 [Repealed 2015, c. 14, s. 31(2). Not in force at date of publication.]

2015, c. 14, s. 31(1) [Not in force at date of publication.]

Proposed Addition — 100.2, 100.3

100.2 (1) Ministry program for the inspection of vehicles and the issuance of certificates — The Minister may establish a program to provide for the inspection of vehicles and the issuance of safety standards certificates, structural inspection certificates, annual inspection certificates and stickers and semiannual inspection certificates and stickers and other types of proof of inspection.

(2) Director of Vehicle Inspection Standards — The Minister may appoint a Director of Vehicle Inspection Standards to administer the program.

(3) Agreements with service providers — The Minister may enter into agreements with service providers to assist with the administration of the program.

(4) Agreements to operate vehicle inspection centres — The Minister may,

(a) enter into agreements that authorize persons to operate vehicle inspection centres under the program; and

(b) authorize one or more service providers to enter into agreements that authorize persons to operate vehicle inspection centres under the program.

(5) **Not a Crown agent** — A vehicle inspection centre is not an agent of the Crown.

(6) **Same** — A service provider is not an agent of the Crown, except as may be provided by the service provider agreement.

(7) **Collection, use and disclosure of information** — A service provider is authorized to collect, use and disclose information, including personal information within the meaning of the *Freedom of Information and Protection of Privacy Act*, for the purpose of providing services under this Act, but the service provider shall exercise this authority solely in accordance with the applicable service provider agreement.

2015, c. 14, s. 32 [Not in force at date of publication.]

100.3 (1) Crown not liable for acts of a vehicle inspection centre or service provider — No action or other proceeding shall be instituted against the Crown, the Minister, the Director of Vehicle Inspection Standards or any other official or employee in the Ministry for any act of a vehicle inspection centre or service provider, or an employee or agent of a vehicle inspection centre or service provider, in the execution or intended execution of a power, duty or responsibility provided for under this Act or for an alleged neglect or default in the execution or intended execution of a power, duty or responsibility provided for under this Act.

(2) **Crown not liable for acts done in good faith under this Act** — No action or other proceeding shall be instituted against the Minister, the Director of Vehicle Inspection Standards or any other official or employee in the Ministry for any act done in good faith in the execution or intended execution of a power or duty under this Act or for any alleged neglect or default in the execution in good faith of a power or duty under this Act.

(3) **Exception** — Despite subsections 5(2) and (4) of the *Proceedings Against the Crown Act*, subsection (2) does not relieve the Crown of liability in respect of a tort committed by a person mentioned in subsection (2) to which it would otherwise be subject.

2015, c. 14, s. 32 [Not in force at date of publication.]

Proposed Addition — 100.4, 100.5

100.4 Prohibitions — (1) **No false statement or inaccurate information** — No person shall make a false statement or include inaccurate information or permit the making of a false statement or the including of inaccurate information,

(a) in any certificate or sticker or other type of proof of inspection referred to in subsection 100.2(1); or

(b) in any application or other document submitted, directly or indirectly, to the Ministry or provided to a customer.

(2) **Registered technicians** — No person shall determine whether or not a vehicle meets the standards for issuance of a certificate or sticker or other type of proof of inspection other than a technician registered with the Director of Vehicle Inspection Standards.

(3) Accredited vehicle inspection centres — No person shall issue, or permit the issuance of, any certificate or sticker or other type of proof of inspection unless,

(a) it is issued by a registered technician after an inspection conducted in accordance with the inspection procedures that are prescribed by regulation or set out in a directive issued under section 100.7 in a vehicle inspection centre accredited by the Director of Vehicle Inspection Standards; and

(b) the vehicle meets the equipment and performance standards that are prescribed by regulation or set out in a directive issued under section 100.7.

(4) Provided or approved forms — No person shall use any form or type of certificate or sticker or other type of proof of inspection other than a form, type or proof provided by or approved by the Ministry.

2015, c. 14, s. 33 [Not in force at date of publication.]

100.5 (1) Inspectors — The Director of Vehicle Inspection Standards may appoint, in writing, one or more persons as vehicle inspection standards inspectors.

(2) Certificate of appointment — The Director shall issue every vehicle inspection standards inspector a certificate of appointment and every inspector who is acting in the execution of his or her duties shall produce his or her certificate of appointment upon request.

(3) Admissibility of copies — A copy of any record of a vehicle inspection centre that purports to be certified by a vehicle inspection standards inspector is admissible in evidence in any proceeding or prosecution as proof, in the absence of evidence to the contrary, of the original.

(4) Obstruction — No person shall obstruct a vehicle inspection standards inspector or withhold, destroy, conceal or refuse to furnish any information or thing required by the inspector for the purposes of carrying out his or her duties.

2015, c. 14, s. 33 [Not in force at date of publication.]

Proposed Addition — 100.6

100.6 (1) Offences — Any person who contravenes subsection 100.1(6), section 100.4 or subsection 100.5(4) is guilty of an offence and on conviction is liable to a fine of not less than $400 and not more than $20,000 or to imprisonment for a term of not more than 30 days, or to both.

(2) Limitation period — No proceeding for an offence under this section may be instituted more than two years after the facts on which the proceeding is based are alleged to have occurred.

(3) Report on conviction to Director — A provincial judge or justice of the peace who makes a conviction for an offence under this section or any regulation made under it, or the clerk of the court in which the conviction is made, shall forthwith certify the conviction to the Director of Vehicle Inspection Standards setting out the name, address and description of the person convicted and the provision contravened under this Act.

2015, c. 14, s. 34 [Not in force at date of publication.]

Proposed Addition — 100.7, 100.8

100.7 (1) Directives — The Director of Vehicle Inspection Standards may make directives,

(a) governing the issuance of safety standards certificates, structural inspection certificates, annual inspection certificates and stickers and semi-annual inspection certificates and stickers and other types of proof of inspection;

(b) governing inspection procedures; and

(c) governing equipment and performance standards that must be met before a certificate, sticker or other proof of inspection mentioned in clause (a) may be issued.

(2) Same — A directive may be general or particular in its application, and may provide for different classes or categories.

(3) Public availability — Every directive,

(a) shall be made available to the public on request; and

(b) shall be publicly posted on at least one Government of Ontario website.

(4) Status — Part III (Regulations) of the *Legislation Act, 2006* does not apply with respect to directives.

(5) Term of agreement — It shall be deemed to be a term and condition of every agreement to operate a vehicle inspection centre that the operator shall comply with all applicable directives.

(6) Admissibility of copies — A copy of a directive or a portion of a directive that purports to be certified by the Director or by an inspector is admissible in evidence in any proceeding or prosecution as proof, in the absence of evidence to the contrary, of the directive or any portion of it.

2015, c. 14, s. 35 [Not in force at date of publication.]

100.8 (1) Regulations — The Minister may make regulations,

(a) governing the payment of fees to the Ministry for anything done by or on behalf of the Minister or the Director of Vehicle Inspection Standards or for any purpose under sections 100.2 to 100.5 and this section;

(b) establishing qualifications and requirements for vehicle inspection centres;

(c) establishing qualifications and requirements for vehicle inspection centre technicians;

(d) providing procedures by which the Director of Vehicle Inspection Standards may,

(i) refuse to accredit a person as a vehicle inspection centre, or

(ii) register a person as a vehicle inspection centre technician or refuse to renew or revoke the person's registration;

(e) governing,

    (i) the issuance of safety standards certificates, structural inspection certificates, annual inspection certificates and stickers and semi-annual inspection certificates and stickers and other types of proof of inspection,

    (ii) inspection procedures, and

    (iii) equipment and performance standards that must be met before a certificate, sticker or other proof of inspection mentioned in subclause (i) may be issued;

(f) defining any term used in sections 100.2 to 100.7.

(2) Amendments to adopted documents — If a regulation made under clause (1)(e) adopts a document by reference, the regulation may adopt the document as it may be amended from time to time.

(3) When adoption of amendment effective — The adoption of an amendment of a document that has been adopted by reference comes into effect upon the amended document being posted on a Government of Ontario website.

2015, c. 14, s. 35 [Not in force at date of publication.]

101. Regulations re accessories and ornaments — The Lieutenant Governor in Council may make regulations,

(a) requiring the use of any accessory, or any type or class thereof, on vehicles, regulating the use thereof and prescribing the specifications thereof;

(b) prohibiting the use on vehicles of any accessory or ornament, or any type or class thereof;

(c) prohibiting the sale or offering for sale of any accessory or ornament, or any type or class thereof, that is designed for use on vehicles;

(d) designating an organization to test and mark its approval of any accessory designated by the regulations, and prohibiting the installation, sale or purchase of any designated accessory that is not marked as approved by the testing organization.

102. (1) Safety devices on vehicles — The Lieutenant Governor in Council may make regulations,

(a) requiring the use or incorporation of any device or any equipment, in or on any vehicle or any class of vehicle, that may affect the safe operation of the vehicle on the highway or that may reduce or prevent injury to persons using the highway, and prescribing the specifications and regulating the installation thereof;

(b) designating devices and designating an organization to test and mark its approval of any device so designated, and prohibiting the incorporation or use in or on a vehicle of any device so designated that is not marked as approved by the testing organization;

(c) prescribing standards or specifications for any vehicles or any class or classes thereof;

(d) providing for and requiring the identification and marking of vehicles or any class or classes thereof;

(e) prescribing the types or classes of vehicles to which subsection (3) applies;

(f) exempting any type or class of vehicle or any class of driver or passenger in a vehicle from the provisions of any regulations made under this section.

(2) **Codes** — Any regulation may adopt by reference, in whole or in part, with the changes that the Lieutenant Governor in Council considers necessary, any code, and may require compliance with any code that is so adopted.

(3) **Prohibition re sale where non-compliance with regulations** — No person shall sell, offer or expose for sale any new vehicle of a type or class prescribed by the regulations made under clause (1)(e) that does not comply with the standards and specifications prescribed by the regulations or that is not marked or identified as prescribed by the regulations.

(4) **Penalty** — Every person who contravenes this section or a regulation made under this section is guilty of an offence and on conviction is liable to a fine of not less than $200 and not more than $1000.

Related Provisions: Motor Vehicle Safety Act, S.C. 1993, c. 16.

103. (1) **Name of owner on commercial vehicles** — Every commercial motor vehicle shall have attached to or painted on both sides of the vehicle in a clearly visible position a sign showing the name of the owner, but the Ministry may by regulation designate any vehicle or classes of vehicles to which this subsection does not apply.

Proposed Amendment — 103(1)

103. **Commercial motor vehicles, further provisions** — (1) **Name of owner on commercial motor vehicles** — Every commercial motor vehicle shall have attached to or painted on both sides of the vehicle in a clearly visible position a sign showing the name of the owner.

2014, c. 9, Sched. 2, s. 32(1) [To come into force January 1, 2017.]

(2) **Reflector** — Every commercial motor vehicle and every trailer shall have securely attached to the back thereof two red reflectors approved by the Ministry, which shall be located as far apart as practicable, at the same height and in such positions as to reflect the light from the headlights of a vehicle approaching from the rear.

(3) **Lamps and reflectors required on rear of new commercial motor vehicles and trailers** — No person shall sell, offer or expose for sale a new commercial motor vehicle or trailer, other than a truck tractor, unless,

(a) there is affixed to each side of the rear thereof in a conspicuous position a lamp, which when lighted shall display a red light only, which shall be clearly visible for a distance of at least 150 metres from the rear of the vehicle; and

(b) there is affixed to each side of the rear thereof and placed in such a position as to reflect the light from the headlamps of a motor vehicle approaching from the rear a red reflector approved by the Ministry.

(4) Name and address of owner on road-building machine — Every road-building machine when on a highway shall have attached to or painted on both sides of the machine in a clearly visible position a sign showing the name and address of the owner.

(5) Exemption to subs. (4) — Subsection (4) does not apply to a road-building machine, operated by or on behalf of an authority having jurisdiction and control of the highway, while engaged in construction or maintenance activities on the highway.

(6) Penalty — Every person who contravenes subsection (3) is guilty of an offence and on conviction is liable to a fine of not less than $200 and not more than $1000.

Proposed Addition — 103(7), (8)

(7) Regulations — The Lieutenant Governor in Council may make regulations,

(a) prescribing requirements, standards and specifications for the identification of commercial motor vehicles, or any class of them, including markings and lights, in addition to the identification requirements in subsection (1);

(b) requiring additional equipment for commercial motor vehicles, or any class of them, prescribing standards and specifications for any equipment required by this Act or by regulation and prescribing standards and specifications for the use, operation and maintenance of any such equipment.

(8) Same — The Minister may by regulation designate any vehicle or class of vehicles to which subsection (1) does not apply.

2014, c. 9, Sched. 2, s. 32(2) [To come into force January 1, 2017.]

Related Provisions: See R.R.O. 1990, Reg. 587, Equipment.

103.1 Power-assisted bicycles — **(1) Equipment, requirements** — Every power-assisted bicycle shall have the prescribed equipment and conform to the prescribed requirements and standards.

(2) Helmet requirement — No person shall ride on, drive or operate a power-assisted bicycle on a highway unless the person is wearing a helmet as required by subsection 104(1) or (2.1).

(3) Regulations — The Minister may make regulations,

(a) prescribing equipment for power-assisted bicycles;

(b) prescribing requirements and standards for power-assisted bicycles;

(c) exempting any class of power-assisted bicycles from subsection (1) or from any provision of the regulations made under this subsection and prescribing conditions and circumstances for any such exemption.

2009, c. 5, s. 35

Related Provisions: See O. Reg. 369/09, Power-assisted Bicycles.

104. (1) **Motorcyclists to wear helmet** — No person shall ride or operate a motorcycle or motor assisted bicycle on a highway unless the person is wearing a helmet that complies with the regulations and the chin strap of the helmet is securely fastened under the chin.

(2) **Idem** — No person shall carry a passenger who is under sixteen years of age on a motorcycle on a highway unless the passenger is wearing a helmet that complies with the regulations and the chin strap of the helmet is securely fastened under the chin.

(2.1) **Bicyclists to wear helmet** — Subject to subsection 103.1(2), no person shall ride or operate a bicycle on a highway unless the person is wearing a bicycle helmet that complies with the regulations and the chin strap of the helmet is securely fastened under the chin.

(2.2) **Duty of parent or guardian** — No parent or guardian of a person under sixteen years of age shall authorize or knowingly permit that person to ride a bicycle, other than a power-assisted bicycle, on a highway unless the person is wearing a bicycle helmet as required by subsection (2.1).

(3) **Regulations** — The Minister may make regulations,

    (a) prescribing standards and specifications for helmets referred to in subsections (1), (2) and (2.1);

    (b) providing for and requiring the identification and marking of the helmets;

    (c) exempting any person or class of persons from the requirements of this section and prescribing conditions for exemptions.

(4) [Repealed 2015, c. 27, Sched. 7, s. 19.]

           1993, c. 18, s. 1; 2009, c. 5, s. 36; 2015, c. 14, s. 36; 2015, c. 27, Sched. 7, s. 19

Case Law

Constitutional

R. v. Pennington (1981), 12 M.V.R. 83, 63 C.C.C. (2d) 343, 128 D.L.R. (3d) 74 (Alta. C.A.); *R. v. Jones*; *R. v. Shannon*, 6 M.V.R. 308, [1980] 2 W.W.R. 364 (Alta. Prov. Ct.) — Provincial legislation requiring motorcycle drivers to wear a helmet was *intra vires*. The legislation did not violate the Alberta Bill of Rights which provided for equality before the law, especially considering that all motorcyclists must wear helmets.

Kittelson v. R. (1981), 10 M.V.R. 31 (Sask. Dist. Ct.) — Such a requirement did not violate the Saskatchewan Human Rights Code which prohibited discrimation generally in respect of "... any other person or class of person."

R. v. Fisher; *R. v. Prest* (1985), 39 M.V.R. 287, 49 C.R. (3d) 222, 23 C.C.C. (3d) 29 (Man. Q.B.) — A challenge under s. 7 of the Charter of Rights and Freedoms was rejected.

R. v. Badesha, 2008 ONCJ 94, 2008 CarswellOnt 1186, 67 M.V.R. (5th) 294, 168 C.R.R. (2d) 164; affirmed 2011 ONCJ 284, 2011 CarswellOnt 4148, 15 M.V.R. (6th) 98 (Ont.

C.J.) — The Sikh motorcycle driver's argument that s. 104(1) of the Act requiring a motorcycle helmet breached s. 2(b) was accepted but the breach was justified by s. 1.

Nature of Offence

R. v. Varga (1983), 24 M.V.R. 256 (B.C. S.C.) — Section 218(2) of the Motor Vehicle Act, R.S.B.C. 1979, c. 288 [re-en. 1980, c. 37, s. 33.1; am. 1982, c. 36, s. 33], was a strict liability offence.

Civil

O'Connell v. Jackson, [1971] 3 W.L.R. 463 (C.A.) — Although the defendant was solely responsible for the collision, the plaintiff's negligence was relevant to the additional injuries and damage which would not have occurred if he had worn a crash helmet. Accordingly, the plaintiff's responsibility was 15% of the assessed damages.

Hildebrand v. Szalai (1979), 1 Man. R. (2d) 438 (C.A.); *MacDonald v. Alderson* (1981), 11 M.V.R. 68 (Man. Q.B.); varied (1982), 14 M.V.R. 212 (Man. C.A.) — It was observed that there was no statutory duty to wear a helmet. No contributory negligence was found as the lack of a helmet did not affect the injuries.

Fraser v. Ortman (1980), 11 Alta. L.R. (2d) 391, 19 A.R. 562 (C.A.); affirming (1978), 19 A.R. 569 (Dist. Ct.) — The defendant's plea of contributory negligence by reason of the plaintiff's defective helmet did not succeed where there was no evidence to suggest any causal connection with the injuries sustained.

Related Provisions: See R.R.O. 1990, Reg. 610, Safety Helmets. See also O. Reg. 473/06, Pilot Project — Power-Assisted Bicycles, s. 3(4); O. Reg. 488/06, Pilot Project — Segways, s. 13.

104.1 (1) Duty of horse riders — No person under the age of 18 years shall ride or be mounted on a horse on a highway unless that person has and is correctly using the following equipment in the manner that it was designed to be used:

> **1. A helmet that complies with the requirements under the *Horse Riding Safety Act, 2001*.**

> **2. Footwear that complies with the requirements under the *Horse Riding Safety Act, 2001*.**

(2) Exception — Paragraph 2 of subsection (1) does not apply to a person equipped with properly functioning and sized hooded stirrups, safety stirrups designed to prevent the rider's foot from passing through or becoming wedged in the stirrups, or stirrups designed to break away when the rider falls from the horse.

(3) Duty of parent or guardian — No parent or guardian of a person under the age of 16 years shall authorize or knowingly permit the person to ride or be mounted on a horse on a highway in contravention of subsection (1).

(4) Rider to identify self — A police officer who finds any person contravening subsection (1) may require that person to stop and to provide identification of himself or herself.

(5) Same — Every person who is required to stop, by a police officer acting under subsection (4), shall stop and identify himself or herself to the police officer.

(6) Same — For the purposes of this section, giving one's correct name and address is sufficient identification.

(7) Same — A police officer may arrest without warrant any person who does not comply with subsection (5).

2001, c. 4, s. 4

Related Provisions: See the Horse Riding Safety Act, 2001, S.O. 2001, c. 4, s. 2.

105. (1) Sale of new vehicles that do not conform to federal standards prohibited — No person who deals in motor vehicles, trailers, conversion units or trailer converter dollies shall sell or offer to sell a new motor vehicle, trailer, conversion unit or trailer converter dolly that does not conform to the standards required under the *Motor Vehicle Safety Act* (Canada) or that does not bear the National Safety Mark referred to in that Act.

Proposed Amendment — 105(1)

(1) Sale of new vehicles that do not conform to federal standards prohibited — No person who deals in motor vehicles, trailers, conversion units or trailer converter dollies shall sell or offer to sell a new motor vehicle, trailer, conversion unit or trailer converter dolly that does not conform to the standards required under the *Motor Vehicle Safety Act* (Canada).

2016, c. 5, Sched. 12, s. 6(1) [Not in force at date of publication.]

(2) Sale of motor assisted bicycles — No person who deals in motor assisted bicycles shall sell a new motor assisted bicycle unless on the delivery of the vehicle to the purchaser, the seller gives to the purchaser a document in a form approved by the Ministry certifying that the vehicle complies with the definition of a motor assisted bicycle.

(3) Penalty — Every person who contravenes subsection (1) is guilty of an offence and on conviction is liable to a fine of not less than $200 and not more than $1000.

Proposed Addition — 105(4)

(4) Regulations — The Lieutenant Governor in Council may make regulations exempting classes of motor vehicles, trailers, conversion units and trailer converter dollies from the application of subsection (1), and prescribing conditions and circumstances for any such exemption.

2016, c. 5, Sched. 12, s. 6(2) [Not in force at date of publication.]

1993, c. 34, s. 1

Related Provisions: See the Motor Vehicle Safety Act, S.C. 1993, c. 16, the Motor Vehicle Fuel Consumption Standards Act, R.S.C. 1985, c. M-9, the Motor Vehicle Safety Regulations, C.R.C., c. 1038, and the Motor Vehicle Tire Safety Regulations, 1995, SOR/95-148.

106. Seat belts — **(1) Seat belt assembly must not be removed or altered** — No person shall drive on a highway a motor vehicle in which a seat belt assembly required under the *Motor Vehicle Safety Act* (Canada) at the time that the vehicle was manufactured or imported into Canada has been removed, rendered partly or wholly inoperative, modified so as to reduce its effectiveness or is not operating properly through lack of maintenance.

(2) **Use of seat belt assembly by driver** — Every person who drives on a highway a motor vehicle in which a seat belt assembly is provided for the driver shall wear the complete seat belt assembly as required by subsection (5).

(3) **Use of seat belt assembly by passenger** — Every person who is at least 16 years old and is a passenger in a motor vehicle on a highway shall,

(a) occupy a seating position for which a seat belt assembly has been provided; and

(b) wear the complete seat belt assembly as required by subsection (5).

(4) **Driver to ensure young passenger uses seat belt assembly** — No person shall drive on a highway a motor vehicle in which there is a passenger who is under 16 years old unless,

(a) that passenger,

(i) occupies a seating position for which a seat belt assembly has been provided, and

(ii) is wearing the complete seat belt assembly as required by subsection (5); or

(b) that passenger is required by the regulations to be secured by a child seating system or child restraint system, and is so secured.

(5) **How to wear seat belt assembly** — A seat belt assembly shall be worn so that,

(a) the pelvic restraint is worn firmly against the body and across the hips;

(b) the torso restraint, if there is one, is worn closely against the body and over the shoulder and across the chest;

(c) the pelvic restraint, and the torso restraint, if there is one, are securely fastened; and

(d) no more than one person is wearing the seat belt assembly at any one time.

(6) **Exception** — Subsections (2) and (3) do not apply to a person,

(a) who is driving a motor vehicle in reverse;

(b) who holds a certificate signed by a legally qualified medical practitioner certifying that the person is,

(i) for the period stated in the certificate, unable for medical reasons to wear a seat belt assembly, or

(ii) because of the person's size, build or other physical characteristic, unable to wear a seat belt assembly; or

(c) who is actually engaged in work which requires him or her to alight from and re-enter the motor vehicle at frequent intervals and the motor vehicle does not travel at a speed exceeding 40 kilometres per hour.

(6.1) [Repealed 2006, c. 25, s. 1.]

(7) Same — Clause (4)(a) does not apply in respect of a passenger if the passenger holds a certificate signed by a legally qualified medical practitioner certifying that the passenger is,

    (a) for the period stated in the certificate, unable for medical reasons to wear a seat belt assembly; or

    (b) because of the person's size, build or other physical characteristic, unable to wear a seat belt assembly.

(8) Regulations — The Lieutenant Governor in Council may make regulations,

    (a) requiring that children or any class of children be secured in child seating systems and child restraint systems in motor vehicles on highways;

    (b) prescribing the specifications of child seating systems and child restraint systems, prescribing different child seating systems and child restraint systems for different classes of children, governing the use of such systems, including prescribing the manner in which a child is to be secured in child seating systems and child restraint systems;

    (c) prescribing classes of children, based on the age, height or weight of a child or the relationship of a child to the driver or owner of the motor vehicle;

    (d) prescribing classes of motor vehicles, drivers and passengers;

    (e) exempting from any of the provisions of this section or the regulations made under this section,

        (i) any class of motor vehicle,

        (ii) any class of driver or passenger, or

        (iii) drivers carrying any prescribed class of passenger,

    and prescribing conditions for any such exemption;

    (f) prescribing circumstances in which drivers, or any class of driver, is exempt from any of the provisions of this section or the regulations made under this section, and prescribing conditions for any such exemption.

(8.1) Police may request passenger's identification — A police officer or officer appointed for carrying out the provisions of this Act may request that a passenger in a motor vehicle who appears to be at least 16 years old identify himself or herself if the officer has reason to believe that the passenger is contravening this section or the regulations made under this section.

(8.2) Same — A passenger who is requested to identify himself or herself under subsection (8.1) shall give the officer reasonable identification of himself or herself and, for such purposes, giving his or her correct name, date of birth and address is reasonable identification.

(8.3) Offence — Every person who contravenes or fails to comply with this section or a regulation made under this section is guilty of an offence and on conviction is liable to a fine of not less than $200 and not more than $1,000.

(9) Definition — In this section,

"seat belt assembly" means a device or assembly composed of straps, webbing or similar material that restrains the movement of a person in order to prevent or mitigate injury to the person and includes a pelvic restraint or a pelvic restraint and a torso restraint.

2004, c. 22, s. 4; 2006, c. 25, ss. 1, 2; 2009, c. 5, s. 37

Commentary

Installed seatbelts must not be modified. Drivers and passengers shall wear seatbelts. Children under 16 must wear seatbelts, or be secured in a child seating system or child restraint system as defined by regulation.

Drivers and passengers must wear a complete seat belt in a properly adjusted and securely fastened manner unless:

(1) the driver is going in reverse;

(2) the person holds a medical certificate containing an exemption; and

(3) the person is engaged in work which requires entering and exiting the vehicle frequently and where the speed does not exceed 40 km/h.

Passengers appearing to be 16 or over need to identify themselves when requested by an officer.

The case law respecting rules relating to contributory negligence is beyond the scope of this book. See Murray D. Segal, *Manual of Motor Vehicle Law* (Toronto: Carswell, 1982), 3 vol. looseleaf. Segal.

Case Law

Constitutional

Paquin v. Montreal (1981), 12 M.V.R. 123 (Que. S.C.); *Léger v. Montréal (Ville)* (1985), 39 M.V.R. 60 (Que. S.C.); affirmed (1986), 41 M.V.R. 85 (Que. C.A.) — Seat belt legislation was properly the province's concern. It did not conflict with ss. 1 and 6 of the Quebec Charter of Rights regarding the rights of each individual to his or her physical well-being and freedom and the right to enjoy property.

R. v. Maier (1989), 21 M.V.R. (2d) 134, 71 Alta. L.R. (2d) 1, [1990] 2 W.W.R. 519, 52 C.C.C. (3d) 419, 101 A.R. 126, 44 C.R.R. 199 (C.A.) — The Court upheld the constitutional validity, considering s. 7 of the Charter of Rights and Freedoms, respecting the requirement for use of a seat belt restraint system by drivers of motor vehicles. No s. 7 infringement was made out.

R. v. Thompson (1986), 41 M.V.R. 158 (B.C. C.A.); affirmed (1986), 45 M.V.R. 136 (B.C. C.A.); *R. v. Settle* (1987), 80 N.S.R. (2d) 274, 200 A.P.R. 274 (Co. Ct.) — Mandatory seat belt legislation does not infringe freedom of religion under s. 2(a) of the Charter of Rights and Freedoms.

R. v. Doucette (1985), 38 M.V.R. 113, 23 C.C.C. (3d) 520 (N.S. Prov. Ct.); affirmed (June 6, 1986), (unreported) (N.S. Co. Ct.); leave to appeal to N.S. C.A. refused (1987), 83 N.S.R. (2d) 450 (note), 210 A.P.R. 450 (note); *Feener v. R.* (1987), 78 N.S.R. (2d) 22, 193 A.P.R. 22, 28 C.R.R. 191 (C.A.) — The accused was charged with operating a motor vehicle without wearing a seat belt. There were exemptions to the mandatory seat belt based on the age, occupation, or health of individuals. The accused argued a contravention of the rights guaranteed under ss. 7 and 15 of the Charter of Rights and Freedoms. It was held that the section did not contravene the Charter.

R. v. Kennedy (1987), 18 B.C.L.R. (2d) 321 (C.A.) — Section 217 of the Motor Vehicle Act (B.C.) requiring the wearing of a seat belt does not infringe s. 7 of the Charter.

R. v. MacIntyre (1989), 22 M.V.R. (2d) 331 (P.E.I. Prov. Ct.) — It was held that s. 91.1 of the Highway Traffic Act, R.S.P.E.I. 1974, c. H-6 requiring use of seat belts did not violate s. 15 of the Charter.

R. v. Powless (1996), 27 M.V.R. (3d) 151 (N.W.T. S.C.) — The Act does not violate s. 15 of the Charter.

Nature of Offence

R. v. Bixby (1987), 7 M.V.R. (2d) 196 (Nfld. S.C.) — The accused was acquitted on a charge of failure to wear a seat belt while operating a motor vehicle. The facts indicated that the accused was suffering from cancer and had been advised by his physician not to wear a seat belt. He produced a physician's certificate to that effect at trial. The relevant statute required a driver to have the certificate on his person in order to avoid conviction. The trial Judge ruled that the circumstances indicated a mere "technical breach" of the law and accordingly entered an acquittal. The Crown appealed. The appeal was allowed. The accused's excuse for failure to wear a seat belt, though valid and sufficient to provide him with an exemption, was of no use to him because he did not have evidence of it with him at the time he was stopped. The statute made no allowance for good excuses which might exempt compliance.

R. v. Merchant (1990), 25 M.V.R. (2d) 234, 87 Sask. R. 309 (Q.B.); *R. v. Folstad* (2001), 22 M.V.R. (4th) 11, 2001 CarswellSask 751 (Prov. Ct.) — The accused was charged with failing to wear a seat belt, contrary to s. 77(1) of The Highway Traffic Act (Sask.). He had been wearing a seat belt, but the trial Judge found that the torso restraint was under the accused's left arm and not over his left shoulder. The accused was convicted and fined $50. The accused appealed. The appeal was allowed; the conviction was quashed and a verdict of not guilty was entered. For a conviction under s. 77(1) of The Highway Traffic Act, it must be established that the accused either was not wearing a seat belt or, if he was, that it was not securely fastened or was not properly adjusted. The accused was wearing a seat belt, and there was no evidence that it was not securely fastened. "Properly adjusted" refers to the degree of snugness of the restraints. In the absence of evidence that the accused's torso restraint was not properly adjusted, he could not be convicted of the offence.

Durham (Regional Municipality) v. Chadband, 2005 CarswellOnt 1274, 2005 ONCJ 111, 19 M.V.R. (5th) 249 (C.J.) — Wearing the upper torso portion of a seatbelt assembly under the arm, rather than over the shoulder, in itself, and without further evidence, does not amount to a violation. "Properly adjusted" refers to the degree of "snugness of the restraints." Where the accused admits that the upper torso straps were not properly adjusted in hanging loosely at the side of his left shoulder, he is guilty.

R. v. Tassone, 2007 CarswellOnt 1736, 222 O.A.C. 121, 2007 ONCA 215, 44 M.V.R. (5th) 81 (C.A.) — "Driving on a highway" did not render the seatbelt requirement inapplicable to a situation where drivers are waiting for a red light. Accidents occur even where vehicles are stopped at a red light. A driver must wear the seatbelt continuously from the time the vehicle is put in motion on a highway to the time a driver leaves the highway, parks the vehicle in position in which the vehicle can be left unattended, or gets out of a vehicle.

R. v. Stewart, 2007 CarswellOnt 1496, 45 M.V.R. (5th) 273 (C.J.) — It is an absolute liability offence subject to the exceptions provided for in the statute. The Crown must prove that the seatbelt was not worn. If it was worn the Crown needs to prove that it was not properly fastened or properly adjusted.

R. v. Bowers, 2007 CarswellSask 300, 2007 SKQB 138, 47 M.V.R. (5th) 311 (Q.B.) — Fresh evidence consisting of pictures and an explanation of how the re-creation took place and what could be seen or not seen was inadmissible.

R. v. Pernala, 2007 CarswellSask 314, 2007 SKPC 60, 298 Sask. R. 311, 51 M.V.R. (5th) 48 (Prov. Ct.) — The accused escaped conviction by the way in which he wore the assembly was not deemed to be improper and the Crown did not leave evidence of heightened risk or that the manner in which it was worn was improper.

R. v. Locke, 2007 CarswellNfld 299, 54 M.V.R. (5th) 141 (Prov. Ct.) — The exemption relating to a person whose work requires him or her to alight frequently while traveling below 50 km/h did not provide a blanket exemption to a taxi driver.

Brampton (City) v. Kanda, 56 M.V.R. (5th) 1, 289 D.L.R. (4th) 304, (sub nom. *R. v. Kanda)* 88 O.R. (3d) 732, [2008] O.J. No. 80, 2008 CarswellOnt 79, 227 C.C.C. (3d) 417, 2008 ONCA 22, 53 C.R. (6th) 331, 233 O.A.C. 118, 41 M.P.L.R. (4th) 199 (C.A.) — The offence is one of strict liability. That classification strikes an appropriate balance between encouraging drivers to be vigilant about the safety of child passengers in their vehicles and not punishing those who exercise due diligence with respect to children's seatbelts.

R. v. Thom, 2010 ONCJ 492, 2010 CarswellOnt 8163, [2010] O.J. No. 4607, 5 M.V.R. (6th) 140 — The requirement that original copies be used if available was a precondition to admissibility of police officer notes into evidence under past recollection recorded but is not a requirement to refresh the witness' memory.

Mississauga (City) v. Vattiata, 2010 ONCJ 588, 2010 CarswellOnt 9341, [2010] O.J. No. 5283, 6 M.V.R. (6th) 128 — It would be unreasonable to not allow police officers to refer to their notes when testifying in matters where they deal with enormous numbers of similar offences.

R. v. Stein (2013), 55 M.V.R. (6th) 63, 2013 BCPC 313, 2013 CarswellBC 3515, [2013] B.C.J. No. 2536 — A house painting manager who made four stops in short succession, was not engaged in the type of activity exempt from the requirement to wear a seatbelt.

R. v. Wilson (2014), 63 M.V.R. (6th) 1, 308 C.C.C. (3d) 350, 2014 ONCA 212, 2014 CarswellOnt 3327, 317 O.A.C. 314, [2014] O.J. No. 1295 — Section 106(2) creates a strict liability offence.

Civil

Reekie v. Messervey (1986), 4 B.C.L.R. (2d) 194 (S.C.); additional reasons at (1986), 10 B.C.L.R. (2d) 231 (S.C.); affirmed (1989), 17 M.V.R. (2d) 94 (B.C. C.A.); leave to appeal to S.C.C. refused (1989), 40 B.C.L.R. (2d) xxxiii (note); leave to appeal reversed in part [1990] 1 S.C.R. 219 — A person who cannot produce the medical certificate required by s. 217(5)(b) of the Motor Vehicle Act (B.C.) is not thereby precluded from raising his or her medical condition as a defence to an allegation of contributory negligence in failing to wear a seat belt. The burden of proof of establishing the validity of the medical excuse is on the person adducing it and the lack of a certificate will affect the weight of his or her evidence.

R. v. Stein (2013), 44 M.V.R. (6th) 150, 2013 BCPC 70, 2013 CarswellBC 920 (B.C. Prov. Ct.) — A project manager for a painting company who alighted 6 times in 12–15 blocks in a 75 minute period did not qualify for the seatbelt exception.

R. v. Wilson (2013), 2013 ONCJ 313, 2013 CarswellOnt 8034, 49 M.V.R. (6th) 320, [2013] O.J. No. 2767 (Ont. C.J.); affirmed 2014 ONCA 212, 2014 CarswellOnt 3327, 308 C.C.C. (3d) 350, 63 M.V.R. (6th) 1, 317 O.A.C. 314, [2014] O.J. No. 1295 — Both s. 106(2) and (4) are strict liability offences.

Related Provisions: See R.R.O. 1990, Reg. 613, Seat Belt Assemblies.

107. (1) Inspection and maintenance of commercial motor vehicles — Every operator shall establish a system, and prepare and keep a written record of that system, to periodically inspect and maintain all commercial motor vehicles and vehicles drawn by commercial motor vehicles that are under the operator's control and that are operated or drawn on the highway.

(2) Same — Every operator shall ensure that periodic inspections and maintenance are carried out in accordance with the system established under subsection (1).

(3) Performance standards — Every operator shall ensure that the commercial motor vehicles operated by the operator on a highway and the vehicles drawn by such commercial motor vehicles meet the prescribed performance standards.

(4) Daily and under-vehicle inspections and reports — Every operator shall, for every commercial motor vehicle operated by the operator and for every vehicle drawn by such a commercial motor vehicle,

    (a) supply the driver of the commercial motor vehicle with the daily inspection schedule for the commercial motor vehicle and the drawn vehicle;

    (b) ensure that daily inspections of the commercial motor vehicle and drawn vehicle are conducted in the prescribed manner;

    (c) ensure that any under-vehicle inspections required by the regulations in respect of the commercial motor vehicle and drawn vehicle are conducted at the times, in the circumstances and in the manner prescribed;

    (d) ensure the accurate completion of daily inspection reports and under-vehicle inspection reports in respect of the commercial motor vehicle and drawn vehicle.

(5) Completion of inspection reports — Every person who conducts a daily inspection or under-vehicle inspection shall accurately complete an inspection report forthwith after completing the inspection.

(6) Driver to carry inspection schedule, reports — At all times while in control of a commercial motor vehicle on a highway, the driver of the vehicle shall have in his or her possession the daily inspection schedule for the commercial motor vehicle and for any vehicle drawn by the commercial motor vehicle and the completed daily inspection reports and under-vehicle inspection reports, if applicable, for the commercial motor vehicle and drawn vehicle.

(7) Driver to surrender reports — The driver of a commercial motor vehicle shall, upon the demand of a police officer or officer appointed for carrying out the provisions of this Act, forthwith surrender the inspection schedule and reports that he or she is required to have in his or her possession by subsection (6).

(8) Report to operator — Every driver of a commercial motor vehicle shall,

(a) make an entry in the daily inspection report forthwith upon any defect coming to his or her attention after the daily inspection is conducted;

(b) report forthwith to the operator, as prescribed, any defect found on the commercial motor vehicle or vehicle drawn by the commercial motor vehicle as a result of the daily inspection or that comes to his or her attention after the daily inspection is conducted; and

(c) submit the completed daily inspection reports and under-vehicle inspection reports to the operator as prescribed.

(9) Prohibition — driving without completing inspections, reports — No person shall drive a commercial motor vehicle on a highway unless a daily inspection of the commercial motor vehicle and any vehicle drawn by the commercial motor vehicle and, if required by the regulations, an under-vehicle inspection or inspections, have been conducted as required by the regulations and an inspection report for each inspection has been completed.

(10) Where inspection conducted by person other than driver — Where a person other than the driver of the commercial motor vehicle conducts the daily inspection or under-vehicle inspection and provides the driver with a completed inspection report, the driver may rely on the inspection report for the purpose of subsection (9) as proof that the inspection to which it relates was conducted as required by the regulations, unless the driver has reason to believe otherwise.

(11) Prohibition — driving with prescribed defect — No person shall drive a commercial motor vehicle on a highway if the commercial motor vehicle or any vehicle drawn by the commercial motor vehicle has a defect prescribed for the purpose of this subsection.

(12) Same — No person shall drive a commercial motor vehicle on a highway if the commercial motor vehicle or any vehicle drawn by the commercial motor vehicle has a defect prescribed for the purpose of this subsection, except as permitted by and in accordance with the regulations.

(13) Records — Every operator of a commercial motor vehicle shall maintain or cause to be maintained the books and records that are prescribed at the prescribed location and shall produce the books and records upon the demand of an officer appointed for carrying out the provisions of this Act.

(14) Electronic documents — Despite the *Electronic Commerce Act, 2000*, electronic documents may only be used for a purpose under this section in compliance with the regulations.

(15) Offence — Every person who contravenes or fails to comply with subsection (1), (2), (3), (4), (11) or (13) is guilty of an offence and on conviction is liable to a fine of not less than $250 and not more than $20,000 or to imprisonment for a term of not more than six months, or to both.

(16) Same — Every person who contravenes or fails to comply with subsection (5), clause (8)(b) or subsection (9) or (12) is guilty of an offence and on conviction is liable to a fine of not less than $200 and not more than $1,000.

(17) Not liable for other offences — It is a defence for a person, other than the operator, charged with an offence under another section of this Act in respect of a defect prescribed for the purpose of subsection (12) that the person complied with the regulations made for the purpose of that subsection.

(18) Regulations — The Lieutenant Governor in Council may make regulations,

(a) defining "commercial motor vehicle" and "operator" for the purposes of this section;

Proposed Amendment — 107(18)(a)

(a) defining "operator" for the purposes of this section;

2014, c. 9, Sched. 2, s. 33 [To come into force January 1, 2017.]

(b) respecting the driving or operation of commercial motor vehicles and the drawing of vehicles by commercial motor vehicles;

(c) prescribing minimum requirements that the system of periodic inspections and maintenance required by subsection (1) must meet, including the content and frequency of the inspections and maintenance;

(d) prescribing performance standards for the purpose of subsection (3);

(e) governing daily inspections and under-vehicle inspections, including prescribing their content, method, and timing, the period for which they are valid and, in respect of under-vehicle inspections, the classes or types of vehicles that require them;

(f) prescribing the qualifications of the persons who may inspect vehicles, and prescribing different qualifications for different kinds of inspections and for different classes or types of vehicles;

(g) prescribing the contents of daily inspection schedules and reports and under-vehicle inspection reports;

(h) governing the making of entries under clause (8)(a);

(i) governing the reporting under clause (8)(b), including operators' responsibilities with respect to reporting;

(j) governing the submission of inspection reports under clause (8)(c);

(k) prescribing defects for the purpose of subsection (11);

(l) prescribing defects and requirements for the purpose of subsection (12);

(m) prescribing and governing books and records to be maintained by operators and prescribing the location where books and records are to be maintained;

(n) governing the use of electronic documents;

(o) exempting any person or class of persons or any vehicle or class or type of vehicles from any provision of this section or of any regulation made under this section and prescribing conditions and circumstances for any such exemption.

(19) Same — A regulation made under subsection (18) may apply in respect of a class or type of vehicle or class of operator or person and may contain different provisions for different classes or types of vehicles and different classes of operators and persons.

1996, c. 20, s. 23; 2005, c. 26, Sched. A, s. 16

Case Law

R. v. Khinda, 66 M.V.R. (5th) 243, 2008 CarswellOnt 847, 2008 ONCJ 45 (C.J.) — The failure to conduct a prescribed inspection on the brakes of a trailer under R.R.O. 1990, Reg. 579, Sched. 1 Part III, para. 11 and R.R.O. 1990, Reg. 587, s. 5(1) provided a reasonable doubt regarding dangerous driving but resulted in a conviction under s. 107(5).

R. v. Zehr, 2011 ONCJ 516, 2011 CarswellOnt 10607, 21 M.V.R. (6th) 322, [2011] O.J. No. 4493 — A hydro truck, a public utility vehicle, on the way to an emergency, was exempt from the requirement in s. 107(7) of the Act.

Related Provisions: See ss. 88–100 regarding inspections of motor vehicles; see O. Reg. 199/07, Commercial Motor Vehicle Inspections; O. Reg. 555/06, Hours of Service; R.R.O. 1990, Reg. 601, Motor Vehicle Inspection Stations; R.R.O. 1990, Reg. 608, Restricted Use of Left Lanes by Commercial Vehicles; R.R.O. 1990, Reg. 612, School Buses; O. Reg. 363/04, Security of Loads; R.R.O. 1990, Reg. 618, Specifications and Standards for Trailer Couplings.

PART VII — LOAD AND DIMENSIONS

108. Definitions — In this Part,

"box length", in a combination of vehicles having more than one trailer, means the external measurement from the front of the foremost trailer to the rear of the rear most trailer, including load, but excluding any portion of auxiliary equipment or machinery that extends beyond the front of the foremost trailer and that is not designed or used for the transportation of goods;

"full trailer" means a trailer designed so that its own weight and any load are carried on its own axles and includes a vehicle combination consisting of a semitrailer and a trailer converter dolly;

"over-dimensional farm vehicle" means a farm tractor, self-propelled implement of husbandry, implement of husbandry, or any combination of them, having a weight, width, length or height in excess of the limits provided in this Part or Part VIII;

"semi-trailer" means a trailer designed so that its forward part rests on or is carried by another vehicle or trailer converter dolly to which it is coupled by means of a fifth wheel assembly.

1993, c. 34, s. 2; 2010, c. 16, Sched. 12, s. 2(2)

Related Provisions: R.R.O. 1990, Reg. 603, Over-Dimensional Farm Vehicles; see also s. 1 of the Act in which trailers are defined.

109. (1) Width of vehicle — Subject to sections 110 and 110.1, no vehicle including load or contents shall have a greater width than 2.6 metres while on a highway except,

(a) traction engines, which may have a total width not exceeding 2.8 metres; or

(b) road service vehicles and, for the purpose of this Part, road service vehicle includes such a vehicle while travelling to and from a maintenance site or repair centre.

(2) Width of load — Subject to sections 110 and 110.1, no load on a vehicle shall have a greater width than 2.6 metres while on a highway except,

(a) loads of raw forest products which shall not exceed a total width of 2.7 metres at point of origin and which shall not exceed a total width of 2.8 metres at any time during transit; or

(b) loads of loose fodder.

(3) Mirrors not included in width — Where a motor vehicle is equipped with one or more mirrors that extend not more than 30 centimetres beyond either side of the vehicle, the amount of the extension shall not be included in determining the width of the vehicle under subsection (1).

(4) Auxiliary equipment, devices not included in width — Where a motor vehicle or trailer is equipped with auxiliary equipment or an auxiliary device that is mounted to the vehicle and that extends beyond either side of the vehicle, the amount of the extension shall not be included in determining the width of the vehicle under subsection (1) if,

(a) the equipment or device is not designed or used to carry a load; and

(b) the equipment or device does not extend more than 10 centimetres from the side of the vehicle.

(5) [Repealed 2010, c. 16, Sched. 12, s. 2(3).]

(6) Length of vehicle — Subject to sections 110 and 110.1, no vehicle, including load, shall exceed the length of 12.5 metres while on a highway.

(6.1) Exception — Subsection (6) does not apply to a fire apparatus, a trailer, a bus, a recreational vehicle or a road service vehicle as described in clause (1)(b).

(6.2) Same — Subject to sections 110 and 110.1 and despite subsection (6.1), no full trailer, including load, shall exceed the length of 12.5 metres while on a highway unless it is in a combination of vehicles whose configuration, weight and dimensions are as prescribed by regulation.

(7) Length of combination — No combination of vehicles, including load, coupled together shall exceed the total length of twenty-three metres while on a highway.

(7.1) Exception — Despite subsection (7), a combination of vehicles whose configuration, weight and dimensions are as prescribed by regulation may have a total length while on a highway, including load, that does not exceed 27.5 metres.

(8) Maximum box length — No combination of vehicles composed of more than one trailer shall have a box length in excess of 18.5 metres while on a highway.

(8.1) Exception — Despite subsection (8), a combination of vehicles whose configuration, weight and dimensions are as prescribed by regulation may have a box length that does not exceed 20 metres while on a highway.

(8.2) [Repealed 2009, c. 33, Sched. 26, s. 3(11).]

(8.3) [Repealed 2009, c. 33, Sched. 26, s. 3(11).]

(9) [Repealed 2009, c. 33, Sched. 26, s. 3(11).]

(10) Maximum length of semi-trailer — Subject to sections 110 and 110.1, no semi-trailer shall have a length with external measurement, excluding any portion of auxillary equipment or machinery that extends beyond the front or rear of the semi-trailer and that is not designed or used to carry a load, that exceeds 14.65 metres while on a highway.

(10.1) Exception — Subsection (10) does not apply to a semi-trailer designed to carry vehicles.

(10.2) Same — Despite subsection (10), a semi-trailer used in a combination of vehicles whose configuration, weight and dimensions are as prescribed by regulation may have a length with an external measurement, excluding any portion of auxiliary equipment or machinery that extends beyond the front of the semi-trailer and that is not designed or used to carry a load, that does not exceed 16.2 metres while on a highway.

(11) Length of bus, recreational vehicle — No bus or recreational vehicle shall exceed the length of 12.5 metres while on a highway, but an increase in the length of a bus or recreational vehicle caused by the addition of a liquid-filled or other energy-absorbing bumper shall not be included in determining the length of the bus or recreational vehicle.

(11.1) Same — Despite subsection (11),

  (a) a recreational vehicle or a bus, other than an articulated bus, that meets the requirements prescribed by regulation may have a length that exceeds 12.5 metres but does not exceed 14 metres; and

  (b) an articulated bus that meets the requirements prescribed by regulation may have a length that exceeds 12.5 metres but does not exceed 25 metres.

(12) Restricting length of combination of vehicles — The council of a municipality that was a city on December 31, 2002 may by by-law prohibit the operation of a combination of vehicles having a total length, including load, in excess of 15.25 metres while on a highway or a portion thereof under its jurisdiction designated in the by-law.

(13) Mirror not included in length — Where a vehicle is equipped with one or more mirrors that extend beyond the front of the vehicle, the amount of the extension shall not be included in determining the length of the vehicle under subsection (6), (11), (11.1) or (12).

(13.1) Aerodynamic device not included in length — Where a commercial motor vehicle, other than a bus or recreational vehicle, or trailer is equipped with an aerodynamic device that extends beyond the rear of the vehicle, the amount of the extension shall not be included in determining the length under subsection (6), (6.2), (7), (7.1), (8), (8.1), (10), (10.2) or (12) if,

(a) any portion of the device that is 1.9 metres or less above the ground does not extend more than 0.305 metres beyond the rear of the vehicle or trailer;

(b) any portion of the device that is more than 1.9 metres above the ground does not extend more than 0.61 metres beyond the rear of the vehicle or trailer;

(c) the device is not designed or used to carry a load; and

(d) the device does not cause the vehicle or trailer to cease to meet any standard under the *Motor Vehicle Safety Regulations* made under the *Motor Vehicle Safety Act* (Canada).

(14) Height of vehicle — Subject to sections 110 and 110.1, no vehicle including load shall have a greater height than 4.15 metres while on a highway.

(14.1) Exception — Despite subsection (14), a vehicle used in a combination of vehicles whose configuration, weight and dimensions are as prescribed by regulation may have a height greater than 4.15 metres but not greater than 4.3 metres while on a highway.

(15) Penalty — Every person who contravenes this section is guilty of an offence and on conviction is liable to a fine of not less than $200 and not more than $1000 and, in addition, the permit issued for the vehicle under section 7 may be suspended for not more than six months.

(15.1) Same — commercial motor vehicle — Despite subsection (15), every person who contravenes this section is guilty of an offence and, if the offence was committed by means of a commercial motor vehicle within the meaning of subsection 16(1), on conviction is liable to a fine of not less than $200 and not more than $20,000 and, in addition, the permit issued for the vehicle under section 7 may be suspended for not more than six months.

Proposed Amendment — 109(15.1)

(15.1) Same — commercial motor vehicle — Despite subsection (15), every person who contravenes this section is guilty of an offence and, if the offence was committed by means of a commercial motor vehicle, on conviction is liable to a fine of not less than $200 and not more than $20,000 and, in addition, the permit issued for the vehicle under section 7 may be suspended for not more than six months.

2014, c. 9, Sched. 2, s. 34 [To come into force January 1, 2017.]

(16) Regulations — The Lieutenant Governor in Council may make regulations,

(a) defining "recreational vehicle" for the purposes of this section;

(b) prescribing equipment and devices that are or are not auxiliary for the purposes of subsection (4);

(c) prescribing configurations, weight and dimensions of vehicles and combinations of vehicles;

(d) setting limits on dimensions of vehicles and combinations of vehicles, except those dimensions already set out in this Act;

(e) prescribing requirements for components and equipment for vehicles and combinations of vehicles;

(f) prescribing requirements for the purpose of subsection (11.1), including prescribing,

    (i) maximum length,

    (ii) bus and recreational vehicle type and use,

    (iii) load distribution,

    (iv) configurations, and

    (v) requirements for components, equipment and safety features;

(g) exempting an aerodynamic device from clause (13.1)(a) or (b) and prescribing conditions and circumstances for any such exemption.

(17) [Repealed 2010, c. 16, Sched. 12, s. 2(15).]

(18) **Same** — The Lieutenant Governor in Council may make regulations exempting any class of vehicles from the application of subsection (10) and prescribing conditions for such exemptions.

1993, c. 34, s. 3; 1994, c. 27, s. 138(9); 1996, c. 20, s. 24; 2002, c. 17, Sched. F, s. 1; 2002, c. 18, Sched. P, s. 25(1)–(4), (6), (7); 2009, c. 33, Sched. 26, s. 3(11); 2010, c. 16, Sched. 12, s. 2(2)–(15); 2015, c. 14, s. 37

Commentary

Width

Subject to a permit being granted under s. 110, no vehicle, including load or contents, shall be wider than 2.6 metres (s. 109(1)). Exceptions are made for road service vehicles (s. 109(1)(b)), loads of raw forest product vehicles (subs. (2)(a)), and loads of loose fodder (subs. (2)(b)). For purposes of calculation in the case of commercial motor vehicles, rear vision mirrors and lamps are excluded (subs. (3)). The calculation in the case of buses is provided in subs. (4). Load covering mechanisms are also excluded (subs. (5)).

Length

Subject to a permit being granted under s. 110, no vehicle, other than a fire apparatus, a semi-trailer or a bus, including load, shall exceed 12.5 metres (subs. (6)). Mirrors are not to be considered in determining length (subs. (13)). No combination of vehicles, including load, when coupled together shall exceed 23 metres (subs. (7)). The back of the driver's compartment to the rearmost of the combination of vehicles shall not exceed 19 metres (subss. (8), (9)). A semi-trailer, as defined in s. 108, except one designed to carry vehicles, shall not exceed 14.65 metres (subs. (10)). A bus, except an articulated bus, shall not exceed 12.5 metres (subs. (11)). Municipalities may by by-law set restrictions on length (subs. (12)).

Height

Subject to a permit being granted under s. 110, no vehicle, including load, shall exceed 4.15 metres in height.

Penalty

An infraction will attract a fine of not less than $200 and not more than $1,000, and, in addition, the permit issued under s. 7 of the Act may be suspended for up to six months.

Case Law

Knox v. Petitpas (1974), 10 N.B.R. (2d) 13 (Q.B.) — The plaintiff struck the defendant's excess load while travelling on the right side of the highway. The defendant was found 60% at fault for not giving the public adequate warning.

Morin v. Brunswick Const. Ltd. (1979), 25 N.B.R. (2d) 505, 51 A.P.R. 505 (Co. Ct.) — Excessive width of a load does not necessarily constitute negligence.

R v. Schneider National Carriers Inc. (2002), 30 M.V.R. (4th) 150, 2002 CarswellOnt 2751 (Ont. C.J.); affirmed (2002), 2002 CarswellOnt 4375 (Ont. C.A.) — The word "designed" relates to the "purpose or function" to be served by the semi-trailer in the carriage of vehicles. "Fit or capable" is not the correct meaning.

Related Provisions: See ss. 108 and 110 of the Act; see R.R.O. 1990, Reg. 577, Covering of Loads; O. Reg. 363/04, Security of Loads; O. Reg. 413/05, Vehicle Weights and Dimensions — For Safe, Productive and Infrastructure-Friendly Vehicles.

110. (1) Permits — **The municipal corporation or other authority having jurisdiction over the highway may, upon application in writing, grant a permit for use of the highway by a vehicle or combination of vehicles in excess of the dimensional limits set out in section 109 or the weight limits set out in Part VIII in order to allow the movement of,**

> **(a) a load, object or structure that cannot reasonably be divided and moved within those limits;**

> **(b) a vehicle that cannot reasonably be divided and moved within those limits and that is not itself carrying a load, object or structure or drawing or carrying a vehicle;**

> **(c) a vehicle or combination of vehicles that is used exclusively to move a load, object or structure or to draw or carry a vehicle as described in clauses (a) and (b).**

(2) Permits, general or limited — **The permit referred to in subsection (1) may be general, or may limit the time and the particular highway that may be used, and may contain conditions relating to the protection of persons and property from injury or damage and the municipal corporation or other authority may require a bond or other security sufficient to cover the cost of repairing any possible damage to the highway.**

(3) Who may issue — **The council of any municipality may by by-law provide that a permit referred to in subsection (1) may be issued by an officer of the corporation named therein.**

(4) Issue of permit by Ministry — In the case of a vehicle for which a permit is required under this section in order to pass over a highway or highways under the jurisdiction of two or more municipalities or other authorities, the permit so to do may be issued by the Ministry, which permit is instead of the several permits to be otherwise obtained from the municipal corporations or other authorities, and the permit may limit the time and the particular highway or highways that may be used, and may contain any special conditions or provisions that may be considered necessary to protect the highways from damage, and the Ministry may require a bond or other security sufficient to cover the cost of repairing possible damage to the highway.

(5) Responsibility for damages caused to highway — The owner, operator or mover of a heavy vehicle, load, object or structure in respect of which a permit is granted under this section is nevertheless responsible for all damages that may be caused to the highway by reason of the driving, operating or moving of any such heavy vehicle, load, object or structure.

(6) Condition of permit — It is a condition of every permit issued under this section that the original of the permit be carried in the vehicle for which the permit was issued and be produced when demanded by a police officer or an officer appointed for carrying out the provisions of this Act.

(7) Penalty — Every person who operates or permits the operation of a vehicle or combination of vehicles contrary to any of the conditions of the permit is guilty of an offence and on conviction is liable to a fine of not less than $200 and not more than $20,000 and, in addition, if the condition contravened is in respect of any weight allowed under the permit, a fine shall be imposed as if the person had not been issued a permit under this section and had been convicted of an offence under section 116, 117 or 118 in respect of any gross vehicle weight, axle unit weight or axle group weight in excess of the maximum allowable weights permitted under this Act or the regulations.

1996, c. 20, s. 25; 2000, c. 26, Sched. O, s. 6

Commentary

The municipality or the province may grant an exemption from the width, length or height requirements found in s. 109 of the Act and weight requirement found in Part VIII of the Act (subss. (1), (3), (4)). The permit may be granted on conditions referable to time and highway, and may limit liability. A bond may be required (subs. (2)).

The owner, operator or driver is responsible for all damages to the highway (subs. (5)).

The original permit must be carried and must be produced on demand (subs. (6)).

Contravention will result in a fine of between $100 and $500. If the contravention is for weight, a fine shall be imposed as if there had been a contravention of s. 116, 117 or 118.

Section 110(6) was introduced in response to *R. v. Nick Dellelce Ltd.* (1977), 34 C.C.C. (2d) 173 (Ont. H.C.), which held that a permit issued under predecessor s. 65 is only subject to the Act and that a condition that the permit be carried in the vehicle and produced on demand was held not to be authorized by the Act and of no validity.

The Red Tape Reduction Act, 2000, S.O. 2000, c. 26, Sched. O. (ss. 1-4, 5(1) and (2) and 14 in force December 6, 2000; ss. 6-13 in force January 1, 2001) re-enacts s. 52 of the

Highway Traffic Act to allow for notice to be given by regular mail for suspensions unrelated to Criminal Code (Canada) offences, and to allow for other prescribed methods of service; amends s. 55.1 to provide that the impoundment history of leased vehicles is linked to the holder of the plate portion of the registration certificate, to extend vehicle impound provisions to persons who are found driving while their licence is under suspension as a result of a court order and to clarify who is responsible for paying storage charges related to impoundment; amends existing provisions dealing with vehicle weights and dimensions to establish a framework for the implementation of an agreement between Ontario and Quebec; and amends s. 175(6)(c) of the Act to clarify when overhead red signal lights and stop arms on school buses must be used.

Case Law

Sunburst Coaches Ltd. v. Romanchuk (1953), 9 W.W.R. (N.S.) 385 (Alta. T.D.) — Apart from the requirement of a permit, the moving of heavy wide loads such as buildings is a lawful and reasonable use of the highway. However, persons driving unwieldy vehicles owe a special duty to keep the vehicle under strict control at all times.

R. v. Lafarge Can. Inc. (1989), 19 M.V.R. (2d) 110 (Ont. Prov. Ct.) — The corporate accused was charged with operating an overweight vehicle. The facts indicated that it had a permit under the provisions of s. 93 [now s. 110] of the Highway Traffic Act (Ont.) permitting it to carry loads up to a specified maximum. When one of its tractor-trailers was stopped by officials of the Ministry of Transportation and Communications and weighed, the load was found to weigh approximately 17,000 kg in excess of its permitted limit. The accused was convicted at trial on the basis that the offence set out in s. 93(7) of the Act was one of absolute liability. The accused appealed on this and other issues. The appeal was dismissed. Section 93(7) of the Act was an offence of strict liability and not one of absolute liability, as found by the trial Judge. The object of the legislation, namely, protecting the highways of the province from damage, and the overall regulatory pattern designed to achieve that end — overweight provisions which expressly authorized permitted exemptions — indicated that the analogy relied upon by the trial Judge between s. 93 and the speeding provisions of the Act was suspect. Moreover, the very complexity of the overweight provisions made it very difficult for transport drivers to understand them, and to construe them as imposing an absolute liability would place an unreasonable burden on such drivers. Finally, nothing in the language of the Act implied an intention on the part of the Legislature to create an absolute liability offence. Although the accused's key submission therefore had merit, a defence of due diligence was not established on the facts.

Related Provisions: See s. 109 and Part VIII of the Act; see O. Reg. 381/98, Special Permits.

110.1 (1) Special permits — **For the purposes set out in subsection (2), the Registrar may, upon application in writing, issue a permit allowing the operation of a vehicle or combination of vehicles that does not comply with,**

> **(a) one or more of the dimensional limits set out in section 109 or a regulation prescribing the configuration, weight and dimensions made for the purpose of subsection 109(7.1), (8.1) or (10.2); or**

> **(b) one or more of the weight limits set out in Part VIII or a regulation made under that Part.**

(2) **Purposes for issuing special permits** — A permit may be issued under subsection (1),

   (a) to harmonize the rules and limits with respect to configurations, weights and dimensions applicable to a class of vehicles or combination of vehicles with those of any other jurisdiction;

   (b) to allow a trial of a vehicle or combination of vehicles;

   (c) to allow a variance from a limit within a geographic area or along routes specified by the Registrar for the movement of a commodity or commodities;

   (d) to allow the use of a vehicle or combination of vehicles for a purpose or in circumstances described in the regulations.

(3) **Classes of permit** — The Registrar may establish different classes of permits for different classes of vehicles or combinations of vehicles.

(4) **Refusal of special permit** — The Registrar may refuse to issue a permit under subsection (1) if the vehicle or combination of vehicles is eligible to be considered for a permit under subsection 110(1), whether or not the applicant has been refused a permit under that subsection.

(5) **Qualifications** — The Registrar may establish qualifications for applicants for a permit under subsection (1).

(6) **Limited number of permits** — The Registrar may limit the number of permits of any class, may adopt any reasonable scheme for allotting the permits within a class and may refuse to issue a permit becasuse the maximum number of permits for the class has already been issued or in accordance with the terms of the allotment scheme.

(7) **Conditions** — The Registrar may attach conditions to a permit that he or she issues as he or she considers appropriate.

(8) **Onus** — The onus is on the applicant to establish that a permit should be granted and the Registrar may refuse any application unless he or she is satisfied that the permit should be granted.

(9) **Submissions and decision** — The Registrar shall consider an applicant's submissions relating to the issuance of a permit and the conditions that attach to the permit, but shall not hold a hearing into the matter, and the Registrar's decision is final.

(10) **Fees** — The Registrar may set fees for the issuance, renewal and replacement of permits issued under this section.

(11) **Same** — The Registrar may set different fees and different validity periods for different classes of vehicles, combinations of vehicles or persons and may exempt classes of vehicles, combinations of vehicles or persons from fees.

2000, c. 26, Sched. O, s. 7

Commentary

The Red Tape Reduction Act, 2000, S.O. 2000, c. 26, Sched. O. (ss. 1-4, 5(1) and (2) and 14 in force December 6, 2000; ss. 6-13 in force January 1, 2001) re-enacts s. 52 of the Highway Traffic Act to allow for notice to be given by regular mail for suspensions unrelated to Criminal Code (Canada) offences, and to allow for other prescribed methods of service; amends s. 55.1 to provide that the impoundment history of leased vehicles is linked to the holder of the plate portion of the registration certificate, to extend vehicle impound provisions to persons who are found driving while their licence is under suspension as a result of a court order and to clarify who is responsible for paying storage charges related to impoundment; amends existing provisions dealing with vehicle weights and dimensions to establish a framework for the implementation of an agreement between Ontario and Quebec; and amends s. 175(6)(c) of the Act to clarify when overhead red signal lights and stop arms on school buses must be used.

Related Provisions: O. Reg. 413/05, Vehicle Weights and Dimensions — For Safe, Productive and Infrastructure-Friendly Vehicles, s. 34.

110.2 (1) Carrying and production of permit — A driver of the vehicle or combination of vehicles in respect of which a permit is issued under section 110.1 shall carry the permit or a copy of it, as specified in the permit, in the vehicle or combination of vehicles and shall produce it on the demand of a police officer or other officer appointed for carrying out the provisions of this Act.

(2) Effect of failure to produce permit — If the permit or copy is not produced in response to a demand under subsection (1), the permit does not apply to the vehicle or combination of vehicles, and the vehicle or combination of vehicles is subject to the dimensional and weight limits that apply as if no permit had been issued.

(3) Offences — Every person who operates or permits the operation of a vehicle or combination of vehicles contrary to any of the conditions of the permit is guilty of an offence and on conviction,

    (a) where no condition with respect to weight is breached, is liable to a fine of not less than $200 and not more than $20,000;

    (b) where the only condition breached is one with respect to weight, is liable to any fine assessed in accordance with section 125; and

    (c) where more than one condition is breached and one of the conditions breached is a condition with respect to weight, is liable to a fine of not less than $200 and not more than $20,000, in addition to any fine assessed in accordance with section 125.

2000, c. 26, Sched. O, s. 7

Commentary

The Red Tape Reduction Act, 2000, S.O. 2000, c. 26, Sched. O. (ss. 1-4, 5(1) and (2) and 14 in force December 6, 2000; ss. 6-13 in force January 1, 2001) re-enacts s. 52 of the Highway Traffic Act to allow for notice to be given by regular mail for suspensions unrelated to Criminal Code (Canada) offences, and to allow for other prescribed methods of service; amends s. 55.1 to provide that the impoundment history of leased vehicles is linked to the holder of the plate portion of the registration certificate, to extend vehicle impound provisions to persons who are found driving while their licence is under suspension as a result of a court order and to clarify who is responsible for paying storage charges related to impoundment; amends existing provisions dealing with vehicle weights and dimensions to establish a framework for the implementation of an agreement between Ontario and Quebec; and amends s. 175(6)(c) of the Act to clarify when overhead red signal lights and stop arms on school buses must be used.

110.3 (1) Suspension, etc., of permit — The Registrar may suspend, refuse to renew, modify or cancel a permit issued under section 110.1 on the grounds of,

    (a) breach of the conditions of the permit or of any other permit held by the holder under that section;

    (b) false or incomplete information in the application for the permit or its renewal or for any other permit held by the holder under that section; or

    (c) an outstanding fee in respect of the permit or any other permit held by the holder under that section, or an outstanding penalty or interest in respect of the fee.

(2) Notice of proposed action — Before taking an action under subsection (1), the Registrar shall notify the permit holder of the proposed action and give the holder an opportunity to make written submissions about the proposed action, and the holder has 15 days from actual or deemed receipt of the notice to make submissions.

(3) Method of giving notice — Notice under subsection (2) is sufficiently given if,

    (a) it is delivered by mail addressed to the permit holder at the latest address for the person appearing on the records of the Ministry;

    (b) it is sent by fax to the person at the latest fax number provided by the person to the Ministry; or

    (c) it is sent by other means prescribed by the regulations.

(4) Same — Unless the person establishes that the person did not, acting in good faith, through absence, accident, illness or other cause beyond the person's control, receive the notice,

    (a) notice given by mail shall be deemed to have been received on the fifth day after it was mailed;

    (b) notice given by fax shall be deemed to have been received on the first business day after it was sent; or

    (c) notice given by a means prescribed by the regulations shall be deemed to have been received on the day prescribed by the regulations.

(5) Submissions and decision — The Registrar shall consider submissions, but shall not hold a hearing into the matter, and the Registrar's decision is final.

(6) Regulations — The Lieutenant Governor in Council may make regulations,

    (a) prescribing other means of giving notice;

(b) governing the giving of notice by a means prescribed under clause (a), including prescribing rules governing when notice is deemed to have been received.

2000, c. 26, Sched. O, s. 7; 2015, c. 27, Sched. 7, s. 21

Commentary

The Red Tape Reduction Act, 2000, S.O. 2000, c. 26, Sched. O. (ss. 1-4, 5(1) and (2) and 14 in force December 6, 2000; ss. 6-13 in force January 1, 2001) re-enacts s. 52 of the Highway Traffic Act to allow for notice to be given by regular mail for suspensions unrelated to Criminal Code (Canada) offences, and to allow for other prescribed methods of service; amends s. 55.1 to provide that the impoundment history of leased vehicles is linked to the holder of the plate portion of the registration certificate, to extend vehicle impound provisions to persons who are found driving while their licence is under suspension as a result of a court order and to clarify who is responsible for paying storage charges related to impoundment; amends existing provisions dealing with vehicle weights and dimensions to establish a framework for the implementation of an agreement between Ontario and Quebec; and amends s. 175(6)(c) of the Act to clarify when overhead red signal lights and stop arms on school buses must be used.

110.4 (1) Additional power of Registrar to suspend, etc. — In addition to taking action under subsection 110.3(1) for a ground listed in that subsection, the Registrar may take action under that subsection with respect to all of the permits of a given class, where in his or her opinion,

(a) the action eliminates or reduces any threat to highway safety;

(b) the action eliminates or reduces any unreasonable wear or damage to the highways and the supporting infrastructure; or

(c) the original reason for granting permits of that class under subsection 110.1(1) no longer exists or is not the same due to a change of circumstances.

(2) Notice of proposed action — Before taking an action under subsection (1), the Registrar shall notify each permit holder of the proposed action and shall give the holders an opportunity to make written submissions about the proposed action, and the holder has 15 days from actual or deemed receipt of the notice to make submissions.

(3) Method of giving notice — Notice under subsection (2) is sufficiently given if,

(a) it is delivered by mail addressed to the permit holder at the latest address for the person appearing on the records of the Ministry;

(b) it is sent by fax to the person at the latest fax number for the person provided by the person to the Ministry; or

(c) it is sent by other means prescribed by the regulations.

(4) Same — Unless the person establishes that the person did not, acting in good faith, through absence, accident, illness or other cause beyond the person's control, receive the notice,

    (a) notice given by mail shall be deemed to have been received on the fifth day after it was mailed;

    (b) notice given by fax shall be deemed to have been received on the first business day after it was sent;

    (c) notice given by a means prescribed by the regulations shall be deemed to have been received on the day prescribed by the regulations.

(5) Submissions and decision — The Registrar shall consider submissions, but shall not hold a hearing into the matter, and the Registrar's decision is final.

(6) Regulations — The Lieutenant Governor in Council may make regulations,

    (a) prescribing other means of giving notice;

    (b) governing the giving of notice by a means prescribed under clause (a), including prescribing rules governing when notice is deemed to have been received.

2000, c. 26, Sched. O, s. 7; 2015, c. 27, Sched. 7, s. 22

Commentary

The Red Tape Reduction Act, 2000, S.O. 2000, c. 26, Sched. O. (ss. 1-4, 5(1) and (2) and 14 in force December 6, 2000; ss. 6-13 in force January 1, 2001) re-enacts s. 52 of the Highway Traffic Act to allow for notice to be given by regular mail for suspensions unrelated to Criminal Code (Canada) offences, and to allow for other prescribed methods of service; amends s. 55.1 to provide that the impoundment history of leased vehicles is linked to the holder of the plate portion of the registration certificate, to extend vehicle impound provisions to persons who are found driving while their licence is under suspension as a result of a court order and to clarify who is responsible for paying storage charges related to impoundment; amends existing provisions dealing with vehicle weights and dimensions to establish a framework for the implementation of an agreement between Ontario and Quebec; and amends s. 175(6)(c) of the Act to clarify when overhead red signal lights and stop arms on school buses must be used.

111. (1) Overhanging load — Every vehicle carrying a load which overhangs the rear of the vehicle to the extent of 1.5 metres or more while on a highway shall display upon the overhanging load at the extreme rear end thereof at any time from one-half hour before sunset to one-half hour after sunrise, or at any other time when there is insufficient light or unfavourable atmospheric conditions, a red light, and at all other times a red flag or a red marker sufficient to indicate the projection of the load.

(2) Proper loading — No person shall operate or permit to be operated upon a highway a motor vehicle that carries a load or draws a vehicle that carries a load unless the load is loaded, bound, secured, contained or covered so that no portion of the load may become dislodged or fall, leak, spill or blow from the vehicle.

(2.1) Same, commercial motor vehicle — No person shall operate or permit to be operated upon a highway a commercial motor vehicle that carries a load or draws a vehicle that carries a load unless the load is loaded, bound, secured, contained or covered in accordance with the regulations.

(2.2) Inspections — No person shall drive upon a highway a commercial motor vehicle that carries a load or a commercial motor vehicle that draws a vehicle carrying a load unless the prescribed inspections have been carried out.

(3) Regulations — The Lieutenant Governor in Council may make regulations,

(a) governing the manner of loading, binding, securing, containing or covering loads on commercial motor vehicles operated on highways;

(b) prescribing standards and specifications of equipment and material used to load, bind, secure, contain or cover loads on commercial motor vehicles;

(c) governing the inspection of,

(i) loads on commercial motor vehicles or on vehicles drawn by a commercial motor vehicle, and

(ii) equipment and material used to load, bind, secure, contain or cover loads on commercial motor vehicles or on vehicles drawn by a commercial motor vehicle;

(d) requiring operators and drivers of commercial motor vehicles to keep the documents and records that may be specified in the regulations and requiring the submission of those documents and records, upon request, to a police officer or officer appointed for carrying out the provisions of this Act;

(e) prescribing things, including the material used to load, bind, secure, contain or cover a load, that are part of a load for the purposes of this section;

(f) exempting any class of vehicle or person from this section or from any provision in a regulation made under this section.

(3.1) Classes — A regulation made under subsection (3) may designate classes of vehicles, highways or persons and may provide that the regulation applies or does not apply to a particular class or applies differently to different classes.

(3.2) Exemptions — The Registrar may exempt any person, vehicle or highway from any provision in the regulations, subject to any conditions that the Registrar considers appropriate.

(3.3) Incorporation by reference — A regulation under clause (3)(a), (b) or (c) that incorporates another document by reference may provide that the reference to the document includes amendments made to the document from time to time after the regulation is made.

(4) Penalty — Every person who contravenes this section or a regulation made under subsection (3) is guilty of an offence and on conviction is liable to a fine of not less than $100 and not more than $200 and, in addition, his or her driver's licence issued under section 32 and the person's permit issued under section 7 may be suspended for a period of not more than sixty days.

(5) Same — commercial motor vehicle — Despite subsection (4), every person who contravenes this section or a regulation made under subsection (3) is guilty of an offence and, if the offence was committed by means of a commercial motor vehicle within the meaning of subsection 16(1), on conviction is liable to a fine of not less than $200 and not more than $20,000 and, in addition, his or her driver's licence issued under section 32 and permit issued under section 7 may be suspended for a period of not more than 60 days.

Proposed Amendment — 111(5)

(5) Same — commercial motor vehicle — Despite subsection (4), every person who contravenes this section or a regulation made under subsection (3) is guilty of an offence and, if the offence was committed by means of a commercial motor vehicle, on conviction is liable to a fine of not less than $200 and not more than $20,000 and, in addition, his or her driver's licence issued under section 32 and permit issued under section 7 may be suspended for a period of not more than 60 days.

2014, c. 9, Sched. 2, s. 35 [To come into force January 1, 2017.]

1996, c. 20, s. 26; 2002, c. 18, Sched. P, s. 26

Commentary

Overhanging loads must bear warnings (subs. (1)). Loads must be firmly bound, sufficiently covered or otherwise secured (subs. (2)). Regulations may be made regarding: loading, securing and covering; designating highways and vehicles (subs. (3)).

Contraventions will attract a fine of between $100 and $200. In addition, the driver's licence under s. 32 and permit under s. 7 may be suspended for up to 60 days.

Case Law

Quasi-Criminal

R. v. Dupont (1986), 42 M.V.R. 138 (Ont. Dist. Ct.) — Section 94(2) [now s. 111(2)] is an offence of strict liability.

Walker-Trowbridge v. D.P.P., [1992] R.T.R. 1822 (Div. Ct.) — In order to decide whether the securing of a load was sufficient, it was necessary to consider the nature of the load, its positioning, the way it was secured and the nature of the journey. As the vehicle had taken a route involving passing under a bridge which the load would inevitably hit, the load was not so secured and in such a position that no danger was likely to be caused by the load falling from the vehicle.

R. v. Burge (1988), 11 M.V.R. (2d) 285, 72 Nfld. & P.E.I.R. 158, 223 A.P.R. 158 (P.E.I. T.D.) — The offence of operating with an unsecured load was one of strict liability.

R. v. Bill Thompson Tpt. Ltd. (1973), 15 C.C.C. (2d) 574 (Ont. Prov. Ct.) — The accused was acquitted of an offence under s. 68(2) [now s. 111(2)] where it was shown that oil drums being carried by the accused were securely tied down but the drums had developed a leak allowing the contents to escape.

R. v. Gray (2004), 5 M.V.R. (5th) 271, [2004] N.B.J. No. 255, 2004 NBPC 18, 2004 CarswellNB 309 (Prov. Ct.) — Where nylon straps holding a heavy load were partially or wholly cut through and where rubber used to prevent chafing had slipped, a conviction could result.

Civil

Eastern Metals Corpn. v. Proteau, [1960] S.C.R. 96; *Wolman v. Wood* (1959), 43 M.P.R. 1 (N.S. T.D.) — Insufficient lighting on overhanging loads.

Farrugia v. Great Western Ry., [1947] 2 All E.R. 565 (C.A.) — The owner of a truck was held liable where a container was knocked from the back of the truck when it passed under a low bridge and injured a boy running along the highway.

N.B. Community College v. Irving Oil Co. (1976), 15 N.B.R. (2d) 361 (Q.B.); affirmed (1977), 18 N.B.R. (2d) 187 (C.A.) — Negligence may be attracted for failure to warn of oversize load.

Morin v. Brunswick Const. Ltd. (1979), 25 N.B.R. (2d) 505, 51 A.P.R. 505 (Co. Ct.) — A defendant was hauling a bulldozer on a float which exceeded prescribed limits for size. He did not obtain an overside load permit and did not comply with the safety measures required for hauling wide loads. The defendant proceeded at dusk with only his park lights and a revolving dome light. The plaintiff struck the blade of the bulldozer on a narrow bridge. The defendant was wholly liable for driving with an oversize load without adequate warnings.

Chiasson v. Doucet (1984), 55 N.B.R. (2d) 145, 144 A.P.R. 145 (Q.B.) — Two truckers were hauling logs on a highway. The logs were transferred to the second truck after the first broke down. The transferred logs were not tied down. A motorcyclist was injured after striking a log that had not been tied down. The truck drivers were 75% liable. The motorcyclist was 25% liable for speeding.

Related Provisions: R.R.O. 1990, Reg. 577, Covering of Loads; O. Reg. 363/04, Security of Loads.

112. (1) Regulations re carriage of explosives, etc. — The Lieutenant Governor in Council may make regulations,

   (a) classifying and defining explosives and dangerous materials;

   (b) regulating or prohibiting the transportation of explosives and dangerous materials or any class thereof by a vehicle on a highway;

   (c) regulating the preparation and packaging of explosives and dangerous materials or any class thereof to be transported by a vehicle on a highway; and

   (d) requiring the labelling of packages and containers of explosives and dangerous materials or any class thereof and prescribing the labels to be attached to such packages and containers.

(2) Code, etc., may be adopted by reference — Any regulation made under subsection (1) may adopt by reference, in whole or in part, with such changes that the Lieutenant Governor in Council considers necessary, any code or standard, or any regulation made by the Government of Canada, and may require compliance with any code, standard or regulation that is so adopted.

(3) Penalty — Every person who contravenes a regulation made under this section is guilty of an offence and on conviction is liable to a fine of not less than $100 and not more than $500 or to imprisonment for a term of not more than three months, or to both.

Case Law

R. v. Carroll (1983), 24 M.V.R. 182 (Alta. Q.B.) — A charge of transporting dangerous goods contrary to a municipal by-law was considered.

Related Provisions: See the Dangerous Goods Transportation Act, R.S.O. 1990, c. D.1; Transportation of Dangerous Goods Act, 1992, S.C. 1992, c. 34.

113. (1) Over-dimensional farm vehicles exempt — This Part, other than regulations made under this section, does not apply to over-dimensional farm vehicles.

(2) Regulations — The Lieutenant Governor in Council may make regulations,

    (a) regulating or prohibiting the movement of over-dimensional farm vehicles or classes thereof on a highway or on classes of highways;

    (b) requiring that escort vehicles or classes of escort vehicles accompany over-dimensional farm vehicles or classes thereof on a highway or classes of highways;

    (c) prescribing the types, specifications and locations of markings, signs and lights that shall be carried by over-dimensional farm vehicles and escort vehicles or classes of either or both of them on a highway or classes of highways;

    (d) prescribing conditions for the movement of over-dimensional farm vehicles on a highway or classes of highways relating to the protection of persons and property from injury or damage.

Related Provisions: R.R.O. 1990, Reg. 603, Over-Dimensional Farm Vehicles.

PART VIII — WEIGHT

114. (1) Definitions — In this Part,

"axle" means an assembly of two or more wheels whose centres are in one transverse vertical plane and which are transmitting weight to the highway;

"axle group weight" means that part of the gross vehicle weight in kilograms transmitted to the highway by a two axle group, three axle group or four axle group;

"axle unit" means any single axle, dual axle or triple axle;

"axle unit weight" means that part of the gross vehicle weight in kilograms transmitted to the highway by an axle unit;

"Class A Highway" means a highway designated as such by the Minister;

"Class B Highway" means a highway not designated by the Minister as a Class A Highway;

"dual axle" means any two consecutive axles whose centres are more than one metre apart and that,

    (a) are articulated from a common attachment to the vehicle, or

    (b) are designed to automatically equalize the load between the two axles;

"four axle group" means four consecutive axles, not including the front axle of a motor vehicle,

>   (a) that are entirely within either a motor vehicle or trailer or semi-trailer, and

>   (b) in which the spacings between the consecutive axles do not exceed 2.5 metres;

"front axle" means the front axle unit of a motor vehicle;

"gross vehicle weight" means the total weight in kilograms transmitted to the highway by a vehicle, or combination or vehicles, and load;

"liftable axle" means an assembly of two or more wheels whose centres are in one transverse vertical plane that is equipped with a device for altering (other than by longitudinal movement of the assembly only) the weight transmitted to the highway surface and that may be able to lift its tires from contact with that surface.

"over-dimensional farm vehicles" means the same as it does in Part VII;

"semi-trailer" means the same as it does in Part VII;

"single axle" means one or more axles whose centres are included between two parallel transverse vertical planes one metre apart;

"tank-truck" means a commercial motor vehicle to which there is attached or upon which there has been placed either permanently or otherwise a closed tank having a capacity of 2.3 kilolitres or more;

"three axle group" means three consecutive axles, not including the front axle of a motor vehicle,

>   (a) that do not form a triple axle within the meaning of the definition of "triple axle",

>   (b) that are entirely within either a motor vehicle or trailer or semi-trailer,

>   (c) in which the spacings between the consecutive axles do not exceed 2.5 metres, and

>   (d) which are not included in a four axle group within the meaning of the definition of "four axle group";

"triple axle" means any three consecutive axles that,

>   (a) have their consecutive centres equally spaced, and

>   (b) have their consecutive centres more than one metre apart,

and that,

>   (c) are articulated from an attachment to the vehicle common to the consecutive axles, or

>   (d) are designed to automatically equalize the load between the three axles under all conditions of loading;

"two axle group" means two consecutive single axles, not including the front axle of a motor vehicle,

>   (a) that are entirely within either a motor vehicle or trailer or semi-trailer,

(b) in which the spacing between the consecutive axles is less than two metres, and

(c) which are not included in a three axle group within the meaning of the definition of "three axle group" or a four axle group within the meaning of the definition of "four axle group".

(2) Designation by Minister — The Minister may designate a highway as a Class A Highway.

(3) Application of Part — This Part does not apply to over-dimensional farm vehicles or to motor vehicles or to road building machines operated by or on behalf of a municipality or other authority having jurisdiction over highways when the vehicle or machine is equipped with a snow clearing device.

(4) Consecutive axles — Where three consecutive axles that are articulated from an attachment to the vehicle common to the consecutive axles are not a triple axle within the meaning of the definition of "triple axle" because their consecutive centres are not equally spaced, that one of the three consecutive axles that is most remote from the centre axle of the consecutive axles shall be deemed to be a single axle and the other two axles shall be deemed to be a dual axle.

(5) Idem — Where three consecutive axles that are not articulated from an attachment to the vehicle common to the consecutive axles are not a triple axle within the meaning of the definition of "triple axle" because their consecutive centres are not equally spaced, any two of the axles that are articulated from an attachment to the vehicle common to the two axles shall be deemed to be a dual axle and the third of the three axles shall be deemed to be a single axle.

(6) Spacing between axles — The spacing between axles is the shortest distance between the centre of rotation of one axle and the centre of rotation of the other.

(7) Axle spacing distance — For the purposes of Tables 1 and 2, the axle spacing is the distance measured between the outer axles forming an axle unit.

(8) Idem — For the purposes of Tables 3, 4 and 5, the axle group spacing is the distance measured between the outer axles forming a two axle group, three axle group or four axle group.

2000, c. 26, Sched. O, s. 8

Commentary

The Red Tape Reduction Act, 2000, S.O. 2000, c. 26, Sched. O. (ss. 1-4, 5(1) and (2) and 14 in force December 6, 2000; ss. 6-13 in force January 1, 2001) re-enacts s. 52 of the Highway Traffic Act to allow for notice to be given by regular mail for suspensions unrelated to Criminal Code (Canada) offences, and to allow for other prescribed methods of service; amends s. 55.1 to provide that the impoundment history of leased vehicles is linked to the holder of the plate portion of the registration certificate, to extend vehicle impound provisions to persons who are found driving while their licence is under suspension as a result of a court order and to clarify who is responsible for paying storage charges related to impoundment; amends existing provisions dealing with vehicle weights and dimensions to establish a framework for the implementation of an agreement between Ontario and Quebec; and amends s. 175(6)(c) of the Act to clarify when overhead red signal lights and stop arms on school buses must be used.

Related Provisions: See section 1(1) of the Act for the definition of "gross weight", See also the following regulations: R.R.O. 1990, Reg. 598, Gross Weight on Bridges, and Standards to Determine Allowable Gross Vehicle Weight for Bridges, O. Reg. 103/97; O. Reg. 413/05, Vehicle Weights and Dimensions — For Safe, Productive and Infrastructure-Friendly Vehicles.

115. (1) Restrictions as to weight on tires — Subject to section 110, no vehicle,

> **(a) equipped with tires of less than 150 millimetres in width where the weight upon any millimetre in the width of the tire exceeds nine kilograms; or**

> **(b) equipped with tires of 150 millimetres or more in width where the weight upon any millimetre in the width of the tire exceeds eleven kilograms,**

shall be operated on a highway.

(2) How tire width ascertained — **For the purpose of this section, where a tire width has been marked thereon by the manufacturer, the width of the tire shall be deemed to be as so marked.**

Related Provisions: See O. Reg. 413/05, Vehicle Weights and Dimensions — For Safe, Productive and Infrastructure-Friendly Vehicles.

116. (1) Maximum allowable axle unit weights — Subject to section 110, no vehicle or combination of vehicles, shall be operated on a Class A Highway where the axle unit weight on an axle unit, whether or not part of any axle group, exceeds,

> **(a) for a single axle with single tires, 9,000 kilograms;**

> **(b) for a single axle with dual tires, 10,000 kilograms;**

> **(c) for a dual axle, that weight shown in Column 2 opposite the corresponding axle spacing shown in Column 1 of Table 1; or**

> **(d) for a triple axle, that weight shown in Column 2 opposite the corresponding axle spacing shown in Column 1 of Table 2.**

(1.1) Other weights set by regulation — **The Lieutenant Governor in Council may make regulations prescribing axle unit weight limits other than those specified or referred to in subsection (1) for any prescribed axle unit on any prescribed class or classes of vehicle or combination of vehicles and, for that purpose, prescribing axle units and classes of vehicles and combinations of vehicles.**

(1.2) Where weights set by regulation apply — **An axle unit weight limit prescribed under subsection (1.1) applies instead of the weights specified or referred to in subsection (1) for a prescribed axle unit on a vehicle or combination of vehicles in a class prescribed under subsection (1.1).**

(2) Restriction of weights allowed under subs. (1) — **Despite subsection (1), the maximum allowable axle unit weight for a dual axle shall not exceed 18,000 kilograms unless the axle is equipped with dual tires.**

(3) Idem — Despite subsection (1), the maximum allowable axle unit weight for a triple axle shall not exceed 27,000 kilograms unless the axle is equipped with dual tires.

(4) Idem — Notwithstanding subsection (1), the maximum allowable axle unit weight for a single front axle shall not exceed 5,000 kilograms unless the driver of the vehicle or combination of vehicles has with him a verification in writing as to the manufacturer's gross axle weight rating for such single front axle.

(5) Production of verification — The driver of a vehicle or combination of vehicles being operated on a Class A Highway who has the verification referred to in subsection (4) shall produce it when so demanded by a police officer or an officer appointed for carrying out the provisions of this Act, and, where it is so demanded and not produced, the driver shall be deemed to not have the verification.

(6) Maximum allowable axle unit weight — Where subsection (4) does not apply because the driver has the verification referred to in subsection (4), then subject to subsection (1), the maximum allowable axle unit weight on the single front axle shall not exceed the manufacturer's gross axle weight rating.

2000, c. 26, Sched. O, s. 9

Commentary

The Red Tape Reduction Act, 2000, S.O. 2000, c. 26, Sched. O. (ss. 1-4, 5(1) and (2) and 14 in force December 6, 2000; ss. 6-13 in force January 1, 2001) re-enacts s. 52 of the Highway Traffic Act to allow for notice to be given by regular mail for suspensions unrelated to Criminal Code (Canada) offences, and to allow for other prescribed methods of service; amends s. 55.1 to provide that the impoundment history of leased vehicles is linked to the holder of the plate portion of the registration certificate, to extend vehicle impound provisions to persons who are found driving while their licence is under suspension as a result of a court order and to clarify who is responsible for paying storage charges related to impoundment; amends existing provisions dealing with vehicle weights and dimensions to establish a framework for the implementation of an agreement between Ontario and Quebec; and amends s. 175(6)(c) of the Act to clarify when overhead red signal lights and stop arms on school buses must be used.

Related Provisions: See R.R.O. 1990, Reg. 579, Designation of Highways; O. Reg. 413/05, Vehicle Weights and Dimensions — For Safe, Productive and Infrastructure-Friendly Vehicles.

117. (1) Maximum allowable axle group weights — Subject to section 110, no vehicle or combination of vehicles, shall be operated on a Class A Highway where any axle group weight exceeds,

    (a) for a two axle group, that weight shown in Column 2 opposite the corresponding axle group spacing shown in Column 1 of Table 3;

    (b) for a three axle group, that weight shown in Column 2 opposite the corresponding axle group spacing shown in Column 1 of Table 4; or

    (c) for a four axle group, that weight shown in Column 2 opposite the corresponding axle group spacing shown in Column 1 of Table 5.

(2) **Other weights set by regulation** — The Lieutenant Governor in Council may make regulations prescribing axle group weight limits other than those specified or referred to in subsection (1) for any prescribed axle group on any prescribed class or classes of vehicle or combination of vehicles and, for that purpose, prescribing axle groups and classes of vehicles and combinations of vehicles.

(3) **Where weights set by regulation apply** — An axle group weight limit prescribed under subsection (2) applies instead of the weights specified or referred to in subsection (1) for a prescribed axle group on a vehicle or combination of vehicles in a class prescribed under subsection (2).

2000, c. 26, Sched. O, s. 10

Commentary

The Red Tape Reduction Act, 2000, S.O. 2000, c. 26, Sched. O. (ss. 1-4, 5(1) and (2) and 14 in force December 6, 2000; ss. 6-13 in force January 1, 2001) re-enacts s. 52 of the Highway Traffic Act to allow for notice to be given by regular mail for suspensions unrelated to Criminal Code (Canada) offences, and to allow for other prescribed methods of service; amends s. 55.1 to provide that the impoundment history of leased vehicles is linked to the holder of the plate portion of the registration certificate, to extend vehicle impound provisions to persons who are found driving while their licence is under suspension as a result of a court order and to clarify who is responsible for paying storage charges related to impoundment; amends existing provisions dealing with vehicle weights and dimensions to establish a framework for the implementation of an agreement between Ontario and Quebec; and amends s. 175(6)(c) of the Act to clarify when overhead red signal lights and stop arms on school buses must be used.

Related Provisions: See R.R.O. 1990, Reg. 579, Designation of Highways; O. Reg. 413/05, Vehicle Weights and Dimensions — For Safe, Productive and Infrastructure-Friendly Vehicles.

118. (1) Maximum allowable gross vehicle weights — Subject to section 110, no vehicle or combination of vehicles, shall be operated on a Class A Highway where the gross vehicle weight exceeds,

(a) the axle unit weight on the front axle, not exceeding the maximum weight permitted on the axle under section 116, plus the sum of the maximum allowable weights for all other axle units of the vehicle or combination of vehicles as set out in section 116;

(b) the axle unit weight on the front axle, not exceeding the maximum weight permitted on the axle under section 116, plus the sum of the maximum allowable weights for any two axle groups, three axle groups or four axle groups, or any combination thereof, as set out in section 117, plus the maximum allowable weight for any axle unit or units excluding the front axle and excluding any axle unit or units which are part of an axle group, as set out in section 116; or

(c) that weight prescribed in the regulations.

(2) Interpretation — Where subsection (1) refers to a weight under or set out in section 116 or 117, the reference includes a weight specified by regulation under subsection 116(1.1) or 117(2).

2000, c. 26, Sched. O, s. 11

Commentary

The Red Tape Reduction Act, 2000, S.O. 2000, c. 26, Sched. O. (ss. 1-4, 5(1) and (2) and 14 in force December 6, 2000; ss. 6-13 in force January 1, 2001) re-enacts s. 52 of the Highway Traffic Act to allow for notice to be given by regular mail for suspensions unrelated to Criminal Code (Canada) offences, and to allow for other prescribed methods of service; amends s. 55.1 to provide that the impoundment history of leased vehicles is linked to the holder of the plate portion of the registration certificate, to extend vehicle impound provisions to persons who are found driving while their licence is under suspension as a result of a court order and to clarify who is responsible for paying storage charges related to impoundment; amends existing provisions dealing with vehicle weights and dimensions to establish a framework for the implementation of an agreement between Ontario and Quebec; and amends s. 175(6)(c) of the Act to clarify when overhead red signal lights and stop arms on school buses must be used.

Related Provisions: See R.R.O. 1990, Reg. 579, Designation of Highways; O. Reg. 413/05, Vehicle Weights and Dimensions — For Safe, Productive and Infrastructure-Friendly Vehicles.

119. (1) Raw forest products allowance during freeze-up — Despite sections 116, 117, 118 and subsection 121(1), during freeze-up the maximum allowable gross vehicle weight for a vehicle or combination of vehicles, while used exclusively for the transportation of raw forest products, shall be 110 per cent of that weight for which a permit has been issued for the vehicle or combination of vehicles in accordance with section 7, provided no axle unit weight, axle group weight or gross vehicle weight exceeds by more than 10 per cent that weight prescribed in this Act or the regulations for such vehicle or combination of vehicles.

(2) Designation of freeze-up — For the purposes of this section, an official of the Ministry authorized by the Minister in writing may designate the date on which a freeze-up shall commence and the date on which a freeze-up shall terminate and the part of the Province to which the designation shall apply.

(3) Part III (Regulations) of the *Legislation Act, 2006* does not apply — A designation under subsection (2) is not a regulation within the meaning of Part III (Regulations) of the *Legislation Act, 2006*.

(4) Prohibition — No vehicle or combination of vehicles having a weight in excess of that authorized in subsection (1) shall be operated on a highway.

2006, c. 21, Sched. F, s. 136(1), Table 1

Case Law

R. v. 779057 Ontario Inc. (1997), 31 M.V.R. (3d) 50 (Ont. Prov. Ct.) — The forwarding of "overweight" scale tickets by a mill to the Ministry did not constitute an unlawful search or seizure of the accused's business records.

120. Prohibition re operation on Class B Highway — Subject to section 110, no vehicle or combination of vehicles shall be operated on a Class B Highway where the weight upon one axle exceeds 8,200 kilograms, or, if the axles are spaced less than 2.4 metres apart, where the weight upon one axle exceeds 5,500 kilograms.

Related Provisions: See R.R.O. 1990, Reg. 579, Designation of Highways.

121. (1) Operating within permitted weight — No vehicle or combination of vehicles having a permit issued in accordance with section 7 of this Act, the fee for which is based upon gross vehicle weight, shall be operated on any highway where the gross vehicle weight exceeds that for which the permit was issued.

(2) Exception to subs. (1) — Despite subsection (1) and subject to sections 116, 117 and 118, where a conversion unit is used to convert a two axle tractor into a three axle tractor and the fee prescribed in the regulations in respect of the conversion unit is paid, the vehicle or combination of vehicles to which the conversion unit is attached may operate on a highway at a maximum gross vehicle weight of 7,000 kilograms in excess of the gross vehicle weight for which a permit was issued for the vehicle or combination of vehicles in accordance with section 7 and the Ministry shall issue a receipt for the fee so prescribed and paid.

(3) Receipt re excess weight payment to be carried — The receipt issued by the Ministry in accordance with subsection (2) shall, whenever a vehicle is on a highway with the conversion unit referred to in subsection (2) attached, be carried by the driver of the vehicle or placed in some readily accessible position in the vehicle and shall be surrendered when demanded by a police officer or an officer appointed for carrying out the provisions of this Act.

(4) Penalty — Every person who contravenes subsection (1) is guilty of an offence and on conviction is liable to a fine as if the person had been convicted under section 125 and the Registrar may suspend the permit issued under section 7 for the vehicle or vehicles involved, and the suspension shall continue until a new permit at the maximum gross vehicle weight allowable has been issued for the vehicle or vehicles and the fee therefor has been paid.

1996, c. 9, s. 26; 2002, c. 18, Sched. P, s. 27

122. (1) Weight load — Subject to section 110, during a reduced load period no commercial motor vehicle or trailer, other than a public vehicle or a vehicle referred to in subsection (2), shall be operated or drawn upon any designated highway where the weight upon an axle exceeds 5,000 kilograms.

(2) Idem — Subject to section 110, during a reduced load period,

    (a) no two axle tank-truck, while used exclusively for the transportation of liquid or gaseous heating fuel;

    (b) no two axle truck, while used exclusively for the transportation of livestock feed; and

    (c) no vehicle transporting live poultry,

shall be operated upon any designated highway where the weight upon an axle exceeds 7,500 kilograms.

(3) Idem — Subject to section 110, during a reduced load period no vehicle having a carrying capacity in excess of 1,000 kilograms, other than a motor vehicle or trailer, shall be operated upon any designated highway where the weight upon any millimetre in the width of a tire exceeds five kilograms.

(4) Exceptions — Subsections (1) and (3) do not apply to,

(a) vehicles operated by or on behalf of a municipality or other authority having jurisdiction and control of a highway, where the vehicles are engaged in highway maintenance, including the carriage and application of abrasives or chemicals to the highway, the stockpiling of abrasives or chemicals for use on a highway, or the removal of snow from a highway;

(b) vehicles used exclusively for the transportation of milk;

(c) fire apparatus;

(d) vehicles operated by or on behalf of a municipality transporting waste; or

(e) public utility emergency vehicles.

(5) Designation — An official of the Ministry authorized by the Minister in writing may designate the date on which a reduced load period shall start or end and the King's Highway or highway in territory without municipal organization, or portion thereof, to which the designation applies.

(6) Part III (Regulations) of the *Legislation Act, 2006* does not apply — A designation under subsection (5) is not a regulation within the meaning of Part III (Regulations) of the *Legislation Act, 2006*.

(7) Designation by municipality — The municipality or other authority having jurisdiction over a highway may by by-law designate the date on which a reduced load period shall start or end and the highway or portion thereof under its jurisdiction to which the designation applies.

2002, c. 17, Sched. F, s. 1; 2006, c. 21, Sched. F, s. 136(1), Table 1

123. (1) Regulations limiting weight on bridges — The Minister may make regulations limiting the gross vehicle weight of any vehicle or any class thereof passing over a bridge forming part of the King's Highway or a highway in territory without municipal organization and notice of the limit of the weights fixed by the regulation, legibly printed, shall be posted up in a conspicuous place at each end of the bridge.

(2) By-laws limiting weight on bridges — The municipality or other authority having jurisdiction over a bridge may by by-law limit the gross vehicle weight of any vehicle or any class thereof passing over the bridge, and the requirements of subsection (1) with respect to the posting up of notice apply thereto.

(3) Same, on connecting links — Despite subsection (2), where the bridge forms part of a highway designated as a connecting link under subsection 21(1) of the *Public Transportation and Highway Improvement Act*, the by-law shall not become operative until it is approved by the Ministry.

(4) Regulations — The Minister may make regulations establishing standards to determine allowable gross vehicle weight for any vehicle or class of vehicle for the purpose of subsection (2).

1996, c. 33, s. 13; 2002, c. 17, Sched. F, s. 1

Related Provisions: See R.R.O. 1990, Reg. 598, Gross Weight on Bridges, and O. Reg. 103/97; R.R.O. 1990, Reg. 615, Signs, s. 41, Standards to Determine Allowable Gross Vehicle Weight for Bridges.

124. (1) Power of officer to have vehicle weighed, examined — A police officer or officer appointed for carrying out the provisions of this Act may stop any vehicle or combination of vehicles, direct the driver to such location as is reasonable in the circumstances, direct the driver to drive the vehicle or combination of vehicles on or off of a scale in order to weigh the vehicle or combination of vehicles using portable or stationary scales, and measure and examine the vehicle or combination of vehicles to determine its nature and dimensions.

(2) Load removed or redistributed — Where it is found that the gross vehicle weight, axle unit weight or axle group weight of any vehicle or combination of vehicles is in excess of the limits permitted under this Act or the regulations, or under the permit issued for the vehicle or combination of vehicles, the police officer or officer appointed for carrying out the provisions of this Act may require the driver to redistribute or remove as much of the load as is necessary to ensure compliance with this Act, the regulations and the permit.

(3) Penalty — Every driver who, when required under subsection (1) to stop, drive to another location or drive the vehicle on or off of a scale, refuses or fails to do so is guilty of an offence and on conviction is liable to a fine of not less than $200 and not more than $1,000 and to the suspension of his or her driver's licence for a period of not more than 30 days.

(4) Same — Every driver is guilty of an offence and on conviction is liable to a fine of not less than $100 and not more than $200 who,

(a) when required under subsection (2) to redistribute or remove part of a load, refuses or fails to do so or to cause it to be done; or

(b) obstructs any weighing, measuring or examination authorized by this section.

(5) Penalty, commercial motor vehicle — Despite subsection (3), every driver of a commercial motor vehicle within the meaning of subsection 16(1) who, when required under subsection (1) to stop, drive to another location, or drive the vehicle on or off of a scale, refuses or fails to do so is guilty of an offence and on conviction is liable to a fine of not less than $200 and not more than $20,000 and to the suspension of his or her driver's licence for a period of not more than 30 days.

Proposed Amendment — 124(5)

(5) Penalty, commercial motor vehicle — Despite subsection (3), every driver of a commercial motor vehicle who, when required under subsection (1) to stop, drive to another location, or drive the vehicle on or off of a scale, refuses or fails to do so is guilty of an offence and on conviction is liable to a fine of not less than $200 and not more than $20,000 and to the suspension of his or her driver's licence for a period of not more than 30 days.

2014, c. 9, Sched. 2, s. 36(1) [To come into force January 1, 2017.]

(6) Same — Despite subsection (4), every driver of a commercial motor vehicle within the meaning of subsection 16(1) is guilty of an offence and on conviction is liable to a fine of not less than $200 and not more than $20,000 who,

Proposed Amendment — 124(6) opening words

(6) Same — Despite subsection (4), every driver of a commercial motor vehicle is guilty of an offence and on conviction is liable to a fine of not less than $200 and not more than $20,000 who,

2014, c. 9, Sched. 2, s. 36(2) [To come into force January 1, 2017.]

(a) when required under subsection (2) to redistribute or remove part of a load, refuses or fails to do so or to cause it to be done; or

(b) obstructs any weighing, measuring or examination authorized by this section.

(6.1) [Repealed 2002, c. 18, Sched. P, s. 28.]

(7) [Repealed 2002, c. 18, Sched. P, s. 28.]

(8) [Repealed 2002, c. 18, Sched. P, s. 28.]

1996, c. 20, s. 27; 2002, c. 18, Sched. P, s. 28

Case Law

R v. 71119 Manitoba Ltd. (2002), 27 M.V.R. (4th) 44, 2002 CarswellMan 19 (Man. Prov. Ct.) — There is no expectation of privacy that bars weighing trucks or requesting information about load.

R. v. B. Gottardo Construction Ltd. (2004), 7 M.V.R. (5th) 186, [2004] O.J. No. 2139, 2004 ONCJ 56, 2004 CarswellOnt 2092 (Ont. C.J.) — Until s. 124 is amended [S.O. 2002, c. 18, Sched. P. s. 28] there is no authority to weigh the vehicle.

R. v. Thivierge, 2010 ABQB 29, 2010 CarswellAlta 68, 486 A.R. 366, 91 M.V.R. (5th) 165 — The key is that the Crown adduce evidence not just that a commercial vehicle went past an inspection station but that the vehicle was subject to a sign requiring it to pull in.

R. v. Martin, 2010 ONCJ 595, 2010 CarswellOnt 9462, 6 M.V.R. (6th) 296 — Where a tractor-trailer driver pulled over for seven minutes before pulling into the truck inspection station to get his papers up to date, he was convicted under s. 216.1(1).

125. (1) Offence and penalty — Every person who contravenes subsection 115(1), section 116, 117 or 118, subsection 119(4), section 120 or subsection 122(1), (2) or (3) or a regulation made under subsection 123(1) or a by-law made under subsection 123(2) is guilty of an offence and on conviction is liable to a fine of,

(a) $5 per 100 kilograms, or part thereof, for any weight in excess of that permitted under this Act or the regulations, where the overweight is less than 2,500 kilograms, but in no case shall the fine be less than $100;

(b) $10 per 100 kilograms, or part thereof, for any weight in excess of that permitted under this Act or the regulations, where the overweight is 2,500 kilograms or more but is less than 5,000 kilograms;

(c) $12 per 100 kilograms, or part thereof, for any weight in excess of that permitted under this Act or the regulations, where the overweight is 5,000 kilograms or more but is less than 7,500 kilograms;

(d) $15 per 100 kilograms, or part thereof, for any weight in excess of that permitted under this Act or the regulations, where the overweight is 7,500 kilograms or more but is less than 10,000 kilograms;

(e) $20 per 100 kilograms, or part thereof, for any weight in excess of that permitted under this Act or the regulations, where the overweight is 10,000 kilograms or more but is less than 15,000 kilograms; and

(f) $25 per 100 kilograms, or part thereof, for any weight in excess of that permitted under this Act or the regulations, where the overweight is 15,000 kilograms or more.

(2) Circumstances where additional fines apply — A person is liable to a fine, in addition to any fine to which the person is liable under subsection (1) or clause 110.2(3)(b) or (c), of not less than $200 and not more than $1,000, under the circumstances set out in subsection (3) or (4) unless the vehicle involved belongs to a class of vehicles or combination of vehicles prescribed by the regulations.

(3) Same — A person is liable in accordance with subsection (2) if,

(a) a liftable axle on a vehicle or combination of vehicles is lifted; and

(b) the person is convicted of an offence under subsection (1) or clause 110.2(3)(b) or (c),

unless,

(c) the offence occurred while the vehicle or combination of vehicles was reversing;

(d) there were no wheels on the axle;

(e) the axle was lifted in compliance with a regulation; or

(f) the axle was reasonably required to be lifted in order to prepare for and carry out completely a safe turn at an intersection or onto or off a highway ramp.

(4) Same — A person is liable in accordance with subsection (2) if,

(a) the person is convicted of an offence referred to in subsection (1) or clause 110.2(3)(b) or (c); and

(b) a liftable axle on the vehicle or combination of vehicles was deployed in such an improper manner that it caused or aggravated the offence.

1996, c. 20, s. 28; 2000, c. 26, Sched. O, s. 12

Commentary

The Red Tape Reduction Act, 2000, S.O. 2000, c. 26, Sched. O. (ss. 1-4, 5(1) and (2) and 14 in force December 6, 2000; ss. 6-13 in force January 1, 2001) re-enacts s. 52 of the Highway Traffic Act to allow for notice to be given by regular mail for suspensions unrelated to Criminal Code (Canada) offences, and to allow for other prescribed methods of service; amends s. 55.1 to provide that the impoundment history of leased vehicles is linked to the holder of the plate portion of the registration certificate, to extend vehicle impound provisions to persons who are found driving while their licence is under suspension as a result of a court order and to clarify who is responsible for paying storage charges related to impoundment; amends existing provisions dealing with vehicle weights and dimensions to establish a framework for the implementation of an agreement between Ontario and Quebec; and amends s. 175(6)(c) of the Act to clarify when overhead red signal lights and stop arms on school buses must be used.

126. Overloading by consignor — Every consignor of goods, or the consignor's agent or employee, who causes a vehicle or combination of vehicles not owned by the consignor to be loaded so that when operated on a highway,

(a) the weight on any millimetre in the width of the tire exceeds a limit set out in subsection 115(1) or in the regulations;

(b) the axle unit weight on an axle unit exceeds a limit set out in section 116 or 119 or in the regulations;

(c) an axle group weight exceeds a limit set out in section 117 or 119 or in the regulations;

(d) the gross vehicle weight exceeds a limit set out in section 118 or 119 or in the regulations; or

(e) the gross vehicle weight exceeds the gross vehicle weight specified in a permit referred to in section 121,

is guilty of an offence and on conviction is liable to a fine as if the consignor had been convicted under section 125.

1994, c. 29, s. 1

127. Regulations — The Lieutenant Governor in Council may make regulations,

(a) describing purposes and circumstances for the purposes of clause 110.1(2)(d);

(b) prescribing other means of giving notice for the purposes of subsections 110.3(3) and 110.4(3), prescribing rules in relation to giving notice by such means and prescribing the day on which notice shall be deemed to have been received when such means are used;

(c) prescribing maximum allowable gross vehicle weights for the purposes of section 118;

(d) exempting classes of vehicles or combinations of vehicles from any provision of this Part and prescribing the weights that are applicable to the exempted vehicles;

(e) exempting classes of vehicles or combinations of vehicles for the purposes of subsection 125(2);

(f) specifying vehicles or combinations of vehicles to which section 118 does not apply and prescribing an alternative means of calculating maximum allowable gross weight;

(g) prescribing maximum allowable weight on a part of a vehicle or combination of vehicles, including weight on a vehicle that forms part of a combination of vehicles;

(h) prescribing maximum allowable loads on vehicles or components of vehicles consistent with the vehicle manufacturer's ratings for the vehicle or components;

(i) providing for the identification and marking of vehicles or any class or classes of vehicle and specifying what class of persons may make such an identification or marking.

1993, c. 34, s. 4; 2000, c. 26, Sched. O, s. 13

TABLE 1 — MAXIMUM ALLOWABLE WEIGHT FOR DUAL AXLE

Column One	Column Two
Axle Spacing (Metres)	Maximum Allowable Weight (Kilograms)
1.0 to less than 1.2	15,400
1.2 to less than 1.3	17,000
1.3 to less than 1.4	17,200
1.4 to less than 1.5	17,500
1.5 to less than 1.6	17,900
1.6 to less than 1.7	18,300
1.7 to less than 1.8	18,700
1.8 or more	19,100

1993, c. 34, s. 5

TABLE 2 — MAXIMUM ALLOWABLE WEIGHT FOR TRIPLE AXLE

Column One	Column Two
Axle Spacing (Metres)	Maximum Allowable Weight (Kilograms)
2.0 to less than 2.4	19,500
2.4 to less than 2.8	21,300
2.8 to less than 2.9	21,700
2.9 to less than 3.0	22,000
3.0 to less than 3.2	23,000
3.2 to less than 3.3	23,100
3.3 to less than 3.4	23,400
3.4 to less than 3.5	23,800
3.5 to less than 3.6	24,100
3.6 to less than 3.7	24,400
3.7 to less than 3.8	24,800

Table 4 — Maximum Allowable Weight for Three Axle Group   **Tab. 4**

Column One	Column Two
Axle Spacing (Metres)	Maximum Allowable Weight (Kilograms)
3.8 to less than 3.9	25,100
3.9 to less than 4.0	25,500
4.0 to less than 4.1	25,800
4.1 to less than 4.2	26,200
4.2 to less than 4.3	26,500
4.3 to less than 4.4	26,900
4.4 to less than 4.5	27,200
4.5 to less than 4.6	27,600
4.6 to less than 4.7	27,900
4.7 to less than 4.8	28,300
4.8 or more	28,600

1993, c. 34, s. 5

TABLE 3 — MAXIMUM ALLOWABLE WEIGHT FOR TWO AXLE GROUP

Column One	Column Two
Axle Spacing (Metres)	Maximum Allowable Weight (Kilograms)
1.0 to less than 1.2	15,000
1.2 to less than 1.3	16,300
1.3 to less than 1.4	16,700
1.4 to less than 1.5	17,000
1.5 to less than 1.6	17,400
1.6 to less than 1.7	17,800
1.7 to less than 1.8	18,200
1.8 to less than 1.9	18,600
1.9 to less than 2.0	19,100

TABLE 4 — MAXIMUM ALLOWABLE WEIGHT FOR THREE AXLE GROUP

Column One	Column Two
Axle Spacing (Metres)	Maximum Allowable Weight (Kilograms)
2.0 to less than 2.4	19,000
2.4 to less than 2.6	20,400
2.6 to less than 2.8	21,000
2.8 to less than 2.9	21,400
2.9 to less than 3.0	21,700
3.0 to less than 3.1	22,000
3.1 to less than 3.2	22,400

Tab. 4   Highway Traffic Act, Part VIII

Column One	Column Two
Axle Spacing (Metres)	Maximum Allowable Weight (Kilograms)
3.2 to less than 3.3	22,700
3.3 to less than 3.4	23,000
3.4 to less than 3.5	23,400
3.5 to less than 3.6	23,700
3.6 to less than 3.7	24,000
3.7 to less than 3.8	24,400
3.8 to less than 3.9	24,700
3.9 to less than 4.0	25,000
4.0 to less than 4.1	25,400
4.1 to less than 4.2	25,700
4.2 to less than 4.3	26,000
4.3 to less than 4.4	26,400
4.4 to less than 4.5	26,700
4.5 to less than 4.6	27,000
4.6 to less than 4.7	27,400
4.7 to less than 4.8	27,700
4.8 to less than 4.9	28,000
4.9 to less than 5.0	28,300
5.0 or more	28,600

TABLE 5 — MAXIMUM ALLOWABLE WEIGHT FOR FOUR AXLE GROUP

Column One	Column Two
Axle Spacing (Metres)	Maximum Allowable Weight (Kilograms)
Less than 3.6	23,500
3.6 to less than 3.7	23,900
3.7 to less than 3.8	24,200
3.8 to less than 3.9	24,600
3.9 to less than 4.0	24,900
4.0 to less than 4.1	25,300
4.1 to less than 4.2	25,700
4.2 to less than 4.3	26,000
4.3 to less than 4.4	26,400
4.4 to less than 4.5	26,700
4.5 to less than 4.6	27,100
4.6 to less than 4.7	27,500
4.7 to less than 4.8	27,800
4.8 to less than 4.9	28,200
4.9 to less than 5.0	28,500
5.0 to less than 5.1	28,900
5.1 to less than 5.2	29,300

Table 5 — Part VIII — Weight   **Tab. 5**

Column One	Column Two
Axle Spacing (Metres)	Maximum Allowable Weight (Kilograms)
5.2 to less than 5.3	29,600
5.3 to less than 5.4	30,000
5.4 to less than 5.5	30,300
5.5 to less than 5.6	30,700
5.6 to less than 5.7	31,100
5.7 to less than 5.8	31,400
5.8 to less than 5.9	31,800
5.9 to less than 6.0	32,100
6.0 to less than 6.1	32,500
6.1 to less than 6.2	32,900
6.2 to less than 6.3	33,200
6.3 to less than 6.4	33,600
6.4 to less than 6.5	33,900
6.5 to less than 6.6	34,300
6.6 to less than 6.7	34,700
6.7 to less than 6.8	35,000
6.8 to less than 6.9	35,400
6.9 to less than 7.0	35,700
7.0 to less than 7.1	36,100
7.1 to less than 7.2	36,500
7.2 to less than 7.3	36,800
7.3 to less than 7.4	37,200
7.4 to less than 7.5	37,600
7.5 or more	38,000

Commentary

The Red Tape Reduction Act, 2000, S.O. 2000, c. 26, Sched. O. (ss. 1-4, 5(1) and (2) and 14 in force December 6, 2000; ss. 6-13 in force January 1, 2001) re-enacts s. 52 of the Highway Traffic Act to allow for notice to be given by regular mail for suspensions unrelated to Criminal Code (Canada) offences, and to allow for other prescribed methods of service; amends s. 55.1 to provide that the impoundment history of leased vehicles is linked to the holder of the plate portion of the registration certificate, to extend vehicle impound provisions to persons who are found driving while their licence is under suspension as a result of a court order and to clarify who is responsible for paying storage charges related to impoundment; amends existing provisions dealing with vehicle weights and dimensions to establish a framework for the implementation of an agreement between Ontario and Quebec; and amends s. 175(6)(c) of the Act to clarify when overhead red signal lights and stop arms on school buses must be used.

Weight

Part VIII of the Act deals with weight.

Section 114 is a definitional section which describes key concepts such as "axle", "axle group weights", "gross vehicle weight" and "Class A and B Highways". The Minister

Tab. 5   Highway Traffic Act, Part VIII

may designate a highway "Class A" (s. 114(2)). Part VIII does not apply to over-dimensional farm vehicles or vehicles operated by a municipality or other authority (s. 114(3)). Irregularly spaced axles are considered in ss. 114(4) and (5). Axle spacing is measured by means of ss. 114(6)–(8).

Section 115 limits weight according to tire width.

Subject to a special permit being granted under s. 110, s. 116 establishes weight restrictions depending on axles. Section 117 provides for maximum weights when axles are grouped. Section 118 limits gross vehicle weights.

Vehicles for the transportation of raw forest products are separately regulated (s. 119). Special weight restrictions are also set out in the case of Class B highways.

Interprovincial carriers must comply with s. 121 of the Act.

The Act provides for weight limits during reduced load periods (s. 122).

The Minister may pass regulations regarding weight on bridges (s. 123).

Offences

A police officer or officer appointed under the Act may cause the vehicle to be weighed at portable or stationary weigh scales, measure distance between axles, and require the driver to redistribute or remove weight (ss. 124(1)–(5)).

Failure to proceed to a scale is punishable by a fine of between $200 and $1,000, and up to a 30-day licence suspension. Failure to redistribute or remove weight or obstruction of any weighing, measuring or examination will attract a fine of between $100 and $200.

Excessive weight contraventions are punishable on an escalating scale (s. 125).

Consignors may be prosecuted under s. 126.

Regulations

Regulations may be made (s. 127).

Tables

The Act includes Tables setting out maximum allowable weights.

Case Law

Quasi-Criminal

R. v. Boyde (1988), 15 M.V.R. (2d) 228 (B.C. Co. Ct.) — The offence of operating an overloaded vehicle was one of strict liability considering the overall regulatory pattern and the maximum penalty of six months' incarceration for nonpayment of fines.

Donline Haulage Inc. v. R. (1980), 4 M.V.R. 241 (Ont. Co. Ct.) — The offence of operating a commercial vehicle with axle weight in excess of the maximum allowable is an offence of strict liability.

R. v. Allen (1979), 3 M.V.R. 203, 59 C.C.C. (2d) 563 (Ont. Dist. Ct.); *R. v. Boyde, supra* — On a charge of operating a commercial motor vehicle with axle unit weight of dual rear axles in excess of allowable weight contrary to the Act, it was held that legislative pattern indicated the offence to be one of absolute liability. It was an open question

Table 5 — Part VIII — Weight **Tab. 5**

whether the defence of commercial impossibility was available, but the defence was not made out by an assertion that compliance with the Act was too expensive.

R. v. Nickel City Transport (Sudbury) Ltd. (1993), 14 O.R. (3d) 115, 22 C.R. (4th) 155, 63 O.A.C. 289, 104 D.L.R. (4th) 340, 47 M.V.R. (2d) 20 (C.A.) — The court was divided on whether s. 116(1)(a) was an offence of strict or absolute liability.

R. v. Laidlaw Tpt. Ltd. (1980), 4 M.V.R. 253 (Ont. Co. Ct.); *Spacemaker Products Ltd. v. R.* (1980), 7 M.V.R. 265 (Ont. Co. Ct.) — The offence under s. 118(1)(a) of exceeding the allowable gross vehicle weight is one of strict, not absolute, liability. Where the vehicle weight would have been permissible had the air-lift middle axle not been in a raised position, the evidence of the driver that the axle had been down when he set out was a good defence.

R. v. Mannion Transportation Ltd. (1985), 31 M.V.R. 246, 38 Sask. R. 152 (Q.B.) — The defendant was charged with operating a commercial vehicle in excess of weight contrary to s. 72(1) of the Highway Act (Sask.). The trial Judge held that the offence charged was one of strict liability. He found that the defendant had exercised due diligence and accordingly dismissed the charge. The Crown appealed; the appeal was dismissed. The offence in question was a public welfare or regulatory offence. It would *prima facie* be a strict liability offence. To show otherwise, it would have to be demonstrated that the Legislature made it clear that "guilt would follow proof merely of the proscribed act." Nothing in the Highway Act suggested that the presumption should be displaced. The statute prohibits certain acts, yet some of those acts were not prohibited absolutely. While the maximum weight of loads was regulated, a person might obtain a permit to exceed the maximum weight. While the Legislature recognized the need to regulate various matters in relation to public highways, it equally recognized the necessity of some flexibility. If the object of the statute was to be achieved, it was not necessary to apply an absolute standard on all occasions. The potential penalties supported the position that the offence was one of strict liability.

George Radford Const. Ltd. v. R. (1980), 6 M.V.R. 295 (Ont. Co. Ct.) — The accused was convicted of carrying gross weight over the amount stated in his commercial vehicle permit. His appeal was allowed where there was no evidence that the vehicles weighed were the same vehicles as identified in the permit.

R. v. Tricil Ltd (1989), 16 M.V.R. (2d) 62 (Ont. Prov. Ct.) — The corporate accused was charged with operating overweight vehicles contrary to a municipal by-law enacted pursuant to the Highway Traffic Act. The facts indicated that the accused had contracts with various commercial establishments to dispose of waste. The Act contained an exception for vehicles operated by, or on behalf of, the municipality transporting waste. Under this provision a competitor of the accused was not charged with operating overweight vehicles engaged in the disposal of residential waste. At trial the accused contended, *inter alia*, that the exception was unconstitutional having regard to s. 15 of the Charter. The charges were stayed. It was held that the purpose of the restrictions was to preserve road conditions, especially during the spring thaw period. However, the exception contained in s. 104(a)(i)(d) of the Act was unrelated to that purpose and was based on the relationship between the owner/operator of the vehicle and the municipality. The statutory scheme, therefore, distinguished between groups carrying on essentially the same activity on a basis not relevant to its purposes. Section 15(1) of the Charter was, therefore, infringed and an appropriate remedy was the staying of the charges in question.

Tab. 5   Highway Traffic Act, Part VIII

R. v. Breau (1989), 19 M.V.R. (2d) 29 (P.E.I. C.A.); reversing (1989), 22 M.V.R. (2d) 300, 78 Nfld. & P.E.I.R. 265, 244 A.P.R. 265 (P.E.I. T.D.); affirming (1989), 15 M.V.R. (2d) 95 (P.E.I. Prov. Ct.) — The accused was charged with the summary conviction offence of operating an overweight vehicle on the highway contrary to regulations made pursuant to the Roads Act (P.E.I.). The provision authorized a peace offer to stop and weigh the vehicles. The trial Judge ruled that the legislation in question was unconstitutional and excluded the evidence under s. 24(2) of the Canadian Charter of Rights and Freedoms. This judgment was affirmed on appeal. On further appeal to the Court of Appeal, the Crown contended that the rulings below were in error in excluding the evidence solely on the basis that the legislation was unconstitutional and without regard to the question of whether the administration of justice would likely be brought into disrepute by the admission of the evidence. The appeal was allowed. It was held that the fact that evidence was obtained as a result of reliance on an unconstitutional legislative provision is not a sufficient basis for exclusion under the Charter. Section 24(2) places an onus on an accused to establish that, considering all the circumstances, the admission of the evidence would likely bring the administration of justice into disrepute. In the case at hand, the trial Judge heard no evidence concerning the detention of the accused under the statute in question. He was, therefore, in no position to rule on the issue of the effect of the admission into evidence. A new trial was ordered.

R. v. Peterson, [1971] 1 O.R. 559, 2 C.C.C. (2d) 154 (C.A.) — The owner may be convicted of "operating" vehicles carrying loads exceeding those for which permits have been issued even though he was not the driver; the offence is the existence on the highway of an overloaded vehicle.

R. v. Strang (1992), 36 M.V.R. (2d) 87, 108 N.S.R. (2d) 238, 294 A.P.R. 238 (C.A.) — A provision which provides that in a prosecution proof of the reading of any scale or weighing device is *prima facie* evidence of the accuracy of the scale or weighing device and of the reading does not offend s. 11(d) of the Charter of Rights.

Ontario (Ministry of Transportation) v. Dagmar Construction Inc. (1995), 12 M.V.R. (3d) 99 (Ont. Prov. Div.) — Where there is evidence with respect to the accuracy of instruments such as weigh scales regarding their efficiency and accuracy, there is prima facie evidence of accuracy which may be rebutted. Prima facie evidence existed where the peace officer testified that he knew the scales were calibrated and adjusted from time to time and that he was familiar with the manner of operation of the scales.

R. v. Dhami, 2006 CarswellOnt 4506, 41 M.V.R. (5th) 192, 2006 ONCJ 271 (Ont. C.J.) — A defence of mistake of fact as part of due diligence was appropriately rejected by the trier.

R. v. Godenir, 2006 CarswellSask 781, 2006 SKQB 481, 41 M.V.R. (5th) 121, 288 Sask. R. 158 (Sask. Q.B.) — A Crown appeal was dismissed where grain was loaded into part of a truck on soft ground and to allow for the possibility of excess weight and inaccurate measurement, the driver did not fill other parts of the truck as much.

Ontario (Ministry of Transportation) v. Underground Services (1983) Ltd., 2006 CarswellOnt 6930, 41 M.V.R. (5th) 252 (Ont. C.J.) — The officer erred in adding the truck's registered gross weight to the trailer's actual weight. The actual weight need be added to the actual weight, and the registered gross weight to the registered gross weight.

R. v. Hart, 2007 CarswellNS 255, 50 M.V.R. (5th) 134, 2007 NSSC 161, 255 N.S.R. (2d) 136, 814 A.P.R. 136 (N.S. S.C.) — It was not an offence to drive a truck whose registered weight was 2800 kg but whose total weight was in excess of 3000 kg where a sign indicated that all trucks with a registered weight of 3000 kg need report to a weigh station.

Civil

Patterson v. Halton, [1954] O.R. 800, [1955] 1 D.L.R. 295 (H.C.) — The mere fact that a vehicle is carrying a load in excess of the permitted maximum when it crashes through a bridge does not bar recovery of damages from the municipality if the main cause of the collapse of the bridge was a state of non-repair.

Hatch v. Fillmore (1968), 1 D.L.R. (3d) 475 (N.S. Co. Ct.) — Where a building being transported by a truck exceeded the permitted height of loads, the operator was liable for damages where the building struck a hydro wire and caused a pole to break and strike plaintiff's house.

Schofield v. Oakville, [1968] 2 O.R. 409, 69 D.L.R. (2d) 441 (C.A.) — It is insufficient compliance with former s. 104(13) to post a load limit sign, which does not even mention a bridge, 700 feet away from the bridge at a place where no bridge can reasonably be seen. The words "at each end of the bridge" mean at the end or close to the end of the structure.

Related Provisions: See s. 1 of the Act for the definition of "gross weight"; see R.R.O. 1990, Reg. 573, Allowable Gross Weight for Designated Class of Vehicles; R.R.O. 1990, Reg. 579, Designation of Highways; O. Reg. 413/05, Vehicle Weights and Dimensions — For Safe, Productive and Infrastructure-Friendly Vehicles; R.R.O. 1990, Reg. 598, Gross Weight on Bridges.

PART IX — RATE OF SPEED

128. (1) Rate of speed — **No person shall drive a motor vehicle at a rate of speed greater than,**

(a) 50 kilometres per hour on a highway within a local municipality or within a built-up area;

(b) despite clause (a), 80 kilometres per hour on a highway, not within a built-up area, that is within a local municipality that had the status of a township on December 31, 2002 and, but for the enactment of the *Municipal Act, 2001*, would have had the status of a township on January 1, 2003, if the municipality is prescribed by regulation;

(b.1) [Repealed 2005, c. 26, Sched. A, s. 17(1).]

(c) 80 kilometres per hour on a highway designated by the Lieutenant Governor in Council as a controlled-access highway under the *Public Transportation and Highway Improvement Act*, whether or not the highway is within a local municipality or built-up area;

(d) the rate of speed prescribed for motor vehicles on a highway in accordance with subsection (2), (5), (6), (6.1) or (7);

(e) the maximum rate of speed set under subsection (10) and posted in a construction zone designated under subsection (8) or (8.1); or

(f) the maximum rate of speed posted on a highway or portion of a highway pursuant to section 128.0.1.

(1.1) Regulation — The Minister may by regulation prescribe the municipalities to which clause (1)(b) applies.

(2) Rate of speed by by-law — The council of a municipality may, for motor vehicles driven on a highway or portion of a highway under its jurisdiction, by by-law prescribe a rate of speed different from the rate set out in subsection (1) that is not greater than 100 kilometres per hour and may prescribe different rates of speed for different times of day.

(3) Same — The rate of speed set under subsection (10) may be any speed that is not greater than 100 kilometres per hour.

(3.1) [Repealed 2006, c. 32, Sched. D, s. 4(5).]

(4) [Repealed 2006, c. 32, Sched. D, s. 4(5).]

(5) Rate in school zones — The council of a municipality may by by-law,

(a) designate a portion of a highway under its jurisdiction that adjoins the entrance to or exit from a school and that is within 150 metres along the highway in either direction beyond the limits of the land used for the purposes of the school; and

(b) for motor vehicles driven, on days on which school is regularly held, on the portion of a highway so designated, prescribe a rate of speed that is lower than the rate of speed otherwise prescribed under subsection (1) or (2) for that portion of highway, and prescribe the time or times at which the speed limit is effective.

(6) Rate on bridges — If the council of a municipality by by-law prescribes a lower rate of speed for motor vehicles passing over a bridge on a highway under its jurisdiction than is prescribed under subsection (1), signs indicating the maximum rate of speed shall be posted in a conspicuous place at each approach to the bridge.

(6.1) Rate on grade — The council of a municipality may by by-law,

(a) designate a portion of a highway under its jurisdiction that includes a grade of 6 per cent or higher; and

(b) prescribe for any class or classes of motor vehicles a lower rate of speed, when travelling down grade on that portion of the highway, than is otherwise prescribed under subsection (1) or (2) for that portion of highway.

(6.2) Same — The portion of a highway designated under clause (6.1)(a) shall not include more than 500 metres on either side of the portion of the highway where the grade is 6 per cent or higher.

(6.3) [Repealed 2006, c. 32, Sched. D, s. 4(9).]

(6.4) [Repealed 2006, c. 32, Sched. D, s. 4(9).]

(7) Rate of speed by regulation — The Minister may make regulations prescribing a rate of speed for,

(a) motor vehicles driven on a highway or portion of a highway within a provincial park;

(b) any class or classes of motor vehicles driven on the King's Highway or portion of the King's Highway whether or not the King's Highway is within a municipality, and the rate of speed may be different for any period or periods of the day or night or direction of travel; and

(c) motor vehicles driven on a highway or portion of a highway in territory without municipal organization.

(8) Construction zones — An official of the Ministry authorized by the Minister in writing may designate any part of the King's Highway as a construction zone, and every construction zone designated under this subsection shall be marked by signs in accordance with the regulations.

(8.1) Same — A person appointed by the municipality for the purpose of this subsection may designate a highway or portion of a highway under the municipality's jurisdiction as a construction zone, and every construction zone designated under this subsection shall be marked by signs in accordance with the regulations.

(8.2) Same — The presence of signs posted under subsection (8) or (8.1) is proof, in the absence of evidence to the contrary, of the designation of the portion of the highway as a construction zone, of the authority of the person authorized under subsection (8) or (8.1) to make the designation and of the speed limit set for the portion of the highway under subsection (10).

(9) Legislation Act, 2006 — A designation under subsection (8) or (8.1) and the setting of a speed limit under subsection (10) are not regulations within the meaning of Part III (Regulations) of the *Legislation Act, 2006*.

(10) Speed limit in construction zones — The person authorized under subsection (8) or (8.1) may set a lower rate of speed for motor vehicles driven in the designated construction zone than is otherwise provided in this section, and the speed limit shall not become effective until the highway or portion of it affected is signed in accordance with subsection (8) or (8.1), as the case may be, and with subsection (10.1).

(10.1) Speed limit signs in construction zones — Signs posting the maximum rate of speed at which motor vehicles may be driven in a designated construction zone may be erected in accordance with the regulations.

(11) By-laws, regulations effective when posted — No by-law passed under this section or regulation made under clause (7)(c) becomes effective until the highway or portion of it affected by the by-law or regulation, as the case may be, is signed in accordance with this Act and the regulations.

(12) Exemption — Where a by-law or regulation passed under this section becomes effective, the rates of speed prescribed in subsection (1) do not apply to the highway or portion of the highway affected by the by-law or regulation.

(13) Fire department vehicles and police vehicles — The speed limits prescribed under this section or any regulation or by-law passed under this section do not apply to,

(a) a fire department vehicle while proceeding to a fire or responding to, but not returning from, a fire alarm or other emergency call;

(b) a police department vehicle being used in the lawful performance of a police officer's duties; or

(c) an ambulance while responding to an emergency call or being used to transport a patient or injured person in an emergency situation.

(14) **Penalty** — Every person who contravenes this section or any by-law or regulation made under this section is guilty of an offence and on conviction is liable, where the rate of speed at which the motor vehicle was driven,

(a) is less than 20 kilometres per hour over the speed limit, to a fine of $3 for each kilometre per hour that the motor vehicle was driven over the speed limit;

(b) is 20 kilometres per hour or more but less than 30 kilometres per hour over the speed limit, to a fine of $4.50 for each kilometre per hour that the motor vehicle was driven over the speed limit;

(c) is 30 kilometres per hour or more but less than 50 kilometres per hour over the speed limit, to a fine of $7 for each kilometre per hour that the motor vehicle was driven over the speed limit; and

(d) is 50 kilometres per hour or more over the speed limit, to a fine of $9.75 for each kilometre per hour that the motor vehicle was driven over the speed limit.

(14.1) **Penalty for speeding in construction zones** — Every person who contravenes this section in a construction zone designated under subsection (8) or (8.1) when there is a worker in the construction zone is liable on conviction, not to the fines set out in subsection (14), but, where the rate of speed at which the motor vehicle was driven,

(a) is less than 20 kilometres per hour over the posted speed limit, to a fine of double the fine set out in clause (14)(a) for each kilometre per hour that the motor vehicle was driven over the speed limit;

(b) is 20 kilometres per hour or more but less than 30 kilometres per hour over the posted speed limit, to a fine of double the fine set out in clause (14)(b) for each kilometre per hour that the motor vehicle was driven over the speed limit;

(c) is 30 kilometres per hour or more but less than 50 kilometres per hour over the posted speed limit, to a fine of double the fine set out in clause (14)(c) for each kilometre per hour that the motor vehicle was driven over the speed limit; and

(d) is 50 kilometres per hour or more over the posted speed limit, to a fine of double the fine set out in clause (14)(d) for each kilometre per hour that the motor vehicle was driven over the speed limit.

(15) **Suspension of licence on conviction** — Subject to subsection 207(7), where a court has convicted a person for a contravention of this section and has determined that the person convicted was driving at a rate of speed of 50 or more kilometres per hour greater than the speed limit, the court may,

(a) suspend the driver's licence of the person for a period of not more than 30 days;

(b) upon the first subsequent conviction where the court determined in respect of each conviction that the person was driving at a rate of speed of 50 or more kilometres per hour greater than the speed limit, suspend the driver's licence of the person for a period of not more than 60 days;

(c) upon the second subsequent conviction or an additional subsequent conviction, where the court determined in respect of each conviction that the person was driving at a rate of speed of 50 or more kilometres per hour greater than the speed limit, suspend the driver's licence of the person for a period of not more than one year.

(15.1) Determining subsequent conviction — In determining whether a conviction is a subsequent conviction for the purposes of subsection (15), the only question to be considered is the sequence of convictions and no consideration shall be given to the sequence of commission of offences or whether any offence occurred before or after any conviction.

(15.2) Five-year limitation — Clauses (15)(b) and (c) do not apply when the subsequent conviction is more than five years after the first conviction.

(15.3) Transition — Despite subsection (15.2), a conviction that was before the date on which this subsection comes into force shall not be taken into account for the purpose of clauses (15)(b) and (c).

(15.4) Certificate of offence not to be amended to charge owner — A certificate of offence that specifies an offence under section 128 against a driver shall not be amended to reflect a charge against that person as an owner.

(16) Definition — In this section, "motor vehicle" includes street car.

1993, c. 31, s. 2(7); 1997, c. 26, s. 137 (Sched.); 2002, c. 17, Sched. C, s. 15(1), (2), Sched. F, s. 1; 2002, c. 18, Sched. P, s. 29(1)–(4); 2005, c. 26, Sched. A, s. 17(1)–(5), (7)–(10); 2006, c. 11, Sched. B, s. 6(2), (4), (5); 2006, c. 21, Sched. F, ss. 115, 139(3); 2006, c. 32, Sched. C, s. 24(4), Sched. D, s. 4(1)–(9); 2009, c. 5, s. 40

Commentary

General

There is an 80 km/h limit for highways not within a city, town, village, built-up area or a highway designated as a controlled-access highway under the Public Transportation and Highway Improvement Act (s. 128(1)(a)).

For highways within cities, etc., the limit is 50 km/h (subs. (1)(b)). The council or trustees of a police village may set higher speed limits (subss. (2), (3)) or, in the case of a park, lower rates (subs. (4)).

The Municipality of Metropolitan Toronto Act regulates speed within the municipality (subss. (1)(e) and (12)).

School zones may be regulated by by-laws designating portions of a highway within 150 metres of a school, and by prescribing speed to 40 km/h between 8:00 a.m. and 5:00 p.m. (subs. (5)).

Special rates of speed apply to: bridges (subs. (6)); provincial parks (subs. (7)(a)); the King's Highway (subs. (7)(b)); and construction zones (subss. (8)–(10)).

Regulations under s. 2, 5 or 6 do not become effective until signs are posted (subs. (11)).

Offences

The following fines apply in the case of speeding:

- $3 for every kilometre up to 20 km/h over the maximum;

- $4.50 for every kilometre between 20 and 34 km/h;

- $7.00 for every kilometre between 35 and 49 km/h; and

- $9.75 for every kilometre over 49 km/h.

In addition, if speeding is in excess of 50 km/h over the limit, up to a 30-day licence suspension may be imposed.

Emergency and Other Vehicles

Speed limits do not apply to: fire engines as defined in s. 61 of the Act proceeding to a fire; a motor vehicle used in the lawful performance of the duties of a police officer; and an ambulance as defined in s. 61 of the Act while responding to an emergency call or being used to transport in an emergency situation (subs. (13)). Streetcars are liable for speeding (subs. (16)).

Case Law

Quasi-Criminal

Nature of Offence

R. v. Stephens (1966), 1 C.R.N.S. 109, 25 M.P.R. 394 (N.S. Co. Ct.); reversed on other grounds (1967), 2 C.R.N.S. 103, 53 M.P.R. 311 (N.S. C.A.); *R. v. Naugler* (1981), 14 M.V.R. 9, 25 C.R. (3d) 392 (N.S. C.A.) — *Mens rea* is not an ingredient of the offence of exceeding the speed limit; the object of the section and the comparative lightness of the penalty indicated that knowledge or awareness of the infraction was not necessary.

R. v. Kennedy (1972), 18 C.R.N.S. 80, 7 C.C.C. (2d) 42 (N.S. Co. Ct.); *R. v. Paul* (1973), 12 C.C.C. (2d) 497 (N.S. Co. Ct.) — A defence of necessity may be sustained in appropriate cases as where a car following too closely did not permit a reduction of speed.

R. v. Walls (1986), 47 M.V.R. 92 (B.C. Co. Ct.) — The accused was charged with speeding and was convicted after the trial Judge rejected her defence of necessity. She appealed. The appeal was dismissed. It was held that the accused claimed that she was speeding because she was being followed closely by a truck. Neither of the police witnesses at trial had observed another vehicle around that of the accused. Her evidence indicated that, while she was annoyed by what she perceived to be tailgating, she was not intimidated nor threatened by it. Accordingly, the defence of necessity was not available to the accused.

R. v. Greening (1991), 40 M.V.R. (2d) 81, 98 Nfld. & P.E.I.R. 267, 311 A.P.R. 267 (Nfld. T.D.) — For necessity to succeed the burden of proof would lay upon the driver to satisfy the court that the action in driving the car at a speed in excess of the limit was the only means open to the driver to avoid an accident.

R. v. Hickey (1976), 13 O.R. (2d) 228, 30 C.C.C. (2d) 416, 70 D.L.R. (3d) 689 (C.A.); *R. v. Lemieux* (1978), 3 C.R. (3d) 284, 41 C.C.C. (2d) 33 (Que. C.A.); *R. v. Gillis* (1974), 18 C.C.C. (2d) 190 (N.S. C.A.) — An honest and reasonable mistake of fact is not a defence to speeding.

R. v. Gillis, supra; R. v. King (1985), 54 Nfld. & P.E.I.R. 286, 160 A.P.R. 286 (Nfld. Dist. Ct.) — A driver exceeding the speed limit is guilty of an offence notwithstanding that he may in good faith have relied on a defective speedometer.

R. v. Canning (1980), 40 N.S.R. (2d) 177, 73 A.P.R. 177 (Co. Ct.) — The offence of speeding under the Motor Vehicle Act, R.S.N.S. 1967, c. 191, s. 96(1), being an absolute liability offence, the defence of due diligence or no negligence was not available to an accused who was exceeding the speed limit despite having set his cruise control correctly.

R. v. Williams (1992), 39 M.V.R. (2d) 315, 14 C.R. (4th) 218, 74 C.C.C. (3d) 160, 114 N.S.R. (2d) 21, 313 A.P.R. 21 (C.A.) — Speeding is an offence of strict not absolute liability. The defences of due diligence and reasonable mistake of fact are available, considering s. 7 of the Charter of Rights.

R. v. Vlajkovic (1994), 5 M.V.R. (3d) 219, 74 O.A.C. 340 (C.A.) — Where speeding and driving while suspended occurred at the same time and were related to the same transaction, the refusal to order severance should not be disturbed.

R. v. Rizzetto (1997), 27 M.V.R. (3d) 270 (N.S. S.C.) — An appeal on the ground of necessity was dismissed where the accused sped to complete overtaking of a vehicle before the end of a passing zone and to prevent a collision with an oncoming vehicle. The vehicle overtaken was near the speed limit and the accused was unfamiliar with roadway. The likelihood of an emergency and breaking of the law were both objectively foreseeable and the creation of the emergency was created by voluntary action.

R. v. Cook (1999), 40 M.V.R. (3d) 124 (Nfld. T.D.) — On a charge of driving at an unreasonable and imprudent speed requires an examination of the conditions present and actual and potential hazards. An objective test involves taking into account a number of factors including the conditions and amount of usage of the highway, the visibility of the driver, speed, posted speed, mechanical fitness, potential hazards and related factors.

R. v. Weber (2003), 39 M.V.R. (4th) 99, 2003 CarswellOnt 1465, 64 O.R. (3d) 126 (Ont. C.J.) — Notwithstanding s. 128(14) (d) of the Act, s. 12(1) of the Provincial Offences Act sets a limit of $500.00.

R. v. Martin (2004), 7 M.V.R. (5th) 219, 248 Sask. R. 202, 2004 SKQB 199, 2004 CarswellSask 364, [2004] S.J. No. 332, [2006] 3 W.W.R. 85 (Q.B.) — The legal principle of providing adequate reasons for decision applies to traffic and by-law courts.

London (City) v. Polewsky (2005), 2005 CarswellOnt 5145, 23 M.V.R. (5th) 63, 202 C.C.C. (3d) 257, [2005] O.J. No. 4500, 138 C.R.R. (2d) 208 (C.A.); leave to appeal refused (2006), 2006 CarswellOnt 3307, 2006 CarswellOnt 3308, [2006] S.C.C.A. No. 37, 138 C.R.R. (2d) 376 (note), 356 N.R. 397 (note), 224 O.A.C. 400 (note) — There is no reason to revisit an earlier holding that the offence is one of absolute liability.

R. v. Wheeler, 2007 CarswellNfld 161, 47 M.V.R. (5th) 39, [2007] N.J. No. 175 (Prov. Ct.) — A disclosure request for other speeding tickets issued by the officer was denied but the Crown was ordered to see if there were operational standards available to indicate how the speed detector was to be operated.

R. v. Crow, 60 M.V.R. (5th) 137, 88 Alta. L.R. (4th) 386, 2007 ABPC 339, 2007 CarswellAlta 1701, 435 A.R. 280 (Prov. Ct.) — The Alberta offence requiring a driver to slow down to 60 kmh or to the posted speed limit if below that speed when passing emergency vehicles with emergency lights flashing while stopped on the same side of the road is a strict liability offence.

R. v. Williams (2008), 69 M.V.R. (5th) 112, 2008 CarswellOnt 1504 (C.J.) — There is no requirement that the operator achieve a certain level of qualification as a prerequisite to accepting the operator's evidence of the rate of speed.

R. v. A. (J.B.), 2008 CarswellOnt 6830, 2008 ONCJ 587, 77 M.V.R. (5th) 97 (C.J.) — Section 128(8) regarding the establishment of construction zones is not an unlawful delegation by the Legislature. It would be unreasonable to have new legislation passed and then revoked each time a temporary construction zone was established.

R. v. Winlow, 2009 CarswellOnt 5208, [2009] O.J. No. 3691, 2009 ONCA 643, 86 M.V.R. (5th) 171, (sub nom. *York (Regional Municipality) v. Winlow)* 99 O.R. (3d) 337, 265 O.A.C. 326 — The fines for speeding in s. 128(4) of the Act are fixed and derived by multiplying the number of kilometres per hour over the speed limit by the appropriate figure. The courts have no discretion to reduce the fines. Under the *Provincial Offences Act*, where the accused is charged with a reduced speed but does not plead guilty, he or she may be found guilty of the correct speed.

R. v. Raham, 2010 CarswellOnt 1546, 2010 ONCA 206, 74 C.R. (6th) 96, 253 C.C.C. (3d) 188, 99 O.R. (3d) 241, 92 M.V.R. (5th) 195, [2010] O.J. No. 1091, 260 O.A.C. 143, 213 C.R.R. (2d) 336 — The offence of stunt driving, stunt driving by speeding 50 kilometres or more over the speed limit, pursuant to s. 172 of the *Act*, and O.Reg. 455/07, s. 3 is an offence of strict liability. Section 172 sets out that the offence may be committed in three ways. Speeding under s. 128 is an included offence under s. 55 of the *Provincial Offences Act* (Ont.).

R. v. Murray, 2010 NSSC 296, 2010 CarswellNS 476, 293 N.S.R. (2d) 264, 98 M.V.R. (5th) 245, 928 A.P.R. 264, [2010] N.S.J. No. 419 — Disclosure would have been as easy as sending a photocopy of the reverse of the ticket to the accused in a speeding case.

R. v. Garbarino, 2010 ONCJ 300, 2010 CarswellOnt 5390, 100 M.V.R. (5th) 150 — In regulatory offences such as speeding, a trial court is entitled to apply the presumption of regularity to the requirements of R.R.O. 1990, Reg. 615, *Signs*.

R. v. Brown, 2011 MBCA 63, 2011 CarswellMan 393, 16 M.V.R. (6th) 13, [2011] M.J. No. 241 (In Chambers). The Crown has to prove that the accused was speeding. The actual rate of speed was not an element of s. 95(1) of the *Highway Traffic Act* (Man.).

R. v. Thom, 2010 ONCJ 492, 2010 CarswellOnt 8163, [2010] O.J. No. 4607, 5 M.V.R. (6th) 140 — The requirement that original copies be used if available was a precondition to admissibility of police officer notes into evidence under past recollection recorded but is not a requirement to refresh the witness' memory.

Mississauga (City) v. Vattiata, 2010 ONCJ 588, 2010 CarswellOnt 9341, [2010] O.J. No. 5283, 6 M.V.R. (6th) 128 — It would be unreasonable to not allow police officers to refer to their notes when testifying in matters where they deal with enormous numbers of similar offences.

R. v. Appiah, 2012 ONCJ 754, 2012 CarswellOnt 15602, 38 M.V.R. (6th) 173, [2012] O.J. No. 5851 (Ont. Ct. J.) — There is no authority to impose a set fine under the *Provincial Offences Act* rather than the statutory fine set under s. 128(14) of the *Highway Traffic Act*.

Judicial Notice

R. v. Cunningham (1979), 1 M.V.R. 223, 45 C.C.C. (2d) 544 (Ont. Div. Ct.) — Where the accused misread posted speed limit signs, it was held that a mistake of law was not a valid defence to a charge of speeding.

R. v. Bland (1974), 6 O.R. (2d) 54, 20 C.C.C. (2d) 332, 17 Crim. L.Q. 193 (C.A.); affirming (1974), 19 C.C.C. (2d) 121 (Ont. H.C.) — Where there is no oral evidence of the speed limit, the court is bound to take judicial notice of the speed limit contained in the regulations.

R. v. Eagles (1976), 31 C.C.C. (2d) 417 (Ont. H.C.); *R. v. Redlick* (1978), 2 C.R. (3d) 380, 41 C.C.C. (2d) 358 (Ont. H.C.) — Where the accused is charged with speeding within a city pursuant to a section that provides that the speed within a city shall not exceed 30 m.p.h. and there is no evidence called that the speeding was within the city, nor evidence called as to the speed limit, the conviction must be quashed as judicial notice cannot be taken that the place of speeding was within the city.

R. v. Joudrey (1992), 39 M.V.R. (2d) 235, 113 N.S.R. (2d) 117, 309 A.P.R. 117 (Prov. Ct.) — The court took judicial nature of textbook passages from a book on speeding and radar.

R. v. Bennett (1971), 15 C.R.N.S. 28, 4 C.C.C. (2d) 55 (N.S. Co. Ct.); *R. v. McGregor* (1895), 26 O.R. 115, 2 C.C.C. 410 (H.C.); *R. v. Cerniuk*, 5 C.R. 234, [1948] 1 W.W.R. 653, 91 C.C.C. 56 (B.C. C.A.); *R. v. Jameson*, [1896] 2 Q.B. 425; *R. v. Potts* (1982), 36 O.R. (2d) 195, 14 M.V.R. 72, 26 C.R. (3d) 252, 134 D.L.R. (3d) 227, 66 C.C.C. (2d) 219 (C.A.); leave to appeal to S.C.C. refused (1982), 66 C.C.C. (2d) 219n, 134 D.L.R. (3d) 227n — Judicial notice may be taken in appropriate circumstances.

R. v. Amyot, [1968] 2 O.R. 626, [1968] 4 C.C.C. 58 (Co. Ct.); *R. v. C.*, [1971] 5 W.W.R. 289 (Alta. Dist. Ct.) — An accused may not be convicted of driving at a specific rate of speed, the offence created by the Act being that of operating a motor vehicle at a greater speed than the existing speed limit.

R. v. Stewart (1997), 30 M.V.R. (3d) 305 (N.B. Q.B.) — Judicial notice of the speed limit contravenes s. 11(d) of the Charter of Rights.

See the cases under *Radar* below.

Durham (Municipality) v. Muia, 2012 ONCJ 229, 2012 CarswellOnt 5592, 32 M.V.R. (6th) 352, [2012] O.J. No. 1711 — Under s. 128(15) of the Act, a license suspension is possible.

R. v. Abrametz (2014), 68 M.V.R. (6th) 95, 2014 SKCA 84, 2014 CarswellSask 490, 442 Sask. R. 86, 616 W.A.C. 86, [2014] S.J. No. 438 — It was permissible to take judicial notice that the highway's limit was 100 kph.

Wording of the Charge

R. v. White, [1957] O.W.N. 491 (C.A.) — An information was laid against the accused charging him with "[b]eing the registered owner of [a] motor vehicle ... [described by licence number] which was driven unlawfully by a person at a greater rate of speed than" the statutory maximum. This was held to be a sufficient indication of the offence charged.

R. v. MacLean (1978), 21 Nfld. & P.E.I.R. 273, 56 A.P.R. 273 (P.E.I. S.C.); *Lawless v. R.* (1981), 11 M.V.R. 296, 33 Nfld. & P.E.I.R. 436, 93 A.P.R. 436 (P.E.I. S.C.); *R. v. McLellan* (1980), 31 Nfld. & P.E.I.R. 79, 87 A.P.R. 79 (P.E.I. S.C.) — On appeal from a conviction for speeding, an appellant argued that the information was a nullity by reason of the fact it did not comply with the form of information prescribed by regulation enacted pursuant to the Act. The officer amended the traffic ticket form by striking out any reference to miles per hour (m.p.h.) and showing the offence to have been committed in terms of kilometres per hour (k.p.h.). It was held that the appeal should have been dismissed with costs. The Act allowed the officer to write in the offence where the offence was not specified on the traffic ticket. This was sufficient authority for the officer to strike out m.p.h. and substitute k.p.h.

R. v. Mockler (1989), 98 N.B.R. 271, 248 A.P.R. 271 (Q.B.) — The appellant was convicted of driving a motor vehicle more than 25 km/h over the speed limit. The appellant appealed from the conviction on the ground that the information was a nullity in that he was charged under the penalty section rather than the substantive section. It was held that the appellant was neither misled nor prejudiced by the information and therefore it was valid.

Obstructing Police

R. v. Solowoniuk (1960), 129 C.C.C. 273 (B.C. C.A.) — Charges of obstructing the police in the execution of their duty have been laid against persons who stop and warn approaching motorists of a police radar trap ahead, but it seems there can be no conviction unless the car warned was proceeding at an illegal speed at the time of the warning.

R. v. Tremblay, [1975] 3 W.W.R. 589, 23 C.C.C. (2d) 179, 58 D.L.R. (3d) 69 (Alta. C.A.) — Appellant was convicted of an offence under s. 144(1) of the Alberta Act, which reads: "No person, whether as a pedestrian or driver, and whether or not with the use or aid of any animal, vehicle or other thing, shall perform or engage in any stunt or other activity upon a highway that is likely to distract, startle or interfere with other users of the highway." The appellant had flashed the headlights of his vehicle on and off a number of times to warn other drivers that they were approaching a police radar trap. It was held that the conviction should be quashed. The evidence failed to establish that the actions of appellant constituted an offence under s. 144(1).

Giffin v. R. (1980), 8 M.V.R. 313, 46 N.S.R. (2d) 541, 89 A.P.R. 541 (Co. Ct.) — Where an officer testifies to speed of 107 km as opposed to 107 km *per hour*, such evidence, while imprecise, is satisfactory.

Included Offences

Smith v. R. (1982), 15 M.V.R. 161, 51 N.S.R. (2d) 539, 102 A.P.R. 539 (C.A.) — Speeding is not included in careless driving.

Charter

R. v. Goreham (1984), 26 M.V.R. 164, 12 C.C.C. (3d) 348, 64 N.S.R. (2d) 68, 143 A.P.R. 68 (C.A.) — The offence was described on the summons as "exceeding prima facie limit". The statute prohibited speeds in excess of 80 km/h on any highway at any time, unless otherwise posted. The abbreviated form of the charge did not violate s. 11(a) of the Charter of Rights and Freedoms.

R. v. Harper (1985), 35 M.V.R. 134, 45 C.R. (3d) 186, 17 C.R.R. 113 (B.C. Co. Ct.); affirmed (1986), 44 M.V.R. 313, 53 C.R. (3d) 185 (B.C. C.A.) — Speeding does not infringe ss. 7 and 11(d) of the Charter of Rights and Freedoms.

R. v. Ellison (1987), 46 M.V.R. 132 (B.C. Co. Ct.) — The accused was convicted of speeding. He appealed on the ground that the denial by the police officer who stopped his car of his request to see the radar reading and the erasure of the reading by the officer contravened the best evidence rule and violated his right to make full answer and defence under s. 7 of the Charter. The appeal was dismissed. It was held that the best evidence rule was confined largely to documentary evidence; apart from documentary evidence it was not usually applied to exclude secondary evidence otherwise admissible. There was no suggestion of an attempt to conceal evidence. The accused had been given the opportunity to make full answer and defence.

R. v. Wilson (1991), 3 M.V.R. (2d) 52 (N.S. Co. Ct.) — The accused was charged with speeding. The Crown refused to comply with repeated requests by counsel for the accused for a copy of the technical manual for the radar machine that had been used to measure the speed of the accused's vehicle. The accused argued that his inability to obtain full disclosure from the Crown had impaired his ability to make full answer and defence contrary to s. 7 of the Charter of Rights and Freedoms. The trial Judge held that there had been a violation of the accused's right to make full answer and defence but that the appropriate remedy was not the stay of proceedings sought by the accused. Instead, he ordered the Crown to deliver the manual and set a date for the trial to continue. On that date, the accused was convicted. He appealed. The appeal was dismissed. The accused's right to make full answer and defence was not infringed by the Crown's refusal to produce the manual. The duty of the Crown is to disclose the evidence which it believes will establish the relevant facts, and the source of that evidence. While any information that may be in the possession of the Crown that could reasonably assist the defence in evaluating the evidence and in preparing for trial should be made available, there must be some reason to think that the information sought could realistically be expected to advance the position of the accused at his trial. The accused failed to establish that the defence was in any way impaired or limited in its ability to challenge the capacity of the radar machine, when operating properly, to record speeds of oncoming vehicles by reason of the reluctance of the Crown to produce the operating manual.

R. v. Hedayat (1992), 41 M.V.R. (2d) 218, 133 A.R. 303 (Q.B.); reversing (1991), 34 M.V.R. (2d) 12 (Alta. Prov. Ct.) — Where the defendant was not served with a violation's ticket until 25 days after the date of the alleged offence, he was not deprived of his right to make full answer and defence and the lower court was in error in finding that there was an abuse of process.

R. v. Longmire (1993), 42 M.V.R. (2d) 21, 119 N.S.R. (2d) 351, 330 A.P.R. 351 (N.S. C.A.) — The Crown's refusal to provide a copy of the radar operation manual did not violate ss. 7 and 11(d) of the Charter of Rights where the appellant did not lay a rational basis or factual foundation for the claim of disclosure.

R. v. Dunne (1998), 33 M.V.R. (3d) 292, 162 Sask. R. 119 (Sask. Q.B.) — The destruction of a videotape activated only once the officer had contacted the accused did not prevent him from making full answer and defence.

R. v. Vellone, 2011 ONCA 785, 2011 CarswellOnt 14646, 108 O.R. (3d) 481, 25 M.V.R. (6th) 1, 250 C.R.R. (2d) 351, 284 O.A.C. 388, [2011] O.J. No. 5708 (Ont. C.A.) — The Attorney General merits notice under s. 109 of the Courts of Justice Act where s. 11(b) of the Charter of Rights is in issue under a municipal prosecution for speeding as systematic issues could be in play.

Signs

R. v. Clark (1974), 3 O.R. (2d) 716, 18 C.C.C. (2d) 52 (C.A.); reversing (1973), 1 O.R. (2d) 210, 24 C.R.N.S. 65, 14 C.C.C. (2d) 73 (H.C.); *R. v. Grace* (1986), 47 M.V.R. 284, 71 N.S.R. (2d) 386, 171 A.P.R. 386 (C.A.); *R. v. Margetis* (1988), 9 M.V.R. (2d) 19 (Ont. H.C.) — On appeal it was held that although the by-law was not proven, the fact that signs regulating speed had been erected was *prima facie* proof of compliance with the regulations under the Highway Traffic Act.

R. v. Redden (1978), 1 M.V.R. 119, 29 N.S.R. (2d) 266, 45 A.P.R. 266 (C.A.) — Although proof of posting a speed sign was required, there need not be a sign at the exact spot where the violation occurred.

R. v. Snodgrass (1980), 32 N.B.R. (2d) 583, 78 A.P.R. 583 (Q.B.) — The accused was charged with driving "in excess of 90 km/h on a highway for which a maximum rate of speed of 90 km was prescribed" in accordance with s. 141 of the Act. The accused contended that in the absence of a speed limit sign on the portion of the highway from where he had turned on to it to where he was stopped, he was entitled to assume that 80 km/h was the speed limit pursuant to s. 117(2) of the 1973 New Brunswick Act and that therefore the charge was improperly constituted. On appeal from conviction, it was held that the appeal should be dismissed. A 90 km speed limit sign was located on the highway just before the intersection where the accused turned onto the highway. Although he could not have seen it by reason of not having passed it, nevertheless, he had a duty upon him of acquainting himself with the prevailing maximum rate and, if in doubt, of governing his speed accordingly.

R. v. Rutledge (1981), 62 C.C.C. (2d) 314 (N.S. Co. Ct.) — Legislation was considered which provided that the fact that the speed limit sign had been "erected and maintained" was *prima facie* evidence that the sign was erected in compliance with the statutory provisions. The word "maintain" was held not to necessarily involve any activity on the part of the traffic authority. The fact that the sign remained standing and clearly visible without a change in its ability to communicate the message was sufficient maintenance within the meaning of the term.

R. v. Strong (1988), 13 M.V.R. (2d) 106, 89 N.S.R. (2d) 232, 227 A.P.R. 232 (Co. Ct.) — The accused was acquitted of a speeding charge. Although the trial Judge accepted the evidence of the police officer with respect to the actual speed of the accused's vehicle as indicated by radar, he entered an acquittal on the basis that the Crown had failed to prove that the accused had passed a speed zone sign indicating the posted speed in the area in question. The Crown appealed. The appeal was allowed. It was held that there was no requirement in the relevant statutory provision that speed zone signs be erected so as to be always visible to a motorist traversing a section of highway covered by the speed approved for that area. Common sense dictated that such could not have been the intention of the Legislature — otherwise such signs would have to be erected at each street intersection and at various intervals along the province's roadways.

Québec (P.G.) c. Lapointe (1989), 22 M.V.R. (2d) 341 (C. Qué.) — The accused was charged with going 101 km/h in a 70 km/h zone. He was travelling on a superhighway, the autoroute. He claimed that in the absence of signs specifying a 70 km/h maximum, he should be able to rely upon the provincial Highway Traffic Act which permits speeds of up to 100 km/h on the autoroute. An acquittal was entered. The signs supported the accused. A representative of the Ministry of Transportation, whose evidence was accepted, testified that the only sign that was nearby was on an entry ramp which the accused did not use. Further, the surplus of 1 km/h was negligible and understandable given that the accused was passing a truck at the relevant time.

R. v. Longmire (1993), 42 M.V.R. (2d) 21, 119 N.S.R. (2d) 351, 330 A.P.R. 351 (N.S. C.A.) — The Act provided that no provisions of the Act for which signs are authorized or required shall be enforced against an alleged violator if, at the time of the alleged violation, the sign was not in the proper position or not discernible by an ordinarily observant person. The burden or exception is on the defendant.

R. v. Christie (1992), 42 M.V.R. (2d) 194, 20 B.C.A.C. 61, 35 W.A.C. 61 (C.A.) — Speeding restrictions in a construction zone do not cease to apply even if no work is being done on the site.

Ontario v. Druce, 2006 CarswellOnt 3102, 2006 ONCJ 183, 32 M.V.R. (5th) 215 (C.J.) — A posted construction zone and speed limit signs were both *prima facie* proof as well as sufficient proof of existence of the speed limit and of the designation of a construction zone.

Chain and Tape Measurement

R. v. Frier (1962), 39 W.W.R. 232 (Sask. Dist. Ct.) — There is no presumption that a tape measure measures distances correctly.

R. v. King (1977), 35 C.C.C. (2d) 424 (Ont. Div. Ct.) — At the trial of an accused on a charge of speeding, a police officer gave evidence of the accused's speed based on the time it took the accused to go past markings on the highway. The police officer stated he had measured the distance between the markings with a chain on which the manufacturer had placed a mark indicating 200 feet. It was held that evidence as to measurements made by the use of the chain, it not being a measuring device, was inadmissible without further evidence as to the accuracy of the measurements. Their accuracy could not be established by the manufacturer's mark since such evidence would be hearsay.

Pacing

R. v. Bland (1974), 6 O.R. (2d) 54, 20 C.C.C. (2d) 332, 17 Crim. L.Q. 193 (C.A.); affirming (1974), 19 C.C.C. (2d) 121 (Ont. H.C.); *Nicholas v. Penny*, [1950] 2 K.B. 466 (C.A.); *R. v. Tait*, [1965] 1 C.C.C. 16 (N.B. Co. Ct.) — If evidence is given that a mechanical device, such as a watch or a speedometer, recorded a particular time or speed which it is the purpose of that instrument to record, that can by itself be *prima facie* evidence on which a court can act of that time or speed, notwithstanding that no evidence is adduced as to the accuracy of the device. If the speed clocked is greatly excessive of the maximum allowed the court would probably convict even in the absence of tests as to accuracy, but it might be otherwise if only small differences were involved.

R. v. Amyot, [1968] 2 O.R. 626, [1968] 4 C.C.C. 58 (Co. Ct.) — A stopwatch reading of a vehicle passing between markers on a highway was made by police in an airplane.

Radar

R. v. Grainger, [1958] O.W.N. 311, 28 C.R. 84, 120 C.C.C. 32 (C.A.); *R. v. Morash* (1972), 10 C.C.C. (2d) 39 (N.S. Co. Ct.) — A conviction may be entered on a charge of speeding on the evidence of data obtained from a radar speedmeter, if evidence is adduced that the equipment was in good working order and was being properly used.

R. v. Lafrentz, [1970] 2 C.C.C. 381 (Sask. Q.B.); *R. v. Waschuk* (1970), 1 C.C.C. (2d) 463 (Sask. Q.B.); *Lawless v. R.* (1981), 11 M.V.R. 296, 33 Nfld. & P.E.I.R. 436, 93 A.P.R. 436 (P.E.I. S.C.) — The speed recorded by a radar device is *prima facie* evidence of that speed and the onus is on the accused to adduce evidence which raises a reasonable doubt as to the accuracy of the radar or the other speed device by which the radar has been tested.

R. v. Wolfe (1979), 3 M.V.R. 143 (B.C. Co. Ct.) — An appeal was allowed where the officer gave evidence that he was trained and that in his opinion the machine was working but where other evidence, including uncertainty of testing procedures, raised a doubt as to whether or not the machine was, in fact, accurate.

R. v. O'Reilly (1979), 10 Alta. L.R. (2d) 199, 3 M.V.R. 228, 16 A.R. 369 (Alta. Dist. Ct.); *R. v. Lehane* (1982), 15 M.V.R. 160 (Alta. Q.B.) — A conviction was set aside where the Crown failed to establish that the tests actually conducted were approved for the particular radar set. Such evidence could have been given by the operator from knowledge which he acquired in his training.

Giffin v. R. (1980), 8 M.V.R. 313, 46 N.S.R. (2d) 541, 89 A.P.R. 541 (Co. Ct.) — The fact was considered that it was not explicitly stated in evidence that the radar machine was capable of recording the speed of the vehicle being tested. It was held that judicial notice could be taken of the use of radar guns although not their exact functioning.

R. v. Martin (1984), 34 Sask. R. 299 (Q.B.) — The operator took a short course in radar operation. He calibrated the machine two hours before the offence, in the presence of the accused and again upon going off duty. The evidence of the operator that the machine was in good working order was sufficient that the machine was recording speed accurately. It is not necessary that the operator be an expert in the field of electronics.

R. v. Bourque (April 16, 1986), Doc. Calgary Appeal 17925 (Alta. C.A.); reversing (1985), 38 M.V.R. 110 (Alta. Q.B.) — When the Crown seeks to rely on electronic devices for convictions, then it must be prepared to establish beyond a reasonable doubt that such devices are operating properly, and are capable of performing the functions for which they are used. At the Queen's Bench level, both proof of the accuracy of the tuning fork and proof that the machine was capable of accurately registering the speed of the accused's vehicle was essential. On appeal, however, it was decided that the Crown is not required to prove the accuracy of the equipment or the tuning fork.

R. v. McDonald (1987), 49 M.V.R. 36 (B.C. Co. Ct.) — The appellant was found guilty of a speeding violation. He appealed on the ground that the police officer who testified at trial as to radar readings was an expert and that the 30 days' notice in writing required by s. 11 of the Evidence Act (B.C.) had not been given. The appeal was dismissed. It was held that the capability and accuracy of radar are a matter of expert opinion. However, the police officer did not give expert evidence as he did not give evidence of radar capability and accuracy. The officer's visual estimation of speed alone provided proof beyond a reasonable doubt.

R. v. Hallett (1988), 8 M.V.R. (2d) 29 (N.S. Co. Ct.) — On appeal the accused contended that the officer's testimony was expert evidence and since no evidence had been led as to the expert qualifications of the officer the evidence was inadmissible. The appeal was dismissed. It was held that the evidence in issue was not opinion evidence and therefore there was no necessity for the prosecution to lead evidence establishing that the officer was an expert. The trial Judge had made findings of fact and credibility regarding the officer's ability to operate the machine and to determine whether it was subject to any inaccuracies on the day of the offence. Moreover it was open to the accused to cross-examine the officer on these matters but he had failed to do so.

Québec (P.G.) v. Rannaud, 9 M.V.R. (2d) 79, [1988] R.J.Q. 2019 (C.S.P. Qué.) — The sole evidence was from a radar operator. The operator testified that he took an instruction course and that he frequently used the device on duty. He indicated that on the night in question he manually and electronically verified the accuracy on three occasions. He also verified the device's operation after stopping the accused. Manual checks were done by means of a tuning fork. The accused was convicted. It was held that no expert was needed to provide evidence regarding calibration. The absence of legislative approval of the use of tuning forks did not invalidate its effectiveness on calibration. If the operator carries out tests correctly and in conformity with recognized methods, he can speak to accuracy of the device and its proper functioning. An operator need not be familiar with the relevant laws of physics. Here, the results of the tests confirmed accuracy.

Masson v. Québec (P.G.) (1988), 9 M.V.R. (2d) 124 (C.S. Qué.) — The accused was convicted of speeding. He appealed challenging the radar evidence. The appeal was dismissed. Leaving aside cases in which calibration, verification of calibration, method of operation, qualifications of the operator or other factors cast a doubt on the evidence of operation and capabilities of a device, the testimony of a qualified operator can found a conviction. Once the conditions precedent are met the fallibilities of the device go to weight. It is unnecessary to show scientifically the principles of radar.

Baie-Comeau (Ville) c. D'Astous (1992), 9 M.V.R. (3d) 189, R.J.Q. 1483, 49 Q.A.C. 99, 74 C.C.C. (3d) 73 (Que. C.A.) — A trial judge may take judicial notice of radar as a device for measuring speed. However, the prosecution is required to establish the accuracy of the particular device in every case. The demonstration that the operator is qualified, that his device is tested before and after its use, and that the test showed that the instrument was accurate establishes prima facie evidence of accuracy.

R. v. Vancrey (2000), 147 C.C.C. (3d) 546, 5 M.V.R. (4th) 302, 135 O.A.C. 89 (C.A.) — The evidence respecting the laser device constituted a prima facie case, and with no evidence to the contrary, the conviction stood. The Crown led evidence of the accuracy and reliability of the particular laser unit, consisting of the performance of the manufacturer's tests for good working order both before and after the use of the device, together with earlier verification of the accuracy of the laser unit for measuring the velocity of moving vehicles on a highway, when compared with an accurate radar unit by a qualified laser and radar operator.

R. v. Mukasa (2000), 10 M.V.R. (4th) 41 (Ont. C.J.); *R v. Le* (2002), 27 M.V.R. (4th) 75, 2002 CarswellOnt 722 (Ont. C.J.) — Laser speed detection devices have been used in Ontario since 1993 and are no longer new and novel technology. Uncontradicted scientific evidence has confirmed the accuracy and reliability of laser speed detection devices. Evidence of readings from a laser speed detection device is admissible.

R. v. Bourne (2001), 17 M.V.R. (4th) 130 (Ont. C.J.) — Despite apparent advances in laser technology, a radar calibration is mandatory.

R. v. Thibault (2003), 216 N.S.R. (2d) 265, 680 A.P.R. 265, 42 M.V.R. (4th) 121, 2003 NSPC 36, 2003 CarswellNS 274 (N.S. Prov. Ct.) — While allowing that a driver may be allowed, after security concerns are addressed, to see the radar readings, the deletion of the readings was found to be necessary because of calibration.

R. v. Sepiashvili (2003), 46 M.V.R. (4th) 254, 2003 CarswellOnt 3985 (Ont. C.J.) — The lower court was entitled to take judicial notice of the general reliability of laser technology to measure speed as a fact established by expert evidence in other cases and accepted by other courts.

R. v. Niewiadomski (2004), 2004 CarswellOnt 597, 4 M.V.R. (5th) 115, [2004] O.J. No. 478 (C.J.) — Cross-examination which elicits the admission of non-compliance with the manufacturer's specifications and directions as to testing and operation should raise a reasonable doubt.

R. v. McLachlan, 2006 CarswellOnt 5370, 37 M.V.R. (5th) 302, 2006 ONCJ 318 (C.J.) — It is not necessary for the laser device to be tested against a conventional random device.

Barrie (City) v. Stocks, 2007 CarswellOnt 125, 2007 ONCJ 13, 41 M.V.R. (5th) 104 (C.J.) — There is no need to test for unacceptable interference if there is no evidence of unacceptable interference.

R. v. Wilkins, 2006 CarswellOnt 8656, 42 M.V.R. (5th) 316, 2006 ONCJ 529 (Ont. C.J.) — An appeal from conviction was allowed where there was no evidence of compliance with the manufacturer's specifications and directions as the officer did not state that the photocopy of the manual used during training was supplied by the manufacturer and there was no evidence that the manual provided with the machine came from the manufacturer.

R. v. Hawkshaw, 2006 CarswellOnt 8721, 45 M.V.R. (5th) 49, 2006 ONCJ 536 (Ont. C.J.) — There is no requirement that because the measurement occurred more than 1000 feet away, expert evidence was necessary.

R. v. House, 2012 ONCJ 517, 2012 CarswellOnt 9877, 37 M.V.R. (6th) 327, [2012] O.J. No. 3772 (Ont. Ct. J.) — The fact that a turning fork is used in other jurisdictions to test the device is irrelevant provided that the device is operated in accordance with the manual.

R. v. Melrose (2013), 44 M.V.R. (6th) 78, 2013 BCSC 526, 2013 CarswellBC 785, [2013] B.C.J. No. 592 (B.C. S.C.); leave to appeal allowed 2014 BCCA 148, 2014 CarswellBC 977, 354 B.C.A.C. 106, 605 W.A.C. 106, [2014] B.C.J. No. 659 — The denial of disclosure regarding the speed measuring device and the constable's qualifications for using that device affected the fairness of the trial.

R. v. Balcom (2013), 46 M.V.R. (6th) 151, 2013 NSPC 26, 2013 CarswellNS 529, 328 N.S.R. (2d) 369, 1039 A.P.R. 369 (N.S. Prov. Ct.) — The accused failed to prove on a balance of probabilities that there was actual prejudice to his ability to make full answer and defence because the officer did not lock in the readings.

Opinion of Officer as to Speed

Crossland v. D.P.P., [1988] 3 All E.R. 712 (Q.B. Div.) — The defendant collided with a pedestrian while accelerating across a junction before the traffic lights turned red. She was charged with driving at a speed exceeding 30 m.p.h. on a restricted road. At the hearing, the only witness as to the defendant's speed was a police officer who inspected the scene of the accident shortly after it had occurred, the damage to the defendant's car and the skid marks made by the defendant's braking, and who carried out speed and braking tests on the defendant's car, from which he calculated that the defendant had been driving at not less than 41 m.p.h. before she started to brake. The defendant was convicted. She appealed by way of case stated, contending that she had been convicted "solely on the evidence of one witness to the effect that, in the opinion of the witness," she had been driving at excessive speed and therefore her conviction could not stand. It was held that although the police officer's evidence included a significant element of expert opinion, his evidence did not amount solely to his opinion that the defendant had been driving at excessive speed since he also described in detail the objectively determined phenomena on which his expert opinion was based, namely the inspections and tests he had carried out at the scene of the accident. Accordingly, the defendant had been properly convicted and her appeal was dismissed.

Opinion of Officer as to Location

R. v. Ross (1981), 11 M.V.R. 8, 47 N.S.R. (2d) 600, 90 A.P.R. 600 (Co. Ct.) — The respondent was charged with speeding in a "residence district". At trial the radar operator testified that he considered the area where he set up his radar a "residential area" because there was "fifty per cent housing in the area." The trial Judge held that the Crown had failed to establish beyond a reasonable doubt that the location at which the respondent was detected travelling in excess of 50 km/h was in "territory contiguous to a highway" where "frontage on the highway for a distance of 100 metres or more" was "*mainly* occupied by dwellings" so as to constitute a "residence district". The Crown appealed. In dismissing the appeal, it was held that penal laws must be given strict interpretation. When an uncertainty or ambiguity in a criminal statute cannot be resolved the uncertainty or ambiguity of meaning must be construed in favour of the accused. In the present case, this rule added weight to the conclusion that the word "mainly" in the legislation should be given its usual meaning, which included the notion of more than one half of whatever was in question. The evidence was also imprecise as to the exact location on the street of the respondent's vehicle when it was picked up on the radar. Having regard to the evidence indicating that parts of the street would not fall within the definition of "residence district" contained in the Motor Vehicle Act, the trial Judge was entitled to have a reasonable doubt as to whether the Crown had established its case.

Radar Camera

R. v. Chow (1991), 83 Alta. L.R. (2d) 113, 68 C.C.C. (3d) 90, 33 M.V.R. (2d) 171, 120 A.R. 124, 8 W.A.C. 124 (C.A.); reversing (1991), 29 M.V.R. (2d) 7, 79 Alta. L.R. (2d) 382, 65 C.C.C. (3d) 162, 118 A.R. 64 (Q.B.) — The accused was charged with being the owner of a motor vehicle, the driver of which was speeding. At trial, the Crown sought to introduce evidence in the form of a photograph generated by a Multanova radar camera depicting a vehicle with an identifiable licence plate and imprinted with a speed, time and date. The trial Judge refused to admit this evidence on the basis that there was no legislative sanction for its acceptance. The charge was dismissed. The Crown appealed. The appeal was dismissed. On further appeal, the appeal was allowed and a conviction entered. The speed as rendered on the photograph and given *viva voce* by the officer was hearsay and *prima facie* inadmissible. The hearsay evidence would be received if it appeared accurate and enjoyed a circumstantial guarantee of trustworthiness. Here the unit had been tested earlier and had been found to be working properly. There was no evidence to the contrary. Evidence of past and consistent performance was admissible and deserving of weight although the officer could not remember the defendant's vehicle. The device provides accurate information and the evidence a right to have been admitted.

R. v. Benias (2000), 6 M.V.R. (4th) 23 (B.C. Prov. Ct.) — The image in the photograph was of poor quality and the licence plate was not legible. The Crown offered no evidence to suggest the officer who signed the certificate had a special expertise in reading illegible images. The court was entitled to form its own view of the photographic evidence.

Identity

R. v. McKay (1978), 18 A.R. 286 (Dist. Ct.) — A driver's licence was held to sufficiently identify the accused so that a charge of speeding could be laid.

Civil

Excessive Speed as Negligence

Wright v. Ruckstuhl, [1955] O.W.N. 728 (H.C.); *Noble v. Stewart* (1923), 51 N.B.R. 94 (C.A.); *Luck v. Toronto Ry.* (1920), 48 O.L.R. 581, 58 D.L.R. 145 (C.A.); *Service Fire Ins. Co. v. Larouche*, [1956] Que. Q.B. 294 — Driving at a speed in excess of the prescribed limit is not actionable negligence resulting in civil liability if there is no causal connection between the speeding and the accident.

MacKenzie v. Robar, [1953] 1 D.L.R. 449 (S.C.C.); *Gemelspach v. Drouillard* (1922), 23 O.W.N. 289 (H.C.) — Even where there is such a speed limit, the obligation of drivers is still to drive at a reasonable speed having regard to the circumstances.

Martin v. Powell, 62 O.L.R. 436, [1928] 4 D.L.R. 149 (C.A.); *Irvine v. Metro. Tpt. Co.*, [1933] O.R. 823, [1933] 4 D.L.R. 682 (C.A.) — The actual rate of speed which will be considered excessive, and which thereby constitutes negligent driving, varies with the nature and condition of the particular highway travelled upon, as well as the amount of traffic which is or may be expected to be upon it. It is always a question of fact dependent upon the circumstances of each case.

Inglis v. Halifax Elec. Tramway Co. (1899), 32 N.S.R. 117; affirmed (1900), 30 S.C.R. 256; *MacKenzie v. Robar, supra*; *Harrison v. Bourn*, [1958] S.C.R. 733; *Morrison v. Dunlap*, [1959] O.W.N. 164, 18 D.L.R. (2d) 393 (C.A.) — The question being one for the jury, an appellate court will not lightly interfere.

Coy v. Godin (1980), 31 N.B.R. (2d) 1, 75 A.P.R. 1 (C.A.) — Exceeding the speed limit by 10 m.p.h. is not in itself negligence.

Bissell v. Rochester, 65 O.L.R. 310, [1930] 3 D.L.R. 825 (H.C.) — In determining what is a reasonable rate of speed, it may be proper to consider that a driver was not familiar with the road, and that there was a sharp curve in the road which could be seen at a considerable distance.

Martin v. Gay's Taxi Ltd., 33 M.P.R. 139, [1954] 2 D.L.R. 394 (N.B. C.A.); *Whiddon v. Wickstrom*, [1948] O.W.N. 336 (C.A.); *Toronto v. Waite*, [1955] O.W.N. 227 (H.C.) — Where there is considerable traffic on the highway a driver must keep a safe distance behind the vehicle ahead, keep a lookout and maintain a reasonable speed, enabling him to stop if the vehicle ahead suddenly stops.

Schram v. Kearns, [1941] 2 W.W.R. 177, [1941] 3 D.L.R. 470 (Sask. C.A.) — It is particularly important to keep a safe distance behind, keep a lookout and maintain a reasonable speed when following another vehicle on a dusty road.

Guidolin v. Voyageur Provincial Inc. (1977), 14 N.R. 495 (S.C.C.) — A bus driver who failed to keep a proper lookout and was travelling too fast in order to bring his vehicle to a stop behind a vehicle stopped ahead was found responsible for the injuries to his passengers when the bus left the roadway and overturned.

Thibodeau v. Doucette (1957), 40 M.P.R. 53 (N.S. C.A.); *Cheratnick v. Williamson and Query*, [1950] 2 W.W.R. 224 (Man. C.A.) — A duty to regulate speeds arises whenever factors exist which limit a driver's range of vision. There is, however, no general rule that a driver's speed must be such as to enable the driver to stop within the limits of vision. The only principle is that a driver must proceed with such care as is reasonable having regard to all existing or foreseeable circumstances, including the physical conditions which affect his ability to see others on the highway or to avoid them when seen. Speed should be restricted, or lookout intensified, in proportion to the apparent difficulties inherent in such obstruction to vision as fog, smoke, dust, rain, falling snow, frost or mud on the windshield, dazzling headlights, objects such as snowbanks or bushes masking a corner, etc., or in the character of the highway, as being wet, icy, etc.

Smith Tpt. Ltd. v. Campbell, [1952] O.R. 479 (H.C.); *Craig v. Struben* (1951), 1 W.W.R. (N.S.) 769 (B.C. C.A.); *Sutherland v. Peart*, 35 M.P.R. 310, [1955] 5 D.L.R. 418 (N.S. C.A.); *Siemens v. Knight* (1955), 1 D.L.R. (2d) 101 (B.C. S.C.) — The existence of a "slow" or "caution" sign or a flashing amber light imposes on the motorist a duty to take special care and reduce speed in order to be able to avoid cross-traffic.

Blackwood Hodge Ltd. v. Tri-Mix Ltd. (1974), 6 Nfld. & P.E.I.R. 438 (P.E.I. S.C.); varied on other grounds (1975), 7 Nfld. & P.E.I.R. 158 (P.E.I. C.A.) — The driver of a truck approached a railway crossing at 40 m.p.h. in a 60 m.p.h. zone. He was held liable for failing to slow down and proceed with caution when approaching the crossings.

Emergency Vehicles

Colwill v. Longman (1928), 33 O.W.N. 284 (H.C.) — An exemption from compliance with speed restrictions does not mean that the issue of negligence may not still arise.

Ryan v. Calgary (1980), 28 A.R. 93 (Q.B.) — The plaintiff's vehicle was struck by a police car when she was attempting to make a left turn out of a mall. The police car was responding to a call. It was unmarked, was not sounding a siren, and was speeding. The Alberta Highway Traffic Act gave the police the qualified right to exceed the speed limit and the right to drive contrary to the rules of the road. The plaintiff was negligent in not keeping a proper lookout and in not yielding to the police car. She had a high duty to watch for traffic situations creating a potential danger of collision. The officer was responsible having in mind the speed at which he was travelling. The plaintiff and the defendant were each found to be 50% at fault.

Crew v. Nicholson (1987), 1 M.V.R. (2d) 284 (Ont. H.C.) — Only in exceptional circumstances is a police officer justified in putting lawful users of the highway at risk by driving at such speeds that he or she might not be able to avoid striking them.

Intersections

Bowell v. Galloway (1922), 22 O.W.N. 56 (H.C.); *Royal Trust Co. v. Toronto Transit Comm.*, [1935] S.C.R. 671, [1935] 3 D.L.R. 420; *Luck v. Toronto Ry.* (1920), 48 O.L.R. 581, 58 D.L.R. 145 (C.A.) — Particular care must be taken at intersections to so regulate one's speed to be able to avoid other traffic entering the intersection.

McLeary v. Eldridge, 30 M.P.R. 241, [1952] 1 D.L.R. 547 (N.S. C.A.); *Curley v. Ottawa Elec. Ry.*, [1946] O.W.N. 597 (C.A.); affirmed [1947] 3 D.L.R. 576 (S.C.C); *Ruttan v. O'Connor-Fenton*, 64 O.L.R. 208, [1929] 4 D.L.R. 62 (C.A.); *Noort v. Oeppen* (1954), 13 W.W.R. 410 (B.C. C.A.) — The above is particularly so where the driver's view is restricted, as by a snowbank or other obstruction.

Bristow v. Marko, [1949] 1 D.L.R. 693 (Ont. C.A.); reversed [1949] 3 D.L.R. 785 (S.C.C.) — Even on a through highway, it has been said that if drivers have not a clear view at intersections of traffic approaching they must reduce their speed.

Boxenbaum v. Wise, [1944] S.C.R. 292, [1944] 4 D.L.R. 199 — A slight increase of speed in crossing with the green light is perfectly normal and reasonable.

Can. Gen. Elec. Co. v. Campbell, [1958] O.W.N. 260 (C.A.) — Starting off from an intersection at a high speed was held to be negligence.

Nyiti v. Leblanc (1982), 53 N.S.R. (2d) 520, 109 A.P.R. 520 (T.D.) — The plaintiff sought damages for loss and personal injuries suffered as a result of a car accident. There was a duty on the defendant to reduce speed when approaching a hazardous intersection. The plaintiff also should have reduced speed. The plaintiff was found 20% responsible and the defendant 80% responsible.

Physical Proof of Speed

Pacific Stages Ltd. v. Jones, [1928] S.C.R. 92; *Gauthier & Co. v. R.*, [1945] S.C.R. 143, [1945] 2 D.L.R. 48; *MacInnis v. Bolduc* (1960), 45 M.P.R. 21, 24 D.L.R. (2d) 661 (N.S. C.A.); *Grant v. Lutes* (1976), 17 N.S.R. (2d) 614 (C.A.) — A skid has been described as a "neutral fact", equally consistent with negligence or no negligence, and for a defendant to go no further than to show that the accident was occasioned by the skidding of the vehicle is not sufficient to rebut a *prima facie* case of negligence.

McKimmie v. Strachan, [1936] O.W.N. 218 (H.C.); *Bijeau v. Gammon* (1940), 15 M.P.R. 198 (N.S. C.A.); *Benjamin v. Mosher*, [1953] 1 D.L.R. 826 (N.S. T.D.) — Likewise, a skid on rounding a corner on a wet morning is not in itself negligence. It must also be shown that under conditions prevailing danger of skidding existed, and that the driver was guilty of not taking reasonable care.

R. v. Johnson (1966), 58 W.W.R. 490 (B.C. C.A.) — The existence of skid marks where a car left the highway did not of itself establish careless driving but merely that brakes were applied while the car was proceeding along the highway.

Ristow v. Wetstein, [1934] S.C.R. 128; *Halase v. Sharpe* (1957), 21 W.W.R. 424 (Alta. Dist. Ct.) — The length of the skid marks, as also the force of the impact, and the vehicle's course following the collision may in each instance be cogent evidence as to the speed of the vehicle.

Kraft Foods Ltd. v. Sushelnitsky, [1949] 1 W.W.R. 67 (Man. C.A.); *Trinidad Leaseholds Ltd. v. Gordon*; *Garman v. Blatt* (1932), 41 O.W.N. 429 (C.A.) — On icy roads a loss of control and skidding may permit an inference of excessive speed or an improper application of the brakes.

Weaver v. Buckle (1983), 19 M.V.R. 227, 42 A.R. 241 (C.A.) — Reliance upon the length of a skid mark to determine speed is unsafe. That is particularly so where this physical evidence is not merely used as confirmation of other evidence leading in the same direction but flies in the face of the other evidence. The table of stopping distances relied on in this case was unsupported by any expert testimony. No effect was given to variations from the specified stopping distance which might have been due to car weight, tire conditions, road surfaces or any other factor. The science of stopping distances, particularly when treated as being synonomous with skid distances, is very inexact. Standard textbooks differ considerably in the tables included. The trial Judge also equated the length of the skid mark with the stopping distance of the car but in so doing did not subtract the length of the car. There was also confusion as to where the skid started. In view of the errors regarding speed and the conclusions drawn from them at trial, the judgment could not stand. The appellant driver had met the onus on him of establishing that the loss or damage did not entirely or solely arise through his negligence or improper conduct.

Related Provisions: See s. 61 of the Highway Traffic Act regarding emergency vehicles; s. 129 of the Act regarding metric conversion; s. 130 of the Act regarding careless driving; s. 131 of the Act regarding unorganized territories; s. 132 of the Act regarding slow driving; ss. 135, 136 of the Act as to right of way at intersections; O. Reg. 556/07, Pilot Project — Emergency Response Vehicles, s. 5(1); O. Reg. 455/07, Races, Contests and Stunts; R.R.O. 1990, Reg. 615, Signs, ss. 1-5.1, 42; R.R.O. 1990, Reg. 619, Speed Limits; R.R.O. 1990, Reg. 620, Speed Limits in Provincial Parks; R.R.O. 1990, Reg. 621, Speed Limits in Territory without Municipal Organization; Public Transportation and Highway Improvement Act, R.S.O. 1990, c. P.50; City of Toronto Act, 1997 (No. 2), S.O. 1997, c. 26, and the Municipal Act, 2001, S.O. 2001, c. 25, s. 170 regarding the authority of municipalities to regulate the racing of motor vehicles and the holding of motor vehicle races.

128.1 Status quo maintained — The repeal of the *Municipal Act* and the resultant amendments to this Act by the *Municipal Statute Law Amendment Act, 2002* do not affect the rates of speed on any highway or the validity of any regulation or by-law passed under section 128 and those rates of speed, regulations and by-laws continue to apply in the same manner as they did on December 31, 2002 until amended or repealed, as the case may be.

2002, c. 17, Sched. C, s. 15(3)

129. Conversion of rate of speed set out in by-laws — Upon the maximum permitted rate of speed in kilometres per hour being marked on the highways or portions thereof affected, the speed limits established under a by-law passed under section 128 that are expressed as a rate of speed in miles per hour set out in Column 1 of the Table shall be deemed to be the rate of speed in kilometres per hour set out opposite thereto in Column 2 of the Table.

Table	
Column 1	**Column 2**
Rate of Speed in Miles per Hour	Rate of Speed in Kilometres per Hour
15	20
20	30
25	40
30	50
35	60
40	60
45	70
50	80
55	90

Table	
Column 1	**Column 2**
Rate of Speed in Miles per Hour	**Rate of Speed in Kilometres per Hour**
60	100

130. Careless driving — Every person is guilty of the offence of driving carelessly who drives a vehicle or street car on a highway without due care and attention or without reasonable consideration for other persons using the highway and on conviction is liable to a fine of not less than $400 and not more than $2,000 or to imprisonment for a term of not more than six months, or to both, and in addition his or her licence or permit may be suspended for a period of not more than two years.

2009, c. 5, s. 41

Case Law

Quasi-Criminal

R. v. De Rosario, 2011 ABPC 294, 2011 CarswellAlta 2187, 26 M.V.R. (6th) 233 — A charge of careless driving was dismissed where the defendant was driving through a "T" intersection when he struck and killed a pedestrian in a crosswalk. The only evidence was his admission that he did not see the pedestrian before it was too late to take evasive action.

R. v. McNally, 2012 SKPC 58, 2012 CarswellSask 325, 33 M.V.R. (6th) 256, 387 Sask. R. 44 — A conviction was entered where the accused was crossing the centre line and weaving within his own lane several times causing other vehicles to take evasive action as the result of entering an address on a GPS device.

Constitutional

R. v. Yolles, [1959] O.R. 206, 30 C.R. 93, 19 D.L.R. (2d) 19, 123 C.C.C. 305 (C.A.); *O'Grady v. Sparling*, [1960] S.C.R. 804; *Mann v. R.*, [1966] S.C.R. 238 — The fact that the Criminal Code touches the subject of negligence does not exclude the province from the whole subject matter of negligence, and this legislation is not in *pari materia* or in conflict with s. 233 [criminal negligence in the operation of a motor vehicle; since repealed] of the Code. The two pieces of legislation are different not only in degree but also in kind. Parliament defined "advertent negligence" as a crime but did not touch "inadvertent negligence", which is dealt with under the provincial legislation in relation to the regulation of highway traffic. Nor is the section rendered *ultra vires* or inoperative by the enactment of s. 233(4) [now s. 249(1)(a)] of the Criminal Code reinstating the offence of dangerous driving. The purpose and effect of s. 233(4) is to make it a criminal offence to drive to the public danger, while the careless driving section is intended to provide appropriate sanctions for the regulation and control of a type of careless and inconsiderate driving falling short of being "dangerous" in the interest of lawful users of the highway.

Burden of Proof

R. v. Gooding (1977), 33 N.S.R. (2d) 98, 57 A.P.R. (2d) 98 (Co. Ct.) — On a charge of careless driving the burden on the Crown is the same as in criminal offences.

R. v. Namink (1979), 27 Chitty's L.J. 289 (Ont. Co. Ct.); *R. v. Marceau* (1978), 2 M.V.R. 202 (Que. S.C.) — Momentary inattention or a simple error of judgment is insufficient to justify a conviction of careless driving.

Wording of Charge

Archer v. R., [1955] S.C.R. 33 — This section originally made it an offence to drive "without due care and attention" or "without reasonable consideration for other persons using the highway," and a charge following the wording of the section was held invalid for duplicity.

R. v. MacKenzie, [1956] O.W.N. 35 (H.C.) — The difficulty in *Archer, supra*, would seem to have been overcome in the present wording of the section, the offence being "driving carelessly" which may be committed in one of two ways. It is sufficient to charge the accused with driving "without due care and attention," and likewise the charge could be for careless driving, without mention of either of the alternative means.

R. v. Toronto Magistrates; Ex parte Bassett, [1966] 2 O.R. 723 (C.A.) — A charge of driving carelessly "at the Municipality of Metropolitan Toronto" is sufficient to identify the transaction in respect of which the charge is laid and is therefore valid.

R. v. Skirzyk (1981), 29 A.R. 291 (Prov. Ct.) — The Crown particularized but the charge was dismissed where the evidence disclosed the alternative mode of driving not mentioned in the information.

R. v. Devereaux (1975), 22 C.C.C. (2d) 568 (Ont. H.C.); *R. v. Nadin*, [1971] 3 W.W.R. 481, 14 C.R.N.S. 201, 3 C.C.C. (2d) 221 (B.C. C.A.); *R. v. Klein*, 64 W.W.R. 513, [1968] 4 C.C.C. 209 (Sask. C.A.); *R. v. Kellett* (April 17, 1978), unreported (Man. C.A.); *R. v. Murphy*, [1971] 4 W.W.R. 318 (Alta. C.A.); *R. v. Henry* (1975), 25 C.C.C. (2d) 71 (Ont. Prov. Ct.); *R. v. Otterbein*, [1967] 2 O.R. 87, 50 C.R. 285, [1967] 3 C.C.C. 128 (H.C.) — It is sufficient to allege a day without specifying the time of day (*Devereaux* and *Henry*, *supra*). It is sufficient to allege that the accused drove a motor vehicle without further describing the vehicle.

Vicarious Liability

R. v. Greenfield, [1954] O.W.N. 292, 18 C.R. 85, 108 C.C.C. 107 (H.C.) — An information alleging that the accused, the owner of an automobile, "unlawfully did permit [it] to be operated ... without due care and attention," etc., does not disclose any offence, since the Act does not make it an offence to "permit" driving contrary to the statute.

R. v. Vaugeois (1959), 29 W.W.R. 368 (B.C. C.A.) — An acquittal on a charge of careless driving because there was insufficient proof of the accused being the driver was held not to be a bar to a later charge against the accused as owner of the car.

Place of Driving

R. v. Wall (1968), 11 Crim. L.Q. 223 (Ont.) — The offence must arise out of driving on a highway, which term does not include a sidewalk.

Double Jeopardy

R. v. Lainey (December 3, 1976), unreported (Ont. H.C.); *R. v. Anthony* (1982), 16 M.V.R. 160, 52 N.S.R. (2d) 456, 106 A.P.R. 456, 69 C.C.C. (2d) 424 (C.A.); *R. v. Landman* (1984), 33 M.V.R. 89 (B.C. Prov. Ct.) — An acquittal on a charge of dangerous driving does not preclude a conviction for careless driving as the two offences have different elements, namely advertent and inadvertent negligence, respectively. It was not an abuse of process for the Crown to proceed on careless driving after an acquittal on dangerous driving. An acquittal or conviction on one offence is not a bar to a prosecution on the other. The plea of *autrefois convict* was not available as a bar to the defendant's trial upon a dangerous driving charge. However, the Crown may be barred by *res judicata*.

Duplicity

R. v. Fry, [1972] 3 O.R. 819, 19 C.R.N.S. 265, 8 C.C.C. (2d) 573 (H.C.); affirmed [1972] 3 O.R. 879n, 19 C.R.N.S. 267n, 9 C.C.C. (2d) 242 (C.A.) — A traffic ticket was held void for duplicity as it charged an accused with careless driving as well as speeding.

Nature of Offence

R. v. Jacobsen (1964), 48 W.W.R. 272, 44 C.R. 24 (B.C. C.A.) — The section, which deals with inadvertent negligence, contains an absolute prohibition and is directed to the regulation of traffic. The offence is committed by the absence of thought, care and attention *per se* and since there are no degrees of inadvertence it is unnecessary to consider the further factors which are essential ingredients of offences under ss. 203 [now s. 220 (criminal negligence causing death)] and 233(1) [criminal negligence in the operation of a motor vehicle; since repealed] of the Criminal Code.

R. v. McIver, [1965] 2 O.R. 475, 45 C.R. 401, [1965] 4 C.C.C. 182 (C.A.); affirmed [1966] S.C.R. 254; *R. v. Lucki* (1955), 17 W.W.R. 446 (Sask. Police Ct.); *R. v. Divizio* (1986), 1 M.V.R. (2d) 226, 32 C.C.C. (3d) 239 (Ont. Dist. Ct.) — As the section is silent as to intent or *mens rea*, the Crown need only prove that the accused committed the prohibited act and the accused will be convicted unless he can show that the forbidden act was done without negligence or fault on his part. Accordingly, a conviction may be based on evidence of a number of conditions and surrounding circumstances from which it appears that unless there was carelessness the collision would not likely have occurred. *Mens rea* was an ingredient of the offence, and that a person who by an involuntary act, for which he was not to blame, got onto the wrong side of the road should not be found guilty of the offence.

R. v. Beauchamp, [1953] O.R. 422, [1953] 4 D.L.R. 340, 16 C.R. 270 (C.A.); *R. v. Seabrook*, [1952] O.R. 471, 14 C.R. 223 (H.C.); *McCrone v. Riding*, [1938] 1 All E.R. 157 (K.B.); *R. v. Parsons* (1952), 15 C.R. 409, 7 W.W.R. (N.S.) 359 (Alta. Dist. Ct.) — The standard is a constantly shifting one, depending on the road, visibility, weather and traffic conditions that exist or may reasonably be expected, and any other conditions that ordinary drivers would take into consideration. It is an objective standard not related to the degree of proficiency or experience of any particular accused, and evidence that the accused has a good record as a careful driver is irrelevant. But concepts of civil negligence are not appropriate, and the conduct of an accused must be of such a nature that it can be considered a breach of duty to the public and deserving of punishment.

R. v. Buchanan (1967), 10 Crim. L.Q. 246 (Mag.); *R. v. Wallings* (1961), 130 C.C.C. 128 (B.C. Co. Ct.) — The Crown is obliged to produce sufficient evidence of pertinent facts to enable the court adequately to assess the conduct of the accused against the objective standard of what the reasonably prudent driver would have done in the situation disclosed by the evidence. It is not sufficient merely to prove the fact of an accident nor the existence of skid marks.

R. v. Rousseau, [1938] O.R. 472, [1938] 3 D.L.R. 574 (C.A.) — The improper driving may be manifested by recklessness on the part of the driver, negligence, or a speed incompatible with the public safety, or any other disregard of the public.

Smallman v. R., 49 M.P.R. 23, [1964] 1 C.C.C. 340 (P.E.I. S.C.) — The existence of actual or potential danger to the public is extraneous and irrelevant to the offence.

R. v. James (1952), 14 C.R. 231 (B.C. Mag. Ct.) — The failure to keep an adequate lookout at a school crossing was held to be careless driving, as was the act of a driver in taking a chance in endeavouring to pass another vehicle.

R. v. Fernets (1963), 42 W.W.R. 309 (Sask. Dist. Ct.) — The motorist was convicted where he had attempted to overtake without ascertaining that the road ahead was clear.

R. v. Buecking (1963), 44 W.W.R. 482 (B.C. S.C.) — A conviction followed where the driver struck a pedestrian in a crosswalk.

R. v. Wilson, [1971] 1 O.R. 349, 1 C.C.C. (2d) 466 (C.A.); *R. v. Turgeon* (1958), 28 C.R. 21, 24 W.W.R. 540, 120 C.C.C. 248 (Sask. Dist. Ct.) — Inadvertent negligence alone or a mere error in judgment is not sufficient to establish the offence.

R. v. Yolles, [1958] O.R. 786, 29 C.R. 195 (H.C.); reversed in part [1959] O.R. 206 (C.A.) — A speed of 80 m.p.h. is not *per se* careless driving.

R. v. Wollf (1966), 57 W.W.R. 702 (Sask. Mag. Ct.) — A driver who was subject to fainting spells or periods of unconsciousness was held guilty of careless driving in driving at a time when he had reason to suspect such an attack.

R. v. Jacobs (1955), 22 C.R. 154, 16 W.W.R. 126, 113 C.C.C. 73 (B.C. C.A.) — The operation of bringing an automobile to a stop is just as much driving it as the operation of accelerating or steering it. A conviction for driving without due care and attention may therefore be properly based on the accused's stopping his car on the wrong side of the road in circumstances that will confuse other persons using the highway.

R. v. Smith (1961), 130 C.C.C. 177 (B.C. Co. Ct.) — The accused, a stranger in the area, crashed into a river dike wall on a dark night. It was held that the mere occurrence of the accident could not give rise to a presumption that it had been caused by very great negligence.

R. v. Johnson (1966), 58 W.W.R. 490 (B.C. C.A.) — The existence of skid marks and the finding of the vehicle 30 feet from the travelled portion of the highway did not establish careless driving.

R. v. Schoemaker (1979), 2 M.V.R. 27 (Ont. Co. Ct.) — An appellant, who was familiar with the crosswalk, and in spite of the fact that he did not have a clear view of the crosswalk, accelerated to a speed of at least 30 m.p.h. to pass the vehicles ahead of him. Such conduct constituted driving without due care and attention and without reasonable consideration for other people using the highway under the circumstances. The result may have been different had the appellant been a stranger in town, unfamiliar with the painted crosswalks.

R. v. Rieswyk (1978), 1 M.V.R. 177, 32 N.S.R. (2d) 602, 54 A.P.R. 602 (Co. Ct.) — An appellant was parked in his car. He accelerated rapidly with tires squealing and entered a service station, rounded the gas pumps and re-entered the street. His speed was estimated 70 to 80 km/h. When he re-entered the street cars were parked on both sides with space for only one car to pass. A dance was finishing, and the people were coming outside from the hall. It was held there was ample evidence to support a conviction taking into account the observations of speed, clocking for a brief time, rapid acceleration and the presence of pedestrians and other vehicles.

Skowronnek v. R. (1980), 9 M.V.R. 36 (Sask. Dist. Ct.) — There were outward and visible signs of the offence including speed, "fishtailing", "kicking up" gravel and something of a chase. The appellant was a highly qualified rally driver, driving a specially equipped car for the purpose of testing before a rally in a somewhat remote area of the city of Saskatoon. The appellant's special skill, equipment and the purpose and place of driving were advanced in defence. To support the charge, the evidence must be such as to prove beyond a reasonable doubt that the accused drove without due care and attention. In some prosecutions, a consideration of standard of skill creeps in, in light of an accident in the background. It is, however, an objective standard of care and attention not related to the degree of proficiency or experience of the particular accused that is involved. It is wrong to assume that there is one standard for ordinary drivers and another for others.

R. v. Peacock (1975), 11 N.B.R. (2d) 579 (Co. Ct.) — A conviction was affirmed where the accused on a motorcycle struck a child in a crosswalk.

R. v. Rogers (1981), 34 N.B.R. (2d) 353, 85 A.P.R. 353 (Q.B.) — Evidence of speeding, passing on the left, failing to yield the right of way and a collision indicated a lack of due care.

R. v. Johnson (1983), 45 N.B.R. (2d) 371, 118 A.P.R. 371 (Q.B.) — A conviction was set aside on appeal where the appellant drove onto the wrong side of the road while attempting to put out a cigarette that had fallen onto the seat, resulting in a collision.

R. v. McDorman (1983), 23 M.V.R. 165 (B.C. Prov. Ct.); affirmed (1984), 27 M.V.R. 37 (B.C. Co. Ct.) — The Court considered lack of sleep, failure to have a gas leak fixed, failure to adjust slack adjusters on the pre-trip inspection, and the missing of truck-route signs by reason of fatigue, and concluded that the cumulative effect was to provide a foundation for a conviction for careless driving.

R. v. Weedon (1987), 7 M.V.R. (2d) 21 (B.C. Co. Ct.) — The *actus reus* is improper driving judged on an objective basis. The lack of due care and attention can then be inferred from the objective indicator. In the case at hand the accused did not have due care for other actual and potential users of the highway. The failure of the accused to consider the risk which he was creating constituted the requisite inadvertence for conviction. His professed superior skill was not relevant given the objective standard used to evaluate an accused's manner of driving.

R. v. Ashton (1985), 36 M.V.R. 100 (Ont. Dist. Ct.) — There was no evidence which supported an inference of careless driving. The fact that the two friends were lying in the middle of the road could not have been foreseen. The accused had a temporary licence which did not permit him to drive in the evening, but there was no logical connection between this breach and the offence charged. Though the accused smelled of alcohol he passed a roadside breath test, and the trace of marihuana in his blood was not sufficient to support an inference that his ability to drive with care was impaired. Individually and cumulatively these facts did not support an inference of careless driving.

Broome v. Perkins, [1987] R.T.R. 321 (Q.B.) — The defence of automatism was unsuccessfully raised in relation to careless driving.

R. v. Yorston (1991), 27 M.V.R. (2d) 27 (N.S. Prov. Ct.); reversed (1991), 106 N.S.R. (2d) 103, 288 A.P.R. 103, 32 M.V.R. (2d) 285 (Co. Ct.) — Making a U-turn on a highway requires the driver to exercise extraordinary care. The duty here was even greater because the police car was fitted with metal framework and bars, which made an over-the-shoulder check of little value. The accused's attention was directed mostly at turning and stopping the speeding vehicle. He paid insufficient attention to other traffic and did not allow enough time after activating his emergency lights for other vehicles to yield the right of way.

R. v. Beauchamp, [1953] O.R. 422, 16 C.R. 270, [1953] 4 D.L.R. 340, 106 C.C.C. 6 (C.A.) — The test, where an accident has occurred, is not whether, if the accused had used greater care or skill, the accident would not have happened. It is whether it is proved beyond reasonable doubt that the accused, in the light of existing circumstances of which he was aware or of which a driver exercising ordinary care should have been aware, failed to use the care and attention or to give to other persons using the highway the consideration that a driver of ordinary care would have used or given in the circumstances. The use of the term "due care", which means care owing in the circumstances, makes it quite clear that, while the legal standard of care remains the same in the sense that it is what the average careful man would have done in like circumstances, the factual standard is a constantly shifting one, depending on road visibility, weather conditions, traffic conditions that exist or may reasonably be expected, and any other conditions that ordinarily prudent drivers would take into consideration. It is a question of fact, depending on the circumstances in each case. Drivers of vehicles cannot be required to regulate their driving as if in constant fear that other drivers who are under observation, and apparently acting reasonably and properly, may possibly act at a critical moment in disregard of the safety of themselves and other users of the road.

R. v. Globoki (1991), 26 M.V.R. (2d) 179 (Ont. Prov. Ct.) — Where an accident has occurred, the fact that serious injury or death has resulted is not, except in unusual cases, relevant to an assessment of whether there has been a departure from the standard of care which would justify a finding of careless driving. The necessity of *mens rea* with respect to careless driving must be taken as referring to something less than advertence by the driver to his or her departure from the standard of care due in the circumstances. *Mere* inadvertent negligence will not necessarily support a conviction for careless driving; the Crown must do more than point to a bare act of negligence, however slight. It must show a sufficient departure from the standard of a prudent and reasonable driver to make the driving "deserving of punishment". Reference to the authorities in relation to dangerous driving and criminal negligence involving motor vehicles is helpful with respect to identifying the approach to be followed in determining whether the conduct of a driver amounted to careless driving, but it must be borne clearly in mind that the standard against which the defendant's driving is to be measured is that contained in s. 111 of the Highway Traffic Act, not that contained in either s. 219 or s. 249(1) of the Criminal Code, R.S.C. 1985, c. C-46.

R. v. Malleck-Lacroix (1991), 35 M.V.R. (2d) 46 (Ont. Prov. Ct.) — There is no special and onerous duty of care on school-bus drivers.

R. v. Chaulk (1995), 11 M.V.R. (3d) 34 (Nfld. Prov. Ct.) — The Crown's argument was rejected that excessive speed over the speed limit was not only prima facie evidence but also conclusive evidence of imprudent driving. Speed above or below the posted speed limits can be either reasonable and prudent or unreasonable and imprudent depending on the existing conditions or potential hazards. Considering that the accused was driving at twice the limit where traffic or pedestrians could be expected, he was guilty.

R. v. Steeden (1995), 12 M.V.R. (3d) 303, 8 B.C.L.R. (3d) 235 (C.A.) — When it is intended to describe conduct in relation to a motor vehicle, the ordinary meaning which attaches to "drive" is one that combines the elements of movement and control: movement of the vehicle and control of that movement by the driver. An act of driving cannot include the failure to set an emergency brake or parking brake before disembarking from a motor vehicle which has been parked with its engine shut off.

R. v. Rose (1996), 26 M.V.R. (3d) 136 (Nfld. T.D.) — Improperly completing a passing manoeuvre or improperly attempting to overtake another vehicle are not included offences.

R. v. Wilson (1997), 34 M.V.R. (3d) 68, 201 N.B.R. (2d) 234, 514 A.P.R. 234; affirmed (1998), 201 N.B.R. (2d) 230, 514 A.P.R. 230 (N.B. Q.B.) — The accused motorcyclist was convicted where he struck and killed a 12-year-old. He was travelling well in excess of the speed limit, saw the victim before the accident and knew that she was riding her bicycle on or close to the edge of a narrow road. She suddenly veered.

R. v. Lawless (1997), 37 M.V.R. (3d) 182, 193 N.B.R. (2d) 81, 493 A.P.R. 31 (N.B. Prov. Ct.) — An R.C.M.P. officer was driving a marked car with emergency equipment activated. When facing a red light the officer drove through the intersection colliding with a vehicle going through on the green and making a left hand turn. Failure to do the visual searches and to slow when proceeding through a red light at a busy and dangerous intersection was careless.

R. v. McCullough (1999), 45 M.V.R. (3d) 126 (Alta. Prov. Ct.) — Falling asleep while in control of a vehicle in a queue for service bays amounted to driving without due care and attention. Due care and attention requires sufficient physical alertness immediately prior to the operation of a motor vehicle to facilitate safe and prudent driving.

R. v. Trigiani (1999), 48 M.V.R. (3d) 228 (Ont. C.J.) — Falling asleep while driving is careless.

R. v. Morrison, 9 M.V.R. (4th) 306 (Y.T. Terr. Ct.); affirmed 2001 CarswellYukon 104 (Y.T. S.C.) — The accused was convicted. He was driving at night on a busy four-lane highway which was not well lit. Pedestrian traffic was generally quite heavy due to the many bars in the area and the weather was snow and sleet. While driving at or approaching the speed limit of 50 kph he hit a person on the road. The accused had a higher duty of caution and prudence and care such that he would be able to stop within a reasonable period in the event an unexpected obstacle emerged.

R. v. Cooke (2001), 21 M.V.R. (4th) 153, 2001 CarswellMan 613 (Man. Prov. Ct.) — The accused was acquitted after his van struck and killed an oblivious pedestrian who was crossing at an inappropriate point. The accused was paying prudent but not exclusive attention to what he believed was a potential danger of children playing off to the side. He took evasive action by slamming on his brakes and at least one other vehicle may have partially obstructed his view.

R v. Vasker (2001), 22 M.V.R. (4th) 264, 2001 CarswellOnt 3416 (Ont. C.J.) — Repeatedly revving a car engine and squealing car tires, "burnouts", near a group of pedestrians supported a conviction.

R v. Januario (2002), 27 M.V.R. (4th) 71, 2002 CarswellOnt 721 (Ont. C.J.) — The phrase "without reasonable consideration" is not the equivalent to "reasonably inconsiderate" in the sense of discourteous or lacking in regard for the feelings of others, which is not the proper meaning.

R. v. Demerchant (2003), 2003 CarswellOnt 4296, 44 M.V.R. (4th) 220 (Ont. C.J.) — A charge of careless driving was stayed for issue estoppel and abuse of process where, in an earlier Criminal Code trial, the trial judge had found that the accident was unavoidable and pursuit of the careless driving charge would necessitate contrary conclusions.

R. v. Lemanski (2003), 2003 CarswellBC 3073, 2003 BCPC 423, 1 M.V.R. (5th) 180 (B.C. Prov. Ct.) — A snowplough operator was acquitted when his properly marked and outfitted vehicle slowly backed up over a pedestrian.

R. v. Monkman, 2005 CarswellYukon 11, 2005 YKTC 19, 16 M.V.R. (5th) 75 (Terr. Ct.) — An RCMP officer was convicted where a suspect who was not belted in died when the police vehicle left the traveled lane when exiting a curve and went down an embankment. The driver performed a shoulder check while in the curve or fell asleep after working 19 hours straight.

R. v. Robertson, 2006 CarswellOnt 8478, 43 M.V.R. (5th) 257, 2006 ONCJ 530 (Ont. C.J.) — A conviction was upheld where the driver of a large pickup truck with a trailer attached on a two-lane highway, was momentarily distracted, failed to notice that traffic had stopped ahead, swerved into oncoming traffic to avoid a collision and collided with an oncoming car, killing two.

R. v. Seguin, 2007 CarswellOnt 619, 2007 ONCJ 40, 44 M.V.R. (5th) 281, [2007] O.J. No. 382 (C.J.) — The trier's decision as to whether disclosure should be ordered in relation to the manual for the radar unit was discretionary. Production would not be appropriate in the absence of relevance.

R. v. Laroche, 2007 CarswellSask 139, 2007 SKPC 21, 46 M.V.R. (5th) 28, 294 Sask. R. 144 (Prov. Ct.) — An acquittal was registered where the court had a reasonable doubt as there was no evidence of the loss of control, the event was of short duration and the officer's observations while he was on foot were hard to validate.

R. v. Champion, 2007 CarswellOnt 4515, 2007 ONCJ 319, 53 M.V.R. (5th) 52, [2007] O.J. No. 2782 (C.J.) — No miscarriage of justice was shown where a statement by the accused that he was the driver was admitted without a voluntariness *voir dire* since there was ample evidence.

R. v. Winfield, 65 M.V.R. (5th) 315, 2008 CarswellYukon 27, 2008 YKTC 30; affirmed 70 M.V.R. (5th) 207, 2008 YKSC 69, 2008 CarswellYukon 72; affirmed 2009 CarswellYukon 86, 2009 YKCA 9, 79 M.V.R. (5th) 19, 273 B.C.A.C. 152, 461 W.A.C. 152 — Passing a large trailer forcing it to the side of the road and almost hitting an oncoming vehicle made out the offence.

R. v. Lozinski, 62 M.V.R. (5th) 111, 2008 CarswellSask 66, 2008 SKPC 6 (Prov. Ct.) — The accused was convicted where his truck hit a wheelchair occupant on a rural highway.

Durham (Regional Municipality) v. Chicoine, 2011 ONCJ 267, 2011 CarswellOnt 3629, [2011] O.J. No. 2329, 16 M.V.R. (6th) 150 (Ont. C.J.). Where the appellant had a minor collision with the back of a car being towed by a tow truck following a rolling stop, the appeal court affirmed an acquittal on careless and conviction for passing on the right not in safety under s. 150(1).

R. v. Beyer, 2011 ABPC 198, 2011 CarswellAlta 1070, [2011] A.J. No. 703, 233 C.R.R. (2d) 1, 17 M.V.R. (6th) 63 (Alta. Prov. Ct.). A conviction resulted where the accused, blinded by the sun, killed a pedestrian.

R. v. Targett, 2011 CarswellNfld 75, [2011] N.J. No. 80, 11 M.V.R. (6th) 310, 312 Nfld. & P.E.I.R. 345, 971 A.P.R. 345 (Prov. Ct.) — A conviction was made out. Speed at 120-130 kph in a 60-80 kph zone pointed toward conviction, but passing numerous cars at high speed cemented it.

Smeltzer v. Merrison, 2012 BCCA 13, 2012 CarswellBC 38, 26 B.C.L.R. (5th) 267, 25 M.V.R. (6th) 186, 315 B.C.A.C. 109, 535 W.A.C. 109 — One cannot pass on the right if there is no lane even though there is enough space to do so.

R. v. Smith, 2012 ONCJ 324, 2012 CarswellOnt 6700, 35 M.V.R. (6th) 163, [2012] O.J. No. 2395 — An application to have a judge assigned instead of a Justice of the Peace for a careless driving charge failed. There were no complex legal or constitutional issues of significant precedent value anticipated. The mere fact of a fatality was not sufficient reason to assign a trial to a judge.

R. v. Stupar, 2015 ONCJ 350, 2015 CarswellOnt 9495, 86 M.V.R. (6th) 331, [2015] O.J. No. 3308 — Driving through a red light at a crosswalk and killing a 6 year- old child resulted in a $25,000 fine and two year prohibition after a guilty plea.

Sentencing

R. v. Martinez (1996), 21 M.V.R. (3d) 106 (Ont. C.A.) — In assessing the fitness of sentence it is appropriate to take into account the fact that the driving caused an accident and death although without intentional or wilful conduct as would be found in a case of dangerous driving causing death.

R. v. Ereddia, 37 M.V.R. (5th) 179, 42 C.R. (6th) 180, 2006 CarswellOnt 5173, 2006 ONCJ 303 (C.J.) — Minimum penalties provided an indication that even a most minor instance within the range of conduct by the offence was intended by the legislation to entail at least some degree of seriousness.

R. v. Pellerin, 2006 CarswellOnt 8374, 2006 ONCJ 503, 43 M.V.R. (5th) 195 (Ont. C.J.) — Appeals by the Crown and accused were dismissed when a victim was killed while riding a bicycle and the sentence was the $1000 maximum fine, the maximum licence suspension of two years, the maximum probation of two years and community service in lieu of incarceration.

R. v. McBride, 2010 YKTC 136, 2010 CarswellYukon 185, [2010] Y.J. No. 176, 6 M.V.R. (6th) 255 — A 30-day conditional sentence, a fine and probation were imposed where a person died. Being extremely tired and getting behind the wheel was almost indistinguishable from drinking and driving.

Related Provisions: See s. 172 of the Act prohibiting racing, contests and stunts and O. Reg. 455/07, Races, Contests and Stunts.

131. (1) Territory without municipal organization — **For the purpose of this Act, the Minister may make regulations providing for the regulation and control of traffic on any highway or portion of a highway in territory without municipal organization where the highway is not under the jurisdiction and control of the Ministry.**

(2) Liability for damages — **With respect to a highway that is not under the jurisdiction and control of the Ministry, no proceeding shall be brought against the Crown for damages caused by any default of the Ministry in maintaining the signs**

regulating and controlling traffic in territories without municipal organization and the Crown is not liable for damages sustained by any person using a highway in a territory without municipal organization.

Related Provisions: R.R.O. 1990, Reg. 621, Speed Limits in Territory without Municipal Organization; R.R.O. 1990, Reg. 624, Stop Signs in Territory without Municipal Organization; R.R.O. 1990, Reg. 631, Yield Right-of-Way Signs in Territory without Municipal Organization.

132. (1) Unnecessary slow driving prohibited — No motor vehicle shall be driven on a highway at such a slow rate of speed as to impede or block the normal and reasonable movement of traffic thereon except when the slow rate of speed is necessary for safe operation having regard to all the circumstances.

(2) Exception — Subsection (1) does not apply to a road service vehicle.

1994, c. 27, s. 138(10)

Case Law

Nova Scotia (A.G.) v. Richard (1986), 45 M.V.R. 127, 75 N.S.R. (2d) 106, 186 A.P.R. 106 (C.A.) — Lack of a rear view mirror would not be negligence unless it was a contributory factor to the collision between the two vehicles. The trial Judge made no finding in this respect. A reading of the evidence before the trial Judge and his decision as a whole, however, made it clear that he considered the damages inherent in the operation of a slow moving, poorly lighted vehicle on a main highway at night under foggy conditions inherently dangerous and that it was a combination of all these factors that contributed to the accident and constituted negligence.

Related Provisions: See s. 147 of the Act as to slow vehicles driving on right side of multi-lane highway; see R.R.O. 1990, Reg. 616, Slow Moving Vehicle Sign.

PART X — RULES OF THE ROAD

133. Definitions — In this Part,

Proposed Addition — 133 "bicycle traffic control signal"

"bicycle traffic control signal" means a traffic control signal where the coloured lenses each display a prescribed bicycle symbol;

2015, c. 14, s. 38(1) [To come into force January 1, 2017.]

"indication" means a signal lens display that is activated by internal illumination;

"road service vehicle" [Repealed 1994, c. 27, s. 138(11).]

"traffic control signal" means that part of a traffic control signal system that consists of one set of no less than three coloured lenses, red, amber and green, mounted on a frame and commonly referred to as a signal head;

Proposed Amendment — 1 "traffic control signal"

"traffic control signal" means that part of a traffic control signal system that consists of one set of no less than three coloured lenses, red, amber and green, mounted

333

on a frame and commonly referred to as a signal head and includes a bicycle traffic control signal;

2015, c. 14, s. 38(2) [To come into force January 1, 2017.]

"**traffic control signal system**" **means all of the signal equipment making up the installation at any location.**

1994, c. 27, s. 138(11)

Related Provisions: R.R.O. 1990, Reg. 626, Traffic Control Signal Systems.

134. (1) **Direction of traffic by police officer** — Where a police officer considers it reasonably necessary,

    (a) to ensure orderly movement of traffic;

    (b) to prevent injury or damage to persons or property; or

    (c) to permit proper action in an emergency,

he or she may direct traffic according to his or her discretion, despite the provisions of this Part, and every person shall obey his or her directions.

(2) **Highway closing** — For the purposes of subsection (1), a police officer may close a highway or any part thereof to vehicles by posting or causing to be posted signs to that effect, or placing or causing to be placed traffic control devices as prescribed in the regulations.

(3) **Driving on closed highway prohibited** — Where signs or traffic control devices have been posted or placed under subsection (2), no person shall drive or operate a vehicle on the closed highway or part thereof in intentional disobedience of the signs or traffic control devices.

(4) **Exception to subs. (3)** — Subsection (3) does not apply to,

    (a) the driver of a road service vehicle, an ambulance, a fire department vehicle, a public utility emergency vehicle or a police department vehicle; or

    (b) a firefighter, as defined in subsection 1(1) of the _Fire Protection and Prevention Act, 1997_, driving a motor vehicle other than one listed in clause (a) while performing his or her duties.

(5) **No Crown or road authority liability** — Every person using a highway closed to traffic in accordance with this section does so at the person's own risk and the Crown or road authority having jurisdiction and control of the highway is not liable for any damage sustained by a person using the highway so closed to traffic.

(6) **Regulations** — The Minister may make regulations providing for the posting of signs and the placing of traffic control devices on any highway or any type or class thereof for the purposes of this section, and prescribing the types of signs and traffic control devices.

2005, c. 26, Sched. A, s. 19; 2009, c. 5, s. 42

Commentary

Where a police officer considers it reasonably necessary, he or she may direct traffic and every person shall obey such directions (s. 134(1)). A police officer may close a highway or part thereof by posting signs or traffic control devices (subs. (2)). Only emergency or road service vehicles may ignore such signs or devices (subss. (3), (4)). Liability is excluded where a driver ignores such signs or devices (subs. (5)). Regulations may be made respecting signs and devices (subs. (6)).

Case Law

R. v. Harms, [1967] 3 C.C.C. 93 (Sask. Prov. Ct.) — *Mens rea* is not necessary to constitute the offence under s. 222 of the Saskatchewan Act of failing to obey a signal of a police officer. However, the signal must be one which to a reasonable person would be open to only one interpretation and given in such a way that he would be able to observe and obey it.

R. v. Walker (1982), 17 M.V.R. 154 (Sask. Prov. Ct.) — Section 222 of the Saskatchewan Act was interpreted to mean that the use of a flashing red light on a public highway of itself clearly denoted, at the least, caution, and at the most, when coupled with other factors, a clear direction to stop. On the facts, the driving of the accused, in the absence of any evidence to the contrary, was evidence leading to the inescapable conclusion that the accused was determined to outrun two vehicles that he knew were driven by the police, who had not signalled him to stop.

R. v. Bothwell (1986), 45 M.V.R. 1 (Ont. C.A.) — The appellant was driving a tractor pulling two hay wagons on a busy highway. The rear wagon was crowding the centre line and did not have a slow-moving vehicle sign. A police officer asked the appellant to pull over, which he briefly did before getting back into the tractor and driving off. The officer followed, repeatedly asking the appellant to pull over. The appellant was charged with obstructing justice and was convicted. His appeal was dismissed. He appealed to the Court of Appeal. The appeal was dismissed. It was held that the way in which the tractor was being operated created a danger on the highway and the officer was empowered by s. 134 of the Highway Traffic Act (Ont.) to require the appellant to pull off the highway. It was clear that the appellant obstructed a police officer in execution of his duty and that he did so wilfully.

R. v. Boehner (1976), 24 N.S.R. (2d) 684, 35 A.P.R. 684 (Co. Ct.) — A motor vehicle inspector suspected that a truck was overweight and ordered the defendant not to dump his load. He dumped the load anyway. He was charged with failing to obey the instructions of a peace officer and was convicted at trial. An appeal was dismissed. Under the New Brunswick Act, the inspector was a peace officer. The defendant was under a duty to obey all reasonable and lawful directions.

Boswell v. Lovett (1970), 2 N.S.R. (2d) 403 (C.A.) — The defendant's failure to see a police officer directing traffic was held to be the sole cause of the accident.

Williams v. R. (1986), 39 M.V.R. 153, 72 N.S.R. (2d) 364, 173 A.P.R. 364 (C.A.) — The accused appealed his conviction on a charge under s. 74(1) of the Motor Vehicle Act (N.S.). Section 74(1) provided that it was an offence to refuse or fail to comply with an order of a peace officer. The road on which the accused lived had been blocked to traffic because of a special event and he was directed by an officer to take another route; instead, the accused drove through the pylons which had been placed across the street. The accused appealed on the grounds that s. 74(1) was too broadly drawn and that the police officer had no specific power to give the accused the direction that he did. The appeal was dismissed. It was held that police officers had implied authority under the Act to give orders arising by necessary implication from the general execution of their duties under the Act, and s. 74(1) was intended to apply to such orders. In the present case, therefore, the officer had the implied authority to direct the accused as he did and the accused was properly convicted under s. 74(1). Even if the officer did not have such implied authority under the Act, he was authorized to give the direction at common law by virtue of the general scope of duties of a police officer to protect life and property by control of traffic.

R. c. Murray (1999), *(*sub nom. *R. v. Murray)* 136 C.C.C. (3d) 197, 32 C.R. (5th) 253, 1 M.V.R. (4th) 24 (Que. C.A.) — A roadblock to apprehend fleeing armed robbers is not arbitrary detention.

R. v. Hamann, 2006 CarswellNfld 335, 41 M.V.R. (5th) 137 (Prov. Ct.) — A doctor on the way to an emergency was convicted of failing to obey an officer where necessity was not made out. An alternate route would have been just as fast.

R. v. Locke, 2007 CarswellNfld 5, 42 M.V.R. (5th) 233 (Prov. Ct.) — Failing to proceed with special care and give way to traffic after stopping at a stop sign is a strict liability offence made out where another vehicle approaching the intersection was made to swerve by the defendant who initially was proceeding without stopping.

R. v. Hemrayeva, 2010 ONCA 194, 2010 CarswellOnt 1409, 92 M.V.R. (5th) 215, 259 O.A.C. 389 ([In Chambers]) — "Traffic" in s. 134(1) refers to one or more vehicles.

R. v. Hajivasilis (2013), 41 M.V.R. (6th) 175, 2013 ONCA 27, 2013 CarswellOnt 508, 114 O.R. (3d) 337, 302 O.A.C. 65, [2013] O.J. No. 253 (Ont. C.A.) — The requirements are not restricted to "highways".

Related Provisions: R.R.O. 1990, Reg. 599, Highway Closings.

134.1 (1) Removal of vehicle, debris blocking traffic — Where a police officer considers it reasonably necessary,

    (a) to ensure orderly movement of traffic; or

    (b) to prevent injury or damage to persons or property,

he or she may remove and store or order the removal and storage of a vehicle, cargo or debris that are directly or indirectly impeding or blocking the normal and reasonable movement of traffic on a highway and shall notify the owner of the vehicle of the location to which the vehicle was removed.

(2) Costs of removal — **The costs and charges for the removal and storage of the vehicle, cargo or debris removed are a debt due by the owner, operator and driver of the vehicle, for which they are jointly and severally liable, and the debt may be recovered in any court of competent jurisdiction and are a lien upon the vehicle, which may be enforced in the manner provided by the *Repair and Storage Liens Act*.**

(3) Conflict with other Acts — **In the event of a conflict with this section, the following prevail:**

    1. Part X of the *Environmental Protection Act* and the regulations made under it, with respect to a pollutant on a highway.

    2. The *Dangerous Goods Transportation Act* and the regulations made under it.

(4) Protection from liability — **No action or other proceeding for damages shall be brought against a police officer, a police force, a police services board, any member of a police services board, the Crown, an employee of the Crown or an agent of**

the Crown for any act done in good faith in the performance or intended performance of a duty under this section, or in the exercise or intended exercise of a power under this section, or any neglect or default in the performance or exercise in good faith of such duty or power.

Proposed Amendment — 134.1(4)

(4) Protection from liability — No action or other proceeding for damages shall be brought against a police officer, a police force, a police services board, any member of a police services board, an employee of the Crown or an agent of the Crown for any act done in good faith in the performance or intended performance of a duty under this section, or in the exercise or intended exercise of a power under this section, or any neglect or default in the performance or exercise in good faith of such duty or power.

2009, c. 5, s. 43(1) [Not in force at date of publication.]

Proposed Addition — 134.1(4.1)–(4.3)

(4.1) Same — No action or other proceeding for damages, other than on account of injury to or the death of any person, shall be brought against a prescribed person or person belonging to a prescribed class of persons who is ordered by a police officer to remove or store a vehicle, cargo or debris under subsection (1) for any act done in good faith in the performance or intended performance of a duty under this section, or any neglect or default in the performance in good faith of such duty.

(4.2) Crown not relieved of liability — Despite subsections 5(2) and (4) of the *Proceedings Against the Crown Act*, subsections (4) and (4.1) do not relieve the Crown of liability in respect of a tort committed by a person mentioned in subsection (4) or (4.1) to which it would otherwise be subject.

(4.3) Regulations — The Minister may make regulations prescribing persons or classes of persons for the purpose of subsection (4.1) and, in doing so, may describe the persons or classes by describing the circumstances or conditions under which they remove or store a vehicle, cargo or debris.

2009, c. 5, s. 43(2) [Not in force at date of publication.]

(5) Definition — In subsection (2),

"operator" means,

(a) operator as defined in subsection 16(1), and

(b) in the absence of evidence to the contrary, where there is no CVOR certificate, as defined in subsection 16(1), or lease applicable to the commercial motor vehicle, the holder of the plate portion of the permit for the commercial motor vehicle.

Proposed Amendment — 134.1(5) "operator" (b)

(b) in the absence of evidence to the contrary, where there is no CVOR certificate, or lease applicable to the commercial motor vehicle, the holder of the plate portion of the permit for the commercial motor vehicle.

2014, c. 9, Sched. 2, s. 37 [To come into force January 1, 2017.]

2005, c. 26, Sched. A, s. 20

135. (1) Application — This section applies where an intersection is not controlled by a stop or yield sign or a traffic control signal system.

(2) Right of way — Every driver approaching an intersection shall yield the right of way to any vehicle in the intersection that has entered it from an intersecting highway.

(3) Idem — When two vehicles enter an intersection from intersecting highways at approximately the same time, the driver on the left shall yield the right of way to the vehicle on the right.

(4) Definitions — In this section, "driver" includes street car operator and "vehicle" includes street car.

Commentary

This section, since an amendment in 1954, creates a positive duty to yield right of way, a breach of which duty will constitute an offence.

Questions of right of way have been a fertile subject of litigation in all jurisdictions, and the statutory provisions relating thereto have undergone considerable amendment. Where intersections are controlled by traffic lights, the provisions of s. 144 apply; at intersections on through highways, s. 136 governs; and where there are yield right of way signs, s. 138 governs. At all other intersections the provisions of s. 135 will be applicable. Up until 1958, the section only applied to create a statutory right of way where two vehicles approached or entered an intersection at the same time, and it was therefore excluded where one vehicle had entered the intersection first. The 1958 amendment clarified the situation by creating two statutory right of ways, one in favour of the vehicle first into the intersection, and the other in favour of the vehicle on the right where the vehicles enter the intersection at approximately the same time. Where the driver with the right of way intends to make a turn at the intersection, the provisions of ss. 141 and 142 should also be kept in mind.

Section 135 governs where there is no stop, yield or traffic control system at an intersection. A driver entering it shall yield the right of way to any vehicle already in the intersection. Where two vehicles enter at about the same time, the vehicle on the left must yield to the vehicle on the right. Street cars are also subject to the rules.

Case Law

Denny v. Brewer, [1961] O.W.N. 161 (Co. Ct.) — This section should be interpreted to mean that the driver of a vehicle approaching an intersection shall yield the right of way to a vehicle that has entered the intersection from a different highway under such circumstances that an accident is not to be reasonably anticipated; and when two vehicles enter an intersection from different highways at approximately the same time in such a way that an accident is to be reasonably anticipated the driver on the left shall yield the right of way to the vehicle on the right.

Brewster v. Spicer (1959), 42 M.P.R. 232, 17 D.L.R. (2d) 505 (N.S. C.A.) — Which of two vehicles enters the intersection first is not necessarily the sole test in determining liability.

Barbery v. Pollard, 24 M.P.R. 276, [1949] 4 D.L.R. 682 (N.B. C.A.); *Ferguson v. Pettipas*, 13 M.P.R. 440, [1939] 1 D.L.R. 295 (N.S. C.A.); *Purdy v. N.S. Light and Power*

Co. (1959), 18 D.L.R. (2d) 356 (N.S. C.A.) — The driver of the vehicle on the left is not justified in proceeding with the intent that he may just reach the intersection first and so obtain the right of way. The driver on the right has the stronger position, and the driver on the left may proceed only if he is reasonably sure that he can do so with safety. Just at what point before actually reaching the intersection and exactly what measures should be taken must depend upon the particular conditions existing at the time.

Hanley v. Hayes, 55 O.L.R. 361, [1925] 3 D.L.R. 782 (C.A.); *Waterfield v. Tazzman*, [1949] 1 D.L.R. 529 (S.C.C.); *Brownlee v. Walker*, [1951] O.W.N. 166 (C.A.); affirmed [1952] 2 D.L.R. 450 (S.C.C.) — If a traveller holding the servient position comes to a crossing and finds no one approaching the crossing on the cross-street within such a distance as to indicate danger of interference or collision, he is under no obligation to stop or to wait, but may proceed to use such crossing as a matter of right.

Hanley v. Hayes, supra; Denny v. Brewer, supra; Gibb v. Sandwich, Windsor and Amherstburg Ry., [1948] O.R. 453, [1948] 3 D.L.R. 739 (C.A.) — It would seem that the test of whether a vehicle has already entered the intersection will be the imminence or reasonable apprehension of a collision. The question is one of fact to be determined in the light of the particular circumstances, but cases on "reasonable and substantial prior entry" may be illustrative of factors such as visibility, speed, etc., which affect the determination.

Lucas v. Kennedy (1961), 31 D.L.R. (2d) 436 (N.S. T.D.) — An inference was drawn from the respective distances travelled by each vehicle into the intersection in determining which had entered first.

Yuan v. Farstad (1967), 62 W.W.R. 645, 66 D.L.R. (2d) 295 (B.C. S.C.) — Where two vehicles entered an intersection at the same time and at the same speed and each driver's view was obstructed until the intersection was reached, the sole responsibility for the ensuing accident rested on the driver approaching from the left.

Higgins v. Tilling (1963), 42 W.W.R. 361 (Sask. Q.B.) — In entering an intersection a driver's vigilance should be concentrated on the area adjacent to the intersection and not dissipated on distant vehicles presenting no apparent danger; he is entitled to assume that distant drivers will use due care and travel at a lawful speed.

Libby v. Fox (1954), 35 M.P.R. 137 (N.B. C.A.) — A motorist approaching an intersection must exercise prudence in relation to traffic which may have the right of way; he need not wait at the intersection indefinitely, he need not cede the right to cross to all traffic no matter how far away such traffic may be from the intersection, but as a prudent driver he should not attempt to cross the intersection if he is aware that the approaching vehicle is at such close proximity that it would be necessary for the driver of such vehicle to cede his right of way in order to avoid a collision.

Cohen and Rudelier v. Bates (1962), 32 D.L.R. (2d) 763 (Man. C.A.) — The right of way rule is not absolute and should not require the driver on the left to treat every intersection as if it were a "stop sign" intersection. But he has no right to enter, even if he reaches the intersection first, unless he has a clear margin of safety and can negotiate the intersection without danger of a collision with traffic approaching from the right. The fact that the driver on the left is driving a large slow-moving delivery van is a factor to be considered in determining whether he did have such a clear margin of safety.

Scheving v. Scott (1960), 32 W.W.R. 234, 24 D.L.R. (2d) 354 (Man. C.A.); *Bell v. Weseen* (1965), 52 W.W.R. 132 (Man. C.A.) — The rule under which the vehicle first entering the intersection had the right of way was considered to be applicable only where the vehicle on the left reached an open intersection substantially in advance of the vehicle on the right. The mere fact that a driver has physically driven his vehicle more than half-way across an intersection does not constitute a pre-emption of the intersection. If he is in the servient position he is under a very heavy onus to avoid a collision with a vehicle approaching from his right.

Reliance on Right of Way

Ludolph v. Palmer and Phillips, [1950] O.R. 821, [1951] 1 D.L.R. 102 (C.A.); *Can. Bread Co. v. Grigg*, [1946] O.W.N. 337, [1946] 2 D.L.R. 374 (C.A.); *Duncan v. Jenks*, [1949] O.W.N. 457 (C.A.); *Prior v. Burton* (1953), 10 W.W.R. 476 (Man. C.A.); *Lumsden v. Martin*, [1938] O.W.N. 201 (C.A.) — Two broad general principles can be deduced from these cases which, when applied to the facts of a particular case, will re-solve many of the issues arising out of collisions at intersections. The first is that a driver in the dominant position has the right to assume that any driver approaching the intersec-tion in the servient position will obey the law and yield him the right of way, as the rule of the road requires. The driver with the right of way has the paramount situation in traffic when his intention to exercise that right is indicated by the surrounding circum-stances and he is not bound to guard against a breach of duty by the other driver.

Swartz Bros. v. Wills, [1935] S.C.R. 628; *Vryenhoek v. Ruel*, [1952] 1 D.L.R. 856, 4 W.W.R. (N.S.) 211 (Man. C.A.); *Man. Motor Transit Ltd. v. McGregor*, [1939] 2 W.W.R. 513, [1939] 3 D.L.R. 419 (Man. C.A.) — The duty to yield to vehicles on the right includes by implication the additional duty of keeping proper lookout for such vehi-cles coming from the right, and the driver cannot be heard to say that he looked and saw nothing, if the approaching vehicle was plainly visible, since not to see what is clearly visible is itself negligence.

B.C. Elec. Ry. Co. v. Farrer, [1955] 5 D.L.R. 161 (S.C.C.); *Heard v. John Erzinger Ltd.*, [1938] 1 W.W.R. 725, [1938] 2 D.L.R. 655 (Sask. C.A.) — The second, and equally im-portant principle, is that the existence of a right of way does not entitle the driver to rush through the intersection regardless of the rights of other parties on the highway or to proceed without taking due care for the safety of himself and others.

Brownlee v. Walker, [1952] 2 D.L.R. 450 (S.C.C.); *Woodward v. Harris*, [1951] O.W.N. 221 (C.A.); *Poirier v. Greenburg* (1946), 19 M.P.R. 243 (N.B. C.A.); *Bashnick v. Mitch-ell* (1981), 13 M.V.R. 110 (Sask. Q.B.) — Even though a driver may have the right of way, he is bound to act so as to avoid a collision if reasonable care on his part will prevent it. The driver ought not to exercise his right of way if the circumstances are such that the result of doing so will be a collision which he reasonably should have foreseen and avoided.

Sinclair v. Catton (1973), 43 D.L.R. (3d) 471 (Man. C.A.) — The statutory right of way merely entitles the driver of the dominant vehicle to rely on the right of way until notic-ing that the driver of the servient vehicle is not permitting him the right of way. The dominant and servient drivers were held equally responsible for the collision.

Brownlee v. Walker, *supra*; *Bothwell v. Gallaway*, [1950] O.R. 377 (H.C.); affirmed [1951] O.R. 50 (C.A.) — How far the two drivers will be found to have fulfilled their respective obligations will depend on the facts of each case, but the mere fact of a colli-sion at an intersection would throw on the driver of the car in the servient position the onus of showing that the other driver, after he became aware, or by the exercise of rea-sonable care should have become aware, of the first driver's disregard of the law, had in fact a sufficient opportunity to avoid the accident of which a reasonably careful and skilful driver would have availed himself. Moreover, in such circumstances any doubts should not be resolved in favour of the first driver whose unlawful conduct was the source of the difficulty.

Smith Tpt. Ltd. v. Campbell, [1952] O.R. 479 (H.C.) — Flashing amber lights at an intersection probably amounted to an abrogation of the right of way provisions, and that, even if they did still apply, there was nevertheless a duty on the driver to exercise "caution" which required something more than a complete reliance on his right of way, otherwise there would be no object in having a warning light.

136. (1) Stop at through highway — Every driver or street car operator approaching a stop sign at an intersection,

(a) shall stop his or her vehicle or street car at a marked stop line or, if none, then immediately before entering the nearest crosswalk or, if none, then immediately before entering the intersection; and

(b) shall yield the right of way to traffic in the intersection or approaching the intersection on another highway so closely that to proceed would constitute an immediate hazard and, having so yielded the right of way, may proceed.

(2) Acquiring right of way — Every driver or street car operator approaching, on another highway, an intersection referred to in subsection (1), shall yield the right of way to every driver or operator who has complied with the requirements of subsection (1).

Commentary

A driver or street car operator, when approaching a stop sign, shall come to a proper and full stop and shall yield the right of way to traffic in or very near the intersection.

Case Law

Quasi-Criminal

Manship v. R. (1983), 22 M.V.R. 257, 48 N.B.R. (2d) 124, 126 A.P.R. 124 (Q.B.) — The accused was convicted of an offence under s. 186(3) of the Motor Vehicle Act (N.B.). That provision required the driver of a motor vehicle approaching a stop sign to bring his vehicle to a full stop at the point nearest the intersection where the driver has a view of approaching traffic on the intersecting highways before entering the intersection. In this case, the stop sign was erected several feet from the intersection at a point where it was impossible to see traffic approaching from a driver's right for an appreciable distance because of the location of a residence close to the street line. Here, the accused stopped at the sign and proceeded slowly and when he saw no traffic he proceeded into the intersection. The appeal was dismissed. While the accused drove carefully and prudently he did not bring his vehicle to a complete stop at a point nearest the intersection where he had a view of approaching traffic and therefore he violated the provision as alleged.

R. v. Ross, [1966] 2 O.R. 273, [1966] 4 C.C.C. 175 (C.A.) — On a charge under s. 136 it is not necessary to prove a by-law or regulation authorizing the erection of a stop sign; the prosecution need only prove that there was a stop sign and, if the charge is under clause (a), that the accused failed to stop at the stop sign; or, if the charge is under clause (b), that the accused failed to yield the right of way.

R. v. Lavelle (1958), 29 C.R. 156, 122 C.C.C. 111 (Ont. H.C.) — Where the by-law is to be proved, the production of a certified copy of the by-law with a form of approval typed on it would appear to be sufficient.

R. v. Lavelle, supra — A *prima facie* case is established by evidence that a stop sign has been erected in a particular location and, in the absence of evidence to the contrary, it will be presumed that the officials of the municipality, acting under instructions, will have so erected the sign in size, colour and location in compliance with the regulations.

R. v. Priest, [1961] O.W.N. 166, 35 C.R. 32 (C.A.) — A driver may be convicted for failing to obey a stop sign that is erected in substantial, though not strict, compliance with the regulations where the visibility of the sign is not affected by the deviation.

R. v. Walker (1979), 5 M.V.R. 114, 48 C.C.C. (2d) 126 (Ont. Co. Ct.) — The offence of going through a stop sign is an absolute liability offence.

R. v. Brennan (1989), 18 M.V.R. (2d) 161, 75 C.R. (3d) 38, 52 C.C.C. (3d) 366, 36 O.A.C. 218 (C.A.) — While it was not necessary to decide the issue, the Court was inclined to agree with *Walker, supra*, that failing to stop at a stop sign fell into the category of absolute liability offences. With respect to s. 25(1) of the Criminal Code, it was held that the question to be asked is not whether the appellant was required or authorized by law to apprehend a driver of a stolen car but rather whether the appellant was required or authorized by law to drive through the stop sign without stopping. Such conduct, as observed in *Walker*, is required or authorized neither by legislative enactment nor at common law. In dismissing the constable's appeal, it was observed that specific exemptions in the Act, such as in relation to speeding (s. 128(12)), and entering an intersection against a red light following a full stop (s. 144(6)), support the dismissal of the constable's appeal.

Ethier v. Insley (1970), 11 C.R.N.S. 222 (Ont. Co. Ct.) — Section 136(1)(b) creates the offence of failing to yield the right of way on entering an intersection and the words "having so yielded the right of way may proceed with caution" do not create a second offence; accordingly, a traffic ticket marked "Highway Traffic Act, s. [116(b)]" and "fail to yield" is not void for duplicity.

R. v. Durnford, [1971] 1 O.R. 657, 2 C.C.C. 116 (C.A.) — This is so notwithstanding that the section does provide for a second offence, but such offence could only be committed by a different person, namely, the driver who began as the dominant driver.

Civil

Nature of Duty

Sorrie v. Cluting, [1955] O.W.N. 946, [1955] 5 D.L.R. 180 (C.A.); *Webb v. Moore's Taxi*, [1942] 3 W.W.R. 294, [1942] 4 D.L.R. 154 (Man. C.A.) — The question arises whether there is any duty to stop before entering a through highway if either no sign has been erected or a sign, though erected, has since fallen down or been removed. A municipality is under no duty to erect stop signs and a by-law constituting a through highway is unenforceable unless and until there are signs or other signals to warn the traffic. If there are no signs, there is no duty to stop. Once signs have been erected there is a duty on the municipality to maintain them and not to remove them without appropriate care. The municipality may be liable in damages if its failure to do so is the cause of an accident.

Patterson v. Cassidy and Preston, [1951] O.W.N. 765, [1951] 4 D.L.R. 846 (C.A.) — The removal of a stop sign by an unauthorized person did not alter the status of a through highway as between two drivers; such status could only be affected by the act of constituted authority. However, s. 136 prescribes duties on a driver "approaching a stop sign at an intersection" and it could hardly be negligence in itself to fail to observe a stop sign that was non-existent.

Kraft v. Prefontaine (1963), 41 W.W.R. 510 (Sask. C.A.) — A stop sign that had been turned 90 degrees was held to be no longer a stop sign since it did not indicate reasonably to people using the road that they were required to stop.

Gonneville v. Bourassa, [1964] Que. S.C. 183 — A stop sign had been knocked down several days before the accident and it was held that no negligence was involved in the driver's failure to stop before entering the through highway.

Kyle v. McCullagh (1969), 71 W.W.R. 206, 8 D.L.R. (3d) 779 (B.C. S.C.); *Levasseur v. Berube* (1970), 2 N.B.R. (2d) 417 (C.A.) — The driver on the through highway was not negligent in not yielding the right of way to the vehicle on the right which had not stopped where the stop sign was missing.

Monarch Broadcasting Co. v. Acorn Tpt. Ltd. (1977), 10 A.R. 107 (Dist. Ct.) — A plaintiff driver turned left onto the Trans Canada Highway. The plaintiff was aware of a tractor-trailer unit approaching from her right. The tractor-trailer unit struck the plaintiff's vehicle. She sued. The action was dismissed. The plaintiff was entirely at fault. Although the tractor-trailer unit was a considerable distance from the intersection when the plaintiff entered, the plaintiff miscalculated in not anticipating the difficulties of stopping or changing the direction of a large vehicle. Furthermore, she was negligent after having made the decision to enter, in not keeping her eye on the approaching vehicle and in not moving to the right of the travelled portion of the southbound lane in order to give the driver of the tractor-trailer unit sufficient room to pass.

Gibbon v. Fortune (1954), 35 M.P.R. 355 (N.B. C.A.); *Krakau v. R.* (1962), 40 W.W.R. 362 (Ex. Ct.) — In a civil action absence of proof of the constituting by-law is not a material issue in determining negligence in failing to observe the stop sign.

Duty to Stop

Griffith v. Luscombe, [1951] O.W.N. 181 (Co. Ct.) — A police car or other emergency vehicle is not in any special position under the Act and must stop at "stop" signs.

Mallet v. Ottawa and Gavan, [1950] O.W.N. 719 (Co. Ct.) — Vehicles in a funeral procession must stop at stop signs.

R. v. Cyr, [1956] Ex. C.R. 161; *Roy v. Carrier et Goulet Enrg.*, [1974] Que. S.C. 360 — The duty to stop is an imperative requirement. A breach thereof will not be easily justified. Therefore, a driver who was unable, due to icy conditions, to bring his vehicle to a stop when approaching a through street and, seeing no other traffic, continued on into the intersection where a collision occurred was held solely responsible for the accident.

McConkey v. Thorn, [1972] S.C.R. 61, 21 D.L.R. (3d) 673 — A driver who merely slowed down at the stop sign and edged across the through highway was held primarily responsible for the ensuing accident.

Martel v. Vandroogenbroek, [1952] Que. S.C. 113 — If a motorist is required to stop before entering the intersection he must stop before the continuation of the sidewalk and is not entitled to proceed to the farther limits of the sidewalk.

Sheehy v. Dumesnil, [1976] 1 S.C.R. 152, 8 N.R. 145 — The defendant failed to stop at a stop sign 51 feet from an intersection although he intended to stop before the intersection. The defendant was absolved of any fault where the collision occurred between the stop sign and the intersection considering ss. 40(14), and (15) of the Quebec Highway Code.

Mudrazia v. Holjevac, [1970] 1 O.R. 275, 8 D.L.R. (3d) 221 (H.C.) — The failure to stop does not *per se* constitute gross negligence.

Entry Into Intersection

Eisenhauer v. Rice (1952), 33 M.P.R. 63 (N.S. C.A.) — The duty of the driver is not discharged simply by stopping and then proceeding without a proper lookout or without regard to the circumstances of probable danger.

Theriault v. Huctwith, [1948] S.C.R. 86; *Donald v. Skibstead* (1954), 12 W.W.R. 657 (Alta. Dist. Ct.); *Summerhayes Lbr. Ltd. v. Bach*, [1949] O.W.N. 739 (C.A.); *Woodward v. Harris*, [1951] O.W.N. 221 (C.A.) — Clearly, a driver need not wait an interminable time for all possible traffic to pass, otherwise the object of facilitating traffic movement would be defeated, but he does have the onus of using reasonable care on entering the highway and of acquiring the right of way at the proper time.

Duret v. Savard (1960), 22 D.L.R. (2d) 755 (Sask. C.A.); *Call v. Smith*, [1938] 3 W.W.R. 539, [1938] 4 D.L.R. 789 (Sask. C.A.); *Johnston Nat. Storage Ltd. v. Mathieson*, [1953] 2 D.L.R. 604 (S.C.C.) — The driver on the through highway will generally be entitled to assume that a driver whom he sees stopped at the intersection will comply with the law and not attempt to enter until it is safe to do so.

Murdock v. Davis, [1939] 2 W.W.R. 621 (B.C. S.C.) — If it is not clear on the evidence that the driver in the servient position had made a sufficient entry to overcome the superior right of way, the doubt should be resolved in favour of the driver on the through highway.

McLeary v. Eldridge, [1953] 1 D.L.R. 547, 30 M.P.R. 241 (N.S. C.A.) — The driver on the through highway who saw the other driver approaching the intersection from behind a snow bank should have taken reasonable precautions and not relied on the other vehicle stopping. He was held contributorily negligent.

Crothers v. Northern Taxi Ltd. (1957), 21 W.W.R. 577, 10 D.L.R. (2d) 87 (Man. C.A.) — However, the greater responsibility of the driver in the servient position should be reflected in the apportionment of degrees of negligence.

Keen v. Stene (1964), 44 D.L.R. (2d) 350 (B.C. C.A.) — An approaching vehicle is an immediate hazard if the circumstances are such as to require its driver to take some sudden or violent action to avoid the threat of collision if the entering vehicle fails to yield the right of way; it is the threat, not the inevitability, of a collision that is to be avoided.

Curley v. Ottawa Elec. Ry., [1946] O.W.N. 597 (C.A.); affirmed [1947] 3 D.L.R. 576 (S.C.C.); *McLeary v. Eldridge, supra* — An entry should not be made into the intersection in order to gain a right of way unless there is an assured margin of safety. If the view in either direction is obstructed the driver must approach the intersection at such speed and with his car under such control that he can stop in a place of safety after he comes to a place where he can see that it is unsafe to proceed.

Davies v. Tuck, [1955] O.W.N. 229, [1955] 3 D.L.R. 353 (C.A.); *Hammond v. Wilkinson*, [1938] 1 W.W.R. 461 (Sask. C.A.) — If an improper entry creates an emergency, the driver so entering will be liable for the reasonable acts of the other driver in combatting that emergency.

Davidson v. Duffett, [1951] O.W.N. 495 (C.A.); *Bristow v. Marko*, [1949] 1 D.L.R. 693 (Ont. C.A.); reversed on other grounds [1949] 3 D.L.R. 785 (S.C.C.); *Arcand v. Kaup*, [1939] 1 W.W.R. 615, [1939] 2 D.L.R. 456 (Alta. C.A.); *Marshall v. Belhumeur*, [1945] Que. K.B. 609 — Although the driver on the through highway does occupy a very favourable position, his right of way is not absolute and he has no vested right to proceed at an unreasonable rate of speed regardless of others who may be entering the intersection. He is subject to the overriding duty to operate his vehicle at all times with due care and reasonable consideration for other users of the highway, particularly since reasonable entry by the servient driver after a stop confers on him the right of way.

Hofbauer v. Byers, [1969] 2 O.R. 389, 5 D.L.R. (3d) 472 (C.A.) — The right of way of the driver on the through highway is not absolute and he may be contributorily negligent in failing to see the other vehicle, particularly at a busy intersection obstructed by traffic.

Rattray v. Kachulak (1957), 21 W.W.R. 107, 7 D.L.R. (2d) 439 (Man. C.A.) — The driver was held to be free of negligence where he commenced to cross with a reasonable margin of safety but was slowed down by pedestrians unlawfully crossing the intersection which he accordingly did not clear before being struck.

Rose v. Belanger, [1984] 2 W.W.R. 505, 25 Man. R. (2d) 277 (Q.B.); reversed in part on other grounds [1985] 3 W.W.R. 612, 31 C.C.L.T. 221, 32 Man. R. (2d) 282 (C.A.) — The plaintiff's wife stopped at a stop sign and proceeded through the intersection without checking further for oncoming traffic on a through street. The defendant was impaired by alcohol and was speeding on the through road. Both the plaintiff's wife and the defendant driver failed to take evasive action when both should have seen each other. The defendant was held 80% responsible.

Nolin v. Tingey (1985), 36 M.V.R. 199 (Ont. H.C.) — The defendant was proceeding at night at normal speed northbound on a through street. The defendant was driving a pick-up truck owned by W and he was grossly impaired. The plaintiff was proceeding westbound and stopped at a stop sign at the intersection. The plaintiff's attention was diverted and he allowed his motorcycle to proceed into the intersection. The defendant's vehicle struck the plaintiff, and the defendant dragged the plaintiff and his motorcycle for several seconds before stopping his vehicle. The plaintiff was found to be negligent in proceeding through the intersection into oncoming traffic. However, even though the defendant was driving at normal speed, it was possible that had he not been impaired, he would have been able to take evasive action. His failure to apprehend the accident for several seconds contributed to the accident. The defendant was found 40% at fault.

Related Provisions: See s. 137 of the Act; see R.R.O. 1990, Reg. 615, Signs, ss. 6-12; R.R.O. 1990, Reg. 623, Stop Signs at Intersections; R.R.O. 1990, Reg. 624, Stop Signs in Territory without Municipal Organization.

137. Stop signs, erection at intersections — In addition to stop signs required at intersections on through highways,

    (a) the council of a municipality may by by-law provide for the erection of stop signs at intersections on highways under its jurisdiction; and

    (b) the Minister may by regulation designate intersections on the King's Highway at which stop signs shall be erected,

and every sign so erected shall comply with the regulations of the Ministry.

2002, c. 17, Sched. F, s. 1

Case Law

R. v. Kinash, 46 M.V.R. (6th) 122, 2013 BCSC 1321, 2013 CarswellBC 2237 (B.C. S.C.) — The presence of a stop sign at an intersection was a condition precedent to a legal requirement to stop at a marked stop line. The stop sign was not at an intersection and accordingly, there was no requirement to stop at a marked stop line.

Fordham v. Dutton-Dunwich (Municipality) (2014), 2014 CarswellOnt 17325, 17 C.C.L.T. (4th) 1, 70 M.V.R. (6th) 1, 2014 ONCA 891, 31 M.P.L.R. (5th) 269, 327 O.A.C. 302 (Ont. C.A.) — Running a stop sign at 80 kph was negligent. Although ordinary rural drivers did not always stop at stop signs, that was not legally relevant.

Related Provisions: See s. 136 of the Act. See also R.R.O. 1990, Reg. 615, Signs, ss. 6-12; R.R.O. 1990, Reg. 623, Stop Signs At Intersections; R.R.O. 1990, Reg. 624, Stop Signs in Territory Without Municipal Organization.

138. (1) Yield right-of-way signs — **The driver or operator of a vehicle or street car approaching a yield right-of-way sign shall slow down to a speed reasonable for the existing conditions or shall stop if necessary as provided in clause 136(1)(a) and shall yield the right of way to traffic in the intersection or approaching on the intersecting highway so closely that it constitutes an immediate hazard and having so yielded may proceed with caution.**

(2) Erection of yield signs — **No yield right-of-way sign shall be erected except in compliance with the regulations.**

Case Law

Quasi-Criminal

R. v. Horban (1959), 31 W.W.R. 139 (Alta. Dist. Ct.) — On a charge of failing to comply with a yield right-of-way sign, the fact the other vehicle was exceeding the speed limit was not held to affect the duty to yield.

Civil

Mulligan v. Morrison Enrg. & Const. Ltd. (1970), 1 Nfld. & P.E.I.R. 155 (P.E.I. S.C.) — The word "yield" means to give to the other party the right of going through the intersection first.

Hammond v. Smith (1964), 45 D.L.R. (2d) 762 (N.S. Co. Ct.) — It is no excuse for not yielding at a yield sign that a driver did not see the other vehicle approaching the intersection.

Doblanko v. J.P. Sunrise Bakery Ltd. (1967), 59 W.W.R. 558 (Alta. Dist. Ct.) — A motorist was not negligent in assuming that he had the right of way in reliance on the normal rules of the road at an intersection normally marked by a "yield" sign which had earlier been knocked down and not replaced and the prior existence of which the motorist had no knowledge.

Krushelnicki v. Kelly's Excavating & Snow Removal Ltd. (1990), 22 M.V.R. (2d) 6, 82 Sask. R. 18 (Q.B.) — The driver of a vehicle has a statutory duty to yield the right of way to oncoming vehicles. Accordingly, if the driver's line of vision is obscured by an object, the driver has a duty not to enter the street until it is safe to do so.

Related Provisions: See R.R.O. 1990, Reg. 615, Signs, ss. 16-19; R.R.O. 1990, Reg. 631, Yield Right-of-Way Signs in Territory without Municipal Organization.

139. (1) Right of way on entering highway from private road — Every driver or street car operator entering a highway from a private road or driveway shall yield the right of way to all traffic approaching on the highway so closely that to enter would constitute an immediate hazard.

(2) Exception to subs. (1) — Subsection (1) does not apply to a driver or operator entering a highway from a private road or driveway controlled by a traffic control signal of a traffic control signal system.

Case Law

Boutilier v. Atton (1964), 50 M.P.R. 131 (N.S. C.A.) — The duty imposed by this section is clearly a high one, and a driver must refrain from entering when vehicles are approaching on the highway until they have passed the driveway.

R. v. Perry (1941), 77 C.C.C. 103 (N.B. Co. Ct.) — However, once an entry has been made, the driver would no longer be "about to enter or cross" and the imperative duty to yield would be replaced by a general duty of reasonable care applicable to all motorists on the highway.

R. v. Hornstein (1973), 11 C.C.C. (2d) 197 (Ont. Prov. Ct.) — The duty of a driver under s. 119 [now s. 139] does not end until his vehicle is safely on the highway; to accept the literal meaning of "about to enter" would place an abstract duty on the driver and would in fact mean that the section could not be violated once the offending vehicle entered any part of the highway.

Berry v. Mapleback (1953), 31 M.P.R. 379 (N.S. C.A.); *Burgoyne v. Indust. Shipping Co.* (1956), 38 M.P.R. 233 (N.S. C.A.); *Pilgrim v. Weston Bakeries*, [1970] 3 O.R. 256, 12 D.L.R. (3d) 692 (C.A.); *Simmons v. Gammon* (1972), 3 Nfld. & P.E.I.R. 161 (P.E.I. S.C.) — A person entering a highway from a private way should be proceeding at a speed at which he would be able to stop in inches, but the driver on the highway may also be guilty of contributory negligence if he is proceeding at an excessive speed, not keeping a proper lookout, driving on the wrong side of the road, etc.

McLatchey v. Harper (1953), 33 M.P.R. 185 (N.B. C.A.) — The car stalled when halfway out of the driveway and was struck by the defendant's vehicle proceeding along the highway. The defendant was held solely responsible for the accident.

R. v. Langille (1980), 7 M.V.R. 294, 31 N.B.R. (2d) 355, 75 A.P.R. 355 (C.A.) — The duty to yield the right of way applies only to a driver about to enter or cross the highway. It does not extend to a driver crossing the highway after a legal entrance.

Shepherd v. Helm (1983), 60 N.S.R. (2d) 93, 128 A.P.R. 93 (T.D.) — The plaintiff's action for damages was dismissed where he had been faced with a vehicle that had exited onto a public street from a private parking lot. The defendant had the responsibility to make the manoeuvre in safety. There is no corresponding duty on a person to drive on a street to ensure he is not interfering with vehicles entering the street from a private lot. The negligence of the defendant was the sole cause of the accident; however, the plaintiff failed to prove any damages.

R. v. Shapero (February 5, 1991), Doc. CA 184/90 (Ont. C.A.) — There is no onus of explanation cast upon a person charged with an offence under s. 139(1) of the Act.

140. Pedestrian crossover — (1) **Duties of driver** — When a pedestrian is crossing on the roadway within a pedestrian crossover, the driver of a vehicle approaching the crossover,

(a) shall stop before entering the crossover;

(b) shall not overtake another vehicle already stopped at the crossover; and

(c) shall not proceed into the crossover until the pedestrian is no longer on the roadway.

(2) [Repealed 2015, c. 14, s. 39(1).]

(3) **Passing moving vehicles within 30 metres of pedestrian crossover** — When a vehicle is approaching a pedestrian crossover and is within 30 metres of it, the driver of any other vehicle approaching from the rear shall not allow the front extremity of his or her vehicle to pass beyond the front extremity of the other vehicle.

(4) **Duty of pedestrian** — No pedestrian shall leave the curb or other place of safety at a pedestrian crossover and walk, run or move into the path of a vehicle that is so close that it is impracticable for the driver of the vehicle to comply with subsection (1).

(5) **Municipal by-laws** — No municipal by-law that purports to designate a pedestrian crossover on a highway on which the speed limit is in excess of 60 kilometres per hour is valid.

(6) **Riding in pedestrian crossover prohibited** — No person shall ride or operate a bicycle across a roadway within a pedestrian crossover.

(7) **Offence** — Every person who contravenes subsection (1) or (3) is guilty of an offence and on conviction is liable to a fine of not less than $150 and not more than $500.

(8) **Regulations** — The Minister may make regulations respecting pedestrian crossovers,

(a) providing for the erection of signs on any highway or any type or class of highway and the placing of markings on the roadway;

(b) prescribing the types of signs and markings and the location on the highway and roadway of each type of sign and marking;

(c) prohibiting the use or erection of any sign or type of sign that is not prescribed.

(9) **Definitions** — In this section,

"pedestrian" includes a person in a wheelchair;

"vehicle" includes a street car.

2005, c. 26, Sched. A, s. 21; 2015, c. 14, s. 39

Commentary

When a pedestrian or a person in a wheelchair is crossing within a pedestrian crossover, drivers shall yield or stop if necessary if the person is in the driver's half of the roadway or about to enter that half (subs. (1)). Overtaking vehicles must cease to do so when the vehicle in front stops (subss. (2), (3)). Persons using a crosswalk should not put drivers in a precarious position (subs. (4)). The speed limit of a highway with a crossover cannot exceed 60 km/h (subs. (5)). Bicycles shall not be ridden through a crossover (subs. (6)).

Case Law

R. v. McLaren (1981), 10 M.V.R. 42 (Ont. C.A.) — Although it is necessary to prove the existence of the by-law designating a crossover, the evidentiary burden may be satisfied by inference from evidence of the existence of such a crossover indicated by signs and markings of the kind that are commonly associated with pedestrian crossovers in the province. There was error in holding that there was no evidence establishing the existence of the by-law.

R. v. Knutson (1989), 13 M.V.R. (2d) 158 (Sask. Q.B.) — The accused was acquitted of failing to yield to pedestrians contrary to s. 54(1) of the Highway Traffic Act (Sask.). The accused's vehicle had struck a member of a school safety patrol who was standing in a crosswalk. The trial Judge ruled that if a person is in the crosswalk but is stationary there is no requirement for a driver to yield the right of way. The Crown appealed. The appeal was allowed. The words "is crossing" in s. 54(1) had to be interpreted in accordance with their common meaning as well as with the objective of the legislation. One purpose of the legislation in issue was to regulate the flow of traffic so as to minimize the risk to the safety of persons who use or are present upon public thoroughfares. Pedestrians were obviously in greater need of protection than vehicles and the statutory provision had to be interpreted with that fact in mind. Moreover, although the usual meaning of the verb "to cross" was to pass from one side to another it was not necessary to complete that process in order to be said to be crossing the highway. One can stop in the middle of the highway and still be said to be crossing it.

R. v. Davis (1996), 21 M.V.R. (3d) 65, 148 N.S.R. (2d) 68, 429 A.P.R. 68 (N.S. C.A.) — The equivalent section of the Nova Scotia Act is one of strict liability.

Irion (Next Friend of) v. Debolt (1999), 48 M.V.R. (3d) 124, (sub nom. *Irion v. Debolt*) 254 A.R. 181 (Q.B.) — The driver of a stopped vehicle allegedly motioned another driver to proceed at a crosswalk. The signal by the other driver did not relieve the defendant of the independent duty not to overtake and pass a vehicle at a crosswalk to permit a pedestrian to pass.

R. v. Gallant (2000), 44 M.V.R. (4th) 213, 2000 CarswellAlta 1728 (Alta. Prov. Ct.) — The defence of due diligence applies to failure to yield the right of way to a pedestrian in a crosswalk.

Ashe v. Werstiuk (2004), 195 B.C.A.C. 35, 319 W.A.C. 35, 48 M.V.R. (4th) 182, 2004 BCCA 75, 2004 CarswellBC 384 (B.C. C.A.) — Where the pedestrian was crossing the street in mid-block and deliberately did not use the crosswalk, liability was apportioned 50% /50%.

Barrie (City) v. Aleem, 2006 CarswellOnt 2334, 2006 ONCJ 131, 32 M.V.R. (5th) 212 (C.J.) — "Path" is not defined in the Act, but means "course along which a person or thing moves or travels." The path includes the area where a vehicle has been, is and where it is going and includes the side of an oncoming vehicle.

Marshall (Litigation Guardian of) v. Annapolis (County) District School Board, 2011 NSCA 13, 2011 CarswellNS 54, (sub nom. *Marshall v. Annapolis County District School Board)* 298 N.S.R. (2d) 373, 6 M.V.R. (6th) 1, 945 A.P.R. 373; reversed in part 2012 SCC 27, 2012 CarswellNS 379, 2012 CarswellNS 380, (sub nom. *Annapolis County District School Board v. Marshall)* [2012] 2 S.C.R. 84, (sub nom. *Marshall v. Annapolis County District School Board)* 319 N.S.R. (2d) 1, 345 D.L.R. (4th) 446, 28 M.V.R. (6th) 42, 1010 A.P.R. 1, 431 N.R. 1 — It was unreasonable to expect a four year old to comply with the Act.

R. v. Calleja, 2013 ONCJ 7, 2013 CarswellOnt 94, 39 M.V.R. (6th) 162, [2013] O.J. No. 116 (Ont. Ct. J.) — The relationship between ss. 140 and 144 was canvassed.

Related Provisions: See R.R.O. 1990, Reg. 615, Signs, ss. 20.1-20.3, 20.7-20.10.

141. (1) Definition — In this section, "centre line" means,

    (a) in the case of a highway on which traffic is permitted to move in opposing directions, the marked line or median that divides traffic moving in opposing directions on the highway or, where there is no marked line or median, the centre of the roadway; and

    (b) in the case of a highway designated for the use of one-way traffic, the left curb or edge of the roadway.

(2) Turns: right at intersection — Where a driver or operator of a vehicle intends to turn to the right into an intersecting highway, he or she shall, where the highway on which he or she is driving has marked lanes for traffic, approach the intersection within the right-hand lane or, where it has no such marked lanes, by keeping immediately to the left of the right curb or edge of the roadway and he or she shall make the right turn by entering the right-hand lane of the intersecting highway where the lane is marked or, where no such lane is marked, by keeping immediately to the left of the right curb or edge of the roadway being entered.

(3) Right, where multiple lanes — Despite subsection (2), where more than one lane of a highway has been designated as a right-turn lane, the driver or operator of a vehicle intending to turn to the right into an intersecting highway shall approach the intersection in one of the lanes and leave the intersection in the lane of the intersecting highway that corresponds to the lane from which the turn was commenced.

(4) Exception — A driver of a road service vehicle entering an intersection within a lane other than one described in subsection (2) or (3) may make a right turn from the approach lane if the turn can be safely made.

(5) Left, across path of approaching vehicle — No driver or operator of a vehicle in an intersection shall turn left across the path of a vehicle approaching from the opposite direction unless he or she has afforded a reasonable opportunity to the driver or operator of the approaching vehicle to avoid a collision.

(6) Left, at intersection — Where a driver or operator of a vehicle intends to turn to the left into an intersecting highway, he or she shall, where the highway on which he or she is driving has marked lanes for traffic, approach the intersection within the left-hand lane provided for the use of traffic moving in the direction in which his or her vehicle is proceeding or, where it has no such marked lanes, by keeping immediately to the right of the centre line of the highway and he or she shall make the left turn by entering the intersection to the right of the centre line or its extension and by leaving the intersection in the left-hand lane provided for the use of traffic moving in the direction in which his or her vehicle is proceeding where the lane is marked or, where no such lane is marked, by passing immediately to the right of the centre line of the intersecting highway.

(7) Left, where multiple lanes — Despite subsection (6), where more than one lane of a highway has been designated as a left-turn lane, the driver or operator of a vehicle intending to turn to the left into an intersecting highway shall approach the intersection in one of the lanes and leave the intersection in the lane of the intersecting highway that corresponds to the lane from which the turn was commenced.

(8) Exception — A driver of a road service vehicle entering an intersection within a left-turn lane may leave the intersection without turning to the left if the movement can be safely made.

(9) Long vehicles — Where, because of the length of a vehicle or combination of vehicles, a turn cannot be made within the confines of the lanes referred to in subsection (2), (3), (6) or (7), a driver, when making such a turn, is not in contravention of any such subsection if he or she complies with the applicable provision as closely as practicable.

Commentary

This section governs: right turns at intersections (subs. (2)); right turns where there are multiple lanes (subss. (3), (4)); left turns across the path of an approaching vehicle (subs. (5)); left turns at intersections (subs. (6)) and where there are multiple lanes (subss. (7), (8)); and turns by extra long vehicles (subs. (9)).

Case Law

Right Turns

Boyd v. McDermid, [1971] 3 O.R. 649, 21 D.L.R. (3d) 385 (C.A.); *Doole v. B.C. Elec. Ry.* (1951), 2 W.W.R. (N.S.) 487 (B.C. S.C.) — Where a driver in making a right turn "cut off" a bus and a passenger in the bus was injured as a result of the bus driver's sudden application of the brakes, the negligence of the driver of the turning car was held to be the primary cause of the accident.

Kirby v. Kalyniak, [1948] S.C.R. 544; *Estabrooks v. Hay*, [1950] 3 D.L.R. 680, 26 M.P.R. 272 (N.B. C.A.) — Blame was apportioned where the turning driver failed to signal his intentions.

Hanmer v. Lucio, [1951] O.W.N. 41 (C.A.) — The defendant, before making a right turn, drove his car to the centre of the highway, and the following driver, assuming that a left turn was to be made, attempted to pass on the right. The resulting collision was held to be the fault of both drivers equally since the following driver should have exercised greater care when he realized that an unusual movement of some kind was to be made by the vehicle ahead.

Theriault v. Bourque (1983), 49 N.B.R. (2d) 389, 129 A.P.R. 389 (T.D.) — The plaintiff motorcycle driver was travelling on the right side of the roadway approaching a car flashing a left turn signal. The car suddenly turned right and a collision occurred. The plaintiff was awarded judgment. The defendant was wholly liable for failing to see the plaintiff and making a sudden turn without signalling. The plaintiff's failure to apply the brakes resulted from lack of time, or distress upon realization of the inevitability of the collision.

Left Turns

Pritchard v. Boucher, [1939] S.C.R. 265, [1939] 3 D.L.R. 129 — A driver making a left turn is required by this section to enter the intersection on his own side of the centre line of the highway, and to leave it in the same manner. He is not required, however, to pass the centre of the intersection before turning.

Edwards v. Stern (1952), 6 W.W.R. (N.S.) 481 (Alta. Dist. Ct.) — In addition to giving such signals as may be required (see s. 142), it is a driver's duty, first, to determine the proper and safe course, and then to turn left only if he can afford the specified opportunity to the other driver.

Mattie v. Delory (1974), 19 N.S.R. (2d) 451 (T.D.) — A left turn signal does not excuse the driver from ensuring that the turn can be made in safety.

Beazley v. Mills Bros. Ltd., 51 B.C.R. 197, [1937] 1 D.L.R. 205 (C.A.); *Gross v. Weaver*, [1946] 3 W.W.R. 440 (Sask. C.A.) — Commencing to turn before reaching the intersection, or cutting the corner, may be negligence contributing to the accident.

Myall v. Quick, [1922] 1 W.W.R. 1, 62 D.L.R. 509 (Alta. S.C.); *Bain v. Fuller* (1917), 29 D.L.R. 113 (N.S. T.D.); affirmed (1970), 51 N.S.R. 55 (C.A.) — If the driver cuts the corner and confronts another driver with the imminent prospect of a collision, he cannot complain if that other adopts an unwise manoeuvre in attempting to avoid it.

Davis v. Hall, [1936] 1 W.W.R. 419 (B.C. S.C.) — A driver is entitled to assume, when approaching an intersection, that the other car will not make a short left turn into the intersecting street.

Payne v. Lane, [1949] O.W.N. 284 (H.C.); *Muffitt v. Fleming*, [1938] O.R. 358, [1938] 3 D.L.R. 84 (C.A.); *Hodge v. Dunn and Ball* (1951), 2 W.W.R. (N.S.) 40 (Sask. C.A.); *Goodwin v. Wrycraft*, [1966] 1 O.R. 26, 52 D.L.R. (2d) 306 (C.A.) — A very heavy onus rests on the driver making a left turn, and he may turn into the path of approaching traffic, even when he is proceeding with a green light, only after having assured himself that he can do so in safety.

Shannon v. Shannon, [1975] W.W.D. 73 (B.C.) — Where a driver was turning left across the line of approaching traffic and collided with a police vehicle which was overtaking cars to their right, the driver of the police vehicle was held 20% at fault.

Raie v. Thorpe (1963), 43 W.W.R. 405 (B.C. C.A.) — The point of time at which the question of immediate hazard and right of way arises is the moment before the driver making the left turn actually commences to make the turn and not some earlier time.

Aherne v. Kaliel, [1945] 1 W.W.R. 331 (Alta. S.C.); affirmed [1945] 3 W.W.R. 524 (Alta. C.A.); *Jessop v. Heffner*, [1949] 2 W.W.R. 696 (B.C. C.A.); *Desjardins v. McGowan* (1973), 6 N.B.R. (2d) 536 (C.A.) — However, the driver in the intersection waiting to turn to the left has only to afford approaching vehicles a "reasonable" opportunity to avoid a collision, and the "through" driver may be wholly or partly responsible for the accident if he is travelling at an excessive speed or on the wrong side of the road, or is not keeping a proper lookout.

R. v. Ball (2004), 2004 CarswellAlta 1859, 2005 ABPC 4, 13 M.V.R. (5th) 61 (Prov. Ct.) — The term "in safety" must mean something more than avoiding a collision, and must mean that a vehicle entering a highway can do without the need of oncoming traffic to take evasive action.

Related Provisions: See s. 142 of the Act regarding signalling turns.

142. (1) Signal for left or right turn — The driver or operator of a vehicle upon a highway before turning to the left or right at any intersection or into a private road or driveway or from one lane for traffic to another lane for traffic or to leave the roadway shall first see that the movement can be made in safety, and if the operation of any other vehicle may be affected by the movement shall give a signal plainly visible to the driver or operator of the other vehicle of the intention to make the movement.

(2) Signal when moving from parked position — The driver or operator of a vehicle parked or stopped on the highway before setting the vehicle in motion shall first see that the movement can be made in safety, and, if in turning the vehicle the operation of any other vehicle may be affected by such movement, shall give a signal plainly visible to the driver or operator of such other vehicle of the intention to make such movement.

(3) Mode of signalling turn — The signal required in subsections (1) and (2) shall be given either by means of the hand and arm in the manner herein specified or by a mechanical or electrical signal device as described in subsection (6).

(4) How to signal manually — When the signal is given by means of the hand and arm, the driver or operator shall indicate his or her intention to turn,

> **(a)** to the left, by extending the hand and arm horizontally and beyond the left side of the vehicle; or

> **(b)** to the right, by extending the hand and arm upward and beyond the left side of the vehicle.

(5) Idem — Despite clause (4)(b), a person on a bicycle may indicate the intention to turn to the right by extending the right hand and arm horizontally and beyond the right side of the bicycle.

(6) Requirements for signalling device — A mechanical or electrical signal device shall clearly indicate the intention to turn, shall be visible and understandable during day-time and night-time from the front and from the rear of the vehicle for a distance of 30 metres, and shall be self-illuminated when used at any time from one-half hour after sunset to one-half hour before sunrise.

(7) Signalling devices to be used only for purpose of indicating turn — No person while operating or in control of a vehicle upon a highway shall actuate the mechanical or electrical device referred to in subsection (6) for any purpose other than to indicate a movement referred to in subsection (1) or (2).

(8) **Signal for stop** — The driver or operator of a vehicle upon a highway before stopping or suddenly decreasing the speed of the vehicle, if the operation of any other vehicle may be affected by such stopping or decreasing of speed, shall give a signal plainly visible to the driver or operator of the other vehicle of the intention to stop or decrease speed,

> (a) **manually** — by means of the hand and arm extended downward beyond the left side of the vehicle; or

> (b) **signalling device** — by means of a stop lamp or lamps on the rear of the vehicle which shall emit a red or amber light and which shall be actuated upon application of the service or foot brake and which may or may not be incorporated with one or more rear lamps.

(9) **Definition** — For the purposes of subsections (1) and (8), "vehicle" includes a street car equipped with turn signals or brake lights, as the case may be.

Commentary

Prior to turning, the driver of the turning vehicle shall first see if the turn can be made in safety and, if the operation of any other vehicle may be affected, shall give a signal plainly visible to the other vehicle (subs. (1)). When moving from a parked position, the driver shall obey the same two requirements (subs. (2)).

Signals shall be given by the hand (subss. (3), (4)) or by a mechanical or electrical signal device (subs. (3), (6)). Cyclists shall use manual signals (subss. (4), (5)). Signalling devices shall only be used to signal (subs (7)). When stopping or suddenly decreasing speed, a hand signal may be required (subs. (8)) if the vehicle does not have stop lamps.

For purposes of turning and stopping, a vehicle includes a street car.

Case Law

Quasi-Criminal

Nature of Duty

R. v. Lebedorf, [1962] O.W.N. 233 (H.C.) — Subsection (1) creates two separate offences: one offence is the failure to see first that such movement can be made in safety; the second offence is failure to give a signal plainly visible to the operator of any other vehicle that may be affected by such movement.

R. v. L. (M.V.) (1988), 12 M.V.R. (2d) 33, 62 Alta. L.R. (2d) 44, 90 A.R. 164 (Prov. Ct.) — The accused was charged under s. 95(2) of the Highway Traffic Act (Alta.). The charge alleged that she made a left turn under conditions in which such a turn could not be completed in safety. The facts indicated that another car was approaching the intersection from the opposite direction with its right turn signal light operating. The accused testified that she saw the car's wheels turn slightly and that the tires kicked up dust and gravel at a point where the right hand turn lane began. The accused also testified that her passenger said, "she is going to turn." The accused's vehicle entered the intersection and was involved in a fatal accident with the approaching vehicle which did not turn. The accused was acquitted. It was held that the offence in question was a strict liability offence. The accused had established on a balance of probabilities that she had exercised reasonable care in the circumstances. Accordingly she was entitled to be acquitted.

R. v. Dillman, 2008 ONCJ 101, 68 M.V.R. (5th) 272, [2008] O.J. No. 1120, 2008 CarswellOnt 1596 (C.J.) — Section 142(1) of the Act is an offence of strict liability. Where the visibility of oncoming traffic is limited, safety required that left turning drivers make allowances for predictable shortcomings and the potential negligence of drivers who may soon appear. Safe left turners are not entitled to assume that all other drivers will strictly adhere to speed limits or pay perfect attention to the road ahead but it would be an unreasonable standard of care and tantamount to imposing absolute liability to hold that a turn was not made in safety because the accident was caused by gross speed or gross inattention of an oncoming driver.

Civil

Patterson v. A.G. Can. (1958), 41 M.P.R. 121 (N.S. C.A.) — The act of turning from one side of a road to the other requires care, caution and adequate warning. It requires an alertness to observe the movement of vehicles approaching from in front and from behind, and the forming of a proper judgment as to what is the best thing to do under the particular circumstances.

Payne v. Lane, [1949] O.W.N. 284 (H.C.); *Stadler v. Blyth* (1951), 1 W.W.R. (N.S.) 830 (Sask. C.A.) — Since the act of turning across the roadway involves the possibility of placing other drivers in a position of jeopardy the onus resting on the turning driver is a particularly heavy one.

Myers v. Vermochin, [1948] 1 D.L.R. 1 (S.C.C.) — The motorist is required by a signal to give warning of his intention to turn, and it therefore follows that such signals must be given in sufficient time to act as a timely warning to the following or approaching traffic.

Sawitsky v. Sielski (1961), 27 D.L.R. (2d) 748 (Sask C.A.) — In the absence of a plainly visible signal of intention to turn, there cannot be any duty on an approaching driver to yield the right of way.

Peek v. S. Cunard & Co. (1958), 40 M.P.R. 236 (N.S. C.A.); *Leonard McLaughlin Motors Ltd. v. Barnes*, [1935] 1 W.W.R. 598 (Man. C.A.) — It is not enough merely to give a signal in order to acquire a right of way to make a turn. Such signal is separate from the additional duty to see that the turn can be made in safety, and the signal may be of no avail if there is an absence of care before and during the turn.

Lloyd v. Henderson, [1963] 2 O.R. 110 (C.A.) — It is negligence to signal and turn without looking to see if other vehicles are approaching from behind.

Guimont v. Williston (1980), 30 N.B.R. (2d) 178, 70 A.P.R. 178 (C.A.); reversing (1980), 29 N.B.R. (2d) 134, 66 A.P.R. 134 (Q.B.) — A driver who turned simultaneously with signalling, colliding with a cyclist whom he had failed to notice passing on the right, was held to have failed in his duty to warn other users of the highway of his intention.

Morrison v. Dunlap, [1959] O.W.N. 164, 18 D.L.R. (2d) 393 (C.A.) — In ascertaining whether the movement can be made in safety, the duty to look cannot be discharged by the driver claiming that he did not see the other car, unless on the evidence there was a reasonable excuse for failure to see it.

Harrison v. Bourn, [1958] S.C.R. 733; *MacKenzie v. Robar*, [1953] 1 D.L.R. 449 (S.C.C.) — Where the other car is clearly in view all the time the turn is being made, it is negligence not to see what is clearly visible.

Weinstein v. Schipper, [1961] O.W.N. 300 (Co. Ct.); *Tiede v. Mifflin*, [1965] 2 O.R. 489, 51 D.L.R. (2d) 200 (Co. Ct.); *Chatten v. Armstrong*, [1968] 1 O.R. 497 (C.A.) — The turn indicators had inadvertently been left operating. It was held to be negligence to leave them on when not intending to make a turn and other drivers were entitled to rely on such indicators within reason.

Harris Tpt. Ltd. v. Cummings (1973), 6 N.B.R. (2d) 77 (C.A.) — The defendant was solely at fault in signalling a left turn and subsequently turning right into plaintiff's path.

Collision With Following Vehicles

Coates v. Toronto St. Catharines Tpt. Ltd., [1941] O.R. 371, [1941] 4 D.L.R. 483 (C.A.) — Although it has been held that a very heavy onus rests on the following driver in the event of a collision with the car ahead (*Ottawa Brick Co. v. Marsh*, [1940] S.C.R. 392), it is also true that an imperative duty rests on the driver ahead, when about to make a left turn, to see that he can do so safely.

R. v. Anderson, [1946] S.C.R. 129; *Hipple v. Registrar of Motor Vehicles*, [1955] O.W.N. 483 (H.C.) — The other party is entitled to rely on the driver complying with the provisions of the section to ascertain if the turn could be made in safety, and also to give a plainly visible signal.

Nicol v. Bowman, [1953] O.R. 624 (C.A.); *Vinegar v Hatheway* (1953), 33 M.P.R. 39 (N.B. C.A.); *McGee v. Smith* (1964), 48 D.L.R. (2d) 476 (N.B. C.A.) — If a driver proposes to turn, he or she must look into the rear vision mirror in ample time before commencing the turn and, if there is traffic approaching, must signal his or her intention to turn in time to give the following driver adequate warning or wait until the other driver has passed. The driver of the following car is entitled to assume that this will be done, and will not be guilty of negligence contributing to the accident if the leading vehicle, without previous signal, suddenly begins to turn at practically the same moment that he or she gives the signal.

Kowalchuk v. Regnier, [1949] 2 W.W.R. 321, [1949] 4 D.L.R. 54 (Man. C.A.); *Auld v. Wallace's Moving & Storage Ltd.* (1973), 6 N.S.R. (2d) 214 (C.A.) — A driver who did not look in his mirror for oncoming traffic at the material time has not taken reasonable care; the fact that he looked at some other time does not cure his fault.

Nicol v. Bowman, *supra* — The fact that there was an intersection close ahead and that the leading vehicle slowed its speed were not sufficient grounds alone upon which to hold that the following driver should have anticipated that the leading vehicle might make a left turn.

Southorn v. Casey (1957), 10 D.L.R. (2d) 333 (Ont. C.A.) — The following driver should have been put on his guard by the movements of the vehicle ahead and liability was apportioned.

Patterson v. A.G. Can. (1958), 41 M.P.R. 121 (N.S. C.A.) — Fault will also be apportioned where, even though a signal has not been given, the turn is not so hurried that avoiding action should not have been taken by the following vehicle.

Auld v. Wallace's Moving & Storage Ltd., [1975] 2 S.C.R. 820, 9 N.S.R. (2d) 434, 2 N.R. 602, 50 D.L.R. (3d) 575; reversing (1973), 6 N.S.R. (2d) 214 (C.A.) — Where the plaintiff pulled left without warning and was struck by the defendant's overtaking truck, the defendant was held 100% at fault by a jury for his failure to signify his intention to pass by sounding his horn.

Pulling Out From Curb

Myers v. Hoffman, [1955] O.R. 965, 1 D.L.R. (2d) 278 (H.C.) — The driver who made a turn across the road from a stopped position without giving a proper signal was held solely responsible for the collision that resulted.

Spratt v. Edmonton, [1942] 2 W.W.R. 456 (Alta. S.C.) — Where a bus pulling out from the curb had to brake suddenly to avoid an overtaking car, the bus operators were held liable for injury to a passenger in the bus injured by the sudden stop.

Schwinghamer v. Dauvin (1956), 19 W.W.R. 280 (Sask. C.A.); *Zaisar v. Nelson* (1953), 9 W.W.R. (N.S.) 47 (Sask. C.A.) — The duty of the driver of a vehicle backing out from the curb into the lane of traffic to take care that he can do so safely is even greater than the duty of one making a turn. At the same time, however, where motor vehicles are parked on both sides of the highway drivers of cars in the centre lane must also be alert to the possibility of parked cars backing away from the curb.

Signalling a Stop (s. 142(8))

Labelle v. Koudriavtzev, [1946] Que. S.C. 335 — A sudden stop is one of the most dangerous moves that a driver can make and can only be excused when it is made for the purpose of protecting life, property or avoiding an accident. The flashing of the rear signal lights can at best be only an indication to the traffic approaching from the rear that the driver intends to slow down or make the usual kind of stop but can in no way be interpreted as an indication that a driver is going to make an abrupt and sudden stop.

Ruetz v. Goetz, [1955] O.W.N. 879 (C.A.) — However, there is no general rule that a driver who stops suddenly without warning when a car is following him is not acting reasonably. There may be circumstances which compel him to stop so suddenly that he cannot reasonably be expected to give warning to cars behind him, and the reasonableness of his actions will depend on the facts of the particular case.

Beaumont v. Ruddy, [1932] O.R. 441 (C.A.); *Bridger v. O'Reilly* (1956), 39 M.P.R. 185 (Nfld. T.D.); *Aylward v. Quillen*, 16 M.P.R. 435, [1943] 2 D.L.R. 399 (N.S. C.A.) — There is a duty on the following driver under s. 136 [now s. 158] not to drive too closely, and a general duty to exercise care and keep a lookout; if he or she collides with the leading vehicle there is a heavy onus on him or her.

O'Brien v. Lawlor (1932), 41 O.W.N. 444 (C.A.) — A jury verdict of negligence on the part of the defendant consisting in "not taking proper precaution of traffic behind" was held not to be too vague where the statement of claim had raised the issue that the defendant's car ought not to have been stopped without warning to traffic behind, and that issue had been dealt with in the directions to the jury.

Cluney v. Bowser (1960), 45 M.P.R. 14, 25 D.L.R. (2d) 387 (N.S. C.A.) — The defendant stopped his truck without any signal just after passing the crest of a hill, and the plaintiff ran into the rear of the truck. Breach of the obligation to give a signal was held to be *prima facie* evidence of negligence and the Court inferred that if a proper signal had been given, the plaintiff would either have avoided the collision or sustained less damage than he did.

Findlay v. Diver (1992), 7 O.R. (3d) 48, 35 M.V.R. (2d) 150, 54 O.A.C. 7 (C.A.) — Modifying *Beaumont v. Ruddy*, *supra*, a correct instruction to a jury is that generally speaking, when one car runs into another from behind, the circumstances can lead to an inference that the driver of the following car was negligent. This is particularly so where the accident did not occur in broad daylight and on dry pavement.

Related Provisions: See O. Reg. 316/03, Operation of Off-Road Vehicles on Highways, s. 24(12).

142.1 (1) Requirement to yield to bus from bus bay — Every driver of a vehicle in the lane of traffic adjacent to a bus bay shall yield the right of way to the driver of a bus who has indicated his or her intention, as prescribed, to re-enter that lane from the bus bay.

(2) Bus not to signal until ready — The driver of a bus shall not indicate his or her intention to re-enter the lane of traffic adjacent to a bus bay until the driver is ready to re-enter traffic.

(3) When bus must wait — No driver of a bus shall re-enter the lane of traffic adjacent to a bus bay and move into the path of a vehicle or street car if the vehicle or street car is so close that it is impractical for the driver to yield the right of way.

(4) Regulations — The Lieutenant Governor in Council may make regulations for the purposes of this section,

(a) defining bus and bus bay;

(b) prescribing the manner in which a bus driver shall indicate his or her intention to re-enter the lane that is adjacent to a bus bay;

(c) prescribing signs, signal devices and markings for bus bays;

(d) prescribing the standards, specifications and location of the signs, signal devices and markings;

(e) prescribing standards for operating and maintaining any signal devices prescribed under clause (c).

1994, c. 27, s. 138(12)

Related Provisions: See O. Reg. 393/02, Definitions and Requirements Under Section 142.1 of The Act (Yielding Right of Way To Buses).

143. U-Turns prohibited — No driver or operator of a vehicle upon a highway shall turn the vehicle so as to proceed in the opposite direction when,

(a) upon a curve where traffic approaching the vehicle from either direction cannot be seen by the driver of the vehicle within a distance of 150 metres;

(b) on a railway crossing or within 30 metres of a railway crossing;

(c) upon an approach to or near the crest of a grade where the vehicle cannot be seen by the driver of another vehicle approaching from either direction within 150 metres; or

(d) within 150 metres of a bridge, viaduct or tunnel where the driver's view is obstructed within such distance.

Case Law

Miles v. Michaud, [1939] 2 W.W.R. 497 (Alta. S.C.); *Ivey v. Guernsey Breeders' Dairy Ltd.* (1941), 56 B.C.R. 342 (C.A.); *Donaher v. Richard* (1981), 37 N.B.R. (2d) 1, 97

A.P.R. 1 (Q.B.) — Even where U-turns are not prohibited, there will clearly be a heavy onus on the driver not to attempt the movement unless it is safe to do so. If he places another driver in jeopardy he will be liable wholly or in part for the consequences of the emergency he has created.

Day v. Toronto Transit Comm., [1940] S.C.R. 433; *Nykiforuk v. McTavish*, [1941] 2 W.W.R. 225, [1941] 3 D.L.R. 332 (Alta. C.A.) — No fault was imputable to the driver making the U-turn.

Arnott v. Schell (1984), 28 M.V.R. 277 (N.B. Q.B.) — An unsafe U-turn was made as the defendant turned without checking her mirror a second time. The plaintiff was an inexperienced motorcyclist driving above the speed limit. The defendant was found 40% liable.

Prasad v. Frandsen (1985), 60 B.C.L.R. 343 (B.C. S.C.) — The driver of the plaintiff's vehicle, which was engaged in an illegal U-turn, was struck by the defendant's speeding vehicle. Both drivers were found equally at fault.

R. v. Dockman (1996), 23 M.V.R. (3d) 67 (Ont. C.A.) — It is an offence to make a U-turn near the crest of a grade without the driver being able to see oncoming vehicles for 150 metres. The unsafe or imprudent nature of the turn is not an element of the offence.

Related Provisions: See R.R.O. 1990, Reg. 615, Signs, s. 23.

144. (1) Definitions — In this section,

"driver" includes an operator of a street car;

"emergency vehicle" means,

(a) a vehicle while used by a person in the lawful performance of his or her duties as a police officer, on which a siren is continuously sounding and from which intermittent flashes of red light or red and blue light are visible in all directions, or

(b) either of the following vehicles, on which a siren is continuously sounding and from which intermittent flashes of red light are visible in all directions:

(i) a fire department vehicle while proceeding to a fire or responding to, but not while returning from, a fire alarm or other emergency call, or

(ii) an ambulance while responding to an emergency call or being used to transport a patient or injured person in an emergency situation;

(c) [Repealed 2007, c. 13, s. 18.]

(d) [Repealed 2007, c. 13, s. 18.]

"intersection" includes any portion of a highway indicated by markings on the surface of the roadway as a crossing place for pedestrians;

"pedestrian" includes a person in a wheelchair;

"vehicle" includes a street car.

(2) [Repealed without coming into force 2006, c. 21, Sched. F, s. 10.1(1).]

(3) [Repealed without coming into force 2006, c. 21, Sched. F, s. 10.1(1).]

(4) Commencement subs. (2), (3) — Subsections (2) and (3) come into force on a day to be named by proclamation of the Lieutenant Governor.

(5) Where to stop — intersection — A driver who is directed by a traffic control signal erected at an intersection to stop his or her vehicle shall stop,

(a) at the sign or roadway marking indicating where the stop is to be made;

(b) if there is no sign or marking, immediately before entering the nearest crosswalk; or

(c) if there is no sign, marking or crosswalk, immediately before entering the intersection.

(6) Where to stop — non-intersection — A driver who is directed by a traffic control signal erected at a location other than at an intersection to stop his or her vehicle shall stop,

(a) at the sign or roadway marking indicating where the stop is to be made;

(b) if there is no sign or marking, immediately before entering the nearest crosswalk; or

(c) if there is no sign, marking or crosswalk, not less than five metres before the nearest traffic control signal.

(7) Yielding to pedestrians — When under this section a driver is permitted to proceed, the driver shall yield the right of way to pedestrians lawfully within a crosswalk.

(8) Yielding to traffic — When under this section a driver is permitted to proceed, he or she shall yield the right of way to traffic lawfully using an intersection or, where traffic control signals are erected where a private road or driveway meets a highway, lawfully using the area controlled by the traffic control signals.

(9) Signs — The provisions of this section are subject to any sign, as prescribed by the regulations, forbidding a left turn, right turn, through movement or combination thereof that is posted at an intersection and every driver shall obey every such sign.

(10) Obeying lane lights — Every driver shall obey every traffic control signal that applies to the lane that he or she is in.

Proposed Amendment — 144(10)

(10) Obeying lane lights — Every driver shall obey every traffic control signal that applies to the lane that he or she is in and, for greater certainty, where both a traffic control signal that is not a bicycle traffic control signal and a bicycle traffic control signal apply to the same lane,

(a) a person riding or operating a bicycle in that lane shall obey the bicycle traffic control signal; and

(b) a person driving a vehicle other than a bicycle in that lane shall obey the traffic control signal that is not a bicycle traffic control signal.

2015, c. 14, s. 40(1) [To come into force January 1, 2017.]

(11) Exception — Despite subsection (10), a driver of a road service vehicle in a left-turn lane may proceed through the intersection without turning to the left if the movement can be safely made, there is showing a circular green or green arrow indication for the through traffic movement and the driver,

(a) where the applicable left-turn traffic control signal is showing a circular red indication, first brings the vehicle to a stop; and

(b) where the operation of any other vehicle may be affected, indicates his or her intention to proceed through the intersection without turning to the left by giving a plainly visible signal to the driver or operator of the other vehicle.

(12) **Green light** — A driver approaching a traffic control signal showing a circular green indication and facing the indication may proceed forward or turn left or right unless otherwise directed.

(13) **Flashing green** — A driver approaching a traffic control signal showing a circular flashing green indication or a solid or flashing left turn green arrow indication in conjunction with a circular green indication and facing the indication may, despite subsection 141(5), proceed forward or turn left or right unless otherwise directed.

(14) **Green arrow** — Every driver approaching a traffic control signal showing one or more green arrow indications only or in combination with a circular red or circular amber indication and facing the indication may proceed only to follow the direction shown by the arrow.

(15) **Amber light** — Every driver approaching a traffic control signal showing a circular amber indication and facing the indication shall stop his or her vehicle if he or she can do so safely, otherwise he or she may proceed with caution.

(16) **Amber arrow** — Every driver approaching a traffic control signal showing an amber arrow indication only or in combination with another indication and facing the indication shall stop his or her vehicle if he or she can do so safely, otherwise he or she may proceed with caution to follow the direction shown by the amber arrow indication.

(17) **Flashing amber** — Every driver approaching a traffic control signal showing a flashing circular amber indication and facing the indication may proceed with caution.

(18) **Red light** — Every driver approaching a traffic control signal showing a circular red indication and facing the indication shall stop his or her vehicle and shall not proceed until a green indication is shown.

(18.1) **Certificate of offence — owner–red light camera evidence** — A person who issues a certificate of offence and offence notice under subsection 3(2) of the *Provincial Offences Act* for a contravention of subsection (18) shall, despite that Act and the regulations under that Act, specify this subsection, instead of subsection (18), as the provision that was contravened, if,

(a) the person who issues the certificate of offence and offence notice believes that the offence was committed on the basis of evidence obtained through the use of a red light camera system; and

(b) the defendant is being charged as the owner of the vehicle.

(18.2) Certificate of offence — driver–red light camera evidence — A person who issues a certificate of offence and offence notice under subsection 3(2) of the *Provincial Offences Act* for a contravention of subsection (18) shall, despite that Act and the regulations under that Act, specify this subsection, instead of subsection (18), as the provision that was contravened, if,

(a) the person who issues the certificate of offence and offence notice believes that the offence was committed on the basis of evidence obtained through the use of a red light camera system; and

(b) the defendant is being charged as the driver of the vehicle.

(18.3) Deemed to specify subs. (18) — A certificate of offence or offence notice that specifies subsection (18.1) or (18.2) as the provision that was contravened shall be deemed to specify that subsection (18) was contravened.

(18.4) No dismissal — No charge shall be dismissed, and no certificate of offence shall be quashed, on the basis that a certificate of offence or offence notice specifies subsection (18.1) or (18.2), instead of subsection (18), as the provision that was contravened.

(18.5) No amendment — A certificate of offence that specifies subsection (18), (18.1) or (18.2) as the provision that was contravened shall not be amended to specify another of those subsection without the consent of the prosecutor and the defendant.

(18.6) Purpose of subss. (18.1) to (18.5) — The purpose of subsections (18.1) to (18.5) is to facilitate the use of computer systems that are maintained by the Government of Ontario for recording and processing information related to provincial offences and that depend, in order to make certain distinctions, on different provision numbers being specified in certificates of offences.

(19) Exception — turn — Despite subsection (18) and subject to subsection (14), a driver, after stopping his or her vehicle and yielding the right of way to traffic lawfully approaching so closely that to proceed would constitute an immediate hazard, may,

(a) turn to the right; or

(b) turn to the left from a one-way street into a one-way street,

without a green indication being shown.

(19.1) Exception — white vertical bar indication — Despite subsection (18), a driver operating a bus or street car on a scheduled transit authority route approaching a traffic control signal showing a white vertical bar indication may, with caution, proceed forward or turn right or left.

(20) Exception — emergency vehicle — Despite subsection (18), a driver of an emergency vehicle, after stopping the vehicle, may proceed without a green indication being shown if it is safe to do so.

(21) Stopping at flashing red light — Every driver approaching a traffic control signal and facing a flashing circular red indication shall stop his or her vehicle, shall yield the right of way to traffic approaching so closely that to proceed would constitute an immediate hazard and, having so yielded the right of way, may proceed.

(22) **Pedestrian crossing** — Where portions of a roadway are marked for pedestrian use, no pedestrian shall cross the roadway except within a portion so marked.

(23) **Pedestrian — green light** — Subject to subsections (24) and (27), a pedestrian approaching a traffic control signal showing a circular green indication or a straight-ahead green arrow indication and facing the indication may cross the roadway.

(24) **Pedestrian — stopping at flashing green light** — No pedestrian approaching a traffic control signal and facing a flashing circular green indication or a solid or a flashing left turn arrow indication in conjunction with a circular green indication shall enter the roadway.

(25) **Pedestrian — stopping at red or amber light** — No pedestrian approaching a traffic control signal and facing a red or amber indication shall enter the roadway.

(26) **Pedestrian control signals — walk** — Where pedestrian control signals are installed and show a "walk" indication, every pedestrian facing the indication may cross the roadway in the direction of the indication despite subsections (24) and (25).

(27) **Pedestrian control signals — don't walk** — No pedestrian approaching pedestrian control signals and facing a solid or flashing "don't walk" indication shall enter the roadway.

(28) **Pedestrian right of way** — Every pedestrian who lawfully enters a roadway in order to cross may continue the crossing as quickly as reasonably possible despite a change in the indication he or she is facing and, for purposes of the crossing, has the right of way over vehicles.

(29) **Riding in crosswalks prohibited** — No person shall ride or operate a bicycle across a roadway within a crosswalk at an intersection or at a location, other than an intersection, which is controlled by a traffic control signal system.

(30) **Symbols** — The "walk" or "don't walk" pedestrian control indications referred to in this section may be shown as symbols as prescribed by the regulations.

(31) **Erection of traffic control signals and signal systems** — Subject to subsection (31.1), no traffic control signal system or traffic control signal used in conjunction with a traffic control signal system shall be erected or installed except in accordance with an approval obtained from a person designated to give such approvals by the municipality or other authority that has jurisdiction over the highway or the intersection.

(31.1) **Same, on connecting links** — No traffic control signal system or traffic control signal used in conjunction with a traffic control signal system shall be erected or installed on a highway designated as a connecting link under subsection 21(1) of the *Public Transportation and Highway Improvement Act* except in accordance with an approval obtained from the Minister or an official of the Ministry authorized by the Minister to grant such approval.

(31.2) Penalty for disobeying amber light — Every person who contravenes subsection (15) is guilty of an offence and on conviction is liable to a fine of not less than $150 and not more than $500.

(31.2.1) Penalty for disobeying red light — Every person who contravenes subsection (18) is guilty of an offence and on conviction is liable to a fine of not less than $200 and not more than $1,000.

(31.3) Offence — Every person who contravenes subsection (7) is guilty of an offence and on conviction is liable to a fine of not less than $150 and not more than $500.

(32) Regulations — The Lieutenant Governor in Council may make regulations,

(a) prescribing the standards or specifications of a traffic control signal system;

(b) prescribing the location of traffic control signals and signal systems;

(c) prescribing standards for operating and maintaining a traffic control signal system;

(d) regulating the use and operation of traffic control signals and signal systems.

Proposed Addition — 144(32)(e)

(e) prescribing a bicycle symbol for bicycle traffic control signals.

2015, c. 14, s. 40(3) [To come into force January 1, 2017.]

1994, c. 27, s. 138(13); 1996, c. 33, s. 14; 1998, c. 5, s. 26; 1998, c. 38, s. 3; 2005, c. 26, Sched. A, s. 22; 2006, c. 19, Sched. T, s. 6; 2006, c. 21, Sched. F, s. 10.1(1); 2007, c. 13, s. 18; 2009, c. 5, s. 44; 2015, c. 14, s. 40(2).

Commentary

A driver who is directed by a traffic signal (light) to stop shall stop where indicated or, in the absence of indication, where it is safe to do so (subs. (5)). Subsection (6) governs where lights are not located at an intersection.

Where a driver is permitted to proceed, he or she shall yield to pedestrians lawfully in the crosswalk (subs. (7)) or vehicles lawfully using the intersection (subs. (8)).

The rules applying to traffic lights are superseded by signs regarding conduct (subs. (10)).

Driver must obey signals applying to their lane (subss. (10), (11)).

Duties are prescribed for drivers approaching a: green light (subs. (12)); flashing green light (subs. (13)); green arrow (subs. (14)); amber light (subs. (15)); amber arrow (subs. (16)); flashing amber (subs. (17)); red light (subs. (18)); amd flashing red light (subs. (21)).

A right turn may be made at a red light under certain circumstances (subs. (19)).

Emergency vehicles must stop and may proceed through a red light when safe to do so (subs. (20)).

Pedestrians must cross only where they are permitted to do so (subs. (22)). The obligations of pedestrians are set out regarding: green lights (subs. (23)); flashing green lights (subs. (24)); red and amber lights (subs. (25)); walk signs (subs. (26)); and don't walk signs (subs. (27)). Pedestrians who lawfully enter intersections have the right of way (subs. (28)).

Cyclists may not ride in a crosswalk (subs. (29)).

As to the erection of signs and signals, see subss. (30)–(32).

The Red Light Camera Pilot Projects Act, 1998, S.O. 1998, c. 38 (in force November 20, 2000) permits evidence obtained from red light cameras to be used in areas designated by regulation for the purpose of enforcing subsection 144(18) of the Highway Traffic Act (failing to stop at a red light or proceeding before the light turns green). O. Reg. 277/99 dealing with the admissibility and use of Red Light Camera System evidence in proceedings under the Act, was brought into force contemporaneously with the Act.

Case Law

Quasi-Criminal

Obedience to Lights

R. v. Potapchuk, [1963] 1 O.R. 40 (H.C.) — On a prosecution for a failure to comply with the provisions of s. 144(6) proof of the existence of a signal light traffic control system at an intersection is *prima facie* evidence that the erection and use of such light has been approved as required by s. 144(31). It was immaterial for purposes of the prosecution whether or not the erection of the lights had been approved, but that any departure from the required specifications would become material and important if the defence established that by reason of such departure the accused did not and, if keeping a reasonable lookout, could not have seen the signal.

R. v. Harrington (1977), 3 B.C.L.R. 217 (Co. Ct.) — The accused on appeal was acquitted as the trial Judge held that the accused had a duty to anticipate when the lights would change from green to amber. The Appeal Court held that there was no such duty but that the accused had to exercise his discretion and the Court should then decide whether his discretion was properly exercised.

R. v. Pszczola (2007), 61 M.V.R. (5th) 25, 2007 CarswellOnt 7966 (C.J.) — There was no authority that supported the concept that control of an intersection existed that would afford a defence to a charge.

Civil

General

Joseph Eva Ltd. v. Reeves, [1938] 2 K.B. 393, [1938] 2 All E.R. 115 (C.A.); *Payne v. Lane*, [1949] O.W.N. 284 (H.C.) — The effect of traffic regulation by traffic lights is to give to the traffic in whose favour the lights are showing the monopoly of the crossing, and such traffic may proceed to cross the intersection on the assumption that any driver approaching against the red light will stop and not enter.

Boxenbaum v. Wise, [1944] S.C.R. 292, [1944] 4 D.L.R. 199 — A driver reaching the intersection at a reasonable rate of speed and seeing the green light will not be negligent in slightly increasing speed as he or she clears the intersection.

Chaschuk (Hurlbert) v. Lebel (1981), 12 M.V.R. 228 (Ont. C.A.) — Traffic lights control the flow of traffic. Drivers of vehicles and pedestrians are entitled to proceed on the supposition that such signals will be obeyed. If that were not the case there would obviously be chaos. To enter into an intersection in the face of a traffic signal which has just turned red may be negligence of the moment. To enter an intersection in the face of a traffic signal that has been red for a significant period of time is negligence that constitutes a marked departure from the standards by which responsible and competent people in charge of motor vehicles habitually govern themselves. It is thus gross negligence.

Flood v. Wellband, 1 W.W.R. (N.S.) 257, [1951] 2 D.L.R. 284 (Man. C.A.) — A driver crossing with the lights is not thereby relieved from the duty to take care. Although he or she is not bound to assume or provide for a disregard of the signals, if the driver sees a vehicle proceeding in disobedience of the signals, he or she ought to take all reasonable steps to avoid a collision.

Vertulia v. Kratz, [1956] O.R. 884 (C.A.); *Horsman v. McGarvey*, [1983] 3 W.W.R. 564 (B.C. C.A.) — If the driver does not see the vehicle until too late to avoid it he or she will not be guilty of negligence.

Elmhurst v. Bobbitt (1962), 41 W.W.R. 153 (Man. C.A.) — A vehicle which enters an intersection on the green light and is delayed by other vehicles from completing the crossing until after the light changes is entitled to complete the crossing in precedence to cross-traffic.

Allen v. Brazeau, [1967] 2 O.R. 665, 65 D.L.R. (2d) 37 (C.A.) — Where both drivers allege that the other went through a red light, the jury should make a finding on this issue. If they fail to do so, a new trial may be ordered.

Muffitt v. Fleming, [1938] O.R. 358, [1938] 3 D.L.R. 84 (C.A.); *Goodwin v. Wrycraft*, [1966] 1 O.R. 26, 52 D.L.R. (2d) 306 (C.A.); *Johnson v. Bitz* (1959), 30 W.W.R. 396, 21 D.L.R. (2d) 733 (Sask. C.A.) — Vehicles proceeding with the green light but seeking to make a left turn in the intersection are in a servient position to the "through" traffic and would also be obliged to comply with the requirements of ss. 141 and 142 as to turns.

Bardos v. Mooring (1974), 9 N.S.R. (2d) 178 (C.A.) — The plaintiff entered the intersection facing a flashing yellow signal light and the defendant had entered the intersection facing a flashing red signal light. Although the defendant had entered before the plaintiff, the defendant was held 100% at fault for failing to yield the right of way.

R. v. Calleja, 2013 ONCJ 7, 2013 CarswellOnt 94, 39 M.V.R. (6th) 162, [2013] O.J. No. 116 (Ont. Ct. J.) — The relationship between ss. 140 and 144 was canvassed.

R. v. Anderson (2012), 40 M.V.R. (6th) 342, 2012 ONCJ 781, 2012 CarswellOnt 16437, [2012] O.J. No. 6217 (Ont. C.J.) — Drivers of vehicles should, when travelling on a road where there are no crosswalks, lights or other pedestrian crossovers, expect to do so without fear of a pedestrian walking in front of the path of the vehicles.

Emergencies

R. v. Fryer (1969), 2 D.L.R. (3d) 704 (B.C. Co. Ct.) — An ambulance carrying an accident victim with clearly apparent head injuries and in need of prompt medical attention is proceeding on an emergency and is therefor an emergency vehicle and the driver is absolved from obeying traffic signals provided he or she exercises due care.

R. v. Hammond (1978), 1 M.V.R. 210 (Ont. Co. Ct.) — In responding to an emergency call, a police officer failed to stop at a red light. The police officer activated the emergency lights on the police vehicle and sounded his horn prior to proceeding through the intersection. It was held that failure to stop at the red light constituted neither an offence of absolute liability nor an offence requiring *mens rea*.

Mahon v. Nova Scotia (A.G.) (1986), 73 N.S.R. (2d) 137, 176 A.P.R. 137 (T.D.) — The plaintiff was found 75% at fault. An ambulance went through a red light and collided with the plaintiff's vehicle going through a green light. The plaintiff had consumed twice the legal limit of alcohol. The defendant disobeyed a light and failed to keep a proper lookout. The plaintiff had a high level of alcohol in his blood which may have precluded him from keeping a proper lookout.

Vysek v. Dennis (1984), 54 A.R. 313 (Q.B.) — An ambulance with its siren going, red light flashing and headlights on stopped at a red light, then proceeded slowly across the intersection while traffic was heavy. The ambulance was struck by a vehicle whose driver was listening to the radio and failed to hear or see it. The parties were each found 50% at fault.

R. v. Kurtzman (1991), 31 M.V.R. (2d) 1, 4 O.R. (3d) 417, 66 C.C.C. (3d) 161, 50 O.A.C. 20 (C.A.) — The words used in s. 144(18) are mandatory and clearly do not anticipate a defence of due diligence or reasonable care. Under s. 144(20), a defence of due diligence may be available to those who, after stopping, exercise all reasonable care to ascertain whether it is safe to proceed. The accused in this case, however, failed to bring his vehicle to a full stop. The language of s. 144(20) is mandatory and absolute and not subject to an inquiry into the reasonableness of the driver's efforts. Even if s. 144(18) created a strict liability offence rather than an offence of absolute liability, the accused ambulance driver did not exercise due diligence.

Atherton v. Boycott (1991), 32 M.V.R. (2d) 69 (Ont. Gen. Div.); additional reasons at (September 20, 1991), Doc. 1327/87 (Ont. Gen. Div.) — The plaintiff, entering an intersection on a green light, was struck by a police cruiser which entered the intersection on a red light with its flashing lights and siren on. The plaintiff did not hear the siren, as he had his radio on. When the police cruiser entered the intersection, the driver slowed from 50 m.p.h. to 30 m.p.h. The plaintiff sued the police officer for damages for personal injuries. The action was allowed in part. Section 144(20) of the Highway Traffic Act permits a driver of an emergency vehicle to proceed without a green indication being shown after stopping the vehicle and if it is safe to proceed. Not only did the defendant fail to stop for the red light, but he entered the intersection at an excessive rate of speed. He failed to discharge the duty of care imposed upon him, and he was negligent in the operation of the police cruiser. The plaintiff, on the other hand, had not been keeping a proper lookout, or he would have realized that it was not safe to proceed. Liability was apportioned 75% to the defendant and 25% to the plaintiff.

Pedestrians

Flood v. Wellband, 1 W.W.R. (N.S.) 257, [1951] 2 D.L.R. 284 (Man. C.A.); *Sinclair v. Snider* (1952), 6 W.W.R. (N.S.) 525 (B.C. S.C.) — Pedestrians, just as much as motorists, are bound to obey traffic lights, and if they choose to try to cross against the lights, or at a point where they are not supposed to cross, they will generally be found at least partly responsible for any collision that results.

Flynn v. Saunders, [1947] O.W.N. 518 (H.C.); affirmed [1947] O.W.N. 975 (C.A.); *Mosher v. Parker*, [1938] 3 W.W.R. 570 (B.C. S.C.); *Mitchell v. Registrar of Motor Vehicles*, [1949] 2 W.W.R. 35 (Man. K.B.) — A pedestrian who has commenced crossing an intersection with the green light in his or her favour is entitled to complete the crossing if the lights change before he or she reaches the other side, and drivers who have stopped for the lights must ascertain that the crossing is free before proceeding.

Salmon v. Stockwell, [1951] O.W.N. 241 (H.C.); *Burton v. Harding*, [1952] O.W.N. 126, [1952] 3 D.L.R. 302 (C.A.) — However, as soon as the lights change, the pedestrian is called upon to use caution to see that he or she would not be struck by or come in contact with any car, the driver of which might assume that it was safe to proceed into the intersection with the green light. If the pedestrian fails to take such care, he or she may be held contributorily negligent.

Bowes v. Stark, [1949] O.W.N. 779 (H.C.) — A driver turning left and colliding with a pedestrian crossing with the green light must assume the onus of providing contributory negligence on the part of the pedestrian.

B.C. Elec. Ry. Co. v. Farrer, [1955] S.C.R. 757, [1955] 5 D.L.R. 161 — The right of a pedestrian to cross an intersection with the green light or "walk" signal in his favour was not an absolute one and, since he had the opportunity to look and if he had looked he would have seen a bus approaching adversely to the light signal, he was partially to blame for the accident but to a relatively minor degree.

Location of Lights

Maxwell v. Routley, [1951] O.W.N. 361 (H.C.) — The provisions of this section concerning the erection and positioning of lights relate to a situation of permanency and not of temporary arrangement which may develop while a road is being repaired. If it were otherwise it would mean that the instant that part of a street or highway was blocked at an intersection because of repair work the municipality would immediately have to install a new set of traffic lights, or be responsible if somebody failed to observe the old ones. Moreover, the section provides only that the traffic light shall be on the right side of the roadway used by the traffic controlled by it, and nothing is stipulated as to where on the right side of that roadway it is to be located.

Related Provisions: See O. Reg. 34/06, Pre-Empting Traffic Control Signal Devices; R.R.O. 1990, Reg. 615, Signs, ss. 21-22; R.R.O. 1990, Reg. 626, Traffic Control Signal Systems.

145. (1) Blocking intersection — The council of a municipality may by by-law prohibit a driver or street car operator approaching, at an intersection, a traffic control signal showing a circular green or green arrow indication from entering the intersection unless traffic in front of him or her is moving in a manner that would reasonably lead him or her to believe he or she can clear the intersection before the signal indication changes to a circular red indication.

(2) Idem — A by-law passed under subsection (1) does not apply to a driver or street car operator who enters an intersection for the purpose of turning to the right or left into an intersecting highway and signals his or her intention to make the turn prior to entering the intersection.

(3) Idem — A by-law passed under subsection (1) shall apply to all signalized intersections of highways under the jurisdiction of the municipality.

146. (1) Portable signal lights — Despite subsection 144(31), during construction or maintenance activities on or adjacent to a highway, a portable lane control signal system may be operated on the highway in accordance with the regulations by the authority having jurisdiction and control of the highway or any person authorized by that authority.

(2) Green light — A driver or a street car operator approaching a portable lane control signal showing a circular green indication and facing the indication may proceed.

(3) Amber light — Every driver or street car operator approaching a portable lane control signal showing a circular amber indication and facing such indication shall stop his or her vehicle or street car if he or she can do so safely, otherwise he or she may proceed with caution.

(4) Red light — Every driver or street car operator approaching a portable lane control signal showing a circular red indication and facing the indication shall stop his or her vehicle or street car and shall not proceed until a circular green indication is shown.

(5) Where to stop — A driver or operator who is required, under this section, to stop his or her vehicle or street car shall do so at a sign or marking on the highway indicating where a stop is to be made or, if there is no such sign or marking, not less than five metres before the nearest portable lane control signal.

(6) Removing, etc., portable system — No person shall without lawful authority remove, deface or otherwise interfere with a portable lane control signal system.

(6.1) Penalty for disobeying amber light — Every person who contravenes subsection (3) is guilty of an offence and on conviction is liable to a fine of not less than $150 and not more than $500.

(6.2) Penalty for disobeying red light — Every person who contravenes subsection (4) is guilty of an offence and on conviction is liable to a fine of not less than $200 and not more than $1,000.

(7) Regulations re portable lane control devices — The Lieutenant Governor in Council may make regulations,

(a) prescribing standards or specifications for portable lane control signal systems;

(b) prescribing locations where portable lane control signal systems may be erected; and

(c) prescribing standards for operating and maintaining portable lane control signal systems.

1998, c. 5, s. 27; 2009, c. 5, s. 45

Related Provisions: See R.R.O. 1990, Reg. 606, Portable Lane Control Signal Systems.

146.1 (1) Traffic control stop and slow signs — A traffic control person on a roadway or adjacent to a roadway where construction or maintenance work is being carried out may display a traffic control stop or slow sign.

(2) Same — firefighters — A firefighter on a roadway or adjacent to a roadway where an accident has occurred may display a traffic control stop or slow sign.

(3) Driver required to stop — Where a traffic control person or firefighter displays a traffic control stop sign, the driver of any vehicle or street car approaching the person shall stop before reaching him or her and shall not proceed until the traffic control person or firefighter stops displaying the traffic control stop sign.

(4) Driver required to slow down — Where a traffic control person or firefighter displays a traffic control slow sign, the driver of any vehicle or street car approaching the person shall approach the person and proceed past him or her and past the construction or maintenance work or scene of an accident with caution and at a slow rate of speed so as not to endanger any person or vehicle on or adjacent to the roadway.

(5) Unauthorized use of sign — No person other than a traffic control person or firefighter shall display on a highway a traffic control stop or slow sign.

(6) Regulations — The Lieutenant Governor in Council may make regulations prescribing the type, design and specifications of traffic control stop and slow signs.

(7) Definitions — In this section,

"construction or maintenance work" includes work by a utility, including a public utility within the meaning of the *Public Utilities Act* or the *Municipal Act, 2001*, or by a transmitter or distributor within the meaning of the *Electricity Act, 1998*;

"firefighter" has the same meaning as in subsection 1(1) of the *Fire Protection and Prevention Act, 1997*;

"traffic control person" means a person who is directing traffic and,

    (a) is employed by,

        (i) the road authority with jurisdiction over the highway,

        (ii) a public utility within the meaning of the *Public Utilities Act* or the *Municipal Act, 2001*,

        (iii) a transmitter or distributor within the meaning of the *Electricity Act, 1998*, or

        (iv) a person under contract with the road authority, public utility, transmitter or distributor to do construction or maintenance work on or adjacent to the roadway, or

    (b) is employed by or under contract with a person who has been issued a permit or written authorization by the road authority with jurisdiction over the highway to occupy a lane or a portion of a highway in order to undertake work on or adjacent to the highway.

2005, c. 26, Sched. A, s. 23

Case Law

R. v. Krahn (2014), 63 M.V.R. (6th) 257, 2014 BCSC 235, 2014 CarswellBC 343, [2014] B.C.J. No. 245 — The test as to whether it is unsafe to stop for a yellow light before entering a marked crosswalk is an objective one.

Related Provisions: See R.R.O. 1990, Reg. 615, Signs, s. 42.1.

147. (1) Slow vehicles to travel on right side — Any vehicle travelling upon a roadway at less than the normal speed of traffic at that time and place shall, where practicable, be driven in the right-hand lane then available for traffic or as close as practicable to the right hand curb or edge of the roadway.

(2) Exception — Subsection (1) does not apply to a driver of a,

(a) vehicle while overtaking and passing another vehicle proceeding in the same direction;

(b) vehicle while preparing for a left turn at an intersection or into a private road or driveway;

(c) road service vehicle; or

(d) bicycle in a lane designated under subsection 153(2) for travel in the opposite direction of traffic.

2015, c. 14, s. 41

Related Provisions: See s. 132 of the Act dealing with slow driving.

148. (1) Passing meeting vehicles — Every person in charge of a vehicle on a highway meeting another vehicle shall turn out to the right from the centre of the roadway, allowing the other vehicle one-half of the roadway free.

(2) Vehicles or equestrians overtaken — Every person in charge of a vehicle or on horseback on a highway who is overtaken by a vehicle or equestrian travelling at a greater speed shall turn out to the right and allow the overtaking vehicle or equestrian to pass.

(3) Exception — Subsections (1) and (2) do not apply to a person in charge of a road service vehicle or a road-building machine or apparatus while the machine or apparatus is engaged in the construction of a highway.

(4) Vehicles meeting bicycles — Every person in charge of a vehicle on a highway meeting a person travelling on a bicycle shall allow the cyclist sufficient room on the roadway to pass.

(5) Vehicles or equestrians overtaking others — Every person in charge of a vehicle or on horseback on a highway who is overtaking another vehicle or equestrian shall turn out to the left so far as may be necessary to avoid a collision with the vehicle or equestrian overtaken, and the person overtaken is not required to leave more than one-half of the roadway free.

(6) Bicycles overtaken — Every person on a bicycle or motor assisted bicycle who is overtaken by a vehicle or equestrian travelling at a greater speed shall turn out to the right and allow the vehicle or equestrian to pass and the vehicle or equestrian overtaking shall turn out to the left so far as may be necessary to avoid a collision.

(6.1) Same — Every person in charge of a motor vehicle on a highway who is overtaking a person travelling on a bicycle shall, as nearly as may be practicable, leave a distance of not less than one metre between the bicycle and the motor vehicle and shall maintain that distance until safely past the bicycle.

(6.2) Same — The one metre distance required by subsection (6.1) refers to the distance between the extreme right side of the motor vehicle and the extreme left side of the bicycle, including all projections and attachments.

(7) Driver unable to turn out is to stop — Where one vehicle is met or overtaken by another, if by reason of the weight of the load on either of the vehicles so meeting or on the vehicle so overtaken the driver finds it impracticable to turn out, he or she shall immediately stop, and, if necessary for the safety of the other vehicle and if required so to do, he or she shall assist the person in charge thereof to pass without damage.

(8) Passing vehicle going in same direction — No person in charge of a vehicle shall pass or attempt to pass another vehicle going in the same direction on a highway unless the roadway,

 (a) in front of and to the left of the vehicle to be passed is safely free from approaching traffic; and

 (b) to the left of the vehicle passing or attempting to pass is safely free from overtaking traffic.

2015, c. 14, s. 42

Commentary

Oncoming vehicles must leave the road clear (subs. (1)). Vehicles being passed should give way (subs. (2)) unless they are a road service or building machine vehicle (subs. (3)). Vehicles shall permit oncoming bicycles to pass (subs. (4)). Vehicles passing other vehicles shall do so in safety (subs. (5)). Bicycles being overtaken should turn out to the right (subs. (6)). If a vehicle being met or overtaken cannot because of the load or otherwise on each vehicle turn aside, it shall stop and assist the other vehicle to pass (subs. (7)). No person shall pass unless it can be done in safety (subs. (8)).

Case Law

Meeting Other Vehicles

Thomas v. Ward (1913), 24 W.L.R. 250 (Alta. S.C.); *Allen v. Lord*, 62 O.L.R. 433, [1928] 4 D.L.R. 62 (C.A.) — The requirements of s. 148 do not mean that a vehicle should always be on the right hand side of the roadway, but only that a driver must, in a reasonable time before actual meeting, turn to the right.

Stamp v. Ont.; Stamp v. Bacon (1984), 47 O.R. (2d) 214, 10 D.L.R. (4th) 687 (C.A.) — Where two motorists, travelling in opposite directions, are both found to have been "crowding" the centre line of the road, the trial Judge is justified in finding them equally responsible for the ensuring collision although he makes no finding as to the side of the road upon which the collision occured.

Thompson v. Fraser, [1955] S.C.R. 419, [1955] 3 D.L.R. 145 — Driving in the middle of the road approaching the crest of a hill was held to be a failure to exercise reasonable care, but not gross negligence.

Gauthier & Co. v. R., [1945] S.C.R. 143, [1945] 2 D.L.R. 48; *Coke and Luker v. Smith*, 3 W.W.R. (N.S.) 559, [1952] 1 D.L.R. 285 (Alta. C.A.); *Jeffs v. Matheson*, [1951] O.R. 743 (C.A.); *Motorways v. Simpson*, [1948] O.R. 360 (H.C.) — A driver must justify being on the wrong side, and a breach of the duty to turn out to the right occasioning damage will establish a *prima facie* case of negligence on the part of the driver of the offending vehicle, casting upon him or her the onus of explanation to show a way in which the accident may have occurred without negligence if he or she is to avoid responsibility.

Fagnan v. Ure (1957), 22 W.W.R. 289, 9 D.L.R. (2d) 480 (Alta. C.A.); affirmed [1958] S.C.R. 377 — The explanation given for being on the wrong side of the road must be a reasonable one, able to be substantiated on the evidence.

Trinidad Leaseholds Ltd. v. Gordon, [1953] O.W.N. 83 (Co. Ct.); *Audet v. Wetsch*, [1928] 3 W.W.R. 655, [1929] 2 D.L.R. 186 (Sask. C.A.) — Where a vehicle is seen to be proceeding on the wrong side of the road, the driver of an approaching vehicle is under a duty to avert by his or her diligence the consequences that must otherwise follow from the non-observance by the first driver, if he or she did not observe, the rule of the road on passing.

Farish & Ellison v. Papp (1957), 23 W.W.R. 690 (Alta. S.C.) — The driver on the proper side of the road should not be held to be negligent unless there is some evidence that he or she had or should have had a reasonable warning of danger, and a reasonable opportunity thereafter of taking evasive action in the face of the oncoming motorist's negligence.

McPhee v. Lalonde, [1946] O.W.N. 373 (H.C.); *Smith v. Cowan and Birks* (1926), 31 O.W.N. 110 (H.C.); *McDonald v. Bezanson*, [1929] 1 D.L.R. 272, 60 N.S.R. 333 (C.A.) — No blame can be attached to the driver for any reasonable course taken to avoid an impending collision even though some other course might have avoided it.

Wotta v. Haliburton Oil Well Cementing Co., [1955] S.C.R. 377, [1955] 2 D.L.R. 785; *Binda v. Waters Const. Co.* (1960), 24 D.L.R. (2d) 431 (Man. C.A.) — Where there is no evidence of which party was on the wrong side of the road at the time of collision, and no evidence to justify a finding of negligence on the part of either, the parties should not be found equally to blame but the action should be dismissed.

Power v. Winter (1952), 30 M.P.R. 131 (Nfld. C.A.); *Carl v. McQueen*, [1962] O.R. 224 (C.A.) — On narrow roads where the width admits of less than two lanes, different considerations may well apply and proper care and prudence may require that one or both drivers stop on meeting and take such steps as may be necessary for a safe passing.

Jackson v. Millar, [1976] 1 S.C.R. 225, 4 N.R. 17, 59 D.L.R. (3d) 246; reversing [1973] 1 O.R. 399, 31 D.L.R. (3d) 263 (C.A.); which reversed [1972] 2 O.R. 197, 25 D.L.R. (3d) 161 (H.C.) — A defendant was found grossly negligent when he attempted to regain the pavement after his right wheels went on to the gravel shoulder. The Court held that, due to his inexperience and fatigue, this novice driver had taken a course of action which inevitably resulted in the accident which occurred.

Graw v. Boucher Logging Ltd., [1977] 4 W.W.R. 421 (Alta. S.C.) — Where two logging vehicles collided on a narrow roadway it was held that the responsibility for the collision rested entirely with the driver of the empty truck who not only did not have control of his vehicle but ought to have given way to the loaded vehicle.

Falkjar v. Buck (1980), 33 N.B.R. (2d) 32, 80 A.P.R. 32 (Q.B.); affirmed (1981), 36 N.B.R. (2d) 193, 94 A.P.R. 193 (C.A.) — The plaintiff was pursued by police at high speed. A second police car approached the plaintiff's vehicle from the other direction and slightly crossed the centre line into the path of the plaintiff's vehicle, resulting in a head-on collision. The officer was held 65% at fault for failing to remain on the proper side of the road. The plaintiff was held 35% contributorily negligent for driving at an excessive speed.

Carol v. Odgen Funeral Home, [1956] O.W.N. 541, 5 D.L.R. (2d) 444 (H.C.) — Even though motorists are required under s. 159 to stop on the approach of an ambulance, nevertheless an ambulance driver has no absolute priority to drive on the wrong side and must exercise care to avoid approaching traffic.

Overtaking

Pluard v. Sheldon, [1951] O.R. 761, [1952] 1 D.L.R. 485 (C.A.); *Moision v. Ricard*, [1955] O.W.N. 469 (C.A.) — The provisions of subss. (4) and (5) of s. 148 apply only where two vehicles are travelling in the same direction and only when both vehicles are in operation and can be turned to the right or left as required. They do not apply to a case where one vehicle is standing wholly or partially on the travelled portion of the highway and cannot be operated because of engine failure.

Empey v. Thurston, 58 O.L.R. 168, [1926] 1 D.L.R. 289 (H.C.) — Necessity rules in the case of a stationary vehicle.

Moision v. Ricard, supra; *Cook v. Boland Bros. Ltd.*, [1942] 1 W.W.R. 306 (Man. K.B.); *Harrison v. Gibson* (1973), 36 D.L.R. (3d) 110 (Sask. Q.B.) — If a moving vehicle runs into a parked car the *res ipsa loquitur* rule applies and the driver is required to advance an explanation for the collision sufficient to negative negligence on his or her part.

Grant v. Fisceatoris, [1950] O.W.N. 91 (C.A.); *Webster v. Craigie* (1931), 40 O.W.N. 226 (C.A.) — There is no provision requiring an overtaking driver to give a signal to a vehicle behind him or her, although there may be a duty at common law to do so.

LeBlanc v. Thibodeau (1969), 1 N.B.R. (2d) 569 (Q.B.); *Rodgers v. Wainwright*, [1933] 3 W.W.R. 620 (Sask. C.A.); *Olson v. Lange* (1957), 24 W.W.R. 59, 13 D.L.R. (2d) 46 (Man. C.A.); *Young v. McKim* (1955), 16 W.W.R. 383 (Man. C.A.) — The overtaking driver was held solely at fault when his vehicle collided with another which had just been involved in a collision with a parked vehicle. The paramount duty of a driver intending to overtake is to be able to see what lies ahead, and if unable to do so he or she should not attempt the movement.

R. v. Lightheart, [1952] Ex. C.R. 12; *McIntyre v. McIntyre*, [1925] 2 W.W.R. 581 (B.C. S.C.) — A driver should not attempt to pass when he or she is following so close as not to afford an opportunity, if the way ahead is not clear, to revert to his or her original position behind the car ahead.

Johnson v. Reisel (1963), 43 W.W.R. 68, 40 D.L.R. (2d) 916 (Man. C.A.) — The defendant in overtaking another vehicle attempted to travel on the passing lane which to his knowledge was covered with snow and heavy slush and he skidded into the oncoming lane of traffic. He was held negligent in undertaking such a risky operation.

Hodge v. Geil (1924), 27 O.W.N. 290 (H.C.); *Johnson v. Riffel*, [1942] 2 D.L.R. 569 (Sask. C.A.); *Putnam v. MacNeill*, [1938] 1 W.W.R. 780 (B.C. S.C.); *Harding v. Edwards*, 64 O.L.R. 98, [1929] 4 D.L.R. 598 (C.A.); affirmed [1931] S.C.R. 167; *Land v.*

Ryan (1968), 1 D.L.R. (3d) 583 (B.C. S.C.); *Beaulieu v. Lavoie* (1973), 6 N.B.R. (2d) 216 (C.A.) — If a driver endeavours to overtake without sufficient room and is forced to "cut-in" sharply in front of the overtaken vehicle, he or she will be responsible for the consequences of that act.

Richards v. Morgan (1974), 5 Nfld. & P.E.I.R. 506 (Nfld. S.C,); varied (1976), 9 Nfld. & P.E.I.R. 370 (Nfld. C.A.) — The defendant driver endeavoured to pass the plaintiff's motor vehicle which was increasing its speed and, although the defendant was successful in passing the plaintiff, the plaintiff lost control and crashed. The plaintiff was found 75% at fault for increasing his speed when the defendant was attempting to pass. The defendant was held 25% at fault for failing to abandon the attempt to pass the plaintiff.

General

Lee Trans. Corp. v. Ontario (Registrar of Motor Vehicles), 2011 ONSC 6003, 2011 CarswellOnt 13367, 24 M.V.R. (6th) 200, [2011] O.J. No. 4820 (Ont. S.C.J.) — Where the Registrar had cancelled and seized licences under s. 47(1)(f) which was confirmed by the Licence Appeal tribunal an appeal was dismissed. The Tribunal's findings of mixed fact and law were entitled to deference. Assuming without deciding that the proposed fresh evidence was admissible, there was no evidence of real steps taken to improve the safety record.

Related Provisions: See s. 166 of the Act regarding overtaking street cars.

149. (1) Driving to left of centre prohibited under certain conditions — No vehicle shall be driven or operated to the left of the centre of a roadway designed for one or more lines of traffic in each direction,

(a) when approaching the crest of a grade or upon a curve in the roadway or within 30 metres of a bridge, viaduct or tunnel where the driver's view is obstructed within that distance so as to create a potential hazard in the event another vehicle might approach from the opposite direction; or

(b) when approaching within 30 metres of a level railway crossing.

(2) Exception — Subsection (1) does not apply,

(a) on a highway divided into clearly marked lanes where there are more such lanes for traffic in one direction than in the other direction;

(b) to a road service vehicle where precautions are taken to eliminate the hazard; or

(c) on a highway while it is designated for the use of one-way traffic.

Case Law

Quasi-Criminal

Plourde v. R. (1981), 14 M.V.R. 27 (N.B. Q.B.) — The defendant appealed a conviction for driving to the left of a solid line, contrary to s. 154(2) of the Motor Vehicle Act, R.S.N.B. 1973, c. M-17. The Act required that lines be clearly visible. The officer conceded that the line was somewhat difficult to see, but if one paid attention one would have seen it that day. The infraction occurred at night. The appellant testified that he knew there was a line there but he believed he had not passed it. The appeal was allowed, holding that the Crown had failed to prove the *actus reus*. Without clear lines, one could not conclude that the responsible authorities wished to control traffic by means of lines. Even if a defendant has a guilty mind, he cannot be found guilty if the lines are not clear.

R. v. Mailman (1990), 24 M.V.R. (2d) 112, 97 N.S.R. (2d) 330, 258 A.P.R. 330 (C.A.) — The defendant was convicted of passing in the face of oncoming traffic contrary to the Motor Vehicle Act, R.S.N.S. 1969, c. 191, s. 105(1)(a) [now R.S.N.S. 1989, c. 293, s. 115(1)(a)]. The conviction was affirmed by the County Court. The defendant applied for leave to appeal, arguing that the Crown did not establish that the safe operation of the oncoming vehicle was impeded in any way because there was no evidence that it was being operated safely. The application for leave to appeal was dismissed. Whether the safe operation of the approaching vehicle was impeded by the actions of the defendant was a question of fact. There was evidence that the oncoming vehicle had to pull over to the side of the road to avoid a collision with the defendant's vehicle. There was no evidence that the oncoming car was not being driven in a proper and prudent manner. The verdict of guilty was reasonable and was amply supported by the evidence.

150. (1) Passing to right of vehicle — **The driver of a motor vehicle may overtake and pass to the right of another vehicle only where such movement can be made in safety and,**

(a) the vehicle overtaken is making or about to make a left turn or its driver has signalled his or her intention to make a left turn;

(b) is made on a highway with unobstructed pavement of sufficient width for two or more lines of vehicles in each direction; or

(c) is made on a highway designated for the use of one-way traffic only.

(2) Driving off roadway prohibited — **No driver of a motor vehicle shall overtake and pass another vehicle by driving off the roadway.**

(3) Non-application of subs. (2) — **Subsection (2) does not apply to,**

(a) a motor vehicle overtaking and passing to the right of another vehicle where the shoulder to the right of the roadway is paved and the vehicle overtaken is making or about to make a left turn or its driver has signalled his or her intention to make a left turn;

(b) an ambulance or fire department vehicle;

(c) a police department vehicle or a vehicle being driven by an officer appointed for carrying out the provisions of this Act;

(d) a tow truck where the driver is responding to a police request for assistance;

(e) a road service vehicle; or

(f) a motor vehicle overtaking and passing to the right of a road service vehicle or road-building machine where a person apparently employed by or on behalf of the authority that is engaged in the highway maintenance operation has directed the driver to pass it and the movement can be made in safety.

1994, c. 27, s. 138(14); 2009, c. 5, s. 46

Case Law

R. v. Worden, [1962] O.W.N. 61 (C.A.) — Section 150(2) creates two separate offences, one if the movement cannot be made in safety, and the other if the driver drives off the roadway.

Hanmer v. Lucio, [1951] O.W.N. 41 (C.A.) — The defendant, before making a right turn, drove first towards the middle of the road and the following car attempted to overtake on the right side. Both drivers were held equally at fault for the resulting collision, since the following driver should have realized that an unusual movement of some kind was contemplated, and it was taking an unreasonable chance to attempt to pass on the right.

Day & Ross Ltd. v. Belanger (1976), 14 N.B.R. (2d) 524 (Q.B.); affirmed *R. v. Belanger* (1976), 16 N.B.R. (2d) 346 (C.A.) — The defendant was found completely to blame for a collision which occurred when the defendant slowed down in order to make a left turn but then suddenly moved to the right colliding with the plaintiff's motor vehicle which was passing on the defendant's right.

151. (1) Highways designated for use of paved shoulder — The Minister may by regulation designate any part of the King's Highway where the paved shoulder may be driven on, and may make regulations,

> (a) regulating the use of the paved shoulder on a designated part of the highway and prescribing conditions and circumstances for that use, including prescribing rules of the road applicable to the use of the paved shoulder, exemptions from any requirement in this Part or in a regulation made under this Part applicable to the use of the paved shoulder and conditions and circumstances for such exemptions;

> (b) providing for the erection of signs and the placing of markings,

>> (i) on any highway approaching any part of a highway designated as having a paved shoulder that may be driven on, and

>> (ii) on any part of a highway designated as having a paved shoulder that may be driven on;

> (c) prescribing the types of the signs and markings referred to in clause (b), instructions to be contained on them and the location of each type of sign and marking.

(2) Classes, types of vehicles, drivers — A regulation made under subsection (1) may prescribe different classes or types of vehicles and different classes of drivers and may define the class or type in relation to any characteristics, including the owner or operator of the vehicle, the purpose for which the vehicle is being used or the employer of or training taken by the driver.

(3) Same — A regulation made under subsection (1) may be general or particular in its application and may apply differently to different classes or types of vehicles or different classes of drivers.

(4) When designation is in effect — No designation made under this section becomes effective until signs are erected in accordance with this section on the designated part of the highway.

(5) **Non-authorized use of paved shoulder prohibited** — No person shall drive on the paved shoulder of any part of the King's Highway designated under this section except in accordance with this section and a regulation made under it.

(6) **Act, regulations otherwise apply** — Except as otherwise provided in a regulation made under this section, the provisions of this Act and its regulations applicable to vehicles apply with necessary modifications to the operation of a vehicle on the paved shoulder of a designated highway.

(7) **Paved shoulder deemed not part of roadway** — A paved shoulder on any part of a highway that is designated under this section shall be deemed not to be part of the roadway within the meaning of the definition of "roadway" in subsection 1(1) or part of the pavement for the purposes of clause 150(1)(b).

2005, c. 26, Sched. A, s. 24; 2015, c. 14, s. 43

Related Provisions: See O. Reg. 618/05, Designation of bus by-pass shoulders on King's Highway; R.R.O. 1990, Reg. 580, Designation of Paved Shoulders on King's Highway.

152. Definition — For the purposes of sections 141, 153 and 154, "designated" means designated by the Minister or by any person authorized by him or her to make the designation or designated by by-law of a municipality.

153. (1) Highway designated for one-way traffic — Where a highway has been designated for the use of one-way traffic only and official signs have been erected accordingly, vehicles and street cars shall be driven only in the direction so designated.

(2) **Exception — bicycle lanes** — A lane on a highway designated for the use of one-way traffic only may be designated for the use of bicycle traffic in the opposite direction and, despite subsection (1), where such a designation is made, a person riding or operating a bicycle in that lane shall travel only in the direction designated for that lane.

(3) **Same** — The designation of a lane for bicycle traffic is not effective until official signs have been erected and the lane has been marked accordingly.

2015, c. 14, s. 44

Related Provisions: See R.R.O. 1990, Reg. 615, Signs.

154. (1) Where highway divided into lanes — Where a highway has been divided into clearly marked lanes for traffic,

> (a) a vehicle shall not be driven from one lane to another lane or to the shoulder or from the shoulder to a lane unless the driver first ascertains that it can be done safely;
>
> (b) in the case of a highway that is divided into three lanes, a vehicle shall not be driven in the centre lane except when overtaking and passing another vehicle where the roadway is clearly visible and the centre lane is clear of traffic within a reasonable safe distance, or in preparation for a left turn, or where the centre lane is at the time designated for the use of traffic moving in the

direction in which the vehicle is proceeding and official signs are erected to indicate the designation;

(c) any lane may be designated for slowly moving traffic, traffic moving in a particular direction or classes or types of vehicles and, despite section 141, where a lane is so designated and official signs indicating the designation are erected, every driver shall obey the instructions on the official signs.

(2) **Exception** — Where safety is not jeopardized, clauses (1)(b) and (c) do not apply to road service vehicles and clause (1)(c) does not apply to road-building machines or apparatus while engaged in the construction of a highway.

2015, c. 14, s. 45

Case Law

Nature of Duty

McConnell v. Alexander & Mitchell, [1954] O.W.N. 61 (H.C.) — Before attempting to overtake another vehicle on a three-lane highway, a driver must be able to see ahead in the centre lane sufficiently past the car in front to permit him or her to move safely into that lane. Failure to take that precaution amounts to negligence.

Gross v. Registrar of Motor Vehicles, [1951] O.W.N. 905 (H.C.) — On multi-lane highways, where two cars have been travelling for some distance in the same position in two lanes, each driver is entitled to assume that the other driver would so continue. Accordingly, if a driver decides to turn from one lane to another following the sounding of a horn in the rear he or she must still exercise care to see that he or she can move in safety with regard to vehicles in the other lane.

R. v. Nekjeu (2000), 8 M.V.R. (4th) 42, 2000 CarswellOnt 4780 (Ont. C.J.) — A conviction under (c) was upheld when the accused drove through an intersection instead of making a right turn as directed by a "right turn must exit" sign. There is no requirement for the sign to state set times.

R. v. Capobianco, 2010 ONCA 589, 2010 CarswellOnt 6692, 1 M.V.R. (6th) 16; leave to appeal refused 2011 CarswellOnt 2151, 2011 CarswellOnt 2152, (sub nom. *York (Regional Municipality) v. Capobianco*) 421 N.R. 398 (note), 286 O.A.C. 399 (note) (S.C.C.) — S. 154(1)(a) contains only one offence. The vehicle must travel as much as possible entirely inside a single lane without leaving it until the driver has assured himself that such a manoeuvre can be executed safely.

Related Provisions: See R.R.O. 1990, Reg. 608, Restricted Use of Left Lanes by Commercial Motor Vehicles; R.R.O. 1990, Reg. 615, Signs, s. 34.

154.1 (1) Regulations for high occupancy vehicle lanes — Where a part of the King's Highway has been divided into clearly marked lanes for traffic, the Minister may by regulation designate any lane as a high occupancy vehicle lane for that part of the King's Highway and may make regulations,

(a) limiting the designation to specified months or times of the year, days, times, conditions or circumstances;

(b) limiting the use of high occupancy vehicle lanes to vehicles, or any class or type of vehicles, with a specified number of occupants, and prescribing conditions and circumstances for such use;

(c) regulating the use of high occupancy vehicle lanes, including prescribing rules of the road applicable to the use of the lanes, exemptions from any requirement in this Part or in a regulation made under this Part applicable to the use of the lanes and conditions and circumstances for such exemptions;

(d) providing for the erection of signs and the placing of markings to identify high occupancy vehicle lanes and the entry and exit points for high occupancy vehicle lanes;

(e) prescribing the types of the signs and markings referred to in clause (d), instructions to be contained on them and the location of each type of sign and marking.

(2) **Regulation may be general or specific** — A regulation made under subsection (1) may be general or specific in its application and may apply differently to different classes or types of vehicles.

(3) **Offence** — No person shall drive a motor vehicle in a high occupancy vehicle lane or enter or exit a high occupancy vehicle lane except in accordance with this section and the regulations made under it.

2005, c. 26, Sched. A, s. 25

Related Provisions: See O. Reg. 620/05, High Occupancy Vehicle Lanes.

154.2 (1) Restricted use of border approach lanes — Where a highway approaches the border between Canada and the United States of America and has been divided into clearly marked lanes for traffic, the Minister or, if the highway is under municipal jurisdiction, the municipality with jurisdiction over the highway may erect signs marking any lane on the highway, or on any part of the highway, as a border approach lane.

(2) **Offence** — No person shall drive a vehicle in a border approach lane except in accordance with the regulations made under this section.

(3) **Authority to stop vehicles** — A police officer may require a driver of a vehicle in a border approach lane to stop and the police officer may demand that the driver and occupants of the vehicle produce for examination the identification or authorization, or both, required under this section.

(4) **Same** — The driver and occupants of a vehicle shall comply with any requirement or demand made by a police officer under subsection (3).

(5) **Regulations** — The Minister may make regulations,

(a) limiting the use of border approach lanes to vehicles, or any class or type of vehicles, that are clearly authorized in accordance with the regulation;

(b) limiting the use of border approach lanes to drivers or occupants of vehicles, or of any class or type of vehicles, or any class of drivers or occupants, who carry identification in accordance with the regulation;

(c) prescribing conditions and circumstances for the use of border approach lanes by vehicles or persons described in clause (a) or (b), including limiting the use of border approach lanes to specified months or times of the year, days or time of day;

(d) prescribing the authorization that is required for a vehicle, or a vehicle belonging to a prescribed class or type of vehicle, to be entitled to use border approach lanes;

(e) prescribing the identification that is required for a person, or a prescribed class of person, to be entitled to use border approach lanes;

(f) governing the erection of signs and the placing of markings to identify border approach lanes;

(g) prescribing the types of the signs and markings referred to in clause (f), instructions to be contained on them and the location of each type of sign and marking;

(h) exempting buses, ambulances, fire department vehicles, commercial motor vehicles as defined in subsection 16(1) that are engaged in highway maintenance or construction and any other type or class of vehicle from any of the limitations in the regulation, and prescribing conditions and circumstances for such exemptions;

Proposed Amendment — 154.2(5)(h)

(h) exempting buses, ambulances, fire department vehicles, commercial motor vehicles that are engaged in highway maintenance or construction and any other type or class of vehicle from any of the limitations in the regulation, and prescribing conditions and circumstances for such exemptions;

2014, c. 9, Sched. 2, s. 38 [To come into force January 1, 2017.]

(i) exempting any class of drivers or occupants from any of the limitations in the regulation, and prescribing conditions and circumstances for such exemptions;

(j) prescribing the maximum length of a border approach lane.

(6) **Regulation may be general or specific** — A regulation made under subsection (5) may be general or specific in its application and may apply differently to different classes or types of vehicles or persons.

2005, c. 26, Sched. A, s. 26; 2009, c. 5, s. 47

Related Provisions: O. Reg. 94/06, Border Approach Lanes.

155. **Times designation applicable** — A designation of a lane for classes or types of vehicles made under clause 154(1)(c) shall apply during the times stated on the official signs.

Related Provisions: See R.R.O. 1990, Reg. 615, Signs.

156. (1) **Moving from roadway to roadway on divided highways** — Where a highway is divided into two separate roadways, no person shall operate or drive a vehicle or lead, ride or drive an animal,

(a) along or on such highway except on the roadway on the right-hand side, having regard to the direction in which the vehicle is being operated or driven or the animal is being led, ridden or driven; or

(b) from one roadway to the other roadway except where a crossing is provided.

(2) Exception — road service vehicles — Despite clause (1)(a), a road service vehicle may be operated or driven on the shoulder of the highway if the vehicle remains on its side of the separation.

(3) Same — bicycles — Despite clause (1)(a), a bicycle may be ridden or operated on the paved shoulder of the highway if the bicycle remains on its side of the separation.

2015, c. 14, s. 46

Case Law

Bland v. R., [1941] O.R. 273, [1941] 4 D.L.R. 414 (C.A.) — Although s. 156 contains certain prohibitions as to vehicles crossing an unpaved boulevard between two parallel paved roadways, there is nothing in the section to restrict the use thereof by pedestrians as part of the highway.

157. (1) Backing prohibited — No driver of a vehicle shall back the vehicle upon the roadway or shoulder of any highway divided by a median strip on which the speed limit is in excess of 80 kilometres per hour.

(2) Exception to subs. (1) — Subsection (1) does not apply to,

(a) an ambulance or fire department vehicle;

(b) a police department vehicle or a vehicle being driven by an officer appointed for carrying out the provisions of this Act;

(c) a person attempting to render assistance to another person; or

(d) a road service vehicle, if the movement is made in safety.

2005, c. 26, Sched. A, s. 27; 2009, c. 5, s. 48

158. (1) Headway of motor vehicles — The driver of a motor vehicle or street car shall not follow another vehicle or street car more closely than is reasonable and prudent having due regard for the speed of the vehicle and the traffic on and the conditions of the highway.

(2) Headway for commercial vehicles — The driver of a commercial motor vehicle when driving on a highway at a speed exceeding 60 kilometres per hour shall not follow within 60 metres of another motor vehicle, but this shall not be construed to prevent a commercial motor vehicle overtaking and passing another motor vehicle.

Case Law

Quasi-Criminal

R. v. Walsh (1960), 33 W.W.R. 91 (Sask. Mag. Ct.) — On charges under this section each case must be decided on its own facts, and there should be evidence of the distance between the two cars; the fact that the driver was not keeping a proper lookout is not in itself ground for a conviction on such a charge.

Re Oskey (1959), 31 C.R. 229, 29 W.W.R. 415 (B.C. S.C.) — The test or measure contained in the words "reasonable or prudent" and the enumerated factors to be taken into account are essential elements of the offence, and it is not sufficient merely to charge a driver with unlawfully allowing his or her vehicle to "follow another too closely".

R. v. Ouseley, [1973] 1 O.R. 729, 10 C.C.C. (2d) 148 (C.A.) — The fact of a rear-end collision did not establish a *prima facie* case of following too closely.

R. v. Ishkanian, [1986] B.C.W.L.D. 634 (Co. Ct.) — The equivalent offence created by s. 164(1) of the Motor Vehicle Act (B.C.) is one of strict liability.

Civil

Dangerfield v. Smith, [1934] 1 W.W.R. 577, [1934] 2 D.L.R. 505 (Man. C.A.) — A person driving a motor vehicle in heavy traffic ought to know that it is not always possible for a car ahead to properly stop and therefore should maintain a distance behind it that will enable him or her to pull up with safety if the car ahead comes to a stop.

De Courcey v. London St. Ry., [1932] O.R. 226, [1932] 2 D.L.R. 319 (C.A.) — A bus operator has no right to drive so closely to the car ahead that, if an emergency in traffic arises, he or she is unable to cope with it without injury to passengers.

Whiddon v. Wickstrom, [1948] O.W.N. 336 (C.A.); *Toronto v. Waite*, [1955] O.W.N. 227 (H.C.) — A driver who ran into the rear of a vehicle in front which made a sudden turn was held at fault for not keeping at a reasonable distance.

Related Provisions: See ss. 128 and 142 of the Act, respectively, regarding speed and signalling for a stop.

159. Approaching, following emergency vehicles — (1) **Stop on approach of vehicle with flashing lights or bell or siren sounding** — The driver of a vehicle, upon the approach of a police department vehicle with its bell or siren sounding or with its lamp producing intermittent flashes of red light or red and blue light, or upon the approach of an ambulance, fire department vehicle or public utility emergency vehicle with its bell or siren sounding or its lamp producing intermittent flashes of red light, shall immediately bring such vehicle to a standstill,

    (a) **as near as is practicable to the right-hand curb or edge of the roadway and parallel therewith and clear of any intersection; or**

    (b) **when on a roadway having more than two lanes for traffic and designated for the use of one-way traffic, as near as is practicable to the nearest curb or edge of the roadway and parallel therewith and clear of any intersection.**

(2) **Slow down on approaching stopped emergency vehicle or tow truck** — Upon approaching an emergency vehicle with its lamp producing intermittent flashes of red light or red and blue light or a tow truck with its lamp producing intermittent flashes of amber light that is stopped on a highway, the driver of a vehicle travelling on the same side of the highway shall slow down and proceed with caution, having due regard for traffic on and the conditions of the highway and the weather, to ensure that the driver does not collide with the emergency vehicle or tow truck or endanger any person outside of the emergency vehicle or tow truck.

(3) **Same** — Upon approaching an emergency vehicle with its lamp producing intermittent flashes of red light or red and blue light or a tow truck with its lamp producing intermittent flashes of amber light that is stopped on a highway with two

or more lanes of traffic on the same side of the highway as the side on which the emergency vehicle or tow truck is stopped, the driver of a vehicle travelling in the same lane that the emergency vehicle or tow truck is stopped in or in a lane that is adjacent to the emergency vehicle or tow truck, in addition to slowing down and proceeding with caution as required by subsection (2), shall move into another lane if the movement can be made safely.

(4) Following fire department vehicle — No driver of a vehicle shall follow in any lane of a roadway at a distance of less than 150 metres a fire department vehicle responding to an alarm.

(5) Stop on approaching emergency vehicle or tow truck — Nothing in subsection (2) or (3) prevents a driver from stopping his or her vehicle and not passing the stopped emergency vehicle or tow truck if stopping can be done safely and is not otherwise prohibited by law.

(6) Offence — Every person who contravenes subsection (1), (2), (3) or (4) is guilty of an offence and on conviction is liable,

(a) for a first offence, to a fine of not less than $400 and not more than $2,000; and

(b) for each subsequent offence, to a fine of not less than $1,000 and not more than $4,000 or to imprisonment for a term of not more than six months, or to both.

(7) Time limit for subsequent offence — An offence referred to in subsection (6) committed more than five years after a previous conviction for an offence referred to in that subsection is not a subsequent offence for the purpose of clause (6)(b).

(8) Driver's licence suspension — If a person is convicted of an offence under subsection (6), the court may make an order suspending the person's driver's licence for a period of not more than two years.

(9) Appeal of suspension — An appeal may be taken from an order under subsection (8) or a decision to not make the order in the same manner as from a conviction or an acquittal under subsection (6).

(10) Stay of order on appeal — Where an appeal is taken under subsection (9) from an order under subsection (8), the court being appealed to may direct that the order shall be stayed pending the final disposition of the appeal or until otherwise ordered by that court.

(11) Definition — In this section,

"emergency vehicle" means,

(a) an ambulance, fire department vehicle, police department vehicle or public utility emergency vehicle,

(b) a ministry vehicle operated by an officer appointed for carrying out the provisions of this Act or the *Public Vehicles Act*, while the officer is in the course of his or her employment,

(c) a vehicle while operated by a conservation officer, fishery officer, provincial park officer or mine rescue training officer, while the officer is in the course of his or her employment,

(d) a vehicle while operated by a provincial officer designated under the *Environmental Protection Act*, the *Nutrient Management Act, 2002*, the *Ontario Water Resources Act*, the *Pesticides Act*, the *Safe Drinking Water Act, 2002* or the *Toxics Reduction Act, 2009*, while the officer is in the course of his or her employment, or

(e) a vehicle as prescribed for the purposes of paragraph 5 of subsection 62(15.1).

2007, c. 13, s. 19; 2009, c. 5, s. 49; 2009, c. 19, s. 68(4); 2015, c. 14, s. 47

Case Law

Nature of Duty

B.C. Elec. Ry. v. Vancouver, [1952] 2 D.L.R. 223, 4 W.W.R. (N.S.) 177 (B.C. C.A.); *Whitehead v. Victoria* (1957), 25 W.W.R. 91, 12 D.L.R. (2d) 599 (B.C. C.A.); *Colwill v. Longman* (1928), 33 O.W.N. 284 (Co. Ct.) — Even where priority of passage is given to emergency vehicles, it is not an absolute right, and there is still a duty to exercise due care, attention and reasonable consideration for other users of the highway.

Fingerote v. Winnipeg (1963), 45 W.W.R. 634 (Man. C.A.) — Drivers of emergency vehicles are under a duty of ordinary care and the duty of others to yield right-of-way is conditional on such others knowing, or having no reasonable excuse for not knowing, of the approach of the emergency vehicle and having a reasonable opportunity to comply with the law.

A.G. Can. v. Prince Albert, [1952] 1 D.L.R. 195, 3 W.W.R. (N.S.) 646 (Sask. C.A.) — The priority of an emergency vehicle may be lost if the siren is not sounded continuously as required.

Samson v. Halifax, [1953] 3 D.L.R. 761 (N.S. T.D.); *Amisson v. Carter* (1950), 27 M.P.R. 360 (N.B. C.A.); *St. John v. City Transit Ltd.*, [1954] 3 D.L.R. 754, 35 M.P.R. 86 (N.B. C.A.); *Krauss v. Vancouver* (1964), 47 W.W.R. 364 (B.C. C.A.) — A heavy onus will lie on a driver who ignores a clearly audible or visible signal of an emergency vehicle and fails to clear the roadway for it.

R. v. Francisty (1997), 27 M.V.R. (3d) 220 (Ont. Prov. Ct.) — The words "upon the approach" must be given their ordinary meaning of "to draw closer to" or "to come very near to" as in "an act or instance of approaching". The section should not be interpreted of restricting from its ambit the angles upon which the emergency vehicle may enter the intersection.

R. v. Quan (2013), 59 M.V.R. (6th) 167, 2013 ONCJ 699, 2013 CarswellOnt 17576, [2013] O.J. No. 5766 — Upon seeing an emergency vehicle on a shoulder of a multi-lane road with its intermittent lights, the driver in the lane next to the shoulder has three obligations: to slow down; proceed with caution; and change lanes if safe to do so.

Bergen v. Guliker Estate, 2015 BCCA 283, 2015 CarswellBC 1678, 75 B.C.L.R. (5th) 351, 21 C.C.L.T. (4th) 28, 79 M.V.R. (6th) 187, [2015] 11 W.W.R. 258, (sub nom. *Bergen v. Guliker)* 374 B.C.A.C. 80, 642 W.A.C. 80 — The trial judge erred in law in imposing a new or novel duty of care on police in advance of a pursuit owed to other drivers.

Related Provisions: See ss. 128(3) and 166(2) in relation to speed limits and passing street cars, respectively.

159.1 [Repealed 2009, c. 5, s. 49.]

160. Towing of persons on bicycles, toboggans, etc., prohibited — No driver of a vehicle or street car shall permit any person riding, riding on or operating a bicycle, coaster, toboggan, sled, skateboard, toy vehicle or any other type of conveyance or wearing roller skates, in-line skates or skis to attach the same, himself or herself to the vehicle or street car on a highway.

2015, c. 14, s. 48

161. Only one vehicle to be drawn on highway — No person shall drive on a highway a motor vehicle, other than a commercial motor vehicle, that is drawing more than one vehicle.

162. Crowding driver's seat — No person shall drive a motor vehicle with persons or property in the front or driver's seat so placed as to interfere with the proper management or control of the motor vehicle.

Case Law

R. v. Patrick (1955), 16 W.W.R. 23 (Sask. Dist. Ct.) — Overcrowding means more persons than will allow the driver to operate the vehicle freely, without interference and safety; *e.g.*, if access to, or use of, the gear-shift lever, brakes, clutch, accelerator or steering wheel are impeded or interfered with, or if the driver's vision is cut down. Numbers alone are not an absolute guide.

Hopcroft v. Bouey (1927), 31 O.W.N. 383 (H.C.) — In this case, even if there was overcrowding, it was not causative of the accident.

163. (1) Vehicles required to stop at railway crossing signal — When the driver of a vehicle is approaching a railway crossing at a time when a clearly visible electrical or mechanical signal device or a flagman is giving warning of the approach of a railway train, he or she shall stop the vehicle not less than 5 metres from the nearest rail of the railway and shall not proceed until he or she can do so safely.

(2) Stop signs at railway crossings — Every driver of a vehicle approaching a stop sign at a railway crossing shall, unless otherwise directed by a flagman, stop the vehicle at the marked stop line or, if none, then not less than five metres from the nearest rail of the railway, and shall not proceed until he or she can do so safely.

2002, c. 18, Sched. P, s. 30

Case Law

Quasi-Criminal

R. v. Holmes (1953), 71 C.C.C. 358 (N.S. Co. Ct.) — When the warning is given, the vehicle must stop and must remain or continue stopped until the apprehended danger is past. The warning is a continuing warning and accordingly the stop must be a continuing stop.

R. v. Wilson (1958), 28 C.R. 356, 25 W.W.R. 550 (Sask. Dist. Ct.) — On a charge under s. 140(2) [now s. 149(2)] of the Saskatchewan Act which prohibits a driver from crossing until the "automatic signal or device indicates that it is safe to do so," it was held that where there were both gates and flashing red lights, there could not be a conviction if either the signal or the gates indicated that it was safe to proceed.

Zsoldos v. Canadian Pacific Railway, 2009 CarswellOnt 253, (sub nom. *Zsoldos v. Canadian Pacific Railway Co.)* 245 O.A.C. 178, 69 C.C.L.I. (4th) 161, 93 O.R. (3d) 321, 2009 ONCA 55, 73 M.V.R. (5th) 167; affirming 2007 CarswellOnt 1511, 45 M.V.R. (5th) 188, 46 C.C.L.I. (4th) 294, [2007] O.J. No. 942 (S.C.J.); leave to appeal refused 2009 CarswellOnt 4370, 2009 CarswellOnt 4371, 262 O.A.C. 399 (note), 400 N.R. 384 (note) (S.C.C.) — The court noted that in *Ryan v. Victoria (City)*, [1999] S.C.J. No. 7, 1999 CarswellBC 79, 1999 CarswellBC 80, 234 N.R. 201, 168 D.L.R. (4th) 513, 117 B.C.A.C. 103, 191 W.A.C. 103, 40 M.V.R. (3d) 1, 44 C.C.L.T. (2d) 1, 59 B.C.L.R. (3d) 81, 50 M.P.L.R. (2d) 1, [1999] 6 W.W.R. 61, [1999] 1 S.C.R. 201, the Supreme Court of Canada abandoned the special rule that placed railway companies in a privileged position within the law of negligence. The special rule was that so long as railway companies complied with government regulations and orders, absent extraordinary circumstances, they were under no further obligation to act in an objectively reasonable manner. After that, companies were subject to the same standard of care as other similarly situated defendants. That did not mean that the regulatory framework is irrelevant. Where a statute authorizes certain activities and strictly defines the manner of performance and the precautions to be taken, it is more likely to be found that compliance with the statute constitutes reasonable care and that no additional measures are required. Where the regulatory framework is general, or permits discretion as to the manner of performance, mere compliance with the statutory framework is unlikely to exhaust the standard of care.

On the review of the trial judgment, CP's failure to carry out night-time inspections of the rural crossing in question was negligent. There were measures available in 1994 that a reasonable railway operator could have employed. The trial judge did not have to set out which of the proposed measures the company should have adopted. The central finding was that it was impossible for a motorist to know that the freight train was in the crossing until it was too late to stop. It was open to the trial judge to draw the common sense inference that had the crossing been illuminated, the accident could have been avoided.

Civil

Duty to Stop at Signal

Armstrong Cartage Co. v. G.T.R. (1918), 42 O.L.R. 660, 43 D.L.R. 122 (C.A.); *Vansantbergen v. Pere Marquette Ry.* (1929), 36 O.W.N. 253 (C.A.) — The fact that the gate on one side of a crossing was not lowered at the time an approaching vehicle had reached a point just outside it was held to be an intimation to the driver that he might safely cross the tracks, and the signalman was negligent in allowing the train to get too near the crossing before lowering the gates.

C.N.R. v. MacEachern, [1947] S.C.R. 64 — Since a motorist, after stopping for a warning signal, is not to proceed until he or she can do so safely, he or she must clearly ascertain that the track is clear even after the train has passed and guard against the possibility of a second train travelling in the opposite direction.

Gordon v. C.N.R., [1944] O.W.N. 505 (C.A.) — Even if the warning bell at a crossing did not ring, the railway will not necessarily be held guilty of negligence if it had complied with the relevant requirements in installing a bell of an approved pattern, maintaining it, and inspecting it frequently.

Unprotected Crossings

Friedman v. C.N.R. (1924), 31 C.R.C. 401; *Reynolds v. C.P.R.*, 59 O.L.R. 396, [1926] 4 D.L.R. 458 (C.A.); reversed [1927] S.C.R. 505 — Before crossing a railway line, a motorist is bound to take reasonable care to know that the way is clear. The reasonable care varies with the circumstances and may be quite different where there is an unobstructed view down the railway line for a long distance than where he or she is approaching a line of which there is no clear view, or is so enclosed in the vehicle as not to be able to hear whistles and bells.

Nicholls v. Great Western Ry. (1868), 27 U.C.Q.B. 382; *C.P.R. v. Smith*, 62 S.C.R. 134, [1921] 3 W.W.R. 300, 59 D.L.R. 373 — A railway track, *per se*, is a warning of danger to those about to go upon it, and they must take reasonable care for their own safety.

Blair v. G.T.R., 53 O.L.R. 405, [1924] 1 D.L.R. 353 (C.A.); *Jewel v. G.T.R.* (1924), 55 O.L.R. 617 (C.A.) — Accordingly, even though there is no mandatory rule of "stop, look and listen," the courts have also considered that it would be just as deplorable if an action lay at the instance of a person who rushed, with eyes open, to his or her own destruction.

Bogle v. C.P.R. (1921), 19 O.W.N. 508 (C.A.); *Storry v. C.N.R.*, [1940] S.C.R. 491, [1940] 3 D.L.R. 554; *Whalen v. C.N.R.* (1946), 19 M.P.R. 87 (N.B. C.A.); affirmed (1946), 60 C.R.T.C. 346 (S.C.C.) — A driver will be responsible for his or her own injury if, owing to flurried mismanagement, he or she stalls the car on a crossing, but for which he or she would have been able to cross in safety.

Highley v. C.P.R., 64 O.L.R. 615, [1930] 1 D.L.R. 630 (C.A.) — The motorist will be solely responsible if there is no excuse for his or her failing to look and listen. Had the driver done so in the above case, he would have seen a train approaching in sufficient time to avoid a collision.

Sullivan v. Dworchuk, [1933] O.W.N. 186 (H.C.); *Wabash Ry. v. Misener* (1906), 38 S.C.R. 94 — The duty to look is not fulfilled by looking when still some distance from the crossing and not looking again before actually entering upon it.

C.N.R. v. Prescesky, [1924] S.C.R. 2, [1924] 2 D.L.R. 504; *Kielb v. C.N.R.*, [1941] O.W.N. 286 (H.C.) — Mere failure to see an approaching train is not conclusive in all circumstances and may be excused by any facts which, in the opinion of the jury or tribunal of fact, furnishes a reasonable excuse for not seeing the train.

C.N.R. v. Clark, [1923] S.C.R. 730, [1923] 3 W.W.R. 938, [1923] 4 D.L.R. 727 — If a motorist approaches a crossing with an obscured view and, because of this, listens with great care for bell and whistle signals, he or she may be justified, upon hearing no signal, in proceeding to cross with only a hurried glance down the track.

Blair v. G.T.R., *supra*; *Dawe v. C.N.R.*, [1946] 2 D.L.R. 585 (N.S. T.D.); *Hendrie v. G.T.R.* (1921), 51 O.L.R. 191, 67 D.L.R. 165 (C.A.); *Flynn v. C.P.R.* (1958), 25 W.W.R. 449, 14 D.L.R. (2d) 114 (Alta. C.A.) — The absence of the proper signals does not relieve a motorist of the duty to keep a lookout and exercise ordinary prudence in approaching a crossing.

Kielb v. C.N.R., [1941] O.W.N. 286 (H.C.); *Armstrong Cartage Co. v. G.T.R.* (1918), 42 O.L.R. 660 (C.A.) — Where the gates at a crossing have not been lowered owing to the neglect of the gateman, and a motorist does not have a clear view down the railway track, he or she will nevertheless be entitled within reason to rely on the "invitation" to cross.

Booth v. Grieve, [1936] O.R. 111, [1936] 1 D.L.R. 682 (C.A.) — Generally speaking, contributory negligence will not be inferred against a passenger for failing to see an approaching train and to warn the driver. The passenger owes no duty to the driver to keep such a lookout, although he or she might be negligent if he or she had in fact observed a train and failed to convey a warning to the driver if it appeared that the driver was unaware of its approach.

Paskivski v. Canadian Pacific Ltd., [1976] 1 S.C.R. 687, [1975] 5 W.W.R. 640, 5 N.R. 1, 57 D.L.R. (3d) 280 — A railway company's duty of care to users of public crossings is limited to the discharge of statutory obligations under the Railway Act and to compliance with orders of the Canadian Transport Commission unless there are special or exceptional circumstances in which even a common law duty of care will require additional precautions or safeguards.

Gavel v. C.N.R., 9 M.P.R. 501, [1935] 2 D.L.R. 627 (N.S. T.D.); *Leviten v. C.N.R.*, 14 M.P.R. 355, [1940] 1 D.L.R. 622 (N.S. T.D.); *Bayda v. C.P.R.*, [1950] 2 W.W.R. 97, [1950] 3 D.L.R. 742 (Sask. C.A.) — Although the Act does not specifically confer on railways a priority of passage over crossings, such a priority, conditioned on the exercise of proper care and compliance with applicable regulations, may readily be inferred from the provisions of the Act and from the decisions of the courts concerning the rights and obligations of both motorist and railway. Accordingly, the engineer of a train has a right to assume that persons approaching a crossing will themselves take at least the most ordinary precautions to avoid injury, and will, within a reasonable distance of the crossing, bring their vehicles to a standstill in order to avoid an accident; in general, he or she is not bound to slacken speed when approaching an obscured crossing, nor to apply the brakes upon observing an approaching motor vehicle.

Adequacy of Protection

G.T.R. v. McKay (1903), 34 S.C.R. 81; *Gagne v. C.N.R.*, [1945] O.W.N. 507, [1945] 4 D.L.R. 273 (C.A.) — The character and extent of the protection which should be given to the public at level crossings is a matter for the determination of the Board of Transport Commissioners and the adequacy of the Board's requirements is not subject to review by the Court or a jury.

Durwood v. C.N.R., [1955] O.W.N. 94 (C.A.); *Anderson v. C.N.R.*, [1944] O.R. 169, [1944] 2 D.L.R. 209 (C.A.) — Under ordinary circumstances, a railway is permitted to carry on its usual operations in the normal way at crossings without other precautions and warnings than are prescribed by the Railway Act or by the Board, and a motorist, in order to recover against the railway, must generally prove a breach of the provisions of the Act or of the orders of the Board.

Train Signals

C.N.R. v. MacEachern, [1947] S.C.R. 64 — There was a municipal by-law prohibiting the blowing of train whistles at the crossing in question. It was held that the by-law substituted for the obligation under s. 248(1) [now s. 250(1)] of the Railway Act an obligation not to sound the whistle at all unless from the particular circumstances at the time a prudent man would consider that in order to prevent an accident the prohibition should be disregarded and the warning given pursuant to a common law duty. But something more than the possibility that the crossing signal would be disregarded by persons at the crossing was required to impose upon the train crew the obligation to blow the whistle.

London v. G.T.R. (1914), 32 O.L.R. 642 (C.A.); *Bayda v. C.P.R.*, [1950] 2 W.W.R. 97, [1950] 3 D.L.R. 742 (Sask. C.A.) — There must be knowledge that the danger is imminent, and not simply knowledge that the danger is possible.

Speed

Bayda v. C.P.R., [1950] 2 W.W.R. 97, [1950] 3 D.L.R. 742 (Sask. C.A.); *G.T.R. v. McKay* (1903), 34 S.C.R. 81 — Apart from the provisions of the Railway Act there is, generally speaking, no duty as to speed on the part of a railway to persons using a crossing, and there can be no right of action for alleged excessive speed.

Preston v. C.N.R., [1951] O.W.N. 373 (C.A.) — Once the railway proved compliance with an order of the Board as to speed, it was not open to the jury to find that additional precautions should have been taken.

Bayda v. C.P.R., *supra*; *Andreas v. C.P.R.* (1905), 37 S.C.R. 1 — "Thickly peopled" (now "thickly populated") as used in s. 249(1) [now s. 251(1)] of the Railway Act means occupied or inhabited or populated by many people; the words imply the existence in the area of dwelling-houses or residences in which people are actually living. The fact that a crossing is used by many people cannot make an adjacent area thickly peopled.

Vynerzenke v. C.N.R. (1922), 22 O.W.N. 1 (C.A.) — It is a question of fact in each case whether an area is thickly peopled.

Inadequately Protected Crossings

Wyatt v. Algoma Central etc. Ry., [1954] O.W.N. 412, [1954] 2 D.L.R. 617 (C.A.); *Eagles v. C.N.R.*, 15 M.P.R. 583, [1941] 2 D.L.R. 744 (N.B. C.A.) — A crossing protected by a watchman on duty 24 hours of the day is a crossing "adequately protected by gates or otherwise" within the meaning of s. 250 [now s. 252] and that section is therefore not applicable to such a crossing.

Crossing Signs

Can. Northern Pac. Ry. v. Chesworth, [1941] S.C.R. 201 — It was alleged that the collision was caused by the failure of the defendant railway to "erect and maintain" signboards as required by s. 207 [now s. 210] of the Railway Act. The action was dismissed since the evidence did not justify a finding that the default in the condition of the crossing sign (it had not been kept painted white) materially contributed to the accident. It was further held that a finding by the Board of Railway Commissioners, made under s. 249 [now s. 251] after the accident, when the crossing was in the same condition as it was at the time of the accident, that the crossing in that condition was not sufficiently protected, was not binding on parties to the action, or upon the Court, and was not admissible evidence upon the issue whether the regulation requiring the placing of the sign at the crossing had been observed.

Related Provisions: See s. 164 of the Act regarding driving under gates and s. 174 of the Act as to the duties of public vehicles to stop at all crossings. The Railway Act, R.S.C. 1985, c. R-1, makes provisions for such matters as the degree of inclination of the highway approaches to a railway crossing, the fencing of such approaches and of the railway, the construction of cattle guards and the erection of signboards; and a General Order of the Canadian Transport Commission [Railway-Highway Crossing at Grade Regulations, SOR/80-748; am. SOR/81-64; SOR/85-75] establishes standard regulations respecting the construction of crossings at grade. In authorizing the construction of a crossing, the Commission may also require that additional protection such as flashing light signals and bell, automatic gates, watchmen, etc., be installed, and such other measures be taken as in the circumstances appear to the Commission best adapted to remove or diminish a danger or obstruction. Where a certain type of protection is directed, reference is made in the Order to the provisions of a General Order applicable to that type of protection giving the detailed specifications therefor, Provisions for the erection of signs is made in s. 210, and the warning signals to be given, and other precautions to be observed, are prescribed by ss. 248–251.

164. Driving of vehicles under crossing gates prohibited — No person shall drive a vehicle through, around or under a crossing gate or barrier at a railway crossing while the gate or barrier is closed or is being opened or closed.

Related Provisions: See ss. 163 and 174 of the Act.

165. (1) Opening of doors of motor vehicles — No person shall,

(a) open the door of a motor vehicle on a highway without first taking due precautions to ensure that his or her act will not interfere with the movement of or endanger any other person or vehicle; or

(b) leave a door of a motor vehicle on a highway open on the side of the vehicle available to moving traffic for a period of time longer than is necessary to load or unload passengers.

(2) Penalty — A person who contravenes subsection (1) is guilty of an offence and on conviction is liable to a fine of not less than $300 and not more than $1,000.

2015, c. 14, s. 49

Case Law

Ryder v. Gray Coach Lines Ltd., [1951] O.W.N. 496 (C.A.); *Frederick v. Northern Taxi Ltd.*, [1949] 1 W.W.R. 49 (Man. K.B.); *Looy v. Elley*, [1940] 2 W.W.R. 238 (B.C. S.C.) — A motorist was held liable for injuries to a cyclist struck by a door opened on the left side.

R. v. Quenneville, 9 M.V.R. (5th) 201, 2004 ONCJ 233, 2004 CarswellOnt 4212 (C.J.) — The offence is one of strict liability.

166. Passing street cars — (1) Standing street car, etc. — Where a person in charge of a vehicle or on a bicycle or on horseback or leading a horse on a highway overtakes a street car or a car of an electric railway, operated in or near the centre of the roadway, which is stationary for the purpose of taking on or discharging passengers, he or she shall not pass the car or approach nearer than 2 metres measured back from the rear or front entrance or exit, as the case may be, of the car on the side on which passengers are getting on or off until the passengers have got on or got safely to the side of the street, as the case may be, but this subsection does

not apply where a safety zone has been set aside and designated by a by-law passed under section 9, 10 or 11 of the *Municipal Act, 2001* or under section 7 or 8 of the *City of Toronto Act, 2006*, as the case may be.

(2) Prohibition as to passing street cars on left-hand side — No person in charge of a vehicle, or on a bicycle or on horseback or leading a horse, overtaking a street car or the car of an electric railway, operated in or near the centre of the roadway, which is stationary or in motion, shall pass on the left side of the car, having reference to the direction in which the car is travelling, but this subsection does not apply to a fire department vehicle while proceeding to a fire or answering a fire alarm call or where the street car or car of an electric railway is being operated on a highway designated for the use of one-way traffic.

2002, c. 17, Sched. F, s. 1; 2006, c. 32, Sched. C, s. 24(6); 2009, c. 5, s. 50

Commentary

As of December 2, 1983, reference to street cars is included in many provisions of the Act, so that the usual rules that apply to motor vehicles will apply to street cars. See s. 1, "motor vehicle", "street car" and "vehicle". Regard should now be had to the specific rule of the road to see if a street car is covered. Even if it is not, regard may be had to the general common law duty of care, which is applicable to street cars, and regard should also be had to the provisions of ss. 229–265 of the Railways Act, R.S.O. 1950, c. 331 (not consolidated in 1960, 1970, 1980 or 1990) governing the operation of street railways along highways, and of appropriate municipal by-laws and the terms of the franchise agreement under which the street railway company operated. Care should be taken when examining the authorities decided below, having in mind the amendments to the Act on December 2, 1983.

Under s. 267 of the Ontario Railways Act, actions against a company are to be commenced within one year after the time when the supposed damage is sustained. When this section bars an action after the stated period against "the railway", the bar is actually against the commencement of an action against the corporate body which is operating the railway at the material time, and the Toronto Transit Commission is such a body: *Lofting v. Toronto Transit Comm.*, [1958] O.W.N. 243, 13 D.L.R. (2d) 268 (C.A.).

Case Law

Passing Street Cars

Wishik v. Brown (1932), 41 O.W.N. 152 (C.A.) — The duty under this section not to pass is imposed only when passengers are getting on and off. Accordingly, a motorist was held not to be in breach of the section where he moved forward after seeing the passengers alight and the doors close, and the doors suddenly opened again and another passenger stepped down.

Ellis v. Hamilton St. Ry. (1920), 48 O.L.R. 380, 57 D.L.R. 33 (C.A.) — The section was passed to protect persons about to board or to alight from cars, but the duties and obligations are put by the Act upon the motorist, and not upon the street car company. There is nothing in the Act that makes the obligation or duty of the motorist less when the street car is stopped at a point other than the regular stopping place.

Katz v. Consol. Motors Ltd., [1930] 1 W.W.R. 305, [1930] 2 D.L.R. 241 (B.C. C.A.); *Walker v. Forbes*, 56 O.L.R. 532, [1925] 2 D.L.R. 725 (H.C.); *Winnipeg Elec. Co. v.*

Starr, [1950] 2 D.L.R. 722 (S.C.C.) — A motorist could not evade the statute by rushing forward to pass a street car which he knew, or ought to have known, was about to stop unless he could pass the car before (not at the time) it reached the stopping point.

Bowler v. Blake, 64 O.L.R. 499, [1930] 1 D.L.R. 683 (H.C.); *Soloway v. Ont. Grape Growing etc. Co.* (1930), 38 O.W.N. 197 (C.A.); *James v. Pieol*, [1932] 3 W.W.R. 365 (B.C. S.C.) — Motorists must be on their guard to avoid pedestrians who step out onto the roadway, or wait on the roadway, for a street car.

Fitzgibbon v. Lehman, [1951] O.W.N. 621 (H.C.) — However, the motorist does have some right to expect that pedestrians stepping out to board a street car will keep some lookout, and he or she will not necessarily be held solely at fault for any accident that occurs.

Rights and Duties of Operators

Gallagher v. Toronto Ry. (1917), 41 O.L.R. 143, 40 D.L.R. 114 (C.A.) — A street car of necessity must have a prior right of way on that portion of the street upon which it alone can travel or the purposes of rapid transit would be defeated.

O'Hearn v. Port Arthur (1902), 4 O.L.R. 209 (Div. Ct.); *Parsons v. Toronto Ry.* (1919), 45 O.L.R. 627 (C.A.); *Fraser v. B.C. Elec. Ry.*, [1919] 2 W.W.R. 513 (B.C. C.A.) — A motorist should keep out of the track of a street car unless satisfied that the passage is clear.

Ewing v. Toronto Ry. (1894), 24 O.R. 694 (Common Pleas) — The superior right of the street railway does not prevent others from driving across or along its tracks at any place or at any time when by so doing they will not interfere with the progress of the street car.

Royal Trust Co. v. Toronto Transit Comm., [1935] S.C.R. 671; *Cornwall St. Ry. v. Mc-Callum*, [1941] O.W.N. 257 (H.C.); *Pronek v. Winnipeg Ry.*, [1933] A.C. 61 (P.C.); *Watson v. Toronto Transit Comm.*, [1949] O.W.N. 431, [1949] 4 D.L.R. 503 (C.A.) — Although a street car operator is generally entitled to assume that a pedestrian or motorist approaching an intersecting street will permit the car to pass by, the circumstances of a preferential right to that part of the highway used by the street railway does not entitle the operator to disregard any apparent danger.

Cooper v. London St. Ry. (1913), 23 O.W.R. 767, 9 D.L.R. 368 (C.A.) — The street car has in fact no right paramount to the ordinary vehicle. Both must travel on the street, and each must exercise its right to use the street with due regard to the rights of the other.

Durie v. Toronto Ry. (1914), 25 O.W.R. 789, 5 O.W.N. 829, 15 D.L.R. 747 (C.A.); *Atkinson v. Toronto Transit Comm.*, [1948] O.W.N. 266 (C.A.); *Tweedie v. Internat. Transit Co.*, [1940] O.W.N. 45, [1940] 1 D.L.R. 731 (C.A.) — It is the duty of the street car company to run their cars under such control, and at such a rate of speed, giving such warning, that when an emergency does arise, such as a vehicle stopped on the tracks, they will be enabled to do everything that reasonable people should do to avoid the accident.

Sim v. Port Arthur (1911), 18 O.W.R. 822, 2 O.W.N. 864 (Div. Ct.) — Merely being or driving on the tracks is not negligence.

Symerose v. Chapman and Toronto Transit Comm., [1949] O.R. 194 (H.C.) — In an action against a street railway for alleged negligent operation of a street car, the plaintiff is entitled to have discovery of any instructions given by the company to instructors of operators, and of any rules, regulations, manuals and other written documents governing the operation of street cars and published by the company. Such documents are relevant to the issue of the operator's negligence as showing the standard of care set up by his or her employer as reasonable, and also to the issue of the company's negligence in employing an incompetent person as operator of a street car.

167. Approaching ridden or driven horses, etc. — **Every person having the control or charge of a motor vehicle or motor assisted bicycle on a highway, when approaching a horse or other animal that is drawing a vehicle or being driven, led or ridden, shall operate, manage and control the motor vehicle or motor assisted bicycle so as to exercise every reasonable precaution to prevent the frightening of the horse or other animal and to ensure the safety and protection of any person driving, leading or riding upon the horse or other animal or being in any vehicle drawn by the horse or other animal.**

Case Law

Nature of Duty

Graham v. K. & E. Tpt. Ltd., [1953] O.W.N. 691 (H.C.) — This section is merely a statutory adoption of the common law duty of a driver of a motor vehicle in relation to horses or other animals on the highway. By analogy a similar duty should apply in relation to animals not on the highway but in a confined area such as a factory yard. The driver of a tractor-trailer was accordingly held liable when he drove unnecessarily close to a team of horses in such a yard, causing them to bolt and thereby injuring the teamster.

Nowitski v. Dutchesen, [1948] 1 W.W.R. 55, [1948] 1 D.L.R. 697 (Sask. C.A.); *Ashick v. Hale* (1911), 20 O.W.R. 606, 3 O.W.N. 372 (H.C.) — Since the duty under this section arises only when a motor vehicle is "approaching" a vehicle drawn by horses, it did not apply to a case where the animals became frightened and bolted when the motor vehicle was passing the horse-drawn vehicle. However, there might still be liability at common law if the motorist did not keep such a watch over the horses as to notice that they were frightened at the car and did not take precautions accordingly.

Stewart v. Steele (1912), 2 W.W.R. 902 (Sask. S.C.); *McIntyre v. Coote* (1909), 19 O.L.R. 9 (Div. Ct.) — Both motorists and persons in charge of horses have an equal right to use the highway, but neither may use it in such a way as to make its use by the other dangerous, and each must use it in conformity with all statutory requirements.

Boyes v. Harris (2000), 7 M.V.R. (4th) 18, 82 B.C.L.R. (3d) 324 (B.C. C.A.) — A motorist should exercise great caution when he sees that a rider is having problems controlling the horse.

168. Use of passing beam — **When on a highway at any time when lighted lamps are required to be displayed on vehicles, the driver of a motor vehicle equipped with multiple beam headlamps shall use the lower or passing beam when,**

> **(a) approaching an oncoming vehicle within 150 metres; or**

> **(b) following another vehicle within 60 metres, except when in the act of overtaking and passing.**

169. (1) Alternating highbeams on emergency vehicles — **Despite section 168, highbeam headlamps that produce alternating flashes of white light may be**

used by a public utility emergency vehicle while responding to an emergency and by an emergency vehicle as defined in subsection 144(1).

(2) Alternating highbeams on other vehicles prohibited — No person shall use highbeam headlamps that produce alternating flashes of white light on any vehicle other than a vehicle referred to in subsection (1).

170. (1) Parking on roadway — No person shall park, stand or stop a vehicle on a roadway,

>   (a) when it is practicable to park, stand or stop the vehicle off the roadway; or

>   (b) when it is not practicable to park, stand or stop the vehicle off the roadway unless a clear view of the vehicle and of the roadway for at least 125 metres beyond the vehicle may be obtained from a distance of at least 125 metres from the vehicle in each direction upon the highway.

(2) Where subs. (1) does not apply — Subsection (1) does not apply to that portion of a roadway within a local municipality, other than a local municipality that was a township on December 31, 2002 and, but for the enactment of the *Municipal Act, 2001*, would have been a township on January 1, 2003.

(3) Idem — Subsection (1) does not apply to that portion of a roadway within a local municipality that was a township on December 31, 2002 and, but for the enactment of the *Municipal Act, 2001*, would have been a township on January 1, 2003 in respect of which there is a by-law prohibiting or regulating parking, standing and stopping.

(4) Idem — Subsection (1) does not apply to a road service vehicle that is parked, standing or stopped safely.

(5) Regulations, parking, etc. — The Minister may make regulations prohibiting or regulating the parking, standing or stopping of vehicles upon a highway or any part of a highway or upon any class or classes thereof.

(6) Effect of regulation on municipal by-law — The part of every municipal by-law that is inconsistent with or has the same effect as a regulation made under subsection (5) is revoked on the day the regulation comes into force.

(7) Removal of vehicle parked at prohibited place — Whenever a police officer, police cadet, municipal law enforcement officer or an officer appointed for carrying out the provisions of this Act finds a vehicle on a highway in contravention of this section or the regulations, he or she may move the vehicle or require the driver or operator or other person in charge of the vehicle to move it.

(8) Disabled vehicle — The provisions of this section do not apply to the driver or operator of a vehicle that is so disabled while on a highway that it is impossible to avoid temporarily a contravention of the provisions.

(9) Precaution against vehicle being set in motion — No person shall park or stand a vehicle on a highway unless he or she has taken the action that may be reasonably necessary in the circumstances to prevent the vehicle from moving or being set in motion.

(10) Warning lights on commercial motor vehicles — Every commercial motor vehicle, when on a highway on which the speed limit is in excess of 60 kilometres per hour at any time when lighted lamps are required to be displayed on vehicles, shall be equipped with a sufficient number of,

(a) flares, lamps or lanterns that have been approved by the Ministry, capable of continuously producing two warning lights, each visible from a distance of at least 150 metres for a period of at least eight hours; or

(b) portable reflectors that have been approved by the Ministry.

(11) Flares on disabled commercial motor vehicle or trailer — When any commercial motor vehicle or trailer is disabled during the period when lighted lamps are required to be displayed on vehicles and the vehicle cannot immediately be removed from the roadway on which the speed limit is in excess of 60 kilometres per hour, the driver or other person in charge of the vehicle shall cause the flares, lamps or lanterns to be lighted, and shall cause them or portable reflectors approved by the Ministry to be placed and maintained on the highway until the time that lighted lamps are not required to be displayed on vehicles or the removal of the vehicle, one at a distance of approximately 30 metres in advance of the vehicle and one at a distance of approximately 30 metres to the rear of the vehicle.

(12) Vehicles interfering with traffic — Despite the other provisions of this section, no person shall park or stand a vehicle on a highway in such a manner as to interfere with the movement of traffic or the clearing of snow from the highway.

(13) Application of subs. (12), where by-law in force — The provisions of subsection (12) with respect to parking or standing in such a manner as to interfere with the movement of traffic or with the clearing of snow from the highway do not apply to a portion of a highway in respect of which a municipal by-law prohibiting or regulating parking or standing in such a manner as to interfere with traffic or with the clearing of snow from the highway, as the case may be, is in force.

(14) Penalty — Every person who contravenes this section is guilty of an offence and on conviction is liable to a fine of not less than $20 and not more than $100.

(15) Powers of officer to remove vehicle — A police officer, police cadet, municipal law enforcement officer or an officer appointed for carrying out the provisions of this Act, upon discovery of any vehicle parked or standing in contravention of subsection (12), of a regulation made under subsection 26(3) of the *Public Transportation and Highway Improvement Act* or of a municipal by-law, may cause it to be moved or taken to and placed or stored in a suitable place and all costs and charges for the removal, care and storage of the vehicle, if any, are a lien upon the vehicle, which may be enforced in the manner provided by the *Repair and Storage Liens Act*.

2002, c. 17, Sched. F, s. 1; 2005, c. 26, Sched. A, s. 28

Commentary

The effect of the provisions of the Act is briefly that vehicles must not be parked on the travelled portion of a highway, not within a city, town or village and not governed by any by-laws: (a) where it is practicable to park off the roadway; (b) at any point where there is not a clear view of the vehicle for 125 metres in either direction; or (c) at any point where the vehicle so parked would interfere with the movement of other traffic or the clearing of snow from the highway. Vehicles offending against these restrictions may be removed by enforcement officers at the expense of the owner. If it is not practicable to park off the roadway, conditions (b) and (c) would still apply; if it is night-time, lights must be shown in accordance with the provisions of s. 62.

An exception applies in favour of disabled vehicles where a temporary contravention of the restrictions is unavoidable, but in such a case lights should be shown in compliance with s. 62, or other precautions taken pursuant to the common law duty of care to warn other users of the highway of the presence of the vehicle in its dangerous position. Disabled commercial motor vehicles must also be protected by flares, lamps, lanterns or approved portable reflectors set out 30 metres each side of the vehicle.

Case Law

Park or Leave Standing

McKee and Taylor v. Malenfant, [1954] S.C.R. 641, [1954] 4 D.L.R. 785 — There is no requirement in the Act that vehicles lawfully using the highway must be kept perpetually in motion. To stop a car for some temporary purpose upon its proper side of the road cannot be negligence *per se*, since vehicles are constantly stopping upon the highway for a variety of purposes. Drivers of other vehicles are aware of this and they must for their own protection keep a vigilant lookout.

Speers v. Griffin, [1939] O.R. 552, [1939] 3 D.L.R. 412 (C.A.) — These words "park or leave standing" import conduct substantially different from the conduct of a driver who drove out of a gateway onto the highway and waited momentarily in his truck until his helper shut the gate and got upon the truck. The word "park" involved more than a momentary stop, and the words "leave standing" were not satisfied by the mere stopping of the truck, the driver remaining in his place and intending to proceed directly.

Colonial Coach Lines Ltd. v. Garland, [1954] 4 D.L.R. 779 (S.C.C.) — A bus stopping to pick up a passenger was not obliged to pull further than it did onto the shoulder.

Brain v. Crinnian, 66 O.L.R. 223, [1931] 1 D.L.R. 546 (C.A.) — A driver has a right at common law to stop temporarily on a road to load or unload his or her vehicle, but this right is limited by the correlative right of others to pass along it. The right of the driver so to stop must be exercised reasonably, and whether the length of time or extent of stoppage is reasonable is a question of fact to be determined by the circumstances of each case.

Gushulak v. Myskiw (1963), 42 W.W.R. 377 (Man. Q.B.) — It is a reasonable act to stop on the travelled portion to assist a disabled vehicle where a gravel ridge rendered it impossible to park off the highway.

Young v. Younger, [1945] O.R. 467, [1945] 3 D.L.R. 195 (C.A.) — A driver stopping in the line of traffic to effect repairs was held to have created an obstruction and a hazard to traffic.

R. v. McIntire (2013), 55 M.V.R. (6th) 159, 2013 YKTC 98, 2013 CarswellYukon 123, [2013] Y.J. No. 115 — A sign at an airport reading "Immediate pickup and drop off only" did not permit parking for five minutes after leaving the car.

R. v. Pike (2013), 56 M.V.R. (6th) 144, 2013 CarswellNfld 403, 341 Nfld. & P.E.I.R. 357, 1061 A.P.R. 357 (Prov. Ct.) — A standing vehicle, which was loading or unloading goods, was not considered parked.

Parking on Travelled Portion

McLean v. McCannell (1936), [1938] O.R. 37 (C.A.); affirmed [1937] S.C.R. 341, [1937] 2 D.L.R. 639; *Gingrich v. Lishman*, [1953] O.W.N. 588 (H.C.) — Non-compliance with the requirement as to parking off the travelled portion of the highway is evidence of negligence and casts on the driver the onus of establishing that it was not practicable to move his or her vehicle off the roadway.

People's Co-op. Ltd. v. Anderson (1963), 46 W.W.R. 95 (Man. C.A.) — The owner of a vehicle left protruding onto the highway was held liable even though the other vehicle which collided with it had strayed across the highway onto the wrong side during a fog.

Windover v. Guest (1958), 15 D.L.R. (2d) 37 (Ont. C.A.) — The improper parking of a car on the roadway may be found to be a contributing cause of collision between two other vehicles, as where the position of the illegally parked car makes it necessary for a vehicle approaching from the rear to cross well over the centre line to pass it.

Bruce v. McIntyre, [1955] S.C.R. 251, [1955] 1 D.L.R. 785 — The Act does not provide that when vehicles are stopped or parked they must be placed on or to the right of the roadway along which they are proceeding, but it is a matter of common knowledge that this is practically the universal procedure.

Disabled Vehicles

Pluard v. Sheldon, [1951] O.R. 761, [1952] 1 D.L.R. 485 (C.A.) — Where a motorist claims the benefit of the exception in s. 170(8) it is good practice that a question should be left expressly to the jury to find whether it was "impossible to avoid temporarily a contravention of the provisions" of the section. Appropriate directions should be given to them that if they answer in the affirmative they should disregard those provisions, whereas if they answer in the negative they must then proceed to consider whether there was a breach of the provisions and whether that breach contributed to cause the loss or damage complained of.

Gingrich v. Lishman, [1953] O.W.N. 588 (H.C.) — The onus is on the driver to show that it was impracticable to park off the highway. Even where that onus is discharged, *e.g.*, by reason of the vehicle being bogged in snow, the requirements of the Act must still be complied with as to lights and flares if the vehicle is left on the highway after dark.

Dawson v. Oberton (1952), 6 W.W.R. 465 (Alta. C.A.) — When a vehicle becomes stalled on the highway, it is the duty of the driver to make use of any available assistance either to move the vehicle to a safer position, or to give warning to other traffic.

Poole & Thompson Ltd. v. McNally, [1934] S.C.R. 717, [1935] 1 D.L.R. 161 — A motorist is clearly justified in stopping on the highway to change a flat tire provided that he or she picks a safe place, *e.g.*, not on a curve.

Rubin v. Steeves (1951), 28 M.P.R. 421 (N.B. C.A.); *Ellis v. Zimmerman*, [1933] 1 W.W.R. 550 (Alta. T.D.) — A driver may be guilty of negligence if he or she leaves a vehicle unnecessarily protruding on the highway and without parking lights at night.

Flares On Commercial Vehicles

Marsden Kooler Tpt. Ltd. v. Pollock, [1953] 1 S.C.R. 66, [1953] 1 D.L.R. 1; *Hill v. Snaychuk*, [1950] 2 W.W.R. 1202 (Alta. T.D.) — A statutory requirement such as putting out flares constitutes a duty that must be performed. If the flares are placed with care they are often an adequate protection, at least for some time. However, the performance of that statutory obligation is the minimum required by law and does not relieve the driver of a truck who left a disabled trailer on the road from exercising the care that a reasonable person would exercise in the circumstances.

Unlighted Vehicles

Keays v. Parks (1950), 27 M.P.R. 296 (N.B. C.A.); *Hill-Venning v. Beszant*, [1950] 2 All E.R. 1151 (C.A.); *City Motors (Nfld.) Ltd. v. Anderson* (1964), 50 M.P.R. 119 (Nfld. T.D.) — The parking of an unlighted vehicle at night on the travelled portion of the highway is, in the absence of some reasonable excuse, negligence at common law. Stopping to repair lights is not such a reasonable excuse where the driver could have parked well to the right.

Bruce v. McIntyre, [1955] S.C.R. 251, [1955] 1 D.L.R. 785 — Persons driving upon the highway at night are entitled to proceed on the assumption that the drivers of other vehicles will comply with the provisions of the Act, and that any vehicle, either parked or temporarily stopped on the highway will exhibit a red light at the rear, though care must still be exercised by the driver of the moving vehicle.

Precautions Against Being Set in Motion (s. 170(9))

Scott v. Philp (1922), 52 O.L.R. 513 (C.A.) — A person lawfully leaving a motor vehicle unattended on a highway must take reasonable means to prevent such mischief as ought to be contemplated as likely to arise from use of the highway, but he or she is not liable for damage caused by his or her property through such interference of third parties as he or she is not bound to anticipate. In this case, a car was left with the wheels towards the curb and the emergency brake unset and a year-old boy got into the car with the result that it was put in motion down an incline and ran into the damaged property. The person so leaving the car was held not to have been negligent as he was not bound to anticipate the interference.

Parking By-Laws

R. v. Anderson, [1960] O.W.N. 189 (Co. Ct.) — The authority under the Municipal Act was restricted to by-laws requiring drivers, and not owners, to use parking meters. A charge could not therefore be laid against the owner as such for non-compliance with the parking meter by-law. The provision was amended in the next session of the Legislature to provide that owners were responsible for infractions of the by-law.

R. v. Brunetti, [1962] O.R. 58, 31 D.L.R. (2d) 21 (C.A.) — The practice of police officers placing chalk-marks on tires of vehicles in order to secure evidence of overparking was considered. The accused was acquitted on a charge of obstructing a police officer where he had erased a chalk-mark from the tire, since it was not shown that the police had any authority to so mark private property, and there was also no evidence to indicate that an offence had been committed or would likely be committed.

R. v. Rogers (1984), 29 M.V.R. 126 (Ont. H.C.) — The accused appealed by way of stated case from his conviction for parking in violation of a municipal by-law. The by-law prohibited individuals from street parking at specified times unless they were holders of specially issued parking permits. At trial, it was held that once the Crown had established ownership of the vehicle, the fact that it was parked at the specified location at the specified time and that no parking permit was displayed in the windshield, caused the onus to shift to the accused under s. 730(2) [now s. 794(2)] of the Criminal Code, to prove that he was, in fact, a permit holder. As the accused called no evidence, it was found that he had not discharged the onus and was convicted. The main question posed on the appeal was whether the Justice of the Peace had erred in finding that the onus lay with the accused to prove that he was the holder of a permit rather than the onus being on the Crown to prove that the accused was not a permit holder. The question was answered in the negative and the appeal was dismissed. Section 730(2) of the Criminal Code placed the burden on the accused to prove that an exception or exemption to an offence was operating in his favour. Proof of possession of a parking permit constituted such an exception and therefore the onus was properly upon the accused. Furthermore, as the accused would have to apply for the permit, the matter was well within his knowledge. Therefore a rational connection existed between the proved facts and the presumed fact with the result that the accused's Charter right to be presumed innocent and his right not to be compellable as a witness against himself were not infringed.

R. v. Timplaru (1987), 49 M.V.R. 41, 58 Sask R. 106 (Q.B.) — The accused was charged with an offence under s. 83(1) of the Vehicles Act (Sask.). The information described the offence as "stopping improperly on a highway." The trial Judge held that s. 83(1) created two offences and, since it was not clear from the information which one the accused had been charged with, the information was duplicitous. The information was quashed. The Crown appealed. The appeal was allowed. The description of the offence as "stopping improperly on a highway" to this case was correct as the relevant section created only one offence and the accused was aware of the case he had to meet. Accordingly, the information was not duplicitous.

McCutcheon v. Corp. of Toronto (City) (1983), 20 M.V.R. 267 (Ont. H.C.) — A challenge under subss. 11(d) and (i) of the Charter of Rights and Freedoms was unsuccessfully mounted against a city by-law that contained a sliding scale of out-of-court payments, which was intended to promote prompt payment.

858579 Ontario Inc. v. QAP Parking Enforcement Ltd. (1995), 11 M.V.R. (3d) 91, 22 O.R. (3d) 346, 122 D.L.R. (4th) 314, 80 O.A.C. 241 (Ont. Div. Ct.) — A towing company, acting at the behest of a private property owner, does not have a lien right.

Related Provisions: See s. 195 regarding the power of municipalities to pass by-laws regulating the parking of vehicles within the municipal area; see also Provincial Offences Act, R.S.O. 1990, c. P.33, Part II; R.R.O. 1990, Reg. 604, Parking; R.R.O. 1990, Reg. 605, Parking of Vehicles in Territory without Municipal Organization; R.R.O. 1990, Reg. 615, Signs, ss. 13-15, 24-27; R.R.O. 1990, Reg. 622, Stopping of Vehicles on Parts of the King's Highway.

171. (1) Tow truck services — **No person shall make or convey an offer of services of a tow truck while that person is within 200 metres of,**

    (a) the scene of an accident or apparent accident; or

    (b) a vehicle involved in an accident,

on the King's Highway.

(2) Idem — No person shall park or stop a tow truck on the King's Highway within 200 metres of,

(a) the scene of an accident or apparent accident; or

(b) a vehicle involved in an accident,

if there is a sufficient number of tow trucks already at the scene to deal with all vehicles that apparently require the services of a tow truck.

(3) Idem — Subsections (1) and (2) do not apply to a person who is at the scene of the accident at the request of a police officer, an officer appointed for carrying out the provisions of this Act, a person engaged in highway maintenance or a person involved in the accident.

Proposed Addition — 171(3.1)

(3.1) Other prohibited activities — No driver of a tow truck, or other person who is in charge of a tow truck, shall engage in an activity prohibited by regulation.

2014, c. 9, Sched. 2, s. 39 [To come into force January 1, 2017.]

(4) Offence — Every person who contravenes any provision in this section is guilty of an offence and on conviction is liable,

(a) for a first offence, to a fine of not less than $200 and not more than $1,000; and

(b) for each subsequent offence, to a fine of not less than $400 and not more than $2,000, or to imprisonment for a term of not more than six months, or to both.

(5) Idem — An offence under this section committed five years or longer after a previous conviction for an offence under this section is not a subsequent offence for the purposes of clause (4)(b).

Proposed Addition — 171(6)

(6) Regulations — The Lieutenant Governor in Council may make regulations,

(a) defining "tow truck" for the purposes of this section;

(b) prescribing prohibited activities for the purpose of subsection (3.1), prescribing conditions and circumstances when the prohibitions apply or do not apply, exempting any class of persons or of vehicles from any such prohibition, and prescribing conditions and circumstances for any such exemption.

2014, c. 9, Sched. 2, s. 39 [To come into force January 1, 2017.]

172. (1) Racing, stunts, etc., prohibited — No person shall drive a motor vehicle on a highway in a race or contest, while performing a stunt or on a bet or wager.

(2) Offence — Every person who contravenes subsection (1) is guilty of an offence and on conviction is liable to a fine of not less than $2,000 and not more than

$10,000 or to imprisonment for a term of not more than six months, or to both, and in addition his or her driver's licence may be suspended,

(a) on a first conviction under this section, for not more than two years; or

(b) on a subsequent conviction under this section, for not more than 10 years.

(3) **Determining subsequent conviction** — In determining whether a conviction is a subsequent conviction for the purposes of subsection (2), the only question to be considered is the sequence of convictions and no consideration shall be given to the sequence of commission of offences or whether any offence occurred before or after any conviction.

(4) **10-year limitation** — A conviction that is more than 10 years after the previous conviction is deemed to be a first conviction for the purpose of subsection (2).

(5) **Police to require surrender of licence, detention of vehicle** — Where a police officer believes on reasonable and probable grounds that a person is driving, or has driven, a motor vehicle on a highway in contravention of subsection (1), the officer shall,

(a) request that the person surrender his or her driver's licence; and

(b) detain the motor vehicle that was being driven by the person until it is impounded under clause (7)(b).

(6) **Administrative seven-day licence suspension** — Upon a request being made under clause (5)(a), the person to whom the request is made shall forthwith surrender his or her driver's licence to the police officer and, whether or not the person is unable or fails to surrender the licence to the police officer, his or her driver's licence is suspended for a period of seven days from the time the request is made.

(7) **Administrative seven-day vehicle impoundment** — Upon a motor vehicle being detained under clause (5)(b), the motor vehicle shall, at the cost of and risk to its owner,

(a) be removed to an impound facility as directed by a police officer; and

(b) be impounded for seven days from the time it was detained under clause (5)(b).

(8) **Release of vehicle** — Subject to subsection (15), the motor vehicle shall be released to its owner from the impound facility upon the expiry of the period of impoundment.

(9) **Early release of vehicle** — Despite the detention or impoundment of a motor vehicle under this section, a police officer may release the motor vehicle to its owner before it is impounded under subsection (7) or, subject to subsection (15), may direct the operator of the impound facility where the motor vehicle is impounded to release the motor vehicle to its owner before the expiry of the seven days if the officer is satisfied that the motor vehicle was stolen at the time that it was driven on a highway in contravention of subsection (1).

(10) **Duty of officer re licence suspension** — Every officer who asks for the surrender of a person's driver's licence under this section shall keep a record of the

licence received with the name and address of the person and the date and time of the suspension and shall, as soon as practicable after receiving the licence, provide the person with a notice of suspension showing the time from which the suspension takes effect and the period of time for which the licence is suspended.

(11) Duty of officer re impoundment — Every officer who detains a motor vehicle under this section shall prepare a notice identifying the motor vehicle that is to be impounded under subsection (7), the name and address of the driver and the date and time of the impoundment and shall, as soon as practicable after the impoundment of the motor vehicle, provide the driver with a copy of the notice showing the time from which the impoundment takes effect, the period of time for which the motor vehicle is impounded and the place where the vehicle may be recovered.

(12) Same — A police officer shall provide a copy of the notice prepared under subsection (11) to the owner of the motor vehicle by delivering it personally or by mail to the address of the owner shown on the permit for the motor vehicle or to the latest address for the owner appearing on the records of the Ministry.

(13) No appeal or hearing — There is no appeal from, or right to be heard before, a vehicle detention, driver's licence suspension or vehicle impoundment under subsection (5), (6) or (7), but this subsection does not affect the taking of any proceeding in court.

(14) Lien for storage costs — The costs incurred by the person who operates the impound facility where a motor vehicle is impounded under this section are a lien on the motor vehicle that may be enforced under the *Repair and Storage Liens Act.*

(15) Costs to be paid before release of vehicle — The person who operates the impound facility where a motor vehicle is impounded under subsection (7) is not required to release the motor vehicle until the removal and impound costs for the vehicle have been paid.

(16) Owner may recover losses from driver — The owner of a motor vehicle that is impounded under this section may bring an action against the driver of the motor vehicle at the time the vehicle was detained under clause (5)(b) to recover any costs or other losses incurred by the owner in connection with the impoundment.

(17) Offence — Every person who obstructs or interferes with a police officer in the performance of his or her duties under this section is guilty of an offence and on conviction is liable to a fine of not less than $200 and not more than $5,000 or to imprisonment for a term of not more than six months, or to both.

(18) Intent of suspension and impoundment — The suspension of a driver's licence and the impoundment of a motor vehicle under this section are intended to promote compliance with this Act and to thereby safeguard the public and do not constitute an alternative to any proceeding or penalty arising from the same circumstances or around the same time.

(18.1) Impoundment concurrent with other administrative impoundments — The impoundment of a motor vehicle under this section runs concurrently with an impoundment, if any, of the same motor vehicle under section 41.4, 48.4, 55.1, 55.2 or 82.1.

(19) [Repealed 2008, c. 17, s. 43.]

(20) Regulations — The Lieutenant Governor in Council may make regulations,

(a) requiring police officers to keep records with respect to licence suspensions and vehicle impoundments under this section for a specified period of time and to report specified information with respect to licence suspensions and vehicle impoundments to the Registrar and governing such records and reports;

(b) exempting any class of persons or class or type of vehicles from any provision or requirement of this section or of any regulation made under this section, prescribing conditions for any such exemptions and prescribing different requirements for different classes of persons or different classes or types of vehicles;

(c) defining the terms "race", "contest" and "stunt" for the purposes of this section.

(21) Definition — In this section,

"driver's licence" includes a driver's licence issued by another jurisdiction.

(22) Same — In this section and in section 172.1,

"motor vehicle" includes a street car, a motorized snow vehicle, a farm tractor, a self-propelled implement of husbandry and a road-building machine.

2007, c. 13, s. 21; 2008, c. 17, s. 43; 2009, c. 5, s. 51

Case Law

Canning v. Wood (1918), 52 N.S.R. 452, 44 D.L.R. 525 (T.D.) — The word "race" as used in this section means a pre-arranged race. The object aimed at is the prevention of the use of the public highway as a race track, such use being likely to attract a number of people and to be accompanied by danger to the public. It would appear, therefore, that merely to speed-up in an attempt to prevent another driver from overtaking would not be within this section, but such conduct might well be an offence against s. 172 requiring an overtaken driver to turn out to the right and allow the other vehicle to pass.

R. v. Smith, [1971] 5 W.W.R. 674 (Sask. Dist. Ct.) — It is not necessary to prove that the accused expressly agreed with another, or others, to embark on a race; this may properly be inferred from observed conduct.

R. v. Tremblay (1974), 1974 CarswellAlta 183, [1975] 3 W.W.R. 589, 23 C.C.C. (2d) 179, 58 D.L.R. (3d) 69 (C.A.) — Flashing headlights or taillights repetitively to warn oncoming vehicles of a police presence did not constitute stunting or other activities on a highway likely to distract, startle or interfere with other users of the highway.

Cavanagh v. Peck (1979), 37 N.S.R. (2d) 94, 67 A.P.R. 94 (T.D.) — The plaintiff was a passenger in a motor vehicle operated by the defendant. The defendant was racing with another car and the plaintiff urged him to go faster. The defendant lost control at 125 m.p.h. and crashed. Gross negligence on the defendant's part was admitted. It was held that the damages should be reduced 25% for her contributory negligence in encouraging the defendant to increase his speed.

R. v. Flannery (1982), 15 M.V.R. 116, 15 Man. R. (2d) 162 (Co. Ct.) — The appellant was convicted of racing contrary to s. 174(1) of the Highway Traffic Act, R.S.M. 1970, c. H60, which reads: "No person shall race a motor vehicle with another motor vehicle upon a highway." The appeal was dismissed. The test a judge must apply is whether from "observed conduct", the conduct and manner of driving constituted racing, in the face of a denial of a scheme or pre-arranged agreement to race. Here, three times the vehicles came abreast and travelled while accelerating on a main street of a hamlet over a distance of two blocks. The repetition of conduct shows an agreement. While the speeds were not atrocious, the manner in which the ultimate speed was attained having regard to the time, location and circumstances existing and the method of accelerating from almost zero to at least 50 km/h in as short a distance as possible while driving abreast connotes only one purpose — to race. Speed is only one element of a race. All the circumstances must be looked at. It is not necessary to show an express agreement to race; such may be inferred from the conduct.

R. v. Beaudoin, 2009 CarswellSask 239, 2009 SKQB 113, 333 Sask. R. 302, 84 M.V.R. (5th) 44 — The phrase "likely to distract, startle or interfere with other users of the highway" in the Saskatchewan *Traffic Safety Act* does not mean that other drivers must be nearly and actually distracted, startled or interfered with.

R. v. White, 2009 CarswellYukon 53, 85 M.V.R. (5th) 118, 2009 YKSC 26 — While a police officer was distracted while investigating another motorist by the loud noise made by after-market headers and exhausts on his truck, drinking was not made out. But see *R. v. Burton* (1984), [1984] S.J. No. 46, 1984 CarswellSask 15, 29 M.V.R. 229, 36 Sask. R. 153 (Q.B.) where a conviction was registered.

R. v. Raham, 2010 CarswellOnt 1546, 2010 ONCA 206, 74 C.R. (6th) 96, 253 C.C.C. (3d) 188, 99 O.R. (3d) 241, 92 M.V.R. (5th) 195, [2010] O.J. No. 1091, 260 O.A.C. 143, 213 C.R.R. (2d) 336 (March 18, 2010) — The offence of stunt driving, stunt driving by speeding 50 kilometres or more over the speed limit, pursuant to s. 172 of the *Act*, and O. Reg. 455/07, s. 3 is an offence of strict liability. Section 172 sets out that the offence may be committed in three ways. Speeding under s. 128 is an included offence under s. 55 of the *Provincial Offences Act* (Ont.).

Related Provisions: See O. Reg. 455/07; Races, Contests and Stunts, O. Reg. 407/08, Reporting to the Registrar: Administrative Suspension of Drivers' Licences.

172.1 (1) Nitrous oxide fuel systems prohibited — No person shall drive or permit to be driven on a highway a motor vehicle manufactured or modified after its manufacture such that nitrous oxide may be delivered into the fuel mixture unless,

(a) the part of the fuel system that may connect to a canister, bottle, tank or pressure vessel capable of containing nitrous oxide can be clearly seen by looking at the interior or exterior of the motor vehicle;

(b) there is no canister, bottle, tank or pressure vessel connected to that part; and

(c) if the part of the fuel system that may connect to a canister, bottle, tank or pressure vessel capable of containing nitrous oxide is located inside the passenger compartment, there is no canister, bottle, tank or pressure vessel capable of containing nitrous oxide in the passenger compartment.

(2) Same — No person shall drive or permit to be driven on a highway a motor vehicle manufactured or modified after its manufacture such that nitrous oxide may be delivered into the fuel mixture unless,

(a) the part of the fuel system that may connect to a canister, bottle, tank or pressure vessel capable of containing nitrous oxide is completely disconnected from the part of the system that connects to the engine;

(b) the disconnection can be clearly seen by looking at the interior or exterior of the motor vehicle; and

(c) the disconnected parts cannot be reconnected from inside the passenger compartment.

(3) Offence — Every person who contravenes subsection (1) or (2) is guilty of an offence and on conviction is liable to a fine of not less than $500 and not more than $2,000 or to imprisonment for a term of not more than six months, or to both.

2007, c. 13, s. 22

173. Horse racing on highway — No person shall race or drive furiously any horse or other animal on a highway.

174. (1) Public vehicles required to stop at railway crossings — The driver of a public vehicle upon approaching on a highway a railway crossing that is not protected by gates or railway crossing signal lights, unless otherwise directed by a flagman, shall,

(a) stop the vehicle not less than 5 metres from the nearest rail of the railway;

(b) look in both directions along the railway track;

(c) open a door of the vehicle and listen to determine if any train is approaching;

(d) when it is safe to do so, cross the railway track in a gear that will not need to be changed while crossing the track; and

(e) not change gears while crossing the railway track.

(2) School buses required to stop it railway crossings — The driver of a school bus, within the meaning of section 175, upon approaching on a highway a railway crossing, whether or not it is protected by gates or railway crossing signal lights, unless otherwise directed by a flagman, shall,

(a) stop the school bus not less than 5 metres from the nearest rail of the railway;

(b) look in both directions along the railway track;

(c) open a door of the school bus and listen to determine if any train is approaching;

(d) when it is safe to do so, cross the railway track in a gear that will not need to be changed while crossing the track; and

(e) not change gears while crossing the railway track.

1997, c. 12, s. 13

Related Provisions: See ss. 163 and 164 of the Act.

175. (1) Definitions — In this section,

"children" means,

    (a) persons under the age of eighteen, and

    (b) in the case where a school bus is being operated by or under a contract with a school board or other authority in charge of a school for the transportation of children to or from school, includes students of the school;

"developmental disability" means a condition of mental impairment, present or occurring during a person's formative years, that is associated with limitations in adaptive behaviour;

"developmental handicap" [Repealed 2001, c. 13, s. 18(1).]

"school" does not include a post-secondary school educational institution;

"school bus" means a bus that,

    (a) is painted chrome yellow, and

    (b) displays on the front and rear thereof the words "school bus" and on the rear thereof the words "do not pass when signals flashing".

(2) Idem — For the purposes of subsection (3), a motor vehicle shall be deemed to be a bus if it is or has been operated under the authority of a permit for which a bus registration or validation fee was paid in any jurisdiction.

(3) Prohibition — No part of a bus, except a bus that at any time during its current validation period is used to transport children or to transport adults who have developmental disabilities, shall be painted chrome yellow.

(3.1) Same — If all or part of a bus operated under the authority of a permit issued under subsection 7(7) is painted chrome yellow, the bus shall also display on its front and rear the words "school bus" and on its rear the words "do not pass when signals flashing".

(4) Idem — No motor vehicle on a highway, other than a school bus, shall have displayed thereon the words "school bus" or the words "do not pass when signals flashing" or be equipped with a school bus stop arm.

(5) Driving motor vehicle, subss. (3), (3.1) and (4) — No person shall drive or operate a motor vehicle on a highway that contravenes subsection (3), (3.1) or (4).

(6) Duty of driver to use signals — Subject to subsection (9), every school bus driver,

    (a) who is about to stop on a highway for the purpose of receiving or discharging children or receiving or discharging adults who have developmental disabilities, shall actuate the overhead red signal-lights on the bus;

    (b) as soon as the bus is stopped for a purpose set out in clause (a), shall actuate the school bus stop arm; and

(c) while the bus is stopped for a purpose set out in clause (a) on a highway, shall continue to operate the overhead red signal-lights and stop arm until the passengers have been received or discharged and until all passengers having to cross the highway have completed the crossing.

(7) **Exception to cl. 170(1)(a)** — Clause 170(1)(a) does not apply to a driver who stops in accordance with subsection (6).

(8) **Restriction on use of signals** — No person shall actuate the overhead red signal-lights or the stop arm on a school bus on a highway under any circumstances other than those set out in subsection (6).

(9) **Idem** — No person shall actuate the overhead red signal-lights or the stop arm on a school bus,

(a) at an intersection controlled by an operating traffic control signal system;

(b) at any other location controlled by an operating traffic control signal system at,

(i) a sign or roadway marking indicating where the stop is to be made,

(ii) the area immediately before entering the nearest crosswalk, if there is no sign or marking indicating where the stop is to be made, or

(iii) a point not less than five metres before the nearest traffic control signal, if there is no sign, marking or crosswalk; or

(c) within sixty metres from a location referred to in clause (a) or (b).

(10) **Bus loading zone** — No person shall stop a school bus on a highway for the purpose of receiving or discharging children or receiving or discharging adults who have developmental disabilities,

(a) opposite a designated school bus loading zone; or

(b) at a designated school bus loading zone, except as close as practicable to the right curb or edge of the roadway.

(11) **Duty of drivers when school bus stopped** — Every driver or street car operator, when meeting on a highway, other than a highway with a median strip, a stopped school bus that has its overhead red signal-lights flashing, shall stop before reaching the bus and shall not proceed until the bus moves or the overhead red signal-lights have stopped flashing.

(12) **Idem** — Every driver or street car operator on a highway, when approaching from the rear a stopped school bus that has its overhead red signal-lights flashing, shall stop at least twenty metres before reaching the bus and shall not proceed until the bus moves or the overhead red signal-lights have stopped flashing.

(13) **Designating bus loading zones** — A council of a municipality may by by-law designate school bus loading zones, in accordance with the regulations, on highways under its jurisdiction and, where it does so, subsection (6) does not apply to a driver about to stop or stopping in a zone so designated.

(14) When effective — No by-law passed under subsection (13) becomes effective until the highways or portions thereof affected have signs erected in compliance with this Act and the regulations.

(15) Regulations — The Lieutenant Governor in Council may make regulations,

(a) respecting the operation of vehicles used for transporting children or for transporting adults who have developmental disabilities;

(b) prescribing the type, design and colour of vehicles referred to in clause (a) and the markings to be displayed thereon;

(c) requiring the use of any equipment on or in vehicles referred to in clause (a) and prescribing the standards and specifications of the equipment;

(d) prescribing the qualifications of drivers of vehicles referred to in clause (a) and prohibiting the operation thereof by unqualified persons;

(e) requiring the inspection of vehicles referred to in clause (a);

(f) respecting the designation of school bus loading zones, the location thereof, the erection of signs and the placing of markings on highways;

(g) prescribing the books and records that shall be kept by persons who operate vehicles used for transporting children or for transporting adults who have developmental disabilities;

(h) requiring the retention of prescribed books and records within vehicles and prescribing the information to be contained and the entries to be recorded in the books or records;

(i) governing the service of offence notices for the purposes of subsections (26), (27) and (28), including authorizing service outside Ontario and deeming service to have been effected on a date determined in accordance with the regulations.

(16) Scope of regulations — Any regulation made under subsection (15) may be general or particular in its application.

(17) Penalty — Every person who contravenes subsection (11) or (12) is guilty of an offence and on conviction is liable,

(a) for a first offence, to a fine of not less than $400 and not more than $2,000; and

(b) for each subsequent offence, to a fine of not less than $1,000 and not more than $4,000 or to imprisonment for a term of not more than six months, or to both.

(18) Time limit for subsequent offence — An offence referred to in subsection (17) committed more than five years after a previous conviction for either of the offences referred to in subsection (17) is not a subsequent offence for the purpose of clause (17)(b).

(19) Certificate of offence — owner — A person who issues a certificate of offence or who prepares an information to be laid under the *Provincial Offences Act* for a contravention of subsection (11) shall, despite that Act and the regulations under that Act, specify this subsection, instead of subsection (11), as the provision that was contravened, if the defendant is being charged as the owner of the vehicle.

(20) **Same** — A person who issues a certificate of offence or who prepares an information to be laid under the *Provincial Offences Act* for a contravention of subsection (12) shall, despite that Act and the regulations under that Act, specify this subsection, instead of subsection (12), as the provision that was contravened, if the defendant is being charged as the owner of the vehicle.

(21) **Deemed to specify subs. (11) or (12)** — A certificate of offence, offence notice, information or summons that specifies subsection (19) or (20) as the provision that was contravened shall be deemed to specify that subsection (11) or (12) was contravened, as the case may be.

(22) **No dismissal** — No charge shall be dismissed, and no certificate of offence or information shall be quashed, on the basis that a certificate of offence, offence notice, information or summons specifies subsection (19) or (20) instead of subsection (11) or (12) as the provision that was contravened.

(23) **No amendment** — A certificate of offence or information that specifies subsection (11) or (12) as the provision that was contravened shall not be amended to specify subsection (19) or (20) and a certificate of offence or information that specifies subsection (19) or (20) as the provision that was contravened shall not be amended to specify subsection (11) or (12), without the consent of the prosecutor and the defendant.

(24) **Purpose of subss. (19) to (23)** — The purpose of subsections (19) to (23) is to facilitate the use of computer systems that are maintained by the Government of Ontario for recording and processing information related to provincial offences.

(25) ***Provincial Offences Act*, Part I** — No summons shall be issued under clause 3(2)(b) of the *Provincial Offences Act* in proceedings alleging an offence under subsection (19) or (20).

(26) **Service of offence notice** — An offence notice issued in proceedings alleging an offence under subsection (19) or (20) may be served in accordance with the regulations, in which case subsections 3(3) to (7) of the *Provincial Offences Act* do not apply.

(27) **Certificate of service** — If the provincial offences officer who issues the certificate of offence also serves the offence notice, that officer shall certify, on the certificate of offence, the fact that he or she took the steps authorized by the regulations to serve the offence notice and the date those steps were taken.

(28) **Evidence** — A certificate referred to in subsection (27) purporting to be signed by the provincial offences officer who issued it shall be received in evidence and is proof of service in the absence of evidence to the contrary.

1997, c. 12, s. 14; 2000, c. 26, Sched. O, s. 14; 2001, c. 13, s. 18; 2004, c. 22, s. 5; 2015, c. 14, s. 50

Commentary

The Red Tape Reduction Act, 2000, S.O. 2000, c. 26, Sched. O. (ss. 1-4, 5(1) and (2) and 14 in force December 6, 2000; ss. 6-13 in force January 1, 2001) re-enacts s. 52 of the Highway Traffic Act to allow for notice to be given by regular mail for suspensions unrelated to Criminal Code (Canada) offences, and to allow for other prescribed methods of service; amends s. 55.1 to provide that the impoundment history of leased vehicles is linked to the holder of the plate portion of the registration certificate, to extend vehicle impound provisions to persons who are found driving while their licence is under suspension as a result of a court order and to clarify who is responsible for paying storage charges related to impoundment; amends existing provisions dealing with vehicle weights and dimensions to establish a framework for the implementation of an agreement between Ontario and Quebec; and amends s. 175(6)(c) of the Act to clarify when overhead red signal lights and stop arms on school buses must be used.

Case Law

McLaughlin v. Morehouse (1975), 10 N.B.R. (2d) 623 (Q.B.) — A driver should anticipate that the driver ahead would stop for a stopped school bus even though the bus' flashing lights were not operating.

R. v. Sabean (1987), 5 M.V.R. (2d) 317, 81 N.S.R. (2d) 370, 203 A.P.R. 370 (C.A.) — The accused was charged with failing to stop for a stopped school bus exhibiting red lights contrary to s. 93(2) of the Motor Vehicle Act. He successfully argued at trial that the information was deficient in that it did not contain the adjective "flashing" before the words "red lights" and the trial Judge dismissed the charge against him. The Crown appealed, contending that the trial Judge erred in failing to allow an amendment to the information. The appeal was allowed. It was held that the information contained sufficient details to enable the accused to know the charge against him, especially considering that it stated the correct statutory reference. Moreover, the amendment sought would not have caused injustice to the accused and he would not have been misled in any way had it been permitted. The trial Judge therefore erred by not exercising the statutory power to amend the information as conferred upon him by s. 529(3) [now s. 601(3)] of the Criminal Code.

McEvay v. Tory (1988), 46 C.C.L.T. 85 (B.C. S.C.); affirmed [1990] 6 W.W.R. 763, 4 C.C.L.T. (2d) 141, 49 B.C.L.R. (2d) 162, 27 M.V.R. (2d) 302 (C.A.) — A bus driver agreed to take the infant plaintiff to school. The driver let the child out of the bus with the instructions that the child cross the road behind the bus at the crosswalk. The child ran in front of the bus and was hit by an oncoming car. The action in negligence against the bus driver was dismissed. The bus driver fully discharged his duty and standard of care in instructing the child where to cross the street. It was beyond the scope of the driver's legal duty to personally escort children across the street. The driver was not liable to specifically alert the child of approaching traffic.

R. v. Kurtz, [2006] O.J. No. 4629, 2006 CarswellOnt 7260, 2006 ONCJ 444, 40 M.V.R. (5th) 306 (C.J.) — Approaching from the rear of a stopped school bus means approaching from the rear of any point behind the lead edge of the front most point of a stopped school bus. The front most point may be a front bumper or object or device attached to or forming part of the school bus which may project past the front bumper of the school bus.

R. v. Brake, 2007 CarswellNfld 118, 46 M.V.R. (5th) 17, [2007] N.J. No. 359 (Prov. Ct.) — An accused was acquitted when there was a reasonable doubt about whether the bus was stopped with the arm extended and lights on.

R. v. Welcher, 2007 CarswellNfld 145, 2007 NLTD 87, 46 M.V.R. (5th) 113, 267 Nfld. & P.E.I.R. 211, 811 A.P.R. 211, [2007] N.J. No. 153 (T.D.) — The wording of the New-foundland section did not seem to consider a vehicle approaching a parked school bus in a parked loading zone that passes to the rear of a bus.

Related Provisions: See s. 174 regarding the necessity of school buses stopping at railway crossings; see also R.R.O. 1990, Reg. 611, Safety Inspections, O. Reg. 468/05, School Bus offence — Service of Offence Notice on Vehicle Owner, R.R.O. 1990, Reg. 612, School Buses; R.R.O. 1990, Reg. 615, Signs, ss. 28-29.

176. (1) Definition — In this section, "school crossing guard" means a person six-teen years of age or older who is directing the movement of persons across a high-way and who is,

(a) employed by a municipality, or

(b) employed by a corporation under contract with a municipality to provide the services of a school crossing guard.

(2) School crossing guard shall display sign — A school crossing guard about to direct persons across a highway with a speed limit not in excess of 60 kilometres per hour shall, prior to entering the roadway, display a school crossing stop sign in an upright position so that it is visible to vehicles approaching from each direction and shall continue to so display the school crossing stop sign until all per-sons, including the school crossing guard, have cleared the roadway.

(3) Vehicles approaching guard displaying sign — Where a school cross-ing guard displays a school crossing stop sign as provided in subsection (2), the driver of any vehicle or street car approaching the school crossing guard shall stop before reaching the crossing and shall remain stopped until all persons, including the school crossing guard, have cleared the roadway and it is safe to proceed.

(4) Display of school crossing stop sign — A school crossing guard shall not display on a highway a school crossing stop sign under any circumstances other than those set out in subsection (2).

(5) Idem — No person other than a school crossing guard shall display on a high-way a school crossing stop sign.

(5.1) Offence — Every person who contravenes subsection (3) is guilty of an of-fence and on conviction is liable to a fine of not less than $150 and not more than $500.

(6) Regulations — The Lieutenant Governor in Council may make regulations prescribing the type, design and specifications of school crossing stop signs.

2005, c. 14, s. 1; 2005, c. 26, Sched. A, s. 29; 2015, c. 14, s. 51

Related Provisions: See R.R.O. 1990, Reg. 615, Signs, ss. 11-12.

177. (1) Soliciting rides prohibited — No person, while on the roadway, shall solicit a ride from the driver of a motor vehicle other than a public passenger conveyance.

(2) Stopping or approaching vehicle prohibited — No person, while on the roadway, shall stop, attempt to stop or approach a motor vehicle for the purpose of offering, selling or providing any commodity or service to the driver or any other person in the motor vehicle.

(3) Exception — Subsection (2) does not apply to the offer, sale or provision of towing or repair services or any other commodity or service, in an emergency.

(3.1) Permitted fund-raising by charities — Subsection (2) does not apply to fund-raising activities that meet the following conditions:

1. They are conducted by a charitable organization registered under the *Income Tax Act* (Canada) on a roadway where the maximum speed limit is 50 kilometres per hour.

2. They are permitted by a by-law of the municipality in which the activities are conducted.

(4) Penalty for contravention of subs. (2) — Every person who contravenes subsection (2) is guilty of an offence and is liable,

(a) on a first conviction, to a fine of not more than $500; and

(b) on each subsequent conviction, to a fine of not more than $1, 000 or to imprisonment for a term of not more than six months, or to both.

(5) s. 171 not affected — Nothing in this section affects the operation of section 171.

1999, c. 8, s. 7(1); 2005, c. 32, s. 2

Commentary

Section 177 was amended as part of the Safe Streets Act, S.O. 1999, c. 8 (Bill 8, in force January 31, 2000). Section 177 should be read in conjunction with that Act. Solicitation in an aggressive manner is prohibited with limited exceptions. Penalties are provided under the Safe Streets Act and the Highway Traffic Act. Section 217 of the Highway Traffic Act has been amended to permit arrest without warrant.

Case Law

R. v. James (2004), 356 A.R. 134, 4 M.V.R. (5th) 231, 2004 CarswellAlta 431 (Prov. Ct.) — Walking through the curb lane to the sidewalk after finishing washing a car window is not a stunt.

R. v. Banks (2005), 2005 CarswellOnt 115, [2005] O.J. No. 98, 17 M.V.R. (5th) 93, 126 C.R.R. (2d) 189, 248 D.L.R. (4th) 118, 192 C.C.C. (3d) 289, 27 C.R. (6th) 296 (S.C.J.); affirming in part 2001 CarswellOnt 2757, 45 C.R. (5th) 23, 55 O.R. (3d) 374, 86 C.R.R. (2d) 104, 205 D.L.R. (4th) 340 (C.J.) — The law respecting squeegee kids was held to be within the province's powers and not infringing the *Charter*.

R. v. Banks, 2007 CarswellOnt 111, [2007] O.J. No. 99, 39 M.V.R. (5th) 1, 216 C.C.C. (3d) 19, 2007 ONCA 19, 275 D.L.R. (4th) 640, 44 C.R. (6th) 244, 84 O.R. (3d) 1, 220 O.A.C. 211, 150 C.R.R. (2d) 239 (C.A.); leave to appeal refused (2007), 2007 Carswell-Ont 5670, 2007 CarswellOnt 5671, [2007] S.C.C.A. No. 139, 156 C.R.R. (2d) 376 (note), 245 O.A.C. 400 (note), 376 N.R. 394 (note) (S.C.C.) — Affirming.

178. Clinging to vehicles, bicycle passengers, etc. — (1) Bicycle riders, etc., clinging to vehicles — A person riding, riding on or operating a motor assisted bicycle, bicycle, coaster, toboggan, sled, skateboard, toy vehicle or any other type of conveyance or wearing roller skates, in-line skates or skis shall not attach it, them, himself or herself to a vehicle or street car on a highway.

(2) Person on bicycle — No person riding or operating a bicycle designed for carrying one person only shall carry any other person thereon.

(3) Person on motor assisted bicycle — No person driving a motor assisted bicycle shall carry any other person thereon.

(4) Persons clinging to vehicles — No person shall attach himself or herself to the outside of a vehicle or street car on a roadway for the purpose of being drawn along the highway.

2015, c. 14, s. 52

179. (1) Duties of pedestrian when walking along highway — Where sidewalks are not provided on a highway, a pedestrian walking along the highway shall walk on the left side thereof facing oncoming traffic and, when walking along the roadway, shall walk as close to the left edge thereof as possible.

(2) Idem — Subsection (1) does not apply to a pedestrian walking a bicycle in circumstances where crossing to the left side of the highway would be unsafe.

Case Law

Walking Along Roadway

Vance v. Drew, [1925] 3 W.W.R. 740 (B.C. S.C.) — Neither the pedestrian nor the driver has a paramount right to the use of the highway, but both have equal rights, subject to the rules of the road and any special regulation for the time being in force for the common safety.

Briand v. Dunphy (1926), 59 N.S.R. 120 (C.A.); *Beauchamp v. Savory* (1921), 30 B.C.R. 429 (C.A.); *Root v. McKinney*, [1930] S.C.R. 337, [1930] 2 D.L.R. 984 — Particularly on country roads, where there are no sidewalks and where persons are necessarily obliged to make use of a part of the travelled way, the driver of a motor vehicle is bound to exercise care in passing or attempting to pass a person on foot.

Stanley v. Nat. Fruit Co., [1931] S.C.R. 60, [1931] 1 D.L.R. 306 — A driver who, in broad daylight, runs down a pedestrian standing still on a street on which he or she knows that pedestrians are in the habit of walking and on which there is no opposing or crossing traffic, assumes a heavy burden when he or she seeks to show that he or she was not guilty of the negligence or improper conduct which caused the accident.

McWhinney v. McCormick, [1946] O.W.N. 231 (H.C.); *Beach v. Healey*, [1943] S.C.R. 272, [1943] 2 D.L.R. 665 — Where there is a sidewalk or usable path to the side of the roadway, it is a matter of common prudence that a pedestrian should use it, although in the absence of specific provision there is no legal obligation on him or her to do so. If the pedestrian is injured while not using an available path or sidewalk, the extent to which this failure was causative of the accident will depend on the particular circumstances.

Cooper v. Temos, [1955] O.W.N. 900, [1955] 5 D.L.R. 548 (H.C.) — Some modification of the common law position has doubtless been effected by the enactment of s. 179 requiring pedestrians to walk on the left of the highway, and a breach of this requirement may afford some evidence of negligence causing or contributing to an accident. The section was designed to ensure that pedestrians will see oncoming traffic and so have an opportunity to avoid it. It does not confer on a pedestrian facing traffic on his or her left side of the pavement a right of way over an approaching motor vehicle on its right side of the road. The pedestrian must yield to such a motor vehicle, but at the same time the duty on the pedestrian does not relieve the motorist from doing what a reasonable person would do to avoid injuring the pedestrian.

Gaetz v. R., [1955] Ex. C.R. 133 — If pedestrians conform to the statutes and by-laws prescribing that they should walk on their left side of the road, so that they can see the oncoming traffic and avoid danger, they cannot be held responsible when they are struck from behind by a motor vehicle travelling in the same direction and whose driver failed to give proper warning of his or her approach or intention to overtake another vehicle.

Crossing Highway at Intersection

Johnson v. Elliott, [1928] 1 W.W.R. 390 (B.C. C.A.); affirmed [1928] S.C.R. 408; *Johnson v. Kwon Poo Wong* (1957), 22 W.W.R. 565 (B.C. S.C.); *Lalonde v. Kahkonen*, [1972] 1 O.R. 91, 22 D.L.R. (3d) 279 (C.A.) — Pedestrians who are crossing a street at the proper place have higher rights than if attempting to cross elsewhere and motorists are under a greater duty to keep a sharp lookout at a street crossing, although pedestrians must also exercise care and not openly expose themselves to danger.

Alter v. Soloway, 66 O.L.R. 610, [1931] 2 D.L.R. 328 (C.A.); *Flynn v. Saunders*, [1947] O.W.N. 518 (H.C.); affirmed [1947] O.W.N. 975 (C.A.); *Barnes v. Consol. Motor Co.*, [1942] 2 W.W.R. 43, [1942] 1 D.L.R. 736 (B.C. S.C.); *Petijevich v. Law*, [1969] S.C.R. 257, 1 D.L.R. (3d) 690 — A pedestrian crossing at an intersection who has exercised care by looking before proceeding to cross, must, once into vehicular traffic and beginning to cross, be allowed to continue crossing in safety and to finish it. A pedestrian has the right to assume that anyone who might come up to the crossing he or she has already entered will exercise care by reducing speed or stopping. It is only when the pedestrian observes approaching traffic at the time when he or she ventures to cross that he or she is bound to exercise care by keeping that traffic in sight.

Graham v. Fowler, [1940] O.W.N. 434 (C.A.); *Beaver v. Brundage*, 18 M.P.R. 398, [1945] 1 D.L.R. 344 (N.S. T.D.); *Cook v. Tully* (1969), 69 W.W.R. 618 (B.C. S.C.); *Lazaroff v. Trischuk* (1964), 49 D.L.R. (2d) 453 (B.C. C.A.) — A pedestrian who ventures into the crossing without looking will generally be held responsible in whole or in part for any ensuing accident.

Knight v. Sampson, [1938] 3 All E.R. 309 (K.B.); *Lerik v. Hampton* (1956), 19 W.W.R. 442 (B.C. S.C.); *Bertrand v. Hall*, [1940] 3 W.W.R. 425 (B.C. S.C.) — Particularly in bad weather conditions, the motorist approaching a pedestrian crossing must, unless he or she can see there is no pedestrian thereon, proceed at such a speed as to be able if necessary to stop before reaching the crossing.

Fullerton v. Hosford (1972), 6 N.B.R. (2d) 403 (Q.B.) — A driver who struck a pedestrian in an unmarked crosswalk at night was held solely at fault in travelling too fast. Where vehicles are turning at an intersection the driver must be on the lookout for pedestrians, and, by an amendment to s. 70(9) [now s. 124(12)] in 1960–61, he or she is required to yield the right of way to pedestrians lawfully within a crosswalk.

Bowes v. Stark, [1949] O.W.N. 779 (H.C.); *Ruston v. Ballard* (1928), 34 O.W.N. 167 (C.A.); *Monrufet v. Burgess* (1959), 28 W.W.R. 313 (B.C. S.C.) — A pedestrian will not be held at fault since he or she could not be expected to assume that a car would turn suddenly without regard for his or her safety on the crosswalk.

Crossing Not at Intersection

Rainey v. Kelley, [1922] 3 W.W.R. 346, 69 D.L.R. 534 (B.C. C.A.); *Roubell v. Kitchener*, [1945] O.W.N. 557, [1945] 3 D.L.R. 577 (C.A.) — In the absence of statutory provisions or by-law a pedestrian is not confined to a street crossing or intersection, and is entitled to cross at any point, although greater care may then be required of him or her in crossing.

Lalonde v. Kahkonen, [1972] 1 O.R. 91, 22 D.L.R. (3d) 279 (C.A.) — The duty on the pedestrian to use greater vigilance arises from the fact that motorists are given the knowledge that there are safety zones for the use of pedestrians which they are ordinarily expected to use. The question is, however, whether the driver could or should have seen the pedestrian in time to avoid a collision.

Rolland v. Warsaba, [1937] 2 W.W.R. 706 (Man. C.A.); *Treftlin v. Donovan*, [1951] O.W.N. 623 (H.C.); affirmed [1951] O.W.N. 879 (C.A.); *Conway v. Dawson* (1956), 39 M.P.R. 156, 6 D.L.R. (2d) 124 (N.S. T.D.); *Russell v. Ryder* (1969), 1 N.B.R. (2d) 572 (Q.B.); affirmed (1970), 2 N.B.R. (2d) 865 (C.A.); *White v. Guptill* (1973), 5 N.S.R. (2d) 638 (C.A.) — Although a motorist is, generally speaking, entitled to assume that pedestrians will obey a by-law as to crossings, he or she is nevertheless not entitled to disregard the movement, even unlawful, of pedestrians if by the exercise of reasonable care he or she could have seen them in time to avoid them.

Ritchie v. Gale, [1934] 3 W.W.R. 703, [1935] 1 D.L.R. 362 (B.C. C.A.); *Levesque v. St. Laurent* (1981), 35 N.B.R. (2d) 315, 88 A.P.R. 315 (Q.B.) — The standard of care owed to children on the highway is the same as that owed to adults, but there may be circumstances which should put motorists on their guard. In a school or playground area or in a built-up residential district, a motorist should drive slowly and carefully, keeping a lookout for children running out into the street.

Teno v. Arnold (1974), 7 O.R. (2d) 276, 55 D.L.R. (3d) 57 (H.C.); varied (1976), 11 O.R. (2d) 585, 67 D.L.R. (3d) 9 (C.A.); varied *Arnold v. Teno*, [1978] 2 S.C.R. 287, (sub nom. *J.B. Jackson Ltd. v. Teno*) 3 C.C.L.T. 272, (sub nom. *Teno v. Arnold*) 19 N.R. 1, 83 D.L.R. (3d) 609 — Where a small child had purchased ice cream from a vendor in a parked truck and then dashed into the street and was struck by a passing motorist, both the vendor and the motorist failed to prove that the child's injuries did not arise as a result of their negligence or improper conduct.

Gilmore v. Butt (1985), 42 M.V.R. 212 (Ont. Dist. Ct.) — The infant plaintiff was 4 years old at the date of the accident, and was permitted by her mother to go to the store with an 11-year-old girl from the neighbourhood. The girl and her escort were standing about 15 feet west of a crosswalk just prior to the accident. The defendant was proceeding east-bound towards the crosswalk. He noticed the girls standing near the crosswalk and close to the curb, and slowed his vehicle to a speed of aproximately 20 km/h. As he proceeded, he realized the girls were standing west of the crosswalk, and he continued driving at the same speed with the right of his vehicle approximately 1-1/2 to 3 feet from the south curb. The plaintiff suddenly ran into the street and was struck by the defendant's vehicle. The defendant denied negligence and in the alternative claimed that the mother was con-tributorily negligent. The action was allowed. The mother was not contributorily negli-gent. The defendant was not keeping a proper lookout. Though the children were not standing at the crosswalk, they were close enough to it to have alerted the defendant that they might attempt to cross the street. There was no reason why the defendant was travel-ling as close to the curb as he was. In all the circumstances, the defendant did not dis-charge the onus on him of proving that the accident did not arise because of his negligence.

Piche v. Longpré (1987), 19 O.A.C. 376 (C.A.); leave to appeal to S.C.C. refused (1987), 23 O.A.C. 320 (note) — The defendant driver slowly approached a construction zone. A school bus was approaching in the opposite direction and stopped to permit the defendant to cross slightly over the centre line and proceed. The plaintiff pedestrian, with vision obscured by a sandpile, backhoe and van, ran into the defendant's car. The trial Judge held the defendant 30% at fault and the plaintiff 70% at fault. The defendant's appeal was allowed. The trial Judge found as a fact that the defendant could not have seen the plain-tiff and, even driving at an extremely slow speed, nothing could have been done to avoid the plaintiff running into the car. The plaintiff was the author of his own misfortune.

Related Provisions: See R.R.O. 1990, Reg. 627, Use of Controlled-Access High-ways by Pedestrians.

180. Littering highway prohibited — Every person who throws or deposits or causes to be deposited any glass, nails, tacks or scraps of metal or any rubbish, re-fuse, waste or litter upon, along or adjacent to a highway, except in receptacles pro-vided for the purpose, is guilty of the offence of littering the highway.

181. Deposit of snow on roadway — No person shall deposit snow or ice on a roadway without permission in writing so to do from the Ministry or the road au-thority responsible for the maintenance of the road.

182. (1) Signs and markings — The Lieutenant Governor in Council may make regulations requiring or providing for the erection of signs and the placing of mark-ings on any highway or any type or class thereof, and prescribing the types of the signs and markings and the location on the highway of each type of sign and mark-ing and prohibiting the use or erection of any sign or type of sign that is not prescribed.

(2) Signs to be obeyed — Every driver or operator of a vehicle or street car shall obey the instructions or directions indicated on any sign so erected.

2002, c. 18, Sched. P, s. 32

Case Law

Quasi-Criminal

R. v. DeBou, [1978] 2 W.W.R. 381 (B.C. Co. Ct.) — An accused was charged under the Motor-vehicle Act, a provincial statute, with failing to obey a traffic sign which had been erected by the Ministry of Transport, a federal department, on federal property. At trial the charge was dismissed. On appeal by the Crown, the appeal was dismissed. The sign was not erected by authority of the Minister of Highways and therefore there was no foundation for a charge under the Motor-vehicle Act.

R. v. Priest, [1961] O.W.N. 166, 35 C.R. 32 (C.A.) — Substantial compliance with the requirements as to erection of stop signs is sufficient if the deviation does not affect the visibility of the sign.

R. v. Fillmore (1977), 26 N.S.R. (2d) 631, 40 A.P.R. 631 (Co. Ct.) — A defendant appealed from his conviction for unlawfully disobeying the instructions of an official traffic control signal. It was held that the appeal should be allowed. The signs were not clear and were open to more than one interpretation, such that a reasonable and competent driver could honestly mistake their meaning.

R. v. Lavelle (1958), 29 C.R. 156, 122 C.C.C. 111 (Ont. H.C.); *R. v. Tsumara* (1960), 128 C.C.C. 280 (B.C. S.C.); *R. v. Podaima* (1962), 39 W.W.R. 173 (Man. C.A.); *R. v. Peterson* (1973), 5 N.S.R. (2d) 850 (C.A.) — Where it is established that a sign has been erected in pursuance of a regulation of an Order in Council and of a by-law, it is a reasonable inference and there must be a presumption that the officials of the municipality acting under instructions have so erected a sign in size, colour and in location in compliance with the regulations.

R. v. Coad (1956), 18 W.W.R. 307, 24 C.R. 264 (Alta. C.A.) — The existence of a built-up area was held to have been proved *prima facie* by the fact that a sign was set up regulating traffic to a speed limit of 30 m.p.h., that of a built-up area.

R. v. Clark (1974), 3 O.R. (2d) 716, 18 C.C.C. (2d) 52 (C.A.); reversing (1973), 1 O.R. (2d) 210, 24 C.R.N.S. 65, 14 C.C.C. (2d) 73 (H.C.); *R. v. McLaren* (1981), 10 M.V.R. 42 (Ont. C.A.); *R. v. Margetis* (1988), 9 M.V.R. (2d) 19 (Ont. H.C.) — Proof of the erection of the signs constituted *prima facie* proof of compliance with the regulation. The Crown was not required to prove in addition the by-law setting the speed limit in order for the Court to register a conviction.

R. v. Pelletier (1963), 50 M.P.R. 81 (N.B. Co. Ct.) — Judicial notice should be taken that the speed limit of motor vehicles is expressed in m.p.h., and the numerals "30" on a traffic sign should therefore be interpreted as "30 m.p.h.".

R. v. Moore (1973), 4 Nfld. & P.E.I.R. 448, 12 C.C.C. (2d) 393 (P.E.I. S.C.) — A sign marked "maximum 40" was held not to comply with the Act which required the words "speed limit" or "maximum speed" to be included.

Civil

Gibbon v. Fortune (1954), 35 M.P.R. 355 (N.B. C.A.); *R. v. Potapchuk*, [1963] 1 O.R. 40 (H.C.) — It would be a most unfortunate thing if the drivers of motor vehicles could ignore stop signs in a city because there might be some flaw in the by-law authorizing them. If the sign is placed irregularly, the remedy is to have it removed, but while it remains it should be obeyed.

Edmundston Bus Line Ltd. v. Berube (1962), 35 D.L.R. (2d) 71 (N.B. C.A.) — The lack of evidence of a by-law authorizing the reservation of a lane for taxis and arrow marks on the pavement had no real bearing on the issue of negligence in failing to observe the signs.

Agnew v. Hayes (1987), 81 N.B.R. (2d) 443, 205 A.P.R. 443 (C.A.) — A and H were driving separate vehicles approaching an intersection. H was driving on a stop street where a sign had been removed by persons unknown. A was driving on a through street. The vehicles collided. A's appeal was allowed. A rightfully assumed H would stop. H had more warning and was not exercising reasonable care.

Greatrex v. Ennismore (Township) (1984), 33 M.V.R. 287 (Ont. H.C.) — The township was found 25% liable because of foliage that partially obscured the stop sign.

Related Provisions: See R.R.O. 1990, Reg. 606, Portable Lane Control Signal Systems; R.R.O. 1990, Reg. 608, Restricted Use of Left Lanes By Commercial Motor Vehicles; s. 184 regarding defacing signs; see R.R.O. 1990, Reg. 615, Signs; R.R.O. 1990, Reg. 623, Stop Signs at Intersections; R.R.O. 1990, Reg. 624, Stop Signs in Territory without Municipal Organization; R.R.O. 1990, Reg. 631, Yield Right-of-Way Signs in Territory without Municipal Organization.

183. (1) Tunnels, regulations re — The Lieutenant Governor in Council may make regulations,

    (a) designating any part of a highway as a tunnel;

    (b) providing for the erection of signs and the placing of markings,

        (i) on any highway approaching any part of a highway designed as a tunnel,

        (ii) on any part of a highway designated as a tunnel,

and prescribing the types of the signs and markings and the location of each type of sign and marking;

    (c) prohibiting or regulating the use of that part of the highway designated as a tunnel by pedestrians, animals or any class or classes of vehicles;

    (d) prohibiting or regulating the transportation of explosives and dangerous materials or any class thereof by a vehicle on that part of a highway designated as a tunnel.

(2) **Signs to be obeyed** — Every driver or operator of a vehicle shall obey the instructions or directions indicated on any sign so erected.

184. Defacing or removing notices or obstructions — Every person who wilfully removes, defaces or in any manner interferes with any notice or obstruction lawfully placed on a highway is guilty of an offence and on conviction is liable to a fine of not less than $200 and not more than $1000 or to imprisonment for a term of not more than six months, or to both.

185. (1) Regulating or prohibiting use of highway by pedestrians, etc. — The Minister may make regulations prohibiting or regulating the use of any highway or part thereof by pedestrians or animals or any class or classes of vehicles.

(2) Prohibiting motor assisted bicycles, etc., on municipal highways — The council of a municipality may by by-law prohibit pedestrians or the use of motor assisted bicycles, bicycles, wheelchairs or animals on any highway or portion of a highway under its jurisdiction.

(3) Removing pedestrians — Where a pedestrian is on a highway in contravention of a regulation made or by-law passed under this section, a police officer may require the pedestrian to accompany him or her to the nearest intersecting highway on which pedestrians are not prohibited and the pedestrian shall comply with the request.

Related Provisions: See s. 179 of the Act, see R.R.O. 1990, Reg. 608 Restricted Use of Left Lanes By Commercial Motor Vehicles; R.R.O. 1990, Reg. 609 Restricted Use of the King's Highway, R.R.O. 1990, Reg. 615, Signs, ss. 37-38; R.R.O. 1990, Reg. 627, Use of Controlled-Access Highways by Pedestrians; R.R.O. 1990, Reg. 630, Vehicles on Controlled-Access Highways, see also The Municipal Act, 2001, c. 25, section 11(1), item 1 which gives single-tier municipalities the power to enact by-laws respecting traffic and parking on highways, and section 41 which speaks to the procedure for enacting by-laws prohibiting motor vehicles on part of a highway.

186. (1) Prohibiting commercial vehicles in left lane — The council of a municipality may by by-law prohibit the operation of,

    (a) a commercial motor vehicle other than a bus; or

    (b) any combination of a commercial motor vehicle and a towed vehicle,

that exceeds 6.5 metres in length, in the left lane of any highway under its jurisdiction that has three or more lanes for traffic in each direction and on which the speed limit is 80 kilometres per hour or more.

(2) When prohibition does not apply — A by-law passed pursuant to subsection (1) does not apply to the use of the left lane of a highway by a commercial motor vehicle,

    (a) that is being used for the maintenance or construction of the highway; or

    (b) in an emergency.

(3) Signs — Where the council of a municipality passes a by-law pursuant to subsection (1), the municipality shall erect signs over the left lane of the highway governed by the by-law so located that they can be seen by the drivers of commercial motor vehicles entering the highway from connecting or intersecting highways.

2005, c. 26, Sched. A, s. 30

Related Provisions: See R.R.O. 1990, Reg. 608, Restricted Use of Left Lanes by Commercial Motor Vehicles.

187. (1) Removal of aircraft from highway after emergency landing — Where an aircraft has made an emergency landing on a highway, the pilot in command thereof, if he or she is physically capable, shall, as soon after landing as is reasonably possible, remove or cause it to be removed from the roadway.

(2) Aircraft and movement along highway subject to Act — Subject to subsection (3), no aircraft shall be driven or drawn along a highway unless the aircraft and the movement thereof comply with the provisions of this Act respecting vehicles and the movement thereof on a highway.

(3) Aircraft take-off from highway — Where an aircraft has landed on a highway because of an emergency related to the operation of the aircraft, the aircraft may take off from the highway provided,

> (a) a licensed commercial pilot, not being the owner of the aircraft, who is qualified to fly that class and category of aircraft, and the pilot in command of the aircraft are both satisfied that the aircraft is airworthy and that there are no physical obstructions on or over the highway which would make such take-off unsafe;

> (b) the pilot in command of the aircraft is satisfied that weather conditions are satisfactory for the purpose and that the minimum requirements are met under the visual flight rules established by the regulations made under the *Aeronautics Act* (Canada) or, if the flight is to be continued under instrument flight rules, that adequate arrangements can be made for obtaining a clearance from an air traffic control unit prior to entering instrument flight weather conditions;

> (c) traffic control is provided by the appropriate police force; and

> (d) the police force consents to the take-off.

(4) Penalty — Every person who contravenes this section is guilty of an offence and on conviction is liable to a fine of not more than $10,000.

(5) No liability where good faith — No proceeding for damages shall be instituted against a police force, police officer or pilot, for an act or an omission done or omitted to be done by it, him or her in respect of the subject-matter of subsection (3) where the force, officer or pilot was acting in good faith.

188. Riding in house or boat trailers prohibited — No driver of a motor vehicle to which a house trailer or boat trailer is attached shall operate the motor vehicle on a highway if the trailer is occupied by any person.

189. Air cushioned vehicles prohibited on highways — No person shall operate a vehicle commonly known as an air cushioned vehicle on a highway.

Proposed Addition — 189.1

189.1 (1) Road-building machines — No person shall drive or permit the operation of a road-building machine on a highway except in accordance with the regulations made under this section.

(2) Offence — A person who contravenes subsection (1) is guilty of an offence and on conviction is liable to a fine of not less than $250 and not more than $20,000.

(3) Regulations — The Lieutenant Governor in Council may make regulations regulating or prohibiting the operation of road-building machines on any highway or class of highway or on any part or parts of any highway.

2016, c. 5, Sched. 12, s. 7 [Not in force at date of publication.]

190. (1) Commercial motor vehicles, driving rules — In this section and in sections 191 and 191.0.1,

"commercial motor vehicle" and "operator" have the same meanings as in subsection 16(1).

Proposed Amendment — 190(1)

(1) Commercial motor vehicles, driving rules — In this section and in sections 191 and 191.0.1,

"operator" has the same meaning as in subsection 16(1).

2014, c. 9, Sched. 2, s. 40 [To come into force January 1, 2017.]

(2) Driving restrictions — No person shall drive a commercial motor vehicle on a highway except in accordance with this section and the regulations made under this section.

(3) Daily log — Every driver shall maintain a daily log and shall carry it at all times while in charge of a commercial motor vehicle on the highway.

(4) Surrender of daily log — Every driver who is required under subsection (3) to carry a daily log shall surrender it to any police officer or officer appointed for the purpose of carrying out the provisions of this Act upon demand by the officer.

(5) One daily log only — No driver shall make or have more than one daily log that records the same time period or overlapping time periods.

(6) Operator's duty — No operator shall permit a person to drive a commercial motor vehicle on a highway except in accordance with this section or the regulations made under this section.

(7) Regulations — The Lieutenant Governor in Council may make regulations,

(a) prescribing the books, logs and records that shall be kept by operators and drivers of commercial motor vehicles;

(b) requiring the retention of books, logs and records, the information to be contained and the entries to be recorded therein and the places where they shall be kept;

(c) prescribing hours of work, periods of rest and other requirements for the purpose of subsection (2), including prescribing different hours or periods for different types of work or driving;

(d) exempting any person or class of persons or any vehicle or class of vehicles from any requirement in this section or any regulation made under this section and prescribing conditions for any such exemption;

(e) [Repealed 2009, c. 5, s. 52.]

(8) Offence and penalty — Every person who contravenes this section or a regulation made under this section is guilty of an offence and on conviction is liable to a fine of not less than $250 and not more than $20,000 or to imprisonment for a term of not more than six months, or to both.

(9) [Repealed 1996, c. 20, s. 29.]

1996, c. 20, s. 29; 2002, c. 18, Sched. P, s. 33; 2009, c. 5, s. 52

Case Law

R. v. Kleysen Transport Ltd. (1990), 31 M.V.R. (2d) 121 (Ont. Prov. Div.) — The defendant, an interprovincial carrier, was charged with permitting a driver to drive a commercial vehicle for more than 13 hours without the required off-duty time contrary to a regulation under the Ontario Highway Traffic Act [O. Reg. 61/89]. The defendant argued that since a regulation under the federal Motor Vehicle Transport Act, 1987, R.S.C. 1985 (3rd Supp.), c. 29, created the same offence, and since the defendant was an interprovincial carrier, the federal law ought to prevail and the provincial legislation was inoperative. The defendant was convicted. *Intra vires* provincial legislation which simply duplicates federal legislation in a particular area without conflicting with it should not be struck down. The provincial legislation in this case was *intra vires* the province and was not in conflict with the federal legislation. It was not inoperative.

R. v. Rioux (2006), 2006 CarswellOnt 7821, 39 M.V.R. (5th) 200 (C.J.) — Just because he was not actually working on these days and spent time at home does not mean that he ceased to be employed as a "driver" for his employer.

R. v. Motovylets, 2011 ONCJ 427, 2011 CarswellOnt 9236, [2011] O.J. No. 4094, 20 M.V.R. (6th) 332 (Ont. C.J.). It would be absurd to conclude that the delivery of inaccurate information recorded and maintained during the fourteen day cycle, should be of no consequence on the date of the demand.

Related Provisions: See s. 191 of the Act; see also Public Vehicles Act, R.S.O. 1990, c. P.54, Truck Transportation Act, R.S.O. 1990, c. T.22, Motor Vehicle Transport Act, 1987, R.S.C. 1985 (3rd Supp.), c. 29, National Transportation Act, 1987, R.S.C. 1985 (3rd Supp.), c. 28; O. Reg. 555/06, Hours of Service.

191. (1) Exemption certificate — An operator may apply in writing to the Registrar for a certificate exempting the operator and any driver employed by or contracted to the operator from any requirement prescribed by the regulations made under clause 190(7)(c) regarding hours of work.

(2) Issuance — On an application under subsection (1), the Registrar may issue the certificate applied for if the Registrar is satisfied that the operator applying for the certificate has a genuine need for it and the issuance of the certificate is unlikely to jeopardize the safety or health of any person.

(3) Conditions — A certificate issued under this section may contain any conditions that the Registrar considers appropriate and a certificate is subject to the conditions set out therein.

(4) Effect of certificate — Subject to subsection (5), a certificate issued under this section exempts the operator to whom it is issued and any driver employed by or contracted to that operator from those requirements prescribed by the regulations made under clause 190(7)(c) that are set out in the certificate.

(5) **Where certificate does not apply** — A certificate issued under this section does not apply to exempt,

   (a) an operator who is in contravention of any condition set out in the certificate;

   (b) a driver who is in contravention of any condition set out in the certificate or who is in contravention of subsection (7); or

   (c) an operator for whom a driver referred to in clause (b) is working.

(6) **Duration** — A certificate is valid during the period set out therein, which period shall not exceed twelve months.

(7) **Certificate to be produced for inspection** — A driver claiming an exemption under a certificate issued under this section shall carry the certificate or a true copy thereof and produce the certificate or copy for inspection upon the demand of a police officer or an officer appointed for the purpose of carrying out the provisions of this Act.

Proposed Amendment — 191

191. (1) **Exemption certificate, hours of work for commercial motor vehicle drivers** — An operator may apply in writing to the Registrar for a certificate exempting the operator and any driver employed by or contracted to the operator from any requirement prescribed by the regulations made under clause 190(7)(a), (b) or (c).

(2) **Issuance** — On an application under subsection (1), the Registrar may issue the certificate applied for granting an exemption from any requirement prescribed by a regulation made under clause 190(7)(c) if the Registrar is satisfied that the operator applying for the certificate has a genuine need for it and the issuance of the certificate is unlikely to jeopardize the safety or health of any person.

(3) **Same** — On an application under subsection (1), the Registrar shall issue a certificate granting the exemptions that are set out in the regulations from requirements prescribed by a regulation made under clauses 190(7)(a), (b) and (c) if the operator applying for the certificate or the vehicle in respect of the which the exemption is to apply belongs to a class specified in the regulations.

(4) **Conditions** — A certificate issued under subsection (2) may contain any conditions that the Registrar considers appropriate and a certificate is subject to the conditions contained in it.

(5) **Same** — A certificate issued under subsection (3) shall contain the conditions that are prescribed in the regulations and a certificate is subject to those conditions.

(6) **Effect of certificate** — Subject to subsection (8), a certificate issued under subsection (2) exempts the operator to whom it is issued and any driver employed by or contracted to that operator from those requirements prescribed by the regulations made under clause 190(7)(c) that are set out in the certificate.

(7) **Same** — Subject to subsection (8), a certificate issued under subsection (3) grants the operator to whom it is issued and any driver employed by or contracted

to that operator the exemptions that are set out in the regulations from requirements made under clauses 190(7)(a), (b) and (c).

(8) Where certificate does not apply — A certificate issued under this section does not apply to exempt,

(a) an operator who is in contravention of any condition set out in the certificate;

(b) a driver who is in contravention of any condition set out in the certificate or who is in contravention of subsection (10); or

(c) an operator for whom a driver referred to in clause (b) is working.

(9) Duration — A certificate is valid during the period set out in the certificate, which period, in the case of a certificate issued under subsection (2), shall not exceed 12 months.

(10) Certificate to be produced for inspection — A driver claiming an exemption under a certificate issued under this section shall carry the certificate or a true copy of it and produce the certificate or copy for inspection upon the demand of a police officer or an officer appointed for the purpose of carrying out the provisions of this Act.

(11) Regulations — The Lieutenant Governor in Council may make regulations,

(a) prescribing classes of operators or vehicles for the purpose of subsection (3);

(b) prescribing the exemptions granted under a certificate issued under subsection (3), and the conditions that apply to such exemptions;

(c) prescribing different requirements that apply to operators or vehicles exempted under a certificate issued under subsection (3) instead of the requirements set out in a regulation made under clause 190(7)(a), (b) or (c), as the case may be.

2016, c. 5, Sched. 12, s. 8 [Not in force at date of publication.]

Related Provisions: See O. Reg. 555/06, Hours of Service.

191.0.1 (1) Contracts of carriage — Every contract of carriage for a person to carry the goods of another person by commercial motor vehicle for compensation shall contain the information required by the regulations and shall be deemed to include the terms and conditions set out in the regulations.

(2) Deemed terms where no contract of carriage — Where a person is hired for compensation to carry the goods of another person by commercial motor vehicle in circumstances where no contract of carriage has been entered into, then a contract of carriage shall be deemed to have been entered into, and the terms and conditions of the deemed contract of carriage shall be as set out in, and shall apply to such persons as are set out in, the regulations.

(3) Money for contract of carriage held in trust — A person who arranges with an operator to carry the goods of another person, for compensation and by commercial motor vehicle, shall hold any money received from the consignor or consignee of the goods in respect of the compensation owed to the operator in a trust account in trust for the operator until the money is paid to the operator.

(4) Other rights unaffected — Nothing in subsection (3) derogates from the contractual or other legal rights of the consignor, the consignee, the operator or the person who arranged for the carriage of the goods with respect to the money that is held in trust under that subsection.

(5) Regulations — The Lieutenant Governor in Council may make regulations,

  (a) prescribing the information to be contained in contracts of carriage;

  (b) prescribing the terms and conditions deemed to be included in every contract of carriage;

  (c) prescribing the terms and conditions deemed to be included in a deemed contract of carriage and the persons to which they apply.

(6) Same — A regulation made under subsection (5) may provide that it applies differently to different classes of contracts of carriage, to different classes of persons or in respect of different classes of goods.

(7) Definitions — In this section,

"compensation" includes any rate, remuneration, reimbursement or reward of any kind paid, payable or promised, or received or demanded, directly or indirectly;

"goods" includes all classes of materials, wares and merchandise and livestock.

Proposed Repeal — 191.0.1(7)

(7) [Repealed 2014, c. 9, Sched. 2, s. 41. To come into force January 1, 2017.]

2002, c. 18, Sched. P, s. 34

PART X.1 — TOLL HIGHWAYS

191.1 Definitions — In this Part,

"electronic toll system" means all of the equipment, including the toll devices prescribed under clause 191.4(a), that is used to electronically determine the amount of tolls owed and who owes them;

"toll highway" means Highway 407 as defined in the *Highway 407 Act, 1998* and any other highway designated as a toll highway under any Act.

1996, c. 1, Sched. E, s. 2(3); 1998, c. 28, s. 67

191.2 (1) Toll device required — No person shall drive a motor vehicle on a toll highway unless a validated toll device, as prescribed under clause 191.4(a), is affixed to the vehicle in accordance with the regulations made under clause 191.4(b).

(2) Validation of toll device — For the purpose of subsection (1), a validated toll device is a toll device that is validated under the *Capital Investment Plan Act, 1993*, the *Highway 407 Act, 1998* or the *Highway 407 East Act, 2012*.

1996, c. 1, Sched. E, s. 2(3); 1998, c. 28, s. 67; 2012, c. 8, Sched. 22, s. 20

Related Provisions: R.R.O. 1990, Reg. 615, Signs; O. Reg. 147/97, Toll Devices.

191.3 (1) Evasion, etc., prohibited — No person shall engage in an activity or use any device or material for the purpose of evading, obstructing or interfering with the effective operation of an electronic toll system.

(2) Powers of police officer — A police officer may at any time, without a warrant, stop, enter and search a motor vehicle that he or she has reasonable grounds to believe is equipped with or carries or contains a device or material contrary to subsection (1) and may seize and take away such device or material found in or upon the motor vehicle.

(3) Forfeiture of device, material — When a person is convicted of an offence under this section, any device or material seized under subsection (2) by means of which the offence was committed is forfeited to the Crown.

(4) Sale of interference device prohibited — No person shall sell, offer or advertise for sale any device or material that is designed or intended to interfere with the effective operation of an electronic toll system.

1996, c. 1, Sched. E, s. 2(3)

191.4 Regulations — The Lieutenant Governor in Council may make regulations,

    (a) prescribing toll devices for the purpose of section 191.2;

    (b) prescribing the manner in which the toll devices shall be affixed in or on a motor vehicle;

    (c) exempting any vehicle or class of vehicles from the application of section 191.2.

1996, c. 1, Sched. E, s. 2(3)

Case Law

R. v. Hopper (2003), 40 M.V.R. (4th) 214, 2003 CarswellOnt 1648 (Ont. C.J.) — While the tailgate was down, there was no evidence that it was down for the purpose of evading, obstructing or interfering with the electronic toll.

Blue Star Trailer Rentals Inc. v. 407 ETR Concession Co., 62 M.V.R. (5th) 180, 239 O.A.C. 162, 91 O.R. (3d) 321, 295 D.L.R. (4th) 83, 2008 CarswellOnt 4179, 2008 ONCA 561 (C.A.); leave to appeal refused (2008), 2008 CarswellOnt 7319, 2008 CarswellOnt 7318, [2008] S.C.C.A. No. 434, 389 N.R. 389 (note) (S.C.C.); reversing (2008), 62 M.V.R. (5th) 161, 2008 CarswellOnt 641, 89 O.R. (3d) 333 (S.C.J.) — A vehicle includes a trailer for purposes of the Highway Traffic Act 407, 1998.

Related Provisions: R.R.O. 1990, Reg. 615, Signs, s. 43.1; O. Reg. 147/97, Toll Devices.

PART X.2 — MEDICAL TRANSPORTATION SERVICES

[Heading repealed 2015, c. 27, Sched. 7, s. 25. Not in force at date of publication.]

191.5 Definitions — In this Part,

"local board" means a local board as defined in section 1 of the *Municipal Affairs Act* and any other body performing a public function that is prescribed by regulation;

"medical transportation service" means a service that is designated by the Minister and that offers transportation to the public, primarily for medical purposes, within, to or from a municipality, but does not include an ambulance service that is licensed under the *Ambulance Act*;

"municipality" [Repealed 2002, c. 17, Sched. F, s. 1.]

Proposed Repeal — 191.5

191.5 [Repealed 2015, c. 27, Sched. 7, s. 25. Not in force at date of publication.]

1996, c. 32, s. 71; 2002, c. 17, Sched. F, s. 1; 2011, c. 9, Sched. 41, s. 3

191.6 (1) By-laws re medical transportation services — A municipality may pass by-laws to set standards for the operation of medical transportation services.

(2) When local boards may pass resolutions — In areas where there is no municipal organization or, where the council of a municipality delegates its power under this section to a local board, a local board may pass resolutions to set standards for the operation of medical transportation services.

(3) Penalty — Every person who contravenes a by-law or resolution passed under this section is guilty of an offence and on conviction is liable to a fine of not more than $10,000.

Proposed Repeal — 191.6

191.6 [Repealed 2015, c. 27, Sched. 7, s. 25. Not in force at date of publication.]

1996, c. 32, s. 71

191.7 Regulations — The Minister may make regulations,

(a) providing that a body that performs a public function is a local board for the purposes of this Part;

(b) designating types of services to be medical transportation services and types of vehicles that may be used to provide medical transportation services

Proposed Repeal — 191.7

191.7 [Repealed 2015, c. 27, Sched. 7, s. 25. Not in force at date of publication.]

1996, c. 32, s. 71

PART X.3 — OFF-ROAD VEHICLES

[Heading added 1999, c. 12, Sched. R, s. 17.]

191.8 (1) Off-road vehicles on highways regulated by regulations, by-laws — No person shall drive an off-road vehicle on a highway except in accordance with the regulations and any applicable municipal by-laws.

(2) Regulations — The Lieutenant Governor in Council may make regulations,

(a) classifying off-road vehicles and drivers;

(b) permitting and regulating the operation of any class of off-road vehicle on any highway, any class of highway or any part or parts of such highway, and permitting any class of driver to drive an off-road vehicle on any highway, any class of highway or any part or parts of such highway, and prescribing conditions for any such permission;

(c) exempting the class of off-road vehicle or of driver that is the subject of a regulation under clause (b) from any requirement in Part II, IV, VI, IX or X of this Act or in any regulation made under those Parts, and prescribing conditions for any such exemption.

(3) Municipal by-laws — The council of a municipality may pass by-laws,

(a) permitting the operation of off-road vehicles with three or more wheels on any highway within the municipality that is under the jurisdiction of the municipality, or on any part or parts of such highway;

(b) prescribing a lower rate of speed for off-road vehicles with three or more wheels than that prescribed for off-road vehicles by regulation on any highway within the municipality that is under its jurisdiction, or on any part or parts of such highway, including prescribing different rates of speed for different highways or parts of highways.

(4) By-laws may regulate times of operation — A by-law passed under subsection (3) may permit the operation of off-road vehicles with three or more wheels on any highway or on any part or parts of a highway only during specified months or hours.

(5) Definition — In this section,

"off-road vehicle" means an off-road vehicle within the meaning of the *Off-Road Vehicles Act*.

1999, c. 12, Sched. R, s. 17; 2002, c. 17, Sched. F, s. 1; 2015, c. 14, s. 53

Commentary

The Red Tape Reduction Act, 1999, S.O. 1999, c. 12, Sched. R. (ss. 1(2), 1(3), 2(1), 2(3), 2(5), 5(1), and 6(1) in force January 1, 2001) amends ss. 6, 7, 12 and 14 of the Highway Traffic Act to facilitate Ontario's participation in the International Registration Plan, which contains reciprocal provisions in respect of commercial motor vehicles that travel across provincial or international borders. The Plan provides for the issuance of IRP cab cards as permits for these vehicles and for the appointment of registration and licence fees in each member jurisdiction on the basis of the distances travelled in each jurisdiction. Persons residing or based in other jurisdictions that are members of the Plan are exempt from the requirements of and fees prescribed under Part II of the Highway Traffic Act.

Related Provisions: O. Reg. 316/03, Operation of Off-Road Vehicles on Highways.

PART XI — CIVIL PROCEEDINGS

191.9 Definition — In this Part,

"lessee" means a person who leases or rents a motor vehicle or street car for any period of time.

Proposed Amendment — 191.9

191.9 Definitions — In this Part,

"lessee" means a person who leases or rents a motor vehicle or street car for any period of time;

"operator" has the same meaning as in subsection 16(1).

2014, c. 9, Sched. 2, s. 42 [To come into force January 1, 2017.]

2005, c. 31, Sched. 10, s. 1

192. (1) Liability for loss or damage — The driver of a motor vehicle or street car is liable for loss or damage sustained by any person by reason of negligence in the operation of the motor vehicle or street car on a highway.

(2) Same — The owner of a motor vehicle or street car is liable for loss or damage sustained by any person by reason of negligence in the operation of the motor vehicle or street car on a highway, unless the motor vehicle or street car was without the owner's consent in the possession of some person other than the owner or the owner's chauffeur.

(3) Same — A lessee of a motor vehicle or street car is liable for loss or damage sustained by any person by reason of negligence in the operation of the motor vehicle or street car on a highway, unless the motor vehicle or street car was without the lessee's consent in the possession of some person other than the lessee or the lessee's chauffeur.

(4) Consent of lessee — Where a motor vehicle is leased, the consent of the lessee to the operation or possession of the motor vehicle by some person other than the lessee shall, for the purposes of subsection (2), be deemed to be the consent of the owner of the motor vehicle.

(5) Liability of operator of commercial motor vehicle — In addition to any liability of an owner or lessee incurred under subsection (2) or (3), the operator of a commercial motor vehicle, as defined in subsection 16(1), is liable for loss or damage sustained by any person by reason of negligence in the operation of the commercial motor vehicle on a highway.

Proposed Amendment — 192(5)

(5) Liability of operator of commercial motor vehicle — In addition to any liability of an owner or lessee incurred under subsection (2) or (3), the operator of a commercial motor vehicle, is liable for loss or damage sustained by any person by reason of negligence in the operation of the commercial motor vehicle on a highway.

2014, c. 9, Sched. 2, s. 43 [To come into force January 1, 2017.]

(6) Joint and several liability — The driver, owner, lessee and operator that are liable under this section are jointly and severally liable.

(7) Application — This section applies where the loss or damage was sustained on or after the day section 2 of Schedule 10 to the *Budget Measures Act, 2005 (No. 2)* comes into force.

(8) Same — This section, as it read immediately before the day section 2 of Schedule 10 to the *Budget Measures Act, 2005 (No. 2)* comes into force, continues to apply where the loss or damage was sustained before that day.

2005, c. 31, Sched. 10, s. 2

Commentary

The meaning of the section is clear, and under its provisions an owner is liable:

    (a) if he is driving the vehicle himself and is negligent;

    (b) if anyone else is driving his vehicle with his knowledge and consent, express or implied, and is negligent;

    (c) if his vehicle is being driven by his chauffeur, whether or not such chauffeur was driving at the time with the knowledge and consent of the owner, and such chauffeur is negligent;

    (d) the consent of the lessee is deemed to be the consent of the owner; and

    (e) liability also extends to the operator of a commercial vehicle.

Section 132(3) of R.S.O. 1970, c. 202, was repealed in 1977 but continued in force in respect of a cause of action arising before 1977, c. 54, s. 16 came into force. The subsection also has application in other provinces. The text of the subsection is as follows:

(3) Notwithstanding subsection 1 [now. s. 192(1)], the owner or driver of a motor vehicle, other than a vehicle operated in the business of carrying passengers for compensation, is not liable for any loss or damage resulting from bodily injury to, or the death of any person being carried in, or upon, or entering, or getting on to, or alighting from the motor vehicle, except where such loss or damage was caused or contributed to by the gross negligence of the driver of the motor vehicle.

This subsection had been one of the most unsatisfactory provisions in the Act, and the endeavours of the courts to apply it to fact situations led to unhappy and inconsistent results. Despite periodic assertions that "the language of [the subsection] is precise and unambiguous and it is the duty of the Court to expound its words in their natural and ordinary sense" (Morden J.A. in *Bohm v. Maurer*, [1958] O.R. 249 at 253 (C.A.)), the courts wavered between a strict interpretation that denied recovery to seemingly deserving plaintiffs and a more liberal construction designed to temper the harshness of the provisions and which resulted in inconsistencies in order to allow recovery to plaintiffs who were equally, but not more, deserving than those whose recovery was held to be barred in other cases.

The difficulties were lessened by the amendment of this subsection in 1966 (c. 64, s. 20), permitting recovery in cases where "gross negligence" was established although that concept itself has also been the subject of much litigation. It would also appear that fewer inconsistencies have arisen in some of the other provinces, the Acts of which have not excluded from the operation of the subsection vehicles "operated in the business of carrying passengers for compensation," but have used other terms such as a "person transported as a guest without payment for the transportation" or "a person transporting passengers for hire or gain" — terms which allow a more equitable application without unnecessarily straining the language.

Case Law

Seegmiller v. Langer (2008), 2008 CarswellOnt 6029, 301 D.L.R. (4th) 454, 77 M.V.R. (5th) 46 (S.C.J.) — The court reviewed the "well-settled principles" regarding s. 192:

1. The question of whether a motor vehicle is in the possession of some person without the consent of the owner is a question of fact to be determined by the evidence in a particular case.

2. The meaning of possession is a question of law but the application of that definition to any particular set of facts is not a question of law alone.

3. Possession is a concept capable of different meanings and there are different types of possession. The primary definition of possession contemplates power, control or dominion over property.

4. Once ownership of a vehicle is established, the onus passes to the owner to establish that the vehicle was, without the consent of the owner, in the possession of some person other than the owner.

5. The owner's vicarious liability under s. 192 is based on possession, as opposed to operation of the vehicle.

6. "[C]onsent to possession of a vehicle is not synonymous with consent to operate it. Public policy considerations reinforce the importance of maintaining that distinction."

7. If possession is given, the owner will be liable even if there is a breach of a condition attached to that possession, including a condition that the person in possession will not operate the vehicle.

8. Breach of conditions placed by the owner on a person's possession of the vehicle, including conditions as to who may operate the vehicle, do not alter the fact of possession.

Liability of Owner

Common Law

Co-operators Ins. Assn. v. Kearney, [1965] S.C.R. 106, 48 D.L.R. (2d) 1 — At common law the driver of an automobile owes a duty to a passenger being carried gratuitously in the automobile to use reasonable care for his or her safety. If, as a result of negligent driving, the passenger is injured the driver is liable to him or her for the damages suffered. If the automobile belongs to someone other than the driver that person is not liable at common law merely because he or she is the owner; the owner's liability, if it exists, must be found in a relationship between the owner and the driver which renders him or her liable for the latter's negligence, or in a relationship between the owner and the passenger which imposes on the former a duty to take care for the safety of the latter.

Purpose of Section

Falsetto v. Brown, [1933] O.R. 645, [1933] 3 D.L.R. 545 (C.A.); *Downs v. Fisher* (1915), 33 O.L.R. 504, 23 D.L.R. 726 (C.A.); *Thompson v. Bourchier*, [1933] O.R. 525, [1933] 3 D.L.R. 119 (C.A.) — The enactment of the predecessor of this section imposed upon the owners of motor cars a civil liability in excess of the common law liability, the aim being to place responsibility where it would be effective, by casting the burden of ensuring safety, so far as possible, upon the owner who has dominion over the vehicle and who has it in his or her power to choose the person to whom it is entrusted, and making the owner responsible for all loss and damage sustained in the operation of the vehicle.

Zago v. Davies (1985), 32 M.V.R. 1, 50 C.P.C. 160, 7 O.A.C. 379, 50 O.R. (2d) 428, 18 D.L.R. (4th) 272 (C.A.) — The plaintiff brought an action for damages arising out of an accident involving a police constable driving a leased vehicle. The constable was protected by the six-month limitation period set out in the Public Authorities Protection Act, but the protection did not extend to the owner. The action was not barred against the owner. It is significant that the section first refers to the owner who is made primarily responsible for the negligent operation of a motor vehicle on a highway. There is no restriction placed on this responsibility. In addition, there is no indication that the owner's liability rests on any particular relationship or deemed relationship with the driver. Rather, the responsibility of the owner derives solely from his or her ownership of that motor vehicle and is activated by the negligence of the driver. The wording of the statute is clear, direct, wide in its scope and remedial in nature. It existed in this form for over 50 years from 1930 to 1983. The section was enacted for compelling social and practical reasons. The negligent operation of a motor vehicle can cause crippling injuries and death leading to crushing financial hardship for the victim. The legislators no doubt considered that the owner of a motor vehicle was more likely to be financially capable of bearing the responsibility for that financial hardship, either through his or her personal holdings or insurance coverage than, for example, a 16-year-old driver using the vehicle with the owner's permission. It is as necessary today as it was in 1930 to ensure, as far as can be done by legislation, that compensation is available to those who suffer loss as a result of the negligent operation of motor vehicles. It is appropriate to provide that compensation by placing responsibility upon the owner as well as the driver of a motor vehicle.

If the driver of a motor vehicle fails within the ambit of s. 11 of the Public Authorities Protection Act, he or she will be shielded from liability if the section against him or her is not commenced within the six-month time limit. The protective shield, however, does not dissolve the negligence of that driver. There is no provision in the Highway Traffic Act to the effect that the passage of a special and unique limitation period exempting the driver from liability also exempts the owner. In the absence of such a provision, there is no reason to exempt the owner from the clear liability imposed by the Highway Traffic Act.

The prime statutory responsibility for damages sustained as a result of the negligent operation of a motor vehicle on a highway rests with the owner. The owner's liability is distinct from that of the driver. That distinct liability arises as a result of the driver's negligence being imputed to the owner. It does not depend on any particular relationship existing or deemed to exist between the owner and driver. On the basis of the clear wording of the statute, an owner remains liable for the negligence of his or her driver, even though the action against the driver must be set aside due to the expiry of the limitation period set out in the Public Authorities Protection Act. There is not a master and servant relationship in existence between the owner and driver. The Highway Traffic Act does not provide that there is any relationship that is deemed to exist between owner and driver. There is nothing in the statute which makes the owner immune from the negligent acts of the driver simply because of the operation of a limitation period in favour of the driver. Rather, the driver's negligent act remains, with all of its consequences, the responsibility of the owner. In the Highway Traffic Act the legislators have provided, as they may, that the liability of the owner for the negligent operation of the vehicle is separate and distinct from that of the driver. It is not and should not be extinguished by the protection afforded to the driver by the Public Authorities Protection Act. The owner remains liable for the negligent act of the driver not by the operation of some principle of the common law but as a result of the legislative enactment set out in the Highway Traffic Act. The aim and purpose of the Highway Traffic Act is to broaden the base of responsibility for damages occasioned by the negligent operation of a motor vehicle on the highway. The words used in the section are clear. The scope of this remedial legislation is broad. It should not be given a narrow and restrictive interpretation.

Tanner v. St. Louis, [1950] 3 D.L.R. 99 (Ont. C.A.) — The driver is, in addition to the owner, also made personally liable for his or her own negligent driving, but the liabilities of owner and driver are concurrent. There is nothing in the section that can be construed to mean that the owner is liable for only 50% of the damages where his or her chauffeur is driving.

Hughes v. McCutcheon, [1952] O.R. 673, [1952] 4 D.L.R. 375 (C.A.); *Carnell's Carriage Factory Ltd. v. Mews Dry Cleaners Ltd.*, 37 M.P.R. 77, [1955] 4 D.L.R. 154 (Nfld. T.D.); *McFee v. Joss* (1925), 56 O.L.R. 578 (C.A.) — In such a case, the owner is not identified with the chauffeur's negligence so as to preclude recovery from him or her, and the driver will be liable both for the damage to the owner's vehicle and to indemnify him or her for any amounts paid to third parties.

McEwen v. Armour, 34 O.W.N. 102, [1928] 2 D.L.R. 958 (H.C.) — On this same basis one owner may recover from a co-owner who was driving the vehicle.

Shallow v. Fort Nelson (Town) (1995), 11 M.V.R. (3d) 248 (B.C. S.C.) — An owner of a car has a duty not to permit persons to drive a car which he knows or ought to know is defective in a way that is likely to cause an accident. An owner does not fail to meet the standard of care where the loss of brake fluid is gradual and there is no warning of impending brake failure.

Barreiro v. Arana (2002), 23 M.V.R. (4th) 174, 2002 CarswellBC 362 (B.C. S.C.); affirmed (2003), 34 M.V.R. (4th) 1, 2003 CarswellBC 235, 10 B.C.L.R. (4th) 316, [2003] 4 W.W.R. 391, 45 C.C.L.I. (3d) 1, 15 C.C.L.T. (3d) 114 (B.C. C.A.) — Where a car rental agent knowingly rented to an underage driver the company was liable too.

Owner's Defences

Buckley and Toronto Transit Comm. v. Smith Tpt. Ltd., [1946] O.R. 798 (C.A.) — The liability of the owner is for "negligence in the operation of the vehicle on the highway," thus he or she is clearly entitled to rely on any defence such as inevitable accident which would negative the existence of any negligence.

Gootson v. R., [1948] 4 D.L.R. 33 (S.C.C.) — Where an accident occurred by reason of insane delusions on the part of the driver, the owner was free from liability: (a) because there was no negligence of the driver that would attach to him; and (b) because he was not himself negligent in entrusting the vehicle to such driver when he had no knowledge of the driver's mental condition.

Nadeau v. Gareau, [1967] S.C.R. 209, 64 D.L.R. (2d) 36 — The similar provision in the Highway Victims Indemnity Act of Quebec did not have the effect of depriving the owner or driver of an automobile which struck a pedestrian of the defence of contributory negligence.

Woodbridge v. Bragg (1956), 5 D.L.R. (2d) 413 (B.C. S.C.) — The owner will not be liable if the negligence of the driver does not take place on the highway, as where a service station attendant in backing a car left for servicing on the service station lot struck and injured two pedestrians.

Bressette v. Wolfe (1984), 48 O.R. (2d) 114 (Co. Ct.) — The provision making the owner of a car liable for the negligence of the driver is applicable to an accident occurring on an Indian Reserve.

Simon v. Savoie (1971), 4 N.B.R. (2d) 354 (Q.B.); *Yarena v. Yaremy*, [1972] 6 W.W.R. 129 (Sask. Dist. Ct.) — The owner is not liable for the operation of vehicles that are not motor vehicles.

Operation

Schuster v. Whitehead, [1960] O.R. 125, 21 D.L.R. (2d) 609 (C.A.); *Temple v. Ottawa Drug Co.*, [1946] O.W.N. 295 (C.A.); *Langel v. Nesbitt*, [1958] O.W.N. 483 (C.A.); *Russell v. Pope* (1975), 20 N.S.R. (2d) 138 (T.D.); *Momney v. R.*, [1972] 2 O.R. 165, 25 D.L.R. (3d) 129 (H.C.) — The word "operation" had to be construed in its strict and primary sense and as not extending beyond the acts and omissions of a person having charge or control of the actual operation or driving of a motor vehicle. An owner could not therefore be held liable for the act of a passenger who negligently opened a car door in the face of an overtaking motorcycle. The position would apparently be otherwise if it was the driver him or herself, and not a passenger, who opened the door.

Drivers

Clapp v. Gallina, [1970] 2 O.R. 91, 10 D.L.R. (3d) 45 (C.A.) — A defendant driver who had admitted liability to the plaintiff had no status to appeal the dismissal of the plaintiff's action against the owner on the finding that the driver was operating the car without the owner's consent.

Hickman Motors Ltd. v. O'Leary (1979), 26 Nfld. & P.E.I.R. 17, 72 A.P.R. 17, 100 D.L.R. (3d) 511 (Nfld. Dist. Ct.); *Gibb v. Schroeder* (1979), 16 B.C.L.R. 169, 106 D.L.R. (3d) 73 (C.A.) — A person driving a motor vehicle is deemed to be in possession of that vehicle with the owner's consent. Once the identity of the owner is proved, the onus shifts to that owner to establish that he or she did not consent to the driver operating the vehicle.

Canada (A.G.) v. Mason (1990), 104 N.B.R. (2d) 130, 261 A.P.R. 130 (Q.B.) — A member of the Canadian Armed Forces suffered injuries following an accident in which the negligent driver of the oncoming vehicle died. The plaintiff brought an action against the defendant owner of the oncoming vehicle for the damages caused to the member. The defendant was liable. While the deceased driver did not have the express consent of the defendant to operate the vehicle, implied consent could, on an objective basis, have been inferred. The statutory onus rested with the defendant to show that the vehicle was, at the time of the negligent operation, in the possession of some person other than the defendant without the defendant's express or implied consent. On the evidence, the defendant failed to meet this onus. It was reasonable, in the circumstances, for the deceased driver to conclude that he was justified in deeming that he had the defendant's implied consent to operate the motor vehicle.

Owner's Liability

Tabata v. Argau (1980), 21 B.C.L.R. 43 (S.C.) — An infant plaintiff suffered injuries when struck while a pedestrian by a vehicle driven by defendant JA. At the time of the accident the plaintiff was running across a street, having just alighted from a parked vehicle operated by defendant KW. Defendants JA and KW were found to be equally at fault. The vehicle driven by KW was owned by her husband, defendant RW, with whose consent she was driving the motor vehicle. On the issue of the husband's liability as owner of the car, the husband was liable. The injuries to the child had been sustained "by reason of a motor-vehicle on any highway" within the meaning of s. 70(1) of the British Columbia Act. It was possible to trace a continuous chain of causation unbroken by the interposition of a new act of negligence and stretching between use and operation of a motor vehicle on the one hand and the injuries sustained by the infant on the other. Defendant KW had been negligent in the operation of the motor vehicle in discharging an infant passenger without adequately instructing her as to what she should do in relation to the automobile once she was out of the car, and in persisting in her decision to move on without delay, causing the child to move herself out of the way and into the path of the other vehicle. The abbreviated instructions to the child and her haste to depart were directly related to the operation of the vehicle and to the injuries of the child.

Ont. Hospital Services Comm. v. Borsoski (1973), 7 O.R. (2d) 83, 54 D.L.R. (3d) 339 (H.C.) — The plaintiff driver took the defendant's car without permission and drove it into a ditch. The plaintiff, defendant and a friend pulled the defendant's car out of the ditch with the defendant's truck. The defendant then instructed the plaintiff, an inexperienced 17-year-old boy, whom he knew to be intoxicated and without a driver's licence, having failed his driver's test three times, to follow the truck. The plaintiff struck the truck while it was turning, causing himself injury. The plaintiff recovered 75%. The defendant was in breach of his common law duty of care to the plaintiff not to put him in a position where foreseeably he could suffer injury.

A.G. Can. v. LaFlamme, [1983] 3 W.W.R. 350, 19 M.V.R. 276, 44 B.C.L.R. 45 (Co. Ct.) — The owner of a stolen vehicle had not complied with s. 192(2)(a) of the Motor Vehicle Act (B.C.) requiring drivers to take precautions against the unauthorized use of their vehicles. At trial, the Judge found the owner negligent and responsible for damages to a police vehicle incurred when police forced the stolen vehicle off the road. The owner appealed. The appeal was allowed. Violation of s. 192(1)(a) of the Act did not constitute negligence. Negligence could still be proven. However, in the present case the owner did not owe a duty of care to the police as an ordinary person would foresee no risk to police resulting from the owner's actions. In addition, there was insufficient causal connection between the owner's actions and the damage to the police vehicle to support the action.

Meaning of Owner

Comer v. Kowaluk, [1938] O.R. 655, [1938] 4 D.L.R. 181 (C.A.); *Singh v. McRae*, [1971] 5 W.W.R. 544, 21 D.L.R. (3d) 634 (B.C. S.C.) — For the purposes of this section, the owner is the person having dominion over, and control of, the motor vehicle in question. The meaning of the term is not fixed but is capable of a flexible interpretation to meet cases as they arise.

Hayduk v. Pidoborozny, [1972] 4 W.W.R. 522 (S.C.C.); *Honan v. Gerhold*, [1975] 2 S.C.R. 866 — It is doubtful whether this is still the law in Ontario.

Edler v. Boyles Tpt. Ltd. (1974), 6 O.R. (2d) 72, 52 D.L.R. (3d) 21 (H.C.) — H purchased a tractor, registered it in the name of BT Ltd. and entered into an agreement with BT Ltd. to haul trailers. Although H might also be an owner by reason of the title in him, BT Ltd. had the necessary degree of dominion and control and was vicariously liable as being the "owner" within the meaning of the Act.

David R. Gillard Ltd. v. Cormier (2000), 6 M.V.R. (4th) 144, 230 N.B.R. (2d) 1, 593 A.P.R. 1 (N.B. C.A.) — A vehicle used for the common benefit of the family was found to be jointly owned by both spouses, regardless of who was the primary driver or registered owner.

Registration

Aubrey v. Harris, [1957] O.W.N. 133, 7 D.L.R. (2d) 545 (C.A.) — Registration is no more than *prima facie* evidence.

Wynne v. Dalby (1913), 30 O.L.R. 67, 16 D.L.R. 710 (C.A.); *Aubrey v. Harris, supra* — Where the registered owner has sold the vehicle under a conditional sale agreement, the purchaser and not the seller is the owner within the meaning of the section, since it was not intended to fix the very serious responsibility which the section imposes upon one who had neither the possession of nor the dominion over the vehicle, although he or she may have been technically the owner of it.

Hartley v. Saunders (1962), 33 D.L.R. (2d) 638 (B.C. S.C.) — There must have been a completed sale before the registered owner will be freed from liability. Where the agreement for sale of the vehicle was conditional upon payment by the purchaser and upon the effecting of certain repairs by the vendor, and no notice of transfer of title had yet been executed, the vendor, and not the purchaser, remained liable as owner even though the car had been handed over to the dealer to sell.

Inwood v. Wilkes and Pett, [1963] 1 O.R. 519, 38 D.L.R. (2d) 10 (H.C.) — The purchaser of a car who took possession of the car, but agreed with the vendor that it would be considered to be "on loan" for a period of 10 days to allow the purchaser to make insurance arrangements, was held to be the "owner" and the vendor was not under any liability under this section.

Duckhorn v. Duckhorn (1977), 2 B.C.L.R. 296 (S.C.) — Defendant F purchased a tractor-trailer unit under a conditional sales contract and leased it to defendant P who operated it commercially and held public utility licences for it. Defendant D, employed by P, was operating the vehicle with his wife and children as passengers and as a result of his negligent driving they were injured. It was held that F was a conditional purchaser under s. 70(2) of the Motor-vehicle Act, R.S.B.C. 1960, c. 253. Under s. 70(1), D was deemed to be F's agent, rendering F liable. P was liable as the registered owner and because it exercised control of the vehicle by way of its commercial licences.

Bois v. McDonald, [1975] 5 W.W.R. 739, 60 D.L.R. (3d) 184 (Alta. C.A.) — A bought a car and was given a bill of sale but asked his mother B to register it in her name and insure it, which she did. It was held that A was the sole owner at the time.

Keizer v. Hanna (1975), 7 O.R. (2d) 327, 55 D.L.R. (3d) 171 (Co. Ct.); affirmed (1975), 10 O.R. (2d) 597, 64 D.L.R. (3d) 193 (C.A.) — Where an unpaid vendor of an automobile allowed the purchaser to take possession of the motor vehicle and the vendor kept the certificate of registration, the vendor was held vicariously liable under the provisions of s. 192 of the Highway Traffic Act.

Haberl v. Richardson, [1951] O.R. 302, [1951] 3 D.L.R. 34 (C.A.); *Ross v. Stone* (1962), 35 D.L.R. (2d) 672 (N.S. T.D.); *Rudney v. Bjornson* (1967), 59 W.W.R. 244 (Man. Q.B.) — A minor, in purchasing a car, had his father appear as the owner for the purpose of obtaining a loan to finance the purchase, but the son bought and paid for the car and always had possession and control. Although the father would be estopped so far as the finance company was concerned, he was not liable under this section.

Honan v. Gerhold, [1975] 2 S.C.R. 866; reversing [1973] 2 O.R. 341, 33 D.L.R. (3d) 675 (C.A.); which affirmed [1972] 1 O.R. 713, 24 D.L.R. (3d) 130 (H.C.); *Raita v. Barbieri* (1981), 11 M.V.R. 158 (Ont. Co. Ct.) — The true owner, in order to avoid his creditors, had his vehicle registered in the name of another who also had the car insured under his policy. The actual owner, as well as the registered owner and nominee, was liable for the negligent acts of the driver.

Wagenstein v. Graham (1954), 13 W.W.R. 392 (B.C. C.A.) — The nominal owner, who had purchased a vehicle under a conditional sale agreement on behalf of another and had in fact had possession of the vehicle for a time, was held liable as "owner".

Henderson v. Michlosky (1963), 42 W.W.R. 618, 39 D.L.R. (2d) 327 (Man. Q.B.) — The wife was liable as owner where the vehicle had been purchased by the husband and placed in her name, there being a presumption of gift in such a case.

Nash v. Wood (1972), 30 D.L.R. (3d) 199 (N.S. T.D.) — The wife had bought and paid for the vehicle but the husband who had registered it in his name and paid the registration fees and insurance premiums was deemed to be the owner.

Powell Lbr. & Hdwe. Ltd. v. Sask. Govt. Ins. Office, [1976] W.W.D. 134 (Sask.) — Where a deposit was paid to insure that the car was not sold to anyone else, and there was no written agreement, it was held that ownership was vested in the vendor.

Gay v. Bourgeois (1979), 25 N.B.R. (2d) 340, 51 A.P.R. 340 (Q.B.) — The purchaser of a new car left his old car at the lot without transferring the registration. Several months later, the car was sold but the registration was not transferred until after the new owner had an accident. The victim sued the original owner and the new owner. Only the new owner was liable. The original owner was not the "owner" at the time of the accident.

Schroth v. Innes, [1976] 4 W.W.R. 225 (B.C. C.A.) — A father was held vicariously liable for damages sustained as a result of the negligence of his son in the operation of a motor vehicle. Although the son had taken out insurance on the automobile, the registration was renewed over several years by the father and there was no definite understanding, let alone any written evidence, of a change of ownership from the father to the son.

Pooley v. Guillet (1975), 8 O.R. (2d) 418, 58 D.L.R. (3d) 194 (H.C.) — Where the defendant purchased a car and had the ownership registered in the name of his co-defendant it was held that the latter was not an owner within the meaning of s. 132(1) [now s. 192(1)] of the Act as she had no interest in the car nor any claim or title to the car.

G.M.S. Egg Grading Co. v. Perkins Motors Ltd. (1975), 7 O.R. (2d) 585, 56 D.L.R. (3d) 161 (H.C.) — The vendor delivered an automobile to the purchaser under an oral agreement. The purchaser failed to pay the deposit or sign the application for transfer of ownership. The purchaser did not arrange financing or provide proof of insurance. When the automobile was involved in a collision the vendor was held vicariously liable as he had not demonstrated an intention to pass the ownership until the financing had been arranged.

Westrop-McKay v. Barrett (2001), 12 M.V.R. (4th) 50, [2001] 8 W.W.R. 342, 93 Alta. L.R. (3d) 120 (Alta. Q.B.) — A failure to take reasonable steps to cancel or transfer registration and insurance left the defendant as owner.

Estates

Ojala v. Sturrock, [1958] O.W.N. 63, 12 D.L.R. (2d) 441 (H.C.) — The administrator of a deceased owner who had consented to the use of the car by the deceased's brother but who had not at that time been appointed administrator was held not to be the "owner" within the meaning of the section.

Re G.B. Wood Ltd., [1932] 3 W.W.R. 525 (Man. K.B.) — The liquidator of a company in process of winding-up who had in his custody and control as such liquidator a car belonging to the company, but who had no personal beneficial interest in the car was not the owner.

Williams v. Swingler, [1975] 2 W.W.R. 34, 56 D.L.R. (3d) 619 (B.C. S.C.); *Tomlinson v. Wurtz* (1981), 129 D.L.R. (3d) 251 (Man. Q.B.) — A father had allowed his daughter to drive his car. After the father's death, but before the administrator of the estate had been appointed, the daughter was involved in an accident while driving her father's car. It was held that the "owner" did not include a person who is deceased at the time of the accident. The father's estate could not be held vicariously liable for the negligence of the daughter.

Municipalities

Aikens v. Kingston, 53 O.L.R. 41, [1923] 3 D.L.R. 869 (H.C.); *Army & Navy Dept. Store Ltd. v. Bruce*, [1971] 4 W.W.R. 312 (B.C. Co. Ct.); *Bd. of Commrs. of Police of London v. Western Freight Lines Ltd.*, [1962] O.R. 948, 34 D.L.R. (2d) 689 (C.A.) — A municipal corporation which, out of its own funds, purchased a motor vehicle for the use of the police department, was held responsible for the consequences of the negligence of a constable by whom it was being driven when an accident occurred.

Beneficial Interest

Meason and Glover v. Michael (1959), 27 W.W.R. 605, 18 D.L.R. (2d) 658 (Sask. C.A.) — The action was dismissed because the person sued, although the nominal and registered owner, had no beneficial interest in the vehicle and had never exercised any dominion or control over it and was not therefore the real owner. It was suggested that a plaintiff seeking to recover damages as a result of a motor car accident examine the defendant for discovery within 6 months of the accident so that he or she may obtain an admission of ownership of the motor car involved before the period of limitation has expired.

Highland Tpt. Ltd. v. Savage (1977), 15 O.R. (2d) 117, 75 D.L.R. (3d) 53 (H.C.) — The registered owner who is not the beneficial owner will have no claim against the person who has negligently caused damage to the vehicle.

Gifts

Budny v. Senechal (1990), 27 M.V.R. (2d) 103 (Ont. Gen. Div.) — RS was the registered owner of a vehicle. He gave the vehicle to his brother, DS, as a gift by a bill of sale on October 7, 1985. DS was responsible for having the vehicle certified, changing registration and transferring insurance. RS's insurance expired October 7, 1985. On December 15, 1985, DS was involved in a collision for which he admitted responsibility. He had not yet had the vehicle certified, changed the registration or transferred the insurance. KB and AB recovered claims from Pilot, KB's insurer, for damages sustained in an accident involving an uninsured third party. In two actions to determine liability, the only issues to be determined at trial were the ownership of the vehicle and whether DS drove without consent of the owner. Judgment was granted against DS and RS in both actions. Because the safety check was not performed, the insurance not placed and the registration not effected in the name of the donee, RS was the registered owner within the meaning of s. 166(1) [now s. 192(1)] of the Highway Traffic Act (Ont.). He allowed the licence plates registered in his name to continue to be affixed to the car, he allowed his insurance to expire rather than cancelling it, and he continued to be concerned whether DS had fulfilled the verbal conditions agreed between them. There was no evidence that RS clearly prohibited DS from driving the vehicle after October 7, 1985; he could have removed the plates but did not. The implication is that RS assumed the risk. The vehicle was therefore being driven by DS with the consent of RS.

Negligence of Chauffeur

D'Alessandro v. Minden, [1943] O.R. 418, [1943] 4 D.L.R. 259 (C.A.) — A clerk who received no compensation for driving the car at any time, but was paid solely for clerical and debt collecting duties, to which driving the car was merely incidental, was not a chauffeur, and the owner was not liable where an accident occurred while the driver was making an unlawful use of the vehicle.

Newman v. Terdik, [1953] O.R. 1, [1953] 1 D.L.R. 422 (C.A.) — A farm employee who was authorized to drive his employer's car between points on the farm was held not to be a chauffeur.

Middlesex v. Bere, [1946] O.W.N. 241 (H.C.) — A taxi driver who was paid on a commission basis was held not to be a chauffeur when he was out on a frolic of his own unconnected with his taxi-driving occupation since he in effect received no compensation for such a pleasure drive.

Clayton v. Raitar Tpt. Ltd., [1948] O.R. 897, [1948] 4 D.L.R. 877 (C.A.) — A truck driver who had been given control of a particular vehicle, and was "on call" at all hours, was held to be still a chauffeur even when he went to his employer's premises after hours and took the vehicle out on a frolic of his own.

Tanner v. St. Louis, [1950] 3 D.L.R. 99 (Ont. C.A.) — Once the status of "chauffeur" is established, the liability of the owner will attach even when the vehicle is in the possession of the chauffeur without the consent of the owner, and the chauffeur is on a frolic of his or her own.

Consent to Possession

Onus

Herron v. Langford, [1949] O.W.N. 753 (H.C.); *Bender v. Ronnenburg*, [1955] O.W.N. 105 (H.C.); *Madere v. Silk*, [1956] O.W.N. 113 729, 6 D.L.R. (2d) 383 (Ont. C.A.) — All that is required of a plaintiff is to establish insofar as the owner of the vehicle is concerned, ownership, negligence and the fact that the vehicle was on the highway and that injury resulted, and the owner will then have the onus, if he or she is to avoid liability, of showing that the car was in the possession of the driver without his or her consent, and that such driver was not a chauffeur.

Barham v. Marsden, [1960] O.W.N. 153 (C.A.) — Where the owner's defence involves the implication of criminal offences on the part of the driver, *e.g.*, taking the car without consent, there is no greater onus on the owner than in ordinary civil actions.

Derrington v. Dom. Ins. Corp. (1962), 39 W.W.R. 257 (Man. C.A.); *Hanes v. Wawanesa Mutual Ins. Co.* (1963), 36 D.L.R. (2d) 718 (S.C.C.) — The onus is the ordinary one and the owner does not have to show beyond a reasonable doubt, but only on the preponderance of evidence, that the vehicle was in the possession of some other person without his or her consent. Where there are co-owners, each or either of them could escape liability by discharging the onus as to him or herself.

Finlayson v. GMAC Leaseco Ltd./GMAC Location Ltée, 2007 CarswellOnt 4953, 2007 ONCA 557, 50 M.V.R. (5th) 1, 53 C.C.L.I. (4th) 84, 284 D.L.R. (4th) 747, 86 O.R. (3d) 481, 228 O.A.C. 17 (C.A.); affirming 2006 CarswellOnt 6079, 38 M.V.R. (5th) 274, 80 O.R. (3d) 554 (Ont. S.C.J.) — Consent to possession is not synonymous with consent to operate. Public policy considerations reinforce the importance of maintaining that distinction.

Henwood v. Coburn, 2007 CarswellOnt 8169, 88 O.R. (3d) 81, 2007 ONCA 882, 54 M.V.R. (5th) 190, 289 D.L.R. (4th) 157, 232 O.A.C. 31 (C.A.); reversing 2006 CarswellOnt 4923, [2006] I.L.R. I-4530, 82 O.R. (3d) 295, 37 M.V.R. (5th) 71 (Ont. S.C.J.) — The owner, a rental agency, alleged that the operator effectively stole the vehicle from the person who had consent to possess it, despite the fact that the person with the consent to possess it was physically in the vehicle at the time of the accident. The owner could be liable even if the person in possession is only a passenger. The matter ought not the have been dealt with in the passenger's favour on a Rule 20 motion.

Consent to Operate

Castilloux v. Sweeny (1975), 8 O.R. (2d) 353, 58 D.L.R. (3d) 49 (Dist. Ct.) — Consent to possession and consent to operate are separate and distinct.

Donald v. Huntley Service Centre Ltd. (1987), 61 O.R. (2d) 257, 7 M.V.R. (2d) 203, 42 D.L.R. (4th) 501 (H.C.) — The owner of the vehicle was the corporate defendant which was a small family-run business. A principal of the corporation, Mrs. W, had forbidden her son to operate the vehicle but permitted him to have possession of the vehicle on the understanding that he would not drive. At the time of the accident he was operating the vehicle. A passenger commenced an action for damages for personal injuries. Judgment was awarded against the corporate defendant. The corporate defendant was liable under s. 166 [now. s. 192] of the Highway Traffic Act. The test was whether a person was in possession of the car with the owner's consent. The fact that the person was forbidden to operate the vehicle was immaterial.

Berube v. Vanest (1991), 32 M.V.R. (2d) 7 (Ont. Gen. Div.); varied (1995), 17 M.V.R. (3d) 1 (Ont. C.A.) — B was injured when he was involved in an accident with a motor vehicle driven by V and owned by C. V was 100% liable for the accident. The question before the Court was whether V was operating the motor vehicle at the time of the accident with the implied consent of C. On the day of the accident, V had expressed an interest in buying C's car and C invited him to take it for a spin sometime. Later that evening, C was drinking with V and a neighbour, H. When H decided to go to the store, accompanied by V, C threw his car keys at H. The keys were caught by V. H drove to the store and back; upon his return, he went inside C's house, and V stayed outside. Sometime later, C noticed that his car was missing. Judgment was granted for B against V and C. Management of a vehicle places an obligation upon an owner to take some care with respect to his or her keys. When C was aware, or should have been aware, that V had caught the keys, he should have taken steps to recover them if he was concerned about V's ability to drive. The invitation to V earlier in the day to take the car for a spin coupled with the throwing of the keys was sufficient to establish an implied consent for V to use the vehicle.

Thorne v. Prets (2003), 2003 CarswellOnt 5211, 45 M.V.R. (4th) 69, 180 O.A.C. 41 (C.A.) — The passenger who was sleeping off alcohol gave no consent to the driver and was surprised to see the vehicle was in motion.

Spouses

Venator v. L'Heureux (1972), 4 N.S.R. (2d) 352, 33 D.L.R. (3d) 467 (C.A.); affirming (1971), 4 N.S.R. (2d) 363, (sub nom. *Venator v. Tackle)* 23 D.L.R. (3d) 340 (T.D.) — Where the husband and wife shared the use of a car owned by the wife, it was held that the husband had implied authority to authorize the use of the car by third persons.

Hydro-Electric Comm. of Kitchener-Wilmot v. Searth (1981), 12 M.V.R. 78 (Ont. Co. Ct.) — Because of the absence of a statutory deeming provision as between husband and wife in Ontario and because of the absence of evidence in *Venator, supra*, of a limitation of authority placed by one spouse on another, a different result was reached.

Daniels v. Ernst (1978), 27 N.S.R. (2d) 365, 41 A.P.R. 365 (C.A.); affirming (1978), 27 N.S.R. (2d) 365, 27 A.P.R. 365 (T.D.) — A husband and wife owned the family car. The wife knew that the husband used the car as he saw fit and allowed other persons to use it. A potential purchaser was involved in an accident while test-driving the car. In an action for damages, it was held that the wife should be found liable. The purchaser was driving the car with the consent of the wife.

McMullin v. MacAulay (1974), 19 N.S.R. (2d) 156 (T.D.) — Where the owner's wife took the car keys to practice driving in the driveway, she lost control of the vehicle and struck a pedestrian. The husband did not meet the onus of proving his lack of authority and the wife was deemed to be driving with his consent.

Family Members

Hamilton v. Rodgers, [1949] O.W.N. 156 (H.C.); *Bickell v. Blewett* (1931), 40 O.W.N. 136 (C.A.); *St. Pierre v. Cie d'Assur. du Club Auto. de Que.*, [1970] I.L.R. 1-359 — The use of a car by members of a family is a consideration that will often lead to the inference of consent on the part of the owner. Consent was implied where the owner's brother had used the car on occasions in the past and took it on the occasion in question assuming that the owner would have given his consent if he had been available.

Walker v. Martin (1919), 45 O.L.R. 504 (H.C.); affirmed (1919), 46 O.L.R. 144, 49 D.L.R. 593 (C.A.) — The implied permission to use the car which would naturally have arisen from the daughter's previous use of it was negatived by the express refusal of the father, on the day of the accident, to allow the daughter to take the car out.

Nash v. Wood (1972), 30 D.L.R. (3d) 199 (N.S. T.D.) — The presumption of authority under the Nova Scotia Act did not extend to the son of the owner's wife by a previous marriage.

Grant v. MacDonnell (1976), 20 N.S.R. (2d) 102 (T.D.) — A father was liable for the negligence of his daughter in the operation of his vehicle even though she had not asked to use the car and it was her practice to do so.

MacCormack v. Spin (1975), 9 Nfld. & P.E.I.R. 283, 63 D.L.R. (3d) 757 (P.E.I. S.C.) — It was held that the owner was not vicariously liable for damage caused by his grandson's negligence where there has been no consent and the grandson is merely a frequent visitor to the owner's home.

Levesque v. Pelletier (1972), 7 N.B.R. (2d) 348 (Q.B.) — An action was dismissed against the owner where the negligent defendant driver had obtained keys to the owner's vehicle from the owner's mother but did not have the owner's consent to possession of the vehicle.

Stewart v. Muise (1976), 16 N.B.R. (2d) 550 (Q.B.) — A son who was home to visit his parents took his father's vehicle without the father's knowledge. The evidence was that the son had previously required permission to drive the vehicle and in this case the lack of consent absolved the owner.

Olsen (Next Friend of) v. Pryde, 421 W.A.C. 269, (sub nom. *Olsen v. Pryde)* 421 A.R. 269, 57 M.V.R. (5th) 167, 2008 CarswellAlta 306, 2008 ABCA 105 (C.A.); affirming 33 M.V.R. (5th) 106, 2006 CarswellAlta 506, 2006 ABQB 310 (Q.B.) — Where the drug addicted son had a habit of taking his father's car to which the father would respond by asking the son to drive it back, the father was responsible for the accident which occurred on the way home.

Insurers

Calverley v. Gore Dist. Mutual Fire Ins. Co., [1959] O.R. 253 (C.A.); *Hall v. Br. Can. Ins. Co.* (1962), 41 W.W.R. 366 (Alta. S.C.) — Problems may arise where the issue is not the liability of the owner, but the liability of the owner's insurer to indemnify the owner for damage to the vehicle wrongfully taken by an employee where the policy excludes such matters as "loss or damage caused by theft by an employee of the insured engaged in the operation, maintenance or repair of the automobile, whether the theft occurred during the hours of such service or employment or not."

Minister of Tpt. (Ont.) v. Can. Gen. Ins. Co., [1970] 2 O.R. 569, 11 D.L.R. (3d) 446 (C.A.) — A general authority granted to one person to drive a vehicle does not give such person the authority to authorize others to drive and the insurer will not be liable where the policy in question was restricted to persons driving with the consent of the insured.

Consent Generally

Vancouver Motors U-Drive Ltd. v. Walker, [1942] S.C.R. 391, [1942] 4 D.L.R. 399 — Consent to possession may be either express or may be implied from the circumstances, such as the relationship of the parties or past dealings between them. An express consent is given when possession is acquired as the result of the free exercise of the owner's will, even though it may have been induced by false representations.

Employer-Employee

Madere v. Silk, [1956] O.W.N. 113 729, 6 D.L.R. (2d) 383 (C.A.); *Baumann v. Springer Const. Ltd.* (1967), 58 W.W.R. 592 (Alta. S.C.) — Possession by an employee will generally be considered to be with the owner's consent unless it is clearly established otherwise.

Adolph v. Rycar, [1943] 3 W.W.R. 324 (Man. K.B.) — The long continued and frequent sustained use of a car, even by a person not within the owner's family, may also be the basis for implying the owner's consent on the occasion in question.

Palsky v. Humphrey, [1964] S.C.R. 580, 48 W.W.R. 38, 45 D.L.R. (2d) 655 — The implied consent of the owner was inferred from the fact that on many occasions the driver had had possession of the car and had driven it both when the owner had been present and when he had not been present. A mild reprimand by the owner the previous day against the driver for taking the car without telling him was not sufficient to revoke the implied consent with respect to subsequent occasions. The Court also considered it proper for the trial Judge to have asked himself whether under all of the circumstances the person who was driving would have been justified in deeming that he had an implied consent to drive.

Stratichuk v. Ouellette (1986), 40 M.V.R. 102 (Ont. Dist. Ct.) — The plaintiffs commenced an action against the defendant for damages sustained to their motor vehicle as a result of an accident which occurred when it was being driven by the defendant. The defendant claimed that he had been driving the vehicle with the implied consent of the plaintiffs. The defendant was a good friend of the son of the plaintiffs and was considered by the plaintiffs to be almost one of the family. The defendant had been allowed to use a boat, snow machine and an all-terrain vehicle owned by the plaintiffs while visiting them at their cottage. Shortly before the accident, the defendant and the plaintiffs' son had left on a camping trip. The mother had specifically instructed both of them that only the son was to use the vehicle on the trip. The plaintiffs' son in the past had always had to ask permission to use the vehicle. The plaintiffs' son fell asleep while he and the defendant were in a cabin, and the defendant used and damaged the vehicle. The defendant did not have implied consent to use the vehicle. The defendant clearly did not have express consent to use the vehicle, and it was a question whether in all the circumstances the owner could be deemed to have consented to the use of his or her vehicle. In the present case, the defendant was aware of the plaintiff's specific instructions that only the son was to drive the vehicle, was aware that even the son needed specific permission to use the family automobile, and he had never in the past asked to use the family automobile. The defendant therefore wrongly assumed that he had implied permission to use the vehicle.

Hefferan v. Hefferan, 60 M.V.R. (5th) 232, 2008 CarswellNfld 30, 842 A.P.R. 48, 275 Nfld. & P.E.I.R. 48, 2008 NLTD 18A (T.D.) — The limitation on a farm worker not to drive off the farm did not vitiate the owner's liability where the employee drove off the farm to get beer and caused an accident.

Consent by Conduct

MacDonald v. Mitchell (1969), 2 N.B.R. (2d) 165, 10 D.L.R. (3d) 240 (C.A.) — The conduct of the owner in leaving the key in the ignition with an intoxicated passenger in the front seat was held not to indicate consent to possession.

Hughes v. McCutcheon, [1952] O.R. 673, [1954] 4 D.L.R. 375 (C.A.) — The owner had given the keys of his car to an intoxicated friend and allowed him to drive, and had subsequently but unsuccessfully endeavoured to prevent him from continuing. It was held that the consent of the owner continued throughout.

Appellate Review

Palsky v. Humphrey, [1964] S.C.R. 580, 48 W.W.R. 38, 45 D.L.R. (2d) 655 — A finding of fact by the trial Judge that the driver of a vehicle had the implied consent of its owner to its possession should not be disturbed where it is apparent that every relevant fact and circumstance has been weighed, unless the inferences drawn are clearly wrong, or unless it appears that the court has acted on some incorrect principle of law.

Lack of Capacity to Consent

Langshur v. Green (1984), 59 N.B.R. (2d) 1, 154 A.P.R. 1 (Q.B.) — A wife allowed her husband to have possession of her vehicle. The husband passed out in the back of the vehicle from intoxication. The husband's companion drove him home. An accident occurred. The plaintiff sued the wife. The action was dismissed. The husband was incapable of exercising his possession and thus could not exercise attributes of persuasion such as directing or requesting anyone else to drive.

Conditional Sales

G.M.S. Egg Grading Co. v. Perkins Motors Ltd. (1975), 7 O.R. (2d) 585, 56 D.L.R. (3d) 161 (H.C.) — The purchaser failed to pay the deposit or sign the application for transfer of ownership. The purchaser did not arrange financing or provide proof of insurance. When the automobile was involved in a collision the vendor was held vicariously liable as he had not demonstrated an intention to pass the ownership until the financing had been arranged.

Collins v. Stafford; Smith v. Stafford (1981), 11 M.V.R. 146, 29 A.R. 473 (Q.B.) — The conditional sales agreement was found never to have been completed. The dealer remained the owner. The dealer's intention to remain in dominion was evidenced by his leaving dealer plates on the vehicle and giving instructions to return the car at a specified time.

Baxter v. State Farm Mutual Automobile Ins. Co. (1989), [1990] I.L.R. 1-2655 (Ont. H.C.) — At issue was whether the individual defendant was the owner of the vehicle which caused a fatal accident while operated by her boyfriend. Prior to the accident, the defendant entered into an agreement to sell the vehicle to her boyfriend for $1,200, $1,000 of which was paid. Despite the purchase of a new vehicle, the defendant, one week prior to the accident, arranged for a 21-day extension of her insurance policy covering the vehicle in question. On the date of the accident, both the vehicle in question and the newly purchased vehicle were registered in the defendant's name. The plaintiff brought an action against the defendant as owner of the motor vehicle in question. The plaintiff was entitled to judgment. A completed transaction of purchase and sale of the vehicle in question had not occurred and, as such, the defendant was an owner of that vehicle at the material time.

Renters

McGrogan v. Hertz Drivurself Stations, [1941] O.R. 348, [1942] 1 D.L.R. 564 (H.C.); *Vancouver Motors U-Drive Ltd. v. Walker*, [1942] S.C.R. 391, [1942] 4 D.L.R. 399 — The renter of a motor vehicle is clearly the owner for the purposes of this section.

Fisher v. Harvey Krotz Ltd. (1984), 26 M.V.R. 32 (Ont. C.A.) — The appellant, the owner of a motor vehicle, had been held liable in damages for injuries suffered by the respondent KF in a motor vehicle accident. The issue raised on the appeal was whether the vehicle was being driven with the consent of the owner at the material time. An unincorporated company owned legally by one B and his father had arranged to lease the appellant's vehicle, presumably for business. The rental agreement provided that the vehicle would not be operated by persons under the age of 25 years and that the authorized drivers were required to have a valid driver's licence. At the time of the accident giving rise to KF's claim, the motor vehicle was being operated by M, an underaged unlicensed driver, with B's consent. The appeal was dismissed. B was in lawful possession of the leased vehicle. Pursuant to s. 192(2) of the Highway Traffic Act, B's consent to the operation of a leased vehicle by M, even though M was a 16-year-old unlicensed driver, was deemed to be the consent of the owner. The right of action against the owner was completely statutory. For reasons of public policy, the Legislature determined that the consent of the lessee to the operation of a leased vehicle was deemed to be the consent of the owner. The restrictions in the rental agreement may well be invoked as between lessor and lessee. However, KF's rights arose by virtue of s. 192, which was enacted for the protection of the public and could not be ousted by the terms of an agreement to which she was not a party.

Ross v. Vayda (1990), 24 M.V.R. (2d) 197, 40 O.A.C. 149, 72 D.L.R. (4th) 700 (C.A.) — The plaintiff was involved in a motor vehicle accident caused by the negligence of a man who identified himself as FV. FV was driving a car owned by F Inc. and leased to PV under a rental agreement which provided that only the lessee was authorized to drive the vehicle. The defendant P Co. was the plaintiff's insurer. The plaintiff obtained judgment against P Co. and FV. The trial Judge found that F Inc. was not liable as the owner of the vehicle under s. 166 [now s. 192] of the Highway Traffic Act (Ont.). Having regard to the facts that the car was not returned to F Inc. for two months despite having been leased for one week, that the lease agreement was not renewed, and that F Inc. had sent registered letters to PV demanding the return of the car, F Inc. had discharged its burden under s. 166(1) [now s. 192(1)] of the Act to prove that its car was in the possession of another person without its consent. P Co. appealed. The appeal was allowed in part. The trial Judge erred in failing to give effect to the provisions of s. 166(2) [now s. 192(2)] of the Act, under which the consent of a lessee of a vehicle to possession of the vehicle by another person is deemed to be the consent of the owner for the purposes of s. 166(1) [now s. 192(1)]. F Inc. failed to discharge the onus placed upon it to rebut the presumption of consent. Accordingly, the judgment below was varied by providing that the plaintiff could recover from FV and F Inc.

Limited Consent

Types of Limitation

In two broad groups of cases limitations imposed by the owner on the possession to which he or she has consented may, in certain circumstances, lead to the owner being freed from liability if those limitations are exceeded. Such cases may involve a limitation of purpose, or a limitation of person.

Limitation of Purpose

Marsh v. Kulchar, [1952] 1 S.C.R. 330, [1952] 1 D.L.R. 593 — Where possession has been given for a particular purpose, the wrongful use of the vehicle for a different purpose may result in the possession being without consent. Thus, where a vehicle was left with a person to "keep his eye on it" and leave it where it was, such person was in the position of a watchman or guard and not of one to whom possession has been given, and where he wrongly drove the car and was involved in an accident, the owner was not liable.

Parking Lots

Baux v. Sauers (1977), 4 Alta. L.R. (2d) 266, 7 A.R. 33 (Dist. Ct.) — Where a car is left at a parking lot with the keys in the ignition, this would probably amount to an implied consent to move the vehicle about the lot in making room for other vehicles to enter or leave, but it is doubtful if such consent would extend to moving the vehicle onto the highway even if the attendant felt this was necessary in re-arranging the location of vehicles on the lot.

Garages

Brent v. Morrison, [1946] O.W.N. 431 636, [1946] 4 D.L.R. 352 (C.A.) — A car left at a garage for repairs was taken to another garage for painting and an accident occurred while it was being returned to the first garage. It was held that the vehicle was not in the possession of the driver with the consent of the owner, since the first garage was given possession of the car for the express purpose of having it repaired, as instructed, and with no authority and, so far as the owner knew, no necessity for taking it off the premises.

LeBar v. Barber and Clarke, 52 O.L.R. 299, [1923] 3 D.L.R. 1147 (C.A.) — A car left in a garage for cleaning, removal of batteries, etc. was wrongly driven by a garage employee.

Bishop v. Bell (1928), 34 O.W.N. 182 (H.C.) — The car was entrusted for the express purpose of having repairs done, after which it was to be returned to the owner. There was consent of the owner to use the car on the highway insofar as necessary for carrying out these purposes.

Hartley v. Saunders (1962), 33 D.L.R. (2d) 638 (B.C. S.C.) — An owner handing a car to a dealer to sell must have expected that it would be driven by salesmen in the course of demonstration to prospective purchasers, and by the mechanic in the course of effecting agreed repairs before sale, but that the implied consent did not extend to the car being moved from the dealer's premises to avoid its being seized as a result of the imminent and expected bankruptcy of the dealer.

Place or Purpose

Newman v. Terdik, [1953] O.R. 1, [1953] 1 D.L.R. 422 (C.A.) — A farm employee was permitted to use his employer's vehicle to travel between points on the farm, but was expressly instructed not to go on the highway. When he did go on the highway, the owner was held not liable because: (a) there was no master and servant relationship since the employee was not acting in the course of his employment; and (b) there was no consent, since the section had reference to possession on a highway, and possession could change from rightful to wrongful, or from possession with consent to possession without consent, without any change in the actual physical possession.

Cooper v. Temos, [1955] O.W.N. 900, [1955] 5 D.L.R. 548 (H.C.); affirmed [1956] O.W.N. 518, 3 D.L.R. (2d) 172 (C.A.); *Murphy v. Faurschou Farms Ltd.*, [1972] 3 W.W.R. 237 (Man. Q.B.) — Once consent to drive on the highway has been given a reasonable excess or disobedience by the driver will not free the owner, and it will be immaterial that the vehicle is being operated at a place on the highway different from that which the owner intended.

Hopcroft v. Bouey (1927), 31 O.W.N. 383 (H.C.) — The owner was held liable for the son's negligence even though the son, to whom the use of the car had been granted, had disobeyed instructions not to drive with others in the car unless his mother or other member of the family was also present with him.

Porter v. Terra Nova Motors (1960), 45 M.P.R. 31, 25 D.L.R. (2d) 728 (Nfld. T.D.) — A car dealer was liable as owner where he had lent a car to a prospective purchaser for a limited time and an accident occurred half an hour after the car was due to have been returned.

McLeod v. Morse (1975), 8 O.R. (2d) 675, 59 D.L.R. (3d) 39 (H.C.) — Where an employee was permitted to take a vehicle home on Saturday night solely for the purpose of cleaning it and returning it on Monday, the owner was held not liable for the negligence occasioned by the employee using the vehicle for personal purposes.

MacLeod v. MacKenzie (1980), 40 N.S.R. (2d) 137, 73 A.P.R. 137 (T.D.) — A vehicle owner lent his car to his son-in-law for a visit to relatives. When the son-in-law used the car to visit taverns instead, it was held that the burden of proving he was not acting as a servant or agent of the owner was discharged.

MacLean v. MacLellan (1975), 21 N.S.R. (2d) 57 (T.D.) — The fact that the defendant permitted his brother to drive on the family farm did not establish a pattern allowing an inference of consent to drive on a public highway on the night in question. The Court was satisfied that had the brother asked permission, it would have been refused.

Meulemeesters v. Smith (1982), 38 O.R. (2d) 735 (H.C.) — At the time of the motor vehicle accident, S was driving a motor vehicle owned by N. N had given S permission to use the motor vehicle for a limited purpose, namely to get groceries and to go on errands. When the accident occurred, S was driving N's vehicle home from a hotel at 1:30 a.m. Neither N nor his wife would have consented to S using the vehicle for this purpose. N should be liable for injuries suffered by the plaintiff. The motor vehicle was in the possession of S with the consent of its owner. Once possession was delivered, with consent to drive on the highway, even for a limited purpose, the owner was liable although the vehicle was driven for some other purpose. If there had been an express prohibition as to a particular use, and that prohibition was violated, then the vehicle might have been said to have been in the possession of the driver without the owner's consent.

Laforme v. Tweedle (1983), 22 M.V.R. 226 (Ont. Co. Ct.) — The defendant K was the owner of a vehicle which was operated by the defendant T at the time of the accident. K parked her car at H's garage when it was not in use. The key was left at the garage as it was sometimes necessary to move K's car and to authorize others, such as T, to move the car about the premises. K never gave T authority beyond that given by H. H had told T never to take the cars off the premises because of T's bad driving record and lack of a licence. T was involved in an accident on the highway a considerable distance away from the garage. An action was brought against K as owner and T as driver. Judgment was awarded against the driver only. K had satisfied the Court on a balance of probabilities through her evidence and the evidence of H that T only had permission to drive her car on garage premises. Generally, once a vehicle is delivered into the possession of another, even for a limited purpose, the owner must accept the responsibility or assume the risk. In view of the lack of consent to drive on the highway and the affirmative prohibition to so drive, the driver T was solely liable.

Gervais v. Richard (1984), 28 M.V.R. 305, 48 O.R. (2d) 191, 30 C.C.L.T. 105, 12 D.L.R. (4th) 738 (Ont. H.C.) — A father satisfied the burden of proving the car was not in his son's possession with the father's consent. The father owned the car. It was usually used by the mother. She used it to teach her 16-year-old to drive. The parents kept the keys. The son had only a learner's permit. The mother allowed her son to drive only with consent of a parent and with a licensed driver. The son made a copy of the keys without the permission or knowledge of the parents. He took it late one night while his parents were asleep. While intoxicated he had an accident.

Dunlop v. Brown (1986), 40 M.V.R. 1 (Ont. Dist. Ct.) — The owner expressly prohibited the driver from driving after consuming alcohol or without the presence of a licensed driver in the vehicle. The driver operated the vehicle alone and after consuming alcohol. The driver was found to be operating the vehicle with the consent of the owner because there was no limitation on the purpose for which the vehicle was to be used.

Limitation of Person

Wellman v. Car-U-Drive Ltd., [1953] O.R. 75, [1953] 1 D.L.R. 643 (H.C.); *Bennetto v. Leslie*, [1950] O.R. 303 (H.C.); *Boyd v. Smith*, [1931] O.R. 361 (C.A.); *King v. Colonial Homes Ltd.*, [1956] S.C.R. 528, 4 D.L.R. (2d) 561; *Martel v. Chartier*, [1935] 1 W.W.R. 306, [1935] 2 D.L.R. 187 (Man. C.A.) — Where a person who has been given possession by the owner without authority gives possession to a third person, the vehicle cannot be said to be in the possession of the third person with the owner's consent.

Marshall v. Mulvie, [1937] O.W.N. 690 (H.C.); *McLennan v. K. & L. Motor Express Ltd.*, [1946] O.W.N. 61 553, [1946] 3 D.L.R. 416 (C.A.) — The owner was not liable where his chauffeur was in the habit of sending his son on errands for the owner without the owner's knowledge or permission.

Usher v. Goncalves (1969), 9 D.L.R. (3d) 15 (B.C. S.C.); *Large v. Platais* (1970), 75 W.W.R. 147 (B.C. S.C.); *Simpson v. Parry* (1968), 65 W.W.R. 606 (B.C. S.C.); *Currie v. McLennan*; *Hewlett v. McLennan* (1984), 54 A.R. 348 (Q.B.) — The owner was held not vicariously liable where the son had borrowed the car with consent but had then loaned the car to a friend contrary to the instructions of his mother who had no reason to believe her instructions would be ignored.

Deakins v. Aarsen, [1971] S.C.R. 609 — Consent to the car being driven by a third party was implied.

Bender v. Ronnenburg, [1955] O.W.N. 105 (H.C.) — If the owner knew of the possession of the third party and took no positive action, consent might be implied.

Thompson v. Bourchier, [1933] O.R. 525, [1933] 3 D.L.R. 119 (C.A.); *Tompkinson v. Ross*, [1953] O.W.N. 105 (H.C.); *Daigle v. Theo Couturier Ltd.* (1973), 6 N.B.R. 679 (C.A.); *Marriage v. Brownlee* (1980), 3 A.C.W.S. (2d) 165 (Ont. H.C.); varied (1982), 13 A.C.W.S. 46 (Ont. C.A.); *Berge v. Langlois* (1982), 138 D.L.R. (3d) 119 (Ont. H.C.); affirmed (1984), 6 D.L.R. (4th) 766n (Ont. C.A.) — There must have been an unlawful handing over, an unauthorized parting with possession, in order to free the owner; merely to allow another to drive will not amount to an abandonment in the sense required. A clear distinction must be made between possession and operation, and it would be placing too narrow a constriction upon the word "possession" to hold that the person to whom a vehicle was loaned or rented was not in possession of it, although present in it, when another person is driving it. The person driving in such a case is in fact merely in possession as the loaner's or renter's guest to operate, subject to the loaner's or renter's possession.

Berge v. Langlois, supra — Where the owner of a car asks one person to drive a second person home and the first person allows the second to drive, the first is acting within the scope of his or her bailment in allowing the second to drive and the owner is liable to the first person for injuries suffered as a result of the second person's driving.

Contois v. Bianchi, [1973] 3 O.R. 180, 36 D.L.R. (3d) 204 (H.C.) — Where the owner had loaned his vehicle to the manager of a finance company and instructed him to sell it there was implied consent to the driving of the vehicle by other parties interested in acquiring it.

Laurentian Motors (Sudbury) Ltd. v. Ford Motor Co. of Can. (1980), 29 O.R. (2d) 466 (H.C.) — A rental agreement which restricts the operation of a leased vehicle to a person over 25 years of age only determines the rights as between the lessor and lessee. The owner is still liable if the loss is caused by the negligent operation of the vehicle by a person 18 years of age driving with the lessee's consent. Nonetheless, once liability is imposed on the lessor, the terms of the agreement may be invoked to bring a claim against the lessee for breach of contract.

Babiuk v. Cutter Laboratories Inc. (1983), 23 Sask. R. 286 (Q.B.) — The plaintiff brought an action to recover for injuries sustained in a motor vehicle accident caused by the negligence of the driver of the defendant's company car. The driver was the common-law wife of the company's employee. Liability was imposed on the company. The driver was not wrongfully in possession of the car. The employee gave the driver the keys and knew that the driver had a valid licence.

Lajeunesse v. Janssens (1983), 44 O.R. (2d) 94, 24 M.V.R. 217, 3 D.L.R. (4th) 163 (H.C.); additional reasons at (1983), 44 O.R. (2d) 99, 3 D.L.R. (4th) 169 (H.C.) — The owner's son was not permitted to allow others to drive. The son remained in the vehicle while another drove. The owner was found liable.

DiFede v. McCarthy (1984), 27 M.V.R. 170, 3 O.A.C. 133 (Ont. H.C.) — The plaintiff appealed from the dismissal of his action in negligence against the defendant Mrs. McC. The plaintiff's vehicle was involved in a collision with a vehicle owned by the defendant Mrs. McC and driven at the time by her husband. The issue in the case was whether the vehicle owned by the defendant was in the possession of her husband without her consent. In this case possession of the motor vehicle had not been specifically entrusted to the husband. The husband was under the influence of alcohol and was arguing with others when his wife re-entered the party leaving her keys on the table. In the course of her trying to calm him down he slipped away taking the car keys. She chased after him and came upon him at a time when he was just pulling away. She entered the vehicle trying to tell him to stop but he would not listen. She had never given him permission to drive as he did not have a licence. In view of his condition and state of mind she exited the vehicle and he continued on, and became involved in the accident. The trial Judge found that the defendant husband was driving without the wife's consent and therefore dismissed the action as against her. The appeal was dismissed. On the wife's evidence it seemed clear that she was in the vehicle only because she was attempting to gain possession. It could not be said that she had actual, physical control of the vehicle, but rather that she was attempting to get physical control or possession of it from her husband. Possession of the vehicle was maintained by him by virtue of at least some duress on his part. He commenced to drive off without her consent and at that time he had possession of it without the consent of the owner. She never did regain possession in the true sense, although she was attempting to do so, and she never did give consent to possession by her husband. It is a rare and unusual case where a motor vehicle can be said to be in possession of some person other than the owner without his or her consent when the owner is in the motor vehicle as a passenger. However, on the findings of the trial Judge in this case, and on the basis that he accepted the evidence of the owner, the defendant owner has satisfied the onus of showing that the motor vehicle was without her consent in the possession of her husband.

Bowie v. Kusan (1985), 34 M.V.R. 72, (sub nom. *Bowie v. McIntyre)* 51 O.R. (2d) 250 (Dist. Ct.) — The owner loaned his car to his daughter from time to time. Each time the daughter wanted to use the car she was required to seek permission from the owner. The owner impressed on her that there was to be no lending of the car to others and no drinking and driving. The daughter was given the car on September 16 and it was to be returned on September 21. On September 20, the owner received a call from his daughter informing him that the car was not working properly. The owner told her to add some transmission fluid and to bring the car home directly. Instead of taking the car to a service station for fluid, the daughter took the car to the house of the defendant's brother-in-law. She gave the car keys to the defendant and the brother-in-law so that the work on the car could be done. The defendant later drove off with the car, without asking for the daughter's consent. The daughter had loaned the car to him on two previous occasions. The defendant, while under the influence of alcohol, veered over from his own lane of traffic and struck the plaintiffs' van. The plaintiffs brought an action against the owner and the defendant for damages arising out of the accident. The action was allowed against the defendant driver only. The owner was not liable because the car was being driven without his knowledge or consent. The owner had placed limitations on the use of the car. He specifically prohibited the lending of the car by his daughter. He was unaware that she had earlier loaned the car to the defendant, and he was unaware of the defendant's use of the car on the night of the accident.

Gunn v. Birch (1986), 47 M.V.R. 212 (Ont. Dist. Ct.); affirmed (April 7, 1987), Doc. 3542/84 (Ont. Div. Ct.) — A departed on a trip and loaned his motor vehicle to his friend B. B did not have a driver's licence, so A stipulated as a condition of the loan of the vehicle that B not drive the vehicle, that the vehicle be driven only by B's sons with either B or his wife in the vehicle, and that the vehicle be used for pleasure driving only. B permitted C, an unlicensed driver, to drive the vehicle while B was an occupant. There was a minor dispute between the two, and by the actions of both of them the vehicle was put in reverse and caused damage to some parked motorcycles. In a subsequent action for damages, the owners of the motorcycles claimed against A as the owner of the motor vehicle. The action against the owner was allowed. The owner of a motor vehicle was liable in such circumstances unless the motor vehicle was at the time without the owner's consent in the possession of some person other than the owner. Here, the motor vehicle was at all times in the possession of B, a possession for which there was express consent and it was again used for pleasure by B, which was a purpose for which there was express consent. The case fell squarely within s. 192(1).

Related Provisions: The Negligence Act, R.S.O. 1990, c. N-1, provides as follows:

Extent of Liability, Remedy Over

1. Where damages have been caused or contributed to by the fault or neglect of two or more persons, the court shall determine the degree in which each of such persons is at fault or negligent, and, where two or more persons are found at fault or negligent, they are jointly and severally liable to the person suffering loss or damage for such fault or negligence, but as between themselves, in the absence of any contract express or implied, each is liable to make contribution and indemnify each other in the degree in which they are respectively found to be at fault or negligent.

Recovery as Between Tortfeasors

2. A tortfeasor may recover contribution or indemnity from any other tortfeasor who is, or would if sued have been, liable in respect of the damage to any person suffering damage as a result of a tort by settling with the person suffering such damage, and thereafter commencing or continuing action against such other tortfeasor, in which event the tortfeasor settling the damage shall satisfy the court that the amount of the settlement was reasonable, and in the event that the court finds the amount of the settlement was excessive it may fix the amount at which the claim should have been settled.

Plaintiff Guilty of Contributory Negligence

3. In any action for damages that is founded upon the fault or negligence of the defendant if fault or negligence is found on the part of the plaintiff that contributed to the damages, the court shall apportion the damages in proportion to the degree of fault or negligence found against the parties respectively.

Where Parties to Be Deemed Equally at Fault

4. If it is not practicable to determine the respective degree of fault or negligence as between any parties to an action, such parties shall be deemed to be equally at fault or negligent.

Adding Parties

5. Wherever it appears that a person not already a party to an action is or may be wholly or partly responsible for the damages claimed, such person may be added as a party defendant to the action upon such terms as are considered just or may be made a third party to the action in the manner prescribed by the rules of court for adding third parties.

Jury to Determine Degrees of Negligence of Parties

6. In any action tried with a jury, the degree of fault or negligence of the respective parties is a question of fact for the jury.

When Plaintiff may be Liable for Costs

7. Where the damages are occasioned by the fault or negligence of more than one party, the court has power to direct that the plaintiff shall bear some portion of the costs if the circumstances render this just.

Limitation of Actions

8. [Repealed 2002, c. 24, Sched. 8, s. 25, item 16]; see also sections 4, 15 and 24 of the Limitations Act, 2002, S.O. 2002, c. 24, Schedule B and the related provisions for s. 206 of the Highway Traffic Act.

193. (1) Onus of disproving negligence — When loss or damage is sustained by any person by reason of a motor vehicle on a highway, the onus of proof that the loss or damage did not arise through the negligence or improper conduct of the owner, driver, lessee or operator of the motor vehicle is upon the owner, driver, lessee or operator of the motor vehicle.

(2) Application — This section does not apply in cases of a collision between motor vehicles or to an action brought by a passenger in a motor vehicle in respect of any injuries sustained while a passenger.

(3) Same — This section applies where the loss or damage was sustained on or after the day section 3 of Schedule 10 to the *Budget Measures Act, 2005 (No. 2)* comes into force.

(4) Same — This section, as it read immediately before the day section 3 of Schedule 10 to the *Budget Measures Act, 2005 (No. 2)* comes into force, continues to apply where the loss or damage was sustained before that day.

(5) Definitions — In this section,

"motor vehicle" includes street car;

"operator" has the same meaning as in subsection 16(1).

Proposed Amendment — 193(5)

(5) Definition — In this section,

"motor vehicle" includes a street car.

2014, c. 9, Sched. 2, s. 44 [To come into force January 1, 2017.]

2005, c. 31, Sched. 10, s. 3

Commentary

The general rule is that negligence must be proved by the party alleging it, but an exception or qualification to this rule has been enacted in s. 193.

Case Law

MacDonald v. Woodard (1973), 2 O.R. (2d) 438, 43 D.L.R. (3d) 182 (Co. Ct.) — This section was clearly enacted in order to overcome difficulties often experienced by plaintiffs in obtaining and presenting sufficient evidence of a motorist's negligence to avoid non-suits at the close of their cases. Knowledge of relevant acts and circumstances leading up to an accident might be in the possession only of the defendant and injustice might result if a plaintiff were unable to overcome the initial obstacle of a *prima facie* case and to avoid having his or her case determined before all the evidence was before the court. Hence the introduction of a type of statutory *res ipsa loquitur* doctrine under which the owner or driver is *prima facie* liable for damage caused by his or her motor vehicle unless he or she satisfies the court on a preponderance of evidence that he or she was not in fact negligent.

Matthews v. Sheffield (1931), 39 O.W.N. 494 (Div. Ct.) — The onus will apply to the driver and also to the owner whether the owner was driving the car or is sued because of the negligence of his or her driver.

Temple v. Ottawa Drug Co., [1946] O.W.N. 295 (C.A.); *Boxenbaum v. Wise*, [1944] S.C.R. 292, [1944] 4 D.L.R. 199; *Maitland v. Mackenzie* (1913), 28 O.L.R. 506 (C.A.) — The section will apply, subject to certain exceptions, when it is shown that loss or damage is sustained by reason of a motor vehicle on a highway. See s. 1 for the meaning of "highway" and "motor vehicle". A plaintiff must therefore show, in order that the section may apply, that the damages were occasioned by the presence of a motor vehicle on the highway, or, in other words, there must necessarily exist a relation between the driver of the motor vehicle and the damage suffered by the victim.

Stewart v. Ottawa Elec. Ry., [1945] O.W.N. 639, [1945] 4 D.L.R. 400 (C.A.); affirmed [1948] 2 D.L.R. 800 (S.C.C.); *Mann v. Hilton*, [1953] O.W.N. 908 (C.A.) — This does not mean that before the onus begins to operate, the plaintiff must first prove that the effective cause of the collision was the conduct of the driver; he or she need only show that the collision — not the conduct of the driver — was the cause of the damage.

Langel v. Nesbitt, [1958] O.W.N. 483 (C.A.) — Once the plaintiff has proved the facts necessary to raise the statutory onus he or she cannot be non-suited.

Maitland v. Mackenzie, supra — There is likewise no power in the court to dismiss the action even though the evidence greatly preponderates in favour of the defendant; it must go to the jury since the statutory presumption is at least equal to oral testimony tending to prove negligence on the part of the owner or driver.

Storry v. C.N.R., [1940] S.C.R. 491, [1940] 3 D.L.R. 554 — The mere presence of a motor vehicle on the highway, although a *causa sine qua non* of the accident, will not of itself constitute the necessary relationship to bring the statutory onus into effect. In this case, a car had been abandoned on the railway track where it had stalled, and it was thrown forward by the train and crushed the plaintiff against a post. It was held that the onus section was not applicable where the role of the automobile was simply that of a projectile moving under the impulse of a blow from a railway train.

Boxenbaum v. Wise, supra; *Honan v. McLean*, 8 W.W.R. (N.S.) 523, [1953] 3 D.L.R. 193 (Sask. C.A.); *Cullen v. Cohen*, [1950] Que. S.C. 94 — It is not necessary that there be a direct contact between the property damaged or the person injured and the motor vehicle; the damage may be attributed to a driver who does not actually hit the victim, but acts in such a way that he or she causes another to run over a pedestrian.

Pollock and Pizel v. Link Mfg. Co., [1955] O.W.N. 463 (Co. Ct.) — Although the section is applied most frequently for the benefit of plaintiff pedestrians, it is also applicable to damage to property, *e.g.*, where an electric sign overhanging the highway was struck by a truck and damaged.

Part XI — Civil Proceedings

Bell Telephone Co. v. Kan Yan Gan Co., [1940] O.R. 510, [1941] 1 D.L.R. 223 (C.A.);
Regnier v. Nelson (1956), 19 W.W.R. 36 (Man. Q.B.); *Long v. Woodworth* (1961), 31
D.L.R. (2d) 532 (N.S. T.D.); *Pageau v. Provincial Tpt. Co.*, [1945] Que. K.B. 431 — The
damage in respect of which action is brought need not necessarily be done on the highway. The onus is cast on the driver of a car which, on the highway, leaves it and does
damage, *e.g.*, to adjacent telephone poles and lines or buildings.

Teno v. Arnold (1974), 7 O.R. (2d) 276, 55 D.L.R. (3d) 57 (H.C.); varied on other
grounds (1976), 11 O.R. (2d) 585, 67 D.L.R. (3d) 9 (C.A.); varied on other grounds
Arnold v. Teno, [1978] 2 S.C.R. 287, (sub nom. *J.B. Jackson Ltd. v. Teno*) 3 C.C.L.T.
272, (sub nom. *Teno v. Arnold*) 19 N.R. 1, 83 D.L.R. (3d) 609 — A small child had
purchased ice cream from a vendor in a parked truck. The child then dashed into the
street and was struck by a passing motorist. The Court held that both the vendor and the
motorist failed to prove the child's injuries did not arise as a result of their negligence or
improper conduct.

A.G. Ont. v. Keller (1978), 23 O.R. (2d) 143, 94 D.L.R. (3d) 632 (C.A.); *Hambley v.
Shepley*, [1967] 2 O.R. 217, 63 D.L.R. (2d) 94 (C.A.); *Miller v. Wolbaum* (1986), 47
M.V.R. 162, 51 Sask. R. 185 (Q.B.); *Moore v. Fanning* (1981), 60 O.R. (2d) 225, 49
M.V.R. 161, 41 C.C.L.T. 67 (H.C.) — Where a police officer is injured when his or her
car goes out of control during a high speed chase of a car where the driver knows he or
she is being being chased, the officer has a cause of action against the driver and s.
133(1) [now s. 193(1)] of the Highway Traffic Act transfers the onus of proof
accordingly.

Sked v. Henry (1991), 28 M.V.R. (2d) 234 (Ont. Gen. Div.) — There was evidence that a
school parking lot was used by the general public on occasion and was therefore a highway for purposes of the Act.

Collision Between Vehicles

Cook v. Boland Bros. Ltd., [1942] 1 W.W.R. 306 (Man. K.B.); *Moision v. Ricard*, [1955]
O.W.N. 469 (C.A.) — Certain exceptions to the application of the onus section are pro-
vided for in s. 193(2), the most important being that of collisions between motor vehicles.
This exception applies where one vehicle is moving and one is stationary.

Sterling Trusts Corp. v. Postma, [1965] S.C.R. 324, 48 D.L.R. (2d) 423 — Section
133(2) [now s. 193(2)] cannot be construed as only applying to the two motor vehicles
which actually collided but to other motor vehicles which, though not directly involved,
are alleged, by reason of their presence on the highway, to have contributed to the
collision.

Martin v. Deutch, [1942] O.W.N. 583, [1942] 4 D.L.R. 529 (C.A.) — The fact of collision between two vehicles may be immaterial where the moving vehicle struck a pedestrian either before or after also striking the other vehicle. In such a case the pedestrian
would be entitled to the benefit of the statutory onus.

Carroll v. Cudney and Bennett, [1963] 1 O.R. 551, 38 D.L.R. (2d) 113 (H.C.) — Where,
as the result of a collision between two vehicles, the driver of one of them is thrown onto
the highway and while lying there is struck by a third vehicle, the statutory onus will not
apply unless a clear line can be drawn between the first and the subsequent collision.
Such a line could not be drawn where the interval between the two occurrences was not
more than one minute.

Carter v. Van Camp, [1930] S.C.R. 156 at 161, [1929] 4 D.L.R. 625 — In this case a collision between two cars resulted in one of them striking and injuring a pedestrian. The application of subsection (1) is not prevented by the provisions of subsection (2) which, excludes from the operation of subsection (1) only cases in which the loss or damage sued for is sustained by an occupant of one of the motor vehicles in collision or by the owner thereof, or, possibly, also by the owner of property being carried in it at the time.

DeGurse v. Henry (1984), 47 O.R. (2d) 172, 44 C.P.C. 309 (H.C.) — The plaintiff was involved in a motor vehicle accident during a snowstorm and had descended from his vehicle to survey the situation when he was struck by another vehicle driven by one of the defendants. It was held that s. 167 [now s. 193] did not apply.

Nolan v. Rhodes (1980), 27 O.R. (2d) 609, 107 D.L.R. (3d) 498 (C.A.) — The benefit of the onus provision does not apply to a snowmobile involved in a collision with a car.

Celniker v. Supt. of Ins. (1981), 12 A.C.W.S. (2d) 74 (Ont. H.C.) — The fact that the occurrence happened on a highway, that motor vehicles used the highway and that injuries sustained might be attributed to a motor vehicle were insufficient by themselves to place the onus on the defendant. The plaintiff must prove that the motor vehicle caused his injuries in order to shift the onus.

Guarantee Co. of North America v. Mercedes-Benz Canada Inc. (2005), 2005 Carswell-Ont 8925, 33 M.V.R. (5th) 147, 83 O.R. (3d) 316 (S.C.J.); affirmed (2006), 2006 Cars-wellOnt 3638, 34 M.V.R. (5th) 21, [2006] O.J. No. 2358, 86 O.R. (3d) 479 (C.A.) — A fire which started under the hood when transmission fluid leaked onto the exhaust manifold was an instance of "damages occasioned by a motor vehicle."

Nature and Discharge of Onus

Winnipeg Elec. Co. v. Geel, [1932] A.C. 690, [1931] S.C.R. 443, [1932] 4 D.L.R. 51, [1932] 2 W.W.R. 305 (P.C.) — The statute creates, as against the owners and drivers of motor vehicles a rebuttable presumption of negligence. The onus of disproving negligence remains throughout the proceedings. If, at the conclusion of the evidence, it is too meagre or too evenly balanced to enable the tribunal to determine this issue, as a question of fact, then, by force of the statute, the plaintiff is entitled to succeed. The onus which the section places on the defendant is not in law a shifting or transitory onus: it cannot be displaced merely by the defendant giving some evidence that he or she was not negligent if that evidence however credible is not sufficient reasonably to satisfy the jury that he or she was not negligent: the burden remains on the defendant until the very end of the case, when the question must be determined whether or not the defendant has sufficiently shown that he or she did not in fact cause the accident by his or her negligence.

Bronson v. Evans, [1943] O.R. 248, [1943] 2 D.L.R. 371 (C.A.); *Long v. Registrar of Motor Vehicles*, [1950] 2 W.W.R. 355, [1950] 4 D.L.R. 587 (Man. C.A.) — It is upon the whole of the evidence submitted at the trial, including all the circumstances and inferences to be drawn therefrom that the defendant must satisfy the jury that the accident was not in fact caused by his or her negligence.

Foster v. Reg. of Motor Vehicles, [1961] O.R. 551, 28 D.L.R. (2d) 561 (C.A.) — Once the onus is placed on the defendant it will not be discharged unless he or she satisfies the court not merely that the damages could have been sustained without negligence for which he or she is responsible, but that the damages were in fact sustained without such negligence.

Bronson v. Evans, supra; *Shapiro v. Wilkinson*, [1943] O.R. 806, [1944] 1 D.L.R. 138 (C.A.); affirmed [1944] S.C.R. 443, [1945] 1 D.L.R. 81 — It is not necessary to find any specific act of negligence against the defendant in order that liability may attach to him or her. If any doubt remains on a consideration of all the evidence as to whether or not the defendant was negligent the plaintiff is entitled to the verdict. This applies where a trial Judge finds him or herself wholly unable to decide with whom the fault lay because the witnesses on both sides all seem to him or her to be worthy of belief, although they are in direct conflict.

Winnipeg Elec. Co. v. Geel, supra; *Williams v. Fedoryshin*, [1959] S.C.R. 248; *Gardam v. R.*, [1948] O.R. 61 641 (C.A.) — The defendant may, however, discharge the onus in various ways as, *e.g.*, by satisfactory proof of a latent defect in his or her vehicle, or by proof that the defendant was the author of his or her own injury, *e.g.*, by placing him or herself in the way of the defendant's vehicle in such a manner that the defendant could not reasonably avoid the impact, or by proof that the circumstances were such that neither party was to blame, because neither could avoid the other.

Walker v. Crago (1951), 4 W.W.R. (N.S.) 64 (Alta. T.D.) — The defendant may likewise give affirmative proof of a course of conduct which establishes the due and proper exercise of that care and caution on his or her part which, in itself, excludes any suggestion of the existence of his or her negligence.

Honan v. McLean, 8 W.W.R. (N.S.) 523, [1953] 3 D.L.R. 193 (Sask. C.A.) — The defendant may show that the accident which, but for his or her negligence, should not have happened in the normal course of events, was caused by an extrinsic fact for which he or she could not be held responsible.

Ontario (Attorney General) v. Williams, 2001 CarswellOnt 584, 9 M.V.R. (4th) 275 (Ont. S.C.J.); additional reasons 2001 CarswellOnt 932 (Ont. S.C.J.) — The plaintiff province sued for the repair of a guardrail located to the left of the left lane of a highway following a single car accident. The accident report, filled in by the police, indicated that the defendant caused the damage. The reverse onus could not be relied upon. It was not intended to absolve the plaintiff, particularly one with resources such as government, from any responsibility for investigating the cause of damage. The defendant's testimony indicated that the accident occurred just as he was about to exit the right lane and did not square with the damage.

Contributory Negligence

Shapiro v. Wilkinson, [1944] S.C.R. 443, [1945] 1 D.L.R. 81; *Dearing v. Hebert*, [1957] S.C.R. 843, 11 D.L.R. (2d) 97 — Since the defendant must show that the loss or damage did not arise through his or her negligence or improper conduct, he or she cannot discharge that onus merely by showing that the plaintiff was guilty of negligence contributing to the accident.

Johnson v. Desharnais, 6 W.W.R. (N.S.) 261 (Alta. C.A.); affirmed [1953] 1 S.C.R. 324, [1953] 2 D.L.R. 401 — Even if the plaintiff was himself negligent he still recovered his damages in full as the defendant motorist did not show that the plaintiff's negligence in fact contributed to the accident, and the defendant could not, by the exercise of reasonable care, have avoided the consequences of such negligence.

Tuckey v. Dyer (1961), 27 D.L.R. (2d) 408 (N.S. T.D.); *Poole & Thompson Ltd. v. McNally*, [1934] S.C.R. 717 — Even if the defendant establishes contributory negligence, there is no onus thereby cast on the plaintiff to establish that the defendant was negligent in order to recover. On the contrary, it will be presumed that the defendant was to blame for the balance of the cause of the accident, and liability will be apportioned accordingly, unless he or she negatives any and all negligence on his or her part as a cause of the accident.

194. [Repealed 2009, c. 33, Sched. 26, s. 3(12).]

PART XII — MUNICIPAL BY-LAWS

195. (1) Inconsistent by-laws may be deemed invalid — If a provision of a municipal by-law passed by the council of a municipality or a police services board for,

    (a) regulating traffic on the highways;

    (b) regulating noise, fumes or smoke created by the operation of motor vehicles on the highways; or

    (c) prohibiting or regulating the operation of motor vehicles or any type or class thereof on the highways,

is inconsistent with this Act or the regulations, the provision of the by-law shall be deemed to be repealed upon the inconsistency arising.

(2) [Repealed 1996, c. 33, s. 15(2).]

(3) Approval of traffic by-laws for connecting links — If the council of a municipality passes a by-law for a purpose mentioned in clause (1)(a) or (c) that affects traffic on a highway designated as a connecting link under subsection 21(1) of the *Public Transportation and Highway Improvement Act*, the clerk of the municipality shall file a copy of the by-law with the Ministry within 30 days of its passing, and the by-law shall not become operative until it is approved by the Ministry.

(4) Approval of traffic by-law in whole or in part — Any by-law for regulating traffic on highways that is submitted to the Ministry for approval may be approved in whole or in part and, where part of a by-law is approved only, that part shall become operative.

(5) Withdrawal of approval by Ministry — The Ministry may withdraw its approval to any by-law or any part thereof by notice sent by registered mail to the clerk of the municipality and the by-law or part thereof shall be deemed to be repealed twenty-one days after the sending of the notice.

1996, c. 33, s. 15; 2002, c. 17, Sched. F, s. 1

Case Law

R. v. Jeffs, [1959] O.R. 150 (H.C.) — The approval under this section of an invalid by-law, *e.g.*, one passed without legislative authority, will not make such by-law valid.

Toronto (City) v. Braganza, 2011 ONCJ 657, 2011 CarswellOnt 13681, [2011] O.J. No. 5445, 21 M.V.R. (6th) 104, 91 M.P.L.R. (4th) 276, 250 C.R.R. (2d) 60. Where a traffic ticket contained the words of the by-law's title "Park-fail to display permit" is sufficient to notify under s. 11(a) of the *Charter*.

PART XIII — SUSPENSION FOR FAILURE TO PAY JUDGMENTS OR MEET SUPPORT OBLIGATIONS

196. Definition — In this Part, "motor vehicle", in addition to the meaning given in section 1, includes "trailer", as defined in section 1.

197. [Repealed 1996, c. 31, s. 69.]

198. (1) Licence suspended for failure to pay judgment — The driver's licence of every person who fails to satisfy a judgment rendered against him or her by any court in Ontario that has become final by affirmation on appeal or by expiry without appeal of the time allowed for appeal, for damages on account of injury to or the death of any person, or on account of damage to property, occasioned by a motor vehicle or street car, within fifteen days from the date upon which the judgment became final shall be suspended by the Registrar upon receiving a certificate of the final judgment from the court in which the same is rendered and after fifteen days notice has been sent to the person of intention to suspend his or her licence unless the judgment is satisfied within the period, and shall remain so suspended and shall not at any time thereafter be renewed, nor shall any new driver's licence be thereafter issued to the person, until the judgment is satisfied or discharged, otherwise than by a discharge in bankruptcy, to the extent of the minimum limits of liability required by the *Insurance Act* in respect of motor vehicle liability policies.

(2) Application where person indebted to fund — Despite subsection (1), the Registrar shall not suspend under subsection (1) the driver's licence of any person who is indebted to the Motor Vehicle Accident Claims Fund.

(3) Payment of judgments in installments — A judgment debtor may, on due notice to the judgment creditor, apply to the court in which the trial judgment was obtained for the privilege of paying the judgment in installments, and the court may, in its discretion, so order, fixing the amounts and times of payment of the installments, and while the judgment debtor is not in default in payment of the installments, he or she shall be deemed not in default in payment of the judgment, and the Minister may restore the driver's licence of the judgment debtor, but the driver's licence shall again be suspended and remain suspended, as provided in subsection (1), if the Registrar is satisfied of default made by the judgment debtor in compliance with the terms of the court order.

(4) Reciprocal effect of subs. (1) with states having similar legislation — The Lieutenant Governor in Council, upon the report of the Minister that a province or state has enacted legislation similar in effect to subsection (1) and that the legislation extends and applies to judgments rendered and become final against residents of that province or state by any court of competent jurisdiction in Ontario, may declare that subsection (1) shall extend and apply to judgments rendered and become final against residents of Ontario by any court of competent jurisdiction in the province or state.

Case Law

Mayhew v. Registrar (1963), 42 D.L.R. (2d) 477 (P.E.I. S.C.) — The plaintiff sought by *mandamus* to compel the Registrar of Motor Vehicles and the Provincial Secretary to restore his driver's licence and motor vehicle registration which had been suspended for non-payment of a judgment rendered against him in Nova Scotia. The plaintiff contended that since he was not the driver of his vehicle at the time of the collision concerned, had not entered an appearance, and had a good defence to the action on the merits, the Nova Scotia judgment was not a final judgment and was not rendered on the determination of all proceedings. It was held that the order should go as asked since the judgment was not final within the meaning of s. 99 of the Prince Edward Island Act. Moreover, the defendants had acted in the capacity of agents to do a particular act and not as servants of the Crown and were amenable to an order in lieu of *mandamus*.

Re Thomaes and Reg. of Motor Vehicles (1978), 18 O.R. (2d) 219, 82 D.L.R. (3d) 305 (Div. Ct.) — Section 198(4) of the Highway Traffic Act and R.R.O. 1990, Reg. 607, provide for reciprocity with regard to suspension of licences where judgments have been obtained in foreign jurisdictions, and can apply even though the defendant did not attorn to that jurisdiction.

Lunel v. Reg. of Motor Vehicles (1980), 4 M.V.R. 183 (Ont. Div. Ct.) — The effect of s. 198 of the Act is to prevent Ontario residents against whom there are outstanding judgments arising from automobile accidents in other jurisdictions from operating motor vehicles on Ontario highways. The date of the judgment is irrelevant as long as it was outstanding when the Ontario legislation went into effect.

Caligiuri v. Co-operators Ins. Assn. (1984), 29 M.V.R. 291, 53 C.B.R. (N.S.) 37 (Ont. Co. Ct.) — The applicant, a discharged bankrupt, applied pursuant to s. 198(3) of the Highway Traffic Act for the privilege of paying an outstanding judgment against him by instalments so that his driving privilege would be reinstated. In light of a potential conflict between the Highway Traffic provision and s. 148(2) of the Bankruptcy Act, as well as the questioned constitutional validity of s. 198(3) of the provincial statute, the Attorney General for Ontario was invited to intervene. It was held that the Highway Traffic provision was constitutionally valid and the applicant was ordered entitled to pay monthly instalments of $150 until the outstanding judgment was discharged. As the impugned provisions dealt with the issuing and cancellation of driving privileges, they were well within the parameters that had been set in s. 92 of the Constitution Act, 1867. Before a court can conclude that a conflict exists between federal and provincial legislation, there must be an explicit contradiction in the sense that both cannot operate at the same time without a necessary clash. Only then will the provincial legislation be deemed inoperative. In this instance, the licensing provisions contemplated in s. 198 of the Highway Traffic Act clearly did not purport to reinstate a debt which may have been extinguished as a result of the operation of the Bankruptcy Act. Section 198 clearly imposed a prerequisite prior to the reinstatement of a licence, which is a matter that provincial authorities have every right to do. Furthermore, a discharged bankrupt would continue to be a "judgment debtor" for the purposes of s. 198, inasmuch as the Bankruptcy Act merely takes away creditors' rights against particular judgment debts without making the "judgment debt" any less of a debt. In setting the amount of the instalments under s. 198, the court must consider the overall amount of the debt as well as the applicant's ability to pay.

Related Provisions: See R.R.O. 1990, Reg. 607, Reciprocal Suspension of Licences.

198.1 (1) Licence suspension on direction of Director of Family Responsibility Office — On receiving a direction under section 37 of the *Family Responsibility and Support Arrears Enforcement Act, 1996* to suspend the driver's licence of a person, the Registrar shall suspend the person's driver's licence, if it is not already under suspension under this section.

(2) Reinstatement — On receiving a direction under section 38 of the *Family Responsibility and Support Arrears Enforcement Act, 1996* to reinstate the driver's licence of a person, the Registrar shall reinstate the licence unless,

(a) the licence is otherwise under suspension;

(b) interest charged or a penalty imposed under subsection 5(2) has not been paid; or

(c) an applicable prescribed administrative fee for handling a dishonoured payment has not been paid.

1996, c. 71, s. 70

198.2 Personal information — The Registrar shall, for purposes related to section 198.1, collect, use and disclose personal information about an identifiable individual disclosed in a direction from the Director of the Family Responsibility Office.

1996, c. 31, s. 70

198.3 (1) Protection from personal liability — No action or other proceeding for damages shall be instituted against the Registrar or any employee of the Ministry for acting in good faith in the execution or intended execution of a duty under this Part.

(2) Crown not relieved of liability — Despite subsections 5(2) and (4) of the *Proceedings Against the Crown Act*, subsection (1) does not relieve the Crown of liability in respect of a tort committed by a person mentioned in subsection (1) to which it would otherwise be subject.

1996, c. 31, s. 70

PART XIV — RECORDS AND REPORTING OF ACCIDENTS AND CONVICTIONS

199. (1) Duty to report accident — Every person in charge of a motor vehicle or street car who is directly or indirectly involved in an accident shall, if the accident results in personal injuries or in damage to property apparently exceeding an amount prescribed by regulation, report the accident forthwith to the nearest police officer and furnish him or her with the information concerning the accident as may be required by the officer under subsection (3).

(1.1) Officer may direct person to report accident at another location — If, on reporting the accident to the nearest police officer under subsection (1), the person is directed by the officer to report the accident at a specified location, the person shall not furnish the officer described in subsection (1) with the information concerning the accident but shall forthwith attend at the specified location and report the accident there to a police officer and furnish him or her with the information concerning the accident as may be required by the officer under subsection (3).

(2) Where person unable to report — Where the person is physically incapable of making a report and there is another occupant of the motor vehicle, the occupant shall make the report.

(3) Duty of police officer — A police officer receiving a report of an accident, as required by this section, shall secure from the person making the report, or by other inquiries where necessary, the particulars of the accident, the persons involved, the extent of the personal injuries or property damage, if any, and the other information as may be necessary to complete a written report concerning the accident and shall forward the report to the Registrar within ten days of the accident.

(4) Report of police officer — The report of a police officer under subsection (3) shall be in the form that is approved by the Minister.

(5) Regulations as to amount of property damage — The Lieutenant Governor in Council may make regulations prescribing the amount of property damage for the purposes of subsection (1).

1997, c. 12, s. 15; 2002, c. 17, Sched. F, s. 1

Commentary

Every person in charge of a motor vehicle or street car who is indirectly or directly involved in an accident shall, if there are personal injuries or damages exceeding an amount set by regulation ($1000), report forthwith to the nearest police officer and furnish the officer with information concerning the accident as may be required (subs. (1)). Where a person is physically unable to report, another occupant shall report (subs. (2)). The police officer shall obtain the particulars of the accident, the names of the persons involved, the extend of the personal injuries or property damage, and any other information as may be necessary to prepare a written report. The report shall be in a form as approved by the Minister (subs. (4)). It shall be forwarded within 10 days of the accident to the Registrar (subs. (3)). The amount of property damage may be changed by regulation (subs. (5)).

Case Law

Duty of Motorist

R. v. Berg, [1956] O.W.N. 653, 116 C.C.C. 204 (Co. Ct.); *Bell v. Fader* (1968), 64 W.W.R. 668, (sub nom. *Bell v. R.)* 4 C.R.N.S. 351, [1969] 2 C.C.C. 9 (Sask. Q.B.); *R. v. Cheadle* (1972), 9 C.C.C. (2d) 111 (Alta. T.D.) — There is nothing in this section to limit its application to accidents occurring on a highway, and it should be interpreted to include every person in charge of a motor vehicle who is involved directly or indirectly in an accident whether the accident occurs on or off the highway.

Gos v. Nicholson (1999), 41 M.V.R. (3d) 308 (Ont. C.A.) — There is no duty on a person involved in a motor vehicle accident to make a statement on her own initiative. The section requires only that a person furnish the investigating officer with information as may be required by the officer.

R. v. Ross (2003), 341 A.R. 196, 44 M.V.R. (4th) 280, 2003 CarswellAlta 1406 (Alta. Prov. Ct.) — A "witness" under the Alberta statute includes the other driver.

R. v. Hajivasilis (2013), 41 M.V.R. (6th) 175, 2013 ONCA 27, 2013 CarswellOnt 508, 114 O.R. (3d) 337, 302 O.A.C. 65, [2013] O.J. No. 253 (Ont. C.A.) — The reporting requirement in s. 199 applies even if the accident does not occur on a "highway".

Obstruct Justice

R. v. Patrick, [1960] O.W.N. 206, 32 C.R. 338 (C.A.) — A person does not become subject to a duty of disclosure unless it is first established that he or she was actually in charge or control of a vehicle involved in an accident. In the absence of such proof, that person cannot be guilty of a criminal offence because he or she refuses to admit an incriminating fact to the police. Accordingly, a charge of obstruction under s. 118 [now s. 129] of the Criminal Code was dismissed where the suspect vehicle was located but the registered owner refused to say when he had last seen or driven his car.

"Forthwith"

R. v. Pearson (1960), 32 W.W.R. 457 (Sask. Mag. Ct.) — The duty to report an accident "forthwith" means within a reasonable time having regard to all the circumstances of the case. A delay of six hours in reporting an accident on a Sunday in which no one was injured and no damage caused except to the driver's own vehicle was considered reasonable.

Bell v. Fader (1968), 64 W.W.R. 668, (sub nom. *Bell v. R.)* 4 C.R.N.S. 351 (Sask. Q.B.) — Where an accident occurred on a construction project off the highway several miles from the nearest town it was sufficient for the driver to report the accident after work, seven hours later.

R. v. Bakker (1986), 41 M.V.R. 190 (Ont. Prov. Ct.) — The accused was involved in an accident at approximately 12:30 a.m., when his vehicle rolled over into a ditch. The accused left the scene of the accident without inspecting the vehicle, and returned to his hotel. The hotel phones were closed for the evening. He returned to the accident scene at 9:00 the next morning and called the police at 9:30. The accused argued on appeal that: the obligation to report did not arise until the damage to the vehicle became apparent; that the damage did not become apparent until the next morning; and that as "forthwith" in s. 173 [now s. 199] meant "as soon as practicable", in the circumstances the accused had fulfilled his obligation under that section. The appeal was dismissed. The driver is not entitled to delay making an assessment of the damage unless he is physically unable to make an assessment. In the present case, even though it was dark, the accused would have been able to assess the damage if he had made an attempt. The fact that the phone lines were closed at the accused's hotel did not afford a defence, because there was no evidence at what time they re-opened the next morning and thus there was no evidence the accused phoned the police "as soon as practicable".

Young Offenders

Person Unknown v. S. (M.) (1986), 43 M.V.R. 306 (Ont. Prov. Ct.) — The applicant pedestrian was injured in a motor vehicle accident and applied to the local police force for a copy of the police accident report. The police refused to release the report on the ground that the driver of the motor vehicle was a young offender within the meaning of the Young Offenders Act (Can.). The applicant applied under s. 40(3)(1) [now s. 44.1(1)(e), R.S.C. 1985, c. Y-1; as am. R.S.C. 1985 (1st Supp.), c. 27] of the Young Offenders Act for an order releasing the report. The application was allowed. Section 40(3)(1) provided that an applicant was required to have a valid interest in the record and that disclosure must be desirable in the proper administration of justice. The applicant clearly had a valid interest in the police accident report, as it contained information which he needed to pursue his civil claim. The right of privacy of the young offender should not take precedence over the rights of the victim. The young offender was not entitled to blanket protection of identity from everyone including the very person he had harmed, and the policy reasons behind protection of a young offender's identity did not extend to afford protection from liability to car owners and their insurance companies. Disclosure of the report was clearly desirable in the interest of the proper administration of justice.

State Farm Mutual Automobile Ins. Co. v. London Police Assn. (1986), 38 M.V.R. 217 (Ont. Dist. Ct.) — The insurance company applied for production in its entirety of an accident report concerning an accident involving a person under 18 years of age. The police force had deleted from the report the name, age and driver's licence of the driver because of their uncertainty over the application of the Young Offenders Act, which forbade the publication of reports concerning offences committed or alleged to have been committed by young persons. The insurance company applied for a declaration that the reports could be published in their entirety, on the grounds, *inter alia*, that a charge under a provincial statute did not constitute an offence under the Young Offenders Act. The application was granted in part. It was held that police officers faced a conflict in that they were required under the Highway Traffic Act to prepare accident reports, yet both the Provincial Offences Act and the Young Offenders Act forbade publication of reports involving offences committed by young persons. In the cases of offences committed under provincial statutes, the police should not complete those portions of the report which contained particulars of any offence laid under a provincial statute as a result of the accident but should complete the remainder of the report including the name and date of birth of anyone under 16. The Young Offenders Act did not apply to offences committed under provincial statutes, and the police could distribute an accident report involving a young offender so long as there was no reference to charges or alleged offences under any federal statute.

Owners

Pelkie v. R. (1980), 4 M.V.R. 186 (Ont. Co. Ct.) — The Crown failed to hold the owner responsible for a driver who was driving the vehicle beyond the scope of the trip for which permission had been granted.

Admissibility of Statements

Marshall v. R., [1961] S.C.R. 123, 26 D.L.R. (2d) 459 — No change in the common law was intended to be effected by this section; a confession is admissible whenever it is proved to have been made voluntarily in the sense that it was not induced by threats or promises. Statements made under compulsion of a statute are not by reason of that fact alone rendered inadmissible in criminal proceedings against the person making them. For purposes of criminal proceedings it is therefore unnecessary to decide whether a statement was made, in whole or in part, under the statutory compulsion.

R. v. Favel (1960), 32 C.R. 287, 30 W.W.R. 582 (Sask. Police Ct.); *R. v. Grosenick* (1969), 72 W.W.R. 76, [1970] 4 C.C.C. 367 (Sask. C.A.) — Statements made pursuant to this section were admissible on a charge of making a false statement in an accident report since this was not a "trial arising out of a motor vehicle accident."

R. v. Arenson (1970), 75 W.W.R. 328 (Man. C.A.) — A conviction for failure to report was based on the accused's own report, made five days after the event, of having struck a parked car.

R. v. Fex (1973), 1 O.R. (2d) 280, 23 C.R.N.S. 368, 14 C.C.C. (2d) 188 (C.A.); affirming [1973] 3 O.R. 242, 21 C.R.N.S. 360, 12 C.C.C. (2d) 239 (H.C.) — The existence of a statutory duty under s. 233(2) [now s. 252(1)] of the Criminal Code does not dispense with the onus on the Crown to establish that a statement made pursuant to that section was not otherwise voluntary.

R. v. Slopek (1974), 21 C.C.C. (2d) 362 (Ont. C.A.) — A statement made by a driver at the scene of an accident with respect to his having the care, charge or control of the car, was not automatically admissible by virtue of the statutory obligation imposed upon him but it is necessary to prove such statement was not otherwise involuntary. Before a statement is admitted it is not necessary for the Crown to establish beyond a reasonable doubt that the accused was in fact the person having the care, charge or control of the car.

R. v. Sarkonak (1990), 23 M.V.R. (2d) 45, 53 C.C.C. (3d) 542, 63 Man. R. (2d) 174 (Q.B.) — The accused was convicted of failing to remain at the scene of an accident contrary to s. 155(2) of the Highway Traffic Act. He attended with his counsel at a police station for the purposes of completing an accident report. Counsel made it clear to a police officer at the station that his client did not wish to make any statement. However, before the accused was permitted to complete the accident report, the police officer required him to identify himself as the driver of the vehicle involved in the accident. At trial, the constable testified that he always imposed such a requirement before he would permit completion of accident reports. The accused's answers to the officer's questions were ruled admissible on the basis that they were "voluntary, separate and apart from the statement itself." The accused appealed. The appeal was allowed. The verbal statements were inadmissible for two reasons. First, being liable for prosecution under the Act and precluded from completing the accident report unless he acknowledged that he was the driver of the vehicle effectively constituted an inducement to the accused to respond to the preliminary questions. Therefore the accused's statements were not voluntary within the meaning of the traditional case law respecting this issue. Second, the preliminary questions were so inextricably linked with the accident report that they constituted, in effect, one transaction.

R. v. White (1999), 42 M.V.R. (3d) 161 (S.C.C.) — Statements made under provincial motor vehicle law were not admissible in a criminal prosecution.

R. v. Lunger (2001), 18 M.V.R. (4th) 311, 2001 CarswellAlta 1319 (Alta. Prov. Ct.); *R. v. Fancey* (2000), 4 M.V.R. (4th) 99, 2000 CarswellNfld 169, 193 Nfld. & P.E.I.R. 79, 582 A.P.R. 79 (Nfld. T.D.) — A false statement regarding identity of the driver would not be immunized.

R. v. Zwicker, 2003 NSCA 140, 2003 CarswellNS 445, 186 C.C.C. (3d) 395, 49 M.V.R. (4th) 69 (C.A.); leave to appeal to S.C.C. refused (2004), 2004 CarswellNS 392, 2004 CarswellNS 393, 335 N.R. 194 (note), 235 N.S.R. (2d) 400 (note), 747 A.P.R. 400 (S.C.C.) — The *Charter* was engaged. It was open to find that an adversarial relationship existed between the accused and the police when the statutorily-compelled statement was made. The statement was properly excluded in the *Motor Vehicle Act* trials.

R. v. Binfet (2014), 2014 CarswellAlta 2623, 601 A.R. 334, 71 M.V.R. (6th) 304, 2014 ABPC 259, [2014] A.J. No. 1478 (Alta. Prov. Ct.) — Noting alcohol on the breath while a driver filled out a traffic accident report did not contravene s. 7 of the *Charter*.

Related Provisions: See s. 200 of the Act; s. 252 of the Criminal Code; R.R.O. 1990, Reg. 596, General (sets the reporting level for accidents at $1000).

199.1 (1) Irreparable vehicles, etc. — In this section,

"irreparable"means, with respect to a vehicle, a vehicle that meets the prescribed criteria for classification as irreparable;

"rebuilt"means, with respect to a vehicle, a vehicle that meets the prescribed criteria for classification as rebuilt;

"salvage"means, with respect to a vehicle, a vehicle that meets the prescribed criteria for classification as salvage;

(2) Application — Subsections (4) to (10), (12) to (18) and (22) to (25) apply with respect to vehicles for which there is a valid permit under this Act.

(3) Exemptions — This section does not apply to such persons as may be prescribed, with respect to such classes of vehicles as may be prescribed or in such circumstances as may be prescribed.

(4) Duty to notify Registrar — If an insurer determines that a vehicle is irreparable or is salvage, the insurer shall notify the Registrar that it is irreparable or is salvage, as the case may be, and shall do so within the prescribed period and shall give the Registrar the prescribed information in the prescribed manner.

(5) Same, other persons — If a person specified in the regulations determines that a vehicle is irreparable or is salvage, the person shall notify the Registrar that it is irreparable or is salvage, as the case may be, and shall do so within the prescribed period and shall give the Registrar the prescribed information in the prescribed manner.

(6) Offence, failure to notify — A person who fails to notify the Registrar in accordance with subsection (4) to (5), as the case may be, is guilty of an offence and on conviction is liable to a fine of not less than $400 and not more than $20,000.

(7) Same, misclassification — A person who notifies the Registrar that a vehicle is irreparable when it is salvage, or who notifies the Registrar that the vehicle is salvage when it is irreparable, is guilty of an offence and on conviction is liable to a fine of not less than $400 and not more than $20,000.

(8) Duty to notify permit holder, etc. — The person required to notify the Registrar under subsection (4) or (5) shall also notify the holder of the vehicle permit for the vehicle or the holder of the vehicle portion of the vehicle permit for the vehicle. The notice must be given in the prescribed manner and within the prescribed period.

(9) Offence — A person who fails to notify the holder of the vehicle permit or of the vehicle portion of the vehicle permit under subsection (8) is guilty of an offence and on conviction is liable to a fine of not less than $400 and not more than $20,000.

(10) Registrar's duty to classify — Upon receiving notice under subsection (4) or (5), the Registrar shall classify the vehicle in the vehicle permit records as irreparable or salvage if the Registrar is satisfied that the prescribed criteria for classifying it as such are met.

(11) Same, classification from another jurisdiction — If a vehicle has a classification equivalent to irreparable or salvage from a jurisdiction that is specified in the regulations, the Registrar may classify the vehicle in the vehicle permit records as irreparable or as salvage.

Proposed Amendment — 199.1(11)

(11) Same, classification from another jurisdiction — If a vehicle has a classification equivalent to irreparable or salvage from a jurisdiction that is specified in the regulations, the Registrar shall classify the vehicle in the vehicle permit records as irreparable or as salvage.

2015, c. 14, s. 54(1) [Not in force at date of publication.]

(12) Submissions re classification — If the person who holds the vehicle permit or the vehicle portion of the vehicle permit for the vehicle disagrees with the decision or action of the Registrar under subsection (10) or (11), the person may make written submissions to the Registrar about the decision or action.

Proposed Amendment — 199.1(12)

(12) Submissions re classification — A person who held the vehicle portion of the permit for the vehicle at the time of the event that led to the vehicle's classification under subsection (10) and who continues to hold the vehicle portion of the permit may make written submissions about the action taken by the Registrar under subsection (10).

2015, c. 14, s. 54(1) [Not in force at date of publication.]

Proposed Addition — 199.1(12.1)

(12.1) Appointment of reviewer — The Registrar may appoint a person as a reviewer to consider any submissions made under subsection (12).

2015, c. 14, s. 54(1) [Not in force at date of publication.]

(13) Same — The submissions must be made within the prescribed period and they must indicate the reasons why the Registrar's decision or action should be changed.

Proposed Amendment — 199.1(13)

(13) Requirements for submissions — The submissions must be made within the prescribed period, must indicate the reasons why the Registrar's action should be changed and must be accompanied by the fee required by the reviewer.

2015, c. 14, s. 54(1) [Not in force at date of publication.]

(14) Written hearing — The Registrar shall consider the submissions, but shall not hold an oral hearing into the matter, and the Registrar's decision or action under subsection (10) or (11) is not stayed by reason of the submissions being made.

Proposed Amendment — 199.1(14)

(14) Written hearing — The reviewer shall consider the submissions, but shall not hold an oral hearing into the matter, and the Registrar's action under subsection (10) is not stayed by reason of the submissions being made.

2015, c. 14, s. 54(1) [Not in force at date of publication.]

(15) Outcome — After considering the submissions, the Registrar may confirm or change his or her decision or action under subsection (10) or (11) and shall notify the person who made the submissions. The Registrar's decision under this subsection is final.

Proposed Amendment — 199.1(15)

(15) Outcome — After considering the submissions, the reviewer may confirm the Registrar's action or direct the Registrar to change his or her action taken under subsection (10) and shall notify the person who made the submissions. The reviewer's decision under this subsection is final.

2015, c. 14, s. 54(1) [Not in force at date of publication.]

(16) Duty to return permit — When the holder of the vehicle permit or of the vehicle portion of the vehicle permit learns or reasonably ought to have learned that the vehicle is irreparable or is salvage, the holder shall return the permit or portion of the permit to the Registrar within the prescribed period.

(17) Offence — A person who fails to return a vehicle permit or the vehicle portion of a vehicle permit to the Registrar in accordance with subsection (16) is guilty of an offence and on conviction is liable to a fine of not less than $200 and not more than $20,000.

(18) Replacement permit — Upon receiving the vehicle permit or the vehicle portion of the vehicle permit under subsection (16), the Registrar may issue a replacement permit or a replacement portion of a permit for the applicable vehicle indicating that the vehicle is classified as irreparable or as salvage, as the case may be.

(19) Prohibition re driving, etc. — No person shall drive or draw on a highway a vehicle classified by the Registrar as irreparable or as salvage or that the regulations specify has an equivalent classification from a jurisdiction that is specified in the regulations, and no person shall permit such a vehicle to be driven or draw on a highway.

(20) Exception — Subsection (19) does not apply,

(a) when the vehicle is being towed for the purposes of repairs;

(b) when the vehicle is being driven or drawn for the purpose of receiving a safety standards certificate; or

(c) in such other circumstances as may be prescribed.

(21) Offence — A person who contravenes subsection (19) is guilty of an offence and on conviction is liable, on a first conviction, to a fine of not less than $100 and not more than $500, and on each subsequent conviction, to a fine of not less than $200 and not more than $1,000.

(22) Rebuilt vehicles — If a vehicle is classified in the vehicle permit records as salvage, the Registrar may reclassify it as rebuilt if the Registrar is satisfied that the prescribed criteria for classifying it as such are met.

(23) Same — A vehicle that is classified in the vehicle permit records as irreparable cannot subsequently be reclassified as rebuilt.

(24) Replacement permit — Subsections (16) and (18) apply, with necessary modifications, with respect to the vehicle permit or the vehicle portion of the vehicle permit for a vehicle that is reclassified as rebuilt.

(25) Limitation — No proceeding for an offence under subsection (6), (7) or (9) shall be instituted more than 24 months after the facts on which the proceeding is based are alleged to have occurred.

(26) [Repealed 2008, c. 17, s. 44.]

(27) Regulations — The Lieutenant Governor in Council may make regulations,

(a) prescribing or specifying such matters as this section requires or permits to be prescribed or specified by regulation;

(b) specifying, for the purposes of subsections (11) and (19), other jurisdictions and their vehicle classifications that are considered to be equivalent to irreparable or salvage for the purposes of those subsections;

(c) defining any word or expression used in this section that is not already expressly defined in this section;

Proposed Addition — 199.1(27)(c.1)

(c.1) governing the fee that a reviewer can require under subsection (13);

2015, c. 14, s. 54(2) [Not in force at date of publication.]

(d) respecting any matter that the Lieutenant Governor in Council considers necessary or advisable to carry out the intent and purpose of this section.

(28) Same — A regulation may establish different requirements or standards for different classes of persons, vehicles, circumstances or other matters.

2000, c. 15, s. 2; 2002, c. 18, Sched. P, s. 35; 2008, c. 17, s. 44

Related Provisions: O. Reg. 376/02, Classification of Vehicles as Irreparable, Salvage and Rebuilt; R.R.O. 1990, Reg. 628, Vehicle Permits, s. 2.1.

200. (1) Duty of person in charge of vehicle in case of accident — Where an accident occurs on a highway, every person in charge of a vehicle or street car that is directly or indirectly involved in the accident shall,

(a) remain at or immediately return to the scene of the accident;

(b) render all possible assistance; and

(c) upon request, give in writing to anyone sustaining loss or injury or to any police officer or to any witness his or her name, address, driver's licence number and jurisdiction of issuance, motor vehicle liability insurance policy in-

surer and policy number, name and address of the registered owner of the vehicle and the vehicle permit number.

(2) Penalty — Every person who contravenes this section is guilty of an offence and on conviction is liable to a fine of not less than $400 and not more than $2,000 or to imprisonment for a term of not more than six months, or to both, and in addition the person's licence or permit may be suspended for a period of not more than two years.

1997, c. 12, s. 16; 2009, c. 5, s. 54

Commentary

The duty of the person in charge of the accident is to: remain at or immediately return to the scene of the accident; render all possible assistance; and, upon request, give to anyone sustaining loss or injury, or to a police officer or witness, his or her name, the owner's name and address, and the number of the permit.

The offence is punishable by a fine of not less than $200 and not more than $1,000 and/or imprisonment up to six months. In addition, the licence or permit may be suspended for up to two years.

Case Law

Information

R. v. Budden, [1964] 2 C.C.C. 290 (Ont. Mag. Ct.) — Only one offence is created by s. 200(1)(a), and a charge of "failing to remain at or immediately return to" the scene of an accident is not void for duplicity.

R. v. Saltys (Soltys) (1979), 6 M.V.R. 31 (B.C. S.C.); affirmed (1980), 8 M.V.R. 59 (B.C. C.A.) — The Crown appealed by way of stated case from a ruling of a Provincial Court judge who had quashed an information charging the accused pursuant to s. 62(1) of the British Columbia Motor Vehicle Act with being the owner of a vehicle the driver of which had failed to remain at the scene of an "incident". The Provincial Court Judge held that in failing to define the word "incident", the Legislature created an offence which is incapable of enforcement because the expression "incident" is so wide in scope that the intention of the Legislature is impossible to determine. In allowing the appeal it was held that the section was valid. Whether or not a person is involved in an "incident" is in each case a question of fact. Certainly a collision resulting in injury to the person or damage to the property of another is an "incident".

R. v. Vanboeyen (1992), 40 M.V.R. (2d) 13, 132 A.R. 326 (Prov. Ct.) — The provincial offence of failing to remain is an included offence in the Criminal Code offence of failing to stop.

Knowledge

R. v. Hill, [1972] 2 O.R. 402, 17 C.R.N.S. 124, 6 C.C.C. (2d) 285 (H.C.); affirmed by the Court of Appeal without written reason; affirmed (1973), 43 D.L.R. (3d) 532, 1 N.R. 136 (S.C.C.) — On a charge under the section it is sufficient to prove that two vehicles have touched; proof of knowledge of damage is not required.

R. v. Racimore (1975), 25 C.C.C. (2d) 143 (Ont. H.C.) — Failing to remain was held not to be an offence requiring *mens rea* but that where the defendant had no knowledge of contact with the other vehicle, he ought to be acquitted as the *actus reus* in failing to remain was involuntary.

R. v. Clarke (1984), 27 M.V.R. 65 (B.C. Co. Ct.) — The accused appealed from her conviction for "failing to remain at the scene of a highway incident," contrary to the Motor Vehicle Act (B.C.), on the ground that she did not possess the requisite mental element for the offence. The evidence at trial indicated that the accused panicked after being involved in an accident. She drove some distance away from the scene of the accident and then stopped. She observed an automobile drive slowly past her vehicle and concluded, erroneously, that it was the other vehicle involved in the accident. Believing that there was no "incident", she did not return to the scene. The appeal was dismissed. The offence in question was a strict liability offence. Accordingly, the test was whether the accused entertained an honest belief in a state of facts, having arrived at that belief responsibly as opposed to negligently, which would have rendered the act an innocent one. On the facts as found by the trial Judge there was no basis for any such "honest belief". Any conclusion of fact which was exculpatory in the mind of the accused arose not from responsible judgment but from a negligent assumption (wishful thinking). The accused possessed the necessary guilty mind required as an ingredient of the offence.

R. v. Hajivasilis (2013), 41 M.V.R. (6th) 175, 2013 ONCA 27, 2013 CarswellOnt 508, 114 O.R. (3d) 337, 302 O.A.C. 65, [2013] O.J. No. 253 (Ont. C.A.) — Section 199.1 is clearly intended to give the Registrar notice of vehicles that have been badly damaged as the use of those vehicles could pose a safety risk. Section 199.1 is not restricted to a "highway".

R. v. Smith, 2015 MBQB 84, 2015 CarswellMan 263, 78 M.V.R. (6th) 216, 317 Man. R. (2d) 158, [2015] M.J. No. 141 — After the Crown made out a *prima facie* case the burden shifted to the accused to establish on a balance of probabilities that her mistake of fact was honest based on reasonable grounds.

Accident

R. v. Hannam (1986), 1 M.V.R. (2d) 361, 86 A.R. 151 (Q.B.) — A *Criminal Code* charge of leaving the scene was considered. Two vehicles had been racing and jockeying for position. It was held that involvement in an accident is not dependent on physical contact between the vehicles.

Constitutional

R. v. Rowley (1986), 43 M.V.R. 290, 6 B.C.L.R. (2d) 280 (C.A.); reversing (1985), 42 M.V.R. 20 (B.C. Co. Ct.) — The accused struck a cyclist and then fled the accident site. He was convicted under s. 62(1) of the Motor Vehicle Act for failing to remain at the scene of an "incident". The accused's appeal of his conviction was allowed on the ground that the word "incident" was so vague as to render s. 62(1) inoperative as contravening s. 7 of the Canadian Charter of Rights and Freedoms. The Crown appealed. The appeal was allowed. It was held that the word "incident" had previously been interpreted by the courts to clearly include the conduct in question of the accused. Section 62(1) was not unconstitutionally vague because it was not impermissibly vague in all its applications. Furthermore, one to whose conduct a statute clearly applied could not successfully challenge the statute for vagueness.

A. G. Que. v. Gagné, [1969] R.L. 534 — Section 61 of the Quebec Highway Code, which is similar to s. 200, was held *intra vires* and not in terms covered by the Criminal Code.

Nature of Duty

R. v. May, [1975] 6 W.W.R. 477, 24 C.C.C. (2d) 505 (Alta. T.D.) — The Alberta section requires the driver of a vehicle involved in an accident to supply to the injured party the information specified therein "or such of that information as requested," and imposes a duty on the driver to supply such information notwithstanding no request is made. The concluding words of the section merely create an alternative to performing the mandatory duty in that the person entitled to the information may waive his or her right to the information, but such waiver must be expressly or impliedly exercised before the driver is relieved of his or her duty under the section.

R. v. Marler (1972), 17 N.B.R. (2d) 663 (Co. Ct.) — The meaning of "apparent extent" of damage in excess of $200 and of compliance "immediately" was considered under the New Brunswick Act.

R. v. Rees (1981), 10 M.V.R. 147 (N.S. Co. Ct.) — The appellant was convicted arising out of his alleged failure to identify himself "to a witness". A taxi driver did not observe the collision between the appellant's vehicle and parked vehicles but his attention was drawn to the scene by the collision. He was not an eyewitness but a close observer of what followed immediately thereafter. The taxi driver followed the appellant, obtained his licence number and reported the matter to the police, leading to the arrest. The appeal was dismissed. Definitions of the term "witness", while of interest, do not answer the question. Many cases in the courts involve cases being proven by circumstantial evidence provided by witnesses. The appellant's submission that the duty to identify to a witness only arises when the other car is occupied could not be accepted. Appellant's final argument was that the Crown had to show that the appellant knew there was a witness in the area. There is no validity to this argument upon a review of the evidence which discloses that the appellant did not make even a cursory search of the area.

R. v. Kirby (1983), 20 M.V.R. 158 (B.C. Co. Ct.) — A driver was acquitted under the relevant British Columbia legislation in circumstances where, as he left his car, the car rolled away and hit another. He was found not to be the "driver."

R. v. Weir (1992), 36 M.V.R. (2d) 118 (Ont. Prov. Ct.) — The Criminal Code offence required an intent to escape civil or criminal liability, while the Act was one of strict liability, to which a defence of due diligence was available. The defendant's departure from the scene after a five-minute delay was a proper exercise of due diligence since he required medical assistance. The Act is intended to deal with a time proximate to the accident. There was no obligation to return to the scene after receiving medical attention.

R. v. DaCosta (2001), 15 M.V.R. (4th) 272 (Ont. S.C.J.) — Statements under the Act and to the insurer under the Insurance Act were found to be compelled.

Identity

R. v. Kennedy (1982), 17 M.V.R. 115 (B.C. Prov. Ct.) — Under the Motor Vehicle Act (B.C.), a driver is required to correctly state his or her name and address to a peace officer upon request. Where that driver is later summoned to court by way of an appearance notice, the trial judge is entitled to take cognizance of the stated name and address on the appearance notice without requiring the Crown to prove the accused driver's identity through a *voir dire*.

Civil

Doucette v. Eddy's Taxi & Bus Service Ltd. (1987), 67 Nfld. & P.E.I.R. 88, 206 A.P.R. 88 (Nfld. T.D.) — The defendant's taxi was stopped at a stop sign and was struck in the rear by a truck skidding along an icy road. The plaintiff was a passenger in the taxi. The defendant driver and the operator of the truck checked on the condition of the vehicles and, upon finding no damage, both left the scene. The defendant driver asked the plaintiff whether any injuries had occurred and a negative reply was received. Later in the day pain and discomfort were felt. The plaintiff commenced an action alleging the defendant driver was negligent in not obtaining the name of the truck driver. The action was dismissed. It was held that ss. 191 and 192 of the Highway Traffic Act (Alta.) did not impose any obligation on the driver of the truck to provide identification if asked. The statute did not create any responsibilities between the plaintiff and the defendant driver, and there was no obligation on the latter to ask for names. The defendant driver acted reasonably. The plaintiff failed to prove negligence.

Related Provisions: See s. 199 of the Act and s. 252 of the Criminal Code.

201. Notification of damage to trees, fences, etc. — Every person who, as a result of an accident or otherwise, operates or drives a vehicle or leads, rides or drives an animal upon a highway and thereby damages any shrub, tree, pole, light, sign, sod or other property on the highway or a fence bordering the highway shall forthwith report the damage to a police officer.

202. (1) Reports by Crown attorneys and police officers — Every Crown Attorney and police officer having knowledge of a fatal accident in which a motor vehicle is involved shall secure the particulars of the accident, the persons involved, and other information as may be necessary to complete a written report to the Registrar on the forms prescribed for that purpose, and shall transmit the report forthwith to the Registrar.

(2) Reports re statistics and traffic control — Every provincial or municipal official or employee, hospital, charitable institution, insurer or other person or organization shall furnish to the Registrar the reports and other information relating to motor vehicle accident statistics and traffic control generally that may be required by the regulations.

(3) Compensation may be allowed — The Lieutenant Governor in Council, by regulation, may allow any person or organization making reports or furnishing information under this section the compensation for so doing that may be considered proper.

Case Law

Spillane (Litigation Guardian of) v. Wasserman (1992), 42 M.V.R. (2d) 144, 13 C.C.L.T. (2d) 267 (Ont. Gen. Div.); additional reasons at (April 1, 1993), Doc. 11625/86, 11629/86 (Ont. Gen. Div.) — Negligence on the part of doctors including a failure to report resulted in forty percent liability.

R. v. Hajivasilis (2013), 41 M.V.R. (6th) 175, 2013 ONCA 27, 2013 CarswellOnt 508, 114 O.R. (3d) 337, 302 O.A.C. 65, [2013] O.J. No. 253 (Ont. C.A.) — The requirements are not restricted to "highways".

203. (1) Report of medical practitioner — Every legally qualified medical practitioner shall report to the Registrar the name, address and clinical condition of every person sixteen years of age or over attending upon the medical practitioner for medical services who, in the opinion of the medical practitioner, is suffering from a condition that may make it dangerous for the person to operate a motor vehicle.

(2) No action for complying with subs. (1) — No action shall be brought against a qualified medical practitioner for complying with this section.

(3) Reports privileged — The report referred to in subsection (1) is privileged for the information of the Registrar only and shall not be open for public inspection, and the report is inadmissible in evidence for any purpose in any trial except to prove compliance with subsection (1).

Proposed Amendment — 203

203. Medical reports — **(1) Mandatory reports** — Every prescribed person shall report to the Registrar every person who is at least 16 years old who, in the opinion of the prescribed person, has or appears to have a prescribed medical condition, functional impairment or visual impairment.

(2) Discretionary reports — A prescribed person may report to the Registrar a person who is at least 16 years old who, in the opinion of the prescribed person, has or appears to have a medical condition, functional impairment or visual impairment that may make it dangerous for the person to operate a motor vehicle.

(3) Authority to make discretionary report prevails over duty of confidentiality — The authority to make a report under subsection (2) prevails over any duty of confidentiality imposed on the prescribed person by or under any other Act or by a standard of practice or rule of professional conduct that would otherwise preclude him or her from providing the information described in that subsection to the Registrar.

(4) Required to meet the person — Subsections (1) and (2) only apply if the prescribed person actually met the reported person for an examination or for the provision of medical or other services, or in the circumstances prescribed by regulation.

(5) Authority to make discretionary report is not a duty — Subsections (2) and (3) do not impose a duty on a prescribed person to report to the Registrar.

2015, c. 14, s. 55 [Not in force at date of publication.]

Case Law

Toms v. Foster (1994), 7 M.V.R. (3d) 34 (Ont. C.A.) — The obligation under s. 203 is mandatory not discretionary.

Cabot v. Newfoundland & Labrador (Registrar of Motor Vehicles), 2009 CarswellNfld 138, 85 M.V.R. (5th) 302, 2009 NLTD 87 — An appeal from the decision of the Registrar was dismissed.

204. (1) Report of optometrist — Every member of the College of Optometrists of Ontario shall report to the Registrar the name, address and clinical condition of every person sixteen years of age or over attending upon the optometrist for optometric services who, in the opinion of the optometrist, is suffering from an eye condition that may make it dangerous for the person to operate a motor vehicle.

(2) No action for compliance with subs. (1) — No action shall be brought against a qualified optometrist for complying with this section.

(3) Reports privileged — The report referred to in subsection (1) is privileged for the information of the Registrar only and shall not be open for public inspection, and the report is inadmissible in evidence for any purpose in any trial except to prove compliance with subsection (1).

Proposed Amendment — 204

204. General rules respecting medical reports — **(1) Contents** — A report required or authorized by section 203 must be submitted in the form and manner specified by the Registrar and must include,

    (a) the name, address and date of birth of the reported person;

    (b) the condition or impairment diagnosed or identified by the person making the report, and a brief description of the condition or impairment; and

    (c) any other information requested by the form.

(2) No liability for compliance — No action or other proceeding shall be brought against a prescribed person required or authorized to make a report under section 203 for making such a report or for reporting to the Registrar in good faith with the intention of reporting under that section.

(3) Reports privileged — A report made under section 203, or made to the Registrar in good faith with the intention of reporting under that section, is privileged for the information of the Registrar only and shall not be open to public inspection.

(4) Regulations — The Lieutenant Governor in Council may make regulations governing reports made under section 203, including regulations,

    (a) prescribing persons for the purpose of subsection 203(1) or (2);

    (b) prescribing medical conditions, functional impairments or visual impairments for the purpose of subsection 203(1);

    (c) prescribing circumstances for the purpose of subsection 203(4).

2015, c. 14, s. 55 [Not in force at date of publication.]

1998, c, 18, Sched. G, s. 56

Case Law

Ferguson Estate v. Burton (1987), 50 M.V.R. 197 (Ont. H.C.) — An epileptic driver lost consciousness while driving, and was involved in an accident which resulted in the death of the driver of the other vehicle. The facts indicated that the epileptic driver had not taken his medication, and was suffering from fatigue and considerable stress. The estate of the deceased sued him and the owner of the vehicle. The defendants joined the family physician who had been treating the driver suffering from epilepsy. In the main action, liability was established in favour of the plaintiffs. Since the physician did not take part in the main proceedings he was bound by this determination by virtue of r. 29.05(5) of the Ontario Rules of Civil Procedure. His argument at the opening of the third-party action alleging that the doctrine of *res judicata* applied was dismissed. In the third-party action, the defendant alleged that the physician was negligent on numerous grounds including his failure to report the driver's medical condition under s. 203 of the Highway Traffic Act. The third-party action was dismissed. The physician had prescribed the proper medication, and had not failed to treat and advise the driver in accordance with the standard expected of an ordinary physician practising as a family practitioner at the relevant time. There was no breach of the guidelines of the Canadian Medical Association which in any event was not mandatory. With respect to the Highway Traffic Act (Ont.), the physician was entitled to take into account the effect of the treatment on his patient in forming his opinion as to whether a patient is suffering from a condition that may make it dangerous for the patient to operate a motor vehicle. Furthermore, a report under s. 203 would not have resulted in a licence suspension since an investigation would have revealed the drug treatment which he had prescribed.

205. (1) Duties of Registrar — The Registrar shall,

(a) **supply of accident report forms** — prepare and supply to police officers and other persons and organizations blank forms approved by the Minister for accident and other reports which shall call for the particulars concerning accidents, the person involved and the extent of the personal injuries and property damage, if any, resulting therefrom, and the other information as may be required by the regulations;

(b) **investigation of accidents** — make such investigation of, and call for the written reports concerning, motor vehicle accidents, traffic conditions and other matters, as he or she may consider necessary and proper, and for that purpose may require the assistance of any police officer;

(c) **keeping of records** — keep,

(i) a record of all motor vehicle accidents in Ontario, reported to him or her or concerning which he or she procures information,

(ii) a record of all convictions for offences under this Act or under the provisions of the *Criminal Code* (Canada) relating to driving on highways, reported to him or her under section 210, and of the other convictions that he or she may consider proper,

(iii) a record of all licences, permits and CVOR certificates issued, suspended, revoked, cancelled or revived under this Act,

Proposed Amendment — 205(1)(c)(iii)

(iii) a record of all licences, permits and CVOR certificates issued, renewed, suspended, revoked, cancelled or revived under this Act,

2014, c. 9, Sched. 2, s. 45(1) [To come into force January 1, 2017.]

Proposed Addition — 205(1)(c)(iii.0.1)

(iii.0.1) a record of all administrative penalties imposed under section 21.1,

2014, c. 9, Sched. 2, s. 45(2) [Not in force at date of publication.]

(iii.1) a record of all safety records for operators determined under clause 22(1)(h) and a record of all safety ratings assigned to operators under section 17.1,

(iii.2) a record of all information relating to the International Registration Plan that is received by the Ministry,

(iv) a record of all unsatisfied judgments rendered against persons holding owners' permits or drivers' licences under this Act, or non-residents reported to him or her pursuant to this Act,

(v) an operating record of every driver, which record shall show all reported convictions of the driver for a contravention of any provision of any statute relating to the operation of motor vehicles, and all reported unsatisfied judgments against the person for any injury or damage caused by the person while operating a motor vehicle and all accidents in which the records of the Registrar indicate the driver has been involved, and the other information that the Registrar may consider proper,

(vi) an operating record of every conviction of every CVOR certificate holder and the holder's agents and employees that is reported to the Registrar under section 210 and the other convictions, whether or not the certificate holder was the person convicted, that the Registrar considers useful for the purpose of the administration and enforcement of this Act, and

(vii) the other records that he or she may be directed to keep by the Minister;

(d) **accident and traffic statistics** — develop adequate uniform methods of accident and traffic statistics, and study accident causes and trends, traffic problems and regulations;

(e) **annual report for Minister** — prepare for the Minister an annual report showing the results of the reporting, collection, analysis and study, and embodying his or her recommendations for the prevention of motor vehicle accidents and the solution of traffic problems, and the report shall be printed and published forthwith upon completion.

(2) **Record keeping** — The records kept under this section shall be kept in any manner or on any medium that allows information to be recorded, stored, retrieved and reproduced.

1993, c. 31, s. 2(8); 1996, c. 33, s. 16; 2002, c. 17, Sched. F, s. 1; 2002, c. 22, s. 100

Case Law

R. v. Hajivasilis (2013), 41 M.V.R. (6th) 175, 2013 ONCA 27, 2013 CarswellOnt 508, 114 O.R. (3d) 337, 302 O.A.C. 65, [2013] O.J. No. 253 (Ont. C.A.) — None of the responsibilities of the Registrar set out in s. 205 are limited to accidents or other traffic related concerns on "highways".

205.0.1 Collection and disclosure of information — (1) Collection by Minister — The Minister may request and collect information from any public body or related government, as he or she considers appropriate, if the Minister considers it necessary for a purpose set out in subsection (5).

(2) Disclosure by Minister — The Minister may disclose information to any public body or related government, as he or she considers appropriate, if the Minister considers it necessary for a purpose set out in subsection (5).

(3) Disclosure to Minister — Upon receipt of a request for information from the Minister under subsection (1), a public body shall disclose to the Minister any information from their records that may assist the Minister with a purpose set out in subsection (5).

(4) Exception — The Minister may not disclose under subsection (2) the measurements used for comparison of photographs as described in section 32.2.

(5) Purposes for collection and disclosure of information — The only purposes for which information may be collected or disclosed under this section are the following:

1. To verify the accuracy of any information provided under this Act by an applicant for or holder of a driver's licence or vehicle permit.

2. To verify the authenticity of any document provided under this Act by an applicant for or holder of a driver's licence or vehicle permit.

3. To detect a false statement in any document provided under this Act by any person.

4. To detect or prevent the improper use of a driver's licence or vehicle permit.

5. To detect or prevent the improper issuance or renewal of a driver's licence or vehicle permit, including by conducting an audit or review of any issuance, renewal or cancellation of a driver's licence or vehicle permit or the conduct of any person or entity involved in issuing, renewing or cancelling a driver's licence or vehicle permit.

6. To provide a public body or related government with the information that the Minister believes is necessary to assist it with a purpose similar to a purpose set out in paragraph 1, 2, 3 or 4 if the holder of a driver's licence or vehicle permit has presented his or her driver's licence or vehicle permit in order to obtain a benefit or service under a legislatively authorized program or service administered or provided by that public body or related government.

(6) Deemed compliance with privacy legislation — Any disclosure of information under this section is deemed to be in compliance with clause 42(1)(e) of the *Freedom of Information and Protection of Privacy Act* and clause 32(e) of the *Municipal Freedom of Information and Protection of Privacy Act.*

(7) Notice under privacy legislation — Any collection by a public body of personal information, as defined in the *Freedom of Information and Protection of Privacy Act* and the *Municipal Freedom of Information and Protection of Privacy Act*, disclosed to the public body under this section is exempt from the application of subsection 39(2) of the *Freedom of Information and Protection of Privacy Act* and subsection 29(2) of the *Municipal Freedom of Information and Protection of Privacy Act.*

(8) **Otherwise authorized collection or disclosure** — The authority to collect and disclose information under this section is in addition to any other authority under this or any other Act for the Ministry to collect and disclose information.

(9) **Regulations** — The Lieutenant Governor in Council may make regulations prescribing a person or entity, or any class of them, as a public body for the purposes of this section.

(10) **Definitions** — In this section,

"public body" means,

(a) any ministry, agency, board, commission, official or other body of the Government of Ontario,

(b) any municipality in Ontario,

(c) a local board, as defined in the *Municipal Affairs Act*, and any authority, board, commission, corporation, office or organization of persons some or all of whose members, directors or officers are appointed or chosen by or under the authority of the council of a municipality in Ontario, or

(d) a prescribed person or entity;

"related government" means,

(a) the Government of Canada and the Crown in right of Canada, and any ministry, agency, board, commission or official of either of them, or

(b) the government of any other province or territory of Canada and the Crown in right of any other province of Canada, and any ministry, agency, board, commission or official of any of them.

2008, c. 17, s. 45

PART XIV.1 — PHOTO-RADAR SYSTEM EVIDENCE

205.1 (1) **Photo-radar system evidence** — Subject to subsection (2), a photograph obtained through the use of a photo-radar system is admissible in evidence in a proceeding under the *Provincial Offences Act* respecting an alleged offence under section 128 of the *Highway Traffic Act* if the alleged offence was committed within an area of Ontario designated by the regulations.

(2) **Conditions** — The photograph must,

(a) show the vehicle and the number plate displayed on the vehicle; and

(b) show or have superimposed upon it an indication of the rate of speed at which the vehicle was being driven when the photograph was taken and the date on which and time at which the photograph was taken.

(3) **Use at trial** — In the absence of evidence to the contrary, the photograph is proof that the vehicle was, on the date and at the time shown or indicated on the photograph, being driven at the rate of speed shown or indicated on the photograph.

(4) Conviction — No person shall be convicted at trial of an offence on the basis of the photograph unless,

(a) the photograph is adduced at trial; or

(b) the person consents to the photograph not being adduced at trial.

1993, c. 31, s. 2(9)

Case Law

Weaver v. Winnipeg (City), 2011 MBQB 309, 2011 CarswellMan 709, 26 M.V.R. (6th) 212, 273 Man. R. (2d) 134 — An action alleging photo-radar in construction zones caused unjust enrichment was struck.

Related Provisions: See O. Reg. 500/94, Photo-Radar System — Part XIV.1 of The Highway Traffic Act.

205.2 Application — Sections 205.3 to 205.13 apply in respect of proceedings based on evidence obtained through the use of a photo-radar system if the proceedings are commenced by filing a certificate of offence under Part I of the *Provincial Offences Act*.

1993, c. 31, s. 2(9)

205.3 (1) *Provincial Offences Act*, Part I — No summons shall be issued under clause 3(2)(b) of the *Provincial Offences Act* in proceedings based on evidence obtained through the use of a photo-radar system.

(2) Application of certain provisions — Sections 5, 5.2, 6, 9, 9.1 and 11 of the *Provincial Offences Act* do not apply to proceedings based on evidence obtained through the use of a photo-radar system.

(3) Service by mail — An offence notice issued in proceedings based on evidence obtained through the use of a photo-radar system may be served in accordance with section 205.5 of this Act, in which case subsections 3(3) to (7) of the *Provincial Offences Act* do not apply.

1993, c. 31, s. 2(9)

205.4 (1) Evidence of ownership — If the proceeding is commenced by filing a certificate of offence, evidence of ownership of the vehicle involved in the alleged offence shall be filed in the court with the certificate.

(2) Same — The evidence of ownership may be contained in the certificate of offence or it may be set out in a separate document.

1993, c. 31, s. 2(9)

205.5 (1) Service by mail — An offence notice may be served by regular prepaid mail if it is mailed within twenty-three days after the occurrence of the alleged offence.

(2) Deemed service — An offence notice that is mailed to the most recent address appearing in the records of the Ministry of Transportation for the person charged shall be deemed to have been served seven days after it is mailed.

(3) Certificate of mailing — If the provincial offences officer who issued the certificate of offence also mails the offence notice or causes it to be mailed, that officer shall certify the fact that the notice was mailed and the date of mailing on the certificate of offence.

(4) Evidence — A certificate referred to in subsection (3) purporting to be signed by the provincial offences officer who issued it shall be received in evidence and is proof of mailing in the absence of evidence to the contrary.

1993, c. 31, s. 2(9)

205.6 Photographic equivalent — A photograph or a photographic equivalent of the photograph obtained through the use of a photo-radar system shall be served with the offence notice.

1993, c. 31, s. 2(9)

205.7 (1) Failure to respond — If fifteen days have elapsed after a defendant is served with an offence notice charging the defendant, as the owner of a vehicle, with a contravention of section 128 and the defendant has not given notice of intention to appear, pleaded guilty or made a payment out of court, as provided by section 5.1, 7 or 8 of the *Provincial Offences Act*, the defendant shall be deemed not to dispute the charge.

(2) Examination by justice — If subsection (1) applies, a justice shall examine the certificate of offence and shall without a hearing enter a conviction in the defendant's absence and impose the set fine for the offence if the certificate is complete and regular on its face and the justice is satisfied that the defendant is the owner of the vehicle involved in the offence.

(3) Quashing proceeding — The justice shall quash the proceeding if he or she is not able to enter a conviction.

1993, c. 31, s. 2(9)

205.8 (1) Challenge to operator's evidence — A defendant who gives notice of an intention to appear in court for the purpose of entering a plea and having a trial of the matter shall indicate on the notice of intention to appear if the defendant intends to challenge the evidence of the person who operated the photo-radar system.

(2) Notification of operator — If the defendant indicates an intention to challenge the evidence of the person who operated the photo-radar system, the clerk of the court shall notify the person.

1993, c. 31, s. 2(9)

205.9 (1) Challenge to officer's evidence — The provincial offences officer who used the evidence obtained through the use of a photo-radar system to identify the owner of the vehicle involved in the alleged offence and who issued the offence notice and certificate of offence shall not be required to give oral evidence at trial unless a summons requiring the officer to attend is issued at trial under section 39 of the *Provincial Offences Act*.

(2) Summons — No summons shall be issued unless a justice is satisfied that the defendant will not be able to have a fair trial if the officer is not required to give oral evidence.

1993, c. 31, s. 2(9)

205.10 (1) Certificate evidence — The certified statements in a certificate of offence are admissible in evidence as proof, in the absence of evidence to the contrary, of the facts stated in it.

(2) Where statements not proof — Subsection (1) does not apply to the statements setting out the evidence of,

(a) the person who operated the photo-radar system if the defendant has indicated, under subsection 205.8(1) or 205.13(3), an intention to challenge the evidence of that person; or

(b) an officer referred to in subsection 205.9(1) in respect of whom a summons has been issued.

1993, c. 31, s. 2(9)

205.11 (1) Failure to appear at trial — If a defendant who has given notice of an intention to appear fails to appear at the time and place appointed for the trial, the defendant shall be deemed not to dispute the charge.

(2) Examination by justice — If subsection (1) applies, section 54 of the *Provincial Offences Act* does not apply, and a justice shall examine the certificate of offence and shall without a hearing enter a conviction in the defendant's absence and impose the set fine for the offence if the certificate is complete and regular on its face and the justice is satisfied that the defendant is the owner of the vehicle involved in the offence.

(3) Quashing proceeding — The justice shall quash the proceeding if he or she is not able to enter a conviction.

1993, c. 31, s. 2(9)

205.12 Adjournment — Despite subsection 49(1) of the *Provincial Offences Act*, the court shall not adjourn a trial for the purpose of having the person who operated the photo-radar system attend to give evidence unless the court is satisfied that the interests of justice require it.

1993, c. 31, s. 2(9)

205.13 (1) Reopening — If a defendant who has been convicted without a hearing attends at the court office during regular office hours within fifteen days of becoming aware of the conviction and appears before a justice requesting that the conviction be struck out, the justice shall strike out the conviction if he or she is satisfied by affidavit of the defendant that, through no fault of the defendant, the defendant was unable to appear for a hearing or a notice or document relating to the offence was not delivered.

(2) If conviction struck out — If the justice strikes out the conviction, he or she shall give the defendant and the prosecutor a notice of trial or proceed under section 7 of the *Provincial Offences Act*.

(3) Trial — If a notice of trial is given, the defendant shall indicate on the notice of intention to appear if the defendant intends to challenge the evidence of the person who operated the photo-radar system.

(4) Notifying officer — If the defendant indicates an intention to challenge the evidence of the person who operated the photo-radar system, the clerk of the court shall notify the person.

(5) Certificate — A justice who strikes out a conviction under subsection (1) shall give the defendant a certificate of the fact in the prescribed form.

1993, c. 31, s. 2(9)

205.14 Regulations — The Lieutenant Governor in Council may make regulations,

    (a) prescribing what constitutes a photo-radar system;

    (b) designating areas of Ontario for purposes of subsection 205.1(1);

    (c) prescribing what constitutes evidence of ownership of a vehicle for purposes of this Part;

    (d) prescribing what constitutes a photographic equivalent of a photograph for the purposes of section 205.6;

    (e) prescribing the form of certificate that a conviction has been struck out.

1993, c. 31, s. 2(9)

Commentary

Photographic evidence obtained through the use of a photo-radar system is admissible in evidence in Provincial Offences Act proceedings respecting alleged speeding offences committed in areas of the province designated by regulation if the evidence indicates the vehicle involved, the number plates on the vehicle, the rate of speed at which the vehicle was travelling and the date and time of the alleged offence. If the proceedings were commenced by the filing of a certificate of offence, certain special procedural rules apply, including provision for service of the offence notice by regular prepaid mail and a requirement that a photographic equivalent of the photographic evidence be served with the notice. Motor vehicle owners are made liable for speeding offences committed with their vehicles where the evidence of the offence is obtained through the use of a photo-radar system, but they would not be liable to imprisonment or licence suspension as a result. It is intended that photo-radar be implemented through pilot projects. If the owner wishes the operator of the photo-radar to be present in court than the owner must so indicate on the notice of intention to appear. Similarly, if the owner desires the presence of the officer who caused the identification to be made from the photo-radar by means of vehicle registration and who issued process, than a summons must be obtained. A fail-safe mechanism exists to reopen, by means of an affidavit, a conviction entered in the absence of the defendant.

Case Law

R. v. Winder (1995), 174 A.R. 170, 102 W.A.C. 170 (C.A.) — Failure to place a sign at a photo-radar location does not infringe s. 11(d) of the Charter. There is nothing in the section which speaks to a timing requirement in terms of notification of the commission of an offence, and reading one into the section could lead to absurd and impractical results.

R. v. Tri-M Systems Inc. (1998), 38 M.V.R. (3d) 265 (B.C. S.C.); appeal dismissed 10 M.V.R. (4th) 232, 87 B.C.L.R. (3d) 212 (B.C. C.A.) — The use of certificates in a photo-radar prosecution does not violate s. 11(d) of the Charter.

R. v. Korlak (1999), 39 M.V.R. (3d) 320 (B.C. S.C.) — The setting of the trigger speed above the posted speed limit is not discriminatory under s. 15 of the Charter. The practice did not single anyone out.

Related Provisions: See O. Reg. 500/94, Photo-Radar System — Part XIV.1 of The Highway Traffic Act as amended by O. Reg. 333/95 which revoked areas designated for the purposes of s. 205.1(1) of the Act.

PART XIV.2 — RED LIGHT CAMERA SYSTEM EVIDENCE

205.15 (1) Red light camera system evidence — Subject to subsection (2), a photograph obtained through the use of a red light camera system shall be received in evidence in a proceeding under the *Provincial Offences Act* respecting an alleged offence under subsection 144(18) of the *Highway Traffic Act* if the alleged offence was committed within an area of Ontario designated by the regulations.

(2) Form and content — The photograph must comply with the requirements of the regulations made under clause 205.25(d).

(3) Certification of photograph — A photograph that purports to be certified by a provincial offences officer as having been obtained through the use of a red light camera system shall be received in evidence as proof, in the absence of evidence to the contrary, that the photograph was obtained through the use of a red light camera system.

(4) Use at trial — In the absence of evidence to the contrary, a photograph of a vehicle obtained through the use of a red light camera system is proof that,

    (a) information shown or superimposed on the photograph that was authorized or required by a regulation made under clause 205.25(d) is true; and

    (b) the vehicle and its driver did not stop and the vehicle and its driver proceeded before a green indication was shown, contrary to subsection 144(18).

(5) Conviction — No person who has entered a plea of not guilty at trial shall be convicted of an offence on the basis of a photograph obtained through the use of a red light camera system unless the photograph is tendered in evidence at trial.

1998, c. 38, s. 4

Commentary

The Red Light Camera Pilot Projects Act, 1998, S.O. 1998, c. 38 (in force November 20, 2000) permits evidence obtained from red light cameras to be used in areas designated by regulation for the purpose of enforcing subsection 144(18) of the Highway Traffic Act (failing to stop at a red light or proceeding before the light turns green). O. Reg. 277/99 dealing with the admissibility and use of Red Light Camera System evidence in proceedings under the Act, was brought into force contemporaneously with the Act.

Case Law

R. v. Yan (2004), 190 O.A.C. 301, (sub nom. *Waterloo (Regional Muncipality) v. Yan)* 72 O.R. (3d) 734 (Eng.), *(*sub nom. *Waterloo (Regional Muncipality) v. Yan)* 72 O.R. (3d) 743 (Fr.), 2004 CarswellOnt 3984, 6 M.V.R. (5th) 60, 244 D.L.R. (4th) 333, 188 C.C.C. (3d) 417 (Ont. C.A.) — The use of certified evidence is designed to save delay and the expense of calling the certifier of the evidence where no basis exists to doubt the accuracy and reliability of the certificate. The onus is on the defence to show some reasonable and legitimate basis to examine the officer. Where photographs did not disclosure on their face in an intelligible way the date, location and time of day they were taken, the photographs ought not to have been admitted.

R. v. Hoem, 2006 CarswellBC 2547, 38 M.V.R. (5th) 281, 2006 BCSC 1530 (S.C.) — The trier did not err in refusing to permit cross-examination of the officer. The fact that the accused did not completely overshoot the red light was not relevant to the offence of failing to stop on a red light before a crosswalk.

R. v. Hykawy, 2007 CarswellMan 1, 2007 MBPC 1, 41 M.V.R. (5th) 207, 211 Man. R. (2d) 98 (Prov. Ct.) — The photographs were admissible as the licence number was clearly visible. The certificates were not. There was an error in identification of the equipment used. The documents were copies. They were not stated to be true copies and although they were said to be certified, the authority to certify was not cited in the document.

R. v. Auto Clearing (1982) Ltd., 2007 CarswellSask 377, 2007 SKPC 69, 53 M.V.R. (5th) 63, 300 Sask. R. 25 (Prov. Ct.) — Owning a vehicle involved in a red light infraction should be read down under s. 11(d) of the *Charter* to permit a due diligence defence. Accused automobile dealers were found to be duly diligent in warning drivers of red light cameras.

Related Provisions: See O. Reg. 277/99, Red Light Camera System Evidence.

205.16 Application — Sections 205.17 to 205.24 apply in respect of proceedings based on evidence obtained through the use of a red light camera system if the proceedings are commenced by filing a certificate of offence under Part I of the *Provincial Offences Act*.

1998, c. 38, s. 4

Commentary

The Red Light Camera Pilot Projects Act, 1998, S.O. 1998, c. 38 (in force November 20, 2000) permits evidence obtained from red light cameras to be used in areas designated by regulation for the purpose of enforcing subsection 144(18) of the Highway Traffic Act (failing to stop at a red light or proceeding before the light turns green). O. Reg. 277/99 dealing with the admissibility and use of Red Light Camera System evidence in proceedings under the Act, was brought into force contemporaneously with the Act.

205.17 (1) *Provincial Offences Act*, Part I — No summons shall be issued under clause 3(2)(b) of the *Provincial Offences Act* in proceedings based on evidence obtained through the use of a red light camera system.

(2) Application of certain provisions — Sections 9, 9.1 and 11 of the *Provincial Offences Act* do not apply to proceedings based on evidence obtained through the use of a red light camera system.

(3) Service of offence notice — An offence notice issued in proceedings based on evidence obtained through the use of a red light camera system may be served in accordance with the regulations, in which case subsections 3(3) to (7) of the *Provincial Offences Act* do not apply.

(4) Certificate of service — If the provincial offences officer who issues the certificate of offence also serves the offence notice, that officer shall certify, on the certificate of offence, the fact that he or she took the steps authorized by the regulations to serve the offence notice and the date those steps were taken.

(5) Evidence — A certificate referred to in subsection (4) purporting to be signed by the provincial offences officer who issued it shall be received in evidence and is proof of service in the absence of evidence to the contrary.

1998, c. 38, s. 4; 2009, c. 33, Sched. 4, s. 3(1), (2)

Commentary

The Red Light Camera Pilot Projects Act, 1998, S.O. 1998, c. 38 (in force November 20, 2000) permits evidence obtained from red light cameras to be used in areas designated by regulation for the purpose of enforcing subsection 144(18) of the Highway Traffic Act (failing to stop at a red light or proceeding before the light turns green). O. Reg. 277/99 dealing with the admissibility and use of Red Light Camera System evidence in proceedings under the Act, was brought into force contemporaneously with the Act.

Related Provisions: See O. Reg. 277/99, Red Light Camera System Evidence, s. 4.

205.18 Evidence of ownership — Evidence of ownership of the vehicle involved in the alleged offence may be contained in the certificate of offence or it may be set out in a separate document.

1998, c. 38, s. 4

Commentary

The Red Light Camera Pilot Projects Act, 1998, S.O. 1998, c. 38 (in force November 20, 2000) permits evidence obtained from red light cameras to be used in areas designated by regulation for the purpose of enforcing subsection 144(18) of the Highway Traffic Act (failing to stop at a red light or proceeding before the light turns green). O. Reg. 277/99 dealing with the admissibility and use of Red Light Camera System evidence in proceedings under the Act, was brought into force contemporaneously with the Act.

205.19 (1) Deemed not to dispute charge — A defendant is deemed to not wish to dispute the charge where,

(a) at least 15 days have elapsed after the defendant was served with the offence notice and the defendant did not give notice of intention to appear under section 5 of the *Provincial Offences Act*, did not request a meeting with the prosecutor in accordance with section 5.1 of that Act and did not plead guilty under section 7 or 8 of that Act;

(b) the defendant requested a meeting with the prosecutor in accordance with section 5.1 of the *Provincial Offences Act* but did not attend the scheduled meeting with the prosecutor; or

(c) the defendant reached an agreement with the prosecutor under subsection 5.1(7) of the *Provincial Offences Act* but did not appear at a sentencing hearing with a justice under subsection 5.1(9) of that Act.

(2) Examination by justice — If subsection (1) applies, a justice shall examine the certificate of offence and shall without a hearing enter a conviction in the defendant's absence and impose the set fine for the offence if the certificate is complete and regular on its face.

(3) Quashing proceeding — The justice shall quash the proceeding if he or she is not able to enter a conviction.

1998, c. 38, s. 4; 2009, c. 33, Sched. 4, s. 3(3)

Commentary

The Red Light Camera Pilot Projects Act, 1998, S.O. 1998, c. 38 (in force November 20, 2000) permits evidence obtained from red light cameras to be used in areas designated by regulation for the purpose of enforcing subsection 144(18) of the Highway Traffic Act (failing to stop at a red light or proceeding before the light turns green). O. Reg. 277/99 dealing with the admissibility and use of Red Light Camera System evidence in proceedings under the Act, was brought into force contemporaneously with the Act.

205.20 (1) Challenge to officer's evidence — The provincial offences officer who used the evidence obtained through the use of a red light camera system to identify the owner or driver of the vehicle involved in the alleged offence and who issued the offence notice and certificate of offence shall not be required to give oral evidence at trial unless a summons requiring the officer to attend is issued at trial under section 39 of the *Provincial Offences Act*.

(2) Same — A provincial offences officer who certifies that a photograph was obtained through the use of a red light camera system shall not be required to give oral evidence at trial unless a summons requiring the officer to attend is issued at trial under section 39 of the *Provincial Offences Act*.

(3) Summons — No summons shall be issued to a provincial offences officer referred to in subsection (1) or (2) unless a justice is satisfied that the defendant will not be able to have a fair trial if the officer is not required to give oral evidence.

1998, c. 38, s. 4

Commentary

The Red Light Camera Pilot Projects Act, 1998, S.O. 1998, c. 38 (in force November 20, 2000) permits evidence obtained from red light cameras to be used in areas designated by regulation for the purpose of enforcing subsection 144(18) of the Highway Traffic Act (failing to stop at a red light or proceeding before the light turns green). O. Reg. 277/99 dealing with the admissibility and use of Red Light Camera System evidence in proceedings under the Act, was brought into force contemporaneously with the Act.

205.21 (1) Certificate evidence — The certified statements in a certificate of offence are admissible in evidence as proof, in the absence of evidence to the contrary, of the facts stated in it.

(2) Where statements not proof — Subsection (1) does not apply to the statements setting out the evidence of an officer referred to in subsection 205.20 (1) in respect of whom a summons has been issued.

1998, c. 38, s. 4

Commentary

The Red Light Camera Pilot Projects Act, 1998, S.O. 1998, c. 38 (in force November 20, 2000) permits evidence obtained from red light cameras to be used in areas designated by regulation for the purpose of enforcing subsection 144(18) of the Highway Traffic Act (failing to stop at a red light or proceeding before the light turns green). O. Reg. 277/99 dealing with the admissibility and use of Red Light Camera System evidence in proceedings under the Act, was brought into force contemporaneously with the Act.

205.22 (1) Failure to appear at trial — If a defendant who has given notice of an intention to appear fails to appear at the time and place appointed for the trial, the defendant shall be deemed not to dispute the charge.

(2) Examination by justice — If subsection (1) applies, section 54 of the *Provincial Offences Act* does not apply, and a justice shall examine the certificate of offence and shall without a hearing enter a conviction in the defendant's absence and impose the set fine for the offence if the certificate is complete and regular on its face.

(3) Quashing proceeding — The justice shall quash the proceeding if he or she is not able to enter a conviction.

1998, c. 38, s. 4

Commentary

The Red Light Camera Pilot Projects Act, 1998, S.O. 1998, c. 38 (in force November 20, 2000) permits evidence obtained from red light cameras to be used in areas designated by regulation for the purpose of enforcing subsection 144(18) of the Highway Traffic Act (failing to stop at a red light or proceeding before the light turns green). O. Reg. 277/99 dealing with the admissibility and use of Red Light Camera System evidence in proceedings under the Act, was brought into force contemporaneously with the Act.

205.23 (1) Reopening — If a defendant who has been convicted without a hearing attends at the court office during regular office hours within 15 days of becoming aware of the conviction and appears before a justice requesting that the conviction be struck out, the justice shall strike out the conviction if he or she is satisfied by the affidavit of the defendant that, through no fault of the defendant, the defendant was unable to appear for a hearing or for a meeting under section 5.1 of the *Provincial Offences Act* or a notice or document relating to the offence was not delivered.

(2) If conviction struck out — If the justice strikes out the conviction, he or she shall give the defendant and the prosecutor a notice of trial or proceed under section 7 of the *Provincial Offences Act*.

(3) Certificate — A justice who strikes out a conviction under subsection (1) shall give the defendant a certificate of the fact in the prescribed form.

1998, c. 38, s. 4; 2009, c. 33, Sched. 4, s. 3(4)

Commentary

The Red Light Camera Pilot Projects Act, 1998, S.O. 1998, c. 38 (in force November 20, 2000) permits evidence obtained from red light cameras to be used in areas designated by regulation for the purpose of enforcing subsection 144(18) of the Highway Traffic Act (failing to stop at a red light or proceeding before the light turns green). O. Reg. 277/99 dealing with the admissibility and use of Red Light Camera System evidence in proceedings under the Act, was brought into force contemporaneously with the Act.

Related Provisions: See O. Reg. 277/99, Red Light Camera System Evidence, s. 5.

205.24 (1) Limitation on penalty: owner — An owner of a motor vehicle convicted, as an owner, of an offence under subsection 144(18) on the basis of evidence obtained through the use of a red light camera system is not liable to,

    (a) a driver's licence suspension under section 46 as a result of default in payment of a fine resulting from that conviction; or

    (b) imprisonment or a probation order under subsection 72(1) of the *Provincial Offences Act* as a result of that conviction or as a result of default in payment of a fine resulting from that conviction.

(2) Same: driver — A driver of a motor vehicle convicted, as a driver, of an offence under subsection 144(18) on the basis of evidence obtained through the use of a red light camera system is not liable to imprisonment or a probation order under subsection 72(1) of the *Provincial Offences Act* as a result of that conviction or as a result of default in payment of a fine resulting from that conviction.

1998, c. 38, s. 4

Commentary

The Red Light Camera Pilot Projects Act, 1998, S.O. 1998, c. 38 (in force November 20, 2000) permits evidence obtained from red light cameras to be used in areas designated by regulation for the purpose of enforcing subsection 144(18) of the Highway Traffic Act (failing to stop at a red light or proceeding before the light turns green). O. Reg. 277/99 dealing with the admissibility and use of Red Light Camera System evidence in proceedings under the Act, was brought into force contemporaneously with the Act.

205.25 Regulations — The Lieutenant Governor in Council may make regulations,

(a) defining "photograph" for the purposes of this Part;

(b) prescribing what constitutes a red light camera system;

(c) designating areas of Ontario for purposes of subsection 205.15(1);

(d) governing the form and content of photographs for the purposes of subsection 205.15(2), including information that may be or must be shown or superimposed on the photographs, and prescribing a system of codes, symbols or abbreviations that may be used to convey the information;

(e) governing the filing of photographs in court for the purposes of this Part;

(f) governing the service of offence notices issued in proceedings based on evidence obtained through the use of red light camera systems, including authorizing service outside Ontario and deeming service to have been effected on a date determined in accordance with the regulations;

(g) prescribing what constitutes evidence of ownership of a vehicle or evidence of the identity of a driver for purposes of this Part;

(h) prescribing the form of certificate that a conviction has been struck out.

1998, c. 38, s. 4; 2015, c. 14, s. 56

Commentary

The Red Light Camera Pilot Projects Act, 1998, S.O. 1998, c. 38 (in force November 20, 2000) permits evidence obtained from red light cameras to be used in areas designated by regulation for the purpose of enforcing subsection 144(18) of the Highway Traffic Act (failing to stop at a red light or proceeding before the light turns green). O. Reg. 277/99 dealing with the admissibility and use of Red Light Camera System evidence in proceedings under the Act, was brought into force contemporaneously with the Act.

Related Provisions: See O. Reg. 277/99, Red Light Camera System Evidence, O. Reg. 277/99.

Part XV — Procedure, Arrests and Penalties

206. [Repealed 2002, c. 24, Sched. B, s. 25, item 11.]

[Editor's Note: The Limitations Act, 2002, *S.O. 2002, c. 24, Schedule B, s. 25, item 11 (in force January 1, 2004) repealed the limitation periods prescribed by s. 206. In their place, the basic two-year and ultimate fifteen-year limitation periods set out in ss. 4 and 15 of the* Limitations Act, 2002 *will apply. Section 206 will continue to apply, however, in certain circumstances provided for under s. 24 of the* Limitations Act, 2002. *Section 24(3) of the Act provides that if the former limitation period expired before January 1, 2004, no proceeding shall be commenced in respect of the claim. Section 24(5) of the Act provides in part that if the former limitation period did not expire before January 1, 2004 and if a limitation period under the* Limitations Act, 2002 *would apply were the claim*

based on an act or omission that took place on or after that date, the former limitation period applies if the claim was discovered before that date. Immediately prior to its repeal, section 206 read as follows:

> 206. (1) **Time limit for instituting civil proceeding** — *Subject to subsections (2) and (3), no proceeding shall be brought against a person for the recovery of damages occasioned by a motor vehicle after the expiration of two years from the time when the damages were sustained.*
>
> (2) **Limitation in case of death** — *Where death is caused, the proceeding may be brought within the time limited by the Family Law Act.*
>
> (3) **Action for damages** — *Despite subsections (1) and (2), when an action is brought within the time limited by this Act for the recovery of damages occasioned by a motor vehicle and a counterclaim, crossclaim or third or subsequent party claim is commenced by a defendant in respect of damages occasioned in the same accident, the lapse of time herein limited is not a bar to the counterclaim, crossclaim or third or subsequent party claim.*

.]

Commentary

The Act prescribes a time limitation of two years for the recovery of damages, running from the time when the damages were sustained. The damages must be occasioned by a motor vehicle (subs. (1)).

Where death is caused, the proceeding may be brought within the time limited by the Family Law Act (subs. (2)).

Bearing in mind that the principal action may be brought on the last day of the two-year period, a counterclaim, cross-claim or third or subsequent party claim is not barred by the lapse of time (subs. (3)).

Note: Some of the cases below refer to the older limitation period, which was one year.

The *Limitations Act, 2002*, S.O. 2002, c. 24, Sched. B, proposes to repeal the limitation period provided for in s. 206. In its place, the basic two-year and ultimate fifteen-year limitation periods set out in ss. 4 and 15 of the *Limitations Act, 2002* will apply. The running of the limitation periods in both cases will be governed by the rules codified in the new Act relating to such matters as attempted resolution, incapacity, litigation guardianship and minority, and in the case of the basic period, discoverability: *see especially* ss. 4 to 9, 11 and 15 of the *Limitations Act, 2002*. Transitional provisions will also apply: *see especially* ss. 24(5) and (8) of the *Limitations Act, 2002*.

Case Law

Application of Section

Want of Prosecution

May v. Johnston, [1964] 1 O.R. 467 (H.C.); *Clairmonte v. Can. Imperial Bank of Commerce*, [1970] 3 O.R. 97, 12 D.L.R. (3d) 425 (C.A.); *Farrar v. McMullen*, [1971] 1 O.R. 709 (C.A.) — The time limitation is referable only to the bringing of an action — namely, the issue of a writ. However, since the purpose of this provision is to protect drivers and owners against stale claims and demands when made after such a lapse of time as to make it difficult, and probably impossible, for them to obtain satisfactory evidence to defend themselves, a party should not be permitted to circumvent the section by issuing a writ and then doing nothing further for a number of years. Such an action will be dismissed for want of prosecution unless the plaintiff can show that no injustice would be done by allowing the action to proceed.

Constitutional

Calzonetti v. Gay (1988), 65 O.R. (2d) 154, 6 M.V.R. (2d) 191, 27 C.P.C. (2d) 93 (H.C.) — In an action for damages for personal injuries, the defendant successfully applied to add C as a third party under s. 206(3) of the Highway Traffic Act. C appealed and, in addition to a procedural argument, challenged the constitutionality of the statutory provision. He contended that it violated s. 15 of the Charter by allowing third-party claims to be brought outside the two-year limitation period set out elsewhere in the Act. C submitted that third-party defendants were thereby discriminated against. The appeal was dismissed. The Act does not create a distinction between two groups of tortfeasors. The two groups — defendants in main actions and third-party defendants — are not constant in their makeup. A person who falls into one group may at another time fall into another. Furthermore, persons in one group or the other do not share anything else with the members of the group except the fact that they are subject to the very legislative distinction being attacked. Moreover, even if the legislation creates two discrete groups, s. 206(3) actually extends to members of both groups since a counterclaim can be asserted against a plaintiff in a two-party situation outside the two-year limitation period. In summary, s. 206(3) is a law of general application.

Federal Crown

A.G. Can. v. Rhode (1957), 21 W.W.R. 128, 8 D.L.R. (2d) 89 (Sask. Dist. Ct.); *R. v. Lightheart*, [1952] Ex. C.R. 12; *R. v. Richardson*, [1947] Ex. C.R. 55; reversed [1948] S.C.R. 57; *A.G. Ont. v. Tombs*, [1946] 4 D.L.R. 516 (Ont. C.A.) — The section is not applicable to a claim made by the Crown in the right of Canada.

Ivey v. R., [1954] Ex. C.R. 200 — The section does apply to a claim commenced by petition of rights against the Crown.

Place of Accident

Viane v. Neyens, [1959] O.W.N. 29 (H.C.); *Dufferin Paving Ltd. v. Anger*, [1940] S.C.R. 174, [1940] 1 D.L.R. 1 — The limitation applies irrespective of whether the accident occurs on or off a highway.

Allard v. Charbonneau, [1953] O.W.N. 381, [1953] 2 D.L.R. 442 (C.A.) — The limitation applies to all actions brought in Ontario even though the accident may have occurred in another province.

Estates

Dressel v. Glaser, [1954] O.W.N. 259, [1954] 1 D.L.R. 655 (C.A.) — The executor or administrator of an estate has the right to set up the defence that the deceased would have had by virtue of this section, and there is nothing in the Trustee Act to deprive him of such right.

Damages Occasioned by Motor Vehicle

Heredi v. Fensom (2002), 25 M.V.R. (4th) 85, 2002 CarswellSask 319, *(sub nom. Fensom v. Kendall)* 213 D.L.R. (4th) 1, [2002] 8 W.W.R. 1, 289 N.R. 88, 19 C.P.C. (5th) 1, 219 Sask. R. 161, 272 W.A.C. 161, 12 C.C.L.T. (3d) 1 (S.C.C.) — "Damages occasioned by a motor vehicle" requires that the presence of a motor vehicle be the dominant feature, or constitute the true nature, of the claim. Conversely, claims, whether framed in contract or in tort, where the presence of a motor vehicle is a fact ancillary to the essence of the action, ought not to be regarded as within the scope of that phrase.

Biggs v. Baker, [1955] O.W.N. 897, [1955] 5 D.L.R. 612 (C.A.); *McLennan Motors Ltd. v. Cotter* (1959), 30 W.W.R. 127 (B.C. Co. Ct.) — The principal criterion for the application of this section is that the action must be for "damages occasioned by a motor vehicle." It is accordingly not applicable to actions to recover damages to a motor vehicle from the person to whom the vehicle has been loaned.

Bonany v. Gratton, [1960] O.W.N. 301, 23 D.L.R. (2d) 591 (C.A.) — The section is not applicable to an action for damages to a vehicle in a collision with a horse straying on the highway.

Lasby v. Everall Enrg. Ltd. (1960), 32 W.W.R. 335 (Sask. Q.B.) — The section is not applicable for damages to a vehicle by a boulder left on the highway.

Northern Alta. Dairy Pool Ltd. v. Strong & Sons Ltd. (1960), 33 W.W.R. 322 (Alta. T.D.) — The section cannot be applied to a claim for damage to goods caused by a fire in the vehicle in which the goods were being carried.

Sask. Govt. Ins. v. Cisna (1986), 39 M.V.R. 242 (Sask. Q.B.) — The plaintiff's automobile, while travelling on a public highway, collided with a cow owned by the defendants. The automobile was damaged and the plaintiff commenced the present action approximately 18 months after the date of the accident. Section 143(1) of the Vehicles Act (Sask.) provides that no action is to be brought against a person for the recovery of damages "occasioned by a motor vehicle" after the expiration of 12 months from the time the damages were sustained. The parties stated a case for a determination of whether the present action involved damages "occasioned by a motor vehicle." It was held that the damages were not occasioned by a motor vehicle. The meaning of the phrase "damages occasioned by a motor vehicle" is damages caused or brought about *by* a motor vehicle, as opposed to damages done *to* a motor vehicle. Hence, in the present case the damages were clearly not occasioned by a motor vehicle.

Bizeau v. C.N.R. and Aziz, 59 O.L.R. 549, [1926] 4 D.L.R. 1066 (C.A.) — Where damages were claimed in respect of the negligence of a driver who had collided with a train at a level crossing, it was said that the damages were not occasioned by a motor vehicle but by the locomotive which was enabled so to occasion them by the negligence of the driver.

Worsley v. Hamilton (1960), 33 W.W.R. 23, 25 D.L.R. (2d) 746 (Sask. C.A.) — The opposite conclusion to *Bizeau, supra*, was reached presumably because it was the negligent operation of the vehicle which resulted in the damages being sustained.

Kozoris v. Thederahn (1964), 50 W.W.R. 435, 47 D.L.R. (2d) 627 (B.C. S.C.) — Damage to a trailer which collided with another vehicle as a result of the negligence of the towing driver who was a bailee for reward of the trailer was damage "occasioned" by a motor vehicle; the damage was caused by the towing vehicle which had been operated negligently. It may be noted that the British Columbia Act (s. 79(1)) was amended in

1963 to refer to damage "occasioned in an occurrence involving a motor-vehicle." This language would appear to widen the application of the limitation period.

Stewart v. Domingos, [1967] 2 O.R. 37, 62 D.L.R. (2d) 282 (C.A.) — The section was not applicable to an action alleging as the cause of the collision negligent repair of a vehicle by a repairer who was neither the owner nor operator of the vehicle.

Ont. Hydro v. Bruell Float Service Ltd. (1973), 1 O.R. (2d) 358, 40 D.L.R. (3d) 342 (H.C.) — A claim framed in contract against a common carrier was held subject to the limitation period since the damage in question had been caused by a motor vehicle.

Molner v. Newman, [1973] 3 O.R. 39, 35 D.L.R. (3d) 672 (H.C.) — The section was applicable where part of a load of scrap metal had fallen from one vehicle and collided with a following vehicle. While the actual physical damage had been caused by the scrap metal, it was only because of the motion of one vehicle that it had been projected onto the other.

Peters v. North Star Oil Ltd. (1965), 53 W.W.R. 321, 54 D.L.R. (2d) 364 (Man. Q.B.) — Damages resulting from the negligent delivery of gasoline from a truck to an underground tank were not damages occasioned by a motor vehicle.

R. A. Beamish Stores Co. v. F. W. Argue Ltd., [1966] 2 O.R. 615, 57 D.L.R. (2d) 691 (C.A.); affirmed [1969] S.C.R. 354, 3 D.L.R. (3d) 290; *Harvey v. Shade Bros. Distributors Ltd.* (1967), 61 W.W.R. 187 (B.C. S.C.) — The section does not apply to the use of auxiliary equipment attached to but not forming part of the vehicle and used for a purpose unrelated to the operation of the vehicle *qua* vehicle.

Hovinga v. Erbsville Enterprises Ltd. (1977), 16 O.R. (2d) 617, 78 D.L.R. (3d) 725 (H.C.) — A go-cart was held not to be a motor vehicle at trial but the decision was reversed on appeal. Section 206(1) of the Highway Traffic Act was held to apply to the case.

L. Blackburn Excavating Ltd. v. Salmon Arm Machine Shop Ltd. (1977), 76 D.L.R. (3d) 190 (B.C. S.C.) — A plaintiff claimed for cost of repairs to and loss of use of his dump truck which was damaged when the hoist with which it was fitted collapsed while it was dumping a load of dirt. The truck could dump while moving but in this instance was stationary, though it was necessary to run the engine of the truck to operate the hoist. It was held that the truck was not a motor vehicle at the time. A motor vehicle was primarily a conveyance. Here, the damage was caused by the use of the hoist, while it was being used to dump material, a purpose unrelated to the operation of the truck as a motor vehicle.

Ont. Hydro v. Bruell Float Service Ltd. (1974), 3 O.R. (2d) 108, 44 D.L.R. (3d) 524 (C.A.); reversing (1973), 1 O.R. (2d) 358, 40 D.L.R. (3d) 342 (H.C.); affirmed [1976] 1 S.C.R. 9, 3 N.R. 508, 55 D.L.R. (3d) 236 — On an appeal it was held that the owner's claim was not for "damages occasioned by a motor vehicle" but for damages for breach of contract to deliver machinery at a specified destination and therefore the statutory limitation period was not applicable to the claim.

Dixon Cable Laying Co. v. Osborne Contracting Ltd., [1974] 6 W.W.R. 431, 49 D.L.R. (3d) 243 (B.C. S.C.) — Where the plaintiff's electric cable had been damaged by defendants' self-propelled backhoe and the action was instituted more than a year after the damage, it was held that the claim was not statute-barred as the motor vehicle was being used as an earth-moving implement at the material time.

Giacomelli v. O'Reilly (1979), 23 O.R. (2d) 469, 9 C.P.C. 65 (M.C.) — Section 206(1) provides a limitation period in which an action must be commenced within two years from the time when damages were sustained. Section 206(3), however, provides that where "a counterclaim is made ... by a defendant in respect of damages occasioned in the same accident, the lapse of time herein limited [by s. 206(1)] is not a bar to the counterclaim. ..." Section 206(3) does not operate so as to bar a late counterclaim unless actual and serious prejudice can be shown. This is so even though the real defendant by counterclaim would be plaintiff's insurer and not plaintiff personally, with the result that by his own action plaintiff was keeping open the insurer's liability for a counterclaim well beyond the two-year limitation period. Since even a stranger to an action may be added by counterclaims, unless actual and serious prejudice is shown, s. 206(3) cannot act as a bar to a late counterclaim against plaintiff's insurer in the absence of such actual and serious prejudice.

Iron Range Bus Lines Ltd. v. Martin Liquid Transfer (Central) Ltd. (1980), 28 O.R. (2d) 321 (H.C.); affirmed (1981), 37 O.R. (2d) 415 (C.A.) — Contamination of water supply by seepage of gasoline from a truck on the highway constituted damage "occasioned by a motor vehicle" within the meaning of s. 206(3) of the Act. On appeal where it was acknowledged by counsel that up to the point of severance the trailer was part of the motor vehicle and the overturn was caused by the failure of the bracket on the fifth wheel of the tractor unit, the Court was not persuaded that the damage complained of was not occasioned by a motor vehicle. The appeal was dismissed with costs.

Byrne v. Goodyear Can. Inc. (1981), 33 O.R. (2d) 800, 125 D.L.R. (3d) 695 (H.C.) — Where a motor vehicle accident occurs as the result of a faulty tire, an action in contract against the vendor of the tire is not subject to the two-year limitation period. Action in negligence against the manufacturer does come within the section.

Fitzgerald v. Eaz-Lift Spring Corp. (Ont.) Ltd. (1981), 45 N.S.R. (2d) 15, 86 A.P.R. 15, 119 D.L.R. (3d) 483 (C.A.) — A cargo trailer overturned on a highway and damaged the car towing it. The owner sued the manufacturer of the sway control bars attached to the trailer for negligent design and manufacture. The action was not one arising out of the ownership, maintenance, operation or use of a motor vehicle.

Fraser v. Peckham (1983), 42 O.R. (2d) 354, 22 M.V.R. 172, 148 D.L.R. (3d) 650 (H.C.) — The plaintiff engaged a taxi cab to convey her to a destination. The plaintiff was injured while alighting from the cab through a defective door which flew open, causing her to fall from the cab, seriously injuring her hip. The defendants, one of whom was the owner and operator of the taxi, moved at the opening of trial for an order that the plaintiff's claim be barred by the provision of s. 206(1) of the Highway Traffic Act (Ont.), and for an order dismissing the action. The action had been launched five years after the events and s. 206(1) barred the recovery of damages occasioned by a motor vehicle after the expiration of two years from the time when the damages were sustained. A declaration was made that the action was barred pursuant to s. 206(1) of the Highway Traffic Act, and the action was dismissed. Whether the action was characterized as being in contract or in negligence, it was barred because the damages were clearly occasioned by a motor vehicle. The Legislature could not have intended different results where the damage was so clearly caught by the section.

Daviault v. Can. Motorcycle Assn. (1985), 49 O.R. (2d) 147 (Ont. H.C.) — The plaintiff who had paid admission to witness a motorcycle race alleged that she was struck by a motorcycle which left the track, causing her injury. The claim in contract appeared not to be governed by the Act.

Clost v. Colautti Construction Ltd. (1985), 52 O.R. (2d) 339, 36 M.V.R. 38, 5 C.P.C. (2d) 11 (H.C.) — The infant plaintiff was injured by a motor vehicle while playing on a toy truck manufactured by the defendant N. The plaintiff sued the owner and driver of the vehicle within the two-year period stipulated in s. 206(1) of the Highway Traffic Act; he then applied to add a claim against N in negligence after the expiration of that period. N made an application to determine whether the two-year period applied to bar the action against it. Section 206(1) of the Act made the limitation period applicable to an action to recover damages "occasioned by a motor vehicle." The action against N was not statute barred. In order to determine whether s. 206(1) of the Act was applicable, it was necessary to examine the substance of the claim being advanced, as opposed to simply considering the cause of the damage. The plaintiffs' action against N was based on the negligence in the design, manufacture and distribution of the toy in question; the fact that the manufacturer's alleged negligence resulted in a car-pedestrian accident was incidental to the substance of the claim against N. Section 206(1) of the Act was never intended to apply to products liability claims where the product involved was not a motor vehicle or an integral part of a motor vehicle.

Hemmerich v. Olinskie (1986), 41 M.V.R. 304, 10 C.P.C. (2d) 1, 29 D.L.R. (4th) 743 (Ont. H.C.) — The plaintiff was injured when the motor vehicle he was driving collided with a vehicle owned and driven by the defendants. The plaintiff commenced his action against the defendants within two years of the accident, but after the expiry of two years, he sought to add a claim in negligence against the tavern which allegedly had allowed him to consume liquor despite his real and apparent intoxication and despite the fact that he was under-age. Claims were also asserted by relatives of the plaintiff against the tavern pursuant to s. 60(4) of the Family Law Act. The issue before the Court was whether the claims against the tavern were statute-barred. Section 206(1) of the Highway Traffic Act (Ont.) provided for a two-year limitation period for "damages occasioned by a motor vehicle," commencing when the damages were sustained. The Family Law Act provided for a two-year limitation period, which was to commence from the time the cause of action arose. The claims were statute-barred. The phrase "damages occasioned by a motor vehicle" has been given a wide interpretation by the courts. While there has been a tendency to restrict the applicability of the section where the claim was founded on contract, the present action was framed in negligence. The crumbling distinction between negligence in tort and breach of contract should result in an expanded application of s. 206(1). The present claim clearly fell within the section. On the facts of the present case, it appeared that the Family Law Act claimants were or should have been aware of the derivative damage they sustained when the plaintiff was first injured, and therefore there were no unusual circumstances to support a finding that the time when the two limitation periods commenced running was different.

Kavanagh v. Don Sloan Equipment Rentals Ltd. (1988), 4 M.V.R. (2d) 34 (Ont. H.C.) — The plaintiff was employed to operate a snow plow on behalf of DSER Ltd. While operating the snow plow he was involved in an accident with another vehicle operated by a third party. At the time of the accident the snow plow was not insured and the third party successfully sued both the plaintiff and DSER Ltd. for damages. The plaintiff subsequently sued DSER Ltd. as well as DS and GS being the sole shareholders, officers and directors of DSER Ltd. The plaintiff alleged negligence on the part of the defendants in failing to insure the vehicle in question. The defendants raised a limitation defence relying on s. 206(1) of the Highway Traffic Act (Ont.) and s. 8(a) of the Negligence Act (Ont.). The facts indicated that the original accident occurred on January 18, 1978, and the consequent judgment was given on January 6, 1981. The plaintiff's action was commenced on October 13, 1982. The action was dismissed. The damages for which the plaintiff had been found liable were occasioned by a motor vehicle. It was the purpose of the present action that the plaintiff recover those damages from the defendants. Such a claim was "for the recovery of damages occasioned by a motor vehicle" within the meaning of the Highway Traffic Act. Furthermore, the plaintiff was seeking indemnity from a joint tortfeasor as contemplated by the Negligence Act. Since the plaintiff had not instituted his claim in a timely manner, his action was statute-barred under both Acts.

Huddle v. Metropolitan Toronto (Municipality) (1991), 34 M.V.R. (2d) 9 (Ont. Gen. Div.) — The one-year limitation period in s. 25 of the Ambulance Act (Ont.) for actions against an ambulance operator, or an employee of an operator, for the recovery of damages occasioned by negligence in the provision of ambulance services applies to the supply of ambulance services to a patient, and not to the operation of the ambulance on a highway. The two-year limitation period in the Highway Traffic Act (Ont.) applies to actions for the recovery of damages occasioned by the negligent operation of an ambulance.

Herbert v. Misuga (1991), 35 M.V.R. (2d) 110, 96 Sask. R. 117, 84 D.L.R. (4th) 645 (Q.B.); varied [1994] 3 W.W.R. 457, 22 C.P.C. (3d) 1, 1 M.V.R. (3d) 221, 116 Sask. R. 292, 59 W.A.C. 292, 111 D.L.R. (4th) 193 (C.A.) — The plaintiff was injured when the defendant deliberately drove his truck into the plaintiff's motocycle with the intention of scaring him. The fact that the tort committed was an assault rather than the negligent operation of a motor vehicle did not oust the limitation period.

Renaud v. OC Transpo (1992), 9 O.R. (3d) 726, 40 M.V.R. (2d) 51, 91 D.L.R. (4th) 755 (Gen. Div.) — The limitation does not apply where a plaintiff slipped on snow and ice on bus steps.

Parekh v. Guelph Air Services '67 Ltd. (1994), 20 O.R. (3d) 1, 5 M.V.R. (3d) 165, 118 D.L.R. (4th) 333, 74 O.A.C. 353 (C.A.) — A snow plow is a motor vehicle for the purposes of s. 206(1).

Dagg v. Abram's Towing & Storage (1994), 11 M.V.R. (3d) 69, 21 O.R. (3d) 377 (Gen. Div.) — The plaintiff was injured while seated in his vehicle which was being towed. The vehicle was damaged. The damages were occasioned by a motor vehicle.

Boertien v. Carter (1995), 13 M.V.R. (3d) 29, 131 Nfld. & P.E.I.R. 8, 408 A.P.R. 8 (P.E.I. T.D.) — The plaintiff sued the defendant for damages for personal injuries arising out of a motor vehicle accident which occurred at the entrance to an arena. The defendant brought a third party claim against the owner of the arena for indemnification. The claim against the arena was founded in occupier's liability negligence and did not relate to damages occasioned by a motor vehicle.

Clark v. 449136 Ontario Inc. (1996), 27 O.R. (3d) 658 (Gen. Div.); aff'd (1997), 30 M.V.R. (3d) 167 (C.A.) — An action against taverners is not within the intended scope or ambit of the Highway Traffic Act.

Dupuis v. Moncton (City), 2005 CarswellNB 215, 2005 CarswellNB 216, [2005] N.B.J. No. 165, 11 C.P.C. (6th) 1, 17 M.V.R. (5th) 13, 10 M.P.L.R. (4th) 36, 2005 NBCA 47, 284 N.B.R. (2d) 97, 742 A.P.R. 97 (C.A.); leave to appeal refused (2005), 2005 CarswellNB 354, 2005 CarswellNB 355, 345 N.R. 393 (note), [2005] S.C.C.A. No. 136, 775 A.P.R. 197 (note), 298 N.B.R. (2d) 197 (note) — Where the claim against the city was based on a belief that the accident was caused by improperly functioning traffic lights, the claim was for damages occasioned by a motor vehicle and not in negligence for faulty installation.

Karakas v. General Motors of Canada Ltd. (2005), 2005 CarswellOnt 2453, 19 M.V.R. (5th) 137 (C.A.); affirming [2004] O.J. No. 5231, 2004 CarswellOnt 5338, 74 O.R. (3d) 273, 10 M.V.R. (5th) 301 (S.C.J.) — Defective wiring causing a parked car to catch fire to a house and contents is occasioned by a motor vehicle.

Longley v. General Motors of Canada Ltd., 68 M.V.R. (5th) 214, 2008 CarswellOnt 1406, 90 O.R. (3d) 536, [2008] O.J. No. 998 (S.C.J.); additional reasons at 68 M.V.R. (5th) 224, 2008 CarswellOnt 2429 (S.C.J.); affirmed 2009 CarswellOnt 5032, 2009 ONCA 627, 84 M.V.R. (5th) 167, 264 O.A.C. 349 — The dominant feature of the claim was not the motor vehicle itself, but was the tailgate and the tailgate latch mechanism when the plaintiff stood on her rear bumper of her parked truck to reach for her jacket and the rear tailgate allegedly collapsed causing her to fall to the ground and hurt her wrist.

Running of Time

Brown v. Croucher, [1931] O.R. 541, [1931] 4 D.L.R. 219 (C.A.); *Switzer v. Kahn*, 64 O.L.R. 219, [1929] 4 D.L.R. 232 (H.C.); *Dormer v. Sumner*, [1934] O.W.N. 145 (H.C.) — In computing the 12-month period [now two years] within which action must be brought, the day on which the event in question occurred is excluded and time begins to run on the next day succeeding. If the time limit expires on a holiday, the time is extended to the day next following.

Shriner v. Mularski (1964), 48 W.W.R. 510 (Man. Q.B.) — An action commenced on March 3 in respect of an accident occurring on March 2 of the previous year was held to be out of time.

Scott v. Thompson (1957), 21 W.W.R. 283, 7 D.L.R. (2d) 655 (Alta. C.A.) — The fact that a person subsequently dies of injuries sustained in a collision does not result in a new cause of action, although the measure of damages may have changed, and the limitation period remains 12 months from the time when the damages were sustained, not 12 months from the date of death.

Greig v. Toronto Transit Comm., [1958] O.W.N. 480 (C.A.) — At a time when an order was required for leave to sue the Registrar, the notice of motion to add the Registrar was required not only to be issued and served but also to be heard within the 12 months.

White v. Proctor, [1936] O.W.N. 268 (H.C.) — The adding of a party defendant within the limitation period stopped the period running, and the amended claim could be filed claiming relief against the added defendant even after the period had expired.

Robinson v. Cornwall, [1951] O.R. 587 (H.C.); *Brown v. Humble*, [1959] O.R. 586 (C.A.); *Mathews v. Wilkes*, [1960] O.W.N. 336 (H.C.); *Beebe v. Brown*, [1963] 1 O.R. 76 (M.C.) — Where a writ has been issued in proper time, but has not been served before its expiry, it may in appropriate circumstances be renewed even though the limitation period has expired.

Medgyes v. Nyznik (1966), 59 W.W.R. 89 (Man. Q.B.); affirmed (1966), 59 W.W.R. 320 (C.A.) — While in Manitoba an extension of time may be granted within which to commence action, such extension will not be lightly granted particularly since the right to commence third-party proceedings would not apply to an action brought within the enlarged time.

Belanger v. Gilbert (1984), 52 B.C.L.R. 197, 8 D.L.R. (4th) 92 (S.C.); affirmed (1984), 58 B.C.L.R. 191, 14 D.L.R. (4th) 428 (C.A.) — The plaintiff commenced an action more than two years after the accident. Less than two years prior to the commencement of the action, the defendant's insurer wrote a letter to the plaintiff inviting settlement and referring to eventual settlement as a certainty. The limitation period was extended as the letter constituted confirmation of the plaintiff's cause of action.

Walton v. Cote (1989), 20 M.V.R. (2d) 171, 69 O.R. (2d) 661, 36 C.P.C. (2d) 113 (H.C.); affirmed (1991), 28 M.V.R. (2d) 1, 1 O.R. (3d) 558 (C.A.) — A motor vehicle accident occurred on October 18, 1986. An action was commenced on October 19, 1988. The question of whether the action was statute-barred by virtue of the two-year limitation period set out in s. 206(1) of the Highway Traffic Act (Ont.) was answered in the negative by the District Court. The defendants appealed. The appeal was allowed. The case law on point established that the period within which an action may be commenced where the limitation period is expressed as a number of years, includes, but ends on, the anniversary of the day of the event giving rise to the action. The principle was clear that the period of one or more years begins to run on the day following the triggering event; in other words, the day of the event itself is excluded. In so doing, a year is complete at the end of the day which is the anniversary of the day of the event.

Jairam v. Bubulal, 75 O.R. (2d) 400, [1990] I.L.R. 1-2670 (Gen. Div.) — A statement of claim seeking damages for the infant and adult passengers of a vehicle involved in an accident was issued within the statutory limitation period. The defendant was added as a party following the expiration of the limitation period. The delay was deliberately based on the erroneous belief that the defendant was uninsured at the time of the accident. The defendant appealed the dismissal of his motion for summary judgment. The appeal was dismissed. The plaintiffs appeared to have a good cause of action against the added defendant. The defendant was unable to demonstrate that he was in any way prejudiced by the delay. The existence of these "special circumstances" justified the extension of the Act's limitation period.

Jenkins v. Bowes Publishing Co. (1991), 30 M.V.R. (2d) 212, 3 O.R. (3d) 154, 50 C.P.C. (2d) 292 (Gen. Div.) — The plaintiff was injured on August 9, 1985, when he was pinned by a forklift truck which an employee of the defendant had negligently parked on an incline. He and an insurance adjuster engaged in settlement negotiations between October 1985 and June 1987. Some time after the plaintiff made an offer in June 1987, the adjuster was advised by his principals that they had consulted a lawyer and that the adjuster was not to contact the plaintiff. In October 1987, the plaintiff was informed by counsel for the defendant's insurer that there was no liability on the defendant's part. The plaintiff brought an action for damages in February 1988. The defendant argued that the damages sustained by the plaintiff were occasioned by a motor vehicle and that the failure of the plaintiff to institute proceedings within the two-year limitation period in s. 206 was a complete defence to the action. The action was allowed. The forklift was a motor vehicle within the meaning of the Highway Traffic Act, and the plaintiff's damages were occasioned as a result of the negligent operation of the forklift as a motor vehicle. Accordingly, the plaintiff's claim was statute-barred unless the defendant was precluded by its conduct from relying on the limitation period. Once the defendant, through its agent the insurance adjuster, entered into settlement negotiations with the plaintiff there was an obligation on it to advise the plaintiff within a reasonable period of time that it was ceasing negotiations. The plaintiff believed that the defendant had accepted liability for the accident and that negotiations would continue in the future, resulting in an eventual settlement. Accordingly, the defendant was estopped from relying on the limitation period in s. 206(1).

Chambo v. Musseau (1993), 49 M.V.R. (2d) 111, 15 O.R. (3d) 305, 19 C.C.L.I. (2d) 66, 106 D.L.R. (4th) 757, 65 O.A.C. 291 (C.A.) — The limitation period applicable to a direct action against the issuer under the uninsured motorist provisions of an insurance police is that under the Insurance Act Regulations, two years from the date on which the insured person knew, or could have known, that the tortfeasor's vehicle was uninsured.

Lancaster v. Middlebro (1996), 21 M.V.R. (3d) 143 (Ont. Gen. Div.) — The limitation period for joining an uninsured motorist claim contained in a policy of insurance is not under the Act but pursuant to the regulations under the Insurance Act.

Peixeiro v. Haberman (1997), 30 M.V.R. (3d) 41 (S.C.C.) — The discoverability rule applies to the section. "Damages were sustained" refers to the time when the damages were perceived to compromise "permanent serious impairment."

Holgate v. Swimmer (1999), 46 O.R. (3d) 599, 2 M.V.R. (4th) 260 (S.C.J.); affirmed (August 21, 2000), Doc. CA C33329 (Ont. C.A.) — A proceeding means one commenced in Ontario, not elsewhere in Canada.

Coutanche v. Napoleon Delicatessen (2003), 44 M.V.R. (4th) 61, 2003 CarswellOnt 1493, 64 O.R. (3d) 634 (Ont. S.C.J.) — After consuming alcohol at what turned out to be an unlicensed premises the deceased took a taxi home and was killed after being dropped off. In assessing the successful request to extend the limitation period it was going too far to say that the deceased's mother ought to have been aware of social host liability issues because she once owned a bar.

Fekrta v. Siavikis, 2008 CarswellOnt 6357, 76 M.V.R. (5th) 218, [2008] O.J. No. 4281 (S.C.J.); affirmed 2009 CarswellOnt 3702, 2009 ONCA 537, 79 M.V.R. (5th) 26, [2009] O.J. No. 2702 — A summary judgment is available to bar an action under s. 206(1) for missing the two-year limitation period.

Infants

Martin v. Kingston City Coach Co., [1947] O.W.N. 110, [1947] 1 D.L.R. 864 (C.A.); *Worsley v. Hamilton* (1960), 33 W.W.R. 23, 25 D.L.R. (2d) 746 (Sask. C.A.) — The suspension of the running of the limitation period with respect to infants is not applicable to the special period under this section, and an action by an infant, suing by his or her next friend, must be brought within the year.

Papamonolopoulos v. Toronto (City) Board of Education (1986), 56 O.R. (2d) 1, 10 C.P.C. (2d) 176, 38 C.C.L.T. 82, (sub nom. *Papamonolopoulos v. Bd. of Education of Toronto*) 16 O.A.C. 249, 30 D.L.R. (4th) 269 (C.A.); leave to appeal to S.C.C. refused (1987), 58 O.R. (2d) 528n, 21 O.A.C. 319n, 35 D.L.R. (4th) 767n, 76 N.R. 240n — Section 47 of the Limitations Act applies to limitation periods prescribed in other statutes as well as to those in the Limitations Act unless its effect is specifically excluded by statute. Section 206(1) of the Highway Traffic Act provides that, "subject to subsections (2) and (3)," the limitation period for the recovery of damages occasioned by a motor vehicle is two years. The ordinary interpretation of that provision is that s. 206(1) is subordinate *only* to subss. (2) and (3) and not to any other section or statute. Section 206 of the Highway Traffic Act, then, specifically excludes the operation of s. 47 of the Limitations

Act. *Martin v. Kingston City Coach Co.*, [1946] O.W.N. 915, [1947] 1 D.L.R. 367 (H.C.); affirmed [1947] O.W.N. 110, [1947] 1 D.L.R. 864 (C.A.), is still the law in Ontario.

Murphy v. Welsh, [1993] 2 S.C.R. 1069, 106 D.L.R. (4th) 404, 66 O.A.C. 240, 14 O.R. (3d) 799n, 156 N.R. 263 (S.C.C.); reversing (1991), 30 M.V.R. (2d) 163, 3 O.R. (3d) 182, 50 O.A.C. 246, 4 C.P.C. (3d) 301, 81 D.L.R. (4th) 475 (C.A.) — Section 47 of the Limitations Act, R.S.O. 1990, c. L.15, which provides that the time for bringing an action under s. 45 of that Act begins to run in the case of an infant when the infant attains majority, does not apply to the two-year limitation period in s. 206(1).

Amendment of Pleadings

Lattimor v. Heaps (1931), 40 O.W.N. 580 (C.A.) — An amendment to the statement of claim after the expiration of the limitation period will not be allowed if the effect is to set up a new cause of action. Thus an amendment cannot be made to add another defendant.

Crozier v. O'Connor, [1960] O.W.N. 352 (C.A.); *Hallier v. Keren* (1968), 63 W.W.R. 204, 66 D.L.R. (2d) 750 (B.C. C.A.) — One cannot add a further party plaintiff.

Bd. of Commrs. of Police of London v. Western Freight Lines Ltd., [1962] O.R. 948, 34 D.L.R. (2d) 689 (C.A.) — One cannot substitute a different entity as plaintiff.

White v. Proctor, [1936] O.W.N. 268 (H.C.) — Where an additional party defendant was added within the time limit, the failure to amend the statement of claim to include a claim against the added defendant until after the expiration of the limitation period did not result in the claim against the added defendant being barred.

Cahoon v. Franks, [1967] S.C.R. 455, 63 D.L.R. (2d) 274 — Personal injury and property damage constitute a single cause of action. The claim for one may be amended to include a claim for the other even after the expiration of the limitation period.

Ont. Hospital Services Comm. v. Registrar of Motor Vehicles, [1969] 1 O.R. 666 (H.C.) — Where an action was commenced by the Ontario Hospital Services Commission to recover the cost of insured services to an infant plaintiff, the pleadings could properly be amended to claim general damages on behalf of the infant even after the limitation period has expired.

Dill v. Alves, [1968] 1 O.R. 58, 65 D.L.R. (2d) 416 (C.A.); *Irving v. Highway King Busses Ltd.* (1930), 37 O.W.N. 362 (H.C.); *Durham v. West*, [1959] O.W.N. 169 (C.A.); *Williamson v. Headley*, [1950] O.W.N. 185 (H.C.) — An amendment may also be permitted solely to correct a misnomer where the writ has been served on the proper party.

Kiselewsky v. Compton (1970), 73 W.W.R. 377 (B.C. C.A.) — Where an action had been commenced against the owner of the vehicle on the basis of his consent to possession by the driver, an amendment could not be made after expiration of the limitation period alleging liability of the owner for the improper conduct of his son who was a passenger in the vehicle at the time of the accident; there was a clear distinction between the liability imposed on the owner by the two sections respectively relied upon.

Uzun v. General Accident Assurance Co. of Can. (1988), 32 M.V.R. (2d) 158 (Ont. C.A.); leave to appeal to S.C.C. refused (1988), 32 M.V.R. (2d) 158 (note) — The plaintiff was injured on July 31, 1982 in a single-vehicle accident while travelling as a passenger in a car owned and driven by her husband. The husband's insurer was notified in February 1983 that the plaintiff would be looking to it for damages for her injuries. A claim against the insurer for s. 3 benefits under the insurance policy was commenced on

July 31, 1984, one day before the limitation period in the Highway Traffic Act expired. No action was brought against the plaintiff's husband. Two years later, the plaintiff moved for an order adding her husband as a party defendant. The motion was dismissed. The plaintiff appealed. The appeal was allowed. The Judge of first instance erred in concluding that the insurer would be prejudiced if the husand were added as a party. The fact of the accident and the nature of the injuries were known to the insurer from the outset. This was a proper case for review of the exercise of the judge's discretion.

Swiderski v. Broy Engineering Ltd. (1992), 11 O.R. (3d) 594, 40 M.V.R. (2d) 228, 16 C.P.C. (3d) 46, 60 O.A.C. 260 (Div. Ct.) — The court has a discretion to add adult defendants after the expiry of the limitation period to an action commenced by adult plaintiffs. The discretion should be exercised sparingly and only in the absence of prejudice to the proposed defendants and in the presence of special circumstances.

Robertson v. O'Rourke (1997), 31 M.V.R. (3d) 102 (Ont. Gen. Div.); affirmed (1998), 35 M.V.R. (3d) 252, 14 C.P.C. (4th) 182 (Ont. C.A.) — The alleged manufacturer of a seatbelt was not added after the expiry of the limitation period when a government agency examining the seatbelt disposed of the vehicle before the limitation period.

Counterclaim and Third-Party Proceedings

Cleave v. Calnan, [1938] O.W.N. 38 (M.C.) — A third-party notice had to be issued within the year, and not just the main action. Since an action may be commenced by a plaintiff on the last day of the limitation period, it is now provided in s. 206(3) that a counterclaim or third-party proceedings may be instituted by a defendant notwithstanding expiration of the limitation period. This is a very necessary provision for the protection of the defendant's rights and it overcomes the difficulty in such cases.

Imbro v. Nagle, [1963] 2 O.R. 570 (C.A.) — Where a default judgment was set aside and leave to defend granted, the right to counterclaim existed by virtue of this section and could not properly be limited by the Court making such order.

Poste v. Gregoire, [1964] 1 O.R. 155 (Master) — The Senior Master confirmed his decision in *Carter v. Dodd*, [1961] O.W.N. 306 (H.C.), but also pointed out that if the limitation period has not expired when the defence is due or is delivered the defendant does not need the benefit of subs. (3) in order to file a counterclaim. However, if such a counterclaim is filed within the limitation period it may be amended after the expiration of the limitation period only if no new cause of action is added, and the subsection does not confer any right to add a new cause of action in such circumstances.

Weir v. Lazarius, [1964] 1 O.R. 158 (M.C.); affirmed [1964] 1 O.R. 205 (H.C.) — The filing of a defence without a counterclaim within the limitation period was not a bar to the filing of a new defence with counterclaim after expiration of the period. It was intimated that the Court still had a discretion under subs. (3) which might be exercised against the application if there was prejudice to the plaintiffs.

Dipasquale v. Muscatello, [1953] O.W.N. 1001 (H.C.) — Where a third-party notice is issued after the limitation period in subs. (1) has expired the defendant can only claim relief over in respect of the plaintiff's claim and cannot add a personal claim against the third-party which has been barred by expiration of the period limited in subs. (1).

Routh v. Levesque, [1963] 1 O.R. 238 (Co. Ct.) — Although the procedure is perhaps unusual, there is no reason why a counterclaim should not be served pursuant to this section even though the plaintiff has not yet delivered his or her statement of claim. *Morley v. Wiggins* (1985), 30 M.V.R. 189, 49 O.R. (2d) 136, 47 C.P.C. 128 (Div. Ct.).

A third party who is not a defendant may counterclaim against the defendant, asserting a claim for relief in relation to his or her own independent damages sustained in the same motor vehicle accident giving rise to the main action. This conclusion is fortified by the familiar principle that it is desirable to resolve in one proceeding all issues arising out of a single incident. It is also a result which would be permitted by the Rules of Civil Procedure. Such a claim may be asserted after the expiry of the limitation period governing the action where the defendant would not be prejudiced.

Morley v. Wiggins, supra — In the aftermath of a motor vehicle accident, the plaintiff sued the defendant for damages. The defendant issued a statement of defence, third-party notice and statement of claim against the third party. The third party delivered a statement of defence to the defendant's claim and a counterclaim against the defendant for damages sustained in the accident. The defendant failed at first instance to strike out the counterclaim and appealed; the appeal was dismissed. Although the Rules of Practice were silent on the possibility of a third party, who was not a defendant, counterclaiming against a defendant who issued the third-party notice, such a possibility had not been excluded in the decided cases and the strictures of R. 167 did not apply to such a counterclaim. Allowing the counterclaim would promote the value of resolving all the issues between the parties in a single proceeding. Furthermore, although the counterclaim was brought more than two years after the date of the accident and would ordinarily be barred by s. 206(1) of the Highway Traffic Act (Ont.), special circumstances relating to the defendant's knowledge of the third party's injuries and the defendant's tardiness in bringing third-party proceedings, justified the Court in considering the counterclaim beyond the limitation period.

Knudsen v. Knudsen (1995), 11 M.V.R. (3d) 226, 22 O.R. (3d) 160 (Gen. Div.); additional reasons at (1995), 11 M.V.R. (3d) 226n, 22 O.R. (3d) 160 at 166 (Gen. Div.) — Special circumstances which would justify adding a defendant after the expiry of the limitation period were not made out where the plaintiff knew of the person's potential liability from the outset, and where the plaintiff attempted to mislead the court in her evidence filed in support of the motion to add the party.

Related Provisions: Reference should also be had to the following limitation provisions: sections, 4, 15, and 24 of the Limitations Act, 2002, S.O. 2002, c. 24, Schedule B, proclaimed in force January 1, 2004, which establish basic two-year and ultimate fifteen-year limitation periods, and prescribe the transitional rules applicable to the limitation periods for a wide range of claims arising in the motor vehicle context; the following provisions were repealed and replaced by the Limitations Act, 2002, but should be referenced in respect of certain acts and omissions which took place before January 1, 2004, in accordance with s. 24 of the Limitations Act, 2002: contribution or indemnity — section 8 of the Negligence Act, R.S.O. 1990, s. 8 — one year from date of judgment or settlement; fatal accidents — dependants' claims for damages — section 61(4) of the Family Law Act, R.S.O. 1990, c. F.3 — two years from the time the cause of action arose; highway disrepair — section 33(5) of the Public Transportation and Highway Improvement Act, R.S.O. 1990, c. P-50 — three months (see supra 1(1) "highway"); highway disrepair — section 44(7) of the Municipal Act, 2001, S.O. 2001, c. 25 — three months (see supra 1(1) "highway"); public authorities — section 7 of the Public Authorities Protection Act, R.S.O. 1990, c. P.38, s. 7 — six months from the date of the act, neglect, or default complained of; Street railways — Subsection 237(1) and (2) of the

Railways Act, R.S.O. 1950, c. 331 — One year; note that the the two-year limitation period prescribed by s. 38(3) of the Trustee Act, R.S.O. 1990, c. T.23 for actions by executors and administrators for torts has been preserved under the Limitations Act, 2002, subject to the new application rules created by the Act.

207. (1) Vehicle owner may be convicted — Subject to subsection (2), the owner of a vehicle may be charged with and convicted of an offence under this Act or the regulations or any municipal by-law regulating traffic for which the driver of the vehicle is subject to be charged unless, at the time of the offence, the vehicle was in the possession of some person other than the owner without the owner's consent and on conviction the owner is liable to the penalty prescribed for the offence.

(2) When owner not liable — The owner of a vehicle, except if the owner is also the driver, shall not be convicted for a contravention of,

    (a) subsection 106(2) or (4);

    (b) sections 129 to 143, subsections 144(1) to (17), subsections 144(19) to (32), sections 145 to 168, section 172, subsections 175(1) to (10), subsections 175(13) to (18) or section 176, 182 or 199;

    (c) a regulation or by-law made or passed under a section or subsection referred to in clause (a) or (b) or under section 106; or

    (d) a by-law passed under any Act regulating or prohibiting turns on a highway.

(3) Permit holder deemed owner — For the purposes of this Act or any municipal by-law regulating or prohibiting parking, standing or stopping, the holder of a permit as defined in section 6 shall be deemed to be the owner of the vehicle referred to in the permit if a number plate bearing a number that corresponds to the permit was displayed on the vehicle at the time an offence was committed unless the number plate was displayed thereon without the holder's consent, the burden of proof of which shall be on the holder.

(4) Exposing number plate — For the purposes of this Act or any municipal by-law regulating or prohibiting parking, standing or stopping, where a number plate issued under section 7 is exposed on a motor vehicle, the holder of the permit corresponding thereto shall be deemed to be the owner of that vehicle unless the number plate was exposed thereon without the permit holder's consent, the burden of proof of which is on the permit holder.

(5) No imprisonment or probation — Any person convicted of an offence pursuant to subsection (1) is not liable to imprisonment or to a probation order under subsection 72(1) of the *Provincial Offences Act* as a result of the conviction or as a result of default in payment of the fine resulting from the conviction.

(6) Where owner not liable — The owner of a motor vehicle shall not be charged as an owner with an offence under section 128 unless the evidence of the offence is obtained through the use of a photo-radar system.

(7) Limitation — An owner of a motor vehicle convicted of an offence under section 128 on the basis of evidence acquired through the use of a photo-radar system or under subsection 175(19) or (20) is not liable to imprisonment, a probation order under subsection 72(1) of the *Provincial Offences Act* or a driver's licence suspension as a result of that conviction or as a result of default in payment of a fine resulting from that conviction.

(8) When owner liable — The owner of a motor vehicle shall not be charged as an owner with an offence under subsection 144(18) unless the evidence of the offence is obtained through the use of a red light camera system in an area designated for the purposes of subsection 205.15(1).

(9) Definition — In this section,

"owner" includes an operator as defined in section 16 or as deemed in section 19.
1993, c. 31, s. 2(10), (11); 1998, c. 38, s. 5; 2004, c. 22, s. 6; 2005, c. 26, Sched. A, s. 31; 2006, c. 25, s. 3

Commentary

The section provides that, subject to exemptions, the owner may be charged with and convicted of an offence under the Act, the regulations, or a by-law regulating traffic unless the vehicle was in another's possession without the owner's consent. On conviction, the owner is liable to the same penalty as the driver (subs. (1)).

However, an owner cannot be convicted, unless he or she is also the driver, of offences relating to:

- seatbelts

- speeding, careless driving and slow driving

- most offences under Part X — Rules of the Road

- reporting an accident

- regulations or by-laws respecting seatbelts or prohibiting turns (subs. (2)).

For purposes of the Act or a by-law respecting parking, standing or stopping, the permit holder is deemed to be the owner, and the holder of the permit corresponding to the plate is deemed the owner unless the number plate was displayed without the permit holder's consent, the burden of proof being on the holder (subss. (3), (4)).

"Owner" includes an operator as defined in ss. 16 and 19 of the Act (subs. (5)).

Prior to 1980, c. 37, s. 20, s. 207 [formerly s. 147] read as follows:

147. (1) Subject to subsection 2, the owner of a vehicle shall incur the penalties provided for any contravention of this Act or of any regulation made by the Lieutenant Governor in Council or of any municipal by-law for regulating traffic approved by the Department unless at the time of the contravention the vehicle was in the possession of some person other than the owner or his chauffeur without the owner's consent, and the driver or operator of a vehicle not being the owner shall also incur the penalties provided for any such contravention.

(2) The owner of a motor vehicle except when he is also the driver shall not incur the penalties provided for any contravention of any of the provisions of sections 82 to 114, 117, 120, 125 and 139 or any regulation or by-law made or passed thereunder or of any of the provisions of any by-law passed under any Act regulating or prohibiting turns on a highway. Motor vehicle owners are made liable to fines for speeding arising from photo-

radar but they would not be liable to imprisonment, a probation order or a licence suspension as a result.

It appears that the section was amended by 1980, c. 37, s. 20, because of the decision in *R. v. Budget Car Rentals (Toronto) Ltd.* (1981), 30 O.R. (2d) 641 at 649, 8 M.V.R. 218 (Div. Ct.), reversing (1981), 30 O.R. (2d) 641 at 642, 7 M.V.R. 72 (H.C.), reversed (1981), 31 O.R. (2d) 161, 9 M.V.R. 52 (C.A.). See, *infra*.

The Red Light Camera Pilot Projects Act, 1998, S.O. 1998, c. 38 (in force November 20, 2000) permits evidence obtained from red light cameras to be used in areas designated by regulation for the purpose of enforcing subsection 144(18) of the Highway Traffic Act (failing to stop at a red light or proceeding before the light turns green). O. Reg. 277/99 dealing with the admissibility and use of Red Light Camera System evidence in proceedings under the Act, was brought into force contemporaneously with the Act.

Case Law

R. v. Vaugeois (1959), 29 W.W.R. 368 (B.C. C.A.); *R. v. Webb* (1961), 36 C.R. 252, 36 W.W.R. 431, 131 C.C.C. 276 (B.C. S.C.) — The offences of owner and driver are separate and distinct and a person might be charged with an offence under the Act either as owner or driver or both.

R. v. Curley, [1953] O.W.N. 603, [1953] 4 D.L.R. 135, 16 C.R. 419 (H.C.) — If the owner has been absolved from blame and acquitted on a charge against the driver, he or she could not be charged again as owner as there would be no "violation of the Act" which could bring him or her as owner within the ambit of this section.

R. v. Lockie, [1950] O.W.N. 589, [1950] 4 D.L.R. 443, 10 C.R. 477 (H.C.); *R. v. Greenfield*, [1954] O.W.N. 292 (H.C.) — If the owner is charged as driver and the prosecution fails to prove that he or she was the driver he or she is not liable on that charge to be convicted as owner.

R. v. Anderson, [1960] O.W.N. 189 (Co. Ct.) — An owner was acquitted on a charge of failing to deposit money in a parking meter, it being held that s. 486 para. 7 [now s. 314(1) para. 8] of the Municipal Act did not authorize an extension of jurisdiction beyond drivers of vehicles to include owners. That section was subsequently amended to permit the imposition of penalties on the owner as well as the driver.

R. v. White, [1957] O.W.N. 491 (C.A.) — Where an information charged the accused with "[b]eing the registered owner of a motor vehicle [described] which was driven unlawfully by a person at a greater speed than" the statutory maximum, the offence had been sufficiently described.

R. v. Reynolds (1977), 34 C.C.C. (2d) 450 (N.W.T. S.C.) — The accused owner was acquitted of a charge of permitting the operation of an unsafe vehicle as the driver, his roommate, had taken the vehicle without the accused's permission.

Donline Haulage Inc. v. R. (1980), 4 M.V.R. 241 (Ont. Co. Ct.) — The accused was convicted of permitting a motor vehicle trailer combination to be operated where the axle weight exceeded the maximum allowable, contrary to s. 72(1)(c), [now s. 116(1)(c)], pursuant to s. 147(1) [now s. 207(1)] of the Act. His appeal was allowed on the ground that the information contained no offence known to law, since the offence created by s. 72(1) was "operating" rather than "permitting". Although an owner could be charged by virtue of s. 147(1), an accused had to be charged directly with the offence.

R. v. Budget Car Rentals (Toronto) Ltd. (1981), 30 O.R. (2d) 641 at 649, 8 M.V.R. 218 (Div. Ct.); reversing (1981), 30 O.R. (2d) 641 at 642, 7 M.V.R. 72 (H.C.); reversed (1981), 31 O.R. (2d) 161, 9 M.V.R. 52 (C.A.) — The respondent was charged as the owner of a vehicle which attracted a parking violation contrary to a municipal by-law. Prior to plea, the respondent successfully moved to quash the information on the ground that it disclosed no offence known to law. The respondent contended that the liability for a penalty assessed against the owner of a vehicle must be proceeded with through means other than the laying of an information charging the owner with an offence. The Crown's appeal by way of stated case was successful (see (1981), 7 M.V.R. 72). The owner's appeal to Divisional Court was successful (see (1981), 8 M.V.R. 218). The Crown brought an application for leave to appeal and an appeal to the Court of Appeal. The Court of Appeal allowed the appeal. It held that the legislation creates an offence with which an owner may be charged and convicted arising out of the illegal parking of a vehicle regardless of whether the owner was the driver. As to the factors to be considered in determining whether the motor vehicle was in the possession of some person other than the owner of his chauffeur without the owner's consent, see s. 192.

R. v. Ron Smith Oilfield Hauling Ltd. (1966), 55 W.W.R. 313 (Alta. S.C.); *R. v. Anger* (1972), 9 C.C.C. (2d) 141 (Alta. T.D.) — A certificate of the Alberta Highway Traffic Board as to registration is sufficient proof of ownership on a charge against the owner, but such certificate will be vitiated for inadequate identification of the vehicle owned if there is a discrepancy in the certificate as to the serial number.

R. v. Arbon (1981), 11 M.V.R. 227, 66 C.C.C. (2d) 11 (Ont. Div. Ct.) — The burden of proving the exception that the vehicle was in the possession of some person other than that owner without the owner's consent rests upon the owner of the vehicle.

R. v. Schnare (1982), 16 M.V.R. 49, 69 C.C.C. (2d) 572, 52 N.S.R. (2d) 354, 106 A.P.R. 354 (C.A.) — The Crown must first prove all the elements of the substantive offence and the owner may raise any defence which would be available to the operator.

Pelkie v. R. (1980), 4 M.V.R. 186 (Ont. Co. Ct.) — A car owner was convicted of failing to remain as the owner of a vehicle involved in an accident where the driver failed to remain. His appeal was allowed on the ground that the driver was on "a frolic of his own" and therefore did not have possession of the vehicle with the owner's consent.

R. v. Pellerin (1988), 10 M.V.R. (2d) 165, 67 C.R. (3d) 305 (Ont. C.A.); affirming (1987), 1 M.V.R. (2d) 204, 59 C.R. (3d) 19 (Ont. Dist. Ct.); affirming (1986), 48 M.V.R. 148 (Ont. Prov. Ct.) — The Court held that s. 207, when relied upon in conjunction with s. 200(1)(a) of the Highway Traffic Act of Ontario, violates s. 7 of the Charter of Rights and Freedoms and was not saved by s. 1. The offence created by s. 18(1) of the Highway Traffic Act is one of absolute liability and not strict liability.

R. v. Wilson (1997), 31 M.V.R. (3d) 238 (N.B. C.A.) — The Act was unconstitutional when it placed the onus on the owner to prove more than he was not in possession. The Act was read down to eliminate the need for an owner to show operation without consent, another had been convicted or that another admits to being the driver at the time.

R. v. Smith (1999), 47 M.V.R. (3d) 135 (B.C. S.C.) — The Crown has the discretion to charge one of the registered owners.

R. v. Miller, 2010 BCCA 39, 2010 CarswellBC 144, 204 C.R.R. (2d) 313, 91 M.V.R. (5th) 1, 251 C.C.C. (3d) 43, 284 B.C.A.C. 9, [2010] B.C.J. No. 121 — The failure to indicate that penalty points upon conviction was not a breach of s. 11(b) of the *Charter of Rights*, but a mere administrative function.

R. v. Jenkins, 2010 ONCA 278, 2010 CarswellOnt 2158, [2010] O.J. No. 1517, 99 O.R. (3d) 561, 260 O.A.C. 296, 212 C.R.R. (2d) 137, 93 M.V.R. (5th) 1, 74 C.R. (6th) 117, 253 C.C.C. (3d) 269; leave to appeal refused 2010 CarswellOnt 7405, 2010 CarswellOnt 7406, 410 N.R. 395 (note), 225 C.R.R. (2d) 374 (note), 279 O.A.C. 399 (note) (S.C.C.) — *Ex parte* proceedings do not violate s. 7 or 11(d) of the *Charter of Rights*.

R. v. Deforest (2013), 41 M.V.R. (6th) 338, 2013 SKPC 30, 2013 CarswellSask 122, 413 Sask. R. 293 (Sask. Prov. Ct.) — It is unreasonable to authorize a long list of relatives who could drive knowing that they were disqualified, and not knowing who was driving and where.

Related Provisions: See s. 192 of the Act.

208. Recovery — **The penalties imposed by or under the authority of this Act for the contravention of this Act or the regulations are recoverable under the *Provincial Offences Act*.**

2002, c. 18, Sched. P, s. 36

Commentary

See the Provincial Offences Act, R.S.O. 1990, c. P.33 which superseded the Summary Convictions Act, R.S.O. 1970, c. 450, in respect of offences under the Highway Traffic Act, setting out a new summary conviction procedure for the prosecution of provincial offences. Part II of the Act, respecting parking infractions, was proclaimed in force on September 1, 1987. The proclamation of Part II of the Provincial Offences Act provided a simplified procedure for the prosecution of parking infractions under provincial legislation and municipal by-laws. It results in large savings in the time expended by enforcement officers and court personnel, since trials are held only when the person charged has requested one. It also allows the court to order that an offender's vehicle permit not be renewed if a parking fine remains unpaid. Police and by-law enforcement officers will no longer be required to serve summonses and to attend trials in the defendants' absence. Upon the receipt of the new parking infraction notice, the owner does not respond to the ticket, a conviction will be entered by the court in the owners' absence.

By S.O. 1992, c. 20, Part II of the Provincial Offences Act was brought into force. On November 5, 1992, Royal Assent was given to Bill 25 — the Parking Infraction Statute Law Amendment Act, 1992. By s. 3 of the Act, the following transitional provision was provided for:

> Part II of the *Provincial Offences Act*, as it read immediately before subsection 1(1) of this Act is proclaimed in force, continues to apply to proceedings that were commenced before subsection 1(1) of this Act is proclaimed in force.

Bill 25 changes the process by which proceedings are determined for persons who are served with parking tickets and who do not respond to those tickets.

Under the present law, if a defendant does not respond to a parking ticket within fifteen days of its issue, the issuer may forward the required information to the clerk of the court, a justice of the peace reviews that information without holding a hearing and, if the justice determines that it is a proper case for a conviction, the justice issues a conviction.

Under the Bill, if a defendant does not respond to a parking ticket within fifteen days of its issue, the issuer may give a further notice of impending conviction to the defendant. If the defendant does not respond to the notice of impending conviction within fifteen days after receiving it, the issuer may forward a certificate to the court clerk requesting a conviction and certifying that it is a proper case for a conviction. Upon receiving such a certificate, the court clerk will issue a conviction.

The Bill also provides as follows:

1. A defendant who is convicted under this process may apply to a justice to have the conviction set aside if the ticket is defective. If the defendant is successful, the justice must require the issuer to pay the defendant $25 in costs.

2. The issue may apply to a justice to have a conviction set aside if the defendant was convicted because of an error made by the issuer.

3. If the regulations so provide, proceedings respecting parking infractions are to be determined by justices of the peace rather than by court clerks.

4. Municipalities authorized to do so by the regulations may collect fines under their parking by-laws.

5. At the time of conviction for a parking infraction, an order may not bew made for imprisonment of the defendant for default in the payment of the fine.

6. A direction for plate denial may be made by an officer of the court rather than a justice of the peace.

In announcing the Bill the Ministry of the Attorney General released a statement which reads in part:

> This Bill should significantly reduce convictions of persons for parking offences because of incorrect identification. All municipalities will now be responsible for giving advance notice of possible conviction to vehicle owners before asking a court for a parking offence court date. Regulations to be made under the *Parking Infractions Statute Law Amendment Act, 1992,* known as Bill 25, will provide increased protection to motorists from wrongful convictions by requiring ticketing officers to include on the ticket the month of renewal on the licence plate sticker. This will allow for a cross check on ownership to screen out most errors. This bill will save the public time and money. Possible convictions based on incorrect identification will be reduced, as will paper being transmitted to the courts. Municipalities will be able to improve their cash flow and take over the collection of fines so that the courts will be freed up for more important work.

When a motorist fails to respond to a parking ticket, and to a follow-up notice of impending conviction, the legislation allows for a conviction once the municipality certifies that the ticket is complete and regular on its face. An examination by a justice of the peace is not required. This procedure will reduce demands on the time of justices of the peace and courts.

The Bill also provides a new method to challenge a conviction. A person convicted may take the ticket to a justice of the peace who, upon finding that it is incomplete, may quash it. In addition, the municipality that requested the conviction based on the defective ticket will have to pay the person $25. This will be an incentive for the municipality to screen out defective tickets before requesting convictions from the court.

Procedures established by Part I of the Provincial Offences Act, dealing with offences under various statutes and by-laws other than parking infractions came into effect on April 1, 1980.

Part I offences are commenced by a certificate of offence filed in court and by serving personally an offence notice indicating a set fine or by a summons. Part III proceedings are commenced by an information followed by a summons or arrest.

Case Law

Agents

R. v. Lawrie & POINTS Ltd. (1987), 59 O.R. (2d) 161, 48 M.V.R. (2d) 189, 19 O.A.C. 81, 32 C.C.C. (3d) 549 (C.A.) — It is permissible for agencies to act for individuals charged with provincial offences.

Amending the Certificate

R. v. Potter (1982), 17 M.V.R. 54 (Ont. H.C.); *Greenspan v. R.* (1982), 17 M.V.R. 57 (Ont. Prov. Ct.); leave to appeal refused (September 16, 1982); *R. v. Arnold* (1982), 17 M.V.R. 61 (Ont. H.C.); *R. v. Matsuba* (1982), 17 M.V.R. 221 (Ont. H.C.); *R. v. Callahan* (1983), 21 M.V.R. 127 (Ont. H.C.) — The omission of a reference to a specific Provincial Offences Court in a Certificate of Offence is not fatal. The Certificate may be amended.

Constitutional

A.G. Ont. v. Town of Kincardine (November 2, 1989), (unreported Toronto), Hayes C.J. (Ont. Prov. Ct.) — The penalty provision of a municipal by-law which formed the basis upon which a set fine was established under the Provincial Offences Act was invalid because the speeding by-law trenched on the applicable section of the *Highway Traffic Act.*

R. v. Carson (1983), 20 M.V.R. 54 (Ont. C.A.) — The appellant was charged under the Highway Traffic Act (Ont.) with driving without a proper headlight. Pursuant to Pt. I of the Provincial Offences Act (Ont.), he was served with an offence notice. The appellant did not respond to the notice. After 15 days had elapsed from the date of service of the notice, the appellant was deemed to not wish to dispute the charge by virtue of s. 9 of the Provincial Offences Act and a conviction was entered in his absence. The appellant appealed his conviction to the Provincial Court and argued that s. 9 of the Provincial Offences Act was unconstitutional in that it contravened his right under s. 11(d) of the Charter of Rights to be presumed innocent until proven guilty according to law in a fair and public hearing by an independent and impartial tribunal. The appeal was dismissed and the appellant obtained special leave to appeal to the Court of Appeal. The Court of Appeal dismissed the appeal, holding that the constitutional validity of s. 9 of the Provincial Offences Act must be considered having regard to the legislative scheme of which it forms an important part. Section 9 is found in Pt. I of the Act which establishes a simple expeditious procedure for dealing fairly and economically with provincial offences. *Prima facie*, s. 9 of the Provincial Offences Act does not contemplate the disposition of a charge in accordance with all the elements of s. 11(d) of the Charter. The issue was whether the limitations in s. 9 on the rights guaranteed by s. 11(d) of the Charter are "reasonable limits prescribed by law" within the meaning of s. 1 of the Charter. Having regard to the type and class of offences, the number of such cases, the reaons for the legislation, the options given to the person charged as to the disposition of his case and the provisions allowing for the quashing of a conviction to avoid any miscarriage of justice, s. 9 of the Provincial Offences Act is a reasonable limitation such as is contemplated by s. 1 of the Charter.

R. v. Felipa (1986), 55 O.R. (2d) 362, 40 M.V.R. 316, 27 C.C.C. (3d) 26, 15 O.A.C. 121 (C.A.) — The *ex parte* procedure under s. 55(1)(a) [now s. 54(1)(a)] of the Provincial

Offences Act (Ont.) where the accused was served with a summons but failed to appear did not contravene ss. 7 and 11(d) of the Charter.

R. v. Richard, [1996] 3 S.C.R. 525, 23 M.V.R. (3d) 1 — In the context of regulatory offences for which imprisonment is not a possibility, s. 11(d) of the Charter does not prevent the legislation from inferring from a defendant's failure to act that the or she waives the right to be presumed innocent and the right to a fair and public hearing by an independent and impartial tribunal, provided the defendant is fully aware of the consequences of failing to act and that the procedural scheme in place provides sufficient safeguards to ensure the conduct was not due to events over which he or she had no control.

R. v. Newton (1996), 23 M.V.R. (3d) 42 (Ont. Prov. Div.); *R. v. Pilipovic* (1996), 23 M.V.R. (3d) 282 (Ont. Prov. Div.) — Applying *R. v. Carson* (1983), 20 M.V.R. 54 (Ont. C.A.), ss. 9 and 9.1 of the Provincial Offences Act were held to be constitutional.

R. v. Vellone, 2011 ONCA 785, 2011 CarswellOnt 14646, 108 O.R. (3d) 481, 25 M.V.R. (6th) 1, 250 C.R.R. (2d) 351, 284 O.A.C. 388, [2011] O.J. No. 5708 (Ont. C.A.) — The Attorney General merits notice under s. 109 of the Courts of Justice Act where s. 11(b) of the Charter of Rights is in issue under a municipal prosecution for speeding as systematic issues could be in play.

R. v. Smith, 2012 ONCJ 324, 2012 CarswellOnt 6700, 35 M.V.R. (6th) 163, [2012] O.J. No. 2395 — An application to have a judge assigned instead of a Justice of the Peace for a careless driving charge failed. There were no complex legal or constitutional issues of significant precedent value anticipated. The mere fact of a fatality was not sufficient reason to assign a trial to a judge.

Eliminating Technicalities

Metropolitan Toronto (Municipality) v. Beck (1990), 23 M.V.R. (2d) 61 (Ont. H.C.) — The accused were issued parking tickets. The Justice of the Peace quashed the certificates of parking infractions on the basis that they were a nullity in that they failed to disclose on their faces the names of the specific persons charged with the offences alleged therein. The municipality applied for an order in the nature of *mandamus* remitting the certificates to the Justice of the Peace. The application was allowed. The approach taken by the Justice of the Peace was overly technical and inappropriate for adjudication with regard to parking infractions. The accused were not misled as to the nature of the charges or prejudiced in their defence. Section 16(1)(b) [now s. 15(1)(b)] of the Provincial Offences Act required that the proceeding be commenced by the filing not only of the certificate of parking infraction but also of evidence of ownership of the vehicle in question. The requirement had been complied with in these cases and, although it may have been preferable to affix the evidence of ownership to the face of the certificate instead of to the face of the filing document, there had been sufficient compliance with s. 7a of Reg. 809 [now R.R.O. 1990, Reg. 200, s. 8] under the Courts of Justice Act, 1984 [now Courts of Justice Act, R.S.O. 1990, c. C.43]. In general, the purpose of the Provincial Offences Act was to create procedures appropriate to the nature of the offence, to eliminate technicalities and to simplify and clarify procedural steps in order to bring proceedings to an expeditious conclusion on the merits while preserving protections which ensure a fair trial.

Identity

R. v. Lively, 9 C.R.N.S. 128, [1970] 3 C.C.C. 119 (N.S. Co. Ct.); *Ellis v. Jones*, [1973] 2 All E.R. 893 (Q.B.) — Evidence that a named person was served with the summons portion of a traffic ticket and that a person with that name was driving the vehicle and appears in court in answer to the summons constitute some evidence of identity.

R. v. McLean (1973), 22 C.R.N.S. 180, 11 C.C.C. (2d) 568 (N.S. Co. Ct.) — The decision in *Lively, supra,* was held not to be the case unless the name was very uncommon.

R. v. Hunt (1986), 45 M.V.R. 124, 18 O.A.C. 78 (C.A.) — The accused was charged with speeding. He was served with and signed the certificate of offence at the scene of the offence. The officer certified on the certificate that he had personally served the offence notice on the person charged. The accused pled not guilty to the charge and returned the offence notice, on which he inserted his new mailing address. The arresting officer testified at trial that he had stopped a motor vehicle for speeding and that the driver had produced a driver's licence bearing the name of the accused, but he did not further identify the accused. The accused's appeal of his conviction was allowed on the ground that the evidence fell short of a *prima facie* case identifying the accused. The Crown appealed. The appeal was allowed. It was held that the scheme of the Provincial Offences Act provided for charging of and service of the offence notice on an accused at the time of his apprehension and securing his attendance before the Court should he, under his signature, elect to plead not guilty and undertake to appear. The scheme depended to a great extent on the signature of the person charged to establish and identify, and s. 10 of the Act provided for proof of the signature. The Court had at all times the power to look at its own records and take notice of their contents. In the circumstances, having regard to the evidence of the police officer and the records of the Court in view of the provisions of the statute referred to, there was sufficient evidence to constitute *prima facie* proof of the identity of the accused as the driver when he appeared in response to the notice of trial to answer the charge. ◆

Certificate of Offence and Informations

R. v. Thompson (1981), 12 M.V.R. 196 (Ont. H.C.) — The failure to describe the provincial offences officer in the certificate as the "issuing officer" is not fatal.

R. v. Elliott (1981), 12 M.V.R. 35 (Ont. C.A.) — The failure of the officer to sign the offence notice does not affect the validity of the proceedings.

R. v. West (1981), 35 O.R. (2d) 179, 13 M.V.R. 70, 64 C.C.C. (2d) 417 (H.C.) — The Provincial Court had quashed an information as being a nullity which charged the respondent that he "did unlawfully operate a motor vehicle on a highway ... when his driver's licence was suspended by operation of the Highway Traffic Act, contrary to the Highway Traffic Act, section 30b." Section 30b [now s. 53] only provided for driving while one's licence was suspended. The Crown brought an application for *mandamus*. The application was granted. It was held that the reference to the section number incorporated the essential element of driving. Although it would have been preferable for the information to be in the words of the section, it did in fact comply with the requirements of an information as set out in s. 26 [now s. 25] of the Provincial Offences Act (Ont.).

Traffic Tickets

R. v. Gregoryk (October 25, 1979), [unreported] (Sask. Q.B.); *R. v. Van Hees*, 27 C.R. 14, [1957] O.W.N. 602 (C.A.); *R. v. Sourwine* (1970), 10 C.R.N.S. 380, 72 W.W.R. 761 (Alta. Dist. Ct.); *R. v. J. D. Irving Ltd.* (1975), 12 N.B.R. (2d) 108, 28 C.C.C. (2d) 242 (C.A.) — In a properly worded charge, the section number is mere surplusage.

R. v. Lemieux (1982), 15 M.V.R. 126 (Ont. C.A.); reversing (1981), 34 O.R. (2d) 691, 11 M.V.R. 307, 63 C.C.C. (2d) 327 (Div. Ct.); which reversed (1978), 1 M.V.R. 27 (Ont. Dist. Ct.) — The use of the abbreviation "H.T.A." does not invalidate a charge in a ticket which alleged that the respondent "did commit the offence of speeding 79 km/h in a 50 km/h zone contrary to H.T.A. section 82, subsection 16."

R. v. Urban (1979), 5 M.V.R. 276 (B.C. S.C.) — A slight deviation in the form of a traffic ticket information from that provided in the regulations was excused.

R. v. Smaill (1979), 6 M.V.R. 167 (B.C. S.C.) — The abbreviations authorized by regulation are not mandatory.

Ortman v. A.G. Saskatchewan (1980), 9 M.V.R. 168, (sub nom. *R. v. Ortman)* 8 Sask. R. 153 (Q.B.) — Placing a check-mark symbol instead of the required "X" was not held to be fatal, not following *R. v. Sullivan*, [1968] 1 O.R. 613, 3 C.R.N.S. 132 (H.C.).

R. v. Wilson (2001), 23 M.V.R. (4th) 296, 2001 CarswellOnt 4374 (Ont. C.J.) — The requirements of a speeding ticket were spelled out.

Toronto (City) v. Braganza, 2011 ONCJ 657, 2011 CarswellOnt 13681, 91 M.P.L.R. (4th) 276, 21 M.V.R. (6th) 104, 250 C.R.R. (2d) 60, [2011] O.J. No. 5445 — Although the lower voluntary amount was no longer available at the time of the issuance, the set fine amount, a requirement, was properly set out and therefore the tickets were valid.

R. v. Smith, 2012 ONCJ 324, 2012 CarswellOnt 6700, 35 M.V.R. (6th) 163, [2012] O.J. No. 2395 — An application to have a judge assigned instead of a Justice of the Peace for a careless driving charge failed. There were no complex legal or constitutional issues of significant precedent value anticipated. The mere fact of a fatality was not sufficient reason to assign a trial to a judge.

209. Right to damages reserved — **No penalty or imprisonment is a bar to the recovery of damages by the injured person.**

210. (1) Notice of conviction to Registrar — **A judge, provincial judge or justice of the peace who makes a conviction in respect of an offence to which this section applies or the clerk of the court in which the conviction is made shall forthwith notify the Registrar of the conviction.**

(1.1) Applicable offences — **This section applies in respect of the following offences:**

> **1. An offence under this Act or under any other Act of the Legislature or the Parliament of Canada or any regulation or order made under any of them committed by means of,**
>
> > **i. a motor vehicle or street car within the meaning of this Act,**
> >
> > **ii. a vessel within the meaning of section 48, or**
> >
> > **iii. a motorized snow vehicle.**
>
> **2. An offence under a municipal by-law regulating traffic on the highways, except convictions for offences for standing or parking.**

(1.2) Contents of notice of conviction — **The notice of conviction under subsection (1) shall set out the name, address and description of the person convicted, the number of his or her driver's licence, the number of the permit of the motor**

vehicle or the registration number of the vessel or motorized snow vehicle, as the case may be, with which the offence was committed, the time the offence was committed and the provision of the Act, regulation, order or by-law contravened.

(2) **Idem** — A judge, provincial judge or justice of the peace who makes a conviction for a prescribed offence or an offence under a prescribed Act of the Legislature or the Parliament of Canada or a regulation or order made under the prescribed Act or the clerk of the court in which the conviction is made shall forthwith notify the Registrar of the conviction setting out the name and address of the person convicted, the date the offence was committed, the provision contravened and the other information that is prescribed.

(3) **Regulations** — The Minister may make regulations prescribing offences and Acts and information to be certified for the purpose of subsection (2).

(4) **Report on accessible parking by-law conviction** — Despite subsection (1), a judge, provincial judge or justice of the peace who makes a conviction under a municipal by-law passed for establishing a system of accessible parking under section 9, 10, 11 or 102 of the *Municipal Act, 2001* or section 7, 8 or 80 of the *City of Toronto Act, 2006* for the improper use of an accessible parking permit issued under section 26 or the clerk of the court in which the conviction is made shall promptly notify the Registrar of the conviction setting out the name and address of the person convicted, the number of the accessible parking permit used in the offence, the name and address of the person or organization in whose name the accessible parking permit is issued, the date the offence was committed and the provision of the by-law contravened.

(5) **Order for conditional discharge** — Where a person pleads guilty to or is found guilty of an offence under the *Criminal Code* (Canada), the *Young Offenders Act* (Canada) or the *Youth Criminal Justice Act* (Canada) referred to in subsection (1) and an order directing that the person be discharged is made under section 736 of the *Criminal Code* (Canada), section 20 or sections 28 to 32 of the *Young Offenders Act* (Canada) or section 42, 59, 94, 95 or 96 of the *Youth Criminal Justice Act* (Canada) including an order in respect of a person on whom an adult sentence is imposed under the *Youth Criminal Justice Act* (Canada), the judge, provincial judge or justice of the peace who makes the order or the clerk of the court in which the order is made shall forthwith notify the Registrar of the order.

(6) **Same** — A notice given under subsection (5) shall set out the name, address and description of the person discharged by the order, the number of the person's driver's licence, the number of the permit of the motor vehicle or the registration number of the motorized snow vehicle with which the offence was committed, the time the offence was committed and the provision of the *Criminal Code* (Canada), the *Young Offenders Act* (Canada) or the *Youth Criminal Justice Act* (Canada) contravened.

(7) **Evidence** — A copy of any document filed in the Ministry under this Act, or any statement containing information from the records required to be kept under this Act, that purports to be certified by the Registrar under the seal of the Ministry as being a true copy of the original shall be received in evidence in all courts without proof of the seal, the Registrar's signature or the manner of preparing the copy or

statement, and is proof, in the absence of evidence to the contrary, of the facts contained in the copy or statement.

(8) Signature of Registrar — The Registrar's signature on a copy or statement described in subsection (7) may be an original signature or an engraved, lithographed, printed or otherwise mechanically or electronically reproduced signature or facsimile signature.

(9) Seal of the Ministry — The seal of the Ministry on a copy or statement described in subsection (7) may be affixed by impression or may be an engraved, lithographed, printed or otherwise mechanically or electronically reproduced seal or facsimile of a seal.

(10) Signature and seal only required on first page — The Registrar's signature on a copy or statement described in subsection (7) need only be on the first page of the copy or statement.

(11) Same — The seal of the Ministry on a copy or statement described in subsection (7) need only be on the first page of the copy or statement if the following pages are sequentially numbered, by hand or otherwise; if the pages following the first page are not sequentially numbered, the seal must be on each page.

(12) Electronic filing in court — A copy or statement described in subsection (7) may be filed in a court by direct electronic transmission in accordance with the regulations.

(13) Regulations — The Lieutenant Governor in Council may make regulations respecting,

    (a) the filing of copies and statements in court by direct electronic transmission; and

    (b) the manner in which the signature of the Registrar and the seal of the Ministry may be represented when such a copy or statement is printed.

    (c) [Repealed 2008, c. 17, s. 46.]

(14) Definition — In this section,

"document" includes a photograph.

1998, c. 38, s. 6; 1999, c. 12, Sched. B, s. 9; 2002, c. 17, Sched. F, s. 1; 2006, c. 19, Sched. D, s. 9(5), (6); 2006, c. 20, s. 5; 2006, c. 32, Sched. C, s. 24(7); 2008, c. 17, s. 46; 2009, c. 5, s. 55; 2009, c. 33, Sched. 26, s. 3(13)

Commentary

Subsection (6) is a significant provision which can be relied upon by the prosecutor to prove the driving record and related information. As long as the signature requirement of the record (subs. (8)) is complied with, the record is admissible. In combination with the federal Evidence Act, the driving record may be used to assist in proving the prior provincial and Criminal Code provisions in a criminal trial.

The Red Light Camera Pilot Projects Act, 1998, S.O. 1998, c. 38 (in force November 20, 2000) permits evidence obtained from red light cameras to be used in areas designated by regulation for the purpose of enforcing subsection 144(18) of the Highway Traffic Act (failing to stop at a red light or proceeding before the light turns green). O. Reg. 277/99 dealing with the admissibility and use of Red Light Camera System evidence in proceedings under the Act, was brought into force contemporaneously with the Act.

Case Law

R. v. Coates (1981), 15 M.V.R. 70, 13 Sask. R. 242 (Q.B.) — A certified copy of registration of a private passenger vehicle as proof of ownership was permitted pursuant to the Saskatchewan Evidence Act, notwithstanding the absence of a provision in the Vehicles Act, similar to s. 210(7) of the Highway Traffic Act (Ont.).

R. v. Johnson (1982), 16 M.V.R. 197 (B.C. Prov. Ct.) — A certificate of the Superintendent of Motor Vehicles set out the fact of the licence suspension and the particulars of 11 previous offences under the Act. The references to the prior convictions were prejudicial and unauthorized, therefore the entire certificate ought not to be admitted.

R. v. Mays (1985), 37 M.V.R. 166 (Ont. C.A.) — The combined operation of s. 210(7) of the Act and ss. 36 and 37 of the Canada Evidence Act may be used to prove a prior Criminal Code conviction to satisfy s. 740 of the Criminal Code [now s. 594].

R. v. Matthes (1985), 32 M.V.R. 303 (B.C. S.C.) — The power of the Deputy Superintendent in British Columbia to sign in place of the Superintendent was referred to.

R. v. Triumbari (1988), 8 M.V.R. (2d) 1, 42 C.C.C. (3d) 481 (Ont. C.A.) — The accused was originally convicted of driving while his driver's licence was under suspension contrary to s. 53 of the Highway Traffic Act. His appeal was allowed in the Provincial Offences Appeal Court. That Court ruled that provisions in two statutes — the Provincial Offences Act and the Highway Traffic Act — which permitted the introduction of certificates of offences and suspensions were unconstitutional. The Charter was said to be violated by not giving the accused notice of intention and copies of the certificates prior to trial. The accused's rights to make full answer and defence were therefore said to be infringed. The Crown appealed. The appeal was allowed. It was held that ss. 210(7), (8) of the Act and s. 57(4) of the Provincial Offences Act (Ont.) did not violate the Charter. Both statutes clearly indicated that the certificates were only *prima facie* evidence of their contents. An accused was not precluded from challenging the accuracy or authenticity of the certificates.

R. v. Vlajkovic (1994), 5 M.V.R. (2d) 219, 74 O.A.C. 340 (Ont. C.A.) — Certified documents may be introduced by the Crown and need not be enforced through the testimony of the officer who ordered them from the Ministry.

R. v. Francis (1996), 22 M.V.R. (3d) 211 (Ont. C.A.) — Under s. 210(7), in the absence of evidence to the contrary, the certificate constitutes conclusive proof of the facts contained therein.

Kennedy v. B.C. (1998), 36 M.V.R. (3d) 73 (B.C. S.C.) — The plaintiff transport driver required an abstract of his driving record in the last five years for his employer. The plaintiff feared he would lose his job if three driving prohibitions were included. He petitioned for an order deleting the references. On a plain reading of the section the record had to contain particulars of any convictions, orders or judgments.

R. v. 2934752 Canada Inc. (1997), 17 M.V.R. (4th) 48 (Ont. Prov. Div.) — The driver produced registration documents and the officer made a note of same. The Crown could not rely on them as they were hearsay against the company. If the Crown could not produce original documents it had the ability to rely upon certified copies under the section which it failed to do here.

R. v. Finnie Distributing (1997) Inc., 2004 CarswellOnt 4529, 11 M.V.R. (5th) 179, 2004 ONCJ 256 (C.J.) — The phrase "in the absence of evidence to the contrary" refers not to the process of certification, but to the facts contained within the certified document. It is not necessary for a witness to identify the certified documents. To require such an identification process neither adds to nor detracts from the accuracy or authenticity. It results in an unnecessary and overly technical interpretation resulting in unnecessary attendance at court for a purely administrative process while defeating the intention of the legislation.

Related Provisions: See O. Reg. 499/94, Electronic Documents.

210.1 (1) Out-of-province evidence re vehicle ownership — A document or copy of a document certified by a provincial offences officer as having been obtained from the government of any province or territory of Canada or from the government of a state of the United States of America, or from a person or entity authorized by any such government to keep records of vehicle permits, number plates or other evidence of vehicle ownership in that jurisdiction, shall be received in evidence in all courts, without proof of the provincial offences officer's signature, of the manner of his or her obtaining, preparing or certifying the document or copy or of the origin of the document or copy, and is proof, in the absence of evidence to the contrary, of the facts contained in the document or copy in the following proceedings:

> **1.** A proceeding relating to the parking, standing or stopping of a vehicle contrary to any Act, regulation or by-law.
>
> **2.** A proceeding relating to a contravention of subsection 175(19) or (20).
>
> **3.** A proceeding that is based on evidence obtained through the use of a red light camera system.

(2) Certificate — The certificate described in subsection (1) must be signed by the provincial offences officer who obtained the document or copy of the document from a government, person or entity described in that subsection and attached to the document or copy.

(3) Signature — The signature of the provincial offences officer on the certificate may be an original signature or an engraved, lithographed, printed or otherwise mechanically or electronically reproduced signature or facsimile signature.

(4) Information re officer's position — The certificate must indicate the clause in the definition of "provincial offences officer" in subsection 1(1) of the *Provincial Offences Act* that describes the provincial offences officer's position as a provincial offences officer and, if his or her position is described in clause (f) of that definition, a copy of the designation must be reproduced in or attached to the certificate.

(5) Evidence attached to certificate of offence, certificate of parking infraction — Despite subsections (2) and (4), where evidence of the ownership of a vehicle obtained as described in subsection (1) is attached to a certificate of offence or to a certificate of parking infraction,

(a) the certificate that is required by subsection (1) may be attached to the certificate of offence or to the certificate of parking infraction or filed as a separate document; and

(b) the copy of the provincial offences officer's designation that is required by subsection (4) to be reproduced in or attached to the certificate that is required by subsection (1) may be attached to the certificate of offence or to the certificate of parking infraction or filed as a separate document.

2015, c. 14, s. 57

211. (1) Definition — In this section, "judge" means a judge, provincial judge or justice of the peace.

(2) Return of suspended driver's licence to Registrar — Subject to subsection (3), a person whose driver's licence is suspended by a judge or by operation of this Act shall immediately forward the driver's licence to the Registrar.

Proposed Amendment — 211(2)

(2) Return of suspended driver's licence to Registrar — Subject to subsections (3) and (4), a person whose driver's licence is suspended shall immediately forward the driver's licence to the Registrar.

2015, c. 14, s. 58(1) [Not in force at date of publication.]

(3) Judge to secure possession — Where a judge makes a conviction and the driver's licence of the person convicted is suspended by the judge or by operation of this Act, the judge shall take the driver's licence and forward it to the Registrar.

(4) [Repealed 2008, c. 17, s. 47.]

Proposed Amendment — 211(4)

(4) Exception — Subsection (2) does not apply to a person whose driver's licence is suspended under a provision or for a reason under this Act that is prescribed by regulation made under subsection (5).

2015, c. 14, s. 58(2) [Not in force at date of publication.]

Proposed Addition — 211(5)

(5) Regulations — The Minister may make regulations prescribing provisions and reasons under this Act for the purpose of subsection (4).

2015, c. 14, s. 58(2) [Not in force at date of publication.]

2008, c. 17, s. 47

Case Law

R. v. Jack (1981), 17 M.V.R. 77 (Ont. Prov. Ct.); *R. v. Boisvenu* (1975), 17 M.V.R. 86 (Ont. H.C.) — This section authorizes a judge to seize an out-of-province licence.

R. v. Ghany (1983), 19 M.V.R. 169 (Ont. C.A.) — For the surrender of a licence to be complete there must be a receipt by the Registrar of the licence for the 30-day period (which, it should be noted, is set out in s. 7 of the regulations and not in s. 185(2) of the statute) to start running. "Surrender" is defined in the *Concise Oxford Dictionary* as meaning "and over, give to another's power or control, relinquish possession of." If the commonly understood meaning of surrender were not accepted, it is difficult to see how the system could be effectively operated and controlled, which is, of course, not conclusive of the matter, but assists in supporting an ordinary and sensible interpretation of the word "surrender" in the context in which it is used in the section.

Related Provisions: See s. 56 of the Act.

212. (1) Police officer may secure possession — Where by or under the provisions of this Act a driver's licence is suspended and the person to whom the suspension applies refuses or fails to surrender his or her licence to the Registrar forthwith, any police officer may take possession of the licence and return it to the Registrar and the Registrar may direct any police officer to take possession of the licence and return it to the Registrar.

> ### Proposed Amendment — 212(1)
>
> **(1) Police officer may secure possession of suspended licence** — Where a person who is required by section 211 to immediately forward his or her suspended driver's licence to the Registrar refuses or fails to do so, any police officer may take possession of the licence and return it to the Registrar and the Registrar may direct any police officer to take possession of the licence and return it to the Registrar.
>
> 2015, c. 14, s. 59 [Not in force at date of publication.]

(2) Penalty — Every person who fails or refuses to surrender his or her driver's licence when required by a police officer under subsection (1) is guilty of an offence and on conviction is liable to a fine of not more than $100.

(3) [Repealed 2008, c. 17, s. 48.]

2008, c. 17, s. 48

213. (1) When owner may appear before justice of the peace — If an owner of a motor vehicle is served with a summons to appear in a local municipality other than that in which the owner resides for an offence against this Act, and the owner's defence is that neither the owner nor the owner's motor vehicle was at the place of the alleged offence at the time the offence occurred, and that the summons must have been issued against the owner through an error of the informant as to the number on the official number plate, then and in that case only the owner may appear before a justice of the peace in the local municipality in which the owner resides and, in the same manner as if the owner were being tried for an offence against this Act, the owner may give evidence corroborated by the evidence of at least two other credible witnesses that neither the owner nor the owner's motor vehicle was at the place of the alleged offence at the time the offence occurred, and that the summons must have been issued against the owner through an error of the informant as to the number on the official number plate.

(2) Certificate — The justice, if satisfied of the truth of the evidence, shall forthwith make out a certificate in English or in French in the form set out in the Schedule to this Act and forward it by registered mail to the justice before whom the summons is returnable.

(3) Dismissal or adjournment — The justice before whom the summons is returnable shall, upon receiving the certificate, thereupon dismiss the charge unless he or she has reason to believe that the testimony is untrue in whole or in part, in which case he or she may adjourn the case and again summon the defendant, who shall then be required to attend before him or her at the place and time mentioned in the summons.

Commentary

Section 213 establishes a mechanism by which cases of mistaken identity may be addressed for offences under the Act. Where an owner is served with a summons to appear in another municipality, and the owner's defence is that neither he or she nor the owner's car were in the other municipality at the relevant time, the owner, supported by two witnesses, may appear before a Justice of the Peace in the local municipality to give evidence. That Justice shall forward a certificate to a Justice of the Peace in the locality to which the summons is returnable, who shall decide to dismiss the charges or adjourn to hear the defendant.

214. (1) General penalty — Every person who contravenes this Act or any regulation is guilty of an offence and on conviction, where a penalty for the contravention is not otherwise provided for herein, is liable to a fine of not less than $60 and not more than $500.

(2) For pedestrian offences — Despite subsection (1), every person, while a pedestrian or a person in a wheelchair, who contravenes Part X or any regulation made thereunder, is guilty of an offence and on conviction, where a penalty for the contravention is not otherwise provided for herein, is liable to a fine of not more than $50.

Related Provisions: The Regulatory Modernization Act, 2007, S.O. 2007, c. 4 provides as follows:

> 15. (1) Previous conviction — This section applies when a person who is convicted of an offence has previously been convicted of an offence under the same or another Act.
>
> (2) Same — The previous conviction may have occurred at any time, including before the day this Act came into force.
>
> (3) Severity of Penalty — Where the prosecuter is of the opinion that the previous conviction is relevant to the determination of the appropriate penalty for the current conviction, he or she may request that the court consider the previous conviction to be an aggravating factor.
>
> (4) Response of court — Where a court recieves a request under subsection (3), the court shall, on imposing the penalty,
>
> > (a) indicate whether it is imposing a more severe penalty having regard to the previous conviction; and
> >
> > (b) if the court decides that the previous conviction does not justify a more severe penalty, give reasons for that decision.

(5) **Other factors still relevant** — Nothing in this section shall be interpreted as limiting any factor, submission or inquiry as to penalty the court is otherwise permitted or required to take into account or make, as the case may be.

.

214.1 (1) **Community safety zone designated on municipal highways** — The council of a municipality may by by-law designate a part of a highway under its jurisdiction as a community safety zone if, in the council's opinion, public safety is of special concern on that part of the highway.

(2) **Community safety zone designated on non-municipal highways** — The Minister of Community Safety and Correctional Services may by regulation designate a part of a provincial highway or of any highway that is not under the jurisdiction of a municipality as a community safety zone if, in his or her opinion, public safety is of special concern on that part of the highway.

(3) **When designation is in effect** — A by-law or regulation designating a community safety zone shall specify the hours, days and months when the designation is in effect.

(4) **Signs** — The municipality or the Minister of Community Safety and Correctional Services, as the case may be, shall ensure that signs denoting a community safety zone are erected in accordance with the regulations.

(5) **Designation not effective until signs are erected** — No by-law or regulation made under this section becomes effective until signs are erected, in accordance with this Act and the regulations, on the designated part of the highway.

(6) **Penalty for speeding in community safety zone** — Every person who commits an offence under section 128 in a community safety zone when it is in effect is liable, on conviction, not to the fines set out in subsection 128(14), but, where the rate of speed at which the motor vehicle was driven,

(a) is less than 20 kilometres per hour over the speed limit, to a fine of double the fine set out in clause 128(14)(a) for each kilometre per hour that the motor vehicle was driven over the speed limit;

(b) is 20 kilometres per hour or more but less than 30 kilometres per hour over the speed limit, to a fine of double the fine set out in clause 128(14)(b) for each kilometre per hour that the motor vehicle was driven over the speed limit;

(c) is 30 kilometres per hour or more but less than 50 kilometres per hour over the speed limit, to a fine of double the fine set out in clause 128(14)(c) for each kilometre per hour that the motor vehicle was driven over the speed limit; and

(d) is 50 kilometres per hour or more over the speed limit, to a fine of double the fine set out in clause 128(14)(d) for each kilometre per hour that the motor vehicle was driven over the speed limit.

(6.1) **Same, construction zone** — Every person who commits an offence under section 128 in a community safety zone, when it is in effect, that is also a construction zone designated under subsection 128(8) or (8.1), when there is a worker in the construction zone, is liable, on conviction, to the penalties set out in subsection (6) and not to an additional penalty under subsection 128(14.1).

(7) Penalty for careless driving or racing in community safety zone — Every person who commits an offence under section 130 or 172 in a community safety zone when it is in effect is liable, on conviction, not to the penalty set out in those sections, but to a fine of not less than double the minimum fine set out in those sections and not more than the maximum fine set out in those sections or to imprisonment for a term of not more than six months, or to both, and in addition his or her licence or permit may be suspended for a period of not more than the maximum period for which his or her licence could be ordered suspended by a court under section 130 or 172, as the case may be.

(8) Penalty for other offences in community safety zone — Every person who commits an offence in contravention of any of section 132 to 164, inclusive (except subsections 140(4) and (6) and subsections 144(22) to (29), inclusive), section 166, 167, 168 or 169, subsection 176(3) or section 182 in a community safety zone when it is in effect is liable, on conviction, not to the penalty otherwise applicable, but to a fine of not less than double the minimum fine otherwise applicable and not more than the maximum fine otherwise applicable.

1993, c. 31, s. 2(12); 1998, c. 6, s. 1; 1999, c. 12, Sched. B, s. 9; 2005, c. 26, Sched. A, s. 32; 2006, c. 19, Sched. T, s. 7; 2007, c. 13, s. 23

Commentary

As of April 2009, the fine was increased to $500. Several other specific offences saw large increases to fines, such as seat belts, careless driving, not stopping at a red light, failing to remain.

Related Provisions: See O. Reg. 510/99, Community Safety Zones; R.R.O. 1990, Reg. 615, Signs, s. 5.2.

215. [Repealed 2009, c. 33, Sched. 26, s. 3(14).]

Commentary

Prior to the re-enactment of s. 215(2) as set out above, the subsection read as follows:

(2) Notwithstanding anything in the *Provincial Offences Act*, where in a designated municipality a justice convicts a person of a prescribed offence and the person, on the recommendation of the justice, attends and successfully completes a driver improvement program conducted by the Ministry, the justice may impose a lesser fine than the fine otherwise provided for by this Act or may order that no fine shall be imposed upon the person in respect of the offence.

The change to the subsection was necessitated by the decision in *R. v. Sortino* (1981), 10 M.V.R. 193, 60 C.C.C. (2d) 166 (Ont. C.A.).

Case Law

R. v. Sortino (1981), 10 M.V.R. 193, 60 C.C.C. (2d) 106 (Ont. C.A.) — The respondent pleaded guilty with an explanation to the offence of speeding. The Justice of the Peace imposed a fine but ordered that the fine be suspended if the respondent would attend the driver improvement centre on or before a fixed date. The respondent agreed to attend but failed to show up. He was sent a notice that the fine was due. He appealed, raising the ground that he had missed the programme due to an illness in his family. On the appeal the sentence was quashed as being one not contemplated by the legislation. The Crown appealed. It was held that s. 152a(2) [now s.215(2)] of the Highway Traffic Act (Ont.) does not contemplate passing a sentence that is suspended subject to the performance of a condition. The Justice must first convict. He or she then may make a recommendation for attendance at a driver improvement programme. The offender must then attend and successfully complete the programme. The driver must then re-attend before the Justice in order for the Justice to determine whether a lesser fine or no fine shall be imposed in respect of the prescribed offence.

R. v. Joe (1992), 41 M.V.R. (2d) 288, 80 Man. R. (2d) 281 (Q.B.); reversed in part (1993), 50 M.V.R. (2d) 179, [1994] 3 W.W.R. 1, 27 C.R. (4th) 79, 92 Man. R. (2d) 8, 87 C.C.C. (3d) 234, 61 W.A.C. 8 (C.A.) — Imprisonment for failure to complete a fine option programme does not violate s. 12 of the Charter of Rights.

Related Provisions: See R.R.O. 1990, Reg. 582, Driver Improvement Program.

216. (1) Power of police officer to stop vehicle — A police officer, in the lawful execution of his or her duties and responsibilities, may require the driver of a motor vehicle to stop and the driver of a motor vehicle, when signalled or requested to stop by a police officer who is readily identifiable as such, shall immediately come to a safe stop.

Proposed Amendment — 216(1)

(1) Power of police officer to stop vehicles — A police officer, in the lawful execution of his or her duties and responsibilities, may require the driver of a vehicle, other than a bicycle, to stop and the driver of a vehicle, when signalled or requested to stop by a police officer who is readily identifiable as such, shall immediately come to a safe stop.

2016, c. 5, Sched. 12, s. 9 [Not in force at date of publication.]

(2) Offence — Every person who contravenes subsection (1) is guilty of an offence and on conviction is liable, subject to subsection (3),

    (a) to a fine of not less than $1,000 and not more than $10,000;

    (b) to imprisonment for a term of not more than six months; or

    (c) to both a fine and imprisonment.

(3) Escape by flight — If a person is convicted of an offence under subsection (2) and the court is satisfied on the evidence that the person wilfully continued to avoid police when a police officer gave pursuit,

    (a) the person is liable to a fine of not less than $5,000 and not more than $25,000, instead of the fine described in clause (2)(a);

    (b) the court shall make an order imprisoning the person for a term of not less than 14 days and not more than six months, instead of the term described in clause (2)(b); and

(c) the court shall make an order suspending the person's driver's licence,

    (i) for a period of five years, unless subclause (ii) applies, or

    (ii) for a period of not less than 10 years, if the court is satisfied on the evidence that the person's conduct or the pursuit resulted in the death of or bodily harm to any person.

(4) Lifetime suspension — An order under subclause (3)(c)(ii) may suspend the person's driver's licence for the remainder of the person's life.

(4.1) Suspension in addition — Except in the case of a suspension for the remainder of the person's life, a suspension under clause (3)(c) is in addition to any other period for which the person's licence is suspended and is consecutive to that period.

(4.2) Notice of suspension — Subject to subsection (4.3), in a proceeding for a contravention of subsection (1) in which it is alleged that the person wilfully continued to avoid police when a police officer gave pursuit, the clerk or registrar of the court, before the court accepts the plea of the defendant, shall orally give a notice to the person to the following effect:

The Highway Traffic Act provides that upon conviction of the offence with which you are charged, in the circumstances indicated therein, your driver's licence shall be suspended for five years.

(4.3) Same: death or bodily harm — In a proceeding for a contravention of subsection (1) in which it is alleged that the person wilfully continued to avoid police when a police officer gave pursuit and that the person's conduct or the pursuit resulted in the death of or bodily harm to any person, the clerk or registrar of the court, before the court accepts the plea of the defendant, shall orally give a notice to the person to the following effect:

The Highway Traffic Act provides that upon conviction of the offence with which you are charged, in the circumstances indicated therein, your driver's licence shall be suspended for not less than 10 years and that it may be suspended for the remainder of your life.

(5) Idem — The suspension of a driver's licence under this section shall not be held to be invalid by reason of failure to give the notice provided for in subsection (4.2) or (4.3).

(6) Appeal of suspension — An appeal may be taken from an order under clause (3)(c) or a decision to not make the order in the same manner as from a conviction or an acquittal under subsection (2).

(7) Stay of order on appeal — Where an appeal is taken from an order under subsection (6), the court being appealed to may direct that the order being appealed from shall be stayed pending the final disposition of the appeal or until otherwise ordered by that court.

1999, c. 13, s. 1

Commentary

Section 216 was introduced along with s. 48 in Bill 178 [en. 1981, c. 72]. Section 216(1) provides for a general power to stop a driver when a police officer is acting in the lawful execution of his or her duties. Section 48(1) provides for a specific power to stop in the drinking and driving area. Introduction of the Bill followed the observation of the Ontario Court of Appeal in *R. v. Dedman*, [1985] 2 S.C.R. 2, affirming (1981), 32 O.R. (2d) 641, 10 M.V.R. 59 (C.A.), which reversed (1980), 30 O.R. (2d) 555, 8 M.V.R. 142 (H.C.), which affirmed (1980), 30 O.R. (2d) 555 at 557, 6 M.V.R. 233 (Prov. Ct.), that the Highway Traffic Act of Ontario did not contain a general power on the part of the police to stop drivers.

Also found in s. 216 is a substantial suspension for escape by flight [subs. (3)] which is aimed at aggravated examples of conduct covered by s. 216(1) that arise in a police chase. A finding of escape by flight may only be made following a conviction for failing to obey a police officer under s. 216(1). It appears that the Crown must allege the particulars of the desired finding in the information. The defendant must be notified in court before plea that the Crown is pursuing the three-year suspension. Following a conviction, the court must be satisfied on the evidence that the conduct falls within s. 216(3). Presumably, the evidence on the s. 216(3) hearing is the same evidence that gave rise to the s. 216(2) conviction. No new evidence may be called. If a breach of s. 216(1) is not alleged there can be no s. 216(3) finding. The defendant has a right of appeal from the s. 216(3) finding [s. 216(6)] and may obtain a stay pending appeal [s. 216(7)]. The Crown has a right of appeal from a decision not to make a s. 216(3) order [s. 216(6)] which may be contrasted with its position under s. 41 of the Highway Traffic Act.

On January 1, 2000, s. 216 was amended by The Sergeant Rick McDonald Memorial Act (Suspect Apprehension Pursuits), 1999, S.O. 1999, c. 13. The Act increased the penalties for failing to stop when requested by a police officer. The minimum fine for the offence committed in ordinary circumstances was increased from $500 to $1,000 and the maximum from $5,000 to $10,000. In circumstances where a driver wilfully continues to avoid police while being pursued, the minimum and maximum fines were introduced at $5,000 and $25,000 respectively with a minimum jail sentence of 14 days. Driving suspensions were increased. The ordinary suspension is 3 years. Where flight occurs it is 5 years. Where bodily harm or death results it is at least 10 years.

Case Law

R. v. Brisson; *R. v. Kennedy* (1986), 37 M.V.R. 313, 13 O.A.C. 27 (C.A.); affirming *R. v. Kennedy* (1984), 29 M.V.R. 145 (Co. Ct.) — Sections 189a(1) and (2) [now ss. 216(1) and (2)] of the Highway Traffic Act make it an offence for a driver to fail to stop in response to the command of a police officer. Section 189a(3) [now s. 216(3)] does not create an offence, but goes to the penalty for a driver who is guilty of the offence created by ss. 189a(1) and (2). If the court finds that a driver who is guilty of failing to stop in response to an order of a police officer wilfully continues to avoid police while a police officer gives pursuit then the court must impose the penalty provided in s. 189a(3). The principle in *Kienapple v. R.*, [1975] 1 S.C.R. 729, does not deal with penalties. The duty to stop in response to an order of a police officer and to avoid police chases is quite different from the duty to drive with care which can, depending on the circumstances, give rise to a conviction of careless driving or perhaps dangerous driving under the Criminal Code. The purpose underlying s. 189a is quite different from that underlying the legislation creating the offence of careless driving or the crime of dangerous driving. The first is to clothe police with authority to stop a driver and make it an offence if the driver fails to obey with special penalties if he or she continues to avoid police pursuit. The legislative purpose with respect to careless or dangerous driving is to protect the public from the danger on the highway of driving in the manner defined and punish those who drive in that way. If a driver is intent on attempting to avoid police after failing to stop in response to their order it does not matter whether he or she drives with care. To drive carefully around the corner and hide in a driveway would be enough to bring down the additional penalty under s. 189a(3).

Ueffing v. R. (1980), 7 M.V.R. 155 (N.S. C.A.) — The appellant was found to have been properly convicted of dangerous driving and the provincial offence of failey to obey the signal of a police officer but the provincial offence was based on conduct preceding the commencement of pursuit and the charge of dangerous driving founded on the manner of driving during the chase.

R. v. Dilorenzo; *R. v. Bancroft* (1984), 26 M.V.R. 259, 45 O.R. (2d) 385, 11 C.C.C. (3d) 13, 2 O.A.C. 62 (C.A.) — *The Standard of Proof* — The burden of proof required to justify a conviction under ss. 189a(1) and (2) [now ss. 216(1) and (2)] of the Highway Traffic Act is lower than that required to justify the imposition of the penalty prescribed by s. 189a(3) [now s. 216(3)]. The offence created by s. 189a(1) was a "strict liability offence" in which there was no necessity for the prosecution to prove the existence of *mens rea*. The doing of the prohibited act *prima facie* imported the offence, leaving it open to the accused to avoid liability by proving that he took all reasonable care. Section 189a(3) did not create a specific offence but rather related to penalty and specified circumstances in which a three-year licence suspension must be ordered. Before the order may be made, the court must be "satisfied" that the person convicted under s. 189a(1) engaged in a particular type of aggravated conduct in that he "wilfully continued to avoid police whiler a police officer gave pursuit." The word "wilfully" used in this context meant with the intention of avoiding the police and must be construed so as to import *mens rea*. The use of the word "satisfied" does not detract from the wilful nature of the conduct against which the subsection was aimed and could be read as having the effect of providing for a test on the balance of probabilities. Section 189a(3) required the prosecution to prove *mens rea* beyond a reasonable doubt as a precondition to the mandatory licence suspension presribed by the subsection.

The "Readily Identifiable" Issue — The defendant knew that the person seeking to stop him was a police officer. This knowledge was not subjective to him or based on anything other than his identification of the officer who at the time was wearing a blue police shirt and identifying shoulder patches plainly visible. Having regard to the objective evidence and the findings made by the trial Judge in his reasons, it was patent that he was satisfied that the police officer was readily identifiable to him and that the prosecution had proved this ingredient of the charge.

Is There a Discretion to Impose Less Than a Three-Year Suspension? — Section 60(1) [now s. 59(1)] of the Provincial Offences Act provided that no penalty was a minimum penalty unless it was specifically declared to be a minimum penalty. The words "the court shall make an order suspending the driver's licence for a period of three years" in s. 189a(3) of the Highway Traffic Act were clear and incapable of misunderstanding. The licence was to be suspended for three years, no more, no less. The Legislature, if not in so many words, had specifically declared the minimum penalty and no basis existed upon which to vary or modify its manifest intention.

The Absence of an Allegation of the Circumstances Set Out in s. 189a(3) — Section 189a(4) [now s. 216(4)] clearly contemplated an allegation of the circumstances set out in s. 189a(3) in the information if s. 189a(3) was to be invoked. Section 189a(4) spoke of "a proceeding for a contravention of subsection (1) *in which the circumstances set out in subsection (3) are alleged*" and provided, in the case of such an allegation, for a form of notice to be given to the defendant before plea, which assumes the inclusion of an allegation of the circumstances set out in s. 189a(3) in the charge. Section 189a(5) [now s. 216(5)] operated to cure a failure to give the s. 189a(4) notice, but this did not eliminate the requirement of the allegation specified in s. 189a(4) which triggered the necessity to give notice. If the Crown seeks the imposition of the further penalty prescribed by s. 189a(3), it must allege the wilful conduct referred to therein in the information. This ensured that a person charged with contravening s. 189a(1) was reasonably informed prior to trial of the additional allegation against him. In neither of the present cases did the informations contain any allegation referable to s. 189a(3).

R. v. Martel (1987), 7 M.V.R. (2d) 33 (Ont. Dist. Ct.) — The accused was convicted of failing to stop her vehicle contrary to s. 216(1) of the Highway Traffic Act. She was sentenced under the provisions of s. 216(3) on the basis that she had "wilfully continued to avoid police while a police officer gave pursuit." The facts revealed that a police officer observed her vehicle being operated late at night with its emergency flashers activated instead of its headlights. The officer pursued the vehicle and turned on his flashing roof light. The accused's vehicle was travelling at a speed of 90 km/h in a 60 km/h zone. On two occasions she stopped her vehicle only to speed off when approached by the officer on foot. She eventually turned into her driveway after a distance of about five miles. The appeal was allowed. The evidence did not indicate that the accused was attempting to avoid the police. She had travelled on two of the busiest streets in the vicinity and her flashers were in continual operation so as to be visible to the police officer. There had been no attempt to avoid the police in the sense of her driving consisting of driving tactics that would allow her to escape or evade the police. The appeal as to the penalty under s. 216(3) was therefore allowed.

R. v. Ladouceur, [1990] 1 S.C.R. 1257, 77 C.R. (3d) 110, 56 C.C.C. (3d) 22, 73 O.R. (2d) 736, 21 M.V.R. (2d) 165, 108 N.R. 171, 40 O.A.C. 1, 48 C.R.R. 112 — The case raised the issue of whether the so-called "routine check" random stops of motorists by police violate s. 7, 8 or 9 of the Canadian Charter of Rights and Freedoms and, if so, whether they can be justified pursuant to s. 1 of the Charter. The random stops conducted under the spot check program and authorized by s. 189a(1) [now s. 216(1)] of the Highway Traffic Act did not violate the Charter. Although the random stop constituted arbitrary detention in violation of s. 9 of the Charter it was justified under s. 1. The random stop did not constitute an unreasonable search and seizure in violation of s. 8 of the Charter. There is no distinction between an organized program of roadside spot checks or the constitutionality of completely random stops conducted by police as part of a routine check which was not part of any organized program. It might well be that since these stops lack any organized structure, they should be treated as constitutionally more suspect than stops conducted under an organized program. Nonetheless, so long as the police officer making the stop is acting lawfully within the scope of a statute, the random stops can be justifiably conducted in accordance with the Charter. The detention was arbitrary, since the decision as to whether the stop should be made lay in the absolute discretion of the police officers. There can thus be no doubt that the routine check random stop constituted an arbitrary detention in violation of s. 9 of the Charter. There is no s. 8 intrusion where a person is required to produce a licence or permit or other documentary evidence of a status or compliance with some legal requirement that is a lawful condition of the exercise of a right or privilege. Since it has been determined that routine check random stops violate s. 9 of the Charter, it was unnecessary to decide whether these random stops infringed s. 7. Routine checks are a justifiable infringement on the rights conferred by s. 9.

R. v. Wilson, [1990] 1 S.C.R. 1291, 77 C.R. (3d) 137, 56 C.C.C. (3d) 142, 74 Alta. L.R. (2d) 1, [1990] 5 W.W.R. 188, 108 W.R. 207, 107 A.R. 321; affirming (1987), 76 A.R. 315 (C.A.) — Released the same date as *R. v. Ladouceur, supra*, the Court came to the same conclusion regarding s. 119 of the Highway Traffic Act (Alta.) in circumstances in which a policeman stopped appellant, even though he had no reason to believe he was doing anything wrong. The stop was not part of Alberta's Checkstop Programme but it was part of floating spotcheck in a given area on the part of the officer. The vehicle was registered out-of-province and was a block away from a small town hotel whose bar had just closed; the officer did not recognize either the vehicle or any of the three men in the front seat. Appellant showed signs of impairment, failed a breathalyzer test, and was charged with and convicted of impaired driving.

R. v. Bunting (1983), 26 M.V.R. 23 (B.C. Co. Ct.) — It would be putting an undue onus upon the Crown to require it to prove beyond a reasonable doubt that an accused knew or saw or was unable to see that a police officer was a person who was readily identifiable as a police officer. It must be conveyed to the person stopped, or to be stopped, that the officer was readily identifiable to him or her as a police officer. On the other hand, having established that all those other matters were readily observable by the reasonable person, if the person being requested or signalled to stop does not do so, the onus is upon him or her to present evidence, either by way of crossexamination or by way of adducing direct evidence of establishing the defence of a reasonable mistake. The only evidence before the trial Judge was very simple. The police officer was dressed in uniform, was driving a police car properly marked as a police car, was flashing wigwag and emergency lights and the accused's car was within four or five lengths of that car. The only inference that could be drawn was that the accused did know and was able to readily recognize that person as being a police officer following him.

R. v. Hisey (1985), 40 M.V.R. 152, 24 C.C.C. (3d) 20, 12 O.A.C. 191 (C.A.); leave to appeal to S.C.C. refused (1986), 40 M.V.R. 152n, 67 N.R. 160 (note), 16 O.A.C. 79 (note) — The issue before the Court was whether s. 189a [now s. 216] of the Highway Traffic Act of Ontario was either *ultra vires* the province or rendered inoperative because it was in conflict with s. 118(a) [now s. 129, obstruct justice] of the Criminal Code. Section 118(a) of the Criminal Code made it an offence to obstruct an officer in the execution of his duties. It was held that section 189a of the Highway Traffic Act was valid. The province had power to regulate motor vehicle traffic under s. 92 subs. 10, 13, and 16 of the Constitution Act, 1867; the fact that s. 189a was not limited to the regulation of trafic on highways was therefore of no consequence as the power of the province in this regard was not so circumscribed. Section 189a did not constitute an intrusion into criminal law, as the *gravamen* of the section was to confer on police officers the power to require motor vehicles to stop and its offence creation feature was subsidiary and ancillary to the conferral of the power to stop. Furthermore, there was no conflict between s. 189a and s. 118(a) of the Criminal Code.

R. v. Leblanc (1988), 4 M.V.R. (2d) 79 (N.B. Q.B.) — Evidence of a marked police car was sufficient to render a peace officer recognizable as such within the meaning of s. 105.1(2) of the New Brunswick Act.

R. v. Smood, [1985] B.C.W.L.D. 1295 (Co. Ct.) — A police officer acting under this section is not required to use any form of manual signalling when requesting a driver to stop. The request to stop may be inferred from the fact of the chase itself and the use of emergency equipment such as flashing lights, without the additional requirement that the officer actually get out of his or her car and order the driver to stop.

R. v. Simpson (1993), 12 O.R. (3d) 182, 43 M.V.R. (2d) 1, 20 C.R. (4th) 1, 79 C.C.C. (3d) 482, 60 O.A.C. 327, 14 C.R.R. (2d) 338 (C.A.) — Only those stops made for the purpose of enforcing driving laws and promoting the safe use of motor vehicles are authorized by s. 216(1), even where those stops are random. A stop and detention under the section to investigate a possible narcotics offence is also not authorized under the common law and s. 8 of the Charter of Rights would be breached. Evidence would have to be excluded under s. 24(2).

R. v. Parker (1992), 41 M.V.R. (2d) 257 (Ont. Gen. Div.) — The fact that an attempt to evade the police may be futile or unsuccessful does not imply that an attempt was not intended to be made.

R. v. MacLennan (1995), 11 M.V.R. (3d) 42, 97 C.C.C. (3d) 69 (N.S. C.A.); reversing (1994), 133 N.S.R. (2d) 196, 380 A.P.R. 196 (S.C.) — Random stops under appropriate provincial legislation infringe s. 9 of the Charter but are justified under s. 1.

R. v. Douglas (1997), 29 M.V.R. (3d) 161 (Ont. Prov. Ct.) — The police gave the defendant a signal to stop while on a paved surface of an apartment building's driveway and parking lot. He was not guilty of failing to obey a lawful signal by a police officer to stop as the paved surface was not a highway.

Brown v. Durham Regional Police Force (1998), 39 M.V.R. (3d) 133, 21 C.R. (5th) 1, 131 C.C.C. (3d) 1, 167 D.L.R. (4th) 672, 116 O.A.C. 126, 43 O.R. (3d) 223 (Ont. C.A.) — Motorcycle club members were stopped on four weekends at checkpoints while on their way to club meetings. Members unsuccessfully brought an action against the police, alleging that their rights under s. 9 of the Charter were violated. Section 216(1) provided lawful authority for checkpoints for highway safety purposes. Section 216 cause is not required under the section to stop.

R. v. Del Ben (2000), 1 M.V.R. (4th) 129, 73 C.R.R. (2d) 175 (Ont. S.C.J.) — Targeted spot checks, for example in relation to a tavern, are not illegal provided the criteria for spot checks are derived from sobriety and/or highway traffic concerns.

R. v. Rempel (2001), 12 M.V.R. (4th) 20 (Sask. Prov. Ct.) — The offence is one of strict liability. Where the accused failed to see lights or hear sirens over 11 blocks, it was due to excessive speed and dangerous driving, which did not amount to a defence.

R. v. Leung (2002), 22 M.V.R. (4th) 53, 2002 CarswellOnt 60 (Ont. S.C.J.) — Once the trial judge rejected the evidence that the driver did not see the officer it was open to conclude that the speed and turns executed by the driver supported a finding that he knew he was being followed and was avoiding the cruiser.

R. v. Coates (2003), 176 C.C.C. (3d) 215, 107 C.R.R. (2d) 293, [2003] O.J. No. 2295, 43 M.V.R. (4th) 241, 2003 CarswellOnt 2203, 172 O.A.C. 330 (Ont. C.A.) — The existence of other lawful police purposes such as investigation of other criminal activity and intelligence gathering, in addition to highway safety concerns, does not taint the lawfulness of the stop.

R. v. Lee (2003), 2003 CarswellOnt 6420, 16 M.V.R. (5th) 30 (S.C.J.) — A trier should take into account that the officer is in plain clothes and in an unmarked vehicle that is most unlike a police vehicle.

Related Provisions: See O. Reg. 340/94, Drivers' Licences, s. 9.

216.1 (1) Power of officer to examine commercial vehicles — Any officer appointed for carrying out the provisions of this Act may, at any time, examine any commercial vehicle and its contents and equipment for the purpose of ascertaining whether this Act, the *Compulsory Automobile Insurance Act* or the *Dangerous Goods Transportation Act*, or the regulations under any of them, are being complied with, and the driver, operator or other person in control of the vehicle shall assist in the examination.

Proposed Amendment — 216.1(1)

(1) Power of officer to examine commercial vehicles, road-building machines — Any officer appointed for carrying out the provisions of this Act may, at any time, examine any commercial vehicle or road-building machine and its contents and equipment for the purpose of ascertaining whether this Act, the *Compulsory Automobile Insurance Act* or the *Dangerous Goods Transportation Act*, or the regulations under any of them, are being complied with, and the driver, operator or other person in control of the vehicle shall assist in the examination.

2016, c. 5, Sched. 12, s. 10(1) [Not in force at date of publication.]

(2) Power to stop commercial vehicles — Any officer appointed for carrying out the provisions of this Act may, for the purpose of an examination under subsection (1), direct, by signals or otherwise, the driver of any commercial vehicle driven on a highway to stop, and the driver, upon being so directed, shall stop the vehicle.

Proposed Amendment — 216.1(2)

(2) Power to stop commercial vehicles, road-building machines — Any officer appointed for carrying out the provisions of this Act, in the lawful execution of his or her duties and responsibilities, including for the purpose of an examination under subsection (1), may direct, by signals or otherwise, the driver of any commercial vehicle or road-building machine driven on a highway to stop, and the driver, upon being so directed, shall stop the vehicle.

2016, c. 5, Sched. 12, s. 10(1) [Not in force at date of publication.]

(3) Surrender of documents — Where a commercial vehicle and its contents and equipment are examined under this section, the officer conducting the examination may require the driver, operator or other person in control of the vehicle to surrender all documents relating to the ownership and operation of the vehicle and to the carriage of the goods, and to furnish all information within that person's knowledge relating to the details of the current trip.

Proposed Amendment — 216.1(3)

(3) Surrender of documents — Where a commercial vehicle or road-building machine and its contents and equipment are examined under this section, the officer conducting the examination may require the driver, operator or other person in control of the vehicle to surrender all documents relating to the ownership and operation of the vehicle and to the carriage of the goods, and to furnish all information within that person's knowledge relating to the details of the current trip.

2016, c. 5, Sched. 12, s. 10(2) [Not in force at date of publication.]

(4) Copies — An officer obtaining a document under subsection (3) may take the document for the purpose of making a copy of it, but the copying shall be done as quickly as reasonably possible and the document copied shall be promptly returned.

(5) Same — Any copy made as provided in subsection (4) and certified to be a true copy by the person making it is admissible in evidence in any proceeding as proof, in the absence of evidence to the contrary, of the original document and of the contents of the original document.

(6) Remove vehicle from the highway until in compliance — Where an officer appointed for carrying out the provisions of this Act is of the opinion, on reasonable and probable grounds, that a commercial vehicle is being operated in contravention of this Act, the *Compulsory Automobile Insurance Act* or the *Dangerous Goods Transportation Act*, or the regulations under any of them, the officer may,

Proposed Amendment — 216.1(6) opening words

(6) Remove vehicle from the highway until in compliance — Where an officer appointed for carrying out the provisions of this Act is of the opinion, on reasonable and probable grounds, that a commercial vehicle or road-building machine is being operated in contravention of this Act, the *Compulsory Automobile Insurance Act* or the *Dangerous Goods Transportation Act*, or the regulations under any of them, the officer may,

2016, c. 5, Sched. 12, s. 10(3) [Not in force at date of publication.]

(a) direct the driver of the vehicle to drive the vehicle to such location as is reasonable in the circumstances and detain it at that location; and

(b) seize the permits and number plates for the vehicle, until the vehicle is able to be operated in compliance with this Act, the *Compulsory Automobile Insurance Act*, the *Dangerous Goods Transportation Act* and the *Public Vehicles Act*, and the regulations under them.

(7) Duty to comply with direction — Every driver who is directed under clause (6)(a) shall comply with the direction.

(8) Offence — Every person who contravenes subsection (1), (2), (3) or (7) is guilty of an offence and upon conviction is liable to a fine of not less than $250 and not more than $20,000.

(9) Definition — For the purposes of this section,

"commercial vehicle" means a commercial motor vehicle and a motor vehicle towing a trailer.

Proposed Addition — 216.1(10)

(10) Regulations — **The Lieutenant Governor in Council may make regulations defining "operator" for the purposes of this section.**

2015, c. 27, Sched. 7, s. 27 [Not in force at date of publication.]

2002, c. 18, Sched. P, s. 37

Case Law

R. v. Nolet, 2010 SCC 24, 2010 CarswellSask 368, [2010] S.C.J. No. 24, [2010] 1 S.C.R. 851, 256 C.C.C. (3d) 1, 320 D.L.R. (4th) 1, 213 C.R.R. (2d) 52, 403 N.R. 1, 76 C.R. (6th) 1, 350 Sask. R. 51, 487 W.A.C. 51, [2010] 8 W.W.R. 1, 95 M.V.R. (5th) 1, 2010 CarswellSask 369, EYB 2010-175730, [2010] A.C.S. No. 24; affirming 2009 SKCA 8, 2009 CarswellSask 39, [2009] S.J. No. 40, 74 M.V.R. (5th) 1, 444 W.A.C. 179, 320 Sask. R. 179, [2009] 4 W.W.R. 604, 245 C.C.C. (3d) 419, 183 C.R.R. (2d) 138 — The court reviewed search powers incident to random stops under the *Highways and Transportation Act* (Sask.).

Related Provisions: See O. Reg. 340/94, Drivers' Licences, s. 9.

217. (1) Assisting officers — **Every person called upon to assist a police officer or officer appointed for carrying out the provisions of this Act in the arrest of a person suspected of having committed any offence mentioned in subsection (2) may assist if he or she knows that the person calling on him or her for assistance is a police officer or officer appointed for carrying out the provisions of this Act, and does not know that there are no reasonable grounds for the suspicion.**

(2) Arrests without warrant — **Any police officer who, on reasonable and probable grounds, believes that a contravention of any of the provisions of subsection 9(1), subsection 12(1), subsection 13(1), subsection 33(3), subsection 47(5), (6), (7) or (8), section 51, 53, subsection 106(8.2), section 130, 172 or 184, subsection 185(3), clause 200(1)(a) or subsection 216(1) has been committed, may arrest, without warrant, the person he or she believes committed the contravention.**

(3) Arresting on view — **Every person may arrest without warrant any person whom he or she finds committing any such contravention.**

(3.1) Arrest without warrant for contravention of subs. 177(2) — **A police officer who believes on reasonable and probable grounds that a person has contravened subsection 177(2) may arrest the person without warrant if,**

 (a) before the alleged contravention of subsection 177(2), the police officer directed the person not to engage in activity that contravenes that subsection; or

 (b) the police officer believes on reasonable and probable grounds that it is necessary to arrest the person without warrant in order to establish the identity of the person or to prevent the person from continuing or repeating the contravention.

(4) Detaining vehicle when arrest is made — **A police officer or officer appointed for carrying out the provisions of this Act, making an arrest without warrant, may detain the motor vehicle with which the offence was committed until the final disposition of any prosecution under this Act or under the *Criminal Code* (Can-**

ada), but the motor vehicle may be released on security for its production being given to the satisfaction of a justice of the peace or judge.

(4.1) Exceptions to release of motor vehicle — A motor vehicle shall not be released under subsection (4) if it was removed, stored, detained or impounded pursuant to any provision of this Act other than subsection (4) of this section.

(5) Care and storage charges — All costs and charges for the care and storage of a motor vehicle detained under subsection (4) are a lien upon the motor vehicle, which may be enforced in the manner provided by the *Repair and Storage Liens Act*.

(6) Duty of person arresting without warrant — A police officer or officer appointed for carrying out the provisions of this Act, making an arrest without warrant, shall, with reasonable diligence, take the person arrested before a justice of the peace or provincial judge to be dealt with according to law.

1993, c. 40, s. 8; 1999, c. 8, s. 7(2); 2007, c. 13, s. 24; 2009, c. 5, s. 56

Commentary

Section 217 allows for a police officer to arrest, on reasonable and probable grounds, any one without warrant whom he or she believes has committed one of the serious enumerated offences in subs. (2). Section 217(1) addresses assisting officers. Anyone can arrest a person who is in the process of committing one of the enumerated offences (subs. (3)). An officer has the power to detain the vehicle of an arrested person pending the outcome of a charge under the Act or the Criminal Code, but a Justice of the Peace or a judge may release the vehicle where security is posted (subs. (4)). Care and storage charges are a lien (subs. (5)). Officers making an arrest must take the person before a Justice of the Peace or a Provincial Court judge with reasonable diligence. Note that failure to stop or to show a licence and failing to stop, ss. 33 and 216, respectively, were added subseqent to the decision in *R. v. Dedman, infra*.

Case Law

R. v. Wentworth Magistrates' Court, [1964] 2 O.R. 316, 43 C.R. 206 (H.C.) — The purpose of s. 217(2) is to give to a police officer a power to arrest without a warrant where the procedure by information and warrant or summons would be likely to be ineffective to secure the attendance of the accused. it was not intended that it should be used as circumventing the limitation period of 21 days for service of summons under s. 6(5) of the Summary Convictions Act, and no arrest should be made after the expiration of that period.

R. v. Matieshin (1963), 44 C.R. 78 (Sask. Mag. Ct.); affirmed (March 19, 1964), unreported (Sask. C.A.) — The Saskatchewan Act, which authorizes the seizure of vehicles illegally operated, does not cover all the offences set out in the Act, but only applies to offences where the use of a vehicle in such a state of disrepair makes it a menace, hazard or danger to other users of the highway or where the vehicle is being operated by a person in a state of disability. Moreover, where the authority to seize is being exercised, as by the removal of keys from a car, the peace officer should inform the operator of the reason or offence before doing so.

R. v. Dedman, [1985] 2 S.C.R. 2; affirming (1981), 32 O.R. (2d) 641, 10 M.V.R. 59 (C.A.); which reversed (1980), 30 O.R. (2d) 555, 8 M.V.R. 142 (H.C.) — Section 153(2) [now s. 217] of the Highway Traffic Act (Ont.), conferring on constables the power to arrest without warrant in respect of certain specified offences against the Act, mentions s. 14(2) [now s. 33(2)] which provides that any person who is unable or refuses to produce his licence in accordance with subs. (1) shall, when requested by a constable, give a reasonable identification of himself. The Act does not, however, unlike the highway traffic legislation in some provinces, empower a constable to arrest without warrant a motorist who fails to obey a signal to stop. However, where the signal to stop constitutes a valid exercise of a police *power* to require a motorist to stop for the purpose of producing his driver's licence, the constable is acting in the execution of a specific duty, and a failure to stop may constitute a wilful obstruction of a peace officer in the execution of his duties in connection with s. 14(1), justifying an arrest for that offence under the Criminal Code. Since the respondent complied with the officer's signal to stop, the Court was not required to decide whether, in the circumstances, the officer in giving a signal to stop was validly exercising an implied power under s. 14 of the Highway Traffic Act, or was validly exercising a power ancillary to his general duties to protect persons and property and to detect crime, thus rendering the respondent, had he not stopped, liable to arrest for wilfully obstructing a peace officer in the execution of his duties.

R. v. Hall (1996), 21 M.V.R. (3d) 85, 89 O.A.C. 43 (C.A.) — Section 217(2) does not grant an absolute discretion to a police officer to make an arrest without warrant. The power of arrest is limited to where an officer has reasonable and probable grounds to believe a person has committed one of a specified number of the more serious offences under the Act. Section 217(2) is not unconstitutionally vague or overbroad in violation of s. 7 of the Charter. Further limiting guidelines or criteria are not necessary to meet s. 7.

R. v. Werhun (1990), 27 M.V.R. (2d) 74, [1991] 2 W.W.R. 344, 62 C.C.C. (3d) 440, 70 Man. R. (2d) 63 (C.A.); reversing 24 M.V.R. (2d) 1, [1990] 5 W.W.R. 729, 67 Man. R. (2d) 59 (Q.B.) — A constitutional challenge to Manitoba's legislation permitting a vehicle to be impounded where the driver was driving while disqualified was unsuccessful.

R. v. Cassidy (2007), 59 M.V.R. (5th) 203, [2007] O.J. No. 4269, 2007 CarswellOnt 7083 (S.C.J.) — The Act does not oblige a bicyclist to carry his or her driver's licence, assuming he or she has one. However, if a bicyclist is stopped by a police officer whom the officer finds contravening the Act, the officer may request the person to stop and provide identification.

218. (1) Cyclist to identify self — A police officer who finds any person contravening this Act or any municipal by-law regulating traffic while in charge of a bicycle may require that person to stop and to provide identification of himself or herself.

(2) Idem — Every person who is required to stop, by a police officer acting under subsection (1), shall stop and identify himself or herself to the police officer.

(3) Idem — For the purposes of this section, giving one's correct name and address is sufficient identification.

(4) Idem — A police officer may arrest without warrant any person who does not comply with subsection (2).

Case Law

R. v. G. (P.) (2000), 10 M.V.R. (4th) 139 (Ont. S.C.J.) — Unlike the motor vehicle sections of the Act, no affirmative obligation exists for a bicycle rider to carry documentation. The wording of the Act implied an oral response would be sufficient. To hold otherwise would produce a result that the young, poor or homeless would be subject to immediate arrest.

219. (1) Suspension of licence upon conviction — Upon the arraignment of a person accused of any of the offences mentioned in subsection 41(1) or sections 42 and 53 and before the court accepts the plea of the person, the clerk or registrar of the court shall orally give notice to the person to the following effect:

> *The Highway Traffic Act provides that upon conviction of the offence with which you are charged, in the circumstances indicated therein, your driver's licence shall be suspended for the period prescribed by statute.*

(2) Idem — The suspension of a driver's licence by operation of this Act shall not be held to be invalid by reason of failure of the clerk or registrar or the court to give the notice provided for in subsection (1).

220. (1) Impounding motor vehicles — In conjunction with a conviction under section 47, 51 or 53 of this Act or section 253, 254 or 255 of the *Criminal Code* (Canada) or with a second conviction under section 252 of the *Criminal Code* (Canada), an order may issue that the motor vehicle driven by or under the care, charge or control of the person convicted at the time of the commission of the offence or second offence, as the case may be, shall be seized, impounded and taken into custody of the law for three months, subject to such conditions and in the manner set out in the order.

(2) Interpretation — For the purpose of subsection (1), a conviction under section 252 of the *Criminal Code* (Canada) that occurs after a conviction under any section referred to in subsection (1) shall be considered as a second conviction under section 252 of the *Criminal Code* (Canada).

(3) Notice to be given — Where a conviction referred to in subsection (1) results because the accused pleads guilty, the order referred to in subsection (1) shall not be issued unless the person has been given notice,

    (a) by a printed or written statement upon or accompanying the summons; or

    (b) orally by the court before the plea of guilty is accepted,

to the following effect:

> *The Highway Traffic Act provides that upon conviction of the offence with which you are charged, in the circumstances indicated therein, an order may be issued that the motor vehicle driven by you or under your care, charge or control at the time of the commission of the offence shall be seized, impounded and taken into the custody of the law.*

(4) When vehicle not to be impounded — An order shall not be issued under subsection (1) in respect of a motor vehicle that is not owned or held under a lease that has less than three months to run by the person convicted unless the person convicted is the principal driver thereof and, if there is a lease of the vehicle, the lease has more than three months to run.

(5) Opportunity to be heard — Before an order is issued under subsection (1), an opportunity shall be given to any person who has an interest in the motor vehicle or is a dependent of or a family member residing with the person convicted to state why the order should not issue.

(6) Undue hardship — Where representation is made under subsection (5), the court shall not issue the order if the court is of the opinion that undue hardship will result thereby.

(7) Change in order — Where an order has been issued under subsection (1), any person referred to in subsection (5) may apply to the court for an amendment to or revocation of the order.

(8) Basis for change — The court, pursuant to an application under subsection (7), may amend or revoke an order that is the subject-matter of the application where there is a relevant change in circumstances since the order was made or information is brought out that was disclosed before the order was made.

(9) Lien — All costs and charges for the care and storage of a motor vehicle impounded under subsection (1) are a lien upon the vehicle.

(10) Effect of lien — A motor vehicle that is subject to a lien under subsection (9) may be retained in the custody of the law so long as the lien remains unpaid or until the motor vehicle is sold by public auction.

(11) Notice of sale — Before a motor vehicle is sold under subsection (10), a reasonable effort shall be made to give the owner two weeks notice of the sale if the owner can be ascertained.

(12) Definition — For the purposes of this section, "court" means a judge or judge of the Ontario Court (Provincial Division).

[Editor's Note: Section 1.1 of the Courts of Justice Act, *R.S.O. 1990, c. C.43 provides in part that a reference in an Act to a court by its former name shall be deemed to be a reference to the new name of that court unless a contrary intention appears. The reference to the Ontario Court (Provincial Division) in this subsection should accordingly be read as a reference to the Ontario Court of Justice.]*

Commentary

The Red Tape Reduction Act, 1999, S.O. 1999, c. 12, Sched. R. (ss. 1(2), 1(3), 2(1), 2(3), 2(5), 5(1), and 6(1) in force January 1, 2001) amends ss. 6, 7, 12 and 14 of the Highway Traffic Act to facilitate Ontario's participation in the International Registration Plan, which contains reciprocal provisions in respect of commercial motor vehicles that travel across provincial or international borders. The Plan provides for the issuance of IRP cab cards as permits for these vehicles and for the appointment of registration and licence fees in each member jurisdiction on the basis of the distances travelled in each jurisdiction. Persons residing or based in other jurisdictions that are members of the Plan are exempt from the requirements of and fees prescribed under Part II of the Highway Traffic Act.

Case Law

McDonald v. Down, [1939] 2 D.L.R. 177 (Ont. H.C.); affirmed [1941] 1 D.L.R. 799 (Ont. C.A.) — This section is *intra vires* since a provision for the impounding of a motor vehicle is not criminal legislation.

Indust. Accept. Corp. v. Simpson, [1950] O.W.N. 205, [1950] 2 D.L.R. 524 (C.A.) — The lien which exists under subs. (4) [now subs. (9)] for storage extends only to reasonable charges therefor and not necessarily to the full amount claimed.

R. v. Werhun (1990), 27 M.V.R. (2d) 74, [1991] 2 W.W.R. 344, 62 C.C.C. (3d) 440, 70 Man. R. (2d) 63 (C.A.); reversing 24 M.V.R. (2d) 1, [1990] 5 W.W.R. 729, 67 Man. R. (2d) 59 (Q.B.) — A constitutional challenge to Manitoba's legislation permitting a vehicle to be impounded where the driver was driving while disqualified was unsuccessful.

R. v. Fiddler (2003), 2003 MBCA 143, 2003 CarswellMan 490, 45 M.V.R. (4th) 15 (C.A.) — An impoundment hearing was not invalidated by the fact that the applicant was not provided with a copy of the police report before the hearing. The applicant did not request a copy and the justice advised the applicant of the essential contents of the report at the hearing.

R. c. Manning, 2013 SCC 1, 2013 CarswellQue 16, 2013 CarswellQue 17, [2013] 1 S.C.R. 3, 290 C.C.C. (3d) 445, 99 C.R. (6th) 36, 353 D.L.R. (4th) 293, 38 M.V.R. (6th) 1, 438 N.R. 216, [2013] S.C.J. No. 1 (S.C.C.) — The court spoke to the availability of s. 490.41(3) of the *Criminal Code*, in addition to highway traffic powers, to impound a vehicle of a drinking driver.

221. (1) Abandoned or unplated vehicles — A police officer or an officer appointed for carrying out the provisions of this Act who discovers a vehicle apparently abandoned on or near a highway or a motor vehicle or trailer without proper number plates may take the vehicle into custody of the law and may cause it to be taken to and stored in a suitable place.

(2) Costs for storage — All costs and charges for removal, care or storage of a vehicle taken or stored under subsection (1) are a lien upon the vehicle that may be enforced in the manner provided by Part III of the *Repair and Storage Liens Act.*

Case Law

R. v. Nicolosi (1998), 36 M.V.R. (3d) 125, 17 C.R. (5th) 134, 127 C.C.C. (3d) 176, 110 O.A.C. 189, 40 O.R. (3d) 417 (C.A.) — The Act authorizes the impounding of the vehicle. Given the need to regulate vehicles and the fundamental importance of licensing to that regulation, a power to remove all improperly licensed vehicles from the roadway is not unreasonable. A seizure of the vehicle does not violate s. 8.

222. Impounding of vehicle on appeal — If a person to whom section 220 applies enters an appeal against the person's conviction and there is filed with the convicting provincial judge sufficient security for the production of the motor vehicle if the appeal should fail, section 220 does not apply unless the conviction is sustained on appeal.

223. (1) Appointment of officers for carrying out provisions of act — The Minister may appoint one or more persons on the staff of the Ministry or any other ministry of the Government of Ontario as an officer or officers for the purpose of carrying out all or any of the provisions of this Act, and any person so appointed has authority to act as a constable throughout Ontario for the purpose.

(2) Certificate of appointment — A person appointed under subsection (1) shall, while carrying out his or her duties under the appointment, have in his or her possession a certificate of appointment under subsection (1) and shall produce such certificate upon request.

224. Service on driver sufficient — In respect of an offence under this Act, the *Compulsory Automobile Insurance Act*, the *Dangerous Goods Transportation Act*, the *Fuel Tax Act* or the *Public Vehicles Act* that involves a commercial motor vehicle, delivery of the offence notice or summons to the driver of the vehicle shall be deemed to be service on the operator of the vehicle as defined in subsection 16(1) or on the owner of the vehicle for the purpose of Part I of the *Provincial offences Act* unless, in the case of the owner, at the time of the offence, the vehicle was in the possession of the driver without the owner's consent.

2002, c. 18, Sched. P, s. 38

225. (1) Inspection of records — An officer of the Ministry may, during normal business hours upon production of his or her designation as an officer, enter any place of business of a person required under this Act or the regulations to keep records for the purpose of inspecting those records.

(2) Idem — An officer of the Ministry, for the purpose of ensuring that this Act and the regulations are being complied with, is authorized to inspect any records required to be kept under this Act or the regulations.

(3) Copies — An officer examining any records under this section may, on giving a receipt therefor, remove any record for the purpose of making copies thereof but the copying must be made quickly and the record promptly returned.

(4) Idem — Any copy made under subsection (3) and certified as a true copy by the person making it is admissible in evidence in any proceeding or prosecution as proof, in the absence of evidence to the contrary, of the record copied and its contents.

(5) Obstruction prohibited — No person shall obstruct any officer from doing anything that he or she is authorized by this section to do or to withhold from the officer or conceal or destroy any record that the officer is authorized to examine or to copy.

(6) Penalty — Every person who contravenes subsection (5) is guilty of an offence and on conviction is liable to a fine of not less than $100 and not more than $1,000 or to imprisonment for a term of not more than six months, or to both.

Case Law

Calgary Police Service v. Alberta (2014), 2014 CarswellAlta 2605, 603 A.R. 316, 86 Admin. L.R. (5th) 288, 10 Alta. L.R. (6th) 298, 72 M.V.R. (6th) 269, 2014 ABQB 791 (Alta. Q.B.) — A ruling by the Privacy Commissioner against the police for giving out personal information including names, addresses and birth dates in an accident report was upheld.

226. [Repealed 1999, c. 12, Sched. R, s. 19.]

Commentary

The Red Tape Reduction Act, 1999, S.O. 1999, c. 12, Sched. R. (ss. 1(2), 1(3), 2(1), 2(3), 2(5), 5(1), and 6(1) in force January 1, 2001) amends ss. 6, 7, 12 and 14 of the Highway Traffic Act to facilitate Ontario's participation in the International Registration Plan, which contains reciprocal provisions in respect of commercial motor vehicles that travel across provincial or international borders. The Plan provides for the issuance of IRP cab cards as permits for these vehicles and for the appointment of registration and licence fees in each member jurisdiction on the basis of the distances travelled in each jurisdiction. Persons residing or based in other jurisdictions that are members of the Plan are exempt from the requirements of and fees prescribed under Part II of the Highway Traffic Act.

Related Provisions: See the Off-Road Vehicles Act, R.S.O. 1990, c. O.4.

227. (1) Where proceeding for offence may be heard — Despite section 29 of the *Provincial Offences Act*, where an offence is committed under this Act, the *Compulsory Automobile Insurance Act*, the *Dangerous Goods Transportation Act*, the *Fuel Tax Act* or the *Public Vehicles Act* in or on a commercial motor vehicle, as defined in subsection 16(1) of this Act, that is employed in a journey, the offence shall be deemed to have been committed in any county or district through which the vehicle passed in the course of the journey on which the offence was committed.

Proposed Amendment — 227(1)

(1) Where proceeding for offence may be heard — Despite section 29 of the *Provincial Offences Act*, where an offence is committed under this Act, the *Compulsory Automobile Insurance Act*, the *Dangerous Goods Transportation Act*, the *Fuel Tax Act* or the *Public Vehicles Act* in or on a commercial motor vehicle, that is employed in a journey, the offence shall be deemed to have been committed in any county or district through which the vehicle passed in the course of the journey on which the offence was committed.

2014, c. 9, Sched. 2, s. 46 [To come into force January 1, 2017.]

(2) Same — For the purpose of subsection (1), where the centre or other part of the road on which the vehicle passed in the course of the journey is the boundary of two or more counties or districts, the offence shall be deemed to have been committed in any of the counties or districts.

1996, c. 33, s. 17; 2002, c. 18, Sched. P, s. 39

PART XVI — PILOT PROJECTS

[Heading added 2005, c. 26, Sched. A, s. 33(1).]

228. (1) Pilot projects — The Lieutenant Governor in Council may by regulation authorize or establish a project for research into or the testing or evaluation of any matter governed by this Act or relevant to highway traffic.

(2) Project may conflict with Acts — Under a project authorized or established under subsection (1),

(a) persons or classes of persons may be authorized to do or use a thing that is prohibited or regulated under this Act, the *Dangerous Goods Transportation Act*, the *Motorized Snow Vehicles Act*, the *Off-Road Vehicles Act* or the *Public Vehicles Act* or to not do or use a thing that is required or authorized by any of those Acts;

(b) the Minister or Ministry or any person authorized or required to do anything under this Act, the *Dangerous Goods Transportation Act*, the *Motorized Snow Vehicles Act*, the *Off-Road Vehicles Act* or the *Public Vehicles Act* may be authorized or required to do anything that is not authorized or required under any of those Acts or to do anything that is authorized or required under any of those Acts in a way that is different from the way it is authorized or required.

(3) Limited to classes — An authorization or requirement described in subsection (2) may be limited to any class of persons, class or type of vehicles, class of equipment, devices or highways, parts of Ontario, time of year or day, activities, matters or any other things.

(4) Regulation to create own scheme of rules — A regulation made under this section may regulate the doing of anything or the use of any thing or prohibit the doing of anything or the using of any thing.

(5) Insurance — A regulation made under this section may require a person or class of persons to carry insurance of a kind and in the amount specified.

(6) Time limit — A regulation made under this section must provide that it is revoked no later than the twelfth anniversary of the day the regulation is filed.

(7) Project prevails over Acts — In the event of a conflict between a regulation made under this section and any provision of this Act, the *Dangerous Goods Transportation Act*, the *Motorized Snow Vehicles Act*, the *Off-Road Vehicles Act* or the *Public Vehicles Act* or of a regulation made under any of those Acts, the regulation made under this section prevails.

(8) Offence — Every person who contravenes a regulation made under this section is guilty of an offence and on conviction is liable to a fine of not less than $250 and not more than $2,500.

2005, c. 26, Sched. A, s. 33

Related Provisions: See Pilot Project — Low-Speed Vehicles; O. Reg. 488/06, Pilot Project — Segways.

SCHEDULE

(Section 213(2))

Certificate of Justice

I, (*name of Justice*), a Justice of the Peace in and for the .... of
.... hereby certify:

1. That (*name of defendant*), of the .... of .... in the ....
   of .... (*occupation*), this day appeared before me and produced to me a
   summons issued by (*name of Justice issuing summons*), a Justice of the Peace
   in and for the .... of .... for an offence against the *Highway Traffic Act*,
   said to have been committed with respect to a car bearing the official plate
   number .... for this year, the offence being alleged to have
   been committed on the .... of .... in the .... of .... on the
   .... day of ....

2. That (*name of defendant*) has deposed before me that neither the defendant
   nor the defendant's motor vehicle was at such place on the
   .... day of ...., 19.........., and that the summons must
   have been issued against the defendant through an error of the informant as
   to the number on the official number plate, and the defendant's testimony in
   this respect has been corroborated by the testimony of two credible witnesses, namely (*here insert the names of two witnesses*).

3. The depositions of the defendant and of the witnesses referred to in paragraph 2 of this certificate are attached hereto.

4. That I am satisfied of the truth of the testimony given before me this day by
   (*name of defendant and two witnesses*), and give this certificate in pursuance
   of subsection 213(2) of the *Highway Traffic Act*.

Dated at .... this .... day of ...., 19..........

.... J.P.

(NOTE. — *Attach depositions of defendant and witnesses to this certificate.*)

HIGHWAY TRAFFIC ACT REGULATIONS

ONT. REG. 581 — ACCESSIBLE PARKING FOR PERSONS WITH DISABILITIES

made under the *Highway Traffic Act*

R.R.O. 1990, Reg. 581, as am. O. Reg. 908/93; 612/05; 543/07; 113/08; 308/10, ss. 1–13, 14 (Fr.); 419/12.

[Note: The title of this Regulation was changed from "Disabled Person Parking Permits" to "Accessible Parking for Persons with Disabilities" by O. Reg. 612/05, s. 1.]

1. In this Regulation,

"person with a disability" means an individual,

(a) who cannot walk without the assistance of another individual or of a brace, cane, crutch, lower limb prosthetic device or similar assistive device or who requires the assistance of a wheelchair,

(b) who suffers from lung disease to such an extent that his or her forced expiratory volume in one second is less than one litre,

(c) for whom portable oxygen is a medical necessity,

(d) who suffers from cardiovascular disease to such an extent that the individual's functional capacity is classified as Class III or Class IV according to Nomenclature and Criteria for Diagnosis of Diseases of the Heart and Great Vessels, ninth edition, published by Little, Brown & Co. in 1994,

(e) whose ability to walk is severely limited due to an arthritic, neurological, musculoskeletal or orthopaedic condition,

(f) whose visual acuity is 20/200 or poorer in the better eye, with corrective lenses if required, or whose maximum field of vision using both eyes has a diameter of 20 degrees or less, or

(g) whose mobility is severely limited by one or more conditions or functional impairments;

"registered nurse in the extended class" means a member of the College of Nurses of Ontario who is a registered nurse holding an extended certificate of registration under the *Nursing Act, 1991*;

"regulated health practitioner" means a person legally qualified to practise in Canada as a physician, chiropodist, chiropractor, occupational therapist, physiotherapist, podiatrist or registered nurse in the extended class;

"traveller permit" means an accessible parking permit for use related to travel issued under subsection 2(4) to an individual holding an unexpired accessible parking permit for general use issued under subsection 2(1).

O. Reg. 612/05, s. 2; 543/07, s. 1; 308/10, s. 1

2. (1) The Minister shall issue an accessible parking permit for general use to every individual who applies for it on a form provided by the Ministry, if a regulated health practitioner certifies the following on the form:

    1. That the applicant is a person with a disability.

    2. The nature of the disability.

    3. Whether the disability is temporary or permanent or whether this fact is unknown.

    4. If the disability is temporary, the anticipated length of time the disability is expected to continue, if known.

(2) If, after January 16, 2006, a regulated health practitioner certifies on an application for an accessible parking permit that the applicant is a person with a permanent disability, no certification from a regulated health practitioner is required on any application for renewal of that permit, despite subsection (1).

(3) If an individual holds an unexpired accessible parking permit for general use issued under subsection (1), the Minister shall not issue another accessible parking permit for general use to the individual under subsection (1).

(4) The Minister shall issue an accessible parking permit for use related to travel to every individual who applies for it and holds an unexpired accessible parking permit for general use issued under subsection (1).

(5) Every accessible parking permit for use related to travel issued under subsection (4) shall specify the locations or circumstances in which it may be used.

(5.1) The Minister shall issue an accessible parking permit for use on a motorcycle or motor assisted bicycle to every individual who applies for it and who,

    (a) owns or leases a motorcycle or motor assisted bicycle;

    (b) holds a Class M or M2 driver's licence; and

    (c) holds an unexpired accessible parking permit for general use that was issued as provided by clause 5(1)(a) or (c).

(6) The Minister shall issue accessible parking permits, other than traveller permits or accessible parking permits for use on a motorcycle or motor assisted bicycle,

    (a) to a corporation, in respect of the number of vehicles that are owned or leased by the corporation primarily to provide transportation services to persons with a disability; and

    (b) to an organization, in respect of the number of vehicles that are owned or leased by the organization and used on a non-profit basis to provide transportation services to persons with a disability.

                          O. Reg. 612/05, s. 2; 113/08, s. 1; 308/10, s. 2

3. The Minister shall issue an accessible parking permit for general use to a visitor to Ontario, if the visitor,

    (a) provides evidence that he or she is the holder of a currently valid permit, number plate or other marker or device bearing the international symbol of access for persons with a disability issued by the visitor's home jurisdiction; or

(b) provides other evidence that he or she is from another jurisdiction and is a person with a disability.

O. Reg. 612/05, s. 2; 113/08, s. 2; 308/10, s. 3

4. If an accessible parking permit is lost or stolen, the Minister shall issue a replacement permit if,

(a) the loss or theft is reported to the Ministry on a form supplied by the Ministry; and

(b) the applicant continues to meet the requirements of section 2 or 3, as applicable.

O. Reg. 308/10, s. 4

5. (1) An accessible parking permit issued to an individual shall be issued,

(a) if the regulated health practitioner certifies that the disability is permanent, for 60 months;

(b) if the regulated health practitioner certifies that the disability is temporary and specifies the anticipated length of time the disability is expected to continue, for the anticipated length of time the disability is expected to continue, up to a maximum of 12 months;

(c) if the regulated health practitioner certifies that it is not possible to determine whether the disability is temporary or permanent, or if the regulated health practitioner certifies that the disability is temporary but of unknown duration, for 60 months;

(d) if the individual is a visitor described in section 3, for the length of the visit, up to a maximum of six months;

(e) if it is a traveller permit, for the lesser of 12 months and the period ending on the date of expiry of the individual's accessible parking permit for general use;

(f) if it is a permit for use on a motorcycle or motor assisted bicycle, for the period ending on the earlier of the date of expiry on the permit, if any, and the date of expiry of the individual's accessible parking permit for general use.

(2) An accessible parking permit issued to a corporation under clause 2(6)(a) shall be issued for a term that reflects the contractual or other obligations of the corporation to provide transportation services to persons with a disability, up to a maximum of 60 months.

(3) An accessible parking permit issued to an organization under clause 2(6)(b) shall be issued for the length of time that the organization anticipates that it will be providing transportation services to persons with a disability, up to a maximum of 60 months.

(4) [Repealed O. Reg. 612/05, s. 3.]

O. Reg. 612/05, s. 3; 543/07, s. 2; 113/08, s. 3; 308/10, s. 5

6. (1) An accessible parking permit ceases to be in force if the holder of the permit ceases to be a person with a disability.

(2) An accessible parking permit issued to an individual is not valid when it is displayed on a vehicle if,

(a) the vehicle is not being used to pick up or transport the holder of the permit; or

(b) the accessible parking permit is a traveller permit and is being used in locations or circumstances not specified on the permit.

(3) An accessible parking permit issued to a corporation or an organization is not valid when it is displayed on a vehicle if the vehicle is not being used to pick up or transport a person with a disability.

(4) An accessible parking permit issued under subsection 2(5.1) for use on a motorcycle or motor assisted bicycle is not valid when it is displayed on a motorcycle or motor assisted bicycle,

(a) in a circumstance described in clause (2)(a);

(b) if the person to whom it was issued does not also have the accessible parking permit for general use that was issued to him or her under subsection 2(1) with him or her; or

(c) if the person to whom it was issued does not hold a valid Class M or M2 driver's licence.

O. Reg. 612/05, s. 3; 113/08, s. 4; 308/10, s. 6

7. (1) Subject to subsection (2), an accessible parking permit shall be displayed on the sun visor or on the dashboard of a vehicle so that the international symbol of access for persons with a disability, the permit number and the expiry date of the permit are clearly visible from the outside of the vehicle.

(2) If the vehicle is a motorcycle or motor assisted bicycle, an accessible parking permit issued under subsection 2(5.1) shall be displayed on the top left corner of the number plate on the vehicle.

O. Reg. 612/05, s. 3; 113/08, s. 5; 308/10, s. 7

8. A vehicle displaying a currently valid permit, number plate or other marker or device bearing the international symbol of access for persons with a disability and issued by another jurisdiction is entitled to the same privileges as a vehicle displaying an accessible parking permit issued under the Act.

O. Reg. 612/05, s. 3; 308/10, s. 8

9. (1) An unexpired accessible parking permit shall be returned to the Ministry promptly if,

(a) the holder is no longer a person with a disability;

(b) the permit is cancelled; or

(c) the permit contains incorrect information.

(2) If the holder of an unexpired accessible parking permit dies, any person who comes into possession of the permit after the holder's death shall promptly return the permit to the Ministry.

(3) An expired accessible parking permit for use on a motorcycle or motor assisted bicycle shall be removed from and not displayed on any motorcycle or motor assisted bicycle.

O. Reg. 612/05, s. 4; 543/07, s. 3; 113/08, s. 6; 308/10, s. 9

10. A parking space designated by a sign under section 11 on land owned and occupied by the Crown may be used only by vehicles displaying a valid accessible parking permit in accordance with this Regulation.

O. Reg. 308/10, s. 10

11. A parking space designated on Crown land or under a municipal by-law for the use of persons with a disability or required by Ontario Regulation 191/11 (*Integrated Accessibility Standards*) made under the *Accessibility for Ontarians with Disabilities Act, 2005* for the use of persons with a disability shall be distinctly indicated by erecting an accessible parking permit sign which shall,

  (a) be not less than forty-five centimetres in height and not less than thirty centimetres in width and bear the markings and have the dimensions as described and illustrated in the following Figure:

or,

(b) **be not less than sixty centimetres in height and not less than thirty centimetres in width and bear the markings and have the dimensions as described and illustrated in the following Figure:**

O. Reg. 166/90, s. 11

O. Reg. 612/05, s. 5; 308/10, s. 11; 419/12, s. 1

12. [Repealed O. Reg. 612/05, s. 6.]

13. (1) A sign that prohibits stopping except the stopping of vehicles displaying a valid accessible parking permit shall be not less than seventy-five centimetres in height and not less than thirty centimetres in width and bear the markings and have the dimensions as described and illustrated in the following Figure:

(2) Despite subsection (1), in an area designated by the *French Language Services Act,* **a sign that prohibits stopping except the stopping of vehicles displaying a valid accessible parking permit shall be not less than seventy-five centimetres in height and not less than thirty centimetres in width and bear the markings and have the dimensions as described and illustrated in the following Figure:**

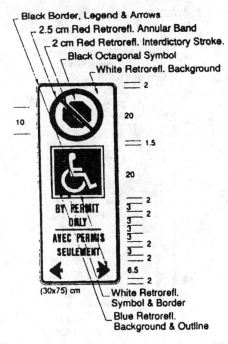

Black Border, Legend & Arrows
2.5 cm Red Retrorefl. Annular Band
2 cm Red Retrorefl. Interdictory Stroke.
Black Octagonal Symbol
White Retrorefl. Background

White Retrorefl. Symbol & Border

Blue Retrorefl. Background & Outline

O. Reg. 908/93, s. 1; 308/10, s. 12

14. (1) A sign that prohibits standing except the standing of vehicles displaying a valid accessible parking permit shall be not less than sixty centimetres in height and not less than thirty centimetres in width and bear the markings and have the dimensions as described and illustrated in the following Figure:

(2) Despite subsection (1), in an area designated by the *French Language Services Act*, a sign that prohibits standing except the standing of vehicles displaying a valid accessible parking permit shall be not less than seventy-five centimetres in height and not less than thirty centimetres in width and bear the markings and have the dimensions as described and illustrated in the following Figure:

O. Reg. 908/93, s. 1; 308/10, s. 13

ONT. REG. 629 — ACCESSIBLE VEHICLES

made under the *Highway Traffic Act*

R.R.O. 1990, Reg. 629, as am. O. Reg. 533/94; 302/95; 184/96; 326/97; 346/02; 49/05; 404/09 (Fr.); 133/10; 172/11, ss. 1–12, 13(1) (Fr.), (2), (3) (Fr.), (4), (5) (Fr.), (6) (Fr.), (7), (8), 14; 170/13.

[Note: The title of this Regulation was changed from "Vehicles for the Transportation of Physically Disabled Passengers" to "Accessible Vehicles" by O. Reg. 172/11, s. 1.]

1. (1) In this Regulation,

"accessible taxicab" means a passenger vehicle that is an accessible vehicle and that is licensed as a taxicab by a municipality;

"accessible urban transit bus" means a bus that is an accessible vehicle and that is operated as part of a service for which a fare is charged for transporting the public by vehicles operated,

(a) by or on behalf of a municipality or a local board as defined in the *Municipal Affairs Act*, or

(b) under an agreement between a municipality and a person, firm or corporation;

"accessible vehicle" means a passenger vehicle or a bus, other than a school bus,

(a) that is designed or modified to be used for the purpose of transporting persons with disabilities and is used for that purpose, whether or not the vehicle is also used to transport persons without disabilities, and

(b) that is operated,

(i) for compensation by, for or on behalf of any person, club, agency or organization, or

(ii) not for compensation by, for or on behalf of any person, club, agency or organization that holds itself out as providing a transportation service to persons with disabilities;

"Canadian Standards Association Standard D409-02" means that Standard and its updates up to and including October, 2004;

"compensation" includes any rate, remuneration, reimbursement or reward of any kind paid, payable, promised, received or demanded, directly or indirectly;

"inter-city bus" means a bus commonly known as a motor coach that has,

(a) motive power mounted to the rear of the front axle,

(b) air-ride or torsion-bar suspension,

(c) a baggage area that is separate from the passenger cabin, and

556

(d) a passenger cabin with reclining seats for passengers;

"LTI accessible taxicab" means an accessible taxicab that,

(a) is manufactured by the London Taxis International division of Manganese Bronze Holdings PLC,

(b) bears the model name TXII, and

(c) is equipped with a ramp and two rear side access doors;

"rear-entry accessible taxicab" means an accessible taxicab with a gross vehicle weight rating of not more than 2,900 kilograms that is equipped with a ramp at the rear, a rear door for wheelchair access and two rear side doors for ambulatory access.

"school bus" [Repealed O. Reg. 170/13, s. 1(2).]

(2) For the purposes of the definition of "accessible vehicle" in subsection (1), "school bus" means a school bus within the meaning of section 175 of the Act.

O. Reg. 184/96, s. 1; 346/02, s. 1; 49/05, s. 1; 172/11, s. 2; 170/13, s. 1

2. (1) Accessible vehicles manufactured on or after January 1, 1986 are prescribed as a class of vehicle for the purposes of subsection 102(3) of the Act.

(2) The standards set out in the Canadian Standards Association Standard D409-M84 are prescribed for all vehicles of the class referred to in subsection (1).

(3) Equipment conforming to the Canadian Standards Association Standard D409-M84 is prescribed and required for use in all vehicles of the class referred to in subsection (1).

(4) This section does not apply to,

(a) rear-entry accessible taxicabs referred to in subsection 8(1);

(b) inter-city buses that are accessible vehicles designed or modified for the purpose of transporting persons in wheelchairs and equipped with a lift or loading ramp;

(c) accessible urban transit buses; or

(d) LTI accessible taxicabs that conform to the standards required under the *Motor Vehicle Safety Act* (Canada) and bear the National Safety Mark referred to in that Act.

O. Reg. 172/11, s. 3

3. (1) Every accessible vehicle shall,

(a) be equipped with an interior mirror designed to provide the driver with a view of the passengers;

(b) be equipped with lights arranged to illuminate all of the interior of the vehicle that shall,

(i) be constantly lit during the loading or unloading of passengers, and

(ii) be sufficient to permit the safe on-board movement of passengers;

(c) be equipped with lights above or beside each passenger access door that shall,

    (i) be constantly lit when the door is open,

    (ii) be shielded to protect the eyes of entering and exiting passengers, and

    (iii) illuminate,

        (A) the ramp, lift or step nosings, and

        (B) in the case of a vehicle manufactured after December 31, 2012, the ground surface for a distance of at least 0.9 metres perpendicular to the outer edge of a lift or the bottom step tread;

(d) be equipped with a means of securing in the open position, each passenger access door or emergency exit door that could be subject to unintentional closing during the loading or unloading of passengers;

(d.1) in the case of a vehicle manufactured after December 31, 2012, be equipped with grab bars, handholds, handrails or stanchions that meet the following requirements:

    (i) they are securely mounted,

    (ii) they are colour-contrasted with their background,

    (iii) they have a slip resistant surface,

    (iv) they have an exterior diameter that permits easy grasping,

    (v) they have sufficient clearance from the surface to which they are attached to permit easy grasping,

    (vi) they are located,

        (A) at each entrance for ambulatory access,

        (B) at each exit for ambulatory access, and

        (C) where passengers are required to pay fares,

    (vii) their location must be distributed within the vehicle to facilitate the safe on-board movement of passengers as appropriate to the design of the vehicle, and

    (viii) when located at an entrance of the vehicle, they are accessible from the ground and are mounted such that they are inside the vehicle when the doors are closed;

(e) have an interior that is free of any sharp projections that may constitute a hazard to passengers;

(f) have floor covering in the aisle and on the steps that,

    (i) is slip resistant, fire-retardant and securely bonded or fastened,

    (ii) produces minimal glare, and

    (iii) is composed of,

        (A) wear-resistant rubber or equivalent material, or

        (B) carpet with a low, firm and level pile or loop;

(g) have steps that,

   (i) have full-width yellow or white step nosings that are colour-contrasted with their background,

   (ii) have closed risers, and

   (iii) have uniform riser heights and tread depths, subject to the structural limitations of the vehicle.

(h) conform with Canada Motor Vehicle Safety Standard 302 regarding flammability;

(i) be equipped with at least one dry-chemical-type fire extinguisher,

   (i) bearing the label of a recognized testing agency,

   (ii) showing a rating of not less than 2-A:10-B:C, and

   (iii) equipped with a pressure gauge indicating that the fire extinguisher is adequately charged,

contained in the extinguisher manufacturer's bracket; and

(j) be equipped with a unitized first aid kit in a sturdy, dustproof removable container containing,

   (i) packets containing hand cleansers and gauze cleansing pads,

   (ii) adhesive dressings, individually wrapped,

   (iii) compress dressings,

   (iv) eye dressing kits,

   (v) gauze dressings,

   (vi) gauze bandages,

   (vii) adhesive tape,

   (viii) triangular bandages,

   (ix) rolled metal splint,

   (x) one pair of scissors,

   (xi) one pair of sliver tweezers, and

   (xii) safety pins.

(k) [Repealed O. Reg. 133/10, s. 1(1).]

(2) The fire extinguisher and first aid kit required by subsection (1) shall be mounted or secured in a location readily accessible to the driver and, if not in plain view, the location thereof shall be plainly marked.

(3) If an accessible vehicle manufactured before January 1, 2013 is equipped with grab bars, handholds, handrails or stanchions, these devices shall meet the requirements set out in subclauses (1)(d.1)(i) to (v).

(4) [Repealed O. Reg. 170/13, s. 2.]

O. Reg. 133/10, s. 1; 172/11, s. 4; 170/13, s. 2

3.1 (1) Every accessible vehicle shall have at least one door for passenger access and an emergency exit door, located on different walls of the vehicle, and the emergency exit door shall be operable from both inside and outside the vehicle.

(2) In the case of an accessible vehicle used for the transportation of persons in wheelchairs, each of the doors referred to in subsection **(1)** shall have a wheelchair passageway that must be at least 762 millimetres wide.

(3) Subsection **(2)** does not apply to an accessible vehicle with a gross vehicle weight rating of not more than 2,900 kilograms that is equipped with two or fewer wheelchair securement devices.

(4) The emergency exit requirements set out in section 6.9.1 of the Canadian Standards Association Standard D409-M84 do not apply to a vehicle referred to in subsection **(3)**.

(5) A vehicle referred to in subsection **(3)** shall have,

   (a) a door for passenger access with a clear opening that must be at least 762 millimetres wide; and

   (b) an emergency exit door with a clear opening that must be at least 724 millimetres wide.

(6) This section does not apply to,

   (a) rear-entry accessible taxicabs referred to in subsection 8(1);

   (b) inter-city buses that are accessible vehicles designed or modified for the purpose of transporting persons in wheelchairs and equipped with a lift or loading ramp; or

   (c) accessible urban transit buses.

(7) Subsections **(2)** and **(5)** do not apply to LTI accessible taxicabs that conform to the standards required under the *Motor Vehicle Safety Act* (Canada) and bear the National Safety Mark referred to in that Act.

O. Reg. 172/11, s. 5

4. (1) Every accessible vehicle used for the transportation of persons in wheelchairs shall display the international symbol of access in a clearly visible position on the rear of the vehicle and on the front of the vehicle in a position other than on the windshield.

(2) The symbol of access required by subsection **(1)** must be at least 15 centimetres high and at least 15 centimetres wide.

O. Reg. 172/11, s. 6

5. (1) Every loading ramp used on an accessible vehicle shall,

   (a) have a slip resistant surface;

   (b) have raised edges of sufficient height to prevent a wheelchair from rolling off the edge of the ramp during the loading or unloading of passengers;

   (c) be secured by means other than a support or lug in the door while the vehicle is operated on a highway; and

   (d) have a coloured-contrasted strip running the full width of the ramp marking the edge of the ramp at the end at which the wheelchair enters from the ground.

(1.1) Clause (1)(b) does not apply to LTI accessible taxicabs that conform to the standards required under the *Motor Vehicle Safety Act* (Canada) and bear the National Safety Mark referred to in that Act.

(2) Every lift used on an accessible vehicle shall,

    (a) have a slip resistant platform surface;

    (b) have the sides of the platform fitted with raised edges extending the full length on each side and of sufficient height to prevent a wheelchair from rolling off the platform during vertical operation of the lift;

    (c) have a retractable lip on the outer edge of the platform of sufficient height to prevent a wheelchair from rolling off the platform during vertical operation of the lift;

    (d) be secured by means other than a support or lug in the door while the vehicle is operated on a highway;

    (e) be capable of raising and lowering a minimum weight of 275 kilograms; and

    (f) have a coloured-contrasted strip running the full width of the platform marking the outer edge of the platform.

(3) Every accessible vehicle manufactured after December 31, 2012 that is equipped with a power-operated loading ramp or a lift or that has a kneeling feature shall also be equipped with both,

    (a) a warning lamp indicator mounted on the exterior of the vehicle near the entrance where the ramp, lift or kneeling feature is used; and

    (b) an audible warning alarm.

(4) The indicator and alarm required by subsection (3) shall function while,

    (a) the power-operated loading ramp is being extended or retracted;

    (b) the lift is being raised or lowered; or

    (c) the vehicle with a kneeling feature is being lowered or raised.

(5) Subsections (3) and (4) do not apply to a vehicle if the permit for the vehicle was issued by a jurisdiction other than Ontario.

(6) [Repealed O. Reg. 170/13, s. 3(4).]

O. Reg. 172/11, s. 7; 170/13, s. 3

5.1 (1) Every designated wheelchair position in an accessible vehicle manufactured after December 31, 2012 shall,

    (a) in the case of a vehicle that has a designated seating capacity of not more than 24 passengers, have an allocated space of 685 millimetres from side to side of the vehicle and 1220 millimetres from front to back of the vehicle; and

    (b) in the case of a vehicle that has a designated seating capacity of more than 24 passengers, have an allocated space of 760 millimetres from side to side of the vehicle and 1220 millimetres from front to back of the vehicle.

(2) A vehicle to which subsection (1) applies may have an overlap between designated wheelchair positions of not more than 150 millimetres from front to back of the vehicle.

O. Reg. 172/11, s. 8; 170/13, s. 4

6. (1) Every accessible vehicle used for the transportation of persons in wheelchairs shall be equipped with wheelchair securement devices that limit the forward, backward, rotational, lateral and vertical motion of every wheelchair in the vehicle at the points of contact of the wheelchair with the vehicle while the vehicle is in normal operation.

(2) For the purpose of subsection (1), normal operation includes full throttle acceleration and maximum braking and cornering.

(3) Every wheelchair securement device in an accessible vehicle shall be,

(a) securely anchored to the vehicle; and

(b) capable of withstanding a load in any direction of not less than 11120 newtons for a period of ten seconds.

(4) Where more than one wheelchair securement device is used to secure a wheelchair in an accessible vehicle, clause (3)(b) applies to the combination of devices used and not to each single device.

(5) This section does not apply to accessible urban transit buses.

O. Reg. 172/11, s. 9

7. (1) Every accessible vehicle shall be equipped with a seat belt assembly, consisting of a pelvic restraint or a pelvic and torso restraint, securely anchored to the vehicle, for each seat in the vehicle intended for use by persons with a mobility impairment.

(2) Every designated wheelchair position in an accessible vehicle shall, in addition to the devices required by section 6, be equipped with an occupant restraint assembly,

(a) securely anchored to the vehicle; or

(b) capable of securing a wheelchair occupant to the wheelchair by encircling both the occupant and wheelchair.

(3) Every seat belt assembly and occupant restraint assembly in an accessible vehicle shall be capable of withstanding a load in any direction of not less than 11120 newtons for a period of ten seconds.

(4) This section does not apply to accessible urban transit buses.

O. Reg. 172/11, s. 10

8. (1) Rear-entry accessible taxicabs manufactured on or after January 1, 1986 are prescribed as a class of vehicle for the purposes of subsection 102(3) of the Act.

(2) The following standards are prescribed for all vehicles of the class referred to in subsection (1):

1. In the case of vehicles manufactured on or after June 30, 2005, the standards set out in the Canadian Standards Association Standard D409-02.

2. In the case of vehicles manufactured on or after January 1, 1986 and before June 30, 2005,

　　i. the standards set out in the Canadian Standards Association Standard D409-02, if the vehicles would have conformed to that Standard had it been in force at the time of their manufacture, or

　　ii. the standards set out in the Canadian Standards Association Standard D409-M84, if the vehicles would not have conformed to the Canadian Standards Association Standard D409-02 had it been in force at the time of their manufacture.

(3) Equipment conforming to the applicable Canadian Standards Association Standard is prescribed and required for use in all vehicles of the class referred to in subsection (1).

(4) Despite subsections (2) and (3), the emergency exit requirements set out in section 6.9.1 of the Canadian Standards Association Standard D409-M84 and those set out in section 6.4 of the Canadian Standards Association Standard D409-02 do not apply to vehicles of the class referred to in subsection (1).

(5) [Repealed O. Reg. 172/11, s. 11.]

(6) [Repealed O. Reg. 172/11, s. 11.]

O. Reg. 49/05, s. 2; 172/11, s. 11

9. [Repealed O. Reg. 172/11, s. 12.]

10. [Repealed O. Reg. 172/11, s. 12.]

11. (1) An accessible urban transit bus is prescribed as a class of vehicle to which subsection 102(3) of the Act applies.

(2) [Repealed O. Reg. 172/11, s. 13(2).]

(3) An accessible urban transit bus shall have,

　　(a) a minimum length of 9.144 metres and a bus chassis as originally provided by the bus manufacturer;

　　(b) at least two passenger doors on the right side, the front door being at least 762 millimetres wide and the other door being at least 813 millimetres wide;

　　(c) [Repealed O. Reg. 172/11, s. 13(4).]

　　(d) a system for securing personal mobility devices consisting of devices anchored to the bus or of compartments, or a combination of both, that limit the forward, backward, rotational, lateral and vertical motion of every personal mobility device in the bus at its points of contact with the bus while it is in normal operation, including full throttle acceleration and maximum braking.

(4) An accessible urban transit bus shall have either,

　　(a) a lift to load a passenger mobility device and passenger onto the bus; or

(b) a mostly level floor that, either by design or by the use of a kneeling feature, is approximately at the level of a typical urban curbside or bus passenger platform during loading or unloading of passengers and is equipped with a ramp having a slope of no more than 4 to 1 to allow passengers to bridge the gap between the bus and the curbside or platform.

(5) [Repealed O. Reg. 172/11, s. 13(8).]

O. Reg. 533/94, s. 1; 302/95, s. 1; 184/96, s. 2; 133/10, s. 2; 172/11, s. 13(2), (4), (7), (8); 170/13, s. 5

12. [Repealed O. Reg. 172/11, s. 14.]

13. [Repealed O. Reg. 172/11, s. 14.]

14. [Repealed O. Reg. 172/11, s. 14.]

ONT. REG. 273/07 — ADMINISTRATIVE PENALTIES

made under the *Highway Traffic Act*

O. Reg. 273/07, as am. O. Reg. 403/08; 244/14.

[Note: The title of this Regulation was changed from "Administrative Monetary Penalties" to "Administrative Penalties" by O. Reg. 244/14, s. 1.]

1. Administrative penalty — A person whose driver's licence is suspended under section 48 or 48.3 of the Act shall pay to the Ministry the following administrative penalty:

1. $150 if the suspension commenced on or before June 30, 2015.

2. $180 if the suspension commenced on or before June 30, 2015 and the suspension is extended after that date by a subsequent suspension under section 48 or 48.3.

3. $180 if the suspension commenced on or after July 1, 2015.

O. Reg. 403/08, s. 1; 244/14, s. 2

2. Licence not reinstated until penalty is paid — (1) **Penalties, reinstatement fees not cumulative** — If the suspension of a person's driver's licence is extended as described in paragraph 2 of section 1 after a penalty was imposed under paragraph 1 of section 1, the person shall be required to pay only one penalty equal to the amount prescribed by paragraph 2 of section 1 and not a penalty equal to the sum of the penalties prescribed by paragraphs 1 and 2 of section 1.

(2) [Repealed O. Reg. 244/14, s. 3(1).]

(3) A person who pays the penalty imposed under section 1 of this Regulation before his or her licence is reinstated is not required to pay a reinstatement fee, in respect of the same reinstatement, under subsection 26(1.1) of Ontario Regulation 340/94 (*Drivers' Licences*) made under the Act.

(4) A person who pays the reinstatement fee under subsection 26(1.1) of Ontario Regulation 340/94 (*Drivers' Licences*) made under the Act before his or her licence is reinstated is not required to pay the penalty, in respect of the same reinstatement, imposed under section 1 of this Regulation.

(5) Despite subsections (3) and (4), where the amount of the penalty imposed under section 1 is different from the amount of the reinstatement fee under subsection 26(1.1) of Ontario Regulation 340/94 (*Drivers' Licences*) made under the Act, the amount that is payable in respect of the same reinstatement is the greater of the two amounts.

O. Reg. 403/08, s. 2; 244/14, s. 3

3. Licence cancelled for failure to pay penalty — If a person owes a penalty imposed under section 1 and does not pay it before his or her driver's licence is reinstated at the end of the suspension, his or her driver's licence may be cancelled upon or after reinstatement.

O. Reg. 403/08, s. 3; 244/14, s. 4

4. Additional penalty — Where payment for a penalty imposed under section 1 is dishonoured, a further penalty of $15 is imposed, and is added to the penalty that is payable under section 1.

O. Reg. 403/08, s. 4

5. Other suspensions unaffected — Nothing in this Regulation affects the operation of another suspension of the person's driver's licence under the Act or any other Act or a regulation made under the Act or under any other Act.

6. Commencement — This Regulation comes into force on the later of June 15, 2007 and the day it is filed.

ONT. REG. 94/06 — BORDER APPROACH LANES

made under the *Highway Traffic Act*

O. Reg. 94/06, as am. O. Reg. 86/15; 425/15 [To come into force January 1, 2017.].

1. Definition — In this Regulation,

"commercial motor vehicle" has the same meaning as in subsection 16(1) of the Act.

Proposed Amendment — 1 "commercial motor vehicle"

"commercial motor vehicle" has the same meaning as in section 3 of Ontario Regulation 419/15 (*Definitions of Commercial Motor Vehicle and Tow Truck*) made under the Act.

O. Reg. 425/15, s. 1 [To come into force January 1, 2017.]

2. Restricted use of border approach lanes — (1) No person shall drive a commercial motor vehicle or a combination of commercial motor vehicle and towed vehicle in a border approach lane unless,

(a) the commercial motor vehicle has displayed in its front windshield a valid placard issued by either the Canadian Border Services Agency or the United States of America's Customs Border Protection as part of the Free and Secure Trade (FAST) program operated by those entities; and

(b) all the occupants of the commercial motor vehicle have valid FAST Commercial Driver identification cards issued by either of the entities described in clause (a) as part of the Free and Secure Trade (FAST) program.

(2) A person may drive a commercial motor vehicle or a combination of commercial motor vehicle and towed vehicle in a border approach lane without complying with subsection (1) if the commercial motor vehicle is,

(a) an emergency vehicle, as defined in section 144 of the Act, operated by a person in the performance of his or her duties;

(b) a vehicle operated by a police officer in the performance of his or her duties;

(c) a vehicle owned or leased by the Crown in right of Ontario operated, in the performance of his or her duties, by an officer appointed for enforcing and carrying out the provisions of the Act;

(d) a road service vehicle engaged in highway maintenance or construction; or

(e) a bus.

(3) A person may drive a commercial motor vehicle or a combination of commercial motor vehicle and towed vehicle in a border approach lane where it is impossible to avoid a temporary contravention of subsection (1),

(a) due to an emergency; or

(b) in order to enter a highway lane or an exit off of the highway that is adjacent to the border approach lane.

3. Signs — (1) The restrictions under subsection 2(1) are in effect only if the border approach lane is marked by signs in accordance with this section.

(2) Border approach lane signs shall be erected at least every 2 kilometres along the length of a border approach lane.

(3) Border approach lane signs may be overhead or ground mounted; an overhead sign shall be erected directly above the border approach lane and a ground mounted sign shall be erected on the side of the highway facing approaching traffic in the border approach lane.

(4) An overhead border approach lane sign shall have the dimensions and bear the markings as illustrated in Figure A and a ground mounted border approach lane sign shall have the dimensions and bear the markings as illustrated in Figure B or C.

(5) Despite subsection (4), in an area designated in the Schedule to the *French Language Services Act*, a border approach lane sign prescribed under that subsection shall be accompanied by an overhead sign that has the dimensions and bears the markings as illustrated in Figure D or by a ground mounted sign that has the dimensions and bears the markings as illustrated in Figure E or F.

(6) The commencement of a border approach lane shall be indicated by an overhead sign that has the dimensions and bears the markings as illustrated in Figure G or a ground mounted sign that has the dimensions and bears the markings as illustrated in Figure H or I.

(7) Despite subsection (6), in an area designated in the Schedule to the *French Language Services Act*, a border approach lane begins sign prescribed under that subsection shall be accompanied by an overhead sign that has the dimensions and bears the markings as illustrated in Figure J or by a ground mounted sign that has the dimensions and bears the markings as illustrated in Figure K or L.

(8) The dimensions of a border approach lane sign or a border approach lane begins sign may differ from those prescribed under this section as long as the dimensions are in the same proportion to each other as the dimensions prescribed under this section.

(9) If a municipality that is in an area designated in the Schedule to the *French Language Services Act* has jurisdiction over a border approach lane, the municipality may erect only the signs prescribed under subsections (4) and (6), and not the signs prescribed under subsections (5) and (7), unless the municipality has passed a by-law under section 14 of that Act and the by-law is in effect.

(10) Despite subsections (4), (5), (6) and (7), a border approach lane sign or border approach lane begins sign may be a sign that displays electronic messages consisting of only the text that is prescribed under those subsections, without regard to the dimensions, markings and other characteristics illustrated in the prescribed signs.

4. Maximum length of border approach lane — The maximum length of a border approach lane is 15 kilometres.

FIGURE A

White Retro-Refl. Background
Black Border, Symbol, Arrow & Legend
Red Retro-Refl. Annular Band
Red Retro-Refl. Interdictory Stroke

EXCEPT

Red Retro-Refl. Logo & Stripe
Blue Retro-Refl. Logo & Legend
(90 x 210) cm

Text alternative: Illustration of an overhead border approach lane sign labelled as "Figure A". The sign contains two rectangles, stacked on top of one another. The top rectangle contains a symbol of a truck inside a circle with an interdictory stroke no symbol. A thick black arrow points down from the no symbol to the bottom rectangle of the sign. The bottom rectangle contains the word "EXCEPT" above a logo. The logo consists of the American flag beside the word "FAST" on top of the Canadian flag beside the word "EXPRES". The following measurements are written below the sign: (90 x 210) cm. The sign appears in black and white, but is surrounded by arrows pointing to its different elements and indicating the colours in which they must appear. This text alternative is provided for convenience only and does not form part of the official law.

FIGURE B

- Black Border, Symbol, Arrow & Legend
- Red Retro-Refl. Annular Band
- Red Retro-Refl. Interdictory Stroke
- White Retro-Refl. Background

- Red Retro-Refl. Logo & Stripe
- Blue Retro-Refl. Logo & Legend

(60 x 150) cm or
(90 x 210) cm

Text alternative: Illustration of a ground-mounted border approach lane sign labelled as "Figure B". The sign contains two rectangles, stacked on top of one another. The top rectangle contains a symbol of a truck inside a circle with an interdictory stroke no symbol. A black arrow points diagonally down and left from the no symbol to the left of the phrase "THIS LANE". The bottom rectangle contains the word "EXCEPT" above a logo. The logo consists of the American flag beside the word "FAST" on top of the Canadian flag beside the word "EXPRES". The following measurements are written below the sign: (60 x 150) cm or (90 x 210) cm. The sign appears in black and white, but is surrounded by arrows pointing to its different elements and indicating the colours in which they must appear. This text alternative is provided for convenience only and does not form part of the official law.

FIGURE C

White Retro-Refl. Background
Black Border, Symbol, Arrow & Legend
Red Retro-Refl. Annular Band
Red Retro-Refl. Interdictory Stroke

Red Retro-Refl. Logo & Stripe
Blue Retro-Refl. Logo & Legend
(60 x 150) cm or
(90 x 210) cm

Text alternative: Illustration of a ground-mounted border approach lane sign labelled as "Figure C". The sign contains two rectangles, stacked on top of one another. The top rectangle contains a symbol of a truck inside a circle with an interdictory stroke: no symbol. A black arrow points diagonally down and right from the no symbol to the right of the phrase "THIS LANE". The bottom rectangle contains the word "EXCEPT" above a logo. The logo consists of the American flag beside the word "FAST" on top of the Canadian flag beside the word "EXPRES". The following measurements are written below the sign: (60 x 150) cm or (90 x 210) cm. The sign appears in black and white, but is surrounded by arrows pointing to its different elements and indicating the colours in which they must appear. This text alternative is provided for convenience only and does not form part of the official law.

FIGURE D

White Retro-Refl. Background
Black Border, Symbol, Arrow & Legend
Red Retro-Refl. Annular Band
Red Retro-Refl. Interdictory Stroke

SAUF

FAST
EXPRES

Red Retro-Refl. Logo & Stripe
Blue Retro-Refl. Logo & Legend
(90 x 210) cm

Text alternative: Illustration of an overhead border approach lane sign labelled as "Figure D". The sign contains two rectangles, stacked on top of one another. The top rectangle contains a symbol of a truck inside a circle with an interdictory stroke no symbol. A thick black arrow points down from the no symbol to the bottom rectangle of the sign. The bottom rectangle contains the word "SAUF" above a logo. The logo consists of the American flag beside the word "FAST" on top of the Canadian flag beside the word "EXPRES". The following measurements are written below the sign: (90 x 210) cm. The sign appears in black and white, but is surrounded by arrows pointing to its different elements and indicating the colours in which they must appear. This text alternative is provided for convenience only and does not form part of the official law.

FIGURE E

Black Border, Symbol, Arrow & Legend
Red Retro-Refl. Annular Band
Red Retro-Refl. Interdictory Stroke
White Retro-Refl. Background

CETTE
VOIE

SAUF
FAST
EXPRES

Red Retro-Refl. Logo & Stripe
Blue Retro-Refl. Logo & Legend
(60 x 150) cm or
(90 x 210) cm

Text alternative: Illustration of a ground-mounted border approach lane sign labelled as "Figure E". The sign contains two rectangles, stacked on top of one another. The top rectangle contains a symbol of a truck inside a circle with an interdictory stroke no symbol. A black arrow points diagonally down and left from the no symbol to the left of the phrase "CETTE VOIE". The bottom rectangle contains the word "EXCEPT" above a logo. The logo consists of the American flag beside the word "FAST" on top of the Canadian flag beside the word "EXPRES". The following measurements are written below the sign: (60 x 150) cm or (90 x 210) cm. The sign appears in black and white, but is surrounded by arrows pointing to its different elements and indicating the colours in which they must appear. This text alternative is provided for convenience only and does not form part of the official law.

FIGURE F

White Retro-Refl. Background
Black Border, Symbol, Arrow & Legend
Red Retro-Refl. Annular Band
Red Retro-Refl. Interdictory Stroke

CETTE VOIE

SAUF
FAST EXPRES

Red Retro-Refl. Logo & Stripe
Blue Retro-Refl. Logo & Legend
(60 x 150) cm or
(90 x 210) cm

Text alternative: Illustration of a ground-mounted border approach lane sign labelled as "Figure F". The sign contains two rectangles, stacked on top of one another. The top rectangle contains a symbol of a truck inside a circle with an interdictory stroke no symbol. A black arrow points diagonally down and right from the no symbol to the right of the phrase "CETTE VOIE". The bottom rectangle contains the word "EXCEPT" above a logo. The logo consists of the American flag beside the word "FAST" on top of the Canadian flag beside the word "EXPRES". The following measurements are written below the sign: (60 x 150) cm or (90 x 210) cm. The sign appears in black and white, but is surrounded by arrows pointing to its different elements and indicating the colours in which they must appear. This text alternative is provided for convenience only and does not form part of the official law.

FIGURE G

White Retro-Refl. Background
Black Border, Symbol, Arrow & Legend
Red Retro-Refl. Annular Band
Red Retro-Refl. Interdictory Stroke

Black Background
White Retro-Refl. Legend
Red Retro-Refl. Logo & Stripe
Blue Retro-Refl. Logo & Legend

(90 x 240) cm

Text alternative: Illustration of an overhead border approach lane begins sign labelled as "Figure G". The sign contains three rectangles stacked on top of one another. The top rectangle contains a symbol of a truck inside a circle with an interdictory stroke no symbol. A thick black arrow points down from the no symbol to the middle rectangle of the sign. The middle rectangle contains the word "EXCEPT" above a logo. The logo consists of the American flag beside the word "FAST" on top of the Canadian flag beside the word "EXPRES". The bottom rectangle has a black background and the word "BEGINS" in white. The following measurements are written below the sign: (90 x 240) cm. The sign appears in black and white, but is surrounded by arrows pointing to its different elements and indicating the colours in which they must appear. This text alternative is provided for convenience only and does not form part of the official law.

FIGURE H

Black Border, Symbol, Arrow & Legend
Red Retro-Refl., Annular Band
Red Retro-Refl. Interdictory Stroke
White Retro-Refl. Background

Black Background
White Retro-Refl. Legend
Red Retro-Refl. Logo & Stripe
Blue Retro-Refl. Logo & Legend

(60 x 170) cm or
(90 x 240) cm

FIGURE I

— White Retro-Refl. Background
— Black Border, Symbol, Arrow & Legend
— Red Retro-Refl. Annular Band
— Red Retro-Refl. Interdictory Stroke

— Black Background
— White Retro-Refl. Legend
— Red Retro-Refl. Logo & Stripe
— Blue Retro-Refl. Logo & Legend

(60 x 170) cm or
(90 x 240) cm

Text alternative: Illustration of a ground-mounted border approach lane begins sign labelled as "Figure I". The sign contains three rectangles, stacked on top of one another. The top rectangle contains a symbol of a truck inside a circle with an interdictory stroke no symbol. A black arrow points diagonally down and right from the no symbol to the right of the phrase "THIS LANE". The middle rectangle contains the word "EXCEPT" above a logo. The logo consists of the American flag beside the word "FAST" on top of the Canadian flag beside the word "EXPRES". The bottom rectangle has a black background and the word "BEGINS" in white. The following measurements are written below the sign: (60 x 170) cm or (90 x 240) cm. The sign appears in black and white, but is surrounded by arrows pointing to its different elements and indicating the colours in which they must appear. This text alternative is provided for convenience only and does not form part of the official law.

FIGURE J

White Retro-Refl. Background
Black Border, Symbol, Arrow & Legend
Red Retro-Refl. Annular Band
Red Retro-Refl. Interdictory Stroke

Black Background
White Retro-Refl. Legend
Red Retro-Refl. Logo & Stripe
Blue Retro-Refl. Logo & Legend

(90 x 240) cm

Text alternative: Illustration of an overhead border approach lane begins sign labelled as "Figure J". The sign contains three rectangles stacked on top of one another. The top rectangle contains a symbol of a truck inside a circle with an interdictory stroke no symbol. A thick black arrow points down from the no symbol to the middle rectangle of the sign. The middle rectangle contains the word "SAUF" above a logo. The logo consists of the American flag beside the word "FAST" on top of the Canadian flag beside the word "EXPRES". The bottom rectangle has a black background and the word "DÉBUT" in white. The following measurements are written below the sign: (90 x 240) cm. The sign appears in black and white, but is surrounded by arrows pointing to its different elements and indicating the colours in which they must appear. This text alternative is provided for convenience only and does not form part of the official law.

579

FIGURE K

Black Border, Symbol, Arrow & Legend
Red Retro-Refl. Annular Band
Red Retro-Refl. Interdictory Stroke
White Retro-Refl. Background

Black Background
White Retro-Refl. Legend
Red Retro-Refl. Logo & Stripe
Blue Retro-Refl. Logo & Legend

(60 x 170) cm or
(90 x 240) cm

Text alternative: Illustration of a ground-mounted border approach lane begins sign labelled as "Figure K". The sign contains three rectangles, stacked on top of one another. The top rectangle contains a symbol of a truck inside a circle with an interdictory stroke no symbol. A black arrow points diagonally down and left from the no symbol to the left of the text "CETTE VOIE". The middle rectangle contains the word "SAUF" above a logo. The logo consists of the American flag beside the word "FAST" on top of the Canadian flag beside the word "EXPRES". The bottom rectangle contains the word "DÉBUT". The following measurements are written below the sign: (60 x 170) cm or (90 x 240) cm. The sign appears in black and white, but is surrounded by arrows pointing to its different elements and indicating the colours in which they must appear. This text alternative is provided for convenience only and does not form part of the official law.

FIGURE L

White Retro-Refl. Background
Black Border, Symbol, Arrow & Legend
Red Retro-Refl. Annular Band
Red Retro-Refl. Interdictory Stroke

Black Background
White Retro-Refl. Legend
Red Retro-Refl. Logo & Stripe
Blue Retro-Refl. Logo & Legend

(60 x 170) cm or
(90 x 240) cm

Text alternative: Illustration of a ground-mounted border approach lane begins sign labelled as "Figure L". The sign contains three rectangles, stacked on top of one another. The top rectangle contains a symbol of a truck inside a circle with an interdictory stroke no symbol. A black arrow points diagonally down and right from the no symbol to the right of the text "CETTE VOIE". The middle rectangle contains the word "SAUF" above a logo. The logo consists of the American flag beside the word "FAST" on top of the Canadian flag beside the word "EXPRES". The bottom rectangle contains the word "DÉBUT". The following measurements are written below the sign: (60 x 170) cm or (90 x 240) cm. The sign appears in black and white, but is surrounded by arrows pointing to its different elements and indicating the colours in which they must appear. This text alternative is provided for convenience only and does not form part of the official law.

O. Reg. 86/15, s. 1

5. Commencement — This Regulation comes into force on the later of March 31, 2006 and the day this Regulation is filed.

ONT. REG. 643/05 — CARRIAGE OF GOODS

made under the *Highway Traffic Act*

O. Reg. 643/05

1. Definitions — In this Regulation,

"household goods" means,

(a) furniture, appliances and personal effects transported as part of the relocation of a household, and includes vehicles and boats moved as part of a household,

(b) uncrated furniture and equipment transported to, and to be furnishings in, an office, store, factory, commercial establishment, museum, hospital or public institution,

(c) stock-in-trade moved as part of the relocation of an office, store or commercial establishment, and

(d) objects of art, displays, exhibits, computers and electronic devices that require specialized handling;

"public truck" means a commercial motor vehicle or the combination of a commercial motor vehicle and trailer or trailers drawn by it, operated by a person to carry the goods of another person for compensation.

2. Goods not covered by this Regulation — This Regulation does not apply to the carriage of the following goods:

1. Goods that are carried solely within a local municipality, excluding a municipality that had the status of a township on December 31, 2002 and, but for the enactment of the *Municipal Act, 2001*, would have had the status of a township on January 1, 2003.

2. Fresh fruit and fresh vegetables grown in continental United States of America or Mexico.

3. Goods used on farms that are carried in a commercial motor vehicle equipped with not more than three axles and that does not draw a trailer.

4. Field crops, fresh fruits, fresh tree nuts, fresh vegetables, horticultural specialities, livestock and animal specialities that are carried in a commercial motor vehicle equipped with not more than three axles and that does not draw a trailer.

5. Skim milk, cream or fresh, unprocessed bulk fluid milk carried on behalf of The Ontario Milk Marketing Board.

6. Milk carried by a co-operative corporation to which the *Co-operative Corporations Act* applies, of which one of the objects is to engage in the transporta-

tion of milk and of which more than three-quarters of the shareholders or members are producers supplying milk to one or more plants.

7. Wheat that is carried by a person appointed to act as agent for the Ontario Wheat Producers' Marketing Board from the agent's premises in a commercial vehicle registered in the agent's name.

8. Ready mixed concrete.

9. Primary forest or raw wood materials that are the products of the forest from which they are being carried.

10. Goods carried by an operator of a commercial vehicle if the goods have been sold, bought, produced, transformed or repaired by, or lent, borrowed, given or leased by, the operator as an integral part of the operator's primary business, which business is not the operation of public trucks.

11. Goods in a bus being operated under the authority of an operating licence issued under the *Public Vehicles Act*.

12. Goods carried by the Ontario Northland Transportation Commission.

3. Liability insurance held by carriers — (1) For each motor vehicle operated by a carrier for the carriage of goods for compensation, the carrier shall provide or effect and carry with an insurer licensed under the *Insurance Act* liability insurance for loss or damage to goods in an amount sufficient to cover the loss or damage of the goods carried.

(2) Subsection (1) does not apply where the cargo is road-construction materials, iron, steel, coal, rough lumber or miscellaneous waste or scrap or materials of an indestructible or non-flammable nature.

4. Information required in contract of carriage — general freight — (1)
A contract of carriage must contain,

    (a) the name of the consignor;

    (b) the name and address of the consignee;

    (c) the originating point of the shipment;

    (d) the destination of the shipment;

    (e) the date of the shipment;

    (f) the name of the originating carrier;

    (g) the names of connecting carriers, if any;

    (h) the particulars of the goods comprising the shipment;

    (i) a space to show the declared valuation of the shipment, if any;

    (j) information as to whether the charges are prepaid or collect;

    (k) a space to show whether the C.O.D. fee is prepaid or collect;

    (l) a space to show the amount to be collected by the carrier on a C.O.D. shipment;

    (m) a space to note any special agreement between the consignor and carrier;

    (n) a statement to indicate that the uniform conditions of carriage apply;

(o) an acknowledgment of receipt of the goods by the carrier or the intermediary indicating whether the goods were received in apparent good order and condition;

(p) an undertaking by the carrier or the intermediary to carry the goods for delivery to the consignee or the person entitled to receive the goods;

(q) the signed acceptance by or on behalf of the originating carrier or intermediary and the consignor of the conditions contained, or deemed to be contained, in the contract of carriage;

(r) a statement of the notice of claim requirements in the uniform conditions of carriage; and

(s) if applicable, a statement, in conspicuous form, that the carrier's liability is limited by a term or condition of another agreement.

(2) The uniform conditions of carriage in Schedule 1 are deemed to be terms and conditions of every contract of carriage to which this section applies.

(3) This section does not apply to a contract of carriage for,

(a) livestock;

(b) animal specialties;

(c) household goods;

(d) road construction materials, garbage, waste or scrap, sod, coal or lumber (rough or dressed); or

(e) a parcel, wrapped or unwrapped, that does not weigh more than 45 kilograms.

5. Information required in contract of carriage — livestock or animal specialties — (1) A contract of carriage for the carriage of livestock or animal specialties must contain,

(a) the name of the consignor;

(b) the name and address of the consignee;

(c) the originating point of the shipment;

(d) the destination of the shipment;

(e) the date of the shipment;

(f) the name of the originating carrier;

(g) the names of connecting carriers, if any;

(h) the particulars of the goods comprising the shipment;

(i) the gross weight of the shipment;

(j) a space to show the declared valuation of the shipment, if any;

(k) information as to whether the charges are prepaid or collect;

(l) a space to show the amount to be collected by the carrier on a C.O.D. shipment;

(m) if applicable, a statement, in conspicuous form, that the carrier's liability is limited by a term or condition of another agreement; and

(n) if applicable, the words "at owner's risk".

(2) The uniform conditions of carriage in Schedule 2 are deemed to be terms and conditions of every contract of carriage to which this section applies.

6. Information required in contract of carriage — household goods —

(1) A contract of carriage for the carriage of household goods must contain,

(a) the name and address of the consignor;

(b) the name, address and telephone number of the consignee;

(c) the originating point of the shipment;

(d) the destination of the shipment;

(e) the date of the shipment;

(f) in a conspicuous place, the name and telephone number of the originating carrier;

(g) in a conspicuous place, the name and telephone number of the destination agent;

(h) the names of connecting carriers, if any;

(i) the inventory of the goods comprising the shipment;

(j) a statement as to whether the goods were received by the carrier in apparent good order and condition, except as noted on the inventory;

(k) a space to show the declared valuation of the shipment;

(l) a space to show the amount of freight and all other charges to be collected by the carrier;

(m) a space to show the date or time period agreed upon for delivery;

(n) a space to note any special services or agreements between consignor and the originating carrier;

(o) a statement to indicate that the uniform conditions of carriage apply;

(p) if applicable, a statement, in conspicuous form, that the carrier's liability is limited by a term or condition of the contract of carriage; and

(q) a statement in conspicuous form that the signature of the consignee for the receipt of goods does not preclude future claim for loss or damage made within the time limits prescribed by the uniform conditions of carriage.

(2) The uniform conditions of carriage in Schedule 3 are deemed to be terms and conditions of every contract of carriage to which this section applies.

7. Commencement — This Regulation comes into force on the later of January 1, 2006 and the day this Regulation is filed.

SCHEDULE 1 — UNIFORM CONDITIONS OF CARRIAGE — GENERAL FREIGHT

1. Liability of Carrier

The carrier of the goods described in this contract is liable for any loss of or damage to goods accepted by the carrier or the carrier's agent except as provided in this Schedule.

2. Liability of Originating and Delivering Carriers

Where a shipment is accepted for carriage by more than one carrier, the originating carrier and the carrier who assumes responsibility for delivery to the consignee (called the delivering carrier in this Schedule), in addition to any other liability under this Schedule, are liable for any loss of or damage to the goods while they are in the custody of any other carrier to whom the goods are delivered and from which liability the other carrier is not relieved.

3. Recovery from Connecting Carriers

    i. The originating carrier or the delivering carrier, as the case may be, is entitled to recover from any other carrier to whom the goods are delivered the amount that the originating carrier or delivering carrier, as the case may be, is required to pay for the loss of or damage to the goods while they were in the custody of such other carrier.

    ii. If there is a concealed damage settlement and the goods were interlined between carriers so that it is not clear as to who had custody of the goods when they were damaged, the originating carrier or delivering carrier, as the case may be, is entitled to recover from each of the connecting carriers an amount prorated on the basis of each carrier's revenue for carriage of the damaged goods.

4. Remedy by Consignor or Consignee

Nothing in Article 2 or 3 deprives a consignor or consignee of any rights the consignor or consignee may have against any carrier.

5. Exceptions from Liability

The carrier shall not be liable for loss, damage or delay to any of the goods described in the contract of carriage caused by an act of God, the Queen's or public enemies, riots, strikes, a defect or inherent vice in the goods, an act or default of the consignor, owner or consignee, authority of law, quarantine or difference in weights of grain, seed or other commodities caused by natural shrinkage.

6. Delay

No carrier is bound to carry goods by any particular public truck or in time for any particular market or otherwise than with due dispatch, unless by agreement that is specifically endorsed in the contract of carriage and signed by the parties.

7. Routing by Carrier

If the carrier forwards the goods by a conveyance that is not a public truck, the liability of the carrier is the same as though the entire carriage were by public truck.

8. Stoppage in Transit

If goods are stopped and held in transit at the request of the party entitled to so request, the goods are held at the risk of that party.

9. Valuation

Subject to Article 10, the amount of any loss or damage for which the carrier is liable, whether or not the loss or damage results from negligence, shall be the lesser of,

i. the value of the goods at the place and time of shipment, including the freight and other charges if paid, and

ii. $4.41 per kilogram computed on the total weight of the shipment.

10. Declared Value

If the consignor has declared a value of the goods on the face of the contract of carriage, the amount of any loss or damage for which the carrier is liable shall not exceed the declared value.

11. Consignor's Risk

i. If it is agreed that the goods are carried at the risk of the consignor, that agreement covers only such risks as are necessarily incidental to the carriage and the agreement does not relieve the carrier from liability for any loss or damage or delay that results from the negligence of the carrier or the carrier's agents or employees.

ii. The burden of proving absence of negligence shall be on the carrier.

12. Notice of Claim

i. No carrier is liable for loss, damage or delay to any goods carried under the contract of carriage unless notice of the loss, damage or delay setting out particulars of the origin, destination and date of shipment of the goods and the estimated amount claimed in respect of such loss, damage or delay is given in writing to the originating carrier or the delivering carrier within 60 days after delivery of the goods or, in the case of failure to make delivery, within nine months after the date of shipment.

ii. The final statement of the claim must be filed within nine months after the date of shipment, together with a copy of the paid freight bill.

13. Articles of Extraordinary Value

i. No carrier is bound to carry any documents, specie or articles of extraordinary value unless by a special agreement to do so.

ii. If such goods are carried without a special agreement and the nature of the goods is not disclosed in the contract of carriage, the carrier shall not be liable for any loss or damage in excess of the maximum liability stipulated in Article 9.

14. Freight Charges

i. If required by the carrier, the freight and all other lawful charges accruing on the goods shall be paid before delivery.

ii. If upon inspection it is ascertained that the goods shipped are not those described in the contract of carriage, the freight charges must be paid upon the goods actually shipped with any additional charges lawfully payable on the freight charges.

iii. If a consignor does not indicate that a shipment is to move prepaid, or does not indicate how the shipment is to move, it will automatically move on a collect basis.

15. Dangerous Goods

Every person, whether as principal or agent, shipping dangerous goods without previous full disclosure to the carrier as required by law shall indemnify the carrier against all loss, damage or delay caused by the failure to disclose and such goods may be warehoused at the consignor's risk and expense.

16. Undelivered Goods

i. If, through no fault of the carrier, the goods cannot be delivered, the carrier shall immediately give notice to the consignor and consignee that delivery cannot be made and shall request disposal instructions.

ii. Pending receipt of disposal instructions,

A. the goods may be stored in the warehouse of the carrier, subject to a reasonable charge for storage, or

B. if the carrier has notified the consignor of this intention, the goods may be removed to and stored in a public or licensed warehouse at the expense of the consignor, without liability on the part of the carrier, and subject to a lien for all freight and other lawful charges, including a reasonable charge for storage.

17. Return of Goods

If a notice has been given by the carrier pursuant to paragraph i of Article 16, and no disposal instructions have been received within 10 days after the date of such notice, the carrier may return to the consignor, at the consignor's expense, all undelivered shipments for which such notice has been given.

18. Alterations

Subject to Article 19, any limitation in the contract of carriage on the carrier's liability and any alteration to the contract of carriage shall be signed or initialled by the consignor and the originating carrier or their agents and, unless signed and initialled, shall be without effect.

19. Weights

i. It shall be the responsibility of the consignor to show correct shipping weights of the shipment on the contract of carriage.

ii. If the actual weight of the shipment does not agree with the weight shown on the contract of carriage, the weight shown on the contract of carriage may be corrected by the carrier.

20. C.O.D. Shipments

i. The carrier shall not deliver a C.O.D. shipment unless payment is received in full.

ii. The charge for collecting and remitting the amount of C.O.D. bills for C.O.D. shipments must be collected from the consignee unless the consignor has instructed otherwise on the contract of carriage.

iii. The carrier shall keep all C.O.D. money in a trust fund or account separate from the other revenues and funds of the carrier's business.

iv. The carrier shall remit all C.O.D. money to the consignor, or person designated by the consignor, within 15 days after collection.

SCHEDULE 2 — UNIFORM CONDITIONS OF CARRIAGE — LIVESTOCK AND ANIMAL SPECIALTIES

1. Liability of Carrier

The carrier of the goods is liable for any loss of or damage or injury to goods accepted by the carrier or the carrier's agent except as provided in this Schedule.

2. Liability of Originating Carrier

Where a shipment is accepted for carriage by more than one carrier, the originating carrier, in addition to any other liability under this Schedule, is liable for any loss of or damage or injury to the goods while they are in the custody of any other carrier to whom the goods are delivered and the onus of proving that the loss, damage or injury was not caused or did not result while the goods were in the custody of another carrier to whom the goods were delivered is upon the originating carrier.

3. Recovery from Connecting Carriers

The originating carrier or the carrier who assumes responsibility for delivery to the consignee (called the delivering carrier in this Schedule), as the case may be, is entitled to recover from any other carrier to whom the goods are delivered the amount that the originating carrier or delivering carrier, as the case may be, is required to pay for the loss of or damage or injury to the goods while they were in the custody of such other carrier.

4. Remedy by Consignor or Consignee

Nothing in Article 2 or 3 deprives a consignor or consignee of any rights the consignor or consignee may have against any carrier.

5. Exceptions from Liability

The carrier shall not be liable for loss, damage, injury or delay to any of the goods described in the contract of carriage caused by an act of God, the Queen's or public enemies, riots, strikes, a defect in the goods, an act or default of the consignor, owner or consignee, authority of law, quarantine or difference in weights of livestock or animal specialties by natural shrinkage.

6. Delay

No carrier is bound to carry goods by any particular public truck or in time for any particular market or otherwise than with due dispatch, unless by agreement that is specifically endorsed in the contract of carriage and signed by the parties.

7. Routing by Carrier

If the carrier forwards the goods by a conveyance that is not a public truck, the liability of the carrier is the same as though the entire carriage were by public truck.

8. Stoppage in Transit

If goods are stopped and held in transit at the request of the party entitled to so request, the goods are held at the risk of that party.

9. Valuation

Subject to Article 10, the amount of any loss, injury or damage for which the carrier is liable, whether or not the loss, injury or damage results from negligence, shall be the lesser of,

> i. the value of the goods at the place and time of shipment including the freight and other charges if paid, and

> ii. $3.31 per kilogram computed on the total weight of the shipment.

10. Declared Value

If the consignor has declared a value of the goods on the face of the contract of carriage, the amount of any loss, injury or damage for which the carrier is liable shall not exceed the declared value.

11. Consignor's Risk

> i. If it is agreed that the goods are carried at the risk of the consignor or owner of the goods, that agreement covers only such risks as are necessarily incidental to the carriage and the agreement does not relieve the carrier from liability for any loss or damage, injury or delay that results from the negligence of the carrier or the carrier's agents or employees.

> ii. The burden of proving absence of negligence shall be on the carrier.

12. Notice of Claim

No carrier is liable for loss, damage, injury or delay to any goods carried under the contract of carriage unless notice of the loss, damage, injury or delay setting out particulars of the origin, destination and date of shipment of the goods and the estimated amount claimed in respect of such loss, damage, injury or delay is given in writing to the originating carrier or the delivering carrier within 90 days after delivery of the goods or, in the case of failure to make delivery, within 90 days after a reasonable time for delivery has elapsed.

13. Articles of Extraordinary Value

> i. No carrier is bound to carry any documents, specie or articles of extraordinary value unless by a special agreement to do so.

> ii. If such goods are carried without a special agreement and the nature of the goods is not disclosed in the contract of carriage, the carrier shall not be liable for any loss, injury, damage or delay in excess of the maximum liability stipulated in Article 9.

14. Freight Charges

> i. If required by the carrier, the freight and all other lawful charges accruing on the goods shall be paid before delivery.

> ii. If upon inspection it is ascertained that the goods shipped are not those described in the contract of carriage, the freight charges must be paid upon the goods actually shipped with any additional charges lawfully payable on the freight charges.

> iii. If a consignor does not indicate that a shipment is to move prepaid, or does not indicate how the shipment is to move, it will automatically move on a collect basis.

15. Undelivered Goods

i. If, through no fault of the carrier, the goods cannot be delivered, the carrier shall immediately give notice to the consignor and consignee that delivery cannot be made and shall request disposal instructions.

ii. Pending receipt of disposal instructions,

A. the goods may be stored in the warehouse of the carrier, subject to a reasonable charge for storage, or

B. if the carrier has notified the consignor in writing of this intention, the goods may be removed to and stored in a public or licensed warehouse at the expense of the consignor, without liability on the part of the carrier, and subject to a lien for all freight and other lawful charges, including a reasonable charge for storage.

16. Alterations

Any limitation in the contract of carriage on the carrier's liability and any alteration to the contract of carriage shall be signed or initialled by the consignor and the originating carrier or their agents and, unless signed and initialled, shall be without effect.

17. C.O.D. Shipments

i. The carrier shall clearly indicate, on the documents accompanying each C.O.D. shipment received and transported, the name and address of the consignor or other person designated as payee to whom the delivering carrier shall remit C.O.D. funds collected upon delivery of the shipment.

ii. The carrier shall keep all C.O.D. money in a trust fund or account separate from the other revenues and funds of the carrier's business.

iii. The carrier shall remit all C.O.D. money to the consignor or person designated by the consignor within 15 days after collection.

iv. If a C.O.D. shipment is not delivered within 10 days of its arrival at its destination, the carrier shall notify the consignor in writing giving reasons for the non-delivery and shall obtain instructions in writing for disposal of the shipment.

SCHEDULE 3 — UNIFORM CONDITIONS OF CARRIAGE — HOUSEHOLD GOODS

1. Liability of Carrier

The carrier of the goods is liable for any loss of or damage to goods accepted by the carrier or the carrier's agent except as provided in this Schedule.

2. Liability of Originating and Delivering Carriers

Where a shipment is accepted for carriage by more than one carrier, the originating carrier and the carrier who assumes responsibility for delivery to the consignee (called the delivering carrier in this Schedule), in addition to any other liability under this Schedule, are liable for any loss of or damage to the goods while they are in the custody of any other carrier to whom the goods are delivered and from which liability the other carrier is not relieved.

3. Recovery from Connecting Carriers

The originating carrier or the delivering carrier, as the case may be, is entitled to recover from any other carrier to whom the goods are delivered the amount that the originating carrier or delivering carrier, as the case may be, is required to pay for the loss of or damage to the goods while they were in the custody of such other carrier.

4. Remedy by Consignor or Consignee

Nothing in Article 2 or 3 deprives a consignor or consignee of any rights the consignor or consignee may have against any carrier.

5. Exceptions from Liability

   i. The carrier shall not be liable for loss, damage or delay to any of the goods described in the contract of carriage caused by an act of God, the Queen's or public enemies, riots, strikes, a defect in the goods, an act or default of the consignor, owner or consignee, authority of law or quarantine.

   ii. Except as a result of the negligence of the carrier or the carrier's agents or employees, the carrier shall not be liable for,

   A. damage to fragile articles that are not packed and unpacked by the contracting carrier or the contracting carrier's agent or employees,

   B. damage to the mechanical, electronic, digital or other operations of radios, televisions, computers, clocks, cameras, audio and visual recording and playing equipment, appliances, musical instruments and other equipment, irrespective of who packed or unpacked such articles, unless servicing and preparation was performed by the contracting carrier or the carrier's agent or employees,

   C. deterioration of or damage to perishable food, plants or pets, or

   D. loss of contents of consignor-packed articles, unless the containers used are opened for the carrier's inspection and articles are listed in the contract of carriage and receipted for by the carrier,

   iii. The carrier shall not be liable for,

   A. damage to or loss of a complete set or unit when only part of such set is damaged or lost, in which event the carrier shall only be liable for repair or replacement of the lost or damaged piece or pieces,

   B. damage to the goods at a place or places of pick-up at which the consignor or the consignor's agent is not in attendance, or

   C. damage to the goods at a place or places of delivery at which the consignee or the consignee's agent is not in attendance and cannot give receipt for goods delivered.

   iv. The burden of proving absence of negligence for the purpose of paragraph ii is on the carrier.

6. Delay

   i. At the time of acceptance of the contract, the originating carrier shall provide the consignor with a date or time period within which delivery is to be made.

ii. Failure by the carrier to effect delivery within the time specified on the face of contract of carriage shall render the carrier liable for reasonable food and lodging expenses incurred by the consignee.

iii. Failure by the consignee to accept delivery when tendered within the time specified in the contract of carriage shall render the consignee liable for reasonable storage in transit, handling and redelivery charges incurred by the carrier.

7. Routing by Carrier

If the carrier forwards the goods by a conveyance that is not a public truck, the liability of the carrier is the same as though the entire carriage were by public truck.

8. Stoppage in Transit

If goods are stopped and held in transit at the request of the party entitled to so request, the goods are held at the risk of that party.

9. Valuation

Subject to Article 10, the amount of any loss or damage for which the carrier is liable, whether or not the loss or damage results from negligence of the carrier or the carrier's employees or agents, shall be the lesser of,

i. the value of the goods at the place and time of shipment, and

ii. the greater of,

A. the value of the goods as represented by the consignor on the face of the contract of carriage, and

B. $4.41 per kilogram computed on the total weight of the shipment.

10. Election

i. If the consignor so elects on the face of the contract of carriage, the maximum liability shall be based on $1.32 per kilogram per article lost or damaged.

ii. If the liability is calculated under Article 9, the consignor shall pay to the carrier any additional charges incurred by the carrier to provide insurance coverage in excess of $1.32 per kilogram per article.

11. Consignor's Risk

i. If it is agreed that the goods are carried at the risk of the consignor, that agreement covers only such risks as are necessarily incidental to the carriage and the agreement does not relieve the carrier from liability for any loss or damage or delay that results from the negligence of the carrier or the carrier's agents or employees.

ii. The burden of proving absence of negligence shall be on the carrier.

12. Notice of Claim

i. No carrier is liable for loss, damage or delay to any goods carried under the contract of carriage unless notice of the loss, damage or delay setting out particulars of the origin, destination and date of shipment of the goods and the estimated amount claimed in respect of such loss, damage or delay is given in writing to the originating carrier or the delivering carrier within 60 days after delivery of the goods or, in the case of failure to make delivery, within nine months after the date of shipment.

ii. The final statement of the claim must be filed within nine months after the date of shipment.

iii. The originating carrier or the delivering carrier, as the case may be, shall acknowledge receipt of the claim within 30 days after receipt.

13. Articles of Extraordinary Value

i. No carrier is bound to carry any documents, specie or articles of extraordinary value unless by a special agreement to do so.

ii. If such goods are carried without a special agreement and the nature of the goods is not disclosed in the contract of carriage, the carrier shall not be liable for any loss or damage in excess of the maximum liability stipulated in Article 9.

14. Freight Charges

i. If required by the carrier, the freight and all other lawful charges accruing on the goods shall be paid before delivery but, if the total charges exceed the estimated charges by more than 10 per cent and if the excess charges are for additional or different goods or services from those to which the estimate applied, the consignee shall pay the difference between the estimated and total charges within 15 days, excluding Saturdays, Sundays and other holidays, after delivery.

ii. The 15-day extension in paragraph i does not apply if the carrier notifies the consignor of the total charges immediately after the goods are loaded or if the consignor signs a waiver of the extension.

iii. If upon inspection it is ascertained that the goods shipped are not those described in the contract of carriage, the freight charges must be paid upon the goods actually shipped with any additional charges lawfully payable on the freight charges.

iv. If a consignor does not indicate that a shipment is to move prepaid, or does not indicate how the shipment is to move, it will automatically move on a collect basis.

15. Dangerous Goods

Every person, whether as principal or agent, shipping dangerous goods without previous full disclosure to the carrier as required by law shall indemnify the carrier against all loss, damage or delay caused by the failure to disclose and such goods may be warehoused at the consignor's risk and expense.

16. Undelivered Goods

i. If, through no fault of the carrier, the goods cannot be delivered, the carrier shall immediately give notice to the consignor and consignee that delivery cannot be made and shall request disposal instructions.

ii. Pending receipt of disposal instructions,

A. the goods may be stored in the warehouse of the carrier, subject to a reasonable charge for storage, or

B. if the carrier has notified the consignor of this intention, the goods may be removed to and stored in a public or licensed warehouse at the expense of the consignor, without liability on the part of the carrier, and subject to a lien for all freight and other lawful charges, including a reasonable charge for storage.

17. Alterations

Subject to Article 18, any limitation in the contract of carriage on the carrier's liability and any alteration to the contract of carriage shall be signed or initialled by the consignor and the originating carrier or their agents and, unless signed and initialled, shall be without effect.

18. Weights

i. It shall be the responsibility of the originating carrier or such carrier's agent to show on the contract of carriage the correct tare and gross and net weights by use of a certified public scale and to attach the weigh scale ticket to such carrier's copy of the contract of carriage.

ii. If there is no certified public scale at the place of origin or within a radius of 16 kilometres of the place of origin, the gross weight shall be deemed to be 112 kilograms per cubic metre of properly loaded van space.

ONT. REG. 376/02 — CLASSIFICATION OF VEHICLES AS IRREPARABLE, SALVAGE AND REBUILT

made under the *Highway Traffic Act*

O. Reg. 376/02, as am. O. Reg. 355/07; 435/12.

1. Definitions — (1) In section 199.1 of the Act and in this Regulation,

"insurer" means,

(a) an insurer, as defined in subsection 1(1) of the *Compulsory Automobile Insurance Act*, or

(b) a person who owns, leases or holds the plate portion of the vehicle permits for 10 or more vehicles the policies of insurance for which do not cover damage caused by all perils;

"irreparable" means, with respect to a vehicle, a vehicle that,

(a) is a total loss and,

(i) has been immersed in liquid to the bottom of its dashboard or higher,

(ii) any major part of its electrical system has been, or appears to have been, immersed in liquid;

(iii) has incurred damage requiring the replacement of,

(A) for a vehicle the occupant compartment of which extends from the front door hinge pillar assemblies to the rear-most cross-member of the vehicle, five or more of the structural assemblies listed in Parts 2, 3 and 4 of the Schedule,

(B) for a vehicle the occupant compartment of which extends from the front-most cross-member of the vehicle to the rear-most cross-member of the vehicle, seven or more of the structural assemblies listed in Parts 1, 2, 3 and 4 of the Schedule,

(C) for a vehicle other than a vehicle described in sub-subclause (A) or (B), three or more of the structural assemblies listed in Parts 2 and 4 of the Schedule, or

(D) its structural fire wall or bulkhead assembly,

(iv) if the vehicle is a motorcycle, has incurred structural damage requiring the replacement by cutting and welding of any integral part of its full frame assembly, or

596

      (v) has been stolen and dismantled such that the retail price for new parts of a like kind to replace those parts missing or damaged exceeds the fair labour cost to install or repair those parts, and,

           (A) a settlement of an insurance claim has been paid for the vehicle as a total loss, or

           (B) the vehicle is owned, leased or the plate portion of its vehicle permit is held by a person who is an insurer within the meaning of clause (b) of the definition of "insurer", or

  (b) is classified by the Registrar as irreparable under subsection 199.1(11) of the Act;

"rebuilt" means, with respect to a vehicle, a vehicle that was classified as salvage by the Registrar under subsection 199.1(10) or (11) of the Act and for which a structural inspection certificate has subsequently been submitted to comply with subsection 2.1(1) of Regulation 628 of the Revised Regulations of Ontario, 1990 (Vehicle Permits);

"salvage" means, with respect to a vehicle, a vehicle that,

  (a) is a total loss and has incurred damage requiring replacement of one or more of the structural assemblies listed in Parts 1, 2, 3 and 4 of the Schedule, but is not irreparable

  (b) is classified by the Registrar as salvage under subsection 199.1(11) of the Act, or

  (c) is a motor vehicle assembled using the body of a motor vehicle with a model year of 1981 or later and the chassis frame assembly of another motor vehicle, both of which were manufactured utilizing a full frame assembly as part of the vehicle's structure;

"salvage value" means the value of a damaged or stolen and dismantled vehicle that is legitimately recoverable through commercial means of disposal and, if the damaged or stolen and dismantled vehicle is purchased by a person described in paragraph 2 of subsection 4(1), that value is the price paid by the person for the vehicle;

"total loss" means, with respect to a vehicle, a vehicle that has been damaged by collision, impact, fire or flood, or has been stolen and dismantled, such that the estimated cost of repairing it exceeds the difference between the fair market value of the vehicle immediately before it was damaged or stolen and its salvage value.

(2) For the purposes of the definitions of "irreparable" and "salvage" and sub-sub-paragraph 2 i A of subsection 4(1), a structural assembly, structural firewall or bulkhead assembly requires replacement if,

  (a) it has been damaged by impact and has been torn, kinked or bent beyond the manufacturer's repair standards or, if there are no manufacturer's repair standards, beyond the commonly accepted standards of the auto body collision repair industry; or

  (b) it has been damaged by heat beyond the manufacturer's repair standards or, if there are no manufacturer's repair standards, beyond the commonly accepted standards of the auto body collision repair industry.

(3) For the purposes of the definition of "irreparable" and sub-subparagraph 2 i B of subsection 4(1), the following are major parts of the electrical system of a vehicle:

1. A fuse panel or breaker panel.

2. A component that monitors, triggers or controls any component of the vehicle's occupant restraint systems.

3. An electronic component that transmits or relays power for use in the heating or cooling of the vehicle's occupant compartment.

4. An electronic component that transmits or relays power for use in the vehicle's defogging or defrosting systems.

5. An electronic component or module that controls the vehicle's primary operating systems.

6. A main wiring harness with unsealed connections that is located in the occupant compartment.

7. An electronic module that controls the vehicle's on board self-diagnostic system, excluding communications, navigational and entertainment systems.

8. An electronic module that controls the vehicle's braking systems or steering systems.

(4) For the purpose of the definition of "total loss", the estimated cost of repairing the vehicle must be calculated using reasonable commercial rates for parts, supplies and labour.

2. Inspection of vehicles — (1) If a person described in paragraph 1 of subsection 4(1) is making the determination that a vehicle, other than a motorcycle, is irreparable or salvage, the determination shall be based on an inspection of the vehicle carried out by a person who,

(a) holds a certificate of qualification, that is not suspended, in the trade of automotive service technician, truck and coach technician or auto body and collision damage repairer issued under the *Ontario College of Trades and Apprenticeship Act, 2009*; and

(b) is employed by a motor vehicle inspection station that is licensed under Regulation 601 of the Revised Regulations of Ontario, 1990 with a Type 6 licence.

(2) If a person described in paragraph 1 of subsection 4(1) is making the determination that a motorcycle is irreparable, the determination shall be based on an inspection of the motorcycle carried out by a person who,

(a) holds a certificate of qualification, that is not suspended, in the trade of motorcycle technician, automotive service technician, truck and coach technician or auto body and collision damage repairer issued under the *Ontario College of Trades and Apprenticeship Act, 2009*; and

(b) is employed by a motor vehicle inspection station that is licensed under Regulation 601 of the Revised Regulations of Ontario, 1990 with a Type 4 or 6 licence.

(3) Every person who carries out an inspection of a vehicle on behalf of an insurer or a person described in paragraph 2 of subsection 4(1) to determine that the vehicle is irreparable or salvage shall provide the insurer or other person on whose behalf the inspection is carried out with a copy of the records used and created in carrying out the inspection and the insurer or other person shall retain the records for two years.

(4) Every motor vehicle inspection station shall retain the records used and created in carrying out an inspection under subsection (1) or (2) for two years.

(5) A person who carries out an inspection under subsection (1) shall only inspect a vehicle that is within the scope of his or her certificate of qualification.

O. Reg. 435/12, s. 1

3. Notification by insurer — (1) An insurer shall notify the Registrar that a vehicle is irreparable or salvage under subsection 199.1(4) of the Act,

(a) if the insurer, within the meaning of clause (a) of the definition of "insurer",

(i) acquires ownership of the vehicle, within six days after the date on which the insurer acquires ownership,

(ii) pays a settlement of the claim to the holder of the permit, but does not acquire ownership of the vehicle, within 14 days after the date on which the insurer pays the settlement; or

(b) if the insurer is an insurer within the meaning of clause (b) of the definition of "insurer", within six days after the date of the incident giving rise to the determination.

(2) Notification of the Registrar by the insurer shall be in the form approved for the purpose by the Minister, fully completed by the insurer.

(3) The form approved by the Minister shall require,

(a) the vehicle identification number;

(b) the insurer's determination that the vehicle is irreparable or salvage;

(c) the name of the holder of the plate portion of the vehicle permit at the time of the incident giving rise to the determination or, if no plate portion has been issued, the name of the holder of the vehicle portion of the vehicle permit;

(d) if applicable, the driver's licence number, date of birth, address and telephone number of the holder described in clause (c);

(e) the date of the incident giving rise to the determination;

(f) if applicable, the insurance claim number for the claim relating to the incident giving rise to the determination;

(g) if applicable, the date the insurer acquired ownership of the vehicle or the date the insurer settled the claim, if the insurer does not acquire ownership of the vehicle, as the case may be;

(h) the name and address of the insurer and the insurer's registrant identification number on the records of the Ministry; and

(i) the name, business address and telephone number of the individual who carried out the inspection and completed the form on behalf of the insurer.

(4) An insurer shall also notify the holder of the vehicle permit or the vehicle portion of the vehicle permit for the vehicle under subsection 199.1(8) of the Act, in writing, that the insurer has determined that the vehicle is irreparable or salvage, within the time limits for notifying the Registrar set out in subsection (1).

4. Notification by other persons — **(1)** The following are required to notify the Registrar under subsection 199.1(5) of the Act:

1. A person other than an insurer who is, at the time of the incident giving rise to the determination that the vehicle is irreparable or salvage, the holder of the plate portion of the vehicle permit for the vehicle or, if no plate portion of the permit has been issued, the holder of the vehicle portion of the vehicle permit and who,

    i. does not have insurance for the, vehicle,

    ii. does have insurance for the vehicle, but the policy of insurance does not cover damage caused by all perils, or

    iii. does have insurance for the vehicle but a settlement of the claim made in relation to the incident giving rise to the determination is not paid by the insurer to the person within 25 days after the incident.

2. A person other than an insurer including an importer, salvager or auctioneer, who buys, sells, wrecks or otherwise deals in used vehicles, who acquires ownership of a vehicle,

    i. that,

        A. appears to have been involved in a collision, impact or fire that caused damage to a structural assembly listed in Part 1, 2, 3 or 4 of the Schedule or that required the replacement of the structural firewall or bulkhead assembly of the vehicle, or

        B. appears to have been immersed in liquid to the bottom of the dashboard or higher, or any major part of its electrical system has been or appears to have been immersed in liquid, and

    ii. the vehicle permit for which has not yet been classified by the Registrar as irreparable or salvage as a result of the damage or apparent immersion in liquid described in sub-subparagraph i A or B.

(2) If a person described in paragraph 1 of subsection (1) determines that a vehicle is irreparable or salvage, that person shall so notify the Registrar under subsection 199.1(5) of the Act within 26 days after the date of the incident giving rise to the determination.

(3) If a person described in paragraph 2 of subsection (1) determines that a vehicle is irreparable or salvage, that person shall so notify the Registrar under subsection 199.1(5) of the Act within six days after acquiring ownership of the vehicle.

(4) Notification by a person described in subsection (1) shall be in the form approved for the purpose by the Minister, fully completed by the person described in subsection (1).

(5) The form approved by the Minister shall require,

(a) the vehicle identification number;

(b) the person's determination that the vehicle is irreparable or salvage;

(c) the name, address and telephone number of the holder of the vehicle portion of the vehicle permit at the time of the determination and the holder's driver's licence number or registrant identification number on the records of the Ministry, as the case may be;

(d) the date of the incident giving rise to the determination, if known; and

(e) the name, business address and telephone number of the individual who carried out the inspection and completed the form on behalf of the person who is required to notify the Registrar.

(6) A person described in paragraph 1 of subsection (1) shall also notify the holder of the vehicle portion of the vehicle permit for the vehicle, if the vehicle portion of the permit is held by another person, under subsection 199.1(8) of the Act, in writing, that the person has determined that the vehicle is irreparable or salvage, within the time limits for notifying the Registrar set out in subsection (2).

5. Submissions re Registrar's classification — The holder of the vehicle permit or the vehicle portion of the vehicle permit for the vehicle must make the submissions under subsection 199.1(12) of the Act within 90 days after the date of the issuance under subsection 199.1(18) of the Act of a replacement permit or a replacement portion of a permit for the vehicle that indicates that the vehicle is classified as irreparable or salvage.

6. Duty to return permit — The holder of the vehicle permit or the vehicle portion of the vehicle permit for the vehicle shall return the permit or portion of the permit to the Registrar as required under subsection 199.1(16) of the Act not later than the date the holder is required to notify the Registrar under subsection 4(2) or (3) or, if the holder is not a person required to notify the Registrar under those subsections, within 10 days after the vehicle is determined by the Registrar to be irreparable or salvage.

7. Equivalent classifications from other jurisdictions — (1) In this section,

"another jurisdiction" means,

(a) another province of Canada,

(b) a territory of Canada,

(c) any state of the United States of America,

(d) Mexico,

(e) any member state of the European Union,

(f) Norway,

(g) Switzerland, or

(h) Japan.

(2) For the purposes of subsections 199.1(11) and (19) of the Act,

(a) another jurisdiction's classification of a vehicle that is or was registered in that jurisdiction that is used by that jurisdiction to indicate that the vehicle has been or may be repaired for continued use as a vehicle is equivalent to the salvage classification in Ontario;

(b) another jurisdiction's classification of a vehicle that is or was registered in that jurisdiction that is used by that jurisdiction to indicate that the vehicle is not fit to be repaired for continued use as a vehicle, including a classification that describes the vehicle as irreparable, scrap, junk, wrecked, dismantled, damaged, totalled, intended for destruction or to be used for parts only is equivalent to the irreparable classification in Ontario;

(c) another jurisdiction's classification of a motorcycle that is or was registered in that jurisdiction that is used by that jurisdiction to indicate that the motorcycle has been or may be rebuilt, including a classification described in clause (a) or (b) or in subsection (3), is equivalent to the irreparable classification in Ontario.

(3) Despite clauses (2)(a) and (b), another jurisdiction's classification of a vehicle that is or was registered in that jurisdiction that describes the vehicle as having been immersed in water to any degree or having been damaged in a fire is equivalent to the irreparable classification in Ontario.

O. Reg. 355/07, s. 1

8. Exemptions — Section 199.1 of the Act does not apply to,

(a) a trailer, traction engine, farm tractor, road-building machine, bicycle, motor assisted bicycle, motorized snow vehicle or street car;

(b) a motorcycle for which a permit was issued under the Act before it was damaged or stolen and dismantled, other than a motorcycle that is irreparable as a result of such damage or theft and dismantling; or

(c) a motor vehicle with a model year of 1980 or earlier.

O. Reg. 355/07, s. 2

9. Commencement — This Regulation comes into force on the day section 199.1 of the Act is proclaimed in force.

SCHEDULE STRUCTURAL ASSEMBLIES

Part 1

Radiator Support Assembly

Upper Rail Assembly — Left

Upper Rail Assembly — Right

Lower Rail Assembly — Left

Lower Rail Assembly — Right

Front Strut Tower/Apron Assembly — Left

Front Strut Tower/Apron Assembly — Right

Cowl Top Panel Assembly

Engine Sub-Frame Assembly

Part 2

Dash Panel Assembly

Windshield "A" Pillar Assembly — Left

Windshield "A" Pillar Assembly — Right

Side Rocker Panel Assembly — Left

Side Rocker Panel Assembly — Right

Centre Hinge "B" Pillar Assembly — Left

Centre Hinge "B" Pillar Assembly — Right

Rear "C" Pillar Assembly — Left

Rear "C" Pillar Assembly — Right

Front Floor Pan Assembly

Rear Floor Pan Assembly

Roof Panel (structural) Assembly

Part 3

Rear Strut Tower/Inner Wheelhouse Assembly — Left

Rear Strut Tower/Inner Wheelhouse Assembly — Right

Inner Quarter Panel Assembly — Left

Inner Quarter Panel Assembly — Right

Rear Cross-Member Assembly

Rear End Panel Assembly — Upper

Rear End Panel Assembly — Lower

Rear Sub Frame Assembly — Left

Rear Sub Frame Assembly — Right

Trunk Floor Pan Assembly

Part 4

Full Frame Vehicle: Complete Full Frame Assembly

ONT. REG. 199/07 — COMMERCIAL MOTOR VEHICLE INSPECTIONS

made under the *Highway Traffic Act*

O. Reg. 199/07, as am. CTR 2 JL 08 - 1; O. Reg. 411/10; 78/11; 171/11; 434/12; 242/14; 256/15 [To come into force July 1, 2016.]; 330/15; 421/15 [To come into force January 1, 2017.].

PART I — INTERPRETATION AND APPLICATION

1. Definitions and interpretation — (1) In section 107 of the Act and in this Regulation,

"commercial motor vehicle" includes a school purposes vehicle but does not include,

(a) a commercial motor vehicle, other than a bus or school purposes vehicle, having a gross weight or registered gross weight of not more than 4,500 kilograms,

(b) an ambulance, a cardiac arrest emergency vehicle, a fire apparatus, a hearse, a casket wagon, a mobile crane, a motor home or a vehicle commonly known as a tow truck,

> **Proposed Amendment — 1(1) "commercial motor vehicle" (b)**
>
> (b) an ambulance, a cardiac arrest emergency vehicle, a fire apparatus, a hearse, a casket wagon, a mobile crane or a motor home,
> O. Reg. 421/15, s. 1(1) [To come into force January 1, 2017.]

> **Proposed Addition — 1(1) "commercial motor vehicle" (b.1)**
>
> (b.1) a tow truck as defined in subsection 4(1) of Ontario Regulation 419/15 (*Definitions of Commercial Motor Vehicle and Tow Truck*) made under the Act,
> O. Reg. 421/15, s. 1(1) [To come into force January 1, 2017.]

(c) a commercial motor vehicle operated under a permit and number plates issued under a regulation made under clause 7(24)(g) or (h) of the Act that is not transporting passengers or goods,

> **Proposed Amendment — 1(1) "commercial motor vehicle" (c)**
>
> (c) a commercial motor vehicle operated under and in accordance with a Dealer permit and number plate or a Service permit and number plate issued under Regulation 628 of the Revised Regulations of Ontario, 1990 (*Vehicle Permits*) made under the Act that is not transporting passengers or goods,
> O. Reg. 421/15, s. 1(1) [To come into force January 1, 2017.]

(c.1) a commercial motor vehicle operated under the terms of a Manufacturer permit and number plate issued under Regulation 628 of the Revised Regulations of Ontario, 1990 (*Vehicle Permits*) made under the Act,

(d) a commercial motor vehicle operated under the authority of an In-Transit permit issued under Regulation 628 of the Revised Regulations of Ontario, 1990 (*Vehicle Permits*) made under the Act,

Proposed Repeal — 1(1) "commercial motor vehicle" (d)

(d) [Repealed O. Reg. 256/15, s. 1(1). To come into force July 1, 2016.]

(e) a commercial motor vehicle leased for 30 days or less by an individual for the purpose of transporting goods for the individual's personal use or for the carriage of passengers for no compensation,

(f) a commercial motor vehicle that is a historic vehicle within the meaning of section 1 of Regulation 628 of the Revised Regulations of Ontario, 1990 (*Vehicle Permits*) made under the Act and that has a vehicle permit for a historic vehicle,

(g) a pick-up truck that,

(i) is being used for personal purposes without compensation, and

(ii) is not carrying, or towing a trailer that is carrying, commercial cargo or tools or equipment of a type normally used for commercial purposes, or

(h) a bus that is used for personal purposes without compensation;

"inter-city bus" means a bus commonly known as a motor coach that has,

(a) motive power mounted to the rear of the front axle,

(b) air-ride or torsion-bar suspension,

(c) a baggage area that is separate from the passenger cabin, and

(d) a passenger cabin with reclining seats for passengers;

Proposed Repeal — 1(1) "inter-city bus"

"inter-city bus" [Repealed O. Reg. 256/15, s. 1(2). To come into force July 1, 2016.]

"operator" means,

(a) in the case of a commercial motor vehicle that is not a school purposes vehicle,

(i) the person directly or indirectly responsible for the operation of the vehicle, including the conduct of the driver of the vehicle and the carriage of goods or passengers, if any, in the vehicle, and

(ii) in the absence of evidence to the contrary, where there is no CVOR certificate, as defined in subsection 16(1) of the Act, national safety code number under the *Motor Vehicle Transport Act* (Canada) or lease applicable to the vehicle, the holder of the plate portion of the permit for the vehicle,

> ### Proposed Amendment — 1(1) "operator" (a)(ii)
>
> **(ii) in the absence of evidence to the contrary, where there is no CVOR certificate, national safety code number under the *Motor Vehicle Transport Act* (Canada) or lease applicable to the vehicle, the holder of the plate portion of the permit for the vehicle,**
>
> O. Reg. 421/15, s. 1(2) [To come into force January 1, 2017.]

(b) in the case of a school purposes vehicle,

(i) the person directly or indirectly responsible for the operation of the vehicle, including the conduct of the driver of the vehicle and the carriage of passengers in the vehicle, and

(ii) in the absence of evidence to the contrary, the holder of the plate portion of the permit for the vehicle.

(2) In this Regulation,

"emergency vehicle" means,

(a) a road service vehicle operated by or on behalf of a road authority,

(b) a vehicle used by a person employed by or on behalf of a police force, or

(c) a vehicle used by or on behalf of a public utility;

"house trailer" includes a cabin trailer, collapsible cabin trailer, tent trailer and camping trailer;

"major defect" means a defect listed in Column 3 of Schedule 1, 2, 3, 5 or 6;

"minor defect" means a defect listed in Column 2 of Schedule 1, 2, 3, 5 or 6;

"motor coach" [Repealed O. Reg. 242/14, s. 1(2).]

> ### Proposed Amendment — 1(2) "motor coach"
>
> **"motor coach" means a bus of monocoque design, designed to provide intercity, suburban, commuter or charter service and equipped with air ride suspension, air brakes, automatic brake adjusters and under-floor baggage storage;**
>
> O. Reg. 256/15, s. 1(3) [To come into force July 1, 2016.]

"pick-up truck" means a commercial motor vehicle that,

(a) has a manufacturer's gross vehicle weight rating of 6,000 kilograms or less, and

(b) is fitted with either,

(i) the original box that was installed by the manufacturer, which has not been modified, or

(ii) a replacement box that duplicates the one that was installed by the manufacturer, which has not been modified;

"principal place of business", for an operator, means the last known address of the operator appearing on the records of the Ministry;

"school purposes bus" means,

(a) a "school bus" as defined in section 175 of the Act, and

(b) a bus, other than an inter-city bus, operated by or under contract with a school board or other authority in charge of a school;

> **Proposed Amendment — 1(2) "school purposes bus" (b)**
>
> **(b)** a bus, other than a motor coach, operated by or under contract with a school board or other authority in charge of a school;
>
>   O. Reg. 256/15, s. 1(4) [To come into force July 1, 2016.]

"school purposes vehicle" means a passenger vehicle, other than a bus, that is operated by or under a contract with a school board or other authority in charge of a school for the transportation of six or more adults with a developmental disability, six or more children or six or more persons from both categories.

(3) For the purposes of Parts II and IV, a trailer converter dolly, if carrying a trailer, shall be considered part of that trailer.

       O. Reg. 242/14, s. 1; 330/15, s. 1

2. Prescribed major and minor defects — (1) The major defects are prescribed as defects for the purpose of subsection 107(11) of the Act.

(2) The minor defects are prescribed as defects for the purpose of subsection 107(12) of the Act.

3. Application to buses — This Regulation applies to buses, whether or not they are used for the transportation of persons.

4. Exemptions — (1) Subsections 107(4) to (12) of the Act and Part II of this Regulation do not apply in respect of the following classes of vehicles, used in the following circumstances:

1. An emergency vehicle while responding to or returning from an emergency.

2. A commercial motor vehicle while providing relief from an earthquake, flood, fire, famine, drought, epidemic, pestilence or other disaster by transporting passengers or goods.

3. A two-axle or three-axle truck, bus or tractor, not drawing a trailer, that is primarily used to transport primary products of a farm, forest, sea or lake produced or harvested by the driver or the driver's employer.

4. A bus that is operated by or on behalf of a municipality as part of the municipality's public transit service, either within the municipality or within 25 kilometres of the boundary of that municipality.

5. A commercial motor vehicle being road-tested, for the purposes of repairs, within 30 kilometres of a repair facility where the vehicle is being repaired by,

     i. the holder of a certificate of qualification, that is not suspended, in the trade of automotive service technician or truck and coach technician issued under the *Ontario College of Trades and Apprenticeship Act, 2009*, or

     ii. an apprentice under that Act.

6. A trailer drawn by a vehicle described in paragraph 1, 2, 4 or 5.

7. A trailer converter dolly that is not carrying a trailer.

(2) Section 107 of the Act and this Regulation do not apply in respect of the following classes of vehicles:

1. A vehicle, other than a trailer or trailer converter dolly, that is drawn by another vehicle.

2. A house trailer, other than a house trailer,

   i. owned or leased by an employer to house the employer's employee,

   ii. carrying commercial cargo or tools or equipment of a type normally used for commercial purposes, or

   iii. carrying animals or non-commercial tools, equipment or vehicles that occupy one-half or more of its floor space.

3. A commercial motor vehicle drawing a house trailer, other than a house trailer,

   i. owned or leased by an employer to house the employer's employee,

   ii. carrying commercial cargo or tools or equipment of a type normally used for commercial purposes, or

   iii. carrying animals or non-commercial tools, equipment or vehicles that occupy one-half or more of its floor space.

(3) Subsection 107(1) of the Act and Part V of this Regulation, other than subsections 18(1), (2) and (3), do not apply in respect of school purposes vehicles.

O. Reg. 434/12, s. 1; 242/14, s. 2

PART II — DAILY INSPECTIONS

5. Daily inspection schedules — (1) The daily inspection schedules apply to different classes of vehicles as follows:

1. Schedule 1 applies to trucks, tractors and trailers drawn by a truck or tractor.

2. Schedule 2 applies to,

   i. buses, including inter-city buses but excluding school purposes buses, and

   ii. trailers drawn by a bus, including an inter-city bus or a school purposes bus.

Proposed Amendment — 5(1), para. 2

2. Schedule 2 applies to,

   i. buses, including motor coaches but excluding school purposes buses, and

   ii. trailers drawn by a bus, including a motor coach or a school purposes bus.

O. Reg. 256/15, s. 2(1) [To come into force July 1, 2016.]

3. Schedule 3 applies to inter-city buses.

Proposed Amendment — 5(1), para. 3

3. Schedule 3 applies to motor coaches.

         O. Reg. 256/15, s. 2(1) [To come into force July 1, 2016.]

4. Schedule 5 applies to school purposes buses, whether or not they are being used for school purposes.

5. Schedule 6 applies to school purposes vehicles.

(2) In supplying a driver with the appropriate daily inspection schedule for each commercial motor vehicle and trailer that the driver will be driving or drawing, as required by clause 107(4)(a) of the Act, an operator may supply the driver of an inter-city bus with either Schedule 2 or 3.

Proposed Amendment — 5(2)

(2) In supplying a driver with the appropriate daily inspection schedule for each commercial motor vehicle and trailer that the driver will be driving or drawing, as required by clause 107(4)(a) of the Act, an operator may supply the driver of a motor coach with either Schedule 2 or 3.

         O. Reg. 256/15, s. 2(2) [To come into force July 1, 2016.]

(3) An operator may include additional information on a schedule to assist the person who will conduct the daily inspection.

(4) An operator may delete a portion of a schedule respecting the inspection of a specific vehicle component if the vehicle to be inspected under that schedule is not required to have and does not have that component.

(5) A schedule supplied to a driver need not include any note to the schedule that is set out in section 19 and that is applicable to that schedule.

         O. Reg. 242/14, s. 3

6. Daily inspections — (1) A daily inspection of a commercial motor vehicle or trailer must include an inspection of every system and component listed in Column 1 of the appropriate daily inspection schedule.

(2) A daily inspection must be adequate to determine whether there is a major or minor defect as set out in the appropriate daily inspection schedule.

(3) A daily inspection is valid for 24 hours.

(4) Despite subsection (3), a daily inspection of an inter-city bus in accordance with Schedule 3 is not valid unless an under-vehicle inspection of the inter-city bus has been conducted in accordance with Part III and is still valid.

Proposed Amendment — 6(4)

(4) Despite subsection (3), a daily inspection of a motor coach in accordance with Schedule 3 is not valid unless an under-vehicle inspection of the motor coach has been conducted in accordance with Part III and is still valid.

         O. Reg. 256/15, s. 3 [To come into force July 1, 2016.]

         O. Reg. 242/14, s. 4

7. Daily inspection report — (1) The report completed when the daily inspection is completed must include the following:

1. The licence plate number and plate jurisdiction of the vehicle.

2. The operator's name.

3. The date and time of the inspection.

4. The city, town, village or highway location where the inspection was conducted.

5. The printed name of the person who conducted the inspection.

6. For a commercial motor vehicle, the odometer reading of the vehicle.

7. Any major and minor defects found during the inspection or, if none were found, a statement that no major or minor defects were found.

8. A statement, signed by the person who conducted the inspection, that the vehicle was inspected in accordance with this Regulation.

(2) If the driver of the commercial motor vehicle is not the person who conducted the daily inspection of the commercial motor vehicle or trailer, the driver shall sign the daily inspection report for the commercial motor vehicle or trailer before driving the commercial motor vehicle or drawing the trailer.

(3) An operator shall supply the driver or other person who conducts daily inspections with daily inspection report forms.

8. On-going monitoring — (1) A driver shall monitor the condition of each commercial motor vehicle and trailer he or she is driving, drawing or in charge of to detect the presence of a major or minor defect.

(2) If a driver detects a major or minor defect while driving, drawing or in charge of a commercial motor vehicle or trailer, the driver shall notify the operator of the defect by any means of communication that is likely to come to the operator's attention quickly, in addition to entering the defect on the daily inspection report as required by clause 107(8)(a) of the Act.

(3) A driver may continue to drive a commercial motor vehicle if the commercial motor vehicle or trailer drawn by it has a minor defect if he or she has entered the defect on the daily inspection report as required by clause 107(8)(a) of the Act.

9. Submission of daily inspection report — (1) A driver shall submit the completed daily inspection report to the operator as soon as possible after the inspection ceases to be valid and, in any event, no later than 20 days after the inspection ceases to be valid.

(2) The completed daily inspection report must be submitted to the operator's principal place of business or to another terminal or business address specified by the operator.

(3) A daily inspection report of a commercial motor vehicle or trailer drawn by it is deemed to be submitted to the operator under this section if it is contained in a book of daily inspection reports that is kept in the commercial motor vehicle and to which the operator has regular access.

(4) Subsection (3) applies only if the driver gave notice, in accordance with subsection 8(2), of any major or minor defects he or she detected after the daily inspection was conducted.

(5) A daily inspection report is considered to be completed for the purpose of this section if, in addition to the entries required by section 7, it contains a record of any major and minor defects detected by the driver after the daily inspection was conducted and entered by the driver as required by clause 107(8)(a) of the Act.

10. Submission of other notices, reports — (1) A driver shall submit to the operator any notice to submit to an inspection or inspection report issued under section 82, 82.1 or 216.1 of the Act or by an enforcement officer or government official of another jurisdiction.

(2) The notices and reports shall be submitted to the operator's principal place of business or another terminal or business address specified by the operator, as soon as possible and, in any event, no later than 20 days after the driver received the notice or report.

PART III — UNDER-VEHICLE INSPECTIONS

11. Under-vehicle inspections — (1) Schedule 4 applies to the under-vehicle inspection of an inter-city bus.

Proposed Amendment — 11(1)

(1) Schedule 4 applies to the under-vehicle inspection of a motor coach.

O. Reg. 256/15, s. 4(1) [To come into force July 1, 2016.]

(2) An under-vehicle inspection must include an inspection of every system and component listed in Column 1 of Schedule 4.

(3) An under-vehicle inspection must be adequate to determine whether there is a defect as set out in Column 2 of Schedule 4.

(4) An under-vehicle inspection must be conducted while the inter-city bus is positioned over a pit or is otherwise raised, in a manner that provides access to all the systems and components of the inter-city bus that must be inspected under Schedule 4.

Proposed Amendment — 11(4)

(4) An under-vehicle inspection must be conducted while the motor coach is positioned over a pit or is otherwise raised, in a manner that provides access to all the systems and components of the motor coach that must be inspected under Schedule 4.

O. Reg. 256/15, s. 4(2) [To come into force July 1, 2016.]

(5) Every defect detected in an under-vehicle inspection must be repaired for the under-vehicle inspection to be considered complete.

(6) An under-vehicle inspection, if it is conducted in Ontario, is valid only if it is conducted by the holder of a certificate of qualification, that is not suspended, in the trade of truck and coach technician issued under the *Ontario College of Trades and Apprenticeship Act, 2009.*

(7) An under-vehicle inspection is valid until the 31st day after it is conducted or until the inter-city bus has been driven 12,000 kilometres, whichever occurs first.

Proposed Amendment — 11(7)

(7) An under-vehicle inspection is valid until the 31st day after it is conducted or until the motor coach has been driven 12,000 kilometres, whichever occurs first.

O. Reg. 256/15, s. 4(3) [To come into force July 1, 2016.]

O. Reg. 434/12, s. 2; 242/14, s. 5

12. Under-vehicle inspection report — (1) The report completed when the under-vehicle inspection is completed must include the following:

1. The licence plate number and the vehicle identification number or unit number of the inter-city bus.

Proposed Amendment — 12(1), para. 1

1. The licence plate number and the vehicle identification number or unit number of the motor coach.

O. Reg. 256/15, s. 5(1) [To come into force July 1, 2016.]

2. The operator's name.

3. The date of the inspection.

4. The address, including the city, town or village, where the inspection was conducted.

5. The printed name of the person who conducted the inspection.

6. The odometer reading of the inter-city bus at the end of the inspection.

Proposed Amendment — 12(1), para. 6

6. The odometer reading of the motor coach at the end of the inspection.

O. Reg. 256/15, s. 5(1) [To come into force July 1, 2016.]

7. A statement, signed by the person who conducted the inspection, that the inter-city bus was inspected in accordance with this Regulation and that at the end of the inspection, there are no defects listed in Column 2 of Schedule 4.

Proposed Amendment — 12(1), para. 7

7. A statement, signed by the person who conducted the inspection, that the motor coach was inspected in accordance with this Regulation and that at the end of the inspection, there are no defects listed in Column 2 of Schedule 4.

O. Reg. 256/15, s. 5(1) [To come into force July 1, 2016.]

(2) A person who conducts an under-vehicle inspection shall also record the following information in the record of the inspections and maintenance of and repairs to the vehicle required by paragraph 2 of subsection 16(1):

1. Any defects listed in Column 2 of Schedule 4 found during the inspection or, if none were found, a statement that no such defects were found.

2. The nature of the repairs carried out, if any.

3. The brake adjustment measurements.

(3) An operator shall give a driver the completed under-vehicle inspection report for each inter-city bus that the driver will be driving that day.

Proposed Amendment — 12(3)

(3) An operator shall give a driver the completed under-vehicle inspection report for each motor coach that the driver will be driving that day.

O. Reg. 256/15, s. 5(2) [To come into force July 1, 2016.]

O. Reg. 242/14, s. 6

13. Submission of under-vehicle inspection reports — (1) A driver shall submit to the operator the completed under-vehicle inspection report that is in his or her possession as soon as possible after the inspection ceases to be valid and, in any event, no later than 20 days after the inspection ceases to be valid.

(2) The completed under-vehicle inspection report must be submitted to the operator's principal place of business or to another terminal or business address specified by the operator.

PART IV — PERFORMANCE STANDARDS

14. Performance standards — (1) The following performance standards are prescribed as vehicle component performance standards for the purpose of subsection 107(3) of the Act:

1. The requirements of Regulation 587 of the Revised Regulations of Ontario, 1990 (*Equipment*) made under the Act.

2. The requirements of Regulation 612 of the Revised Regulations of Ontario, 1990 (*School Buses*) made under the Act.

3. The performance standards set out in Schedules 1 and 2 of Regulation 611 of the Revised Regulations of Ontario, 1990 (*Safety Inspections*) made under the Act.

Proposed Amendment — 14(1), para. 3

3. The performance standards set out in Schedules 1, 2, 3, 4, 5, 6 and 7 to this Regulation.

O. Reg. 256/15, s. 6(1) [To come into force July 1, 2016.]

4. The performance standards set out in Schedules 1, 2, 3, 4, 5 and 6 of this Regulation.

Proposed Amendment — 14(1), para. 4

4. The requirements of Regulation 625 of the Revised Regulations of Ontario, 1990 (*Tire Standards and Specifications*) **made under the Act.**

O. Reg. 256/15, s. 6(1) [To come into force July 1, 2016.]

(2) For the purpose of paragraph 4 of subsection (1), the schedules shall be read as if the absence of a specified defect is a performance standard.

Proposed Amendment — 14(2)

(2) For the purpose of paragraph 3 of subsection (1), the schedules shall be read as if the absence of a specified defect is a performance standard.

O. Reg. 256/15, s. 6(2) [To come into force July 1, 2016.]

O. Reg. 78/11, s. 1

PART V — RECORDKEEPING

15. Daily inspection reports — An operator shall keep the daily inspection reports submitted by drivers for at least six months.

16. Other records — (1) An operator shall keep the following records, in respect of each commercial motor vehicle, trailer and trailer converter dolly operated by the operator:

1. Identification records for the vehicle, including,

   i. the vehicle's unit number, if any,

   ii. the vehicle's year and make,

   iii. the vehicle's vehicle identification number, and

   iv. if the vehicle is not owned by the operator, the name of the person that supplies the vehicle to the operator, and the first and last dates on which the vehicle was operated by the operator.

2. A record of the inspections and maintenance of and repairs to the vehicle, including,

   i. the nature of the inspections, maintenance and repairs,

   ii. the name of the person who conducted each inspection and performed each maintenance or repair,

   iii. if an inspection, maintenance or repair was conducted or performed by someone other than the operator or a person employed by the operator, the invoice or other record of the inspection, maintenance or repair provided by the person who conducted or performed it,

   iv. if a part was purchased and used in maintenance or in a repair, the invoice or receipt for the part, and

   v. if the vehicle has an odometer, the odometer reading of the vehicle at the end of the inspection, maintenance or repair.

3. The types and frequency of inspections and maintenance required to be carried out on the vehicle under the operator's system of periodic inspections and maintenance.

4. A record of any axle or suspension modifications of the vehicle that affect the manufacturer's gross vehicle weight rating or gross axle weight rating.

5. Copies of safety standards certificates and annual inspection certificates issued in respect of the vehicle, and copies of equivalent documents from other jurisdictions issued in respect of the vehicle.

6. In the case of an inter-city bus, every under-vehicle inspection report for the inter-city bus submitted to the operator under section 13.

Proposed Amendment — 16(1), para. 6

6. In the case of a motor coach, every under-vehicle inspection report for the motor coach submitted to the operator under section 13.

O. Reg. 256/15, s. 7 [To come into force July 1, 2016.]

7. Copies of the notices and reports submitted to the operator under section 10.

(2) An operator shall retain the records described in subsection (1) for at least two years or, if a record relates to a vehicle that ceases to be operated by the operator, for six months after the vehicle ceases to be operated by the operator, whichever period is shorter.

CTR 2 JL 08 -1; O. Reg. 242/14, s. 7

17. Records kept at operator's business — Any record or document that an operator is required by this Regulation to keep shall be kept at the operator's principal place of business or another terminal or business address of the operator.

18. Electronic records — **(1)** Any record or document that is required to be created, kept or surrendered by section 107 of the Act or this Regulation may be made, kept or surrendered in electronic format if it meets the requirements of this section.

(2) An electronic record or document must meet every requirement of section 107 of the Act and of this Regulation, except that it is not required to have a signature.

(3) Upon demand of a police officer or officer appointed for the purpose of carrying out the provisions of the Act, a driver who carries a daily inspection report, under-vehicle inspection report or inspection schedule in electronic format shall produce, at the driver's option,

  (a) an electronic display of the report or schedule, that is readable from outside the vehicle;

  (b) a printed copy of the report or schedule, signed by the driver; or

  (c) a handwritten copy of the report or schedule, signed by the driver.

(4) Despite section 17, an operator may keep a record or document that is in electronic format at any place if it can be readily accessed by the operator from the operator's principal place of business in a format that would allow a printed copy of the record or document to be generated as required by subsection (5).

(5) Upon demand of a police officer or officer appointed for the purpose of carrying out the provisions of the Act, an operator who has in their possession a record or document in electronic format shall generate a printed copy of the record or document, signed by the person who makes the copy.

O. Reg. 242/14, s. 8

PART VI — NOTES TO THE SCHEDULES

19. Notes to the schedules — The following notes apply to the schedules to this Regulation:

[1]Adjustment limits are in section 5 of Regulation 587 of the Revised Regulations of Ontario, 1990 (*Equipment*) made under the Act.

[2]Limit is prescribed by Schedule 1 to Regulation 611 of the Revised Regulations of Ontario, 1990 (*Safety Inspections*) made under the Act.

[3]Cargo securement device and load covering requirements are prescribed by section 111 of the Act and by Ontario Regulation 363/04 (*Security of Loads*) made under the Act and Regulation 577 of the Revised Regulations of Ontario, 1990 (*Covering of Loads*) made under the Act.

[4]Prescribed limit is 12.7 mm of fore and aft horizontal movement between the upper and lower halves of the fifth wheel assembly.

[5]Requirements are under the *Dangerous Goods Transportation Act* and the *Transportation of Dangerous Goods Act, 1992* (Canada).

[6]Mirror requirements are in section 66 of the Act.

[7]View requirements are in sections 66 and 74 of the Act and in section 1 of Schedule 1 to Regulation 611 of the Revised Regulations of Ontario, 1990 (*Safety Inspections*) made under the Act.

[8]Lamp requirements are in section 62 of the Act.

[9]Reflector requirements are in section 103 of the Act.

[10]Limit is prescribed by Schedule 1 to Regulation 611 of the Revised Regulations of Ontario, 1990 (*Safety Inspections*) made under the Act.

[11]Wear limit is prescribed by section 3 of Regulation 625 of the Revised Regulations of Ontario, 1990 (*Tire Standards and Specifications*) made under the Act.

[12]Emergency exit requirements are in section 25 of the *Public Vehicles Act*.

[13]Interior lamp requirements are in section 20 of Regulation 982 of the Revised Regulations of Ontario, 1990 (*General*) made under the *Public Vehicles Act*.

[14]Passenger and mobility device restraints requirements are in section 106 of the Act and in sections 6 and 7 of Regulation 629 of the Revised Regulations of Ontario, 1990 (*Accessible Vehicles*) made under the Act.

[15]As required by manufacturer's specifications.

[16]View requirements are in section 74 of the Act and in section 1 of Schedule 1 to Regulation 611 of the Revised Regulations of Ontario, 1990 (*Safety Inspections*) made under the Act.

[17]Alarm requirements are in section 2 of Regulation 612 of the Revised Regulations of Ontario, 1990 (*School Buses*) made under the Act.

[18]Fire extinguisher requirements are in sections 2 and 4 of Regulation 612 of the Revised Regulations of Ontario, 1990 (*School Buses*) made under the Act.

[19]First aid kit requirements are in sections 2 and 3 of Regulation 612 of the Revised Regulations of Ontario, 1990 (*School Buses*) made under the Act.

[20]Sticker requirements are in section 10 of Regulation 611 of the Revised Regulations of Ontario, 1990 (*Safety Inspections*) made under the Act.

[21]Interior and exterior lamp requirements are in section 62 of the Act and in sections 2 and 4 of Regulation 612 of the Revised Regulations of Ontario, 1990 (*School Buses*) made under the Act.

[22]View requirements are in section 66 of the Act and in section 3 of Regulation 612 of the Revised Regulations of Ontario, 1990 (*School Buses*) made under the Act.

[23]Passenger and mobility device restraint system requirements are in section 106 of the Act and in sections 6 and 7 of Regulation 629 of the Revised Regulations of Ontario, 1990 (*Accessible Vehicles*) made under the Act and section 2 of Regulation 612 of the Revised Regulations of Ontario, 1990 (*School Buses*) made under the Act.

[24]View requirements are in section 66 of the Act.

Proposed Amendment — 19

19. Notes to the schedules — The following notes apply to the schedules to this Regulation:

[1]Adjustment limits are in section 5 of Regulation 587 of the Revised Regulations of Ontario, 1990 (*Equipment*) made under the Act.

[2]Air loss rate limit is prescribed by Schedule 7 to this Regulation.

[3]Cargo securement device and load covering requirements are prescribed by section 111 of the Act and by Ontario Regulation 363/04 (*Security of Loads*) made under the Act and Regulation 577 of the Revised Regulations of Ontario, 1990 (*Covering of Loads*) made under the Act.

[4]Prescribed limit is 12.7 mm of fore and aft horizontal movement between the upper and lower halves of the fifth wheel assembly.

[5]Requirements are under the *Dangerous Goods Transportation Act* and the *Transportation of Dangerous Goods Act, 1992* (Canada).

[6]Mirror requirements are in section 66 of the Act.

[7]View requirements are in sections 66 and 74 of the Act and in section 1 of Schedule 7 to this Regulation.

[8]Lamp requirements are in section 62 of the Act.

[9]Reflector requirements are in section 103 of the Act.

[10]Steering lash (free play) limit is prescribed by Schedule 7 to this Regulation.

[11]Wear limit is prescribed by section 3 of Regulation 625 of the Revised Regulations of Ontario, 1990 (*Tire Standards and Specifications*) made under the Act.

[12]Emergency exit requirements are in section 25 of the *Public Vehicles Act*.

[13]Interior lamp requirements are in section 20 of Regulation 982 of the Revised Regulations of Ontario, 1990 (*General*) made under the *Public Vehicles Act*.

[14]Passenger and mobility device restraints requirements are in section 106 of the Act and in sections 6 and 7 of Regulation 629 of the Revised Regulations of Ontario, 1990 (*Accessible Vehicles*) made under the Act.

[15]As required by manufacturer's specifications.

[16]View requirements are in section 74 of the Act and in section 1 of Schedule 1 to Regulation 611 of the Revised Regulations of Ontario, 1990 (*Safety Inspections*) made under the Act.

[17]Alarm requirements are in section 2 of Regulation 612 of the Revised Regulations of Ontario, 1990 (*School Buses*) made under the Act.

[18]Fire extinguisher requirements are in sections 2 and 4 of Regulation 612 of the Revised Regulations of Ontario, 1990 (*School Buses*) made under the Act.

[19]First aid kit requirements are in sections 2 and 3 of Regulation 612 of the Revised Regulations of Ontario, 1990 (*School Buses*) made under the Act.

[20]Sticker requirements are in section 10 of Regulation 611 of the Revised Regulations of Ontario, 1990 (*Safety Inspections*) made under the Act.

[21]Interior and exterior lamp requirements are in section 62 of the Act and in sections 2 and 4 of Regulation 612 of the Revised Regulations of Ontario, 1990 (*School Buses*) made under the Act.

[22]View requirements are in section 66 of the Act and in section 3 of Regulation 612 of the Revised Regulations of Ontario, 1990 (*School Buses*) made under the Act.

[23]Passenger and mobility device restraint system requirements are in section 106 of the Act and in sections 6 and 7 of Regulation 629 of the Revised Regulations of Ontario, 1990 (*Accessible Vehicles*) made under the Act and section 2 of Regulation 612 of the Revised Regulations of Ontario, 1990 (*School Buses*) made under the Act.

[24]View requirements are in section 66 of the Act.

O. Reg. 256/15, s. 8 [To come into force July 1, 2016.]

O. Reg. 411/10, s. 1; 171/11, s. 1

PART VII — REVOCATION AND COMMENCEMENT

20. Revocation — Regulation 575 of the Revised Regulations of Ontario, 1990 is revoked.

21. Commencement — This Regulation comes into force on the later of the day section 16 of Schedule A to the *Transportation Statute Law Amendment Act, 2005* comes into force and the day this Regulation is filed.

SCHEDULE 1 — DAILY INSPECTION OF TRUCKS, TRACTORS AND TRAILERS

Column 1	Column 2	Column 3
Systems and Components	Minor Defects	Major Defects
Part 1. Air Brake System	(a) audible air leak. (b) slow air pressure build-up rate.	(a) pushrod stroke of any brake exceeds the adjustment limit.[1] (b) air loss rate exceeds prescribed limit.[2] (c) inoperative towing vehicle (tractor) protection system. (d) low air warning system fails or system is activated. (e) inoperative service, parking or emergency brake.
Part 2. Cab	(a) occupant compartment door fails to open.	(a) any cab or sleeper door fails to close securely.
Part 3. Cargo Securement	(a) insecure or improper load covering.	(a) insecure cargo. (b) absence, failure, malfunction or deterioration of required cargo securement device or load covering.[3]
Part 4. Coupling Devices	(a) coupler or mounting has loose or missing fastener.	(a) coupler is insecure or movement exceeds prescribed limit.[4] (b) coupling or locking mechanism is damaged or fails to lock. (c) defective, incorrect or missing safety chain or cable.
Part 5. Dangerous Goods		(a) dangerous goods requirements not met.[5]

Column 1	Column 2	Column 3
Systems and Components	Minor Defects	Major Defects
Part 6. Driver Controls	(a) accelerator pedal, clutch, gauges, audible and visual indicators or instruments fail to function properly.	
Part 7. Driver Seat	(a) seat is damaged or fails to remain in set position.	(a) seatbelt or tether belt is insecure, missing or malfunctions.
Part 8. Electric Brake System	(a) loose or insecure wiring or electrical connection.	(a) inoperative breakaway device. (b) inoperative brake.
Part 9. Emergency Equipment and Safety Devices	(a) emergency equipment is missing, damaged or defective.	
Part 10. Exhaust System	(a) exhaust leak, except as described in Column 3.	(a) leak that causes exhaust gas to enter the occupant compartment.
Part 11. Frame and Cargo Body	(a) damaged frame or cargo body.	(a) visibly shifted, cracked, collapsing or sagging frame member.
Part 12. Fuel System	(a) missing fuel tank cap.	(a) insecure fuel tank. (b) dripping fuel leak.
Part 13. General		(a) serious damage or deterioration that is noticeable and may affect the vehicle's safe operation.
Part 14. Glass and Mirrors	(a) required mirror[6] or window glass fails to provide the required view[7] to the driver as a result of being cracked, broken, damaged, missing or maladjusted.	

Column 1	Column 2	Column 3
Systems and Components	Minor Defects	Major Defects
	(b) required mirror[6] or glass has broken or damaged attachments onto vehicle body.	
Part 15. Heater / Defroster	(a) control or system failure.	(a) defroster fails to provide unobstructed view through the windshield.
Part 16. Horn	(a) vehicle has no operative horn.	
Part 17. Hydraulic Brake System	(a) brake fluid level is below indicated minimum level. (b) [Repealed O. Reg. 242/14, s. 9(2).]	(a) brake boost or power assist is not operative. (b) brake fluid leak. (c) brake pedal fade or insufficient brake pedal reserve. (d) activated (other than ABS) warning device. (e) brake fluid reservoir is less than $\frac{1}{4}$ full. (f) parking brake is inoperative.
Part 18. Lamps and Reflectors	(a) required lamp does not function as intended.[8] (b) required reflector is missing or partially missing.[9]	*When use of lamps is required*: (a) failure of both low-beam headlamps. (b) failure of both rearmost tail lamps. *At all times*: (a) failure of a rearmost turn-indicator lamp. (b) failure of both rearmost brake lamps.
Part 19. Steering	(a) steering wheel lash (free-play) is greater than normal.	(a) steering wheel is insecure, or does not respond normally.

Column 1	Column 2	Column 3
Systems and Components	**Minor Defects**	**Major Defects**
		(b) steering wheel lash (free-play) exceeds prescribed limit.[10]
Part 20. Suspension System	(a) air leak in air suspension system.	(a) damaged (patched, cut, bruised, cracked to braid or deflated) air bag or insecurely mounted air bag.
	(b) a broken spring leaf.	(b) cracked or broken main spring leaf or more than one broken spring leaf.
	(c) suspension fastener is loose, missing or broken.	(c) part of spring leaf or suspension is missing, shifted out of place or is in contact with another vehicle component.
		(d) loose U-bolt.
Part 21. Tires	(a) damaged tread or sidewall of tire.	(a) flat tire.
		(a.1) tire leaking, if leak can be felt or heard.
	(b) tire leaking, if leak cannot be heard.	(b) tire tread depth is less than wear limit.[11]
		(c) tire is in contact with another tire or any vehicle component other than mud-flap.
		(d) tire is marked "Not for highway use".
		(e) tire has exposed cords in the tread or outer sidewall area.
Part 22. Wheels, Hubs and Fasteners	(a) hub oil below minimum level (when fitted with sight glass).	(a) wheel has loose, missing or ineffective fastener.
	(b) leaking wheel seal.	(b) damaged, cracked or broken wheel, rim or attaching part.
		(c) evidence of imminent wheel, hub or bearing failure.
Part 23. Windshield Wiper / Washer	(a) control or system malfunction.	*When use of wipers or washer is required:*

Column 1	Column 2	Column 3
Systems and Components	Minor Defects	Major Defects
	(b) wiper blade is damaged, missing or fails to adequately clear driver's field of vision.	(a) wiper or washer fails to adequately clear driver's field of vision in area swept by driver's side wiper.

O. Reg. 242/14, s. 9

SCHEDULE 2 — DAILY INSPECTION OF BUSES AND OF TRAILERS DRAWN BY BUSES

Column 1	Column 2	Column 3
Systems and Components	Minor Defects	Major Defects
Part 1. Accessibility Devices	*Accessibility device may not be used if*: (a) alarm fails to operate. (b) equipment malfunctions. (c) interlock system malfunctions.	(a) vehicle fails to return to normal level after kneeling. (b) extendable lift, ramp or other passenger-loading device fails to retract.
Part 2. Air Brake System	(a) audible air leak. (b) slow air pressure build-up rate.	(a) pushrod stroke of any brake exceeds the adjustment limit.[1] (b) air loss rate exceeds prescribed limit.[2] (c) inoperative towing vehicle (tractor) protection system. (d) low air warning system fails or system is activated. (e) inoperative service, parking or emergency brake.
Part 3. Cargo Securement	(a) insecure or improper load covering.	(a) insecure cargo. (b) absence, failure, malfunction or deterioration of required cargo securement device or load covering.[3]

623

Column 1	Column 2	Column 3
Systems and Components	**Minor Defects**	**Major Defects**
▸**Part 4. Coupling Devices**	(a) coupler or mounting has loose or missing fastener.	(a) coupler is insecure or movement exceeds prescribed limit.[4] (b) coupling or locking mechanism is damaged or fails to lock. (c) defective, incorrect or missing safety chain or cable.
Part 5. Dangerous Goods		(a) dangerous goods requirements not met.[5]
Part 6. Doors and Emergency Exits	(a) door, window or hatch fails to open or close securely. (b) alarm inoperative.	*When carrying passengers:* (a) required emergency exit fails to function as intended.[12]
Part 7. Driver Controls	(a) accelerator pedal, clutch, gauges, audible and visual indicators or instruments fail to function properly.	*When carrying passengers:* (a) accelerator sticking and engine fails to return to idle.
Part 8. Driver Seat	(a) seat is damaged or fails to remain in set position.	(a) seatbelt or tether belt is insecure, missing or malfunctions.
Part 9. Electric Brake System	(a) loose or insecure wiring or electrical connection.	(a) inoperative breakaway device. (b) inoperative brake.
Part 10. Emergency Equipment and Safety Devices	(a) emergency equipment is missing, damaged or defective.	
Part 11. Exhaust System	(a) exhaust leak except as described in Column 3.	(a) leak that causes exhaust gas to enter the occupant compartment.
Part 12. Exterior Body and Frame	(a) insecure or missing body parts.	(a) visibly shifted, cracked, collapsing or sagging frame member.

Column 1	Column 2	Column 3
Systems and Components	**Minor Defects**	**Major Defects**
	(b) insecure or missing compartment door. (c) damaged frame or body.	
Part 13. Fuel System		(a) missing fuel tank cap. (b) insecure fuel tank. (c) dripping fuel leak.
Part 14. General		(a) serious damage or deterioration that is noticeable and may affect the vehicle's safe operation.
Part 15. Glass and Mirrors	(a) required mirror[6] or window glass fails to provide the required view[7] to the driver as a result of being cracked, broken, damaged, missing or maladjusted. (b) required mirror[6] or glass has broken or damaged attachments onto vehicle body.	*When carrying passengers:* (a) driver's view of the road is obstructed in the area swept by the windshield wipers.
Part 16. Heater / Defroster	(a) control or system failure.	(a) defroster fails to provide unobstructed view through the windshield.
Part 17. Horn	(a) vehicle has no operative horn.	
Part 18. Hydraulic Brake System	(a) brake fluid level is below indicated minimum level. (b) [Repealed O. Reg. 242/14, s. 10(1).]	(a) brake boost or power assist is not operative. (b) brake fluid leak. (c) brake pedal fade or insufficient brake pedal reserve. (d) activated (other than ABS) warning device. (e) brake fluid reservoir is less than ¼ full.

625

Column 1	Column 2	Column 3
Systems and Components	**Minor Defects**	**Major Defects**
		(f) parking brake is inoperative.
Part 19. Lamps and Reflectors	(a) required interior lamp does not function as intended.[13] (b) required reflector is missing or partially missing.[9] (c) passenger safety or access lamp does not function.	*When use of lamps is required*: (a) failure of both low-beam headlamps. (b) failure of both rearmost tail lamps. *At all times*: (a) failure of a rearmost turn-indicator lamp. (b) failure of both rearmost brake lamps.
Part 20. Passenger Compartment	(a) stanchion padding is damaged. (b) damaged steps or floor. (c) insecure or damaged overhead luggage rack or compartment. (d) malfunction or absence of required passenger or mobility device restraints.[14] (e) passenger seat is insecure.	*When affected position is occupied*: (a) malfunction or absence of required passenger or mobility device restraints.[14] (b) passenger seat is insecure.
Part 21. Steering	(a) steering wheel lash (free-play) is greater than normal.	(a) steering wheel is insecure, or does not respond normally. (b) steering wheel lash (free-play) exceeds prescribed limit.[10]

Column 1	Column 2	Column 3
Systems and Components	**Minor Defects**	**Major Defects**
Part 22. Suspension System	(a) air leak in air suspension system. (b) a broken spring leaf. (c) suspension fastener is loose, missing or broken.	(a) damaged (patched, cut, bruised, cracked to braid or deflated) air bag or insecurely mounted air bag. (b) cracked or broken main spring leaf or more than one broken spring leaf. (c) part of spring leaf or suspension is missing, shifted out of place or in contact with another vehicle component. (d) loose U-bolt.
Part 23. Tires	(a) damaged tread or sidewall of tire. (b) tire leaking, if leak cannot be heard.	(a) flat tire. (a.1) tire leaking, if leak can be felt or heard. (b) tire tread depth is less than wear limit.[11] (c) tire is in contact with another tire or any vehicle component other than mud-flap. (d) tire is marked "Not for highway use". (e) tire has exposed cords in the tread or outer sidewall area.
Part 24. Wheels, Hubs and Fasteners	(a) hub oil below minimum level. (when fitted with sight glass). (b) leaking wheel seal.	(a) wheel has loose, missing or ineffective fastener. (b) damaged, cracked or broken wheel, rim or attaching part. (c) evidence of imminent wheel, hub or bearing failure.
Part 25. Windshield Wiper / Washer	(a) control or system malfunction.	*When use of wipers or washer is required*:

Column 1	Column 2	Column 3
Systems and Components	Minor Defects	Major Defects
	(b) wiper blade is damaged, missing or fails to adequately clear driver's field of vision.	(a) wiper or washer fails to adequately clear driver's field of vision in area swept by driver's side wiper.

O. Reg. 242/14, s. 10

SCHEDULE 3 — DAILY INSPECTION OF INTER-CITY BUSES [Heading amended O. Reg. 242/14, s. 11(1). Amended to "Daily Inspection of Motor Coaches", O. Reg. 256/15, s. 9. To come into force July 1, 2016.]

Column 1	Column 2	Column 3
Systems and Components	Minor Defects	Major Defects
Part 1. Accessibility Devices	*Accessibility device may not be used if*: (a) alarm fails to operate. (b) equipment malfunctions. (c) interlock system malfunctions.	(a) vehicle fails to return to normal level after kneeling. (b) extendable lift, ramp or other passenger-loading device fails to retract.
Part 2. Air Brake System	(a) audible air leak. (b) slow air pressure build-up rate.	(a) there is any indication of a brake adjustment problem. (b) air loss rate exceeds prescribed limit.[2] (c) inoperative towing vehicle (tractor) protection system. (d) low air warning system fails or system is activated. (e) inoperative service, parking or emergency brake.
Part 3. Coupling Devices	(a) coupler or mounting has loose or missing fastener.	(a) coupler is insecure or movement exceeds prescribed limit.[4] (b) coupling or locking mechanism is damaged or fails to lock.

628

Column 1	Column 2	Column 3
Systems and Components	**Minor Defects**	**Major Defects**
		(c) defective, incorrect or missing safety chain or cable.
Part 4. Dangerous Goods		(a) dangerous goods requirements not met.[5]
Part 5. Doors and Emergency Exits	(a) door, window or hatch fails to open or close securely. (b) alarm inoperative.	*When carrying passengers*: (a) required emergency exit fails to function as intended.[12]
Part 6. Driver Controls	(a) accelerator pedal, clutch, gauges, audible and visual indicators or instruments fail to function properly.	*When carrying passengers*: (a) accelerator sticking and engine fails to return to idle.
Part 7. Driver's Seat	(a) seat is damaged or fails to remain in set position.	(a) seatbelt or tether belt is insecure, missing or malfunctions.
Part 8. Emergency Equipment and Safety Devices	(a) emergency equipment is missing, damaged or defective.	
Part 9. Exhaust System	(a) exhaust leak except as described in Column 3.	(a) leak that causes exhaust gas to enter the occupant compartment.
Part 10. Exterior Body	(a) insecure or missing body parts. (b) insecure or missing compartment door.	
Part 11. Fuel System		(a) missing fuel tank cap. (b) insecure fuel tank. (c) dripping fuel leak.
Part 12. General		(a) serious damage or deterioration that is noticeable and may affect the vehicle's safe operation.

Column 1	Column 2	Column 3
Systems and Components	Minor Defects	Major Defects
Part 13. Glass and Mirrors	(a) required mirror[6] or window glass fails to provide the required view[7] to the driver as a result of being cracked, broken, damaged, missing or maladjusted.	*When carrying passengers*:
	(b) required mirror[6] or glass has broken or damaged attachments onto vehicle body.	(a) driver's view of the road is obstructed in the area swept by the windshield wipers.
Part 14. Heater / Defroster	(a) control or system failure.	(a) defroster fails to provide unobstructed view through the windshield.
Part 15. Horn	(a) vehicle has no operative horn.	
Part 16. Lamps and Reflectors	(a) required interior lamp does not function as intended.[13]	*When use of lamps is required*:
	(b) required reflector is missing or partially missing.[9]	(a) failure of both low-beam headlamps.
	(c) passenger safety or access lamp does not function.	(b) failure of both rearmost tail lamps.
		At all times:
		(a) failure of a rearmost turn-indicator lamp.
		(b) failure of both rearmost brake lamps.
Part 17. Passenger Compartment	(a) stanchion padding is damaged.	*When affected position is occupied*:
	(b) damaged steps or floor.	(a) malfunction or absence of required passenger or mobility device restraints.[14]

Column 1	Column 2	Column 3
Systems and Components	Minor Defects	Major Defects
	(c) insecure or damaged overhead luggage rack or compartment. (d) malfunction or absence of required passenger or mobility device restraints.[14] (e) passenger seat is insecure.	(b) passenger seat is insecure.
Part 18. Suspension System	(a) air leak in air suspension system.	(a) damaged (patched, cut, bruised, cracked to braid or deflated) air bag or insecurely mounted air bag.
Part 19. Steering	(a) steering wheel lash (free-play) is greater than normal.	(a) steering wheel is insecure, or does not respond normally. (b) steering wheel lash (free-play) exceeds prescribed limit.[10]
Part 20. Tires	(a) damaged tread or sidewall of tire. (b) tire leaking, if leak cannot be heard.	(a) flat tire. (a.1) tire leaking, if leak can be felt or heard. (b) tire tread depth is less than wear limit.[11] (c) tire is in contact with another tire or any vehicle component other than mud-flap. (d) tire is marked "Not for highway use". (e) tire has exposed cords in the tread or outer sidewall area.
Part 21. Wheels, Hubs and Fasteners	(a) hub oil below minimum level. (when fitted with sight glass). (b) leaking wheel seal.	(a) wheel has loose, missing or ineffective fastener. (b) damaged, cracked or broken wheel, rim or attaching part.

Column 1	Column 2	Column 3
Systems and Components	**Minor Defects**	**Major Defects**
		(c) evidence of imminent wheel, hub or bearing failure.
Part 22. Windshield Wiper Blades / Washer	(a) control or system malfunction. (b) wiper blade is damaged, missing or fails to adequately clear driver's field of vision.	*When use of wipers or washers is required:* (a) wiper or washer fails to adequately clear driver's field of vision in area swept by driver's side wiper.

O. Reg. 242/14, s. 11

SCHEDULE 4 — UNDER-VEHICLE INSPECTION OF INTER-CITY BUSES [Heading amended O. Reg. 242/14, s. 12(1). Amended to "Under-Vehicle Inspection of Motor Coaches", O. Reg. 256/15, s. 10. To come into force July 1, 2016.]

Column 1	Column 2
Systems and Components	**Defects**
Part 1. Air Brake System	(a) audible air leak. (b) brake pushrod stroke is beyond the adjustment limit.[1] (c) clearance between disc brake pads and rotor exceeds manufacturer's specified limit. (d) clearance between a brake calliper piston and the disc pad backing plate exceeds manufacturer's specified limit. (e) wedge brake shoe movement exceeds manufacturer's specified limit. (f) excessive discharge of fluids from air reservoir. (g) air compressor, mounts or attachments damaged or defective. (h) compressor drive-belt loose or damaged. (i) air line or fitting damaged or insecure. (j) air tank defective, damaged or insecure. (k) air tank drain or moisture ejector device inoperable. (l) brake chamber, brake linkage or other brake component is defective, damaged or insecure. (m) [Repealed O. Reg. 242/14, s. 12(2).]

Column 1	Column 2	
Systems and Components	**Defects**	
	(n)	spring brake is broken or malfunctions.
	(o)	inoperative service, parking or emergency brake.
Part 2. Exhaust System	(a)	exhaust leak.
	(b)	exhaust system component insecure, damaged or perforated.
Part 3. Frame and Underbody	(a)	any frame member or fastener is damaged, cracked or insecure.
	(b)	any component mount is damaged or insecure.
Part 4. Fuel System	(a)	fuel leak.
	(b)	insecure fuel tanks, fuel tank mounts or guards.
	(c)	fuel line or fitting damaged or insecure.
Part 5. Steering	(a)	steering linkage is damaged or insecure.
	(b)	power steering fluid is leaking, contaminated or low.
	(c)	power steering component damaged or insecure.
Part 6. Suspension System	(a)	air leak or malfunction of air suspension system or component.
	(b)	damage or deterioration of any suspension component including:
		(i) spring and air bag,
		(ii) axle or frame attaching component,
		(iii) axle supporting or aligning component,
		(iv) suspension or component fastener,
		(v) shock absorber or attachments.
Part 7. Tires	(a)	tire inflation less than required.[15]
	(b)	tire tread is less than wear limit.[11]
	(c)	damage to tread or sidewall of tire.
	(d)	retread or rebuilt tire is used on front axle.
Part 8. Wheels and Fasteners	(a)	loose, missing, damaged or ineffective wheel fastener.
	(b)	damaged wheel or wheel component.

O. Reg. 242/14, s. 12

SCHEDULE 5 — DAILY INSPECTION OF SCHOOL PURPOSES BUSES

Column 1	Column 2	Column 3
Systems and Components	Minor Defects	Major Defects
Part 1. Air Brake System	(a) audible air leak. (b) slow air pressure build-up rate.	(a) brake is beyond its adjustment limit.[1] (b) air loss rate exceeds prescribed limit.[2] (c) low air warning system fails or system is activated. (d) inoperative service, parking or emergency brake.
Part 2. Alternating Overhead Lamps	(a) a lamp is missing or inoperative. (b) lamps do not alternate. (c) a lamp is not of the proper colour.	*When use of lamp is required*: (a) a lamp is missing or inoperative. (b) lamps do not alternate. (c) a lamp is not of the proper colour.
Part 3. Doors and Windows, other than Emergency Exits	(a) a window or door fails to open or close securely.	*When carrying passengers*: (a) door fails to open or close securely. *At all times*: (a) window fails to provide the required view[16] to the driver as a result of being cracked, broken, damaged, missing, maladjusted, clouded or fogged.
Part 4. Driver Controls	(a) accelerator pedal, clutch, gauges, audible and visual indicators or instruments fail to function properly.	(a) accelerator is sticking and the engine fails to return to idle.
Part 5. Emergency Exits	(a) required alarm is inoperative.[17]	*When carrying passengers*: (a) window fails to open from inside or close securely.

Column 1	Column 2	Column 3
Systems and Components	**Minor Defects**	**Major Defects**
		(b) door fails to open freely from inside and outside. (c) a required door alarm is inoperative.[17]
Part 6. Emergency Flares, Lamps or Reflectors	(a) missing or insecure.	
Part 7. Exhaust System	(a) exhaust leak except as described in Column 3.	(a) exhaust leak that causes exhaust gas to enter the occupant compartment.
Part 8. Exterior Body and Frame	(a) insecure or missing body parts. (b) insecure or missing compartment door. (c) damaged frame or body.	(a) one or more visibly shifted, cracked, collapsing or sagging frame member.
Part 9. Fire Extinguisher	(a) fire extinguisher missing. (b) the gauge on any required fire extinguisher indicates an empty condition or a complete lack of pressure.[18] (c) fire extinguisher is not securely mounted or stored in a manner that prevents the extinguisher from being a projectile object.	*When carrying passengers:* (a) fire extinguisher missing. (b) the gauge on any required fire extinguisher indicates an empty condition or a complete lack of pressure.[18]
Part 10. First Aid Kit	(a) required first aid kit is missing.[19] (b) kit is incomplete.	*When carrying passengers:* (a) required first aid kit is missing.[19]
Part 11. Fuel System		(a) missing fuel tank cap. (b) insecure fuel tank. (c) dripping fuel leak.

Column 1	Column 2	Column 3
Systems and Components	Minor Defects	Major Defects
Part 12. General		(a) serious damage or deterioration that is noticeable and may affect the vehicle's safe operation.
Part 13. Heater / Defroster	(a) control or system failure.	(a) defroster fails to provide an unobstructed view through the windshield and through the side windows to the left and right of the driver's seat.
Part 14. Horn	(a) no operative horn.	
Part 15. Hydraulic Brake System	(a) brake fluid level is below indicated minimum level.	(a) brake boost or power assist is not operative. (b) brake fluid leak. (c) brake pedal fade or insufficient brake pedal reserve. (d) activated (other than ABS) warning device. (e) brake fluid reservoir is less than $\frac{1}{4}$ full. (f) inoperative service or parking brake.
Part 16. Inspection Stickers		(a) a required sticker is missing, unreadable or is invalid.[20]
Part 17. Lamps and Reflectors	(a) required interior or exterior lamp does not operate or function as intended.[21] (b) required reflector is missing or partially missing.[9]	*At all times*: (a) vehicle does not have at least one left and one right rear turn signal lamp. (b) vehicle does not have at least one brake lamp. *When use of lamps is required*: (a) vehicle does not have at least one low-beam headlamp. (b) vehicle does not have at least one tail lamp.

Column 1	Column 2	Column 3
Systems and Components	Minor Defects	Major Defects
Part 18. Mirrors	(a) a mirror fails to provide the required view to the driver as a result of being cracked, damaged or maladjusted.[22] (b) a mirror has broken or damaged attachments onto vehicle body.	(a) a mirror is missing or broken. (b) the glass surface of a mirror has an aggregate non-reflective area exceeding 6.5 square centimetres.
Part 19. Mobility Device Lift		(a) extendable lift, ramp or other passenger-loading device fails to retract.
Part 20. Mobility Device Ramp		(a) ramp will not attach securely to vehicle when positioned to load or unload passengers in mobility devices or will not remain in the stored position. (b) ramp structure is weak, damaged or worn.
Part 21. Passenger Compartment	(a) stanchion padding is damaged. (b) damaged steps or floor. (c) insecure or damaged overhead luggage rack or compartment.	
Part 22. Pedestrian-Student Safety Crossing Arm	(a) the arm is missing or fails to function as intended.	
Part 23. Seats and Seat Belts	(a) driver's seat fails to remain in set position. (b) required restraint system or component of required restraint system is missing.[23]	*When affected position is occupied*: (a) required restraint system or component of restraint system is missing.[23]

Column 1	Column 2	Column 3
Systems and Components	**Minor Defects**	**Major Defects**
	(c) restraint system or component of restraint system is defective.	(b) restraint system or component of restraint system is defective.
	(d) seat is insecure.	(c) seat is insecure.
	(e) restraint system for passenger in mobility device or mobility device restrain system or component of either system is missing or defective.	*When affected position is occupied with a mobility device or a passenger in a mobility device:*
		(a) passenger restraint system, mobility device restraint system or component of either system is missing or defective.
		When affected position or position behind it is occupied:
		(a) passenger seat or passenger protection barrier is insecure.
		(b) seat back or passenger protection barrier padding is missing, partially missing or has shifted from position so as not to be effective.
Part 24. Steering	(a) steering wheel lash (free-play) is greater than normal.	(a) steering wheel is insecure or does not respond normally.
		(b) steering wheel lash (free-play) exceeds prescribed limit.[10]
Part 25. Stop Arm	(a) if equipped with flashing lamps to illuminate letters of the word "STOP", any lamp is partially or wholly inoperative.	*When use of stop arm or stop sign is required:*

Column 1	Column 2	Column 3
Systems and Components	**Minor Defects**	**Major Defects**
	(b) stop arm or stop sign is missing.	(a) stop arm or stop sign is missing.
	(c) stop arm or stop sign is damaged so as to significantly affect visibility.	(b) stop arm or stop sign is damaged so as to significantly affect visibility.
	(d) will not extend fully or stay fully extended.	(c) will not extend fully or stay fully extended.
	(e) either light on stop arm is inoperative or lights do not alternate or lights are not red.	(d) either light on stop arm is inoperative or lights do not alternate or lights are not red.
Part 26. Suspension System	(a) air leak in air suspension system.	(a) damaged (patched, cut, bruised, cracked to braid or deflated) air bag or insecurely mounted air bag.
	(b) one broken spring leaf.	(b) cracked or broken main spring leaf or more than one broken spring leaf.
	(c) suspension fastener is loose, missing or broken.	(c) part of spring leaf or suspension is missing, shifted out of place or in contact with another vehicle component.
		(d) loose U-bolt.
		(e) broken spring on other than a leaf spring system.
Part 27. Tires	(a) damaged tread or sidewall of tire.	(a) flat tire.
		(a.1) tire leaking, if leak can be felt or heard.
	(b) tire leaking, if leak cannot be heard.	(b) tire tread depth is less than wear limit.[11]
		(c) tire is in contact with another tire or any vehicle component other than mud-flap.
		(d) tire is marked "Not for highway use".
		(e) tire has exposed cords in the tread or outer sidewall area.

Column 1	Column 2	Column 3
Systems and Components	Minor Defects	Major Defects
Part 28. Wheels, Hubs, Fasteners and Bearings	(a) hub oil below minimum level (when fitted with sight glass). (b) leaking wheel seal.	(a) wheel has loose, missing or ineffective fastener. (b) damaged, cracked or broken wheel, rim or attaching part. (c) evidence of imminent wheel, hub or bearing failure.
Part 29. Windshield Wiper / Washer	(a) control or system malfunction. (b) wiper blade is damaged, missing or ineffective. (c) wiper or washer fails to adequately clear the windshield in the areas swept by both wipers.	*When use of wipers or washers is required*: (a) control or system malfunction. (b) wiper is damaged, missing or ineffective. (c) wiper or washer fails to adequately clear the windshield in the areas swept by both wipers.

O. Reg. 411/10, s. 2; 242/14, s. 13

SCHEDULE 6 — DAILY INSPECTION OF SCHOOL PURPOSES VEHICLES

Column 1	Column 2	Column 3
Systems and Components	Minor Defects	Major Defects
Part 1. Doors and Windows	(a) window or door fails to open or close securely.	*When carrying passengers*: (a) door fails to open or close securely. *At all times*:

Column 1	Column 2	Column 3
Systems and Components	**Minor Defects**	**Major Defects**
		(a) window fails to provide the required view[24] to the driver as a result of being cracked, broken, damaged, missing, maladjusted, clouded or fogged.
Part 2. Driver Controls	(a) accelerator pedal, clutch, gauges, audible and visual indicators or instruments fail to function properly.	(a) accelerator is sticking and the engine fails to return to idle.
Part 3. Exhaust System	(a) exhaust leak except as described in Column 3.	(a) leak that causes exhaust gas to enter the occupant compartment.
Part 4. Exterior Body and Frame	(a) insecure or missing body parts. (b) damaged frame or body.	(a) one or more visibly shifted, cracked, collapsing or sagging frame member.
Part 5. Fuel System		(a) missing fuel tank cap. (b) insecure fuel tank. (c) dripping fuel leak.
Part 6. General		(a) serious damage or deterioration that is noticeable and may affect the vehicle's safe operation.
Part 7. Heater / Defroster	(a) control or system failure.	(a) defroster fails to provide unobstructed view through the windshield and through the side windows to left and right of driver's seat.
Part 8. Horn	(a) no operative horn.	
Part 9. Hydraulic Brake System	(a) brake fluid level is below indicated minimum level.	(a) brake boost or power assist is not operative. (b) brake fluid leak. (c) brake pedal fade or insufficient brake pedal reserve. (d) activated (other than ABS) warning device.

Column 1	Column 2	Column 3
Systems and Components	**Minor Defects**	**Major Defects**
		(e) brake fluid reservoir is less than ¼ full.
		(f) inoperative service or parking brake.
Part 10. Inspection Stickers		(a) a required sticker is missing, unreadable or invalid.[20]
Part 11. Lamps	(a) required exterior lamp does not operate or function as intended.[8]	*At all times*: (a) does not have at least one left and one right rear turn signal lamp. *When use of lamps is required*: (a) does not have at least one low-beam headlamp. (b) does not have at least one tail lamp.
Part 12. Mirrors	(a) a mirror fails to provide the required view[24] to the driver as a result of being cracked, broken, damaged, missing or maladjusted. (b) a mirror has broken or damaged attachments onto vehicle body.	(a) mirror is missing or broken. (b) the glass surface of a mirror has an aggregate non-reflective area exceeding 6.5 square centimetres.
Part 13. Mobility Device Lift		(a) extendable lift, ramp or other passenger-loading device fails to retract.
Part 14. Mobility Device Ramp		(a) ramp will not attach securely to vehicle when positioned to load or unload passengers in mobility devices, or will not remain in the stored position. (b) ramp structure is weak, damaged or worn.

Column 1	Column 2	Column 3
Systems and Components	**Minor Defects**	**Major Defects**
Part 15. Seats and Seat Belts	(a) driver's seat fails to remain in set position. (b) required restraint system or component of required restraint system is missing.[14] (c) restraint system or component of restraint system is defective. (d) seat is insecure (e) restraint system for passenger in mobility device or mobility device restraint system or component of either system is missing or defective.	*When affected position is occupied*: (a) required restraint system or component of required system is missing.[14] (b) restraint system or component of restraint system is defective. (c) seat is insecure. *When affected position is occupied with a mobility device or a passenger in a mobility device*: (a) passenger restraint system, mobility device restraint system or component of either system is missing or defective.
Part 16. Steering	(a) steering wheel lash (free-play) is greater than normal.	(a) steering wheel is insecure or does not respond normally. (b) steering wheel lash (free-play) exceeds prescribed limit.[10]
Part 17. Suspension System	(a) air leak in air suspension system. (b) one broken spring leaf.	(a) damaged (patched, cut, bruised, cracked to braid or deflated) air bag or insecurely mounted air bag. (b) cracked or broken main spring leaf or more than one broken spring leaf.

Column 1	Column 2	Column 3
Systems and Components	Minor Defects	Major Defects
	(c) suspension fastener is loose, missing or broken.	(c) part of spring leaf or suspension is missing, shifted out of place or in contact with another vehicle component. (d) loose U-bolt. (e) broken spring on other than a leaf spring system.
Part 18. Tires	(a) damaged tread or sidewall of tire. (b) tire leaking, if leak cannot be heard.	(a) flat tire. (a.1) tire leaking, if leak can be felt or heard. (b) tire tread depth is less than wear limit.[11] (c) tire is in contact with any vehicle component other than mud-flap. (d) tire is marked "Not for highway use". (e) tire has exposed cords in the tread or outer sidewall area.
Part 19. Wheels, Hubs, Fasteners and Bearings	(a) leaking wheel seal.	(a) visual or audible evidence of a loose, missing or ineffective fastener. (b) damaged, cracked or broken wheel, rim or attaching part. (c) evidence of imminent wheel, hub or bearing failure.
Part 20. Windshield Wipers / Washer	(a) control or system malfunction. (b) wiper blade is damaged, missing or ineffective. (c) wiper or washer fails to adequately clear the windshield in the areas swept by both wipers.	*When use of wipers and washers is required:* (a) control or system malfunction. (b) wiper is damaged, missing or ineffective.

Column 1	Column 2	Column 3
Systems and Components	**Minor Defects**	**Major Defects**
		(c) wiper or washer fails to adequately clear the windshield in the areas swept by both wipers.

O. Reg. 242/14, s. 14

Proposed Addition — Sched. 7

SCHEDULE 7 — PERFORMANCE STANDARDS UNDER SUBSECTION 107(3) OF THE ACT [Heading added O. Reg. 256/15, s. 11. To come into force July 1, 2016.]

GENERAL
[Heading added O. Reg. 256/15, s. 11. To come into force July 1, 2016.]

1. (1) Body, Sheet Metal and Equipment — The body, sheet metal and equipment shall meet the following standards:

1. No bumper, fender or mudguard shall have been removed.

2. Each bumper shall be securely mounted.

3. Each mud flap, where applicable, shall be in position.

4. No bumper, fender, molding or other part shall have a broken, bent or sharp edge that protrudes in such a way as to constitute a hazard to persons or vehicles.

5. No hood latch shall be missing or fail to hold the hood closed and no safety catch, in the case of a front opening hood, shall be missing or inoperative.

6. No tilt cab latch shall be missing or fail to hold the tilt cab latched and no safety catch shall be missing or inoperative.

7. Every occupant seat shall be securely mounted and shall maintain its position and adjustment.

8. Where a seat belt assembly is required under the provisions of the *Motor Vehicle Safety Act* (Canada), no seat belt assembly or its anchorages shall have been removed, rendered partly or wholly inoperative, or modified so as to reduce their effectiveness.

9. If fitted with a seat belt assembly or assemblies, each belt anchorage shall be secure, each buckle and retractor shall operate as intended and no belt webbing shall be visibly damaged so as to reduce its effectiveness.

10. If fitted with a driver's sun visor, the sun visor shall function as intended.

11. If fitted with an overhead package shelf or shelves, each overhead package shelf shall be securely mounted and not have any broken, missing, excessively worn or excessively stretched package retaining components.

12. In the case of a bus or accessible vehicle, the floor and stepwell covering shall not be so cracked, curled, loose or worn as to present a tripping hazard.

13. In the case of a bus or accessible vehicle, each stanchion, grab handle, guard rail and guard panel shall be securely mounted and fastening parts shall not be missing.

14. In the case of a bus or accessible vehicle, where originally installed by the manufacturer, no energy-absorbing material shall be missing from stanchions and guard rails or from the tops or sides of seat backs.

15. In the case of an accessible vehicle,

> i. if fitted with wheelchair securement devices, each device anchorage shall be secure, each component part shall operate as intended, and no component part shall have damage, apparent on visual inspection, that would reduce its effectiveness,
>
> ii. if fitted with occupant restraint assemblies, each component part of an occupant restraint assembly shall operate as intended, and no component part shall have damage, apparent on visual inspection, that would reduce its effectiveness,
>
> iii. if fitted with occupant restraint assemblies anchored to the vehicle, each restraint assembly anchorage shall be secure, and
>
> iv. no plate, cover or energy-absorbing material required to protect persons from sharp edges or corners shall be missing or worn or damaged so as to reduce its effectiveness.

(2) **Occupant Compartment Doors and Emergency Exits** — The occupant compartment door or doors shall meet the following standards:

1. Each occupant compartment door shall open freely when its release mechanism is actuated and shall close securely, and if originally fitted with flexible material on vertical closing edges, the flexible material shall not be missing or excessively loose or torn.

2. In the case of a motor vehicle having a separate exit door, other than a door to be used only in an emergency,

> i. when the driver's door control is in the "closed" position and the exit door is fully closed, and a moderate amount of manual force is applied in an attempt to open the door, it shall not open, and if fitted with an audible or visual warning device, the device shall function,
>
> ii. when the driver's door control is in the position to open the exit door, if fitted with brake and accelerator interlock systems, the systems shall automatically apply the rear brakes and hold them in the applied position and the engine speed will be prevented from exceeding idle speed until the door control is moved to the "closed" position and the door has closed, and

iii. when the exit door is fitted with sensitive edges, and the door is not fully closed, manual pressure applied to the edge of each sensitive edge shall cause the door to reopen,

> A. if fitted with an audible or visual warning device, the device shall function,

> B. if fitted with brake and accelerator interlock systems, the systems shall automatically apply the rear brakes and hold them in the applied position and the engine speed will be prevented from exceeding idle speed until the door control is moved to the "closed" position and the door has closed.

3. In the case of a bus, other than an accessible vehicle or a bus used for the purpose of transporting prisoners or other persons held in custody, an emergency exit,

i. if a door, shall have a clear passageway to it and be located at the rear of the vehicle or near the rear on the left side of the vehicle, and the release mechanism when actuated shall function from inside the vehicle, as well as from outside the vehicle where fitted with outside release, and the door shall open freely and close securely, and if originally fitted with an emergency door audible or visible warning device, the device shall function,

ii. if a hinged pushout window, shall open outwards when the release mechanism is actuated and adequate directions for the emergency use of the pushout window shall be displayed on or adjacent to the pushout window, and if originally fitted with an emergency warning device, it shall function,

iii. if a non-hinged pushout window, shall have adequate directions for the emergency use of the pushout window displayed on or adjacent to it, and

iv. if a roof hatch, shall open outwards when the release mechanism is actuated and a reasonable amount of manual force is applied, and adequate directions for the emergency use of the roof hatch shall be displayed on or adjacent to it.

4. In the case of an accessible vehicle,

i. all devices used to secure passenger access or emergency exit doors in the open position shall operate as intended and shall not have damage, apparent on visual inspection, that would reduce their effectiveness,

ii. if fitted with an emergency exit door, the door shall have no fixed obstructions blocking the passage of persons or, in the case of a vehicle used for the transportation of persons in wheelchairs, blocking the passage of wheelchairs, and the door release mechanism when actuated shall function from inside and outside the vehicle,

iii. if fitted with a ramp or power lift, the means of attachment of the ramp or power lift to the vehicle shall be secure with no fastening parts missing and when the ramp or power lift is in the stored position, it shall be secured, by means other than a support or lug in the door, in such manner as to not pose a potential hazard to occupants of the vehicle, and

iv. if fitted with a power lift, the lift platform shall rise and descend smoothly when activated by the appropriate controls.

(3) **Exterior Compartment Door** — If fitted with an exterior compartment door or doors, each exterior compartment door shall meet the following standards:

1. The door shall be securely attached to the body.

2. The door shall be equipped with a lock, latch or spring device that shall hold the door closed.

(4) **Chassis Frame, Underbody and Body Mounts** — The chassis frame, underbody and body mounts shall meet the following standards:

1. No chassis frame member or structural member of a unitized or monocoque body shall be visibly cracked or perforated by corrosion.

2. No chassis frame member or structural member of a unitized or monocoque body shall have loose or missing connecting fasteners that may degrade the safety of the vehicle or jeopardize its handling characteristics.

3. The underbody, excluding the underbody of a separate cargo body, shall not be visibly perforated by rust or otherwise damaged, or have any opening other than those intended by the manufacturer or required for the installation of an alternative fuel system.

(5) **Drive Shaft Hanger** — The drive shaft hanger brackets and guards shall meet the following standards:

1. No fasteners shall be missing, loose or damaged.

2. No drive shaft guard or hanger bracket shall be insecure or missing.

(6) **Mirrors** — Mirrors required under the Act and regulations shall meet the following standards:

1. Each mirror shall be securely mounted and maintain a set adjustment.

2. No mirror shall have any significant reduction in reflecting surface owing to deterioration of the silvering.

3. In the case of a motor vehicle where there is no rear window, or the view through the rear window is restricted in such a way as not to afford a driver a clear view to the rear of the motor vehicle, the outside rear view mirror or mirrors shall not be missing.

(7) **Windshield and Windows** — The windshield and windows shall meet the following standards:

1. Where glass is used, there shall be no evidence of the glass being any glass other than safety glass.

2. Any manufacturer's marking,

i. on the windshield shall be AS1 or AS10,

ii. on the side and rear windows at levels requisite for driving visibility shall be AS1, AS2, AS4, AS6, AS10 or AS11, and

iii. on windows for standing passengers, in interior partitions or in openings in the roof shall be AS1, AS2, AS3, AS4, AS5, AS6, AS7, AS10, AS11, AS12 or AS13.

3. No material that obstructs the driver's view of the highway or an intersecting highway shall be fitted in the windshield opening or in a side window opening to the left or right of the driver's seat.

4. No material other than safety glass shall be used for a windshield.

5. No safety glass in the windshield or in any side window to the left or right of the driver's seat shall be crazed, clouded or fogged so as to materially impair vision.

6. No safety glass shall have exposed sharp edges or be missing in part.

7. There shall be no crack that extends through both layers of glass or be any length that extends more than 50 mm within the area swept by the windshield wipers.

8. There shall be no stone chip that is larger than 13 mm in diameter within the area swept by the windshield wipers.

9. Any window to the left of the driver's seat that is suitable for the purpose of permitting a signal by means of the hand or arm shall open readily.

(8) Fuel System — In the fuel system, no mounting or attachment shall be missing.

(9) Exhaust System — The exhaust system, including exhaust manifolds, shall meet the following standards:

1. No exhaust pipe, muffler or tail pipe shall be missing or insecurely mounted.

2. No component of the exhaust system shall be so located as to cause charring or other heat damage to any wiring, fuel line, brake line or combustible material of the vehicle.

3. No component of the exhaust system shall pass through the occupant compartment.

4. No component of the exhaust system shall be so located or unguarded that an individual may be burned by it on entering or leaving the vehicle.

5. No exhaust system shall be shortened or modified from original equipment so as to fail to direct the exhaust beyond the underbody of the occupant compartment or luggage compartment, and in no case shall the distance between the outlet and periphery of the underbody, past which it directs the exhaust, exceed 15 cm.

(10) Fifth Wheel — Where a fifth wheel coupling device is installed, it shall meet the following standards:

1. The fifth wheel shall be fastened securely to the vehicle.

2. In the case of a fifth wheel secured to the vehicle frame by means of U-bolts, there shall be positive stops that prevent the fifth wheel from shifting on the frame.

3. The jaw closure mechanism and locking system shall be in good working order and shall not be broken, cracked or excessively worn.

4. If fitted with a slider mechanism, the slider mechanism shall lock securely and shall not show any signs of failure or excessive wear.

(11) **Trailer Hitch** — Where a trailer hitch is installed, the trailer hitch, hitch mounting and connecting devices for safety cables and chains shall meet the following standards:

1. No trailer hitch or towing structure to which a trailer hitch is attached shall be insecurely mounted.

2. No latch mechanism shall fail to close securely.

3. No part shall be missing, cracked, broken, excessively bent, seized or excessively worn.

4. No cast or forged hitch shall show any indication that repairs have been made by means of brazing or welding.

5. No connecting devices provided at the rear of a vehicle for the attachment of a safety chain or cable shall be insecurely fastened, missing, cracked, broken or excessively worn.

O. Reg. 256/15, s. 11 [To come into force July 1, 2016.]

BRAKES

[Heading added O. Reg. 256/15, s. 11. To come into force July 1, 2016.]

2. (1) **Hydraulic, Vacuum and Air System Components** — Hydraulic, vacuum and air system components which are external to the wheel brakes, including reservoirs, fittings, valves, supports, hose clamps, connections, air chambers, air cleaners, hoses and tubes, other than any portions of such components that are within structures and not visible, shall meet the following standards:

1. With vacuum, hydraulic or air boost systems fully charged, there shall be no hydraulic or vacuum leak in the service brake system while the service brakes are fully applied or released.

2. No hydraulic, air or vacuum hose or tube shall be abraded, restricted, crimped, cracked or broken.

3. No hydraulic, air or vacuum hose or tube shall be located so as to chafe against any part of the vehicle.

4. No hydraulic, air or vacuum hose or tube shall have damaged or missing clamps or supports.

5. The brake tubing shall not show any indication of leakage or heavy corrosion scaling.

6. The hydraulic fluid level in any reservoir shall not be below the minimum level as specified by the manufacturer, or where there is no minimum level specified by the manufacturer, no more than 10 mm below the lowest edge of each filler opening.

7. The air cleaner of the vacuum system or air compressor shall not be clogged.

(2) **Air-Boosted Hydraulic Brakes or Full Air Brakes** — In the case of a motor vehicle equipped with air-boosted hydraulic brakes or full air brakes, the air system shall meet the following standards:

1. If fitted with a compressor drive belt, the compressor drive belt shall have correct tension, and shall not be cut, frayed or excessively worn.

2. The air pressure gauge shall be operative.

3. With the engine running at a fast idle, the time required to build air pressure from 50 to 90 pounds per square inch gauge measure shall not exceed three minutes.

4. With the air system fully charged and the engine running, each air reservoir drain valve shall be actuated and shall function.

5. The governor cut-in and cut-out pressures shall not be lower or higher than those specified by the vehicle manufacturer, or if not specified by the vehicle manufacturer, 80 pounds per square inch gauge measure and 135 pounds per square inch gauge measure, respectively.

6. With the air brake system fully charged and immediately after the engine is stopped, the compressed air reserve shall be sufficient to permit one full service brake application from fully charged system pressure without lowering reservoir pressure more than 20 per cent.

7. With the air brake system fully charged and engine stopped, air pressure drop shall not exceed,

   i. with the service brakes released, two pounds per square inch in one minute, and

   ii. with the service brakes fully applied, three pounds per square inch in one minute.

8. The low pressure warning device shall operate when system pressure is reduced to 55 pounds per square inch gauge measure.

(3) **Vacuum-Boosted Hydraulic Brakes with Vacuum Gauge** — In the case of a motor vehicle equipped with vacuum-boosted hydraulic brakes and fitted with a vacuum gauge and low vacuum warning device, the gauge and warning device shall meet the following standards:

1. The vacuum gauge shall be operative.

2. With the engine stopped, the warning device shall operate before the vacuum reserve drops to less than eight inches of mercury.

(4) **Vacuum-Boosted Hydraulic Brakes without Vacuum Gauge** — In the case of a motor vehicle equipped with vacuum-boosted hydraulic brakes and fitted with a low vacuum warning device but not fitted with a vacuum gauge, there shall be at least one boosted brake application available after the warning device operates.

(5) **External Mechanical Components** — No mechanical component of the service, parking and emergency brake systems which is external to the wheel or drive shaft brakes shall be misaligned, insecure, excessively worn, broken, binding, seized, missing, frayed or disconnected.

(6) Internal Components — Wheel brake internal components shall meet the following standards:

1. No drum or disc shall have any external crack or cracks on the friction surface, other than normal heat-check cracks, that reach the edge of the drum bore or periphery of the disc.

2. No drum or disc shall have any mechanical damage to the friction surface, other than that which may be attributed to normal wear.

3. No ventilated disc shall have broken or visibly cracked cooling fins.

4. No inside diameter of a drum shall be greater than the dimension stamped on the drum, or where the dimension is not stamped on the drum, the vehicle manufacturer's wear limit.

5. No thickness of a disc shall be less than the dimension stamped on the disc, or where the dimension is not stamped on the disc, the vehicle manufacturer's wear limit.

6. The thickness of a hydraulic brake lining, measured at the lining edge, shall not be less than,

   i. in the case of a drum brake, 2 mm for a bonded lining or 3 mm for a riveted lining,

   ii. in the case of disc brake, 3 mm for a bonded pad or 5 mm for a riveted pad.

7. The thickness of an electric brake lining, measured at the lining edge, shall not be less than 2 mm.

8. The thickness of an air brake lining, measured at the lining edge, shall not be less than,

   i. in the case of a drum brake, 5 mm for a continuous strip lining or 8 mm for block-type lining,

   ii. in the case of disc brake, 3 mm for a bonded pad or 5 mm for a riveted pad.

9. No brake lining shall be broken, cracked or loose on its shoe or pad.

10. No brake lining shall show evidence of contamination such as to affect braking performance.

11. No hydraulic brake cylinder shall show evidence of leakage.

12. No mechanical or structural parts shall be misaligned, badly worn, cracked, broken, binding, seized, disconnected, missing or insecure, and no grease retainer shall be missing or leaking.

13. If fitted with an automatic adjuster, the automatic adjuster shall not be inoperative.

14. No hydraulic brake piston shall fail to move when moderate pressure is applied to the brake pedal.

(7) Hydraulic System — In the case of a motor vehicle equipped with hydraulic service brakes, the hydraulic system and related warning devices shall meet the following standards:

1. A hydraulic master cylinder push rod shall be properly adjusted.

2. In the case of a vehicle equipped with dual circuit hydraulic brakes, the brake failure warning lamp shall be operative.

3. With moderate foot force maintained on the service brake pedal for 10 seconds and, in the case of power-boosted brakes, with the engine running, the service brake pedal shall not move towards the applied position.

4. With heavy foot force applied to the service brake pedal and, in the case of power-boosted brakes, with the engine running,

    i. the total pedal travel shall not exceed 80 per cent of the total available travel, and

    ii. on a vehicle equipped with dual circuit hydraulic brakes, the brake failure warning lamp shall not come on.

5. For the purpose of paragraph 4, where a motor vehicle is equipped with a HYDRA BOOST braking system, the foot force applied to the pedal shall not exceed 60 pounds.

(8) **Power-Boosted Hydraulic Brakes** — In the case of a motor vehicle equipped with power-boosted hydraulic brakes, after the engine has been stopped and the vacuum, air or hydraulic boost has been depleted, and while holding moderate pressure on the service brake pedal and starting the engine, the pedal shall move towards the applied position.

(9) **Hydraulically-Boosted with Electric Pump Backup Hydraulic Brakes** — In the case of a motor vehicle equipped with hydraulically-boosted hydraulic brakes and electrically-driven hydraulic pump for the reserve power system, after the engine has been stopped and the hydraulic boost has been depleted, and while holding moderate pressure on the service brake pedal and moving the ignition switch to the "ON" position, the pump shall meet the following standards:

1. The pump shall start and run.

2. The brake pedal shall move towards the applied position.

(10) **Service Brake Operation Test** — When the unloaded vehicle is stopped from a speed of between 15 and 20 kilometres per hour, with heavy pedal force, on a substantially level, dry, smooth, paved surface free from loose material, the service brake system shall meet the following standards:

1. There shall be no brake pull either to the left or to the right.

2. No component shall fail.

3. Each wheel brake shall release immediately after the pedal force is removed.

O. Reg. 256/15, s. 11 [To come into force July 1, 2016.]

ENGINE CONTROLS AND STEERING

[Heading added O. Reg. 256/15, s. 11. To come into force July 1, 2016.]

3. (1) **Accelerator Control System** — Except in the case of a trolley bus, the complete accelerator control system shall meet the following standards when tested

while the engine is running, the vehicle is stationary and the transmission is in neutral:

1. The engine speed shall drop to idle when the accelerator pedal is released.

2. Where the engine is equipped with an emergency stopping device, the engine shall stop when the control is actuated while the engine is idling.

(2) **Power Control System** — In the case of a trolley bus, the complete power control system shall meet the following standards when tested while the reverser is in the neutral position:

1. The system shall function as intended.

2. The controller shall turn off positively when the power pedal is released.

(3) **Power-Boosted Steering** — In the case of power-boosted steering, the power steering drive belt, reservoir fluid level and system operation shall meet the following standards:

1. The power steering drive belt shall not be missing, cut, frayed or excessively worn, and shall have correct tension.

2. The fluid in the power steering reservoir shall not be lower than the minimum level specified by the vehicle manufacturer.

3. With the engine running,

   i. the power steering system shall operate as intended, and

   ii. the hydraulic system shall not show excessive fluid leakage.

(4) **Steering Column and Box** — The steering column and box or boxes shall meet the following standards:

1. The steering column and box or boxes shall not be loose in their mountings to the body and frame.

2. No bolt or nut shall be loose or missing from a mounting.

3. Steering shaft couplings and splines shall not have excessive play.

4. If fitted with a steering column energy-absorbing section, the section shall not be visibly damaged so as to reduce its effectiveness.

(5) **Wheel Alignment** — While all wheels are on the ground and the front wheels are in the straight ahead position, they shall not be visibly out of alignment.

(6) **Steering Lash (Free Play)** — While the front wheels are on the ground in the straight ahead position, the steering mechanism shall meet the following standards:

1. Steering lash (free play) shall not exceed the limit designated by the vehicle manufacturer.

2. Where the limit is not designated by the vehicle manufacturer,

   i. in the case of a vehicle with a power steering system, with the engine running, steering lash (free play) shall not exceed,

      A. 75 mm for a steering wheel diameter of 500 mm or less,

      B. 87 mm for a steering wheel diameter of more than 500 mm.

ii. in the case of a vehicle with a manual steering system, steering lash (free play) shall not exceed,

    A. 87 mm for a steering wheel diameter of 500 mm or less,

    B. 100 mm for a steering wheel diameter of more than 500 mm.

(7) Steering Interference — While the front wheels are on the ground and, in the case of a vehicle equipped with power-boosted steering, with the engine running, the front wheels shall turn from full right to full left and back again without interference or indication of roughness in the mechanism.

(8) Steering Linkage System — The steering linkage system shall meet the following standards:

1. No part shall be damaged, repaired or modified so as to visibly weaken the linkage system or affect the proper steering of the vehicle.

2. No nut, bolt or cotter pin shall be loose, excessively worn or missing.

3. There shall not be excessive play in any steering linkage joint.

(9) Front Wheel Play — While the front wheels are off the ground and the vehicle is supported so that the steering linkage assumes its normal attitude, the steering linkage shall meet the following standard:

1. Without movement of the opposite wheel, no front wheel shall have play about a vertical axis of,

    i. six mm for a tire diameter designation of 16 or less,

    ii. nine mm for a tire diameter designation that is larger than 16 but not larger than 18, or

    iii. 12 mm for a tire diameter designation that is larger than 18,

as measured at the extreme front or rear of the tire tread face.

O. Reg. 256/15, s. 11 [To come into force July 1, 2016.]

SUSPENSION

[Heading added O. Reg. 256/15, s. 11. To come into force July 1, 2016.]

4. (1) Inner Control Arm Pivots, etc. — Inner control arm pivots, king pins, wheel and axle bearings, and ball joints, other than wear-indicating ball joints, when inspected for wear and damage with the wheels of the vehicle off the ground so that the suspension joints are not under load, shall meet the following standards:

1. No non-load-carrying ball joint shall show any perceptible play other than that specified by the manufacturer.

2. No load-carrying ball joint shall have play in excess of that specified by the vehicle manufacturer.

3. In the case of king pins, no front wheel shall have a rocking play about a horizontal axis in excess of,

    i. six mm for a tire diameter designation of 16 or less,

    ii. nine mm for a tire diameter designation that is larger than 16 but not larger than 18, or

iii. 12 mm for a tire diameter designation that is larger than 18,

as measured at the extreme top or bottom of the tire tread face.

4. No control arm inner pivot shall have excessive play.

5. No wheel or axle bearing shall give any indication of excessive wear or damage when the bearing is rotated.

6. No wheel or axle bearing shall be maladjusted so as to result in excess play or binding.

(2) **Wear-indicating Ball Joints** — When wear-indicating ball joints are under load with the wheels on the ground, they shall not show any excessive wear.

(3) **Strut Suspension System** — With the front wheels off the ground and the vehicle supported so that the suspension assumes its normal attitude, no front wheel shall have a rocking play about a horizontal axis in excess of 5 mm as measured at the extreme top or bottom of the tire tread face.

(4) **Suspension Components** — Front and rear springs, shackles, U-bolts, centrebolts, radius rods, control arms, shock-absorbers, equalizers, stabilizers, their supports and attachments shall not be loose, bent, cracked, broken, disconnected, perforated by corrosion or missing.

(5) **Axle Tracking** — The rear axle or axles and their wheels shall not be tracking improperly so as to adversely affect control of the vehicle.

(6) **Air Suspension System** — If fitted with an air suspension system, not including air booster bags added to light vehicles to provide added carrying capacity, the air suspension system shall meet the following standards:

1. In the case of a vehicle equipped with full air brakes, when the engine is started with zero gauge air pressure in the entire air system including air brake system, air shall not begin to flow into the suspension system before 55 pounds per square inch gauge is reached in the brake system.

2. When the air suspension system is fully charged, no air leakage shall occur.

3. If fitted with a pusher or tag axle, no air leakage shall occur when the pusher or tag axle is tested in either load or reduced load sharing mode with air in the suspension system at normal operating pressure.

4. If fitted with a pusher or tag axle, the pusher or tag axle, with air in the suspension system at normal operating pressure, shall respond properly to its load sharing control switch or valve.

5. With air in the suspension system at normal operating pressure, the vehicle body and chassis frame shall be supported clear of all axles and shall appear to be level.

6. No suspension joints of a variable load-sharing axle with independent suspension shall be worn beyond the manufacturer's specified safe limits.

O. Reg. 256/15, s. 11 [To come into force July 1, 2016.]

ELECTRICAL

[Heading added O. Reg. 256/15, s. 11. To come into force July 1, 2016.]

5. (1) Horn — The horn shall not be loose on its mounting.

(2) Heating and Defrosting System — The heating and defrosting system shall meet the following standards:

1. The heating system shall function as intended.

2. The visible portions of the hoses and piping for the interior heaters routed within the occupant compartment shall not be abraded, cracked or leaking.

3. The defrosting system shall deliver heated air to the windshield and, where fitted with a defrosting system for the side windows to the left and right of the driver's seat, to those side windows.

(3) Engine Starter Safety Feature — If originally fitted with a clutch pedal safety switch or neutral safety switch, the switch shall meet the following standards:

1. It shall not have been removed or rendered inoperative.

2. It shall function as intended.

(4) Speedometer — The speedometer shall be in good working order.

O. Reg. 256/15, s. 11 [To come into force July 1, 2016.]

LIGHTING

[Heading added O. Reg. 256/15, s. 11. To come into force July 1, 2016.]

6. Lamps and Reflectors — Lamps and reflectors required under the Act and regulations shall meet the following standards:

1. The operation of any lighting circuit shall not interfere with the operation of any other circuit.

2. Each lens and reflex reflector shall be correctly installed and shall not be discoloured or missing in whole or in part.

3. Each lamp and reflector shall be securely mounted on the vehicle and none shall be missing.

4. The turn signal lamps and the flasher unit shall operate properly.

5. No headlamp shall be coated or covered with a coloured material except as permitted by section 4.1 of Regulation 596 of the Revised Regulations of Ontario, 1990 (*General*) made under the Act.

6. No headlamp shall be modified by the attachment to the lamp or to the vehicle or any device that reduces the effective area of the lens or brightness of the light.

7. All headlamps shall be properly aligned.

8. Each headlamp shutter or retracting headlamp shall operate over the full range of movement or shall be secured in the fully open position.

9. In the case of a bus or an accessible vehicle, all interior lamps, including stepwell lamps, shall light when the appropriate switch is in the "ON" position.

10. In the case of an accessible vehicle, the lights provided to illuminate the loading equipment and step nosings shall light when the appropriate switch is in the "ON" position or when the doors are opened.

O. Reg. 256/15, s. 11 [To come into force July 1, 2016.]

WHEELS

[Heading added O. Reg. 256/15, s. 11. To come into force July 1, 2016.]

7. Wheels — Wheels shall meet the following standards:

1. No wheel fastener shall have insufficient thread engagement.

2. No disc wheel assembly shall have any visible crack, elongated bolt hole, indication of repair by welding, or be so bent or damaged as to affect the safe operation of the vehicle.

3. No wheel rim or lock ring shall be mismatched, bent, sprung, or otherwise damaged so as to affect the safe operation of the vehicle.

4. No cast wheel shall show evidence of excessive wear in the clamp area.

5. No wheel spoke shall be missing, loose or broken.

O. Reg. 256/15, s. 11 [To come into force July 1, 2016.]

ONT. REG. 424/97 — COMMERCIAL MOTOR VEHICLE OPERATORS' INFORMATION

made under the *Highway Traffic Act*

O. Reg. 424/97, as am. O. Reg. 197/99; 640/05; 247/07; 397/08; 281/12; 436/12; 331/15; 420/15 [To come into force January 1, 2017.].

[Note: The title of this Regulation was changed from "Commercial Vehicle Operator's Registration Certificates" to "Commercial Motor Vehicle Operators' Information" by O. Reg. 197/99, s. 1.]

PART I — CVOR CERTIFICATES

1. (1) In this Regulation,

"audit" means an inspection of the records pertaining to the transportation enterprise of an operator and an assessment of the operator's safety performance and practices;

"auditor" means,

(a) an officer appointed for the purpose of carrying out the provisions of the Act,

(b) a person engaged as an auditor by an organization recognized by the Registrar, or

(c) a person recognized as an auditor by another jurisdiction who, in the Registrar's opinion, performs audits similar to those performed in Ontario in an acceptable form and manner;

Proposed Addition — 1(1) "commercial motor vehicle"

"commercial motor vehicle" has the same meaning as in section 3 of Ontario Regulation 419/15 *(Definitions of Commercial Motor Vehicle and Tow Truck)* made under the Act;

O. Reg. 420/15, s. 1 [To come into force January 1, 2017.]

"commercial motor vehicle", **"CVOR certificate"** and **"operator"** have the same meanings as in subsection 16(1) of the Act;

Proposed Repeal — 1(1) "commercial motor vehicle", "CVOR certificate" and "operator"

"commercial motor vehicle", **"CVOR certificate"** and **"operator"** [Repealed O. Reg. 420/15, s. 1. To come into force January 1, 2017.]

"fleet" means all the commercial motor vehicles operated in Ontario by the holder of a CVOR certificate for which number plates have been issued by Ontario or by a state of the United States of America.

Proposed Addition — 1(1) "operator"

"operator" has the same meaning as in subsection 16(1) of the Act.

O. Reg. 420/15, s. 1 [To come into force January 1, 2017.]

(2) In this Regulation and for the purpose of subsection 18(2) of the Act,

"fleet size" means the total number of commercial motor vehicles operated in Ontario by the holder of a CVOR certificate for which number plates have been issued by Ontario or by a state of the United States of America.

O. Reg. 197/99, ss. 1–3; 397/08, s. 1

1.0.1 A commercial motor vehicle is exempt from the requirements of section 16 of the Act if it is operated under the terms of a Manufacturer permit and number plate issued under Regulation 628 of the Revised Regulations of Ontario, 1990 (*Vehicle Permits*) made under the Act.

Proposed Amendment — 1.0.1

1.0.1 A commercial motor vehicle is exempt from the requirements of section 16 of the Act if it is operated under and in accordance with,

(a) a special permit issued under Regulation 628 of the Revised Regulations of Ontario, 1990 (*Vehicle Permits*) made under the Act;

(b) a permit for which temporary validation has been issued under Regulation 628 of the Revised Regulations of Ontario, 1990 (*Vehicle Permits*) made under the Act; or

(c) a Manufacturer permit and number plate issued under Regulation 628 of the Revised Regulations of Ontario, 1990 (*Vehicle Permits*) made under the Act.

O. Reg. 420/15, s. 2 [To come into force January 1, 2017.]

O. Reg. 331/15, s. 1

1.1 (1) A commercial motor vehicle for which number plates have been issued by another Canadian jurisdiction is exempt from the requirements of section 16 of the Act if,

(a) it is operated under the authority of a valid safety fitness certificate, within the meaning of the *Motor Vehicle Transport Act* (Canada), issued by the other jurisdiction; or

(b) it is required by the *Motor Vehicle Transport Act* (Canada) or the laws of the other jurisdiction to have a safety fitness certificate issued by the other jurisdiction.

(2) It is a condition of the exemption in clause (1)(a) that the driver of the commercial motor vehicle surrender the safety fitness certificate referred to in that subsec-

tion, or a copy of it, and, if the vehicle is leased, the lease or a copy of it, on the demand of a police officer.

(3) If the commercial motor vehicle has been issued number plates from a jurisdiction that does not issue safety fitness certificate documentation, the driver of the commercial vehicle may provide the police officer with the safety fitness certificate number and sufficient information to check its validity instead of surrendering the safety fitness certificate as required by subsection (2).

(4) The lease referred to in subsection (2) must identify the leased vehicle, the parties to the lease and their addresses, the operator of the vehicle and the operator's safety fitness certificate number.

O. Reg. 640/05, s. 1; 247/07, s. 1

1.2 (1) A pick-up truck is exempt from the requirements of section 16 of the Act if,

(a) it is being used for personal purposes without compensation; and

(b) it is not carrying, or towing a trailer that is carrying, commercial cargo or tools or equipment of a type normally used for commercial purposes.

(2) In this section,

"pick-up truck" means a commercial motor vehicle that,

(a) has a manufacturer's gross vehicle weight rating of 6,000 kilograms or less, and

(b) is fitted with either,

(i) the original box that was installed by the manufacturer, which has not been modified, or

(ii) a replacement box that duplicates the one that was installed by the manufacturer, which has not been modified.

O. Reg. 247/07, s. 2

1.3 (1) A CVOR certificate shall not be issued to an operator unless an individual, on behalf of the operator, has successfully completed an examination described in subsection (2) not more than six months before the operator's application for a CVOR certificate is received by the Ministry.

(2) The examination shall be set or approved by the Ministry for the purpose of testing knowledge of the safe operation of commercial motor vehicles and of the statutory and regulatory requirements applicable to the operation of commercial motor vehicles.

(3) For the purposes of subsection (1), the following are individuals who may take the examination on behalf of an operator:

1. If the operator is a sole proprietor, the operator.

2. If the operator is a corporation, an officer of the corporation.

3. If the operator is an unincorporated organization, an employee of the operator who has responsibility for the operator's safety management.

(4) Despite paragraph 2 of subsection (3), if the Registrar considers it impractical for an officer to take the examination on behalf of a corporate operator, the Registrar may waive that requirement; in that case, an employee of the corporation who has responsibility for the operator's safety management may take the examination on behalf of the operator.

(5) For greater certainty, an individual is considered to have successfully completed the examination only on behalf of the operator applying for the CVOR certificate. An individual who has successfully completed the examination on behalf of an operator is not considered to have successfully completed the examination on behalf of another operator.

(6) The following operators are exempt from the examination requirement of this section:

  1. **An operator seeking renewal of a CVOR certificate.**

  2. **An operator that held a valid CVOR certificate at any time within the previous three years before the application is received by the Ministry.**

  3. **An operator whose principal place of business is not in Ontario.**

(7) The fee for taking the examination, whether or not it is successfully completed, is $32.

(8) This section applies to applications for CVOR certificates received on or after October 1, 2013.

O. Reg. 281/12, s. 1

2. (1) Subject to subsection (2), a CVOR certificate that is issued on or after December 1, 2008 expires,

  (a) on the second anniversary of the date of its issue if it is issued before December 1, 2009;

  (b) on the first anniversary of the date of its issue if it is issued on or after December 1, 2009.

(2) A CVOR certificate that is issued on or after December 1, 2008 subject to terms and conditions expires on a date assigned by the Registrar, which must be between six months and 24 months after the date of its issue.

O. Reg. 397/08, s. 2

2.1 (1) Subject to subsections (2) and (3), a renewed CVOR certificate expires on the next anniversary of the CVOR certificate's expiry date.

(2) If a CVOR certificate to which the Registrar assigned an expiry date under subsection 17(5.1) of the Act is renewed, the expiry date of the renewed CVOR certificate is,

  (a) the second anniversary of the CVOR certificate's expiry date, if the expiry date was assigned before December 1, 2009;

  (b) the first anniversary of the CVOR certificate's expiry date, if the expiry date was assigned on or after December 1, 2009.

662

(3) If, at the time a CVOR certificate is renewed, the operator's safety rating is Excellent or Satisfactory, or if the Registrar has sent a notice under subsection 17.1(2) of the Act proposing a safety rating of Excellent or Satisfactory, the renewed CVOR certificate expires on the second anniversary of the CVOR certificate's expiry date.

(4) Subsection (3) does not apply if the application for renewal is completed after the expiry of the CVOR certificate.

O. Reg. 397/08, s. 2

3. (1) Notice of an expiry date assigned under subsection 17(5.1) of the Act and notice of a proposed revocation of a CVOR certificate under subsection 17.0.1(2) of the Act may be served on the operator at the most recent address or fax number for the operator in the Ministry's records,

(a) personally;

(b) by regular mail; or

(c) by fax.

(2) The notice shall be deemed to have been served on the operator,

(a) on the day it was personally served;

(b) on the fifth day after it was mailed;

(c) on the day it was sent by fax, if sent before 5 p.m.;

(d) on the day after it was sent by fax, if sent at or after 5 p.m.

(3) If the day described in clause (2)(b), (c) or (d) is a holiday, the notice shall be deemed to have been served on the next day that is not a holiday.

O. Reg. 397/08, s. 2

3.1 It is a term of every CVOR certificate that it is a safety fitness certificate for the purpose of the *Motor Vehicle Transport Act* (Canada).

O. Reg. 640/05, s. 1

4. The following fees shall be paid to the Ministry for:

1. An uncertified copy of an operator's CVOR record $5.00

2. A certified copy of an operator's CVOR record $10.00

5. (1) The safety record of an operator shall contain a record of the following information:

1. Any suspension or cancellation of the plate portion of the permit under clause 47(1)(a) of the Act.

2. Any suspension or cancellation of the operator's CVOR certificate under clause 47(1)(c) of the Act.

3. Any restriction imposed under subsection 47(2) of the Act on the number of commercial motor vehicles that may be operated by the operator.

4. Any order under subsection 47(8.1) or (10) of the Act for the seizure of the plate portion of permits, permits or number plates.

5. Any notice sent to the operator under section 47.1 of the Act.

6. Any warning letters sent by, or interviews held with, Ministry officials relating to the operator's safety performance and practices.

7. Any conviction related to the operation of a commercial motor vehicle or a vehicle drawn by it, for an offence committed by an operator, its agents or employees,

    i. under this Act or under any other Act of the Legislature or the Parliament of Canada or any regulation or order made under any of them, or

    ii. for an offence under a municipal by-law regulating traffic on the highways, or orders made under any of them, except convictions for offences for standing or parking.

8. The particulars of any accident involving a commercial motor vehicle operator by the operator or a vehicle drawn by it.

9. The results of any inspection under section 82 or 82.1 of the Act or any similar inspection of a commercial motor vehicle operated by the operator, or a vehicle drawn by it.

10. The result of any investigation or inspection of the record of the operator,

    i. under the Act, the *Compulsory Automobile Insurance Act*, the *Dangerous Goods Transportation Act*, the *Public Vehicles Act*, the *Truck Transportation Act*, the *Fuel Tax Act*, the *Apprenticeship and Certification Act, 1998*, the *Ontario College of Trades and Apprenticeship Act, 2009* or the *Motor Vehicle Transport Act* (Canada), or

    ii. under any other Act of the Legislature or the Parliament of Canada or any regulation or order made under any of them if, in the Registrar's opinion, the results of the investigation or inspection contain information described in paragraphs 14, 15 or 16, or relate to the safe operation of its commercial motor vehicles or vehicles drawn by them.

11. Any safety rating that has been assigned to the operator.

12. The results of any audits of the operator.

13. Any record from another jurisdiction in respect of the operator that is comparable to that described in any of paragraphs 1 to 12.

14. The operator's fleet size.

15. The total kilometres travelled by the fleet operated by the operator in each of,

    i. Ontario,

    ii. Canada outside Ontario, and

    iii. outside Canada.

16. The total kilometres of projected travel by the fleet operated by the operator, as reported by the operator at any time, in each of,

    i. Ontario,

    ii. Canada outside Ontario, and

    iii. outside Canada.

17. Any compilations or analyses of any of the information in paragraphs 1 to 16.

(2) The following do not form part of a safety record:

1. A record that is not in the possession of the Registrar.

2. A record originating outside of Ontario that, in the Registrar's opinion, is unreasonably difficult to refer to (because of its form or medium of storage, or for any other reason).

3. A record described in paragraphs 1 to 7 of subsection (1) if, in the Registrar's opinion, the record does not relate to the safe operation of the operator's commercial motor vehicles, or vehicles drawn by them.

O. Reg. 197/99, s. 4; 397/08, s. 3; 436/12, s. 1

6. Every holder of a CVOR certificate shall notify the Registrar of the holder's fleet size for the previous 12 months within 15 days after the day the holder's fleet size is 20 per cent greater or less than it was when the fleet size was last reported to the Registrar.

O. Reg. 397/08, s. 4

7. (1) The Registrar may at any time request that a holder of a CVOR certificate provide any or all of the following information or records to the Registrar:

1. The holder's fleet size.

2. The number of buses, trucks or other types or classes of commercial motor vehicles, as specified by the Registrar, in the holder's fleet.

3. The total kilometres travelled by the holder's fleet in the period specified by the Registrar.

4. The total kilometres of projected travel by the holder's fleet in the period specified by the Registrar.

5. Any change in the information provided by the operator in the operator's application for a CVOR certificate or pursuant to a previous request under this section.

6. Documentation to support the information provided by the operator under section 6 or under this section.

(2) A request from the Registrar under subsection (1) shall be made in writing and shall be sent to the holder of the CVOR certificate by mail, courier or fax at the holder's most recent address or fax number in the Ministry's records.

(3) Upon receipt of a request made under subsection (1), a holder of a CVOR certificate shall provide the requested information or records within the time or by the date specified by the Registrar, which may not be less than 15 days after the date of the request.

(4) Compliance with subsection (3) is a condition of retaining a CVOR certificate.

O. Reg. 397/08, s. 4

PART II — SAFETY RATINGS

8. This Part applies to the assignment of safety ratings under section 17.1 of the Act.

O. Reg. 197/99, s. 5

9. In this Part, the date on which an audit is completed is the most recent date on which an auditor has completed the audit report or an amendment to it.

O. Reg. 197/99, s. 5

10. (1) The Registrar shall assign to an operator one of the following safety ratings, as determined in this Part:

1. Excellent.

2. Satisfactory.

3. Satisfactory Unaudited.

4. Conditional.

5. Unsatisfactory.

(2) A safety rating set out in a paragraph of subsection (1) is a higher rating than a rating set out in a later paragraph.

O. Reg. 197/99, s. 5

10.1 (1) The Registrar shall recognize the safety rating for an operator issued by another province or territory of Canada instead of assigning a safety rating under this Regulation if the operator is an extra-provincial motor carrier undertaking and the Registrar has not issued number plates for any of its commercial motor vehicles.

(2) If the Registrar, before January 1, 2006, assigned a safety rating for an operator described in subsection (1), that safety rating is cancelled as of January 1, 2006.

O. Reg. 640/05, s. 2

11. (1) The Registrar may assign an Excellent rating to an operator where, in the Registrar's opinion, the operator's safety record shows that the operator's performance and practices are excellent with respect to the safe operation of its commercial motor vehicles and vehicles drawn by them.

(2) The Registrar shall not assign an Excellent rating to an operator unless,

(a) the operator's safety record contains the results of an audit completed within the previous 36 months; and

(b) the operator,

(i) has held a CVOR certificate for the previous 24 months, or

(ii) has satisfied the Registrar that the operator has been operating in Ontario for the previous 24 months and has obtained a CVOR certificate.

(c) [Repealed O. Reg. 397/08, s. 5.]

(3) The Registrar shall not assign an Excellent rating to an operator whose rating had previously been reduced from Excellent unless,

(a) more than six months have passed since the rating was reduced from Excellent; and

(b) the operator satisfies clauses (2)(a) and (b).

O. Reg. 197/99, s. 5; 397/08, s. 5

12. (1) The Registrar may assign a Satisfactory rating to an operator where, in the Registrar's opinion, the operator's safety record shows that the operator's performance and practices are satisfactory with respect to the safe operation of its commercial motor vehicles and vehicles drawn by them.

(2) The Registrar shall not assign a Satisfactory rating to an operator rated Conditional or Satisfactory Unaudited unless,

(a) the operator's safety record contains the results of an audit completed within the previous 36 months; and

(b) the operator,

(i) has held a CVOR certificate for the previous six months, or

(ii) has satisfied the Registrar that the operator has been operating in Ontario for the previous six months and has obtained a CVOR certificate.

O. Reg. 197/99, s. 5; 397/08, s. 6

13. (1) The Registrar may assign a Satisfactory Unaudited rating to an operator if the operator has not been audited and, in the Registrar's opinion, the operator's safety record shows that the operator's performance and practices are satisfactory with respect to the safe operation of its commercial motor vehicles and vehicles drawn by them.

(2) For the purpose of subsection (1), an operator shall be deemed not to have been audited if,

(a) the operator has a conditional rating;

(b) the most recent audit in the operator's safety record was completed more than 36 months ago; and

(c) the results of that audit are satisfactory in the Registrar's opinion.

O. Reg. 197/99, s. 5

14. (1) The Registrar may assign a Conditional rating to an operator where, in the Registrar's opinion, the operator's safety record shows that the operator's performance and practices are less than satisfactory with respect to the safe operation of its commercial motor vehicles and vehicles drawn by them.

(2) The Registrar shall assign a Conditional rating to an operator when nothing described in paragraphs 1, 2 or 3 of subsection 15(1) which resulted in an Unsatisfactory rating under subsection 15(1), is any longer in effect.

(3) The Registrar shall not assign to an operator a higher rating sooner than six months after the Registrar assigns to the operator a Conditional rating.

O. Reg. 197/99, s. 5

15. (1) The Registrar shall assign an Unsatisfactory rating to an operator on the first day when any of the following comes into effect, for reasons which, in the Registrar's opinion, relate to the safe operation of the operator's commercial motor vehicles or vehicles drawn by them:

　1. The plate portion of the operator's permit is suspended or cancelled under clause 47(1)(a) of the Act.

　2. The operator's CVOR certificate is suspended or cancelled under clause 47(1)(c) of the Act.

　3. The time period specified in an order under subsection 47(10) of the Act during which an operator's permit or number plate may be seized, is in effect.

(2) The Registrar shall not assign to an operator a rating higher than Unsatisfactory while anything described in paragraphs 1, 2 or 3 of subsection (1) is in effect.

O. Reg. 197/99, s. 5

15.1 (1) The Registrar may assign an Unsatisfactory rating to an operator if the Registrar has reason to believe that the operator does not have the minimum liability insurance coverage required by law in respect of bodily injury, death or loss or damage to property of other persons, other than cargo.

(2) Failure by the operator to promptly and adequately respond to a request by the Registrar that the operator prove that it has the required insurance is sufficient reason for the Registrar to believe that the operator does not have the required insurance for the purpose of subsection (1).

(3) After assigning an Unsatisfactory rating to an operator, the Registrar shall not assign a different rating to the operator unless the operator proves to the Registrar that it does have the required insurance.

(4) If, after being assigned an Unsatisfactory rating under this section, the operator proves to the Registrar that it has the required insurance, the Registrar may assign a higher rating to the operator immediately after the assignment of an Unsatisfactory rating under this section.

(5) If the Registrar assigns a Conditional rating to an operator immediately after assigning the operator an Unsatisfactory rating under this section, the Registrar may, despite subsection 14(3), assign a new rating to replace the Conditional rating at any time that the Registrar considers appropriate.

(6) In this section,

"required insurance" means the minimum liability insurance coverage required by law in respect of bodily injury, death or loss or damage to property of other persons, other than cargo.

O. Reg. 640/05, s. 2

16. (1) In assigning a safety rating, the Registrar shall have regard to the operator's safety record.

(2) In assigning a safety rating, the Registrar,

　(a) may have regard to the safety record of a person related to the operator;

(b) need not consider audit results from an audit completed less than six months after the date on which a previous audit was completed; and

(c) need not consider audit results where he or she is of the view that the records audited do not adequately reflect the operator's safety performance and practices in Ontario.

(3) Subsection 17(4) of the Act applies, with necessary modifications, for the purpose of determining who are related persons under clause (2)(a).

O. Reg. 197/99, s. 5

ONT. REG. 510/99 — COMMUNITY SAFETY ZONES

made under the *Highway Traffic Act*

O. Reg. 510/99, as am. O. Reg. 628/99; 220/00; 458/00; 1/01; 68/01; 375/01; 412/01; 262/02; 46/03; 87/03; 178/03; 445/04; 493/05; 368/06; 22/07; 95/08; 112/08 [Corr. by CTR 12 MA 08 - 1]; 380/08; 145/10; 24/12; 199/12; 243/12; 264/13; 175/14; 5/15; 379/15; 2/16.

1. The part of a highway described in a schedule to this Regulation is designated as a community safety zone for the hours, days and months specified in the schedule.

O. Reg. 220/00, s. 1

SCHEDULE 1 — TOWN OF WHITBY [Heading amended O. Reg. 220/00, s. 2.]

1. (1) That part of the King's Highway known as No. 12 in the Town of Whitby in The Regional Municipality of Durham lying between a point situate 20 metres measured southerly from its intersection with the centre line of the roadway known as Winchester Road (Durham Regional Road No. 3) and extending northerly through the intersection of the roadway known as Winchester Road (Durham Regional Road No. 3) along that part of the King's Highway known as No. 7 and No. 12, to a point situate 30 metres measured northerly from its intersection with the centre line of the roadway known as Carnwith Drive.

(2) This designation is effective 24 hours a day, seven days a week and every month of the year.

O. Reg. 628/99, s. 1

SCHEDULE 2 — TOWNSHIP OF RAMARA

1. (1) That part of the King's Highway known as No. 12 in the Township of Ramara in the County of Simcoe lying between a point situate 740 metres measured southerly from its intersection with the centre lines of the roadways known as Ramara Road 47/Ramara Concession Road 4 and a point situate 640 metres measured northerly from its intersection with the centre lines of the roadways known as Ramara Road 47/Ramara Concession Road 4.

(2) This designation is effective 24 hours a day, seven days a week and every month of the year.

O. Reg. 220/00, s. 3; 412/01, s. 1

SCHEDULE 3 — TOWNSHIP OF SPRINGWATER

670

**1. (1) That part of the King's Highway known as No. 93 in the Township of Spr-
ingwater, formerly known as the Police Village of Hillsdale, in the County of Simcoe
lying between a point situate 235 metres measured southerly from its intersection
with the centre line of the roadway known as Martin Street and a point situate 150
metres measured northerly from its intersection with the centre line of the roadway
known as Robert Boulevard.**

**(2) This designation is effective 24 hours a day, seven days a week and every month
of the year.**

O. Reg. 458/00, s. 1

SCHEDULE 4 — TOWNSHIP OF MCDOUGALL

**1. (1) That part of the King's Highway known as No. 69 in the Township of McDou-
gall in the Territorial District of Parry Sound lying between a point situate 250 metres measured northerly from its intersection with the northerly limit of the roadway known as Hammel Avenue and a point situate 350 metres measured northerly
from its intersection with the centre line of the roadway known as Bayside Drive.**

**(2) That part of the King's Highway known as No. 124 in the Township of McDou-
gall in the Territorial District of Parry Sound beginning at a point situate 40 metres
measured easterly from its intersection with the centre line of the roadway known as
Burnside Bridge Road and extending easterly for a distance of 820 metres.**

**(3) The designations set out in subsections (1) and (2) are effective 24 hours a day,
seven days a week and every month of the year.**

O. Reg. 1/01, s. 1

SCHEDULE 5 — TOWNSHIP OF SEGUIN

**1. (1) That part of the King's Highway known as No. 141 in the Village of Rosseau in
the Township of Seguin in the Territorial District of Parry Sound lying between a
point situate 190 metres measured westerly from its intersection with the centre line
of the roadway known as McCarthy Street and a point situate 140 metres measured
westerly from its intersection with the centre line of the roadway known as Clifford
Street.**

**(2) That part of the King's Highway known as No. 141 in the settlement known as
Humphrey in the Township of Seguin in the Territorial District of Parry Sound lying between a point situate 170 metres measured westerly from its intersection with
the centre line of the roadway known as Sandy Plains Road and a point situate 255
metres measured westerly from its intersection with the centre line of the roadway
known as Laughing Loon Lane.**

**(3) That part of the King's Highway known as No. 518 in the Township of Seguin in
the Territorial District of Parry Sound lying between a point situate 100 metres
measured westerly from its intersection with the centre line of the roadway know as
Isabella Lake Road and a point situate 200 metres measured northerly from its intersection with the centre line of the roadway known as James Street.**

(4) This designation is effective 24 hours a day, seven days a week and every month of the year.

O. Reg. 68/01, s. 1; 2/16, s. 1

SCHEDULE 6 — TOWN OF CALEDON

1. (1) That part of the King's Highway known as No. 10 in the Town of Caledon lying between a point situate 100 metres measured northerly from its intersection with the centre line of the roadway known as Highwood Road and a point situate 1,450 metres measured northerly from its intersection with the centre line of the roadway known as Highwood Road.

(2) This designation is effective 24 hours a day, seven days a week and every month of the year.

O. Reg. 375/01, s. 1

SCHEDULE 7 — MUNICIPALITY OF CLARINGTON [Heading added O. Reg. 262/02, s. 1.]

1. (1) That part of the east side of the King's Highway known as Nos. 35/115 in the Municipality of Clarington lying between a point situate 110 metres measured northerly from its intersection with the centre line of the roadway known as Concession Road 3 and a point situate 100 metres measured southerly from its intersection with the centre line of the roadway known as Concession Road 4.

(2) This designation is effective 24 hours a day, seven days a week and every month of the year.

O. Reg. 262/02, s. 1

SCHEDULE 8 — TOWNSHIP OF SIOUX NARROWS NESTOR FALLS [Heading added O. Reg. 46/03, s. 1.]

1. (1) That part of the King's Highway known as No. 71 in the Township of Sioux Narrows Nestor Falls in the Territorial District of Kenora lying between a point situate at its intersection with the centre line of the roadway known as Fadden Road and a point situate 350 metres measured northerly from its intersection with the northerly abutment of the Sioux Narrows Bridge.

(2) This designation is effective between 6 a.m. and 10 p.m., seven days a week and every month of the year.

O. Reg. 46/03, s. 1

SCHEDULE 9 — MUNICIPALITY OF NORTHERN BRUCE PENINSULA [Heading added O. Reg. 87/03, s. 1.]

1. (1) That part of the King's Highway known as No. 6 in the Municipality of Northern Bruce in the County of Bruce beginning at a point situate 405 metres measured southerly from its intersection with the centre line of the roadway known as Bruce Road 9 and extending northerly for a distance of 923 metres.

(2) This designation is effective 24 hours a day, seven days a week and every month of the year.

O. Reg. 87/03, s. 1

SCHEDULE 10 — MUNICIPALITY OF TEMAGAMI [Heading added O. Reg. 178/03, s. 1.]

1. (1) That part of the King's Highway known as No. 11 in the Municipality of Temagami in the Territorial District of Nipissing lying between a point situate 85 metres measured southerly from its intersection with the centre line of the roadway known as Lakeshore Drive and a point situate 125 metres measured northerly from its intersection with the centre line of the roadway known as Second Avenue West.

(2) This designation is effective 24 hours a day, seven days a week and every month of the year.

O. Reg. 178/03, s. 1

SCHEDULE 11 — DISTRICT OF ALGOMA [Heading added O. Reg. 445/04, s. 1.]

1. (1) That part of the King's Highway known as No. 17B in the Garden River Indian Reserve in the District of Algoma lying between a point situate 1250 metres measured easterly from its intersection with the centre line of the bridge over Garden River and a point situate 1460 metres measured westerly from its intersection with the centre line of the bridge over the Garden River.

(2) This designation is effective 24 hours a day, seven days a week and every month of the year.

O. Reg. 445/04, s. 1; 199/12, s. 1

SCHEDULE 12 — TOWN OF ORANGEVILLE [Heading added O. Reg. 493/05, s. 1.]

1. (1) That part of the King's Highway known as No. 9 in the Town of Orangeville in the Country of Dufferin lying between a point situate 270 metres measured westerly from its intersection with the centre line of the roadway known as Rolling Hills Drive and a point situate 450 metres measured easterly from its intersection with the centre line of the roadway known as Rolling Hills Drive.

(2) This designation is effective 24 hours a day, seven days a week and every month of the year.

O. Reg. 493/05, s. 1

SCHEDULE 13 — TOWNSHIP OF CHATSWORTH [Heading added O. Reg. 368/06, s. 1.]

1. (1) That part of the King's Highway known as No. 10 in the Township of Chatsworth in the County of Grey lying between a point situate **490** metres measured southerly from its intersection with the centre line of the roadway known as Glendale Airport Road and a point situate **610** metres measured northerly from its intersection with the centre line of the roadway known as Glendale Airport Road.

(2) This designation is effective 24 hours a day, seven days a week and every month of the year.

O. Reg. 368/06, s. 1

SCHEDULE 14 — MUNICIPALITY OF WHITESTONE [Heading added O. Reg. 22/07, s. 1.]

1. (1) That part of the King's Highway known as No. 124 in the Municipality of Whitestone in the Territorial District of Parry Sound lying between a point situate **160** metres measured easterly from its intersection with the easterly limit of the bridge over Whitestone Lake and a point situate **85** metres measured westerly from its intersection with the centre line of the roadway known as Percy Lane.

(2) This designation is effective 24 hours a day, seven days a week and every month of the year.

O. Reg. 22/07, s. 1

SCHEDULE 15 — TOWNSHIP OF CHAMPLAIN [Heading added O. Reg. 95/08, s. 1.]

1. (1) That part of the King's Highway known as No. 34 in the Township of Champlain in the United Counties of Prescott and Russell lying between a point situate **187** metres measured northerly from its intersection with the centre line of the roadway known as Happy Hollow Road and a point situate at its intersection with the northerly limits of the Town of Vankleek Hill.

(2) This designation is effective 24 hours a day, seven days a week and every month of the year.

O. Reg. 95/08, s. 1

SCHEDULE 16 — TOWNSHIP OF SCUGOG [Heading added O. Reg. 112/08, s. 1. Corrected by CTR 12 MA 08 -1]

1. (1) That part of the King's Highway known as No. 12 in the Hamlet of Greenbank in the Township of Scugog lying between a point situate **800** metres measured southerly from its intersection with the centre line of the roadway known as Cragg Road and a point situate **700** metres measured northerly from its intersection with the centre line of the roadway known as Cragg Road.

(2) This designation is effective 24 hours a day, seven days a week and every month of the year.

O. Reg. 112/08, s. 1 [Corr. by CTR 12 MA 08 - 1]

SCHEDULE 17 — TOWNSHIP OF TEHKUMMAH [Heading added O. Reg. 380/08, s. 1.]

1. (1) That part of the King's Highway known as No. 6 in the Corporation of the Township of Tehkummah in the Territorial District of Manitoulin lying between a point situate 120 metres measured sourtherly from its intersection with the centre line of the roadway known as Green Street and a point situate 20 metres measured northerly from its intersection with the centre line of the roadway known as Water Street.

(2) This designation is effective 24 hours a day, seven days a week and every month of the year.

O. Reg. 380/08, s. 1

SCHEDULE 18 — MUNICIPALITY OF GILLIES, DISTRICT OF THUNDER BAY [Heading added O. Reg. 145/10, s. 1.]

1. (1) That part of the King's Highway known as No. 595 in the Municipality of Gillies in the District of Thunder Bay beginning at a point situate 700 metres measured southerly from its intersection with the centre line of the King's Highway known as No. 608 and extending northerly for a distance of 1400 metres.

(2) That part of the King's Highway known as No. 608 in the Municipality of Gillies in the District of Thunder Bay beginning at a point situate at its intersection with the centre line of the King's Highway known as No. 595 and extending easterly for a distance of 700 metres.

(3) That part of the King's Highway known as No. 595 in the Municipality of Gillies in the District of Thunder Bay beginning at a point situate at its intersection with the centre lines of the roadways known as Pee Dee Road and Main Street and extending southerly for a distance of 1300 metres.

(4) That part of the King's Highway known as No. 595 in the Municipality of Gillies in the District of Thunder Bay beginning at a point situate at its intersection with the centre lines of the roadways known as Pee Dee Road and Main Street and extending easterly for a distance of 700 metres.

(5) This designation is effective 24 hours a day, seven days a week and every month of the year.

O. Reg. 145/10, s. 1

SCHEDULE 19 — COUNTY OF NORFOLK [Heading added O. Reg. 24/12, s. 1.]

1. (1) That part of the King's Highway known as No. 6 in the County of Norfolk lying between a point situate 25 metres measured easterly from its intersection with the centre line of the roadway known as Erie Street and a point situate 25 metres measured easterly from its intersection with the centre line of the roadway known as Lakeview Avenue.

(2) This designation is effective 24 hours a day, seven days a week and every month of the year.

O. Reg. 24/12, s. 1

SCHEDULE 20 — TOWNSHIP OF SOUTHWEST OXFORD [Heading added O. Reg. 243/12, s. 1.]

1. (1) That part of the King's Highway known as No. 19 in the Township of Southwest Oxford lying between a point situate 400 metres measured northerly from its intersection with the centre line of the roadway known as Highway 18 and a point situate 500 metres measured southerly from its intersection with the centre line of the roadway known as Highway 18.

(2) This designation is effective 24 hours a day, seven days a week and every month of the year.

O. Reg. 243/12, s. 1

SCHEDULE 21 — TOWNSHIP OF PUSLINCH [Heading added O. Reg. 264/13, s. 1.]

1. (1) That part of the King's Highway known as No. 6 in the Township of Puslinch lying between a point situate at its intersection with the centre lines of the roadways known as Currie Drive and Telfer Glen Street and a point situate 340 metres measured southerly from its intersection with the centre line of the roadway known as Church Street.

(2) This designation is effective 24 hours a day, seven days a week and every month of the year.

O. Reg. 264/13, s. 1; 5/15, s. 1

SCHEDULE 22 — TOWNSHIP OF IGNACE [Heading added O. Reg. 175/14, s. 1.]

1. (1) That part of the King's Highway known as No. 17 in the Township of Ignace in the Territorial District of Kenora lying between a point situate 305 metres measured easterly from its intersection with the centre line of the roadway known as Pine Street and a point situate 215 metres measured westerly from its intersection with the centre line of the roadway known as West Street.

(2) This designation is effective 24 hours a day, seven days a week and every month of the year.

O. Reg. 175/14, s. 1

SCHEDULE 23 — MUNICIPALITY OF CENTRAL MANITOULIN [Heading added O. Reg. 379/15, s. 1.]

1. (1) That part of the King's Highway known as No. 542 in the Village of Sandfield in the Municipality of Central Manitoulin in the Territorial District of Manitoulin lying between a point situate 377 metres measured southerly from its intersection with the centre line of the roadway known as Hutchinson Road and a point situate 1050 metres measured northerly from its intersection with the centre line of the roadway known as Hutchinson Road.

(2) That part of the King's Highway known as No. 542 in the Village of Spring Bay in the Municipality of Central Manitoulin in the Territorial District of Manitoulin lying between a point situate 510 metres measured easterly from its intersection with the centre line of the roadway known as Grimesthorpe Road and a point situate 385 metres measured westerly from its intersection with the centre line of the roadway known as Grimesthorpe Road.

(3) This designation is effective 24 hours a day, seven days a week and every month of the year.

O. Reg. 379/15, s. 1

ONT. REG. 287/08 — CONDUCT REVIEW PROGRAMS

made under the *Highway Traffic Act*

O. Reg. 287/08, as am. O. Reg. 405/08; 163/10.

[Note: The title of this Regulation was changed from "Remedial Measures Conduct Review Program for Drivers Suspended for Certain Offences Related to Impaired Driving" to "Conduct Review Programs" by O. Reg. 405/08, s. 1.]

PART I — REMEDIAL MEASURES CONDUCT REVIEW PROGRAM FOR DRIVERS SUSPENDED FOR CONDUCT RELATED TO IMPAIRED DRIVING

[Heading added O. Reg. 405/08, s. 2.]

1. Features of remedial measures conduct review program — **(1)** A remedial measures conduct review program for drivers suspended for conduct related to impaired driving consists of a preliminary assessment of the extent to which a person is affected by or suffers from substance abuse and, based on the results of the preliminary assessment, appropriate remedial education or treatment programs.

(2) The preliminary assessment may utilize assessment tools to determine the appropriate remedial education or treatment program or programs for the participant, including any tools, tests, scales or inventories from, or suitable for use in, the field of substance abuse assessment.

(3) A preliminary assessment and remedial programs must be conducted or provided by a person authorized or required by the Minister to do so.

O. Reg. 405/08, s. 3

2. Criteria to participate in program — The following persons may be required to participate in a remedial measures conduct review program under this Regulation:

    1. A person whose driver's licence has been suspended under,

        i. clause 41(1)(b.1) of the Act,

        ii. clause 41(1)(c) of the Act,

        iii. clause 41(1)(d) of the Act,

        iv. clause 41(1)(e) of the Act, or

        v. any other clause of subsection 41(1) of the Act, if the person's driver's licence was previously suspended under any of clauses 41(1)(b.1), (c), (d) or (e) of the Act.

2. A person whose driver's licence has been suspended under section 48 of the Act in respect of a second or subsequent suspension under that section.

3. A person who is required to participate in an ignition interlock conduct review program under Part IV of this Regulation.

O. Reg. 405/08, s. 4; 163/10, s. 1

3. Attendance, participation and conduct standards — (1) A person who, as part of a remedial measures conduct review program under this Regulation, conducts a preliminary assessment or conducts or provides a remedial education or treatment program shall notify each participant of the attendance, participation and conduct standards for the assessment or remedial program before beginning the assessment or remedial program, as the case may be.

(2) Notification under subsection (1) may be provided to each participant individually, or may be made on any written or electronic material that is provided to participants or that participants are required to read.

(2.1) Participants who receive written or electronic material under this section are required to read it.

(3) A participant will be required to leave the assessment or remedial program if his or her attendance, participation or conduct does not meet the standards for the assessment or remedial program, as the case may be.

O. Reg. 405/08, s. 5

4. Successful completion of program — A participant has successfully completed a remedial measures conduct review program under this Regulation if,

(a) the person who conducted the preliminary assessment reports to the Registrar that the participant successfully completed the assessment; and

(b) for each remedial education or treatment program the participant was required to take, the person who conducted or provided the program reports to the Registrar that the participant successfully completed such remedial program.

5. Failure to complete program — (1) A person who is required to leave a preliminary assessment or remedial program as described in section 3 or who otherwise fails to successfully complete a remedial measures conduct review program under this Regulation is required to retake the entire remedial measures conduct review program, beginning at the preliminary assessment, regardless of how much of the program he or she previously participated in or successfully completed.

(2) The driver's licence of a person described in paragraph 2 of section 2 who is required by the Registrar to participate in a remedial measures conduct review program shall be suspended under section 57 of the Act if the person fails to successfully complete the program within,

(a) 120 days from the date the person's driver's licence is suspended, in the case of a person whose driver's licence was suspended under section 48 of the Act for a second time; or

(b) **180 days from the date the person's driver's licence is suspended, in the case of a person whose driver's licence was suspended under section 48 of the Act for a third or subsequent time.**

(3) **The suspension under subsection (2) continues until the Registrar is satisfied that the person has successfully completed the program.**

O. Reg. 405/08, s. 6

6. Public list of providers — The Ministry shall make available to the public a list of the persons or classes of persons authorized or required by the Minister to conduct preliminary assessments and to conduct or provide remedial programs as part of a remedial measures conduct review program under this Regulation.

7. Equivalent program outside Ontario — Despite section 1, the Registrar may permit a person who resides in another province or territory of Canada or in a state of the United States of America and who is required to complete a remedial measures conduct review program under this Regulation to complete instead a program provided in his or her province, territory or state that the Registrar considers equivalent to a remedial measures conduct review program under this Regulation.

7.1 Exemption — Despite section 1 and clause 4(a), a person who is not required by the Registrar to complete a preliminary assessment is exempt from the requirement for a preliminary assessment.

O. Reg. 405/08, s. 7

8. Programs may vary across province — A remedial measures conduct review program under this Regulation, or any feature of such program, may differ in its content, duration and method of delivery in different parts of Ontario.

PART II — IGNITION INTERLOCK CONDUCT REVIEW PROGRAMS — GENERAL

[Heading added O. Reg. 405/08, s. 8. Amended O. Reg. 163/10, s. 2.]

[Heading repealed O. Reg. 163/10, s. 2.]

9. Definitions — In this Part,

"approval sticker" means a sticker in the form approved by the Minister for the purposes of this Part;

"authorized person" means a person authorized by the Minister to install, inspect and maintain ignition interlock devices for the purposes of this Part.

O. Reg. 405/08, s. 8

9.1 Application — This Part applies to all participants in an ignition interlock conduct review program under this Regulation.

O. Reg. 163/10, s. 3

10. Ignition interlock conduct review program — An ignition interlock conduct review program is hereby established.

O. Reg. 405/08, s. 8

11. Licence subject to condition — (1) The driver's licence of a person required to participate in an ignition interlock conduct review program under this Regulation is subject to the condition that he or she is prohibited from driving any motor vehicle that is not equipped with an ignition interlock device.

(2) The ignition interlock device referred to in subsection (1) shall be installed by an authorized person and shall bear an approval sticker.

O. Reg. 405/08, s. 8; 163/10, s. 4

12. Approved ignition interlock device — An ignition interlock device that meets the following requirements is an approved ignition interlock device for the purposes of section 41.2 of the Act:

1. The device was installed pursuant to a request or requirement under this Regulation.

2. The device meets the requirements of section 2 of Ontario Regulation 251/02 (*Ignition Interlock Devices*) made under the Act.

O. Reg. 405/08, s. 8; 163/10, s. 4

13. Programs may vary across province — An ignition interlock conduct review program under this Regulation, or any feature of such a program, may differ in its content, duration and method of delivery in different parts of Ontario.

O. Reg. 405/08, s. 8; 163/10, s. 4

14. Equivalent program outside Ontario — Despite anything in this Part, the Registrar may permit a person who resides in another province or territory of Canada or in a state of the United States of America and who is or could be required to complete an ignition interlock conduct review program under this Part to complete instead a program provided in his or her province, territory or state that the Registrar considers equivalent to an ignition interlock conduct review program under this Part.

O. Reg. 405/08, s. 8

15. Performance standards — (1) A person who, as part of an ignition interlock conduct review program under this Regulation, carries out the installation, inspection or maintenance of an ignition interlock device, shall notify each participant of the attendance and performance standards for the program before beginning the installation.

(2) Notification under subsection (1) may be provided to each participant individually, or may be provided on any written or electronic material that is provided to participants.

(3) Participants who receive written or electronic material under this section are required to read it.

O. Reg. 405/08, s. 8; 163/10, s. 5

16. Request for installation to be in writing — (1) A person whom the Registrar has required to participate in an ignition interlock conduct review program under Part III may request an authorized person to install the device in the motor vehicle and the request shall be made in writing.

(1.1) A person whom the Registrar has required to participate in an ignition interlock conduct review program under Part IV shall request an authorized person to install the device in the motor vehicle and the request shall be made in writing.

(2) The request shall include an acknowledgement by the participant that he or she,

    (a) has received notification of the attendance and performance standards of the program;

    (b) understands how to operate the ignition interlock device properly; and

    (c) understands that he or she is solely responsible for ensuring,

        (i) that the device is not tampered with by any person,

        (ii) that the device is not removed without authorization, and

        (iii) that the performance standards referred to in section 15 are met.

(3) An authorized person shall affix an approval sticker to an ignition interlock device if the request to install the device was made by a person required to participate in the program by the Registrar.

O. Reg. 405/08, s. 8; 163/10, ss. 6, 7

17. Inspection and maintenance of device — (1) A participant shall ensure that the motor vehicle in which an ignition interlock device has been installed is brought to the authorized person that installed the device for inspection and maintenance as and when required by the attendance and performance standards, or at least once every 60 days.

(2) Despite subsection (1), if the ignition interlock device installed in a motor vehicle is designed to be inspected and maintained by removing a component from it, the participant shall, at least once every 60 days, ensure that,

    (a) the component is removed, in accordance with the instructions of the authorized person who installed the device, and is delivered to that authorized person for inspection and maintenance; and

    (b) the replacement component provided to the participant by the authorized person is installed in the device in accordance with the authorized person's instructions.

O. Reg. 405/08, s. 8

18. Records — (1) Every authorized person shall maintain a record with respect to the installation, inspection and maintenance of an ignition interlock device carried out by the person.

(2) A record under subsection (1) shall include,

    (a) the name, address and driver's licence number of the person who requested the installation of the device;

(b) the make, model and vehicle identification number of the motor vehicle in which it was installed; and

(c) the results of any inspection of the device, including any information obtained from the device itself.

(3) The authorized person shall, upon request, submit the records maintained under this section to the Registrar.

O. Reg. 405/08, s. 8

19. Ignition interlock providers publicly listed — The Ministry shall make publicly available a list of the persons or classes of persons authorized by the Minister to provide an ignition interlock device under this Part.

O. Reg. 405/08, s. 8

PART III — IGNITION INTERLOCK LICENCE CONDITION IMPOSED FOR SUSPENSION UNDER SECTION 48 OF THE ACT

[Heading added O. Reg. 405/08, s. 8. Amended O. Reg. 163/10, s. 8.]

20. Definition — In this Part,

"authorized person" means a person authorized by the Minister to install, inspect and maintain ignition interlock devices for the purposes of this Part.

O. Reg. 405/08, s. 8; 163/10, s. 9

20.1 Required participation in program — A person whose driver's licence has been suspended under section 48 of the Act may be required, if the suspension is the person's third or subsequent suspension under that section, to participate in an ignition interlock conduct review program under this Part.

O. Reg. 163/10, s. 9

21. Length of participation in program — (1) A person who is required to participate in an ignition interlock conduct review program under this Part shall participate in the program for six months.

(2) The six-month period referred to in subsection (1) may be extended by six months from the date the Registrar is satisfied that,

(a) the ignition interlock device has been tampered with or has been removed without authorization;

(b) the participant has failed to comply with section 17; or

(c) the participant has failed to comply with the ignition interlock condition referred to in subsection 11(1).

(3) If more than one period of extension applies to a person, the person is required to participate in the program until the end of the period of extension imposed most recently by the Registrar.

(4) The period of required participation, including any extension, under this section runs concurrently with the period of time, if any, during which an ignition interlock condition is imposed on a person's driver's licence where the driver's licence has been reinstated pursuant to subsection 41.1(1) of the Act and the person has been convicted of an offence under section 253, 254 or 255 of the *Criminal Code* (Canada).

(5) A person to whom subsection (4) applies is not eligible to apply to remove the ignition interlock condition under subsection 41.2(2) or (6) of the Act until the person meets the requirements for successful completion of the ignition interlock conduct review program under section 22.

(6) The period of required participation, including any extension, continues until the requirements for successful completion of the program are met.

O. Reg. 405/08, s. 8; 163/10, s. 10

22. Successful completion of program — A participant in an ignition interlock conduct review program under this Part completes it successfully if the Registrar is satisfied that,

(a) the participant has successfully completed any examinations under clause 15(1)(e) of Ontario Regulation 340/94 (*Drivers' Licences*) made under the Act that he or she is required to complete pursuant to subsection 32(5) of the Act;

(b) the person has complied with the ignition interlock condition described in subsection 11(1); and

(c) the participant has successfully completed the period of required participation, including any extension.

O. Reg. 405/08, s. 8; 163/10, s. 11

PART IV — REINSTATEMENT UNDER SUBSECTION 41(4.1) OF THE ACT AND MANDATORY INSTALLATION OF AN IGNITION INTERLOCK DEVICE

[Heading added O. Reg. 163/10, s. 12.]

23. Ignition interlock conduct review program — The ignition interlock conduct review program described in this Part is established for the purposes of subsection 259(1.1) of the *Criminal Code* (Canada).

O. Reg. 163/10, s. 12

24. Exemption from certain provisions of Act — A person who is required to participate in an ignition interlock conduct review program under this Part is exempt from subsections 41.2(1), (5) and (9) of the Act.

O. Reg. 163/10, s. 12

25. Required participation in program — (1) A person may be required to participate in an ignition interlock conduct review program under this Part if,

    (a) on or after August 3, 2010, the person's driver's licence is suspended for a period of one year pursuant to clause 41(1)(f) of the Act for an offence that is described in clause 41(1)(b.1) or (c) of the Act; and

    (b) the Registrar is satisfied that,

        (i) the circumstances of the offence did not involve impairment of the person caused by a drug other than alcohol, or caused by a combination of substances that included drugs other than alcohol,

        (ii) an order was made under section 259 of the *Criminal Code* (Canada) concerning the person and the order does not exclude the person from participating in an ignition interlock conduct review program under this Part,

        (iii) the person has completed and signed the written request referred to in subsection 16(1.1),

        (iv) the person has completed the preliminary assessment referred to in subsection 1(1),

        (v) the person's driver's licence has not been suspended under section 42 of the Act within the five years preceding the suspension referred to in clause (a),

        (vi) the person's driver's licence was not, on the date of the offence, subject to a condition requiring the use of an ignition interlock device, and

        (vii) the person's driver's licence has not previously been reinstated under subsection 41.1(2) of the Act.

(2) Despite clause (1)(a), a person is not eligible to participate in an ignition interlock conduct review program under this Part if the suspension referred to in clause (1)(a) is for an offence under section 255 of the *Criminal Code* (Canada) as described in clause 41(1)(b.1) of the Act and the offence involves the causation of bodily harm or death.

(3) A person is not eligible to participate in an ignition interlock conduct review program under this Part until after the later of,

    (a) the expiry of the minimum absolute prohibition period described in subsection 259(1.2) of the *Criminal Code* (Canada); and

    (b) a day that is at least six months after the person is made subject to an order under section 259 of the *Criminal Code* (Canada).

(4) Where a person meets the following requirements, the date described in clause (3)(b) shall instead be a day that is at least three months after the person is made subject to an order under section 259 of the *Criminal Code* (Canada):

    1. The person enters a plea of guilty to the offence.

    2. The person is then made subject to an order under section 259 of the *Criminal Code* (Canada) and the order is made within 90 days of the date of the offence.

3. Within the minimum absolute prohibition period described in subsection 259(1.2) of the *Criminal Code* (Canada), the person submits an application under subsection 41(4.1) of the Act that is satisfactory to the Registrar.

(5) Where the date of the offence is earlier than August 3, 2010 and a person meets the following requirements, the date described in clause (3)(b) shall instead be a day that is at least three months after the person is made subject to an order under section 259 of the *Criminal Code* (Canada):

1. The person enters a plea of guilty to the offence.

2. The person is then made subject to an order under section 259 of the *Criminal Code* (Canada) and the order is made on or before November 1, 2010.

3. Within the minimum absolute prohibition period described in subsection 259(1.2) of the *Criminal Code* (Canada), the person submits an application under subsection 41(4.1) of the Act that is satisfactory to the Registrar.

O. Reg. 163/10, s. 12

26. Installation required after reinstatement — A person required to participate in an ignition interlock conduct review program under this Part shall, within 30 days of the reinstatement of his or her driver's licence, have an ignition interlock device installed in a motor vehicle by an authorized person.

O. Reg. 163/10, s. 12

27. Installation period — (1) A person required to participate in an ignition interlock conduct review program under this Part shall have an ignition interlock device installed in a motor vehicle,

(a) for a minimum of nine months, if the person,

(i) enters a plea of guilty to the offence,

(ii) is then made· subject to an order under section 259 of the *Criminal Code* (Canada) and the order is made within 90 days of the date of the offence, and

(iii) within the minimum absolute prohibition period described in subsection 259(1.2) of the *Criminal Code* (Canada), submits an application under subsection 41(4.1) of the Act that is satisfactory to the Registrar; or

(b) for a minimum of 12 months, in any other case.

(2) Despite subsection (1), where the date of the offence is earlier than August 3, 2010, the person shall have an ignition interlock device installed in a motor vehicle,

(a) for a minimum of nine months, if the person,

(i) enters a plea of guilty to the offence,

(ii) is then made subject to an order under section 259 of the *Criminal Code* (Canada) and the order is made on or before November 1, 2010, and

(iii) within the minimum absolute prohibition period described in subsection 259(1.2) of the *Criminal Code* (Canada), submits an application under subsection 41(4.1) of the Act that is satisfactory to the Registrar; or

(b) for a minimum of 12 months, in any other case.

(3) The installation period continues until the requirements for successful completion of the program are met.

(4) The Registrar may extend the installation period by three months after any date on which the Registrar is satisfied that,

(a) the ignition interlock device has analyzed a sample of breath that shows that the driver had a level of blood alcohol concentration greater than the level allowed by the performance standards referred to in section 15; or

(b) the ignition interlock device prompted the driver to provide a breath sample and no sample was provided.

O. Reg. 163/10, s. 12

28. Licence suspension — **(1)** A participant's driver's licence may be suspended under section 57 of the Act if the Registrar is satisfied that,

(a) the participant failed to install an ignition interlock device within 30 days of the date of reinstatement of his or her driver's licence under subsection 41(4.1) of the Act;

(b) the ignition interlock device has been tampered with or has been removed without authorization;

(c) the participant has failed to comply with the driver's licence condition referred to in subsection 11(1);

(d) the participant has failed to comply with section 17;

(e) the participant's driver's licence is suspended under section 41 or 42 of the Act;

(f) the participant's driver's licence is suspended under section 48 or 48.3 of the Act; or

(g) the participant is convicted of an offence under the Act, or under the regulations made under the Act, for having a level of blood alcohol concentration in excess of a limit prescribed by the Act or the regulations made under the Act.

(2) The suspension of a participant's driver's licence under subsection (1) shall continue for a period of time that is the same as the period of time for which the driver's licence suspension under section 41 of the Act would have continued had the person's driver's licence not been reinstated under subsection 41(4.1) of the Act.

(3) The suspension of a participant's driver's licence under subsection (1) shall continue until such time as the person completes the remedial measures program under Part I.

(4) A person whose driver's licence is suspended under subsection (1) is not eligible to re-apply for admission into, or to continue to participate in, an ignition interlock program under this Part, other than for the purposes of complying with subsection (5).

(5) Upon reinstatement of a person's driver's licence at the end of a suspension under subsection (1),

(a) the licence is subject to the condition referred to in subsection 11(1) for a period of at least one year; and

(b) the Registrar shall not remove that condition until at least 12 months have passed after any date on which the Registrar is satisfied that,

(i) the person failed to comply with the ignition interlock condition referred to in subsection 11(1),

(ii) the ignition interlock device had been tampered with or had been removed without authorization, or

(iii) the person failed to comply with section 17.

O. Reg. 163/10, s. 12

29. Successful completion of program — A participant in an ignition interlock conduct review program under this Part completes it successfully if the Registrar is satisfied that,

(a) the authorized person who conducted the installation, inspection and maintenance of the ignition interlock device has reported that the participant successfully completed the program;

(b) the participant has successfully completed the installation period applicable to him or her, including any extension;

(c) the participant has complied with the ignition interlock condition described in subsection 11(1);

(d) on the day of the last appointment for the inspection and maintenance required under section 17, the participant's driver's licence is not suspended;

(e) the participant has successfully completed any examinations under clause 15(1)(e) of Ontario Regulation 340/94 (*Drivers' Licences*) made under the Act that he or she is required to complete pursuant to subsection 32(5) of the Act; and

(f) the participant has successfully completed any remedial measures conduct review program in which he or she was required to participate under Part I.

O. Reg. 163/10, s. 12

ONT. REG. 577 — COVERING OF LOADS

made under the *Highway Traffic Act*

R.R.O. 1990, Reg. 577, as am. O. Reg. 402/09 (Fr.).

1. In this Regulation,

"clear aggregate" means gravel, crushed stone or slag in the form of particles that are not less than 3/8 inch in diameter or more than 1 1/2 inches in diameter;

"registered gross weight" means the weight for which a permit has been issued under the Act, the fee for which permit is based upon the weight of the vehicle or combination of vehicles and load;

"waste" means ordinary waste associated with municipal collection systems, including ashes, garbage, refuse and domestic waste.

2. (1) Subject to subsection (2), where a commercial motor vehicle or a combination of a commercial motor vehicle and trailer or trailers is being operated on a highway and is carrying a load that is,

    (a) sand, gravel, crushed stone, slag, salt or any mixture thereof, where such substances are in the form of particles of up to 1 1/2 inches in diameter;

    (b) waste; or

    (c) shredded scrap metal,

the portion of the load that is not enclosed by the vehicle or load container shall be covered with a covering that is made of tarpaulin, canvas, netting or other material capable of confining the load within the vehicle container or load container.

(2) Subsection (1) does not apply where the commercial motor vehicle or the combination of a commercial motor vehicle and trailer or trailers is being operated,

    (a) in the course of applying sand, salt, a mixture of sand and salt or any similar substance to the highway for the purpose of winter highway maintenance;

    (b) in the course of collecting waste;

    (c) in the course of carrying waste where the vehicle does not have a gross weight or registered gross weight in excess of 10,000 pounds;

    (d) in the course of carrying a load that is not waste and the vehicle does not have a gross weight or registered gross weight in excess of 18,000 pounds;

    (e) in the course of carrying sand, gravel, crushed stone or slag, of which not less than 90 per cent is clear aggregate, where the highest point of the load does not extend above the top of the vehicle container or load container, and the perimeters of the load are not less than twelve inches beneath the top of the vehicle container or load container;

(f) in the course of carrying sand, gravel, crushed stone, slag, salt or any mixture thereof in December, January, February or March where the highest point of the load does not extend above the top of the vehicle container or load container, and the perimeters of the load are not less than twelve inches beneath the top of the vehicle container or load container;

(g) in the course of carrying agricultural products, where such vehicle is owned by a farmer;

(h) on a highway with,

    (i) an untreated gravel or crushed stone surface,

    (ii) an earth surface, or

    (iii) a surface treated solely for dust abatement purposes;

(i) while proceeding across a highway in order to proceed on a highway as described in clause (h), or in proceeding across a highway in order to enter onto private property abutting the highway; or

(j) within the limits of a highway construction contract.

ONT. REG. 512/97 — CRITICAL DEFECTS OF COMMERCIAL MOTOR VEHICLES

made under the *Highway Traffic Act*

O. Reg. 512/97, as am. O. Reg. 130/10; 410/10; 166/12.

[Note: The title of this Regulation was changed from "Suspension and Impoundment of Commercial Motor Vehicles For Critical Defects under Section 82.1 of The Act" to "Critical Defects of Commercial Motor Vehicles" by O. Reg. 130/10, s. 1.]

PART 1 — GENERAL

Certification of Officers

1. A police officer or officer appointed for carrying out the provisions of the Act must hold a Critical Inspection Certificate issued by the Registrar in order to carry out inspections under section 82.1 of the Act.

O. Reg. 130/10, s. 2

Prescribed Period

2. For the purpose of subsection 82.1(8) of the Act, the prescribed period is two years.

O. Reg. 410/10, s. 1

Service of An Order to Impound and Suspend

3. [Repealed O. Reg. 410/10, s. 2.]

Security

4. (1) For the purpose of subsection 82.1(23) of the Act, the security ordered to be deposited with the court may be in the form of a bond, letter of credit, certified cheque, bank draft or money order.

(2) If the security is in the form of a bond, it shall be given by an insurer licensed under the *Insurance Act* to write surety and fidelity insurance and shall remain in force until the security is released to the owner under subsection (9) or transferred to the Minister of Finance under subsection (11).

(3) If the security is in the form of a letter of credit, it shall be irrevocable, shall be given by a loan or trust corporation registered in Ontario or by a bank named in Schedule I or II of the *Bank Act* (Canada) and shall remain in force until the secur-

ity is released to the owner under subsection (9) or transferred to the Minister of Finance under subsection (11).

(4) All security deposited with the court shall be made payable to the Accountant of the Superior Court of Justice.

(5) The Accountant of the Superior Court of Justice shall not release the security to the owner except in accordance with a court order or on consent and shall not transfer the security to the Crown except in accordance with a certificate of forfeiture.

(6) An owner who seeks the release of the security shall obtain an order of the court that ordered that the security be deposited or the consent of the Registrar to the release of the security.

(7) An owner who seeks the release of the security in accordance with a court order shall file with the Accountant of the Superior Court of Justice,

   (a) a requisition for the release of the security;

   (b) a certified copy of the court order; and

   (c) an affidavit stating that the time prescribed by the Rule of Civil Procedure for an appeal from the court order directing the release of the security has expired and no appeal is pending.

(8) An owner who seeks the release of the security on consent shall file with the Accountant of the Superior Court of Justice,

   (a) a requisition for the release of the security; and

   (b) the consent of the owner and the Registrar, or their solicitors.

(9) Upon receipt of the materials required by subsection (7) or (8), the Accountant of the Superior Court of Justice shall release the security to the owner with accrued interest, if any.

(10) Upon the forfeiture of the security to the Crown under subsection 50.3(4) or (7) of the Act, the Registrar may file with the Accountant of the Superior Court of Justice a certificate of forfeiture in a form approved by the Minister, without notice to the owner.

(11) Upon receipt of the certificate of forfeiture, the Accountant of the Superior Court of Justice shall transfer the security with accrued interest, if any, to the Minister of Finance.

O. Reg. 130/10, s. 3

PART II — CRITICAL DEFECTS

Interpretation

5. (1) In this Part,

"broken", when used to refer to a vehicle component, means that the component or any of its sub-components is split into more than one part;

"cracked", when used to refer to a vehicle component, means that the component is not broken but has a split that penetrates completely through the component or any of its sub-components;

"steering axle" means any axle of a commercial motor vehicle that is controlled by the driver to provide direction to the motor vehicle.

(2) For the purposes of determining if a commercial motor vehicle or trailer has a critical defect under section 82.1 or 84 of the Act,

(a) a liftable axle, being an axle that is designed to be adjusted vertically and to lift its tires from contact with the surface of the highway when in a raised position, shall be considered part of a vehicle;

(b) a conversion unit shall be considered part of the vehicle that it converts; and

(c) a trailer converter dolly, if carrying a trailer, shall be considered part of that trailer.

O. Reg. 130/10, s. 4

Brakes

6. In section 7 and 8, "rotor" includes a disc.

Air Brakes

7. (1) In this section, the measurement of travel of a push rod out of a service brake chamber shall be taken with the vehicle engine turned off, an initial air system pressure between 90 and 100 psi (620 and 690 kPa), the park brakes released and the service brake actuator fully applied.

(2) A commercial motor vehicle or trailer, if the trailer is required by subsection 64(5) of the Act to have brakes, equipped with an air brake system other than an air-over-hydraulic brake system has a critical defect for the purposes of sections 82.1 and 84 of the Act if one or more of the following defects is present on more than 50 per cent of the wheel brakes of the vehicle:

1. A drum or rotor is cracked, broken or missing.

2. A chamber housing, chamber support, chamber push rod, slack adjuster, cam shaft, or cam shaft support bracket is broken or missing.

3. A shoe, shoe lining, shoe block, pad, pad lining or pad block is missing.

4. The push rod travel out of the service brake chamber is 1/4 inch (6.3 mm) or more beyond the measurement listed in Column 2 of Schedule 1 for the type of chamber listed in Column 1 of Schedule 1 if the brake is cam or disc type.

5. When the brake actuator is applied,

i. there is no movement of the chamber push rod, slack adjuster or cam shaft,

ii. neither one of the two shoes moves, or

iii. neither one of the two shoe linings contacts the drum.

O. Reg. 130/10, s. 5; 166/12, s. 1

Hydraulic Brakes

8. (1) A commercial motor vehicle or trailer, if the trailer is required by subsection 64(5) of the Act to have brakes, equipped with hydraulic or air-over-hydraulic brakes has a critical defect for the purposes of sections 82.1 and 84 of the Act if two or more of the following defects are present on the vehicle:

1. Brake fluid can be seen coming out of any location in the system upon full brake application with the vehicle engine turned on or the depth of hydraulic brake fluid in any reservoir of the master cylinder is less than 1/4 inch (6.3 mm) at its deepest point.

2. A brake drum or rotor is cracked, broken or missing.

3. The actuator, linkages or cables of the parking brake system are broken or missing or any cables are seized such that there is no movement of the cables to both rear wheel brakes when the brake actuator is applied.

(2) If a commercial motor vehicle or trailer has two or more defects of the type described in paragraph 2 of subsection (1), the two or more defects under that paragraph constitute a critical defect for the purposes of sections 82.1 and 84 of the Act.

O. Reg. 130/10, s. 6

Steering

9. A commercial motor vehicle has a critical defect for the purposes of sections 82.1 and 84 of the Act if either of the following defects is present:

1. With the wheels of the steering axle on the ground in the straight ahead position and the engine turned on, the circumference of the steering wheel moves in excess of the measurements contained in Column 2 for the application diameter shown in Column 1 of Schedule 2, with no accompanying movement of the left front wheel.

2. With the vehicle having been stopped with the wheels of the steering axle on the ground in the straight ahead position, with hand force alone applied, a steering linkage ball and socket joint relating to the steering axle moves other than rotationally by more than ¼ inch (6.3 mm).

O. Reg. 130/10, s. 7

Wheels and Rims

Definitions

10. (1) In this section,

"fastener" means a component used to secure a vehicle's disc wheels or spoke wheel rims to the vehicle and may include a wheel stud, rim clamp stud, inner cap nut,

outer cap nut, two-piece flange nut, ball seat nut, flat nut or any combination of them;

"loose", when applied to a fastener, means that there is visually observable space between the fastener and its contact point on the disc wheel or spoke wheel rim or that the fastener can be moved using hand force only;

"wheel assembly" means disc wheels, spoke wheels and fastener on one side of one axle.

(2) A commercial motor vehicle or trailer has a critical defect for the purposes of sections 82.1 and 84 of the Act if one or more of the following defects is present on two or more of its wheel assemblies;

    1. A disc wheel or component of it is broken.

    2. 50 per cent or more of the stud holes in a stud piloted disc wheel are visibly elongated or 50 per cent or more of the stud holes in a hub piloted disc wheel are visible when the nuts are seated against the disc wheel.

    3. A spoke wheel, including a cast wheel, or a component of it, is broken.

    4. On a wheel with 10 or more fastener positions, any three fasteners or any two adjacent fasteners are cracked, broken, missing or loose.

    5. On a wheel with 9 or fewer fastener positions, any two fasteners are cracked, broken, missing or loose.

O. Reg. 130/10, s. 8

Tires

11. (1) In this section,

"bias ply tire" includes belted bias ply tire;

"cord" means the strands of material used to strengthen a tire;

"radial ply tire" includes belted radial ply tire;

"sidewall" means the portion of a tire between the tread and the bead;

"tread" means the portion of a tire designed to come into contact with the road.

(2) A commercial motor vehicle or trailer has a critical defect for the purposes of sections 82.1 and 84 of the Act if one or more of the following defects is present on four or more of its tires:

    1. A steering axle tire,

        i. has no tread remaining across 75 per cent or more of the width of the tire at any location on the tire, or

        ii. has exposed cord.

    2. In a bias ply tire, other than a steering axle tire,

        i. two or more layers of cord are exposed, or

        ii. five square inches (32.3 square centimetres) or more of the outermost layer of cords are exposed.

3. In a radial ply tire, other than a steering axle tire,

　　i. two or more layers of cord are exposed in the tread area, or

　　ii. six square inches (38.7 square centimetres) of cord is exposed in the sidewall.

4. A tire,

　　i. is contacting a vehicle component, other than a tire, with the vehicle stopped in the straight ahead position,

　　ii. is void of air pressure or has an air leak that is audible or tangible, or

　　iii. is marked "not for highway use" or "farm use only" or bears the letters "SL", "NHS", "K", "AT", "DH", "VA" OR "TG" as part of the tire designation or on any other location on the tire.

O. Reg. 130/10, s. 9

Suspension and Frame

12. (1) In this section,

"helper leaf spring" means a leaf spring designed for auxiliary load resistance;

"leaf spring assembly" means an assembly of four or more leaf springs, not including helper leaf springs;

"leaf spring" means a long narrow plate of spring steel designed for load resistance.

(2) A commercial motor vehicle or trailer has a critical defect for the purposes of sections 82.1 and 84 of the Act if on one or more of its leaf spring assemblies 50 per cent or more of the leaf springs, including the helper leaf springs if in use, are broken.

(3) A commercial motor vehicle or trailer has a critical defect for the purposes of sections 82.1 and 84 of the Act if any of its frame members or other structural support members is broken, bent or perforated by corrosion resulting in the shifting of the vehicle's body onto any component of the vehicle's steering, clutch, fifth wheel, engine, transmission or suspension systems.

O. Reg. 130/10, s. 10

13. This Regulation comes into force on February 2, 1998.

SCHEDULE 1

COLUMN 1		COLUMN 2	
Service Brake Chambers Clamp Type Brake Chamber Data		Push Rod Travel	
Type	Outside Diameter		
6	4 1/2" (114.3mm)	1 1/4"	(31.75mm)
9	5 1/4" (133.35mm)	1 3/8"	(34.93mm)

COLUMN 1			COLUMN 2	
12	5 11/16"	(144.46mm)	1 3/8"	(34.93mm)
12 Long Stroke	5 11/16"	(144.46mm)	1 3/4"	(44.45mm)
16	6 3/8"	(161.93mm)	1 3/4"	(44.45mm)
16 Long Stroke	6 3/8"	(161.93mm)	2"	(50.8mm)
20	6 25/32"	(172.24mm)	1 3/4"	(44.45mm)
20 Long Stroke	6 25/32"	(172.24mm)	2"	(50.8mm)
24	7 7/32"	(183.36mm)	1 3/4"	(44.45mm)
24 Long Stroke	7 7/32"	(183.36mm)	2"	(50.8mm)
24 Long Stroke with Square Inlet Port or with Square Raised Embossment on Lid	7 7/32"	(183.36mm)	2 1/2"	(63.5mm)
30	8 3/32"	(205.58mm)	2"	(50.8mm)
30 Long Stroke with Square Inlet Port or with Square Raised Embossment on Lid	8 3/32"	(205.58mm)	2 1/2"	(63.5mm)
36	9"	(228.6mm)	2 1/4"	(57.15mm)
Bolt Type Chamber Data				
Type	Outside Diameter			
A	6 15/16"	(176.21mm)	1 3/8"	(34.93mm)
B	9 3/16"	(233.36mm)	1 3/4"	(44.45mm)
C	8 1/16"	(204.79mm)	1 3/4"	(44.45mm)
D	5 1/4"	(133.35mm)	1 1/4"	(31.75mm)
E	6 3/16"	(157.16mm)	1 3/8"	(34.93mm)
F	11"	(279.4mm)	2 1/4"	(57.15mm)
G	9 7/8"	(250.83mm)	2"	(50.8mm)
Rotochamber Type Chamber Data				
Type	Outside Diameter			
9	4 9/32"	(108.74mm)	1 1/2"	(38.1mm)
12	4 13/16"	(122.23mm)	1 1/2"	(38.1mm)
16	5 13/32"	(137.32mm)	2"	(50.8mm)
20	5 15/16"	(150.81mm)	2"	(50.8mm)
24	6 13/32"	(162.72mm)	2"	(50.8mm)
30	7 1/16"	(179.39mm)	2 1/4"	(57.15mm)

COLUMN 1			COLUMN 2	
36	7 5/8"	(193.68mm)	2 3/4"	(69.85mm)
50	8 7/8"	(225.43mm)	3"	(76.2mm)
Tie Rod Piston Type Chamber Data				
Type	**Outside Diameter**			
30 Long Stroke with Square Inlet Port	6 1/2"	(165.1mm)	2 1/2"	(63.5mm)
DD-3 Type Chamber Data				
Type	**Outside Diameter**			
30	8 1/8"	(206.37mm)	2 1/4"	(57.15mm)

SCHEDULE 2

Column 1	Column 2
Steering Wheel Diameter	**Free movement**
Less than 16 inches (40.6cm)	8 inches (20.3cm)
16 inches (40.6cm) and larger but less than 18 inches (45.7cm)	9 inches (22.8cm)
18 inches (45.7cm) and larger but less than 19 inches (48.2cm)	10 inches (25.4cm)
19 inches (48.2cm) and larger but less than 20 inches (50.8cm)	11 inches (29.7cm)
20 inches (50.8cm) and larger but less than 21 inches (53.3cm)	12 inches (30.4cm)
21 inches (53.3cm) and larger but less than 22 inches (55.8cm)	13 inches (33cm)
22 inches and larger (55.8cm)	14 inches (35.5cm)

ONT. REG. 393/02 — DEFINITIONS AND REQUIREMENTS UNDER SECTION 142.1 OF THE ACT (YIELDING RIGHT OF WAY TO BUSES)

made under the *Highway Traffic Act*

O. Reg. 393/02, as am. O. Reg. 87/15.

1. Definitions — (1) For the purposes of section 142.1 of the Act,

"bus" means a bus that,

(a) is used for the transportation of passengers or passengers and express freight for compensation,

(b) is at least 25 feet long and 8 feet wide, and

(c) has a sign affixed as close as possible to its rear left turn signal light that has the dimensions and bears the markings as illustrated in the following Figure:

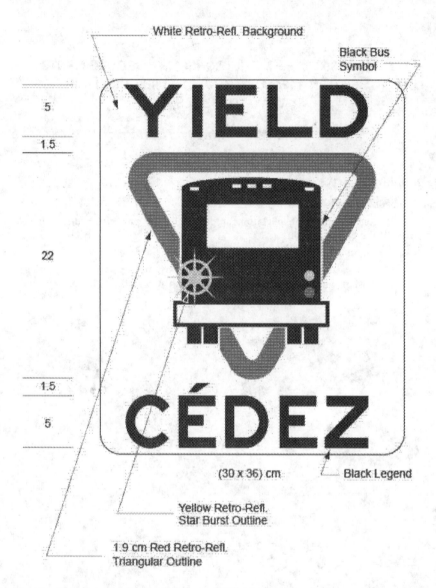

White Retro-Refl. Background

Black Bus Symbol

5

1.5

22

1.5

5

(30 x 36) cm

Black Legend

Yellow Retro-Refl. Star Burst Outline

1.9 cm Red Retro-Refl. Triangular Outline

"bus bay" means that portion of the highway beside a bus stop sign that is used by buses for the boarding and alighting of passengers, the use of which portion of the highway requires buses to exit from and subsequently re-enter an adjacent lane of traffic.

(2) The dimensions of the sign referred to in clause (c) of the definition of "bus" in subsection (1) may be greater than the dimensions prescribed and illustrated in the Figure to that definition so long as each dimension is increased and, when increased, has the same relation to the other dimensions of the sign as the dimensions prescribed and illustrated in that Figure have to each other.

O. Reg. 87/15, s. 1

2. Signalling intention to re-enter traffic — The driver of a bus shall indicate his or her intention to re-enter the lane of traffic adjacent to a bus bay,

(a) by the use of a mechanical or electrical signal device as described in subsection 142(6) of the Act; or

(b) by means of the hand and arm in accordance with subsection 142(4) of the Act.

3. Commencement — This Regulation comes into force on the day subsection 138(12) of the *Statute Law Amendment Act (Government Management and Services), 1994* is proclaimed in force.

ONT. REG. 419/15 — DEFINITIONS OF COMMERCIAL MOTOR VEHICLE AND TOW TRUCK

made under the *Highway Traffic Act*

O. Reg. 419/15 [ss. 1–5 to come into force January 1, 2017.]

Unproclaimed Text — 1–5

COMMERCIAL MOTOR VEHICLE

1. Definition of commercial motor vehicle, generally — For the purpose of every provision of the Act and the regulations, "commercial motor vehicle" includes a motor vehicle commonly known as a tow truck even if it does not have a truck or delivery body attached to it.

2. Definition of commercial motor vehicle for specified provisions — (1) For the purposes of the following provisions of the Act, "commercial motor vehicle" is defined in section 3 of this Regulation:

    1. Section 16.

    2. Subsections 20(1) and (2).

    3. Subsection 32(17).

    4. Clause 41.2(13)(a).

    5. Subsection 57(20).

    6. Subsection 62(33).

    7. Subsection 64(9).

    8. Subsection 66(6).

    9. Subsection 70(4.1).

    10. Subsection 80(2).

    11. Subsections 82(3) and (10).

    12. Section 82.1.

    13. Subsection 84(2).

    14. Subsection 109(15.1).

    15. Subsection 111(5).

    16. Subsections 124(5) and (6).

    17. Section 190.

    18. Section 191.0.1.

    19. Subsection 192(5).

20. Section 227.

(2) Despite subsection (1) and clause (b) of the definition of "commercial motor vehicle" in subsection 3(1), "commercial motor vehicle" in section 190 of the Act and in Ontario Regulation 555/06 (*Hours of Service*) made under the Act does not include a tow truck as defined in section 4 of this Regulation.

3. (1) In the provisions of the Act listed in subsection 2(1),

"commercial motor vehicle" means,

(a) a commercial motor vehicle, as defined in subsection 1(1) of the Act, other than a vehicle excluded by subsection (2) or (3),

(b) a tow truck as defined in section 4, other than a vehicle excluded by subsection (3), and

(c) a commercial motor vehicle, as defined in subsection 1(1) of the Act, with a flatbed that can tilt to load, other than a vehicle excluded by subsection (3) or (4).

(2) The following vehicles are excluded from clause (a) of the definition of "commercial motor vehicle" in subsection (1):

1. A commercial motor vehicle, as defined in subsection 1(1) of the Act, other than a bus, having a gross weight or registered gross weight of not more than 4,500 kilograms.

2. A bus that is used for personal purposes without compensation.

3. An ambulance, a fire apparatus, a hearse, a casket wagon or a motor home.

(3) The following vehicles are excluded from clauses (a), (b) and (c) of the definition of "commercial motor vehicle" in subsection (1):

1. A commercial motor vehicle, as defined in subsection 1(1) of the Act, leased for no longer than 30 days by an individual for the transportation of goods kept for that individual's personal use or the gratuitous carriage of passengers.

2. A commercial motor vehicle, as defined in subsection 1(1) of the Act, operated under and in accordance with a Dealer permit and number plate, a Service permit and number plate or a Manufacturer permit and number plate issued under Regulation 628 (*Vehicle Permits*) made under the Act that is not transporting passengers or goods.

(4) The following vehicles are excluded from clause (c) of the definition of "commercial motor vehicle" in subsection (1):

1. A vehicle described in clause (b) of the definition of "tow truck" in subsection 4(1).

(5) Nothing in this section excludes a commercial motor vehicle, as defined in this section, from the definition of "commercial motor vehicle" in subsection 1(1) of the Act.

4. Tow truck defined for s. 3 definition of commercial motor vehicle — (1) For the purpose of clause (b) of the definition of "commercial motor vehicle" in subsection 3(1),

"tow truck" means,

(a) a motor vehicle commonly known as a tow truck,

(b) a commercial motor vehicle, as defined in subsection 1(1) of the Act, with a flatbed that can tilt to load and that is used exclusively to tow or transport other motor vehicles, and

(c) a motor vehicle, other than a motor vehicle excluded by subsection (2), that is designed, modified, configured or equipped so that it is capable of towing other motor vehicles.

(2) The following motor vehicles are excluded from clause (c) of the definition of "tow truck" in subsection (1):

1. An off-road vehicle, as defined in section 1 of the *Off-Road Vehicles Act*.

2. A motor vehicle that is used for personal purposes only and that is used infrequently to tow, for no compensation, another motor vehicle that is also used for personal purposes only.

3. A motor home that is used for personal purposes only and that is towing another motor vehicle that is for the use of the driver of the motor home for personal purposes only.

4. A commercial motor vehicle, as defined in subsection 1(1) of the Act, towing one or more motor vehicles using the saddlemount configuration.

(3) In clause (c) of the definition of "tow truck" in subsection (1),

"towing" means drawing another motor vehicle by means of a boom, hook, hoist, pulley, stinger, sling, belt, fork or other similar device that elevates part of the drawn motor vehicle, with or without the use of a dolly or other similar device.

(4) A reference in this section to a motor vehicle being towed or transported includes a motor vehicle being towed or transported that is damaged, incomplete or inoperable.

Tow Truck

5. Definition of tow truck in s. 171 of the Act — For the purpose of section 171 of the Act, "tow truck" has the same meaning as in section 4 of this Regulation.

Commencement

6. Commencement — (1) Subject to subsections (2) and (3), this Regulation comes into force on the day it is filed.

(2) Sections 1 to 4 come into force on the later of the day subsection 1(3) of Schedule 2 to the *Fighting Fraud and Reducing Automobile Insurance Rates Act, 2014* comes into force and the day this Regulation is filed.

(3) Section 5 comes into force on the later of the day section 39 of Schedule 2 to the *Fighting Fraud and Reducing Automobile Insurance Rates Act, 2014* comes into force and the day this Regulation is filed.

ONT. REG. 339/94 — DEMERIT POINT SYSTEM

made under the *Highway Traffic Act*

O. Reg. 339/94, as am. O. Reg. 164/96; 331/97; 538/97; 637/99; 124/01; 107/03; 197/05; 596/05; 615/05; 64/06; 521/06; 428/09; 204/10; 226/15; 403/15; 53/16.

INTERPRETATION

1. (1) In this Regulation,

"accumulated demerit points" means the total demerit points in a person's record acquired as a result of offences committed within any period of two years, less any points deducted for that period under this Regulation;

"probationary driver" [Repealed O. Reg. 204/10, s. 1(1).]

(2) A reference in this Regulation to a class of driver's licence is a reference to the class of licence as prescribed in Ontario Regulation 340/94.

(3) A reference in this Regulation to "fully licensed driver", "level 1 exit test", "level 2 exit test", "novice driver" and "valid driver's licence" is a reference to those expressions as defined in Ontario Regulation 340/94.

(4) A reference in this Regulation to the surrender of a licence does not include the surrender of a licence card that has been marked by the Ministry as valid only to show the driver's photograph.

(5) The short descriptions in Column 3 of the Table to this Regulation indicate, for convenience of reference only, the general nature of the offences under the provisions in Column 1 of the Table and shall not be construed to limit the offences for which demerit points are imposed.

O. Reg. 204/10, s. 1

GENERAL

2. If a person is convicted of an offence under a provision of an Act, regulation or municipal by-law set out in Column 1 of the Table to this Regulation and the penalty imposed by the court for the conviction does not include a period of licence suspension, the Registrar shall record in respect of the person, as of the date of commission of the offence, the number of demerit points set out opposite thereto in Column 2.

3. (1) If a person is convicted of an offence or two or more offences arising out of the same circumstances and the penalty imposed by the court includes a period of licence suspension, no demerit points shall be recorded.

(2) If a person is convicted of two or more offences arising out of the same circumstances and the penalty imposed by the court does not include a period of licence suspension, demerit points shall only be recorded for the conviction carrying the greatest number of points.

O. Reg. 204/10, s. 2

4. (1) If a resident of Ontario is convicted or forfeits bail in another province or territory of Canada or in one of the states of the United States of America for an offence that, in the opinion of the Registrar, is in substance and effect equivalent to an offence for which demerit points would be recorded upon conviction in Ontario, the Registrar may record the demerit points for the conviction as if the conviction had been entered or the bail forfeited in Ontario for the equivalent offence.

(2) For the purposes of subsection (1), "conviction" includes a plea of guilty or a finding of guilt.

(3) Any accumulated demerit points of a new Ontario resident who becomes a fully licensed driver or a novice driver here, including a person classed as a novice driver under subsection 28(1) of Ontario Regulation 340/94 shall be reduced, from the day on which he or she becomes a fully licensed driver or a novice driver,

    (a) to seven, if the driver becomes a fully licensed driver and his or her accumulated demerit points total eight or more;

    (b) to four, if the driver becomes a novice driver and his or her accumulated demerit points total five or more.

(4) After a reduction under subsection (3), the accumulated demerit points that remain shall be those recorded for the most recently committed offences.

O. Reg. 204/10, s. 3

5. (1) If a person convicted of an offence set out in Column 1 of the Table appeals the conviction and notice of the appeal is served on the Registrar, the conviction and the demerit points related to it shall not be entered on the person's record unless the conviction is sustained on appeal.

(2) If a conviction referred to in subsection (1) and related demerit points have been recorded prior to service of notice of an appeal on the Registrar, the conviction and demerit points shall be removed from the record, and any suspension imposed as a result of the conviction shall be stayed, as of the date notice is served on the Registrar, unless the conviction is sustained on appeal.

6. (1) The notice of suspension sent to a person in respect of a suspension under this Regulation shall state the effective date of the suspension.

(2) [Revoked O. Reg. 124/01, s. 1.]

(3) The period of licence suspension is concurrent with the unexpired portion of any other licence suspension under this or any other authority.

O. Reg. 124/01, s. 1

DEMERIT POINTS: FULLY LICENSED DRIVERS

7. (1) If a person who is a fully licensed driver in Ontario in one or more licence classes or a person who is not a resident of Ontario has six, seven or eight accumulated demerit points, the Registrar shall mail a notice setting out the number of points to the person at his or her latest address appearing on the records of the Ministry.

(2) A failure to give notice under subsection (1) does not render any further proceeding under this Regulation ineffective.

8. (1) If a person who is a fully licensed driver in Ontario in one or more licence classes or a person who is not a resident of Ontario has 9, 10, 11, 12, 13 or 14 accumulated demerit points, the Registrar may require the person to attend an interview before a Ministry official and to provide information or other evidence to show cause why his or her driver's licence should not be suspended.

(2) The Minister may suspend or cancel the person's driver's licence,

    (a) if the person fails to attend the required interview; or

    (b) if the person does not comply with the Ministry's requirements as a result of the interview; or

    (c) if, in the Minister's opinion, the person has not shown cause at the interview why the licence should not be suspended.

(2.1) The Minister may cancel the person's driver's licence if the person fails to pay a fee required under subsection 56(4) of the Act.

(3) A licence suspended under subsection (2) shall not be reinstated until such period as the Minister considers advisable has elapsed from the date the licence was surrendered on account of the suspension or two years have elapsed from the date of the suspension, whichever occurs first.

O. Reg. 204/10, s. 4; 403/15, s. 1

9. (1) If a person who is a fully licensed driver in Ontario in one or more licence classes or a person who is not a resident of Ontario has 15 or more accumulated demerit points, the Registrar shall, after giving notice, suspend the person's driver's licence.

(2) A licence suspended under subsection (1) shall not be reinstated until,

    (a) in the case of a first suspension, 30 days have elapsed from the date the licence was surrendered on account of the suspension or two years have elapsed from the date of the suspension, whichever occurs first; or

    (b) in the case of a subsequent suspension, six months have elapsed from the date the licence was surrendered on account of the suspension or two years have elapsed from the date of the suspension, whichever occurs first.

(3) For the purpose of clause (2)(b), a suspension is a subsequent suspension only if it occurs as a result of a conviction for an offence committed within two years after the expiry of a prior suspension under this section.

(4) If a suspension is imposed on a person who, at the time of the suspension, is a fully licensed driver in Ontario in one or more licence classes or a person who is not a resident of Ontario, the person's accumulated demerit points for convictions for offences that occurred prior to the effective date of the suspension shall be reduced to seven on that date and the remaining points shall be those recorded for the most recently committed offences.

[Heading repealed O. Reg. 204/10, s. 5.]

10.–14. [Repealed O. Reg. 204/10, s. 5.]

DEMERIT POINTS: NOVICE DRIVERS

15. (1) The Registrar shall mail a notice to a novice driver at his or her latest address on the records of the Ministry setting out the reason for the notice, the circumstances under which his or her licence may be suspended and any other action the Ministry may take if, within any two-year period, the novice driver accumulates two, three, four or five demerit points.

(2) A failure to give notice under subsection (1) does not render any further proceeding under this Regulation ineffective.

(3) [Repealed O. Reg. 204/10, s. 6.]

O. Reg. 204/10, s. 6

16. (1) The Registrar may require a novice driver to attend an interview before a Ministry official at a designated time and place if, within any two-year period, the novice driver accumulates six, seven or eight demerit points.

(2) The Minister may suspend or cancel the person's driver's licence,

    (a) if the person does not attend the required interview;

    (b) if the person does not comply with the Ministry's requirements as a result of the interview; or

    (c) if, in the Minister's opinion, the person has not shown cause at the interview why the licence should not be suspended.

(2.1) The Minister may cancel the person's driver's licence if the person fails to pay a fee required under subsection 56(4) of the Act.

(3) A licence suspended under subsection (2) shall not be reinstated until such period as the Registrar considers advisable has elapsed from the date the licence was surrendered on account of the suspension or two years have elapsed from the date of the suspension, whichever occurs first.

O. Reg. 204/10, s. 7; 403/15, s. 2

17. (1) If a novice driver has nine or more accumulated demerit points, the Registrar shall, after giving notice, suspend his or her driver's licence.

(2) A licence suspended under subsection (1) shall not be reinstated until,

(a) in the case of a first suspension, 60 days have elapsed from the date the licence was surrendered on account of the suspension or two years have elapsed from the date of the suspension, whichever occurs first; or

(b) in the case of a subsequent suspension, six months have elapsed from the date the licence was surrendered on account of the suspension or two years have elapsed from the date of the suspension, whichever occurs first.

(3) For the purpose of clause (2)(b), a suspension is a subsequent suspension only if it occurs as a result of a conviction for an offence committed within two years after the expiry of a prior suspension under this section.

(4) If a suspension is imposed on a person who, at the time of the suspension, is a novice driver, the person's accumulated demerit points for convictions for offences that occurred prior to the effective date of the suspension shall be reduced to four on that date and the remaining points shall be those recorded in respect of the most recently committed offences.

(5) If a suspension is imposed on a person who, at the time of the suspension, is no longer a novice driver, the person's accumulated demerit points for convictions for offences that occurred prior to the effective date of the suspension shall be reduced to seven on that date and the remaining points shall be those recorded in respect of the most recently committed offences.

18. (1) Sections 7 to 9 apply, and not sections 15, 16 and 17, to a driver who holds a licence that includes more than one licence class, only one of which is novice class, if he or she is a fully licensed driver in the other licence class or classes.

(2) [Repealed O. Reg. 204/10, s. 8.]

O. Reg. 204/10, s. 8

19. Regulation 578 of the Revised Regulations of Ontario, 1990 and Ontario Regulations 316/91, 694/92 and 611/93 are revoked.

20. This Regulation comes into force on June 6, 1994.

TABLE

ITEM	COLUMN 1	COLUMN 2	COLUMN 3
	Provisions for Offences	Number of Demerit Points	Short Description of Offences for Convenience of Reference only
1	Section 200 of the *Highway Traffic Act*	7	Failing to remain at scene of accident
1.1	Section 216 of the *Highway Traffic Act*, except where a suspension order is made under subsection 216(3)	7	Driver failing to stop when signalled or requested to stop by a police officer

ITEM	COLUMN 1	COLUMN 2	COLUMN 3
2	Section 130 of the *Highway Traffic Act*	6	Careless driving
3	Section 172 of the *Highway Traffic Act*	6	Racing
4	Section 128 of the *Highway Traffic Act*; subsection 13(3) of Regulation 829 of the Revised Regulations of Ontario, 1990; any provision of the National Capital Commission Traffic and Property Regulations CRC 1978, c. 1044 made under the *National Capital Act* (Canada) fixing maximum rates of speed and any municipal by-law fixing maximum rates of speed where the rate of speed is exceeded by,		
	(a) 50 km/h or more	6	Exceeding speed limit by 50 km/h or more
	(b) 30 km/h or more and less than 50 km/h	4	Exceeding speed limit by 30 to 49 km/h
	(c) more than 15 km/h and less than 30 km/h	3	Exceeding speed limit by 16 to 29 km/h
5	Subsections 174(1) and (2) of the *Highway Traffic Act*	5	Driver of public vehicle or school bus failing to stop at railway crossings
6	Section 164 of the *Highway Traffic Act*	3	Driving through, around or under railway crossing barrier
7	Subsections 135(2) and (3), clause 136(1)(b), subsection 136(2), subsection 138(1), subsection 139(1), subsection 141(5) and subsections 144(7), (8) and (21) of the *Highway Traffic Act*	3	Failing to yield right of way

ITEM	COLUMN 1	COLUMN 2	COLUMN 3
8	Clause 136(1)(a), subsections 144(14), (15), (16), (17), (18) and (21), subsections 146(3) and (4) and section 163 of the *Highway Traffic Act*, any municipal by-law requiring a driver to stop for a stop sign or signal light, and the National Capital Commission Traffic and Property Regulations CRC 1978, c. 1044 made under the *National Capital Act* (Canada) requiring a driver to stop for a stop sign	3	Failing to obey a stop sign, signal light or railway crossing signal
9	Subsection 134(1) of the *Highway Traffic Act*	3	Failing to obey directions of police constable
10	Subsection 134(3) of the *Highway Traffic Act*	3	Driving or operating a vehicle on a closed highway
11	Subsections 199(1) and (1.1) of the *Highway Traffic Act*	3	Failing to report an accident
12	Subsection 148(8), sections 149, 150 and 166 of the *Highway Traffic Act*	3	Improper passing
13	Section 154 of the *Highway Traffic Act*	3	Improper driving where highway divided into lanes
14	Subsections 175(11) and (12) of the *Highway Traffic Act*	6	Failing to stop for school bus
15	Section 158 of the *Highway Traffic Act*	4	Following too closely
16	Section 162 of the *Highway Traffic Act*	3	Crowding driver's seat
17	Clause 156(1)(a) of the *Highway Traffic Act*	3	Drive wrong way — divided highway
18	Clause 156(1)(b) of the *Highway Traffic Act*	3	Cross divided highway — no proper crossing provided
19	Section 153 of the *Highway Traffic Act*	3	Wrong way in one way street or highway
20	Subsection 157(1) of the *Highway Traffic Act*	2	Backing on highway
21	Subsections 140(1) and (3) of the *Highway Traffic Act*	3	Pedestrian crossover
22	Subsections 148(1), (2), (4), (5), (6) and (7) of the *Highway Traffic Act*	2	Failing to share road
23	Subsections 141(2) and (3) of the *Highway Traffic Act*	2	Improper right turn
24	Subsections 141(6) and (7) of the *Highway Traffic Act*	2	Improper left turn

ITEM	COLUMN 1	COLUMN 2	COLUMN 3
25	Subsections 142(1), (2) and (8) of the *Highway Traffic Act*	2	Failing to signal
26	Section 132 of the *Highway Traffic Act*	2	Unnecessary slow driving
27	Section 168 of the *Highway Traffic Act*	2	Failing to lower headlamp beam
28	Subsection 165(1) of the *Highway Traffic Act*	3	Improper opening of vehicle door
29	Section 143 and subsection 144(9) of the *Highway Traffic Act* and any municipal by-law prohibiting turns	2	Prohibited turns
30	Section 160 of the *Highway Traffic Act*	2	Towing of persons on tobog-gans, bicycles, skis, etc., pro-hibited
31	Subsection 182(2) of the *Highway Traffic Act*	2	Failing to obey signs pre-scribed by regulation under subsection 182(1)
32	Subsection 106(2) of the *Highway Traffic Act*	2	Driver failing to properly wear seat belt
33	Subclause 106(4)(a)(i) of the *Highway Traffic Act*	2	Driving while passenger under 16 fails to occupy po-sition with seat belt
33.1	Subclause 106(4)(a)(ii) of the *Highway Traffic Act*	2	Driving while passenger under 16 fails to properly wear seat belt
33.2	Clause 106(4)(b) of the *Highway Traffic Act*	2	Driving while child passen-ger not properly secured
34	Subsection 8(2) of Regulation 613 of the Revised Regula-tions of Ontario, 1990	2	Driver failing to ensure in-fant passenger is secured as prescribed
34.1	Subsection 8(3) of Regulation 613 of the Revised Regula-tions of Ontario, 1990	2	Driver failing to ensure tod-dler passenger is secured as prescribed
34.2	Subsection 8(4) of Regulation 613 of the Revised Regula-tions of Ontario, 1990	2	Driver failing to ensure child passenger is secured as pre-scribed
35	Clause 159(1)(a) of the *High-way Traffic Act*	3	Failing to stop on right for emergency vehicle
36	Clause 159(1)(b) of the *High-way Traffic Act*	3	Failing to stop — nearest curb — for emergency vehi-cle
36.1	Clause 159(1)(b) of the *High-way Traffic Act*	3	Failing to stop — nearest edge of roadway — for emer-gency vehicle

ITEM	COLUMN 1	COLUMN 2	COLUMN 3
36.2	Subsection 159(2) of the *Highway Traffic Act*	3	Failing to slow down and proceed with caution for emergency vehicle or tow truck
36.3	Subsection 159(3) of the *Highway Traffic Act*	3	Failing to move into another lane for emergency vehicle or tow truck — if safe to do so
36.4	Subsection 159(4) of the *Highway Traffic Act*	3	Following fire department vehicle too closely
37	Subsection 79(2) of the *Highway Traffic Act*	3	Motor vehicle equipped with or carrying a speed measuring warning device
38	Subsection 154.1(3) of the *Highway Traffic Act*	3	Improper use of high occupancy vehicle lane
39	Subsection 146.1(3) of the *Highway Traffic Act*	3	Failing to obey traffic control stop sign
40	Subsection 146.1(4) of the *Highway Traffic Act*	3	Failing to obey traffic control slow sign
41	Subsection 176(3) of the *Highway Traffic Act*	3	Failing to obey school crossing stop sign
42	Section 78 of the *Highway Traffic Act*	3	Driving with display screen visible to driver
43	Section 78.1 of the *Highway Traffic Act*	3	Driving while holding or using hand-held device
44	Subsection 148(6.1) of the *Highway Traffic Act*	2	Failing to leave one metre while passing bicycle

O. Reg. 164/96, s. 1; 331/97, s. 1; 538/97, s. 1; 637/99, s. 1; 107/03, s. 1; 197/05, s. 1; 596/05, s. 1; 615/05, s. 1; 64/06, s. 1; 521/06, s. 1; 428/09, s. 1; 226/15, s. 1; 53/16, s. 1

ONT. REG. 618/05 — DESIGNATION OF BUS BY-PASS SHOULDERS ON KING'S HIGHWAY

made under the *Highway Traffic Act*

O. Reg. 618/05, as am. O. Reg. 263/12; 149/14; 88/15; 174/15; 41/16.

1. Designation of bus by-pass shoulders — (1) Those parts of the King's Highway described in Schedule 1 are designated as having paved shoulders for use by a bus operated in accordance with a licence issued under the *Public Vehicles Act* and an authorization provided by the Ministry by,

(a) the Greater Toronto Transit Authority, also known as GO Transit; or

(b) Mississauga Transit.

(1.1) Those parts of the King's Highway described in Schedule 2 are designated as having paved shoulders for use by a bus operated in accordance with a licence issued under the *Public Vehicles Act* and an authorization provided by the Ministry by,

(a) the OC Transpo Corporation, also known as OC Transpo; or

(b) a bus line operator operating on behalf of the OC Transpo Corporation, but only with respect to those of its buses in which a valid placard issued by the OC Transpo Corporation is displayed in its front windshield.

(1.2) Those parts of the King's Highway described in Schedule 3 are designated as having paved shoulders for use by a bus operated in accordance with a licence issued under the *Public Vehicles Act* and an authorization provided by the Ministry by Grand River Transit, also known as GRT.

(2) A paved shoulder on a part of the King's Highway designated under this section may also be used by,

(a) an emergency vehicle, as defined in section 144 of the Act, being driven by a person in the performance of his or her duties;

(b) a vehicle being driven by a police officer in the lawful performance of his or her duties;

(c) a vehicle owned or leased by the Crown in right of Ontario being driven, in the lawful performance of his or her duties, by an officer appointed for enforcing and carrying out the provisions of the Act; and

(d) a road service vehicle actively engaged in road construction or maintenance activities on or near the paved shoulder.

(3) No person shall drive or stop a vehicle on a paved shoulder of a part of the King's Highway designated under subsection (1), (1.1) or (1.2), except as permitted under subsection (1), (1.1) or (1.2), as applicable, or subsection (2).

715

(4) Subsection (3) does not apply where it is impossible to avoid a temporary contravention of it due to,

    (a) an emergency; or

    (b) a vehicle being disabled while on a highway.

O. Reg. 263/12, s. 1; 149/14, s. 1; 41/16, s. 1

2. Signs marking bus by-pass shoulders — (1) A paved shoulder on a part of the King's Highway designated under section 1 shall be marked with the following ground mounted signs:

    1. A sign that has the dimensions and bears the markings illustrated in Figure 1.

    2. In an area designated in the Schedule to the *French Language Services Act*, a sign that has the dimensions and bears the markings illustrated in Figure 2, in addition to a sign described in paragraph 1.

FIGURE 1

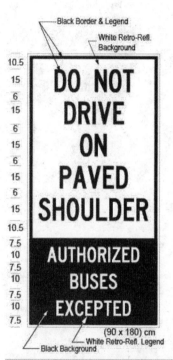

Black Border & Legend

White Retro-Refl. Background

10.5
15
6
15
6
15
6
15
6
15
10.5

DO NOT DRIVE ON PAVED SHOULDER

7.5
10
7.5
10
7.5
10
7.5

AUTHORIZED BUSES EXCEPTED

(90 x 180) cm
White Retro-Refl. Legend
Black Background

Text alternative: Illustration of a ground-mounted sign labelled as "Figure 1". The sign contains two rectangles, stacked on top of one another. The top rectangle contains the words "DO NOT DRIVE ON PAVED SHOULDER" in black lettering on a white reflective background. The bottom rectangle contains the words "AUTHORIZED BUSES EXCEPTED" in white lettering on a black reflective background. The following measurements are written below the sign: (90 x 180) cm. The sign is surrounded by dimensions of its different elements. This text alternative is provided for convenience only and does not form part of the official law.

FIGURE 2

Text alternative: Illustration of a ground-mounted sign labelled as "Figure 2". The sign contains two rectangles, stacked on top of one another. The top rectangle contains the words "INTERDIT DE CIRCULER SUR L'ACCOTEMENT" in black lettering on a white reflective background. The bottom rectangle contains the words "EXCEPTÉ AUTOBUS AUTORISÉS" in white lettering on a black reflective background. The following measurements are written below the sign: (90 x 180) cm. The sign is surrounded by dimensions of its different elements. This text alternative is provided for convenience only and does not form part of the official law.

(2) The commencement of a paved shoulder on a part of the King's Highway designated under section 1 shall be marked with the following ground mounted signs:

   1. A sign that has the dimensions and bears the markings illustrated in Figure 3.

2. In an area designated in the Schedule to the *French Language Services Act*, a sign that has the dimensions and bears the markings illustrated in Figure 4, in addition to a sign described in paragraph 1.

FIGURE 3

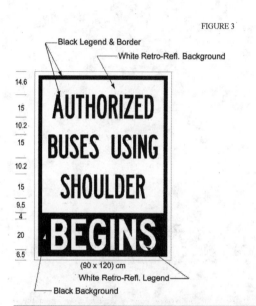

Black Legend & Border

White Retro-Refl. Background

14.6

15

10.2

15

10.2

15

9.5

4

20

6.5

AUTHORIZED BUSES USING SHOULDER

BEGINS

(90 x 120) cm

White Retro-Refl. Legend

Black Background

Text alternative: Illustration of a ground-mounted sign labelled as "Figure 3". The sign contains two rectangles, stacked on top of one another. The top rectangle contains the words "AUTHORIZED BUSES USING SHOULDER" in black lettering on a white reflective background. The bottom rectangle contains the words "BEGINS" in white lettering on a black reflective background. The following measurements are written below the sign: (90 x 120) cm. The sign is surrounded by dimensions of its different elements. This text alternative is provided for convenience only and does not form part of the official law.

FIGURE 4

Black Legend & Border   White Retro-Refl. Background

9.5
12.5
ÉMPRUNT DE
8.6
12.5
L'ACCOTEMENT
8.6
12.5
PAR AUTOBUS
8.6
12.5
AUTORISÉS
4.5
8.2
20
DÉBUT
4

(120 x 120) cm

White Retro-Refl. Legend
Black Background

Text alternative: Illustration of a ground-mounted sign labelled as "Figure 4". The sign contains two rectangles, stacked on top of one another. The top rectangle contains the words "EMPRUNT DE L'ACCOTEMENT PAR AUTOBUS AUTORISÉS" in black lettering on a white reflective background. The bottom rectangle contains the words "DÉBUT" in white lettering on a black reflective background. The following measurements are written below the sign: (120 x 120) cm. Measurements for the height of the lettering and horizontal spacing between the lines of text appear to the left of the sign. This text alternative is provided for convenience only and does not form part of the official law.

(3) The end of a paved shoulder on a part of the King's Highway designated under section 1 shall be marked with the following ground mounted signs:

1. A sign that has the dimensions and bears the markings illustrated in Figure 5.

2. In an area designated in the Schedule to the *French Language Services Act*, a sign that has the dimensions and bears the markings illustrated in Figure 6, in addition to a sign described in paragraph 1.

FIGURE 5

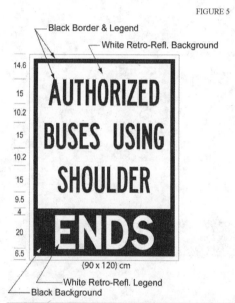

(90 x 120) cm

Text alternative: Illustration of a ground-mounted sign labelled as "Figure 5". The sign contains two rectangles, stacked on top of one another. The top rectangle contains the words "AUTHORIZED BUSES USING SHOULDER" in black lettering on a white reflective background. The bottom rectangle contains the words "ENDS" in white lettering on a black reflective background. The following measurements are written below the sign: (90 x 120) cm. Measurements for the height of the lettering and horizontal spacing between the lines of text appear to the left of the sign. This text alternative is provided for convenience only and does not form part of the official law.

FIGURE 6

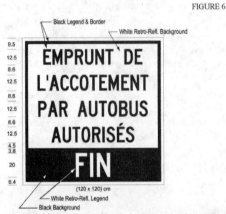

Text alternative: Illustration of a ground-mounted sign labelled as "Figure 6". The sign contains two rectangles, stacked on top of one another. The top rectangle contains the words "EMPRUNT DE L'ACCOTEMENT PAR AUTOBUS AUTORISÉS" in black lettering on a white reflective background. The bottom rectangle contains the words "FIN" in white lettering on a black reflective background. The following measurements are written below the sign: (120 x 120) cm. Measurements for the height of the lettering and horizontal spacing between the lines of text appear to the left of the sign. This text alternative is provided for convenience only and does not form part of the official law.

(4) The dimensions of a sign may be greater than the dimensions prescribed in subsection (1), (2) or (3) so long as each dimension is increased and, when increased, has the same relation to the other dimensions of the sign as the prescribed dimensions have to each other.

(5) A ground mounted sign shall be erected on the side of the highway facing approaching traffic.

O. Reg. 88/15, s. 1

3. Revocation — Regulation 580 of the Revised Regulations of Ontario, 1990 is revoked.

4. Commencement — This Regulation comes into force on the later of December 1, 2005 and the day this Regulation is filed.

SCHEDULE 1 — HIGHWAY NO. 403

1. That portion of the King's Highway known as Highway No. 403 in the City of Mississauga in The Regional Municipality of Peel,

(a) in the eastbound direction, between a point situate 260 metres measured easterly from the intersection of Highway No. 403 with the centre line of Erin Mills Parkway and a point situate 607 metres measured westerly from the intersection of Highway No. 403 with the centre line of Mavis Road;

(b) in the westbound direction, between a point situate 737 metres measured westerly from the intersection of Highway No. 403 with the centre line of Mavis Road and a point situate 210 metres measured easterly from the intersection of Highway No. 403 with the centre line of Erin Mills Parkway.

SCHEDULE 2 — HIGHWAY NO. 417 [Heading added O. Reg. 263/12, s. 2.]

1. That portion of the King's Highway known as Highway No. 417 in the City of Ottawa,

(a) in the eastbound direction, between a point situate 590 metres measured easterly from the intersection of Highway No. 417 with the centre line of Eagleson Road and a point situate 750 metres measured westerly from the intersection of Highway No. 417 with the centre line of Moodie Drive;

(b) in the westbound direction, between a point situate 875 metres measured westerly from the intersection of Highway No. 417 with the centre line of Moodie Drive and a point situate 1150 metres measured easterly from the intersection of Highway No. 417 with the centre line of Eagleson Road;

(c) in the eastbound direction, between a point situate 288 metres measured easterly from the intersection of Highway No. 417 with the centre line of Nicholas Street and a point situate 782 metres measured westerly from the intersection of Highway No. 417 with the centre line of Vanier Parkway;

(d) in the eastbound direction, between a point situate 519 metres measured easterly from the intersection of Highway No. 417 with the centre line of Vanier Parkway and a point situate 701 metres measured westerly from the intersection of Highway No. 417 with the centre line of St. Laurent Boulevard;

(e) in the eastbound direction, beginning at a point situate 1157 metres measured easterly from the intersection of Highway No. 417 with the centre line of St. Laurent Boulevard and extending easterly for a distance of 523 metres to the westerly limit of Ottawa Road 174;

(f) in the westbound direction, between a point situate 438 metres measured westerly from the intersection of Highway No. 417 with the centre line of St. Laurent Boulevard and a point situate 900 metres measured easterly from the intersection of Highway No. 417 with the centre line of Vanier Parkway.

O. Reg. 263/12, s. 2; 174/15, s. 1; 41/16, s. 2

SCHEDULE 3 — HIGHWAY NO. 8 [Heading added O. Reg. 149/14, s. 2.]

1. That portion of the King's Highway known as Highway No. 8 in the City of Kitchener,

(a) in the eastbound direction, between a point situate 800 metres measured easterly from the intersection of Highway No. 8 with the centre line of Fairway Road and a point situate 1900 metres measured westerly from the intersection of Highway No. 8 with the centre line of Sportsworld Drive;

(b) in the eastbound direction, beginning at a point situate 300 metres measured westerly from the intersection of Highway No. 8 with the centre line of Sportsworld Drive and extending westerly for a distance of 1100 metres;

(c) in the westbound direction, beginning at a point situate 300 metres measured westerly from the intersection of Highway No. 8 with the centre line of Sportsworld Drive and extending westerly for a distance of 750 metres;

(d) in the westbound direction, between a point situate 1300 metres measured westerly from the intersection of Highway No. 8 with the centre line of Sportsworld Drive and a point situate 800 metres measured easterly from the intersection of Highway No. 8 with the centre line of Fairway Road.

O. Reg. 149/14, s. 2

ONT. REG. 579 — DESIGNATION OF HIGHWAYS

made under the *Highway Traffic Act*

R.R.O. 1990, Reg. 579, as am. O. Reg. 374/09 (Fr.).

1. The following highways are designated as Class A highways:

1. The King's Highway.

2. Every highway within a city, town or incorporated village, except those on which heavy traffic is prohibited by municipal by-law.

3. Every hard-surfaced county and township highway, except those designated by by-law of a county or township.

2. The King's Highway is designated as a through highway.

ONT. REG. 366/09 — DISPLAY SCREENS AND HAND-HELD DEVICES

made under the *Highway Traffic Act*

O. Reg. 366/09, as am. O. Reg. 253/12; 424/15 [To come into force January 1, 2017.].

DEFINITIONS

1. Definitions — In this Regulation,

> **Proposed Addition — 1 "commercial motor vehicle"**
>
> "commercial motor vehicle" has the same meaning as in section 3 of Ontario Regulation 419/15 (*Definitions of Commercial Motor Vehicle and Tow Truck*) made under the Act;
>
> O. Reg. 424/15, s. 1 [To come into force January 1, 2017.]

"hand microphone or portable radio" means a wireless communication device, consisting of a hand-held unit that is both receiver and microphone, that is operated by a push-to-talk function on a set frequency and that allows for voice communication but not for the transmission and receipt of voice communication at the same time;

"mobile data terminal" means a computerized device that is used exclusively to communicate with a dispatcher or control centre;

"two-way radio" means a wireless communication device, consisting of a main receiver unit and a separate hand-held microphone, that is operated by a push-to-talk function on a set frequency and that allows for voice communication but not for the transmission and receipt of voice communication at the same time.

DISPLAY SCREENS

2. Exemption for law enforcement officers — The following persons, while engaged in the performance of their duties, may drive a motor vehicle on a highway with a display screen of a computer or other device in the motor vehicle visible to the driver:

1. Police officers, within the meaning of the *Police Services Act*.

2. Special constables appointed under section 53 of the *Police Services Act*.

3. Auxiliary members of a police force.

4. First Nations Constables appointed under subsection 54(1) of the *Police Services Act*.

5. Persons appointed under a statute of the Parliament of Canada and who are peace officers within the meaning of section 2 of the *Criminal Code* (Canada).

6. Persons appointed as police constables under section 44 of the *Railway Safety Act* (Canada).

7. Persons designated as park wardens by the Minister of Natural Resources or under the *Canada National Parks Act* (Canada).

8. Park wardens under the *Provincial Parks and Conservation Reserves Act, 2006.*

9. Conservation officers under section 87 of the *Fish and Wildlife Conservation Act, 1997.*

3. Exemption for other enforcement officers — The following persons, while engaged in the performance of their duties, may drive a motor vehicle on a highway with a computer display screen in the motor vehicle visible to the driver:

1. Provincial offences officers designated under subsection 1(3) of the *Provincial Offences Act.*

2. Municipal law enforcement officers appointed under section 15 of the *Police Services Act.*

3. The Fire Marshal and Deputy Fire Marshal appointed under the *Fire Protection and Prevention Act, 1997.*

4. Municipal fire chiefs and deputy fire chiefs.

5. Guards appointed under the *Public Works Protection Act.*

4. Exemption for certain evaluation and monitoring functions — (1) Drivers employed by or on contract to a road authority and engaged in collecting data and viewing pavement evaluation indices may drive a motor vehicle equipped with an automatic road analyser on a highway with a computer display screen in the motor vehicle visible to the driver.

(2) Persons appointed as spectrum management officers under the *Radiocommunication Act* (Canada) and engaged in frequency spectrum management may drive a motor vehicle on a highway with a computer display screen in the motor vehicle that is connected to equipment used to monitor radio frequencies and is visible to the driver.

(3) Persons employed by or on contract to a telecommunication enterprise and engaged in monitoring service levels may drive a motor vehicle on a highway with a computer display screen in the motor vehicle that is connected to equipment used to monitor service levels and disruptions and is visible to the driver.

(4) Persons employed as automobile technicians or mechanics may test drive a motor vehicle on a highway with a computer display screen that provides diagnostic information about the vehicle's performance in the motor vehicle visible to the driver.

5. Exemption for other public functions — (1) The following persons, while engaged in the performance of their duties, may drive a motor vehicle on a highway with a mobile data terminal display screen in the motor vehicle visible to the driver:

  1. Employees of and persons contracted to a public utility within the meaning of the *Public Utilities Act*, the *Municipal Act, 2001* or the *City of Toronto Act, 2006*.

  2. Employees of and persons contracted to a transmitter or distributor within the meaning of the *Electricity Act, 1998*.

(2) Employees of or persons contracted to a road authority, while they are engaged in road patrol, repair, maintenance or construction activities, may drive a motor vehicle on a highway with a mobile data terminal display screen in the motor vehicle visible to the driver.

6. Exemption for certain commercial activities — (1) Drivers of commercial motor vehicles, within the meaning of subsection 16(1) of the Act, may drive a commercial motor vehicle on a highway with a mobile data terminal display screen in the vehicle visible to the driver.

Proposed Amendment — 6(1)

(1) Drivers of commercial motor vehicles, may drive a commercial motor vehicle on a highway with a mobile data terminal display screen in the vehicle visible to the driver.

O. Reg. 424/15, s. 2(1) [To come into force January 1, 2017.]

(2) The following persons, while engaged in the performance of their duties, may drive a motor vehicle on a highway with a mobile data terminal display screen in the motor vehicle visible to the driver:

  1. Drivers of motor vehicles clearly identified as courier delivery vehicles.

  2. Drivers of tow trucks or roadside assistance service vehicles.

Proposed Amendment — 6(2), para. 2

  2. Drivers of roadside assistance service vehicles.

O. Reg. 424/15, s. 2(2) [To come into force January 1, 2017.]

  3. Drivers of taxicabs and limousines licensed by a municipality or airport authority to provide passenger service.

7. Exempt devices — The display screens of the following devices may be visible to any driver in a motor vehicle driven on a highway:

  1. A device that displays,

      i. information on the conditions, use and immediate environment of the vehicle, or

      ii. information on road or weather conditions.

  2. An ignition interlock device.

  3. A car audio control that displays only text or static images.

4. A hand-held device that displays only text or static images and is connected directly into and operates using the audio system controls of the motor vehicle.

8. Requirement that display screens be secure — The exemptions in sections 2, 3, 4, 5, 6 and 7 apply only if the display screen of the computer, mobile data terminal or other device is placed securely in or mounted to the motor vehicle so that it does not move while the vehicle is in motion.

HAND-HELD DEVICES

9. Exemption for law enforcement officers — The following persons, while engaged in the performance of their duties, may drive a motor vehicle on a highway while holding or using a hand-held wireless communication device:

1. Police officers, within the meaning of the *Police Services Act*.

2. Special constables appointed under section 53 of the *Police Services Act*.

3. Auxiliary members of a police force.

4. First Nations Constables appointed under subsection 54(1) of the *Police Services Act*.

5. Persons appointed under a statute of the Parliament of Canada and who are peace officers within the meaning of section 2 of the *Criminal Code* (Canada).

6. Persons appointed as police constables under section 44 of the *Railway Safety Act* (Canada).

7. Persons designated as park wardens by the Minister of Natural Resources or under the *Canada National Parks Act* (Canada).

8. Park wardens under the *Provincial Parks and Conservation Reserves Act, 2006*.

9. Conservation officers under section 87 of the *Fish and Wildlife Conservation Act, 1997*.

10. Exemption for other enforcement officers — The following persons, while engaged in the performance of their duties, may drive a motor vehicle on a highway while holding or using a two-way radio:

1. Provincial offences officers designated under subsection 1(3) of the *Provincial Offences Act*.

2. Municipal law enforcement officers appointed under section 15 of the *Police Services Act*.

3. The Fire Marshal and Deputy Fire Marshal appointed under the *Fire Protection and Prevention Act, 1997*.

4. Municipal fire chiefs and deputy fire chiefs.

5. Guards appointed under the *Public Works Protection Act*.

11. Time-limited exemption for other public functions — (1) The following persons, while engaged in the performance of their duties, may drive a motor vehicle on a highway while holding or using a two-way radio:

1. Employees of and persons contracted to a public utility within the meaning of the *Public Utilities Act*, the *Municipal Act, 2001* or the *City of Toronto Act, 2006*.

2. Employees of and persons contracted to a transmitter or distributor within the meaning of the *Electricity Act, 1998*.

(2) Employees of or persons contracted to a road authority, while they are engaged in road patrol, repair, maintenance or construction activities, may drive a motor vehicle on a highway while holding or using a two-way radio.

(3) This section is revoked on January 1, 2018.

O. Reg. 253/12, s. 1

12. Time-limited exemption for certain commercial activities — (1) Drivers of commercial motor vehicles, within the meaning of subsection 16(1) of the Act, may drive a commercial motor vehicle on a highway while holding or using a two-way radio.

Proposed Amendment — 12(1)

(1) Drivers of commercial motor vehicles, may drive a commercial motor vehicle on a highway while holding or using a two-way radio.

O. Reg. 424/15, s. 3(1) [To come into force January 1, 2017.]

(2) The following persons, while engaged in the performance of their duties, may drive a motor vehicle on a highway while holding or using a two-way radio:

1. Drivers of motor vehicles clearly identified as courier delivery vehicles.

2. Drivers of tow trucks or roadside assistance service vehicles.

Proposed Amendment — 12(2), para. 2

2. Drivers of roadside assistance service vehicles.

O. Reg. 424/15, s. 3(2) [To come into force January 1, 2017.]

3. Drivers of taxicabs and limousines licensed by a municipality or airport authority to provide passenger service.

4. Drivers of street cars.

5. Drivers of road-building machines.

(3) Subsection (1) does not apply if the driver is using the commercial motor vehicle for personal purposes without compensation.

(4) This section is revoked on January 1, 2018.

O. Reg. 253/12, s. 2

13. Time-limited exemption for amateur radio operators — (1) Drivers who hold a valid radio operator certificate issued under the *Radiocommunication*

Act (Canada) may drive a motor vehicle on a highway while holding or using a two-way radio.

(2) This section is revoked on January 1, 2018.

O. Reg. 253/12, s. 3

14. Exemption for pressing buttons — **(1)** A person may drive a motor vehicle on a highway while pressing a button on a hand-held wireless communication device to make, answer or end a cell phone call or to transmit or receive voice communication on a two-way radio if the device is placed securely in or mounted to the motor vehicle so that it does not move while the vehicle is in motion and the driver can see it at a quick glance and easily reach it without adjusting his or her driving position.

(2) A person may drive a motor vehicle on a highway while pressing a button on a device that is worn on his or her head or hung over or placed inside his or her ear or is attached to his or her clothing and is linked to a hand-held wireless communication device to make, answer or end a cell phone call or to transmit or receive voice communication on a two-way radio or a hand microphone or portable radio.

COMMENCEMENT

15. [Repealed O. Reg. 253/12, s. 4.]

ONT. REG. 341/94 — DRIVER LICENCE EXAMINATIONS

made under the *Highway Traffic Act*

O. Reg. 341/94, as am. O. Reg. 672/98; 90/00; 338/00; 339/00; 356/05 [Corrected Ont. Gaz. 9/7/05 Vol. 138:28.]; 599/05; 101/08; 75/11; 144/15.

1. Subject to sections 2 to 6, an applicant for a driver's licence must take the applicable examinations prescribed in Ontario Regulation 340/94 unless the applicant has been exempted by the Minister.

O. Reg. 90/00, s. 1; 144/15, s. 1

2. (1) A resident of Ontario who applies for a Class A, C, D, F, G or M driver's licence and pays the prescribed fee is not required to take the applicable examinations under clauses 15(1)(a) and (b) of Ontario Regulation 340/94 if he or she,

    (a) holds a valid driver's licence of an equivalent class that is not subject to special conditions and restrictions and that is issued by another province or a territory of Canada; and

    (b) surrenders that licence.

(2) A resident of Ontario who applies for a Class A, C, D, F or G driver's licence and an air brake endorsement to that licence and pays the prescribed fee is not required to take the applicable examinations under clause 15(1)(c) of Ontario Regulation 340/94 if he or she,

    (a) holds a valid driver's licence of an equivalent class with, if applicable, an air brake endorsement that authorizes the operation of a motor vehicle equipped with air brakes, or a combination of such a vehicle and towed vehicles, that is not subject to special conditions and restrictions and that is issued by another province or a territory of Canada having an air brake endorsement program recognized by Ontario; and

    (b) surrenders that licence.

(3) A resident of Ontario who applies for a Class B or E licence and pays the prescribed fee may be issued a Class C or F driver's licence, as applicable, without being required to take the applicable examinations under clauses 15(1)(a) and (b) of Ontario Regulation 340/94 if he or she,

    (a) holds a valid driver's licence that is equivalent to a Class B or E driver's licence, is not subject to special conditions and restrictions and is issued by another province or a territory of Canada; and

    (b) surrenders that licence.

(4) A resident of Ontario who applies for a Class G or M driver's licence, pays the prescribed fee and provides the information required by the Minister is not re-

quired to take the applicable examinations under clauses 15(1)(a) and (b) of Ontario Regulation 340/94 if he or she,

(a) holds a valid driver's licence that authorizes the operation of the relevant class of motor vehicle, is not subject to special conditions and restrictions and is issued by a state of the United States of America, the United States Department of State or Canada Forces Europe; and

(b) surrenders that licence.

(5) A resident of Ontario who applies for a Class G driver's licence and pays the prescribed fee is not required to take the applicable examinations under clauses 15(1)(a) and (b) of Ontario Regulation 340/94 if he or she,

(a) holds a driver's licence that authorizes the operation of that class of motor vehicle, is not subject to special conditions and restrictions and,

(i) is issued by a jurisdiction which is a party to a valid and subsisting agreement with Ontario respecting the reciprocal exchange of driver's licences, or

(ii) is issued by Japan and is certified as valid by a Japanese diplomatic or consular official or is accompanied by a valid international driver's permit from Japan; and

(b) surrenders that licence or permit.

(6) An applicant for a Class G driver's licence under subsection (1), (2), (4) or (5) of section 3 or an applicant for a Class M driver's licence under subsection (1) or (4) who meets the requirements set out in section 28 of Ontario Regulation 340/94 for exemption from novice conditions is not required to take the applicable examinations under subsection 15(2) of that Regulation.

(7) In addition to the requirements set out in subsections (1) to (6), an applicant for a Class A, B, C, D, E, F, G or M driver's licence under those subsections must have held a valid driver's licence for at least 24 months during the three years immediately before making the application.

O. Reg. 672/98, s. 1; 339/00, s. 1

2.1 An applicant for a Class A driver's licence shall be issued a Class A driver's licence subject to the condition described in section 3 of Ontario Regulation 340/94 (*Drivers' Licences*) made under the Act if,

(a) subsection 2(1) or (2) of this Regulation applies to the applicant; and

(b) the applicant previously held a Class A driver's licence issued by Ontario and the last such Class A driver's licence held by the applicant was subject to that condition.

O. Reg. 101/08, s. 1

3. (1) An applicant for a Class D, G or M driver's licence who meets all other qualifications for the issuing of such a licence may be issued a new licence,

(a) without taking the applicable examinations under sections 15, 17 and 18 of Ontario Regulation 340/94 if he or she held a licence issued under the Act that expired within one year of the making of the application; or

(b) without taking the applicable examinations under section 15 of Ontario Regulation 340/94 if he or she held a licence issued under the Act that expired between one and three years before the making of the application.

(2) An applicant for a Class A, B, C, E or F driver's licence who meets all other qualifications for such a licence may be issued a new licence without taking the applicable examinations under clause 15(1)(b) or (c) of Ontario Regulation 340/94 if he or she held a licence issued under the Act that expired within three years of the making of the application.

(3) A holder of a Class M or M2 driver's licence who is eligible to take a level 1 exit test to obtain a Class G2 licence and applies therefor is not required to take the applicable examinations under clause 15(1)(a) of Ontario Regulation 340/94 if he or she applies to take the level 1 exit test within five years of being issued the Class M or M2 licence.

(4) [Repealed O. Reg. 75/11, s. 1.]

O. Reg. 75/11, s. 1

4. (1) The following persons are not required to take the applicable examinations under clauses 15(1)(a) and (b) or subsection 15(2) of Ontario Regulation 340/94 on applying for a Class G driver's licence:

1. The Governor General.

2. The Lieutenant Governor.

3. A representative of a foreign government who possesses a valid foreign driver's licence at the time of application and who has taken a post in Ontario in the capacity of,

    i. ambassador, high commissioner or chargé d'affaires,

    ii. head of delegation or head of office,

    iii. minister-counsellor or minister,

    iv. counsellor,

    v. first, second or third secretary,

    vi. attaché,

    vii. military, air or naval attaché or advisor,

    viii. assistant military, air or naval attaché or advisor, or

    ix. consul-general, consul, vice-consul or consular agent.

4. The spouse of a representative referred to in paragraph 3 if the spouse possesses a valid foreign driver's licence at the time of application.

4.1 The child of a representative referred to in paragraph 3 if the child possesses a valid foreign driver's licence at the time of application.

5. A person serving or employed on the technical or support staff of a diplomatic or consular mission or high commission if the person,

    i. is authorized as eligible for exempt status by the Department of External Affairs (Canada),

    ii. is not a Canadian citizen or permanent resident of Canada as defined in the *Immigration Act* (Canada),

    iii. is assigned to duty from the foreign government being represented and not engaged locally by the mission or commission, and

    iv. is the holder of a valid foreign driver's licence at the time of application.

6. The spouse or child of any person described in paragraph 5, if the spouse or child meets the requirements set out in subparagraph ii of paragraph 5, is from a reciprocating country and possesses a valid foreign driver's licence at the time of application.

7. A member of a force or of a civilian component of a force of one of the Contracting Parties to the North Atlantic Treaty Organization Status of Forces Agreement who,

    i. has taken a post in Ontario under the Agreement,

    ii. is from a reciprocating country,

    iii. is not a Canadian citizen or permanent resident of Canada as defined in the *Immigration Act* (Canada), and

    iv. is the holder of a valid driver's licence issued by a reciprocating country at the time of application.

7.1 The spouse or child of any person described in paragraph 7, if the spouse or child meets the requirements set out in subparagraphs 7 ii, iii and iv.

8. A representative of an international organization who has taken a post in Ontario and,

    i. is authorized as eligible for exempt status by the Department of External Affairs (Canada),

    ii. is not a Canadian citizen or permanent resident of Canada as defined in the *Immigration Act* (Canada),

    iii. is assigned to duty from the international organization and is not engaged locally by it, and

    iv. is the holder of a valid foreign driver's licence at the time of application.

9. The spouse or child of any person described in paragraph 8 if the spouse or child meets the requirements set out in subparagraph ii of paragraph 8 and possesses a valid foreign driver's licence at the time of application.

10. A Canadian counterpart to persons referred to in paragraphs 3 and 4 returning to Canada as a resident of Ontario from assigned duty abroad.

10.1 A Canadian counterpart to persons referred to in paragraphs 4.1, 5, 6, 7, 7.1, 8 and 9 returning to Canada as a resident of Ontario from assigned duty abroad.

(1.1) In addition to the requirements set out in paragraphs 4.1, 5, 6, 7, 7.1, 8, 9 and 10.1 of subsection (1), an applicant for a Class G driver's licence under those paragraphs must hold a valid foreign driver's licence and must have held a valid driver's licence or a valid driver's licence issued by another jurisdiction, or a combi-

nation of such driver's licences, for at least 24 months during the three years immediately before making the application.

(2) In this section,

"spouse" has the same meaning as in Part III of the *Family Law Act*.
O. Reg. 90/00, s. 2; 338/00, s. 1; 356/05, s. 1 [Corrected Ont. Gaz. 9/7/05 Vol. 138:28.]

5. (1) A person described in paragraph 4.1, 5, 6, 7, 7.1, 8, 9 or 10.1 of subsection 4(1)
who has not held a valid driver's licence as required by subsection 4(1.1) for at least
24 months during the three years before making the application may obtain a Class
G2 driver's licence without examination, but in order to be issued a Class G driver's
licence, the person must comply with the time requirements under section 28 of Ontario Regulation 340/94 and must successfully pass the applicable level 2 exit test.

(2) A person described in subsection (1) shall be credited with the length of time he
or she has held a valid driver's licence or a valid driver's licence issued by another
jurisdiction within the three years prior to the application toward the length of time
the applicant is classed as a novice driver and toward the prescribed time limits to
take the level 2 exit test.
O. Reg. 338/00, s. 2

6. (1) A resident of Ontario who applies for a Class A, C, D, F or G driver's licence
and, if applicable, an air brake endorsement to that licence and pays the prescribed
fee is not required to take the applicable examinations under clauses 15(1)(a) to (d)
and subsection 15(2) of Ontario Regulation 340/94 (*Drivers' Licences*) made under
the Act if,

(a) the applicant is the holder or former holder of a DND 404 permit of an
equivalent class with, if applicable, an air brake endorsement or certification
that authorizes the operation of a motor vehicle equipped with air brakes, or a
combination of such a vehicle and towed vehicles;

(b) the DND 404 permit with, if applicable, the endorsement or certification is
not subject to special conditions and restrictions; and

(c) the applicant meets the requirements set out in subsection (2).

(2) The applicant must meet the following requirements:

1. The applicant must be a member or former member of the Canadian Armed
Forces.

2. The applicant must have held a DND 404 permit for at least 24 months.

3. In the case of an applicant who is the holder of a DND 404 permit with, if
applicable, an air brake endorsement or certification, the permit must not be
suspended or cancelled.

4. In the case of an applicant who is the former holder of a DND 404 permit
with, if applicable, an air brake endorsement or certification,

i. the permit must not have been suspended or cancelled at the time it was
surrendered to the Department of National Defence (Canada) or at the
time the applicant was released from the Canadian Armed Forces, and

ii. the applicant must have held the permit with, if applicable, the endorsement or certification within the three years prior to the application.

5. For each province or territory of Canada that issued to the applicant a driver's licence with, if applicable, an air brake endorsement, the most recent driver's licence issued to the applicant by that province or territory must not be suspended or cancelled.

(3) In this section,

"DND 404 permit" means a permit issued by the Department of National Defence (Canada) authorizing persons to drive its vehicles.

O. Reg. 144/15, s. 2

ONT. REG. 340/94 — DRIVERS' LICENCES

made under the *Highway Traffic Act*

O. Reg. 340/94, as am. O. Reg. 727/94; 75/95; 306/96; 484/96; 149/97; 251/97;
416/97; 509/97; 19/98; 94/98; 460/98; 490/98; 578/98; 633/98; 671/98; 494/99;
89/00; 304/00; 336/00; 337/00; 125/01; 67/02; 191/02; 115/03; 207/04; 305/04;
83/05; 176/05; 196/05; 355/05; 575/05; 597/05; 110/08; 288/08; 205/10
[Amended O. Reg. 452/10.]; 453/10; 74/11; 291/11; 42/12, ss. 1–3, 4 (Fr.);
169/12; 251/12; 242/13; 246/14; 145/15; 227/15; 257/15 [s. 1(1) to come into
force January 1, 2017.]; 134/16, ss. 1 (Fr.), 2.

1. (1) In this Regulation,

"air brakes" includes air over hydraulic brakes;

"corrective lenses" means lenses that correct visual acuity but does not include extraordinary optical devices that enhance or modify vision or that interfere with the horizontal visual field, such as telescopic lenses, prism lenses or sidebar prisms;

"Demerit Point Regulation" means Ontario Regulation 339/94 (*Demerit Point System*) made under the Act;

"fully licensed driver" means a person authorized to drive a class of motor vehicle on a highway and who, while operating a vehicle of that class, is not subject to novice conditions;

"level 1 exit test" means a test designed to demonstrate a person's ability to drive a Class G1 or M1 motor vehicle safely;

"level 2 exit test" means a test designed to demonstrate a person's ability to drive a Class G2 or M2 motor vehicle at a level beyond the minimum standard required to qualify for a Class G2 or M2 driver's licence;

"limited-speed motorcycle" means,

    (a) a motorcycle that,

        (i) has sufficient power to attain a rate of speed of more than 32 kilometres per hour on level ground within a distance of 1.6 kilometres from a standing start,

        (ii) has a maximum attainable speed of 70 kilometres per hour or less, measured in accordance with International Organization for Standardization standard ISO 7117:1995 entitled "Motorcycles — Measurement of Maximum Speed",

        (iii) has steering handlebars that are completely restrained from rotating in relation to the axle of only one wheel in contact with the ground,

        (iv) has a minimum seat height, when unladen, of 650 millimetres,

(v) has a minimum wheel rim diameter of 250 millimetres and a minimum wheelbase of 1,016 millimetres, and

(vi) has an engine displacement of 50 cubic centimetres or less, or

(b) a motorcycle manufactured on or after September 1, 1988 to which the manufacturer has affixed a compliance label pursuant to section 6 of the *Motor Vehicle Safety Regulations* under the *Motor Vehicle Safety Act* (Canada) that identifies the motor vehicle as a limited-speed motorcycle and that continues to meet the requirements for a limited-speed motorcycle that were in force at the time that the motorcycle was manufactured;

"novice driver" means a person classed as such under section 29;

"registered gross weight" means the weight for which a permit has been issued under the Act, the fee for which is based on the weight of the vehicle or combination of vehicles and load;

"same-sex partner" [Repealed O. Reg. 355/05, s. 1.]

"school purposes bus" means a school bus as defined in subsection 175(1) of the Act or any other bus operated by or under contract with a school board or other authority in charge of a school while they are being used to transport adults with a developmental disability or children;

"spouse" has the same meaning as in Part III of the *Family Law Act*;

"valid driver's licence" means a driver's licence that is not expired, cancelled or under suspension.

(2) A reference in this Regulation to the expressions "children", "developmental disability" and "school" is a reference to those expressions as defined in subsection 175(1) of the Act.

(3) A reference in this Regulation to the expression "accumulated demerit points" is a reference to that expression as defined in the *Demerit Point Regulation.*

(4) For the purposes of this Regulation, time that is not continuous may be included in determining the length of time a person has held a driver's licence.
O. Reg. 89/00, s. 1; 67/02, s. 1; 83/05, s. 1; 355/05, s. 1; 597/05, s. 1; 205/10, s. 1

2. (1) Subject to subsection (6) and sections 3, 5, 6, 7 and 25, a driver's licence of the class prescribed in Column 1 of the Table is authority to drive a motor vehicle of the corresponding class prescribed in Column 2 and the classes of motor vehicles prescribed in Column 3.

COLUMN 1	COLUMN 2	COLUMN 3
Class of Licence	Class of Motor Vehicle	Other Classes of Motor Vehicle the Driving of which is Authorized
Class A	Class A — any combination of a motor vehicle and towed vehicles where the towed vehicles exceed a total gross weight of 4,600 kilograms, but not a bus carrying passengers	Class D and G

COLUMN 1	COLUMN 2	COLUMN 3
Class B	Class B — any school purposes bus having a designed seating capacity for more than 24 passengers	Class C, D, E, F and G
Class C	Class C — any bus having a designed seating capacity for more than 24 passengers, but not a school purposes bus carrying passengers	Class D, F and G
Class D	Class D — any motor vehicle exceeding 11,000 kilograms gross weight or registered gross weight, and any combination of a motor vehicle exceeding a total gross weight or registered gross weight of 11,000 kilograms and towed vehicles not exceeding a total gross weight of 4,600 kilograms, but not a bus carrying passengers	Class G
Class E	Class E — any school purposes bus having a designed seating capacity for not more than 24 passengers	Class F and G
Class F	Class F — any ambulance, and any bus having a designed seating capacity for not more than 24 passengers, but not a school purposes bus carrying passengers	Class G
Class G	Class G — any motor vehicle not exceeding 11,000 kilograms gross weight or registered gross weight and any combination of a motor vehicle not exceeding a total gross weight or registered gross weight of 11,000 kilograms and towed vehicles where the towed vehicles do not exceed a total gross weight of 4,600 kilograms, but not,	
	(a) a motorcycle or motor assisted bicycle;	
	(b) a bus carrying passengers; or	
	(c) an ambulance in the course of providing ambulance service as defined in the *Ambulance Act*	
Class G1	Class G1 — any motor vehicle in Class G and any combination of a motor vehicle in Class G and towed vehicles, except,	
	(a) Class D farm vehicles deemed to be Class G vehicles under subsection 2(3);	

COLUMN 1	COLUMN 2	COLUMN 3
	(b) Class F vehicles deemed to be Class G vehicles under subsection 2(4);	
	(c) a vehicle equipped with air brakes	
Class G2	Class G2 — any motor vehicle in Class G and any combination of such a vehicle and towed vehicles, except a vehicle equipped with air brakes	
Class M	Class M — a motorcycle, including a limited-speed motorcycle, and a motor assisted bicycle	subject to Class G1 conditions, any motor vehicle in Class G1 and any combination of such a vehicle and towed vehicles
Class M1	Class M — a motorcycle, including a limited-speed motorcycle, and a motor assisted bicycle	
Class M2	Class M — a motorcycle, including a limited-speed motorcycle, and motor assisted bicycle	subject to Class G1 conditions, any motor vehicle in Class G1 and any combination of such a vehicle and towed vehicles

(2) A Class D or G motor vehicle that is designed and used as a tow truck shall be deemed not to be a Class A motor vehicle when it is towing a disabled or unsafe motor vehicle or trailer on a highway.

(3) A Class D motor vehicle shall be deemed to be a Class G motor vehicle if,

(a) it is owned or leased by a farmer and used for his or her personal transportation or the transportation of farm products, supplies or equipment without compensation to or from a farm; and

(b) the fee paid for the vehicle permit was determined under Schedule 2 to Regulation 628 of the Revised Regulations of Ontario, 1990.

(4) A Class F motor vehicle shall be deemed to be a Class G motor vehicle when being operated by,

(a) a police officer in the performance of police duties; or

(b) a peace officer who, in the course of his or her duties, is transporting prisoners or other persons held in custody.

(5) A Class F motor vehicle, other than an ambulance or car pool vehicle as defined in the *Public Vehicles Act*, with a designed seating capacity for not more than 11 passengers that is used for personal purposes without compensation shall be deemed to be a Class G motor vehicle.

(6) No driver's licence provides authority to drive a motor vehicle equipped with air brakes unless the licence bears an air brake endorsement.

O. Reg. 83/05, s. 2; 597/05, s. 2; 110/08, s. 1; 42/12, s. 1

2.1 (1) Where the Minister changes the class of a Class A, B, C or E driver's licence, the driver's licence may only be changed to,

(a) a Class G driver's licence; or

(b) a Class C, D, E or F driver's licence, if the Minister is satisfied that the holder of the driver's licence meets the qualifications for that class of driver's licence.

(2) Subsection (1) applies despite the *Human Rights Code*.

O. Reg. 251/12, s. 1

3. The Minister may, based on the results of an examination under clause 15(1)(b) or (c), including the combination of vehicles driven during the examination by the holder of or applicant for a Class A driver's licence, impose a condition on the person's Class A driver's licence that the person not drive,

(a) a combination of vehicles that constitutes a Class A vehicle consisting of a motor vehicle and more than one trailer; or

(b) a combination of vehicles that constitutes a Class A vehicle consisting of,

(i) a motor vehicle, and

(ii) a single trailer that is equipped with air brakes.

O. Reg. 110/08, s. 2

4. (1) In this section,

"house trailer" includes a cabin trailer, collapsible cabin trailer, tent trailer and camping trailer;

"pick-up truck" means a commercial motor vehicle that,

(a) has a manufacturer's gross vehicle weight rating of 6,000 kilograms or less, and

(b) is fitted with either,

(i) the original box that was installed by the manufacturer, which has not been modified, or

(ii) a replacement box that duplicates the one that was installed by the manufacturer, which has not been modified.

(2) A combination of a pick-up truck towing one house trailer that would, but for this section, be a Class A motor vehicle is deemed to be a Class G motor vehicle when driven by a person who is a fully licensed driver holding a Class B, C, D, F or G driver's licence if all of the following conditions are satisfied:

1. The only reason the combination of the pick-up truck and house trailer is not a Class G motor vehicle is because the total gross weight of the house trailer exceeds 4,600 kilograms.

2. The combination of pick-up truck and house trailer is being driven and used for personal purposes without compensation.

3. The combination of the pick-up truck and the house trailer,

i. has a fifth wheel assembly that attaches the house trailer to the pick-up truck, and

ii. complies with the applicable dimensional limits under Part VII of the Act, the applicable weight limits under Part VIII of the Act and the regulations made under those parts.

4. The pick-up truck has no more than two axles.

5. Neither the pick-up truck nor the house trailer is equipped with air brakes.

6. The house trailer bears,

i. a compliance label as required under the *Motor Vehicle Safety Regulations* (Canada) and, either on the compliance label or on a label applied to the vehicle beside the compliance label, the national safety mark required under those regulations,

ii. a compliance label containing a statement that complies with subsection 6(2) of the *Motor Vehicle Safety Regulations* (Canada), confirming that the vehicle conformed to all applicable standards under those regulations that were in effect when the vehicle was manufactured,

iii. a Canadian Statement of Compliance (SOC) label issued by the Canadian Registrar of Imported Vehicles, or

iv. a vehicle licence plate issued by a state in the United States and a label indicating that the house trailer was manufactured in compliance with federal vehicle safety standards applicable at that time in the United States.

7. The house trailer bears a label indicating that it was manufactured to Canadian Standards Association Standard Z240 RV or to United States Recreation Vehicle Industry Association standard NFPA 1192 or ANSI A119.2.

8. The house trailer,

i. is not owned or leased by an employer to house the employer's employee, and

ii. is not carrying commercial cargo or tools or equipment of a type normally used for commercial purposes.

9. Less than one-half of the floor space of the house trailer is occupied by animals, non-commercial tools, non-commercial equipment, vehicles or a combination of them.

O. Reg. 83/05, s. 3; 291/11, s. 1

NOVICE LICENCE CONDITIONS

5. (1) The holder of a Class G1 driver's licence may drive a Class G1 motor vehicle on a highway if a holder of a Class A, B, C, D, E, F or G driver's licence or its equivalent authorizing the holder to drive the motor vehicle, who qualifies as an accompanying driver, occupies the seat beside the driver for the purpose of giving

him or her instruction in driving the motor vehicle and the following additional conditions are met:

1. [Repealed O. Reg. 205/10, s. 2(1).]

2. The accompanying driver's blood alcohol concentration must be less than 50 milligrams of alcohol in 100 millilitres of blood while the novice driver is operating the motor vehicle.

3. No person other than the novice driver and the accompanying driver shall occupy a front seat in the motor vehicle.

4. The number of passengers in the seats other than the front seats of the motor vehicle must not exceed the number of operable seat belt assemblies in those other seats.

5. The motor vehicle may not be driven on a highway designated by subsection (4).

6. The motor vehicle may not be driven by the novice driver between midnight and 5 a.m.

(2) A person is qualified to act as an accompanying driver if he or she,

(a) is a fully licensed driver in a Class G motor vehicle;

(b) has been licensed in Ontario or another jurisdiction for at least four years; and

(c) meets the applicable requirements of the Act and the regulations, including any requirement to wear corrective lenses but not including any requirement for any special or modified controls applicable to the accompanying driver's licence.

(3) [Repealed O. Reg. 205/10, s. 2(3).]

(4) The following highways are designated for the purposes of paragraph 5 of subsection (1):

1. Those parts of the King's Highway known as Nos. 400, 400A, 401, 402, 403, 404, 405, 406, 409, 410, 412, 416, 417, 420 and 427 with posted speed limits greater than 80 kilometres per hour.

1.1 All of the King's Highway known as Highway 407 East.

1.2 All of the private toll highway known as Highway 407.

2. All of the King's Highway known as the Queen Elizabeth Way.

3. Those parts of the highway known as the Don Valley Parkway, the Gardiner Expressway and the E. C. Row Expressway.

4. That part of the King's Highway known as the Conestoga Parkway from its westerly limit at its intersection with the King's Highway known as Nos. 7 and 8 to its northerly limit at its intersection with the King's Highway known as No. 86.

(5) Paragraph 5 of subsection (1) does not apply if the accompanying driver is a driving instructor licensed in Ontario.

(6) Subsection (1) does not apply to the driving of a motor assisted bicycle.

O. Reg. 149/97, s. 1; 83/05, s. 4; 205/10, s. 2; 134/16, s. 2

6. **(1)** The holder of a Class G2 driver's licence may drive a Class G2 motor vehicle on a highway subject to the following conditions:

    1. [Repealed O. Reg. 205/10, s. 3(1).]

    2. The number of passengers in the motor vehicle must not exceed the number of operable seat belt assemblies installed in it.

    3. Between the hours of midnight and 5 a.m., there must not be more than one passenger in the motor vehicle who is under the age of 20, other than a person who is a member of the novice driver's immediate family.

(1.1) Despite subsection (1), the holder of a Class G2 driver's licence who has held a valid G2 driver's licence for at least six months may drive a Class G2 motor vehicle on a highway subject to the following conditions:

    1. [Repealed O. Reg. 205/10, s. 3(2).]

    2. The number of passengers in the motor vehicle must not exceed the number of operable seat belt assemblies installed in it.

    3. Between the hours of midnight and 5 a.m., there must not be more than three passengers in the motor vehicle who are under the age of 20, other than a person who is a member of the novice driver's immediate family.

(2) Subsections (1) and (1.1) do not apply to the driving of a motor assisted bicycle.

(3) For the purpose of subsection (1.1), the requirement that a novice driver has held a valid G2 licence for at least six months means that, at the time the novice driver is driving, he or she held a valid G2 licence for at least the immediately preceding six months.

(4) Paragraph 3 of subsection (1) and paragraph 3 of subsection (1.1) do not apply to,

    (a) a novice driver who is at least 20 years old; or

    (b) any novice driver if a person who qualifies as an accompanying driver, as described in subsection 5(2), and who meets the condition for an accompanying driver as set out in paragraph 2 of subsection 5(1), occupies the seat beside the driver and no person other than the novice driver and the accompanying driver occupies a front seat in the motor vehicle.

(5) The age distinctions in paragraph 3 of subsection (1), paragraph 3 of subsection (1.1) and clause (4)(a) apply despite the *Human Rights Code*.

(6) In paragraph 3 of subsection (1) and paragraph 3 of subsection (1.1), immediate family includes the novice driver's guardian and immediate family who are related by blood, marriage, conjugal relationship outside marriage or adoption.

                                        O. Reg. 196/05, s. 1; 205/10, s. 3

7. The holder of a Class M1 driver's licence may drive a motorcycle on a highway subject to the following conditions:

    1. [Repealed O. Reg. 205/10, s. 4.]

    2. The motorcycle may only be driven from one-half hour before sunrise to one-half hour after sunset.

3. No passenger may be carried on the motorcycle.

4. The motorcycle may not be driven on a highway with a speed limit in excess of 80 kilometres per hour other than those parts of the King's Highway known as Nos. 11, 17, 61, 69, 71, 101, 102, 144 and 655.

O. Reg. 205/10, s. 4

8. [Repealed O. Reg. 205/10, s. 5.]

9. (1) The Registrar shall, after giving notice, suspend or cancel the driver's licence of a novice driver as provided in subsection (2) in the following circumstance:

1. The novice driver is convicted of any of the offences described in subsection (3).

(2) Subject to subsections (4) and 10(5), the Registrar shall,

(a) upon a novice driver's first conviction for any of the offences, suspend the driver's licence of the person for 30 days;

(b) upon a novice driver's second conviction for any of the offences, suspend the driver's licence of the person for 90 days; and

(c) upon a novice driver's third conviction for any of the offences, cancel the driver's licence of the person.

(3) Subsection (1) applies with respect to any of the following offences:

1. An offence under subsection 44.1(3) of the Act.

2. A contravention of any of the conditions specified in section 5, 6 or 7 of this Regulation.

3. An offence under the Act set out in Column 1 of the Table to the *Demerit Point Regulation* for which the number of demerit points set out opposite thereto in Column 2 is four or more, regardless of whether or not demerit points have been recorded.

4. An offence under subsection 216(3) of the Act.

5. An offence under section 78 or 78.1 of the Act.

(4) If a novice driver is convicted of two or more offences arising out of the same circumstances and two or more of these offences are offences described in subsection (3), only one conviction shall be counted for the purposes of subsection (2).

(5) In determining whether a conviction is a second, third or subsequent conviction for the purposes of this section and section 10, the only question to be considered is the sequence of the convictions and no consideration shall be given to the sequence of commission of offences or whether any offence occurred before or after any conviction.

O. Reg. 125/01, s. 1; 205/10, s. 6; 227/15, s. 1

10. (1) Subsection 9(1) does not apply with respect to a conviction for an offence, if the offence occurs after a person's driver's licence is cancelled as described in clause 9(2)(c) but before the person reapplies for a class G1 or M1 driver's licence, as the case may be.

(2) Subsection 9(1) does not apply with respect to a conviction that occurred before the day section 6 of Ontario Regulation 205/10 comes into force.

(2.1) Subsection 9(1) does not apply with respect to a conviction for an offence described in paragraph 5 of subsection 9(3), if the offence occurred before the day section 1 of Ontario Regulation 227/15 comes into force.

(3) Subsection 9(1) does not apply with respect to a conviction for an offence described in paragraph 3, 4 or 5 of subsection 9(3), if at the time of the offence,

(a) the holder of a Class G1 or G2 driver's licence also holds a Class M driver's licence; or

(b) the holder of a Class M1 or M2 driver's licence also holds a Class A, B, C, D, E, F or G driver's licence.

(4) Clause 9(2)(b) or (c) does not apply when the second, third or subsequent conviction is more than five years after the previous conviction.

(5) If the holder of a Class G1 or G2 driver's licence is a fully licensed driver in Class M or if the holder of a Class M1 or M2 driver's licence is a fully licensed driver in Class A, B, C, D, E, F or G, as the case may be, the Registrar shall only cancel the person's Class G1, G2, M1 or M2 driver's licence, as the case may be, as described in clause 9(2)(c).

(6) If the holder of a Class G1, G2, M1 or M2 driver's licence is convicted of a third offence described in subsection 9(3) and subsequently becomes a fully licensed driver in Class G or M, as the case may be, before the Registrar receives notice of the person's third conviction, the Registrar shall not cancel the person's driver's licence as described in clause 9(2)(c) but shall instead suspend the licence for 90 days.

O. Reg. 83/05, s. 5; 205/10, s. 6; 227/15, s. 2

11. **(1)** The Registrar shall state the effective date of the licence suspension or cancellation in the notice given under subsection 9(1).

(2) The period of licence suspension under subsection 9(1) is concurrent with the unexpired portion of any other licence suspension under the Act or this Regulation or under any other authority.

(3) A licence suspended under subsection 9(1) shall not be reinstated,

(a) in the case of a suspension described in clause 9(2)(a), until 30 days have elapsed from the date the licence is surrendered on account of the suspension or two years have elapsed from the date of the suspension, whichever occurs first; or

(b) in the case of a suspension described in clause 9(2)(b), until 90 days have elapsed from the date the licence is surrendered on account of the suspension or two years have elapsed from the date of the suspension, whichever occurs first.

(4) Despite anything in this Regulation, a person whose Class G1, G2, M1 or M2 driver's licence has been cancelled as described in clause 9(2)(c),

(a) shall be required to reapply for a driver's licence; and

(b) shall be classed as a G1 or M1 driver without the benefit of any time previously earned in Class G1 or M1, as the case may be.

(5) Fees paid by a person under subsection 26(1) with respect to a Class G1, G2, M1 or M2 driver's licence that is cancelled as described in clause 9(2)(c) are not refundable and may not be credited towards any subsequent fee payable by the person for any driver's licence applied for by the person.

(6) If a driver's licence is suspended or cancelled under subsection 9(1) in respect of a conviction for an offence described in paragraph 3 of subsection 9(3), no demerit points shall be recorded in respect of that conviction, despite section 2 and subsection 3(2) of the *Demerit Point Regulation*.

(7) If a person is convicted of an offence described in paragraph 3 of subsection 9(3) that occurs after the person's driver's licence is cancelled as described in clause 9(2)(c) but before the person reapplies for a class G1 or M1 driver's licence, as the case may be, no demerit points shall be recorded in respect of that conviction, despite section 2 and subsection 3(2) of the *Demerit Point Regulation*.

O. Reg. 83/05, s. 5; 205/10, s. 6

11.1 The following information is prescribed for the purposes of section 57.1.1 of the Act:

1. The passenger's date of birth.

2. The nature of the familial relationship between the passenger and the driver of the motor vehicle, and the name and address of the person or persons through whom the driver and the passenger are related, if any.

O. Reg. 196/05, s. 2

LICENCES: GENERAL

12. (1) An applicant for a Class A, B, C, D, E or F driver's licence must hold or have held a driver's licence issued by a province or territory of Canada.

(2) A Class G1, G2, M, M1 or M2 driver's licence or an equivalent licence or an instruction permit issued by the Province of Ontario or another province or territory of Canada, shall be deemed not to be a driver's licence for the purposes of subsection (1).

(3) Subsection (1) does not apply to an applicant for a Class A, C, D or F driver's licence who is a member or former member of the Canadian Armed Forces and who meets the requirements of section 6 of Ontario Regulation 341/94 (*Driver Licence Examinations*) made under the Act.

(4) An applicant for a Class B or E driver's licence must be at least 21 years old at the time of application.

(5) An applicant for a Class A, C, D or F driver's licence must be at least 18 years old at the time of application.

(6) An applicant for a Class G, G1, G2, M, M1 or M2 driver's licence must be at least 16 years old at the time of application.

(7) The age requirement in subsection (4) applies despite the *Human Rights Code*.
O. Reg. 509/97, s. 1; 83/05, s. 6; 145/15, s. 1

13. (1) An applicant for a Class B or E driver's licence shall meet the following requirements:

1. The applicant shall provide evidence satisfactory to the Minister that he or she has, not more than five years before the date of application, successfully completed a driver improvement course approved by the Minister.

2. The applicant shall not have accumulated more than six demerit points in his or her driving record.

3. The applicant shall not hold a Class G1 or G2 driver's licence.

(2) An applicant for or a holder of a Class B or E driver's licence shall meet the following requirements:

1. The person's driver's licence shall not have been under suspension at any time within the preceding 12 months as a result of the person having been convicted or found guilty of an offence referred to in section 53, subsection 128(15), section 130, 172, 200 or 216 of the Act, or an offence under the *Criminal Code* (Canada) committed by means of a motor vehicle or while driving or having the care or control of a motor vehicle as defined in the Act.

2. The person shall not have been convicted or found guilty within the preceding five years of two or more offences under the *Criminal Code* (Canada) committed on different dates by means of a motor vehicle or while driving or having the care or control of a motor vehicle.

3. The person shall not have been convicted or found guilty within the preceding five years of an offence under section 151, 152, 153, 155, 159, 160, 163, 167, 168, 170, 171, 172, 173, 212, 271, 272 or 273 of the *Criminal Code* (Canada), under section 4, 5 or 6 of the *Controlled Drugs and Substances Act* (Canada) or under section 4 or 5 of the *Narcotics Control Act* (Canada).

4. The person shall not have been convicted or found guilty within the preceding five years of more than one offence referred to in paragraph 1.

(3) A holder of a Class B or E driver's licence shall not have accumulated more than eight demerit points in his or her driving record and not be classed as a probationary driver.

(4) Although not convicted or found guilty under subsection (2), an applicant for or a holder of a Class B or E driver's licence must not have been convicted or found guilty of an offence for conduct that affords reasonable grounds for believing that the person will not properly perform his or her duties or is not a proper person to have custody of children while having control of a school purposes bus.
O. Reg. 205/10, s. 7

14. (1) An applicant for or a holder of a driver's licence must not,

(a) suffer from any mental, emotional, nervous or physical condition or disability likely to significantly interfere with his or her ability to drive a motor vehicle of the applicable class safely; or

(b) be addicted to the use of alcohol or a drug to an extent likely to significantly interfere with his or her ability to drive a motor vehicle safely.

(2) In determining whether an applicant for or a holder of a driver's licence of any class meets the qualifications described in subsection (1), the Minister,

(a) may take into consideration the relevant medical standards for applicants or holders of that class of driver's licence set out in the *CCMTA Medical Standards for Drivers*; and

(b) may require the applicant or holder to provide evidence satisfactory to the Minister that he or she is able to drive a motor vehicle of the applicable class safely, including,

(i) any reports of examinations under section 15, and

(ii) any additional medical information.

(3) Despite clause (2)(a) and unless otherwise provided in this Regulation, if there is a difference between a medical standard set out in the *CCMTA Medical Standards for Drivers* and a medical standard set out in this Regulation, the Minister shall take into consideration the standard set out in this Regulation instead of the standard set out in the *CCMTA Medical Standards for Drivers*.

(4) In this section, the *CCMTA Medical Standards for Drivers* means the document entitled *CCMTA Medical Standards for Drivers*, published by the Canadian Council of Motor Transport Administrators and dated March 2009, as it may be amended from time to time, that is available on the Internet through the website of the Canadian Council of Motor Transport Administrators.

O. Reg. 83/05, s. 7; 453/10, s. 1

15. (1) An examination of an applicant for or a holder of any class of driver's licence, including a driver's licence with or without any endorsement, condition or waiver, or an examination in relation to any endorsement, condition or waiver may include,

(a) an examination of the person's knowledge of the Act and the regulations under it;

(b) a demonstration of the person's ability to drive safely a motor vehicle of a class authorized to be driven by the class of licence applied for or held;

(c) a demonstration of the person's ability to operate safely a motor vehicle of a class authorized to be driven by the class of licence applied for and that is equipped with air brakes, or a combination of such a motor vehicle and towed vehicles;

(d) an examination of a person's knowledge of air brakes, their functions and safe operation for the class of licence applied for or held; and

(e) medical and physical examinations, tests and procedures to determine the person's fitness to drive or to determine whether the person meets the qualifications prescribed by section 14, 17, 18, 21.1 or 21.2.

(1.1) It is a condition of a driver's licence that the holder submit to the examinations required under subsection (1) at such times as the Minister may require.

(2) An examination under subsection (1) may include the applicable level 2 exit test in the case of a person fully licensed to operate a Class G or M motor vehicle or in the case of an applicant for a Class G or M driver's licence or a driving instructor's licence.

(3) The applicable level 2 exit test may be taken in a Class G motor vehicle, including one equipped with air brakes, in the case of any person fully licensed to operate a Class G vehicle.

(4) If an examination referred to in this section includes a demonstration of the person's ability to drive safely a motor vehicle, the applicant shall be deemed to be fully licensed in that class of vehicle for the purpose of the examination.

(5) Where the horizontal visual field of a driver is to be determined under an examination conducted pursuant to clause (1)(e),

(a) it shall be measured without the aid of extraordinary optical devices that enhance or modify vision or that interfere with the horizontal visual field, such as telescopic lenses, prism lenses or sidebar prisms;

(b) the visual field representation must include the central visual fixation point at its centre;

(c) the continuous horizontal visual field shall not include the natural blind spot; and

(d) the continuous degrees of the horizontal visual field that are required above and below fixation shall be continuous throughout the required continuous degrees along the horizontal meridian.
O. Reg. 490/98, s. 1; 83/05, s. 8; 205/10, s. 8; 42/12, s. 2

16. The Minister may require that,

(a) any holder of a Class G or M driver's licence who has reached the age of 80 complete successfully the applicable examinations prescribed in section 15 every two years and demonstrate every two years that he or she continues to meet the qualifications prescribed in section 14;

(b) any holder of a driver's licence who has reached the age of 70 and is involved in an accident complete successfully the applicable examinations prescribed in section 15 and demonstrate that he or she continues to meet the qualifications prescribed in section 14;

(c) any holder of a Class A, B, C, D, E or F driver's licence who has reached the age of 65 but has not yet reached the age of 80 and is involved in an accident or accumulates more than two demerit points complete successfully the applicable examinations prescribed in section 15 and demonstrate that he or she continues to meet the qualifications prescribed in section 14;

(d) any holder of a Class A, B, C, E or F driver's licence who is under the age of 46 complete successfully the examination prescribed in clause 15(1)(a) every five years and demonstrate every five years that he or she continues to meet the qualifications prescribed in section 14;

(e) any holder of a Class A, B, C, E or F driver's licence who has reached the age of 46 but has not yet reached the age of 65 complete successfully the examination prescribed in clause 15(1)(a) every five years and demonstrate every three years that he or she continues to meet the qualifications prescribed in section 14;

(f) any holder of a Class A, B, C, E or F driver's licence who has reached the age of 65 but has not yet reached the age of 80 complete successfully the examination prescribed in clause 15(1)(a) every five years and demonstrate every year that he or she continues to meet the qualifications prescribed in section 14;

(g) any holder of a Class D driver's licence who has reached the age of 65 but has not yet reached the age of 80 complete successfully the examination prescribed in clause 15(1)(a) every five years and demonstrate every five years that he or she continues to meet the qualifications prescribed in subsection 18(3);

(h) any holder of a Class A, B, C, D, E or F driver's licence who has reached the age of 80 complete successfully the applicable examinations prescribed in section 15 every year and demonstrate every year that he or she continues to meet the qualifications prescribed in section 14; and

(i) any holder of a driver's licence with an air brake endorsement complete successfully the examinations prescribed in clauses 15(1)(c) and (d),

   (i) at any time that he or she is required under any of clauses (a) to (h) to take an examination prescribed in clause 15(1)(a) or (b), or

   (ii) every five years.
                     O. Reg. 484/96, s. 1; 304/00, s. 1; 305/04, s. 1; 453/10, s. 2; 251/12, s. 2

17. An applicant for or a holder of a Class B, C, E or F driver's licence whose hearing in one ear is better than in the other must be able to perceive in the better ear, with or without a hearing aid, a forced whisper at a distance of 1.5 metres or, if an audiometer is used to test the person's hearing, must not have a loss in the better ear of more than 40 decibels at 500, 1,000 and 2,000 hertz.
                     O. Reg. 83/05, s. 9; 453/10, s. 3

18. (1) An applicant for or a holder of a Class M, M1 or M2 driver's licence must have,

   (a) a visual acuity as measured by Snellen Rating that is not poorer than 20/50, with both eyes open and examined together with or without the aid of corrective lenses; and

   (b) a horizontal visual field of at least 120 continuous degrees along the horizontal meridian and at least 15 continuous degrees above and below fixation, with both eyes open and examined together.

(2) An applicant for or a holder of a Class G, G1 or G2 driver's licence must have,

   (a) a visual acuity as measured by Snellen Rating that is not poorer than 20/50 with both eyes open and examined together with or without the aid of corrective lenses; and

(b) a horizontal visual field of at least 120 continuous degrees along the horizontal meridian and at least 15 continuous degrees above and below fixation, with both eyes open and examined together.

(3) An applicant for or a holder of a Class A, B, C, D, E or F driver's licence must have,

(a) a visual acuity as measured by Snellen Rating that is not poorer than 20/30 with both eyes open and examined together and not poorer than 20/100 in the weaker eye, with or without the aid of corrective lenses; and

(b) a horizontal visual field of at least 150 continuous degrees along the horizontal meridian and at least 20 continuous degrees above and below fixation, with both eyes open and examined together.

O. Reg. 83/05, s. 10; 453/10, s. 4

19. The examinations and qualifications required of an applicant for or a holder of a driver's licence by sections 14, 16 and 17, subsection 18(1), clause 18(2)(a), subsection 18(3) and sections 21.1 and 21.2 apply despite the *Human Rights Code*.

O. Reg. 83/05, s. 11; 453/10, s. 5

20. If the Minister waived under this section any of the qualifications set out in section 17, as this section and section 17 read before January 1, 2011, with respect to an applicant for or a holder of any class of driver's licence, the Minister may renew the waiver of those qualifications for the holder requesting a renewal of his or her licence, as if those qualifications still applied to the holder, if,

(a) the holder provides evidence satisfactory to the Minister, including the reports of any examinations which the Minister may require, that he or she can safely drive motor vehicles in the class authorized to be driven by the class of licence for which a renewal has been applied; and

(b) there has been no worsening of the condition that would have disqualified the holder had the waiver not been granted.

O. Reg. 453/10, s. 6

21. [Repealed O. Reg. 453/10, s. 7.]

21.1 If the Minister waived under this section a qualification set out in clause 17(1)(j) or (k), as this section and as those clauses read before January 1, 2011, for an applicant for or a holder of a Class A or D driver's licence, the Minister may renew the waiver of the qualification set out in clause 18(3)(a) or (b), as applicable, for the holder requesting a renewal of his or her licence if,

(a) the holder can safely drive motor vehicles in the class authorized to be driven by the class of licence for which a renewal is requested;

(b) there is no worsening of the condition that would have disqualified the holder had the prior waiver not been granted;

(c) the holder provides evidence that he or she has successfully completed the tests, procedures and examinations that the Minister may require to demonstrate that the conditions in clauses (a) and (b) are satisfied; and

(d) the holder does not have a medical condition or disability that requires a Ministerial waiver from the qualifications for obtaining any class of driver's licence prescribed in the Act or the regulations other than the waiver under this section.

O. Reg. 306/96, s. 1; 578/98, s. 1; 83/05, s. 12; 453/10, s. 8

21.2 (1) The Minister may waive the qualification set out in clause 18(2)(b) for an applicant for or a holder of a Class G, G1 or G2 driver's licence if,

(a) the applicant or holder provides evidence that he or she has successfully completed the tests, procedures and examinations that the Minister may require; and

(b) the applicant or holder,

(i) meets all of the other qualifications set out in this Regulation for the applicable class of driver's licence,

(ii) has not been able to meet the qualification set out in clause 18(2)(b) for a period of at least three months immediately before the application,

(iii) does not have a medical or visual condition or disability that, alone or combined with a reduced horizontal visual field, may significantly impair his or her ability to drive, including,

(A) a neurological deficit or disorder, including epilepsy,

(B) diabetes that requires insulin for control,

(C) hypotension, or

(D) an impairment resulting from dementia, stroke, brain tumour, brain surgery, head trauma or arthritis,

(iv) does not have accumulated more than six demerit points on his or her driving record,

(v) did not have his or her driver's licence under suspension at any time within the preceding five years pursuant to section 53, subsection 128(15) or section 130, 172, 200 or 216 of the Act or as a result of a conviction under the *Criminal Code* (Canada) for an offence committed by means of a motor vehicle or while driving or having the care, charge or control of a motor vehicle, and

(vi) has not, within the preceding five years and within the period of time he or she has been unable to meet the requirements of clause 18(2)(b), been involved in a collision the circumstances of which also gave rise to a conviction for contravening or failing to comply with section 128, 136, 138, 140, 141, 147, 148, 154, 156, 158 or 172 or subsection 175(11) of the Act.

(2) The Minister may revoke a waiver given under subsection (1) at any time if the holder no longer meets the requirements of subclause (1)(b)(i), (iii), (iv), (v) or (vi).

(3) If the applicant's or holder's horizontal visual field is so fragmented or incomplete that the size, shape, nature or relative position of the defects in it or along the

754

horizontal meridian or above or below fixation may significantly impair his or her ability to drive, then the Minister shall not grant the waiver under this section.

O. Reg. 306/96, s. 1; 578/98, s. 2; 336/00, s. 1; 191/02, s. 1; 83/05, s. 13

22. Any class of driver's licence, except a Class G1, G2, M, M1 or M2 driver's licence, is authority for,

(a) a police officer or an officer appointed for carrying out the provisions of the Act to drive a motor vehicle of any class including a vehicle equipped with air brakes, other than a motorcycle, on a highway in an emergency and in the performance of his or her duties under the Act;

(a.1) a firefighter, as defined in subsection 1(1) of the *Fire Protection and Prevention Act, 1997*, to drive a motor vehicle of any class including a vehicle equipped with air brakes, other than a motorcycle, on a highway in an emergency and in the performance of his or her duties under that Act; and

(b) a motor vehicle mechanic to drive a motor vehicle of any class including a vehicle equipped with air brakes, other than a motorcycle, on a highway while carrying out a road test of the vehicle in the course of servicing it.

O. Reg. 115/03, s. 1; 83/05, s. 14

23. (1) Subject to subsection (3), a Class A, B, C, D, E, F or G driver's licence is authority to drive on a highway any motor vehicle other than a motorcycle for the purpose of receiving instruction in driving it, as long as a person who holds a driver's licence authorizing the person to drive the motor vehicle occupies a seat beside the driver for the purpose of giving him or her instruction.

(1.1) Subsection 2(6) does not apply to prevent a driver referred to in subsection (1) from receiving instruction in driving a motor vehicle equipped with air brakes for the purpose of obtaining an air brake endorsement.

(1.2) The driver's licence of a person who is giving instruction to a driver in the circumstances described in subsection (1) must bear an air brake endorsement if the motor vehicle is equipped with air brakes.

(1.3) A person may give instruction to a driver in the circumstances described in subsection (1) if the person holds a class of licence equivalent to a Class A, B, C, D, E, F or G driver's licence that is issued by another province or territory of Canada of which the person is a resident and that authorizes the person to drive the motor vehicle in which instruction is being given, including an equivalent air brake endorsement if the motor vehicle is equipped with air brakes.

(2) A Class M or M2 driver's licence is authority to drive on a highway any motor vehicle of a class that may be driven by a holder of a Class G1 driver's licence for the purpose of receiving instruction in driving it, and section 5 applies.

(3) It is a condition attaching to every licence that the holder, while receiving instruction in driving a bus, not drive the bus on a highway while the bus is carrying passengers other than passengers who are giving or receiving instruction in driving it.

O. Reg. 75/95, s. 1; 110/08, s. 3

23.1 A driver's licence, other than a class G1, G2, M1 or M2 driver's licence, may be renewed for a specified period of not less than 12 months and not more than 84 months after the expiry date shown on the licence.

O. Reg. 484/96, s. 2

24. (1) The Minister or any person authorized by the Minister may issue to an applicant for a driver's licence a temporary licence valid for up to 90 days permitting him or her to drive a motor vehicle in the class shown on the temporary licence while the Ministry is investigating and assessing the application.

(1.1) [Revoked O. Reg. 94/98, s. 1.]

(2) The Minister or any person authorized by the Minister may issue a temporary Class B or E driver's licence for a period of 90 days to an applicant who, although not meeting the requirements of paragraph 1 of subsection 13(1), is otherwise qualified for such a licence, and may reissue it for a further period of 90 days.

(3) Despite subsection (1), the Minister or any person authorized by the Minister may not issue a temporary Class B or E driver's licence to an applicant who is otherwise qualified for such a licence for a period exceeding 45 days while the Ministry is investigating whether the applicant meets the requirements of subsection 13(2).

(4) Despite subsection (1), the Minister or any person authorized by the Minister may issue a temporary driver's licence for a period of up to six months to the holder of an Ontario driver's licence who may be out of the Province and is required to appear in person in order to satisfy licence renewal requirements and cannot return prior to the expiry of the driver's licence.

(5) A temporary driver's licence issued under this section expires upon the issue or refusal of a driver's licence or the expiry date of the temporary licence, whichever occurs first.

O. Reg. 416/97, s. 1; 94/98, s. 1

25. The Minister may impose conditions on a driver's licence appropriate to the holder's driving ability in respect of the type of motor vehicle and the special mechanical control devices required on any motor vehicle that the holder may drive, or such other conditions as are appropriate to ensure that the holder drives the motor vehicle safely.

25.1 A decision made by the Minister under subclause 32(5)(b)(i) of the Act is prescribed as a kind of decision a person may appeal under section 50 of the Act.

O. Reg. 205/10, s. 9

26. (1) The following fees shall be paid:

 1. For a Class A, B, C, D, E or F driver's road test **85.00**

 2. For a Class A, B, C, E or F driver's road test for drivers having attained the age of 65 years or over **14.00**

 3. For a level 2 Class G2 or M2 driver's road test **85.00**

 4. For a level 1 Class G1 or M1 road test **50.00**

5. For an air brake endorsement practical test 50.00

5.1 [Repealed O. Reg. 575/05, s. 1(1).]

6. For an examination of a person's knowledge of the Act and the regulations under it 15.00

6.1 [Repealed O. Reg. 575/05, s. 1(1).]

7. For an application for the replacement of a driver's licence 28.00

Proposed Amendment — 26(1), para. 7

7. For an application for the replacement of a driver's licence 31.00
O. Reg. 257/15, s. 1(1) [To come into force January 1, 2017.]

7.1 [Repealed O. Reg. 575/05, s. 1(1).]

8. For information on whether a specific driver's licence is valid, together with verification of such information,

    i. if the information is requested and given on the telephone 2.50

    ii. if the information is requested and given on the Internet 2.00

8.1 [Repealed O. Reg. 575/05, s. 1(1).]

9. For each search of driver records by driver licence number or name of driver 12.00

10. For a copy of any writing, paper or document filed in the Ministry or any statement containing information from the records 6.00

11. For certification of a copy of any writing, paper or document filed in the Ministry or any statement containing information from the records ... 6.00

11.1 [Repealed O. Reg. 575/05, s. 1(1).]

12. For each six-month period or part thereof during which a driver's licence is valid 6.65

12.1 [Repealed O. Reg. 575/05, s. 1(1).]

13. [Repealed O. Reg. 575/05, s. 1(1).]

14. [Repealed O. Reg. 575/05, s. 1(1).]

15. [Repealed O. Reg. 575/05, s. 1(1).]

16. [Repealed O. Reg. 575/05, s. 1(1).]

(1.0.1) [Repealed O. Reg. 74/11, s. 1(1).]

(1.0.2) The fee for a test under paragraph 1, 2, 3, 4 or 5 of subsection (1) is due when the test is booked and is payable even if the time booked for taking the test passes without the test being taken.

(1.1) A fee described in subsection (1.4) is payable to the Ministry for the reinstatement of a driver's licence that was suspended for any of the following reasons:

1. A conviction under the Act or a regulation.

2. The default in payment of a fine for a conviction referred to in section 46 of the Act.

3. An unsatisfied judgment, as permitted under section 198 of the Act.

4. The accumulation of demerit points, as prescribed under the *Demerit Point Regulation*.

5. A conviction under the *Criminal Code* (Canada).

6. A payment out of the Motor Vehicle Accident Claims Fund under subsection 4(4) or 10(1) of the *Motor Vehicle Accident Claims Act*, a default in repayment of an amount owing to the Fund under subsection 4(8) or 11(3) of that Act, including a failure to satisfy the proof of financial responsibility condition of the restoration of a licence under the regulations made under section 11 of that Act.

7. An unpaid support order that was made under the *Family Responsibility and Support Arrears Enforcement Act, 1996*.

8. A conviction under the *Compulsory Automobile Insurance Act*.

(1.2) Despite subsection (1.1), no fee is payable if a reinstatement is made following a suspension resulting from a conviction referred to in that subsection and an appeal of the conviction is filed; however, the fee is payable if the conviction is sustained on appeal.

(1.3) The fee is payable only once for a reinstatement of a licence that has more than one suspension recorded against it at the same time for any of the reasons set out in subsection (1.1).

(1.4) The fee payable under subsection (1.1) is,

    (a) $150 if the suspension commenced on or before June 30, 2015 and,

        (i) is not extended after that date by a subsequent suspension, or

        (ii) the holder is not subject after that date to a provision of the Act that would impose a suspension if the licence were not already suspended;

    (b) $180 if the suspension commenced on or before June 30, 2015 and,

        (i) is extended after that date by a subsequent suspension, or

        (ii) the holder is subject after that date to a provision of the Act that would impose a suspension if the licence were not already suspended;

    (c) $180 if the suspension commenced on or after July 1, 2015.

(2) Despite subsection (1), there is no fee for a driver's re-examination required in the following circumstances:

1. The driver has reached the age of 80.

2. The driver has reached the age of 70 and has been requested under clause 15(1)(b) or subsection 15(2) to demonstrate his or her ability to operate a motor vehicle.

3. The driver suffers from a reported medical condition and has been requested to take a re-examination by the Minister.

4. In the case of a pilot field test, the Ministry may waive the fee for a retest.

(3) The fee for a Class A, B, C, D, E or F road test and an air brake endorsement practical test is the fee set out in paragraph 1 or 2 of subsection (1), as the case may be.

(4) A fee paid under subsection (1.0.2) for a test described in any of paragraphs 1 to 5 of subsection (1) for a test that was not taken is not refundable except as follows:

1. The fee may be fully refunded or fully credited towards a subsequent fee payable by the individual for a test described in subsection (1) within the same licence class or for the same endorsement as the test the individual failed to take if the applicant provides notice or reason satisfactory to the Minister.

2. Half of the fee may be refunded or credited towards a subsequent fee payable by the individual for a test described in subsection (1) within the same licence class or for the same endorsement if the individual attended the test, but failed to take the test because the vehicle to be used by the individual in the test was considered by the Minister to be unsatisfactory for use in a road test.

3. Half of the fee may be refunded or credited towards a subsequent fee payable by the individual for a test described in subsection (1) within the same licence class or for the same endorsement if the individual attended the test, but failed to take or complete the test because a person authorized by the Minister to make such determination determined that the test could not be taken or completed.

(5) Subsection (1) does not apply to,

(a) the Governor General;

(b) the Lieutenant Governor;

(c) a representative of a foreign government who has taken a post in Ontario in the capacity of,

(i) ambassador, high commissioner or chargé d'affaires,

(ii) head of delegation or head of office,

(iii) minister-counsellor or minister,

(iv) counsellor,

(v) first, second or third secretary,

(vi) attaché,

(vii) military, air or naval attaché or advisor,

(viii) assistant military, air or naval attaché or advisor,

(ix) consul-general, consul, vice-consul or consular agent;

(d) the spouse or child of a representative referred to in clause (c);

(e) a person serving or employed on the technical staff of a diplomatic or consular mission or high commission as long as the person,

(i) is authorized as eligible for exempt status by the Department of Foreign Affairs and International Trade of Canada,

(ii) is not a Canadian citizen or permanent resident of Canada as defined in the *Immigration and Refugee Protection Act* (Canada), and

(iii) is assigned to duty from the foreign government being represented and not engaged locally by the mission or commission; or

(f) a representative of an international organization who has taken a post in Ontario and,

(i) is authorized as eligible for exempt status by the Department of Foreign Affairs and International Trade of Canada,

(ii) is not a Canadian citizen or permanent resident of Canada as defined in the *Immigration and Refugee Protection Act* (Canada),

(iii) is assigned to duty from the international organization being represented and not engaged locally by the organization;

(g) the spouse or child of any person in clause (f) as long as the spouse or child meets the requirements set out in subclause (f)(ii).

O. Reg. 484/96, s. 3; 251/97, s. 1; 19/98, s. 1; 460/98, s. 1; 633/98, s. 1; 89/00, s. 2; 207/04, s. 1; 355/05, s. 2; 575/05, s. 1; 205/10, s. 10; 74/11, s. 1; 42/12, s. 3; 169/12, s. 1; 242/13, s. 1; 246/14, s. 1; 257/15, s. 1(2)

26.0.1 (1) A recognized authority shall pay a fee of $20 to the Ministry for the Ministry to enrol a driver trainee in the Ontario Driver Certification Program.

(2) The fee to enrol a driver trainee is due and payable when the recognized authority submits to the Ministry the results of examinations of the driver trainee under the Ontario Driver Certification Program.

(3) Despite subsection (1), there is no enrolment fee payable with respect to a driver trainee if the driver trainee does not successfully complete the training and testing under the Ontario Driver Certification Program.

(4) For the purposes of this section,

"Ontario Driver Certification Program" means the Ontario Driver Certification Program administered by the Ministry, under which the Ministry,

(a) monitors the training and testing of driver trainees by recognized authorities, and

(b) recognizes the results of examinations of driver trainees under section 15 that are submitted to the Ministry by recognized authorities;

"recognized authority" means a corporation or other entity that is recognized by the Ministry as competent to both train and test driver trainees under the Ontario Driver Certification Program.

O. Reg. 246/14, s. 2

FEE ADJUSTMENT — CONSUMER PRICE INDEX

[Heading added O. Reg. 169/12, s. 2.]

26.1 (1) Beginning on September 1, 2014, and on every September 1 after that, the fees prescribed in paragraphs 1, 3, 4 and 6 of subsection 26(1) are the fees for the previous 12-month period adjusted by the percentage change in the Ontario Consumer Price Index between the previous two calendar years.

(2) The actual fees prescribed in paragraphs 1, 3, 4 and 6 of subsection 26(1) are the amounts determined by the calculation described in subsection (1) rounded to the nearest quarter of a dollar.

(3) If the percentage change in the Ontario Consumer Price Index between the previous two calendar years results in a negative amount, the fees prescribed in paragraphs 1, 3, 4 and 6 of subsection 26(1) shall remain at the same level as the previous year.

(4) In this section, the percentage change in the Ontario Consumer Price Index between two calendar years is the percentage change in the Consumer Price Index for Ontario (All-Items) between those years as published by Statistics Canada under the authority of the *Statistics Act* (Canada).

O. Reg. 169/12, s. 2

PENALTIES

[Heading added O. Reg. 169/12, s. 3.]

27. (1) A person shall pay a penalty of 10 per cent of the amount owing if,

(a) the person purports to pay by cheque, whether separately or together with another payment, a fee payable under this Regulation and the payment is dishonoured;

(b) the person fails to pay the amount owing within 30 days after the date of a letter from the Ministry informing him or her that the payment was dishonoured; and

(c) the amount of the payment is $50 or more.

(2) Subsection (1) does not apply if an equal penalty is payable with respect to the same payment under the authority of another regulation made under the Act.

NOVICE DRIVERS' LICENCES

28. (1) A person who resides in Ontario but who has never held an Ontario driver's licence may only apply for a Class G1 or M1 driver's licence, unless the person is licensed in another jurisdiction and either meets the requirements set out in Ontario Regulation 341/94 for an exchange licence or is wholly or partially exempted under section 29.

(2) A qualified applicant shall be issued a Class G1 driver's licence valid for a period of five years.

(3) A qualified applicant shall be issued a Class M1 driver's licence valid for a period of 90 days.

(4) A novice driver shall hold a valid driver's licence for a minimum period in each novice level before becoming eligible to advance to the next highest level, as follows:

1. In the case of Class G1 and G2, 365 days.

2. In the case of Class M1, 60 days.

3. In the case of Class M2, 670 days.

(5) If a Class G1 driver successfully completes a Ministry-approved driver education course and provides evidence of that fact satisfactory to the Minister, the minimum period of 365 days referred to in paragraph 1 of subsection (4) as it applies to Class G1 is reduced to 245 days.

(6) If a Class M1 or M2 driver successfully completes a Ministry-approved motorcycle training course and provides evidence satisfactory of that fact to the Minister, the minimum period of 670 days referred to in paragraph 3 of subsection (4) is reduced to 550 days.

(7) A person who has been issued a Class M1 driver's licence and who has completed a Ministry-approved motorcycle training course offered by a municipal police force or the Ontario Provincial Police is not required to take a Ministry-conducted level 1 exit test under clause 15(1) (b) and, despite paragraph 2 of subsection (4) and subsection (13), is immediately eligible,

  (a) to obtain a Class M2 driver's licence; and

  (b) to take the Ministry-conducted level 2 exit test under clause 15(1)(b).

(7.1) A person to whom a Class M2 driver's licence is issued under subsection (7) must hold the Class M2 licence for the period of time required by subsection (6) before obtaining his or her Class M driver's licence but, despite subsection (13), is not required to take the level 2 exit test again after the expiry of the period of time required by subsection (6) in order to obtain a Class M driver's licence.

(8) A person who has been issued a Class M1 driver's licence and who has completed a Ministry-approved motorcycle training course offered by an organization other than a municipal police force or the Ontario Provincial Police is not required to take a Ministry-conducted level 1 exit test under clause 15(1)(b) in order to obtain a Class M2 driver's licence.

(9) For the purpose of a reduction under subsection (5) or (6), a certificate obtained on successful completion of a driver education or motorcycle training course is valid for two years from the date of issue of the course certificate.

(10) For the purpose of an exemption from the level 1 exit test under subsection (7) or (8), or for the right under subsection (7) to take the level 2 exit test at an earlier date than required by subsection (13), the certificate obtained on successful completion of a motorcycle training course is valid for up to six months from the date of issue of the course certificate.

(10.1) A person who applies for a Class M1 driver's licence before November 28, 2008, held a valid driver's licence at any time between November 27, 2002 and November 28, 2005 and satisfies the Ministry that he or she was an experienced driver of a motor assisted bicycle for which a valid permit had been issued is exempt from the requirement in paragraph 2 of subsection (4) and is immediately eligible to take the level 1 exit test under clause 15(1)(b).

(11) A novice driver who holds a Class G1 or M1 driver's licence for the period of time required under this section and whose licence is currently valid may take the applicable level 1 exit test.

(12) A novice driver who successfully completes the applicable test under subsection (11) shall be issued, as applicable, a Class G2 driver's licence valid for the remainder of the five-year period for which the Class G1 licence was valid or a Class M2 licence valid for a period of five years.

(13) A novice driver who holds a Class G2 or M2 driver's licence for the period of time required under this section and whose licence is currently valid may take the applicable level 2 exit test.

(14) A driver who successfully completes the applicable test under subsection (13) shall be issued, as applicable, a Class G or M driver's licence for the remainder of the period for which the Class G2 or M2 driver's licence was valid.

(15) A driver who holds a Class G1 driver's licence may requalify within the six-month period prior to the five year licence expiry date, and every five years thereafter, by taking the applicable examinations set out in clause 15(1)(a) or, if eligible, may qualify as a Class G2 driver by taking the applicable examinations set out in clause 15(1)(b).

(16) A driver who holds a Class G2 driver's licence after first obtaining a Class G1 driver's licence, or if issued a Class G2 driver's licence initially on application, may requalify within the six-month period prior to the five year expiry date of the licence, and every five years thereafter, by taking the applicable examinations set out in clause 15(1)(b) or, if eligible, may qualify as a Class G driver by taking the applicable examinations set out in subsection 15(2).

(17) A driver who holds a Class M2 driver's licence may requalify within the six-month period prior to the five year licence expiry date, and every five years thereafter, by taking the applicable examinations set out in clause 15(1)(b) or, if eligible, may qualify as a Class M driver by taking the applicable examinations set out in subsection 15(2).

(18) A driver who successfully completes the applicable requalification examinations within 12 months prior to the expiry of the requalification period is not required to take them again in order to requalify.

(19) A Class G1, G2 or M2 driver's licence is not renewable except in accordance with subsections (15), (16), (17) and (18).

(20) A Class M1 driver's licence is not renewable but it may be stamped valid for the date of a road test that is after the licence's expiry date if the holder makes the appointment for the test before the expiry of the licence.

O. Reg. 727/94, s. 1; 83/05, s. 15; 176/05, s. 1; 597/05, s. 3

29. (1) A driver of a motor vehicle, other than a motorcycle or a motor assisted bicycle, on a highway shall be classed as a novice driver in Class G1 or G2 unless he or she,

(a) is a fully licensed driver who has held at any time in the last three years a valid driver's licence, other than a Class G1, G2, M, M1 or M2 driver's licence, issued under the Act;

(b) is the equivalent of a fully licensed driver in Ontario, other than in Class M, and has held for at least 24 months in the last three years a valid driver's licence, other than a driver's licence equivalent to a Class M1 or M2 driver's licence, issued by,

> (i) another province or territory of Canada, Canada Forces Europe, a state of the United States of America or Japan, or

> (ii) a jurisdiction which is a party to a valid and subsisting agreement with Ontario respecting the reciprocal exchange of driver's licences; or

(c) is a member or former member of the Canadian Armed Forces who meets the requirements of section 6 of Ontario Regulation 341/94 (*Driver Licence Examinations*) made under the Act.

(2) A driver of a motorcycle on a highway shall be classed as a novice driver in Class M1 or M2 unless he or she,

(a) has held at any time in the last three years a valid driver's licence in Class M issued under the Act; or

(b) is the equivalent of a fully licensed driver in Ontario in Class M and has held for at least 24 months in the last three years a valid driver's licence in a class equivalent to Class M, M1 or M2 issued by another province or territory of Canada, a state of the United States of America or Canada Forces Europe.

(3) Despite subsections (1) and (2), the period of time during which an equivalent licence must be held under those subsections may be reduced by the period of time that the driver held the equivalent of a Class G1 driver's licence, to a maximum of 12 months, and by the period of time that the driver held the equivalent of a Class M1 driver's licence, to a maximum of 60 days.

(4) A driver classed as a novice driver under subsection (1) or (2) shall remain classed in the applicable novice driver class until the driver has successfully completed a level 1 or level 2 exit test, as the case may be, for the applicable class of vehicle and has met any other requirements under this Regulation.

(5) Subsections (1) to (4) do not apply to,

(a) the Governor General;

(b) the Lieutenant Governor;

(c) a representative of a foreign government who has taken a post in Ontario in the capacity of,

> (i) ambassador, high commission or chargé d'affaires,

> (ii) head of delegation or head of office,

> (iii) minister-counsellor or minister,

> (iv) counsellor,

> (v) first, second or third secretary,

> (vi) attaché,

> (vii) military, air or naval attaché or advisor,

> (viii) assistant military, air or naval attaché or advisor,

> (ix) consul-general, consul, vice-consul or consular agent;

(d) the spouse of a representative referred to in clause (c);

(e) Canadian counterparts of the persons referred to in clauses (c) and (d) who return to Canada as residents of Ontario from assigned duty abroad;

(f) a person who is a resident of any province or territory of Canada, other than Ontario, or of another country or state and who holds a valid driver's licence in accordance with the laws of that province, country or state.

(6) An applicant for a driver's licence who was previously licensed in Ontario more than three years but less than ten years before the time of application and provides evidence satisfactory to the Minister of that fact shall be classed as a novice driver but shall be exempt from the prescribed time limits on eligibility to take the level 1 and 2 exit tests.

(7) Subject to subsection (3), any driver who has held for less than 24 months in the last three years before the time of application a valid driver's licence issued by a jurisdiction described in subclause (1)(b)(i) or (ii) shall be entitled to a credit for the period of time he or she held the licence and shall qualify for placement in level 2 without the necessity of a level 1 exit test.

(8) A driver under subsection (7) may take a level 2 exit test upon holding a licence for two years and the period of licensed time referred to in subsection (7) may be included as part of that two-year period.

(9) An applicant for a driver's licence who has not held a licence in the applicable licence class for at least 24 months within the last three years shall be credited with the length of time he or she has held a driver's licence within that period toward the length of time the driver is classed as a novice driver and toward the prescribed time limits on eligibility to take the level 1 and 2 exit tests if the applicant provides evidence satisfactory to the Minister that he or she is from a jurisdiction other than Ontario or one referred to in clause (1)(b) or (2)(b) and of the length of time during which he or she held the licence.

(10) An applicant for a driver's licence may take the applicable level 2 exit test without being subject to the prescribed time limits if the applicant provides evidence satisfactory to the Minister that he or she is from a jurisdiction other than Ontario or one referred to in clause (1)(b) or (2)(b) and has held a driver's licence in the applicable licence class for at least 24 months in the last three years.

(11) [Repealed O. Reg. 83/05, s. 16(3).]

(12) An applicant referred to in subsection (10) who does not complete the level 2 exit test successfully on the first attempt must take and successfully complete the level 1 and 2 exit tests but shall be exempt from the prescribed time limits on eligibility to take the tests.

(13) Upon successful completion of the level 2 exit test, the applicant shall be issued a Class G or M driver's licence, as applicable, if all other requirements have been met.

O. Reg. 671/98, s. 1; 89/00, s. 3; 337/00, s. 1; 83/05, s. 16; 355/05, s. 3; 205/10, s. 11; 145/15, s. 2

30. (1) The Minister or any person authorized by the Minister may issue,

(a) a temporary Class G1 driver's licence, for a period of up to 90 days;

(b) a temporary Class G2 or M2 driver's licence, for a period of up to 365 days.

(2) A temporary licence under subsection (1) may not be issued for a period beyond the day on which the licence holder is scheduled to take a road test if, on the day he or she schedules the test, he or she holds a Class G1, G2 or M2 driver's licence and the applicable licence expires prior to the day of the road test.

O. Reg. 494/99, s. 1; 83/05, s. 17

NOVICE CONDITIONS: RESIDENTS OF THE JAMES BAY AREA

31. [Repealed O. Reg. 83/05, s. 18.]

32. [Repealed O. Reg. 83/05, s. 18.]

REMEDIAL PROGRAMS AND REQUIREMENTS TO REINSTATE SUSPENDED DRIVERS' LICENCES

32.1 (1) A person whose driver's licence has been suspended under clauses 41(1)(a), (b), (d) or (e) of the Act shall attend an interview with an official of the Ministry before his or her driver's licence may be reinstated.

(2) As a result of the interview, the Ministry may require that the person successfully complete one or more remedial education or training programs for the purpose of improving his or her ability to drive safely.

(3) This section does not apply if the person is required to participate in a remedial measures conduct review program under Ontario Regulation 287/08 (*Remedial Measures Conduct Review Program For Drivers Suspended for Certain Offences related to Impaired Driving*) made under the Act.

O. Reg. 490/98, s. 2; 288/08, s. 1

32.2 The Registrar shall not reduce the period of suspension and reinstate the driver's licence of a person whose driver's licence has been suspended indefinitely under clause 41(1)(h) of the Act for a second subsequent conviction unless the Registrar is satisfied that the person,

(a) has successfully completed the remedial program or programs he or she is required to complete under subsection 32.1(2) or under Ontario Regulation 287/08 (*Remedial Measures Conduct Review Program For Drivers Suspended for Certain Offences related to Impaired Driving*) made under the Act;

(b) has successfully completed any examinations under clause 15(1)(e) that he or she is required to complete pursuant to subsection 32(5) of the Act;

(c) has not pleaded guilty or been found guilty or convicted under a provision referred to in subsection 42(1) of the Act during the ten-year period immediately before applying for a reduction in the period of the suspension and reinstatement of his or her driver's licence; and

(d) has not contravened the suspension during the ten-year period immediately before applying for a reduction in the period of the suspension and reinstatement of his or her driver's licence.

O. Reg. 490/98, s. 2; 288/08, s. 1

32.3–32.11 [Repealed O. Reg. 288/08, s. 1.]

MISCELLANEOUS

33. (1) The holder of a driver's licence who changes his or her address shall, within six days after the change, send by registered mail or have filed with the Ministry a notice in writing, or electronically in a format designated by the Ministry, of the change giving the former address, the present address and the number of his or her driver's licence.

(2) The holder of a driver's licence who changes his or her name shall, within six days after the change, provide evidence satisfactory to the Minister of the change of name.

(3) [Repealed O. Reg. 205/10, s. 12.]

O. Reg. 205/10, s. 12

34. It is a condition of every driver's licence that the holder's signature be written in ink in the appropriate place on the licence.

35. Regulation 585 of the Revised Regulations of Ontario, 1990 and Ontario Regulations 317/91, 706/92, 402/93, 819/93, 193/94 and 194/94 are revoked.

36. This Regulation comes into force on June 6, 1994.

ONT. REG. 499/94 — ELECTRONIC DOCUMENTS [REPEALED]

made under the *Highway Traffic Act*

O. Reg. 499/94, as am. O. Reg. 77/11.

[Note: Electronic Documents *repealed by O. Reg. 77/11, s. 1.]*

1. In this Regulation, "electronic document" means any statement, document or record filed in the Ministry that is maintained in an electronic format and includes any such statement, document or record that,

(a) is a copy of another electronic document, or

(b) has been transferred into an electronic format from any paper or written format.

2. An electronic document is properly made if the information set out in the document can be examined or retrieved in an intelligible form by electronic means.

3. (1) An electronic document that is a copy is properly made if the copy accurately reproduces the information set out in the document even if the copy displays the information differently from the way the information is displayed in the document.

(2) An electronic document that is a copy may encrypt, summarize, reformat or compress the information set out in the document if the copy displays the information accurately when the copy is examined or retrieved by electronic means.

4. An electronic document is properly certified and sealed if the document, or the electronic transmission of which it forms a part,

(a) originates in the Ministry;

(b) states that the information set out in the document has been obtained from Ministry records; and

(c) bears the signature of the Registrar under the seal of the Ministry.

5. (1) An electronic document is properly filed in the Ministry if the transmission of which the document forms a part is completely and accurately received and recorded in an electronic format.

(2) An electronic document is properly filed in a court if,

(a) the document is made, certified and sealed in accordance with this Regulation; and

(b) the information required by Form 1 of Ontario Regulation 500/94 is completely and accurately received and recorded such that it can be examined or retrieved in an intelligible form by electronic means.

6. (1) An electronic document may be printed by any means that produces the document on paper.

(2) In an electronic document or a printed copy of an electronic document, the seal of the Ministry may be represented by an asterisk.

(3) A printed copy of an electronic document filed in a court shall be deemed to have been filed as the original document if it has been printed in accordance with Ontario Regulation 497/94.

7. This Regulation comes into force on the day the *Provincial Offences Statute Law Amendment Act, 1993* comes into force.

ONT. REG. 587 — EQUIPMENT

made under the *Highway Traffic Act*

R.R.O. 1990, Reg. 587, as am. O. Reg. 229/95; 276/99; 305/00; 115/08; 396/08; 375/09; 73/11.

BRAKES

1. [Repealed O. Reg. 73/11, s. 1.]

2. (1) Where the vehicle has a clutch, a brake test shall be made with the clutch disengaged.

(2) Where the vehicle has no clutch, a brake test shall be made without motive power being applied to the driving wheels, except in the case of electrical brakes.

O. Reg. 73/11, s. 2

3. (1) The brakes required by section 64 of the Act and this Regulation shall be adequate to stop the vehicle or combination of vehicles referred to in column 1 of the Table within a distance not greater than the distance set opposite the vehicle or combination of vehicles in column 2 while being operated at a rate of speed of

twenty miles per hour on a dry, smooth, hard asphalt or other paved surface free
from loose material and having not more than 1 per cent gradient.

	COLUMN 1	COLUMN 2
Item	Vehicle	Distance
1.	A motor vehicle having a seating capacity for less than 10 persons	25 feet
1.1	A motor tricycle	25 feet
2.	A motorcycle other than a motor tricycle	30 feet
3.	A commercial motor vehicle having a registered gross weight of 10,000 pounds or less	30 feet
4.	A commercial motor vehicle having a registered gross weight of more than 10,000 pounds	40 feet
5.	A combination of a motor vehicle and a trailer where the trailer has a gross weight of 3,000 pounds or less	40 feet
6.	A combination of a motor vehicle and a trailer where the trailer has a gross weight of more than 3,000 pounds or a combination of a motor vehicle and more than one trailer	50 feet
7.	A combination of a motor vehicle and a mobile home	50 feet

(2) A testing device that measures stopping distance based on peak deceleration
shall be used for the purposes of subsection (1).

O. Reg. 115/08, s. 1; 73/11, s. 3

4. Every mobile home when on a highway shall be equipped with brakes adequate to
stop and to hold the vehicle as required by this Regulation, and all such brakes and
braking systems shall be maintained in good working order.

5. (1) The push rod stroke of the service brake chamber of a vehicle equipped with
wheel brake air chambers shall be not more than the push rod stroke listed in Column 2 of the Schedule for the type of chamber listed in Column 1 of the Schedule if
the wheel brake has cam or disc type brakes.

(2) The push rod stroke of the service brake chamber of a vehicle equipped with
wheel brake air chambers shall be not more than the vehicle manufacturer's maximum push rod stroke if the brake chamber type does not appear in Column 1 of the
Schedule.

(3) If the wheel brakes of a vehicle equipped with wheel brake air chambers have
wedge type brakes, the combined movement of both brake shoe linings shall not
exceed one-eighth of an inch.

(4) Measurements of wheel brakes under subsections (1), (2) and (3) shall be taken with the vehicle engine turned off, an initial air system pressure between 90 and 100 psi, the park brakes released and the service brake actuator fully applied.

(5) All the wheels of a vehicle manufactured after April 30, 1995 that is equipped with wheel brake air chambers shall have wheel brakes each of which is automatically adjustable.

(6) Each wheel brake referred to in subsection (5) that is equipped with an external adjustment mechanism and has an exposed push rod shall have an indicator that indicates the condition of service brake under adjustment.

(7) The indicator referred to in subsection (6) must be visible to a person with 20/40 vision who is adjacent to or underneath the vehicle.

(8) No wheel brake shall be removed, rendered partly or wholly inoperable, modified so as to reduce its effectiveness or shall operate improperly.

(9) Brakes shall be adjusted so that the braking power is applied as equally as possible to the wheels on opposite sides of the vehicle.

(10) A motorcycle shall be equipped with two independently actuated service brake systems, one applying at least the front wheel brakes and the other applying at least the rear wheel brakes, unless the motorcycle was manufactured solely with a split-service brake system, within the meaning of Canada Motor Vehicle Safety Standard 122 of the *Motor Vehicle Safety Regulations* (Canada), and the split-service brake system,

    (a) met the requirements of that Standard at the time it was manufactured;

    (b) has a single actuator; and

    (c) has been maintained in its original condition.

O. Reg. 229/95, s. 1; 276/99, s. 1; 115/08, s. 2

REFLECTORS

6. A motor vehicle or trailer having a width in excess of eighty inches may display a reflector approved by the Ministry instead of a clearance lamp on the rear of the vehicle.

7. (1) A trailer shall be equipped with conspicuity markings as follows:

    1. On and after June 1, 2000 and before January 1, 2002, a trailer manufactured after December 1, 1993 whose overall width is greater than 2.05 metres and whose gross vehicle weight rating is greater than 4,500 kilograms shall be equipped with conspicuity markings in accordance with United States Federal Motor Vehicle Safety Standard 108 S. 5.7 that became effective on December 1, 1993 or with Canadian Motor Vehicle Safety Standard 108 that became effective on January 24, 1997.

    2. On and after January 1, 2002, every trailer whose overall width is greater than 2.05 metres and whose gross vehicle weight rating is greater than 4,500 kilograms shall be equipped with conspicuity markings in accordance with

United States Federal Motor Vehicle Safety Standard 108 S. 5.7 that became effective on December 1, 1993 or with Canadian Motor Vehicle Safety Standard 108 that became effective on January 24, 1997.

(2) Subsection (1) does not apply to a trailer designed exclusively for living or office use.

O. Reg. 229/95, s. 1; 305/00, s. 1

NON-APPLICATION OF SECTION 103 OF THE ACT

8. Subsection 103(1) of the Act does not apply to,

(a) a commercial motor vehicle, or a trailer drawn by it, registered in the name of or operated under any form of contract on behalf of,

(i) a department of a provincial government,

(ii) a department of the government of Canada,

(iii) a board or commission the members of which are appointed by the Governor General in Council or a Lieutenant Governor in Council,

(iv) a municipality,

(v) a board or commission the members of which are appointed by a municipality, or

(vi) a public service corporation, board or commission,

if the vehicle or trailer bears a mark or sign indicating ownership;

(b) a commercial motor vehicle registered in the name of or operated under any form of contract on behalf of a funeral director;

(c) a motor vehicle classified for registration purposes as a dual-purpose vehicle other than one licensed as a public vehicle or public truck;

(d) a commercial motor vehicle operated under a written lease or a written agreement for the exclusive use of a person other than the owner where the vehicle bears a mark or sign indicating ownership;

(e) a motor vehicle designed, equipped and used exclusively for living accommodation, commonly known as a motorized mobile home;

(f) a commercial motor vehicle to which is attached temporarily or permanently, a structure designed, used and maintained as a mobile dwelling unit commonly known as a camper; or

(g) a commercial motor vehicle having a registered gross weight of up to and including 18,000 pounds, other than one licensed as a public vehicle or a public truck.

NON-APPLICATION OF SECTION 78 OF THE ACT

9. [Repealed O. Reg. 375/09, s. 1.]

DAYTIME RUNNING LIGHT SYSTEMS

10. (1) No person shall sell or offer for sale a daytime running light system that does not conform to the requirements of the Canadian Standards Association Standard CAN/CSA-D603-88, Daytime Running Light Systems.

(2) For the purpose of subsection (1), a daytime running light system means a group of electrical components including the control unit designed for installation on a motor vehicle to automatically activate lights used to improve the conspicuity of the vehicle viewed from the front at all times other than when headlights are required.

11. (1) In this section,

"motor tricycle" means a motorcycle that,

(a) is designed to travel on three wheels in contact with the ground,

(b) has seating on which all occupants must sit astride,

(c) has not more than four designated seating positions,

(d) has a manufacturer's gross vehicle weight rating of 1,000 kilograms or less,

(e) has a minimum wheel rim diameter of 250 millimetres,

(f) has a minimum wheel base of 1,016 millimetres, and

(g) does not have a structure partially or fully enclosing the driver and passenger, other than that part of the vehicle forward of the driver's torso and the seat backrest.

(2) For the purpose of determining the number of wheels on a motorcycle, two wheels are considered to be one wheel if they are mounted on the same axle and the distance between the centres of their areas of contact with the ground is less than 460 millimetres.

(3) A motorcycle with two front wheels shall not be operated on the highway unless it is a motor tricycle that,

(a) bears the manufacturer's compliance label issued under section 6 of the *Motor Vehicle Safety Regulations* (Canada) specifying the type of vehicle as "TRI" for motor tricycle or, in the case of an imported motor tricycle, a compliance label or other label as provided for in section 12 of those Regulations; and

(b) continues to meet the regulatory standards that applied to it at the time it was manufactured or imported.

(4) A motor tricycle shall not have more seating positions than it had when originally manufactured.

(5) A motor tricycle originally manufactured for sale in Canada shall not have more than two seating positions unless the motor tricycle,

(a) was originally manufactured with more than two seating positions; and

(b) bears the manufacturer's compliance label issued under section 6 of the *Motor Vehicle Safety Regulations* (Canada) specifying the type of vehicle as "TRI" for motor tricycle.

(6) An imported motor tricycle shall not have more than two seating positions unless the motor tricycle,

> **(a)** was originally manufactured as a motor tricycle with more than two seating positions; and

> **(b)** bears a compliance label or other label to prove conformity as provided for in section 12 of the *Motor Vehicle Safety Regulations* (Canada).

(7) A motor tricycle shall be fitted with at least two mirrors that conform to the requirements set out in Canada Motor Vehicle Safety Standard 111 under the *Motor Vehicle Safety Regulations* (Canada).

(8) Every motor tricycle shall have a parking brake adequate to hold the vehicle stationary for a few seconds when tested at light throttle in low forward gear and in reverse.

(9) None of the original controls of the brake system of a motor tricycle, including the anti-lock brake controls, shall have been removed, modified or replaced so that their effectiveness is reduced.

(10) In the case of a motor tricycle originally fitted with an electronic stability control system, such system shall not be missing and there shall be no indication of a malfunction in the system.

O. Reg. 115/08, s. 3

Speed-Limiting Systems
[Heading added O. Reg. 396/08, s. 1.]

12. For the purposes of section 68.1 of the Act,

"commercial motor vehicle" means a commercial motor vehicle as defined in subsection 1(1) of the Act.

O. Reg. 396/08, s. 1

13. (1) A commercial motor vehicle is exempt from subsections 68.1(1), (2), (3) and (6) of the Act if it is,

> **(a)** a bus;

> **(b)** a mobile crane;

> **(c)** a motor home;

> **(d)** a vehicle manufactured before 1995;

> **(e)** a vehicle with a manufacturer's gross vehicle weight rating under 11,794 kilograms; or

> **(f)** an ambulance, a cardiac arrest emergency vehicle, or a fire apparatus.

(2) For the purposes of clauses 1(d) and (e), the date that a commercial motor vehicle was manufactured and its manufacturer's gross vehicle weight rating shall be deemed, in the absence of evidence to the contrary, to be,

> **(a)** the date and weight on the commercial motor vehicle's compliance label; or

(b) where a commercial motor vehicle does not have a compliance label affixed or the label is illegible, a document from the vehicle's manufacturer that is carried by the driver and that references the vehicle's vehicle identification number and indicates its year of manufacture and gross vehicle weight rating.

(3) A commercial motor vehicle is exempt from subsection 68.1(1) of the Act if,

(a) it is not equipped with an electronic control module capable of being programmed to limit vehicle speed;

(b) it is engaged in providing relief in an emergency, being a situation or impending situation that constitutes a danger of major proportions to life, property or the environment, whether caused by forces of nature, an accident, an intentional act or otherwise; or

(c) it is operated by or on behalf of a municipality, road authority, public utility or of the government of Ontario or of Canada while responding to a situation or impending situation that constitutes an imminent danger, though not one of major proportions, to life, property or the environment, whether caused by forces of nature, an accident, an intentional act or otherwise.

(4) A driver of a commercial motor vehicle is exempt from subsection 68.1(1) of the Act if the vehicle is leased for 30 days or less by an individual for the transportation of the goods kept for the individual's personal use.

O. Reg. 396/08, s. 1

14. (1) The speed-limiting system of a commercial motor vehicle shall be properly set at a maximum speed of 105 kilometres per hour.

(2) A speed-limiting system is properly set for the purposes of subsection (1) if it prevents a driver, by means of accelerator application, from accelerating to or maintaining a speed greater than permitted under subsection (1).

(3) The maximum speed under subsection (1) shall be set by means of the electronic control module that limits the feed of fuel to the engine.

(4) A commercial motor vehicle is exempt from subsection (3) if it is equipped with an equally effective system, not dependent on the electronic control module, that allows limitation of vehicle speed, remotely or not, but does not allow the driver to deactivate or modify the system in Ontario so that it does not comply with subsections (1) and (2).

O. Reg. 396/08, s. 1

15. (1) A speed-limiting system shall be in good working order.

(2) Without limiting the generality of subsection (1), all aspects of a commercial motor vehicle's computer system or systems, computer programs, components, equipment and connections that are capable of playing a role in preventing a driver from increasing the speed of a commercial motor vehicle beyond a specified value shall be in good working order.

O. Reg. 396/08, s. 1

16. A commercial motor vehicle's electronic control module shall contain information that accurately corresponds with any component or feature of the vehicle referred to in the module, including information regarding the tire rolling radius, axle gear ratio and transmission gear ratio.

O. Reg. 396/08, s. 1

17. The prescribed speed for the purposes of subsection 68.1(9) of the Act is 115 kilometres per hour.

O. Reg. 396/08, s. 1

18. The following devices are prescribed for the purposes of clause 68.1(3)(a) of the Act:

1. A device that causes inaccurate information to be transmitted to the electronic control module about a commercial motor vehicle's actual speed.

2. A device that causes inaccurate information to be sent to the electronic control module about the revolutions per minute of the engine.

O. Reg. 396/08, s. 1

SCHEDULE 1

COLUMN 1		COLUMN 2
Service Brake Chambers		Push Rod Travel
Clamp Type Brake Chamber Data		
Type	Outside Diameter	
6	4 1/2"(114.3mm)	1 1/4"(31.75mm)
9	5 1/4"(133.35mm)	1 3/8"(34.93mm)
12	5 11/16"(144.46mm)	1 3/8"(34.93mm)
12 Long Stroke	5 11/16"(144.46mm)	1 3/4"(44.45mm)
16	6 3/8"(161.93mm)	1 3/4"(44.45mm)
16 Long Stroke	6 3/8"(161.93mm)	2"(50.8mm)
20	6 25/32"(172.24mm)	1 3/4"(44.45mm)
20 Long Stroke	6 25/32"(172.24mm)	2"(50.8mm)
24	7 7/32"(183.36mm)	1 3/4"(44.45mm)
24 Long Stroke	7 7/32"(183.36mm)	2"(50.8mm)
24 Long Stroke with Square Inlet Port or with Square Raised Embossment on Lid	7 7/32"(183.36mm)	2 1/2"(63.5mm)
30	8 3/32"(205.58mm)	2"(50.8mm)
30 Long Stroke with Square Inlet Port or with Square Raised Embossment on Lid	8 3/32"(205.58mm)	2 1/2"(63.5mm)
36	9"(228.6mm)	2 1/4"(57.15mm)
Bolt Type Chamber Data		
Type	Outside Diameter	

COLUMN 1		COLUMN 2
Service Brake Chambers		Push Rod Travel
Clamp Type Brake Chamber Data		
Type	Outside Diameter	
A	6 15/16"(176.21mm)	1 3/8"(34.93mm)
B	9 3/16"(233.36mm)	1 3/4"(44.45mm)
C	8 1/16"(204.79mm)	1 3/4"(44.45mm)
D	5 1/4"(133.35mm)	1 1/4"(31.75mm)
E	6 3/16"(157.16mm)	1 3/8"(34.93mm)
F	11"(279.4mm)	2 1/4"(57.15mm)
G	9 7/8"(250.83mm)	2"(50.8mm)
Rotochamber Type Chamber Data		
Type	Outside Diameter	
9	4 9/32"(108.74mm)	1 1/2"(38.1mm)
12	4 13/16"(122.23mm)	1 1/2"(38.1mm)
16	5 13/32"(137.32mm)	2"(50.8mm)
20	5 15/16"(150.81mm)	2"(50.8mm)
24	6 13/32"(162.72mm)	2"(50.8mm)
30	7 1/16"(179.39mm)	2 1/4"(57.15mm)
36	7 5/8"(193.68mm)	2 3/4"(69.85mm)
50	8 7/8"(225.43mm)	3"(76.2mm)
Tie Rod Piston Type Chamber Data		
Type	Outside Diameter	
30 Long Stroke with Square In-let Port	6 1/2"(165.1mm)	2 1/2"(63.5mm)
DD-3 Type Chamber Data		
Type	Outside Diameter	
30	8 1/8"(206.37mm)	2 1/4"(57.15mm)

O. Reg. 229/95, s. 2; 276/99, s. 2

ONT. REG. 588 — EXEMPTION FROM SECTION 7 OF THE ACT — AMERICAN STATES [REVOKED]

made under the *Highway Traffic Act*

R.R.O. 1990, Reg. 588, as am. O. Reg. 496/93; 21/94; 187/94; 432/95; 85/98; 667/00.

[Note: Exemption from Section 7 of the Act — American States *revoked by O. Reg. 667/00.]*

ONT. REG. 589 — EXEMPTION FROM SECTIONS 7 AND 11 OF THE ACT — STATES OF THE UNITED STATES OF AMERICA [REVOKED]

made under the *Highway Traffic Act*

R.R.O. 1990, Reg. 589, as am. O. Reg. 188/94; 431/95; 667/00.

[Note: Exemption from Sections 7 and 11 of the Act — States of the United States if America *revoked by O. Reg. 667/00.]*

ONT. REG. 590 — EXEMPTION FROM SECTIONS 7 AND 11 OF THE ACT — STATE OF ILLINOIS [REVOKED]

made under the *Highway Traffic Act*

R.R.O. 1990, Reg. 590, as am. O. Reg. 667/00.

[Note: Exemption from Sections 7 and 11 of the Act — State of Illinois *revoked by O. Reg. 667/00.]*

ONT. REG. 591 — EXEMPTION FROM SECTIONS 7 AND 11 OF THE ACT — STATE OF MICHIGAN [REVOKED]

made under the *Highway Traffic Act*

R.R.O. 1990, Reg. 591, as am. O. Reg. 667/00.

[Note: Exemption from Sections 7 and 11 of the Act — State of Michigan *revoked by O. Reg. 667/00.]*

ONT. REG. 592 — EXEMPTION FROM SECTIONS 7 AND 11 OF THE ACT — STATE OF SOUTH DAKOTA [REVOKED]

made under the *Highway Traffic Act*

R.R.O. 1990, Reg. 592, as am. O. Reg. 667/00.

[Note: Exemption from Sections 7 and 11 of the Act — State of South Dakota *revoked by O. Reg. 667/00.]*

ONT. REG. 595 — GARAGE LICENCES

made under the *Highway Traffic Act*

R.R.O. 1990, Reg. 595, as am. O. Reg. 435/06 (Fr.).

1. (1) The following fees shall be paid to the Ministry:

    1. For a licence to deal in motor vehicles or trailers and operate a used car lot, for each separate premises **$25.00**

    2. For a licence to buy and wreck motor vehicles, for each separate premises **25.00**

    3. For the replacement of a licence in the case of loss or destruction of original **5.00**

(2) Where a licence referred to in paragraph 1 or 2 of subsection (1) is for a business commenced on or after the 1st day of September in a year, one half of the fee shall be paid for the licence for that year.

(3) A licence remains in force only during the calendar year in which it is issued.

(4) Where the ownership of premises in respect of which a licence under this Regulation has been issued is transferred, the licence shall be returned to the Ministry by the vendor and the new owner shall make application for a new licence.

(5) The Ministry may require that the applicant for a garage licence provide proof that the proposed operation will not be in contravention of any by-law of the municipality in which it will be located.

2. The records prescribed in subsection 60(1) of the Act shall be kept on the business premises of the person required to keep the records, in the book supplied by the Ministry for that purpose, for a period of two years.

3. Every person who engages in the business of wrecking or dismantling vehicles shall forthwith, when the person wrecks or dismantles a motor vehicle or trailer,

    (a) clearly mark the permit for the motor vehicle or trailer "WRECKED";

    (b) sign the permit;

    (c) print the number of the person's licence on the permit if the person is licensed under the Act to buy and wreck motor vehicles; and

    (d) send the permit and the number plates for the vehicle to the Ministry.

4. Every person who engages in the business of operating a garage, repair shop, or used car lot or the business of wrecking or dismantling motor vehicles shall maintain for a period of two years a record of every motor vehicle in which the person installs an engine or cylinder block and the record shall include the serial number of

the engine or cylinder block removed from and the serial number of the engine or cylinder block installed in the vehicle.

ONT. REG. 596 — GENERAL

made under the *Highway Traffic Act*

R.R.O. 1990, Reg. 596, as am. O. Reg. 537/97; 213/03; 406/09 (Fr.); 228/15.

Headlamps

1. (1) In this section and in sections 2, 3 and 4,

"beam" means the light projected from a pair of lighted headlamps.

(2) In this section and in sections 2, 3, 4 and 4.1,

"headlamp" means one of the lamps on the front of a motor vehicle required by subsection 62(1) of the Act.

O. Reg. 213/03, s. 1

2. (1) Subject to section 3, the headlamps on a motor vehicle shall be capable of projecting at least two beams, so controlled that only one beam can be selected for use by the driver of the motor vehicle at any one time according to the requirements of traffic.

(2) One beam shall be a lower or passing beam so aimed that none of the high intensity portion of the beam that is directed,

(a) to the left of the vehicle, is higher than 127 millimetres below; or

(b) to the right of the vehicle, is higher than,

the horizontal line through the centre of the headlamp from which it comes, at a distance of 7.6 metres ahead of the headlamp, when the vehicle is not loaded, and the high intensity portion of the lower or passing beam shall not rise higher than 1.07 metres above the level on which the vehicle stands at a distance of 22.9 metres ahead of the vehicle.

3. Headlamps on motor vehicles manufactured and sold before the 1st day of August, 1939, may provide a single beam of light if the single beam complies with the following requirements and limitations:

1. The headlamps shall be so aimed that when the vehicle is not loaded, none of the high intensity portion of the light shall, at a distance of 7.6 metres ahead of the vehicle, rise higher than a level of 127 millimetres below the horizontal centre of the headlamp from which it comes and, at a distance of 22.9 metres ahead, shall not rise higher than 1.07 metres above the level on which the vehicle stands.

2. No lighting device of more than thirty-two mean spherical candela shall be used in a single beam headlamp.

4. No lighting device of over four mean spherical candela shall be carried on a motor vehicle unless it is equipped with a device for the elimination of glare approved by the Minister.

4.1 (1) A headlamp that emits a white light only may be coated or covered with a coloured material if the headlamp,

(a) is a halogen sealed beam lamp,

(i) that complies with,

(A) the U.S. Federal Motor Vehicle Safety Standards 49CFR571.108, as it reads on the day this section comes into force, including being marked by the manufacturer with the manufacturer's name or trademark and the DOT symbol, or

(B) clause 108.1(a)(iii) of the *Motor Vehicle Safety Regulations* SOR/78-257 made under the *Motor Vehicle Safety Act* (Canada), as it reads on the day this section comes into force, including being marked by the manufacturer with the manufacturer's name or trademark, the ECE symbol (a circle surrounding the letter E) and a designation commencing with the letter H, and

(ii) that was manufactured with a coating or covering of coloured material; or

(b) contains one or more replaceable halogen bulbs,

(i) that comply with,

(A) the U.S. Federal Motor Vehicle Safety Standards 49CFR571.108, as it reads on the day this section comes into force, including being marked by the manufacturer with the manufacturer's name or trademark, the DOT symbol and the bulb type, or

(B) clauses 108.1(a)(i) and (ii) of the *Motor Vehicle Safety Regulations* SOR/78-257 made under the *Motor Vehicle Safety Act* (Canada), as it reads on the day this section comes into force, including being marked by the manufacturer with the manufacturer's name or trademark, the ECE symbol (a circle surrounding the letter E) and a designation commencing with the letter H, and

(ii) that were manufactured with a coating or covering of coloured material.

(2) Sub-subclauses (1)(a)(i)(B) and (1)(b)(i)(B) apply with necessary modifications to a replacement halogen sealed beam lamp or a replacement halogen bulb as if it were a halogen sealed beam lamp or a halogen bulb connected to a headlamp assembly by the manufacturer of the motor vehicle.

(3) Subsection (1) does not apply if the halogen sealed beam lamp or replaceable halogen bulb,

(a) is connected to a headlamp assembly or installed on a motor vehicle for which it is not designed;

(b) is coated or covered with a coloured material after its manufacture; or

(c) is altered after its manufacture, other than as described in clause (b).

O. Reg. 213/03, s. 2

Width of Tires

5. (1) Except as provided in subsection (2), commercial motor vehicles having a gross weight in column 1 of the following Table with rear tires of less than the widths set opposite thereto in column 2 shall not be operated upon a highway:

Item	Column 1	Column 2
1	2090 kg or less	88 mm
2	More than 2090 kg but not more than 2410 kg	101 mm
3	More than 2410 kg but not more than 2750 kg	114 mm
4	More than 2750 kg but not more than 3040 kg	127 mm
5	More than 3040 kg but not more than 4360 kg	152 mm
6	More than 4360 kg but not more than 5080 kg	177 mm
7	More than 5080 kg but not more than 5810 kg	203 mm
8	More than 5810 kg but not more than 7260 kg	254 mm
9	More than 7260 kg but not more than 8200 kg	304 mm
10	More than 8200 kg but not more than 10,000 kg	355 mm
11	More than 10,000 kg but not more than 10,890 kg	406 mm
12	More than 10,890 kg but not more than 11,230 kg	419 mm
13	More than 11,230 kg but not more than 12,250 kg	457 mm
14	More than 12,250 kg but not more than 12,700 kg	508 mm

(2) In the case of a trailer, a four-wheeled commercial motor vehicle that has its gross weight distributed approximately evenly on all wheels and a commercial motor vehicle that has more than four wheels, the Minister may authorize tires of less width than is prescribed in subsection (1).

Hydraulic Brake Fluid

6. For the purpose of section 65 of the Act, the prescribed standards and specifications for hydraulic brake fluid and hydraulic system mineral oil are those set out in Canadian Motor Vehicle Safety Standard 116 issued by the Road and Motor Vehicle Traffic Safety Branch of Transport Canada or United States Motor Vehicle Safety Standard 116 issued by the National Highway Traffic Safety Administration of the United States Department of Transport.

7. For the purpose of section 65 of the Act, the prescribed standards for hydraulic brake fluid containers are those set out in S5.2 of United States Federal Motor Vehicle Safety Standard 116 except that,

(a) S5.2.2.1(d) and S5.2.2.2.(a) shall be deemed to read "Certification that the brake fluid conforms to Canadian Motor Vehicle Safety Standard 116";

(b) S5.2.2.1(c) shall be deemed to read "The minimum wet boiling point in Celsius or in Fahrenheit and Celsius of the fluid";

(c) S5.2.2(f) shall be deemed to read "The minimum wet boiling point in Celsius or in Fahrenheit and Celsius of the DOT brake fluid in the container"; and

(d) S5.2.2(g)(4) shall be deemed to read "CAUTION: DO NOT REFILL CONTAINER, AND DO NOT USE FOR OTHER LIQUIDS. (Not required for containers with a capacity in excess of 20 litres)".

8. For the purpose of section 65 of the Act, the prescribed colour of hydraulic brake fluid and hydraulic system mineral oil is that set out in S5.1.14 of United States Federal Motor Vehicle Safety Standard 116.

Safety Seat Belt

9. (1) In this section and in the Schedule, "safety seat belt" means a single-occupancy lap-type safety seat belt for use in a motor vehicle.

(2) The manufacturer of a safety seat belt shall not sell the belt or offer it for sale in Ontario unless the belt conforms to the standard of performance set out in the Schedule and bears the mark SAE J4.

(3) A manufacturer shall not mark a belt under subsection (2) unless it conforms to the standard of performance set out in the Schedule.

(4) No person shall sell or offer for sale a safety seat belt unless the belt is marked SAE J4.

(5) A safety seat belt bearing a Canadian Standards Association monogram shall be deemed to be marked in compliance with subsections (2), (3) and (4).

(6) No person shall mark a safety seat belt except in accordance with this section.

10. (1) No person shall operate upon a highway a motorcycle or motor assisted bicycle equipped with handlebars that are more than 380 millimetres in height above the

uppermost portion of the seat provided for the operator when the seat is depressed by the weight of the operator.

(2) No person shall be carried as a passenger on a motorcycle operated on a highway except,

    (a) in a side car designed to carry a passenger; or

    (b) subject to subsection (3), on a seat that is situated to the rear of the seat provided for the operator and that is securely fastened to the motorcycle, which shall be equipped with foot rests for the passenger.

(3) A person who is a passenger on a motorcycle operated on a highway and who is occupying the seat referred to in clause (2)(b) shall sit astride the seat in such a manner that his or her feet are placed upon the foot rests referred to in clause (2)(b).

Damage to Property Accident Report

11. For the purpose of subsection 199(1) of the Act, the prescribed amount for damage to property is $2,000.

O. Reg. 537/97, s. 1; 228/15, s. 1

SCHEDULE

1. (1) The assembled safety seat belt shall withstand a static loop load of not less than 1815 kilograms.

(2) After the assembled safety seat belt has withstood the static loop load referred to in subsection (1),

    (a) the release mechanism of the buckle shall be operable; and

    (b) the force required to open the buckle shall not exceed 20 kilograms.

2. (1) The part of the belt webbing that is likely to come into contact with the wearer shall be not less than 48 millimetres wide under no load and not less than 46 millimetres wide when subjected to a test load of 1815 kilograms.

(2) When subjected to a test load of 1135 kilograms the elongation of the webbing shall not exceed 25 per cent.

3. Slippage of the webbing in the adjusting mechanism at or near the buckle, in the release mechanism and at the attachment fittings shall not exceed a total of 25 millimetres under the static loop load specified in section 1.

ONT. REG. 598 — GROSS WEIGHT ON BRIDGES

made under the *Highway Traffic Act*

R.R.O. 1990, Reg. 598, as am. O. Reg. 768/92; 207/93; 353/93; 401/93; 600/93; 209/95; 336/95; 503/95; 75/96; 366/96; 74/98; 361/99; 139/00; 193/01; 470/01; 54/02; 151/02; 230/02; 47/03; 383/03; 63/04; 362/04; 474/05; 141/07; 18/08; 401/08; 169/09; 434/09; 435/09; 483/09; 7/10; 168/10; 17/11; 417/11; 433/12; 48/13; 143/13; 236/13; 311/14.

1. No person shall move a vehicle or combination of vehicles of a class described in Column 1 of the Table in a Schedule to this Regulation on, over or upon the bridge described in the Schedule if the gross weight of the vehicle or combination of vehicles is greater than the weight in tonnes set opposite in Column 2 of the Table in the Schedule.

O. Reg. 207/93, s. 1; 353/93, s. 1; 205/95, s. 1; 336/95, s. 1; 503/95, s. 1; 361/99, s. 1; 139/00, s. 1; 193/01, s. 1; 54/02, s. 1; 383/03, s. 1; 63/04, s. 1; 362/04, s. 1; 474/05, s. 1; 141/07, s. 1; 18/08, s. 1; 401/08, s. 1; 169/09, s. 1; 483/09, s. 1; 433/12, s. 1; 311/14, s. 1

2. [Repealed O. Reg. 311/14, s. 1.]

. . . . .

Ont. Reg. 620/05 — High Occupancy Vehicle Lanes

made under the *Highway Traffic Act*

O. Reg. 620/05, as am. O. Reg. 356/07; 367/09; 236/10 [s. 2 to come into force July 1, 2016. Amended O. Reg. 99/15, s. 6.]; 435/10; 459/11; 177/12 [s. 1(2) to come into force July 1, 2016. Amended O. Reg. 99/15, s. 7.]; 205/14; 89/15; 99/15, ss. 1–5; 101/15.

1. Designation of high occupancy vehicle lanes — The left lane of the part of the King's Highway described in a schedule to this Regulation is designated as a high occupancy vehicle lane for the hours, days and months specified in the schedule.

2. Use of high occupancy vehicle lanes — No person shall operate a motor vehicle or a commercial motor vehicle in a high occupancy vehicle lane unless one of the following circumstances exists:

1. In the case of a motor vehicle, the vehicle has at least two persons occupying seating positions.

2. In the case of a commercial motor vehicle,

    i. the vehicle has at least two persons occupying seating positions, and

    ii. the length of the vehicle or the total length of the vehicle and any vehicle being towed is less than 6.5 metres.

3. The vehicle is a bus.

4. The person is operating an emergency vehicle, as defined in section 144 of the Act, in the performance of his or her duties.

5. The person is operating the vehicle in the lawful performance of his or her duties as a police officer.

6. The person is operating a vehicle owned or leased by the Province of Ontario in the lawful performance of his or her duties as an officer appointed for carrying out the provisions of the Act.

7. The person is operating a vehicle engaged in road construction or maintenance activities in or near the high occupancy vehicle lane.

8. The person is operating a tow truck that has been requested to provide towing or repair services to a disabled vehicle in or near a high occupancy vehicle lane by a police officer, an officer appointed for carrying out the provisions of the Act, or a person driving the disabled vehicle, and operating the tow truck in the high occupancy vehicle lane is necessary to attend at and depart from the location of the disabled vehicle.

9. The person is operating a motor vehicle to which are attached valid number plates that,

    i. are issued by the Ministry,

    ii. have green lettering on a white background, and

    iii. display the words "GREEN VEHICLE" or "VÉHICULE ÉCOLOGIQUE".

Proposed Repeal — 2, para. 9

9. [Repealed O. Reg. 236/10, s. 2. To come into force July 1, 2016.]

10. The vehicle is a taxicab or limousine that,

    i. is being operated by a person who has a valid licence, permit or authorization issued by a municipality or airport authority to operate the vehicle for the purpose of providing passenger transportation services, and

    ii. has mounted on the rear of the vehicle a valid plate bearing an identification number issued by the municipality or airport authority for the use of the vehicle for that purpose.

Proposed Repeal — 2, para. 10

10. [Repealed O. Reg. 177/12, s. 1(2). To come into force July 1, 2016.]

O. Reg. 236/10, s. 1; 177/12, s. 1(1)

3. **Buffer zones** — (1) Entry and exit points at which vehicles may enter or exit high occupancy vehicle lanes are located between buffer zones, illustrated in Figure A in section 4.

(2) No person shall operate a motor vehicle or commercial motor vehicle to enter or exit a high occupancy vehicle lane by crossing a buffer zone, unless the movement can be made safely and one of the following circumstances exists:

1. The person is directed to make the movement by a police officer.

2. The person is operating an emergency vehicle, as defined in section 144 of the Act, in the performance of his or her duties.

3. The person is operating the vehicle in the lawful performance of his or her duties as a police officer.

4. The person is operating a vehicle owned or leased by the Province of Ontario in the lawful performance of his or her duties as an officer appointed for carrying out the provisions of the Act.

5. The person is operating a vehicle engaged in road construction or maintenance activities in or near the high occupancy vehicle lane.

6. The person is operating a tow truck that has been requested to provide towing or repair services to a disabled vehicle in or near a high occupancy vehicle lane by a police officer, an officer appointed for carrying out the provisions of the Act, or a person driving the disabled vehicle, and crossing the buffer zone is necessary to attend at and depart from the location of the disabled vehicle.

7. The person is complying with the requirements of section 159 of the Act.

(3) Subsection 148(2) of the Act does not apply to a person operating a vehicle in a high occupancy vehicle lane.

(4) [Repealed O. Reg. 99/15, s. 1(5).]

O. Reg. 99/15, s. 1

4. Roadway markings — A high occupancy vehicle lane shall have the following roadway markings, as illustrated in Figure A:

1. Painted white diamond markings on the surface of the roadway of the high occupancy vehicle lane, placed periodically along the length of the lane.

2. Painted white buffer zone markings on the surface of the roadway separating high occupancy vehicle lanes from other highway lanes.

3. Painted white continuity lane markings on the surface of the roadway between buffer zones indicating points at which vehicles may enter or exit a high occupancy vehicle lane.

FIGURE A

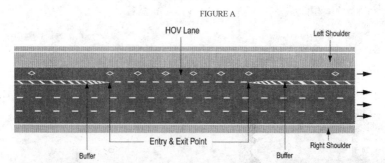

Text alternative: Illustration of "Figure A" showing an overhead plan of a divided highway with the high occupancy vehicle lane as the leftmost lane on a highway. The lane has white diamond markings on the roadway and broken white lines indicating the entry and exit points. Diagonal lines painted between solid lines before and after the entry and exit points indicate the buffer between the high occupancy vehicle lane and the lane beside it. The left shoulder is indicated to the left of the high occupancy vehicle lane. This text alternative is provided for convenience only and does not form part of the official law.

O. Reg. 89/15, s. 1

5. Signs — **(1) The commencement of a high occupancy vehicle lane shall be indicated by an overhead sign that has the dimensions and bears the markings as illustrated in Figure B.**

FIGURE B

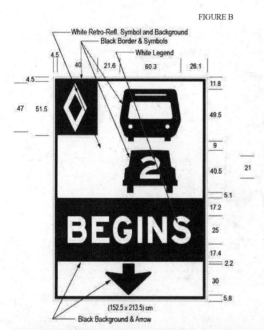

Text alternative: Illustration of an overhead high occupancy vehicle lane sign labelled as "Figure B". The sign contains three rectangles, stacked on top of one another. The top rectangle has a white reflective background and contains a symbol of a bus on top of a symbol of a car with the number "2" inside it. A white diamond shape in a small black rectangle appears in the upper left corner of this rectangle. The middle rectangle contains the word "BEGINS" in white letters on a reflective black background. The bottom rectangle has a white reflective background and contains a thick black arrow pointing down. The following measurements are written below the sign: (152.5 x 213.5) cm. The sign is surrounded by measurements of its different elements. This text alternative is provided for convenience only and does not form part of the official law.

(2) Despite subsection (1), in an area designated in the Schedule to the *French Language Services Act*, the commencement of a high occupancy vehicle lane shall be indicated by an overhead sign that has the dimensions and bears the markings as illustrated in Figure C.

FIGURE C

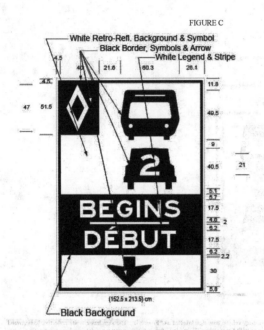

Text alternative: Illustration of an overhead high occupancy vehicle lane sign labelled as "Figure C". The sign contains three rectangles, stacked on top of one another. The top rectangle has a white reflective background and contains a symbol of a bus on top of a symbol of a car with the number "2" inside it. A white diamond shape in a small black rectangle appears in the upper left corner of this rectangle. The middle rectangle contains the word "BEGINS/DÉBUT" in white letters on a reflective black background. The bottom rectangle has a white reflective background and contains a thick black arrow pointing down. The following measurements are written below the sign: (152.5 x 213.5) cm. The sign is surrounded by measurements of its different elements. This text alternative is provided for convenience only and does not form part of the official law.

(3) High occupancy vehicle lane signs shall be erected along the length of a high occupancy vehicle lane and shall have the dimensions and bear the markings as illustrated in Figure D:

FIGURE D

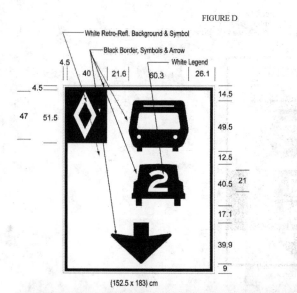

(152.5 x 183) cm

Text alternative: Illustration of an overhead high occupancy vehicle lane sign labelled as "Figure D". The sign has a white reflective background and contains a symbol of a bus on top of a symbol of a car with the number "2" inside it, below which appears a thick black arrow pointing down. A white diamond shape in a small black rectangle appears in the upper left corner of this rectangle. The following measurements are written below the sign: (152.5 x 183) cm. The sign is surrounded by measurements of its different elements. This text alternative is provided for convenience only and does not form part of the official law.

(4) High occupancy vehicle lane signs shall not be more than four kilometres apart from each other.

(5) The end of a high occupancy vehicle lane shall be indicated by an overhead sign that has the dimensions and bears the markings as illustrated in Figure E or by a

ground mounted sign that has the dimensions and bears the markings as illustrated in Figure F.

FIGURE E

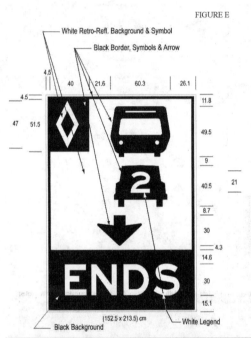

Text alternative: Illustration of an overhead high occupancy vehicle lane sign labelled as "Figure E". The sign contains two rectangles, stacked on top of one another. The top rectangle has a white reflective background and contains a symbol of a bus on top of a symbol of a car with the number "2" inside it, below which appears a thick black arrow pointing down. A white diamond shape in a small black rectangle appears in the upper left corner of this rectangle. The bottom rectangle contains the word "ENDS" in white letters on a reflective black background. The following measurements are written below the sign: (152.5 x 213.5) cm. The sign is surrounded by measurements of its different elements. This text alternative is provided for convenience only and does not form part of the official law.

FIGURE F

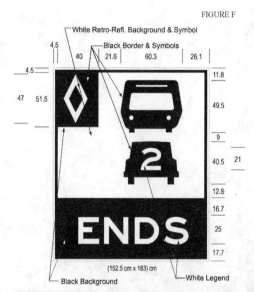

(152.5 cm x 183) cm

Black Background — White Legend

White Retro-Refl. Background & Symbol

Black Border & Symbols

Text alternative: Illustration of a ground mounted high occupancy vehicle lane sign labelled as "Figure F". The sign contains two rectangles, stacked on top of one another. The top rectangle has a white reflective background and contains a symbol of a bus on top of a symbol of a car with the number "2" inside it, below which appears a thick black arrow pointing down. A white diamond shape in a small black rectangle appears in the upper left corner of this rectangle. The bottom rectangle contains the word "ENDS" in white letters on a reflective black background. The following measurements are written below the sign: (152.5 x 183) cm. The sign is surrounded by measurements of its different elements. This text alternative is provided for convenience only and does not form part of the official law.

(6) Despite subsection (5), in an area designated in the Schedule to the *French Language Services Act*, the end of a high occupancy vehicle lane shall be indicated by an overhead sign that has the dimensions and bears the markings as illustrated in Figure G or by a ground mounted sign that has the dimensions and bears the markings as illustrated in Figure H.

801

FIGURE G

White Retro-Refl. Background & Symbol

Black Border, Symbols & Arrow

White Legend & Stripe

(152.5 x 213.5) cm

Black Background

Text alternative: Illustration of an overhead high occupancy vehicle lane sign labelled as "Figure G". The sign contains two rectangles, stacked on top of one another. The top rectangle has a white reflective background and contains a symbol of a bus on top of a symbol of a car with the number "2" inside it, below which appears a thick black arrow pointing down. A white diamond shape in a small black rectangle appears in the upper left corner of this rectangle. The bottom rectangle contains the word "ENDS/FIN" in white letters on a reflective black background. The following measurements are written below the sign: (152.5 x 213.5) cm. The sign is surrounded by measurements of its different elements. This text alternative is provided for convenience only and does not form part of the official law.

FIGURE H

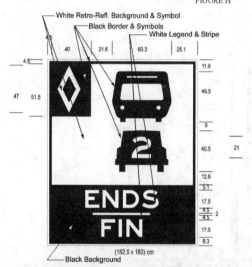

Text alternative: Illustration of a ground mounted high occupancy vehicle lane sign labelled as "Figure H". The sign contains two rectangles, stacked on top of one another. The top rectangle has a white reflective background and contains a symbol of a bus on top of a symbol of a car with the number "2" inside it. A white diamond shape in a small black rectangle appears in the upper left corner of this rectangle. The bottom rectangle contains the word "ENDS/FIN" in white letters on a reflective black background. The following measurements are written below the sign: (152.5 x 183) cm. The sign is surrounded by measurements of its different elements. This text alternative is provided for convenience only and does not form part of the official law.

(7) A sign prohibiting the crossing of a buffer zone shall have the dimensions and bear the markings as illustrated in,

    (a) Figure I or J, if the sign is an overhead sign; or

    (b) Figure K or L, if the sign is a ground mounted sign.

FIGURE I

Text alternative: Illustration of an overhead buffer zone sign labelled as "Figure I". The sign contains an image on the left of a buffer zone as diagonal lines painted between solid lines and on the right contains the words "Do Not Cross". The sign has a white reflective background with the buffer zone image and words appearing in black. The following measurements are written below the sign: (152.5 x 152.5) cm. The sign is surrounded by measurements of its different elements. This text alternative is provided for convenience only and does not form part of the official law.

FIGURE J

(152.5 x 152.5) cm
Black Border & Legend
White Retro-Refl. Background   Black Symbol

Text alternative: Illustration of an overhead buffer zone sign labelled as "Figure J". The sign contains an image on the right of a buffer zone as diagonal lines painted between solid lines and on the left contains the words "Do Not Cross". The sign has a white reflective background with the buffer zone image and words appearing in black. The following measurements are written below the sign: (152.5 x 152.5) cm. The sign is surrounded by measurements of its different elements. This text alternative is provided for convenience only and does not form part of the official law.

FIGURE K

(90 x 120) cm

Black Border &Legend

Black Symbol

White Retro-Refl. Background

Text alternative: Illustration of a ground mounted buffer zone sign labelled as "Figure K". The sign contains an image on the left of a buffer zone as diagonal lines painted between solid lines and on the right contains the words "Do Not Cross". The sign has a white reflective background with the buffer zone image and words appearing in black. The following measurements are written below the sign: (90 x 120) cm. The sign is surrounded by measurements of its different elements. This text alternative is provided for convenience only and does not form part of the official law.

FIGURE L

(90 x 120) cm

Black Symbol
Black Border & Legend
White Retro-Refl. Background

Text alternative: Illustration of a ground mounted buffer zone sign labelled as "Figure L". The sign contains an image on the right of a buffer zone as diagonal lines painted between solid lines and on the left contains the words "Do Not Cross". The sign has a white reflective background with the buffer zone image and words appearing in black. The following measurements are written below the sign: (90 x 120) cm. The sign is surrounded by measurements of its different elements. This text alternative is provided for convenience only and does not form part of the official law.

(8) Despite subsection (7), in an area designated in the Schedule to the *French Language Services Act*, a sign prohibiting the crossing of a buffer zone shall have the dimensions and bear the markings as illustrated in,

  (a) Figure M or N, if the sign is an overhead sign; or

  (b) Figure O or P, if the sign is a ground mounted sign.

FIGURE M

Text alternative: Illustration of an overhead buffer zone sign labelled as "Figure M". The sign contains an image on the left of a buffer zone as diagonal lines painted between solid lines and on the right contains the words "Do Not Cross/Ne pas traverser". The sign has a white reflective background with the buffer zone image and words appearing in black. The following measurements are written below the sign: (152.5 x 152.5) cm. The sign is surrounded by measurements of its different elements. This text alternative is provided for convenience only and does not form part of the official law.

FIGURE N

Text alternative: Illustration of an overhead buffer zone sign labelled as "Figure N". The sign contains an image on the right of a buffer zone as diagonal lines painted between solid lines and on the left contains the words "Do Not Cross/Ne pas traverser". The sign has a white reflective background with the buffer zone image and words appearing in black. The following measurements are written below the sign: (152.5 x 152.5) cm. The sign is surrounded by measurements of its different elements. This text alternative is provided for convenience only and does not form part of the official law.

FIGURE O

(90 x 120) cm

Text alternative: Illustration of a ground mounted buffer zone sign labelled as "Figure O". The sign contains an image on the left of a buffer zone as diagonal lines painted between solid lines and on the right contains the words "Do Not Cross/Ne pas traverser". The sign has a white reflective background with the buffer zone image and words appearing in black. The following measurements are written below the sign: (90 x 120) cm. The sign is surrounded by measurements of its different elements. This text alternative is provided for convenience only and does not form part of the official law.

FIGURE P

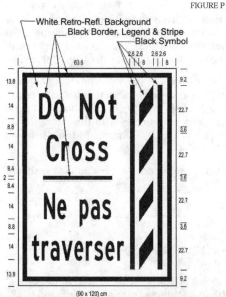

(90 x 120) cm

(9) The dimensions of a sign may differ from those prescribed in this section as long as the dimensions are in the same proportion to each other as the dimensions prescribed in this section are to each other.

(10) An overhead sign shall be erected directly above the high occupancy vehicle lane and a ground mounted sign shall be erected on the side of the highway facing approaching traffic.

O. Reg. 89/15, s. 2

6.–10. [Repealed O. Reg. 99/15, s. 2(2).]

SCHEDULE A — HIGHWAY NO. 404

1. (1) That part of the King's Highway known as No. 404 (southbound) lying between a point situate 1,100 metres measured southerly from its intersection with the centre line of the roadway known as 16th Avenue in The Regional Municipality of York, and a point situate 1,090 metres measured southerly from its intersection with the centre line of the roadway known as Sheppard Avenue in the City of Toronto.

(2) That part of the King's Highway known as No. 404 (northbound) lying between a point situate 210 metres measured northerly from its intersection with the centre line of the roadway known as Van Horne Avenue in the City of Toronto and a point situate 567 metres measured southerly from its intersection with the centre line of the roadway known as Regional Road Highway 7 in The Regional Municipality of York.

(3) This designation is effective 24 hours a day, seven days a week and every month of the year.

(4) [Repealed O. Reg. 99/15, s. 3(2).]

O. Reg. 356/07, s. 1; 99/15, s. 3

SCHEDULE B — HIGHWAY NO. 403

1. (1) That part of the King's Highway known as No. 403 (eastbound) in the City of Mississauga in The Regional Municipality of Peel lying between a point situate 886 metres measured westerly from its intersection with the centre line of the roadway known as Winston Churchill Boulevard, and a point situate 30 metres measured southerly from its intersection with the centre line of the roadway known as Matheson Boulevard.

(2) That part of the King's Highway known as No. 403 (westbound) in the City of Mississauga in The Regional Municipality of Peel lying between a point situate 150 metres measured easterly from its intersection with the centre line of the roadway known as Matheson Boulevard, and a point situate 520 metres measured easterly from its intersection with the centre line of the roadway known as Winston Churchill Boulevard.

(3) This designation is effective 24 hours a day, seven days a week and every month of the year.

SCHEDULE C — HIGHWAY NO. 417 [Heading added O. Reg. 367/09, s. 1.]

1. (1) That part of the King's Highway known as No. 417 (eastbound) in the City of Ottawa lying between a point situate 415 metres measured westerly from its intersection with the centre line of the roadway known as Palladium Drive and a point situate 14 metres measured westerly from its intersection with the centre line of the roadway known as Moodie Drive.

(2) This designation is effective 24 hours a day, seven days a week and every month of the year.

O. Reg. 367/09, s. 1; 205/14, s. 1

2. (1) That part of the King's Highway known as No. 417 (westbound) in the City of Ottawa lying between a point situate 1,105 metres measured westerly from its intersection with the centre line of the roadway known as Moodie Drive and a point situate 465 metres measured easterly from its intersection with the centre line of the roadway known as Palladium Drive.

(2) This designation is effective 24 hours a day, seven days a week and every month of the year.

O. Reg. 205/14, s. 1

SCHEDULE D — QUEEN ELIZABETH WAY AND HIGHWAY
NO. 403 [Heading added O. Reg. 435/10, s. 1.]

1. (1) That part of the King's Highway known as Queen Elizabeth Way and No. 403 (eastbound) in The Regional Municipality of Halton lying between a point situate 39 metres measured westerly from its intersection with the centre line of the roadway known as Guelph Line in the City of Burlington and a point situate 101 metres measured westerly from its intersection with the centre line of the roadway known as Trafalgar Road in the Town of Oakville.

(2) That part of the King's Highway known as Queen Elizabeth Way/Highway 403 (westbound) in The Regional Municipality of Halton lying between a point situate 185 metres measured easterly from its intersection with the centre line of the roadway known as Trafalgar Road and in the Town of Oakville and a point situate 380 metres measured easterly from its intersection with the centre line of the roadway known as Guelph Line in the City of Burlington.

(3) This designation is effective 24 hours a day, seven days a week and every month of the year.

(4) [Repealed O. Reg. 99/15, s. 4(2).]

O. Reg. 435/10, s. 1; 459/11, s. 1; 99/15, s. 4

SCHEDULE E [Repealed O. Reg. 99/15, s. 5(2).]

1. [Repealed O. Reg. 99/15, s. 5(2).]

SCHEDULE F [Repealed O. Reg. 99/15, s. 5(2).]

1. [Repealed O. Reg. 99/15, s. 5(2).]

SCHEDULE G [Repealed O. Reg. 99/15, s. 5(2).]

1. [Repealed O. Reg. 99/15, s. 5(2).]

ONT. REG. 599 — HIGHWAY CLOSINGS

made under the *Highway Traffic Act*

R.R.O. 1990, Reg. 599, as am. O. Reg. 643/92; 94/08.

1. For the purposes of section 134 of the Act, a police officer may close a highway or any part thereof by either of the following methods:

1. By,

i. posting or causing to be posted a Do Not Enter sign as prescribed in subsection 2(1) in such a manner that the sign faces approaching traffic and that the bottom edge of the sign is not less than one metre above the roadway, and

ii. placing or causing to be placed not fewer than three traffic control devices of the type prescribed in clause 2(2)(a) or two traffic control devices of the type prescribed in clauses 2(2)(b) and (c) in such a manner that the control devices stand in a line at right angles to approaching traffic with not more than one metre separating each pair of control devices.

2. By deploying or causing to be deployed across the roadway a highway ramp gate traffic control device as prescribed in subsection 2(3) that was installed by the road authority having jurisdiction and control of the highway and locking it in place.

O. Reg. 643/92, s. 1; 94/08, s. 1

2. (1) A Do Not Enter sign shall,

(a) be square or rectangular in shape and shall be not less than sixty centimetres in width and sixty centimetres in height; and

(b) bear the markings and have the minimum dimensions as prescribed and illustrated in Figure 1.

(2) A traffic control device may,

(a) be conical in shape, not less than 45 centimetres in height, have a white retro-reflective collar and bear the markings and have the minimum dimensions as prescribed and illustrated in Figure 2;

(b) be rectangular in shape, not less than 90 centimetres in height and not less than 20 centimetres in width and bear the markings and have the minimum dimensions as prescribed and illustrated in Figure 3;

(c) be a barricade, not less than 100 centimetres in width and 100 centimetres in height and bear the markings and have the minimum dimensions as prescribed and illustrated in Figure 4; or

(d) be rectangular in shape, not less than 20 centimetres in height and not less than 90 centimetres in width, with black bars on an orange retro-reflective

815

background and bear the markings and have the minimum dimensions as prescribed and illustrated in Figure 5.

(3) A highway ramp gate traffic control device shall,

(a) be a barrier that extends across the width of the roadway when deployed
such that it blocks vehicular access to the highway;

(b) be capable of being locked in place;

(c) have on it at least one Do Not Enter sign, as prescribed in subsection (1), in
such a manner that the sign faces approaching traffic and the bottom edge of
the sign is not less than one metre above the roadway; and

(d) have at least two traffic control devices, as prescribed in clause (2)(d), on
the same plane on either side of the Do Not Enter sign in such a manner that
the long edges of the control devices are horizontal to the roadway and facing
approaching traffic.

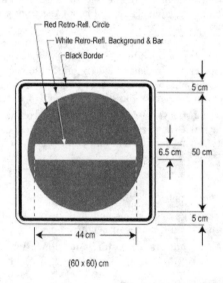

Red Retro-Refl. Circle

White Retro-Refl. Background & Bar

Black Border

5 cm

6.5 cm   50 cm

5 cm

44 cm

(60 x 60) cm

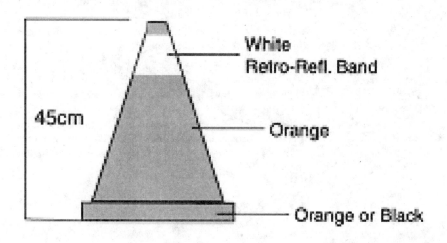

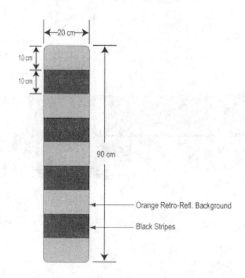

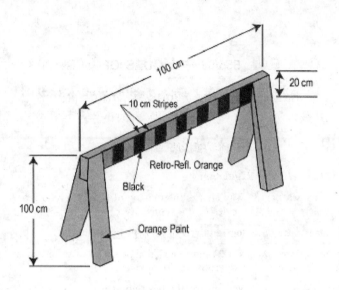

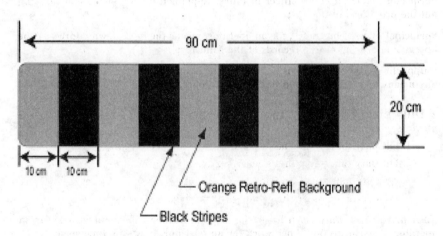

O. Reg. 94/08, s. 2

ONT. REG. 555/06 — HOURS OF SERVICE

made under the *Highway Traffic Act*

O. Reg. 555/06, as am. O. Reg. 405/07; 114/09; 43/12 (Fr.).

INTERPRETATION, APPLICATION

1. Definitions — In this Regulation,

"co-driver" means a person who shares the driving of a commercial motor vehicle with another driver and who rides in the vehicle as a passenger when not driving;

"daily log" means the daily log required to be kept by section 17;

"day", for any driver, means a 24-hour period that starts at midnight or at such other hour designated by the operator for the driver;

"home terminal" for any driver, means the location at which the driver ordinarily reports for work, including an operator's place of business;

"inspector" means a police officer or officer appointed for the purpose of carrying out the provisions of the Act;

"principal place of business", for an operator, means the last known address of the operator appearing on the records of the Ministry;

"supporting document" means a document or information, recorded and stored by any means, that could be used to determine compliance with this Regulation.

2. Duty status time — (1) There are four categories of duty status time for the purpose of this Regulation:

    1. Off-duty time, other than time spent in a sleeper berth.

    2. Off-duty time spent in a sleeper berth.

    3. On-duty time spent driving.

    4. On-duty time, other than time spent driving.

(2) A driver is on duty when he or she drives a commercial motor vehicle for an operator or performs any other work for an operator, including time spent,

    (a) inspecting, servicing, repairing, cleaning and warming up a commercial motor vehicle;

    (b) travelling in a commercial motor vehicle as a co-driver, when the time is not spent in the sleeper berth;

    (c) participating in the loading and unloading of a commercial motor vehicle;

    (d) inspecting and checking the load of a commercial motor vehicle;

(e) waiting for a commercial motor vehicle to be serviced, loaded, unloaded and dispatched;

(f) waiting for a commercial motor vehicle or its load to be inspected; and

(g) waiting at an en-route point because of an accident or other unplanned occurrence or situation.

(3) A driver is off duty when he or she is not on duty.

(4) Despite subsection (2), a driver is off duty when he or she drives a commercial motor vehicle if,

(a) he or she is driving the vehicle for personal use that has no commercial purpose;

(b) the vehicle has been unloaded;

(c) any trailers have been unhitched;

(d) he or she does not drive the vehicle more than 75 kilometres in a day; and

(e) an entry is made in the "Remarks" section of the daily log or on the time record required by subsection 18(3),

(i) stating that the driver used the vehicle for personal use, and

(ii) setting out the odometer readings at the start and the end of the personal use driving.

(5) Despite clause (2)(b), if a driver travels as a passenger to a location where he or she is to start driving a commercial motor vehicle and takes eight consecutive hours of off-duty time at the location before starting to drive, the time spent as a passenger getting to the location is counted as off-duty time.

3. Exemptions from Regulation — (1) Subject to subsection (3), a driver and operator are exempt from this Regulation while the driver is driving a commercial motor vehicle of a type and in the circumstances described in any of the following paragraphs:

1. A two or three-axle commercial motor vehicle, or combination of a two-axle commercial motor vehicle and a one-axle trailer, being used,

i. to transport the primary products of a farm, forest, sea or lake, if the driver or the operator is the owner and producer or harvester of the products, or

ii. to return after transporting the primary products of a farm, forest, sea or lake, if the vehicle is empty or is transporting supplies and equipment used for the production of primary products of a farm, forest, sea or lake.

2. A vehicle being used by a person in the lawful performance of his or her duties as an inspector.

3. A cardiac arrest emergency vehicle operated by or under the authority of a hospital.

4. A vehicle engaged in providing relief in an emergency, being a situation or impending situation that constitutes a danger of major proportions to life, property or the environment, whether caused by forces of nature, an accident, an intentional act or otherwise.

4.1 A vehicle operated by or on behalf of a municipality, road authority or public utility while responding to a situation or impending situation that constitutes an imminent danger, though not one of major proportions, to life, property or the environment, whether caused by forces of nature, an accident, an intentional act or otherwise.

5. A bus that is operated by or on behalf of a municipality as part of the municipality's public transit service, either within the municipality or within 25 kilometres of the boundary of the municipality.

(2) This Regulation does not apply to a driver, or the operator of such driver, while driving a pick-up truck that,

(a) is being used for personal purposes without compensation; and

(b) is not carrying, or towing a trailer that is carrying, commercial cargo or tools or equipment of a type normally used for commercial purposes.

(3) A driver's on-duty time and off-duty time, within the meaning of this Regulation, when he or she is exempt from this Regulation under subsection (1) shall nonetheless be included in the calculations of a driver's hours of off-duty and on-duty time for the purposes of complying with this Regulation on the days when the driver is not exempt under subsection (1).

(4) In this section,

"emergency" [Repealed O. Reg. 405/07, s. 1(2).]

"pick-up truck" means a commercial motor vehicle that,

(a) has a manufacturer's gross vehicle weight rating of 6,000 kilograms or less, and

(b) is fitted with either,

(i) the original box that was installed by the manufacturer, which has not been modified, or

(ii) a replacement box that duplicates the one that was installed by the manufacturer, which has not been modified.

O. Reg. 405/07, s. 1

3.1 Exemption for volunteer firefighters — (1) A driver and operator are exempt from this Regulation while the driver is performing duties as a volunteer firefighter, as defined in the *Fire Protection and Prevention Act, 1997*, but no matter how many hours the driver actually performs duties as a volunteer firefighter, the exemption shall not exceed,

(a) two consecutive hours a day; or

(b) two consecutive hours in the mandatory off-duty time period required by section 9.

(2) The exemption period under subsection (1) shall be included as off-duty time in the calculations of the driver's hours of off-duty and on-duty time for the purposes of complying with this Regulation when the driver is not exempt under subsection (1).

O. Reg. 114/09, s. 1

DAILY REQUIREMENTS

4. Designation of driver's day — (1) The operator shall designate the hour at which the driver's day starts if it does not start at midnight and shall notify the driver of the designation.

(2) The designation shall apply for the duration of the driver's cycle.

5. Daily driving time — (1) After a driver has accumulated 13 hours of driving time in a day, the driver shall not drive again on the same day.

(2) After a driver has accumulated 14 hours of on-duty time in a day, the driver shall not drive again on the same day.

6. Daily off-duty time — (1) A driver shall take at least 10 hours of off-duty time in a day.

(2) Off-duty time under subsection (1) that is in addition to the mandatory eight consecutive hours of off-duty time required by section 9 may be distributed throughout the day in blocks of no less than 30 minutes each.

(3) The off-duty time referred to in subsection (2) shall be at least two hours and may be added to the mandatory eight consecutive hours of off-duty time but cannot form part of it.

7. Deferral of off-duty time — A driver may split the off-duty time required by section 6 over any two consecutive days by deferring a maximum of two hours of the daily off-duty time from the first day to the second day and increasing the total of the driving and on-duty times in the first day by not more than two hours if,

    (a) the deferred off-duty time does not form part of the mandatory period of eight consecutive hours of off-duty time required by section 9;

    (b) before the end of the second day, the driver takes a consecutive period of off-duty time consisting of the eight consecutive hours required by section 9 plus the off-duty time deferred from the first day;

    (c) the total off-duty time taken in the two days is at least 20 hours;

    (d) the total driving time in the two days does not exceed 26 hours;

    (e) the total on-duty time in the two days does not exceed 28 hours;

    (f) the driver is not splitting off-duty time under section 11 at any time during the two days; and

    (g) an entry is made in the "Remarks" section of the daily log or on the record required by subsection 18(3) clearly indicating the day from which the off-duty time has been deferred and the day to which it was deferred.

SHIFT REQUIREMENTS

8. Requirements for sleeper berth — For the purposes of sections 10 and 11, a sleeper berth must,

(a) be designed to be used as sleeping accommodation;

(b) not be located in or on a trailer;

(c) be located,

(i) in the cab of the commercial motor vehicle or immediately adjacent to the cab and be securely fixed to it,

(ii) in the cargo space of the commercial motor vehicle and be separated from the remainder of the cargo space by a solid physical barrier, or

(iii) in the case of a bus, in the passenger compartment of the bus and be separated from the passenger area of the passenger compartment by a solid physical barrier that is equipped with a door that can be locked;

(d) in the case of a bus,

(i) be at least 1.9 metres long, 60 centimetres wide and 60 centimetres high,

(ii) provide privacy for the occupant, and

(iii) be equipped with a means to significantly limit the amount of light entering the area;

(e) in the case of a commercial motor vehicle other than a bus,

(i) be rectangular in shape,

(ii) be at least 1.9 metres long,

(iii) be at least 60 centimetres wide, and

(iv) be at least 60 centimetres high, measured from the top of the sleeping mattress to the highest point of the area;

(f) be constructed so that there are no impediments to ready entrance to or exit from the area;

(g) have a direct and readily accessible means of passing from it into the driver's seat or compartment;

(h) be protected against leaks and overheating from the vehicle's exhaust system;

(i) be equipped to provide adequate heating, cooling and ventilation;

(j) be reasonably sealed against dust and rain;

(k) be equipped with a mattress that is at least 10 centimetres thick and adequate bedding so that the occupant can get restful sleep; and

(l) be equipped with a means of preventing ejection of the occupant during deceleration of the commercial motor vehicle, the means being designed, installed and maintained to withstand a total force of 2,700 kilograms applied toward the front of the vehicle and parallel to the longitudinal axis of the vehicle.

9. Mandatory off-duty time — (1) After a driver has accumulated 13 hours of driving time from the end of the most recent period of eight or more consecutive hours of off-duty time, the driver shall not drive again unless he or she takes at least eight consecutive hours of off-duty time.

(2) After a driver has accumulated 14 hours of on-duty time from the end of the most recent period of eight or more consecutive hours of off-duty time, the driver shall not drive again unless he or she takes at least eight consecutive hours of off-duty time.

(3) After 16 hours have elapsed from the end of the most recent period of eight or more consecutive hours of off-duty time, the driver shall not drive again unless he or she takes at least eight consecutive hours of off-duty time.

10. Exception to mandatory off-duty time — travelling by ferry — (1) A driver travelling for more than five hours by a ferry may meet the mandatory off-duty time requirement of section 9 by spending a minimum of eight hours resting in two or more of,

> (a) a sleeper berth while waiting at the terminal to board the ferry;
>
> (b) rest accommodations on the ferry; and
>
> (c) a rest stop that is no more than 25 kilometres from the point of disembarkation from the ferry.

(2) For the purposes of section 9,

> (a) off-duty time taken under this section is deemed to begin at the start of the last period of off-duty time described in subsection (1); and
>
> (b) the elapsed time referred to in subsection 9(3) must not include the periods of off-duty time described in subsection (1) that precede the start of the last period of off-duty time described in subsection (1).

(3) The driver shall record the hours spent as described in subsection (1) in the daily log as off-duty time spent in a sleeper berth and shall retain the receipts for the crossing and rest accommodation fees as supporting documents.

11. Splitting off-duty time — (1) A driver may meet the off-duty time requirement of section 9 in a sequence of sleeper berth periods under subsection (2) or (3) until the sequence of sleeper berth periods ends with a period of at least eight consecutive hours of off-duty time, if all the sleeper berth periods in the sequence meet the requirements of subsection (2) or (3), as the case may be.

(2) A driver who is driving a commercial motor vehicle fitted with a sleeper berth may meet the mandatory off-duty time requirement of section 9 by accumulating off-duty time in no more than two periods where,

> (a) neither period of off-duty time is less than two hours;
>
> (b) the total of the two periods of off-duty time is at least 10 hours;
>
> (c) the off-duty time is spent resting in the sleeper berth; and

(d) the driver does not drive again when,

(i) the total of the driving times before and after each sleeper berth period in a sequence referred to in subsection (1) exceeds 13 hours,

(ii) the total of the on-duty times before and after each sleeper berth period in a sequence referred to in subsection (1) exceeds 14 hours, and

(iii) the total of the elapsed times before and after each sleeper berth period in a sequence referred to in subsection (1) exceeds 16 hours.

(3) Where a team of two or more co-drivers are driving a commercial motor vehicle fitted with a sleeper berth, each driver may meet the mandatory off-duty time requirement of section 9, not by accumulating off-duty time as provided by subsection (2), but by accumulating off-duty time in no more than two periods where,

(a) neither period of off-duty time is less than four hours;

(b) the total of the two periods of off-duty time is at least eight hours;

(c) the off-duty time is spent resting in the sleeper berth; and

(d) the driver does not drive again when,

(i) the total of the driving times before and after each sleeper berth period in a sequence referred to in subsection (1) exceeds 13 hours,

(ii) the total of the on-duty times before and after each sleeper berth period in a sequence referred to in subsection (1) exceeds 14 hours, and

(iii) the total of the elapsed times before and after each sleeper berth period in a sequence referred to in subsection (1) exceeds 16 hours.

(4) For the purpose of subsection (3), each driver must record in the "Remarks" section of the daily log the times when a co-driver, other than a co-driver described in subsection 2(5), enters the commercial motor vehicle.

CYCLE REQUIREMENTS

12. 7 or 14-day cycle — (1) An operator shall require that each driver follows either a 7-day or a 14-day cycle, as designated by the operator for the driver.

(2) A driver shall follow the cycle designated for him or her by the operator.

(3) An operator shall not change a driver's cycle except as provided by section 14.

13. Off-duty requirements — (1) Subject to section 14, a driver shall not drive unless the driver has taken at least 24 consecutive hours of off-duty time in the preceding 14 days.

(2) A driver who is following a 7-day cycle shall not drive again in that cycle after accumulating 70 hours of on-duty time during any period of seven days or during the period beginning on the day on which the cycle was reset under section 14, whichever is less.

(3) A driver who is following a 14-day cycle shall not drive again in that cycle after accumulating 120 hours of on-duty time during any period of 14 days or during the

period beginning on the day on which the cycle was reset under section 14, which-ever is less.

(4) A driver who is following a 14-day cycle shall not drive again in that cycle after accumulating 70 hours of on-duty time without having taken at least 24 consecutive hours of off-duty time during the period when the 70 hours were accumulated.

14. Cycle reset — off-duty time — (1) An operator may end a driver's 7-day cycle and designate a new 7-day or 14-day cycle for the driver if the driver takes at least 36 consecutive hours of off-duty time before starting the new cycle.

(2) An operator may end a driver's 14-day cycle and designate a new 14-day or 7-day cycle if the driver takes at least 72 consecutive hours of off-duty time before starting the new cycle.

(3) For the purpose of the cycle requirements of this Regulation, a driver's accumulated hours at the start of each new cycle are deemed to be zero and the driver's hours start to accumulate again at the start of the new cycle.

ADVERSE DRIVING CONDITIONS

15. Increased driving and on-duty times in adverse driving conditions — (1) A driver who encounters adverse driving conditions while driving a commercial motor vehicle may,

   (a) increase the driving time permitted by section 5 by up to two hours and the on-duty time permitted by that section by up to two hours and reduce the off-duty time required by subsection 6(2) by a corresponding amount; and

   (b) increase the driving time permitted by sections 9 and 11 by up to two hours and the on-duty times permitted by those sections by up to two hours if the 16 hour elapsed time required by subsection 9(3) is not exceeded.

(2) If, as a result of subsection (1), the driver exceeds the on-duty time for the cycle permitted by sections 12 to 14, the cycle requirements under those sections must be met by the end of the following day.

(3) If a driver extends his or her driving or on-duty times under subsection (1), the reason for the extension must be entered in the "Remarks" section of the daily log or on the time record required by subsection 18(3).

(4) In this section,

"adverse driving conditions" means significantly impaired driving conditions that were not known, or could not reasonably have been known, to a driver or an operator dispatching a driver immediately before the driver began driving.

RECORD-KEEPING

16. Records to be in local time — (1) Time recorded in a driver's daily log and in the operator's record required by subsection 18(3) must be the local time at the driver's home terminal at the start of each cycle.

(2) The same local time applies for the duration of a driver's cycle.

17. Daily log requirement — (1) Every driver shall keep a daily log each day that accounts for all of the driver's on-duty time and off-duty time for that day in accordance with this Regulation.

(2) An operator shall require every driver to keep a daily log in accordance with this Regulation.

18. Exception to daily log requirement — (1) A driver is not required to keep a daily log for a day if the driver,

(a) on the operator's instructions, drives a commercial motor vehicle solely within a radius of 160 kilometres of the location at which the driver starts the day; and

(b) returns at the end of the day to the same location from which he or she started.

(2) Subsection (1) does not apply to a driver who is driving under a permit issued under section 191 of the Act.

(3) If a driver is not required to keep a daily log for a day pursuant to subsection (1), the operator shall keep a record for the day showing,

(a) the date, the driver's name and the location at which the driver starts and ends the day;

(b) the cycle that the driver is following;

(c) the hour at which each duty status starts and ends and the total number of hours spent in each duty status; and

(d) the number of hours of on-duty time and the number of hours of off-duty time, within the meaning of this Regulation, that the driver accumulated each day during the 14 days immediately before the start of the day, for which the driver was exempt from this Regulation and not required to keep a daily log.

(4) For the purpose of clause (3)(c), if the driver is on duty within a municipality such that a number of periods of driving time are interrupted by a number of periods of other on-duty time of less than one hour each, the periods of driving time may be combined and the periods of other on-duty time may be combined.

19. Contents of daily log — (1) A driver shall, at the start of each day, enter the following information in the daily log:

1. The driver's name.

2. The date.

3. The name of the driver's co-drivers, if any.

4. The start time of the day being recorded, if the day does not start at midnight.

5. The cycle that the driver is following.

6. The odometer reading, at the start of the day, of the commercial motor vehicle to be operated by the driver.

7. The number of hours of on-duty time and the number of hours of off-duty time, within the meaning of this Regulation, that the driver accumulated each day during the 14 days immediately before the start of the day, for which the driver was exempt from this Regulation and not required to keep a daily log, recorded in the "Remarks" section of the daily log.

8. The number plate of each commercial motor vehicle to be driven and each trailer to be drawn by the driver on the day.

9. The name of the operator for whom the driver is to drive during the day.

10. The addresses of the driver's home terminal and of the principal place of business of the operator for whom the driver is to drive during the day.

(2) A driver shall, over the course of each day, enter the following information in the daily log:

1. The start and end times for each duty status during the day.

2. Each city, town, village or highway location and the province or state where the driver's duty status changes.

(3) A driver shall, at the end of each day, enter the following information in the daily log:

1. The total time spent in each duty status during the day.

2. The odometer reading at the end of the day.

3. The total distance driven by the driver.

(4) A driver is not required to record the information described in paragraph 7 of subsection (1) for any day for which the driver carries copies of the records required to be kept by the operator under subsection 18(3).

(5) If the driver is on duty within a municipality such that a number of periods of driving time are interrupted by a number of periods of other on-duty time of less than one hour each,

(a) instead of recording the information described in paragraph 1 of subsection (2), the periods of driving time may be combined and the periods of other on-duty time may be combined;

(b) the driver is not required to record the information described in paragraph 2 of subsection (2) with respect to the periods that have been combined under clause (a); and

(c) the driver shall enter on the graph grid of Form 1 the municipality in which he or she is on duty.

20. Handwritten daily log — (1) If the daily log is handwritten, the entries required by section 19 must be made legibly.

(2) If the daily log is handwritten, the driver shall sign each page at the end of the day, attesting to the accuracy of the information recorded on it.

(3) A handwritten daily log must include a duty status graph grid in Form 1.

21. Computer-generated daily log — (1) A driver may make a daily log by entering all the information required by section 19 into a computer at the start of, over the course of and at the end of the day as required by that section.

(2) If a driver uses a computer to make the daily log, the computer must be capable of printing the daily log in an understandable format and the driver must be able to prepare a handwritten daily log from the information recorded in the computer.

(3) If a driver prints a daily log from the computer or prepares a handwritten daily log from the information stored in the computer, he or she shall date and sign each page, attesting to the accuracy of the information recorded on it.

(4) A daily log printed from the computer shall include a duty status graph grid in Form 1.

(5) For greater certainty, the information stored in the computer is itself a daily log for the purposes of this Regulation.

22. Recording device-generated daily log — (1) A driver may make a daily log by using a recording device installed in a commercial motor vehicle, if the device,

    (a) automatically records time and movement for the vehicle;

    (b) automatically records and indicates the number of times it is disconnected and keeps a record of the time and date of these occurrences;

    (c) keeps track of and records the total on-duty time remaining in the driver's cycle and the total on-duty time accumulated in the driver's cycle;

    (d) stores all the information required to be kept under section 19, as well as the information required to be recorded by clauses (a), (b) and (c); and

    (e) can display the stored information in a readable and understandable format on demand.

(2) The recording device may be an electric, electronic, telematic or other device.

(3) If a driver uses a recording device to make a daily log, the driver shall enter into the device all the information required by section 19, at the start of, over the course of and at the end of the day as required by that section, that is not automatically recorded and stored by the device.

(4) If a driver uses a recording device to make the daily log, the device must be capable of printing the daily log in an understandable format or the driver must be able to prepare a handwritten daily log from the information stored in the device.

(5) If a driver prints a daily log from the recording device or prepares a handwritten daily log from the information stored in the device, he or she shall date and sign each page, attesting to the accuracy of the information recorded on it.

(6) A handwritten daily log generated from the information stored in a recording device must include a duty status graph grid in Form 1.

(7) For greater certainty, the information stored in the recording device is itself a daily log for the purposes of this Regulation.

23. Required to carry and surrender daily logs and supporting documents — (1) A driver who is required to keep a daily log shall not drive unless the driver has in his or her possession,

(a) a copy of the daily logs or a copy of the record required to be kept under subsection 18(3), for the preceding 14 days;

(b) the daily log for the current day, completed up to the time at which the last change in the driver's duty status occurred; and

(c) any supporting documents.

(2) A driver shall forthwith surrender the documents referred to in subsection (1) for inspection upon the demand of an inspector.

(3) If a driver is using a recording device to make a daily log or did use a recording device to make a daily log for any of the preceding 14 days, the driver shall,

(a) forthwith surrender, upon demand of an inspector, a printed or handwritten daily log generated from the information stored in the device for each of such days; and

(b) show, upon demand of an inspector,

(i) a readable display from the device of the required information stored in the device for each of such days, and

(ii) a readable display from the device indicating that it has not been disconnected during any of the previous 14 days that it has been used to make a daily log.

(4) An operator shall not request, require or allow a driver to drive in contravention of subsection (1).

24. Documents forwarded to operator — (1) A driver shall, within 20 days after completing a daily log, forward the original daily log and supporting documents to a place of business of the operator.

(2) An operator shall ensure that every driver complies with subsection (1).

25. Retention of documents by operator — (1) An operator shall,

(a) deposit each daily log and its supporting documents at its principal place of business within 30 days after receiving them; and

(b) keep, for at least six months, at its principal place of business,

(i) all the daily logs and supporting documents for each driver, in chronological order,

(ii) the records required by subsection 18(3) in respect of each driver, and

(iii) the records required by section 28.

(2) Despite subsection (1), where any of the documents described in that subsection are in an electronic, digital or other form other than handwritten or printed form,

the operator may retain them at a place where they can be readily accessed by the operator from the operator's principal place of business in a format,

(a) that can produce a readable and understandable display of the information; and

(b) from which a printed or handwritten version of the information can be produced.

26. Daily log requirements — driver works for multiple operators —
(1) Where a driver works for more than one operator in a day, the driver shall,

(a) enter in the daily log the name of each operator and the address of the principal place of business of each operator;

(b) designate in the daily log one operator as the principal operator; and

(c) for the purpose of subsection 24(1),

(i) forward the original daily log to a place of business of the principal operator and a copy of the daily log to a place of business of each of the other operators, and

(ii) forward the supporting documents to a place of business of the operator to whom it relates.

(2) For the purpose of section 4, the designation of the hour at which a driver's day starts shall be made by the principal operator.

(3) For the purpose of subsection 12(1), the designation of a 7-day or 14-day cycle shall be made by the principal operator.

(4) Section 18 does not apply where a driver works for more than one operator in a day.

27. Integrity of daily logs — (1) No person shall enter inaccurate information in a daily log or falsify, mutilate or deface a daily log or any supporting documents.

(2) An operator shall not request, require or allow a driver to contravene this section.

28. Operators to monitor drivers' compliance — (1) An operator shall monitor each driver's compliance with this Regulation.

(2) If an operator determines that a driver has failed to comply with any provision of this Regulation, the operator shall record the details of the non-compliance and of the remedial action taken by the operator in response to it.

REVOCATION AND COMMENCEMENT

29. Revocation — Ontario Regulation 4/93 is revoked.

30. Commencement — This Regulation comes into force on the later of January 1, 2007 and the day this Regulation is filed.

Form 1 — Duty Status Graph Grid
Highway Traffic Act

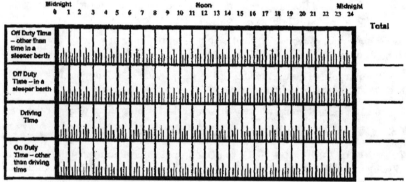

The pre-printed times at the top of the graph grid are for illustration purposes only and should be replaced by the correct times by those drivers for whom the operator has chosen a day that starts at some time other than midnight.

Instructions

Fill out the grid as follows:

    1. For each duty status,

        (a) mark the start time and the end time; and

        (b) draw a continuous line between the time markers and duty status.

    2. Record the name of each city, town, village or highway location and the province or state where the driver's duty status changes.

    3. If the driver is on duty within a municipality such that a number of periods of driving time being interrupted by a number of periods of other on-duty time of less than one hour each, the periods of driving time may be combined and the periods of other on-duty time may be combined.

    4. Enter on the right of the grid the total number of hours of each period of duty status, which total must equal 24 hours.

ONT. REG. 251/02 — IGNITION INTERLOCK DEVICES

made under the *Highway Traffic Act*

O. Reg. 251/02

1. Definitions — In this Regulation,

"approval sticker" means a sticker in the form approved by the Minister for the purpose of this Regulation;

"authorized person" means a person authorized under subsection 41.2(14) of the Act to install, maintain and remove approved ignition interlock devices;

"ignition interlock condition" means a condition on a person's driver's licence prohibiting that person from driving any motor vehicle that is not equipped with an approved ignition interlock device.

2. Approved devices — An ignition interlock device is an approved ignition interlock device for the purpose of section 41.2 of the Act if,

    (a) it uses alcohol-specific sensing technology that will not permit a false reading based on the introduction of another substance;

    (b) it meets one of the following standards:

        1. "Model Specifications for Breath Alcohol Ignition Interlock Devices (BAIIDs)", published by the National Highway Traffic Safety Administration (NHTSA), Department of Transportation, Washington, D.C., Docket No. 91-07, Notice 2, April 7, 1992.

        2. "Qualification Test Specification for Breath Alcohol Ignition Interlock Devices for Use in the Province of Alberta", published by the Solicitor General of Alberta, 1993; and

    (c) it has an approval sticker affixed to it.

3. Requirements for affixing approval sticker on installation — (1) An authorized person shall not affix an approval sticker to an ignition interlock device that meets the criteria set out in clauses 2(a) and (b) unless,

    (a) a person whose driver's licence is subject to an ignition interlock condition requests the installation of the device in writing; and

    (b) the authorized person is satisfied that the person's driver's licence is subject to an ignition interlock condition.

(2) The written request required by clause (1)(a) shall include an acknowledgement by the person that he or she understands how to operate the device and that he or she is responsible for ensuring that the device is properly operated and maintained and is not tampered with by any person.

(3) If the authorized person receives the request as required by subsections (1) and (2) and is satisfied that the person's driver's licence is subject to an ignition interlock condition, the authorized person shall affix an approval sticker to the handset part of the ignition interlock device so that the sticker is plainly visible after the device is installed.

(4) The authorized person shall make and retain a copy of the person's driver's licence if the authorized person affixes the approval sticker to the ignition interlock device.

4. Inspection and maintenance of device — (1) A person who has had an approved ignition interlock device installed into a motor vehicle must ensure that the motor vehicle is brought to the authorized person that installed the device for inspection and maintenance at least once every 60 days.

(2) Despite subsection (1), if the approved ignition interlock device installed into a motor vehicle is designed to be inspected and maintained by removing a component from it, the person who had the device installed must, at least once every 60 days,

    (a) ensure that the component is removed, in accordance with the instructions of the authorized person that installed the device, and is delivered to that authorized person for inspection and maintenance; and

    (b) ensure that the replacement component provided to the person by the authorized person is installed into the device in accordance with the instructions of the authorized person.

5. Records — (1) Every authorized person shall maintain a record of the approved ignition interlock devices installed, inspected, maintained or removed by the person.

(2) The record shall show the name, address, date of birth and driver's licence number of the person who requested the installation of the approved ignition interlock device and the make, model and vehicle identification number of the motor vehicle into which it was installed.

(3) The record shall also show the results of each inspection carried out under section 4, including any information obtained from an ignition interlock device.

(4) The authorized person shall notify the Registrar if the person determines from an inspection of an ignition interlock device that the device has been tampered with.

(5) The authorized person shall, upon request, submit the records maintained under this section to the Registrar.

6. Criteria for removal of ignition interlock condition — (1) The Registrar shall remove the ignition interlock condition under subsection 41.2(4) of the Act if,

    (a) the person whose driver's licence is subject to the condition has not been convicted of an offence under subsection 41.2(11) or (13) of the Act in the preceding 12 months; and

(b) where the person whose driver's licence is subject to the condition requested the installation of an approved ignition interlock device,

(i) the person has complied with section 4, and

(ii) the person has ensured that the device was not tampered with, as shown by the records from the inspections carried out under section 4.

(2) The Registrar shall remove the ignition interlock condition under subsection 41.2(8) of the Act if,

(a) the person whose driver's licence is subject to the condition has not been convicted of an offence under subsection 41.2(11) or (13) of the Act in the preceding 36 months; and

(b) where the person whose driver's licence is subject to the condition requested the installation of an approved ignition interlock device,

(i) the person has complied with section 4, and

(ii) the person has ensured that the device was not tampered with, as shown by the records from the inspections carried out under section 4.

7. This Regulation comes into force on December 23, 2002.

ONT. REG. 11/04 — INTERNATIONAL REGISTRATION PLAN

made under the *Highway Traffic Act*

O. Reg. 11/04

1. Application for IRP cab cards — An application for IRP cab cards for each of the vehicles in a fleet shall include,

(a) the applicant's name, business address, mailing address, telephone number and contact person;

(b) the IRP account number previously assigned to the applicant by the Ministry, if there is one;

(c) the applicant's CVOR certificate number, international fuel tax account number and Canada Customs and Revenue Agency business number;

(d) whether the applicant is a private carrier, a carrier for hire, a carrier of household goods or a daily rental carrier;

(e) whether the application is a first application for a fleet, an application to validate existing IRP cab cards, an application to add a jurisdiction to existing IRP cab cards, an application to add a vehicle to or remove a vehicle from the applicant's fleet, an application to cancel a fleet's IRP cab cards or an application to change a vehicle's registered gross vehicle weight or weight group number;

(f) the IRP registration identification number (RIN) previously assigned to the applicant by the Ministry, if there is one;

(g) the number assigned by the applicant to the fleet that is the subject of the application;

(h) for applications other than a first application for a fleet, the effective and expiry dates of the IRP cab cards currently issued in respect of the fleet;

(i) the insurers for the fleet and for each vehicle in the fleet and the insurance policy numbers and expiry dates;

(j) the other IRP jurisdictions in which the applicant intends to operate the fleet in the 12-month period to which the application applies;

(k) for a first application for a fleet, the estimated distance the applicant intends to operate the fleet in each jurisdiction in the 12-month period to which the application applies;

(l) for applications other than those described in clause (k), the actual distance the applicant operated the fleet in each jurisdiction in the previous 12-month period;

(m) each vehicle's vehicle identification number and its colour, model year, make, fuel type and vehicle type;

(n) the unit number assigned to each vehicle by the applicant;

(o) the plate number of each vehicle, if applicable;

(p) the name of the holder of the vehicle portion of the IRP cab card, if different from the holder of the plate portion, for each vehicle;

(q) the number of truck axles and trailer axles on each vehicle;

(r) each vehicle's tare weight;

(s) each vehicle's registered gross vehicle weight for each jurisdiction and, if there is a variance of 10 per cent or more between any two jurisdictions, an explanation of the variance;

(t) each vehicle's weight group number for each jurisdiction;

(u) the purchase price or lease capital cost of each vehicle;

(v) the date of the purchase or lease of each vehicle;

(w) if the vehicle is leased, whether it is leased from the lessor by the applicant or by a third party that is the owner or operator of the vehicle;

(x) if the vehicle is leased, the name of the lessor and the registration identification number (RIN) assigned to the lessor by the Ministry, if any;

(y) if the vehicle is owned or leased by a third party that is the owner or operator of the vehicle, the registration identification number (RIN) assigned to the owner or operator by the Ministry, if any, and the international fuel tax account number, if applicable, of the owner or operator.

2. Records to be maintained — For the purpose of section 7.2 of the Act, every holder of an IRP cab card shall maintain and preserve the following records:

1. Records of the distance travelled in each trip taken by the vehicle, in accordance with Article XV of the International Registration Plan and the International Registration Plan Audit Procedures Guidelines.

2. All the records relating to the purchase or lease of the vehicle.

3. All the records relating to any capital improvements made to the vehicle.

3. Interest rate — The rate of interest payable to the Minister under section 7.7 of the Act shall be determined in accordance with section 9 of Ontario Regulation 22/97 made under the *Fuel Tax Act*.

4. Manner of serving objections — An objection under subsection 7.8(1) or 7.11(7) of the Act may be served on the Minister personally or by facsimile transmission, courier or registered mail.

ONT. REG. 484/07 — LAMPS — USE OF FLASHING RED OR GREEN LIGHTS

made under the *Highway Traffic Act*

O. Reg. 484/07, as am. O. Reg. 76/11.

1. Definitions — In this Regulation,

"ambulance" [Repealed O. Reg. 76/11, s. 1.]

"emergency" and "emergency response vehicle" [Repealed O. Reg. 76/11, s. 1.]

"municipal emergency plan" means an emergency plan formulated by a municipality under section 3 of the *Emergency Management and Civil Protection Act*.

O. Reg. 76/11, s. 1

2. Use of flashing red lights — In addition to the vehicles listed in paragraphs 1 to 4 of subsection 62(15.1) of the Act, the following are vehicles that may carry lamps that cast a red light to the front:

1. A Ministry of Revenue vehicle operated by a provincial offences officer designated under the *Provincial Offences Act* for the purposes of enforcing the *Fuel Tax Act*, the *Gasoline Tax Act* and the *Tobacco Tax Act*, while the officer is in the course of his or her employment.

2. An aviation and forest fire management vehicle operated by an officer designated under the *Forest Fires Prevention Act*, while the officer is responding to a fire or other emergency.

3. [Repealed O. Reg. 76/11, s. 2.]

O. Reg. 76/11, s. 2

3. Use of flashing green lights — (1) In addition to the persons described in paragraph 1 of subsection 62(16) of the Act, the volunteer medical responders listed in subsection (3) may carry on or in a vehicle and operate a lamp that produces intermittent flashes of green light while,

(a) proceeding and responding to, but not returning from, a medical emergency call to which a police officer, firefighter or ambulance has also been dispatched;

(b) transporting a patient at the request of a government or government agency; or

(c) performing duties assigned in a municipal emergency plan to the volunteer medical response organization of which the volunteer medical responder is a member.

(2) While using flashing green lights as permitted under subsection (1), a volunteer medical responder shall carry the original or a copy of his or her photo identification of membership issued by the volunteer medical response organization and, upon the demand of a police officer or officer appointed for carrying out the provisions of the Act, shall surrender it for reasonable inspection.

(3) This section applies to the following volunteer medical responders:

    1. A member of Hatzoloh Toronto.

    2. A member of St. John Ambulance.

4. Commencement — This Regulation comes into force on the later of September 30, 2007 and the day this Regulation is filed.

ONT. REG. 473/07 — LICENCES FOR DRIVING INSTRUCTORS AND DRIVING SCHOOLS

made under the *Highway Traffic Act*

O. Reg. 473/07, as am. O. Reg. 473/07, s. 37; 347/08; 110/12; 173/12; 245/13.

PART I — INTERPRETATION

1. Interpretation — (1) In this Regulation,

"Class G motor vehicle" means a Class G motor vehicle within the meaning of the Table to subsection 2(1) of O. Reg. 340/94;

"driver education certificate" [Repealed O. Reg. 347/08, s. 1(1).]

"driver education student record" [Repealed O. Reg. 347/08, s. 1(3).]

"electronic driver education certificate" means an electronic record, maintained by the Ministry, of a student's successful completion of a course of driving instruction provided by a driving school;

"old regulation" means Regulation 586 of the Revised Regulations of Ontario, 1990 (*Driving Instructor's Licence*) made under the Act, as it read on November 30, 2007;

"paper driver education certificate" means a certificate provided by the Ministry to a driving school on or after December 1, 2007 and before November 1, 2008 for the purpose of being issued by the driving school to a student on successful completion of a course of driving instruction provided by the driving school.

"O. Reg. 340/94" means Ontario Regulation 340/94 (*Drivers' Licences*) made under the Act.

(2) A reference in this Regulation to a prescribed class of driving instruction is to a class of driving instruction prescribed under section 2 or 15, as the case may be.

(3) For greater certainty, a school board that provides driving instruction as a business or as part of a driver education course approved by the Ministry is a driving school.

O. Reg. 347/08, s. 1

841

PART II — DRIVING INSTRUCTOR LICENCES

Class of Instruction

2. Prescribed class of driving instruction — In-vehicle driving instruction in the operation of a Class G motor vehicle provided to a holder of a Class G1, G2 or G driver's licence is a class of driving instruction that an individual must be authorized to provide for the purpose of subsection 58(1) of the Act.

3. Authorization to provide driving instruction — The holder of a valid driving instructor licence is authorized to provide instruction in the prescribed class of in-vehicle driving instruction.

Issuance and Renewal of Licences

4. Requirements for driving instructor licence — (1) An applicant must satisfy the following requirements for the issue of a driving instructor licence:

1. The applicant has the ability to operate, and to instruct in the safe operation of, a Class G motor vehicle.

2. The applicant meets the requirements of subsection 5(2) of O. Reg. 340/94 to be an accompanying driver, other than by virtue of being licensed as a driving instructor in Ontario.

3. The applicant successfully completed, not more than one year before the date of the application, the examinations referred to in clauses 15(1)(a) and (b) and subsection 15(2) of O. Reg. 340/94.

4. The applicant satisfies the Minister, not more than one year before the date of the application, that he or she meets the requirements of subsection 18(2) of O. Reg. 340/94.

5. The applicant does not have any accumulated demerit points on his or her driving record.

6. The applicant's driver's licence has not been under suspension at any time in the preceding two years,

   i. as a result of being found guilty or convicted of an offence under section 9 or 53, subsection 128(15) or section 130, subsection 172(2) or section 200 or 216 of the Act,

   ii. as a result of being found guilty or convicted of an offence under section 2 of the *Compulsory Automobile Insurance Act*,

   iii. as a result of being found guilty or convicted of an offence under the *Criminal Code* (Canada) committed by means of a motor vehicle or while driving or having the care or control of a motor vehicle, or of a comparable offence in another jurisdiction, or

   iv. pursuant to section 48 or 48.3 or subsection 172(6) of the Act.

7. The applicant is not, on the date of the application, subject to a charge for an offence under section 151, 152, 153, 153.1, 155, 160, 162, 163, 163.1, 167, 168,

170, 171, 172, 172.1, 173, 212, 271, 272 or 273 of the *Criminal Code* (Canada) or of a comparable offence in another jurisdiction.

8. The applicant has never been convicted or found guilty of an offence under the *Criminal Code* (Canada) listed in paragraph 7, or of a comparable offence in another jurisdiction.

9. The applicant has not been convicted or found guilty in the preceding five years of an offence under the *Criminal Code* (Canada), not including an offence listed in paragraph 7, or of a comparable offence in another jurisdiction.

10. The applicant has never been convicted or found guilty of an offence under section 5, 6 or 7 of the *Controlled Drugs and Substances Act* (Canada) or section 4 or 5 of the *Narcotic Control Act* (Canada), or of a comparable offence in another jurisdiction.

11. The applicant has not been convicted or found guilty in the preceding five years of an offence under the *Controlled Drugs and Substances Act* (Canada) or the *Narcotic Control Act* (Canada), not including an offence listed in paragraph 10, or of a comparable offence in another jurisdiction.

12. The applicant is not subject to a court order, conditions of parole or an undertaking to an officer in charge prohibiting him or her from,

    i. possessing a weapon, or

    ii. being alone with, in the presence of or in proximity to persons under any age that may be specified in the order, conditions or undertaking.

13. The applicant has successfully completed, not more than five years before the date of the application, a course for in-vehicle driving instructors approved by the Ministry.

14. Where the applicant has been licensed by another jurisdiction, the applicant's driving record in that jurisdiction is comparable to that required by paragraph 5.

15. The applicant is a fit and proper person to be a driving instructor, having regard to the applicant's character, integrity and past conduct.

(2) Subject to section 35, the Minister shall refuse to issue a driving instructor licence to a person who does not satisfy the requirements of paragraphs 1 to 15 of subsection (1) and shall serve written notice of the refusal on the person.

O. Reg. 110/12, s. 1

5. Application for driving instructor licence — (1) An applicant for a driving instructor licence shall submit, together with the application,

    (a) [Repealed O. Reg. 110/12, s. 2.]

    (b) the fees required by subsection 8(1); and

    (c) any other material that the Minister may require as evidence that the applicant satisfies the requirements of subsection 4(1).

(2) An applicant for a driving instructor licence who has twice failed an examination for such licence under subsection 15(2) of O. Reg. 340/94 is not eligible to take the examination again until one year has passed since the last failed examination.

(3) An applicant for a driving instructor licence who has twice failed an examination for such licence under clause 15(1)(a) of O. Reg. 340/94 is not eligible to take the examination again until one year has passed since the last failed examination.

O. Reg. 347/08, s. 2; 110/12, s. 2

6. Term of initial driving instructor licence — (1) The term of a driving instructor licence issued to an applicant for the first time under this Regulation shall be at least 13 months and shall expire on March 31 of the year in which it expires.

(2) Despite subsection (1), a driving instructor licence that is deemed to be issued under section 9 expires on the date set out in the licence that was issued under the old regulation.

7. Renewal of driving instructor licence — (1) Every renewal of a driving instructor licence shall be for a term of three years and shall expire on March 31 of the year in which it expires.

(2) A driving instructor licence that is not renewed within one year after its expiry is not renewable and must be applied for again.

(3) Section 6 applies with necessary modifications to a driving instructor licence that is applied for again as required by subsection (2).

8. Fees — (1) The following fees are payable in respect of the issue, renewal or replacement of a driving instructor licence:

1.	For examinations under clauses 15(1)(a) and (b) and subsection 15(2) of O. Reg. 340/94	$100
1.1	For the administration of examinations under clauses 15(1)(a) and (b) and subsection 15(2) of O. Reg. 340/94 described in paragraph 1	$10
2.	For the issue or renewal of a driving instructor licence, per month, to the date of its expiry	$1.33
3.	[Repealed O. Reg. 245/13, s. 1(1).]	
4.	For replacement of a lost or destroyed driving instructor licence	$28

(2) The fees under paragraphs 1 and 1.1 of subsection (1) are due when the examinations are booked and are payable even if the time booked for taking the examinations passes without the examinations being taken.

O. Reg. 173/12, s. 1; 245/13, s. 1

8.1 Fee adjustment — Consumer Price Index — (1) Beginning on September 1, 2014, and on every September 1 after that, the fee prescribed in paragraph 1 of subsection 8(1) is the fee for the previous 12-month period adjusted by the percentage change in the Ontario Consumer Price Index between the previous two calendar years.

(2) The actual fee prescribed in paragraph 1 of subsection 8(1) is the amount determined by the calculation described in subsection (1) rounded to the nearest quarter of a dollar.

(3) If the percentage change in the Ontario Consumer Price Index between the previous two calendar years results in a negative amount, the fee prescribed in paragraph 1 of subsection 8(1) shall remain at the same level as the previous year.

(4) In this section, the percentage change in the Ontario Consumer Price Index between two calendar years is the percentage change in the Consumer Price Index for Ontario (All-Items) between those years as published by Statistics Canada under the authority of the *Statistics Act* (Canada).

O. Reg. 173/12, s. 2

9. Transition — A person who holds a valid driving instructor's licence under the old regulation on November 30, 2007 is deemed to be issued a driving instructor licence under this Regulation on December 1, 2007.

Refusal to Renew and Revocation of a Licence

10. Refusal to renew or revocation of driving instructor licence — (1) Subject to section 35, the Minister may refuse to renew or may revoke a driving instructor licence if,

(a) the licensee made a false or inaccurate statement on his or her application for the licence under this Regulation, on his or her application for a licence under the old regulation or on his or her application for renewal of a licence that was issued or deemed to be issued under this Regulation;

(b) the licensee did not satisfy a requirement of subsection 4(1) at the time the application for the licence was made or the licence was issued;

(c) if the licensee holds a licence deemed to be issued under section 9, the licensee did not satisfy a requirement of section 3 of the old regulation at the time the application for a driving instructor's licence was made or the licence was issued under the old regulation or at the time the licence was deemed to be issued under section 9 of this Regulation;

(d) at any time while licensed as a driving instructor,

(i) under this Regulation,

(A) the licensee ceases to meet the requirements of subsection 5(2) of O. Reg. 340/94 to be an accompanying driver, other than by virtue of being licensed as a driving instructor in Ontario,

(B) the licensee has more than three accumulated demerit points on his or her driving record,

(C) the licensee is convicted or found guilty of an offence under the *Criminal Code* (Canada) or of a comparable offence in another jurisdiction,

(D) the licensee is convicted or found guilty of an offence under the *Controlled Drugs and Substances Act* (Canada) or the *Narcotic Control Act* (Canada) or of a comparable offence in another jurisdiction,

(E) the licensee is subject to a court order, conditions of parole or an undertaking to an officer in charge, prohibiting him or her from possessing a weapon, or

(F) the licensee is subject to a court order, conditions of parole or an undertaking to an officer in charge, prohibiting him or her from being alone with, in the presence of or in proximity to persons under any age that may be specified in the order, conditions or undertaking, or

(ii) under the old regulation, grounds existed for the suspension or revocation of the licence under section 9 of that regulation;

(e) at any time while licensed as a driving instructor under this Regulation or, in the case of subclauses (i) and (ii), while licensed as a driving instructor under the old regulation,

(i) the licensee does not or did not operate motor vehicles safely,

(ii) the licensee does not or did not provide adequate instruction to his or her students or treats his or her students in an inappropriate manner,

(iii) the licensee contravenes or fails to comply with section 58, 58.1 or 58.2 of the Act or any provision of this Regulation or breaches a condition of his or her licence, or

(iv) the licensee is not a fit and proper person to be a driving instructor, having regard to his or her character, integrity and past conduct; or

(f) on or after December 1, 1997, whether while licensed as a driving instructor under this Regulation or the old regulation or while not so licensed, the licensee is or was convicted or found guilty of an offence under section 151, 152, 153, 153.1, 155, 160, 162, 163, 163.1, 167, 168, 170, 171, 172, 172.1, 173, 212, 271, 272 or 273 of the *Criminal Code* (Canada) or a comparable offence in another jurisdiction; or

(g) on or after December 1, 1997, whether while licensed as a driving instructor under this Regulation or the old regulation or while not so licensed, the licensee is or was convicted or found guilty of an offence under section 5, 6 or 7 of the *Controlled Drugs and Substances Act* (Canada), section 4 or 5 of the *Narcotic Control Act* (Canada) or a comparable offence in another jurisdiction.

(2) Despite sub-subclause (1)(d)(i)(B), the Minister shall not revoke or refuse to renew a driving instructor licence of a licensee who was licensed as a driving instructor under the old regulation on November 30, 2007 and who had more than three accumulated demerit points on his or her driving record on November 30, 2007, unless,

(a) the licensee acquires any demerit points on or after December 1, 2007 as a result of an offence that was committed on or after that day;

(b) having had his or her accumulated demerit points reduced on or after December 1, 2007 to three or fewer, he or she has more than three accumulated demerit points on his or her driving record at any time after that day; or

(c) the licensee has more than eight accumulated demerit points on his or her driving record at any time on or after December 1, 2007.

(3) [Repealed O. Reg. 347/08, s. 3(2).]

(4) [Repealed O. Reg. 347/08, s. 3(2).]

(5) Despite sub-subclause (1)(d)(i)(E), the Minister shall not revoke or refuse to renew a driving instructor licence of a licensee who was licensed as a driving instructor under the old regulation on November 30, 2007 and who was subject to an order, condition or undertaking described in that sub-subclause made on or before that date.

(6) Nothing in subsection (2) or (5) prevents the Minister from revoking or refusing to renew a driving instructor licence for any other reason under subsection (1).

(7) The Minister shall serve written notice of a refusal to renew or a revocation of a license on the licensee.

(8) A licence revocation shall be effective on the date set out in the notice.

O. Reg. 347/08, s. 3

Obligations of Licensees

11. Licence to be displayed — Every licensed driving instructor shall display his or her driving instructor licence in the motor vehicle in which he or she is providing driving instruction so that the licence is plainly visible to a person sitting in the driver's seat.

12. Instruction must be for licensed driving school — (1) A licensed driving instructor shall not provide instruction to the holder of a Class G1 driver's licence except pursuant to a written contract between the instructor and a licensed driving school for the employment or services of the instructor to provide driving instruction.

(2) [Repealed O. Reg. 473/07, s. 37.]

O. Reg. 473/07, s. 37

12.1 Consent to Ministry — Every licensed driving instructor shall give each licensed driving school with which he or she is under contract to provide driving instruction a written consent to the Ministry to notify the school if the instructor's licence is or may be revoked.

O. Reg. 347/08, s. 4

13. Information to Ministry — Every licensed driving instructor shall respond forthwith to any inquiries from the Ministry for information relating to his or her qualifications to hold a driving instructor licence.

14. Students' licences not to be retained — If a licensed driving instructor asks to see a student's driver's licence, the instructor may retain the student's driver's licence only for as long as is necessary to make a copy of it and must ensure that the licence is returned to the student immediately after it is copied.

O. Reg. 347/08, s. 5

PART III — DRIVING SCHOOL LICENCES

Classes of Instruction

15. Prescribed classes of driving instruction — The following are prescribed as classes of driving instruction that a person must be authorized to provide for the purpose of subsection 58.1(2) of the Act:

1. In-vehicle driving instruction in the operation of a Class G motor vehicle provided to a holder of a Class G1, G2 or G driver's licence in a driver education course approved by the Ministry.

2. Classroom driving instruction in the operation of a Class G motor vehicle provided to a person who does not hold a driver's licence or who holds a Class G1 or G2 driver's licence in a driver education course approved by the Ministry.

16. Authorization to operate driving school — (1) The holder of a driving school licence is authorized to operate a driving school that provides instruction in the classes of driving instruction prescribed by section 15.

(2) [Repealed O. Reg. 473/07, s. 37.]

(3) [Repealed O. Reg. 473/07, s. 37.]

O. Reg. 473/07, s. 37

Issuance and Renewal of Licences

17. Licence specific to school — A driving school licence is valid only in respect of the premises specified in the driving school licence.

18. Requirements for driving school licence — (1) An applicant must satisfy the following requirements for the issue of a driving school licence:

1. The applicant is competent to operate a driving school.

2. The applicant satisfies the Minister that it holds all other applicable licenses that are required for the applicant to engage in a business and to operate a driving school.

3. The applicant owns or leases premises for the driving school's office and classrooms.

4. The applicant satisfies the Minister that the driving school's office and classrooms are in compliance with all applicable zoning restrictions.

5. The driving school's classrooms are appropriate for the purpose of providing driving instruction, including being appropriately equipped and maintained for that purpose.

5.1 The motor vehicles to be used to provide driving instruction comply with section 27.

6. The curriculum for the driving school's proposed driver education course is satisfactory to the Ministry.

7. The applicant maintains general liability insurance in the amount of at least $2,000,000 with respect to any one incident that occurs in a classroom.

8. The applicant has entered into a written contract for the employment or services of one or more licensed driving instructors to provide driving instruction.

9. If the applicant is an individual, the applicant is a fit and proper person to operate a driving school, having regard to his or her character, integrity and past conduct.

10. If the applicant is a partnership or corporation, the partners of the partnership or officers and directors of the corporation are fit and proper persons to operate a driving school, having regard to their character, integrity and past conduct.

11. Any person related to the applicant satisfies the requirements of paragraph 9 or 10, as the case may be.

(2) For the purpose of paragraph 11 of subsection (1), a person is related to an applicant in any of the following circumstances:

1. The applicant and the person are individuals connected by blood relationship, marriage, common-law partnership, within the meaning of the *Income Tax Act* (Canada), or adoption.

2. The applicant is a partnership and the person is or was a partner of the partnership, or the person is a partnership and the applicant is or was a partner of the partnership.

3. The applicant and the person are or were partners of the same partnership.

4. Both the applicant and the person are corporations and,

    i. the applicant controls, directly or indirectly, or manages the person,

    ii. the applicant controlled, directly or indirectly, or managed the person,

    iii. the person controls, directly or indirectly, or manages the applicant, or

    iv. the person controlled, directly or indirectly, or managed the applicant.

5. Both the applicant and the person are corporations and they are or were controlled, directly or indirectly, or managed by the same person.

6. Both the applicant and the person are corporations and they have or have had common officers or directors.

(3) Subject to section 35, the Minister shall refuse to issue a driving school licence to an applicant that does not satisfy the requirements of paragraphs 1 to 11 of subsection (1), and shall serve written notice of the refusal on the person.

O. Reg. 347/08, s. 6

19. Term of initial driving school licence — The term of a driving school licence issued to an applicant for the first time under this Regulation shall be at least one year and shall expire on the date set out in the licence.

20. Renewal of driving school licence — (1) Every renewal of a driving school licence shall be for a term of three years and shall expire on the date that is the third anniversary of the date of the renewal.

(2) A driving school licence that is not renewed within six months after its expiry is not renewable and must be applied for again.

(3) Section 18 applies with necessary modifications to a driving school licence that is applied for again as required by subsection (2).

Refusal to Renew and Revocation of a Licence

21. Refusal to renew or revocation of driving school licence — (1) Subject to section 35, the Minister may refuse to renew or may revoke a driving school licence if,

(a) the licensee made a false or inaccurate statement on the application for the licence or on the application for renewal of the licence;

(b) the licensee did not satisfy a requirement of section 18 at the time the application for the licence was made or the licence was issued;

(c) the licensee ceases to satisfy a requirement of section 18 at any time after the licence is issued;

(d) the driving school does not provide adequate instruction to its students or treats its students, or permits its driving instructors to treat its students, in an inappropriate manner;

(e) the licensee, or a partner, officer or director of the licensee, contravenes or fails to comply with section 58, 58.1 or 58.2 of the Act or any provision of this Regulation or breaches a condition of its licence;

(f) the licensee, or a partner, officer or director of the licensee, is not a fit and proper person to operate a driving school, having regard to his or her character, integrity and past conduct; or

(g) the driving school is not in operation and has not been in operation for a period of one year.

(2) The Minister shall serve written notice of a refusal to renew or a revocation of a license on the licensee.

(3) A licence revocation shall be effective on the date set out in the notice.

Obligations of Licensees

22. Licence to be displayed — Every licensee that operates a licensed driving school shall display a copy of the driving school licence in every classroom used to provide driving instruction so that it is plainly visible to the students in the classroom.

23. Approval for premises — A licensed driving school shall obtain the Ministry's prior approval for the premises it proposes to use for its office and classrooms.

24. Driving instructors — A licensee that operates a licensed driving school shall not permit any person to provide instruction in the prescribed class of in-vehicle driving instruction or the prescribed class of classroom driving instruction unless,

(a) the person holds a driving instructor licence issued or deemed to be issued under this Regulation;

(b) the person is under written contract with the school for his or her employment or services to provide driving instruction; and

(c) the person has given the school a written consent to the Ministry to notify the school if his or her instructor's licence expires or is or may be revoked and the school has given the consent to the Ministry, in the form and manner specified by the Ministry.

O. Reg. 347/08, s. 7

25. Requirements re classroom driving instruction — (1) A licensee that operates a licensed driving school shall not permit any person to provide the prescribed class of classroom driving instruction unless,

(a) the person and the school satisfy the requirements of section 24; and

(b) the person,

(i) has successfully completed a course in classroom driving instruction approved by the Ministry, or

(ii) in the case of person who is certified by the Ontario College of Teachers to provide classroom driving instruction, has successfully completed before September 29, 2008 a course in classroom driving instruction approved by a school board.

(2) The holder of a valid driving instructor licence who satisfies the requirements of subsection (1) is authorized to provide instruction in both the prescribed class of in-vehicle driving instruction and the prescribed class of classroom driving instruction.

(3) [Repealed O. Reg. 347/08, s. 8.]

(4) [Repealed O. Reg. 347/08, s. 8.]

(5) [Repealed O. Reg. 347/08, s. 8.]

O. Reg. 347/08, s. 8

26. Requirements re driver education course — (1) Every licensed driving school shall provide instruction in a prescribed class of driving instruction in accordance with the curriculum of the driver education course that is satisfactory to the Ministry as required by paragraph 6 of subsection 18(1).

(2) A driver education course must be completed in one year.

27. Vehicles — Every licensee that operates a licensed driving school shall ensure that each motor vehicle used by the driving school to provide driving instruction satisfies the following requirements:

1. It has a currently validated vehicle permit.

2. It has number plates displayed in accordance with the Act.

3. It is equipped with a properly functioning service brake actuator that may be operated by the driving instructor.

4. A safety standards certificate has been issued in respect of the motor vehicle within the previous year.

5. It is insured by a policy of automobile insurance, as defined in subsection 1(1) of the *Compulsory Automobile Insurance Act*, with a limit for personal injury or damage to property of not less than $2,000,000 exclusive of interest and costs in respect of any one accident, and the policy contains a driving training school endorsement in a form approved by the Superintendent of Financial Services.

28. Students' licences not to be retained — If a licensed driving school asks to see a student's driver's licence, the school may retain the student's driver's licence only for as long as is necessary to make a copy of it and must return the licence to the student immediately after copying it.

29. Driver education certificates — (1) Electronic driver education certificates and paper driver education certificates are prescribed as driver education certificates for the purpose of subsection 58.1(6) of the Act.

(2) A licensed driving school shall not issue a driver education certificate to a student and a person authorized to sign a paper driver education certificate by subsection 29.2(2) shall not do so until the student has successfully completed both the prescribed class of classroom driving instruction and the prescribed class of in-vehicle driving instruction that comprise the school's driver education course.

(3) Every licensed driving school shall return its unused paper driver education certificates, if it has any, to the Ministry on or before the first anniversary of the day Ontario Regulation 347/08 is filed and shall not issue any paper driver education certificates after that date.

(4) [Repealed O. Reg. 347/08, s. 9.]

(5) [Repealed O. Reg. 347/08, s. 9.]

(6) [Repealed O. Reg. 347/08, s. 9.]

O. Reg. 347/08, s. 9

29.1 Issuance of electronic driver education certificates — (1) A licensed driving school issues an electronic driver education certificate to a student upon the successful completion of the school's driver education course by notifying the Ministry electronically, in the form and manner specified by the Ministry, that the student has successfully completed the school's driver education course and by paying to the Ministry the fee prescribed under subsection 30(2).

(2) An electronic driver education certificate is not considered issued under subsection (1) until the Ministry acknowledges to the driving school receipt of the notification and of the fee required under section 30.

(3) A licensed driving school that has issued an electronic driver education certificate to a student in error may, with the consent of the Ministry, cancel the certifi-

cate electronically, in the form and manner specified by the Ministry, and the Ministry shall acknowledge the cancellation to the driving school.

(4) The Registrar shall include on the driver records that he or she maintains for every person who holds a driver's licence the fact that the person was issued,

(a) an electronic driver education certificate under this Regulation; or

(b) a paper driver education certificate or driver education student record issued to him or her under this Regulation or the old regulation, if the person submits a copy of the paper driver education certificate or driver education student record to the Ministry.

O. Reg. 347/08, s. 9

29.2 Issuance of paper driver education certificates — (1) A licensed driving school may issue a paper driver education certificate to a student upon the successful completion of the school's driver education course by giving the certificate to the student.

(2) A paper driver education certificate issued to a student under subsection (1) must be signed by,

(a) a licensed driving instructor under contract with the school for his or her employment or services;

(b) if the licensee that operates the licensed driving school is a partnership, one of the partners;

(c) if the licensee that operates the licensed driving school is a corporation, one of the officers or directors previously identified to the Ministry as an officer or director; or

(d) if the driver education course is provided by a school board, a full-time employee of the board designated in writing by the board.

(3) A licensed driving school may issue a replacement paper driver education certificate to a former student of the school only if the school still has a record of that student's enrolment in and successful completion of the school's driver education course.

(4) Every licensee that operates a licensed driving school shall keep the school's unused paper driver education certificates in a secure location and shall notify the Ministry immediately of the loss, theft or destruction of any such certificates.

O. Reg. 347/08, s. 9

30. Fees for driver education certificates — (1) Every licensee that operates a licensed driving school shall pay $15 to the Ministry for each paper driver education certificate provided by the Ministry to the licensee.

(2) Every licensee that operates a licensed driving school shall pay $15 to the Ministry for each electronic driver education certificate issued by the licensee on and after September 29, 2008.

(3) The Ministry shall refund a licensee $2.25 for each unused paper driver education certificate provided by the Ministry to the licensee that the licensee returns to

the Ministry and for each electronic driver education certificate that the licensee notifies the Ministry is cancelled.

(4) [Repealed O. Reg. 347/08, s. 10.]

O. Reg. 347/08, s. 10

31. Information to Ministry — (1) Every licensee that operates a licensed driving school shall notify the Ministry within 15 days after any change in the information provided by it to the Ministry with its licence application or thereafter, and shall provide the Ministry with supporting documents relevant to such change.

(1.1) Every licensee that operates a licensed driving school shall notify the Ministry immediately, in the form and manner specified by the Ministry,

(a) upon entering into a written contract with a licensed driving instructor for his or her employment or services to provide driving instruction; and

(b) upon such instructor's ceasing to provide driving instruction for the school for any reason.

(2) Despite subsection (1), a licensee shall obtain prior approval from the Ministry for any new premises it proposes to use for its office or for a classroom.

(3) On the day a driver education course provided by a licensed driving school starts, the licensee that operates the school shall submit to the Ministry the following information in the form and manner required by the Ministry:

1. The name of the licensed driving school.

2. The licence number issued to the school by the Ministry.

3. The start date of the course.

3.1 The list of licensed driving instructors who will provide classroom instruction in the course.

3.2 The list of licensed driving instructors who will provide in-vehicle instruction in the course.

4. The list of students enrolled in the course, including each student's name, gender, date of birth, address and telephone number.

5. For each student who holds a driver's licence before the start of the course, the number of the licence.

(4) At the end of a driver education course provided by a licensed driving school, the licensee that operates the school shall submit to the Ministry the list of students who successfully completed the course and,

(a) a copy of each paper driver education certificate issued by the school;

(b) for each successful student, a copy of his or her driver's licence;

(c) the list of licensed driving instructors who provided classroom instruction in the course; and

(d) the list of licensed driving instructors who provided in-vehicle instruction in the course.

(5) Every licensee that operates a licensed driving school shall respond forthwith to any inquiries from the Ministry for information relating to its qualifications to hold a driving school licence.

O. Reg. 347/08, s. 11

32. Recordkeeping — (1) Every licensee that operates a licensed driving school shall keep and retain the following records at its office:

1. The original driving school licence for the school.

2. The list of students enrolled in each driver education course provided by the school, as described in paragraph 4 of subsection 31(3).

3. For each student who holds a driver's licence before the start of the course, the number of the licence.

4. The name of each licensed driving instructor under contract with the school for his or her employment or services who provided classroom or in-vehicle instruction for each course provided by the school, the number and expiry date of his or her driver's licence and the number and expiry date of his or her driving instructor licence issued or deemed to be issued under this Regulation.

5. A classroom training record sheet for each student enrolled in a driver education course provided by the school, which must contain,

  i. the student's name,

  ii. the dates, times and duration of each classroom training session attended by the student,

  iii. the student's classroom test results,

  iv. the signature of the student, and

  v. the name and signature of the licensed driving instructor who provided the classroom instruction.

6. An in-vehicle training record sheet for each student enrolled in a driver education course provided by the school, which must contain,

  i. the student's name,

  ii. the dates and times of each in-vehicle training session attended by the student and the duration of the student's actual driving time during each session,

  iii. the student's in-vehicle test results,

  iv. the signature of the student, and

  v. the name and signature of the licensed driving instructor who provided the in-vehicle instruction.

6.1 A record of each electronic driver education certificate issued by the school to a student on successful completion of a driver education course provided by the school, including a record of the Ministry's acknowledgment that it was notified of such issuance, and a record of the cancellation of any such electronic driver education certificate that was issued in error and of the Ministry's acknowledgment of the cancellation.

7. Copies of each paper driver education certificate issued by the school to a student on successful completion of a driver education course provided by the school.

8. [Repealed O. Reg. 347/08, s. 12(3).]

9. A list of the licensed driving instructors who enter into a written contract with the school for their employment or services, including a record of the days and hours worked by each such instructor and a record of his or her earnings.

10. Copies of each written contract for employment or services entered into by a licensed driving instructor and the school.

(2) The records described in paragraphs 2 to 8 of subsection (1) shall be kept for three years from the date they are created.

(3) The list of instructors described in paragraph 9 of subsection (1) shall be kept for three years from the date it ceases to be current.

(4) A contract described in paragraph 10 of subsection (1) shall be kept for three years from the date the instructor ceases to be under contract with the school for his or her employment or services.

(5) No student or instructor shall sign a training record sheet under either paragraph 5 or 6 of subsection (1) until after the student has successfully completed that portion of the driver education course.

(6) [Repealed O. Reg. 473/07, s. 37.]

O. Reg. 473/07, s. 37; 347/08, s. 12

33. Electronic records — (1) Any record required to be kept or retained by section 32 may be kept or retained in electronic form if,

(a) it contains all the information required by section 32; and

(b) upon the demand of an inspector appointed under section 58.2 of the Act, the record can be viewed electronically and a paper copy can be produced for inspection and copying.

(2) For the purposes of clause (1)(a), the requirement that a record be signed is satisfied by an electronic signature if,

(a) the electronic signature is reliable for the purpose of identifying the person; and

(b) the association of the electronic signature with the electronic document is reliable.

(3) A licensee that operates a licensed driving school may submit any document to the Ministry in electronic form only with the prior approval of the Ministry and in the form and manner specified by the Ministry.

34. Return of records, etc. on ceasing to be licensed — A licensee that is notified that the Minister is revoking or refusing to renew its driving school licence shall, forthwith upon notification,

(a) return its original licence and all of its unused paper driver education certificates to the Ministry;

(b) provide the Ministry with all records in the licensee's possession that the Ministry may require regarding students currently enrolled in the school's driver education courses; and

(c) provide to the Ministry any records listed under subsection 32(1) that it possesses at the close of business on the last day that it is licensed.

O. Reg. 347/08, s. 13

PART IV — RIGHT TO BE HEARD

35. Right to be heard — circumstances — (1) An applicant for a driving instructor licence or person who holds a driving instructor licence, including a licence deemed to have been issued under section 9, has no right to be heard before the Minister makes a decision to refuse to issue the licence or to revoke or refuse to renew the licence except in the following circumstances:

1. Where the Minister proposes to refuse to issue a licence because the applicant fails to satisfy a requirement under paragraph 1 or 15 of subsection 4(1).

2. Where the Minister proposes to revoke a licence or refuse to renew a licence under clause 10(1)(b) because the licensee did not satisfy a requirement set out in paragraph 1 or 15 of subsection 4(1).

3. Where the Minister proposes to revoke a licence or refuse to renew a licence under clause 10(1)(c) because the licensee did not satisfy a requirement set out in clause 3(1)(a) or (h) of the old regulation.

4. Where the Minister proposes to revoke a licence or refuse to renew a licence under subclause 10(1)(d)(ii) because the licensee did not satisfy a requirement set out in clause 3(1)(a) or (h) of the old regulation.

5. Where the Minister proposes to revoke a licence or refuse to renew a licence under subclause 10(1)(e)(i), (ii) or (iv).

(2) An applicant for a driving school licence or person who holds a driving school licence has no right to be heard before the Minister makes a decision to refuse to issue the licence or to revoke or refuse to renew the licence except in the following circumstances:

1. Where the Minister proposes to refuse to issue a licence because the applicant fails to satisfy a requirement under paragraph 1, 9, 10 or 11 of subsection 18(1).

2. Where the Minister proposes to revoke or to refuse to renew a licence under clause 21(1)(b) because the licensee failed to satisfy a requirement set out in paragraph 1, 9, 10 or 11 of subsection 18(1).

3. Where the Minister proposes to revoke or to refuse to renew a licence under clause 21(1)(c) because the applicant fails to satisfy a requirement set out in paragraph 1, 9, 10 or 11 of subsection 18(1).

4. Where the Minister proposes to revoke or to refuse to renew a licence under clause 21(1)(d) or (f).

(3) Prior to making a decision described in paragraph 1, 2, 3, 4 or 5 of subsection (1) or paragraph 1, 2, 3 or 4 of subsection (2), the Minister shall serve a notice of his or her proposed decision on the applicant or licensee, together with a summary of the reasons for such proposed decision.

(4) An applicant or licensee may, within 30 days after being served with a notice under subsection (3), submit in writing to the Minister any information that the applicant or licensee considers relevant to the Minister's proposed decision.

(5) The Minister shall review and consider any information submitted under subsection (4) before making a decision described in paragraph 1, 2, 3, 4 or 5 of subsection (1) or paragraph 1, 2, 3 or 4 of subsection (2).

(6) There is no right to appeal a decision of the Minister made under section 58 or 58.1 of the Act or under this Regulation, but nothing in this Regulation prevents the taking of a proceeding in court to review such a decision.

PART V — GENERAL

36. (1) Service — Any notice required to be served under this Regulation is sufficiently served if delivered personally or sent by mail addressed to the person upon whom service is to be made at the last address for service appearing on the records of the Ministry.

(2) **Same** — Service made by mail is deemed to be made on the seventh day after the day of mailing.

PART VI — REVOCATIONS AND COMMENCEMENT

37. Revocation of provisions of this Regulation — Subsections 12(2), 16(2) and (3) and 32(6) are revoked on September 1, 2008.

38. Revocation of current regulation — Regulation 586 of the Revised Regulations of Ontario, 1990 is revoked.

39. Commencement — (1) Subject to subsection (2), this Regulation comes into force on the later of September 1, 2007 and the day this Regulation is filed.

(2) Part II and section 38 come into force on December 1, 2007.

Ont. Reg. 8/03 — Local Municipalities Where 80 Kilometres Per Hour Speed Limit Applies

made under the *Highway Traffic Act*

O. Reg. 8/03

1. Application of 80 km/hr speed limit — The local municipalities listed in the Table are prescribed for the purpose of clause 128(1)(b) of the Act.

2. Commencement — This Regulation comes into force on the later of the day it is filed and January 1, 2003.

TABLE

Addington Highlands
Adelaide-Metcalfe
Adjala-Tosorontio
Admaston/Bromley
Alberton
Alfred and Plantagenet
Algonquin Highlands
Alnwick-Haldimand
Amaranth
Armour
Armstrong
Arran-Elderslie
Ashfield-Colbome-Wawanosh
Asphodel-Norwood
Assiginack
Athens
Atikokan
Augusta
Baldwin
Barrie Island
Bathurst Burgess Sherbrooke
Bayham
Beckwith
Billings
Black River-Matheson
Blandford-Blenheim
Bonfield
Bonnechere Valley

Brethour
Brock
Brockton
Brooke-Alvinston
Brudenell, Lynoch and Raglan
Burpee and Mills
Callander
Calvin
Carling
Carlow/Mayo
Casey
Cavan-Millbrook-North Monaghan
Central Elgin
Central Frontenac
Central Huron
Central Manitoulin
Centre Hastings
Centre Wellington
Chamberlain
Champlain
Chapleau
Chapple
Chatsworth
Chisholm
Clearview
Cockburn Island
Coleman
Conmee
Cramahe
Dawn-Euphemia
Dawson
Dorion
Douro-Dummer
Drummond-North Elmsley
Dubreuilville
Dutton-Dunwich
Dymond
Dysart et al
Ear Falls
East Ferris
East Garafraxa
East Hawkesbury
East Luther Grand Valley
East Zorra-Tavistock
Edwardsburgh/Cardinal
Elizabethtown-Kitley
Emo
Enniskillen
Essa

Evanturel
Faraday
Fauquier-Strickland
Front of Yonge
Frontenac Islands
Galway-Cavendish and Harvey
Gauthier
Georgian Bay
Georgian Bluffs
Gillies
Gordon
Greater Madawaska
Grey Highlands
Guelph/Eramosa
Hamilton
Harley
Harris
Hastings Highlands
Havelock-Belmont-Methuen
Head, Clara and Maria
Highlands East
Hilliard
Hilton
Hornepayne
Horton
Howick
Hudson
Huron Shores
Huron-Kinloss
Ignace
James
Jocelyn
Johnson
Joly
Kerns
Killaloe, Hagarty and Richards
Kincardine
King
La Vallee
Laird
Lake of Bays
Lake of The Woods
Lanark Highlands
Larder Lake
Laurentian Valley
Leeds and the Thousand Islands
Limerick
Loyalist
Lucan Biddulph

Macdonald Meredith et al
Machar
Machin
Madawaska Valley
Madoc
Magnetawan
Malahide
Manitouwadge
Mapleton
Marmora and Lake
Matachewan
Mattawan
Mattice-Val Cote
McDougall
McGarry
McKellar
McMurrich-Monteith
McNab-Braeside
Melancthon
Michipicoten
Middlesex Centre
Minden Hills
Montague
Moonbeam
Morley
Morris-Tumberry
Mulmur
Muskoka Lakes
Nairn and Hyman
Neebing
Nipigon
Nipissing
North Algona-Wilberforce
North Dumfries
North Dundas
North Frontenac
North Glengany
North Grenville
North Huron
North Kawartha
North Middlesex
North Stormont
Northern Bruce Peninsula
Norwich
O'Connor
Oliver Paipoonge
Opasatika
Oro-Medonte
Otonabee-South Monaghan

Papineau-Cameron
Pelee
Perry
Perth East
Perth South
Pickle Lake
Plummer Additional
Prince
Puslinch
Ramara
Red Rock
Rideau Lakes
Russell
Ryerson
Sables-Spanish Rivers
Schreiber
Scugog
Seguin
Severn
Shedden
Shuniah
Sioux Narrows-Nestor Falls
Smith-Ennismore-Lakefield
South Algonquin
South Bruce
South Dundas
South Frontenac
South Glengarry
South Stormont
Southgate
Southwest Middlesex
South-West Oxford
Southwold
Springwater
St. Clair
St. Joseph
Stirling-Rawdon
Stone Mills
Strathroy-Caradoc
Strong
Tarbutt and Tarbutt Additional
Tay
Tehkummah
Terrace Bay
Thames Centre
The Archipelago
The Nation
The North Shore
Tiny

Tudor and Cashel
Tweed
Tyendinaga
Uxbridge
Val Rita-Harty
Wainfleet
Warwick
Wellesley
Wellington North
West Elgin
West Grey
West Lincoln
West Perth
White River
Whitestone
Whitewater Region
Wilmot
Wollaston
Woolwich
Zorra

ONT. REG. 631/98 — LONG-TERM VEHICLE IMPOUNDMENT UNDER SECTION 55.1 OF THE ACT

made under the *Highway Traffic Act*

O. Reg. 631/98, as am. O. Reg. 439/01; 412/10; 456/10; 44/12 (Fr.).

[Note: The title of this regulation was changed from "Orders to Impound or Release Motor Vehicles under Section 55.1 of the Act" to "Long-Term Vehicle Impoundment under Section 55.1 of the Act" by O. Reg. 412/10, s. 1.]

INTERPRETATION
[Heading added O. Reg. 456/10, s. 1.]

0.1 In this Regulation,

"**Tribunal**" means the Licence Appeal Tribunal.

O. Reg. 456/10, s. 1

PRESCRIBED PERIOD

1. For the purpose of subsection 55.1(3) of the Act, the prescribed period is two years.

RELEASE OF VEHICLE BEFORE END OF IMPOUND PERIOD
[Heading added O. Reg. 439/01, s. 1.]

1.1 For the purposes of subsection 55.1(14) of the Act (release of vehicle before end of impound period), the prescribed class of persons and prescribed class of motor vehicles are:

1. Persons who,

    i. carry on the business of renting motor vehicles to the public, and

    ii. are the holder of the plate portion of the permit for the impounded motor vehicle.

2. Motor vehicles that are the subject of a rental agreement,

    i. for a term of 30 days or less,

    ii. between a person described in paragraph 1 and a person other than the person whose driving of the motor vehicle as described in subsection 55.1(1) of the Act is the reason for the impoundment of the vehicle, and

    iii. that does not name as an authorized additional driver or additional permitted driver the person whose driving of the motor vehicle as de-

scribed in subsection 55.1(1) of the Act is the reason for the impoundment of the vehicle.

O. Reg. 439/01, s. 1; 412/10, s. 2

[Heading repealed O. Reg. 412/10, s. 3.]

2. [Repealed O. Reg. 412/10, s. 3.]

3. [Repealed O. Reg. 412/10, s. 3.]

3.1 [Repealed O. Reg. 412/10, s. 3.]

4. [Repealed O. Reg. 412/10, s. 3.]

EXEMPTIONS

5. Ambulances, fire department vehicles and police department vehicles are exempt from section 55.1 of the Act.

6. If a police officer or officer appointed for carrying out the provisions of the Act is of the opinion that a motor vehicle's drawn vehicle or load cannot be safely or practically removed in a timely manner before the vehicle is removed to an impound facility under clause 55.1(2)(a) of the Act, the operator and owner of the motor vehicle are exempt from the requirement under subsection 55.1(10) of the Act to have the drawn vehicle or load removed forthwith.

O. Reg. 412/10, s. 4

7. If a police officer or officer appointed for carrying out the provisions of this Act considers a motor vehicle necessary to an investigation into the contravention of any Ontario or federal law or for another law enforcement purpose, and directs that the motor vehicle be removed to a place other than an impound facility for the investigation or other law enforcement purpose, the motor vehicle is exempt from clause 55.1(2)(a) of the Act for the time it is needed by the police officer or officer, and any person driving, operating or removing the motor vehicle in accordance with such direction of a police officer or officer is exempt from subsection 55.1(32) of the Act.

O. Reg. 412/10, s. 5

8. [Repealed O. Reg. 412/10, s. 6.]

APPEALS UNDER SECTION 50.2 OF THE ACT

[Heading added O. Reg. 456/10, s. 2.]

9. An appeal to the Tribunal under section 50.2 of the Act with respect to the impoundment of a motor vehicle under section 55.1 of the Act shall be commenced by filing with the Tribunal a notice of appeal, together with the fee established by the

Tribunal, within 15 days after the day the vehicle was detained under subsection 55.1(1) of the Act.

O. Reg. 456/10, s. 2

10. (1) In determining whether exceptional hardship will result from an impoundment under section 55.1 of the Act, the Tribunal shall consider whether no alternative to the impounded motor vehicle is available and, if no alternative is available, whether the impoundment will result in,

(a) a threat to the health or safety of any person ordinarily transported by the motor vehicle; or

(b) a threat to the public health and safety or to the environment or property of a community in whose service the motor vehicle is ordinarily used.

(2) In determining whether exceptional hardship will result from an impoundment under section 55.1 of the Act, the Tribunal shall not, subject to subsection (3), consider whether the impoundment will result in,

(a) inconvenience to any person;

(b) financial or economic loss to any person;

(c) loss of employment or employment opportunity to any person; or

(d) loss of education or training or of an educational or training opportunity to any person.

(3) The Tribunal may consider the criteria set out in clauses (2)(b), (c) and (d) if the owner demonstrates that,

(a) no alternative to the impounded motor vehicle is available;

(b) the loss will be immediate, significant and lasting;

(c) the impact of the loss will be upon a person ordinarily transported by the motor vehicle; and

(d) the impact of the loss,

(i) will be upon a person other than the person whose driving while his or her driver's licence was under suspension resulted in the impoundment of the motor vehicle, and

(ii) will not be a result of a loss by the suspended driver of the type set out in clause (2)(b), (c) or (d).

(4) In order to show that no alternative to the impounded motor vehicle is available under subsection (1) or clause (3)(a), the owner must demonstrate that every reasonable option has been considered and inquired into that could eliminate or adequately mitigate any threat or loss to the person, including using another vehicle and making arrangements to do without any motor vehicle during the impound period.

O. Reg. 456/10, s. 3

ONT. REG. 601 — MOTOR VEHICLE INSPECTION STATIONS

made under the *Highway Traffic Act*

R.R.O. 1990, Reg. 601, as am. O. Reg. 761/91; 185/92; 559/92; 180/93; 818/93; 372/98; 377/02; 117/08; 474/09; 79/11; 437/12; 243/14; 255/15, ss. 1–6, 7 (Fr.) [To come into force July 1, 2016.].

INTERPRETATION

1. (1) In this Regulation,

"annual inspection certificate", "annual inspection report", "annual inspection sticker", "NSC Standard 11B", "salvage motor vehicle", "semi-annual inspection certificate", "semi-annual inspection report", "semi-annual inspection sticker" and "structural inspection certificate" have the same meanings as in Regulation 611;

"proof of brake inspection document" means a document that meets the requirements of Section 3: Brake Systems of NSC Standard 11B with respect to qualification of a prior inspection;

"Regulation 611" means Regulation 611 of the Revised Regulations of Ontario, 1990 (*Safety Inspections*) made under the Act.

Proposed Amendment — 1(1)

(1) In this Regulation,

"annual inspection certificate", "annual inspection report", "annual inspection sticker", "Passenger/Light-Duty Vehicle Inspection Standard", "salvage motor vehicle", "semi-annual inspection certificate", "semi-annual inspection report", "semi-annual inspection sticker" and "structural inspection certificate" have the same meanings as in section 1 of Regulation 611;

"NSC Standard 11B" has the same meaning as in subsection 2.1(1) of Regulation 611;

"proof of brake inspection document" means a document that meets the requirements of Section 3: Brake Systems of NSC Standard 11B with respect to qualification of a prior inspection;

"Regulation 611" means Regulation 611 of the Revised Regulations of Ontario, 1990 (*Safety Inspections*) made under the Act.

O. Reg. 255/15, s. 1 [To come into force July 1, 2016.]

(2) In this Regulation, a reference to a Schedule is a reference to that Schedule as set out in Regulation 611.

O. Reg. 761/91, s. 1; 818/93, s. 1; 372/98, s. 1; 474/09, s. 1; 79/11, s. 1; 243/14, s. 1

CLASSES OF MOTOR VEHICLE INSPECTION STATIONS

2. Motor vehicle inspection stations are classified as follows:

1. Class F is a fleet station.

2. Class G is a station operated by Her Majesty the Queen in right of Canada or Ontario, a municipality or a school board or commission on behalf of a municipality.

3. Class P is any station other than a Class F or Class G station.

O. Reg. 818/93, s. 1

MOTOR VEHICLE INSPECTION STATION LICENCES

3. Motor vehicle inspection station licences are classified as follows:

1. [Repealed O. Reg. 474/09, s. 2(1).]

2. A Type 1 or Type 2 licence is authority to inspect and certify trailers, trailer converter dollies and motor vehicles in accordance with the inspection requirements and performance standards set out in Schedule 1, 2, 6 or 6.1 or in NSC Standard 11B as modified by Schedule 3, 4 or 5, as appropriate to the class or type of vehicle inspected.

Proposed Amendment — 3, para. 2

2. A Type 1 or Type 2 licence is authority to inspect and certify trailers, trailer converter dollies and motor vehicles in accordance with the inspection requirements and performance standards set out in,

i. Schedule 6 or 6.1,

ii. NSC Standard 11B as modified by Schedule 3, or

iii. the Passenger/Light-Duty Vehicle Inspection Standard.

O. Reg. 255/15, s. 2(1) [To come into force July 1, 2016.]

3. A Type 3 licence is authority to inspect and certify trailers and trailer converter dollies in accordance with the inspection requirements and performance standards set out in NSC Standard 11B (Trailer) as modified by Schedule 4.

Proposed Amendment — 3, para. 3

3. A Type 3 licence is authority to inspect and certify trailers and trailer converter dollies in accordance with the inspection requirements and performance standards set out in NSC Standard 11B (Trailer) as modified by Schedule 3.

O. Reg. 255/15, s. 2(2) [To come into force July 1, 2016.]

4. A Type 4 licence is authority to inspect and certify motorcycles in accordance with the inspection requirements and performance standards set out in Schedules 6 and 6.1.

5. [Repealed O. Reg. 474/09, s. 2(3).]

6. A Type 6 licence is authority to inspect a salvage motor vehicle in accordance with the inspection requirements and performance standards set out in Schedule 9.

O. Reg. 761/91, s. 2; 818/93, s. 1; 372/98, s. 2; 117/08, s. 1; 474/09, s. 2; 79/11, s. 2

4. (1) It is a condition of a Type 1, 2, 3 or 4 licence that the licensee ensure that premises in which inspections are carried out,

(a) have sufficient internal space or external hard standing area for the inspection of at least one vehicle of the class that the licensee is licensed to inspect;

(b) be equipped with a mechanic's common hand tools and a hoist or jack suitable for the weight of the vehicle to be inspected;

(c) be equipped with devices appropriate to the class or type of vehicle to be inspected for,

(i) aiming headlights,

(ii) measuring wear in brake system components,

(iii) measuring tire tread depth,

(iv) measuring play or wear in steering and suspension systems,

(v) detecting leaks in compressed fuel systems;

(vi) measuring the torque of wheel and rim fasteners;

Proposed Addition — 4(1)(c)(vii)

(vii) measuring window tint;

O. Reg. 255/15, s. 3(1) [To come into force July 1, 2016.]

(d) be maintained in a clean and safe condition.

Proposed Addition — 4(1.0.1)

(1.0.1) Despite clause (1)(c), in respect of a Type 3 licence, a motor vehicle inspection station is not required to ensure that the premises are equipped with devices for aiming headlights or measuring window tint and, in respect of a Type 4 licence, a motor vehicle inspection station is not required to ensure that the premises are equipped with devices for measuring window tint.

O. Reg. 255/15, s. 3(2) [To come into force July 1, 2016.]

(1.1) It is a condition of a Type 6 licence that the licensee ensure that premises in which inspections are carried out,

(a) have sufficient internal space for the inspection of at least one vehicle of the class that the licensee is licensed to inspect;

(b) be equipped with industry-accepted equipment capable of making three-dimensional measurements on unibody and non-unibody vehicles;

(c) be equipped with devices suitable for safely supporting the vehicle during inspection;

(d) be maintained in a clean and safe condition.

(1.2) It is a condition of a Type 6 licence that the licensee keep on the licensed premises copies of, or copies of relevant excerpts from, the manuals used as a source of the manufacturer's specifications for vehicle dimensions for every make, model and year of vehicle for which the station has prepared a structural inspection certificate, together with a copy of the actual measurements taken for each vehicle.

(2) It is a condition of a licence that the licensee ensure that the equipment referred to in clauses (1)(c) and (1.1)(b) be kept in proper working order and that all measuring or testing devices be calibrated to a degree of accuracy consistent with the performance standards prescribed by Regulation 611.

O. Reg. 761/91, s. 3; 818/93, s. 1; 372/98, s. 3; 474/09, s. 3; 79/11, s. 3

5. It is a condition of a licence that the licensee,

(a) own or lease the premises in which the inspections are carried out;

(b) display the licence in a conspicuous position in the station;

(c) issue a safety standards certificate, annual inspection certificate, semi-annual inspection certificate or structural inspection certificate only on a form supplied to the licensee by the Ministry; and

(d) issue a safety standards certificate, annual inspection certificate, semi-annual inspection certificate or structural inspection certificate for a vehicle inspected in accordance with the inspection requirements and complying with the performance standards prescribed by Regulation 611, if the inspection fee charged by the licensee is paid.

O. Reg. 761/91, s. 4; 818/93, s. 1; 372/98, s. 4; 79/11, s. 4

6. (1) It is a condition of a licence that the licensee not charge an additional inspection fee if,

(a) a vehicle is inspected at a station;

(b) repairs or adjustments to the vehicle or its equipment are required to qualify it for a safety standards certificate or for an annual inspection sticker or a semi-annual inspection sticker;

(c) the inspection fee charged by the licensee is paid;

(d) the required repairs or adjustments to the vehicle or its equipment are made at a place other than the station; or

(e) the vehicle is brought back to the station for issuance of the certificate or affixing of a sticker within ten days after the original inspection.

(2) An additional fee may be charged if a second inspection of a wheel brake assembly must be carried out before a safety standards certificate is issued or before an annual inspection sticker is affixed to the vehicle.

O. Reg. 761/91, s. 5; 818/93, s. 1; O. Reg. 79/11, s. 5

7. (1) It is a condition of a Class G licence that the licensee not issue or authorize any person to issue a safety standards certificate, an annual inspection certificate or a semi-annual inspection certificate for a vehicle unless a permit for the vehicle has been issued in the licensee's name or, in the case of an annual inspection certificate or a semi-annual inspection certificate, unless the vehicle is a bus.

(2) It is a condition of a Class G licence that the licensee not affix or authorize any person to affix an annual inspection sticker or a semi-annual inspection sticker unless a permit for the vehicle has been issued in the licensee's name or unless the vehicle is a bus.

O. Reg. 761/91, s. 6; 818/93, s. 1; 79/11, s. 6

REGISTRATION OF MOTOR VEHICLE INSPECTION MECHANICS

8. (1) It is a condition of the registration of a motor vehicle inspection mechanic, except a mechanic who only inspects trolley buses, that the mechanic hold a certificate of qualification, that is not suspended, in the trade of automotive service technician, truck and coach technician, motorcycle technician, truck-trailer service technician or auto body and collision damage repairer issued under the *Ontario College of Trades and Apprenticeship Act, 2009.*

(2) It is a condition of the registration of a motor vehicle inspection mechanic who only inspects trolley buses that a transit authority designate the mechanic as a person who may inspect trolley buses and notify the Director of the designation.

(3) It is a condition of the registration of a motor vehicle inspection mechanic who holds only a certificate of qualification in the trade of motorcycle technician that the mechanic only issue safety standards certificates for motorcycles.

(4) It is a condition of the registration of a motor vehicle inspection mechanic who does not hold a certificate of qualification in the trade of motorcycle technician that the mechanic not issue safety standards certificates for motor tricycles within the meaning of Regulation 611 of the Revised Regulations of Ontario, 1990 (*Safety Inspections*) made under the *Highway Traffic Act.*

(5) It is a condition of the registration of a motor vehicle inspection mechanic who holds only a certificate of qualification in the trade of truck-trailer service technician that the mechanic,

   (a) only issue safety standards certificates for trailers; and

   (b) only issue annual inspection certificates and affix annual inspection stickers for trailers and trailer converter dollies.

(5.1) It is a condition of the registration of a motor vehicle inspection mechanic who holds only a certificate of qualification in the trade of auto body and collision damage repairer that the mechanic only issue structural inspection certificates for rebuilt motor vehicles.

(6) In subsections (1) and (2), "trolley bus" means a bus propelled by electric power obtained from overhead wires.

O. Reg. 761/91, s. 7; 818/93, s. 1; 372/98, s. 5; 117/08, s. 2; 79/11, s. 7; 437/12, s. 1

9. If the employment of a motor vehicle inspection mechanic registered with a licensee is terminated or the licensee requests the termination of the registration, the licensee shall promptly report the mechanic's name, trade code, certificate number and termination date to the Ministry in writing.

O. Reg. 818/93, s. 1

OPERATING A MOTOR VEHICLE INSPECTION STATION

Proposed Addition — 9.1, 9.2

9.1 A motor vehicle inspection mechanic conducting an inspection using the Passenger/Light-Duty Vehicle Inspection Standard shall accurately complete an inspection report that contains the following information:

1. The date of inspection.

2. The make, model year, model and vehicle identification number of the vehicle.

3. The odometer reading of the vehicle at the end of the inspection.

4. The name of the mechanic and his or her trade certification number under the *Ontario College of Trades and Apprenticeship Act, 2009.*

5. The name, licence number, address and telephone number of the licensee.

6. Whether or not the vehicle passed the inspection.

7. The number of any safety standards certificate issued.

8. Whether or not the inspection is an additional or second inspection described in section 6.

9. All of the information regarding the inspection required by the Passenger/Light-Duty Vehicle Inspection Standard.

O. Reg. 255/15, s. 4 [To come into force July 1, 2016.]

9.2 A licensee shall provide each person that has had a vehicle inspected using the Passenger/Light-Duty Vehicle Inspection Standard with the completed inspection report required by section 9.1.

O. Reg. 255/15, s. 4 [To come into force July 1, 2016.]

10. (1) A licensee shall keep on the licensed premises,

(a) a copy of each safety standards certificate, annual inspection certificate and semi-annual inspection certificate issued by the licensee for a period of one year from the date of issue;

Proposed Addition — 10(1)(a.1)

(a.1) a copy of each inspection report prepared under section 9.1 for a period of one year from the date of inspection;

O. Reg. 255/15, s. 5 [To come into force July 1, 2016.]

(b) a record of all vehicles inspected together with the measurements and any other information required to be recorded by the Schedules and by NSC Standard 11B as modified by the Schedules and, where applicable, a list of defects, recommended repairs and actual repairs carried out by the licensee, for a period of one year from the date of inspection;

(c) a written record of all persons authorized by the licensee to countersign safety standards certificates, annual inspection certificates, semi-annual inspection certificates or structural inspection certificates or to affix annual in-

873

spection stickers or semi-annual inspection stickers on behalf of the licensee, for a period of one year from the date of termination of such authority;

(d) in respect of every vehicle to which an annual inspection sticker has been affixed and for a period of one year from the date of affixing the sticker on the vehicle, an annual inspection report, being a report signed by the motor vehicle inspection mechanic inspecting the vehicle and the licensee or a person authorized in writing by the licensee showing,

    (i) the date of inspection,

    (ii) the vehicle identification number,

    (iii) the annual inspection sticker number, and

    (iv) the information recorded under clause (b);

(e) in respect of every vehicle to which a semi-annual inspection sticker has been affixed and for a period of one year from the date of affixing the sticker on the vehicle, a semi-annual inspection report, being a report signed by the motor vehicle inspection mechanic inspecting the vehicle and the licensee or a person authorized in writing by the licensee showing,

    (i) the date of inspection,

    (ii) the vehicle identification number,

    (iii) the semi-annual inspection sticker number, and

    (iv) the information recorded under clause (b); and

(f) in respect of every vehicle inspected based upon proof of a prior brake inspection, a copy of the proof of brake inspection document, for a period of one year from the date of the inspection relying upon proof of a prior brake inspection.

(2) [Repealed O. Reg. 243/14, s. 2(2).]

O. Reg. 761/91, s. 8; 818/93, s. 1; 372/98, s. 6; 79/11, s. 8; 243/14, s. 2

10.1 (1) A licensee shall, within seven days after issuing a structural inspection certificate in respect of a motor vehicle, send to the Director the following information and documents:

1. The structural inspection certificate issued.

2. The completed Rebuilt Vehicle Parts Audit Form.

3. The name and address of the person who carried out the rebuilding of the salvage motor vehicle.

4. The name and address of the vehicle owner, if different from that of the person who carried out the rebuilding.

5. The name and address of the insurer of the vehicle who paid out the claim for the salvage motor vehicle, or the name and address of the person, other than an insurer, who declared the vehicle a total loss.

6. The make, model year and vehicle identification number of the vehicle.

7. A list of the major components used in rebuilding the vehicle, including the name of the supplier, the date of their purchase from the supplier by the per-

son who carried out the rebuilding and the vehicle identification numbers of the vehicles that the major components came from.

8. The invoice for the purchase of each major component used in rebuilding the vehicle, clearly showing the information set out in paragraph 7.

9. The estimate of repairs required, as prepared by the insurer or other person who declared the vehicle a total loss, or documentation, provided by the insurer or other person who declared the vehicle a total loss, that fully describes the damaged components and the extent of their damage.

10. The invoice for the purchase of a vehicle chassis, clearly showing the vehicle identification number of the vehicle from which the chassis came.

11. Two colour photographs clearly showing the damage to the front, rear and sides of the salvage motor vehicle, taken before rebuilding it, or, if the vehicle was rebuilt at a premises other than the motor vehicle inspection station and photographs were not taken, a written statement by the insurer or other person who declared the vehicle a total loss that such photographs are not available.

12. One colour photograph of the salvage motor vehicle taken in a frame alignment bench.

13. If the wheel alignment is inspected at a premises other than the motor vehicle inspection station, a statement that the wheel alignment meets the manufacturer's specifications, and including in the statement the vehicle identification number of the vehicle, the applicable manufacturer's specifications, the actual measurements taken for the vehicle, the name, address and signature of the person at the other premises who is making the statement and his or her trade certification number under the *Ontario College of Trades and Apprenticeship Act, 2009*.

14. The relevant excerpts from the manuals used as a source of the manufacturer's specifications for vehicle dimensions for the make, model and year of the vehicle.

15. The actual measurements taken for the vehicle.

(1.1) The documents required by subsection (1) shall be originals or, if originals do not exist or cannot reasonably be obtained, copies.

(1.2) Despite subsection (1), if the motor vehicle for which the structural inspection certificate is issued is a reassembled motor vehicle, the licensee is not required to send to the Director the following:

1. The information required by paragraphs 5 and 9 of subsection (1).

2. The information and documents required by paragraphs 7, 8 and 10 of subsection (1), if the components and chassis for the reassembled vehicle are acquired from a donor vehicle registered to the owner of the reassembled vehicle.

3. The photographs required by paragraph 11 of subsection (1), if the licensee sends to the Director photographs in sufficient number to display all of the major components that were used in reassembling the vehicle.

(2) No structural inspection certificate shall be issued unless the licensee or the person authorized by the licensee to countersign structural inspection certificates, and

the mechanic who inspects the vehicle are satisfied that there is a complete record of all the information, documents and photographs required under this section.

(3) Subsection (2) does not apply to a vehicle imported into Ontario, the permit for which was issued by a jurisdiction listed in Column 1 of the Table to this section and that is classified by that jurisdiction with a classification that is set out in Column 2 of the Table as equivalent to rebuilt for that jurisdiction.

(3.1) For a vehicle described in subsection (3), the licensee shall send to the Director the structural inspection certificate issued and a copy of the vehicle permit issued by the other jurisdiction showing the classification of the vehicle.

(4) The mechanic who performs the inspection shall use the photographs and information provided in the record to establish that the vehicle is the one described in the record.

(5) The major components referred to in paragraph 7 of subsection (1) include, if they are not from the salvage motor vehicle itself, the engine, transmission, transaxle, transfer case, rear axle or drive unit, front axle or drive unit, hood, fenders, bumpers, side or quarter panels, trunk lid, doors, hatches, seats, dashboard, frame, full or partial frame rail, radiator grill, body roof, front and rear bumper covers, front pillar, center pillar, lock pillar, door pillar, body shell, tailgate, alloy wheels, truck cab and box, and motorcycle forks and fairing.

(6) For the purpose of subsection (1.2),

"reassembled motor vehicle" means a motor vehicle that has been assembled using the body of a motor vehicle with a model year of 1981 or later and the chassis frame assembly of another motor vehicle, both of which were manufactured utilizing a full frame assembly as part of the vehicle's structure.

TABLE

COLUMN 1	COLUMN 2
Jurisdiction	Equivalent to Rebuilt
Canada	
Alberta	Repaired
British Columbia	Rebuilit
Manitoba	Rebuilit
New Brunswick	Rebuilit
Newfoundland and Labrador	Rebuilit
Nova Scotia	Rebuilit
Prince Edward Island	Rebuilit
Quebec	Reconstruit
Saskatchewan	Rebuilit
United States of America	
Alabama	Reconstructed
Alaska	Reconstructed Vehicle
Arizona	Restored Salvage
Arkansas	Reconstructed, "REC"

TABLE

COLUMN 1	COLUMN 2
Jurisdiction	Equivalent to Rebuilt
California	Salvage, or Salvaged, or Rebuilt
Colorado	Code "R", Rebuilt
Connecticut	Code "A"
Florida	Rebuilt
Georgia	Rebuilt
Idaho	Reconstructed Vehicle
Illinois	Reconstructed Vehicle
Indiana	Rebuilt Vehicle
Iowa	Prior salvage
Kentucky	Rebuilt Vehicle
Massachusetts	Reconstructed
Michigan	Rebuilt
Minnesota	Prior salvage, Rebuilt
Missouri	Prior salvage
Montana	Rebuilt salvage
Nebraska	Previously salvaged
Nevada	Rebuilt
New York	Rebuilt salvage
North Carolina	Code "SVR"
North Dakota	Previous salvage
Ohio	Rebuilt salvage
Texas	Reconditioned, Rebuilt salvage
Vermont	Rebuilt
Virginia	Salvage rebuilt
West Virginia	Reconstructed
Wisconsin	Repaired salvage
Wyoming	Code "R"

O. Reg. 372/98, s. 7; 377/02, s. 1; 437/12, s. 2

11. (1) A licensee operating a Class P station shall identify the station by displaying an identifying sign provided by the Ministry in a conspicuous position, visible to the public.

(2) The sign remains the property of the Crown and shall be returned to the Ministry when the licensee ceases to hold a Class P licence or to operate a station.

(3) A sign identifying a Class P station shall not be displayed at a Class F or G station.

O. Reg. 761/91, s. 9; 818/93, s. 1; 372/98, s. 8; 474/09, s. 4

12. (1) If annual inspection stickers with corresponding annual inspection certificate forms, semi-annual inspection stickers with corresponding semi-annual inspection certificate forms and safety standards certificate forms have not been used and are in the same condition as they were when they were received, a licensee may return them to the Ministry for a refund of the fees paid for them.

(2) A licensee who ceases to operate a motor vehicle inspection station or whose licence expires or is revoked shall return to the Ministry, along with the materials referred to in subsection (1), a copy of every safety standards certificate, annual inspection certificate or semi-annual inspection certificate kept under clause 10(1)(a).

O. Reg. 818/93, s. 1; 79/11, s. 9

13.

Proposed Addition — 13(0.1)

(0.1) A licensee shall keep annual inspection stickers, annual inspection certificate forms, semi-annual inspection stickers, semi-annual inspection certificate forms and safety standards certificate forms that have not been used in a secure place on the licensed premises.

O. Reg. 255/15, s. 6 [To come into force July 1, 2016.]

(1) A licensee shall promptly report to the Director the loss, theft or destruction of any certificate form or inspection sticker provided by the Ministry.

(2) The licensee shall include in the report the serial numbers of the certificates or stickers and all available information relevant to the loss, theft or destruction.

(3) The licensee who, after having given a report to the Director, recovers a lost or stolen form or sticker, shall promptly forward it to the Ministry.

O. Reg. 818/93, s. 1; 372/98, s. 9; 79/11, s. 10

FEES

14. (1) The following fees shall be paid to the Ministry:

1. For a Class F or P motor vehicle inspection station licence　..... $50.00

2. For a Class F licence replacing a subsisting Class P licence or for a Class P licence replacing a subsisting Class F licence 5.00

3. For a duplicate of a Class F or P licence in case of loss or destruction of the original 5.00

4. For a safety standards certificate form or a structural inspection certificate form supplied to a Class F or P station 5.00

5. For the registration of a motor vehicle inspection mechanic by a Class F or P station 14.00

6. For an annual inspection sticker with accompanying annual inspection certificate supplied to a Class F or P station or a replacement in case of damage or destruction of the original 2.50

7. For a semi-annual inspection sticker with accompanying semi-annual inspection certificate supplied to a Class F or P station or a replacement in case of damage or destruction of the original 1.00

8. [Repealed O. Reg. 474/09, s. 5.]

9. [Repealed O. Reg. 474/09, s. 5.]

(2) No fee is payable for the registration of a motor vehicle inspection mechanic who replaces a registered mechanic at the same station.

(3) The fees in paragraphs 1 and 5 of subsection (1) are reduced by one-half if an application for a license or registration is made after June 30 in the year for which it is issued.

O. Reg. 761/91, s. 10; 818/93, s. 1; 372/98, s. 10; 474/09, s. 5; 79/11, s. 11

15. (1) An application for a licence shall be in the form provided by the Minister.

(2) A safety standards certificate, a structural inspection certificate, an annual inspection certificate and a semi-annual inspection certificate shall be in the forms provided by the Minister.

(3) [Repealed O. Reg. 474/09, s. 6.]

O. Reg. 761/91, s. 11; 818/93, s. 1; 372/98, s. 11; 474/09, s. 6; 79/11, s. 12

16. [Revoked O. Reg. 818/93, s. 1.]

17. [Revoked O. Reg. 818/93, s. 1.]

18. [Revoked O. Reg. 180/93, s. 2.]

Form 1 [Revoked O. Reg. 180/93, s. 3.]

[Revoked O. Reg. 180/93, s. 3.]

Form 2 [Revoked O. Reg. 180/93, s. 3.]

[Revoked O. Reg. 180/93, s. 3.]

Form 3 [Revoked O. Reg. 180/93, s. 2.]

[Revoked O. Reg. 818/93, s. 2.]

Form 4 [Repealed O. Reg. 474/09, s. 7.]

[Repealed O. Reg. 474/09, s. 7.]

Form 5 [Repealed O. Reg. 474/09, s. 7.]

[Repealed O. Reg. 474/09, s. 7.]

ONT. REG. 361/98 — MOTOR VEHICLES

made under the *Environmental Protection Act*

O. Reg. 361/98, as am. O. Reg. 401/98; 86/99; 438/99; 641/00; 78/01; 237/01; 343/01; 445/03; 587/05; 191/10; 41/13.

DEFINITIONS

1. (1) In this Regulation,

"catalytic converter" means a device through which exhaust from a motor is passed in order to prevent or lessen the emission of a contaminant;

"conditional emissions inspection report" means a report issued under subsection 9.1(3);

"Drive Clean Guide" means the Ministry of the Environment publication entitled "Drive Clean Guide" and dated February 1, 1999, as amended from time to time;

"emissions inspection report" means a report issued under subsection 2(7);

"expanded program area" means the areas set out in Schedule 3, and includes every place that has the same postal code as a place in one of those areas;

"Greater Toronto Area" means the areas set out in Schedule 1, and includes every place that has the same postal code as a place in one of those areas;

"grey market vehicle" means a motor vehicle imported into Canada and manufactured to emission standards that at the time of manufacture were less stringent than those applicable to the same or similar categories of new vehicles in Canada;

"GVWR" stands for the gross vehicle weight rating and means the value specified by the vehicle manufacturer as the loaded weight of a single vehicle;

"heavy vehicle" means a motor vehicle with a GVWR of more than 4,500 kilograms;

"hot rod" means a motor vehicle in which the original motor has been replaced with a motor of a type not installed by the manufacturer on that model of motor vehicle for the model year designated for the motor vehicle by the manufacturer;

"kit car" means a motor vehicle that has been constructed using a new and complete body of a motor vehicle that is supplied without a motor, chassis or drive train;

"leaded gasoline" [Repealed O. Reg. 191/10, s. 1(3).]

"light duty truck" [Revoked O. Reg. 343/01, s. 1(7).]

"light vehicle" means a motor vehicle with a GVWR of 4,500 kilograms or less;

"model year", when used with respect to a motor vehicle, a motor or a chassis, means the model year designated by the manufacturer or, if there is no such designation, the calendar year in which the manufacture is completed;

"Ontario Drive Clean repair facility" means a facility accredited by the Director as an Ontario Drive Clean repair facility;

"Ontario Drive Clean testing facility" means a facility accredited by the Director as an Ontario Drive Clean testing facility;

"passenger vehicle" [Revoked O. Reg. 343/01, s. 1(10).]

"rebuilt car" means a motor vehicle that has been constructed using various used or new component parts, such as a body, chassis or frame, obtained from other vehicles or from auto wreckers, dealers or manufacturers;

"urban and commuter areas" means the areas set out in Schedule 2, and includes every place that has the same postal code as a place in one of those areas.

"unleaded gasoline" [Repealed O. Reg. 191/10, s. 1(3).]

(2) Despite the definition of "model year" in subsection (1),

(a) the model year of a grey market vehicle or hot rod shall be deemed to be,

(i) the model year designated by the manufacturer for the vehicle, if the manufacturer designated the model year of the vehicle to be 2000 or a later year,

(ii) the calendar year in which the manufacture of the vehicle was completed, if the manufacture of the vehicle was completed in 2000 or a later year and the manufacturer did not designate a model year for the vehicle, or

(iii) 1980, in any other case; and

(b) the model year of a kit car or rebuilt car shall be deemed to be the model year of the motor.

O. Reg. 86/99, s. 1; 438/99, s. 1; 343/01, s. 1; 191/10, s. 1

DRIVE CLEAN INSPECTORS AND REPAIR TECHNICIANS
[Heading added O. Reg. 343/01, s. 2.]

1.1 (1) A person is a Drive Clean inspector for light vehicles for the purposes of this Regulation if he or she has successfully completed, within the previous 24 months, a course satisfactory to the Director with respect to the testing of air emissions and on-board diagnostic systems of light vehicles.

(2) A person is a Drive Clean inspector for heavy vehicles for the purposes of this Regulation if he or she has successfully completed, within the previous 24 months, a course satisfactory to the Director with respect to the testing of air emissions and on-board diagnostic systems of heavy vehicles.

(3) A person is a Drive Clean repair technician for the purposes of this Regulation if,

(a) the person holds a certificate of qualification as an automotive service technician issued under the *Ontario College of Trades and Apprenticeship Act, 2009*;

(b) the person has successfully completed, within the previous 36 months, a course satisfactory to the Director with respect to the repair of on-board diagnostic systems, emission control systems and components of light vehicles; or

(c) the person has qualifications that the Director considers equivalent to the qualifications referred to in clause (a) or (b).

(3.1) If the Director is satisfied that a Drive Clean repair technician has incompetently performed repairs intended to bring a vehicle more nearly into compliance with the maximum emissions standards or test standards prescribed by this Regulation, the Director may, by giving written notice to the repair technician, require the repair technician to successfully complete one or more courses satisfactory to the Director to address the incompetence.

(3.2) Despite subsections (1) and (2) and clause (3)(b), if a person is a Drive Clean inspector referred to in subsection (1) or (2) or a Drive Clean repair technician referred to in clause (3)(b) on December 31, 2010 and that person would be required to complete a course referred to in subsection (1), (2) or clause (3)(b) during the period beginning on January 1, 2011 and ending on December 31, 2012, that person is required to complete the applicable course referred to in subsection (1), (2) or clause (3)(b) no later than December 31, 2012.

(4) Despite subsections (1) to (3), a person is not a Drive Clean inspector or Drive Clean repair technician for the purposes of this Regulation if the Director gives the person written notice indicating that the Director is satisfied that,

(a) the person has submitted false or misleading personal information to the Director;

(b) the person has been convicted within the preceding 48 months of an offence under the Act or the regulations that relates to motor vehicles or to a lack of honesty or integrity in dealing with customers;

(c) the person has created, distributed or used a document that,

(i) indicates that a motor vehicle complies with standards prescribed in section 7, 8, 9.0.1, 10, 11 or 12 when the vehicle does not comply with those standards or has not been tested in accordance with this Regulation for compliance with those standards, or

(ii) indicates that a motor vehicle is not required to comply with the standards prescribed in section 8 or 9.0.1 when the vehicle is required to comply with those standards; or

(d) the person has previously been given notice under subsection (3.1) and the Director is satisfied that the person has, on an occasion other than the occasion that is the subject matter of that previous notice, incompetently performed repairs intended to bring a vehicle more nearly into compliance with the standards prescribed in this Regulation.

(5) The Director shall not give a person notice under subsection (3.1) or (4) unless the Director has advised the person in writing of the proposal to give notice and has

afforded the person a reasonable opportunity to make written or oral submissions to the Director.

(6) A notice under subsection (4) may provide that the notice does not apply to the person after a date specified by the Director in the notice.

(7) The Director may revoke a notice given under subsection (4) on a date specified by the Director, and the notice does not apply to the person after that date.

O. Reg. 343/01, s. 2; 587/05, s. 1; 191/10, s. 2; 41/13, s. 1

FALSE REPORTS

[Heading added O. Reg. 587/05, s. 2. Amended O. Reg. 191/10, s. 3(1).]

1.2 No person shall create, distribute or use a document that,

(a) indicates that a motor vehicle complies with standards prescribed in section 7, 8, 9.0.1, 10, 11 or 12 when the vehicle does not comply with those standards or has not been tested in accordance with this Regulation for compliance with those standards; or

(b) indicates that a motor vehicle is not required to comply with the standards prescribed in section 8 or 9.0.1 when the vehicle is required to comply with those standards.

O. Reg. 587/05, s. 2; 191/10, s. 3

TESTING MOTOR VEHICLES WITH RESPECT TO AIR EMISSIONS

[Heading added O. Reg. 343/01, s. 3.]

2. (1) For the purpose of enforcing the Act and this Regulation, no person other than a Drive Clean inspector for light vehicles or a Drive Clean inspector for heavy vehicles shall determine compliance with the maximum emission standards prescribed in sections 7 and 10.

(2) For the purpose of enforcing the Act and this Regulation, no person other than a Drive Clean inspector for light vehicles shall determine compliance with the standards prescribed in sections 8, 9.0.1 and 11.

(2.1) [Repealed O. Reg. 191/10, s. 4(3).]

(3) Despite subsection (2), a Drive Clean inspector for heavy vehicles may determine compliance with the maximum emission standards prescribed in section 11 if compliance is achieved pursuant to subsection 11(4.1).

(4) For the purpose of enforcing the Act and this Regulation, no person other than a Drive Clean inspector for heavy vehicles shall determine compliance with the maximum emission standards prescribed in section 12.

(5) The testing to determine compliance with the standards prescribed in section 7, 8, 9.0.1, 10, 11 and 12 for the purpose of enforcing the Act and this Regulation shall take place at an Ontario Drive Clean testing facility.

(6) Despite subsections (1), (2), (4) and (5), a provincial officer or police officer may determine compliance with the standards prescribed in this Regulation for the purpose of enforcing the Act and this Regulation and may do so at any location.

(7) If testing conducted in accordance with this Regulation confirms compliance with standards prescribed in section 7, 8, 9.0.1, 10, 11 or 12, an Ontario Drive Clean testing facility may issue a report indicating that the vehicle complies with the standards.

(8) If a motor vehicle of a model year after 1997 is manufactured with an on-board diagnostic system designed to identify motor or emission control system problems and regulate motor or emission control system operations, testing to determine compliance with maximum emission standards prescribed in the Regulation may include an advisory test of the on-board diagnostic system in accordance with the Drive Clean Guide.

(9) A person who, with the consent of the Director, alters a vehicle and submits it to an Ontario Drive Clean testing facility or an Ontario Drive Clean repair facility for the purpose of assessing the quality of the facility and the competence of staff at the facility is exempt from subseciton 22(3) and section 23 of the Act and from sections 5, 6 and 7 of this Regulation.

O. Reg. 343/01, s. 3; 191/10, s. 4

APPLICATION

3. (1) Section 6 of this Regulation applies with respect to every motor vehicle operating in Ontario.

(2) This Regulation applies with respect to every motor vehicle operating in Ontario for which a permit under the *Highway Traffic Act* is in effect.

(3) This Regulation, other than sections 8, 9.0.1 and 11, applies with respect to every heavy vehicle.

O. Reg. 343/01, s. 4; 191/10, s. 5

EMISSION CONTROL EQUIPMENT FOR KIT CARS, REBUILT CARS AND HOT RODS

4. (1) A kit car or a rebuilt car that receives its first permit under the *Highway Traffic Act* on or after January 1, 1999, shall include, as part of a system to prevent or lessen the emission of contaminants, all of the original pollution control systems and components, or equivalent replacements, included or usually included with the motor of the rebuilt car or kit car by the manufacturer of the motor.

(2) A hot rod that receives a motor replacement on or after January 1, 1999, shall receive a motor designed to meet emission standards at least as stringent as those achieved by the original motor with all its original emission control equipment attached and functioning, and the replacement motor shall have the original catalytic converter and all the original emission control equipment, or equivalent replace-

ments, included or usually included with the replacement motor by the manufacturer of the motor.

O. Reg. 86/99, s. 3

CATALYTIC CONVERTERS

5. (1) [Repealed O. Reg. 191/10, s. 6.]

(2) [Repealed O. Reg. 191/10, s. 6.]

(3) If a motor or motor vehicle is manufactured with a catalytic converter, no person shall alter or cause or permit the alteration of the motor or motor vehicle in a manner that permits exhaust emissions to bypass the catalytic converter.

(4) No person shall operate or cause or permit the operation of a motor of motor vehicle that was manufactured with a catalytic converter if the catalytic converter, or any replacement for the catalytic converter.

(a) is not capable of performing the function for which the catalytic converter was intended; or

(b) is disconnected, removed or otherwise altered so that it is not capable of performing the function for which the catalytic converter was intended.

O. Reg. 86/99, s. 4; 191/10, s. 6

VISIBLE EMISSIONS

6. (1) No person shall operate or cause or permit the operation of a light vehicle from which there is a visible emission for more than 15 seconds in any five-minute period.

(2) No person shall operate or cause or permit the operation of a heavy vehicle from which there is a visible emission for more than 15 seconds in any five-minute period.

O. Reg. 86/99, s. 5; 343/01, s. 5

EMISSION CONTROL SYSTEMS OR DEVICES

6.1 The following types of systems and devices are prescribed for the purpose of subsection 22(4) of the Act:

1. A system or device that is manufactured by the manufacturer of the system or device that is being replaced and,

i. is identical to or equivalent to the system or device that is being replaced, or

ii. is manufactured as a replacement for the system or device that is being replaced.

2. A system or device that is approved by the Bureau of Automobile Repair, the California Air Resources Board, the United States Environmental Protection Agency or another body specified by the Director as a replacement for the system or device that is being replaced.

O. Reg. 86/99, s. 6

7. (1) If a motor or motor vehicle is manufactured with a system or device to prevent or lessen the emission of any contaminant, including an on-board diagnostic system designed to identify motor or emissions control system problems and regulate motor or emission control system operations, the following standards are prescribed as additional maximum emission standards for the vehicle:

1. The system or device, or any replacement therefor, must be maintained or kept in such a state of repair that it is capable of performing the funciton for which it was intended.

2. The system or device, or any replacement therefor, must be kept installed on, attached to or incorporated in the motor or motor vehicle in such a manner that, when the motor or motor vehicle is operating, the system or device functions in the manner in which it was intended to function.

(2) Every motor vehicle for which emission standards are prescribed in this section shall comply with those standards.

(3) No person shall operate or cause or permit the operation of a motor vehicle that does not comply with subsection (2).

O. Reg. 401/98, s. 1; 86/99, s. 7; 343/01, s. 6; 191/10, s. 7

TWO SPEED IDLE TEST GASOLINE FUELLED LIGHT VEHICLES (AND OTHER FUELS EXCEPT DIESEL)

8. (1) This section applies with respect to a light vehicle that operates on a fuel other than diesel fuel.

(2) If a motor vehicle fuelled by natural gas is tested for compliance with the maximum emission standards prescribed in this section for hydrocarbons, methane found in the emissions shall be excluded.

(3) The maximum emission standards set out in Table 8 of the Drive Clean Guide for motor vehicles of a model year and GVWR set out in that Table are prescribed for those vehicles.

(4) The procedure to be used for testing a motor vehicle's compliance with the maximum emission standards prescribed in this section is the preconditioned two speed idle test, as described in the Drive Clean Guide, or a test that the Director considers equivalent.

(5) The maximum emission standards prescribed in this section do not apply with respect to a motor vehicle if the design or configuration of the motor vehicle,

(a) is incompatible with the performance of the tests referred to in subsection (4); or

(b) would render the performance of the tests referred to in subsection (4) unsafe.

(6) Every motor vehicle for which emission standards are prescribed in this section shall comply with those standards.

(7) No person shall operate or cause or permit the operation of a motor vehicle that does not comply with subsection (6).

O. Reg. 401/98, s. 2; 86/99, ss. 8, 9; 343/01, s. 7

DYNAMOMETER TEST GASOLINE FUELLED LIGHT VEHICLES (AND OTHER FUELS EXCEPT DIESEL)

[Heading added O. Reg. 343/01, s. 9.]

9. [Repealed O. Reg. 191/10, s. 8.]

ON-BOARD DIAGNOSTIC SYSTEM TEST (ALL LIGHT VEHICLES)

[Heading added O. Reg. 191/10, s. 9(1).]

9.0.1 (1) This section applies to a light vehicle of a model year after 1997 that was manufactured with an on-board diagnostic system designed to identify motor or emission control system problems and regulate motor or emission control system operations if the design or configuration of the motor vehicle,

(a) is compatible with the performance of the test referred to in subsection (4); and

(b) would not render the performance of the test referred to in subsection (4) unsafe.

(2) This section applies in the following areas:

1. The Greater Toronto Area.

2. The urban and commuter areas.

3. The expanded program area.

(3) The on-board diagnostic system test standards set out in Table 9.0.1B of the Drive Clean Guide are prescribed as standards for motor vehicles to which this section applies.

(4) The procedure to be used for testing a motor vehicle's compliance with the standards prescribed in subsection (3) is the on-board diagnostic system test as described in the Drive Clean Guide or a test that the Director considers equivalent.

(5) Subject to subsection (6), if this section applies to a vehicle, the procedure prescribed in subsection (4) shall be used before a procedure prescribed in subsection 8(4) or 11(3).

(6) During the period beginning on November 1, 2011 and ending on December 31, 2012, subsection (5) applies only if the Ontario Drive Clean testing facility at which the vehicle is tested has the equipment to perform the procedure mentioned in subsection (4) and a Drive Clean inspector who has successfully completed the course satisfactory to the Director with respect to the testing of air emissions and on-board diagnostic systems of light vehicles is available at the facility to perform the procedure.

(7) A motor vehicle to which this section applies that does not operate on diesel fuel is deemed to comply with section 8 if it complies with the standards prescribed in subsection (3).

(8) A motor vehicle to which this section applies that operates on diesel fuel is deemed to comply with section 11 if it complies with the standards prescribed in subsection (3).

(9) Every motor vehicle to which this section applies shall comply with the on-board diagnostic system test standards.

(10) No person shall operate or cause or permit the operation of a motor vehicle that does not comply with subsection (9).

O. Reg. 191/10, s. 9

REPAIR COST LIMIT FOR LIGHT VEHICLES

[Heading added O. Reg. 343/01, s. 9. Amended O. Reg. 191/10, s. 10(1).]

9.1 (1) Subsections 8(6) and 9.0.1(9) do not apply to a motor vehicle if all of the following criteria are satisfied:

1. The vehicle is tested by an Ontario Drive Clean testing facility and the test results indicate non-compliance with prescribed standards.

2. After the test,

i. the vehicle is taken to an Ontario Drive Clean repair facility that has been provided with a copy of the test results and work costing $450 or more has been performed by or under the supervision of a Drive Clean repair technician to bring the vehicle more nearly into compliance with the maximum emission standards or the standards prescribed in section 9.0.1, or

ii. the vehicle is taken to an Ontario Drive Clean repair facility that has been provided with a copy of the test results and the facility certifies in writing that, in their professional opinion,

A. no work costing less than $450 will bring the vehicle more nearly into compliance with the maximum emission standards or the standards prescribed in section 9.0.1 by a significant amount, or

B. they have performed as much work as possible, costing less than $450, to bring the vehicle more nearly into compliance with the maximum emission standards or the standards prescribed in section 9.0.1.

3. If work has been performed under subparagraph 2 ii, within 60 days after the date of the test, the vehicle is returned to an Ontario Drive Clean testing facility and retested, and the test results again indicate non-compliance with prescribed standards.

4. The work done to the vehicle to bring it into compliance is not covered by a warranty.

(2) An exemption from subsections 8(6) and 9.0.1(9) pursuant to subsection (1) applies only until the earlier of the following dates:

    1. The second anniversary of the retest referred to in paragraph 3 of subsection (1).

    2. The day on which the vehicle is next tested for compliance with prescribed standards after the retest referred to in paragraph 3 of subsection (1).

(3) If, pursuant to subsection (1), subsections 8(6) and 9.0.1(9) do not apply to a vehicle, the Ontario Drive Clean testing facility referred to in paragraph 3 of subsection (1) may issue a report indicating that the vehicle is not required to comply with the standards prescribed in sections 8 and 9.0.1.

(4) [Revoked O. Reg. 445/03, s. 2.]

(5) [Repealed O. Reg. 191/10, s. 10(9).]

O. Reg. 343/01, s. 9; 445/03, s. 2; 191/10, s. 10

[Heading repealed O. Reg. 191/10, s. 11.]

9.2 [Repealed O. Reg. 191/10, s. 11.]

TWO SPEED IDLE TEST GASOLINE FUELLED HEAVY VEHICLES (AND OTHER FUELS EXCEPT DIESEL)

10. (1) This section applies with respect to a heavy vehicle that operates on a fuel other than diesel fuel.

(1.1) [Revoked O. Reg. 343/01, s. 10.]

(1.2) [Revoked O. Reg. 343/01, s. 10.]

(2) If a motor vehicle fuelled by natural gas is tested for compliance with the maximum emission standards prescribed in this section for hydrocarbons, methane found in the emissions shall be excluded.

(3) The maximum emission standards set out in Table 10 of the Drive Clean Guide for motor vehicles of a model year set out in that Table are prescribed for those vehicles.

(4) The procedure to be used for testing a motor vehicle's compliance with the maximum emission standards prescribed in this section is the preconditioned two speed idle test, as described in the Drive Clean Guide, or a test that the Director considers equivalent.

(5) The maximum emission standards prescribed in this section do not apply with respect to a motor vehicle if the design or configuration of the motor vehicle,

    (a) is incompatible with the performance of the tests referred to in subsection (4); or

    (b) would render the performance of the tests referred to in subsection (4) unsafe.

(6) [Revoked O. Reg. 86/99, s. 13.]

(7) Every motor vehicle for which emission standards are prescribed in this section shall comply with those standards.

(8) No person shall operate or cause or permit the operation of a motor vehicle that does not comply with subsection (7).

(9) [Revoked O. Reg. 445/03, s. 3.]

(10) [Revoked O. Reg. 445/03, s. 3.]

O. Reg. 401/98, s. 4; 86/99, ss. 12, 13; 438/99, s. 2; 343/01, s. 10; 445/03, s. 3

OPACITY TEST DIESEL FUELLED LIGHT VEHICLES

11. (1) This section applies with respect to a light vehicle that operates on diesel fuel.

(2) The maximum emission standard set out in Table 11 of the Drive Clean Guide for an area and for motor vehicles of a model year set out in that Table is prescribed for those vehicles in that area.

(3) The procedure to be used for testing a motor vehicle's compliance with the maximum emission standard prescribed in this section is the opacity test for diesel fuelled light vehicles, as described in the Drive Clean Guide, or a test that the Director considers equivalent.

(3.1) The maximum emission standards prescribed in this section do not apply with respect to a motor vehicle if the design or configuration of the motor vehicle,

(a) is incompatible with the performance of the applicable tests referred to in subsection (3); or

(b) would render the performance of the applicable tests referred to in subsection (3) unsafe.

(4) Every motor vehicle for which emission standards are prescribed in this section shall comply with those standards.

(4.1) A motor vehicle shall be deemed to comply with the emission standards prescribed in this section if, when tested in accordance with subsection 12(3), it complies with the maximum emission standard set out in Table 12 of the Drive Clean Guide for a heavy vehicle of the same model year that operates on diesel fuel.

(5) No person shall operate or cause or permit the operation of a motor vehicle that does not comply with subsection (4).

O. Reg. 401/98, s. 5; 86/99, s. 14; 343/01, s. 11; 445/03, s. 4

OPACITY TEST DIESEL FUELLED HEAVY VEHICLES

12. (1) This section applies with respect to a heavy vehicle that operates on diesel fuel.

(1.1) [Revoked O. Reg. 343/01, s. 12.]

(1.2) [Revoked O. Reg. 343/01, s. 12.]

(2) The maximum emission standard set out in Table 12 of the Drive Clean Guide for motor vehicles of a type and a model year set out in that Table and for a period set out in the Table is prescribed for those vehicles for that period.

(3) The procedure to be used for testing a motor vehicle's compliance with the maximum emission standards prescribed in this section is the opacity test for diesel fuelled heavy vehicles, as described in the Drive Clean Guide, or a test that the Director considers equivalent.

(4) Every motor vehicle for which emission standards are prescribed in this section shall comply with those standards.

(5) No person shall operate or cause or permit the operation of a motor vehicle that does not comply with subsection (4).

(6) [Revoked O. Reg. 445/03, s. 5(2).]

(7) [Revoked O. Reg. 445/03, s. 5(2).]

O. Reg. 401/98, s. 6; 86/99, s. 15; 438/99, s. 3; 343/01, s. 12; 445/03, s. 5

SUBMISSION OF VEHICLE FOR TESTING

13. (1) A provincial officer designated for the purpose of carrying out Part III of the Act or a police officer may, by written notice in a form approved by the Minister, require the driver or owner of a motor vehicle to submit it for testing and inspection.

(2) Every driver or owner of a motor vehicle shall comply with a written notice given under subsection (1).

(3) A notice under subsection (1) may be given to the owner of a vehicle by leaving a copy of the notice with the driver of the vehicle.

O. Reg. 401/98, s. 7; 343/01, s. 13

ORDERS UNDER SECTION 18 OF THE ACT

13.1 An order under section 18 of the Act may be given to a person who owns or has management or control of one or more motor vehicles by leaving a copy of the order with the driver of any of the vehicles.

O. Reg. 401/98, s. 8

[Note: Tables 1–9 revoked O. Reg. 86/99, s. 16.]

[Note: Form 1 revoked O. Reg. 343/01, s. 15.]

SCHEDULE 1 — GREATER TORONTO AREA

The following areas are the areas referred to in the definition of "Greater Toronto Area" in subsection 1(1):

1.   The Regional Municipality of Durham.

2.   The Regional Municipality of Halton.

3.   The City of Hamilton.
4.   The Regional Municipality of Peel.
5.   The City of Toronto.
6.   The Regional Municipality of York.

O. Reg. 343/01, s. 14

SCHEDULE 2 — URBAN AND COMMUTER AREAS

The following areas, as they existed on June 26, 1998, are the areas referred to in the definition of "urban and commuter areas" in subsection 1(1):

1.   The City of Barrie, the City of Brantford, the City of Cambridge, the Town of Clearwater, the City of Guelph, the City of Kitchener, the City of London, the City of Niagara Falls, the City of Peterborough, the Village of Point Edward, the City of Sarnia, the City of St. Catharines, the City of Waterloo, the City of Welland and the City of Windsor.

2.   The County of Brant, the County of Essex, The Regional Municipality of Niagara, the County of Oxford and The Regional Municipality of Waterloo.

3.   The following parts of the County of Dufferin: Township of Amaranth, Township of East Garafraxa, Township of Mono, Township of East Luther Grand Valley, Town of Orangeville, Town of Shelburne.

4.   The following parts of the County of Elgin: Township of Southwold, Township of Malahide, Municipality of Central Elgin, City of St. Thomas.

5.   The following parts of The Regional Municipality of Haldimand-Norfolk: City of Nanicoke, Town of Haldimand, Town of Dunnville, Town of Simcoe.

6.   The following parts of the County of Lambton: Township of Enniskillen, Township of Plympton, Township of Moore, Village of Oil Springs, Town of Petrolia, Village of Wyoming, Town of Forest.

7.   The following parts of the County of Middlesex: Township of Middlesex Centre, Township of London, Township of North Dorchester, Township of Caradoc, Township of West Nissouri, Town of Strathroy.

8.   The following parts of the County of Northumberland: Town of Cobourg, Township of Hope, Town of Port Hope, Township of Hamilton.

9.   The following parts of the County of Perth: Township of Perth East, Township of South Easthope, City of Stratford, Township of Perth South, Town of St. Marys.

10.   The following parts of the County of Peterborough: Township of Cavan-Millbrook-North Monaghan, Township of Smith-Ennismore, Township of Douro-Dummer, Township of Otonabee-South Monaghan, Village of Lakefield.

11.   The following parts of the County of Simcoe: Township of Adjala-Tosorontio, Town of Bradford-West Gwillimbury, Township of Essa, Township of Oro-Medonte, Township of Severn, Town of New Tecumseth, Town of Innisfil, Township of Springwater, Town of Wasaga Beach, City of Orillia.

12. The following parts of the County of Victoria: Town of Lindsay, Township of Ops, Township of Eldon, Township of Emily, Township of Mariposa, Village of Omemee, Village of Woodville, Township of Manvers.

13. The following parts of the County of Wellington: Township of Mapleton (including Township of Mayborough), Town of Erin, Township of Mount Forest-Arthur-West Luther-Arthur, Township of Puslinch, Township of Guelph-Eramosa, Township of Centre Wellington.

O. Reg. 343/01, s. 14

SCHEDULE 3 — EXPANDED PROGRAM AREA

The following areas are the areas referred to in the definition of "expanded program area" in subsection 1(1):

1. The parts of the following areas that are not included in the urban and commuter areas:
    i   The County of Dufferin.
    ii.   The County of Elgin.
    iii. Haldimand County.
    iv.   The City of Kawartha Lakes.
    v.   The County of Lambton.
    vi.   The County of Middlesex.
    vii. Norfolk County.
    viii. The County of Northumberland.
    ix.   The County of Perth.
    x.   The County of Peterborough.
    xi.   The County of Simcoe.
    xii. The County of Wellington.
2. The Municipality of Chatham-Kent.
3. The geographic area of the Frontenac Management Board, as set out in paragraph 3.3(b) of an Order made under section 25.2 of the *Municipal Act* on January 7, 1997 and published in *The Ontario Gazette* dated February 15, 1997.
4. The County of Hastings.
5. The City of Kingston.
6. The County of Lanark.
7. The United Counties of Leeds and Grenville.
8. The County of Lennox and Addington.
9. The City of Ottawa.
10. The United Counties of Prescott and Russell.
11. The County of Prince Edward.
12. The United Counties of Stormont, Dundas and Glengarry.

O. Reg. 343/01, s. 14

ONT. REG. 316/03 — OPERATION OF OFF-ROAD VEHICLES ON HIGHWAYS

made under the *Highway Traffic Act*

O. Reg. 316/03, as am. O. Reg. 455/10; 122/11; 134/15; 135/15; 333/15.

PART I — DEFINITIONS

1. Definitions — In this Regulation,

"all-terrain vehicle" means an off-road vehicle that,

(a) has four wheels, the tires of which are all in contact with the ground,

(b) has steering handlebars,

(c) has a seat that is designed to be straddled by the driver, and

(d) is designed to carry,

(i) a driver only and no passengers, or

(ii) a driver and only one passenger, if the vehicle,

(A) has one passenger seat that is designed to be straddled by the passenger while sitting facing forward behind the driver, and

(B) is equipped with foot rests for the passenger that are separate from the foot rests for the driver;

"multi-purpose off-highway utility vehicle" means an off-road vehicle that,

(a) has four or more wheels, the tires of which are all in contact with the ground,

(b) has a steering wheel for steering control,

(c) has seats that are not designed to be straddled, and

(d) has a minimum cargo capacity of 159 kilograms;

"off-road vehicle" has the same meaning as in the *Off-Road Vehicles Act*;

"recreational off-highway vehicle" means an off-road vehicle that,

(a) has four or more wheels, the tires of which are all in contact with the ground,

(b) has a steering wheel for steering control,

(c) has seats that are not designed to be straddled, and

(d) has an engine displacement equal to or less than 1,000 cubic centimetres;

894

"seat belt assembly" means a device or assembly composed of a strap or straps, webbing or similar material that restrains the movement of a person in order to prevent or mitigate injury to the person.

O. Reg. 135/15, s. 1

PART II — OPERATION ON CLASSES OF HIGHWAYS

2. Operation on highways generally prohibited — An off-road vehicle shall not be driven on any highway except,

(a) as specified in this Part;

(b) as permitted by Part IV; or

(c) as permitted by clause 2(2)(a) of the *Off-Road Vehicles Act*.

3. Prohibited highways — Except as permitted by section 28, no off-road vehicle shall be driven on a highway listed in Schedule A.

4. Permitted provincial highways for certain off-road vehicles — (1) Subject to subsection (2), no off-road vehicle shall be driven on a highway listed in Schedule B.

(2) All-terrain vehicles, multi-purpose off-highway utility vehicles and recreational off-highway vehicles may be driven on a highway listed in Schedule B if the requirements of Part III are met.

O. Reg. 135/15, s. 2

4.1 Permitted municipal highways for certain off-road vehicles — (1) Subject to subsection (2), an off-road vehicle may be driven on a highway or part of a highway in a municipality if,

(a) a by-law made by the municipality under subsection 191.8(3) of the Act permits the operation of the off-road vehicle on the highway or part of the highway;

(b) the off-road vehicle is driven only during the months or hours specified in the by-law, in the case where the by-law limits the operation of the off-road vehicle on the highway or part of the highway within the municipality to certain months or hours; and

(c) the requirements of Part III are met.

(2) Subsection (1) does not apply to an off-road vehicle other than,

(a) an all-terrain vehicle;

(b) a multi-purpose off-highway utility vehicle; and

(c) a recreational off-highway vehicle.

O. Reg. 135/15, s. 2

5. Highways on Crown lands or within provincial parks or conservation reserves — An off-road vehicle may be driven on a highway or part of a highway that is on Crown land administered under the *Public Lands Act* or that is within a provincial park or conservation reserve within the meaning of the *Provincial Parks and Conservation Reserves Act, 2006*, unless the operation of the off-road vehicle on the highway or part of the highway is prohibited by the road authority or is otherwise prohibited by law.

O. Reg. 135/15, s. 2

PART III — REGULATION OF OFF-ROAD VEHICLES ON HIGHWAYS

6. Conditions for off-road vehicles to be operated on highways — An off-road vehicle shall not be operated on a highway unless it meets the requirements of sections 7 to 15 and it is operated in accordance with sections 16 to 24.

Equipment Requirements

7. Weight and width of multi-purpose off-highway utility vehicles, etc. — (1) If the off-road vehicle is a multi-purpose off-highway utility vehicle, it must,

   (a) weigh 1,814 kilograms or less; and

   (b) have an overall width not greater than 2.03 metres, excluding mirrors.

(2) If the off-road vehicle is a recreational off-highway vehicle, it must,

   (a) weigh 1,700 kilograms or less; and

   (b) have an overall width not greater than 2.03 metres, excluding mirrors.

O. Reg. 135/15, s. 3

7.1 Weight of all-terrain vehicles — (1) If the off-road vehicle is an all-terrain vehicle that was manufactured after December 31, 2001, the weight carried on the all-terrain vehicle must not exceed the maximum weight capacity as shown on the overloading warning label affixed by the manufacturer.

(2) For the purposes of subsection (1), the weight carried on the all-terrain vehicle includes the weight of the driver, any passenger, the cargo and accessories, and the trailer tongue weight, if any, but does not include the vehicle curb weight.

O. Reg. 135/15, s. 3

8. Tires — All the tires on the off-road vehicle must be inflated to the manufacturer's recommended settings for normal operation.

O. Reg. 135/15, s. 3

9. Motor vehicle safety standards — If the off-road vehicle is an all-terrain vehicle, it must meet the motor vehicle safety standards prescribed for restricted-use motorcycles in the *Motor Vehicle Safety Regulations* made under the *Motor Vehicle Safety Act* (Canada) applicable when the vehicle was manufactured.

O. Reg. 135/15, s. 3

10. Equipment configuration and performance requirements — If the off-road vehicle was manufactured after December 31, 2001, it must meet the equipment configuration and performance requirements set out in at least one of the following standards that are applicable to that class of off-road vehicle:

1. ANSI/SVIA-1-2001, entitled *American National Standard for Four Wheel All-Terrain Vehicles — Equipment, Configuration, and Performance Requirements*, approved by the American National Standards Institute, Inc. on February 15, 2001 and published by the Specialty Vehicle Institute of America.

2. ANSI/SVIA 1-2007, entitled *American National Standard for Four Wheel All-Terrain Vehicles*, approved by the American National Standards Institute, Inc. on July 23, 2007 and published by the Specialty Vehicle Institute of America.

3. ANSI/SVIA 1-2010, entitled *American National Standard for Four Wheel All-Terrain Vehicles*, approved by the American National Standards Institute, Inc. on December 23, 2010 and published by the Specialty Vehicle Institute of America.

4. ANSI/ROHVA 1-2011, entitled *American National Standard for Recreational Off-Highway Vehicles*, approved by the American National Standards Institute, Inc. on July 11, 2011 and published by the Recreational Off-Highway Vehicle Association.

5. COHV 1-2012, entitled *Canadian Off-Highway Vehicle Distributors Council Standard for Four Wheel All-Terrain Vehicles*, approved on September 26, 2012 and published by the Canadian Off-Highway Vehicle Distributors Council.

6. COHV 2-2012, entitled *Canadian Off-Highway Vehicle Distributors Council Standard for Recreational Off-Highway Vehicles*, approved on September 26, 2012 and published by the Canadian Off-Highway Vehicle Distributors Council.

7. ANSI/OPEI B71.9-2012, entitled *American National Standard for Multipurpose Off-Highway Utility Vehicles*, approved by the American National Standards Institute, Inc. on March 6, 2012 and published by the American National Standards Institute, Inc.

8. COHV 3-2013, entitled *Canadian Off-Highway Vehicle Distributors Council Standard for Multipurpose Off-Highway Utility Vehicles*, approved on April 3, 2013 and published by the Canadian Off-Highway Vehicle Distributors Council.

9. ANSI/ROHVA 1-2014, entitled *American National Standard for Recreational Off-Highway Vehicles*, approved by the American National Standards Institute, Inc. on September 24, 2014 and published by the Recreational Off-Highway Vehicle Association.

O. Reg. 135/15, s. 3

10.1 Safety equipment for multi-purpose off-highway utility vehicles and recreational off-highway vehicles — (1) If the off-road vehicle is a multi-purpose off-highway utility vehicle, it must be equipped with an occupant protective structure and comply with subsection (3).

(2) If the off-road vehicle is a recreational off-highway vehicle, it must be equipped with a roll-over protective structure and comply with subsection (3).

(3) A multi-purpose off-highway utility vehicle or a recreational off-highway vehicle must be equipped,

>   **(a)** with a handle or device that may be grasped by an occupant to provide support and to assist the occupant in keeping his or her arms and hands within the vehicle;

>   **(b)** for each seating position, with a seat belt assembly that is in good working order and that includes a strap or straps sufficient to restrain both the pelvis and the torso; and

>   **(c)** with a rear view mirror.

O. Reg. 135/15, s. 3

11. Equipment installed at time of manufacture and manufacturer's label — **(1)** A component, equipment or other feature of the off-road vehicle that was part of the vehicle when manufactured and that is required by section 9, 10 or 10.1 must operate properly and must not be missing, partly or wholly inoperable or modified so as to reduce its effectiveness.

(2) A component, equipment or other feature of the off-road vehicle that is specified in the definition of "all-terrain vehicle", "multi-purpose off-highway utility vehicle" or "recreational off-highway vehicle" in section 1 or that is required by section 9, 10 or 10.1 must have been installed at the time the vehicle was manufactured.

(3) If the off-road vehicle was manufactured after December 31, 2001, it must display in plain view the label that was affixed to the vehicle at the time of its manufacture to show the manufacturer's certification of the standard or standards listed in section 10 to which the vehicle conforms.

(4) If the off-road vehicle is an all-terrain vehicle manufactured after December 31, 2001, it must display in plain view the overloading warning label that was affixed to the vehicle at the time of its manufacture to show the maximum weight capacity.

O. Reg. 135/15, s. 3

12. Braking system — **(1)** The off-road vehicle must be equipped with service brakes that comply with the requirements set out in at least one of the standards listed in section 10 that are applicable to that class of off-road vehicle.

(2) The off-road vehicle must be equipped with a parking brake or parking mechanism that complies with the requirements set out in at least one of the standards listed in section 10 that are applicable to that class of off-road vehicle.

O. Reg. 135/15, s. 3

13. Lamps — **(1)** Despite subsection 62(1) of the Act, the off-road vehicle must be equipped with one or two lamps that emit a white light on the front of the vehicle and one or two lamps that emit a red light at the rear of the vehicle.

(2) The lamps required by subsection (1) must be lit at all times the off-road vehicle is operated on the highway.

(3) The subsections of section 62 of the Act that refer to lamps required under subsections (1), (2) or (3) of that section shall be read as if referring to the lamps required under subsection (1) of this section.

(4) The lamps required on the front of an off-road vehicle by subsection (1) must be aimed such that the high intensity portion of the beam is directed below the horizontal line through the centre of the lamp from which it comes, at a distance of 7.6 metres ahead of the lamp, when the vehicle is not loaded.

(5) If the off-road vehicle was manufactured after January 1, 1998, it must be equipped with a stop lamp or lamps on the rear of the vehicle that emit a red light when any service brake is applied.

(6) A stop lamp required under subsection (5) may be incorporated with a rear lamp or may be a separate lamp.

(7) The off-road vehicle must be equipped with,

    (a) one yellow reflex reflector on each side at the front;

    (b) one red reflex reflector on each side at the rear; and

    (c) one or more red reflex reflectors on the rear.

(8) The reflex reflectors required by subsection (7) must comply with the requirements of the *Motor Vehicle Safety Regulations* made under the *Motor Vehicle Safety Act* (Canada) if those requirements were applicable to the vehicle when the vehicle was manufactured.

O. Reg. 135/15, s. 4

14. Windshield — The off-road vehicle need not be equipped with a windshield, but if it is, the windshield must satisfy the requirements prescribed for a motorcycle windshield under subsection 1(10) of Schedule 6 to Regulation 611 of the Revised Regulations of Ontario, 1990.

15. No obstruction of view — **(1)** There must not be any object or non-transparent material placed on or attached to the off-road vehicle that obstructs the driver's view of traffic approaching from any direction at an intersection, or of traffic approaching from the rear of the vehicle.

(2) If the off-road vehicle is towing a trailer, the trailer or load must not obstruct the driver's view of traffic approaching from any direction at an intersection, or of traffic approaching from the rear of the vehicle.

Operation Requirements

16. Permit — **(1) Permit** — The off-road vehicle shall not be operated on a highway unless a permit under section 5 of the *Off-Road Vehicles Act* has been issued in respect of that vehicle and a number plate showing the number of the permit is displayed on the vehicle as required under that Act.

(2) Subsection (1) does not apply to an off-road vehicle operated under the authority of a permit issued under section 7 of the *Highway Traffic Act*, as provided by section 7 of the *Off-Road Vehicles Act*.

O. Reg. 135/15, s. 5

17. Insurance — The off-road vehicle shall be insured in accordance with section 2 of the *Compulsory Automobile Insurance Act* and section 15 of the *Off-Road Vehicles Act*.

18. Driver's licence conditions — (1) The driver of the off-road vehicle shall hold a valid Class A, B, C, D, E, F, G, G2, M or M2 driver's licence issued under the Act unless he or she is exempt, under section 34 of the Act, from the application of section 32 of the Act.

(2) If the driver of the off-road vehicle holds a Class G2 or Class M2 driver's licence and is under the age of 20, there must not be, between the hours of midnight and 5 a.m., more than one passenger on the off-road vehicle who is under the age of 20, other than a person who is a member of the novice driver's immediate family, as defined in subsection 6(6) of Ontario Regulation 340/94 (*Drivers' Licences*) made under the Act.

(3) Despite subsection (2), if the holder of the Class G2 or Class M2 driver's licence has held a valid driver's licence of that class for the immediately preceding six months or longer, the maximum number of passengers under the age of 20 allowed is three.

(4) The age distinctions in this section apply despite the *Human Rights Code*.

(5) Subsections (2) and (3) are subject to the requirements with respect to passengers set out in sections 19.1, 19.2 and 19.3.

O. Reg. 135/15, s. 6

19. Helmet — (1) The driver of the off-road vehicle and every passenger on the vehicle shall wear a helmet that complies with section 19 of the *Off-Road Vehicles Act*.

(2) No person shall drive an off-road vehicle on a highway with a passenger on the vehicle unless the passenger is wearing a helmet as required by subsection (1).

O. Reg. 135/15, s. 6

19.1 Seat belts on multi-purpose off-highway utility vehicles or recreational off-highway vehicles — (1) Every passenger on a multi-purpose off-highway utility vehicle or a recreational off-highway vehicle on a highway shall,

    (a) occupy a seating position for which a seat belt assembly has been provided; and

    (b) wear the complete seat belt assembly as required by subsection (4).

(2) No person shall drive a multi-purpose off-highway utility vehicle or a recreational off-highway vehicle on a highway unless he or she is wearing a complete seat belt assembly as required by subsection (4).

(3) No person shall drive a multi-purpose off-highway utility vehicle or a recreational off-highway vehicle on a highway with a passenger on the vehicle, unless the passenger is,

    (a) occupying a seating position for which a seat belt assembly has been provided; and

    (b) wearing the complete seat belt assembly as required by subsection (4).

(4) A seat belt assembly shall be worn so that,

    (a) the strap of each restraint is securely fastened and worn firmly against the body in the intended position; and

    (b) no more than one person is wearing any strap of the seat belt assembly at any one time.

O. Reg. 135/15, s. 6

19.2 Passengers on all-terrain vehicles — No person shall drive an all-terrain vehicle on a highway with a passenger on the vehicle unless,

    (a) the vehicle is designed to carry both a driver and a passenger; and

    (b) the passenger is straddling the passenger seat behind the driver while facing forward with his or her feet securely on the separate foot rests intended for the passenger.

O. Reg. 135/15, s. 6

19.3 No passengers under the age of eight — No person shall drive an off-road vehicle on a highway with a passenger on the vehicle who is under the age of eight.

O. Reg. 135/15, s. 6

19.4 No riding on a trailer — No person shall drive an off-road vehicle on a highway while it is towing a trailer or any other attachment if there is a passenger on the trailer or other attachment.

O. Reg. 135/15, s. 6

20. Application of *Highway Traffic Act* — (1) Except as otherwise provided in this Regulation, the provisions of the Act and its regulations applicable to motor vehicles apply with necessary modifications to the operation of an off-road vehicle on a highway.

(2) Subsection 62(19), sections 64 and 66 and subsection 76(1) of the Act do not apply to the operation of an off-road vehicle on a highway.

21. Application of *Off-Road Vehicles Act* — The *Off-Road Vehicles Act* and the regulations made under that Act that apply to the operation of off-road vehicles off the highway apply with necessary modifications to the operation of an off-road vehicle on a highway.

22. Maximum speed — (1) The off-road vehicle shall not be driven at a rate of speed greater than,

(a) 20 kilometres per hour, if the speed limit established under the Act for that part of the highway is not greater than 50 kilometres per hour; or

(b) 50 kilometres per hour, if the speed limit established under the Act for that part of the highway is greater than 50 kilometres per hour.

23. Environmental protection — (1) The off-road vehicle shall not be operated in such a manner as to,

(a) discharge a contaminant or cause or permit the discharge of a contaminant into the natural environment that may have an adverse effect on the environment or impair the quality of any waters; or

(b) contravene any conditions, restrictions and prohibitions imposed by any legislation and related regulations enacted to protect the environment.

(2) The off-road vehicle shall not be operated in such a manner that it causes or is likely to cause,

(a) a risk to the safety of any person;

(b) harm or material discomfort to any person from dust, emissions or noise;

(c) harm, injury or damage, either directly or indirectly, to any property, flora or fauna; or

(d) alteration, disruption or destruction to the natural environment, including erosion damage or degradation of the right of way.

(3) The off-road vehicle shall not be driven in or through a river, stream or other watercourse on a highway if doing so would or would be likely to alter, disrupt or destroy any fish habitat.

24. Rules of the road — (1) The off-road vehicle shall be driven on the shoulder of the highway in the same direction as the traffic using the same side of the highway.

(2) Despite subsection (1), the off-road vehicle may be driven on the roadway in the same direction as the traffic using the same side of the highway if,

(a) there is no shoulder;

(b) the shoulder of the highway is obstructed and cannot be used by the off-road vehicle; or

(c) the shoulder is not wide enough to allow the off-road vehicle to be driven with all of its tires remaining completely off of the roadway.

(3) Despite subsection (1), the off-road vehicle shall not be driven on the shoulder but shall be driven on the roadway in the same direction as the traffic using the same side of the highway if it is being driven across a level railway crossing.

(4) When driven on the shoulder of the highway, the off-road vehicle shall be driven as close to and parallel with the right edge of the shoulder as can be done practicably and safely.

(5) When driven on the roadway pursuant to subsection (2), the off-road vehicle shall be driven as close to and parallel with the right edge of the roadway as can be done practicably and safely.

(6) When entering the shoulder or the roadway, the off-road vehicle shall yield the right of way to vehicles already using the shoulder or the roadway, as the case may be, and shall enter the shoulder or roadway only when it is safe to do so.

(7) The off-road vehicle shall not be driven in the median strip of the highway.

(8) The off-road vehicle shall not be driven on any part of the highway that is designated as a construction zone under subsection 128(8) of the Act or on any other part of the highway where construction work or highway maintenance is being carried out, unless the off-road vehicle is operating as a vehicle described in subsection 128(13) of the Act or as a road service vehicle.

(9) If part or all of the highway is closed under subsection 134(2) of the Act, the off-road vehicle shall not be driven on any adjacent part of the highway that may be open, unless the off-road vehicle is operating as a vehicle described in subsection 128(13) of the Act or as a road service vehicle.

(10) The off-road vehicle shall not overtake and pass any moving motor vehicle or motorized snow vehicle at any time when both the off-road vehicle and the other vehicle are travelling on the same shoulder or roadway of the highway.

(11) Despite subsection (10), an off-road vehicle may overtake and pass another off-road vehicle when both are travelling on the shoulder if the movement can be made in safety while remaining on the shoulder and to the left of the off-road vehicle being overtaken and passed.

(12) If the off-road vehicle is an all-terrain vehicle, the person driving the all-terrain vehicle on the highway may, despite clause 142(4)(b) of the Act, indicate the intention to turn right by extending the right hand and arm horizontally beyond the right side of the vehicle.

(13) Before commencing a left turn in the manner required by subsection 141(5), (6) or (7) of the Act, the off-road vehicle shall, without interfering with the movement of traffic travelling in the same direction as the off-road vehicle, move away from the shoulder or from the right edge of the roadway, as the case may be, and be positioned on the roadway in the position from which the left turn is to be made.

(14) Upon completing a left turn, the off-road vehicle shall, without interfering with the movement of traffic travelling in the same direction as the off-road vehicle, move back to the right edge of the roadway or shoulder, as the case may be.

O. Reg. 135/15, s. 7

PART IV — EXEMPTIONS

25. Definitions — In this Part,

"emergency" means a situation that constitutes a danger to life or property;

"employee" means,

(a) a person employed in the service of the Crown or any agency of the Crown,

(b) a police officer, conservation officer or other person appointed for the preservation and maintenance of the public peace or any officer appointed for enforcing or carrying out the provisions of this Act or the *Off-Road Vehicles Act*,

(c) a firefighter as defined in the *Fire Protection and Prevention Act, 1997*,

(d) an employee of an ambulance service as defined in the *Ambulance Act*,

(e) an employee of a municipality or of a local board as defined in the *Municipal Affairs Act*,

(f) an employee of a board, commission or other local authority exercising any power with respect to municipal affairs or purposes, or

(g) an employee or agent of the operator of a water, gas, electric heat, light or power works, telegraph and telephone lines, a railway, a street railway, works for the transmission of gas, oil, water or electrical power or energy or any similar works supplying the general public with necessaries or conveniences.

26. **Crossing a highway** — Part III of this Regulation does not apply to a person who drives an off-road vehicle directly across a highway pursuant to clause 2(2)(a) of the *Off-Road Vehicles Act*.

27. **Farmers and trappers** — (1) Sections 7, 8, 9, 10, 10.1, 11 and 18 do not apply to the operation of an off-road vehicle as described in clause 2(2)(b) of the *Off-Road Vehicles Act* if,

(a) the driver of the vehicle holds a valid driver's licence; and

(b) the number of passengers on the off-road vehicle does not exceed the number of seating positions that were installed at the time the vehicle was manufactured.

(2) Despite sections 4 and 4.1, an off-road vehicle may be operated as described in clause 2(2)(b) of the *Off-Road Vehicles Act* on any highway other than a highway listed in Schedule A if the conditions described in clauses (1)(a) and (b) are met.

O. Reg. 135/15, s. 8

28. **Public work functions** — (1) An employee who is acting in the course of his or her employment or in response to an emergency may operate an off-road vehicle on a highway, including a highway listed in Schedule A or B, in accordance with this Regulation despite any provision that would provide otherwise in Parts II, IV and VI of the Act.

(2) Sections 7, 8, 9, 10, 10.1, 11 and 18 do not apply to the operation of an off-road vehicle on a highway by an employee who is driving the off-road vehicle in the course of his or her employment or in response to an emergency if,

(a) the employee holds a valid driver's licence; and

(b) the number of passengers on the off-road vehicle does not exceed the number of seating positions that were installed at the time the vehicle was manufactured.

(3) Sections 4 and 4.1 do not apply to the operation of an off-road vehicle permitted under subsection (1).

(4) Despite section 24, an employee who is permitted under subsections (1) and (2) to operate an off-road vehicle on a highway listed in Schedule A may only drive the off-road vehicle on a part of the highway that is not the roadway or the shoulder.

O. Reg. 135/15, s. 9

29. Far northern Ontario and unorganized territory — (1) A person may operate an off-road vehicle on a highway in an area of the province described in Schedule C in accordance with this Regulation despite any provision that would provide otherwise in Parts II, IV and VI of the Act.

(2) Sections 9, 10, 10.1, 11, 16 and 18 do not apply to the operation of an off-road vehicle on a highway in an area of the province described in Schedule C if,

(a) the driver of the off-road vehicle is at least 16 years old;

(b) the driver of the off-road vehicle holds a valid driver's licence or motorized snow vehicle operator's licence; and

(c) the number of passengers on the off-road vehicle does not exceed the number of seating positions that were installed at the time vehicle was manufactured.

(3) Despite sections 4 and 4.1, an off-road vehicle may be operated on any highway other than a highway listed in Schedule A in an area of the province described in Schedule C if the conditions described in clauses (2)(a), (b) and (c) are met.

(4) This section does not apply with respect to a highway or part of a highway that is under the jurisdiction of a municipality if the municipality has by by-law prohibited the operation of the off-road vehicle on the highway or part of the highway.

(5) This section does not apply with respect to a highway or part of a highway that is described in section 5 if the operation of the off-road vehicle is prohibited on the highway or part of the highway.

O. Reg. 135/15, s. 10

PART V — REVOCATION, COMMENCEMENT

30. Revocation — Ontario Regulation 195/97 is revoked.

31. Commencement — This Regulation comes into force on the later of the day it is filed and the day Part X.3 of the Act is proclaimed in force.

SCHEDULE A — HIGHWAYS PROHIBITED TO ALL OFF-ROAD VEHICLES

1. That part of the King's Highway known as Nos. 400, 401, 402, 403, 404, 405, 406, 409, 410, 412, 416, 417, 420 and 427 and the Queen Elizabeth Way.

1.1 That part of the King's Highway known as Highway 407 East.

1.2 The private toll highway known as Highway 407.

2. That part of the King's Highway known as No. 6 where that highway is contiguous with the King's Highway known as No. 403.

3. That part of the King's Highway known as No. 24 where that highway is contiguous with the King's Highway known as No. 403.

4. That part of the King's Highway known as No. 35 where that highway is contiguous with the King's Highway known as No. 115.

5. That part of the King's Highway known as No. 58 where that highway is contiguous with the King's Highway known as No. 406.

6. That part of the King's Highway known as No. 3 lying between a point situate at its intersection with the eastern limit of the roadway known as Ron McNeil Line (also known as Elgin County Road 52) where Ron McNeil Line continues as the roadway known as Ford Drive in the Township of Southwold and a point situate at its intersection with the west junction of the roadway known as Centennial Avenue in the Municipality of Central Elgin.

7. That part of the King's Highway known as No. 3 (also known as Huron Church Road) in the County of Essex lying between a point situate at its intersection with the westerly limit of the roadway known as Outer Drive in the Town of Tecumseh and a point situate at its intersection with the easterly limit of the roadways known as Industrial Drive and Northwood Street in the City of Windsor.

8. That part of the King's Highway known as No. 6 in the County of Haldimand lying between a point situate at its intersection with the roadway known as Argyle Street South and a point situate at its intersection with the southern limit of the roadway known as Seneca Greens Road.

9. That part of the King's Highway known as No. 6 lying between a point situate at its intersection with the King's Highway known as No. 401 in the Township of Puslinch and a point situate at its intersection with the south junction of the King's Highway known as No. 7 where King's Highway No. 7 continues as the roadway known as Wellington Street (also known as Wellington County Road 124) in the City of Guelph.

10. That part of the King's Highway known as Nos. 6 and 7 in the City of Guelph lying between a point situate at its intersection with the south junction of the King's Highway known as No. 7 where King's Highway No. 7 continues as the roadway known as Wellington Street (also known as Wellington County Road 124) and a point situate at its intersection with the north junction of the King's Highway known as No. 7 where King's Highway No. 7 continues as the roadway known as Woodlawn Road.

11. That part of the King's Highway known as No. 7 lying between a point situate at its intersection with the King's Highway known as No. 417 in the City of Ottawa and a point situate 150 metres measured easterly from its intersection with the centre line of the roadway known as McNeely Avenue in the Town of Carleton Place.

12. That part of the King's Highway known as No. 7 in the City of Kitchener lying between a point situate at its intersection with the roadway known as Victoria Street and a point situate at its intersection with the east junction of the King's Highway known as No. 8 where King's Highway No. 8 continues as the roadway known as King Street.

13. That part of the King's Highway known as Nos. 7 and 8 lying between a point situate at its intersection with the eastern limit of the roadway known as Waterloo Road 5 in the Township of Wilmot and a point situate at its intersection with the east junction of the King's Highway known as No. 8 where King's Highway No. 8 continues as the roadway known as King Street in the City of Kitchener.

14. That part of the King's Highway known as Nos. 7 and 115 lying between a point situate at its intersection with the west junction of the King's Highway known as No. 7 in the Township of Cavan Monaghan and a point situate at its intersection with the east junction of the King's Highway known as No. 7 in the City of Peterborough.

15. That part of the King's Highway known as No. 8 in the City of Kitchener lying between a point situate at its intersection with the King's Highway known as No. 401 and a point situate at its intersection with the east junction of the King's Highway known as No. 7 where King's Highway No. 7 continues as the roadway known as King Street.

16. That part of the King's Highway known as No. 11 in the City of Orillia lying between a point situate at its intersection with the roadway known as Memorial Avenue and a point situate at its intersection with the roadway known as Laclie Street.

17. That part of the King's Highway known as No. 11 lying between a point situate at its intersection with the south junction of the King's Highway known as No. 17 in the City of North Bay and a point situate at its intersection with the centre line of the roadway known as Muskoka Road 169 (also known as Bethune Drive) in the Town of Gravenhurst in The District Municipality of Muskoka.

18. That part of the King's Highway known as No. 26 in the County of Simcoe lying between a point situate 50 metres measured westerly from its intersection with the centre line of the King's Highway known as No. 7149 in the Town of Wasaga Beach and a point situate 50 metres measured easterly from its intersection with the centre line of the roadway known as Poplar Sideroad in the Town of Collingwood.

19. That part of the King's Highway known as Nos. 11 and 17 in the City of North Bay lying between a point situate at its intersection with the roadway known as Seymour Street and a point situate at its intersection with the King's Highway known as No. 11 (also known as Algonquin Avenue).

20. That part of the King's Highway known as Nos. 11 and 17 lying between a point situate at its intersection with the centre line of the roadway known as Lakeshore Drive in the Municipality of Shuniah and a point situate at its intersection with the centre line of the King's Highway known as No. 130 in the Municipality of Oliver Paipoonge.

21. That part of the King's Highway known as No. 17 in the City of North Bay lying between a point situate at its intersection with the King's Highway known as No. 11 (also known as Algonquin Avenue) and a point situate at its intersection with the roadway known as Gormanville Road.

22. That part of the King's Highway known as No. 17 in the City of Greater Sudbury lying between a point situate at its intersection with the middle junction of the roadway known as Municipal Road 55 and a point situate 1100 metres measured westerly from its intersection with the west junction of the roadway known as Municipal Road 55.

23. That part of the King's Highway known as No. 58 in the City of Thorold lying between a point situate at its intersection with the King's Highway known as No. 406 and a point situate at its intersection with the westerly limit of the roadway known as Niagara Regional Road No. 57 (also known as Thorold Stone Road).

24. That part of the King's Highway known as No. 61 in the City of Thunder Bay lying between a point situate at its intersection with the King's Highway known as No. 11 and a point situate at its intersection with the roadway known as Chippewa Road.

25. That part of the King's Highway known as No. 69 in the Territorial District of Sudbury lying between a point situate 1890 metres measured southerly from its intersection with the centre line of the King's Highway known as No. 637 in the Township of Servos and a point situate 1585 metres measured southerly from its intersection with the centre line of the roadway known as Estaire Road in the City of Greater Sudbury.

26. That part of the King's Highway known as No. 85 lying between a point situate at its intersection with the King's Highway known as No. 7 (also known as Victoria Street) in the City of Kitchener and a point situate 385 metres measured northerly from its intersection with the centre line of the roadway known as Waterloo Regional Road 15 (also known as King Street) in the Township of Woolwich.

27. That part of the King's Highway known as No. 115 lying between a point situate at its intersection with the King's Highway known as Nos. 35 and 115 in the Municipality of Clarington and a point situate at its intersection with the King's Highway known as No. 7 in the Township of Cavan Monaghan.

28. That part of the King's Highway known as No. 137 lying between a point situate at its intersection with the King's Highway known as No. 401 in the Township of Leeds and The Thousand Islands and a point situate 15 metres measured southerly from the south abutment of the Thousand Island Bridge.

29. That part of the King's Highway known as No. 7087 (also known as E. C. Row Expressway) in the City of Windsor in the County of Essex lying between a point situate at its intersection with the northerly limit of the King's Highway known as No. 7902 (also known as Ojibway Parkway) and a point situate 365 metres measured easterly from its intersection with the centre line of the King's Highway known as No. 3 (also known as Huron Church Road).

30. All of the King's Highway known as No. 7274 (also known as Highway 6/Airport Road Connection).

31. That part of the King's Highway known as No. 7902 (also known as Ojibway Parkway) in the City of Windsor in the County of Essex lying between a point situate at its intersection with the northerly limit of the south junction of the roadway known as Broadway Street and a point situate at its intersection with the easterly limit of the Essex Terminal Railway right-of-way.

32. That part of the King's Highway known as No. 7908 (also known as Essex County Road 9/Howard Avenue Diversion) in the Town of Tecumseh in the County of Essex lying between a point situate at its intersection with the southerly limit of the King's Highway known as No. 3 and a point situate at its intersection with the northerly limit of the roadways known as Laurier Parkway and South Talbot Road

where the King's Highway known as No. 7908 continues as the roadway known as Essex County Road 9.

O. Reg. 455/10, s. 1; 122/11, s. 1; 134/15, s. 1; 333/15, s. 1

SCHEDULE B — HIGHWAYS PERMITTED TO ALL-TERRAIN VEHICLES, MULTI-PURPOSE OFF-HIGHWAY UTILITY VEHICLES AND RECREATIONAL OFF-HIGHWAY VEHICLES [Heading amended O. Reg. 135/15, s. 11(1).]

1. All of the Secondary and Tertiary highways known as and numbered 500 to 899, but not including that part of the Secondary highway known as No. 587 south of a point situate 3.6 km southerly from its intersection with the highway known as Pass Lake Cross Road in the Municipality of Shuniah, in the District of Thunder Bay, being within the boundary of Sleeping Giant Provincial Park.

2. All of the King's Highways known as and numbered 7041, 7104, 7181, 7182, 7241.

3. All of the King's Highways known as Nos. 94, 105, 125, 127, 130 and 141.

4. That part of the King's Highway known as No. 4 lying between a point situate at its intersection with the highway known as Huron County Road 12 (also known as Kippen Road) in the Municipality of Huron East, in the County of Huron, and a point situate at the north end of the structure known as the Bayfield River Bridge (at the southern boundary of the former Town of Clinton) in the Municipality of Central Huron, in the County of Huron.

5. That part of the King's Highway known as No. 6 lying between a point situate at its intersection with the south junction of the highway known as Bruce County Road No. 9 (also known as Colpoy Bay Road) in the Town of South Bruce Peninsula, in the County of Bruce, and a point situate 400 metres measured north of the centre line of the roadway known as Dyers Bay Road in the Municipality of Northern Bruce Peninsula, in the County of Bruce.

6. That part of the King's Highway known as No. 6 lying between a point situate at its intersection with the highway known as Water Street in the Township of Tehkummah, in the District of Manitoulin, and a point situate 2,000 metres measured northerly from the centre line of the highway known as Whites Point Road in the Town of Northeastern Manitoulin and the Islands, in the District of Manitoulin.

7. That part of the King's Highway known as No. 6 lying between a point situate at 330 metres measured southerly from the middle of the swing bridge over the Little Current North Channel in the Town of Northeastern Manitoulin and the Islands in the District of Manitoulin and a point situate at its intersection with the highway known as Foster Drive in the Town of Espanola in the District of Sudbury.

8. That part of the King's Highway known as No. 8 lying between a point situate 1.3 kilometres measured westerly from the centre line of the west most intersection with the King's Highway known as No. 23, in the Municipality of West Perth, in the County of Perth, and a point situate at its intersection with the highway known as Centennial Drive in the Municipality of Huron East, in the County of Huron.

9. That part of the King's Highway known as No. 8 lying between a point situate 100 metres measured easterly from the centre line of the highway known as Huron

909

Street in the Municipality of West Perth, in the County of Perth, and a point situate at its intersection with the highway known as Ransford Street in the Municipality of Central Huron, in the County of Huron.

10. That part of the King's Highway known as No. 9 lying between a point situate at its intersection with the highway known as Wellington Road 1 in the Township of Howick, in the County of Huron, and a point situate 500 metres measured southerly from the centre line of the roadway known as Bruce Road 24 (also known as Absalom Street) in the Municipality of South Bruce, in the County of Bruce.

11. That part of the King's Highway known as No. 9 lying between a point situate 600 metres measured northerly from the intersection with the highway known as Bruce Road 24 (also known as Absalom Street) in the Municipality of South Bruce, in the County of Bruce, and a point situate at its intersection with the King's Highway known as No. 21 in the Municipality of Kincardine, in the County of Bruce.

12. That part of the King's Highway known as No. 11 lying between a point situate at its western most intersection with the King's highway known as No. 71 east of the Settlement Area of Barwick, in the Township of Chappel, in the Reserve of the Manitou Rapids First Nation in the District of Rainy River, and a point situate 300 metres measured easterly from the centre line of the highway known as Miller Street North at the eastern most boundary of the Town of Rainy River, in the District of Rainy River.

13. That part of the King's Highway known as No. 11B lying between a point situate at its northern most intersection with the King's Highway known as No. 11 in the Township of Atikokan, in the District of Rainy River, and a point situate at its intersection with the Secondary Highway known as No. 622 in the District of Rainy River.

14. That part of the King's Highway known as No. 23 lying between a point situate at its intersection with the King's Highway known as No.7 in the Township of Lucan Biddulph, in the County of Middlesex, and a point situate 1.1 kilometres measured southerly from its intersection with the King's Highway known as No. 8 in the Municipality of West Perth, in the County of Perth.

15. That part of the King's Highway known as No. 23 lying between a point situate at its intersection with a point measured 1.1 kilometres northerly from the King's Highway known as No. 8 in the Municipality of West Perth, in the County of Perth, and a point situate at its intersection with the roadway known as West Perth Line No. 44 in the Town of North Perth, in the County of Perth.

16. That part of the King's Highway known as No. 28 lying between a point situate at its intersection with the highway known as Peterborough County Road 504 in the Township of North Kawartha, in the County of Peterborough, and a point situate at its intersection with the King's Highway known as No. 121 in the Town of Bancroft, in the County of Hastings.

17. That part of the King's Highway known as No. 28 lying between a point situate 880 metres measured easterly from the centre line of the highway known as Hastings Street in the Town of Bancroft, in the County of Hastings, and a point situate at its intersection with the King's Highway known as No. 41 in the Township of Addington Highlands, in the County of Lennox and Addington.

18. That part of the King's Highway known as No. 35 lying between a point situate at its northern most intersection with the King's Highway known as No. 118 in the Township of Minden Hills, in the County of Haliburton, and a point situate at its intersection with the King's Highway known as No. 60 in the Township of Lake of Bays, in the District of Muskoka.

19. That part of the King's Highway known as No. 41 lying between a point situate at the Frontenac and the Lennox and Addington County Boundary (Bon Echo Provincial Park North Boundary) in the Township of Addington Highlands, in the County of Lennox and Addington, and a point situate at its intersection with the highway known as Renfrew County Road 512 (also known as Foymount Road) in the Municipality of Bonnechere Valley, in the County of Renfrew.

20. That part of the King's Highway known as No. 41 lying between a point situate 800 metres measured northerly from the centre line of its southern most intersection with the King's Highways known as No. 60 (also known as Bonnechere Street) in the Municipality of Bonnechere Valley, in the County of Renfrew, and a point situate at its intersection with the King's Highway known as No.17 in the Township of Laurentian Valley, in the County of Renfrew.

21. That part of the King's Highway known as No. 60 lying between a point situate at its intersection with the highway known as Cotieville Road in the Township of Horton, in the County of Renfrew, and a point situate at its intersection with a point measured 500 metres westerly from the centre line of the highway known as Ott Road in the Municipality of Bonnechere Valley, in the County of Renfrew.

22. That part of the King's Highway known as No. 60 in the County of Renfrew lying between a point situate 800 metres measured northerly from its intersection with the roadway known as Bridge Street in the Municipality of Bonnechere Valley and a point situate 800 metres measured easterly from its intersection with the roadway known as Renfrew County Road 62 South in the Township of Madawaska Valley.

23. That part of the King's Highway known as No. 60 lying between a point situate 500 metres measured westerly from the centre line of its western-most intersection with County Road No. 62 in the Township of Madawaska Valley, in the County of Renfrew, and a point situate 300 metres measured southerly from the middle of the Headstone Creek Bridge (at the east entrance of Algonquin Provincial Park) in the District of Nipissing.

24. That part of the King's Highway known as No. 60 lying between a point situate at its intersection with the northern most boundary of the Township of Algonquin Highlands (being the westerly boundary of Algonquin Park), in the County of Haliburton, and a point situate at its intersection with the King's Highway known as No. 35 in the Township of Lake of Bays, in the District of Muskoka.

25. That part of the King's Highway known as No. 61 lying between a point situate with the international boundary between Canada and the United States of America in the Municipality of Neebing, in the District of Thunder Bay, and a point situate at its intersection with the King's Highway known as No. 130 in the Municipality of Oliver Paipoonge, in the District of Thunder Bay.

26. That part of the King's Highway known as No. 62 lying between a point situate at its intersection with the King's Highway known as No. 7 in the Township of Madoc, in the County of Hastings, and a point situate 300 metres measured south-

erly from the centre line of the highway known as Bay Lake Road in the Town of Bancroft, in the County of Hastings.

27. That part of the King's Highway known as No. 62 lying between a point situate at its intersection with the highway known as Hybla Road in the Municipality of Hastings Highlands, in the County of Hastings, and a point situate at its intersection with the King's Highway known as No.127 in the Municipality of Hastings Highlands, in the County of Hastings.

28. That part of the King's Highway known as No. 63 lying between a point situate at its intersection with the highway known as Peninsula Road in the City of North Bay, in the District of Nipissing, and a point situate at its intersection with the boundary of the Province of Ontario and the Province of Quebec in the District of Nipissing.

29. That part of the King's Highway known as No. 64 lying between a point situate at its intersection with the King's Highway known as No. 69 in the Municipality of French River, in the District of Sudbury, and a point situate at its western most intersection with the King's Highway known as No. 17 in the Municipality of West Nipising, in the District of Nipissing.

30. That part of the King's Highway known as No. 64 lying between a point situate at its intersection with the highway known as Sabourin Road in the Municipality of West Nipissing, in the District of Nipissing, and a point situate at its intersection with the King's Highway known as No. 11 in the District of Nipissing.

31. That part of the King's Highway known as No. 65 lying between a point situate at its intersection with the boundary of the Province of Ontario and the Province of Quebec in the District of Timiskaming and a point situate at its intersection with the northern most intersection with the King's Highway known as No. 11B in the Town of New Liskeard, in the District of Timiskaming.

32. That part of the King's Highway known as No. 65 lying between a point situate at its intersection with the southern most intersection with the Kings Highway known as No. 11B in the Town of New Liskeard in the District of Timiskaming and a point situate at its intersection with the King's Highway known as No. 66 in the Township of Matachewan in the District of Timiskaming.

33. That part of the King's Highway known as No. 66 lying between a point situate at its intersection with King's Highway known as Highway No. 11 in the District of Timiskaming and a point situate at its intersection with the Secondary Highway known as No. 566 in the Township of Matachewan, in the District of Timiskaming.

34. That part of the King's Highway known as No. 72 lying between a point situate at its intersection with the King's Highway known as No. 17 in the District of Kenora and a point situate at its intersection with the railway tracks of the Canadian National Railway in the Town of Sioux Lookout, in the District of Kenora.

35. That part of the King's Highway known as No. 89 lying between a point situate at its intersection with a point measured 800 metres westerly from the centre line of its western most intersection with the King's Highway known as No. 10 in the Town of Shelburne, in the County of Dufferin, and a point situate 1.4 kilometres measured east from the centre line of the King's Highway known as No. 6 in the Township of Wellington North, in the County of Wellington.

36. That part of the King's Highway known as No. 89 lying between a point situate at its intersection with a point situate 1.8 km west of its intersection with the King's Highway known as No. 6 in the Township of Wellington North, in the County of Wellington, and a point situate at the intersection with the highway known as Wellington Road No. 2 in the Town of Minto, in the County of Wellington.

37. That part of the King's Highway known as No. 101 lying between a point situate at its intersection with the boundary of the Province of Ontario and the Province of Quebec in the Township of Black River-Matheson, in the District of Cochrane, and a point situate at the middle of the bridge over the Black River in the Township of Black River-Matheson, in the District of Cochrane.

38. That part of the King's Highway known as No. 101 lying between a point situate at its western most intersection with the King's Highway known as No. 11 in the Township of Black River-Matheson, in the District of Cochrane, and a point situate at its intersection with the Tertiary Highway known as No. 803 the City of Timmins, in the District of Cochrane.

39. That part of the King's Highway known as No. 101 lying between a point situate at its intersection with the King's Highway known as No. 144 in the City of Timmins, in the District of Cochrane, and a point situate 120 metres measured easterly from the centre line of the highway known as Watson's Skyway Road in the Township of Michipicoten, in the District of Algoma.

40. That part of the King's Highway known as No. 108 lying between a point situate at its intersection with the King's Highway known as No. 17 in the Township of The North Shore, in the District of Algoma, and a point situate at its intersection with the highway known as Eastern Drive South in the City of Elliot Lake, in the District of Algoma.

41. That part of the King's Highway known as No. 112 lying between a point situate at its intersection with the King's Highway known as No. 11 in the District of Timiskaming and a point situate at its intersection with the King's Highway known as No. 66 in the Town of Kirkland Lake, in the District of Timiskaming.

42. That part of the King's Highway known as No. 118 lying between a point situate at its intersection with the highway known as Haliburton Road 14 (also known as Eagle Lake Road) in the Municipality of Dysart et al, in the County of Halibuton, and a point situate at its intersection with the King's Highway known as No. 11 in the Town of Bracebridge, in the District of Muskoka.

43. That part of the King's Highway known as No. 118 lying between a point situate at its intersection with a point measured 500 easterly from the centre line of the highway known as Dover Spring Road in the Municipality of Dysart et al, in the County of Haliburton, and a point situate at its intersection with the King's Highway known as No. 28 in the Township of Faraday, in the County of Hastings.

44. That part of the King's Highway known as No. 124 lying between a point situate at its intersection with the highway known as Hurdville Road South in the Township of McDougall, in the District of Parry Sound, and a point situate at its intersection with the King's Highway known as No. 11 in the Township of Strong, in the District of Parry Sound.

45. That part of the King's Highway known as No. 129 lying between a point situate 900 metres measured north of the centre line of the highway known as River Street in the Town of Thessalon, in the District of Algoma, and a point situate at 500 metres measured north of the centre line of the highway known as Eastern Drive South in the Township of Chapleau, in the District of Sudbury.

46. That part of the King's Highway known as No. 132 lying between a point situate at 1.5 kilometres measured west of the centre line of the highway known as Renfrew County Road 33 (also known as Lochiel Avenue) in the Town of Renfew in the County of Renfrew and a point situate at its intersection with the King's Highway known as No. 41 in the Township of Bonnechere Valley in the County of Renfrew.

47. That part of the King's Highway known as No. 144 lying between a point situate at its intersection with the highway known as Cartier East Entrance Road in the Geographic Township of Cartier, in the District of Sudbury, and a point situate at its intersection with the King's Highway known as No. 101 in the City of Timmins, in the District of Cochrane.

48. [Repealed O. Reg. 135/15, s. 11(5).]

O. Reg. 135/15, s. 11

SCHEDULE C — AREAS IN FAR NORTHERN ONTARIO AND UNORGANIZED TERRITORY

1. The areas in the districts of Kenora and Thunder Bay north of the railway tracks of the Canadian National Railways passing through the municipalities of Malachi, Minaki, Quibell, Sioux Lookout, Savant Lake, Armstrong and Nakina.

2. The area in the Territorial District of Cochrane north of 50 degrees latitude.

3. The area in the Territorial District of Algoma north of the railway tracks of the Canadian Pacific Railway passing through the municipalities of Amyot, Franz and Missanabie.

4. All highways that are in unorganized territory and that are under the jurisdiction and control of a road authority other than the Ministry.

ONT. REG. 603 — OVER-DIMENSIONAL FARM VEHICLES

made under the *Highway Traffic Act*

R.R.O. 1990, Reg. 603, as am. O. Reg. 150/97; 437/06 (Fr.); 454/10; 171/15; 334/15.

1. No over-dimensional farm vehicle shall be driven or drawn on a highway described in the Schedule.

O. Reg. 150/97, s. 1; 334/15, s. 1

2. (1) Subject to subsection (5), every over-dimensional farm vehicle while being driven or drawn on a highway from one-half hour after sunset to one-half hour before sunrise or at any other time when, due to insufficient light or unfavourable atmospheric conditions, persons and vehicles on the highway are not clearly discernible at a distance of 150 metres or less, shall carry a lamp at each side of the front and at each side of the rear, each of which shall,

(a) produce intermittent flashes of amber light;

(b) be placed not more than 150 millimetres from the side of the permanent structure of the vehicle; and

(c) be visible at a distance of 150 metres from the front and rear respectively of the vehicle.

(2) Subject to subsections (5) and (6), every over-dimensional farm vehicle that exceeds 3.8 metres in width while being driven or drawn on a highway from one-half hour after sunset to one-half hour before sunrise or at any other time when, due to insufficient light or unfavourable atmospheric conditions, persons and vehicles on the highway are not clearly discernible at a distance of 150 metres or less, shall be equipped with an illuminated rotating amber light mounted on the uppermost part of the vehicle and producing intermittent flashes of amber light visible at a distance of 150 metres to the front and to the rear.

(3) Subject to subsection (5), every over-dimensional farm vehicle that exceeds 3.8 metres in width while being driven or drawn on a highway at times other than the time specified in subsections (1) and (2) shall be equipped with the lamps described in subsection (1) or with the light described in subsection (2).

(4) Subject to subsection (5), every over-dimensional farm vehicle that exceeds 4.8 metres in width, while being driven or drawn on a highway from one-half hour after sunset to one-half hour before sunrise or at any other time when, due to insufficient light or unfavourable atmospheric conditions, persons and vehicles on the highway are not clearly discernible at a distance of 150 metres or less shall be,

(a) preceded by an escort vehicle at a distance of approximately 60 metres; and

(b) followed by an escort vehicle at a distance of approximately 60 metres.

(5) Subsections (1), (2), (3) and (4) do not apply to a vehicle that is directly crossing the highway.

(6) Subsection (2) does not apply to an over-dimensional farm vehicle that does not exceed 4.8 metres in width while being driven or drawn on a highway and is,

(a) preceded by an escort vehicle at a distance of approximately 60 metres; and

(b) followed by an escort vehicle at a distance of approximately 60 metres.

3. Escort vehicles required under this Regulation shall,

(a) have in operation vehicular hazard warning signal lamps commonly known as four-way flashers; or

(b) carry an illuminated rotating amber light mounted on the uppermost part of the vehicle and producing intermittent flashes of amber light visible at a distance of 150 metres to the front and to the rear.

SCHEDULE

1. That part of the King's Highway known as Nos. 400, 401, 402, 403, 404, 405, 409, 410, 412, 416, 417 and 427.

O. Reg. 334/15, s. 2

1.1 That part of the King's Highway known as Highway 407 East.

O. Reg. 334/15, s. 2

1.2 The private toll highway known as Highway 407.

O. Reg. 334/15, s. 2

2. That part of the King's Highway known as No. 406 lying between a point at its intersection with the King's Highway known as the Queen Elizabeth Way in the City of St. Catharines and a point at its intersection with the roadway known as Holland Road in the Town of Thorold.

3. That part of the King's Highway known as No. 420 in the City of Niagara Falls lying between a point at its intersection with the King's Highway known as the Queen Elizabeth Way and a point at its intersection with the roadway known as Stanley Avenue.

4. All of the King's Highway known as the Queen Elizabeth Way.

5. All of the King's Highway known as No. 2A in the City of Scarborough.

6. That part of the King's Highway known as No. 2 in the Town of Ancaster lying between a point at its intersection with the King's Highway known as No. 403 and a point at its intersection with the King's Highway known as No. 2/53.

7. That part of the King's Highway known as No. 2/53 in the Town of Ancaster lying between a point at its intersection with the King's Highway known as No. 2 and a point at its intersection with the western boundary of the Regional Municipality of Hamilton Wentworth.

8. That part of the King's Highway known as No. 5 lying between a point at its intersection with the King's Highway known as No. 403 at the Halton Region boundary and a point at its intersection with the King's Highway known as No. 6 in the Town of Flamborough.

9. That part of the King's Highway known as No. 6 lying between a point at its intersection with the King's Highway known as No. 403 at the Town of Dundas boundary and a point at its intersection with the King's Highway known as No. 401 in Wellington County.

10. That part of the King's Highway known as No. 6 lying between a point at its intersection with the southern boundary of the Regional Municipality of Hamilton Wentworth and the roadway known as Alderlea Avenue in the Township of Glanbrook.

11. That part of the King's Highway known as No. 7 in the City of Brampton lying between a point at its intersection with the King's Highway known as No. 7/410 (Heart Lake Road) and a point at its western intersection with the roadway known as Chinguacousy Road (Second Line Road West).

12. That part of the King's Highway known as No. 7/410 (Heart Lake Road) in the City of Brampton lying between a point at its northern intersection with the King's Highway known as No. 7 (Bovaird Drive) and a point at its southern intersection with the King's Highway known as No. 7 (Queen Street East).

13. That part of the King's Highway known as No. 7 lying between a point at its intersection with the King's Highway known as No. 7/410 (Heart Lake Road) in the City of Brampton and a point at its intersection with the King's Highway known as the Markham By-Pass in the Regional Municipality of York.

14. That part of the King's Highway known as No. 7 lying between a point at its intersection with the King's Highway known as No. 28/115 in the City of Peterborough and a point at its intersection with the eastern boundary of the City of Peterborough.

15. That part of the King's Highway known as No. 7 lying between a point at its intersection with the western limit of the King's Highway known as No. 417 in the Township of West Carlton and a point at its intersection with the King's Highway known as No. 15 in the Township of Beckwith.

16. That part of the King's Highway known as No. 7 lying between a point at its intersection with the roadway known as Victoria Street in the City of Kitchener and a point at its intersection with the King's Highway known as No. 8.

17. That part of the King's Highway known as No. 7/8 lying between a point at its intersection with the eastern limit of the roadway known as Waterloo Road No. 5 in the Township of Wilmot and a point at its intersection with the King's Highway known as No. 8 in the City of Kitchener.

18. That part of the King's Highway known as No. 7187 lying between a point at its intersection with the King's Highway known as No. 401 and a point at its intersection with the King's Highway known as No. 8 (King Street) in the City of Kitchener.

19. That part of the King's Highway known as No. 8 lying between a point at its intersection with the King's Highway known as No. 7187 and a point at its intersection with the King's Highway known as No. 7/8 in the City of Kitchener.

20. That part of the King's Highway known as No. 11 in the City of Orillia lying between a point at its intersection with the roadway known as Memorial Avenue and a point at its intersection with the roadway known as Laclie Street.

21. That part of the King's Highway known as No. 9 lying between a point at its intersection with the King's Highway known as No. 11 in the Town of Newmarket and a point at its intersection with the King's Highway known as No. 10 in the Township of Mono.

22. That part of the King's Highway known as No. 10 lying between a point at its intersection with the roadway known as Burnhamthorpe Road in the City of Mississauga and a point at its intersection the northern boundary of the City of Brampton (Mayfield Road).

23. That part of the King's Highway known as No. 20 (Centennial Parkway) in the City of Stoney Creek lying between a point at its intersection with the King's Highway known as No. 53 (Rymals Road) and a point at its intersection with the roadway known as King Street.

24. That part of the King's Highway known as No. 27 lying between a point at its intersection with the roadway known as Eglinton Avenue in the City of Etobicoke and a point at its intersection with the roadway known as Regional Road No. 49 (Nashville Road) in the City of Vaughan.

25. That part of the King's Highway known as No. 28/115 lying between a point at its intersection with the King's Highway known as No. 7A/115 at the western boundary of the Township of North Monagan and a point at its intersection with the King's Highway known as No. 7 in the City of Peterborough.

26. That part of the King's Highway known as No. 35/115 in Durham Region lying between a point at its intersection with the King's Highway known as No. 401 and a point at its intersection with the King's Highway known as No. 35 and the King's Highway known as No. 115.

27. That part of the King's Highway known as No. 48 lying between a point at its intersection with the King's Highway known as No. 401 in the City of Scarborough and a point situated at its intersection with the roadway known as Elgin Mills Road in the Town of Markham.

28. That part of the King's Highway known as No. 50 lying between a point at its intersection with the King's Highway known as No. 27 in the City of Etobicoke and a point at its intersection with the roadway known as Columbia Way East in the Town of Caledon.

29. That part of the King's Highway known as No. 58 in the City of Thorold lying between a point at its intersection with the King's Highway known as No. 406 and a point at its intersection with the westerly limit of the roadway known as Niagara Regional Road No. 57 (Thorold Stone Road).

30. That part of the King's Highway known as No. 86 lying between its intersection with the King's Highway known as No. 7 (Victoria Street) in the City of Kitchener and a point at its intersection with the roadway known as Waterloo Road No. 17 in the Township of Woolwich.

31. That part of the King's Highway known as No. 115 lying between a point at its intersection with the King's Highway known as No. 35/115 in Durham Region and a point at its intersection with the King's Highway known as No. 7A/115 in Cavan Township.

32. That part of the King's Highway known as No. 137 lying between a point at its intersection with the King's Highway known as No. 401 in the Township of the Front of Leeds and Lansdowne and a point at its intersection with the Border between Canada and The United States of America.

O. Reg. 150/97, s. 2

33. That part of the King's Highway known as No. 3 (Huron Church Road) in the County of Essex lying between a point situate 625 metres measured easterly from the centre line of the roadway known as Howard Avenue in the Town of Tecumseh and a point situate at its intersection with the easterly limit of the roadways known as Industrial Drive and Northwood Street in the City of Windsor.

O. Reg. 454/10, s. 1; 171/15, s. 1

34. That part of the King's Highway known as No. 7087 (E. C. Row Expressway) in the City of Windsor in the County of Essex lying between a point at its intersection with the northerly limit of the King's Highway known as No. 7902 (Ojibway Park-

way) and a point situate 365 metres measured easterly from its intersection with the centre line of the King's Highway known as No. 3 (Huron Church Road).

O. Reg. 454/10, s. 1

35. That part of the King's Highway known as No. 7902 (Ojibway Parkway) in the City of Windsor in the County of Essex lying between a point at its intersection with the northerly limit of the south junction of the roadway known as Broadway Street and a point at its intersection with the easterly limit of the Essex Terminal Railway right-of-way.

O. Reg. 454/10, s. 1

ONT. REG. 604 — PARKING

made under the *Highway Traffic Act*

R.R.O. 1990, Reg. 604, as am. O. Reg. 431/91; 530/91; 28/92; 59/92; 61/92; 137/92; 338/92; 471/92; 558/92; 625/92; 650/92; 23/93; 106/93; 181/93; 275/93; 487/93; 633/93; 724/93; 803/93; 24/94; 227/94; 292/94; 450/94; 459/94; 563/94; 36/95; 67/95; 188/95; 306/95; 337/95; 356/95; 71/96; 329/96; 370/96; 411/96; 476/96; 139/97; 193/97; 339/97; 30/98; 417/98; 716/98; 55/99; 360/99; 406/99; 433/99; 434/99; 506/99; 444/00; 482/00; 332/01; 333/01; 335/01; 354/01; 355/01; 293/02; 294/02; 9/03; 79/03; 119/04; 454/05; 455/05; 534/05; 230/06; 309/06; 391/06; 457/06; 479/06; 535/06; 456/07; 520/07; 548/07; 43/08; 50/08; 170/08; 311/08; 358/08; 381/08; 452/08; 502/10; 4/11; 386/11; 413/11; 64/12; 154/12; 361/12; 122/13; 215/13; 227/13; 220/14; 184/15; 210/15; 275/15; 366/15.

PARKING OF VEHICLES ON THE KING'S HIGHWAY AND TOLL HIGHWAYS

[Heading amended O. Reg. 366/15, s. 1.]

1. This Regulation applies to the King's Highway and to that part of any other highway within 100 metres of its intersection with the King's Highway, except where a by-law regulating or prohibiting parking has been passed by the council or trustees of the municipality or police village having jurisdiction over the highway.

2. Subject to section 3, where a person parks a vehicle off the roadway of the King's Highway, he or she shall park the vehicle,

(a) on the right side of the highway having reference to the direction in which the vehicle has been travelling; and

(b) so that the left side of the vehicle is parallel to the edge of the roadway.

3. (1) Where a person parks a vehicle in an area off the roadway of the King's Highway marked by signs, erected and maintained by the Ministry to indicate that the area may be used for parking vehicles at an angle to the edge of the roadway, he or she shall park the vehicle,

(a) in the case of an area clearly marked into parking spaces, within a parking space so that no part of the vehicle encroaches on a contiguous parking space; and

(b) in all other cases, between the signs and on the right hand side of the highway having reference to the direction in which the vehicle has been travelling and so that,

(i) the travelled portion of the highway is to the rear of the vehicle, and

(ii) the line formed to the left hand side of the vehicle intersects the pavement edge line at an angle of not less than 40 degrees, and not greater than 50 degrees.

(2) The signs under subsection (1) shall bear the words "angle parking" and in addition clearly indicate the extent of the parking area.

4. (1) No person shall park a vehicle on the King's Highway,

(a) in such a manner as to obstruct,

(i) a sidewalk,

(ii) a crosswalk,

(iii) an entrance on the highway to, or from, a private road or lane, or

(iv) an entrance-way for vehicles to pass between the highway and land contiguous to the highway;

(b) within three metres of a point in the edge of the roadway and nearest a fire hydrant;

(c) on or within 100 metres of a bridge over, under or across which the highway passes;

(d) within six metres of a point at the edge of the roadway and nearest to a public entrance to,

(i) a hotel as defined in the *Hotel Fire Safety Act*, or

(ii) a place where film, as defined in the *Film Classification Act, 2005*, is exhibited and where the place is open to the public, or

(iii) a public hall as defined in the *Public Halls Act*, while the hall is open to the public;

(e) subject to clause (f), within nine metres of an intersection on the highway;

(f) where there is a signal-light traffic control system installed at an intersection on the highway, within fifteen metres of the intersection;

(g) within fifteen metres of the nearest rail of a level railway crossing;

(h) in a position or place that prevents or is likely to prevent the removal of any vehicle already parked on the highway; or

(i) for a longer period of time than three hours between 12 midnight and 7 a.m.

(2) No person shall park a vehicle on a highway where the Ministry erects and maintains a sign or signs indicating a prohibited parking area,

(a) within an area on the highway and up to 100 metres from an intersection on the highway; and

(b) in the case of a fire hall with an entrance-way to the highway for the use of fire fighting vehicles,

(i) 7.5 metres from the entrance-way on the same side of the highway as the fire hall, and

(ii) 100 metres from the entrance-way on the opposite side of the highway to that of the fire hall; and

(c) in the case of a school under the *Education Act*, on both sides of the highway contiguous to the limit of the land used for school purposes while the school is open for educational purposes.

(3) Signs in respect of schools under clause (2)(c) shall bear an additional inscription indicating the times at which the parking prohibition is in effect.

O. Reg. 455/05, s. 1

5. (1) No person shall park a vehicle on a part of the King's Highway described in a Schedule to Appendix A.

(2) No person shall park a vehicle on a part of the King's Highway described in Column 1 of a Schedule to Appendix B between the limits set out in Column 2 thereof during the period set out in Column 3 thereof for a longer period of time than that set out in Column 4 thereof.

(3) Except in an emergency, no person shall park a vehicle on a part of the King's Highway described in a Schedule to Appendix C where the Ministry erects and maintains a sign or signs indicating emergency parking only.

6. Sections 2, 3, 4 and 5 do not apply to a vehicle parked by a person in the lawful performance of their duty as a police officer or by a person in the lawful performance of their duty on behalf of a road authority.

7. Sections 1 to 6 apply with necessary modifications to private toll highways.

O. Reg. 366/15, s. 2

(Appendices containing Schedules are omitted.)

Ont. Reg. 605 — Parking of Vehicles in Territory Without Municipal Organization

made under the *Highway Traffic Act*

R.R.O. 1990, Reg. 605, as am. O. Reg. 10/92; 276/93; 225/97; 118/99; 438/06 (Fr.).

1. No person shall park a vehicle on a part of a highway in a territory without municipal organization described in the Schedule if signs indicating a prohibited parking area are posted along the affected part.

2. If a highway is referred to in the Schedule by a number or name, the reference is to that part of the highway in a territory without municipal organization that is known thereby.

3. Section 1 does not apply to a vehicle,

(a) parked by a person in the performance of his or her duty as a police officer;

(b) parked by a person in the performance of his or her duty on behalf of a road authority; or

(c) parked by the driver of a vehicle that is so disabled while on a highway that it is impossible to avoid temporarily a contravention of section 1.

. . . . .

ONT. REG. 402/15 — PEDESTRIAN CROSSOVER SIGNS

made under the *Highway Traffic Act*

O. Reg. 402/15

INTERPRETATION AND APPLICATION

1. Interpretation — In this Regulation,

(a) the word "text" in the provisions refers to "legend" in the Figures; and

(b) the word "markings" in the provisions refers to "background", "border", "outline", "stripe" and "symbol" in the Figures and to roadway markings in the diagrams.

2. Level 1 and Level 2 pedestrian crossover signs — For the purpose of this Regulation and section 140 of the Act, a pedestrian crossover may be indicated,

(a) by the Level 1 pedestrian crossover signs described and illustrated in section 3 and erected in accordance with section 4 and by the markings described and illustrated in section 5; or

(b) by the Level 2 pedestrian crossover signs described and illustrated in section 6 and erected in accordance with section 7 and by the markings described and illustrated in section 8.

LEVEL 1 PEDESTRIAN CROSSOVER SIGNS

3. Level 1 pedestrian crossover signs — (1) Following are the Level 1 pedestrian crossover signs:

1. A sign, not less than 75 centimetres high and not less than 60 centimetres wide, bearing the text and markings and having the dimensions illustrated in the following Figure:

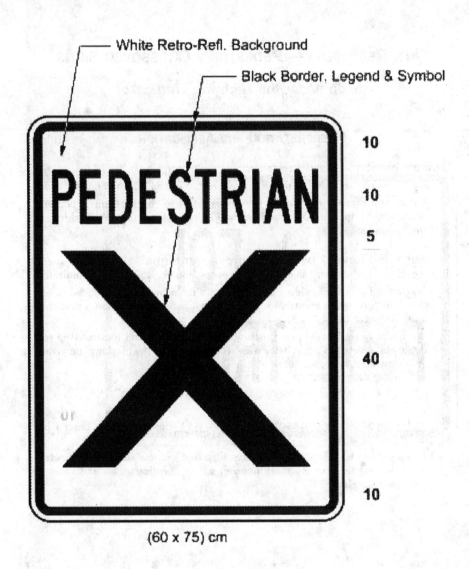

White Retro-Refl. Background

Black Border, Legend & Symbol

PEDESTRIAN

10

10

5

40

10

(60 x 75) cm

2. A sign, not less than 45 centimetres high and not less than 60 centimetres wide, bearing the text and markings and having the dimensions illustrated in the following Figure:

926

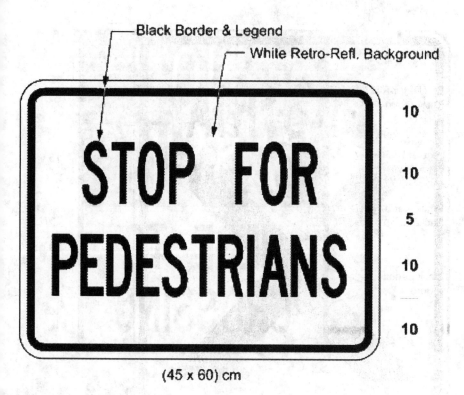

(45 x 60) cm

3. A sign, not less than 75 centimetres high and not less than 60 centimetres wide, bearing the text and markings and having the dimensions illustrated in the following Figure:

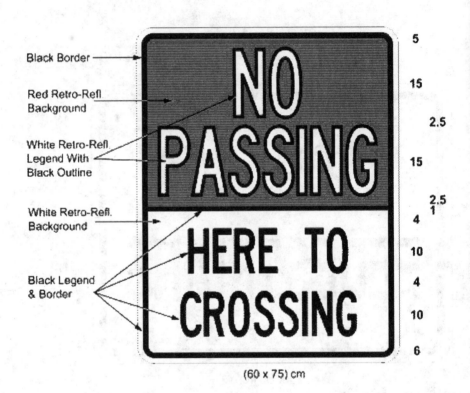

(60 × 75) cm

4. One or more double-sided signs, rectangular in shape, as near as practicable to 40 centimetres high and either 180 centimetres or 90 centimetres wide, each side being translucent, bearing opaque markings and having the dimensions described and illustrated in the following Figures:

Figure 1

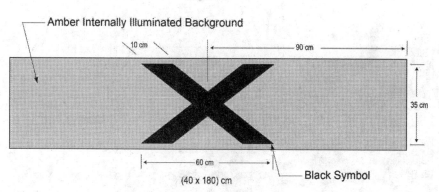

Amber Internally Illuminated Background

10 cm

90 cm

35 cm

60 cm

(40 x 180) cm

Black Symbol

Figure 2

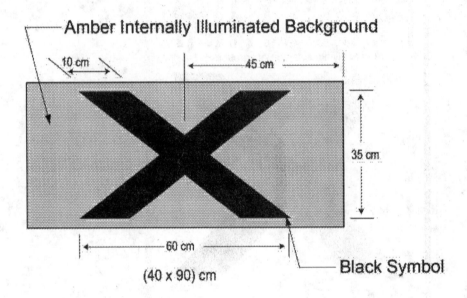

Amber Internally Illuminated Background

10 cm   45 cm   35 cm

60 cm

(40 x 90) cm

Black Symbol

(2) Despite subsection (1), in an area designated by the *French Language Services Act*, the Level 1 pedestrian crossover signs are the following:

　　1. Instead of the sign illustrated in paragraph 1 of subsection (1), a sign, not less than 90 centimetres high and not less than 60 centimetres wide, bearing the

text and markings and having the dimensions illustrated in the following Figure:

2. Instead of the sign illustrated in paragraph 2 of subsection (1), a sign, not less than 60 centimetres high and not less than 60 centimetres wide, bearing the

text and markings and having the dimensions illustrated in the following Figure:

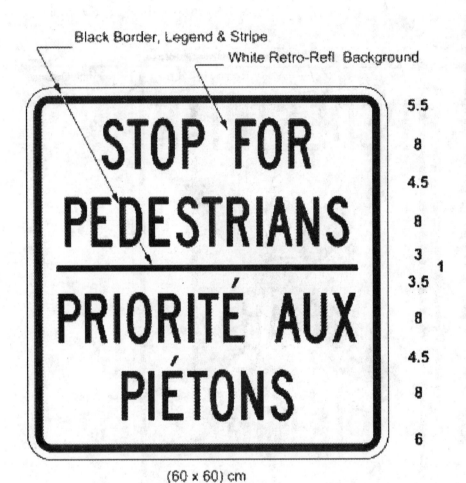

(60 x 60) cm

3. In addition to the sign illustrated in paragraph 3 of subsection (1), a sign, not less than 75 centimetres high and not less than 60 centimetres wide, bearing the

text and markings and having the dimensions illustrated in the following Figure:

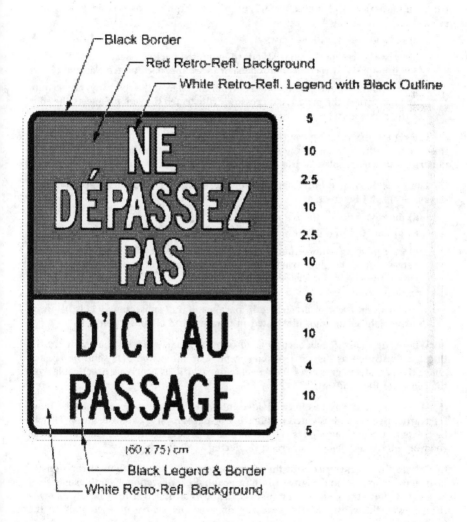

4. One or more signs illustrated in paragraph 4 of subsection (1).

(3) The signs illustrated in paragraph 4 of subsection (1) shall be continuously illu-minated on both sides from the inside and shall project light downward to illumi-nate the pedestrian crossing from one edge of the roadway to the other.

4. Erection of Level 1 pedestrian crossover signs — (1) The sign illus-trated in paragraph 1 of subsection 3(1) or in paragraph 1 of subsection 3(2) shall be erected,

   (a) on both sides of the highway;

   (b) in two places on the same standard, mounted back to back, so that the signs face in opposite directions and one sign faces approaching traffic; and

   (c) at a point not more than 4 metres from the edge of the roadway, adjacent to the place where the pedestrian crossover illustrated in section 5 meets the edge of the roadway.

(2) The sign illustrated in paragraph 2 of subsection 3(1) or paragraph 2 of subsec-tion 3(2) shall be erected in the same manner as and immediately below the sign illustrated in paragraph 1 of the same subsection.

(3) The signs illustrated in paragraph 3 of subsection 3(1) and paragraph 3 of sub-section 3(2) shall be erected,

   (a) on both sides of the highway;

   (b) in one place on the standard so that they face approaching traffic;

   (c) at a point not more than 4 metres from the edge of the roadway and 30 metres before the place where, from the perspective of approaching vehicular traffic, the pedestrian crossover illustrated in section 5 meets the edge of the roadway; and

   (d) such that the sign illustrated in paragraph 3 of subsection 3(2) is below or to the right of the sign illustrated in paragraph 3 of subsection 3(1).

(4) Where the roadway has been divided into two clearly marked lanes for traffic, the sign illustrated as Figure 1 of paragraph 4 of subsection 3(1) shall be erected above the pedestrian crossover facing vehicular traffic as nearly as practicable over the centre of the roadway.

(5) Where the roadway has been divided into more than two clearly marked lanes for traffic, two signs illustrated as Figure 1 of paragraph 4 of subsection 3(1) shall be erected such that one sign is erected as nearly as practicable over each half of the roadway above the pedestrian crossover facing vehicular traffic.

(6) Where the characteristics of the highway require a combination of the signs il-lustrated as Figure 1 and Figure 2 in paragraph 4 of subsection 3(1), the signs shall be erected above the pedestrian crossover facing vehicular traffic as nearly as prac-ticable over the centre of the roadway or over the centre of each half of the roadway.

(7) A sign erected under subsection (4) shall have four circular pedestrian-activated flashing amber beacons such that there are two beacons, mounted back to back, on each end of the sign.

(8) Signs erected under subsection (5) or (6) shall have a total of four circular pedestrian-activated flashing amber beacons such that there are two beacons, mounted back to back, near the inside end of each sign and as close as practicable to the centre of the roadway.

(9) For each direction of travel on the roadway, the beacons required by subsection (7) or (8) shall be illuminated and flash alternately when activated by a push button or other device, and shall not otherwise be illuminated or flash.

5. Roadway markings for Level 1 pedestrian crossover signs — (1)
Where Level 1 pedestrian crossover signs are used, a pedestrian crossover that is at an intersection on the highway shall have markings on the surface of the roadway having the dimensions and being the distance from each other illustrated in the following diagram:

STROKE WIDTH OF
SOLID OR OUTLINED X
IS 30 TO 50 cm.
OUTLINED Xs MUST
HAVE A MINIMUM LINE
WIDTH OF 10 cm.

Text alternative: Diagram of an overhead view of a pedestrian crossover at an intersection on a four-lane roadway. Two "X" markings of 2.5 x 6 m size appear on the roadway in the two lanes approaching the crossover and are set 30 m back from the crosswalk lines. The crossover has double crosswalk bars marking the roadway in the southern leg of the intersection that measure 15 cm to 20 cm wide and 15 cm to 20 cm apart. The space between the two sets of double bars is not less than 2.5 m wide. The stroke width of solid "x" markings is 30 to 50 cm and outlined "X"s must have a minimum line width of 10 cm. This text alternative is provided for convenience only and does not form part of the official law.

(2) Where Level 1 pedestrian crossover signs are used, a pedestrian crossover that is not at an intersection shall have markings on the surface of the roadway having the dimensions and being the distance from each other illustrated in the following diagram:

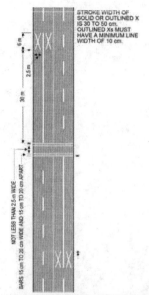

STROKE WIDTH OF
SOLID OR OUTLINED X
IS 30 TO 50 cm.
OUTLINED Xs MUST
HAVE A MINIMUM LINE
WIDTH OF 10 cm.

6 m

2.5 m

30 m

NOT LESS THAN 2.5 m WIDE

BARS 15 cm TO 20 cm WIDE AND 15 cm TO 20 cm APART

Text alternative: Diagram of an overhead view of a mid-block pedestrian crossover on a four-lane roadway. Two "X" markings of 2.5 x 6 m size appear on the roadway in the two lanes approaching the crossover and are set 30 m back from the crosswalk lines. The crossover has double crosswalk bars marking the roadway that measure 15 cm to 20 cm wide and 15 cm to 20 cm apart. The space between the two sets of double bars is not less than 2.5 m wide. The stroke width of solid "x" markings is 30 to 50 cm and outlined "X"s must have a minimum line width of 10 cm. This text alternative is provided for convenience only and does not form part of the official law.

LEVEL 2 PEDESTRIAN CROSSOVER SIGNS

6. Level 2 pedestrian crossover signs — (1) Following are the Level 2 pedestrian crossover signs:

1. Two signs, each not less than 75 centimetres high and not less than 60 centimetres wide, bearing the markings and having the dimensions illustrated in the following Figures:

FIGURE 1

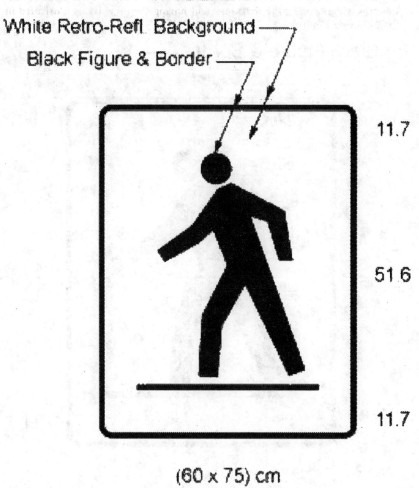

White Retro-Refl. Background

Black Figure & Border

11.7

51.6

11.7

(60 x 75) cm

FIGURE 2

White Retro-Refl. Background

Black Figure & Border

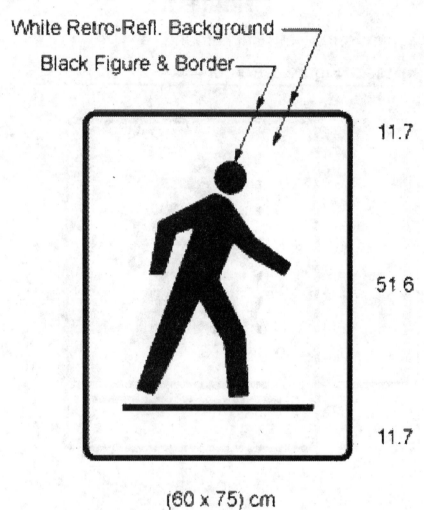

11.7

51.6

11.7

(60 x 75) cm

2. A sign, not less than 45 centimetres high and not less than 60 centimetres wide, bearing the text and markings and having the dimensions illustrated in the following Figure:

Black Border & Legend

White Retro-Refl. Background

STOP FOR
PEDESTRIANS

10

10

5

10

10

(45 x 60) cm

3. A sign, not less than 75 centimetres high and not less than 60 centimetres wide, bearing the text and markings and having the dimensions illustrated in the following Figure:

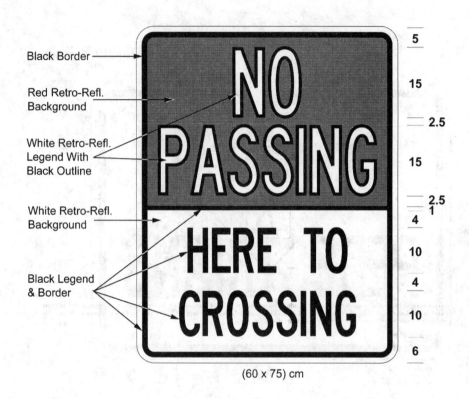

Black Border

Red Retro-Refl. Background

White Retro-Refl. Legend With Black Outline

White Retro-Refl. Background

Black Legend & Border

NO PASSING

HERE TO CROSSING

5
15
2.5
15
2.5
1
4
10
4
10
6

(60 x 75) cm

4. A sign, not less than 60 centimetres high and not less than 60 centimetres wide, bearing the markings and having the dimensions illustrated in the following Figure:

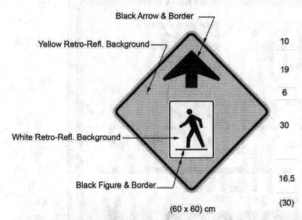

Black Arrow & Border

Yellow Retro-Refl. Background

White Retro-Refl. Background

Black Figure & Border

10

19

6

30

16.5

(30)

(60 x 60) cm

Text alternative: Illustration of diamond-shaped sign, with a yellow background and black arrow pointing up and, at its centre, a sign with the symbol in black of a person crossing the road from right to left on a white background. Sign size indicated (60 x 60 cm). This text alternative is provided for convenience only and does not form part of the official law.

(2) Despite subsection (1), in an area designated by the *French Language Services Act*, the Level 2 pedestrian crossover signs are the following:

    1. The signs illustrated in paragraph 1 of subsection (1).

    2. Instead of the sign illustrated in paragraph 2 of subsection (1), a sign, not less than 60 centimetres high and not less than 60 centimetres wide, bearing the

text and markings and having the dimensions illustrated in the following Figure:

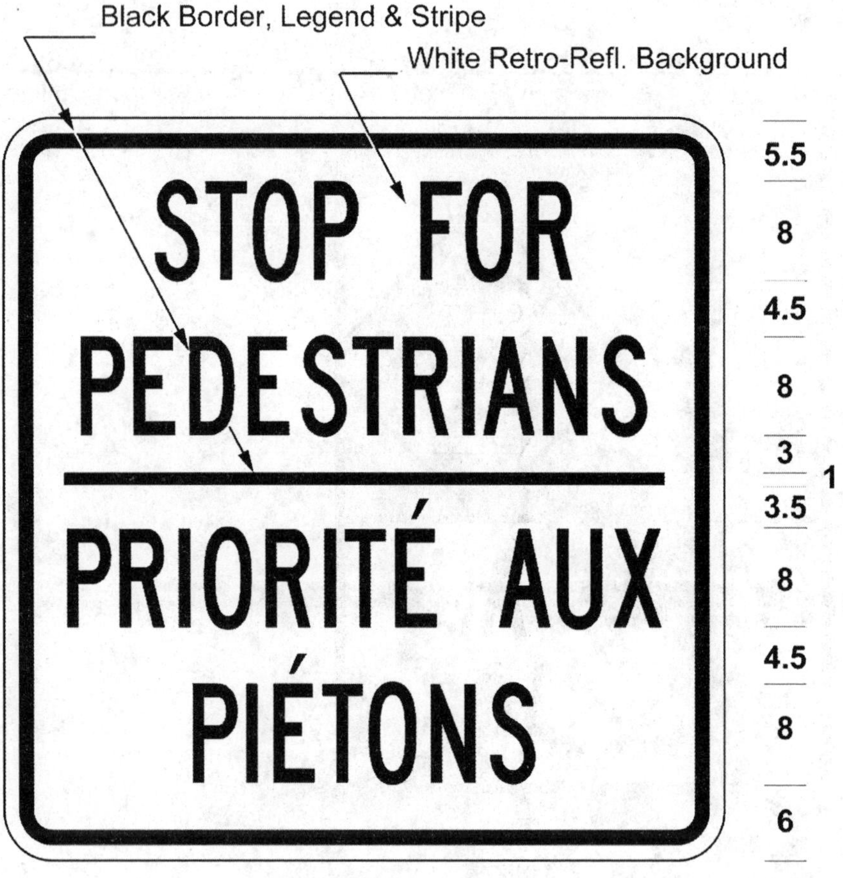

Black Border, Legend & Stripe

White Retro-Refl. Background

STOP FOR PEDESTRIANS

PRIORITÉ AUX PIÉTONS

5.5

8

4.5

8

3

3.5

8

4.5

8

6

1

(60 x 60) cm

3. In addition to the sign illustrated in paragraph 3 of subsection (1), a sign, not less than 75 centimetres high and not less than 60 centimetres wide, bearing the

text and markings and having the dimensions illustrated in the following Figure:

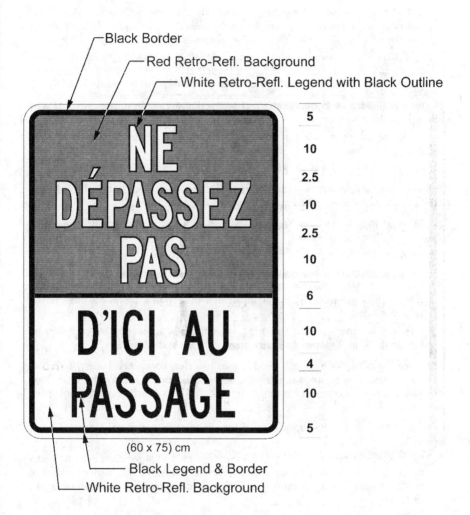

Black Border

Red Retro-Refl. Background

White Retro-Refl. Legend with Black Outline

5

10

2.5

10

2.5

10

6

10

4

10

5

(60 x 75) cm

Black Legend & Border

White Retro-Refl. Background

4. The sign illustrated in paragraph 4 of subsection (1).

7. Erection of Level 2 pedestrian crossover signs — (1) The signs illustrated in paragraph 1 of subsection 6(1) shall be erected as follows:

1. For each direction of travel, each sign shall be erected in two places on the same standard, mounted back to back, so that the signs face in opposite directions and one sign faces approaching traffic.

2. Each sign shall be at a point not more than 4 metres from the edge of the roadway, adjacent to the place where the pedestrian crossover described and illustrated in section 8 meets the edge of the roadway.

3. Where the highway is divided into two separate roadways, the sign illustrated as Figure 2 shall be erected on the left side of each roadway facing traffic at a point not more than 4 metres from the edge of the roadway.

(2) The sign illustrated in paragraph 2 of subsection 6(1) or in paragraph 2 of subsection 6(2) shall be erected,

(a) in the same manner as and immediately below the signs illustrated in paragraph 1 of subsection 6(1); and

(b) with the bottom of the sign not less than 1.5 metres from the ground.

(3) Subsection (2) does not apply to the signs illustrated in paragraph 1 of subsection 6(1) that are mounted overhead as set out in subsection (5) or (6).

(4) The signs illustrated in paragraph 3 of subsection 6(1) and in paragraph 3 of subsection 6(2) shall be erected,

(a) on the right side of the highway facing approaching traffic;

(b) at a point not more than 4 metres from the edge of the roadway and 30 metres before the place where, from the perspective of approaching vehicular traffic, the pedestrian crossover illustrated in section 8 meets the edge of the roadway; and

(c) such that the sign illustrated in paragraph 3 of subsection 6(2) is below or beside the sign illustrated in paragraph 3 of subsection 6(1).

(5) Where the roadway has been divided into two clearly marked lanes for traffic, the sign illustrated as Figure 1 in paragraph 1 of subsection 6(1) may also be erected above the pedestrian crossover facing vehicular traffic as nearly as practicable over the centre of each lane.

(6) Where the roadway has been divided into more than two clearly marked lanes for traffic,

(a) the sign illustrated as Figure 1 in paragraph 1 of subsection 6(1) may also be erected above the pedestrian crossover on the right side facing vehicular traffic as nearly as practicable over each half of the roadway for each direction of travel; and

(b) the sign illustrated as Figure 2 in paragraph 1 of subsection 6(1) may also be erected above the pedestrian crossover on the left side facing vehicular traffic approaching on the right side of the roadway as nearly as practicable over each half of the roadway for each direction of travel.

(7) A rapid rectangular pedestrian-activated flashing amber beacon may be erected directly above the signs illustrated in paragraph 1 of subsection 6(1) as illustrated in section 8.

(8) For each direction of travel where a rectangular beacon described in subsection (7) is erected, each indication shall be illuminated and flash alternately when activated by a push button or other device, and shall not otherwise be illuminated or flash.

(9) The sign illustrated in paragraph 4 of subsection 6(1) may be erected on the right side of the highway facing approaching traffic no more than 100 metres before the sign illustrated in paragraph 3 of that subsection.

8. Roadway markings and sign placement for Level 2 pedestrian crossover signs — (1) Where Level 2 pedestrian crossover signs are used, a pedestrian crossover that is at an intersection on the highway shall have markings on the surface of the roadway having the dimensions and being the distance from each other illustrated in the following diagram and may have the signs and flashing beacons illustrated in the following diagram:

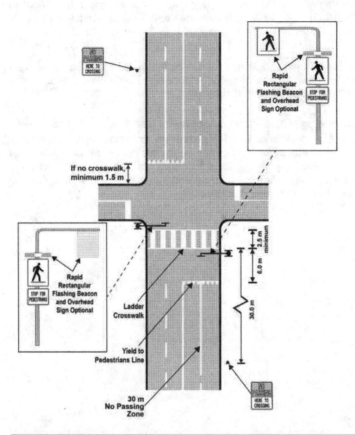

Text alternative: Diagram of an overhead view of a pedestrian crossover at an intersection on a four-lane roadway. A ladder crosswalk, consisting of many parallel bars positioned between two horizontal outer lines and with a minimum width of 2.5 m, runs from one edge of the roadway to the other. A yield to pedestrians line, known as shark teeth, is positioned on each side of the crossing 6 m back from the outer crosswalk lines. No passing zones are indicated with solid pavement markings in the traffic lanes starting at the yield to pedestrians lines and continuing for a distance of 30 m. The placement of the signs described in paragraphs 1, 2 and 3 of subsection 6 (1) and in subsection 7 (5) and of rapid rectangular flashing beacons described in subsection 7 (7) are shown. This text alternative is provided for convenience only and does not form part of the official law.

(2) Where Level 2 pedestrian crossover signs are used, a pedestrian crossover that is not at an intersection shall have markings on the surface of the roadway having the dimensions and being the distance from each other illustrated in the following diagram and may have the signs and flashing beacons illustrated in the following diagram:

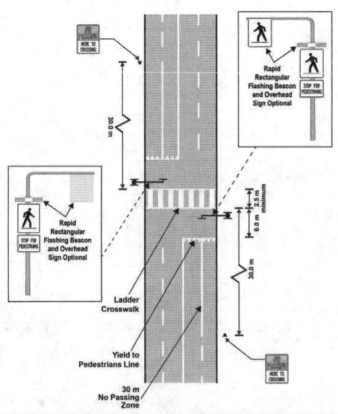

Text alternative: Diagram of an overhead view of a mid-block pedestrian crossover on a four-lane roadway. A ladder crosswalk, consisting of many parallel bars positioned between two horizontal outer lines and with a minimum width of 2.5 m, runs from one edge of the roadway to the other. A yield to pedestrians line, known as shark teeth, is positioned on each side of the crosswalk 6 m back from the outer crosswalk lines. No passing zones are indicated with solid pavement markings in the traffic lanes starting at the yield to pedestrians lines and continuing for a distance of 30 m. The placement of the signs described in paragraphs 1, 2 and 3 of subsection 6 (1) and in subsection 7 (5) and of rapid rectangular flashing beacons described in subsection 7 (7) are shown. This text alternative is provided for convenience only and does not form part of the official law.

(3) The ladder crosswalks and shark teeth yield to pedestrians lines illustrated in the diagrams in subsections (1) and (2) shall meet the requirements set out in the following Figures:

Figure 1

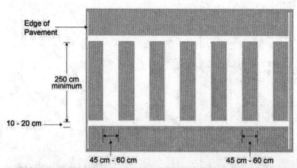

Edge of Pavement

250 cm minimum

10 - 20 cm

45 cm - 60 cm   45 cm - 60 cm

Text alternative: Illustration of pavement markings for a ladder crosswalk. This is a line of parallel bars separated by spaces and positioned between two horizontal bars. Each parallel bar and each space is between 45 and 60 cm wide. This text alternative is provided for convenience only and does not form part of the official law.

Figure 2

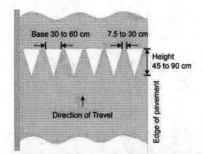

Base 30 to 60 cm   7.5 to 30 cm

Height
45 to 90 cm

Direction of Travel

Edge of pavement

Text alternative: Illustration of pavement markings for a shark teeth yield to pedestrians line. This is a line of triangles with the bottom points facing the direction of approaching traffic. The base of each triangle is between 30 and 60 cm wide and the space between each triangle at the base is between 7.5 and 30 cm wide. This text alternative is provided for convenience only and does not form part of the official law.

COMMENCEMENT

9. Commencement — This Regulation comes into force on the later of the day subsection 39(4) of the *Transportation Statute Law Amendment Act (Making Ontario's Roads Safer), 2015* comes into force and the day this Regulation is filed.

ONT. REG. 500/94 — PHOTO-RADAR SYSTEM — PART XIV.1 OF THE HIGHWAY TRAFFIC ACT

made under the *Highway Traffic Act*

O. Reg. 500/94, as am. O. Reg. 333/95.

1. (1) In this section, "subject motor vehicle" means a motor vehicle the rate of speed of which is measured by a photo-radar system.

(2) A photo-radar system is a device that,

(a) calculates in kilometres per hour the rate of speed at which a subject motor vehicle is being driven by measuring the relative movement between the device and the subject motor vehicle;

(b) takes a photograph of the subject motor vehicle, whether or not other vehicles are in the camera's field of view, at the moment of calculation of the rate of speed at which the subject motor vehicle is being driven;

(c) shows or superimposes on the photograph the rate of speed at which the subject motor vehicle is being driven, together with the date and time at which the photograph is taken and the rate of speed calculated.

(3) A photograph obtained through the use of a photo-radar system may show or have superimposed on it information in addition to that referred to in clause (2)(c), but the inclusion or omission of such additional information does not prevent the photograph from being used for its intended purpose under this or any other Act.

(4) The following device constitutes a photo-radar system:

1. Gatsometer Gatso Radar Type 24 with traffic camera types AUS or AUS-D for mobile and stationary controls.

2. [Revoked O. Reg. 333/95, s. 1.][1]

3. (1) A statement containing information from the records of the Ministry certified by the Registrar of Motor Vehicles under the seal of the Ministry constitutes evidence of ownership of a vehicle for the purposes of Part XIV.1 of the Act.

(2) If the statement is made by electronic means in an electronic format, the information contained in the statement may be displayed in Form 1.

---

[1] O. Reg. 333/95 revoked areas designated for the purposes of subsection 205.1(1) of the *Highway Traffic Act*.

4. (1) A likeness in all material respects of a photograph, including the information shown or superimposed upon the photograph pursuant to clause 205.1(2)(b) of the Act, is a photographic equivalent of the photograph for the purposes of section 205.6 of the Act.

(2) The photographic equivalent may be reproduced by electronic, optical, chemical or any other means.

5. A certificate of striking out conviction shall be in Form 103 of Regulation 200 of the Revised Regulations of Ontario, 1990.

Form 1 — Highway Traffic Act

Form 1 — Certificate of Ownership

Form 1

Highway Traffic Act

CERTIFICATE OF OWNERSHIP

This is to certify that:

Name: ....

Address: ....

Province: .... Postal Code ....

is the person in whose name the plate portion of a permit (as defined in section 6 of the *Highway Traffic Act*) was issued and was the owner of the motor vehicle referred to in the permit on the following date:

Plate Number: ....

"*(Seal)*"   ....

        Date   Registrar of Motor Vehicles

ONT. REG. 306/15 — PILOT PROJECT — AUTOMATED VEHICLES

made under the *Highway Traffic Act*

O. Reg. 306/15, as am. O. Reg. 306/15, s. 18 [To come into force January 1, 2026.].

[Note: Pilot Project — Automated Vehicles *repealed by O. Reg. 306/15, s. 18. To come into force January 1, 2026.]*

INTERPRETATION AND APPLICATION

1. Interpretation — **(1) In this Regulation,**

"approval" means approval to test automated vehicles issued under section 9;

"automated driving system" means a system that performs dynamic driving tasks to operate a vehicle with limited or no need for any dynamic driving task to be performed by a human driver;

"automated vehicle" means a motor vehicle or a street car, excluding a motorcycle or motor-assisted bicycle, with an automated driving system that operates at driving automation Level 3, 4 or 5;

"drive", in relation to an automated vehicle, includes driving or causing the operation of the automated vehicle, with or without the automated driving system being engaged;

"dynamic driving task" includes a task required for the operational aspect of driving, such as steering, braking, accelerating and monitoring the vehicle and roadway, and a task required for the tactical aspect of driving, such as responding to events and determining when to change lanes, turn or use signals, but does not include a task required for the strategic aspect of driving, such as determining destinations;

"Level" means an automated driving system's level of driving automation for on-road vehicles, as defined in SAE Standard J3016;

"owner", in the case of a commercial motor vehicle, includes the operator, within the meaning of subsection 16(1) of the Act;

"Registrar" means the Registrar of Motor Vehicles;

"SAE Standard J3016" means SAE International Standard J3016: Taxonomy and Definitions for Terms Related to On-Road Motor Vehicle Automated Driving Systems, issued on January 16, 2014 and available on SAE International's website.

(2) The Levels of driving automation are the following:

1. Level 0 — no automation.

2. Level 1 — driver assistance.

3. Level 2 — partial automation.

4. Level 3 — conditional automation.

5. Level 4 — high automation.

6. Level 5 — full automation.

(3) A person seated in the driver's seat of an automated vehicle is considered to be driving the automated vehicle, and to be the driver of the vehicle, with or without the automated driving system being engaged.

2. Application — (1) This Regulation applies to an automated vehicle, with or without the automated driving system being engaged.

(2) This Regulation does not apply to a motor vehicle with an automated driving system that operates at driving automation Level 0, 1 or 2.

PILOT PROJECT

3. Pilot project established — (1) A pilot project to evaluate the use of automated vehicles on highways is established.

(2) The Minister shall conduct and complete an evaluation of the use of automated vehicles on highways under the pilot project before the tenth anniversary of the day this Regulation comes into force.

(3) The Minister may from time to time during the course of the pilot project conduct interim evaluations of the use of automated vehicles with an automated driving system that operates at driving automation Level 3 or 4 to determine if there is a need to continue to evaluate such vehicles under the pilot project.

PROHIBITION AND PERMITTED USE

4. Prohibition — No person shall drive or permit the operation of an automated vehicle on a highway, except as permitted by this Regulation.

5. Permitted use of automated vehicles — A person may drive or permit the operation of an automated vehicle on a highway if,

(a) the owner of the vehicle has been approved under section 9 to test automated vehicles;

(b) the vehicle meets the requirements of sections 11 and 12;

(c) the vehicle is in good working order;

(d) the driver holds any of the following that authorizes him or her to drive the vehicle:

(i) A valid Class A, B, C, D, E, F or G driver's licence.

   (ii) A valid driver's licence issued by another jurisdiction.

   (iii) A valid International Driver's Permit;

(e) the driver complies with section 13; and

(f) the vehicle is being driven only for testing purposes under the pilot project established by this Regulation.

6. Application of Act — The Act applies to the operation of an automated vehicle, to a person who drives an automated vehicle and to the owner of an automated vehicle.

APPROVAL TO TEST AUTOMATED VEHICLES

7. Who may apply for approval — (1) The owner of one or more automated vehicles, if the requirements of subsection (2) or (3) are satisfied, may apply to the Registrar for approval to test the vehicles under the pilot project.

(2) For vehicles that were originally manufactured as automated vehicles,

   (a) the owner must also be the original manufacturer of the vehicles; and

   (b) the owner must be a company, within the meaning of the *Motor Vehicle Safety Act* (Canada), that,

      (i) is authorized under that Act to apply a national safety mark to the vehicles, or

      (ii) is a foreign manufacturer registered under that Act.

(3) For vehicles that were not originally manufactured as automated vehicles but were converted into automated vehicles,

   (a) the owner must also be the person that converted the vehicles into automated vehicles;

   (b) the owner must be an original manufacturer of automated vehicles or a technology company, an academic or research institution or a manufacturer of parts, systems, equipment or components for automated driving systems; and

   (c) the Registrar must be satisfied that the owner has the expertise to properly convert vehicles into automated vehicles.

8. Required information and documents — (1) An application for approval must include the following information and documents:

1. The name and business address of the applicant.

2. The name, business address, business telephone number, business fax number and business e-mail address of the applicant's contact person for the purposes of this Regulation.

3. Proof satisfactory to the Registrar of the applicant's ownership of the vehicles.

4. The total number of vehicles of any make, model and class to be tested.

5. Declaration by the applicant that the vehicles are covered by automobile insurance, as defined in subsection 1(1) of the *Compulsory Automobile Insurance Act*, in respect of any one accident, to the limit of at least $5,000,000, exclusive of interest and costs, against liability resulting from bodily injury to or the death of one or more persons and loss of or damage to property.

6. Declaration by the applicant that the vehicles,

>   i. comply with the requirements of sections 11 and 12,

>   ii. are in good working order,

>   iii. meet the statutory and regulatory requirements applicable to motor vehicles or street cars, as the case may be, and

>   iv. are capable of being driven safely in Ontario.

7. Declaration that the applicant will conduct the testing of the vehicles safely and in accordance with the law.

8. Any other information relevant to the applicant, the vehicles, the testing or the drivers that the Registrar may request.

(2) If requested to do so by the Registrar, an applicant shall demonstrate that an automated vehicle complies with subparagraph 6 iii or iv of subsection (1).

9. Approval of application

— (1) The Registrar may approve an application that meets the requirements of section 11 subject to any conditions that the Registrar may impose, including any condition that the Registrar considers necessary to ensure that the testing will be conducted safely and in accordance with the law.

(2) The Registrar may refuse to approve an application if he or she is not satisfied that the testing will be conducted safely and in accordance with the law.

(3) If the Registrar imposes conditions in an approval, the owner shall comply with the conditions and shall ensure that the testing is conducted in compliance with the conditions.

10. Revocation of approval

— (1) The Registrar may revoke an approval if, in his or her opinion,

(a) false or inaccurate information, or information that was incomplete in a material respect, was provided in the application;

(b) the person to whom the approval was issued,

>   (i) does not comply with a condition of the approval, or

>   (ii) ceases to meet the requirements set out in section 7;

(c) the testing of the vehicles has not been conducted,

>   (i) in compliance with this Regulation, or

>   (ii) in compliance with any conditions of the approval; or

(d) the testing of the vehicles has not been or will not be conducted safely and in accordance with the law.

(2) Notice of the revocation of an approval is sufficiently given if it is given to the owner's contact person referred to in paragraph 2 of subsection 8(1) by any of the following methods:

    1. Personal delivery to the contact person at the latest address for that person provided by the owner.

    2. Regular mail addressed to the contact person at the latest address for that person provided by the owner.

    3. Fax to the contact person at the latest fax number for that person provided by the owner.

    4. E-mail to the contact person at the latest e-mail address for that person provided by the owner.

(3) Unless the contact person establishes that he or she did not, acting in good faith, through absence, accident, illness or other cause beyond the person's control, receive the notice,

    (a) notice given by regular mail is deemed to have been received on the fifth day after it was mailed; and

    (b) notice given by fax or by e-mail is deemed to have been received on the first business day after it was sent.

(4) The approval is revoked on the day the notice of the revocation is received or deemed to have been received.

AUTOMATED DRIVING SYSTEM

11. Automated driving system requirements — (1) For a vehicle that was originally manufactured as an automated vehicle, its automated driving system,

    (a) must comply with any applicable requirements of the Act and the regulations;

    (b) must comply with any requirements of the *Motor Vehicle Safety Act* (Canada) that apply to automated driving systems for the vehicle's year of manufacture; and

    (c) must comply with SAE Standard J3016.

(2) For a vehicle that was not originally manufactured as an automated vehicle but was converted into an automated vehicle, its automated driving system,

    (a) must comply with any applicable requirements of the Act and the regulations;

    (b) must not render the vehicle non-compliant in any respect with the *Motor Vehicle Safety Act* (Canada) or the *Motor Vehicle Safety Regulations* made under that Act; and

    (c) must comply with SAE Standard J3016.

12. Mechanisms and systems included in automated driving system — For every automated vehicle, its automated driving system must be equipped with the following mechanisms and system:

1. A mechanism, easily accessible to the driver, that engages and disengages the automated driving system.

2. A system that,

    i. safely alerts the driver if a failure of the automated driving system is detected while it is engaged, and

    ii. does either of the following when an alert is given:

        A. requires the driver to take over all the dynamic driving tasks required to operate the vehicle, or

        B. if the driver does not or is unable to take over all the dynamic driving tasks required to operate the vehicle, causes the vehicle to safely move out of traffic and come to a complete stop.

3. A mechanism that allows the driver to take over all the dynamic driving tasks required to operate the vehicle if the automated driving system fails or if the driver disengages the automated driving system.

DRIVER'S DUTIES

13. Driver's duties — (1) The driver of an automated vehicle shall remain at all times in the driver's seat of the vehicle and shall monitor the vehicle's operation.

(2) The driver of an automated vehicle shall carry a copy of the approval in the vehicle.

(3) The driver of an automated vehicle shall present a copy of the approval upon the demand of any police officer or officer appointed for enforcing or carrying out the provisions of the Act.

(4) In the event of a collision or traffic stop, the driver of an automated vehicle shall advise the attending police officer or officer appointed for enforcing or carrying out the provisions of the Act that the vehicle is an automated vehicle and is being tested under the pilot project established by this Regulation.

REPORTS AND RECORDS

14. Changes in information — (1) An owner to whom an approval has been issued shall notify the Registrar of any change in the information provided to the Registrar in the application for approval no later than 10 days after the day the change occurs.

(2) Without limiting the generality of subsection (1), an owner to whom an approval has been issued shall notify the Registrar,

    (a) if a vehicle listed in the original application for approval, identified by its make, model and class, is no longer being tested;

(b) if a vehicle not listed in the original application for approval, identified by its make, model and class, is being tested; and

(c) if a vehicle described in clause (b), identified by its make, model and class, is no longer being tested.

15. Collision reports — An owner to whom an approval has been issued shall notify the Registrar of any collision involving an automated vehicle no later than 10 days after the day the collision occurs and shall include the following information respecting the particulars of the collision:

1. The vehicles involved, identified by their vehicle identification numbers.

2. The persons involved.

3. The location of the collision.

4. The apparent cause of the collision.

5. The details and extent of any personal injury or damage to property caused by the collision.

6. Any other relevant information that the Registrar may request.

16. Records retention — (1) An owner to whom an approval has been issued shall retain any record that relates to its use of automated vehicles, including information requested under section 15, until the third anniversary of the day this Regulation is revoked.

(2) The owner shall retain the records at its principal place of business in Ontario, if any, or, if the owner has notified the Registrar that it keeps records at other specified premises in Ontario, at those other premises.

(3) Despite subsection (2), records in electronic form need not be retained at the premises described in that subsection if those records can be retrieved in a usable electronic or paper form promptly upon request.

(4) The owner shall ensure that it maintains the capacity to retrieve its electronic records throughout the retention period described in subsection (1).

17. Reports to Minister — (1) If requested to do so by the Minister, an owner to whom an approval has been issued shall report in writing to the Minister on its use of automated vehicles under the pilot project, or on any aspect of that use that may be specified by the Minister.

(2) If requested to do so by the Minister, the owner shall give the Minister any record referred to in subsection 16(1) that the Minister may require to evaluate the pilot project.

REVOCATION AND COMMENCEMENT

18. Revocation — This Regulation is revoked on the tenth anniversary of the day it comes into force.

19. Commencement — This Regulation comes into force on the later of January 1, 2016 and the day this Regulation is filed.

ONT. REG. 488/06 — PILOT PROJECT — SEGWAYS

made under the *Highway Traffic Act*

O. Reg. 488/06, as am. O. Reg. 488/06, ss. 19, 21 [s. 21 to come into force
October 19, 2018.]; 292/11; 277/13.

[Note: Pilot Project — Segways *repealed by O. Reg. 488/06, s. 21. To come into force
October 19, 2018.]*

1. Definitions — **(1) In this Regulation,**

"public park" means a provincial park within the meaning of the *Provincial Parks
and Conservation Reserves Act, 2006* **or land designated by a municipality for use as
a park;**

**"Segway" means a device known as the Segway Personal Transporter or the Segway
Human Transporter that is manufactured by Segway Inc.**

(2) A Segway is deemed not to be a motor vehicle under the Act.

**(3) Despite subsection (2), a Segway is a motor vehicle for the purpose of a munici-
pal by-law that governs or prohibits the operation of motor vehicles on or along any
sidewalk, trail, path or walkway or in any public park or exhibition ground, unless
the by-law provides otherwise.**

O. Reg. 488/06, s. 19

2. Pilot project re Segways — **A pilot project to evaluate the use and operation
of Segways is established.**

3. Prohibition — **(1) Under this project, no person shall operate a Segway on a
highway, trail, path or walkway or in a public park or exhibition ground except as
permitted by this Regulation.**

**(2) No person shall operate a Segway on a highway, trail, path or walkway or in a
public park or exhibition ground if the Segway has been modified after its
manufacture.**

**(3) Subsection (2) does not prohibit the operation of a Segway if a basket, bag or
other thing customarily attached as an accessory to a bicycle, or a bell, horn or lamp
to comply with section 12, has been added to the Segway after its manufacture.**

4. Segways permitted — **(1) A person permitted by section 5 or 6 to use a
Segway may operate a Segway on any roadway or on the shoulder of a highway in
accordance with this Regulation.**

(2) Subject to any municipal by-law, a person may operate a Segway on a sidewalk, trail, path or walkway or in a public park or exhibition ground in accordance with this Regulation.

(3) No licence or permit is required in order to operate a Segway on a roadway, the shoulder of a highway, a sidewalk, trail, path or walkway or in a public park or exhibition ground.

5. Use by police officers, letter carriers — (1) A police officer may, in the course of his or her duties, operate a Segway that is owned or leased by the police force of which he or she is a member.

(2) A letter carrier who is an employee of Canada Post Corporation may, while engaged in door-to-door delivery of mail, operate a Segway that is owned or leased by Canada Post Corporation.

6. Use by persons with limited mobility — A person who is 14 years old or older may operate a Segway if his or her mobility is limited by one or more disabilities, conditions or functional impairments.

7. Prohibited on controlled-access highways — A Segway shall not be operated on,

(a) those parts of the controlled-access highways described in Schedule 1 to Regulation 627 of the Revised Regulations of Ontario, 1990 (*Use of Controlled-Access Highways by Pedestrians*) made under the Act;

(b) those parts of the controlled-access highways described in the Schedule to Regulation 630 of the Revised Regulations of Ontario, 1990 (*Vehicles on Controlled-Access Highways*) made under the Act; or

(c) any highway to which access by pedestrians or bicycles is prohibited under any Act, regulation or by-law.

8. Sidewalk or roadway use — (1) Where sidewalks are provided on a highway, a Segway shall only be operated on the sidewalk and not on the roadway.

(2) Despite subsection (1), a Segway may not be operated on a sidewalk where such operation is prohibited by municipal by-law, except where the highway is located in a tunnel or underpass.

(3) Where sidewalks are not provided on a highway or where the operation of Segways on sidewalks is prohibited by municipal by-law, a Segway shall only be operated,

(a) if there is a shoulder on the highway, on the shoulder as close to the right edge of the shoulder as possible;

(b) if there is no shoulder on the highway, on the right side of the roadway as close to the edge of the roadway as possible.

9. Application of the Act — (1) Parts II, IV, VI and X.3, sections 142, 179 and 199 and subsection 214(2) of the Act do not apply to the operation of a Segway or to a person who operates a Segway.

(2) Section 140 and subsections 144(22) to (28) of the Act apply to a Segway as if the Segway were a pedestrian.

(3) When a Segway is being operated on a sidewalk, trail, path or walkway or in a public park or exhibition ground, the provisions of the Act, other than the Parts and sections listed in subsection (1), apply to the operation of the Segway and to the operator of the Segway as if the Segway and the operator were a pedestrian.

(4) When a Segway is being operated on a roadway or on the shoulder of a highway, the provisions of the Act, other than the Parts and sections listed in subsection (1) or the provisions listed in subsection (2), apply to the operation of the Segway and to the operator of the Segway as if the Segway were a bicycle and the operator a rider.

(5) Despite subsection (4), the operator of a Segway shall not make a left turn at an intersection as if the Segway were a bicycle and the operator a rider, but shall instead cross the intersecting highways as if the Segway and the operator were a pedestrian.

10. Safe operation — (1) The operator of a Segway shall keep a safe distance from pedestrians and other users of the roadway, shoulder, sidewalk, trail, path, walkway, public park or exhibition ground at all times and shall give way to a pedestrian or bicycle by slowing or stopping, as necessary, where there is insufficient space for the pedestrian or bicycle and the Segway to pass.

(2) A Segway shall not be operated on a sidewalk, trail, path or walkway or in a public park or exhibition ground at a speed that is markedly greater than the speed of the pedestrians who are proximate to the Segway.

(3) A Segway shall not be operated in such a manner that it may harm, injure or damage, either directly or indirectly, any person or property.

11. General rules re operation of Segway — (1) The person operating a Segway shall be the only person on the Segway.

(2) A Segway shall not be operated when towing another person, vehicle or device.

(3) The person operating a Segway shall stand at all times while the Segway is in motion.

12. Equipment — (1) Every Segway shall be equipped with a bell or horn which shall be kept in good working order and sounded whenever it is reasonably necessary to notify pedestrians or others of its approach.

(2) When operated at any time from one-half hour before sunset to one-half hour after sunrise and at any other time when, due to insufficient light or unfavourable atmospheric conditions, persons and vehicles are not clearly discernible at a distance of 150 metres or less, every Segway shall carry a lighted lamp displaying a

white or amber light at the front of the Segway and a lighted lamp displaying a red light at the rear of the Segway.

(3) The lamps may be attached to the Segway or may be carried or worn by the operator on his or her person.

(4) A Segway and all of its components shall be maintained in good working order at all times.

13. Helmets — A person who is under 18 years old shall wear a bicycle helmet that complies with the requirements of subsection 104(2.1) of the Act when operating a Segway.

14. Insurance — If Canada Post Corporation or a police force owns or leases one or more Segways for the use of its employees or members, it shall maintain a policy of insurance for each such Segway that provides the coverage required for a motor vehicle under the *Compulsory Automobile Insurance Act*.

15. Operator to stop for police officer — Every operator of a Segway shall stop when required to do so by a police officer and shall, on the demand of the police officer,

　　(a) surrender his or her driver's licence, if he or she has one and has it in his or her possession, for reasonable inspection by the officer; or

　　(b) provide the officer with his or her correct name, address and date of birth.

16. Duty to report accident — (1) Where a Segway is involved in an accident with a pedestrian, animal or vehicle that results in personal injury or property damage, the operator of the Segway shall forthwith report the accident to a police officer and furnish him or her with the information concerning the accident as may be required by the officer under subsection (2).

(2) A police officer receiving a report of an accident, as required by this section, shall secure from the person making the report, or by other inquiries where necessary, the particulars of the accident, the persons involved, the extent of the personal injuries or property damage, if any, and the other information that may be necessary to complete a written report concerning the accident and shall forward the report to the Registrar within 10 days of the accident.

(3) The report of a police officer under subsection (2) shall be in the form that is approved by the Minister.

17. Reports to Minister — (1) If Canada Post Corporation or a police force owns or leases one or more Segways for the use of its employees or members, it shall, if requested by the Minister, report to the Minister on the use of Segways by its employees or members under this Regulation, or on any aspect of such use as may be specified by the Minister.

(2) Any municipality in which Segways are being used shall, if requested by the Minister, report to the Minister on the use of Segways in the municipality under this Regulation, or on any aspect of such use as may be specified by the Minister.

18. Exemptions from this Regulation — (1) A police officer who is permitted to operate a Segway by subsection 5(1) is exempt from subsection 3(2), sections 7, 8 and 9, subsections 10(1) and (2) and 12(2) and section 15.

(2) A letter carrier who is permitted to operate a Segway by subsection 5(2) is exempt from subsection 3(2) and section 8.

19. Amendment — The definition of "public park" in section 1 of this Regulation is revoked and the following substituted:

"public park" means a provincial park within the meaning of the *Provincial Parks and Conservation Reserves Act, 2006* or land designated by a municipality for use as a park;

20. Commencement — (1) Subject to subsection (2), this Regulation comes into force on the day it is filed.

(2) Section 19 comes into force on the day section 65 of the *Provincial Parks and Conservation Reserves Act, 2006* comes into force.

21. Revocation — This Regulation is revoked on October 19, 2018.

O. Reg. 292/11, s. 1; 277/13, s. 1

ONT. REG. 28/16 — PILOT PROJECT — THREE-WHEELED VEHICLES

made under the *Highway Traffic Act*

O. Reg. 28/16 [s. 12 to come into force July 1, 2016.], as am. O. Reg. 28/16, ss. 12, 13 [s. 12 to come into force July 1, 2016; s. 13 to come into force March 1, 2026.].

[Note: Pilot Project — Three-Wheeled Vehicles *repealed by O. Reg. 28/16, s. 13. To come into force March 1, 2026.]*

INTERPRETATION

1. Definitions — In this Regulation,

"**Ontario Regulation 340/94**" means Ontario Regulation 340/94 (*Drivers' Licences*) made under the Act;

"**Ontario Regulation 376/02**" means Ontario Regulation 376/02 (*Classification of Vehicles as Irreparable, Salvage and Rebuilt*) made under the Act;

"**Regulation 587**" means Regulation 587 of the Revised Regulations of Ontario, 1990 (*Equipment*) made under the Act;

"**Regulation 601**" means Regulation 601 of the Revised Regulations of Ontario, 1990 (*Motor Vehicle Inspection Stations*) made under the Act;

"**Regulation 610**" means Regulation 610 of the Revised Regulations of Ontario, 1990 (*Safety Helmets*) made under the Act;

"**Regulation 611**" means Regulation 611 of the Revised Regulations of Ontario, 1990 (*Safety Inspections*) made under the Act;

"**Regulation 613**" means Regulation 613 of the Revised Regulations of Ontario, 1990 (*Seat Belt Assemblies*) made under the Act;

"**Regulation 628**" means Regulation 628 of the Revised Regulations of Ontario, 1990 (*Vehicle Permits*) made under the Act.

"**three-wheeled vehicle**" means a motor vehicle, other than a motor tricycle as defined in Regulation 587, that,

  (a) is designed to travel on three wheels in contact with the ground,

  (b) has not more than four designated seating positions, and

  (c) has a manufacturer's gross vehicle weight rating of 1,000 kilograms or less or, if it does not have a manufacturer's gross vehicle weight rating, the sum of its unloaded vehicle mass and the product obtained by multiplying its seating capacity by 68 kilograms is 1,000 kilograms or less.

PILOT PROJECT

2. Pilot project established — (1) A pilot project to evaluate the use of three-wheeled vehicles on highways is established.

(2) The Minister shall conduct and complete an evaluation of the use of three-wheeled vehicles on highways under the pilot project before the tenth anniversary of the day this Regulation comes into force.

PROHIBITIONS AND PERMITTED USE

3. Prohibitions — (1) No person shall drive or permit the operation of a three-wheeled vehicle on a highway, except as permitted by this Regulation.

(2) No person shall drive or permit the operation of a three-wheeled vehicle on a highway with a passenger who is classified as an infant, toddler or pre-school to primary grade child under subsection 8(1) of Regulation 613.

4. Permitted use of three-wheeled vehicles — A person may drive or permit the operation of a three-wheeled vehicle on a highway if the vehicle,

    (a) bears,

        (i) in the case of a three-wheeled vehicle manufactured or built in Canada, the manufacturer's compliance label issued under section 6 of the *Motor Vehicle Safety Regulations* (Canada) specifying the type of vehicle as "TWV/VTR" or,

        (ii) in the case of an imported three-wheeled vehicle, a compliance label or other label as provided for in section 12 of those Regulations;

    (b) continues to meet the regulatory standards that applied to it at the time it was manufactured or imported;

    (c) is in good working order;

    (d) is not equipped with a side car or trailer; and

    (e) is driven by a driver who holds a valid Class A, B, C, D, E, F or G driver's licence that authorizes him or her to drive the vehicle or is a resident of another province, country or state, or a resident of Ontario for less than 60 days, who is authorized to drive the vehicle under subsection 34(1) or (2) of the Act.

APPLICATION OF ACT AND REGULATIONS

5. Application of Act — The Act and the regulations apply to three-wheeled vehicles as provided in this Regulation.

6. Three-wheeled vehicle generally deemed not a motorcycle — Subject to sections 7, 8 and 9, a three-wheeled vehicle operated in accordance with this

Regulation is deemed not to be a motorcycle for the purposes of the Act and the regulations, including, for greater certainty, for the purposes of Ontario Regulation 340/94.

7. Three-wheeled vehicle is a motorcycle for registration purposes —
A three-wheeled vehicle is a motorcycle, and shall be treated as such, for the purposes of the following:

1. Part II (Permits) of the Act.

2. Regulation 628.

8. Three-wheeled vehicle is a motorcycle for helmet requirements —
A three-wheeled vehicle is a motorcycle, and shall be treated as such, for the purposes of section 104 of the Act and Regulation 610.

9. Three-wheeled vehicle is a motorcycle for classification as irreparable, etc. — (1) A three-wheeled vehicle is a motorcycle, and shall be treated as such, for the purposes of Ontario Regulation 376/02, other than subsections 2(1) and (2) of that Regulation, which do not apply to a three-wheeled vehicle.

(2) If a person described in paragraph 1 of subsection 4(1) of Ontario Regulation 376/02 is making the determination that a three-wheeled vehicle is irreparable, the determination shall be based on an inspection of the vehicle carried out by a person described in subsection 2(1) or (2) of that Regulation.

(3) The definition of "irreparable" in subsection 1(1) of Ontario Regulation 376/02 is modified in respect of three-wheeled vehicles as follows:

   1. For a three-wheeled vehicle with a full frame assembly,

   "irreparable" means a vehicle that,

      (a) is a total loss and,

         (i) has incurred structural damage requiring the replacement by cutting and welding of any integral part of its full frame assembly, or

         (ii) has been stolen and dismantled such that the retail price for new parts of a like kind to replace those parts missing or damaged exceeds the fair labour cost to install or repair those parts, and,

            (A) a settlement of an insurance claim has been paid for the vehicle as a total loss, or

            (B) the vehicle is owned, leased or the plate portion of its vehicle permit is held by a person who is an insurer within the meaning of clause (b) of the definition of "insurer", or

      (b) is classified by the Registrar as irreparable under subsection 199.1(11) of the Act.

   2. For a three-wheeled vehicle with a unibody assembly,

"irreparable" means a vehicle that,

    (a) is a total loss and,

        (i) has been immersed in liquid to the bottom of its dashboard or higher,

        (ii) any major part of its electrical system has been, or appears to have been, immersed in liquid,

        (iii) has incurred damage requiring the replacement of one or more of the structural assemblies listed in Part 1, 2, 3 or 4 of the Schedule, or

        (iv) has been stolen and dismantled such that the retail price for new parts of a like kind to replace those parts missing or damaged exceeds the fair labour cost to install or repair those parts, and,

           (A) a settlement of an insurance claim has been paid for the vehicle as a total loss, or

           (B) the vehicle is owned, leased or the plate portion of its vehicle permit is held by a person who is an insurer within the meaning of clause (b) of the definition of "insurer", or

    (b) is classified by the Registrar as irreparable under subsection 199.1(11) of the Act.

10. Inspection requirements — (1) Despite section 3 of Regulation 611, the inspection requirements and performance standards contained in Schedules 1 and 2 to that Regulation that apply to a three-wheeled vehicle are subject to the following modification:

    1. The chain, belt or driven sprocket shall not be excessively worn, frayed or loose and no fasteners in connection with those parts shall be missing, loose, cut or damaged.

Proposed Amendment — 10(1)

(1) Inspection requirements — Despite section 3 of Regulation 611, the inspection requirements and performance standards that apply to a three-wheeled vehicle are contained in the Passenger/Light-Duty Vehicle Inspection Standard, subject to the following modifications:

    1. The provisions dealing with electronic stability controls do not apply to a three-wheeled vehicle not manufactured with a stability control system.

    2. The chain, belt or driven sprocket shall not be excessively worn, frayed or loose and no fasteners in connection with those parts shall be missing, loose, cut or damaged.

        O. Reg. 28/16, s. 12(1) [To come into force July 1, 2016.]

(2) Despite section 3 of Regulation 601, a Type 1, 2 or 4 licence is authority to inspect and certify three-wheeled vehicles in accordance with the inspection requirements and performance standards contained in Schedules 1 and 2 to Regulation 611 as modified by subsection (1).

Proposed Amendment — 10(2)

(2) Despite section 3 of Regulation 601, a Type 1, 2 or 4 licence is authority to inspect and certify three-wheeled vehicles in accordance with the inspection requirements and performance standards contained in the Passenger/Light-Duty Vehicle Inspection Standard as modified by subsection (1).

O. Reg. 28/16, s. 12(1) [To come into force July 1, 2016.]

(3) Despite subsection 8(3) of Regulation 601, a motor vehicle inspection mechanic who holds only a certificate of qualification in the trade of motorcycle technician may issue safety standards certificates for three-wheeled vehicles.

Proposed Addition — 10(4)

(4) In this section,

"Passenger/Light-Duty Vehicle Inspection Standard" means the Reference Handbook entitled "Passenger/Light-Duty Vehicle Inspection Standard" in English and "Norme d'inspection des véhicules de tourisme et des véhicules utilitaires légers" in French, dated October 2015, published by the Ministry and available on a Government of Ontario website.

O. Reg. 28/16, s. 12(2) [To come into force July 1, 2016.]

REPORTS

11. **Reports to Minister** — If requested to do so by the Minister, an owner of a three-wheeled vehicle shall report to the Minister on the owner's use of the vehicle under the pilot project, or on any aspect of that use that may be specified by the Minister.

AMENDMENT, REVOCATION AND COMMENCEMENT

Unproclaimed Text — 12

12. **Amendment** — (1) Subsections 10(1) and (2) are revoked and the following substituted:

(1) **Inspection requirements** — Despite section 3 of Regulation 611, the inspection requirements and performance standards that apply to a three-wheeled vehicle are contained in the Passenger/Light-Duty Vehicle Inspection Standard, subject to the following modifications:

1. The provisions dealing with electronic stability controls do not apply to a three-wheeled vehicle not manufactured with a stability control system.

2. The chain, belt or driven sprocket shall not be excessively worn, frayed or loose and no fasteners in connection with those parts shall be missing, loose, cut or damaged.

(2) Despite section 3 of Regulation 601, a Type 1, 2 or 4 licence is authority to inspect and certify three-wheeled vehicles in accordance with the inspec-

tion requirements and performance standards contained in the Passenger/Light-Duty Vehicle Inspection Standard as modified by subsection (1).

(2) Section 10 is amended by adding the following subsection:

(4) In this section,

"Passenger/Light-Duty Vehicle Inspection Standard" means the Reference Handbook entitled "Passenger/Light-Duty Vehicle Inspection Standard" in English and "Norme d'inspection des véhicules de tourisme et des véhicules utilitaires légers" in French, dated October 2015, published by the Ministry and available on a Government of Ontario website.

13. Revocation — This Regulation is revoked on the tenth anniversary of the day it comes into force.

14. Commencement — (1) Subject to subsection (2), this Regulation comes into force on the later of March 1, 2016 and the day this Regulation is filed.

(2) Section 12 comes into force on July 1, 2016.

ONT. REG. 606 — PORTABLE LANE CONTROL SIGNAL SYSTEMS

made under the *Highway Traffic Act*

R.R.O. 1990, Reg. 606, as am. O. Reg. 443/93; 442/06 (Fr.); 90/15.

1. Every portable lane control signal system shall consist of at least one set of green, amber and red signal-lights for each direction from which traffic to be controlled by the system approaches.

2. (1) Each set of signal-lights in a portable lane control signal system shall be arranged vertically in the following order, commencing at the bottom: green, amber and red.

(2) A portable lane control signal system shall not be operated in such a manner as to show the green and amber signal-lights illuminated simultaneously.

(3) Each lamp and each lens in a signal-light shall be maintained in such a manner that the signal-light, when illuminated, is clearly visible to approaching traffic at a distance of at least 100 metres.

(4) Each signal-light lens shall be at least twenty centimetres in diameter and the signal head containing the set of signal-lights shall be mounted on a yellow backboard not less than 100 centimetres in height and not less than fifty centimetres in width, as illustrated in the following figure:

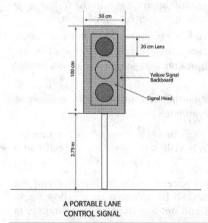

A PORTABLE LANE
CONTROL SIGNAL

Text alternative: Illustration of portable lane control signal as described in subsection 2 (4). Bottom of signal backboard is 2.75 m above ground. The yellow backboard for the traffic signal head is rectangular in shape measuring 100 cm high and 50 cm wide. Each of the three circular lenses is 20 cm in diameter. This text alternative is provided for convenience only and does not form part of the official law.

O. Reg. 90/15, s. 1

3. (1) Each set of signal-lights in a portable lane control signal system shall be placed to the right of, facing and clearly visible to approaching traffic.

(2) The bottom edge of the backboard of each set of signal-lights shall be not less than 2.75 metres above the level of the roadway.

(3) A portable lane control signal system shall not be located at an intersection or pedestrian crossover.

(4) A portable lane control signal system shall not be located in any place or manner so as to conflict with any signal-light traffic control system.

4. (1) Three signs described in subsection (2) and having retro-reflective backgrounds shall be erected for each direction from which traffic to be controlled by the portable lane control signal system approaches.

(2) The signs shall be erected in front of a set of signal-lights to the right of, facing and clearly visible to approaching traffic and shall be arranged in the following sequence, commencing farthest from the portable lane control signal system:

> **1.** A DO NOT PASS SIGN, as prescribed in Regulation 615 of Revised Regulations of Ontario, 1990.

> **2.** A warning sign with an orange background indicating that a set of signal-lights is ahead.

> **3.** A sign indicating the location at which a driver approaching a set of signal-lights is to bring his or her vehicle to a stop,

as illustrated in the following diagram:

SIGN LAYOUT REQUIRED
FOR PORTABLE LANE
CONTROL SIGNAL SYSTEM

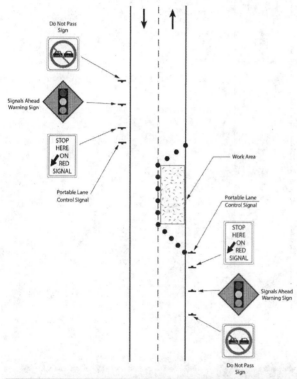

Text alternative: Diagram of the placement of a portable lane control signal system placed on the right side facing each direction of traffic on a highway along with three signs erected prior to the portable lane control signal and facing traffic. The outermost sign is a "DO NOT PASS" sign, followed by a "SIGNALS AHEAD" warning sign and finally a "STOP HERE ON RED SIGNAL" sign that has a thick, black arrow pointed diagonally and downward. The last sign is placed the closest to the portable lane control signal system in front of the coned off work area which is blocking half of the roadway in the diagram. This text alternative is provided for convenience only and does not form part of the official law.

(3) In an area designated under the *French Language Services Act*, the signs described in subsection **(2)** shall be erected as illustrated in the following diagram:

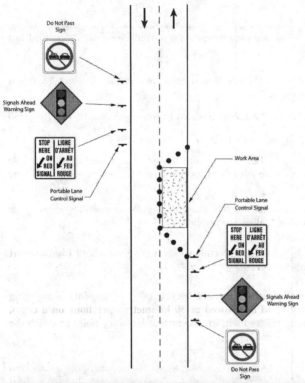

SIGN LAYOUT REQUIRED FOR PORTABLE LANE CONTROL SIGNAL SYSTEM

Text alternative: Diagram of the placement of a portable lane control signal system placed on the right side facing each direction of traffic on a highway along with three signs erected prior to the portable lane control signal and facing traffic. The outermost sign is a "DO NOT PASS" sign, followed by a "SIGNALS AHEAD" warning sign and finally a "STOP HERE ON RED SIGNAL / LIGNE D'ARRÊT AU FEU ROUGE" sign that has a thick, black arrow pointed diagonally and downward. The last sign is placed the closest to the portable lane control signal system in front of the coned off work area which is blocking half of the roadway in the diagram. This text alternative is provided for convenience only and does not form part of the official law.

(4) A municipality that is situated in a designated area but that has not passed a by-law under subsection 14(1) of the *French Language Services Act* is not required to erect the signs illustrated in subsection (3).

O. Reg. 443/93, s. 1; 90/15, s. 2

ONT. REG. 369/09 — POWER-ASSISTED BICYCLES

made under the *Highway Traffic Act*

O. Reg. 369/09

1. Maximum weight — The unladen weight of a power-assisted bicycle must not be more than 120 kilograms.

2. Wheel width, diameter — (1) The wheels of a power-assisted bicycle must not be less than 35 millimetres wide.

(2) The diameter of the wheels of a power-assisted bicycle must not be less than 350 millimetres.

3. Battery and motor — (1) The battery and motor of a power-assisted bicycle must be securely fastened to the bicycle to prevent them from moving while the bicycle is in motion.

(2) The motor of a power-assisted bicycle must disengage if pedalling ceases, the accelerator is released or the brakes are applied.

4. Electric terminals — All electric terminals on a power-assisted bicycle must be completely insulated and covered.

5. Brakes — The brakes of a power-assisted bicycle must be capable of bringing the bicycle, while being operated at a speed of 30 kilometres per hour on a clean, paved and level surface, to a full stop within nine metres from the point at which the brakes were applied.

6. No modifications — A power-assisted bicycle must not be ridden on, driven or operated if it has been modified after its manufacture in any way that may result in increasing its power or its maximum speed beyond the limits set out in clause (d) of the definition of "power-assisted bicycle" in section 2 of the *Motor Vehicle Safety Regulations* made under the *Motor Vehicle Safety Act* (Canada).

7. Good working order — A power-assisted bicycle must not be ridden on, driven or operated unless it is in good working order.

8. Commencement — This Regulation comes into force on the latest of,

    (a) October 3, 2009;

    (b) the day section 35 of the *Road Safety Act, 2009* comes into force; and

    (c) the day this Regulation is filed.

ONT. REG. 34/06 — PRE-EMPTING TRAFFIC CONTROL SIGNAL DEVICES

made under the *Highway Traffic Act*

O. Reg. 34/06, as am. O. Reg. 359/11.

1. Definitions — In this Regulation,

"emergency vehicle" means an ambulance, a fire department vehicle or a police department vehicle;

"public transit vehicle" means,

    (a) a vehicle operated by or on behalf of a municipality under the authority of an operating licence issued under the *Public Vehicles Act*, or

    (b) a bus operated by the Greater Toronto Transit Authority, also known as GO Transit;

"traffic signal maintenance vehicle" means a vehicle that is used by or on behalf of a road authority to maintain traffic control signal systems.

O. Reg. 359/11, s. 1

2. Exemptions from prohibition — The following vehicles are exempt from the prohibition in subsection 79.1(1) of the Act against pre-empting traffic control signal devices:

    1. Public transit vehicles.

    2. Emergency vehicles.

    3. Traffic signal maintenance vehicles, so long as the pre-empting traffic control signal device is being used only to test traffic control signal systems or to test the pre-empting traffic control signal device.

O. Reg. 359/11, s. 2

3. Commencement — This Regulation comes into force on the later of February 15, 2006 and the day this Regulation is filed.

ONT. REG. 455/07 — RACES, CONTESTS AND STUNTS

made under the *Highway Traffic Act*

O. Reg. 455/07, as am. O. Reg. 406/08; 175/09 (Fr.); 360/11 (Fr.).

1. [Repealed O. Reg. 406/08, s. 1.]

2. Definition, "race" and "contest" — (1) For the purposes of section 172 of the Act, "race" and "contest" include any activity where one or more persons engage in any of the following driving behaviours:

> **1.** Driving two or more motor vehicles at a rate of speed that is a marked departure from the lawful rate of speed and in a manner that indicates the drivers of the motor vehicles are engaged in a competition.

> **2.** Driving a motor vehicle in a manner that indicates an intention to chase another motor vehicle.

> **3.** Driving a motor vehicle without due care and attention, without reasonable consideration for other persons using the highway or in a manner that may endanger any person by,

>> **i.** driving a motor vehicle at a rate of speed that is a marked departure from the lawful rate of speed,

>> **ii.** outdistancing or attempting to outdistance one or more other motor vehicles while driving at a rate of speed that is a marked departure from the lawful rate of speed, or

>> **iii.** repeatedly changing lanes in close proximity to other vehicles so as to advance through the ordinary flow of traffic while driving at a rate of speed that is a marked departure from the lawful rate of speed.

(2) In this section,

"marked departure from the lawful rate of speed" means a rate of speed that may limit the ability of a driver of a motor vehicle to prudently adjust to changing circumstances on the highway.

3. Definition, "stunt" — For the purposes of section 172 of the Act, "stunt" includes any activity where one or more persons engage in any of the following driving behaviours:

> **1.** Driving a motor vehicle in a manner that indicates an intention to lift some or all of its tires from the surface of the highway, including driving a motorcycle with only one wheel in contact with the ground, but not including the use of lift axles on commercial motor vehicles.

2. Driving a motor vehicle in a manner that indicates an intention to cause some or all of its tires to lose traction with the surface of the highway while turning.

3. Driving a motor vehicle in a manner that indicates an intention to spin it or cause it to circle, without maintaining control over it.

4. Driving two or more motor vehicles side by side or in proximity to each other, where one of the motor vehicles occupies a lane of traffic or other portion of the highway intended for use by oncoming traffic for a period of time that is longer than is reasonably required to pass another motor vehicle.

5. Driving a motor vehicle with a person in the trunk of the motor vehicle.

6. Driving a motor vehicle while the driver is not sitting in the driver's seat.

7. Driving a motor vehicle at a rate of speed that is 50 kilometres per hour or more over the speed limit.

8. Driving a motor vehicle without due care and attention, without reasonable consideration for other persons using the highway or in a manner that may endanger any person by,

    i. driving a motor vehicle in a manner that indicates an intention to prevent another vehicle from passing,

    ii. stopping or slowing down a motor vehicle in a manner that indicates the driver's sole intention in stopping or slowing down is to interfere with the movement of another vehicle by cutting off its passage on the highway or to cause another vehicle to stop or slow down in circumstances where the other vehicle would not ordinarily do so,

    iii. driving a motor vehicle in a manner that indicates an intention to drive, without justification, as close as possible to another vehicle, pedestrian or fixed object on or near the highway, or

    iv. making a left turn where,

        (A) the driver is stopped at an intersection controlled by a traffic control signal system in response to a circular red indication;

        (B) at least one vehicle facing the opposite direction is similarly stopped in response to a circular red indication; and

        (C) the driver executes the left turn immediately before or after the system shows only a circular green indication in both directions and in a manner that indicates an intention to complete or attempt to complete the left turn before the vehicle facing the opposite direction is able to proceed straight through the intersection in response to the circular green indication facing that vehicle.

4. Exceptions — (1) Despite section 2, "race" and "contest" do not include,

    (a) a rally, navigational rally or similar event that is conducted,

        (i) under the supervision of the Canadian Association of Rally Sport,

        (ii) under the supervision of a club or association approved in writing by the Ministry, or

      (iii) **with the written approval of the road authority or road authorities having jurisdiction over the highway or highways used;**

  (b) **motor vehicle owners engaged in a tour, scenic drive, treasure hunt or other similar motoring event in which the participants drive responsibly and in a manner that indicates an overall intention to comply with the provisions of the Act; or**

  (c) **an event held on a closed course with the written approval of the road authority having jurisdiction over the highway, including any event lawfully using any of the trademarks "CART", "Formula One", "Indy", "IndyCar", "IRL" or "NASCAR".**

(2) Despite sections 2 and 3, "race", "contest" and "stunt" do not include any activity required for the lawful operation of motor vehicles described in subsections 62(15.1) or 128(13) of the Act, or the lawful operation of an emergency vehicle as defined in subsection 144(1) of the Act.

5. Commencement — This Regulation comes into force on the later of the day section 21 of the *Safer Roads for a Safer Ontario Act, 2007*, comes into force and the day this Regulation is filed.

ONT. REG. 37/93 — RECIPROCAL SUSPENSION OF DRIVER'S LICENCE

made under the *Highway Traffic Act*

O. Reg. 37/93, as am. O. Reg. 558/96; 111/03; 404/08.

1. Pursuant to subsection 42(5) of the Act, each offence provision in Column 2 of the Table that has been enacted by the state of the United States of America mentioned in Column 1 opposite the provision is designated for the purposes of sections 41 and 42 of the Act:

Item	Column 1 State	Column 2 Offence
1.	New York	The operation of a motor vehicle while under the influence of alcohol or drugs under section 1192 of the *Vehicle and Traffic Law*.
2.	New York	Criminal negligence or manslaughter resulting from the operation of a motor vehicle under article 125 of the *Penal Law*.
3.	New York	Reckless or dangerous driving under section 1212 of the *Vehicle and Traffic Law*.
4.	Michigan	Manslaughter resulting from the operation of a motor vehicle, under *Michigan Compiled Law*, Section 750.321.
5.	Michigan	Failure to stop at the scene of an accident involving injury or death of a person, under *Michigan Compiled Law*, Sections 257.617 and 257.617a.
6.	Michigan	Operation of a motor vehicle while impaired by or under the influence of an intoxicating liquor or a controlled substance, or a combination of them, under *Michigan Compiled Law*, Section 257.625(3).
7.	Michigan	Operation of a motor vehicle with over .08 grams or more of alcohol per 100 millilitres of blood, per 210 litres of breath or per 67 millilitres of urine, under *Michigan Compiled Law*, Section 625(1)(b).

	Column 1	Column 2
Item	**State**	**Offence**
8.	Michigan	**Refusal to provide a chemical breath analysis, under** *Michigan Compiled Law*, **Section 257.625a.**
9.	Michigan	**Operation of a motor vehicle while under the influence of intoxicating liquor, controlled substance or a combination of them, causing serious impairment to a person, under** *Michigan Compiled Law*, **Section 257.725(5).**
10.	Michigan	**Operation of a motor vehicle while impaired by or under the influence of an intoxicating liquor or a controlled substance, or a combination of them, under** *Michigan Compiled Law*, **Section 257.625(4).**

O. Reg. 558/96, s. 1; 111/03, s. 1; 404/08, s. 1

ONT. REG. 607 — RECIPROCAL SUSPENSION OF LICENCES

made under the *Highway Traffic Act*

R.R.O. 1990, Reg. 607, as am. O. Reg. 441/06 (Fr.).

1. Subsection 198(1) of the Act extends and applies to judgments rendered and become final against residents of Ontario by any court of competent jurisdiction in the following provinces:

1. Alberta
2. British Columbia
3. Manitoba
4. New Brunswick
5. Newfoundland
6. Nova Scotia
7. Prince Edward Island
8. Quebec
9. Saskatchewan

2. Subsection 198(1) of the Act extends and applies to judgments rendered and become final against residents of Ontario by any court of competent jurisdiction in the following states:

1. Alabama
2. Arizona
3. Arkansas
4. Colorado
5. Connecticut
6. Delaware
7. Idaho
8. Illinois
9. Indiana
10. Iowa
11. Kansas
12. Kentucky
13. Louisiana
14. Maryland
15. Michigan
16. Minnesota
17. Mississippi
18. Missouri
19. Montana
20. Nebraska
21. New Hampshire
22. New Jersey
23. New Mexico
24. New York
25. North Carolina
26. North Dakota
27. Ohio
28. Oklahoma
29. Oregon
30. Pennsylvania
31. Rhode Island
32. South Carolina
33. Tennessee
34. Texas
35. Utah
36. Virginia
37. Washington
38. West Virginia
39. Wisconsin
40. Wyoming

41. District of Columbia

ONT. REG. 277/99 — RED LIGHT CAMERA SYSTEM EVIDENCE

made under the *Highway Traffic Act*

O. Reg. 277/99, as am. O. Reg. 569/00; 605/00; 606/00; 607/00; 608/00; 609/00; 610/00; 345/04; 245/07; 487/07; 328/12; 404/15.

DEFINITIONS AND APPLICATION
[Heading added O. Reg. 245/07, s. 1.]

1. (1) For the purposes of Part XIV.2 of the Act,

"photograph" includes,

    (a) any form of electronically recorded image,

    (b) a reproductin of all or part of a photograph, and

    (c) an enlargement of all or part of a photograph.

(2) In this Regulation,

"detectable speed" means the speed at which a red light camera system is programmed to detect the movement of a vehicle;

"intersection" includes any portion of a highway indicated by markings on the surface of the roadway as a crossing place for pedestrians.

O. Reg. 569/00, s. 1

1.1 The areas set out in the Table are designated for the purpose of subsection 205.15(1) of the Act.

TABLE

Halton, The Regional Municipality of

Hamilton, City of

Ottawa, City of

Peel, The Regional Municipality of

Toronto, City of

Waterloo, The Regional Municipality of

York, The Regional Municipality of

O. Reg. 605/00, s. 1; 606/00, s. 1; 607/00, s. 1; 608/00, s. 1; 609/00, s. 1; 610/00, s. 1; 328/12, s. 1

2. (1) For the purposes of Part XIV.2 of the Act, a red light camera system is the combination of one or more cameras and other equipment of a type described in

subsection (1.1) that is installed at an intersection controlled by a traffic control signal such that,

    (a) it is capable of photographing all or part of the intersection; and

    (b) it takes a first photograph of a vehicle when the vehicle approaches the intersection at or above a detectable speed when a red indication is shown and it then takes one or more further photographs in succession.

(1.1) A red light camera system may be either of the following systems:

    1. Gatsometer RLC, model number 36mST-MC-GL4-ONT, referred to in this Regulation as Gatsometer.

    2. TraffiStar SR 520-ONT, referred to in this Regulation as TraffiStar.

(2) A further photograph referred to in clause (1)(b) may be taken when the green indication is shown.

(3) A red light camera system may take the sequence of photographs described in clause (1)(b) from the same or different angles.

(4) A red light camera system may be permanently or temporarily installed at an intersection.

O. Reg. 569/00, s. 2; 245/07, s. 2

INFORMATION ON PHOTOGRAPHS
[Heading added O. Reg. 245/07, s. 3.]

3. (1) A photograph taken by a red light camera system may show or have superimposed on it any of the following information:

    1. The date when it was taken.

    2. The municipality where it was taken.

    3. The time of day when it was taken.

    4. The length of time that the indication was showing red before the photograph was taken.

    5. The length of time that the indication was showing amber before the photograph was taken.

    6. The speed at which the vehicle shown in the photograph was travelling when the first photograph in a series of photographs was taken.

(2) The information may be conveyed using the system of codes, symbols and abbreviations described in section 3.1 or 3.2 and in section 3.3.

(3) [Revoked O. Reg. 345/04, s. 1(1).]

(4) Nothing in subsection (1) precludes a photograph from showing or having superimposed on it any other information, if that information is shown or superimposed on the photograph when it is certified by a provincial offences officer for the purposes of subsection 205.15(3) of the Act.

(5) In order to be received in evidence, an enlargement of a photograph must clearly show the number plate of the vehicle that is the subject of the photograph and as

much of the rest of the photograph as is necessary to show that the enlargement is of part of that photograph.

(6) An enlargement or reproduction of a photograph or part of a photograph taken by a red light camera system is not required to show or have superimposed on it any information, if the enlargement or reproduction is tendered in evidence together with the photograph of which it is an enlargement or reproduction.

(7) If a defendant who has been served with an offence notice based on evidence obtained through the use of a red light camera system does not give notice of intention to appear, it is not necessary to file any photograph in court.

O. Reg. 569/00, s. 3; 345/04, s. 1; 245/07, s. 4

3.1 (1) On the first photograph of a series of photographs taken by a Gatsometer red light camera system, the information described in subsection 3(1) may appear as a box containing three rows and 12 columns of characters interpreted as follows:

1. In the top row, reading from left to right,

   i. the first four characters are the time that the photograph was taken, in hours and minutes expressed in 24-hour clock format,

   ii. the next eight characters are the date that the photograph was taken, in numbers, with the first two being the day of the month, the second two being the month and the last four being the year.

2. In the middle row, reading from left to right,

   i. the first character is a lane identifier,

   ii. the second character is "Y", which means that the next two characters indicate the length of time that the indication was showing amber before the photograph was taken,

   iii. the third and fourth characters are the number of seconds, to the tenth of a second, for which the indication was showing amber before the photograph was taken,

   iv. the fifth to eighth characters are the code identifying the municipality in which the red light camera system is located,

   v. the ninth character is "R", which means that the next two characters indicate the length of time that the indication was showing red before the photograph was taken,

   vi. the tenth, eleventh and twelfth characters are the number of seconds, to the tenth of a second, for which the indication was showing red before the photograph was taken.

3. In the bottom row, reading from left to right,

   i. the first character is "A", which means that this is the first in the series of photographs taken,

   ii. the second, third and fourth characters are the frame set number on the roll of film used,

   iii. the fifth to eighth spaces are blank,

iv. the ninth to twelfth characters are the roll number assigned to the roll of film.

(2) On the second photograph of a series of photographs taken by a Gatsometer red light camera system, the information described in subsection 3(1) may appear as a box containing three rows and 12 columns of characters interpreted as follows:

1. In the top row, reading from left to right,

i. the first four characters are the time that the photograph was taken, in hours and minutes expressed in 24-hour clock format,

ii. the next eight characters are the date that the photograph was taken, in numbers, with the first two being the day of the month, the second two being the month and the last four being the year.

2. In the middle row, reading from left to right,

i. the first character is a lane identifier,

ii. the second character is "Y", which means that the next two characters indicate the length of time that the indication was showing amber before the photograph was taken,

iii. the third and fourth characters are the number of seconds, to the tenth of a second, for which the indication was showing amber before the photograph was taken,

iv. the fifth to eighth characters are the code identifying the municipality in which the red light camera system is located,

v. the ninth character is "R", which means that the next two characters indicate the length of time that the indication was showing red before the photograph was taken,

vi. the tenth, eleventh and twelfth characters are the number of seconds, to the tenth of a second, for which the indication was showing red before the photograph was taken.

3. In the bottom row, reading from left to right,

i. the first character is "B", which means that this is the second in the series of photographs taken,

ii. the second, third and fourth characters are the frame set number on the roll of film used,

iii. the fifth character is "V", which means that the following characters in the row indicate the speed at which the vehicle was travelling when the first photograph in the series of photographs was taken, or this space may be blank,

iv. the sixth character is "=" or "V", which means that the following characters in the row indicate the speed at which the vehicle was travelling when the first photograph in the series of photographs was taken,

v. the seventh, eighth and ninth characters are the speed at which the vehicle was travelling when the first photograph in the series of photographs was taken, in kilometres per hour,

vi. the tenth, eleventh and twelfth characters are, respectively, "k", "m" and "h", which means kilometres per hour.

(3) The time that the photograph was taken, as described in subparagraph 1 i of subsection (1) and in subparagraph 1 i of subsection (2), appears with the minutes as a superscript, so for example, the time 19:47 appears as 19^{47}.

(4) The length of time that the indication was showing amber before the photograph was taken, as described in subparagraph 2 iii of subsection (1) and in subparagraph 2 iii of subsection (2), although they are to the tenth of the second, do not show the decimal point that should appear to the left of the last digit and the digit representing the number of the tenth of seconds appears as a superscript, so for example, 3.7 seconds appears as 3^7.

(5) The length of time that the indication was showing red before the photograph was taken, as described in subparagraph 2 vi of subsection (1) and in subparagraph 2 vi of subsection (2), although they are to the tenth of the second, do not show the decimal point that should appear to the left of the last digit and the digit representing the number of the tenth of seconds appears as a superscript, so for example, 3.7 seconds appears as 03^7.

(6) [Repealed O. Reg. 245/07, s. 5(4).]

O. Reg. 345/04, s. 2; 245/07, s. 5

3.2 (1) On the first photograph of a series of photographs taken by a TraffiStar red light camera system, the information described in subsection 3(1) may appear as a box containing two rows and eight columns of characters interpreted as follows:

1. In the top row, reading from left to right, are the column headings, "Time", "Date", "Lane", "Amber", "Code", "Red", "Photo" and "Speed".

2. In the bottom row,

i. in the first column is the time that the photograph was taken, in hours and minutes expressed in 24-hour clock format,

ii. in the second column is the date that the photograph was taken, in numbers, with the first two being the day of the month, the second two being the month and the last four being the year,

iii. in the third column is a lane identifier,

iv. in the fourth column is the number of seconds, to the tenth of a second, for which the indication was showing amber before the photograph was taken,

v. in the fifth column is the code identifying the municipality in which the red light camera system is located,

vi. in the sixth column is the number of seconds, to the tenth of a second, for which the indication was showing red before the photograph was taken,

vii. in the seventh column,

A. the first three characters are the frame set numbers, and

B. the fourth character is "A", which means that this is the first in the series of photographs taken,

viii. in the eighth column is the speed at which the vehicle was travelling when the first photograph in the series of photographs was taken, in kilometres per hour.

(2) On the second photograph of a series of photographs taken by a TraffiStar red light camera system, the information described in subsection 3(1) may appear as a box containing two rows and eight columns of characters interpreted as follows:

1. In the top row, reading from left to right, are the column headings, "Time", "Date", "Lane", "Amber", "Code", "Red", "Photo" and "Speed".

2. In the bottom row,

i. in the first column is the time that the photograph was taken, in hours and minutes expressed in 24-hour clock format,

ii. in the second column is the date that the photograph was taken, in numbers, with the first two being the day of the month, the second two being the month and the last four being the year,

iii. in the third column is a lane identifier,

iv. in the fourth column is the number of seconds, to the tenth of a second, for which the indication was showing amber before the photograph was taken,

v. in the fifth column is the code identifying the municipality in which the red light camera system is located,

vi. in the sixth column is the number of seconds, to the tenth of a second, for which the indication was showing red before the photograph was taken,

vii. in the seventh column,

A. the first three characters are the frame set numbers, and

B. the fourth character is "B", which means that this is the second in the series of photographs taken,

viii. in the eighth column is the speed at which the vehicle was travelling when the first photograph in the series of photographs was taken, in kilometres per hour.

O. Reg. 245/07, s. 6; 487/07, s. 1

3.3 The key for the code identifying the municipality in which a red light camera system is located, which appears on the photographs pursuant to subparagraph 2 iv

of subsection 3.1(1), subparagraph 2 iv of subsection 3.1(2), subparagraph 2 v of subsection 3.2(1) and subparagraph 2 v of subsection 3.2(2), is as follows:

TABLE 1
REGIONAL MUNICIPALITY OF HALTON

2000 to 2099

TABLE 2
CITY OF HAMILTON

0067	0099	0162
0175	0221	0252
0288	0329	1200 to 1399

TABLE 3
CITY OF OTTAWA

5000 to 6900

TABLE 4
REGIONAL MUNICIPALITY OF PEEL

1000 to 1169

TABLE 5
CITY OF TORONTO

0033	0039	0049
0105	0124	0128
0131	0143	0188
0294	0321	0325
0407	0409	0420
0431	0434	0437
0452	0454	0463
0471	0488	0534
0565	0589	0619
0675	0698	0702
0786	0869	1170
1191	1407	1541

TABLE 5
CITY OF TORONTO

1570	1608	2500 to 2999

TABLE 6
REGIONAL MUNICIPALITY OF WATERLOO

0104	0742	0752	0881	1700 to 1799

TABLE 7
REGIONAL MUNICIPALITY OF YORK

3000 to 3200

O. Reg. 245/07, s. 6; 328/12, s. 2

SERVICE OF OFFENCE NOTICE
[Heading added O. Reg. 245/07, s. 7.]

4. (1) An offence notice issued in a proceeding based on evidence obtained through the use of a red light camera system may be served by sending the offence notice by regular prepaid mail to the person charged within 23 days after the occurrence of the alleged offence.

(2) Subject to subsections (4), (5) and (5.1), the offence notice shall be sent to the address of the person charged as it appears on the Ministry's records on the date of the alleged offence.

(3) If the provincial offences officer who issued the certificate of offence also mails the offence notice or causes it to be mailed, that officer shall certify, on the certificate of offence, the fact that the offence notice was mailed and the date it was mailed.

(4) If the person is charged as the owner of the vehicle, the address of the person as it appears on the Ministry's records respecting the holder of the plate portion of the vehicle permit shall be used.

(5) If the person is charged as the driver of the vehicle, the address of the person as it appears in the Ministry's records respecting the person's driver's licence shall be used.

(5.1) Where the provincial offences officer who issued the certificate of offence believes that the person charged resides or, in the case of a corporation, has its principal place of business, outside Ontario, the address outside Ontario at which the officer believes the person resides or has its principal place of business shall be used.

(6) Service of an offence notice mailed in accordance with this section shall be deemed to be effected on the seventh day following the day on which it was mailed.

O. Reg. 404/15, s. 1

CERTIFICATE STRIKING OUT A CONVICTION

[Heading added O. Reg. 245/07, s. 8.]

5. A certificate striking out a conviction under Part XIV.2 of the Act shall be in Form 103 of Regulation 200 of the Revised Regulations of Ontario, 1990 made under the *Courts of Justice Act*.

6. This Regulation comes into force on the day section 4 of the *Red Light Cameras Pilot Projects Act, 1998* comes into force.

ONT. REG. 407/08 — REPORTING TO THE REGISTRAR: ADMINISTRATIVE SUSPENSION OF DRIVERS' LICENCES

made under the *Highway Traffic Act*

O. Reg. 407/08

1. Reporting to Registrar under various provisions of the Act — (1) A police officer, acting under subsection 48.3(1) of the Act, shall notify the Registrar in accordance with this section.

(2) A police officer who requests a person to surrender his or her driver's licence under subsection 48(2) or (3) or clause 172(5)(a) of the Act shall notify the Registrar of the request and provide the person with the notice of suspension required under subsection 48(11) or subsection 172(10) of the Act, as the case may be.

(3) A police officer may cause another police officer or a person employed by a police service to notify the Registrar for the purpose of subsections (1) and (2).

(4) Notification shall be given to the Registrar by any means of telecommunication.

(5) Notification under subsection (1) shall be given within 90 days after the day on which the person who is the subject of the notification was driving or had care, charge or control of the relevant motor vehicle.

(6) Notification given under subsection (1), (2) or (3) shall be confirmed by the police officer who gave or caused the notification to be given by completing the form provided by the Registrar for that purpose and submitting it to the Registrar electronically at the time of the notification or as soon as practicable thereafter, electronically or otherwise.

2. Commencement — This Regulation comes into force on the later of May 1, 2009 and the day it is filed.

ONT. REG. 608 — RESTRICTED USE OF LEFT LANES BY COMMERCIAL MOTOR VEHICLES

made under the *Highway Traffic Act*

R.R.O. 1990, Reg. 608, as am. O. Reg. 442/93; 74/94; 105/97; 717/98; 432/99 [Corrected Gazette 16/10/99 Vol. 132:42.]; 218/00; 523/00; 370/04; 619/05; 42/08; 384/08; 366/11; 408/11; 460/11; 285/12; 9/13; 299/13; 204/14; 216/14; 91/15; 183/15; 1/16.

1. (1) Subject to subsection (2), no person shall operate a commercial motor vehicle or any combination of a commercial motor vehicle and a towed vehicle that exceeds 6.5 metres in length, except a bus, an ambulance or a fire apparatus, in the left lane or, where the left lane has been designated as a high occupancy vehicle lane, in the lane adjacent to the high occupancy vehicle lane of those portions of the King's Highway described in the Schedules.

(2) Subsection (1) does not apply to a commercial motor vehicle engaged in maintenance or construction or where an emergency requires the use of the lane by a commercial motor vehicle.

O. Reg. 619/05, s. 1

2. (1) A sign indicating that commercial motor vehicles are prohibited in a lane of a highway shall be in the form and dimensions prescribed and illustrated in the following Figure:

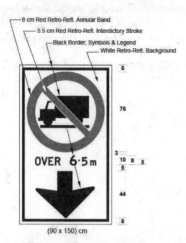

(90 x 150) cm

Text alternative: Illustration of an overhead sign containing an image at the top of a truck in a circle with an interdictory stroke "no" symbol. Below that appear the words "OVER 6.5 m" and a black arrow appears at the bottom of the sign pointing down. The sign has a white reflective background with the truck image, arrow and words appearing in black. The circular "no" symbol is in red. The following measurements are written below the sign: (90 x 150) cm. The sign is surrounded by measurements of its different elements. This text alternative is provided for convenience only and does not form part of the official law.

(1.1) Despite subsection (1), in an area designated under the *French Language Services Act*, a sign indicating that commercial motor vehicles are prohibited in a lane of a highway shall be in the form and dimensions prescribed and illustrated in the following Figure:

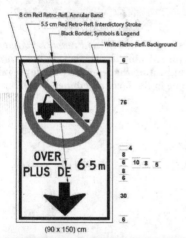

(90 x 150) cm

Text alternative: Illustration of an overhead sign containing an image at the top of a truck in a circle with an interdictory stroke "no" symbol. Below that appear the words "OVER/PLUS DE 6.5 m" and a black arrow appears at the bottom of the sign pointing down. The sign has a white reflective background with the truck image, arrow and words appearing in black. The circular "no" symbol is in red. The following measurements are written below the sign: (90 x 150) cm. The sign is surrounded by measurements of its different elements. This text alternative is provided for convenience only and does not form part of the official law.

(2) The sign referred to in subsection (1) or (1.1) shall be erected directly above the lane on those portions of the King's Highway described in the Schedules.

O. Reg. 442/93, s. 1; 619/05, s. 2; 91/15, s. 1

3. (1) Where the conditions make it impracticable to place a sign in accordance with the requirements of section 2, a sign indicating that commercial motor vehicles are prohibited in a lane of a highway shall be in the form and dimensions illustrated in the following Figure:

(90 x 150) cm

Text alternative: Illustration of a ground mounted sign containing an image at the top of a truck in a circle with an interdictory stroke "no" symbol. Below that appear the words "OVER 6.5 m". At the bottom of the sign on the left side appear the words "THIS LANE" and on the right side appears a black arrow pointing down and diagonally to the right. The sign has a white reflective background with the truck image, arrow and words appearing in black. The circular "no" symbol is in red. The following measurements are written below the sign: (90 x 150) cm. The sign is surrounded by measurements of its different elements. This text alternative is provided for convenience only and does not form part of the official law.

(1.1) Despite subsection (1), in an area designated under the *French Language Services Act*, where the conditions make it impracticable to place a sign in accordance with the requirements of section 2, a sign indicating that commercial motor vehicles are prohibited in a lane of a highway shall be in the form and dimensions illustrated in the following Figure:

8 cm Red Retro-Refl. Annular Band
5.5 cm Red Retro-Refl. Interdictory Stroke
Black Border, Symbol & Legend
White Retro-Refl. Background

(90 x 150) cm

Text alternative: Illustration of a ground mounted sign containing an image at the top of a truck in a circle with an interdictory stroke "no" symbol. Below that appear the words "PLUS DE 6.5 m". At the bottom of the sign on the left side appear the words "CETTE VOIE" and on the right side appears a black arrow pointing down and diagonally to the right. The sign has a white reflective background with the truck image, arrow and words appearing in black. The circular "no" symbol is in red. The following measurements are written below the sign: (90 x 150) cm. The sign is surrounded by measurements of its different elements. This text alternative is provided for convenience only and does not form part of the official law.

(2) The sign referred to in subsection (1) shall be erected not less than 1.5 metres or more than 2.5 metres above the level of the King's Highway described in the Schedules.

(3) The sign referred to in subsection (1.1) shall be erected not less than 1.5 metres or more than 2.5 metres above the level of the King's Highway described in the Schedules and shall be erected in combination with the sign required by subsection (1), below it, to the right of it or up to 100 metres beyond it.

O. Reg. 442/93, s. 2; 619/05, s. 3; 91/15, s. 2

. . . . .

ONT. REG. 609 — RESTRICTED USE OF THE KING'S HIGHWAY AND TOLL HIGHWAYS

made under the *Highway Traffic Act*

R.R.O. 1990, Reg. 609, as am. O. Reg. 754/93; 44/08; 312/08; 234/09; 474/10; 503/10; 414/11; 357/12; 185/15; 369/15.

[Note: The title of this Regulation was changed from "Restricted Use of the King's Highway" to "Restricted Use of the King's Highway and Toll Highways" by O. Reg. 369/15, s. 1.]

1. (1) No person shall operate or ride the following on those parts of a highway described in Schedule 1:

1. A farm tractor.

2. A self-propelled implement of husbandry.

3. A motor vehicle towing an implement of husbandry.

4. A motor vehicle designed as a farm implement for drawing ploughs, mowing machines and other implements of husbandry and used for hauling a load.

5. A vehicle or combination of vehicles with a slow moving vehicle sign attached to it.

6. A horse.

7. A vehicle drawn by a horse.

(2) Subsection (1) does not apply to,

(a) a person who owns, occupies or is hired by the owner or occupier to work on lands adjoining the highway to which lands there is no other means of access by highway while such person is engaged in gaining access to or egress from such lands if in gaining such access or egress the person proceeds by the shortest route over such highway to the lands; or

(b) a vehicle used for the maintenance of the highway.

O. Reg. 754/93, s. 1; 234/09, s. 1; 369/15, s. 2

2. Where the highway is referred to in Schedule 1 by a number or name, the reference is to that part of the King's Highway or to the private toll highway that is known thereby.

O. Reg. 234/09, s. 2; 369/15, s. 3

SCHEDULE 1

1. All of the King's Highways known as Nos. 400, 401, 402, 403, 404, 405, 406, 409, 410, 412, 416, 417, 420 and 427 and the Queen Elizabeth Way.

1.1 All of the King's Highway known as Highway 407 East.

1.2 All of the private toll highway known as Highway 407.

2. All of the King's Highway known as Nos. 69 and 400.

3. All of the King's Highway known as Nos. 6 and 403.

4. All of the King's Highway known as Nos. 24 and 403.

5. All of the King's Highway known as Nos. 35 and 115.

6. All of the King's Highway known as Nos. 58 and 406.

7. That part of the King's Highway known as No. 3 lying between a point situate at its intersection with the eastern limit of the roadway known as Ron McNeil Line (also known as Elgin County Road 52) where Ron McNeil Line continues as the roadway known as Ford Drive in the Township of Southwold and a point situate at its intersection with the west junction of the roadway known as Centennial Avenue in the Municipality of Central Elgin.

8. That part of the King's Highway known as No. 6 lying between a point situate at its intersection with the King's Highway known as No. 401 in the Township of Puslinch and a point situate at its intersection with the south junction of the King's Highway known as No. 7 where King's Highway No. 7 continues as the roadway known as Wellington Street (also known as Wellington County Road 124) in the City of Guelph.

9. That part of the King's Highway known as No. 6 in the City of Hamilton lying between a point situate at its intersection with the King's Highway known as No. 403 and a point situate at its intersection with the King's Highway known as No. 7273 (also known as Old Highway 6).

10. That part of the King's Highway known as Nos. 6 and 7 in the City of Guelph lying between a point situate at its intersection with the south junction of the King's Highway known as No. 7 where King's Highway No. 7 continues as the roadway known as Wellington Street (also known as Wellington County Road 124) and a point situate at its intersection with the north junction of the King's Highway known as No. 7 where King's Highway No. 7 continues as the roadway known as Woodlawn Road.

11. That part of the King's Highway known as No. 7 lying between a point situate at its intersection with the centre line of the King's Highway known as No. 417 in the City of Ottawa and a point situate at its intersection with the centre line of the roadway known as McNeeley Avenue in the Town of Carleton Place.

12. That part of the King's Highway known as No. 7 in the City of Kitchener lying between a point situate at its intersection with the roadway known as Victoria Street and a point situate at its intersection with the east junction of the King's Highway known as No. 8 where King's Highway No. 8 continues as the roadway known as King Street.

13. That part of the King's Highway known as Nos. 7 and 8 lying between a point situate at its intersection with the eastern limit of the roadway known as Waterloo Road 5 in the Township of Wilmot and a point situate at its intersection with the east junction of the King's Highway known as No. 8 where King's Highway No. 8 continues as the roadway known as King Street in the City of Kitchener.

14. That part of the King's Highway known as Nos. 7 and 115 lying between a point situate at its intersection with the west junction of the King's Highway known as No. 7 in the Township of Cavan-Millbrook-North Monaghan and a point situate at its intersection with the east junction of the King's Highway known as No. 7 in the City of Peterborough.

15. That part of the King's Highway known as No. 8 in the City of Kitchener lying between a point situate at its intersection with the King's Highway known as No. 401 and a point situate at its intersection with the east junction of the King's Highway known as No. 7 where King's Highway No. 7 continues as the roadway known as King Street.

16. That part of the King's Highway known as No. 11 in the City of Orillia lying between a point situate at its intersection with the roadway known as Memorial Avenue and a point situate at its intersection with the roadway known as Laclie Street.

17. That part of the King's Highway known as No. 58 in the City of Thorold lying between a point situate at its intersection with the King's Highway known as No. 406 and a point situate at its intersection with the westerly limit of the roadway known as Niagara Regional Road No. 57 (also known as Thorold Stone Road).

18. That part of the King's Highway known as No. 85 lying between a point situate at its intersection with the King's Highway known as No. 7 (also known as Victoria Street) in the City of Kitchener and a point situate at its intersection with the roadway known as Waterloo Regional Road 15 (also known as King Street) in the Township of Woolwich.

19. That part of the King's Highway known as No. 115 lying between a point situate at its intersection with the King's Highway known as Nos. 35 and 115 in the Municipality of Clarington and a point situate at its intersection with the King's Highway known as No. 7 in the Township of Cavan-Millbrook-North Monaghan.

20. That part of the King's Highway known as No. 137 lying between a point situate at its intersection with the King's Highway known as No. 401 in the Township of Leeds and The Thousand Islands and a point situate at its intersection with the border between Canada and the United States of America.

21. All of the King's Highway known as No. 7274 (also known as Highway 6/Airport Road Connection).

22. That part of the King's Highway known as No. 3 (also known as Huron Church Road) in the County of Essex lying between a point situate 625 metres measured easterly from its intersection with the centre line of the roadway known as Howard Avenue in the Town of Tecumseh and a point situate at its intersection with the easterly limit of the roadways known as Industrial Drive and Northwood Street in the City of Windsor.

23. That part of the King's Highway known as No. 7087 (also known as E. C. Row Expressway) in the City of Windsor in the County of Essex lying between a point situate at its intersection with the northerly limit of the King's Highway known as No. 7902 (also known as Ojibway Parkway) and a point situate 365 metres measured easterly from its intersection with the centre line of the King's Highway known as No. 3 (also known as Huron Church Road).

24. That part of the King's Highway known as No. 7902 (also known as Ojibway Parkway) in the City of Windsor in the County of Essex lying between a point situ-

ate at its intersection with the northerly limit of the south junction of the roadway known as Broadway Street and a point situate at its intersection with the easterly limit of the Essex Terminal Railway right-of-way.

25. That part of the King's Highway known as No. 26 in the County of Simcoe lying between a point situate 50 metres measured westerly from its intersection with the centre line of the King's Highway known as No. 7149 in the Town of Wasaga Beach and a point situate 50 metres measured easterly from its intersection with the centre line of the roadway known as Poplar Sideroad in the Town of Collingwood.

O. Reg. 754/93, s. 2; 44/08, s. 1; 312/08, s. 1; 474/10, s. 1; 503/10, s. 1; 414/11, s. 1; 357/12, s. 1; 185/15, s. 1; 369/15, s. 4

ONT. REG. 610 — SAFETY HELMETS

made under the *Highway Traffic Act*

R.R.O. 1990, Reg. 610, as am. O. Reg. 411/95; 38/03; 405/09 (Fr.); 101/12 (Fr.); 102/12.

1. A helmet worn by a person,

    (a) riding on or operating a motorcycle; or

    (b) operating a motor assisted bicycle,

on a highway shall,

    (c) have a hard, smooth outer shell lined with protective padding material or fitted with other energy absorbing material and shall be strongly attached to a strap designed to be fastened under the chin of the wearer; and

    (d) be undamaged from use or misuse.

2. The helmet referred to in section 1 shall conform to the requirements of the,

    (a) Canadian Standards Association Standard D230 Safety Helmets for Motorcycle Riders and shall bear the monogram of the Canadian Standards Association Testing Laboratories;

    (b) Snell Memorial Foundation and shall have affixed thereto the certificate of the Snell Memorial Foundation;

    (c) British Standards Institute and shall have affixed thereto the certificate of the British Standards Institute;

    (d) United States of America Federal Motor Vehicle Safety Standard 218 and shall bear the symbol DOT constituting the manufacturer's certification of compliance with the standard; or

    (e) United Nations Economic Commission for Europe Regulation No. 22, "Uniform Provisions Concerning the Approval of Protective Helmets and of Their Visors for Drivers and Passengers of Motor Cycles and Mopeds", and shall have affixed thereto the required international approval mark.

O. Reg. 102/12, s. 1

3. A helmet worn by a person operating or riding a bicycle on a highway shall,

    (a) have a smooth outer surface, be constructed so that the helmet is capable of absorbing energy on impact and be strongly attached to a strap designed to be fastened under the chin of the wearer; and

    (b) be undamaged from use or misuse.

O. Reg. 411/95, s. 1

4. (1) The helmet referred to in section 3 shall conform to the requirements of one or more of the following standards:

1. Canadian Standards Association CAN/CSA D113.2-M89 (Cycling Helmets).

2. Snell Memorial Foundation B-95 (1995 Standard for Protective Headgear for Use with Bicycles).

3. Snell Memorial Foundation B-90 (1990 Standard for Protective Headgear for Use in Bicycling).

4. Snell Memorial Foundation B-90S (1994 Supplementary Standard for Protective Headgear for Use with Bicycles).

5. American National Standards Institute ANSI Z90.4-1984 (American National Standard for Protective Headgear for Bicyclists).

6. American Society for Testing and Materials ASTM F1447-94 (Standard Specification for Protective Headgear Used in Bicycling).

7. British Standards Institute BS 6863:1989 (British Standard Specification for Pedal Cyclists' Helmets).

8. Standards Association of Australia AS 2063.2-1990 (Part 2: Helmets for Pedal Cyclists).

9. Snell Memorial Foundation N-94 (1994 Standard for Protective Headgear: for Use in Non-Motorized Sports).

10. United States Consumer Product Safety Commission (CPSC) 16 CFR Part 1203 Safety Standards for Bicycle Helmets.

(2) The helmet shall bear the mark of the standards authority or the mark of the manufacturer showing that the helmet meets the prescribed standard.

(3) A reference to a standard in subsection (1) includes any amendments made to the standard, whether made before or after February 11, 2003.

O. Reg. 411/95, s. 1; 38/03, s. 1

5. A person who is 18 years old or older is not required to comply with subsection 104(2.1) of the Act.

O. Reg. 411/95, s. 1

ONT. REG. 611 — SAFETY INSPECTIONS

made under the *Highway Traffic Act*

R.R.O. 1990, Reg. 611, as am. O. Reg. 318/91; 762/91; 510/97; 373/98; 330/01; 65/02; 378/02; 214/03; 114/08; 42/09; 476/09; 407/10; 413/10; 80/11 [Corrected Ont. Gaz. 23/04/11 Vol. 144:17.]; 241/14; 254/15 [To come into force July 1, 2016.]; 329/15; 356/15 [To come into force July 1, 2016.].

DEFINITIONS

1. In this Regulation,

"accessible vehicle" means a passenger vehicle or a bus,

> (a) that is designed or modified to be used for the purpose of transporting persons with disabilities and is used for that purpose, whether or not the vehicle is also used to transport persons without disabilities, and

> (b) that is operated,

>> (i) for compensation by, for or on behalf of any person, club, agency or organization, or

>> (ii) not for compensation by, for or on behalf of any person, club, agency or organization that holds itself out as providing a transportation service to persons with disabilities;

"annual inspection certificate" means a vehicle inspection record evidencing compliance with the inspection requirements and performance standards set out in NSC Standard 11B as modified by sections 1 and 2 of Schedule 3;

"annual inspection report" means, in relation to a vehicle inspection that results in the issuance of an annual inspection sticker, a report containing the information required by clause 10(1)(d) of Regulation 601 of the Revised Regulations of Ontario, 1990 (*Motor Vehicle Inspection Stations*) made under the Act;

"annual inspection sticker" means a vehicle inspection sticker evidencing compliance with the inspection requirements and performance standards set out in NSC Standard 11B as modified by sections 1 and 2 of Schedule 3;

"bus" [Repealed O. Reg. 80/11, s. 1(3).]

"commercial vehicle" means a commercial motor vehicle and any trailer or trailer converter dolly drawn by the commercial motor vehicle, but does not include a bus, a school purposes vehicle or an accessible vehicle;

"compensation" includes any rate, remuneration, reimbursement or reward of any kind paid, payable, promised, received or demanded, directly or indirectly;

"dual fuel" [Repealed O. Reg. 476/09, s. 1.]

"dump vehicle" [Repealed O. Reg. 476/09, s. 1.]

"dump vehicle inspection sticker" [Repealed O. Reg. 476/09, s. 1.]

"historic vehicle" means a motor vehicle that,

    (a) is at least 30 years old, and

    (b) is substantially unchanged or unmodified from the original manufacturer's product;

"licence" means a motor vehicle inspection station licence issued under section 91 of the Act;

"licensee" means a person who is a holder of a motor vehicle inspection station licence issued under section 91 of the Act;

"motor tricycle" means a motorcycle that,

    (a) is designed to travel on three wheels in contact with the ground,

    (b) has seating on which all occupants must sit astride,

    (c) has not more than four designated seating positions,

    (d) has a manufacturer's gross vehicle weight rating of 1,000 kilograms or less,

    (e) has a minimum wheel rim diameter of 250 millimetres,

    (f) has a minimum wheel base of 1,016 millimetres, and

    (g) does not have a structure partially or fully enclosing the driver and passenger, other than that part of the vehicle forward of the driver's torso and the seat backrest;

"original equipment manufacturer propane fueled motor vehicle" [Repealed O. Reg. 476/09, s. 1.]

Proposed Addition — 1 "Passenger/Light-Duty Vehicle Inspection Standard"

"Passenger/Light-Duty Vehicle Inspection Standard" means the Reference Handbook entitled "Passenger/Light-Duty Vehicle Inspection Standard" dated July 2015, published by the Ministry and available on a Government of Ontario website;

Proposed Amendment — 1 "Passenger/Light-Duty Vehicle Inspection Standard"

"Passenger/Light-Duty Vehicle Inspection Standard" means the Reference Handbook entitled "Passenger/Light-Duty Vehicle Inspection Standard" in English and "Norme d'inspection des véhicules de tourisme et des véhicules utilitaires légers" in French, dated October 2015, published by the Ministry and available on a Government of Ontario website;

                    O. Reg. 356/15, s. 1 [To come into force July 1, 2016.]
                    O. Reg. 254/15, s. 1 [To come into force July 1, 2016.]

"physically-disabled-passenger vehicle" [Repealed O. Reg. 80/11, s. 1(5).]

"propane fueled motor vehicle" [Repealed O. Reg. 476/09, s. 1.]

"propane vehicle inspection sticker" [Repealed O. Reg. 476/09, s. 1.]

"safety inspection sticker" [Repealed O. Reg. 80/11, s. 1(5).]

"salvage motor vehicle" means a motor vehicle whose vehicle permit indicates that it is classified as salvage;

"school purposes vehicle" means a passenger vehicle, other than a bus, that is operated by or under contract with a school board or other authority in charge of a school for the transportation of adults with a developmental disability or children;

"semi-annual inspection certificate" means a vehicle inspection record evidencing compliance with the inspection requirements and performance standards set out in NSC Standard 11B as modified by sections 1, 2 and 3 of Schedule 3;

"semi-annual inspection report" means, in relation to a vehicle inspection that results in the issuance of a semi-annual inspection sticker, a report containing the information required by clause 10(1)(e) of Regulation 601 of the Revised Regulations of Ontario, 1990 (*Motor Vehicle Inspection Stations*) made under the Act;

"semi-annual inspection sticker" means a vehicle inspection sticker evidencing compliance with the inspection requirements and performance standards set out in NSC Standard 11B as modified by sections 1, 2 and 3 of Schedule 3;

"structural inspection certificate" means a safety standards certificate issued after an inspection of a salvage motor vehicle that has been rebuilt evidencing compliance with the inspection requirements and performance standards set out in Schedule 9. O. Reg. 762/91, s. 1; 373/98, s. 1; 330/01, s. 1; 65/02, s. 1; 378/02, s. 1; 114/08, s. 1; 476/09, s. 1; 80/11, s. 1; 241/14, s. 1

1.1 [Revoked O. Reg. 762/91, s. 1.]

2. For purposes of this Regulation, "children", "developmental disability" and "school" have the same meaning as in subsection 175(1) of the Act.

O. Reg. 762/91, s. 1; 65/02, s. 2

APPLICATION OF NSC STANDARD 11B
[Heading added O. Reg. 80/11, s. 2.]

2.1 (1) In this Regulation,

"NSC Standard 11B" means Part B, entitled "Periodic Commercial Motor Vehicle Inspections (PMVI)", of the National Safety Code Standard 11, entitled "Maintenance and Periodic Inspection Standards", published by the Canadian Council of Motor Transport Administrators and dated October 2014, as amended from time to time.

(2) A reference in this Regulation to Schedule 3 modifying NSC Standard 11B is a reference to Schedule 3 to this Regulation.

(3) The inspection requirements and performance standards that NSC Standard 11B states are applicable to a truck apply, with the modifications set out in Schedule

3, to inspections of commercial motor vehicles, other than buses, school purposes vehicles and accessible vehicles, under section 4, 4.4 or 8 of this Regulation.

(4) The inspection requirements and performance standards that NSC Standard 11B states are applicable to a trailer apply, with the modifications set out in Schedule 3, to inspections of trailers under section 4.3 of this Regulation and inspections of trailers and trailer converter dollies under section 8 of this Regulation.

(5) The inspection requirements and performance standards that NSC Standard 11B states are applicable to a bus apply, with the modifications set out in Schedule 3, to inspections of buses, school purposes vehicles and accessible vehicles under section 4.1, 4.2, 4.4 or 10 of this Regulation.

(6) Where Schedule 3 provides that an inspection requirement or performance standard set out in NSC Standard 11B does not apply to a type of inspection of any class of vehicle or applies only in a modified manner, the vehicle must be inspected in accordance with the inspection requirements set out in NSC Standard 11B as modified by Schedule 3 and must comply with the performance standards set out in NSC Standard 11B as modified by Schedule 3.

(7) For the purposes of this Regulation, in NSC Standard 11B,

"authorized inspector" or "authorized technician" means, in relation to an inspection conducted in Ontario, a motor vehicle inspection mechanic registered by the Director of Vehicle Inspection Standards under section 92 of the Act and, in relation to an inspection conducted in a Canadian jurisdiction other than Ontario, means any person authorized by that jurisdiction to conduct the inspection.

O. Reg. 80/11, s. 2; 241/14, s. 2

APPLICATION

[Heading added O. Reg. 80/11, s. 2.]

2.2 (1) Sections 4, 4.1, 4.2, 4.3, 4.4, 8 and 10 do not apply in respect of the following classes of vehicles:

    1. A motor vehicle commonly known as a recreational vehicle or as a motor home, other than a motor vehicle,

        i. carrying commercial cargo or tools or equipment of a type normally used for commercial purposes, or

        ii. carrying animals or non-commercial tools, equipment or vehicles that occupy one-half or more of its floor space.

    2. A house trailer, other than a house trailer,

        i. owned or leased by an employer to house the employer's employee,

        ii. carrying commercial cargo or tools or equipment of a type normally used for commercial purposes, or

        iii. carrying animals or non-commercial tools, equipment or vehicles that occupy one-half or more of its floor space.

(2) In paragraph 2 of subsection (1), "house trailer" includes a cabin trailer, collapsible cabin trailer, tent trailer and camping trailer.

Proposed Repeal — 2.2

2.2 [Repealed O. Reg. 254/15, s. 2. To come into force July 1, 2016.]

O. Reg. 80/11, s. 2

SAFETY STANDARDS CERTIFICATE

3. A safety standards certificate shall not be issued in respect of a motor vehicle, other than a vehicle referred to in section 4, 4.1, 4.2, 4.4, 5 or 5.1, unless the vehicle has been inspected in accordance with the inspection requirements and complies with the performance standards set out in Schedules 1 and 2.

Proposed Amendment — 3

3. (1) A safety standards certificate shall not be issued in respect of a motor vehicle unless the vehicle has been inspected in accordance with the inspection requirements and complies with the performance standards set out in the Passenger/Light-Duty Vehicle Inspection Standard.

(2) For greater certainty, subsection (1) does not apply to a vehicle referred to in section 4, 4.1, 4.2, 4.3.1, 5 or 5.1 but does apply to a motor vehicle, not equipped with air brakes, that is commonly known as a recreational vehicle or as a motor home.

O. Reg. 254/15, s. 3 [To come into force July 1, 2016.]

O. Reg. 762/91, s. 1; 476/09, s. 2; 80/11, s. 3

4. If a vehicle is a commercial motor vehicle that is required to display an annual inspection sticker under section 8, a safety standards certificate shall not be issued in respect of the vehicle unless it has been inspected in accordance with the inspection requirements and complies with the performance standards set out in NSC Standard 11B as modified by section 1 of Schedule 3.

O. Reg. 762/91, s. 1; 80/11, s. 4; 241/14, s. 3

4.1 If a vehicle is a school purposes vehicle that is required to display an annual inspection sticker under section 10, a safety standards certificate shall not be issued in respect of the vehicle unless it has been inspected in accordance with the inspection requirements and complies with the performance standards set out in NSC Standard 11B as modified by sections 1 and 2 of Schedule 3.

O. Reg. 80/11, s. 4; 241/14, s. 4

4.2 A safety standards certificate shall not be issued in respect of a bus or an accessible vehicle unless it has been inspected in accordance with the inspection requirements and complies with the performance standards set out in NSC Standard 11B as modified by sections 1 and 2 of Schedule 3.

O. Reg. 80/11, s. 4; 241/14, s. 5

4.3 A safety standards certificate shall not be issued in respect of a trailer unless it has been inspected in accordance with the inspection requirements and complies with the performance standards set out in NSC Standard 11B as modified by section 1 of Schedule 3.

O. Reg. 80/11, s. 4; 241/14, s. 6

Proposed Addition — 4.3.1

4.3.1 A safety standards certificate shall not be issued in respect of a motor vehicle, equipped air brakes, that is commonly known as a recreational vehicle or as a motor home unless it has been inspected in accordance with the inspection requirements and complies with the performance standards applicable to trucks set out in NSC Standard 11B as modified by section 1 of Schedule 3.

O. Reg. 254/15, s. 4 [To come into force July 1, 2016.]

4.4 For purposes of the issuance of a safety standards certificate, the owner or lessee of a commercial motor vehicle or school purposes vehicle that is not required to display an annual inspection sticker under section 8 or 10 may request that the vehicle be inspected in accordance with the inspection requirements referred to in section 4 or 4.1, as appropriate to the type of vehicle, instead of those referred to in section 3.

O. Reg. 80/11, s. 4

5. A safety standards certificate shall not be issued in respect of a motorcycle, other than a motorcycle with two front wheels, unless the motorcycle has been inspected in accordance with the inspection requirements and complies with the performance standards in Schedule 6.

O. Reg. 762/91, s. 1; 114/08, s. 2

5.1 A safety standards certificate shall not be issued in respect of a motorcycle with two front wheels, unless it is a motor tricycle that has been inspected in accordance with the inspection requirements and complies with the performance standards in Schedule 6.1.

O. Reg. 114/08, s. 3

5.2 For the purpose of determining the number of wheels on the front of a motorcycle referred to in sections 5 and 5.1, two wheels are considered to be one wheel if they are mounted on the same axle and the distance between the centres of their areas of contact with the ground is less than 460 millimetres.

O. Reg. 114/08, s. 3

6. [Repealed O. Reg. 476/09, s. 3.]

7. [Repealed O. Reg. 476/09, s. 3.]

STRUCTURAL INSPECTION CERTIFICATE

7.1 (1) A structural inspection certificate shall only be issued in respect of a salvage motor vehicle but shall not be issued in respect of a salvage motor vehicle unless the vehicle has been inspected in accordance with the inspection requirements and complies with the performance standards set out in Schedule 9.

(2) No structural inspection certificate shall be issued in respect of a motor vehicle if the licensee or mechanic is satisfied that a vehicle permit marked "irreparable" has been issued in respect of the vehicle.

O. Reg. 373/98, s. 2; 378/02, s. 2

INSPECTION STICKER AND CERTIFICATE

Commercial Vehicles

8. (1) A commercial vehicle is prescribed as a type or class of vehicle to which section 85 of the Act applies if it has a combined gross weight exceeding 4,500 kilograms.

(2) For purposes of subsection (1), the combined gross weight of a commercial vehicle is the total of the gross weight, registered gross weight or manufacturer's gross vehicle weight rating of each commercial motor vehicle, trailer or trailer converter dolly included within the commercial vehicle.

(3) Commercial vehicles shall be inspected in accordance with the inspection requirements set out in NSC Standard 11B as modified by section 1 of Schedule 3.

(4) If a commercial vehicle has been inspected in accordance with the inspection requirements and complies with the performance standards referred to in subsection (3), the licensee of the station in which the vehicle was inspected, a person authorized in writing by the licensee or the motor vehicle inspection mechanic who inspected the vehicle shall promptly,

(a) complete the annual inspection certificate and annual inspection report and provide copies of them to the owner or lessee;

(b) indicate the month and year of inspection and the vehicle type on the annual inspection sticker corresponding to the certificate; and

(c) remove or cover any annual inspection sticker relating to a previous inspection and affix the current annual inspection sticker,

(i) for a commercial motor vehicle, to the outer surface of the lower left hand corner of the windshield, or to a conspicuous position on the left side of the truck cab, or

(ii) for a trailer or trailer converter dolly, to its outer surface, on the left side and as close as practicable to the front of it.

(5) An annual inspection sticker described in subsection (4) is valid until the end of the twelfth month after the month of inspection indicated on the sticker.

(6) If a commercial vehicle is issued with a safety standards certificate in accordance with section 4, 4.3 or 4.4, the licensee of the station in which the vehicle was inspected, a person authorized in writing by the licensee or the motor vehicle inspection mechanic who inspected the vehicle shall at the time of issuing the safety standards certificate also issue an annual inspection certificate and an annual inspection

report and affix to the vehicle an annual inspection sticker in the manner described in subsection (4).

(7) Subsections (1) and (2) do not apply to an unladen commercial vehicle while it is being operated,

    (a) under the terms of a special permit issued to a manufacturer or dealer under Regulation 628 of the Revised Regulations of Ontario, 1990 (*Vehicle Permits*) made under the Act; or

    (b) under the terms of a dealer number plate, service number plate or manufacturer number plate issued under that regulation.

(8) Subsections (1) and (2) do not apply to a commercial vehicle while it is being towed under the terms of a dealer number plate or a service number plate issued under Regulation 628 of the Revised Regulations of Ontario, 1990 (*Vehicle Permits*) made under the Act,

    (a) to a location where its load will be removed as required by section 82.1 of the Act; or

    (b) to an impound facility pursuant to section 82.1 of the Act.

Proposed Addition — 8(9)

(9) Subsections (1) and (2) do not apply to the following classes of vehicles:

    1. A motor vehicle commonly known as a recreational vehicle or as a motor home, other than a motor vehicle,

        i. carrying commercial cargo or tools or equipment of a type normally used for commercial purposes, or

        ii. carrying animals or non-commercial tools, equipment or vehicles that occupy one-half or more of its floor space.

    2. A house trailer, including a cabin trailer, collapsible cabin trailer, tent trailer and camping trailer, other than a house trailer,

        i. owned or leased by an employer to house the employer's employee,

        ii. carrying commercial cargo or tools or equipment of a type normally used for commercial purposes, or

        iii. carrying animals or non-commercial tools, equipment or vehicles that occupy one-half or more of its floor space.

            O. Reg. 254/15, s. 5 [To come into force July 1, 2016.]

O. Reg. 762/91, s. 1; 510/97, s. 1; 476/09, s. 4; 407/10, s. 1; 80/11, s. 5; 241/14, s. 7; 329/15, s. 1

[Heading repealed O. Reg. 476/09, s. 5.]

9. [Repealed O. Reg. 476/09, s. 5.]

Buses, School Purposes Vehicles and Accessible Vehicles

[Heading amended O. Reg. 80/11, s. 6.]

10. (1) A bus carrying passengers is prescribed as a type or class of vehicle to which section 85 of the Act applies.

(2) Subsection (1) does not apply to a bus that is used for personal purposes without compensation unless the bus has a manufacturer's gross vehicle weight rating of more than 4,500 kilograms.

(3) A school purposes vehicle is prescribed as a type or class of vehicle to which section 85 of the Act applies while it is being used for the transportation of,

> (a) six or more adults with a developmental disability;

> (b) six or more children; or

> (c) six or more persons referred to in clause (a) or (b).

(4) An accessible vehicle carrying passengers is prescribed as a type or class of vehicle to which section 85 of the Act applies.

(5) A bus, a school purposes vehicle and an accessible vehicle shall be inspected in accordance with the inspection requirements set out,

> (a) in NSC Standard 11B as modified by sections 1 and 2 of Schedule 3 for purposes of the issuance of an annual inspection certificate; and

> (b) in NSC Standard 11B as modified by sections 1, 2 and 3 of Schedule 3 for purposes of the issuance of a semi-annual inspection certificate.

(6) If a bus, a school purposes vehicle or an accessible vehicle has been inspected in accordance with the inspection requirements and complies with the performance standards set out in NSC Standard 11B as modified by sections 1 and 2 of Schedule 3, the licensee of the station in which the vehicle was inspected, a person authorized in writing by the licensee or the motor vehicle inspection mechanic who inspected the vehicle shall promptly,

> (a) complete the annual inspection certificate and annual inspection report and provide copies of them to the owner or lessee;

> (b) indicate the month and year of inspection and the vehicle type on the annual inspection sticker corresponding to the certificate; and

> (c) remove or cover any annual inspection sticker relating to a previous inspection and affix the current annual inspection sticker to the outer surface of the lower right hand corner of the windshield, on a fixed side window as close as practicable to the front of the vehicle or to a conspicuous position on the right side of the vehicle body close to the front of the vehicle.

(7) An annual inspection sticker described in subsection (6) is valid,

> (a) until the end of the twelfth month after the month of inspection indicated on the sticker, if the vehicle also displays a valid semi-annual inspection sticker; or

(b) until the end of the sixth month after the month of inspection indicated on the sticker, if the vehicle does not also display a valid semi-annual inspection sticker.

(8) If a bus, a school purposes vehicle or an accessible vehicle has been inspected in accordance with the inspection requirements and complies with the performance standards set out in NSC Standard 11B as modified by sections 1, 2 and 3 of Schedule 3, the licensee of the station in which the vehicle was inspected, a person authorized in writing by the licensee or the motor vehicle inspection mechanic who inspected the vehicle shall promptly,

(a) complete the semi-annual inspection certificate and semi-annual inspection report and provide copies of them to the owner or lessee;

(b) indicate the month and year of inspection on the semi-annual inspection sticker corresponding to the certificate; and

(c) remove or cover any semi-annual inspection sticker relating to a previous inspection and affix the current sticker to the outer surface of the lower right hand corner of the windshield, on a fixed side window as close as practicable to the front of the vehicle or to a conspicuous position on the right side of the vehicle body close to the front of the vehicle.

(9) A semi-annual inspection sticker affixed under subsection (8) is valid until the end of the sixth month after the month of inspection indicated on the sticker.

(10) If a bus, a school purposes vehicle or an accessible vehicle is issued with a safety standards certificate in accordance with section 4.1, 4.2 or 4.4, the licensee of the station in which the vehicle was inspected, a person authorized in writing by the licensee or the motor vehicle inspection mechanic who inspected the vehicle shall at the time of issuing the safety standards certificate also issue an annual inspection certificate and an annual inspection report and affix to the vehicle an annual inspection sticker in the manner described in subsection (6).

(11) [Repealed O. Reg. 241/14, s. 8(4).]

Proposed Amendment — 10(11)

(11) Subsections (1), (2), (3) and (4) do not apply to a motor vehicle commonly known as a recreational vehicle or as a motor home, other than a motor vehicle,

(a) carrying commercial cargo or tools or equipment of a type normally used for commercial purposes; or

(b) carrying animals or non-commercial tools, equipment or vehicles that occupy one-half or more of its floor space.

O. Reg. 254/15, s. 6 [To come into force July 1, 2016.]

O. Reg. 762/91, s. 1; 65/02, s. 3; 80/11, s. 6 [Corrected Ont. Gaz. 23/04/11 Vol. 144:17.]; 241/14, s. 8

[Heading repealed O. Reg. 80/11, s. 6.]

11. [Repealed O. Reg. 80/11, s. 6.]

11.1 [Repealed O. Reg. 42/09, s. 1.]

Historic Vehicles

[Heading repealed O. Reg. 476/09, s. 5. Re-enacted O. Reg. 80/11, s. 7.]

12. An historic vehicle inspected under section 3, 4, 4.1, 4.2, 4.4, 5, 5.1, 8 or 10, as applicable, shall be inspected and tested in accordance with the inspection requirements referred to in that section and shall be in a functional condition relative to its design, construction and operation.

O. Reg. 476/09, s. 5; 80/11, s. 7

REPLACEMENT CERTIFICATE OR STICKER

13. (1) If an annual inspection certificate or an annual inspection sticker is damaged or destroyed during its period of validity, a replacement certificate and sticker shall be issued and affixed by the station that issued the original certificate and sticker or by the Ministry, containing the same information as the original certificate and sticker.

(2) If a semi-annual inspection certificate or a semi-annual inspection sticker is damaged or destroyed during its period of validity, a replacement certificate and sticker shall be issued and affixed by the station that issued the original certificate and sticker or by the Ministry, containing the same information as the original certificate and sticker.

(3) If a certificate or sticker is replaced by a station referred to in subsection (1) or (2), the licensee shall indicate on the station record that the certificate or sticker is a replacement.

O. Reg. 762/91, s. 1; 476/09, s. 6; 80/11, s. 8

EXEMPTIONS

14. A commercial vehicle, bus, school purposes vehicle or accessible vehicle displaying or carrying valid evidence of compliance with the periodic inspection requirements of any Canadian jurisdiction other than Ontario is exempt from the requirements of section 85 of the Act.

O. Reg. 762/91, s. 1; 80/11, s. 9

15. A commercial vehicle, bus, school purposes vehicle or accessible vehicle displaying or carrying valid evidence of compliance with the periodic inspection requirements contained in Part 396, Title 49, Code of Federal Regulations of the United States Department of Transportation based on an inspection carried out in the United States of America is exempt from the requirements of section 85 of the Act.

O. Reg. 762/91, s. 1; 80/11, s. 10

16. Sections 14 and 15 do not apply if the evidence of compliance with periodic inspection requirements is based on a roadside inspection performed by or on behalf of a governmental authority.

O. Reg. 762/91, s. 1

. . . . .

ONT. REG. 468/05 — SCHOOL BUS OFFENCE — SERVICE OF OFFENCE NOTICE ON VEHICLE OWNER

made under the *Highway Traffic Act*

O. Reg. 468/05, as am. O. Reg. 405/15.

1. Service of offence notice — (1) An offence notice issued in a proceeding against an owner of a motor vehicle for an offence under subsection 175(19) or (20) of the Act may be served by regular prepaid mail to the person charged, at the address of the holder of the plate portion of the permit as it appears in the Ministry's records, within 23 days after the occurrence of the alleged offence.

(1.1) Where the provincial offences officer who issued the certificate of offence for an offence described in subsection (1) believes that the person charged resides or, in the case of a corporation, has its principal place of business, outside Ontario, the offence notice may be served by regular prepaid mail to the person charged, at the address outside Ontario at which the officer believes the person resides or has its principal place of business, within 23 days after the occurrence of the alleged offence.

(2) Service of an offence notice that has been mailed in accordance with subsection (1) or (1.1) shall be deemed to have been effected on the seventh day after the day it was mailed.

O. Reg. 405/15, s. 1

2. Certifying service on certificate of offence — If the provincial offences officer who issued the certificate of offence also serves the offence notice on the person charged, that officer shall certify on the certificate of offence the fact that the offence notice was mailed and the date it was mailed.

3. Affidavit of service — Where an offence notice is served in accordance with this Regulation by a person other than the provincial offences officer who issued the certificate of offence, the person shall complete an affidavit of service.

4. Commencement — This Regulation comes into force on the later of the day subsection 5(1) of the *Highway Traffic Statute Law Amendment Act (Child and Youth Safety), 2004* comes into force and the day this Regulation is filed.

ONT. REG. 612 — SCHOOL BUSES

made under the *Highway Traffic Act*

R.R.O. 1990, Reg. 612, as am. O. Reg. 319/91; 307/00; 66/02; 308/04; 129/07; 198/07; 450/08; 129/10; 169/13, ss. 1–7, 8 (Fr.); 92/15.

INTERPRETATION
[Heading added O. Reg. 169/13, s. 1.]

1. Interpretation — (1) In this Regulation,

"accessible school bus" means a school bus that is designed or modified to be used for the purpose of transporting a person in a wheelchair and is used for that purpose, whether or not the school bus is also used to transport persons who are not in a wheelchair;

"CSA Standard D250" means the Canadian Standards Association Standard D250, *School Buses*, and includes CSA-D250-M1982, CSA-D250-M1985, CSA-D250-98, CSA-D250-03, CSA-D250-07, CSA-D250-12 and any subsequent CSA-D250 that takes effect on or after June 1, 2013;

"CSA Standard D409-M84" means the Canadian Standards Association Standard D409-M84, *Motor Vehicles for the Transportation of Physically Disabled Persons*;

"school bus" means a school bus as defined in subsection 175(1) of the Act;

"school purposes bus" means,

(a) a school bus, or

(b) any other bus operated by or under contract with a school board or other authority in charge of a school while it is being used to transport adults with a developmental disability or children.

(1.1) [Repealed O. Reg. 129/10, s. 1.]

(1.2) [Repealed O. Reg. 129/10, s. 1.]

(1.3) [Repealed O. Reg. 129/10, s. 1.]

(1.4) [Repealed O. Reg. 129/10, s. 1.]

(2) For the purposes of this Regulation, the date that a school bus was manufactured is deemed, in the absence of evidence to the contrary, to be the date on the school bus's compliance label.

(3) [Repealed O. Reg. 129/10, s. 1.]

(3.1) [Repealed O. Reg. 129/10, s. 1.]

(4) [Repealed O. Reg. 198/07, s. 1.]

O. Reg. 319/91, s. 1; 307/00, s. 1; 66/02, s. 1; 308/04, s. 1; 129/07, s. 1; 198/07, s. 1; 450/08, s. 1; 129/10, s. 1; 169/13, s. 2

1.1 Conflicts between standards and regulation — Where the requirements prescribed in a Canadian Standards Association Standard referred to in this Regulation are different from the requirements set out in this Regulation, the requirements set out in this Regulation prevail unless otherwise specified in this Regulation.

O. Reg. 129/10, s. 1

SCHOOL BUSES

[Heading added O. Reg. 169/13, s. 3.]

2. (1) CSA Standard D250 — No person shall operate or permit the operation of a school bus registered in Ontario and manufactured before June 1, 2013 unless the school bus was manufactured in accordance with the following standards:

1. In the case of a school bus manufactured on or after December 1, 1982 and before September 1, 1987, either CSA-D250-M1982 or CSA-D250-M1985.

2. In the case of a school bus manufactured on or after September 1, 1987 and before June 1, 2000, either CSA-D250-M1985 or CSA-D250-98.

3. In the case of a school bus manufactured on or after June 1, 2000 and before January 1, 2005, either CSA-D250-98 or CSA-D250-03.

4. In the case of a school bus manufactured on or after January 1, 2005 and before November 1, 2010, either CSA-D250-03 or CSA-D250-07.

5. In the case of a school bus manufactured on or after November 1, 2010 and before June 1, 2013, either CSA-D250-07 or CSA-D250-12.

(1.1) No person shall operate or permit the operation of a school bus registered in Ontario and manufactured on or after June 1, 2013 unless the school bus was manufactured in accordance with the following standards:

1. CSA-D250-12 or, in the case of a school bus manufactured on or after the effective date prescribed in a subsequent CSA-D250, that subsequent CSA-D250.

2. Despite paragraph 1, in the case of a school bus manufactured on or after the date of publication of a subsequent CSA-D250 but before the effective date prescribed in that subsequent CSA-D250, either one of the following:

   i. that subsequent CSA-D250, or

   ii. the CSA-D250 in effect when the school bus was manufactured.

(2) Subsection (1) does not apply to a school bus that was registered in a jurisdiction other than Ontario before it was registered in Ontario and that was registered in Ontario on December 1, 2008 if the school bus has been modified to comply with the appropriate CSA Standard D250 for the school bus depending on its date of manufacture, as set out in subsection (1).

(3) On and after August 15, 2009, no person shall operate or permit the operation of a school bus described in subsection (2) unless the school bus has been inspected by a person approved by the Minister or belonging to a class of persons approved by the Minister and certified by that person to have been modified to comply with the appropriate CSA Standard D250 for the school bus depending on its date of manufacture, as set out in subsection (1).

(4) The inspection and certification required by subsection (3) must be completed and issued before November 1, 2009.

(5) No person shall operate or permit the operation of a school bus registered in Ontario and manufactured in accordance with or modified to comply with CSA-D250-98, CSA-D250-03 or CSA-D250-07 unless the school bus continues to meet the CSA Standard D250 to which it was manufactured or modified.

(5.1) No person shall operate or permit the operation of a school bus registered in Ontario and manufactured in accordance with CSA-D250-12 or a subsequent CSA Standard D250 unless the school bus continues to meet the CSA Standard D250 to which it was manufactured.

(6) No person shall operate or permit the operation of a school bus registered in Ontario, manufactured before June 1, 2000 and manufactured in accordance with or modified to comply with CSA-D250-M1982 or CSA-D250-M1985 unless the school bus continues to comply with the colour and identification requirements prescribed,

    (a) in Clauses 3.6, 4.7 and 4.18 of CSA-D250-M1982, in the case of a school bus manufactured in accordance with or modified to comply with CSA-D250-M1982; or

    (b) in Clauses 4.6, 5.7 and 5.18 of CSA-D250-M1985, in the case of a school bus manufactured in accordance with or modified to comply with CSA-D250-M1985.

O. Reg. 307/00, s. 2; 308/04, s. 2; 450/08, s. 2; 129/10, s. 2; 169/13, s. 4

3. **Equipment** — (1) Every school bus registered in Ontario shall,

    (a) be equipped with red only overhead signal lights,

        (i) that have,

            (A) at least four signal lights that comply with CSA-D250-M1982, CSA-D250-M1985 or CSA-D250-98, in the case of a school bus manufactured before January 1, 2005, or

            (B) eight signal lights that comply with the appropriate CSA Standard D250 for the school bus depending on its date of manufacture, as set out in subsection 2(1) or (1.1), in the case of a school bus manufactured on or after January 1, 2005, and

        (ii) that are actuated by a control device accessible to the driver and equipped to give the driver a clear and unmistakable signal either visible or audible when the signal lights are operating;

(b) be equipped with a first aid kit that complies with,

   (i) the appropriate CSA Standard D250 for the school bus depending on its date of manufacture, as set out in subsection 2(1) or (1.1), or

   (ii) a subsequent CSA Standard D250;

(c) be equipped with a system of mirrors that comply with the appropriate CSA Standard D250 for the school bus depending on its date of manufacture, as set out in subsection 2(1) or (1.1), except that,

   (i) a school bus manufactured before November 30, 1997 may comply with the mirror requirements prescribed in CSA-D250-98 or CSA-D250-03, and

   (ii) a school bus manufactured on or after November 30, 1997 and before January 1, 2005 shall comply with the mirror requirements prescribed in CSA-D250-98 or CSA-D250-03;

(d) display the words "SCHOOL BUS" in upper case letters on the front and rear of the bus in a manner that complies with the requirements of the appropriate CSA Standard D250 for the school bus depending on its date of manufacture, as set out in subsection 2(1) or (1.1); and

(e) display the words "DO NOT PASS WHEN SIGNALS FLASHING" in upper case letters on the rear of the bus in a manner that complies with the requirements of the appropriate CSA Standard D250 for the school bus depending on its date of manufacture, as set out in subsection 2(1) or (1.1).

(2) Every school bus registered in Ontario shall be equipped with a stop arm device that,

(a) displays on the front and rear of the device the word "STOP" in upper case letters; and

(b) complies with,

   (i) CSA-D250-98 or CSA-D250-03, in the case of a school bus manufactured before January 1, 2005, or

   (ii) the appropriate CSA Standard D250 for the school bus depending on its date of manufacture, as set out in subsection 2(1) or (1.1), in the case of a school bus manufactured on or after January 1, 2005.

(3) Every school bus registered in Ontario that was manufactured before January 1, 2005 shall be equipped with a pedestrian-student safety crossing arm that complies with the requirements of CSA-D250-07.

(4) Every school bus registered in Ontario shall display,

(a) a sign affixed to the bottom of the left window on the rear of the school bus that has the dimensions and bears the markings as illustrated in Figure 1; and

(b) a sign affixed to the bottom of the right window on the rear of the bus that has the dimensions and bears the markings as illustrated in Figure 2.

FIGURE 1

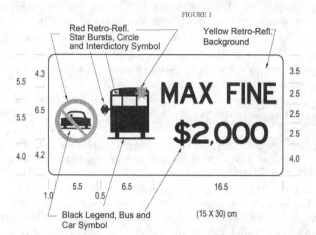

Red Retro-Refl. Star Bursts, Circle and Interdictory Symbol

Yellow Retro-Refl. Background

Black Legend, Bus and Car Symbol

(15 X 30) cm

Text alternative: Illustration of a sign labelled as Figure 1. The sign contains the "no passing" circle symbol with an interdictory stroke on the left side. Beside that is a solid black image of a stopped school bus with its stop arm extended. On the right side of the sign appear the words "MAX FINE $2,000". The following measurements are written below the sign: (15 x 30) cm. The sign has a yellow reflective background and the symbols and wording appear in black. The sign is surrounded by measurements of its different elements. This text alternative is provided for convenience only and does not form part of the official law.

FIGURE 2

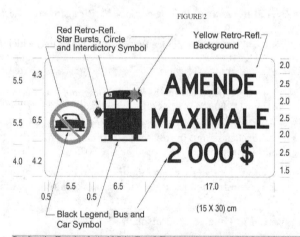

Red Retro-Refl. Star Bursts, Circle and Interdictory Symbol

Yellow Retro-Refl. Background

Black Legend, Bus and Car Symbol

(15 X 30) cm

Text alternative: Illustration of a sign labelled as Figure 2. The sign contains a "no passing" circle symbol with an interdictory stroke on the left side. Beside that is a solid black image of a stopped school bus with its stop arm extended. On the right side of the sign appear the words "AMENDE MAXIMALE 2 000 $". The following measurements are written below the sign: (15 x 30) cm. The sign has a yellow reflective background and the symbols and wording appear in black. The sign is surrounded by measurements of its different elements. This text alternative is provided for convenience only and does not form part of the official law.

(5) If the dimensions of the left or right window on the rear of a school bus cannot accommodate either or both of the signs as required by subsection (4), both signs shall be affixed to the rear bumper directly below the locations prescribed by clauses (4)(a) and (b).

(6) The signs affixed in accordance with subsection (4) or (5) must be visible at all times to vehicles approaching from the rear of the school bus and shall not be obstructed by any part of or attachment to the school bus.

(7) The signs required by subsection (4) must meet the performance requirements of any of the types of sheeting specified in the American Society for Testing and Materials Standard D 4956-01a and the sheeting must have a Luminance Factor (Y%) of at least 15.

O. Reg. 319/91, s. 2; 307/00, s. 3; 66/02, s. 2; 129/10, s. 3; 169/13, s. 5; 92/15, s. 1

SCHOOL PURPOSES BUSES

[Heading added O. Reg. 169/13, s. 6.]

4. School purposes buses — **(1)** No person shall operate or permit the operation of a school purposes bus in Ontario unless it is equipped with,

(a) a light or lights arranged to provide light to the whole of the interior except the driver's position, and that are constantly lighted during darkness when there are passengers in the vehicle;

(b) an adequate fire extinguisher securely mounted in such a manner and place as to be readily accessible;

(c) tire chains or snow tires for each driving wheel that is not of the dual type that are placed on the wheels when the conditions of the highway require their use; and

(d) at least one door or exit and,

(i) a door or exit for emergency use situated at the rear of the vehicle or near the rear on the left side of the vehicle and which has a door lock equipped with an interior handle which releases the lock when lifted up, or

(ii) at least three pushout windows on each side of the passenger compartment of the vehicle each of which,

(A) has a minimum height of 500 millimetres and a minimum width of 760 millimetres,

(B) is designed, constructed and maintained to open outwards when a reasonable amount of manual force is applied to the inside of the window, and

(C) displays on or adjacent to the window adequate directions for its emergency use.

(2) A school purposes bus that is equipped in accordance with subclause (1)(d)(ii) must be equipped with an additional pushout window located in the rear of the bus.

O. Reg. 198/07, s. 2; 129/10, s. 3

ACCESSIBLE SCHOOL BUSES

[Heading added O. Reg. 169/13, s. 7.]

5. Application of ss. 6 and 7 — Sections 6 and 7 apply with respect to accessible school buses and are in addition to any other provisions of this Regulation that apply with respect to school buses.

O. Reg. 198/07, s. 2; 169/13, s. 7

6. CSA Standards: accessible school buses — (1) No person shall operate or permit the operation of an accessible school bus registered in Ontario and manufactured on or after January 1, 1986 and before June 1, 2013 unless,

(a) the accessible school bus was,

(i) manufactured in accordance with or modified to comply with CSA Standard D409-M84 and,

(A) manufactured in accordance with the appropriate CSA Standard D250 for the school bus depending on its date of manufacture, as set out in subsection 2(1), or

(B) in the case of a school bus referred to in subsection 2(2), modified to comply with the appropriate CSA Standard D250 for the school bus depending on its date of manufacture, as set out in subsection 2(1), or

(ii) manufactured in accordance with CSA-D250-12; and

(b) the accessible school bus continues to meet the CSA Standards referred to in subclause (a)(i) or (ii).

(2) No person shall operate or permit the operation of an accessible school bus registered in Ontario and manufactured on or after June 1, 2013 unless the accessible school bus,

(a) was manufactured in accordance with the appropriate CSA Standard D250 for the accessible school bus depending on its date of manufacture, as set out in subsection 2(1.1); and

(b) continues to meet the CSA Standard D250 to which it was manufactured.

O. Reg. 129/10, s. 4; 169/13, s. 7

7. Equipment: accessible school buses — (1) This section applies to all accessible school buses registered in Ontario and manufactured on or after January 1, 1986.

(2) Every accessible school bus shall,

(a) be equipped with lights above or beside each passenger access door that shall,

(i) be shielded to protect the eyes of entering and exiting passengers, and

(ii) in the case of an accessible school bus manufactured after December 31, 2012, illuminate the ground surface for a distance of at least 0.9 metres perpendicular to the outer edge of the lift or the bottom step tread;

(b) have floor covering in the aisle and on the steps that produces minimum glare; and

(c) conform to Canada Motor Vehicle Safety Standard 302 under the *Motor Vehicle Safety Act* (Canada) regarding flammability.

(3) Every accessible school bus shall have at least one door for passenger access and an emergency exit door, located on different walls of the school bus, and the emergency exit door shall be operable from both inside and outside the school bus.

(4) Each of the doors referred to in subsection (3) shall have a wheelchair passageway that must be at least 760 millimetres wide.

(5) Every lift used on an accessible school bus shall,

(a) have a coloured-contrasted strip running the full width of the lift platform marking the outer edge of the platform; and

(b) be secured by means other than a support or lug in the door while the school bus is being operated on a highway.

(6) Every accessible school bus shall display the international symbol of access in a clearly visible position on the rear of the school bus and on the front of the school bus in a position other than on the windshield.

(7) The symbol of access required by subsection (6) must be at least 15 centimetres high and at least 15 centimetres wide.

O. Reg. 169/13, s. 7

. . . . .

Ont. Reg. 613 — Seat Belt Assemblies

made under the *Highway Traffic Act*

R.R.O. 1990, Reg. 613, as am. O. Reg. 195/05; 443/06 (Fr.); 522/06; 236/09; 362/11.

1. Correctional Service of Canada vehicles that are modified to facilitate the transportation of persons held in custody and police department vehicles are exempt from the requirement that,

   (a) torso restraints;

   (b) seat belt assemblies in the centre front seat seating position; and

   (c) seat belt assemblies in the rear seat seating positions,

not be removed, rendered partly or wholly inoperative or modified so as to reduce their effectiveness.

O. Reg. 522/06, s. 1

2. A police officer or peace officer who in the lawful performance of his or her duty is transporting a person in his or her custody is exempt from subsections 106(2), (3) and (4) of the Act.

O. Reg. 522/06, s. 2

3. A person who is in the custody of a police officer or peace officer is exempt from subsection 106(3) of the Act.

O. Reg. 522/06, s. 3

4. An employee or agent of Canada Post while engaged in rural mail delivery is exempt from subsection 106(2) of the Act.

O. Reg. 522/06, s. 4

5. An ambulance attendant or any other person transported in the patient's compartment of an ambulance as defined in subsection 1(1) of the Act is exempt from subsection 106(3) of the Act where attendance to a patient makes it impracticable to wear a seat belt assembly.

O. Reg. 522/06, s. 5; 362/11, s. 1

6. A firefighter occupying a seating position behind the driver's cab in a fire department vehicle, as defined in subsection 1(1) of the Act, is exempt from subsection 106(3) of the Act where the performance of work activities makes it impracticable to wear a seat belt assembly.

O. Reg. 522/06, s. 6; 362/11, s. 2

6.1 A co-driver, as defined in Ontario Regulation 555/06 (*Hours of Service*) made under the Act, is exempt from subsection 106(3) of the Act when he or she is occupying a sleeper berth that meets the requirements of section 8 of that regulation.

O. Reg. 236/09, s. 1

7. (1) In this Regulation "taxicab" means,

(a) a motor vehicle licensed as a cab by a municipality; or

(b) a motor vehicle designed for carrying less than ten passengers and operated under the authority of an operating licence issued under the *Public Vehicles Act.*

(2) Taxicabs are exempt from the requirement that,

(a) torso restraints for drivers' seating positions; and

(b) seat belt assemblies in the centre front seat seating positions,

not be removed, rendered partly or wholly inoperative or modified so as to reduce their effectiveness.

(3) The driver of a taxicab while transporting for hire a passenger is exempt from subsection 106(2) of the Act.

O. Reg. 522/06, s. 7

8. (1) Passengers under eight years old are classified as follows for the purposes of this section:

1. Children weighing less than nine kilograms are classified as infants.

2. Children weighing nine kilograms or more but less than 18 kilograms are classified as toddlers.

3. Children weighing 18 kilograms or more but less than 36 kilograms and who are less than 145 centimetres tall are classified as pre-school to primary grade children.

(2) The driver of a motor vehicle on a highway is required to ensure that an infant passenger is secured as set out in subsection (5) or (5.1).

(3) The driver of a motor vehicle on a highway is required to ensure that a toddler passenger is secured as set out in subsection (6) or (7.1).

(4) The driver of a motor vehicle on a highway is required to ensure that a pre-school to primary grade child passenger is secured as set out in subsection (7) or (7.1) and subsection (8).

(5) An infant shall be secured in a rearward-facing child restraint system that,

(a) conforms to the requirements of Standard 213.1 (Infant Restraint Systems) made under the *Motor Vehicle Safety Act* (Canada);

(b) is secured by a seat belt assembly in the manner recommended by the manufacturer of the child restraint system, unless the child restraint system was designed to be and is secured by means of a universal anchorage system; and

(c) has all harnesses, straps and buckles designed to secure the infant in the child restraint system properly adjusted and securely fastened.

(5.1) Despite clause (5)(a), an infant may be secured in a restraint system that conforms to the requirements of Standard 213.5 (Restraint Systems for Infants with Special Needs) made under the *Motor Vehicle Safety Act* (Canada) if he or she is an infant with special needs as defined in the *Motor Vehicle Restraint Systems and Booster Cushions Safety Regulations* made under the *Motor Vehicle Safety Act* (Canada).

(6) A toddler shall be secured,

    (a) in a child restraint system that,

        (i) conforms to the requirements of,

            (A) Standard 213 (Child Restraint Systems) made under the *Motor Vehicle Safety Act* (Canada), or

            (B) Standard 213.4 (Built-in Child Restraint Systems and Built-in Booster Cushions) made under the *Motor Vehicle Safety Act* (Canada),

        (ii) is secured by a seat belt assembly in the manner recommended by the manufacturer of the child restraint system, unless the child restraint system was designed to be and is secured by means of a universal anchorage system,

        (iii) is secured by all the anchorage straps and devices recommended by the manufacturer of the child restraint system, if the motor vehicle was manufactured on or after January 1, 1989, and

        (iv) has all harnesses, straps and buckles designed to secure the toddler in the child restraint system properly adjusted and securely fastened; or

    (b) in a child restraint system described in subsection (5), if the manufacturer's specifications permit or recommend the system for use by children who weigh nine kilograms or more and not less than the weight of the toddler.

(7) A pre-school to primary grade child shall be secured,

    (a) if there is a seating position in the motor vehicle that has a seat belt assembly consisting of a pelvic restraint and a torso restraint, in that position,

        (i) on a child booster seat that is used in the manner recommended by its manufacturer and that conforms to,

            (A) Standard 213.2 (Booster Cushions) made under the *Motor Vehicle Safety Act* (Canada), or

            (B) Standard 213.4 (Built-in Child Restraint Systems and Built-in Booster Cushions) made under the *Motor Vehicle Safety Act* (Canada), and

        (ii) by the motor vehicle's complete seat belt assembly, worn as described in subsection (9);

    (b) if all the seating positions in the motor vehicle have a seat belt assembly consisting only of a pelvic restraint, by the pelvic restraint, worn as described in subsection (9); or

    (c) in a child restraint system described in clause (6)(a), if the manufacturer's specifications permit or recommend the system for use by children who weigh

18 kilograms or more and not less than the weight of the pre-school to primary grade child.

(7.1) Despite subclause (6)(a)(i), clause (6)(b), subclause (7)(a)(i) and clause (7)(c), a toddler or pre-school to primary grade child may be secured in a restraint system that conforms to the requirements of Standard 213.3 (Restraint Systems for Disabled Persons) made under the *Motor Vehicle Safety Act* (Canada) if he or she,

   (a) is a mobility-impaired occupant as defined in the *Motor Vehicle Restraint Systems and Booster Cushions Safety Regulations* made under the *Motor Vehicle Safety Act* (Canada); or

   (b) has a developmental disability as defined in section 175 of the Act.

(8) Despite subsections (7) and (7.1), a pre-school to primary grade child shall not be secured in a seating position if the seating position has a front air bag that has not been turned off or cannot be turned off.

(9) For the purpose of clauses (7)(a) and (b), a seat belt assembly shall be worn so that,

   (a) the pelvic restraint is worn firmly against the body and across the hips;

   (b) the torso restraint, if there is one, is worn closely against the body and over the shoulder and across the chest; and

   (c) the pelvic restraint, and the torso restraint, if there is one, are securely fastened.

(10) Clause (9)(b) does not apply to child booster seats, such as abdominal shield booster seats, that are designed to be secured in place by the pelvic restraint of the seatbelt assembly only.

(11) The driver of a motor vehicle that is registered in a state of the United States of America is deemed to have complied with the appropriate standard under the *Motor Vehicle Safety Act* (Canada) required by subsection (5), (5.1), (6), (7) or (7.1) if the child is secured in a child restraint system that meets Federal Motor Vehicle Safety Standard 213 made under Title 49 of the *United States Code*, Chapter 301, Motor Vehicle Safety, in a manner recommended by the manufacturer of the child restraint system.

O. Reg. 195/05, s. 1; 522/06, s. 8; 236/09, s. 2

8.1 (1) The following are exempt from complying with subsections 8(2), (3) and (4):

   1. The driver of a taxicab, bus or public vehicle, while transporting a passenger for hire.

   2. The driver of an ambulance.

   3. [Repealed O. Reg. 236/09, s. 3(1).]

(2) Despite paragraph 1 of subsection (1), the following are not exempt from complying with subsections 8(2), (3) and (4) while transporting children to or from school:

   1. The driver of a taxicab that is operated by or under contract with a school board or other authority in charge of a school for the transportation of children.

2. The driver of a public vehicle with a seating capacity of less than 10 persons that is operated by or under contract with a school board or other authority in charge of a school for the transportation of children.

(3) [Repealed R.R.O. 1990, Reg. 613, s. 8.1(4).]

(4) Subsection (3) is revoked on the fifth anniversary of the day Ontario Regulation 236/09 comes into force.

O. Reg. 195/05, s. 1; 236/09, s. 3

9. Where a motor vehicle that was manufactured in or imported into Canada prior to the 1st day of January, 1974 is driven on a highway,

(a) the driver and passengers are exempt from the requirement to wear the torso restraint component of a seat belt assembly; and

(b) the driver is exempt from the provisions of subsection 106(4) of the Act with respect to the requirement that a passenger wear the torso restraint component of a seat belt assembly.

O. Reg. 522/06, s. 9

10. Where a motor vehicle manufactured without seat belt assemblies for each seating position and not modified so that there is a seat belt assembly for each seating position is driven on a highway,

(a) the driver is exempt from the requirement of subsection 106(2) of the Act to wear a seat belt assembly if there is no seat belt assembly at the driver's seating position;

(b) a passenger is exempt from the requirement of subsection 106(3) of the Act to wear a seat belt assembly if the passenger occupies a position without a seat belt assembly and there is no other available seating position with a seat belt assembly; and

(c) the driver is exempt from clause 106(4)(a) of the Act with respect to any passenger described in clause (b).

O. Reg. 522/06, s. 10

ONT. REG. 363/04 — SECURITY OF LOADS

made under the *Highway Traffic Act*

O. Reg. 363/04, as am. O. Reg. 165/12.

PART 1 — GENERAL

1. Interpretation — (1) In this Regulation,

"commercial motor vehicle" includes a combination of a commercial motor vehicle and a trailer or trailers;

"gross combination weight rating", in respect of a combination of a commercial motor vehicle and a trailer or trailers means the greatest of,

    (a) the total of the gross vehicle weight of the commercial motor vehicle and the greater of the manufacturer's gross vehicle weight rating and the gross vehicle weight of each trailer and trailer converter dolly in the combination,

    (b) the total of the manufacturer's gross vehicle weight rating of the commercial motor vehicle and the greater of the manufacturer's gross vehicle weight rating and the gross vehicle weight of each trailer and trailer converter dolly in the combination, and

    (c) the total of the registered gross weight of the commercial motor vehicle and the greater of the manufacturer's gross vehicle weight rating and the gross vehicle weight of each trailer and trailer converter dolly included in the combination;

"gross vehicle weight" means the total weight in kilograms transmitted to the highway by a vehicle, or combination of vehicles, and load;

"National Standard" means the National Safety Code Standard 10 entitled "Cargo Securement", published by the Canadian Council of Motor Transport Administrators and dated September 2010, as amended from time to time and available on the Ministry's website.

(2) For the purposes of this Regulation,

    (a) terms used in this Regulation and defined in the National Standard have the same meaning as in the National Standard;

    (b) except in the term "working load limit", the term "load" has the same meaning as "cargo" in the National Standard.

O. Reg. 165/12, s. 1

2. Compliance with National Standard — (1) Every commercial motor vehicle carrying a load on a highway must be in compliance with Division 3 (Requirements for Cargo Securement System) and Division 4 (Tiedowns) of Part 1 of the National Standard.

(2) A tiedown or securing device that is marked by its manufacturer shall be deemed to have a working load limit equal to the working load limit determined in accordance with the National Standard.

(3) A tiedown or securing device that is not marked by its manufacturer shall be deemed to have a working load limit equal to zero.

O. Reg. 165/12, s. 2

3. Permit load securement conditions prevail — A vehicle carrying a load on a highway under the authority of a permit issued under section 110 of the Act that contains load securement requirements that conflict with any requirements of this Regulation must be in compliance with the permit requirements and not with the conflicting requirements of this Regulation.

PART 2 — COMMERCIAL MOTOR VEHICLES OF 4,500 KILOGRAMS OR LESS

4. Application of Part — This Part applies to commercial motor vehicles for which each of the gross vehicle weight, registered gross weight, manufacturer's gross vehicle weight rating and gross combination weight rating is 4,500 kilograms or less.

5. Securement of load — (1) A load carried on a commercial motor vehicle on a highway must be secured by means of,

(a) sides, sideboards or stakes and rear stakes, endgate or endboard that,

(i) are securely attached to the vehicle,

(ii) are strong enough and high enough to ensure that the load will not shift on or fall from the vehicle, and

(iii) have no opening large enough to permit any of the load to pass through;

(b) at least one tiedown that meets the requirements of subsection 2(1) for each 3.04 linear metres of lading or fraction thereof, and as many additional tiedowns that meet the requirements of subsection 2(1) as are necessary to secure each part of the load, either by direct contact between the load and the tiedown or by contact between the load and dunnage; or

(c) any other means that prevents a load from shifting or falling that is similar to and at least as effective as the means specified in clause (a) or (b).

(2) A tiedown or dunnage in contact with exterior, topmost items of a load and securely holding each interior and lower item shall be deemed to comply with the requirements for contact in clause (1)(b).

(3) If the load may shift in transit, the load must be blocked, restrained or contained in such a manner that it will not shift in a forward direction when the vehicle decelerates at a rate of six metres per second per second or more and must be,

(a) securely blocked or braced against the sides, sideboards or stakes of the vehicle; or

(b) secured by devices that conform to the requirements set out in clause (1)(b) or (c).

(4) This section does not apply to,

(a) a vehicle carrying a load that, because of its size, shape or weight, must be carried on a special-purpose vehicle or must be fastened by special methods, if the load is securely and adequately fastened to the vehicle; or

(b) a motor vehicle or road-building machine operated by or on behalf of an authority having jurisdiction and control of a highway while the vehicle or machine is engaged in construction, maintenance or marking activities.

6. Tiedowns — (1) The working load limit of a tiedown shall be deemed to be the working load limit of its weakest component.

(2) [Repealed O. Reg. 165/12, s. 3.]

(3) The strength of anchor points must be at least as strong as the tiedown when the connector is loaded in any direction in which the tiedown may load it.

(4) A tiedown shall not be used if,

(a) the active portion has knots in it;

(b) any component of it exhibits stretch, deformation, wear or damage beyond the limits specified by the manufacturer; or

(c) it has been repaired or shortened other than in accordance with the manufacturer's specifications.

(5) Where an "over-the-centre" type of tiedown tensioner is used, the handle must be locked in place and secured by an adequate secondary means to prevent its inadvertent release.

(6) Except in the case of steel, fibre or synthetic strapping that is permanently crimped, tiedowns used on a commercial motor vehicle to secure the load against movement in any direction must be designed, constructed and maintained in such a manner that the driver of the vehicle can tighten the tiedown in transit.

O. Reg. 165/12, s. 3

7. Material used for load securement — Material used on or in a vehicle as dunnage, chocks or cradles or for blocking or bracing must be strong enough that it will not be split or crushed by the load or the tiedowns.

O. Reg. 165/12, s. 4

PART 3 — COMMERCIAL MOTOR VEHICLES OVER 4,500 KILOGRAMS

8. Application of Part — This Part applies to commercial motor vehicles having a gross vehicle weight, registered gross weight, manufacturer's gross vehicle weight rating or gross combination weight rating exceeding 4,500 kilograms.

9. Compliance with National Standard — (1) Every commercial motor vehicle carrying a load on a highway must be in compliance with Part 1 of the National Standard.

(2) Every commercial motor vehicle on a highway carrying a load that is described in Division 1,2,3, 4, 5, 6, 7, 8 or 9 of Part 2 of the National Standard must be in compliance with that Part.

10. Inspection — Every driver of a commercial motor vehicle operating on a highway shall inspect the vehicle as prescribed by Part 1 of the National Standard.

11. Exemption — Subsections 5(1) and (2) and section 9 of the National Standard do not apply to,

    (a) a vehicle carrying a load that, because of its size, shape or weight, must be carried on a special-purpose vehicle or must be fastened by special methods, if the load is securely and adequately fastened to the vehicle; or

    (b) a motor vehicle or road-building machine operated by or on behalf of an authority having jurisdiction and control of a highway while the vehicle or machine is engaged in construction, maintenance or marking activities.

PART 4 — REVOCATION, COMMENCEMENT

12. Revocation — Regulation 614 of the Revised Regulations of Ontario, 1990 is revoked.

13. Commencement — This Regulation comes into force on the day section 26 of Schedule P to the *Government Efficiency Act, 2002* is proclaimed in force.

ONT. REG. 415/10 — SHORT-TERM VEHICLE IMPOUNDMENT UNDER SECTION 55.2 OF THE ACT

made under the *Highway Traffic Act*

O. Reg. 415/10, as am. O. Reg. 423/15 [To come into force January 1, 2017.].

1. Exemptions from s. 55.2 of the Act, ambulances, etc. — Ambulances, fire department vehicles and police department vehicles are exempt from section 55.2 of the Act.

2. Exemptions from s. 55.2 of the Act, commercial motor vehicles — A commercial motor vehicle within the meaning of subsection 16(1) of the Act is exempt from section 55.2 of the Act if the driver's licence suspension took effect less than 100 days before the day on which the driving while under suspension takes place.

Proposed Amendment — 2

2. Exemptions from s. 55.2 of the Act, commercial motor vehicles — A commercial motor vehicle, as defined in section 3 of Ontario Regulation 419/15 (*Definitions of Commercial Motor Vehicle and Tow Truck*) made under the Act, is exempt from section 55.2 of the Act if the driver's licence suspension took effect less than 100 days before the day on which the driving while under suspension takes place.

O. Reg. 423/15, s. 1 [To come into force January 1, 2017.]

3. Commencement — This Regulation comes into force on the later of the day section 25 of the *Road Safety Act, 2009* comes into force and the day this Regulation is filed.

ONT. REG. 615 — SIGNS

made under the *Highway Traffic Act*

R.R.O. 1990, Reg. 615, as am. O. Reg. 699/92; 444/93; 519/93; 909/93; 148/97; 332/98 [Corrected Gazette 1/8/98 Vol. 131:31.]; 380/98; 380/02; 246/03; 63/06; 175/08 [s. 5(8) corr. by CTR 13 JN 08 - 1] [ss. 9(2), 10(2) repealed O. Reg. 339/09, s. 39.]; 261/08; 339/09; 93/15; 335/15; 407/15.

SPEED LIMIT SIGNS

1. A speed limit sign,

    (a) shall be not less than 60 centimetres in width and 75 centimetres in height;

    (b) shall bear the word "maximum" in black letters not less than 10 centimetres in height on a white retro-reflective background;

    (c) shall display in black numerals not less than 30 centimetres in height on a white retro-reflective background the prescribed maximum rate of speed; and

    (d) may display a tab sign not less than 20 centimetres in height and not less than 60 centimetres in width immediately below the speed limit sign and the tab sign shall bear the legend "km/h" in white retro-reflective letters not less than 10 centimetres in height on a black background,

as illustrated in the following Figure:

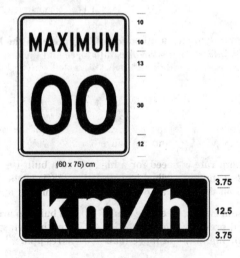

or a speed limit sign shall,

(e) be not less than 60 centimetres in width and 90 centimetres in height;

(f) bear the word "maximum" in black letters not less than 10 centimetres in height on a white retro-reflective background;

(g) display in black numerals not less than 30 centimetres in height on a white retro-reflective background the prescribed maximum rate of speed; and

(h) bear the legend "km/h" in white retro-reflective letters not less than 7.5 centimetres in height on a black background,

as illustrated in the following Figure:

(60 x 90) cm

O. Reg. 339/09, s. 1

2. (1) Subject to section 4, where a maximum rate of speed other than that prescribed by subsection 128(1) of the Act is prescribed for a highway in a local municipality or built-up area, speed limit signs shall be erected on the highway, in each direction of travel,

(a) not more than 600 metres apart where the speed limit prescribed is 60 kilometres per hour or less; and

(b) not more than 900 metres apart where the speed limit prescribed is greater than 60 kilometres per hour and not more than 70 kilometres per hour.

(2) Where the maximum rate of speed for a highway in a built-up area more than 1,500 metres in length is that prescribed by subsection 128(1) of the Act, speed limit signs shall be erected on the highway not more than 900 metres apart.

(3) Where the maximum rate of speed for a highway in a built-up area 1,500 metres or less in length is that prescribed by subsection 128(1) of the Act, speed limit signs shall be erected on the highway not more than 300 metres apart.

O. Reg. 175/08, s. 1

3. (1) The commencement of the part of a highway for which a maximum rate of speed is prescribed shall be indicated by a speed limit sign accompanied immediately below by a sign bearing the markings and having the dimensions as illustrated in the following Figure:

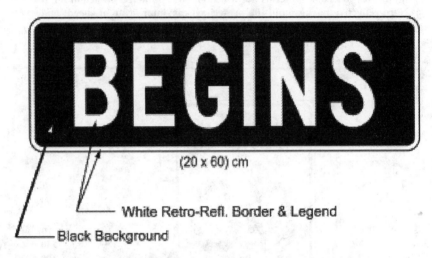

(20 x 60) cm

White Retro-Refl. Border & Legend

Black Background

(2) Despite subsection (1), in an area designated by the *French Language Services Act*, the commencement of the part of a highway for which a maximum rate of speed is prescribed shall be indicated by a speed limit sign accompanied immediately below by a sign bearing the markings and having the dimensions as illustrated in the following Figure:

(45 x 60) cm

White Retro-Refl. Border & Legend
Black Background

O. Reg. 175/08, s. 2; 339/09, s. 2

4. A speed limit sign shall be erected on the right side of the highway, facing approaching traffic, not more than 4.5 metres from the roadway, and the bottom edge of the sign shall be not less than 1.5 metres or more than 2.5 metres above the level of the roadway.

5. (1) Where the council of a municipality designates a portion of a highway under subsection 128(5) of the Act, a speed limit sign,

    (a) that,

        (i) has the dimensions and bears the markings as illustrated in Figure A,

        (ii) is electrically illuminated from within the sign and legible to approaching drivers only when the sign is illuminated, or

        (iii) is a mechanically operated louvered type sign which displays the prescribed markings only during the period of operation; or

    (b) that,

        (i) has the dimensions and bears the markings as illustrated in Figure B, or

        (ii) is similar to the sign referred to in subclause (i) except that it does not include a tab sign bearing the legend "km/h",

shall be erected in accordance with section 4 at the commencement of the portion of the highway so designated.

Figure A

Figure B

(1.0.1) [Repealed O. Reg. 175/08, s. 3(7).]

(1.1) Despite subsection (1), where the council of a municipality that is in an area designated by the *French Language Services Act* designates a portion of a highway under subsection 128(5) of the Act, there shall be erected in accordance with section 4 at the commencement of the designated portion a speed limit sign,

    (a) that,

        (i) has the dimensions and bears the markings as illustrated in Figure A to subsection (1), and

(ii) is either electrically illuminated from within and legible to approaching drivers only when illuminated or is a mechanically operated louvered type sign that displays the prescribed markings only during the period of operation; or

(b) that,

(i) has the dimensions and bears the markings as illustrated in Figure C, or

(ii) is similar to the sign in Figure C except that it does not include a tab sign bearing the legend "km/h".

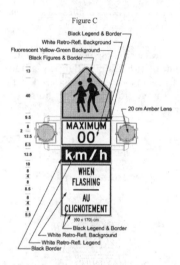

Figure C

(1.2) [Repealed O. Reg. 175/08, s. 3(7).]

(2) A sign referred to in clause (1)(a) or (1.1)(a) shall be illuminated or actuated and legible during the hours prescribed by by-law under subsection 128(5) of the Act on days during which school is regularly held.

(3) The flashing amber signals on a sign referred to in clause (1)(b) or (1.1)(b) shall be actuated during the hours prescribed by by-law under subsection 128(5) of the Act on days during which school is regularly held.

(4) [Repealed O. Reg. 175/08, s. 3(5).]

(5) A sign referred to in clauses (1)(a) and (b) shall be not less than 30 centimetres in height and not less than 60 centimetres in width and bear the legend "MAXIMUM" in black letters not less than 8 centimetres in height and display the speed limit prescribed by by-law in black numerals not less than 12.5 centimetres in height on a white background.

(5.1) A sign referred to in clauses (1.1)(a) and (b) shall be not less than 30 centimetres in height and not less than 60 centimetres in width, shall bear the legend

"MAXIMUM" in black letters not less than 8 centimetres in height and shall display the speed limit prescribed by by-law in black numerals not less than 12.5 centimetres in height on a white background.

(6) A speed limit sign as prescribed in section 1 shall be erected at the termination of the designated portion of the highway, except that the maximum speed shown thereon shall be the appropriate speed limit for the adjoining portion of the highway.

(7) Sections 1, 2 and 3 do not apply to a sign erected under subsection (1) or (1.1).

(8) [Repealed O. Reg. 175/08, s. 3(7).].
          O. Reg. 444/93, s. 1; 246/03, s. 1; 175/08, s. 3 [Corr. by CTR 13 JN 08 - 1]; 339/09, s. 3

[Editor's Note: Section 5.1 was incorrectly printed in the Ontario Gazette as 5. It has been corrected in this publication.]

5.1 (1) If the Minister prescribes a rate of speed of 60 kilometres per hour for motor vehicles driven on a portion of the King's Highway adjacent to a school, a speed limit sign shall be erected in accordance with section 4 at the start of the portion of the highway designated and have the dimensions and bear the markings as illustrated in the following Figure:

(1.1) Despite subsection (1), if the Minister prescribes a rate of speed of 60 kilometres per hour for motor vehicles driven on a portion of the King's Highway adjacent to a school that is in an area designated by the *French Language Services Act*, a speed limit sign shall be erected in accordance with section 4 at the start of the portion of the highway designated and have the dimensions and bear the markings as illustrated in the following Figure:

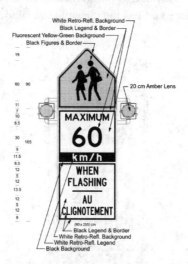

(1.2) [Repealed O. Reg. 175/08, s. 4(4).]

(2) If a sign referred to in subsection (1) or (1.1) is erected, the flashing amber signals on the sign shall be actuated on days during which school is regularly held between the hours specified in section 7 of Regulation 619 of the Revised Regulations of Ontario, 1990.

(3) A sign referred to in subsection (1) or (1.1) shall be not less than 210 centimetres in height and not less than 90 centimetres in width, bear the legend MAXIMUM in black letters not less than 10 centimetres in height and display in black numerals not less than 30 centimetres in height on a white background the numerals "60".

(4) A speed limit sign as prescribed in section 1 shall be erected at the end of the designated portion of the highway, except that the maximum speed shown shall be the appropriate speed limit for the adjoining portion of the highway.

(5) Sections 1, 2 and 3 do not apply to a sign erected under subsection (1) or (1.1).

(6) [Repealed O. Reg. 175/08, s. 4(4).]

O. Reg. 519/93, s. 1; 332/98, s. 1; 246/03, s. 2; 175/08, s. 4; 339/09, s. 4

COMMUNITY SAFETY ZONE SIGNS

5.2 (1) Where a part of a highway is designated as a community safety zone under subsection 214.1(1) or (2) of the Act, signs shall be erected in accordance with this section.

(2) A sign shall be erected at the commencement of the community safety zone that,

    (a) faces approaching traffic on the right side of the highway at the commencement of the portion of the highway so designated;

(b) is not less than 60 centimetres in width and 90 centimetres in height; and

(c) bears the markings and has the dimensions as illustrated in the following Figure:

(3) In an area designated by the *French Language Services Act*, an additional sign shall be erected at the commencement of the community safety zone that,

(a) faces approaching traffic on to the right of the sign prescribed in subsection (2);

(b) is not less than 75 centimetres in width and 90 centimetres in height; and

(c) bears the markings and has the dimensions as illustrated in the following Figure:

(4) A sign shall be erected at the end of the community safety zone that,

    (a) faces approaching traffic on the right side of the highway at the end of the portion of the highway so designated;

    (b) is not less than 60 centimetres in width and 90 centimetres in height; and

    (c) bears the markings and has the dimensions as illustrated in the following Figure:

(5) In an area designated under the *French Language Services Act*, an additional sign shall be erected at the end of the community safety zone that,

   (a) faces approaching traffic on the right of the sign prescribed in subsection (4);

   (b) is not less than 75 centimetres in width and 90 centimetres in height; and

   (c) bears the markings and has the dimensions as illustrated in the following Figure:

(6) If the part of the highway designated as a community safety zone is 1,000 metres long or more, signs shall be erected in accordance with subsection (8) that,

   (a) face approaching traffic in each direction of travel on the right side of the highway;

   (b) are not less than 60 centimetres in width and 90 centimetres in height; and

   (c) bear the markings and have the dimensions as illustrated in the following Figure:

(7) If the part of the highway designated as a community safety zone is 1,000 metres long or more in an area designated under the *French Language Services Act*, additional signs shall be erected in accordance with subsection (8) that,

(a) face approaching traffic on the right of each sign prescribed in subsection (6);

(b) are not less than 75 centimetres in width and 90 centimetres in height; and

(c) bear the markings and have the dimensions as illustrated in the following Figure:

(8) Signs erected under subsections (6) and (7) shall be not more than 300 metres apart from each other where the speed limit for the part of the highway on which the sign is erected is 60 kilometres an hour or less, and not more than 2 kilometres apart from each other where the speed limit for the part of the highway on which the sign is erected is more than 60 kilometres an hour.

O. Reg. 380/98, s. 1; 339/09, s. 5

STOP SIGNS

6. (1) A stop sign erected before August 1, 1993 shall,

(a) be octagonal in shape, not less than 60 centimetres in height and width and bear the word "stop" in white retro-reflective letters not less than 20 centimetres in height on a background of red retro-reflective material; or

(b) be octagonal in shape, not less than 60 centimetres in height and width and bear the words "stop" and "arrêt" in white retro-reflective letters on a background of red retro-reflective material.

(2) A stop sign erected on or after August 1, 1993 shall be as described in clause (1)(a) and illustrated in the following Figure:

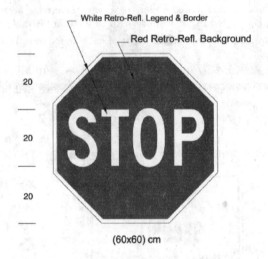

White Retro-Refl. Legend & Border

Red Retro-Refl. Background

20

20

20

(60x60) cm

(3) On or after August 1, 2015, no stop sign shall be valid except as described and illustrated in subsection (2).

O. Reg. 444/93, s. 2; 261/08, s. 1; 339/09, s. 6

7. A stop sign shall be erected on the right side of the highway, facing approaching traffic, at a point not less than 1.5 metres and not more than 15 metres from the intersecting roadway or the nearest rail at a railway crossing.

O. Reg. 63/06, s. 1

8. A stop sign shall be erected so that the left edge of the sign shall be not more than 4 metres from the edge of the roadway.

O. Reg. 63/06, s. 2

9. A stop sign shall be erected so that the bottom edge is not less than 1.5 metres and not more than 2.5 metres above the level of the roadway.

10. When all approaches to an intersection are controlled by stop signs, an All-Way tab sign,

(a) as illustrated in the following Figure, may be appended to the stop signs, directly below them:

(15 × 30) cm

(b) as illustrated in the following Figure, may be appended to the stop signs, directly below them, in an area designated by the *French Language Services Act*:

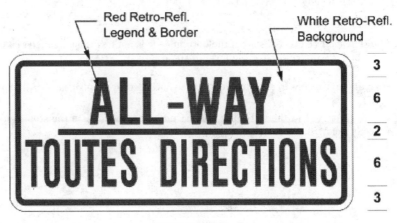

(20 x 45) cm

O. Reg. 444/93, s. 3; 339/09, s. 7

11. (1) A school crossing stop sign shall be octagonal in shape, not less than 30 centimetres in height and not less than 30 centimetres in width.

(2) Each face of a school crossing stop sign shall bear the word "stop" in white retro-reflective letters not less than 12.5 centimetres in height on a background of red retro-reflective material.

(3) Each face of a school crossing stop sign may bear a single flashing red light centred above or below the word "stop" that is visible to the traffic approaching the sign.

O. Reg. 380/02, s. 1; 63/06, s. 3

12. Sections 45 and 46 do not apply to a school crossing stop sign.

STOPPING SIGNS

13. A sign prohibiting stopping shall,

> **(a) be not less than 30 centimetres in height and not less than 30 centimetres in width; and**

> **(b) bear the markings and have the dimensions prescribed in the following Figure:**

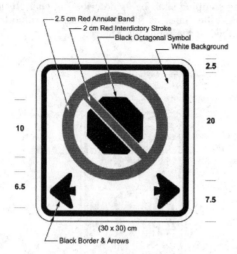

O. Reg. 339/09, s. 8

14. (1) A sign restricting stopping shall,

(a) be not less than 45 centimetres in height and not less than 30 centimetres in width; and

(b) bear the markings and indicate the times at which stopping is prohibited and have the dimensions as prescribed in the following Figure:

(2) Despite subsection (1), in an area designated by the *French Language Services Act,* **a sign restricting stopping shall be as described in clause (1)(a) and bear the markings and indicate the times at which stopping is prohibited and have the dimensions as prescribed in the following Figure:**

O. Reg. 449/93, s. 4; 339/09, s. 9

15. (1) Every sign erected on or after the 28th day of March, 1986 that prohibits standing shall,

    (a) be not less than 30 centimetres in height and 30 centimetres in width; and

    (b) bear the markings and have the dimensions as illustrated in the following Figure:

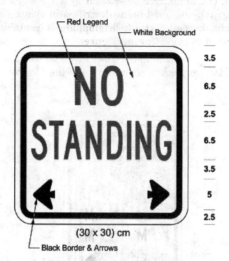

(30 x 30) cm

(1.1) Despite subsection (1), in an area designated by the *French Language Services Act*, a sign that prohibits standing shall,

　　(a) be not less than 60 centimetres in height and not less than 30 centimetres in width; and

　　(b) bear the markings and have the dimensions as illustrated in the following Figure:

(30 x 60) cm

(2) Every sign erected on or after the 28th day of March, 1986 that restricts standing shall,

(a) be not less than 45 centimetres in height and not less than 30 centimetres in width; and

(b) bear the markings, indicating the times at which standing is prohibited and have the dimensions as illustrated in the following Figure:

(30 x 45) cm

(2.1) Despite subsection (2), in an area designated by the *French Language Services Act*, a sign that restricts standing shall,

(a) be not less than 75 centimetres in height and not less than 30 centimetres in width; and

(b) bear the markings and indicate the times at which standing is prohibited and have the dimensions as illustrated in the following Figure:

(3) On or after the 1st day of December, 1992, no sign restricting or prohibiting standing shall be valid except as prescribed and illustrated in subsection (1) or (2).

O. Reg. 699/92, s. 1; 444/93, s. 5; 339/09, s. 10

YIELD RIGHT-OF-WAY SIGNS

16. A yield right-of-way sign may be erected on a highway that intersects another highway.

17. A yield right-of-way sign shall,

(a) be in the shape of an equilateral triangle with sides not less than 75 centimetres in length;

(b) bear the marking and have the dimensions as prescribed and illustrated in the following Figure:

75 x 75 cm TRIANGULAR

10

75

2 cm White Retro-Refl. Border
10 cm Red Retro-Refl. Triangular Outline
White Retro-Refl. Centre

(c) be erected so that the bottom point is not less than 1.5 metres and not more than 2.5 metres above the level of the roadway; and

(d) be erected facing approaching traffic on the right side of the highway at a point not less than 1.5 metres and not more than 15 metres from the roadway of the intersecting highway or on a median not less than 1.5 metres and not more than 15 metres from a roadway of the intersecting divided highway.

O. Reg. 339/09, s. 11

18. (1) A yield right-of-way sign referred to in section 17 may be accompanied immediately below by a tab sign bearing the markings and having the dimensions as illustrated in the following Figure:

Red Retro-Refl. Border & Legend

White Retro-Refl. Background

6.25

10

6.25

(22.5 x 45) cm

(2) In an area designated by the *French Language Services Act*, a yield right-of-way sign referred to in section 17 may be accompanied immediately below by a tab sign bearing the markings and having the dimensions as illustrated in the following Figure:

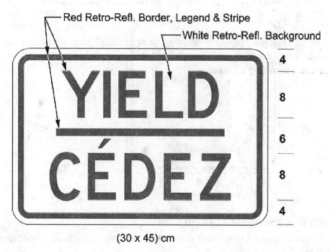

Red Retro-Refl. Border, Legend & Stripe

White Retro-Refl. Background

4

8

6

8

4

(30 x 45) cm

O. Reg. 444/93, s. 6; 339/09, s. 12

19. A yield right-of-way sign shall be erected so that the left edge of the sign is not more than 4 metres from the edge of the roadway.

O. Reg. 175/08, s. 5

PEDESTRIAN CROSSOVER

20. [Revoked R.R.O. 1990, Reg. 615, s. 20.10.]

20.1–20.3 [Repealed O. Reg. 407/15, s. 1.]

20.4–20.6 [Revoked R.R.O. 1990, Reg. 615, s. 20.10.]

20.7–20.9 [Repealed O. Reg. 175/08, s. 8.]

20.10 [Repealed O. Reg. 407/15, s. 1.]

TURN SIGNS

21. (1) A no right turn sign shall,

    (a) be not less than 60 centimetres in height and not less than 60 centimetres in width; and

    (b) include the markings and the dimensions as described and illustrated in the following Figure:

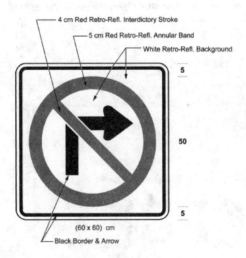

(2) Every sign that restricts a right turn shall,

    (a) be not less than 90 centimetres in height and not less than 60 centimetres in width; and

    (b) bear the markings and indicate the times at which a right turn is prohibited and have the dimensions as illustrated in the following Figure:

Text alternative: Illustration of a sign with a no right turn symbol consisting of a right turn black arrow inside a red circle with an interdictory stroke, on white retro-reflective background with a black border and the text "7 AM - 9 AM", "4 PM - 6 PM", "MON-FRI". Size indicated (60 x 90) cm. This text alternative is provided for convenience only and does not form part of the official law.

(2.1) Despite subsection (2), a sign that restricts a right turn in an area designated by the *French Language Services Act* shall be as described in clause (2)(a) and bear the markings and indicate the times at which a right turn is prohibited and have the dimensions as illustrated in the following Figure:

Text alternative: Illustration of a sign with a no right turn symbol consisting of a right turn black arrow inside a red circle with an interdictory stroke, on white retro-reflective background with a black border and the text "7 AM - 9 AM", "4 PM - 6 PM", "MON-FRI / LUN-VEN". Size indicated (60 x 90) cm. This text alternative is provided for convenience only and does not form part of the official law.

(3) Every sign erected on or after September 1, 1998 that prohibits a vehicle from making a right turn at a signalized intersection when the signal indication is red shall,

    (a) be not less than 90 centimetres in height and not less than 60 centimetres in width; and

    (b) include the markings and dimensions as illustrated in the following Figure:

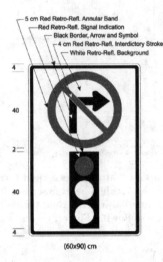

(60x90) cm

(3.1) On or after January 1, 2003, no sign prohibiting a right turn at a signalized intersection when the signal indication is red shall be valid except as prescribed and illustrated in subsection (3).

(3.2) Before January 1, 2003, no sign prohibiting a right turn at a signalized intersection when the signal indication is red, other than a sign as prescribed and illustrated in subsection (3), shall be valid unless it was authorized by this Regulation immediately before September 1, 1998.

(4) A no left turn sign shall,

    (a) be not less than 60 centimetres in height and not less than 60 centimetres in width; and

    (b) include the markings and the dimensions as described and illustrated in the following Figure:

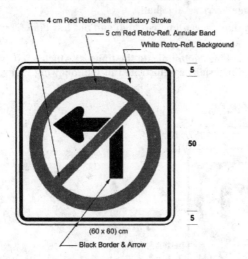

(5) Every sign that restricts a left turn shall,

(a) be not less than 90 centimetres in height and not less than 60 centimetres in width; and

(b) bear the markings and indicate the times at which a left turn is prohibited and have the dimensions as illustrated in the following Figure:

(5.1) Despite subsection (5), a sign that restricts a left turn in an area designated by the *French Language Services Act* shall,

> **(a) be not less than 90 centimetres high and not less than 60 centimetres wide; and**

> **(b) bear the markings and indicate the times at which a left turn is prohibited and have the dimensions as illustrated in the following Figure:**

Text alternative: Illustration of a sign with a no left turn symbol consisting of a left turn black arrow inside a red circle with an interdictory stroke, on white retro-reflective background with a black border and the text "7 AM - 9 AM", "4 PM - 6 PM", "MON-FRI/LUN-VEN". Size indicated (60 x 90) cm. This text alternative is provided for convenience only and does not form part of the official law.

(6) Every sign erected on or after September 1, 1998 that prohibits a vehicle from making a left turn at a signalized intersection when the signal indication is red shall,

> **(a) be not less than 90 centimetres in height and not less than 60 centimetres in width; and**

> **(b) include the markings and dimensions as illustrated in the following Figure:**

(6.1) On or after January 1, 2003, no sign prohibiting a left turn at a signalized intersection when the signal indication is red shall be valid except as prescribed and illustrated in subsection (6).

(6.2) Before January 1, 2003, no sign prohibiting a left turn at a signalized intersection when the signal indication is red, other than a sign as prescribed and illustrated in subsection (6), shall be valid unless it was authorized by this Regulation immediately before September 1, 1998.

O. Reg. 699/92, s. 3; 443/93, s. 9; 332/98, s. 2; 339/09, s. 15; 93/15, s. 1

22. (1) A sign that prohibits a vehicle from making a right turn or proceeding straight through an intersection shall,

(a) be not less than 60 centimetres in height and not less than 60 centimetres in width; and

(b) include the markings and the dimensions as described and illustrated in the following Figure:

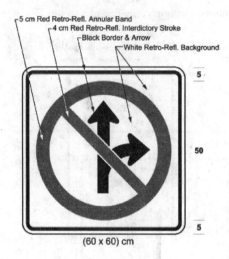

(60 x 60) cm

(2) A sign that prohibits a vehicle from making a left turn or proceeding straight through an intersection shall,

    (a) be not less than 60 centimetres in height and not less than 60 centimetres in width; and

    (b) include the markings and the dimensions as described and illustrated in the following Figure:

(60 x 60) cm

(3) A no turn sign shall,

    (a) be not less than 60 centimetres in height and not less than 60 centimetres in width; and

    (b) include the markings and the dimensions as described and illustrated in the following Figure:

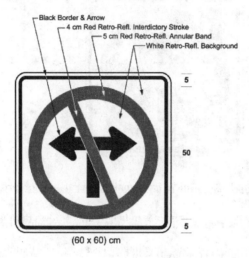

(60 x 60) cm

(4) No sign that,

    (a) prohibits a vehicle from making a right turn or proceeding straight through an intersection shall be valid except as prescribed and illustrated in subsection (1);

    (b) prohibits a vehicle from making a left turn or proceeding straight through an intersection shall be valid except as prescribed and illustrated in subsection (2); and

    (c) prohibits both a left and a right turn shall be valid except as prescribed and illustrated in subsection (3).

(5) Every sign that prohibits a vehicle from proceeding straight through an intersection shall,

    (a) be not less than 60 centimetres in height and not less than 60 centimetres in width; and

    (b) include the markings and the dimensions as illustrated in the following Figure:

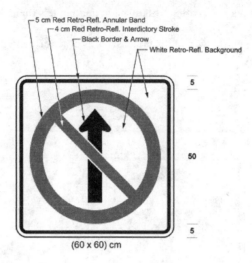

(6) Subsection (5) does not apply to a DO NOT ENTER sign as prescribed and illustrated in section 31.

(7) Every sign that restricts a vehicle from proceeding straight through an intersection shall,

    (a) be not less than 90 centimetres in height and not less than 60 centimetres in width; and

    (b) include the markings and the dimensions as illustrated in the following Figure:

Text alternative: Illustration of a sign with a no proceeding straight symbol consisting of a black arrow proceeding straight, inside a red a circle with an interdictory stroke on white retro-reflective background with a black border, and the text "7 AM - 9 AM", "4 PM - 6 PM", and "MON-FRI". Indicated size (60 x 90) cm. This text alternative is provided for convenience only and does not form part of the official law.

(7.1) Despite subsection (7), a sign erected in an area designated by the *French Language Services Act* that restricts a vehicle from proceeding straight through an intersection shall,

    (a) be not less than 90 centimetres in height and not less than 60 centimetres in width; and

    (b) include the markings and the dimensions as illustrated in the following Figure:

4 cm Red Retro-Refl. Interdictory Stroke
Black Border, Legend & Arrow
5 cm Red Retro-Refl. Annular Band
White Retro-Refl. Background

(60 x 90) cm

Text alternative: Illustration of a sign with a no proceeding straight symbol consisting of a black arrow proceeding straight, inside a red a circle with an interdictory stroke on white retro-reflective background with a black border, and the text "7 AM - 9 AM", "4 PM - 6 PM", and "MON-FRI/LUN-VEN". Indicated size (60 x 90) cm. This text alternative is provided for convenience only and does not form part of the official law.

(8) [Repealed O. Reg. 332/98, s. 3.]

(9) [Repealed O. Reg. 332/98, s. 3.]

        O. Reg. 699/92, s. 4; 444/93, s. 10; 332/98, s. 3; 339/09, s. 16; 93/15, s. 2

NO U TURN SIGN

23. A No U Turn sign shall,

    (a) be rectangular in shape and shall be not less than 60 centimetres in height and not less than 60 centimetres in width; and

    (b) bear the markings and have the dimensions as prescribed and illustrated in the following Figure:

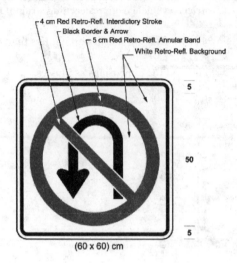

4 cm Red Retro-Refl. Interdictory Stroke
Black Border & Arrow
5 cm Red Retro-Refl. Annular Band
White Retro-Refl. Background

5

50

5

(60 x 60) cm

O. Reg. 339/09, s. 17

PARKING CONTROL SIGNS

24. A sign prohibiting parking shall,

(a) be not less than 30 centimetres in height and not less than 30 centimetres in width; and

(b) bear the markings and have the dimensions as described and illustrated in the following Figure:

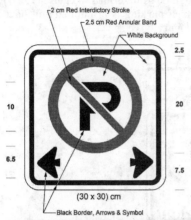

Text alternative: Illustration of a sign with a no parking symbol consisting of a black letter "P" inside a red circle with an interdictory stroke above two black arrows pointing left and right, on a white background with a black border. Indicated size (30 x 30) cm. This text alternative is provided for convenience only and does not form part of the official law.

O. Reg. 339/09, s. 18; 93/15, s. 3

25. (1) A sign restricting parking shall,

    (a) be not less than 45 centimetres in height and not less than 30 centimetres in width; and

    (b) bear the markings and indicate the times at which parking is prohibited and have the dimensions as described in the following Figure:

(2) Despite subsection (1), a sign erected in an area designated by the *French Language Services Act* that restricts parking shall be as described in clause (1)(a), bear the markings and indicate the times at which parking is prohibited and have the dimensions as illustrated in the following Figure:

O. Reg. 444/93, s. 11; 339/09, s. 19

26. (1) A sign permitting parking for a specified period of time shall,

(a) be not less than 45 centimetres in height and not less than 30 centimetres in width; and

(b) bear the markings, indicate the times at which parking is permitted, the maximum period during which a vehicle may be parked and have the dimensions as prescribed in the following Figure:

(2) Despite subsection (1), a sign erected in an area designated by the *French Language Services Act* that permits parking for a specified period of time shall be as described in clause (1)(a) and bear the markings, indicate the times at which parking is prohibited, indicate the maximum period during which a vehicle may be parked and have the dimensions as prescribed in the following Figure:

O. Reg. 444/93, s. 12; 63/06, s. 4; 339/09, s. 20

27. (1) A sign prohibiting parking except in an emergency shall,

(a) be not less than 90 centimetres in height and not less than 60 centimetres in width; and

(b) bear the markings and have the dimensions as described and illustrated in the following Figure:

(2) Despite subsection (1), a sign erected in an area designated by the *French Language Services Act* that prohibits parking except in an emergency shall be as described in clause (1)(a), be erected in combination with it, below it or to the right of it or up to 100 metres beyond it, and have the dimensions as illustrated in the following Figure:

4 cm Red Retro-Refl. Interdictory Stroke
Black Letter "P"
6 cm Red Retro-Refl. Annular Band
White Retro-Refl. Background

6.5

21

42

3.5
8
4
8
4
8
6

STATIONNEMENT
D'URGENCE
SEULEMENT

(60 x 90) cm
Black Border & Legend

Text alternative: Illustration of a sign with a no parking symbol consisting of a black letter "P" inside a red circle with an interdictory stroke, above the text "STATIONNEMENT D'URGENCE SEULEMENT", on white retro-reflective background with a black border. Indicated size (60 x 90) cm. This text alternative is provided for convenience only and does not form part of the official law.

O. Reg. 444/93, s. 13; 339/09, s. 21; 93/15, s. 4

SCHOOL BUS LOADING ZONE

28. School bus loading zones may be designated only,

    (a) on one side of a highway; and

    (b) on the side of the highway on which,

        (i) a school is situated, or

        (ii) a building or facility is situated which is frequently visited by school children under supervision of their teachers.

29. **(1)** A school bus loading zone sign shall,

    (a) be not less than 45 centimetres in height and not less than 30 centimetres in width;

    (b) bear the words "school bus loading zone" in black letters not less than 4 centimetres in height on a white retro-reflective background; and

    (c) bear a single headed or double headed arrow in black not less than 5.5 centimetres in height,

as illustrated in the following Figure:

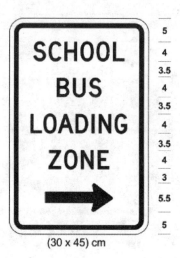

(30 x 45) cm

(1.1) Despite subsection (1), a school bus loading zone sign erected in an area designated by the *French Language Services Act* shall,

(a) be not less than 45 centimetres in height and not less than 60 centimetres in width;

(b) bears the words "school bus loading zone — zone d'arrêt des autobus scolaires" in black letters not less than 4 centimetres in height on a white retro-reflective background;

(c) bear two single headed arrows in black not less than 5.5 centimetres in height; and

(d) be as illustrated in the following Figure:

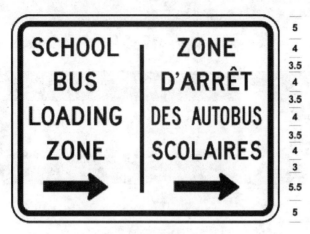

(45 x 60) cm

(2) One sign with a single headed arrow pointing towards the loading zone shall be erected at each end of a school bus loading zone and, where the length of the loading zone exceeds 60 metres, signs with double headed arrows shall be erected at intervals of no more than 45 metres.

O. Reg. 444/93, s. 14; 339/09, s. 22

ONE-WAY SIGN

30. (1) A One-Way sign shall,

(a) be rectangular in shape and shall be not less than 30 centimetres in height and not less than 90 centimetres in width; and

(b) bear the marking and have the dimensions as prescribed and illustrated in the following Figure:

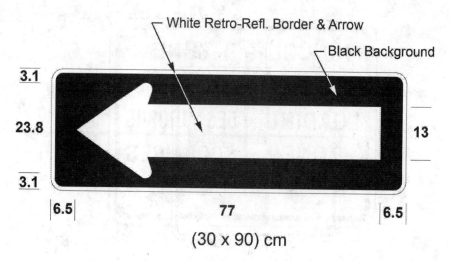

(30 x 90) cm

(2) A One-Way Sign shall be used, with the arrow pointing in the appropriate direction, to indicate the highways upon which traffic is allowed to travel in one direction only.

O. Reg. 339/09, s. 23; 93/15, s. 5

31. **A Do Not Enter Sign shall,**

(a) be rectangular in shape and shall be not less than 60 centimetres in width and 60 centimetres in height; and

(b) bear the markings and have the dimensions as prescribed and illustrated in the following Figure:

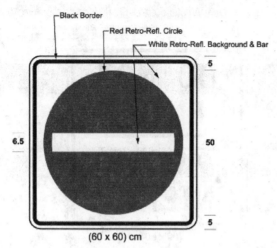

(60 x 60) cm

O. Reg. 339/09, s. 24

32. (1) A sign referred to in section 31 may be accompanied immediately below by a tab bearing the markings and having the dimensions as illustrated in the following Figure:

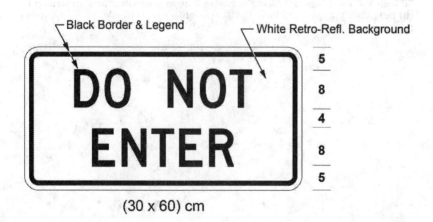

(30 x 60) cm

(2) A sign referred to in section 31 that is erected in an area designated by the *French Language Services Act* may be accompanied immediately below by a tab sign bearing the markings and having the dimensions illustrated in the following Figure:

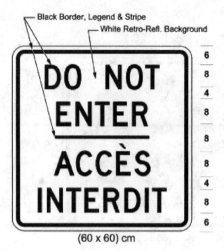

(60 x 60) cm

O. Reg. 444/93, s. 15; 339/09, s. 25; 93/15, s. 6

TRUCK SIGN

33. A No Heavy Trucks Sign shall,

(a) be not less than 60 centimetres in width and not less than 60 centimetres in height; and

(b) bear the markings and have the dimensions as prescribed and illustrated in the following Figure:

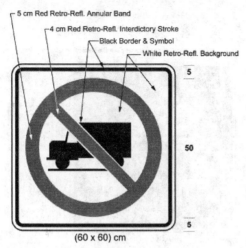

5 cm Red Retro-Refl. Annular Band

4 cm Red Retro-Refl. Interdictory Stroke

Black Border & Symbol

White Retro-Refl. Background

5

50

5

(60 x 60) cm

O. Reg. 339/09, s. 26

34. (1) A Lane Designation Sign shall be used to indicate by means of a single arrow or a combination of arrows the only permitted movement or movements by vehicles on one or more lanes of a highway marked with the sign.

(2) A Lane Designation Sign shall,

(a) in the case of Figures 1 to 6 and Figure 8, be not less than 60 centimetres in height and not less than 60 centimetres in width;

(b) in the case of Figure 7, be not less than 90 centimetres in height and not less than 90 centimetres in width;

(c) in the case of Figures 9 and 10, be not less than 150 centimetres in height and not less than 90 centimetres in width; and

(d) bear the markings and have the dimensions as prescribed and illustrated in one of the following Figures:

Figure 1

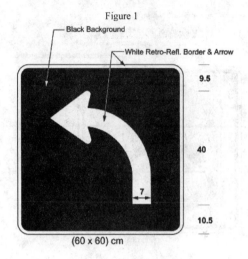

Figure 1
— Black Background
— White Retro-Refl. Border & Arrow
9.5
40
7
10.5
(60 x 60) cm

Figure 2

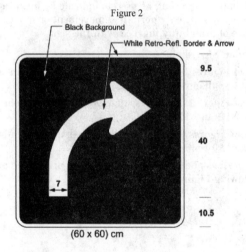

Figure 2
— Black Background
— White Retro-Refl. Border & Arrow
9.5
40
7
10.5
(60 x 60) cm

Figure 3

Figure 3

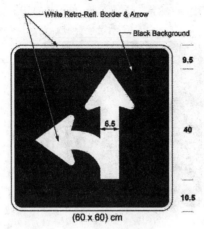

White Retro-Refl. Border & Arrow

Black Background

9.5

6.5

40

10.5

(60 x 60) cm

Figure 4

Figure 4

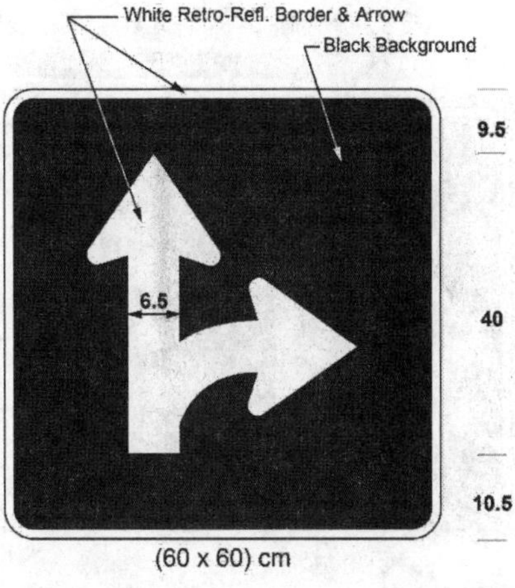

White Retro-Refl. Border & Arrow

Black Background

9.5

6.5

40

10.5

(60 x 60) cm

Figure 5

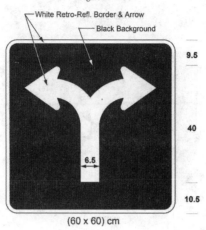

Figure 5

(60 x 60) cm

Figure 6

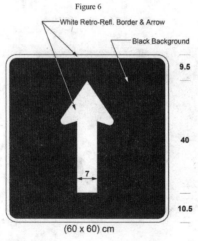

Figure 6

(60 x 60) cm

Figure 7

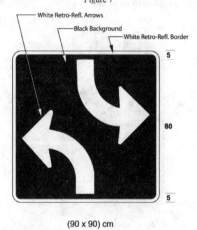

Figure 7

White Retro-Refl. Arrows

Black Background

White Retro-Refl. Border

5

80

5

(90 x 90) cm

Figure 8

Figure 8

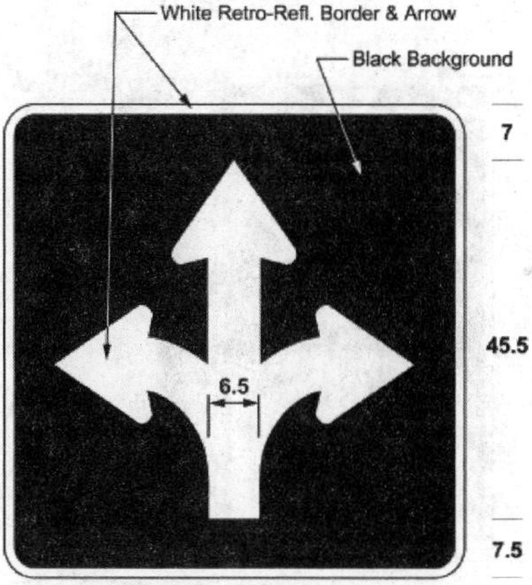

White Retro-Refl. Border & Arrow

Black Background

7

45.5

6.5

7.5

(60 x 60) cm

Figure 9

Figure 9
White Retro-Refl. Border & Arrows
Black Background

CENTRE
LANE
ONLY

(90 x 150) cm

White Retro-Refl. Background
Black Border & Legend

Figure 10

Figure 10
White Retro-Refl. Border, Arrow & Background
Black Background

VOIE
MÉDIANE
SEULEMENT

(90 x 150) cm

Black Border & Legend

(3) A Lane Designation Sign in Figure 7 signifies that the lane marked with the sign shall be used by a vehicle for the purpose only of making a left turn.

(4) A Lane Designation sign,

    (a) may, in the case of Figures 1 to 6 and Figure 8, be erected over the lane or be ground mounted;

    (b) shall, in the case of Figure 7, be erected directly over a two-way left turn lane;

(c) shall, in the case of Figure 9, be ground mounted to the right of the highway, facing the approaching traffic; and

(d) shall, in the case of Figure 10, be ground mounted to the right of the highway, facing the approaching traffic, directly below or up to 100 metres beyond the sign in Figure 9.

(5) Figures 1 and 2 of clause (2)(d) may display a tab sign not less than 30 centimetres in height and not less than 60 centimetres in width immediately below Figures 1 and 2 and shall,

(a) in the case of Figure 1, bear the legend "Left Lane"; and

(b) in the case of Figure 2, bear the legend "Right Lane".

Figure 1

Figure 1

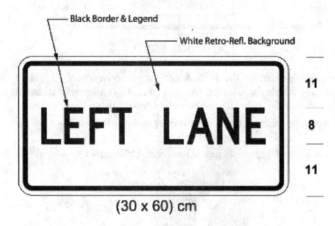

Black Border & Legend

White Retro-Refl. Background

11

8

11

(30 x 60) cm

Figure 2

Figure 2

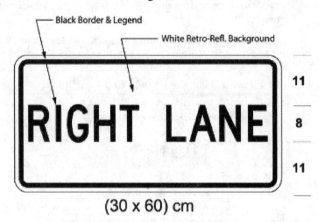

(30 x 60) cm

(6) In an area designated by the *French Language Services Act*, Figures 1 and 2 of clause (2)(d) may display a tab sign not less than 45 centimetres in height and not less than 60 centimetres in width immediately below those Figures that,

> **(a)** in the case of Figure 1, bears the legend "Left Lane — Voie de gauche"; and

> **(b)** in the case of Figure 2, bears the legend "Right Lane — Voie de droite".

Figure 1

(45 x 60) cm

Figure 2

Figure 2

Black Border, Legend & Stripe

White Retro-Refl. Background

(45 x 60) cm

O. Reg. 444/93, s. 16; 909/93; 339/09, s. 27; 93/15, s. 7

DO NOT PASS SIGN

35. (1) A Do Not Pass Sign erected on or after the 28th day of March, 1986 shall,

(a) be not less than 60 centimetres in height and not less than 60 centimetres in width; and

(b) bear the markings and have the dimensions illustrated in the following Figure:

Figure 3

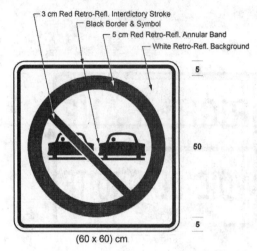

(60 x 60) cm

O. Reg. 339/09, s. 28; 93/15, s. 8

NO BICYCLES SIGN

36. A Bicycle Prohibition Sign erected on or after the 28th day of March, 1986 shall,

(a) be not less than 60 centimetres in height and not less than 60 centimetres in width; and

(b) bear the markings and have the dimensions as illustrated in the following Figure:

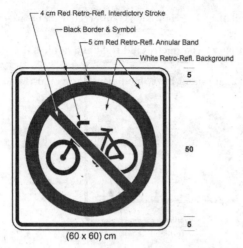

(60 x 60) cm

O. Reg. 339/09, s. 29; 93/15, s. 9

37. A Pedestrian Prohibition Sign erected on or after the 28th day of March, 1986 shall,

(a) be not less than 60 centimetres in height and not less than 60 centimetres in width; and

(b) bear the markings and have the dimensions as illustrated in the following Figure:

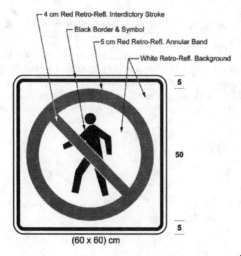

(60 x 60) cm

O. Reg. 339/09, s. 30

PEDESTRIAN AND BICYCLE PROHIBITION SIGN

38. A Pedestrian and Bicycle Prohibition Sign erected on or after the 28th day of March, 1986 shall,

(a) be not less than 60 centimetres in height and not less than 60 centimetres in width; and

(b) bear the markings and have the dimensions as illustrated in the following Figure:

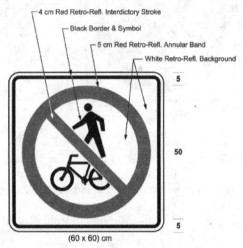

(60 x 60) cm

O. Reg. 339/09, s. 31

INTERDICTORY AND PERMISSIVE SYMBOLS

39. (1) An annular red band with a diagonal red stroke running through the centre of the band at 45 degrees to the horizontal, as illustrated in the following Figures or as close to as practicable so as not to obliterate the symbol, is an interdictory symbol and where an interdictory symbol is used on the sign prescribed by this Regulation, the symbol signifies that whatever is depicted within the symbol is prohibited:

5 cm RED REFL. ANNULAR BAND
WITH 4 cm INTERDICTORY STROKE

(2) An annular green band as illustrated in the following Figure is a symbol that when used on a sign prescribed by this Regulation signifies that whatever is depicted within the symbol is permitted.

Symbol

5 cm GREEN REFL. ANNULAR BAND

O. Reg. 339/09, s. 32

LOAD RESTRICTION SIGN

40. (1) A Load Restriction sign erected on or after January 1, 2015 shall bear the markings and have the dimensions as illustrated in the following Figure:

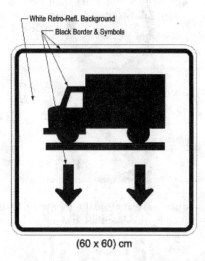

(60 x 60) cm

(2) A Load Restriction sign described in subsection (1) shall have one or both of the following Figures appended to it:

(30 x 60) cm

(30 x 60) cm

(3) [Repealed O. Reg. 175/08, s. 9(3).]

(4) On and after January 1, 2015, every Load Restriction sign shall bear the markings and have the dimensions as prescribed and illustrated in subsection (1).

O. Reg. 175/08, s. 9(1), (3); 339/09, s. 33

40.1 (1) A Load Restriction sign erected on or after January 1, 2015 in an area designated by the *French Language Services Act* shall bear the markings and have the dimensions as prescribed and illustrated in subsection 40(1).

(2) A Load Restriction sign described in subsection (1) shall have one or both of the following Figures appended to it:

(30 x 60) cm

(3) [Repealed O. Reg. 175/08, s. 10(3).]

(4) On and after January 1, 2015, every Load Restriction sign in an area designated by the *French Language Services Act* shall bear the markings and have the dimensions as prescribed and illustrated in subsection 40(1).

O. Reg. 444/93, s. 17; 175/08, s. 10(1), (3); 339/09, s. 34

GROSS WEIGHT ON BRIDGES SIGN

41. (1) A gross weight on bridges sign shall,

(a) in the case of Figure 1,

(i) be not less than 75 centimetres in height and not less than 60 centimetres in width,

(ii) bear the words "MAXIMUM" and indicate the prescribed maximum gross vehicle weight in tonnes of a vehicle or combination of vehicles permitted on the bridge, and

(iii) bear the markings and have the dimensions as prescribed and illustrated in Figure 1:

Figure 1

White Retro-Refl. Background

Black Legend & Border

MAXIMUM

00

tonnes

10

25

10

(60 x 75) cm

(a.1) [Repealed O. Reg. 246/03, s. 3(3).]

(b) in the case of Figure 2,

   (i) be not less than 150 centimetres in height and not less than 90 centimetres in width,

   (ii) bear the words "MAXIMUM",

   (iii) indicate the prescribed maximum gross vehicle weight in tonnes of a single vehicle permitted on the bridge, opposite the marking of a single vehicle,

   (iv) indicate the prescribed maximum gross vehicle weight in tonnes of a combination of two vehicles permitted on the bridge, opposite the marking of a combination of two vehicles,

   (v) indicate the prescribed maximum gross vehicle weight in tonnes of a combination of three vehicles permitted on the bridge, opposite the marking of a combination of three vehicles, and

   (vi) bear the markings and have the dimensions prescribed and illustrated in Figure 2:

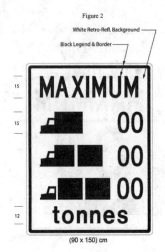

Figure 2

(90 x 150) cm

(b.1) [Repealed O. Reg. 246/03, s. 3(6).]

(1.1) [Repealed O. Reg. 175/08, s. 11(2).]

(2) The prescribed maximum gross vehicle weight indicated on a sign prescribed by this section shall be such weight as is prescribed by a regulation or by-law made under section 123 of the Act.

O. Reg. 444/93, s. 18; 246/03, s. 3; 175/08, s. 11; 339/09, s. 35; 93/15, s. 10

CONSTRUCTION ZONE SIGN

42. (1) A part of a highway that has been designated as a construction zone shall be marked at the commencement and at the end of the construction zone with construction zone signs erected on the right side of the highway, facing approaching traffic and not more than 4.5 metres from the roadway, with the bottom edge of the sign not less than 1.5 metres or more than 2.5 metres above the level of the roadway.

(2) The commencement of a designated construction zone shall be indicated by a sign that has the dimensions and bears the markings as illustrated in the following Figure:

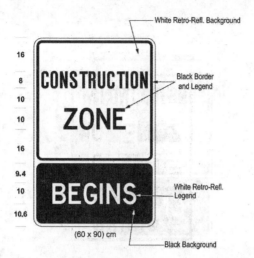

(3) Despite subsection (2), in an area designated in the Schedule to the *French Language Services Act*, the commencement of a designated construction zone shall be indicated by a sign that has the dimensions and bears the markings as illustrated in the Figure to subsection (2) and a sign that has the dimensions and bears the markings as illustrated in the following Figure:

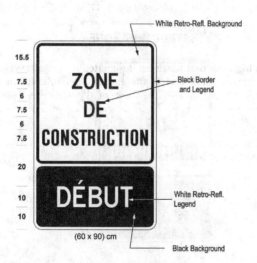

(4) The end of a designated construction zone shall be indicated by a sign that has the dimensions and bears the markings as illustrated in the following Figure:

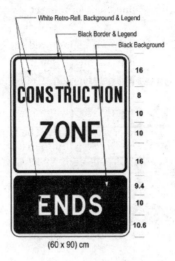

(60 x 90) cm

(5) Despite subsection (4), in an area designated in the Schedule to the *French Language Services Act*, the end of a designated construction zone shall be indicated by a sign that has the dimensions and bears the markings as illustrated in the Figure to subsection (4) and a sign that has the dimensions and bears the markings as illustrated in the following Figure:

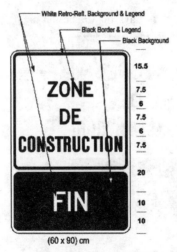

(60 x 90) cm

O. Reg. 63/06, s. 5; 175/08, s. 12; 339/09, s. 36; 93/15, s. 11

42.1 (1) A traffic control stop or slow sign used by a traffic control person or a firefighter in accordance with section 146.1 of the Act shall,

    (a) be octagonal in shape;

    (b) measure 450 millimetres between opposite sides;

    (c) be mounted on a pole that is 1.2 metres long;

    (d) be made of material with at least the rigidity of plywood that is six millimetres thick; and

    (e) be maintained in a clean and legible condition.

(2) One side of a traffic control stop or slow sign shall be high-intensity retro-reflective grade red in colour with the word "stop" in the centre of the sign written in legible high-intensity retro-reflective grade white upper case letters 150 millimetres high.

(3) The other side of a traffic control stop or slow sign shall be retro-reflective fluorescent yellow-green in colour with a black diamond-shaped border that is at least 317 millimetres by 317 millimetres and the word "slow" in the centre of the sign written in legible black upper case letters 120 millimetres high.

O. Reg. 63/06, s. 5; 175/08, s. 13

BUSES EXCEPTED

43. (1) A Buses Excepted Tab Sign erected on or after the 28th day of March, 1986 shall,

    (a) be not less than 30 centimetres in height and not less than 60 centimetres in width; and

    (b) bear the markings and have the dimension as illustrated in the following Figure:

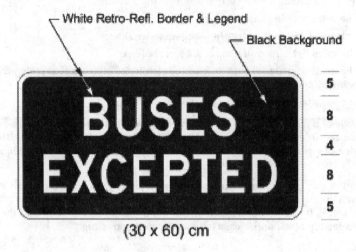

(30 x 60) cm

(1.1) Despite subsection (1), a Buses Excepted Tab Sign in an area designated by the *French Language Services Act* shall,

(a) be not less than 60 centimetres in height and not less than 60 centimetres in width; and

(b) bear the markings and have the dimensions as illustrated in the following Figure:

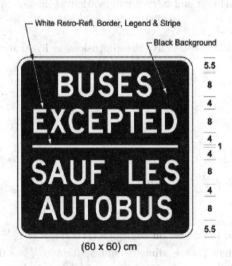

(60 x 60) cm

(2) A Buses Excepted tab sign as prescribed and illustrated in subsection (1) or (1.1) may be erected immediately below a sign prescribed in section 21, 22 or 34.

O. Reg. 444/93, s. 19; 175/08, s. 14; 339/09, s. 37

TOLL HIGHWAYS

[Heading added O. Reg. 335/15, s. 1.]

43.0.1 Definition — In sections 43.1, 43.2, 43.3 and 43.4,

"heavy vehicle" means a vehicle that has a gross weight or a registered gross weight greater than 5,000 kilograms.

O. Reg. 335/15, s. 1

43.1 (1) A sign on a controlled-access highway requiring that a heavy vehicle be equipped with a valid toll device on Highway 407 shall,

(a) be not less than 240 centimetres in height and not less than 540 centimetres in width; and

(b) bear the markings and have the dimensions as illustrated in Figure 1.

(2) In addition to the sign referred to in subsection (1), in an area designated by the *French Language Services Act*, **a sign on a controlled-access highway requiring that a heavy vehicle be equipped with a valid toll device on Highway 407 shall,**

(a) be not less than 240 centimetres in height and not less than 810 centimetres in width; and

(b) bear the markings and have the dimensions as illustrated in Figure 2.

(3) A sign on a highway other than a controlled-access highway requiring that a heavy vehicle be equipped with a valid toll device on Highway 407 shall,

(a) be not less than 120 centimetres and height and not less than 240 centimetres in width; and

(b) bear the markings and have the dimensions as illustrated in Figure 3.

(4) In addition to the sign referred to in subsection (3), in an area designated by the *French Language Services Act*, **a sign on a highway other than a controlled-access highway requiring that a heavy vehicle be equipped with a valid toll device on Highway 407 shall,**

(a) be not less than 180 centimetres in height and not less than 240 centimetres in width; and

(b) bear the markings and have the dimensions as illustrated in Figure 4.

(5) [Repealed O. Reg. 335/15, s. 2(5).]

O. Reg. 148/97, s. 1; 339/09, s. 38; 93/15, s. 12; 335/15, s. 2

43.2 (1) A sign on a controlled-access highway requiring that a heavy vehicle be equipped with a valid toll device on Highway 407 East shall,

(a) be not less than 274.5 centimetres in height and not less than 549 centimetres in width; and

(b) bear the markings and have the dimensions as illustrated in the following Figure:

274.5 x 549 cm

Text alternative: Illustration of sign with "407" inside a Crown symbol above the word "Toll" and the text "Vehicles Over 5 Tonnes Must Have Valid Transponder". The word "Toll" is on a yellow retro-reflective background and the rest of the sign is a white retro-reflective background with a black border. Indicated sign size: (274.5 x 549 cm). This text alternative is provided for convenience only and does not form part of the official law.

(2) A sign on a highway other than a controlled-access highway requiring that a heavy vehicle be equipped with a valid toll device on Highway 407 East shall,

(a) be not less than 180 centimetres in height and not less than 240 centimetres in width; and

(b) bear the markings and have the dimensions as illustrated in the following Figure:

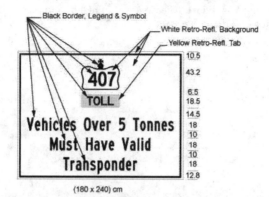

(180 x 240) cm

O. Reg. 335/15, s. 3

43.3 (1) A sign on a controlled-access highway requiring that a heavy vehicle be equipped with a valid toll device on Highway 412 shall,

(a) **be not less than 274.5 centimetres in height and not less than 549 centimetres in width; and**

(b) **bear the markings and have the dimensions as illustrated in the following Figure:**

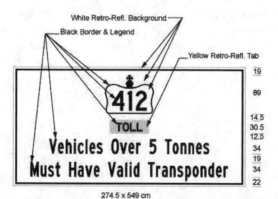

274.5 x 549 cm

(2) A sign on a highway other than a controlled-access highway requiring that a heavy vehicle be equipped with a valid toll device on Highway 412 shall,

    (a) be not less than 180 centimetres in height and not less than 240 centimetres in width; and

    (b) bear the markings and have the dimensions as illustrated in the following Figure:

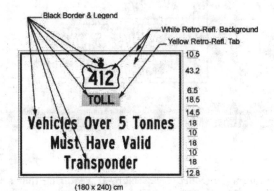

(180 x 240) cm

Text alternative: Illustration of sign with "412" inside a Crown symbol above the word "Toll" and the text "Vehicles Over 5 Tonnes Must Have Valid Transponder". The word "Toll" is on a yellow retro-reflective background and the rest of the sign is a white retro-reflective background with a black border. Indicated sign size: (180 x 240 cm). This text alternative is provided for convenience only and does not form part of the official law.

O. Reg. 335/15, s. 3

43.4 A sign on Highway 401 requiring that a heavy vehicle be equipped with a valid toll device on Highway 407 East and on Highway 412 shall

    (a) be not less than 274.5 centimetres in height and not less than 549 centimetres in width; and

    (b) bear the markings and have the dimensions as illustrated in the following Figure:

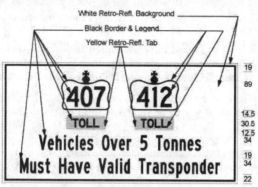

White Retro-Refl. Background
Black Border & Legend
Yellow Retro-Refl. Tab

274.5 x 549 cm

Text alternative: Illustration of sign with "407" and "412", each inside a Crown symbol and each above the word "Toll" and the text "Vehicles Over 5 Tonnes Must Have Valid Transponder". The word "Toll" is on a yellow retro-reflective background and the rest of the sign is a white retro-reflective background with a black border. Indicated sign size: (274.5 x 549 cm). This text alternative is provided for convenience only and does not form part of the official law.

O. Reg. 335/15, s. 3

GENERAL

44. The dimensions of a sign may be greater than the dimensions prescribed and illustrated in this Regulation so long as each dimension is increased and, when increased, has the same relation to the other dimensions of the sign as the dimensions prescribed and illustrated in this Regulation have to each other.

45. A sign prescribed by this Regulation, other than a sign prescribed by section 13, 14, 15, 24, 25, 26 or 27, shall be so placed as to be visible at all times for a distance of at least 60 metres to the traffic approaching the sign.

O. Reg. 175/08, s. 15

46. No person, other than a municipal corporation or other authority having jurisdiction over a highway, shall erect or maintain a sign prescribed by the Act and regulations.

47. Where the characteristics of a highway make it impracticable to place a sign or pavement markings as specified in this Regulation, the sign or pavement markings shall be placed so as to comply as nearly as practicable with those requirements.

O. Reg. 699/92, s. 5

48. No speed limit sign bearing the words "speed limit" is valid.

49. Where a sign is erected in accordance with sections 21, 22, 23 and 34 and the sign is internally illuminated, or changed by means of dot or disc matrix or louvers, the sign shall only be legible to approaching drivers during the time of operation and shall comply as nearly as practicable with those requirements and dimensions as prescribed.

50. (1) A sign prescribed by a provision of this Regulation may show days and times other than those shown in the Figure to that provision.

(2) A sign prescribed by a provision of this Regulation shall show the prescribed speed and not 00 km/h, if that is the speed shown in the Figure to that provision.

(3) The signs prescribed by clauses 41(1)(a) and (b) shall show the prescribed number of tonnes and not 00 tonnes as shown in the Figures to those clauses.

O. Reg. 699/92, s. 6; 175/08, s. 16

51. For the purposes of this Regulation, an area designated by the *French Language Services Act* means an area designated in Schedule 1 to that Act.

O. Reg. 444/93, s. 20

52. A municipality situated in an area designated by the *French Language Services Act* is not required to comply with the sign requirements for such areas unless it has passed a by-law under section 14 of that Act.

O. Reg. 444/93, s. 20

ONT. REG. 616 — SLOW MOVING VEHICLE SIGN

made under the *Highway Traffic Act*

R.R.O. 1990, Reg. 616, as am. O. Reg. 423/96; 407/09 (Fr.); 94/15.

1. (1) The slow moving vehicle sign to be attached to a slow moving vehicle as defined in subsection 76(2) of the Act shall be in the shape of a base-down equilateral triangle, fluorescent yellow-orange in colour with a dark red retro-reflective border, and shall be of the dimensions and size as prescribed and illustrated in the following Figure:

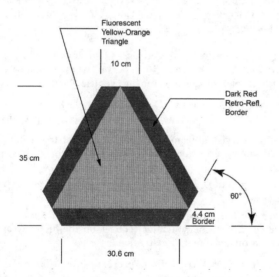

(2) The sign referred to in subsection (1) shall be bonded to a durable rigid weatherproof-base surface.

(3) The brightness of the retro-reflective material referred to in subsection (1) shall comply with the requirements of the Schedule.

O. Reg. 423/96, s. 1; 94/15, s. 1

2. (1) The sign referred to in section 1 shall be mounted,

(a) base down in a plane perpendicular to the direction of travel of the vehicle;

(b) where practicable, on the rear of the vehicle or combination of vehicles at the centre of mass; and

(c) not less than one-half metre or more than 2 metres above the roadway.

(2) The sign shall be clearly visible for a distance of not less than 150 metres from the rear of the vehicle or combination of vehicles.

O. Reg. 423/96, s. 2

3. The sign referred to in section 1 shall be free from dirt and obstruction and shall be so affixed as to be plainly visible at all times and the view of the sign shall not be obscured or obstructed by any part of the vehicle or any attachment thereto or by the load carried.

4. The dimensions of a slow moving vehicle sign may be greater than the dimensions prescribed and illustrated in section 1 so long as each dimension is increased and, when increased, has the same relation to the other dimensions of the sign as the dimensions prescribed and illustrated have to each other.

5. A slow-moving vehicle sign shall be deemed to meet the requirements of this Regulation if the sign is marked with the monogram of the Canadian Standards Association Testing Laboratories.

6. (1) Subsection 76(1) of the Act and sections 1 to 5 of this Regulation do not apply to a horse-drawn vehicle when driven by a person whose religious convictions or beliefs prohibit the display of the slow moving vehicle sign.

(2) A person described in subsection (1) shall not drive a horse-drawn vehicle on a highway unless a marker is displayed on the vehicle in accordance with this section.

(3) The marker shall be visible from a distance of at least 150 metres when illuminated by a lighted lamp on a vehicle that is approaching or overtaking the horse-drawn vehicle during,

(a) the period beginning one-half hour before sunset and ending one-half hour after sunrise; and

(b) any other period during which, due to insufficient light or unfavourable atmospheric conditions, persons and vehicles on the highway are not clearly discernible at a distance of 150 metres or less.

(4) The marker shall consist of five strips of grey, silver or white reflective material, each at least 2.5 centimetres wide.

(5) Four of the strips shall be affixed to the outside perimeter of the rear of the vehicle in accordance with the following rules:

1. One strip shall be affixed to the top of the rear of the vehicle, be placed horizontally and be at least 56 centimetres long.

2. One strip shall be affixed to each of the two sides of the rear of the vehicle, be placed vertically and be at least 42 centimetres long.

3. One strip shall be affixed to the bottom of the rear of the vehicle, be placed horizontally and be at least 28 centimetres long.

(6) The fifth strip shall be affixed as high as possible on the left side of the front of the vehicle, be placed vertically and be at least 14 centimetres long.

(7) The marker shall be free from dirt and obstruction and shall be affixed so as to be plainly visible at all times and the view of the marker shall not be obscured or obstructed by any part of the vehicle, by any attachment to the vehicle or by the load carried.

O. Reg. 423/96, s. 3

SCHEDULE BRIGHTNESS OF REFLECTIVE MATERIAL

Item	Column 1 Angle of incidence (degrees)	Column 2 Minimum brightness if angle of divergence is 0.2 degrees (average candle power/foot candle/square foot of material)	Column 3 Minimum brightness if angle of divergence is 0.5 degrees (average candle power/foot candle/square foot of material)
1	0	10.0	5.0
2	15	7.0	4.0
3	30	5.0	2.0
4	45	1.0	0.5

O. Reg. 94/15, s. 2

ONT. REG. 381/98 — SPECIAL PERMITS

made under the *Highway Traffic Act*

O. Reg. 381/98, as am. O. Reg. 440/06 (Fr.); 172/12; 243/13; 259/15.

1. (1) Subject to subsection (2), if the Ministry issues a permit under section 110 of the Act authorizing the moving of heavy vehicles, loads, objects or structures in excess of the dimensional or weight limits set out in section 109 and Part VIII of the Act, respectively, the following fees shall be paid to the Ministry:

1.	For an annual term	**$440.00**
2.	For a project	**286.00**
3.	For a single trip where the vehicle, load, object or structure is in excess of dimensional limits	**65.00**
4.	For a single trip where the vehicle, load, object or structure is in excess of weight or weight and dimensional limits, and the gross vehicle weight does not exceed 120,000 kilograms and,	
	i. the permit is issued for a distance of less than or equal to 100 kilometres	**125.00**
	ii. the permit is issued for a distance of greater than 100 kilometres but less than or equal to 500 kilometres	**200.00**
	iii. the permit is issued for a distance of greater than 500 kilometres	**260.00**
5.	For a single trip where the vehicle, load, object or structure is in excess of weight or weight and dimensional limits and the gross vehicle weight exceeds 120,000 kilograms	**700.00**
6.	For a replacement permit in case of the loss or destruction of the original	**25.00**
7.	For an amendment to an existing permit, where the amendment does not significantly alter the restriction on the amount of the load being moved or the length of the term of the permit	**16.50**

(2) No fee is payable where a permit referred to in subsection (1) is applied for by a Ministry of the Government of Ontario.

(3) The fee for a permit referred to in subsection (1) is the fee that is in effect on the day the permit becomes effective.

O. Reg. 172/12, s. 1; 243/13, s. 1; 259/15, s. 1

2. Regulation 617 of the Revised Regulations of Ontario, 1990 is revoked.

Ont. Reg. 618 — Specifications and Standards for Trailer Couplings

made under the *Highway Traffic Act*

R.R.O. 1990, Reg. 618, as am. O. Reg. 403/09 (Fr.).

1. In this Regulation,

"fifth wheel assembly" means a coupling device having its lower-half mounted on the rear portion of a vehicle frame or the frame of a trailer converter dolly and its upper-half fastened to the underside of the forward portion of a semi-trailer for the purpose of supporting and towing the semi-trailer;

"full trailer" means a vehicle that is towed by another vehicle and is so designed and used that the whole of its weight and load is carried on its own axles and includes a combination consisting of a semi-trailer and a trailer converter dolly;

"semi-trailer" means a vehicle that is towed by another vehicle and is so designed and used that a substantial part of its weight and load rests on or is carried by the other vehicle or a trailer converter dolly through a fifth wheel assembly;

"tow bar" means a towing structure that is connected to the chassis frame of the forward axle of a full trailer and which includes an eye or equivalent device for the purpose of coupling with a trailer hitch;

"trailer converter dolly" means a device consisting of one or more axles, a fifth wheel lower-half and a tow bar used to convert a semi-trailer into a full trailer; and

"trailer hitch" means a coupling device mounted on the rear of a truck tractor or trailer to which a tow bar may be attached for the purpose of towing a full trailer.

2. Where a truck tractor and one or more trailers are operated in combination, the coupling devices connecting the truck tractor and trailer or trailers shall be designed, constructed and installed and the truck tractor, trailer or trailers shall be designed and constructed so that when they are operated in combination in a straight line on a level, smooth, paved surface, the path of the trailer or trailers does not swing or deviate more than 76 millimetres to either side of the path of the truck tractor.

3. (1) The lower-half of a fifth wheel assembly on a truck tractor, trailer or trailer converter dolly shall be attached to the frame of the truck tractor, trailer or trailer converter dolly with a mounting that,

    (a) has,

        (i) brackets, mounting plates or angles, and

(ii) bolts or equivalent devices,

which together will withstand a force, applied at the coupling point of the fifth wheel assembly, equivalent to the gross weight of the trailer or trailers being towed without residual deformation to the mounting parts;

(b) is installed so that the frame of the truck tractor, trailer or converter dolly does not crack or become deformed; and

(c) is installed so as to prevent shifting of the lower-half of the fifth wheel assembly on the frame to which it is attached.

(2) Where the upper-half of a fifth wheel assembly is attached to a semi-trailer it shall be attached to the underside of the semi-trailer so as to prevent,

(a) warping or cracking of the upper-half of the fifth wheel assembly or the underside of the semi-trailer; and

(b) separation of the upper-half of the fifth wheel assembly from the semi-trailer.

(3) A fifth wheel assembly shall be equipped with a locking device that prevents separation of its upper-half from its lower-half.

(4) Where a fifth wheel assembly includes a manual release system, the fifth wheel assembly shall be equipped with a locking device or devices which applies automatically on the coupling of a semi-trailer to a truck tractor, trailer converter dolly or to another semi-trailer.

(5) The lower-half of a fifth wheel assembly on a truck tractor, trailer or trailer converter dolly shall be so mounted in relation to the axles of the truck tractor, trailer or trailer converter dolly that,

(a) the load distribution does not unduly interfere with the steering, braking or maneuverability of the truck tractor, trailer or trailer converter dolly; and

(b) the combination operates safely.

4. (1) A full trailer shall be equipped with a tow bar that is of sufficient strength to withstand a force through its attachments equivalent to the gross weight of the trailer or trailers being towed, without residual deformation to the tow bar.

(2) Where a tow bar is used to tow a full trailer it shall be connected to the full trailer with an attachment that,

(a) has a strength equal to or greater than that of the tow bar;

(b) in the case of a hinged tow bar, has the minimum clearance necessary for adequate articulation; and

(c) is attached in the manner for which it was designed.

(3) Where a truck tractor or trailer is equipped with a trailer hitch, the trailer hitch shall,

(a) be of sufficient strength to withstand a force applied at the point to which the tow bar is connected, equivalent to the gross weight of the trailer or trailers being towed, without residual deformation to the trailer hitch;

(b) provide the minimum clearance necessary for adequate articulation in its connection to the trailer being towed; and

(c) be provided with a locking device to prevent accidental separation of the truck tractor or trailer from the trailer being towed.

(4) The attachment of a trailer hitch to the towing structure of a truck tractor or trailer shall have a strength that is equal to or greater than that of the trailer hitch.

(5) A towing structure to which a trailer hitch is attached, shall have a strength equal to or greater than that of the trailer hitch.

(6) The attachment of a towing structure to a truck tractor or trailer shall,

(a) be reinforced or braced to prevent distortion of the frame of the truck tractor or trailer; and

(b) have a strength equal to or greater than that of the trailer hitch.

5. (1) A full trailer shall be coupled to the frame or an extension of the frame of a truck tractor or trailer with a safety connecting device that will prevent the full trailer from breaking loose in the event the tow bar fails or becomes disconnected.

(2) The safety connecting device referred to in subsection (1) shall,

(a) not be attached to any part of a trailer hitch that would render the safety connecting device ineffective should the trailer hitch or its attachment to the towing structure fail;

(b) have the minimum slack necessary for adequate articulation;

(c) have an ultimate strength not less than the gross weight of the trailer or trailers being towed and where the safety connecting device consists of two chains, two cables or two other links, each chain, cable or other link and its attachments shall have an ultimate strength equal to the gross weight of the trailer or trailers being towed;

(d) be connected in such a manner so as to prevent the tow bar from dropping to the ground, and to keep the swing of the full trailer within safe limits in the event the tow bar fails or becomes disconnected;

(e) be equipped with a hook or hooks or other means of attachment that will not become disconnected accidentally;

(f) where it is used in conjunction with a hinged tow bar and where the safety connecting device consists of two chains, two cables or two other links, be attached to the forward axle or chassis frame of the forward axle of the full trailer at two points as far apart as the configuration of the axle or frame permits and equidistant from the centreline of the full trailer;

(g) where it is used in conjunction with a hinged tow bar and where the safety connecting device consists of a single chain or single cable,

(i) have its ends attached to the forward axle or chassis frame of the forward axle of the full trailer at two points as far apart as the configuration of the axle or frame permits and equidistant from the centreline of the full trailer,

(ii) lead along each side of the tow bar, and

(iii) be formed into a bridle by using a thimble and twin-base clamps and include a single means of attachment;

(h) where it is used in conjunction with a non-hinged tow bar,

(i) consist of two chains, two cables or two other links attached to the tow bar at a single point on the centreline of the tow bar or at two points equidistant from the centreline of the tow bar such that the attachment is behind the eye of the tow bar, or

(ii) consist of a single chain, cable or other link attached to the tow bar on the centreline of the tow bar at any point behind the eye of the tow bar;

(i) where it consists of two chains, two cables or two other links attached at separate points, the separate points shall be equidistant from the centreline of the truck tractor or towing trailer; or

(j) where it consists of two chains, two cables or two other links attached to the same point or where a bridle, single chain, single cable or other single link is used, be attached to a point on the centreline of the truck tractor or towing trailer.

ONT. REG. 619 — SPEED LIMITS

made under the *Highway Traffic Act*

R.R.O. 1990, Reg. 619, as am. O. Reg. 2/91; 4/91; 41/91; 75/91; 170/91; 221/91; 233/91; 419/91; 428/91; 483/91; 502/91; 563/91; 637/91; 642/91; 27/92; 138/92; 308/92; 339/92; 445/92; 470/92; 481/92; 626/92; 633/92; 767/92; 20/93; 63/93; 136/93; 206/93; 277/93; 306/93; 474/93; 488/93; 520/93; 661/93; 725/93; 895/93; 932/93; 25/94; 75/94; 293/94; 449/94; 564/94; 611/94; 661/94; 695/94; 4/95; 65/95; 123/95; 189/95; 269/95; 376/95; 495/95; 29/96; 30/96; 148/96; 325/96; 328/96; 396/96; 424/96; 466/96; 477/96; 44/97; 115/97; 140/97; 141/97; 194/97; 208/97; 209/97; 327/97; 356/97; 366/97; 432/97; 434/97; 26/98; 27/98; 28/98; 109/98; 206/98; 207/98; 208/98; 443/98; 511/98; 512/98; 541/98; 718/98; 2/99; 203/99; 223/99; 224/99; 225/99; 255/99; 362/99; 363/99; 364/99; 405/99; 440/99; 466/99; 467/99; 468/99; 634/99; 223/00; 232/00; 239/00; 290/00; 291/00; 292/00; 320/00; 442/00; 443/00; 445/00; 466/00; 481/00; 519/00; 625/00; 149/01 [Corrected Gazette 09/06/01 Vol. 134:23.]; 208/01; 376/01; 9/02; 53/02; 55/02; 152/02; 221/02; 227/02; 303/02; 78/03; 351/03; 385/03; 386/03; 387/03; 388/03; 65/04; 151/04; 152/04; 256/04; 435/04; 436/04; 437/04; 90/05; 164/05; 206/05; 424/05; 473/05; 495/05; 497/05; 498/05; 621/05; 110/06; 117/06; 145/06; 235/06; 392/06; 446/06; 450/06; 451/06; 15/07; 16/07; 20/07; 140/07; 142/07; 200/07; 428/07; 457/07; 521/07; 546/07; 549/07; 553/07; 38/08; 47/08; 54/08; 89/08; 169/08; 228/08; 255/08; 269/08; 270/08; 359/08; 360/08; 383/08; 399/08; 400/08; 451/08; 10/09; 39/09; 40/09; 50/09; 51/09; 53/09; 64/09; 142/09; 143/09; 144/09; 145/09; 149/09; 171/09; 201/09; 248/09; 280/09; 323/09; 324/09; 408/09; 430/09; 432/09; 433/09; 60/10; 140/10; 154/10; 302/10; 304/10; 326/10; 409/10; 471/10; 473/10; 501/10; 64/11; 65/11; 66/11; 93/11; 281/11; 406/11; 409/11; 411/11; 415/11; 449/11; 450/11; CTR 22 SE 11 - 1; 5/12; 27/12; 29/12; 37/12; 49/12; 112/12; 114/12; 116/12; 152/12; 155/12; 156/12; 158/12; 192/12; 202/12; 231/12; 235/12; 238/12; 239/12; 244/12; 290/12; 303/12; 324/12; 336/12; 344/12; 356/12; 392/12; 396/12; 40/13; 126/13; 191/13; 206/13; 226/13; 248/13; 316/13; 320/13; 150/14; 151/14; 152/14; 218/14; 32/15; 33/15; 98/15; 100/15; 130/15; 186/15; 239/15; 243/15; 244/15; 245/15; 248/15; 263/15; 308/15; 377/15; 380/15; 22/16; 23/16; 24/16; 60/16.

Schedules omitted.

1. The speed limit on those parts of the King's Highway described in,

    (a) Part 1 of each Schedule is prescribed as 100 kilometres per hour;

    (b) Part 2 of each Schedule is prescribed as 90 kilometres per hour;

    (c) Part 3 of each Schedule is prescribed as 80 kilometres per hour;

    (d) Part 4 of each Schedule is prescribed as 70 kilometres per hour;

    (e) Part 5 of each Schedule is prescribed as 60 kilometres per hour;

(f) Part 6 of each Schedule is prescribed as 50 kilometres per hour;

2. Despite section 1, the speed limit on those parts of the King's Highway that are within truck inspection stations established and maintained by the Ministry is prescribed as 40 kilometres per hour.

3. Where a highway is referred to in a Schedule by a number or name, the reference is to that part of the King's Highway that is known thereby.

4. (1) In a Schedule,

"township", when used with reference to a township in a territorial district, means a geographic township, except where otherwise provided.

(2) Where a part of the King's Highway is referred to in a Schedule as being in a municipality that, by reason of a municipal reorganization, has become another municipality or a part thereof, the reference shall be deemed to be a reference to that part of the King's Highway in that other municipality or part thereof.

5. No person shall operate a commercial motor vehicle, except a bus, at a greater rate of speed than 50 kilometres per hour, northbound, on that part of the King's Highway known as No. 20 in The Regional Municipality of Hamilton-Wentworth lying between a point situate at its intersection with the southerly limit of the roadway known as King Street in the City of Hamilton and a point situate 45 metres measured southerly from its intersection with the northerly limit of the roadway known as Green Mountain Road in the Torn of Stoney Creek.

6. [Revoked O. Reg. 442/00, s. 1.]

7. (1) Despite paragraph 8 of Part 3 of Schedule 53, no person shall operate a motor vehicle at a greater rate of speed than 60 kilometres per hour on days during which school is regularly held between the hours of 7:15 a.m. to 8:15 a.m. and 2:15 p.m. to 3:15 p.m. on that part of the King's Highway known as No. 48 in the Town of Georgina in the Regional Municipality of York beginning at a point situate 105 metres measured westerly from its intersection with the westerly limit of the roadway known as Weir's Road and extending westerly for a distance of 750 metres.

(2) Despite paragraph 9 of Part 3 of Schedule 2, no person shall operate a motor vehicle at a greater rate of speed than 60 kilometres per hour on days during which school is regularly held between the hours of 8:00 a.m. to 9:00 a.m. and 3:00 p.m. to 4:00 p.m. on that part of the King's Highway known as No. 3 in the Township of Malahide, in the County of Elgin, beginning at a point situate 100 metres measured easterly from its intersection with the centre line of the roadway known as County Road 40 (Springfield Road) and extending westerly for a distance of 750 metres.

(3) Despite paragraph 13 of Part 3 of Schedule 16, no person shall operate a motor vehicle at a greater rate of speed than 60 kilometres per hour on days during which school is regularly held between the hours of 8:00 a.m. to 9:00 a.m. and 2:45 p.m. to 3:45 p.m. on that part of the King's Highway known as No. 12 and No. 48 in the Township of Brock in The Regional Municipality of Durham beginning at a point

situate 199 metres measured northerly from its intersection with the centre line of the roadway known as Beaver Avenue and extending northerly for a distance of 750 metres.

(4) Despite paragraph 10 of Part 3 of Schedule 53, no person shall operate a motor vehicle at a greater rate of speed than 60 kilometres per hour on days during which school is regularly held between the hours of 8:00 a.m. to 9:00 a.m. and 2:45 p.m. to 3:45 p.m. on that part of the King's Highway known as No. 12 and No. 48 in the Township of Brock in The Regional Municipality of Durham beginning at a point situate 199 metres measured northerly from its intersection with the centre line of the roadway known as Beaver Avenue and extending northerly for a distance of 750 metres.

(5) Despite paragraph 1 of Part 4 of Schedule 120, no person shall operate a motor vehicle at a greater rate of speed than 60 kilometres per hour on days during which school is regularly held between the hours of 7:30 a.m. to 9:30 a.m. and 2:30 p.m. to 4:30 p.m. on that part of the King's Highway known as No. 141 in the Village of Humphrey in the Township of Seguin in the Territorial District of Parry Sound beginning at a point situate 75 metres measured westerly from its intersection with the centre line of the roadway known as Sandy Plains Road and extending easterly for a distance of 410 metres.

O. Reg. 488/93; 520/93; 140/97; 443/98; 255/99; 473/05, s. 1; 324/09, s. 1; 5/12, s. 1

Ont. Reg. 620 — Speed Limits in Provincial Parks

made under the *Highway Traffic Act*

R.R.O. 1990, Reg. 620, as am. O. Reg. 166/94; 439/06 (Fr.).

1. In this Regulation,

"areas of high pedestrian use" means picnic areas, swimming areas, play grounds, sports fields, trails, walkways, boat launching areas, parking areas, visitor centres, park offices, comfort stations and other commonly used recreational facilities where there is a potential for conflict between pedestrian and vehicular traffic;

"campground" means an area where camp-sites as defined in the *Provincial Parks Act* are operated.

O. Reg. 166/94, s. 1

2. No person shall drive a motor vehicle on that part of a highway, other than the King's Highway, lying within an area set apart as a provincial park under the *Provincial Parks Act* at a greater rate of speed than,

    (a) in the case of those parts of highways set out in the Schedules, 70 kilometres per hour;

    (b) in the case of areas of high pedestrian use and campgrounds, where signs are posted, 20 kilometres per hour; and

    (c) in any other case, 40 kilometres per hour.

O. Reg. 166/94, s. 1

SCHEDULE 1

That part of the roadway known as Lake Traverse Road in Algonquin Park lying between a point situate at its intersection with the Sand Lake gate and a point situate at its intersection with the bridge over the Petawawa River at Lake Traverse.

SCHEDULE 2

[Revoked O. Reg. 166/94, s. 2.]

ONT. REG. 621 — SPEED LIMITS IN TERRITORY WITHOUT MUNICIPAL ORGANIZATION

made under the *Highway Traffic Act*

R.R.O. 1990, Reg. 621, as am. O. Reg. 40/91; 429/91; 140/92; 337/92; 447/92; 621/92; 26/93; 107/93; 278/93; 426/93; 510/93; 634/93; 147/96; 595/98; 438/00; 334/01; 255/02; 11/03; 378/03; 257/04; 373/09 (Fr.).

(Schedules omitted.)

1. No person shall drive a motor vehicle on that part of a highway located in territory without municipal organization described in paragraph 1 of each Schedule at a greater rate of speed than that prescribed in paragraph 2 of each Schedule.

ONT. REG. 103/97 — STANDARDS TO DETERMINE ALLOWABLE GROSS VEHICLE WEIGHT FOR BRIDGES

made under the *Highway Traffic Act*

O. Reg. 103/97, as am. O. Reg. 159/02.

1. In this Regulation,

"bridge" [Revoked O. Reg. 159/02, s. 1(1).]

"Canadian Highway Bridge Design Code" means the "Canadian Highway Bridge Design Code" designated as CAN/CSA-S6-00 published by the Canadian Standards Association and the "Commentary on CAN/CSA-S6-00, the Canadian Highway Bridge Design Code" published by the Canadian Standards Association, as they may be amended from time to time;

"Ontario Highway Bridge Design Code" [Revoked O. Reg. 159/02, s. 1(3).]

"professional engineer" means a person who holds a licence or a temporary licence issued under the *Professional Engineers Act* to engage in the practice of professional engineering, but does not include a person who holds a limited licence issued under that Act.

O. Reg. 159/02, s. 1

2. For the purpose of subsection 123(2) of the Act, a determination of a limit on the gross vehicle weight of vehicles passing over a bridge shall,

(a) be made in accordance with the provisions of the Canadian Highway Bridge Design Code;

(b) be signed and sealed by two professional engineers who have determined and set out the maximum allowable load limit at which the bridge may be posted, and the period of time for which the determination remains valid; and

(c) precede the enactment of any by-law, where the by-law comes into force after the date on which this Regulation comes into force.

O. Reg. 159/02, s. 2

3. This Regulation comes into force on April 1, 1997.

ONT. REG. 623 — STOP SIGNS AT INTERSECTIONS

made under the *Highway Traffic Act*

R.R.O. 1990, Reg. 623, as am. O. Reg. 234/91; 529/91; 9/92; 62/92; 472/92;
142/93; 511/93; 804/93; 26/94; 80/94; 363/94; 35/95; 450/96; 29/98; 418/98;
596/98; 119/99; 263/00; 440/00; 337/01; 254/02; 379/03; 148/04; 57/05; 425/05;
519/05; 480/06; 481/06; 482/06; 5/07; 9/07; 138/07; 458/07; 550/07; 40/08;
41/08; 171/08; 58/09; 316/09; 307/10; 313/10; 452/11; 157/12; 358/12; 321/13;
157/14; 161/14; 339/15; 21/16.

(Schedules omitted.)

1. The intersections on the King's Highway that are described in paragraph 1 of each Schedule are designated as intersections at which stop signs shall be erected to face traffic travelling in the direction referred to in paragraph 2 of each Schedule.

2. Where a highway is referred to in a Schedule by a number or name, the reference is to that part of the King's Highway that is known thereby.

3. (1) Every intersection of a controlled-access King's Highway exit ramp and a highway that is not otherwise controlled by a traffic light or yield sign is designated as an intersection at which a stop sign shall be erected.

(2) A stop sign at an intersection described in subsection (1) shall face the traffic on the exit ramp.

O. Reg. 157/14, s. 1

ONT. REG. 624 — STOP SIGNS IN TERRITORY WITHOUT MUNICIPAL ORGANIZATION

made under the *Highway Traffic Act*

R.R.O. 1990, Reg. 624, as am. O. Reg. 1/91; 430/91; 11/92; 63/92; 192/92; 766/92; 108/93; 143/93; 427/93; 489/93; 635/93; 27/94; 294/94; 565/94; 124/95; 149/96; 152/96; 371/96; 375/97; 120/99; 415/99; 436/99; 439/00; 338/01; 425/01; 253/02; 256/02; 257/02; 296/02; 384/03; 64/04; 139/07; 303/10; 223/11; 234/12; 236/12; 296/12; 393/12; 162/14; 108/15; 109/15; 155/15; 237/15.

1. The intersections on highways in territory without municipal organization that are described in paragraph 1 of each Schedule are designated as intersections at which stop signs shall be erected to face traffic travelling in the direction referred to in paragraph 2 of each Schedule.

2. Where a highway is referred to in a Schedule by a number or name, the reference is to that part of the highway in a territory without municipal organization that is known thereby.

[Schedules omitted.]

ONT. REG. 622 — STOPPING OF VEHICLES ON PARTS OF THE KING'S HIGHWAY

made under the *Highway Traffic Act*

R.R.O. 1990, Reg. 622, as am. O. Reg. 233/00; 336/01; 496/05; 525/07; 247/08; 44/09; 52/09; 170/09; 410/09; 482/09; 478/10; 407/11; 410/11; 451/11; 457/11; 30/12; 188/12; 241/12; 289/12; 295/12; 394/12; 432/12; 123/13; 190/13; 219/14; 182/15; 92/16.

(Appendices omitted.)

1. (1) No person shall stop a vehicle on a part of the King's Highway described in a Schedule to Appendix A.

(2) No person shall stop a vehicle on a part of the King's Highway described in Column 1 of a Schedule to Appendix B between the limits set out in Column 2 during the period set out in Column 3 for a longer period of time than that set out in Column 4.

2. Where a highway is referred to in a Schedule by number or name, the reference is to that part of the King's Highway known by it.

ONT. REG. 381/02 — TESTING, REPAIR AND COMPLIANCE REQUIREMENTS FOR UNSAFE VEHICLES UNDER SECTION 82 OF THE ACT

made under the *Highway Traffic Act*

O. Reg. 381/02

1. Evidence of repair and compliance — (1) The following may be required as evidence, for the purpose of clause 82(4)(b) or subsection 82(5) of the Act, that a vehicle and its equipment have been repaired as required by subsection 82(4) or (5) of the Act and comply with the requirements of the Act and the regulations:

1. Repair orders, work orders and parts invoices.

2. A safety standards certificate.

3. A certificate, in a form approved by the Minister, issued by a motor vehicle inspection station, as defined in section 88 of the Act, indicating that the part of the vehicle or of its equipment that was required to be repaired under subsection 82(4) or (5) of the Act has been repaired and complies with the Act and the regulations.

4. Supporting documentation, including examination or test results and measurements.

(2) The evidence of repair and compliance may be required in the form of original documents or photocopies.

(3) The evidence of repair and compliance shall be submitted by a method specified in the notice served pursuant to subsection 82(6) of the Act.

(4) The notice may specify that the evidence be submitted to the person or office specified in the notice,

(a) personally;

(b) by registered mail;

(c) by courier; or

(d) by fax.

(5) The evidence must be received by the person or office specified in the notice by the date specified in the notice.

2. Exemption if vehicle plates and permit surrendered or "unfit" permit issued — (1) An owner of a vehicle or operator of a commercial motor vehicle upon receiving a notice to have the vehicle examined and tested under subsection 82(3) of the Act or repaired under subsection 82(4) or (5) of the Act may, instead of having the vehicle or its equipment examined and tested or repaired, surrender the number plates and permit for the vehicle to the person or office specified in the notice or provide that person or office with proof that a vehicle permit marked "unfit" has been issued for the vehicle.

(2) The requirements in subsections 82(3), (4) and (5) of the Act that an owner or operator have a vehicle examined and tested or repaired and submitted for further examinations and tests and that the owner or operator submit evidence that the vehicle and its equipment comply with the Act and the regulations do not apply to a person who complies with the alternative requirements set out in subsection (1).

(3) Subsections 1(2), (3), (4) and (5) apply, with necessary modifications, to the proof required to be submitted under this section.

3. Rules for service of notices — (1) A notice required under subsection 82(6) of the Act shall be served on the owner of a vehicle either by serving the driver as provided in subsection 82(7) of the Act or,

(a) at the most recent address or fax number for the owner in the Ministry's records;

(b) at the address or fax number appearing on the certificate of registration for the vehicle or, where the certificate of registration consists of a vehicle portion and plate portion, at the address or fax number appearing on the plate portion; or

(c) at any address or fax number at which the police officer or officer appointed for the purpose of carrying out the provisions of the Act who serves the notice reasonably believes the order will come to the owner's notice, including the address or fax number of any of the owner's places of business.

(2) A notice required under subsection 82(6) of the Act shall be served on the operator of a commercial motor vehicle either by serving the driver as provided in subsection 82(7) of the Act or,

(a) at the most recent address or fax number for the operator in the Ministry's records;

(b) at the address or fax number appearing on the CVOR certificate, produced by the driver or other person in charge of the commercial motor vehicle;

(c) at the address or fax number appearing in the lease or contract described in subsection 16(3) of the Act that is produced by the driver or other person in charge of the commercial motor vehicle;

(d) at the address or fax number appearing in the certificate of registration for the commercial motor vehicle or, where the certificate of registration consists of a vehicle portion and plate portion, at the address or fax number appearing on the plate portion; or

(e) at any address or fax number at which the police officer or officer appointed for the purpose of carrying out the provisions of the Act who serves the notice reasonably believes that the order will come to the operator's notice, including the address or fax number of any of the operator's places of business.

(3) A notice may be served on the owner or operator of the vehicle,

(a) personally;

    (b) by registered mail;

    (c) by regular mail;

    (d) by courier; or

    (e) by fax.

(4) A notice shall be deemed to have been served on an owner or operator of the vehicle,

    (a) on the day it was personally served;

    (b) on the fifth day after it was mailed;

    (c) on the second day after it was given to the courier;

    (d) on the day it was sent by fax, if sent before 5 p.m.;

    (e) on the day after it was sent by fax if sent at or after 5 p.m.

(5) If the day described in clause (4)(b), (c), (d) or (e) is a holiday, the notice shall be deemed to have been served on the next day that is not a holiday.

4. Revocation — Regulation 602 of the Revised Regulations of Ontario, 1990 is revoked.

5. Commencement — This Regulation comes into force on the day section 14 of Schedule R to the *Red Tape Reduction Act, 1999* is proclaimed in force.

ONT. REG. 625 — TIRE STANDARDS AND SPECIFICATIONS

made under the *Highway Traffic Act*

R.R.O. 1990, Reg. 625, as am. O. Reg. 495/93; 382/02; 318/03; 617/05; 107/06; 116/08; 243/10; 168/14.

1. In this Regulation,

"aspect ratio" means the height of the tire section divided by the overall width of the tire, multiplied by 100;

"bead" means the part of a tire that is shaped to fit the rim;

"cord" means the strands forming a ply in a tire;

"groove" means the space between two tread ribs;

"Northern Ontario" means the Territorial Districts of Algoma, Cochrane, Kenora, Manitoulin, Nipissing, Parry Sound, Rainy River, Sudbury, Timiskaming and Thunder Bay;

"ply" means the layer of parallel cords used in forming the tire carcass;

"sidewall" means the portion of a tire between the tread and the bead;

"siping" means small, straight, angular or curved slits, other than grooves, molded or cut in the tread surface of a tire;

"studded tire" means a tire that has a tread embedded with devices that project beyond the tread and have a hardness of greater than seven on the Mohs scale;

"tread" means the portion of a tire that comes in contact with the road;

"tread rib" means a tread section running circumferentially around a tire;

"TSMI" means the Tire Stud Manufacturing Institute.

O. Reg. 617/05, s. 1; 107/06, s. 1

2. A tire,

    (a) shall have no exposed cord;

    (b) shall have no tread or sidewall cuts or snags deep enough to expose the cords;

    (c) shall have no abnormal visible bump, bulge or knot; and

    (d) other than a tire specifically designed for regrooving or recutting and marked as being so designed shall not be regrooved or recut.

3. (1) Subject to subsection (2), a tire shall not be worn to the extent that in any two adjacent major grooves at three equally spaced intervals around the circumference of the tire,

(a) the tread wear indicators contact the road; or

(b) less than 1.5 millimetres of tread depth remains.

(2) A front tire on a motor vehicle having a gross vehicle weight rating of more than 4,500 kilograms shall not be worn to the extent that less than three millimetres of tread depth remains in any two adjacent major grooves at three equally spaced intervals around the circumference of the tire.

(3) For the purposes of subsections (1) and (2), siping on a tire, other than a tire forming part of a dual tire set on an urban transit bus, does not constitute tread.

(4) Where the tread pattern on a tire is of such a design that no major grooves are present, the tread depth shall be determined by measurements at the locations designated by the tire manufacturer for this purpose at three equally spaced intervals around the circumference of the tire.

4. (1) Tires shall be installed on a vehicle so as to avoid,

(a) a mixture of construction types consisting of radial ply tires on the front and bias ply or belted bias ply tires on the rear;

(b) a mixture consisting of 50 or 60 aspect ratio tires on the front with any aspect ratio of tires other than 50 or 60 aspect ratio, on the rear;

(c) a combination of construction types or sizes of tires on an axle, except where such types or sizes are equivalent by tire industry standards; or

(d) contact between tires in a dual set or a difference in overall diameter between tires in a dual set of more than thirteen millimetres or a difference in circumference of more than forty-one millimetres.

(2) Clause 1(a) does not apply to tires fitted on a vehicle with dual rear tires.

(3) Clause 1(c) does not apply to a temporary use spare tire, specified by a vehicle manufacturer as suitable for emergency use, if not more than one temporary use spare tire is installed on a vehicle.

5. A tire fitted on a vehicle shall not,

(a) be of a smaller size than the vehicle manufacturer's specified minimum size; or

(b) contact any vehicle component so as to affect the safe operation of the vehicle.

5.1 (1) In this section,

"motor tricycle" means a motorcycle that,

(a) is designed to travel on three wheels in contact with the ground,

(b) has seating on which all occupants must sit astride,

(c) has not more than four designated seating positions,

(d) has a manufacturer's gross vehicle weight rating of 1,000 kilograms or less,

(e) has a minimum wheel rim diameter of 250 millimetres,

(f) has a minimum wheel base of 1,016 millimetres, and

(g) does not have a structure partially or fully enclosing the driver and passenger, other than that part of the vehicle forward of the driver's torso and the seat backrest.

(2) For the purpose of determining the number of wheels on a motorcycle, two wheels are considered to be one wheel if they are mounted on the same axle and the distance between the centres of their areas of contact with the ground is less than 460 millimetres.

(3) A motor tricycle with two front wheels shall not be fitted with a tire of a size or type not intended for operation on a motor tricycle.

O. Reg. 116/08, s. 1

6. A tire shall not be installed on a motor vehicle or trailer that bears,

(a) the words "not for highway use", "farm use only" or "competition circuit use only";

(b) the letters "SL", "NHS" or "TG" after the tire designation; or

(c) any other wording or lettering indicating that the tire was not designed for highway use.

7. (1) No person shall operate on a highway a motor vehicle, trailer, device or apparatus equipped with tires that,

(a) bear the words "not for highway use", "farm use only" or "competition circuit use only";

(b) bear the letters "SL", "NHS" or "TG" after the tire designation;

(c) bear any other wording or lettering indicating that the tire was not designed for highway use; or

(d) were not manufactured to comply with the standards prescribed under the *Motor Vehicle Tire Safety Act* (Canada) and the regulations made thereunder as they existed on the 28th day of February, 1985.

(2) Subsection (1) does not apply to an off-road vehicle being operated under Ontario Regulation 316/03 ("Operation of Off-Road Vehicles on Highways") made under the *Highway Traffic Act* or under subsection 2(2) of the *Off-Road Vehicles Act*.

O. Reg. 318/03, s. 1

8. (1) A front tire on a bus shall not have been altered by the addition of material to produce a new tread surface.

(2) Subsection (1) does not apply to a tire on a trolley bus.

O. Reg. 495/93, s. 1

9. (1) No person shall operate a vehicle equipped with studded tires on a highway unless all of the following conditions are met:

1. The vehicle is operated during the period starting on September 1 and ending on May 31.

2. The permit holder of the vehicle is,

  i. a resident of Northern Ontario,

  ii. a corporation with a business premise in Northern Ontario, as shown by the address on the plate portion of the vehicle permit,

  iii. a municipal corporation having jurisdiction and control of a highway or portion of a highway located in Northern Ontario,

  iv. a road authority having jurisdiction and control of a highway or portion of a highway located in Northern Ontario,

  v. a district school board in Northern Ontario,

  vi. a school authority in Northern Ontario,

  vii. Her Majesty the Queen in right of Ontario, or

  viii. not a resident of Ontario and the vehicle is in Ontario for no longer than 30 days.

3. In the case of a vehicle with a gross vehicle weight rating equal to or less than 3,500 kilograms, all vehicle wheels are equipped with studded tires.

4. In the case of a vehicle with a gross vehicle weight rating greater than 3,500 kilograms, studded tires are either on all vehicle wheels or on only the vehicle wheels on one axle, and the vehicle is,

  i. an ambulance, police vehicle or fire department vehicle,

  ii. a school bus,

  iii. a public utility emergency vehicle, or

  iv. a road service vehicle.

5. The studs meet the specifications listed in paragraph i or ii as follows:

  i. The studs,

    A. are evenly embedded during tread manufacture,

    B. do not protrude more than 2.0 millimetres,

    C. have an aggregate object exposed surface area of 3 per cent of the tread surface area or less, and

    D. have an exposed surface area variability between tires of the same size of no greater than 25 per cent.

  ii. The studs,

    A. are securely and safely embedded after tread manufacture in pinholes moulded in any part of the tread other than the middle one-third,

    B. are inserted in a tire that after manufacturing or remoulding has never been driven on a vehicle,

    C. have only one peak per stud and no hollow part, and

D. meet the stud specifications applicable to the gross vehicle weight rating of the vehicle on which the studded tires are mounted, as set out in the Table.

TABLE: STUD SPECIFICATIONS

	Gross vehicle weight rating	Maximum protrusion of stud when newly installed	Maximum protrusion of stud when in use	Maximum stud weight and maximum static force	Maximum number of studs per tire	Material of studs
1.	2,500 kilograms or less	1.2 millimetres	2.0 millimetres	1.12 grams and 120 newtons	90 for TSMI sizes #13 or lower 110 for TSMI size #15 130 for TSMI sizes #16 and higher	Any, except steel
2.	more than 2,500 kilograms but not exceeding 3,500 kilograms	1.2 millimetres	2.0 millimetres	2.3 grams and 180 newtons	90 for TSMI sizes #13 or lower 110 for TSMI size #15 130 for TSMI sizes #16 and higher	Any, except steel
3.	3,500 kilograms or more	1.5 millimetres	2.5 millimetres	3 grams and 340 newtons	150	Any
4.	3,500 kilograms or more	1.5 millimetres	2.5 millimetres	1.12 grams and 120 newtons	250	Any

(2) Where the condition set out in subparagraph 2viii of subsection (1) is met, the vehicle is exempt from the requirements of paragraphs 3 and 5 of that subsection.

O. Reg. 495/93, s. 1; 617/05, s. 2; 243/10, s. 1; 168/14, s. 1

10. [Revoked O. Reg. 382/02, s. 1.]

11. [Revoked O. Reg. 495/93, s. 1.]

Ont. Reg. 147/97 — Toll Devices

made under the *Highway Traffic Act*

O. Reg. 147/97, as am. O. Reg. 15/14.

1. The following toll devices are prescribed for the purposes of section 191.2 of the Act:

    1. A toll device that bears the trademark "ETR Express Toll Route" and the label "Heavy Vehicle 4".

    2. A toll device that bears the trademark "CANTOLL" and the label "Heavy Vehicle 4".

O. Reg. 15/14, s. 1

2. (1) Where a toll device is required, it shall be mounted at least 5 centimetres from any metal object.

(2) Where a toll device is required, it shall be mounted on the inside of the front windshield of the vehicle, in the centre of the windshield, such that the top of the toll device is at least 5 centimetres and not more than 10 centimetres from the top of the windshield.

(3) Despite subsection (2), if the vehicle's front windshield is divided in the centre by a vertical metal strip, the toll device shall be mounted as described in that subsection except that it shall be located at least 5 centimetres to the right of the vertical metal strip.

3. (1) Subject to subsection (2), all vehicles are exempt from the application of section 191.2 of the Act.

(2) Section 191.2 of the Act applies to all heavy vehicles except those that are emergency vehicles as defined in subsection 144(1) of the Act, road building machines and motor vehicles registered to the Department of National Defence.

(3) In this section,

"heavy vehicle" means a vehicle that has a gross weight or a registered gross weight greater than 5,000 kilograms.

Ont. Reg. 626 — Traffic Control Signal Systems

made under the *Highway Traffic Act*

R.R.O. 1990, Reg. 626, as am. O. Reg. 213/92; 88/93; 65/96; 85/15; 408/15 [s. 1(2), (3) to come into force January 1, 2017.].

1. (1) Every traffic control signal shall consist of one circular amber and one circular red indication in combination with,

(a) a circular green indication;

(b) a circular green indication and one or more green arrow indications;

(c) a circular green indication, one or more green arrow indications and one or more amber arrow indications; or

(d) one or more green arrow indications.

(2) Green arrow, amber arrow, circular green, circular amber, circular red and white vertical bar indications may be used for traffic control signals and, where they are used, they shall be arranged vertically from the bottom, as follows:

right turn green arrow, right turn amber arrow, left turn green arrow, left turn amber arrow, straight through green arrow, circular green, circular amber, circular red and white vertical bar.

Proposed Addition — 1(2.1)–(2.4)

(2.1) Despite subsection (1), a bicycle traffic control signal shall consist of three opaque circular indications, each with a oloured translucent bicycle symbol, arranged vertically from the bottom as follows:

green, amber, red

(2.2) A green arrow indication on an opaque circular indication may be used for bicycle traffic control signals and, where is used, it shall be arranged vertically below the three opaque circular indications described in subsection (2.1).

(2.3) An amber arrow indication, on the same opaque circular indication that is used for the green arrow indication escribed in subsection (2.2) or on a separate opaque circular indication, may be used for bicycle traffic control signals and, where a separate opaque circular indication is used, it shall be arranged vertically above the green arrow indication.

(2.4) For the purpose of subsection (2.1), the bicycle symbol shall be as illustrated in the following Figure:

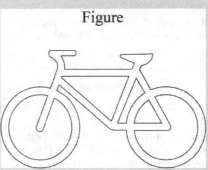

Figure

O. Reg. 408/15, s. 1(2) [To come into force January 1, 2017.]

(3) No traffic control signal system shall be operated so as to show more than one circular indication simultaneously on the same traffic control signal.

(4) Every traffic control signal system that is installed shall have at least two traffic control signals located on the far side of the intersection from which vehicles are approaching, at least one of which shall be located on the far right side.

(4.1) Despite subsection (4), a traffic control signal system installed at a crosswalk at an intersection for the purpose of assisting pedestrians to cross the roadway shall have,

(a) at least two traffic control signals facing the directions from which vehicles on the roadway approach the crossing; and

(b) at least one stop sign facing vehicles approaching the intersection from the other intersecting roadway.

Proposed Addition — 1(4.2)

(4.2) A bicycle traffic control signal installed at an intersection shall be located on the far side of the intersection from which vehicles are approaching and an additional bicycle traffic control signal may be located on the near side of the intersection from which vehicles are approaching.

O. Reg. 408/15, s. 1(2) [To come into force January 1, 2017.]

(5) Traffic control signals, where installed, shall be not less than 2.75 metres above the level of the roadway when adjacent to the travelled portion of the roadway and not less than 4.5 metres above the level of the roadway when suspended over the travelled portion of the roadway.

Proposed Addition — 1(5.1)

(5.1) Despite subsection (5), a bicycle traffic control signal, where installed, shall be not less than 2.5 metres above the level of the roadway when adjacent to the travelled portion of the roadway and not less than 4.5 metres above the level of the roadway when suspended over the travelled portion of the roadway.

O. Reg. 408/15, s. 1(2) [To come into force January 1, 2017.]

(6) Despite subsection (5), where a traffic control signal system is installed at a freeway entrance ramp as part of a traffic management system,

   (a) one traffic control signal shall be located to the left side of the roadway, not less than one metre above the level of the roadway; and

   (b) one traffic control signal shall be located to the right side of the roadway, not less than 2.75 metres above the level of the roadway.

(7) A symbol "don't walk" pedestrian control indication shall,

   (a) be rectangular in shape and shall not be less than thirty centimetres in height or width; and

   (b) consist of an orange silhouette of a hand on an opaque background as illustrated in the following Figure:

FIGURE

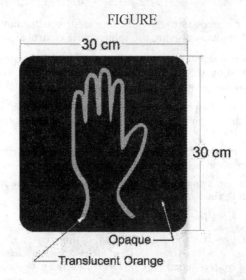

(8) A symbol "walk" pedestrian control indication shall be rectangular in shape and shall be not less than thirty centimetres in height or width and shall consist of,

   (a) in the case of a lens that cannot provide a solid symbol, an outlined symbol of a walking pedestrian in lunar white on an opaque background as illustrated in Figure 1; or

   (b) in the case of a lens that can provide a solid symbol, a solid symbol of a walking pedestrian in lunar white on an opaque background as illustrated in Figure 2.

FIGURE 1

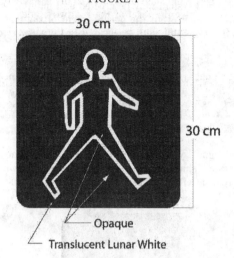

Opaque

Translucent Lunar White

FIGURE 2

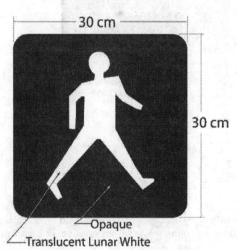

Opaque

Translucent Lunar White

(9) The positions of the symbol pedestrian control indications referred to in subsections (7) and (8) shall be as provided in any one of the following paragraphs:

    1. The symbols are mounted vertically with the hand outline on top.

    2. The symbols are within the same lens and are superimposed over each other.

3. The symbols are side by side within the same lens with the hand outline to the left.

(10) A traffic control signal system may be erected and maintained at a place other than an intersection, in which event the arrangement of the traffic control signals shall comply as nearly as possible with the provisions of subsections (4) and (5).

Proposed Amendment — 1(10)

(10) A traffic control signal system may be erected and maintained at a place other than an intersection, in which event the arrangement of the traffic control signals shall comply as nearly as possible with the provisions of subsections (4), (5) and (5.1).

O. Reg. 408/15, s. 1(3) [To come into force January 1, 2017.]

(11) A traffic control signal system that operates as a simultaneous protected and permissive left turn system shall display a left turn amber arrow indication immediately after the display of a left turn green arrow indication.

O. Reg. 213/92, s. 1; 65/96, 1; 85/15, s. 1; 408/15, s. 1(1)

ONT. REG. 627 — USE OF CONTROLLED-ACCESS HIGHWAYS BY PEDESTRIANS

made under the *Highway Traffic Act*

R.R.O. 1990, Reg. 627, as am. O. Reg. 171/91; 139/92; 25/93; 467/96; 230/97; 416/98; 255/04; 39/08; 313/08; 408/10; 475/10; 453/11; 113/12; 194/12; 232/12; 242/12; 359/12; 228/13; 370/15; 25/16.

1. (1) Subject to subsection (2), pedestrians are prohibited from using those parts of the controlled-access highways described in Schedule 1.

(2) Subsection (1) does not apply to pedestrians,

(a) engaged in police, highway maintenance, highway construction or vehicle inspection duties;

(b) within commuter parking lots established and maintained by the Ministry or proceeding directly between such lots and adjacent intersecting highways;

(c) within truck inspection stations or pulp load check areas established and maintained by the Ministry;

(d) making use of a controlled-access highway where the use is necessary because of an emergency; or

(e) crossing at a traffic control signal or a crosswalk.

O. Reg. 255/04, s. 1

2. Where a highway is referred to in a schedule by a number or name, the reference is to that part of the King's Highway or to the private toll highway that is known thereby.

O. Reg. 370/15, s. 1

SCHEDULE 1

1. All of the King's Highways known as Nos. 401, 402, 403, 404, 405, 406, 409, 410, 412, 416, 417 and 427 and the Queen Elizabeth Way.

1.1 All of the King's Highway known as Highway 407 East.

1.2 All of the private toll highway known as Highway 407.

2. All of the King's Highway known as No. 400, except for that part of King's Highway No. 400 known as Rose Street in the City of Barrie in the County of Simcoe beginning at a point situate at its intersection with the centre line of the roadway known as Simcoe County Road 27 (also known as Bayfield Street) and extending northerly for a distance of 230 metres.

3. All of the King's Highway known as Nos. 6 and 403.

4. All of the King's Highway known as Nos. 35 and 115.

5. All of the King's Highway known as Nos. 24 and 403.

6. All of the King's Highway known as Nos. 58 and 406.

7. That part of the King's Highway known as No. 420 in the City of Niagara Falls lying between a point situate at its intersection with the King's Highway known as the Queen Elizabeth Way and a point situate 91 metres measured westerly from its intersection with the centre line of the westerly limit of the roadway known as Stanley Avenue.

8. That part of the King's Highway known as No. 3 lying between a point situate at its intersection with the eastern limit of the roadway known as Ron McNeil Line (also known as Elgin County Road 52) where Ron McNeil Line continues as the roadway known as Ford Drive in the Township of Southwold and a point situate at its intersection with the west junction of the roadway known as Centennial Avenue in the Municipality of Central Elgin.

9. That part of the King's Highway known as No. 6 in the County of Haldimand lying between a point situate at its intersection with the roadway known as Argyle Street South and a point situate at its intersection with the southern limit of the roadway known as Seneca Greens Road.

10. That part of the King's Highway known as No. 6 lying between a point situate at its intersection with the King's Highway known as No. 401 in the Township of Puslinch and a point situate at its intersection with the south junction of the King's Highway known as No. 7 where King's Highway No. 7 continues as the roadway known as Wellington Street (also known as Wellington County Road 124) in the City of Guelph.

11. That part of King's Highway known as No. 6 in the City of Hamilton lying between a point situate at its intersection with the centre line of the King's Highway known as No. 403 and a point situate 50 metres measured northerly from its intersection with the centre line of the King's Highway known as No. 7273 (also known as Old Highway 6), except for 50 metres measured north and 50 metres measured south of its intersection with centre line of Book Road.

12. That part of the King's Highway known as Nos. 6 and 7 in the City of Guelph lying between a point situate at its intersection with the south junction of the King's Highway known as No. 7 where King's Highway No. 7 continues as the roadway known as Wellington Street (also known as Wellington County Road 124) and a point situate at its intersection with the north junction of the King's Highway known as No. 7 where King's Highway No. 7 continues as the roadway known as Woodlawn Road.

13. That part of the King's Highway known as No. 7 in the City of Ottawa lying between a point situate at its intersection with the King's Highway known as No. 417 and a point situate 150 metres measured easterly from its intersection with the centre line of the roadway known as McNeely Avenue in the Town of Carleton Place.

14. That part of the King's Highway known as No. 7 in the City of Kitchener lying between a point situate at its intersection with the roadway known as Victoria Street and a point situate at its intersection with the east junction of the King's Highway known as No. 8 where King's Highway No. 8 continues as the roadway known as King Street.

15. That part of the King's Highway known as Nos. 7 and 8 lying between a point situate at its intersection with the eastern limit of the roadway known as Waterloo Road 5 in the Township of Wilmot and a point situate at its intersection with the east junction of the King's Highway known as No. 8 where King's Highway No. 8 continues as the roadway known as King Street in the City of Kitchener.

16. That part of the King's Highway known as Nos. 7 and 115 lying between a point situate at its intersection with the west junction of the King's Highway known as No. 7 in the Township of Cavan-Millbrook-North Monaghan and a point situate 30 metres measured westerly from its intersection with the centre line of the roadway known as Landsdowne Street East in the City of Peterborough.

17. That part of the King's Highway known as No. 8 in the City of Kitchener lying between a point situate at its intersection with the King's Highway known as No. 401 and a point situate at its intersection with the east junction of the King's Highway known as No. 7 where King's Highway No. 7 continues as the roadway known as King Street.

18. That part of the King's Highway known as No. 11 in the City of Orillia lying between a point situate at its intersection with the roadway known as Memorial Avenue and a point situate at its intersection with the roadway known as Laclie Street.

19. That part of the King's Highway known as No. 11 lying between a point situate at its intersection with the south junction of the King's Highway known as No. 17 in the City of North Bay and a point situate at its intersection with the centre line of the roadway known as Muskoka Road 169 (also known as Bethune Drive) in the Town of Gravenhurst in The District Municipality of Muskoka.

20. That part of the King's Highway known as No. 26 in the County of Simcoe lying between a point situate 50 metres measured westerly from its intersection with the centre line of the King's Highway known as No. 7149 in the Town of Wasaga Beach and a point situate 50 metres measured easterly from its intersection with the centre line of the roadway known as Poplar Sideroad in the Town of Collingwood.

21. That part of the King's Highway known as Nos. 11 and 17 in the City of North Bay lying between a point situate at its intersection with the roadway known as Seymour Street and a point situate at its intersection with the King's Highway known as No. 11 (also known as Algonquin Avenue).

22. That part of the King's Highway known as Nos. 11 and 17 lying between a point situate at its intersection with the centre line of the roadway known as Lakeshore Drive in the Municipality of Shuniah and a point situate at its intersection with the centre line of the King's Highway known as No. 130 in the Municipality of Oliver Paipoonge.

23. That part of the King's Highway known as No. 17 in the City of North Bay lying between a point situate at its intersection with the King's Highway known as No. 11 (also known as Algonquin Avenue) and a point situate at its intersection with the roadway known as Gormanville Road.

24. That part of the King's Highway known as No. 17 in the City of Greater Sudbury lying between a point situate at its intersection with the middle junction of the roadway known as Municipal Road 55 and a point situate at its intersection with the west junction of the roadway known as Municipal Road 55.

25. That part of the King's Highway known as No. 58 in the City of Thorold lying between a point situate at its intersection with the King's Highway known as No. 406 and a point situate at its intersection with the westerly limit of the roadway known as Niagara Regional Road No. 57 (also known as Thorold Stone Road).

26. That part of the King's Highway known as No. 61 in the City of Thunder Bay lying between a point situate at its intersection with the King's Highway known as No. 11 and a point situate at its intersection with the roadway known as Broadway Avenue.

26.1 That part of the King's Highway known as No. 69 in the Territorial District of Sudbury lying between a point situate 2438 metres measured southerly from its intersection with the centre line of the roadway known as Crooked Lake Road in the Township of Cox and a point situate 1585 metres measured southerly from its intersection with the centre line of the roadway known as Estaire Road in the City of Greater Sudbury.

27. That part of the King's Highway known as No. 85 lying between a point situate at its intersection with the King's Highway known as No. 7 (also known as Victoria Street) in the City of Kitchener and a point situate 385 metres measured northerly from its intersection with the centre line of the roadway known as Waterloo Regional Road 15 (also known as King Street) in the Township of Woolwich.

28. That part of the King's Highway known as No. 115 lying between a point situate at its intersection with the King's Highway known as Nos. 35 and 115 in the Municipality of Clarington and a point situate at its intersection with the King's Highway known as No. 7 in the Township of Cavan-Millbrook-North Monaghan.

29. That part of the King's Highway known as No. 137 lying between a point situate at its intersection with the King's Highway known as No. 401 in the Township of Leeds and The Thousand Islands and a point situate at its intersection with the border between Canada and the United States of America.

30. All of the King's Highway known as No. 7274 (also known as Highway 6/Airport Road Connection).

31. That part of the King's Highway known as No. 7087 (also known as E. C. Row Expressway) in the City of Windsor in the County of Essex lying between a point situate at its intersection with the northerly limit of the King's Highway known as No. 7902 (also known as Ojibway Parkway) and a point situate 365 metres measured easterly from its intersection with the centre line of the King's Highway known as No. 3 (also known as Huron Church Road).

32. That part of the King's Highway known as No. 7902 (also known as Ojibway Parkway) in the City of Windsor in the County of Essex lying between a point situate at its intersection with the northerly limit of the south junction of the roadway known as Broadway Street and a point situate at its intersection with the easterly limit of the Essex Terminal Railway right-of-way.

O. Reg. 39/08, s. 1; 313/08, s. 1; 408/10, s. 1; 475/10, s. 1; 453/11, s. 1; 113/12, s. 1; 194/12, s. 1; 232/12, s. 1; 242/12, s. 1; 359/12, s. 1; 228/13, s. 1; 370/15, s. 2; 25/16, s. 1

ONT. REG. 601/93 — USED VEHICLE INFORMATION PACKAGE

made under the *Highway Traffic Act*

O. Reg. 601/93, as am. O. Reg. 246/95; 497/95; 88/00; 357/05; 636/05; 445/09; 212/10.

1. In this Regulation,

"used motor vehicle" means,

(a) any motor vehicle having a registered empty vehicle weight of 2,200 kilograms or less as recorded on the vehicle's most recent permit, which permit must have been issued under section 7 of the Act, except a bus or motor-assisted bicycle or an off-road vehicle as defined in the *Off-Road Vehicles Act*,

(b) a motorized mobile home, regardless of its gross weight, the most recent permit for which has been issued under section 7 of the Act;

"used vehicle information package" means an information package issued by the Ministry of Consumer and Commercial Relations or the Ministry of Transportation containing information on registrations relating to a used motor vehicle made under the *Personal Property Security Act* and the *Repair and Storage Liens Act* and the Ontario registration history of the vehicle.

O. Reg. 497/95, s. 1

2. The following classes of sellers or transferors are exempt from providing used vehicle information packages under subsection 11.1(1) of the Act:

1. An owner of a used motor vehicle who transfers it to a person who transports the goods of other persons for compensation under an agreement for use of the vehicle that provides for the transfer of the vehicle back to the owner on termination of the agreement.

2. A person who transports the goods of other persons for compensation who transfers a used motor vehicle back to the owner of the vehicle on termination of an agreement for use of the vehicle.

3. A person who transfers a used motor vehicle from an estate to any person legally entitled to the vehicle.

4. A corporation that sells or transfers a used motor vehicle forming part of its assets to a shareholder of the corporation.

5. A person who transfers a used motor vehicle for no consideration to a member of his or her family.

6. A spouse or former spouse who transfers to his or her spouse or former spouse a used motor vehicle under a separation agreement or divorce judgment.

6.1 [Repealed O. Reg. 357/05, s. 1.]

7. A person who sells or transfers a used motor vehicle to a hospital, local services board, municipality, school board, university or college.

8. A person who transfers a used motor vehicle to an insurer as defined in the *Insurance Act* on receiving payment under an insurance policy as a result of the vehicle having been stolen or wrecked.

9. A corporation carrying out multiple transfers of used motor vehicles to another corporation.

10. A motor vehicle dealer who is registered under the *Motor Vehicle Dealers Act, 2002*, other than a dealer registered as a broker.

10.1 A person who sells or transfers a used motor vehicle to a motor vehicle dealer who is registered under the *Motor Vehicle Dealers Act, 2002*, other than a dealer registered as a broker.

10.2 A motor vehicle dealer who meets the following requirements:

    i. the dealer was registered under the *Motor Vehicle Dealers Act* on December 31, 2009, and

    ii. the dealer is exempted from the *Motor Vehicle Dealers Act, 2002* and its regulations under paragraph 18, 19 or 21 of subsection 2(1) of Ontario Regulation 333/08 (*General*) made under that Act.

10.3 A motor vehicle dealer who meets the following requirements:

    i. the dealer was not registered under the *Motor Vehicle Dealers Act* on December 31, 2009,

    ii. the dealer is exempted from the *Motor Vehicle Dealers Act, 2002* and its regulations under paragraph 18, 19 or 21 of subsection 2(1) of Ontario Regulation 333/08 (*General*) made under that Act, and

    iii. the dealer satisfies the Ministry of that exemption.

10.4 A person who sells or transfers a used motor vehicle to a motor vehicle dealer referred to in paragraph 10.2 or 10.3.

11. An owner of a used motor vehicle who transfers the vehicle to a holder of a taxicab owner's licence issued under a municipal by-law pursuant to an agreement for use of the vehicle as a taxicab that provides for the transfer of the vehicle back to the owner on termination of the agreement.

12. A holder of a taxicab owner's licence issued under a municipal by-law who transfers a used motor vehicle back to the owner of the vehicle on termination of an agreement for use of the vehicle as a taxicab.

13. A person who transfers a used motor vehicle for no consideration to a religious, charitable or benevolent organization as defined in the *Income Tax Act* (Canada).

14. A person who transfers a used motor vehicle under a security agreement as defined in the *Personal Property Security Act*.

15. A person who transfers a used motor vehicle into that person's name pursuant to the *Repair and Storage Liens Act.*

16. A person who transfers a used motor vehicle to any person pursuant to the rules of a licensed lottery.

17. A person who as trustee transfers a used motor vehicle to a person having a beneficial interest in it.

18. A person who sells or transfers a used motor vehicle for the purposes of wrecking or dismantling it to a holder of a Class C licence issued by the Ministry.

O. Reg. 246/95, s. 1; 497/95, s. 2; 88/00, s. 1; 357/05, s. 1; 636/05, s. 1; 445/09, s. 1; 212/10, s. 1

3. The following classes of purchasers or transferee are exempt from delivering used vehicle information packages under subsection 11.1(3) of the Act:

1. An owner of a used motor vehicle that is transferred back to the owner by a person who transports the goods of other persons for compensation on termination of an agreement for use of the vehicle.

2. A person who transports the goods of other persons for compensation to whom a used motor vehicle is transferred by the owner of the vehicle under an agreement for use of the vehicle.

3. A person to whom a used motor vehicle is transferred from an estate for no consideration.

4. A shareholder of a corporation to whom a used motor vehicle forming part of the corporation's assets is sold or transferred by the corporation.

5. A member of his or her family to whom the transferor transfers a used motor vehicle for no consideration.

6. A spouse or former spouse to whom a used motor vehicle is transferred by his or her spouse or former spouse under a separation agreement or divorce judgment.

6.1 [Repealed O. Reg. 357/05, s. 2.]

7. A hospital, local services board, municipality, school board, university or college to which a used motor vehicle is sold or transferred.

8. An insurer as defined in the *Insurance Act* to whom a person transfers a used motor vehicle on receiving payment under an insurance policy as a result of the vehicle having been stolen or wrecked.

9. A corporation to which another corporation has made multiple transfers of used motor vehicles.

10. A motor vehicle dealer who is registered under the *Motor Vehicle Dealers Act, 2002*, other than a dealer registered as a broker, to whom a used motor vehicle is sold or transferred.

10.1 A person to whom a used motor vehicle is sold or transferred by a motor vehicle dealer who is registered under the *Motor Vehicle Dealers Act, 2002*, other than a dealer registered as a broker.

10.2 A motor vehicle dealer referred to in paragraph 10.2 or 10.3 of section 2 to whom a used motor vehicle is sold or transferred.

10.3 A person to whom a used motor vehicle is sold or transferred by a motor vehicle dealer referred to in paragraph 10.2 or 10.3 of section 2.

11. An owner of a used motor vehicle to whom the vehicle is transferred back on termination of an agreement for use of the vehicle as a taxicab by a holder of a taxicab owner's licence issued under a municipal by-law.

12. A holder of a taxicab owner's licence issued under a municipal by-law to whom a used motor vehicle is transferred by the owner of the vehicle under an agreement for use of the vehicle as a taxicab.

13. A religious, charitable or benevolent organization as defined in the *Income Tax Act* (Canada) to which a used motor vehicle has been transferred for no consideration.

14. A person to whom a used motor vehicle is sold or transferred by a person under a security agreement as defined in the *Personal Property Security Act*.

15. A person into whose name a used motor vehicle is transferred under the *Repair and Storage Liens Act*.

16. A person to whom a used motor vehicle is transferred pursuant to the rules of a licensed lottery.

17. A person having a beneficial interest in a used motor vehicle to whom the vehicle is transferred by the trustee.

18. A holder of a Class C licence issued by the Ministry to whom a used motor vehicle has been sold or transferred for the purpose of wrecking or dismantling it.

O. Reg. 246/95, s. 2; 497/95, s. 3; 88/00, s. 2; 357/05, s. 2; 636/05, s. 2; 445/09, s. 2; 212/10, s. 2

4. (1) For the purpose of paragraph 5 of sections 2 and 3, "member of his or her family" means the spouse, father, mother, grandfather, grandmother, son, daughter, grandson, granddaughter, son-in-law, daughter-in-law, father-in-law or mother-in-law of the transferor or transferee, as the case may be.

(2) For the purpose of subsection (1) and paragraphs 5 and 6 of sections 2 and 3, "spouse" has the same meaning as in Part III of the *Family Law Act*.

O. Reg. 88/00, s. 3; 357/05, s. 3

5. A fee of $20 shall be paid for a used vehicle information package.

ONT. REG. 628 — VEHICLE PERMITS

made under the *Highway Traffic Act*

R.R.O. 1990, Reg. 628, as am. O. Reg. 198/91; 309/92; 590/92; 404/93; 820/93; 576/94; 245/95; 332/95; 337/97; 343/97; 508/97; 540/98; 654/98; 71/99; 254/99; 299/99; 437/99; 87/00; 146/00; 193/00; 262/00; 508/00; 666/00; 691/00; 123/01; 331/01; 353/01; 379/02; 423/03; 437/03; 290/04; 367/04; 398/04; 15/05; 183/05; 358/05; 588/05; 637/05; 71/08; 303/08; 446/09; 211/10; 414/10; 62/11; 188/11; 344/11; 41/12 (Fr.); 119/12; 168/12; CTR 23 JL 12 - 1; 312/12, s. 1; 244/13; 214/14; 245/14 [s. 1(2), (6) to come into force November 1, 2016; s. 1(1), (3)–(5), (7), (8) to come into force January 1, 2017.]; 271/14; 78/15; 258/15 [s. 1(1) to come into force January 1, 2018; s. 2 to come into force December 1, 2016; ss. 3, 4 to come into force January 1, 2017] [s. 5 repealed O. Reg. 328/15, s. 8.]; 328/15, ss. 1–7; 422/15 [To come into force January 1, 2017.].

INTERPRETATION

1. (1) In this Regulation,

"carrying capacity" means,

(a) in the case of a school bus, the weight in kilograms that is obtained when the seating capacity of the bus is multiplied by forty, and

(b) in the case of a bus, other than a school bus, the weight in kilograms that is obtained when the seating capacity of the bus is multiplied by sixty;

"emissions inspection report" and "conditional emissions inspection report" have the same meanings as in Ontario Regulation 361/98 made under the *Environmental Protection Act*;

"expanded program area" has the same meaning as in Ontario Regulation 361/98 made under the *Environmental Protection Act*;

"farmer" means a farming business within the meaning of the *Farm Registration and Farm Organizations Funding Act, 1993* that,

(a) has a current registration number under that Act,

(b) is not required to file a farming business registration form under that Act pursuant to an order by the Agriculture, Food and Rural Affairs Appeal Tribunal that the requirement be waived, or

(c) meets the requirements set out in one of the paragraphs of subsection 8(3) of Ontario Regulation 282/98 (*General*) made under the *Assessment Act*;

"farm products" does not include products preserved by freezing, pickling, cooking, smoking or curing, other than cured tobacco leaves;

"Greater Toronto Area" has the same meaning as in Ontario Regulation 361/98 made under the *Environmental Protection Act*;

"gross weight" means,

(a) in the case of a bus, the combined weight and carrying capacity of the bus, and

(b) in the case of a commercial motor vehicle, other than a bus, the combined weight of the motor vehicle and load or, where a commercial motor vehicle is drawing a trailer or trailers, the combined weight of the motor vehicle, trailer or trailers and load but, where a trailer transmits to the highway a total weight of 2,800 kilograms or less, that weight shall not be included in determining gross weight;

"historic vehicle" means, despite the definition in subsection 7(1.1) of the Act, a motor vehicle that,

(a) is at least 30 years old,

(b) is operated on a highway in parades, for purposes of exhibition, tours or similar functions organized by a properly constituted automobile club or for purposes of repair, testing or demonstration for sale,

(c) is substantially unchanged or unmodified from the original manufacturer's product, and

(d) does not have attached to it year-of-manufacture plates;

"hybrid vehicle" means a motor vehicle that is equipped by its manufacturer with an internal combustion engine as a source of power and an electric motor as an auxiliary source of power;

"kit car" has the same meaning as in Ontario Regulation 361/98 made under the *Environmental Protection Act*;

"reassembled motor vehicle" means a motor vehicle assembled using the body of a motor vehicle with a model year of 1981 or later and the chassis frame assembly of another motor vehicle, both of which were manufactured utilizing a full frame assembly as part of the vehicle's structure;

"registered gross weight" has the same meaning as in Ontario Regulation 340/94 made under the Act;

"resident of Northern Ontario" means a person, other than a corporation, who ordinarily resides in the Territorial District of Algoma, Cochrane, Kenora, Manitoulin, Nipissing, Parry Sound, Rainy River, Sudbury, Timiskaming or Thunder Bay;

"RUO sticker" means a sticker that is evidence of validation effected under subsection 5(4).

"special permit" means a permit issued under section 12;

"temporary validation" means validation issued under section 5.2;

"urban and commuter areas" has the same meaning as in Ontario Regulation 361/98 made under the *Environmental Protection Act*.

"year-of-manufacture plates" means number plates that are described in subsection 7(7.2) of the Act.

(2) For the purposes of sections 5.2 and 12 and subsection 17(1), a commercial motor vehicle is considered to be laden in the following circumstances:

1. It is towing another motor vehicle.

2. It is carrying any goods or cargo.

3. It is drawing a trailer that is carrying any goods or cargo.

4. It is drawing a trailer chassis that is carrying an inter-modal shipping container.

5. It is a bus carrying two or more passengers.

(3) Despite subsection (2), a commercial motor vehicle described in paragraph 1, 2, 3 or 4 of that subsection is considered to be unladen if its gross weight is 4,500 kilograms or less.
O. Reg. 337/97; 540/98, s. 1; 654/98, s. 1; 508/00, s. 1; 691/00, s. 1; 331/01, s. 1; 353/01, s. 1; 379/02, s. 1; 398/04, s. 1; 183/05, s. 1; 71/08, s. 1; 271/14, s. 1

PERMITS

2. (1) It is a requirement for receiving a permit for a used motor vehicle or for a motor vehicle classified as salvage or rebuilt,

(a) that the applicant submit a safety standards certificate issued upon an inspection of the vehicle that was completed within the preceding 36 days;

(b) if the application is in respect of a motor vehicle with a registered gross weight of 4,500 kilograms or less, that the Ministry is satisfied that an emissions inspection report has been issued in respect of the vehicle within the preceding 12 months; and

(b.1) [Revoked O. Reg. 423/03, s. 1(1).]

(c) if the application is in respect of a motor vehicle with a registered gross weight of more than 4,500 kilograms, that the Ministry is satisfied that an emissions inspection report has been issued in respect of the vehicle within the preceding 12 months.

(2) Subject to subsection (2.1), subsection (1) does not apply,

(a) where the permit applied for is a CAVR cab card or an IRP cab card;

(b) where the applicant is the spouse or the estate of the person who is registered in Ontario as the owner of the vehicle or the spouse of the person whose estate is registered in Ontario as the owner of the vehicle;

(b.1) [Repealed O. Reg. 358/05, s. 1(1).]

(c) where the applicant is a motor vehicle dealer who is registered under the *Motor Vehicle Dealers Act, 2002*, other than a dealer registered as a broker;

(c.1) where the applicant is a motor vehicle dealer who,

(i) was registered under the *Motor Vehicle Dealers Act* on December 31, 2009, and

(ii) is exempted from the *Motor Vehicle Dealers Act, 2002* and its regulations under paragraph 18, 19 or 21 of subsection 2(1) of Ontario Regulation 333/08 (*General*) made under that Act;

(c.2) where the applicant is a motor vehicle dealer who,

(i) was not registered under the *Motor Vehicle Dealers Act* on December 31, 2009,

(ii) is exempted from the *Motor Vehicle Dealers Act, 2002* and its regulations under paragraph 18, 19 or 21 of subsection 2(1) of Ontario Regulation 333/08 (*General*) made under that Act, and

(iii) satisfies the Ministry of that exemption;

(d) to an application for a permit for a motor vehicle that has been operated 6,000 kilometres or less and for which a permit has been issued under section 7 of the Act in the name of a motor vehicle dealer exempted under clause (c), (c.1) or (c.2) and has not been in the name of a person other than such a dealer;

(e) where the vehicle portion of the permit applied for is to be issued in the name of the person who is registered in Ontario as the owner of the vehicle;

(f) to an application for a permit for a commercial motor vehicle, other than a dump truck, that is registered in another jurisdiction, where the person applying to be the permit holder does not reside in Ontario;

(g) to an application for a permit for a motor vehicle that is registered in another jurisdiction, where the applicant has, within the preceding twelve months, been the holder of a currently validated permit that was issued for the vehicle by the Province of Ontario; or

(h) where the permit applied for is in respect of a vehicle being transferred by one leasing company to another leasing company and, at the time of the transfer, the vehicle is in the possession of a lessee under a lease agreement.

(2.1) Unless an emissions inspection report required under clause (1)(b) or (c) has been issued in respect of a motor vehicle, evidence of validation shall not be furnished for the motor vehicle where,

(a) any of clauses (2)(a) to (g) applies to the motor vehicle; and

(b) an emissions inspection report would be required under section 8.1 or 8.2.

(3) Clause (1)(a) does not apply in respect of a motor assisted bicycle.

(4) Clause (1)(b) does not apply in respect of,

(a) a motor vehicle the model year of which is 1987 or older;

(b) a current model year motor vehicle or a future model year motor vehicle;

(c) a motorcycle or a motor assisted bicycle;

(d) a vehicle to which paragraph 2 of subsection 19(1) applies;

(e) any motor vehicle that does not use an internal combustion engine as its source of power;

(f) a kit car;

(g) a hybrid vehicle; or

(h) an historic vehicle.

(4.1) Clause (1)(b) does not apply,

(a) where the permit applied for is in respect of a vehicle being transferred to the applicant by a member of his or her family; or

(b) where the permit applied for is in respect of a vehicle being transferred to the applicant by a leasing company under a lease agreement between the applicant and the leasing company.

(5) Clause (1)(b) only applies in respect of an application if the applicant's address, as shown on the plate portion of the permit, is within the Greater Toronto Area, the urban and commuter areas or the expanded program area.

(5.1) Clause (1)(c) does not apply in respect of,

(a) a motor vehicle that does not use an internal combustion engine as its source of power;

(a.1) a hybrid vehicle; or

(b) a current model year motor vehicle or a future model year motor vehicle.

(5.2) Clause (1)(c) only applies in respect of an application respecting a motor vehicle that uses fuel other than diesel fuel if the applicant's address, as shown on the plate portion of the permit, is within the Greater Toronto Area, the urban and commuter areas or the expanded program area.

(6) The emissions inspection report required under clause (1)(b) or (c) shall be based on the emissions test for the relevant motor vehicle as set out in Ontario Regulation 361/98 made under the *Environmental Protection Act*.

(6.1) [Revoked O. Reg. 691/00, s. 2(5).]

(7) Where a person to whom subsection (1) applies does not submit the safety standards certificate with the application, a permit marked "unfit motor vehicle" may be issued.

(8) Where a permit marked "unfit motor vehicle" has been issued for a vehicle, nothing in subsection (2) shall be construed so as to allow a permit that is not marked "unfit motor vehicle" to be issued for the vehicle unless the applicant submits a safety standards certificate issued upon an inspection of the vehicle that was completed within the preceding 36 days.

(9) Where the Ministry is not satisfied that an emissions inspection report has been issued in respect of a vehicle where clause (1)(b) or (c) applies to the applicant, the vehicle portion of a permit may be issued, but no number plates shall be attached to the vehicle and no evidence of validation for the permit shall be furnished unless the requirement set out in clause (1)(b) or (c) is met.

(10) Where a permit is issued under subsection (9) while the requirement set out in clause (1)(b) or (c) is unmet, nothing in subsection (2) shall be construed so as to allow a plate portion of the permit to be issued.

(11) In this section,

"member of his or her family" means, in relation to an applicant, the following persons, whether related to the applicant by blood or adoption:

1. The applicant's spouse.

2. The applicant's parent, step-parent, grandparent or step-grandparent.

3. The applicant's child, step-child, grandchild or step-grandchild.

4. The applicant's sibling or half-sibling.

5. The applicant's father-in-law, mother-in-law, son-in-law, daughter-in-law, brother-in-law or sister-in-law;

"spouse" has the same meaning as in Part III of the *Family Law Act*.
   O. Reg. 309/92, s. 1; 245/95, s. 1; 540/98, s. 2; 654/98, s. 2; 299/99, s. 1; 87/00, s. 1; 666/00, s. 1; 691/00, s. 2; 353/01, s. 2; 379/02, s. 2; 423/03, s. 1; 183/05, s. 2; 358/05, s. 1; 588/05, s. 1; 446/09, s. 1; 211/10, s. 1; 188/11, s. 1

2.1 (1) It is a requirement for receiving a permit for a motor vehicle for the first time after it was reclassified as rebuilt under subsection 199.1(22) of the Act that the applicant submit a structural inspection certificate issued for the vehicle.

(2) Subsection (1) does not apply to a motor vehicle for which the applicant held, at any time in the 12 months immediately before the application for the permit is made, a currently validated permit issued under the Act for the vehicle and that is registered in another jurisdiction at the time of the application for the permit.
   O. Reg. 379/02, s. 3

3. Where a vehicle for which a permit is currently validated is modified so that it does not correspond to the description of the vehicle on the permit, the owner of the vehicle shall apply to the Ministry for a new permit for the vehicle within six days after the modification.

3.1 If there is a change to the name or address of the owner of a vehicle for which a permit is currently validated so that the owner's name or address does not correspond to the name or address on the permit, the owner of the vehicle shall apply to the Ministry for a new permit for the vehicle within six days after the change occurs.
   O. Reg. 168/12, s. 1

4. (1) For the purposes of clause 7(1)(a) of the Act, a permit for a motor vehicle ceases to be currently validated with the expiration of the expiry day, month and year shown on the permit or, in the case of a permit bearing evidence of validation, on the expiration of the expiry day shown on the permit in the month and year shown on the evidence of validation.

(2) Subsection (1) does not apply to a permit issued for,

   (a) a motor vehicle where the permit holder is the Government of the Province of Ontario; or

   (b) a commercial motor vehicle to which section 5 applies.

(3) Subsection (1) does not apply to a permit issued for a commercial motor vehicle where the permit holder is a municipal fire department.

(3.1) Subsection (1) does not apply to a special permit or temporary validation of a permit.

(4) A permit issued to a permit holder referred to in clause (2)(a) and subsection (3) ceases to be currently validated when surrendered to the Ministry.

O. Reg. 71/08, s. 2

5. (1) For the purpose of clause 7(1)(a) of the Act, a permit for a commercial motor vehicle ceases to be currently validated with the expiration of the month and year shown on the permit or, in the case of a permit bearing evidence of validation, on the expiration of the month and year shown on the evidence of validation.

(2) Subject to subsections (3), (4) and (5), the period for which a permit for a commercial motor vehicle may be validated is any number of consecutive months between a minimum of three and a maximum of fifteen.

(3) A bus permit that expires before the 1st day of August may be validated in that year for July and August or August only of that year if the bus,

    (a) is operated under the authority of a public vehicle licence issued under the *Public Vehicles Act* that restricts the use of the bus to school purposes only or is operated for school purposes only within the corporate limits of one urban municipality;

    (b) is primarily used for the purpose of transporting children to or from school;

    (c) is operated under a contract with a school board or other authority in charge of a school or if the permit holder is a municipality or school board; and

    (d) during the period of validation authorized by the RUO sticker, is intended to be,

        (i) occupied by the driver only, or

        (ii) used only for driver examination or driver training, and the trainer holds a proper driver's licence.

(4) A permit referred to in subsection (3) is validated when a RUO sticker is issued in respect of the permit and such sticker is affixed to the number plate in accordance with subsection 9(2).

(5) Subject to subsection (6), where the fee for a permit is prorated under a reciprocity agreement or arrangement with another jurisdiction, the period for which the permit may be validated is,

    (a) in the case of a conversion or new registration, any number of consecutive months between a minimum of three and a maximum of fifteen; and

    (b) in the case of a renewal, twelve consecutive months.

(5.1) [Repealed O. Reg. 62/11, s. 1.]

(5.2) [Repealed O. Reg. 62/11, s. 1.]

(6) This section does not apply to a special permit or temporary validation of a permit.

(7) This section does not apply to a permit for a commercial motor vehicle that has a gross weight of 3,000 kilograms or less unless the vehicle is a bus.

          O. Reg. 146/00, s. 1; 666/00, s. 2; 71/08, s. 3; 62/11, s. 1

5.1 (1) A permit for a passenger car, a motorized mobile home, an historic vehicle, a motorcycle, a motor assisted bicycle, a commercial motor vehicle with a gross weight of not more than 3,000 kilograms or a combination of a commercial motor vehicle and a trailer with a gross weight of not more than 3,000 kilograms may be validated for a period of not less than three months and not more than 24 months.

(1.1) A Dealer permit, a Service permit, a Dealer and Service permit or a Manufacturer permit may be validated for a period of not less than three months and not more than 24 months.

(2) Validation of a permit upon renewal shall not be issued for a period of time beyond the date upon which the vehicle would next require proof of having complied with the emissions requirements of Ontario Regulation 361/98 made under the *Environmental Protection Act* in order to obtain validation.

(3) Subject to subsection (2), a permit is validated until the expiry date set out on it and, after renewal, a permit is validated until the first, second or third anniversary date of the original expiry date, as set out on the renewed permit.

(4) Subsection (3) does not apply to a permit to which subsection 8.1(8) applies.

   O. Reg. 337/97, s. 2; 540/98, s. 3; 71/99, s. 1; 254/99, s. 1; 262/00, s. 1; 367/04, s. 1; 62/11, s. 2; 328/15, s. 1

5.2 (1) A permit for any motor vehicle may be temporarily validated for a period of 10 days.

(2) Subject to subsection (3), temporary validation may not be issued more than twice to the same holder of a permit for the same vehicle.

(3) If, after being issued one or two consecutive temporary validations of a permit for a vehicle, the permit is validated on payment of a fee prescribed under section 18 or 19, the permit may again be temporarily validated one or two consecutive times.

(4) Temporary validation shall not be issued for a motor vehicle if the permit for the motor vehicle is marked "unfit motor vehicle" or, in the case of a permit issued by another jurisdiction, the equivalent of unfit in that jurisdiction.

(5) Temporary validation shall not be issued for a motor vehicle if the permit for the motor vehicle indicates that the motor vehicle is classified as irreparable or salvage or, in the case of a permit issued by another jurisdiction, the equivalent of irreparable or salvage in that jurisdiction.

(6) Evidence of temporary validation shall be affixed to the number plate that corresponds to the temporary permit, in accordance with subsection 9(1).

(7) Evidence of temporary validation shall not be displayed on the number plate of a commercial motor vehicle that is laden.

(8) Section 2 does not apply to the furnishing of evidence of temporary validation issued under this section.

O. Reg. 71/08, s. 4

6. (1) A permit for a motor vehicle shall be validated by means of evidence of validation provided by the Ministry.

(2) Evidence of validation for a permit shall be affixed to a number plate for the vehicle in accordance with this Regulation, and the portion of the evidence of validation not intended for the number plate may be affixed in the appropriate space provided on the permit for the vehicle.

O. Reg. 119/12, s. 1

7. A permit for a trailer expires when it is surrendered to the Ministry or replaced by a permit issued by another jurisdiction.

8. (1) It is a condition applying to every permit, other than an IRP cab card or a special permit, that it bear the signature of the holder thereof, written in ink.

(2) Where the permit holder is a corporation, the signature of a person authorized to sign on behalf of the corporation is in compliance with subsection (1).

O. Reg. 666/00, s. 3; 71/08, s. 5; 62/11, s. 3

8.0.1 (1) This section applies to applications for the issuance of number plates or evidence of validation for use on a number plate for,

    (a) a bus; or

    (b) a commercial motor vehicle, other than a bus, having a registered gross weight of more than 4,500 kilograms.

(2) Number plates or evidence of validation for use on a number plate shall not be issued in respect of a motor vehicle to which this section applies unless the Ministry is satisfied that the person whose name is to appear or appears on the plate portion of the permit is the holder of a valid CVOR certificate.

(3) Despite subsection (2), number plates or evidence of validation for use on a number plate may be issued even if the person whose name is to appear or appears on the plate portion of the permit is not the holder of a valid CVOR certificate, provided the Ministry is satisfied that the vehicle will be operated in accordance with the law.

(4) This section does not apply to applications for temporary validation of a permit.

(5) In this section,

"valid CVOR certificate" means a CVOR certificate, as defined in subsection 16(1) of the Act, that,

> **Proposed Amendment — 8.0.1(5) "valid CVOR certificate" opening words**
>
> "valid CVOR certificate" means a CVOR certificate, that,
>
> O. Reg. 422/15, s. 1 [To come into force January 1, 2017.]

(a) is not under suspension,

(b) has not expired,

(c) has not been revoked or cancelled, and

(d) has not been terminated by the holder of the certificate.

O. Reg. 214/14, s. 1

8.1 (1) This section applies to applications for the renewal of a motor vehicle permit for motor vehicles,

(a) that use an internal combustion engine as their source of power; and

(b) that have a registered gross weight of 4,500 kilograms or less.

(1.1) [Revoked O. Reg. 423/03, s. 2.]

(2) This section does not apply in respect of,

(a) a kit car;

(a.1) a hybrid vehicle;

(b) a motorcycle or a motor assisted bicycle;

(c) a vehicle to which paragraph 2 of subsection 19(1) applies; or

(d) an historic vehicle.

(3) Despite anything in this Regulation, no motor vehicle permit, other than a special permit, shall be renewed or evidence of validation, other than evidence of temporary validation, shall be furnished in respect of a motor vehicle to which this section applies unless the Ministry is satisfied that an emissions inspection report or a conditional emissions inspection report has been issued in respect of the vehicle within 12 months before the permit expires or, if the application for renewal is made after the expiry of the permit, within 12 months before the application for renewal.

(4) Subsection (3) applies in respect of a motor vehicle the model year of which is 1988 or later in the seventh calendar year after its model year and in every second calendar year after that.

(5) Subsection (3) only applies to an application for renewal if the applicant's address, as shown on the plate portion of the permit, is within the Greater Toronto Area, the urban and commuter areas or the expanded program area.

(6) The emissions inspection report or conditional emissions inspection report required under this section shall be based on the emissions tests that are applicable to the vehicle in respect of which the application for renewal is made, as set out in Ontario Regulation 361/98 made under the *Environmental Protection Act*.

(6.1) An emissions inspection report issued in respect of a vehicle more than 12 months before the permit expires or, if the application for renewal is made after the expiry of the permit, more than 12 months before the application for renewal, may be used in satisfaction of the requirement set out in subsection (3) if the report,

(a) was issued on or after January 1 of the calendar year immediately preceding the calendar year in which the application for renewal is made; and

(b) was issued in satisfaction of the requirement set out in clause 2(1)(b) and used only once for that purpose.

(7) No permit shall be validated for a period that ends more than 36 months after the date on which the emissions inspection report or conditional emissions inspection report required under this section was issued.

(8) Despite anything in this section, a permit may be renewed or validated without the required emissions inspection report or conditional emissions inspection report if the Ministry is satisfied that it was not reasonably possible for the permit holder to have the vehicle tested for emissions.

(9) Subsection (8) may be applied only one time in respect of a permit holder for a vehicle.

Table
Application of Subsection 8.1(1)
[Revoked O. Reg. 423/03, s. 2.]

O. Reg. 540/98, s. 4; 654/98, s. 3; 299/99, s. 2; 437/99, s. 1; 691/00, s. 3; 353/01, s. 3; 423/03, s. 2; 183/05, s. 3; 588/05, ss. 2, 3; 71/08, s. 6; 188/11, s. 2

8.2 (1) This section applies to applications for the renewal of a motor vehicle permit for motor vehicles,

    (a) that use an internal combustion engine as their source of power; and

    (b) that have a registered gross weight of more than 4,500 kilograms.

(1.1) This section does not apply in respect of a hybrid vehicle.

(2) Despite anything in this Regulation, no motor vehicle permit, other than a special permit, shall be renewed or evidence of validation, other than evidence of temporary validation, shall be furnished in respect of a motor vehicle described in subsection (1) unless the Ministry is satisfied that an emissions inspection report has been issued in respect of the vehicle within 12 months before the permit expires or, if the application for renewal is made after the expiry of the permit, within 12 months before the application for renewal.

(3) Subsection (2) applies in respect of a motor vehicle in the seventh calendar year after its model year and in every calendar year after that, but only once in any 12-month period.

(4) Subsection (2) does not apply to an application for renewal that is made in, or in respect of a permit that expires in, an eligible year in respect of a vehicle that uses diesel fuel if the Ministry is satisfied that the last emissions inspection report for the vehicle,

    (a) was issued within 24 months before the permit expires or, if the application for renewal is made after the expiry of the permit, within 24 months before the application for renewal; and

    (b) indicates that the vehicle achieved opacity of 20 per cent or less in the opacity test required for that emissions inspection report.

(5) Subsection (2) only applies to an application for renewal in respect of a vehicle that uses fuel other than diesel fuel if the applicant's address, as shown on the plate portion of the permit, is within the Greater Toronto Area, the urban and commuter areas or the expanded program area.

(6) The emissions inspection reports required under this section shall be based on the emissions tests that are applicable to the vehicle in respect of which the application for renewal is made, as set out in Ontario Regulation 361/98 made under the *Environmental Protection Act.*

(7) Despite anything in this section, a permit may be renewed or validated without the required emissions inspection report if the Ministry is satisfied that it was not reasonably possible for the permit holder to have the vehicle tested for emissions.

(8) For the purposes of subsection (4),

"eligible year" means,

   (a) for a vehicle with an odd-numbered model year, 2005 and every second calendar year after that,

   (b) for a vehicle with an even-numbered model year, 2006 and every second calendar year after that.

Table
Application of Subsection 8.2(1)

[Revoked O. Reg. 423/03, s. 2.]

O. Reg. 299/99, s. 3; 437/99, s. 2; 691/00, s. 4; 423/03, s. 2; 183/05, s. 4; 588/05, s. 4; 71/08, s. 7; 188/11, s. 3

8.3 (1) This section applies to applications for evidence of validation of a motor vehicle permit in respect of a year or part of a year when there is in force a City of Toronto by-law levying a tax in respect of motor vehicles.

(2) Despite anything in this Regulation, evidence of validation of a motor vehicle permit, other than evidence of validation of a special permit or evidence of temporary validation, shall not be furnished in respect of a motor vehicle unless the Ministry is satisfied that the tax levied in respect of the motor vehicle by the by-law described in subsection (1) has been paid.

(3) Subsection (2) does not apply where the person applying for the evidence of validation of a motor vehicle permit is exempt under section 20 or subsection 21(2) from paying a fee for validation of a motor vehicle permit or for evidence of validation of a motor vehicle permit.

O. Reg. 303/08, s. 1

NUMBER PLATES

9. (1) Evidence of validation issued for use on a number plate shall be affixed,

   (a) where the permit is for a commercial motor vehicle, in the upper right corner of the number plate exposed on the front of the motor vehicle; and

(b) in all other cases, in the upper right corner of the number plate exposed on the rear of the motor vehicle.

(2) Despite subsection (1), a RUO sticker shall be affixed in the upper left corner of the number plate exposed on the front of the bus.

(3) The number plates for a motor vehicle, other than a motorcycle or a motor assisted bicycle, shall be attached to and exposed in a conspicuous position on the front and rear of the motor vehicle.

(3.1) Where the number plates attached to the vehicle are year-of-manufacture plates, and only one plate was issued by the Ministry in that year for display on a motor vehicle, that plate shall be attached to and exposed in a conspicuous position at the rear of the vehicle.

(4) The number plate for a motorcycle, motor assisted bicycle or trailer shall be attached to and exposed in a conspicuous position on the rear of the vehicle.

(5) This section does not apply in respect of Dealer permits and number plates, Service permits and number plates, Dealer and Service permits and number plates or Manufacturer permits and number plates.

O. Reg. 331/01, s. 2; 367/04, s. 2; 328/15, s. 2

10. (1) For the purpose of subsection 11(3) of the Act, a number plate may be affixed to a trailer and number plates, one of which bears evidence of current validation, may be affixed to a motor vehicle where the permit holder is in possession of,

(a) the vehicle portion of the permit issued for the vehicle and the transfer application completed and signed by both the person named in the vehicle portion and the new owner;

(b) the plate portion of the permit that corresponds with the number plates to be affixed to the vehicle; and

(c) in the case of a used motor vehicle, a safety standards certificate issued upon an inspection of the vehicle that was completed within the preceding thirty-six days.

(2) Clause (1)(b) does not apply where the permit that corresponds with the number plates is a permit that was issued before the 1st day of December, 1982.

(3) Clause (1)(c) does not apply where a safety standards certificate would not be required to be submitted to the Ministry in order to obtain a permit other than a permit marked "unfit motor vehicle".

(4) Where a plate holder, as the first owner or first lessee of the vehicle, takes possession of a motor vehicle from a motor vehicle dealer registered under the *Motor Vehicle Dealers Act, 2002*, other than a dealer registered as a broker or outside Ontario dealer or registered only as an exporter,

(a) a copy of the dealer's bill of sale or some other document establishing ownership; or

(b) a copy of the dealer's bill of sale and a copy of the lease agreement,

may be substituted for the requirement under clause 10(1)(a).

(4.1) Subsection (4) applies with necessary modifications where a plate holder, as the first owner or first lessee of the vehicle, takes possession of a motor vehicle from a motor vehicle dealer referred to in clause 2(2)(c.1) or (c.2).

(5) Where a corporation signs the transfer application referred to in clause 10(1)(a), the signature of a person authorized to sign on behalf of the corporation is a sufficient signing of the transfer application.

(6) A person driving a motor vehicle or drawing a trailer on a highway under the authority of subsection 11(4) of the Act is required to carry the applicable documents referred to in subsection (1) or true copies thereof, and must surrender them for inspection upon a demand made under the Act.

O. Reg. 446/09, s. 2; 211/10, s. 2; 119/12, s. 2

[Heading repealed O. Reg. 71/08, s. 8.]

11. (1) A year-of-manufacture plate shall not be used on a commercial motor vehicle,

    (a) if the commercial motor vehicle has a gross weight of more than 3,000 kilograms; or

    (b) if the commercial motor vehicle is not used primarily for personal transportation.

(2) A permit shall not be issued or validated for a commercial motor vehicle described in clause (1)(a) or (b) on which a year-of-manufacture plate is used.

O. Reg. 71/08, s. 8; 62/11, s. 4

EVIDENCE OF VALIDATION EXEMPTION
[Heading added O. Reg. 119/12, s. 3.]

11.1 (1) Despite clauses 7(1)(a) and (c) of the Act and despite subsections 4(1) and 5(1), section 6 and subsection 9(1) of this Regulation, a motor vehicle may be driven on a highway after evidence of validation for the permit has been purchased but before it has been affixed to the number plate, if the following conditions are met:

    1. The evidence of validation was purchased by means of an electronic transaction,

        i. no later than on the expiry date of the old evidence of validation, and

        ii. no earlier than nine days before the expiry date of the old evidence of validation.

    2. A printed copy of the receipt for the electronic transaction is carried in the vehicle and is surrendered by the driver with the permit for the vehicle upon a demand made under the Act.

    3. The number plates required for the vehicle remain properly displayed on the vehicle.

    4. The old evidence of validation remains properly affixed to the number plate.

(2) The exemption described in subsection (1) is valid for a period of 10 days after the expiry date of the old evidence of validation.

(3) In this section,

"electronic transaction" means a transaction completed over the internet;

"old evidence of validation" means the evidence of validation in force at the time the new evidence of validation was purchased.

O. Reg. 119/12, s. 3

RESTRICTED PERMITS
[Heading added O. Reg. 71/08, s. 8.]

12. (1) A special permit that is valid for 10 days may be issued for the following motor vehicles:

    1. A commercial motor vehicle.

    2. A motor vehicle or trailer owned by a manufacturer or dealer in motor vehicles or trailers.

    3. A motor vehicle or trailer bought at an auction if the Ministry has authorized the issuance of special permits at the auction.

    4. A motor vehicle or trailer that is entering Ontario solely for the purpose of passing through Ontario.

    5. A motor vehicle or trailer that is being taken out of Ontario.

    6. A motor vehicle that is a roadworthy prototype vehicle.

(2) A special permit shall not be issued if the applicant has not complied with subsection 11(2) of the Act.

(3) A person to whom a special permit is issued for a vehicle may be issued only one further special permit for the same vehicle in any 12-month period.

(4) Subsection (3) does not apply in respect of a special permit for which the fee prescribed under subparagraph 15 iv, v, vi or vii of subsection 17(1) is paid.

(5) A special permit shall be affixed in a clearly visible position,

    (a) to the windshield of the motor vehicle; or

    (b) in the case of a special permit issued for a trailer, to the windshield of the motor vehicle drawing the trailer.

(6) Despite subsection (5), if a special permit provides for another method for affixing or carrying the special permit, it shall be affixed or carried as stated and not as provided by subsection (5).

(7) A special permit shall not be issued for a motor vehicle or trailer if the permit for the motor vehicle or trailer is marked "unfit motor vehicle" or "unfit" or, in the case of a permit issued by another jurisdiction, the equivalent of unfit in that jurisdiction.

(8) A special permit shall not be issued for a motor vehicle or trailer if the permit for the motor vehicle or trailer indicates that it is classified as irreparable or salvage or, in the case of a permit issued by another jurisdiction, the equivalent of irreparable or salvage in that jurisdiction.

(9) A special permit shall not be displayed on a laden commercial motor vehicle unless the fee paid for the special permit was the fee prescribed by subparagraph 15 v, vi or vii of subsection 17(1).

(10) Subsection (9) does not apply to a special permit issued for a trailer if,

(a) the trailer is drawn by a motor vehicle for which the vehicle permit was not issued under this section; and

(b) the trailer and the motor vehicle drawing it are in compliance with subsection 121(1) of the Act.

(11) Clauses 7(1)(b) and (c) of the Act do not apply in respect of a motor vehicle for which a special permit is issued while the special permit is valid.

(12) Clause 7(4)(b) of the Act does not apply in respect of a trailer with a valid special permit.

(13) Section 2 does not apply to the issuance of a special permit.

O. Reg. 71/08, s. 8

13. (1) Upon filing satisfactory evidence as to the need for it, a Dealer permit and number plate may be issued to a dealer in motor vehicles, other than motorcycles and motor assisted bicycles, who,

(a) is a motor vehicle dealer registered under the *Motor Vehicle Dealers Act, 2002*; or

(b) is a motor vehicle dealer referred to in clause 2(2)(c.1) or (c.2).

(2) A Dealer number plate may be used only on a motor vehicle that is owned, by the person to whom the Dealer permit corresponding to the Dealer number plate is issued, as part of the inventory that is offered for sale by the person and only for private use in Ontario or for purposes related to the sale of the motor vehicle.

(2.1) [Repealed O. Reg. 367/04, s. 3(1).]

(3) A Dealer number plate may be used only on a commercial motor vehicle that is owned, by the person to whom the Dealer permit corresponding to the Dealer number plate is issued, as part of the inventory that is offered for sale by the person and only for purposes related to the sale of the commercial motor vehicle.

(4) A Dealer number plate shall not be used on a motor vehicle, including a commercial motor vehicle, that is kept for private use or for hire.

(5) A Dealer number plate shall not be used on a commercial motor vehicle that is loaded with goods.

(6) [Repealed O. Reg. 367/04, s. 3(1).]

O. Reg. 309/92, s. 2; 590/92, s. 1; 508/97, s. 1; 367/04, s. 3(1); 211/10, s. 3

13.1 (1) Upon filing satisfactory evidence as to the need for it, a Service permit and number plate may be issued to a person engaged in the business of repairing, customizing, modifying or transporting trailers or motor vehicles other than motorcycles and motor assisted bicycles or to a person engaged in the business of manufacturing or selling trailers.

(2) A Service number plate may be used on a trailer or motor vehicle other than a motorcycle or motor assisted bicycle only,

(a) for purposes related to the repair, road testing, customization or modification of the vehicle, if the vehicle is in the possession of the person to whom the Service permit corresponding to the Service number plate is issued;

(b) for the purpose of transporting the vehicle by a person engaged in the business of transporting vehicles;

(c) for purposes related to the manufacture or sale of a trailer; or

(d) for the purpose of towing the vehicle by a person engaged in the business of transporting vehicles,

(i) to a location where its load will be removed as required by section 82.1 of the Act, or

(ii) to an impound facility pursuant to section 82.1 of the Act.

(3) A Service number plate may be used only on a commercial motor vehicle owned by or in the possession of the person to whom the Service permit corresponding to the Service number plate is issued and only,

(a) for purposes related to the repair, road testing, customization or modification of the commercial motor vehicle; or

(b) in the case of a person engaged in the business of transporting commercial motor vehicles, for purposes of transporting the commercial motor vehicle.

(4) A Service number plate shall not be used on a vehicle, including a commercial motor vehicle, that is kept for private use or for hire.

(5) Except as permitted by subclause (2)(d)(i), a Service number plate shall not be used on a commercial motor vehicle or trailer that is loaded with goods.

O. Reg. 367/04, s. 3(1); 414/10, s. 1

13.2 (1) Upon filing satisfactory evidence as to the need for it, a Dealer and Service permit and number plate may be issued,

(a) to a manufacturer of motorcycles or motor assisted bicycles;

(b) to a dealer in motorcycles or motor assisted bicycles who,

(i) is a motor vehicle dealer registered under the *Motor Vehicle Dealers Act, 2002*, or

(ii) is a motor vehicle dealer referred to in clause 2(2)(c.1) or (c.2); or

(c) to a person engaged in the business of repairing, customizing, modifying or transporting motorcycles or motor assisted bicycles.

(2) A Dealer and Service permit and number plate may be used only on a motorcycle or motor assisted bicycle,

(a) that is owned by the person to whom the Dealer and Service permit corresponding to the Dealer and Service number plate is issued as part of the inventory that is offered for sale by the person and only for private use in Ontario or for purposes related to the sale of the motorcycle or motor assisted bicycle;

(b) for purposes related to the repair, road testing, customization or modification of the motorcycle or motor assisted bicycle, if the motorcycle or motor assisted bicycle is in the possession of the person to whom the Dealer and Service permit corresponding to the Dealer and Service number plate is issued; or

(c) for the purpose of transporting the motorcycle or motor assisted bicycle by a person engaged in the business of transporting motorcycles or motor assisted bicycles.

(3) A Dealer and Service number plate shall not be used on a motorcycle or motor assisted bicycle that is kept for private use or for hire.

O. Reg. 367/04, s. 3(1); 211/10, s. 4

13.2.1 (1) Upon filing satisfactory evidence as to the need for it, a Manufacturer permit and number plate may be issued to a person engaged in the business of manufacturing motor vehicles, other than motor assisted bicycles, or components for motor vehicles, other than motor assisted bicycles.

(2) A Manufacturer number plate may be used only on a motor vehicle,

(a) that is owned by the person to whom a Manufacturer permit is issued; and

(b) that was manufactured by the person to whom a Manufacturer permit is issued or the components of which were manufactured by the person to whom a Manufacturer permit is issued.

(3) A Manufacturer number plate may be used on a motor vehicle only for purposes of exhibiting, demonstrating, evaluating or testing the motor vehicle.

(4) Despite subsection (3), a Manufacturer number plate may be used on a motor vehicle that was imported into Canada pursuant to a declaration made under Schedule VII of the *Motor Vehicle Safety Regulations* (Canada) made under the *Motor Vehicle Safety Act* (Canada) only for,

(a) purposes permitted by subsection (3); or

(b) other purposes permitted by Schedule VII of the *Motor Vehicle Safety Regulations* (Canada) made under the *Motor Vehicle Safety Act* (Canada).

(5) A Manufacturer number plate shall not be used on a motor vehicle that is kept for hire.

(6) A Manufacturer number plate shall not be used on a commercial motor vehicle that is loaded with goods or that is drawing a vehicle that is loaded with goods.

O. Reg. 328/15, s. 3

13.3 (1) A Dealer number plate or a Service number plate shall be attached to and exposed in a conspicuous position on the rear of the rear-most vehicle being towed or operated under the authority of the corresponding permit.

(1.1) A Manufacturer number plate shall be attached to and exposed in a conspicuous position on the rear of the motor vehicle.

(2) A Dealer and Service number plate for a motorcycle or motor assisted bicycle shall be attached to and exposed in a conspicuous position on the rear of the motorcycle or motor assisted bicycle.

(3) Where a Dealer permit, a Service permit, a Dealer and Service permit or a Manufacturer permit is validated, evidence of validation shall be affixed in the upper right corner of the number plate that corresponds with the permit.

(4) Subsections 11(3) and (4) of the Act do not apply to a manufacturer, dealer or other person referred to in subsection 13(1), 13.1(1) or 13.2(1) with respect to vehicles that are in the person's possession for purposes related to the sale, repair, customization or modification of the vehicles or, in the case of a person engaged in the business of transporting vehicles, for purposes of transporting the vehicles.

O. Reg. 367/04, s. 3(1); 328/15, s. 4

13.4 [Repealed O. Reg. 367/04, s. 3(2).]

COMMERCIAL VEHICLE EXEMPTIONS

14. (1) A commercial motor vehicle is exempt from section 7 of the Act while the vehicle is being driven or operated in Ontario, if it,

    (a) is registered in a reciprocating province that grants exemptions for commercial motor vehicles similar to the exemptions granted by this section; and

    (b) is owned or leased by a resident of the reciprocating province.

(2) Subsection (1) does not apply to a bus operating on a regular route or schedule between a place in Ontario and a place in any other province.

O. Reg. 637/05, s. 1

15. (1) A commercial motor vehicle that,

    (a) is registered in a reciprocating state of the United States of America that grants exemptions for commercial motor vehicles similar to the exemptions granted by this section; and

    (b) is owned or leased by a resident of the reciprocating state,

is exempt from the provisions of section 7 of the Act while the vehicle is being driven or operated in Ontario if the vehicle is,

    (c) a hearse or ambulance;

    (d) a motor vehicle commonly known as a motorized mobile home that is designed, equipped and used exclusively for living accommodation;

    (e) a public vehicle operated on a scheduled service in Ontario within sixteen kilometres of its point of entry on the international boundary line between

Canada and the United States of America or operated on a chartered trip originating outside Ontario;

(f) a commercial motor vehicle having a gross weight of 2,800 kilograms or less, or a combination of a commercial motor vehicle and trailer or trailers where the trailer or trailers transmit to the highway a total weight of 2,800 kilograms or less, that is being operated in Ontario for the purpose of transporting goods owned by the owner or lessee of the commercial motor vehicle;

(g) being operated in Ontario for the purpose of transporting from a farm natural products of a farm or livestock, or both, owned by the owner or lessee of the commercial motor vehicle;

(h) being operated in Ontario for the purpose of transporting objects and materials used in the production of cultural presentations or exhibitions, if the presentations or exhibitions are not carried on solely for the purpose of financial gain; or

(i) a commercial motor vehicle having a gross weight of 8,200 kilograms or less, or a combination of a commercial motor vehicle and trailer or trailers having a gross weight of 8,200 kilograms or less, that is being operated in Ontario for the purpose of transporting used household goods owned by the owner or lessee of the commercial motor vehicle.

(2) Clauses (1)(g) and (h) do not apply to provide an exemption for a commercial motor vehicle being operated in Ontario on a continuous trip originating at a point outside Ontario and destined to a point outside Ontario.

15.1 [Repealed O. Reg. 62/11, s. 5.]

16. A trailer in Ontario that displays a valid number plate issued by another province or a state of the United States of America or that is in compliance with the provisions of the law, in respect of registration of trailers, of the jurisdiction in which the owner or lessee of the trailer resides is exempt from section 7 of the Act.
O. Reg. 666/00, s. 5

16.1 (1) Subject to subsections (2), (3) and (4), the following classes of vehicle are exempt from subsections 7(1), (4) and (5) of the Act:

1. Commercial motor vehicles and vehicles that are used for hauling,

i. raw forest products, or

ii. materials, supplies or equipment required for, or used in a process related to, the harvesting or processing of raw forest products.

2. Vehicles with a manufacturer's gross vehicle weight rating exceeding 63,500 kilograms that are used exclusively for transporting between steel production facilities,

i. steel slabs, steel coils or related partly-processed or finished goods, or

ii. steel production equipment.

3. New vehicles that are owned by their manufacturer and that, upon being completed, are driven away from the place at which their manufacture was completed.

(2) The exemption in paragraph 1 of subsection (1) applies only while the following conditions are satisfied:

1. The driver, owner and operator of the commercial motor vehicle and vehicle are complying with the Act, other than subsections 7(1), (4) and (5), the *Compulsory Automobile Insurance Act* and the *Dangerous Goods Transportation Act*, and with the regulations under those Acts.

2. The commercial motor vehicle and vehicle are not being operated on a highway other than to cross it directly at the intersection of a private road and,

   i. The King's Highway known as No. 105 in the Township of Ear Falls in the District of Kenora, or

   ii. the King's Highway known as No. 657 in the Township of Ear Falls in the District of Kenora.

3. There is an outstanding permit issued under clause 34(2)(f) of the *Public Transportation and Highway Improvement Act* permitting the use of the private road as a means of access to the highways referred to in paragraph 2.

4. There is a vehicle portion of the permit for both the commercial motor vehicle and the vehicle.

5. The driver of the commercial motor vehicle shall surrender the vehicle portion of the permits for the commercial motor vehicle and vehicle, or a copy of them, upon a demand made under the Act.

(3) The exemption in paragraph 2 of subsection (1) applies only while the following conditions are satisfied:

1. The vehicle is only operated in the City of Hamilton,

   i. while directly crossing the roadway known as Depew Street at a point 320 metres south of the roadway known as Burlington Street East and 48 metres north of the roadway known as Gertrude Street, or

   ii. on the following parts of highways:

      A. That part of the roadway known as Kenilworth Avenue North lying between its northern limit and a point at its intersection with the roadway known as Dofasco Road.

      B. That part of the roadway known as Dofasco Road lying between a point at its intersection with the roadway known as Kenilworth Avenue North and a point at its intersection with the roadway known as Beach Road.

      C. That part of the roadway known as Ottawa Street North lying between its northern limit and a point at its intersection with the roadway known as Beach Road.

      D. That part of the roadway known as Beach Road lying between a point at its intersection with the roadway known as Kenilworth Avenue North to a point 200 metres west of the roadway known as Ottawa Street North.

      E. That part of the roadway known as Burlington Street East lying between a point at its intersection with the roadway known as Ottawa Street North and a point at its intersection with the roadway known as Strathearne Avenue.

F. That part of the roadway known as Strathearne Avenue lying between its northern limit and a point at its intersection with the roadway known as Brampton Street.

2. There is a current written agreement between the City of Hamilton and the operator of the vehicle relating to the use of vehicles as described in paragraph 2 of subsection (1) on the parts of highways described in subparagraphs 1 i and ii.

3. The operator of the vehicle is in compliance with the agreement described in paragraph 2.

(4) The exemption in paragraph 3 of subsection (1) applies only while the following conditions are satisfied:

1. The vehicle is in transit between the place at which its manufacture was completed and the yard at which it is to be kept prior to shipping.

2. The distance between the place at which the vehicle's manufacture was completed and the yard at which it is to be kept prior to shipping is not more than eight kilometres.

3. The driver of the vehicle is the holder of a valid driver's licence for that class of vehicle.

4. The vehicle is insured under a contract of automobile insurance in accordance with section 2 of the *Compulsory Automobile Insurance Act*.

O. Reg. 343/97; 123/01, s. 1; 119/12, s. 4; 78/15, s. 1

GENERAL FEES

17. (1) The following fees shall be paid to the Ministry:

1. For a permit for a motor vehicle or trailer $20

Proposed Amendment — 17(1), para. 1

1. For a permit for a motor vehicle or trailer $32
O. Reg. 245/14, s. 1(1) [To come into force January 1, 2017.]

2. For a permit and number plates for a motor vehicle 40

Proposed Amendment — 17(1), para. 2

2. For a permit and number plates for a motor vehicle $45
O. Reg. 245/14, s. 1(2) [To come into force November 1, 2016.]

Proposed Amendment — 17(1), para. 2

2. For a permit and number plates for a motor vehicle $57
O. Reg. 245/14, s. 1(3) [To come into force January 1, 2017.]

Proposed Amendment — 17(1), para. 2

2. For a permit and number plates for a motor vehicle, ... $59.
O. Reg. 258/15, s. 1(1) [To come into force January 1, 2018.]

2.1 For a Dealer permit and number plate for a motor vehicle other than a motorcycle or motor assisted bicycle 30

2.2 For a Manufacturer permit and number plate, ... $30.

3. For a permit and number plate for a trailer 59

> **Proposed Amendment — 17(1), para. 3**
>
> **3.** For a permit and number plate for a trailer $72
> O. Reg. 245/14, s. 1(4) [To come into force January 1, 2017.]

4. For a permit and number plates for a commercial motor vehicle, where a municipal fire department will be operating the vehicle and is applying to be the permit holder 35

5. For a duplicate validated permit for a motor vehicle or a duplicate permit for a trailer, in case of loss or destruction 20

> **Proposed Amendment — 17(1), para. 5**
>
> **5.** For a duplicate validated permit for a motor vehicle or a duplicate permit for a trailer, in case of loss or destruction $32
> O. Reg. 245/14, s. 1(5) [To come into force January 1, 2017.]

6. For a duplicate validated permit, number plates and evidence of validation for a motor vehicle, in case of loss or destruction 40

> **Proposed Amendment — 17(1), para. 6**
>
> **6.** For a duplicate validated permit, number plates and evidence of validation for a motor vehicle, in case of loss or destruction $45
> O. Reg. 245/14, s. 1(6) [To come into force November 1, 2016.]

> **Proposed Amendment — 17(1), para. 6**
>
> **6.** For a duplicate validated permit, number plates and evidence of validation for a motor vehicle, in case of loss or destruction $57
> O. Reg. 245/14, s. 1(7) [To come into force January 1, 2017.]

6.0.0.1 For a duplicate permit and number plate for a trailer, in case of loss or destruction 35

> **Proposed Amendment — 17(1), para. 6.0.0.1**
>
> **6.0.0.1** For a duplicate permit and number plate for a trailer, in case of loss or destruction $48
> O. Reg. 245/14, s. 1(8) [To come into force January 1, 2017.]

6.0.1 For replacement of a Dealer permit and number plate and evidence of validation in case of loss or destruction 30

6.0.2 For replacement of a Manufacturer permit and number plate in case of loss or destruction, ... $30.

6.1 For a motor vehicle permit and number plates bearing a requested graphic 75

6.2 For a duplicate validated motor vehicle permit, number plates bearing the same requested graphic and evidence of validation, in case of loss or destruction 50

7. For a motor vehicle permit and number plates bearing a requested number
.... **$276.64**

7.1 For a motor vehicle permit and number plates bearing a requested number
and graphic **300**

7.2 For a permit issued under subsection 7(7.1) of the Act to match existing
number plates for a historic vehicle, where a permit has not previously been
issued under that subsection matching those specific number plates for that
specific historic vehicle **225**

8. For a motor vehicle permit and number plates bearing an amateur radio call
sign **30**

9. For the replacement of number plates bearing a requested number, with or
without a requested graphic, with number plates bearing the same number and
graphic, if any,

    i. in the case of loss or destruction **90**

    ii. in the case of the plates being stolen and a police report submitted
.... **50**

9.1 For the replacement of number plates bearing a requested number with
number plates bearing the same number and adding a requested graphic
.... **125**

9.2 For the replacement of number plates bearing a requested number and
graphic with number plates bearing the same number but a different graphic
.... **125**

9.3 For a sample number plate **15**

9.4 For a sample number plate bearing a requested graphic **30**

10. For the replacement of number plates bearing an amateur radio call sign
with number plates bearing the same amateur radio call sign, in case of loss or
destruction **15**

11. For evidence of validation only, in case of loss or destruction **7**

12. For a permit for a motor vehicle or trailer that is issued to a person licensed under the Act to deal in motor vehicles or trailers, where the vehicle for
which the permit is issued is held for resale **5**

12.1 For a permit for a motor vehicle or trailer that is issued to a motor vehicle
dealer registered under the *Motor Vehicle Dealers Act, 2002*, other than a
dealer registered as a broker, where the vehicle for which the permit is issued
is held for resale **5**

12.2 For a permit for a motor vehicle or trailer that is issued to a motor vehicle
dealer referred to in clause 2(2)(c.1) or (c.2), where the vehicle for which the
permit is issued is held for resale **5**

13. To increase by 7,000 kilograms the permitted gross weight of a vehicle in
accordance with subsection 121(2) of the Act, for an annual term from the 1st
day of April to the 31st day of March **300**

14. [Repealed O. Reg. 62/11, s. 6(3).]

15. For a special permit for,

    i. a trailer 23

    ii. a motor vehicle that is not a commercial motor vehicle 23

    iii. an unladen commercial motor vehicle for which temporary validation is not issued 23

    iv. a roadworthy prototype vehicle 23

    v. a laden commercial motor vehicle not drawing a trailer 114

    vi. a commercial motor vehicle drawing a trailer, either or both of which are laden 201

    vii. a commercial motor vehicle on whose chassis there is a machine or apparatus that is not designed or used primarily for the transportation of persons or property 201

16. For each search of vehicle records by plate number, vehicle identification number, name or identification number of registered owner or permit holder
.... 12

17. For a copy of any writing, paper or document, other than an accident report, filed in the Ministry or any statement containing information from the records 6

18. For a copy of an accident report 12

19. For a certification of a copy of any writing, paper or document filed in the Ministry or any statement containing information from the records 6

20. For administrative costs associated with the issuance or validation of a permit, the fee for which is prorated under a reciprocity agreement or arrangement with another jurisdiction 25

(2) Despite paragraphs 9.3 and 9.4 of subsection (1), no fee is payable for a sample plate or a sample plate with a requested graphic issued to the Government of Ontario or for non-commercial use.

(3) No fee is payable under paragraph 6.1, 6.2, 9, 9.1, 9.2 or 9.4 of subsection (1) where the number plates referred to in that paragraph bear a veteran graphic and are issued to a person who is certified by the Royal Canadian Legion — Ontario Command to be a veteran.

(4) Despite paragraph 7.1 of subsection (1), the fee payable under that paragraph for a motor vehicle permit and number plates bearing a requested number and a veteran graphic issued to a person who is certified by the Royal Canadian Legion — Ontario Command to be a veteran is $251.65.

(5) In subsections (3) and (4),

"veteran graphic" means a graphic honouring veterans that is made available by the Ministry.

O. Reg. 193/00, s. 1; 437/03, s. 1; 290/04, s. 1; 367/04, s. 4; 15/05, s. 1; 71/08, s. 9; 446/09, s. 3; 211/10, s. 5; 62/11, s. 6; 168/12, s. 2; 312/12, s. 1; 244/13, s. 1; 245/14, s. 1(9), (10); 258/15, s. 1(2); 328/15, s. 5

VALIDATION FEES

17.1 The fee for temporary validation of a permit is $15.

O. Reg. 71/08, s. 10

18. (1) For validation of a permit referred to in Schedule 4, the following fees shall be paid to the Ministry:

  1. If the validation period is 12 months, the applicable annual fee for the appropriate permit number set out in Schedule 4.

  2. If the validation period is 24 months, an amount equal to twice the applicable annual fee for the appropriate permit number set out in Schedule 4.

  3. If the validation period is at least three months but not 12 or 24 months, the fee determined under subsection (2).

(2) If the validation period of the permit is at least three but not 12 or 24 months, the validation fee for that number of months is the amount calculated according to the following formula and rounded up or down to the nearest nickel:

$$A \times (\frac{B}{12})$$

in which,

"A" is the number of months, and

"B" is the applicable annual fee for the appropriate permit number set out in Schedule 4.

(3) For the purposes of determining the validation fee payable for a number of months under this section, a part of a month shall count as a full month.

(4) Upon renewal of the validation of a permit referred to in Schedule 4, the following fees shall be paid to the Ministry:

  1. If the validation period is at least three but not more than 12 months, the applicable annual fee for the appropriate permit number set out in Schedule 4.

  2. If the validation period is more than 12 but not more than 24 months, an amount equal to twice the applicable annual fee for the appropriate permit number set out in Schedule 4.

(5) Despite subsection (4), if a person demonstrates to the Ministry that it was not possible to operate the vehicle during any period before the application for renewal was made, the Ministry shall refund to the person the difference between the amount paid for renewal of the permit validation and the amount of the fee, determined under subsection (2), payable for the number of months for which the vehicle could be operated, less a $5 administrative fee.

(6) If a person surrenders plates for a permit referred to in Schedule 4 to the Ministry at least three months before the end of a period of validation purchased on renewal, subsection (4) does not apply and the Ministry shall refund to the person in respect of the remaining full months of validation the amount of the fee, determined under subsection (2), payable for that number of months, less a $5 administrative fee.

(6.1) Despite subsections (5) and (6), a person is not eligible for a refund of fees under those subsections if,

(a) the person has received compensation under section 17.2 of the *Ministry of Government Services Act*;

(b) the compensation is in respect of a service standard not having been met in connection with the issuance of evidence of validation for a permit to the person in respect of a validation period; and

(c) the fees that would otherwise be refunded are all or part of the fees the person paid for the validation period in respect of which the compensation was received.

(7) Subsections (1) and (2) apply, and subsection (4) does not apply, to the renewal of the validation period for,

(a) a permit to which subsection 8.1(8) applies;

(b) a Dealer permit, a Service permit, a Dealer and Service permit or a Manufacturer permit; and

(c) a permit for which the anniversary date of its expiry date has been changed.

(8) If the portion of a commercial motor vehicle designed to carry a load is occupied solely by a self-contained dwelling unit designed, equipped and used exclusively for living accommodation, the weight of the unit is not included in determining the gross weight of the vehicle for the purpose of ascertaining fees for permit numbers 10 and 11.
O. Reg. 337/97, s. 3; 71/99, s. 2; 254/99, s. 2; 262/00, s. 2; 331/01, s. 3; 367/04, s. 5; 637/05, s. 2; 62/11, s. 7; 344/11, s. 1; 328/15, s. 6

19. (1) For validation of a permit for a commercial motor vehicle, the following fees shall be paid to the Ministry:

1. For a commercial motor vehicle or a combination of a commercial motor vehicle and trailer or trailers, other than a bus, having a gross weight of more than 3,000 kilograms,

    i. if the validation period is 12 months, the applicable annual fee set out in Schedule 1,

    ii. if the validation period is at least three but less than 12 months, the fee determined under subsection (2), or

    iii. if the validation period is 13, 14 or 15 months, the fee determined under subsection (3).

2. For a commercial motor vehicle or a combination of a commercial motor vehicle and trailer or trailers, other than a bus, having a gross weight of more than 3,000 kilograms, where the permit holder is a farmer and the vehicle is used for any of the purposes set out in subsection (5),

    i. if the validation period is 12 months, the applicable annual fee set out in Schedule 2,

    ii. if the validation period is at least three but less than 12 months, the fee determined under subsection (2), or

iii. if the validation period is 13, 14 or 15 months, the fee determined under subsection (3).

3. For a bus, including a school bus described in subsection 5(3),

i. if the validation period is 12 months, the applicable annual fee set out in Schedule 3,

ii. if the validation period is at least three but less than 12 months, the fee determined under subsection (2), or

iii. if the validation period is 13, 14 or 15 months, the fee determined under subsection (3).

(2) If the validation period is at least three but less than 12 months, the validation fee for that number of months is the amount calculated according to the following formula and rounded up to the nearest dollar:

$$[(A \times 8) + 4] \times (\frac{B}{100})$$

in which,

"A" is the number of months, and

"B" is the applicable annual fee set out in Schedule 1, 2 or 3, as applicable.

(3) If the validation period is 13, 14 or 15 months, the validation fee for that number of months is the amount calculated according to the following formula and rounded up to the nearest dollar:

$$A \times (\frac{B}{12})$$

in which,

"A" is the number of months, and

"B" is the applicable annual fee set out in Schedule 1, 2 or 3, as applicable.

(4) For the purposes of determining the validation fee payable for a number of months under this section, a part of a month shall count as a full month.

(5) The purposes referred to in paragraph 2 of subsection (1) are,

(a) the farmer's personal transportation;

(b) the uncompensated transportation of farm products, supplies or equipment; or

(c) the compensated transportation of farm products, supplies or equipment in the month of September, October or November.

(6) The fee for validation of a permit for a commercial motor vehicle is one-half the fee payable under paragraph 1 of subsection (1), if,

(a) the commercial motor vehicle is used exclusively for the transportation of road building machinery owned by the permit holder; or

(b) the commercial motor vehicle,

    (i) has a machine or apparatus mounted upon the chassis thereof that is not designed or used primarily for the transportation of persons or property, and

    (ii) is only incidentally operated or moved over the highways.

(7) Despite paragraph 3 of subsection (1), a permit for a school bus described in subsection 5(3) shall not be issued or validated if the bus has a gross weight of more than 20,000 kilograms.

O. Reg. 62/11, s. 7

FEE EXEMPTIONS

20. (1) No fee is payable for a permit, number plates or evidence of validation issued for a motor vehicle where the permit holder or person applying to be the permit holder is,

(a) the Governor General;

(b) the Lieutenant Governor;

(c) the government of a province or of Canada;

(d) a foreign government or a representative of a foreign government who has taken a post in Ontario in the capacity of,

    (i) ambassador, high commissioner or chargé d'affaires,

    (ii) head of delegation or head of office,

    (iii) minister-counsellor or minister,

    (iv) counsellor,

    (v) first, second or third secretary,

    (vi) attaché,

    (vii) military, air or naval attaché or advisor,

    (viii) assistant military, air or naval attaché or advisor,

    (ix) consul-general, consul, vice-consul or consular agent;

(e) the spouse or child of any representative referred to in clause (d);

(f) a person serving or employed on the technical or support staff of a diplomatic or consular mission or high commission provided that the person,

    (i) is authorized as eligible for exempt status by Foreign Affairs and International Trade Canada,

    (ii) is not a Canadian citizen or permanent resident within the meaning of the *Immigration and Refugee Protection Act* (Canada), and

    (iii) is assigned to duty from the foreign government being represented and not engaged locally by the mission or commission;

(g) the spouse or child of any person described in clause (f), provided that the spouse or child meets the requirements set out in subclause (f)(ii);

(h) an international organization that is authorized as eligible for exempt status by Foreign Affairs and International Trade Canada;

(i) a representative of an international organization described in clause (h) who is posted in Ontario and,

  (i) is authorized as eligible for exempt status by Foreign Affairs and International Trade Canada,

  (ii) is not a Canadian citizen or permanent resident within the meaning of the *Immigration and Refugee Protection Act* (Canada), and

  (iii) is assigned to the post from the international organization and is not engaged locally by it; or

(j) the spouse or child of any person described in clause (i), if the spouse or child meets the requirements set out in subclause (i)(ii).

(2) In this section,

"spouse" has the same meaning as in Part III of the *Family Law Act*.

O. Reg. 309/92, s. 4; 87/00, s. 2; 358/05, s. 2; 62/11, s. 8

21. (1) No fee is payable for validation of a permit for,

(a) a commercial motor vehicle, where the permit holder is a band, as defined by and to which the *Indian Act* (Canada) applies, and the vehicle's operation outside a reserve is exclusively for the carriage of goods owned by the band;

(b) a commercial motor vehicle, where the permit holder is the Canadian Red Cross Society or any branch thereof or the Order of St. John;

(c) a commercial motor vehicle, where the permit holder is a municipal fire department; or

(d) a bus, where the permit holder is a church Sunday school, church day school, a non-denominational school or a religious organization.

(2) No fee is payable for the validation of a permit issued in Ontario for a validation period coinciding with the balance of the period of validity of a permit issued by another jurisdiction to the same permit holder in respect of the same motor vehicle where,

(a) the permit holder is a member of the Canadian Armed Forces who has moved into Ontario and surrendered the permit for the vehicle issued by the other jurisdiction; or

(b) the permit holder is a member of the armed forces of the United States of America who has been assigned to duty in Ontario for a period exceeding three months and surrendered the permit for the vehicle issued by the other jurisdiction.

21.1 (1) The fee set out in paragraph 1 of subsection 17(1) does not apply with respect to a permit for a vehicle applied for under section 3.1 as a result of a change of address of the owner of the vehicle.

(2) The fee set out in paragraph 1 of subsection 17(1) does not apply with respect to a permit for a vehicle applied for under section 3.1 as a result of a change of name of the owner of the vehicle,

(a) if the permit is held by the owner as an individual; or

(b) if the permit would be exempt under subsection 21(1).

O. Reg. 168/12, s. 3

22. **(1)** The fees set out in paragraphs 1, 2 and 3 of subsection 17(1) do not apply with respect to,

(a) a permit and number plate, where the fee for the permit is prorated under a reciprocity agreement or arrangement with another jurisdiction;

(b) a permit for a commercial motor vehicle, where the person applying to be the permit holder is the Canadian Red Cross Society or any branch thereof or the Order of St. John;

(c) a permit and number plate, where the number plate is issued as a replacement for a number plate that bears the international symbol of access for the disabled;

(d) a permit issued to a person licensed under the Act to wreck vehicles, where the vehicle for which the permit is issued is held for wrecking;

(e) a permit that is issued to correct information contained thereon.

(2) The fee set out in paragraph 7 of subsection 17(1) does not apply with respect to a permit and number plate bearing a requested number where the number plate is issued as a replacement for a number plate bearing a requested number and the international symbol of access for the disabled.

CTR 23 JL 12 – 1

22.1 The fee set out in paragraph 20 of subsection 17(1) does not apply to the conversion of the registration of a commercial motor vehicle from the Canadian Agreement on Vehicle Registration to the International Registration Plan.

O. Reg. 666/00, s. 6

PENALTY

23. If a person purports to pay a vehicle-related fee or tax, other than a tax described in section 8.3 by a cheque that is not honoured, and the fee or tax is not paid within thirty days after the date of a letter from the Ministry notifying the person that the cheque was not honoured, the person shall pay a penalty of the greater of,

(a) 10 per cent of the amount of the fee or tax outstanding, and

(b) $5 for each number plate or permit.

O. Reg. 303/08, s. 2

. . . . .

Ont. Reg. 413/05 — Vehicle Weights and Dimensions — For Safe, Productive and Infrastructure-Friendly Vehicles

made under the *Highway Traffic Act*

O. Reg. 413/05, as. am. O. Reg. 435/08 [ss. 14–17 repealed O. Reg. 457/10, s. 31.]; 457/10, ss. 1–30; 167/12; 16/14; 8/16.

Application and Interpretation

1. Application — (1) Subject to any by-law made under subsection 109(12) of the Act, this Regulation sets out dimensional limits for the purposes of section 109 of the Act.

(2) This Regulation sets out weight limits for the purposes of sections 115 to 118 of the Act.

O. Reg. 457/10, s. 1

2. Definitions — (1) The definitions in sections 108 and 114 of the Act apply to this Regulation.

(2) In this Regulation,

"A-train double" means a vehicle combination composed of a tractor, a semi-trailer and,

(a) a trailer converter dolly that is towed from a single hitch, as shown in Figure 1, on the centre line of the semi-trailer and another semi-trailer, or

(b) a full trailer attached to the semi-trailer as if a trailer converter dolly were used and towed from a single hitch, as shown in Figure 1, on the centre line of the semi-trailer;

Figure 1: A-train double

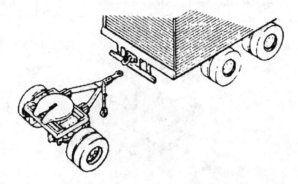

"aggregate vehicle" means a vehicle or vehicle combination that is designed for dumping or spreading sand, gravel, crushed or uncut rock, asphalt, slag or rubble or any mixture of such materials and that is transporting a load consisting mostly of any of these materials;

"axle spread" means the longitudinal distance between the centres of the foremost and rearmost axles of an axle unit;

"B-train double" means a vehicle combination composed of a tractor and two semi-trailers, the rearmost of which is attached by a fifth wheel assembly whose lower half is mounted on the rear of the foremost semi-trailer, as shown in Figure 2;

Figure 2: B-train double

"base length" means the distance measured between the centres of the first axle of the front axle of a vehicle or vehicle combination and the last axle of a vehicle or vehicle combination;

"C-train double" means a vehicle combination consisting of a tractor and two semi-trailers, the second of which is attached to the first by a trailer converter dolly that has a frame rigid in the horizontal plane and that is towed from two hitches located in a horizontal transverse line on the foremost semi-trailer that preclude any rotation in the horizontal plane about the hitch point, as shown in Figure 3;

Figure 3: C-train double

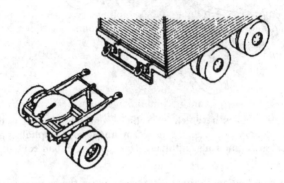

"carbon dioxide tank semi-trailer" means a tank semi-trailer that is used regularly to transport carbon dioxide, was manufactured to Transport Canada specification TC331 or United States Department of Transportation specification MC331 and bears the appropriate specification number on the compliance label or manufacturer's identification plate affixed to the vehicle;

"combination" and **"vehicle combination"** mean a combination of vehicles;

"cryogenic tank semi-trailer" means a tank semi-trailer that was manufactured to United States Compressed Gas Association specification CGA341 or Transport Canada specification TC341 and bears the appropriate specification number on the compliance label or manufacturer's identification plate affixed to the vehicle;

"designated bus or recreational vehicle", when followed by a number, means the designated bus or recreational vehicle identified by the same number in the Table to section 3.1;

"designated combination" [Repealed O. Reg. 457/10, s. 2(2).]

"designated tractor-trailer combination", when followed by a number, means the designated tractor-trailer combination identified by the same number in the Table to section 3;

"designated truck", when followed by a number, means the designated truck identified by the same number in the Table to section 3.2;

"designated truck-trailer combination", when followed by a number, means the designated truck-trailer combination identified by the same number in the Table to section 3.3;

"drawbar" means a towing structure that is connected to a trailer or a trailer converter dolly and that includes an eye or equivalent device for coupling to a trailer hitch;

"drive axle" means an axle unit that is connected to the power source of a motor vehicle and that transmits tractive power to the wheels;

"end dump semi-trailer" means a semi-trailer to which is permanently attached a body or box that is hinged and that can be raised to dump from the rear of the semi-trailer;

"fifth wheel assembly" means a plate-type coupling device comprised of a kingpin, locking jaws and plates, the lower half of which is mounted on the rear portion of a vehicle frame or the frame of a trailer converter dolly and the upper half of which is fastened to the underside of the forward portion of a semi-trailer for the purpose of supporting and towing the semi-trailer;

"forced-steer auxiliary pusher axle" means an axle that articulates in response to forces generated through mechanisms and linkages operated by the driver, but does not include not the front axle of a vehicle or vehicle combination;

"full trailer" means a trailer designed so that the whole of its own weight and of any load are carried on its own axles and includes a vehicle combination consisting of a semi-trailer and a trailer converter dolly;

"inter-axle spacing" means the longitudinal distance separating two consecutive axle units within a vehicle or vehicle combination, measured from the centre of the rearmost axle of the foremost axle unit to the centre of the foremost axle of the other axle unit;

"inter-vehicle-unit distance", for a vehicle combination, means,

    (a) the distance between the centres of the last axle of the motor vehicle or road building machine and the first axle of the towed vehicle, and

    (b) the distance between the centres of the last axle of the first towed vehicle and the first axle of the second towed vehicle,

but in subsection 38(2), Schedules 11, 12 and 13 and Vehicle Weight Tables 3 to 29, it means the lesser of clauses (a) and (b);

"long combination" means a tractor-trailer combination to which one or more of the following applies:

    1. The total length, including load, exceeds the 23 metre limit specified in subsection 109(7) of the Act.

    2. The box length of a combination including more than one trailer exceeds the 18.5 metre limit specified in subsection 109(8) of the Act.

    3. The semi-trailer length, excluding any portion of auxiliary equipment or machinery that extends beyond the front or rear of the semi-trailer and that is not designed or used for the transportation of goods, exceeds the 14.65 metre limit specified in subsection 109(10) of the Act;

"non-designated", with reference to a truck, bus, recreational vehicle or vehicle combination means a truck, bus, recreational vehicle or vehicle combination that is not, respectively, a designated truck, a designated bus or recreational vehicle, a designated tractor-trailer combination, a designated truck-trailer combination or a designated saddlemount combination;

"open-top hopper dump semi-trailer" means a semi-trailer to which is permanently attached an open-top body or box with bottom hoppers that can be opened to dump from the bottom of the semi-trailer;

"pony trailer" means a trailer that is designed and used so that the preponderance of the trailer's weight and load is carried on its own axles and that is equipped with a drawbar rigidly attached to the trailer;

"quadruple axle" means a four axle group in which the axles,

   (a) have their consecutive centres equally spaced,

   (b) have their consecutive centres more than one metre apart,

   (c) do not include a liftable axle or a self-steering axle,

   (d) have the same number of tires at each wheel position, and

   (e) are articulated from an attachment to the vehicle common to the consecutive axles or are designed to automatically equalize the load between the four axles under all conditions of loading;

"self-steering axle" means an assembly of two or more wheels whose centres are in one transverse vertical plane and whose wheels can articulate in response to forces generated between the tires and the road or through mechanisms and linkages that operate independently of the driver;

"single semi-trailer" means a semi-trailer that is the only trailer in a tractor-trailer combination;

"tag-axle tank semi-trailer" means a tank semi-trailer,

   (a) that is not more than 14.65 metres in length,

   (b) that is equipped with a rear single axle and a front tandem axle, whose inter-axle spacing is more than 2.5 metres,

   (c) whose single axle,

       (i) is a self-steering axle capable of turning 20 degrees in either direction, and

       (ii) is not a liftable axle, and

   (d) whose axles automatically equalize its load such that the weight on the self-steering axle is not more than 500 kilograms greater or less than the average weight per axle of the tandem axle;

"tandem axle" means a dual axle as defined in section 114 of the Act that does not include a liftable axle or a self-steering axle and that has the same number of tires at each wheel position;

"tank full trailer" means a full trailer that is permanently attached to a closed tank having a capacity of 2.3 kilolitres or more;

"tank pony trailer" means a pony trailer that is permanently attached to a closed tank having a capacity of 2.3 kilolitres or more;

"tank semi-trailer" means a semi-trailer that is permanently attached to a closed tank having a capacity of 2.3 kilolitres or more;

"tractor" means a commercial motor vehicle designed to draw one or more semi-trailers, or a semi-trailer and a full trailer, to which it is coupled by means of a fifth wheel assembly;

"tridem axle" means a triple axle as defined in section 114 of the Act that does not include a liftable axle or a self-steering axle and that has the same number of tires at each wheel position;

"tri-drive axle" means a drive axle composed of a tridem axle in which each axle of the tridem axle transmits tractive power to its wheels;

"truck" does not include a tractor or a bus;

"turn centre" means the geometric centre,

(a) on a semi-trailer consisting only of one axle unit, of the axle unit,

(b) on a semi-trailer consisting of more than one axle unit, of the axle unit containing more axles,

(c) on a semi-trailer containing a quadruple axle, of the quadruple axle,

(d) on a tractor, full trailer or pony trailer, of the rear axle unit,

(e) on a truck, bus or recreational vehicle, of the drive axle unit;

"vehicle combination" [Repealed O. Reg. 457/10, s. 2(13).]

"wheelbase" means the longitudinal distance,

(a) from the centre of the kingpin to the turn centre, in the case of a semi-trailer or in the case of a full trailer without a turntable in designated truck-trailer combination 3,

(b) from the centre of articulation of the turntable to the turn centre, in the case of a full trailer with a turntable in designated truck-trailer combination 3,

(c) from the centre of the kingpin to the geometric centre of the tridem axle, in the case of the front portion of a hinged semi-trailer, and from the articulation point of the forward hinge to the geometric centre of the tandem axle, in the case of the rear portion of a hinged semi-trailer,

(d) from the centre of the front axle to the turn centre, in the case of a tractor, truck, bus or recreational vehicle,

(e) from the centre of the hitching device to the turn centre, in the case of a pony trailer or of a full trailer, other than a full trailer in designated truck-trailer combination 3.

(3) For the purposes of this Regulation, where a tire width has been marked on the tire by the manufacturer, the width of the tire shall be deemed to be as marked.

(4) For the purposes of this Regulation, the month and year when a vehicle was manufactured or built is the earliest month and year on any incomplete vehicle manufacturer's information label or manufacturer's compliance label on the vehicle.

O. Reg. 457/10, s. 2; 167/12, s. 1; 16/14, s. 1; 8/16, s. 1

DESIGNATED VEHICLES AND COMBINATIONS

[Heading amended O. Reg. 457/10, s. 3.]

3. Designated tractor-trailer combinations — The Table to this section sets out 15 tractor-trailer combinations that are designated tractor-trailer combinations if the vehicle combination meets the configuration description in the correspondingly numbered Schedule and complies with the dimensional limits of the Schedule and with all the relevant preconditions for the designated combination in the Schedule and in sections 5 to 14.

TABLE OF DESIGNATED TRACTOR-TRAILER COMBINATIONS

Schedule	Designated Tractor-Trailer Combination	Type of Tractor-Trailer Combination
1	1	Tractor Fixed Axle Semi-trailer
2	2	Tractor Self-steer Triaxle Semi-trailer
3	3	Tractor Self-steer Quad Semi-trailer
4	4	Tractor Self-steer 5-Axle Semi-trailer (1-3-1)
5	5	Tractor Self-steer 5-Axle Semi-trailer (1-1-3)
6	6	Tractor Self-steer 6-Axle Semi-trailer (1-4-1)
7	7	Tractor Self-steer 6-Axle Semi-trailer (1-1-4)
8	8	Tri-drive Tractor Fixed Axle Semi-trailer
9	9	Tri-drive Tractor Self-steer Triaxle Semi-trailer
10	10	Tri-drive Tractor Self-steer Quad Semi-trailer
11	11	Tractor A-train Double Trailers
12	12	Tractor B-train Double Trailers
13	13	Tractor C-train Double Trailers
14	14	Stinger-Steer Tractor Semi-trailer Auto Carrier
15	15	Tractor Hinged Semi-trailer

O. Reg. 457/10, s. 3

3.1 Designated buses and recreational vehicles — The Table to this section sets out three buses and two recreational vehicles that are designated buses or recreational vehicles if the vehicle meets the configuration description in the correspondingly numbered Schedule and complies with the dimensional limits of the

Schedule and with all the relevant preconditions for the designated vehicle in the Schedule and in section 8.

TABLE OF DESIGNATED BUSES OR RECREATIONAL VEHICLES

Schedule	Designated Bus or Recreational Vehicle	Type of Bus or Recreational Vehicle
16	1	Standard Bus or Comparable Recreational Vehicle
17	2	Inter-city Bus or Comparable Recreational Vehicle
18	3	Articulated Bus

O. Reg. 457/10, s. 3

3.2 Designated trucks — The Table to this section sets out seven trucks that are designated trucks if the vehicle meets the configuration description in the correspondingly numbered Schedule and complies with the dimensional limits of the Schedule and with all the relevant preconditions for the designated vehicle in the Schedule and in sections 5 to 14.

TABLE OF DESIGNATED TRUCKS

Schedule	Designated Truck	Type of Truck
19	1	2-Axle Truck
20	2	Tandem-axle Truck
21	3	3-Axle Truck with Auxiliary Axle
22	4	Twin-steer Tandem-drive Truck
23	5	Self-steer Triaxle Truck
24	6	Tri-drive 4-Axle Truck
25	7	Twin-steer Tri-drive 5-Axle Truck

O. Reg. 457/10, s. 3

3.3 Designated truck-trailer combinations — The Table to this section sets out five truck-trailer combinations that are designated truck-trailer combinations if the vehicle combination meets the configuration description in the correspondingly numbered Schedule and complies with the dimensional limits of the Schedule and with all the relevant preconditions for the designated vehicle in the Schedule and in sections 5 to 14.

TABLE OF DESIGNATED TRUCK-TRAILER COMBINATIONS

Schedule	Designated Truck-Trailer Combination	Type of Truck-Trailer Combination
26	1	Truck and Fixed Axle Pony Trailer
27	2	Truck and Self-steer Triaxle Pony Trailer
28	3	Truck and Full Trailer
29	4	Truck and Self-steer Triaxle Full Trailer
30	5	Truck and Tridem-axle Full Trailer

O. Reg. 457/10, s. 3

3.4 Designated saddlemount combination — A saddlemount combination is a designated saddlemount combination if it meets the configuration description in Schedule 31 and complies with the dimensional limits of the Schedule and with all of the relevant preconditions for the designated saddlemount combination in the Schedule.

O. Reg. 457/10, s. 3

4. Weight limit chart not determinative of designated vehicle or combination — A vehicle or vehicle combination described in sections 3 to 3.4 is a designated vehicle or a designated combination even if it does not meet the limits in the weight limit chart of the corresponding Schedule.

O. Reg. 457/10, s. 4

4.1 [Repealed O. Reg. 457/10, s. 4.]

PRECONDITIONS FOR DESIGNATED VEHICLES OR DESIGNATED COMBINATIONS

[Heading amended O. Reg. 457/10, s. 5(1).]

5. Liftable axles and controls — (1) A designated vehicle or designated vehicle combination may have axles in addition to those specified in the corresponding Schedule, but the additional axles must remain in the raised position.

(2) A designated truck or a tractor in a designated combination may not be equipped with or have controls, whether remote or manual, that would allow the driver from the cab of the truck or tractor to lift, deploy or alter the weight on a self-steering axle of the truck or of any drawn trailer unless,

(a) the truck, truck-trailer combination or tractor-trailer combination is designed to carry raw forest products; or

(b) the controls,

(i) do not activate unless the emergency 4-way flashers are activated,

(ii) contain a device that prevents lifting the axle or altering the axle weight when the truck or vehicle combination is travelling at a speed over 60 kilometres per hour, and

(iii) in the case of a tractor-trailer combination, operate only on the most forward self-steering axle of the semi-trailer.

(3) The tractor in a designated tractor-trailer combination 12 may not be equipped with or have controls, whether remote or manual, that would allow the driver to lift, deploy or alter the weight on the tandem or tridem axles in the combination, unless the controls,

(a) operate only on the forward axle of the lead trailer's tridem axle;

(b) do not activate unless the emergency 4-way flashers are activated; and

(c) contain a device that prevents lifting the axle or altering the axle weight when the combination is travelling at a speed over 60 kilometres per hour.

(3.1) A designated truck may be equipped with,

(a) manual controls mounted outside the cab of the truck to lift or deploy its self-steering axle or forced-steer auxiliary pusher axle;

(b) manual controls mounted outside the cab of the truck to alter the weight on its self-steering axle or forced-steer auxiliary pusher axle, but only for use outside of Ontario;

(c) automatic controls that lift its self-steering axle when reversing and deploy it again when moving forward; and

(d) automatic controls that lift or deploy its self-steering axle or forced-steer auxiliary pusher axle, depending on whether the truck is heavily or lightly loaded.

(3.2) A trailer in a designated combination may be equipped with,

(a) manual controls to lift or deploy its self-steering axles;

(b) manual controls to alter the weight on its self-steering axles, but only for use outside Ontario;

(c) automatic controls that lift its self-steering axles when reversing and deploy them again when moving forward; and

(d) automatic controls that lift or deploy its self-steering axles, depending on whether the trailer is heavily or lightly loaded.

(4) In subsection (3) and in Schedule 12,

"tridem axle" means a triple axle as defined in section 114 of the Act that does not include a self-steering axle and that has the same number of tires at each wheel position, and includes an axle unit that is equipped with a device for altering the weight transmitted to the highway surface.

O. Reg. 457/10, s. 5(2)

6. Rear impact guards — (1) The rearmost trailer of any designated tractor-trailer combination that is a long combination must be equipped with a rear impact guard meeting the requirements of subsection (2) if,

(a) the trailer was manufactured after July 14, 1993 and before January 27, 1998;

(b) the trailer has an axle unit that can slide or is fixed so that the rear of the rearmost tire is more than 0.3 metres in front of the rear of the trailer; and

(c) the trailer's rear structure is more than 0.56 metres above the ground when the trailer is unladen on a level surface.

(2) A rear impact guard, must consist of a single horizontal beam that is rigidly attached to the trailer and that,

(a) extends within 0.1 metres of each side of the trailer;

(b) is not more than 0.3 metres in front of the rear of the trailer and is as close to the rear as possible; and

(c) is not more than 0.56 metres above the ground when the trailer is unladen on a level surface.

(3) The rearmost trailer in a combination described in subsection (5) must be equipped with a rear impact guard that meets one of the following standards, as that standard read on the date of the trailer's manufacture:

1. United States Federal Motor Vehicle Safety Standard 224.

2. Standard 223 under the *Motor Vehicle Safety Act* (Canada).

(4) Subsection (3) does not apply if one of the standards described in that subsection exempts the rearmost trailer in a combination described in subsection (5) from having a rear impact guard.

(5) Subsection (3) applies to,

(a) any designated tractor-trailer combination that is a long combination whose rearmost trailer was manufactured after January 26, 1998;

(b) designated tractor-trailer combination 2, 3, 4, 5, 6, 7, 9 or 10;

(c) any designated tractor-trailer combination that includes a trailer that was manufactured after 2005; or

(d) any designated truck-trailer combination that includes a trailer that was manufactured after August 31, 2007.

O. Reg. 457/10, s. 6

7. Brakes — (1) [Repealed O. Reg. 457/10, s. 7(1).]

(2) [Repealed O. Reg. 457/10, s. 7(1).]

(3) The following brake requirements apply to designated tractor-trailer combinations 4, 5, 6, 7 and 15:

1. The semi-trailer service brake system must be constructed so that a single leakage failure in any component of the system, except the tubing or fittings in the control line, does not render the brakes on more than three axles inoperative.

2. The semi-trailer must be equipped with a low air pressure warning system constructed so that, in the event the air pressure in any one of the service brake reservoirs falls below 483 kPa or 70 psi, a red LED warning lamp will illuminate. The lamp must be side-facing, located on the outside of the semi-trailer near the front side marker lamp, within the field of view of the tractor's rear view mirror, and must include a bulb check feature.

3. The semi-trailer supply and control gladhands must be equipped with screens that will prevent any particle larger than 0.33 millimetres or 0.013 inches from entering the gladhand beyond a point where it remains visible from the opening. A label indicating that the vehicle is equipped with gladhand screens and stating that the gladhand screens must be inspected regularly and kept clean to prevent brake system malfunction must be placed adjacent to the gladhands.

4. The semi-trailer must be equipped with an antilock brake system that directly or indirectly controls each wheel of the semi-trailer.

5. The semi-trailer must display a clearly visible label with the name and telephone number of the semi-trailer manufacturer and the appropriate brake system circuit diagram number.

O. Reg. 457/10, s. 7

8. Tires — The tires of a designated vehicle or vehicle combination must be at least 150 millimetres wide.

O. Reg. 457/10, s. 8

9. Wheel cut — (1) Every designated vehicle with a self-steering axle and every designated vehicle combination with a self-steering axle, other than a self-steering tag axle in designated bus or recreational vehicle 1 or 2, must comply with the wheel cut requirements of the Table to this section.

(2) In this section,

"wheel cut" means the number of degrees the wheels of a self-steering axle are capable of turning in either direction from the straight ahead position.

TABLE
MINIMUM REQUIRED SELF-STEERING AXLE WHEEL CUT

Distance from Turn Centre to Self-steering Axle	Minimum Degrees of Wheel Cut
4.65 metres or less	20°
More than 4.65 metres and less than or equal to 5.85 metres	25°
More than 5.85 metres and less than or equal to 7.10 metres	28°
More than 7.10 metres	30°

O. Reg. 457/10, s. 9

10. Self-steering axle locking device — (1) In designated tractor-trailer combinations 2 and 9, if the axle spread of the tandem axle of the semi-trailer exceeds 1.85 metres, the designated combination must be equipped with an automatic device that locks the self-steering axle in the straight ahead position when the combination is travelling at a speed over 60 kilometres per hour.

(2) Designated tractor-trailer combinations 4 and 6 must be equipped with an automatic device that locks the rearmost self-steering axle in the straight ahead position when the combination is travelling at a speed over 60 kilometres per hour.

O. Reg. 457/10, s. 10

11. Tri-drive locking device — Any differential locks on a tri-drive axle of any designated vehicle or vehicle combination must remain unlocked while the vehicle or combination is operated on a highway.

O. Reg. 457/10, s. 11

12. C-train equipment — (1) The foremost semi-trailer of a designated tractor-trailer combination 13 must be equipped with a hitch that meets the requirements of section 904 of the *Motor Vehicle Safety Regulations* made under the *Motor Vehicle Safety Act* (Canada).

(2) [Repealed O. Reg. 457/10, s. 12(2).]

(3) The trailer converter dolly of a designated tractor-trailer combination 13 must meet the requirements of section 903 of the *Motor Vehicle Safety Regulations* made under the *Motor Vehicle Safety Act* (Canada).

O. Reg. 457/10, s. 12

13. Labelling — (1) The semi-trailer in designated tractor-trailer combinations 2, 3, 4, 5, 6, 7, 9, 10 and 15, the trailer in designated truck-trailer combinations 2 and 4 and designated trucks 3 and 5 must bear their original compliance labels and comply with subsections (2) and (3).

(2) The original compliance label or the manufacturer's identification plate on the truck or trailer must,

> (a) contain the notation "SPIF", signifying that the truck or trailer is safe, productive and infrastructure-friendly and was manufactured to meet the specifications of this Regulation;

> (b) identify the company authorized under the *Motor Vehicle Safety Act* (Canada) to apply a national safety mark, the foreign manufacturer registered under that Act or the authorized dealer of either of them, that manufactured the truck or trailer; and

> (c) indicate the gross vehicle and axle weight ratings.

(3) If a truck or trailer was not manufactured to meet the specifications of this Regulation, but was converted to meet such specifications, it must bear a label adjacent to the original compliance label,

(a) containing the notation "SPIF", signifying that the truck or trailer is safe, productive and infrastructure-friendly and was converted to meet the specifications of this Regulation;

(b) identifying the company authorized under the *Motor Vehicle Safety Act* (Canada) to apply a national safety mark, the foreign manufacturer registered under that Act or the authorized dealer of either of them, that converted the truck or trailer; and

(c) indicating the revised gross vehicle and axle weight ratings.

(4) If a semi-trailer was manufactured or converted before 2006, the label required by subsection (2) or (3) may bear the notation "Reg 597 (Ont) — 3" or "Reg 597 (Ont) — 4" instead of the notation "SPIF".

O. Reg. 457/10, s. 13

14. Weight requirements — (1) Weight requirements — The following designated vehicles and vehicles within designated combinations must be designed to load equalize within the meaning of subsection (2):

1. Designated trucks 3 and 5.

2. The semi-trailer in designated tractor-trailer combinations 2 to 7, 9, 10 and 15.

3. The pony trailer in designated truck-trailer combination 2.

(2) A vehicle load equalizes if,

(a) in the case of designated truck 3, the weight of the auxiliary self-steering axle or forced-steer auxiliary pusher axle is not more than 500 kilograms greater or less than 33 per cent of the weight on the tandem axle;

(b) in the case of designated truck 5, the weight of the self-steering axle is not more than 500 kilograms greater or less than the average weight per axle of the tandem axle;

(c) in the case of the semi-trailer in designated tractor-trailer combinations 2 to 7, 9 and 10, the weight of each self-steering axle is not more than 500 kilograms greater or less than the average weight per axle of the tandem, tridem or quadruple axle;

(d) in the case of the semi-trailer in designated tractor-trailer combination 15, the weight of the tandem axle is not more than 500 kilograms greater or less than 67 per cent of the weight of the tridem axle; and

(e) in the case of the pony trailer in designated truck-trailer combination 2, the weight of the self-steering axle is not more than 500 kilograms greater or less than the average weight per axle of the tandem axle.

(3) [Repealed O. Reg. 457/10, s. 14(1).]

(4) [Repealed O. Reg. 457/10, s. 14(1).]

(5) A semi-trailer forming part of designated tractor-trailer combinations 3, 4, 5, 6, 7, 10 and 15 must be equipped with,

(a) a device that accurately displays the total weight on the trailer axles in kilograms; or

(b) a device and a table or chart, from the combined use of which the total weight on the trailer axles in kilograms may be readily and accurately obtained.

(6) [Repealed O. Reg. 457/10, s. 14(3).]

(7) [Repealed O. Reg. 457/10, s. 14(3).]

(8) [Repealed O. Reg. 457/10, s. 14(3).]

O. Reg. 457/10, s. 14

RULES APPLICABLE TO DESIGNATED VEHICLES AND DESIGNATED COMBINATIONS

[Heading amended O. Reg. 457/10, s. 15(1).]

15. Dimensional limits for long combinations — **(1) A designated tractor-trailer combination that is a long combination shall comply with the dimensional limits in the corresponding Schedule and not with the dimensional limits specified in section 109 of the Act, if the dimensional limits in the Schedule are greater than those in section 109 of the Act.**

(2) A long combination that is a designated tractor-trailer combination 4, 6 or 7 in every respect except that both self-steering axles are raised shall comply with the dimensional limits in the corresponding Schedule and not with the dimensional limits specified in section 109 of the Act, if the dimensional limits in the Schedul e are greater than those in section 109 of the Act and if the gross vehicle weight of the long combination does not exceed the amount permitted in Vehicle Weight Table 32.

(3) A designated truck-trailer combination 3, a designated bus or recreational vehicle 2 or 3 and a designated saddlemount combinaton shall comply with the dimensional limits in the corresponding Schedule and not with the dimensional limits specified in section 109 of the Act, if the dimensional limits in the Schedule are greater than those in section 109 of the Act.

O. Reg. 457/10, s. 15(2)

16. [Repealed O. Reg. 457/10, s. 16.]

17. Axle unit weight limits — **The axle unit weight for a designated vehicle or combination is that specified in the corresponding Schedule instead of the axle unit weight specified or referred to in subsection 116(1) of the Act.**

O. Reg. 457/10, s. 17

18. [Repealed O. Reg. 457/10, s. 18.]

19. Axle group weight limits — The axle group weight for a quadruple axle in a designated tractor-trailer combination 6 or 7 is that specified in the corresponding Schedule instead of the axle group weight for a four axle group referred to in clause 117(1)(c) of the Act.

O. Reg. 457/10, s. 19

20. Maximum allowable gross vehicle weight — designated vehicles and combinations — (1) Clauses 118(1)(a) and (b) of the Act do not apply to designated vehicles and combinations.

(2) For the purpose of clause 118(1)(c) of the Act,

(a) the maximum allowable gross vehicle weight of a designated vehicle or vehicle combination is the amount prescribed by the weight limit chart of the appropriate Schedule; and

(b) where the weight limit chart of the appropriate Schedule refers to a Vehicle Weight Table, the appropriate Vehicle Weight Table, determined in accordance with section 38, applies.

(3) [Repealed O. Reg. 457/10, s. 20.]

(4) [Repealed O. Reg. 457/10, s. 20.]

O. Reg. 457/10, s. 20

RULES APPLICABLE TO NON-DESIGNATED VEHICLES AND COMBINATIONS

[Heading added O. Reg. 457/10, s. 21.]

21. Maximum allowable gross vehicle weight — non-designated vehicles and combinations — (1) Clauses 118(1)(a) and (b) of the Act do not apply to non-designated vehicles and combinations, except as provided in section 22 of this Regulation.

(2) For the purpose of clause 118(1)(c) of the Act,

(a) the maximum allowable gross vehicle weight for non-designated vehicles and combinations, other than B-train combinations, is the amount prescribed in Vehicle Weight Table 32;

(b) the maximum allowable gross vehicle weight for non-designated B-train combinations is the amount prescribed in Vehicle Weight Table 33.

(3) [Repealed O. Reg. 457/10, s. 21.]

(4) [Repealed O. Reg. 457/10, s. 21.]

(5) [Repealed O. Reg. 457/10, s. 21.]

O. Reg. 457/10, s. 21

22. Maximum allowable gross vehicle weight — transition for non-designated vehicles and combinations — (1) For the purpose of section 118 of the Act, the maximum allowable gross vehicle weight for a non-designated vehicle or vehicle combination described in subsection (2) and before the date specified in that subsection is the lowest of,

(a) the amount calculated under clause 118(1)(a) of the Act;

(b) the amount calculated under clause 118(1)(b) of the Act; and

(c) the maximum allowable gross vehicle weight under the appropriate Vehicle Weight Table from Vehicle Weight Tables 1 to 29, as determined in accordance with section 38.

(2) Subsection (1) applies to the following non-designated vehicles and vehicle combinations before the specified date:

1. Before January 1, 2016, a tractor-trailer combination that includes a single semi-trailer, if the semi-trailer has four or more deployed axles, was manufactured before 2006 and is not an end dump semi-trailer or an open-top hopper dump semi-trailer.

2. Before January 1, 2016, a tractor-trailer combination with two trailers, if both trailers were manufactured before 2006.

3. Before January 1, 2021, a tractor-trailer combination that includes a single carbon dioxide tank semi-trailer, cryogenic tank semi-trailer or tag-axle tank semi-trailer, if the semi-trailer has three or fewer deployed axles.

4. Before January 1, 2021, a truck, bus or recreational vehicle, if the truck, bus or recreational vehicle was manufactured before July 1, 2011.

5. Before January 1, 2021, a truck-trailer combination if both the truck and trailer were manufactured before July 1, 2011.

6. Subject to subsection (4), before January 1, 2021, a truck-trailer combination if,

i. either the truck or the trailer, but not both, was manufactured before July 1, 2011, and

ii. the other vehicle is a designated truck or is a trailer that meets all of the requirements in order to be part of a designated truck-trailer combination.

(3) Before January 1, 2021, subsection (1) applies to a non-designated tractor-trailer combination that includes a single tank semi-trailer with three or fewer axles deployed, other than a carbon dioxide tank semi-trailer, cryogenic tank semi-trailer or tag-axle tank semi-trailer, except that the maximum allowable gross vehicle weight is determined by subtracting 3,000 kilograms from the weight determined under that subsection.

(4) Before January 1, 2021, subsection (1) applies to a non-designated truck-trailer combination that is composed of a twin-steer tandem axle truck and trailer and that meets the requirements in subparagraphs 6 i and ii of subsection (2), except that the maximum allowable gross vehicle weight is determined by subtracting the following amount from the weight determined under subsection (1):

1. If the trailer is a triaxle pony trailer or a triaxle full trailer, 2,500 kilograms.

2. If the trailer is a pony trailer with a wheelbase of 8.75 metres or more or a full trailer with a wheelbase of 7.25 metres or more and the trailer is not a triaxle trailer,

> i. **5,500 kilograms, if its base length is less than 18.25 metres,**

> ii. **4,500 kilograms, if its base length is 18.25 metres or more but less than 18.75 metres,**

> iii. **3,500 kilograms, if its base length is 18.75 metres or more but less than 19.25 metres, or**

> iv. **2,500 kilograms, if its base length is 19.25 metres or more.**

3. If the trailer is a pony trailer with a wheelbase of less than 8.75 metres or a full trailer with a wheelbase of less than 7.25 metres and the trailer is not a triaxle trailer,

> i. **5,500 kilograms, if it has one axle,**

> ii. **8,500 kilograms, if it has two axles, or**

> iii. **9,500 kilograms, if it has three or more axles.**

(5) In subsection (4),

"triaxle" with reference to a trailer, means a trailer with a single self-steer axle in the front and a tandem axle in the rear;

"twin-steer tandem axle truck" means a 4-axle truck with a front tandem axle and a rear tandem drive axle.

O. Reg. 457/10, s. 21; 167/12, s. 2

23. [Repealed O. Reg. 457/10, s. 21.]

[Heading repealed O. Reg. 457/10, s. 21.]

24. [Repealed O. Reg. 457/10, s. 21.]

[Heading repealed O. Reg. 457/10, s. 22(1).]

25. Aggregate vehicles — **(1) This section applies to aggregate vehicles, but does not apply to designated vehicles and combinations or to non-designated vehicles and combinations to which section 21 applies.**

(2) Clauses 118(1)(a) and (b) of the Act do not apply to aggregate vehicles.

(3) The maximum allowable gross vehicle weight of an aggregate vehicle shall be determined by subtracting, in the case of a two-axle aggregate vehicle, 1,000 kilograms or, in the case of an aggregate vehicle of three or more axles, 1,500 kilograms from,

> **(a) the maximum weight permitted on the front axle under section 116 of the Act plus the sum of the maximum allowable weights for all other axle units of the vehicle or vehicle combination as set out in section 116 of the Act;**

(b) the maximum weight permitted on the front axle under section 116 of the Act plus the sum of the maximum allowable weights for any two axle groups, three axle groups or four axle groups, or any combination of them, as set out in section 117 of the Act, plus the maximum allowable weight for any axle unit or units excluding any axle unit or units that are part of an axle group, as set out in section 116 of the Act; or

(c) the maximum allowable gross vehicle weight prescribed by clause 22(1)(c) of this Regulation.

(4) Where the calculation of front axle weight for an aggregate vehicle powered by a tractor results in a weight over 6,500 kilograms, the front axle weight shall be deemed to be 6,500 kilograms.

(5) In this section and in Vehicle Weight Tables 1 to 29

"front axle weight", in respect of an aggregate vehicle, means,

(a) for a single front axle, the maximum weight permitted under section 116 of the Act for a single axle, and

(b) for a dual front axle, one-half the maximum weight permitted under section 116 of the Act for a dual axle.

O. Reg. 457/10, s. 22

26. [Repealed O. Reg. 457/10, s. 23.]

27. [Repealed O. Reg. 457/10, s. 23.]

28. [Repealed O. Reg. 457/10, s. 23.]

29. [Repealed O. Reg. 457/10, s. 23.]

30. [Repealed O. Reg. 457/10, s. 23.]

31. [Repealed O. Reg. 457/10, s. 23.]

32. [Repealed O. Reg. 457/10, s. 23.]

33. [Repealed O. Reg. 457/10, s. 23.]

34. **Permits** — (1) Despite section 21, the Registrar may issue permits under clause 110.1(1)(b) of the Act allowing the operation of the following non-designated vehicles and of the following vehicles that form part of a non-designated vehicle combination in compliance with the maximum allowable gross vehicle weights specified in subsection 22(1) or section 25:

1. After December 31, 2010, an end-dump semi-trailer or open-top hopper dump semi-trailer that was manufactured before 2003 and is part of a tractor-trailer combination.

2. After December 31, 2015, a single semi-trailer, other than a dump semi-trailer, with four or more deployed axles that was manufactured before 2006 and is part of a tractor-trailer combination.

3. After December 31, 2015, a trailer that forms part of a tractor-trailer combination with two trailers, if both trailers were manufactured before 2006.

4. After December 31, 2020, a truck, bus or recreational vehicle that was manufactured before July 1, 2011.

5. After December 31, 2020, a trailer in a truck-trailer combination, if the trailer was manufactured before July 1, 2011.

(2) A permit described in subsection (1) may be issued for the purpose of allowing the continued use of a vehicle by itself or in a combination referred to in subsection (1), but the permit shall be limited to the normal operating life of the vehicle and shall not be valid,

(a) in the case of an open-top hopper dump semi-trailer, for longer than 20 years after the year of its manufacture;

(b) in the case of a tank full trailer or a tank pony trailer, for longer than 20 years after the year of its manufacture;

(b.1) in the case of a tank semi-trailer, for longer than 25 years after the year of its manufacture;

(c) in the case of a semi-trailer, other than a tank semi-trailer, with four or more axles, for longer than 20 years after the year of its manufacture;

(d) in the case of a semi-trailer, other than a tank semi-trailer, that forms part of a tractor-trailer combination with two trailers, for longer than 20 years after the year of its manufacture;

(e) in the case of a truck that is a concrete mixer fitted with a revolving drum, for longer than 20 years after the year of its manufacture;

(f) in the case of a vehicle not referred to in clause (a), (b), (c), (d) or (e), for longer than 15 years after the year of its manufacture.

(3) [Repealed O. Reg. 457/10, s. 24.]

(4) [Repealed O. Reg. 457/10, s. 24.]

O. Reg. 457/10, s. 24; 16/14, s. 2

34.1 Axle weight limits — (1) For the purposes of section 116 of the Act, if a non-designated vehicle or a vehicle that is part of a non-designated combination is manufactured after June 30, 2011, the weight on an axle unit shall not exceed the manufacturer's gross axle weight rating if the manufacturer's gross axle weight is less than the amount otherwise permitted by the Act and this Regulation.

(2) If the driver of the vehicle or vehicle combination does not have with him or her verification in writing of the manufacturer's gross axle weight ratings of the axles of the vehicle or combination, or if the driver does not provide that verification when demanded by a police officer or officer appointed for carrying out the provisions of this Act, the axle unit weight on an axle unit shall not exceed,

(a) for the front axle, the lower of 5,000 kilograms and the sum of the maximum tire load ratings specified on the tire side walls; and

(b) for other axles, the sum of the maximum tire load ratings specified on the tire side walls.

O. Reg. 457/10, s. 25

[Heading repealed O. Reg. 457/10, s. 26(1).]

35. Tractor tandem axle weight increases — (1) Tandem axles with an axle spread of at least 1.2 metres and less than 1.6 metres are prescribed axle units for the purposes of section 116 of the Act when they form part of a three-axle tractor that is not part of a designated combination, that has both a front single axle equipped with single tires and a rear tandem axle and that has no other axles deployed.

(2) Instead of the maximum allowable axle unit weights specified in Table 1 of Part VIII of the Act, the prescribed weight for the axle units prescribed in subsection (1) is 18,000 kilograms.

O. Reg. 457/10, s. 26(2)

MISCELLANEOUS
[Heading added O. Reg. 8/16, s. 2.]

36. Flexible aerodynamic devices not included in length — (1) An aerodynamic device with which a commercial motor vehicle or trailer is equipped is exempt from clauses 109(13.1)(a) and (b) of the Act if the device meets all of the following conditions:

1. The device is a flexible aerodynamic device.

2. When the device is not deployed, the device is capable of being folded so that no portion of it extends more than 0.305 metres beyond the rear of the vehicle or trailer.

3. When the device is deployed, no portion of the device that is 1.9 metres or less above the ground extends beyond a transverse vertical plane that,

   i. starts from the rear bottom of the vehicle or trailer, and

   ii. intersects the point that is 1.74 metres above the ground and 1.21 metres beyond the rear of the vehicle or trailer, as shown in Figure 4.

4. When the device is deployed, no portion of the device that is more than 1.9 metres above the ground extends more than 1.52 metres beyond the rear of the vehicle or trailer, as shown in Figure 4.

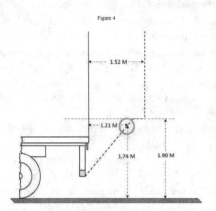

Figure 4

(2) In subparagraph 3 i of subsection (1),

"rear bottom of the vehicle or trailer" means,

(a) **if the vehicle or trailer is equipped with a rear impact guard, the rear bottom edge of the rear impact guard, or**

(b) **if the vehicle or trailer is not equipped with a rear impact guard, the rear bottom edge of its rearmost component having structural properties, including the deck, stairs or ramp, but excluding auxiliary equipment or machinery.**

O. Reg. 8/16, s. 2

36.1 [Repealed O. Reg. 457/10, s. 27.]

36.2 Exemption from all maximum weights — fire apparatus — A fire apparatus is exempt from sections 116, 117 and 118 of the Act if the fire apparatus does not exceed the axle unit, axle group or gross vehicle weight ratings specified by the manufacturer.

O. Reg. 435/08, s. 2

SCHEDULES OF DESIGNATED VEHICLES AND COMBINATIONS

[Heading amended O. Reg. 457/10, s. 28.]

37. Interpretation for Schedules — (1) The following interpretive rules apply to Schedules 1 to 31:

1. **The column heading "Ref" refers to a reference number associated with a dimension of the designated vehicle or combination. Some of the dimensions are set out in the diagram at the top of the Schedule identified by their reference number.**

2. **A reference to an axle unit in a Configuration Description is to a deployed axle unit. If an axle unit is not referred to in a Configuration Description, the**

designated combination does not have that axle unit unless it is an additional axle described in subsection 5(1).

3. Where a tire weight limit is expressed as weight per millimetre, the reference is to a millimetre of tire width.

4. The sum of the maximum tire load ratings shall be determined by adding the highest tire load ratings of the tires as specified on the tire side walls.

5. A vehicle that is required to comply with subsection 109(2) of the Act and that does comply with that subsection shall be deemed to be in compliance with the width limits in Schedules 1 to 31.

6. Maximum width shall be determined in accordance with subsections 109 (1), (3) and (4) of the Act.

7. Maximum length shall be determined in accordance with section 109 of the Act, excluding subsection 109(10.1) of the Act.

8. "Not controlled" means that no measurement is prescribed.

9. "Overall" refers to the total combination.

10. In calculating allowable gross vehicle weight, where a Schedule refers to the actual weight on the front axle, if that weight exceeds maximum allowable weight for the axle, the maximum allowable weight must be used in the calculation.

(2) In Schedules 1 to 31,

"AGVW" means allowable gross vehicle weight;

"allowable gross vehicle weight" means the maximum permissible weight of a vehicle or vehicle combination for the purpose of section 118 of the Act;

"bed length" means the external measurement of a trailer from the front of its cargo carrying space to the rear of its cargo carrying space, but excluding any portion of auxiliary equipment or machinery that extends beyond the front of the trailer and that is not designed for the transportation of goods;

"box length", in a truck-trailer combination, means the external measurement from the front of the load-carrying portion of the truck to the rear of the trailer, including load, but excluding any portion of auxiliary equipment or machinery that extends beyond the front of the load-carrying portion of truck and that is not designed or used for the transportation of goods;

"converter dolly drawbar length" means the longitudinal distance from the centre of the hole in the fifth wheel of a converter dolly to the centre of its eye or equivalent device;

"effective rear overhang", except where otherwise specified, means the longitudinal distance from the turn centre of the vehicle to its rearmost point, including any load;

"effective wheelbase" means the longitudinal distance between the geometric centres of front and rear axle units of a truck;

"GAWR" means manufacturer's gross axle weight rating;

"hitch offset",

(a) in the case of an A-train or C-train, means the longitudinal distance from the turn centre of the foremost semi-trailer to the articulation point of the hitch used to tow the rearmost trailer, and

(b) in the case of truck or tractor, means the longitudinal distance from the turn centre of the truck or tractor to the articulation point of the hitch or coupling device used to tow a trailer;

"inter-city bus" means a bus commonly known as a motor coach that has,

(a) motive power mounted to the rear of the front axle,

(b) air-ride or torsion-bar suspension,

(c) a baggage area that is separate from the passenger cabin, and

(d) a passenger cabin with 15 or more reclining seats for passengers;

"kg" means kilograms;

"load equalized" means that a vehicle that is required by subsection 14(1) to be designed to load equalize actually does load equalize within the meaning of subsection 14(2);

"m" means metres;

"Max." means maximum;

"Min." means minimum;

"mm" means millimeters;

"na" means not applicable;

"not load equalized" means that a vehicle that is required by subsection 14(1) to be designed to load equalize does not actually load equalize within the meaning of subsection 14(2);

"quadruple spread" means the longitudinal distance between the centres of the foremost and rearmost axles of the quadruple axle;

"RV" means recreational vehicle;

"self-steer", with respect to an axle, means self-steering axle;

"swing radius" means the greatest horizontal distance from the vertical axis through the centre of the kingpin to any point on the semi-trailer ahead of the kingpin, including load and any extension to the length caused by auxiliary equipment or machinery;

"tag axle" means the rearmost axle of a bus or recreational vehicle that forms part of a two axle group with a drive axle;

"tandem" means tandem axle;

"track width" means the width of an axle across the outside faces of the tires measured at any point above the lowest point of the rim;

"tridem" means tridem axle;

"tri-drive" means tri-drive axle;

"verified" means that the driver of the vehicle or vehicle combination has with him or her verification in writing of the manufacturer's gross axle weight ratings of the axles of the vehicle or combination and provides that verification when demanded by a police officer or officer appointed for carrying out the provisions of the Act;

"wheelbase" [Repealed O. Reg. 167/12, s. 3.]

O. Reg. 457/10, s. 28; 167/12, s. 3; 16/14, s. 3

[Heading repealed O. Reg. 457/10, s. 28.]

38. Application of Vehicle Weight Tables — (1) The following rules apply to the application of the Vehicle Weight Tables:

1. The appropriate Vehicle Weight Table from Vehicle Weight Tables 1 to 29 applies to a non-designated vehicle or combination to which section 22 applies.

2. If a Schedule specifies one of Vehicle Weight Tables 1 to 29, the specified Vehicle Weight Table applies to a designated vehicle or combination.

3. If a Schedule specifies Vehicle Weight Table 30 or 31, the specified Vehicle Weight Table applies to a designated truck-trailer combination.

4. Vehicle Weight Tables 32 and 33 apply to non-designated vehicles and combinations to which section 22 does not apply.

(2) Where one of Vehicle Weight Tables 1 to 29 applies, the appropriate table is determined based on the number of axles and the inter-vehicle-unit distance or intra-vehicle-unit distance, with the following exceptions:

1. The maximum allowable gross vehicle weight for a 5-axle A-train double or C-train double is as prescribed in Vehicle Weight Table 8.

2. The maximum allowable gross vehicle weight for a 7-axle vehicle without a drawn vehicle is as prescribed in Vehicle Weight Table 16.

3. The maximum allowable gross vehicle weight for an eight or more axle vehicle without a drawn vehicle is as prescribed in Vehicle Weight Table 23.

(3) In the case of non-designated combinations, if the gross weight transmitted to the highway by the rearmost vehicle of the combination is not at least five per cent of the gross weight of the combination, the axles of the rearmost vehicle are not included in calculating the base length and the number of axles when determining the combination's maximum allowable gross vehicle weight under a Vehicle Weight Table; instead, the maximum allowable gross vehicle weight of the combination is determined by adding the weight derived from the appropriate Vehicle Weight Table and the actual weight of the rearmost vehicle.

(4) If the determination of the maximum allowable gross vehicle weight under subsection (3) produces a result greater than 63,500 kilograms, the maximum allowable gross vehicle weight for the non-designated combination is 63,500 kilograms.

(5) In this section and in the Vehicle Weight Tables,

"front axle weight", in respect of a vehicle or vehicle combination that is not an aggregate vehicle, means,

> (a) for a single front axle, the axle unit weight on the front axle or, if that weight is more than the maximum weight permitted for a single axle under section 116 of the Act, the maximum weight permitted for a single axle under section 116 of the Act,

> (b) for a dual front axle, one-half of the axle unit weight on the dual front axle or, if that weight is more than one-half of the maximum weight permitted for a dual axle under section 116 of the Act, one-half of the maximum weight permitted for a dual axle under section 116 of the Act, and

> (c) for a triple front axle, one-third of the axle unit weight for the triple front axle or, if that weight is more than one-third of the maximum weight permitted for a triple axle under section 116 of the Act, one-third of the maximum weight permitted for a triple axle under section 116 of the Act.

"intra-vehicle-unit distance", for a five or six-axle vehicle without a drawn vehicle, means the greater of,

> (a) the distance between the centres of the second and third axles from the front of the vehicle, and

> (b) the distance between the centres of the third and fourth axles from the front of the vehicle;

"number of axles" means the total number of axles on a vehicle or vehicle combination that are deployed.

(6) In Vehicle Weight Tables 1 to 29, subsections 25(4) and (5) apply and subsection (5) of this section does not apply in determining front axle weight on an aggregate vehicle.

O. Reg. 457/10, s. 28

SCHEDULE 1 — DESIGNATED TRACTOR-TRAILER COMBINATION 1 — TRACTOR FIXED AXLE SEMI-TRAILER [Heading amended O. Reg. 457/10, s. 29.]

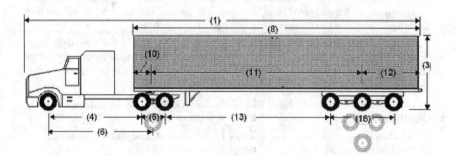

Configuration Description

Designated Tractor-Trailer Combination 1 is composed of a tractor and a single semi-trailer. The front axle of the tractor is a single axle with single tires. The drive axle of the tractor is either a single or tandem axle. The semi-trailer has one axle unit that is either a single, tandem or tridem axle.

Qualifying Preconditions

Equipment and components, see ss. 5, 6 and 8

Exceptions

Until January 1, 2020, the dimensional limits for Wheelbase (11), Effective Rear overhang (12), Inter-vehicle-unit distance (13) and Track Width (19) do not apply if the semi-trailer was built before 2006 and is not more than 14.65 metres long.

DIMENSIONAL LIMIT CHART

Vehicle	Ref.	Feature	Dimensional Limit
Overall	(1)	Overall Length	Max. 23.0m
Overall	(2)	Width	Max. 2.6m
Overall	(3)	Height	Max. 4.15m
Tractor	(4)	Inter-axle Spacing	Min. 3.0m
Tractor	(5)	Tandem Axle Spread	1.2 to 1.85m

DIMENSIONAL LIMIT CHART

Vehicle	Ref.	Feature	Dimensional Limit
Tractor	(6)	Wheelbase	Max. 7.2m if tractor built after 2005
Tractor	(6)	Wheelbase — (long combination)	Max. 7.2m
Semi-Trailer	(8)	Length	Max. 16.2m
Semi-Trailer	(9)	End-Dump Semi-Trailer Bed Length	Max. 14.65m
Semi-Trailer	(10)	Swing Radius	Max. 2.0m
Semi-Trailer	(11)	Wheelbase — If tractor wheelbase is 6.2m or less	6.25m to 12.50m
Semi-Trailer	(11)	Wheelbase — If tractor wheelbase is >6.2m to 6.3m	6.25m to 12.47m
Semi-Trailer	(11)	Wheelbase — If tractor wheelbase is >6.3m to 6.4m	6.25m to 12.40m
Semi-Trailer	(11)	Wheelbase — If tractor wheelbase is >6.4m to 6.5m	6.25m to 12.33m
Semi-Trailer	(11)	Wheelbase — If tractor wheelbase is >6.5m to 6.6m	6.25m to 12.27m
Semi-Trailer	(11)	Wheelbase — If tractor wheelbase is >6.6m to 6.7m	6.25m to 12.20m
Semi-Trailer	(11)	Wheelbase — If tractor wheelbase is >6.7m to 6.8m	6.25m to 12.13m
Semi-Trailer	(11)	Wheelbase — If tractor wheelbase is >6.8m to 6.9m	6.25m to 12.07m
Semi-Trailer	(11)	Wheelbase — If tractor wheelbase is >6.9m to 7.0m	6.25m to 12.00m
Semi-Trailer	(11)	Wheelbase — If tractor wheelbase is >7.0m to 7.1m	6.25m to 11.93m
Semi-Trailer	(11)	Wheelbase — If tractor wheelbase is >7.1m to 7.2m	6.25m to 11.87m
Semi-Trailer	(12)	Effective Rear Overhang	Max. 35% of wheelbase
Semi-Trailer	(13)	Inter-vehicle-unit Distance — single to single, tandem or tridem	Min. 3.0m
Semi-Trailer	(13)	Inter-vehicle-unit Distance — tandem to tandem	Min. 5.0m

DIMENSIONAL LIMIT CHART

Vehicle	Ref.	Feature	Dimensional Limit
Semi-Trailer	(13)	Inter-vehicle-unit Distance — tandem to tridem	Min. 5.5m
Semi-Trailer	(16)	Tandem Spread	1.2 to 3.1m
Semi-Trailer	(16)	Tridem Spread	2.4 to 3.7m
Semi-Trailer	(19)	Track Width — trailer with single tires built before 2010	2.3 to 2.6m
Semi-Trailer	(19)	Track Width — trailer with single tires built after 2009	2.45 to 2.6m
Semi-Trailer	(19)	Track Width — all other trailers	2.5 to 2.6m

WEIGHT LIMIT CHART

Feature	Weight Limit	
Front Axle Maximum: (lowest of a, b and c)		
a) by manufacturer's axle rating or default	i. GAWR (if verified), or	
	ii. If GAWR not verified, the lower of:	
	1. 5,000 kg, and	
	2. the sum of the maximum tire load ratings	
b) by tire width	11 kg × combined tire widths in mm	
c) by axle unit description	Single Axle	7,700 kg
Other Axle Maximums: (lowest of a, b and c)		
a) by manufacturer's axle rating or default	i. GAWR (if verified), or	
	ii. If GAWR not verified, the sum of the maximum tire load ratings	
b) by tire width	10 kg × combined tire widths in mm	
c) by axle unit description	Other Tractor Axles and Trailer Axles:	
	Single Axle (Single Tires)	9,000 kg
	Single Axle (Dual Tires)	10,000 kg

WEIGHT LIMIT CHART

Feature	Weight Limit	
	Tandem Axle by axle spread:	
	— 1.2 < 1.8m	**18,000 kg**
	— 1.8m or more (Single Tires)	**18,000 kg**
	— 1.8m or more (Dual Tires)	**19,100 kg**
	Tridem Axle — by axle spread:	
	— 2.4 < 3.0m	**21,300 kg**
	— 3.0 < 3.6m	**24,000 kg**
	— 3.6 to 3.7m	**26,000 kg**
Allowable Gross Vehicle Weight: (lower of i and ii)	i. actual weight on the front axle plus other axle maximums	
	ii. Until January 1, 2020, maximum weight in appropriate Vehicle Weight Table (1–15), if semi-trailer Wheelbase (11) or Inter-vehicle-unit Distance (13), as provided in Exceptions note, are less than the minimums specified in the Dimensional Limit Chart	

WEIGHT LIMIT CHART

Feature	Weight Limit	
Front Axle Maximum: (lowest of a, b and c)		
a) by manufacturer's axle rating or default	i. GAWR (if verified), or	
	ii. If GAWR not verified, the lower of:	
	1. 5,000 kg, and	
	2. the sum of the maximum tire load ratings	

WEIGHT LIMIT CHART

Feature	Weight Limit	
b) by tire width	**11 kg × combined tire widths in mm**	
c) by axle unit description	**Single Axle**	**7,700 kg**
Other Axle Maximums: (lowest of a, b and c)		
a) by manufacturer's axle rating or default	**i. GAWR (if verified), or**	
	ii. If GAWR not verified, the sum of the maximum tire load ratings	
b) by tire width	**10 kg × combined tire widths in mm**	
c) by axle unit description	**Other Tractor Axles and Trailer Axles:**	
	Single Axle (Single Tires)	**9,000 kg**
	Single Axle (Dual Tires)	**10,000 kg**
	Tandem Axle by axle spread:	
	— 1.2 < 1.8m	**18,000 kg**
	— 1.8m or more (Single Tires)	**18,000 kg**
	— 1.8m or more (Dual Tires)	**19,100 kg**
	Tridem Axle — by axle spread:	
	— 2.4 < 3.0m	**21,300 kg**
	— 3.0 < 3.6m	**24,000 kg**
	— 3.6 to 3.7m	**26,000 kg**
Allowable Gross Vehicle Weight: (lower of i and ii)	**i. actual weight on the front axle plus other axle maximums**	

WEIGHT LIMIT CHART

Feature	Weight Limit
	ii. **Until January 1, 2020, maximum weight in appropriate Vehicle Weight Table (1–15), if semi-trailer Wheelbase (11) or Inter-vehicle-unit Distance (13), as provided in Exceptions note, are less than the minimums specified in the Dimensional Limit Chart**

O. Reg. 435/08, s. 3; 457/10, s. 29; 167/12, s. 4; 16/14, s. 4

SCHEDULE 2 — DESIGNATED TRACTOR-TRAILER COMBINATION 2 — TRACTOR SELF-STEER TRIAXLE SEMI-TRAILER [Heading amended O. Reg. 457/10, s. 29.]

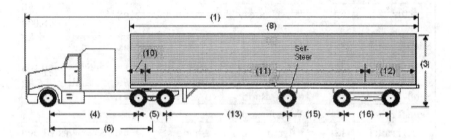

Configuration Description

Designated Tractor-Trailer Combination 2 is composed of a tractor and a single semi-trailer. The front axle of the tractor is a single axle with single tires. The drive axle of the tractor is a tandem axle. The semi-trailer has two axle units: a single self-steer axle (in front) and a tandem axle (in the rear).

Qualifying Preconditions

Weight, see s. 14

Equipment and components, see ss. 5, 6, 8, 9,10

1211

Labelling, see s. 13

Exceptions

Until January 1, 2020, the dimensional limits for Wheelbase (11) and Track width (19) do not apply if the semi-trailer was built before 2006 and is not more than 14.65 metres long.

Alternatives

A vehicle combination that meets every requirement to be Designated Tractor-Trailer Combination 2 except that the self-steer axle of the semi-trailer is not deployed is Designated Tractor-Trailer Combination 1.

DIMENSIONAL LIMIT CHART

Vehicle	Ref.	Feature	Dimensional Limit
Overall	(1)	Overall Length	Max. 23.0m
Overall	(2)	Width	Max. 2.6m
Overall	(3)	Height	Max. 4.15m
Tractor	(4)	Inter-axle Spacing	Min. 3.0 m
Tractor	(5)	Tandem Axle Spread	1.2 to 1.85m
Tractor	(6)	Wheelbase	Max. 6.2m if tractor built after 2005
Tractor	(6)	Wheelbase — (long combination)	Max. 6.2m
Semi-Trailer	(8)	Length	Max. 16.2m
Semi-Trailer	(9)	End-Dump Semi-Trailer Bed Length	Max. 14.65m
Semi-Trailer	(10)	Swing Radius	Max. 2.0m
Semi-Trailer	(11)	Wheelbase	6.25 to 12.5m
Semi-Trailer	(12)	Effective Rear Overhang	Max. 35% of wheelbase
Semi-Trailer	(13)	Inter-vehicle-unit Distance	Min. 4.0m if trailer built after 2005
Semi-Trailer	(15)	Inter-axle Spacing	> 2.5 to 3.0m
Semi-Trailer	(16)	Tandem Spread	1.2 to 2.8m
Semi-Trailer	(19)	Track Width — tandem — trailer with single tires built before 2010	2.3 to 2.6m
Semi-Trailer	(19)	Track Width — tandem — trailer with single tires built after 2009	2.45 to 2.6m

DIMENSIONAL LIMIT CHART

Vehicle	Ref.	Feature	Dimensional Limit
Semi-Trailer	(19)	Track Width — tandem — all other trailers	2.5 to 2.6m

WEIGHT LIMIT CHART

Feature	Weight Limit	
Front Axle Maximum: (lowest of a, b and c)		
a) by manufacturer's axle rating or default	i. GAWR (if verified), or	
	ii. If GAWR not verified, the lower of:	
	1. 5,000 kg, and	
	2. the sum of the maximum tire load ratings	
b) by tire width	11 kg × combined tire widths in mm	
c) by axle unit description	Single Axle	7,700 kg
Other Axle Maximums: (lowest of a, b and c)		
a) by manufacturer's axle rating or default	i. GAWR if verified), or	
	ii. If GAWR not verified, the sum of the maximum tire load ratings	
b) by tire width	Self-steer axle	11 kg × combined tire widths in mm
	Not self-steer axle	10 kg × combined tire widths in mm
c) by axle unit description	Tractor Tandem Drive Axle by axle spread:	
	—1.2 < 1.8m	18,000 kg
	—1.8m or more (Single Tires)	18,000 kg
	—1.8m or more (Dual Tires)	19,100 kg
	Trailer Axles:	
	i. If tandem axle spread is 1.2 < 1.8m or there are single tires on any wheel of trailer:	
	1. self-steer axle (load equalized)	9,000 kg

WEIGHT LIMIT CHART

Feature	Weight Limit	
	2. self-steer axle (not load equalized)	7,500 kg
	3. tandem axle (load equalized)	18,000 kg
	4. tandem axle (not load equalized)	15,000 kg
	ii. If tandem axle spread is 1.8 to 2.8m and there are no single tires on any wheel of trailer:	
	1. self-steer axle (load equalized)	9,550 kg
	2. self-steer axle (not load equalized)	8,000 kg
	3. tandem axle (load equalized)	19,100 kg
	4. tandem axle (not load equalized)	16,000 kg
Allowable Gross Vehicle Weight: (lowest of i, ii and iii)	i. actual weight on the front axle plus other axle maximums	
	ii. maximum weight based on base length:	
	Base length	Maximum
	< 13m	46,000 kg
	13m < 13.75m	49,000 kg
	13.75m < 14.5m	51,000 kg
	14.5m < 15m	53,000 kg
	15m or more	55,000 kg
	iii. Until January 1, 2020, maximum weight in appropriate Vehicle Weight Table (9-15), if Semi-trailer Wheelbase (11), as provided in Exceptions note, is less than the minimum specified in the Dimensional Limit Chart	

O. Reg. 435/08, s. 3; 457/10, s. 29; 16/14, s. 5

SCHEDULE 3 — DESIGNATED TRACTOR-TRAILER COMBINATION 3 — TRACTOR SELF-STEER QUAD SEMI-TRAILER [Heading amended O. Reg. 457/10, s. 29.]

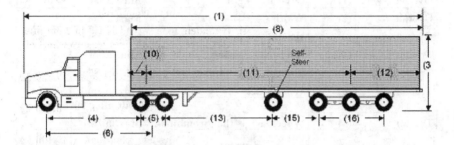

Configuration Description

Designated Tractor-Trailer Combination 3 is composed of a tractor and a single semi-trailer. The front axle of the tractor is a single axle with single tires. The drive axle of the tractor is a tandem axle. The semi-trailer has two axle units: a single self-steer axle in front and a tridem axle in the rear.

Qualifying Preconditions

Weight, see s. 14

Equipment and components, see ss. 5, 6, 8, 9

Labelling, see s. 13

Exceptions

Until January 1, 2020, the dimensional limits for Wheelbase (11), Inter-vehicle-unit Distance (13) and Track Width (19) do not apply if the semi-trailer was built before 2006 and is not more than 14.65 metres long and the Inter-vehicle-unit Distance (13) is not less than 4.5 metres.

Alternatives

A combination that meets every requirement to be Designated Tractor-Trailer Combination 3 except that the self-steer axle of the semi-trailer is not deployed is Designated Tractor-Trailer Combination 1.

DIMENSIONAL LIMIT CHART

Vehicle	Ref.	Feature	Dimensional Limit
Overall	(1)	Overall Length	Max. 23.0m
Overall	(2)	Width	Max. 2.6m
Overall	(3)	Height	Max. 4.15m
Tractor	(4)	Inter-axle Spacing	Min. 3.0m
Tractor	(5)	Tandem Axle Spread	1.2 to 1.85m
Tractor	(6)	Wheelbase	Max. 6.2m if tractor built after 2005
Tractor	(6)	Wheelbase — (long combination)	Max. 6.2m
Semi-Trailer	(8)	Length	Max. 16.2m
Semi-Trailer	(9)	End-Dump Semi-Trailer Bed Length	Max. 14.65m
Semi-Trailer	(10)	Swing Radius	Max. 2.0m
Semi-Trailer	(11)	Wheelbase	6.25 to 12.5m
Semi-Trailer	(12)	Effective Rear Overhang	Max. 35% of wheelbase
Semi-Trailer	(13)	Inter-vehicle-unit Distance — if tridem spread is 3.0 < 3.6m	Min. 6.0m
Semi-Trailer	(13)	Inter-vehicle-unit Distance — if tridem spread is 3.6 to 3.7m	Min. 5.5m
Semi-Trailer	(15)	Inter-axle Spacing	> 2.5 to 3.0m
Semi-Trailer	(16)	Tridem Spread	3.0 to 3.7m
Semi-Trailer	(19)	Track Width — tridem — trailer with single tires built before 2010	2.3 to 2.6m
Semi-Trailer	(19)	Track Width — tridem — trailer with single tires built after 2009	2.45 to 2.6m

DIMENSIONAL LIMIT CHART

Vehicle	Ref.	Feature	Dimensional Limit
Semi-Trailer	(19)	Track Width — tridem — all other trailers	2.5 to 2.6m

WEIGHT LIMIT CHART

Feature	Weight Limit		
Front Axle Maximum: (lowest of a, b and c)			
a) by manufacturer's axle rating or default	i. GAWR (if verified), or		
	ii. If GAWR not verified, the lower of:		
	1. 5,000 kg, and		
	2. the sum of the maximum tire load ratings		
b) by tire width	11 kg × combined tire widths in mm		
c) by axle unit description	Single Axle		7,700 kg
Other Axle Maximums: (lowest of a, b and c)			
a) by manufacturer's axle rating or default	i. GAWR (if verified), or		
	ii. If GAWR not verified, the sum of the maximum tire load ratings		
b) by tire width	Self-steer axle		11 kg × combined tire widths in mm
	Not self-steer axle		10 kg × combined tire widths in mm
c) by axle unit description	Tractor Drive Axle — by tandem axle spread:		
	— 1.2 > 1.8m		18,000 kg
	— 1.8 to 1.85m (Single Tires)		18,000 kg
	— 1.8 to 1.85m (Dual Tires)		19,100 kg
	Trailer Axles — by tridem axle spread:		

WEIGHT LIMIT CHART

Feature	Weight Limit		
	i.	tridem axle spread is 3.0 > 3.6m:	
		1. self-steer axle (load equalized)	8,000 kg
		2. self-steer axle (not load equalized)	6,900 kg
		3. tridem axle (load equalized)	24,000 kg
		4. tridem axle (not load equalized)	20,700 kg
	ii.	tridem axle spread is 3.6 to 3.7m:	
		1. self-steer axle (load equalized)	8,500 kg
		2. self-steer axle (not load equalized)	7,400 kg
		3. tridem axle (load equalized)	25,500 kg
		4. tridem axle (not load equalized)	22,200 kg
Allowable Gross Vehicle Weight: (lowest of i, ii and iii)	i.	actual weight on the front axle plus other axle maximums	
	ii.	Maximum weight based on base length:	
		Base length	Maximum
		> 16.5	54,000 kg
		16.5m > 17.5m	56,000 kg
		17.5m > 18.25m	58,000 kg
		18.25m > 18.75m	59,000 kg
		18.75m > 19.25m	60,000 kg
		19.25m or more	60,800 kg

WEIGHT LIMIT CHART

Feature	Weight Limit
	iii. **Until January 1, 2020, maximum weight in appropriate Vehicle Weight Table (16-22), if Semi-trailer Wheelbase (11) or Inter-vehicle-unit Distance (13), as provided in Exceptions note, are less than the minimums specified in the Dimensional Limit Chart**

O. Reg. 435/08, s. 3; 457/10, s. 29; 16/14, s. 6

SCHEDULE 4 — DESIGNATED TRACTOR-TRAILER COMBINATION 4 — TRACTOR SELF-STEER 5-AXLE SEMI-TRAILER (1-3-1) [Heading amended O. Reg. 457/10, s. 29.]

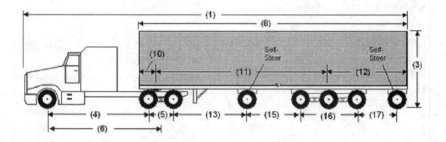

Configuration Description

Designated Tractor-Trailer Combination 4 is composed of a tractor and a single semi-trailer. The front axle of the tractor is a single axle with single tires. The drive axle of the tractor is a tandem axle. The semi-trailer has three axle units: a single self-steer axle in front, a tridem axle in the middle, and a single self-steer axle in the rear.

Qualifying Preconditions

Weight, see s. 14

Equipment and components, see ss. 5 to 10

Labelling, see s. 13

DIMENSIONAL LIMIT CHART

Vehicle	Ref.	Feature	Dimensional Limit
Overall	(1)	Overall Length	Max. 23.0m
Overall	(2)	Width	Max. 2.6m
Overall	(3)	Height	Max. 4.15m
Tractor	(4)	Inter-axle Spacing	Min. 3.0m
Tractor	(5)	Tandem Axle Spread	1.3 to 1.85m
Tractor	(6)	Wheelbase	Max. 6.2m if tractor built after 2005
Tractor	(6)	Wheelbase — (long combination)	Max. 6.2m
Semi-Trailer	(8)	Length	Max. 16.2m
Semi-Trailer	(9)	End-Dump Semi-Trailer Bed Length	Max. 14.65m
Semi-Trailer	(10)	Swing Radius	Max. 2.0m
Semi-Trailer	(11)	Wheelbase	Min. 9.5m
Semi-Trailer	(12)	Effective Rear Over-hang	Max. Lesser of 53% of wheelbase or 5.1m
Semi-Trailer	(13)	Inter-vehicle-unit Distance	Min. 3.0m
Semi-Trailer	(15)	Inter-axle Spacing	3.0 to 4.0m
Semi-Trailer	(16)	Tridem Spread	3.0 to 3.1m
Semi-Trailer	(17)	Inter-axle Spacing	2.1 to 2.8m
Semi-Trailer	(19)	Track Width — tridem axle — trailer with single tires built before 2010	2.3 to 2.6m
Semi-Trailer	(19)	Track Width — tridem axle — trailer with single tires built after 2009	2.45 to 2.6m

DIMENSIONAL LIMIT CHART

Vehicle	Ref.	Feature	Dimensional Limit
Semi-Trailer	(19)	Track Width — tridem axle — all other trailers	2.5 to 2.6m

WEIGHT LIMIT CHART

Feature	Weight Limit	
Front Axle Maximum: (lowest of a, b and c)		
a) by manufacturer's axle rating or default	i. GAWR (if verified), or	
	ii. If GAWR not verified, the lower of:	
	1. 5,000 kg, and	
	2. the sum of the maximum tire load ratings	
b) by tire width	11 kg × combined tire widths in mm	
c) by axle unit description	Single Axle	7,700 kg
Other Axle Maximums: (lowest of a, b and c)		
a) by manufacturer's axle rating or default	i. GAWR (if verified), or	
	ii. If GAWR not verified, the sum of the maximum tire load ratings	
b) by tire width	Self-steer axle	11 kg × combined tire widths in mm
	Not self-steer axle	10 kg × combined tire widths in mm
c) by axle unit description	Tractor Drive Axle — By tandem axle spread:	
	—1.2 < 1.8m	18,000 kg
	—1.8 to 1.85m (Single Tires)	18,000 kg
	—1.8 to 1.85m (Dual Tires)	19,100 kg
	Trailer Axles:	
	1) self-steer axle (load equalized)	7,500 kg

WEIGHT LIMIT CHART

Feature	Weight Limit			
	2) self-steer axle (not load equalized)	6,600 kg		
	3) tridem axle (load equalized)	22,500 kg		
	4) tridem axle (not load equalized)	19,800 kg		
Allowable Gross Vehicle Weight: (lower of i and ii)	i. actual weight on the front axle plus other axle maximums			
	ii. maximum weight based on base length and inter-vehicle-unit distance:			
	Base length	**Inter-vehicle-unit Distance**		
		3.0m<3.3m	3.3m<3.6m	3.6m or more
	< 17.75m	55,000 kg	56,000 kg	57,000 kg
	17.75m < 18.5m	57,500 kg	59,000 kg	59,500 kg
	18.50m < 19.25m	59,000 kg	60,500 kg	61,000 kg
	19.25m or more	60,000 kg	62,000 kg	63,500 kg

O. Reg. 435/08, s. 4; 457/10, s. 29; 16/14, s. 7

SCHEDULE 5 — DESIGNATED TRACTOR-TRAILER COMBINATION 5 — TRACTOR SELF-STEER 5-AXLE SEMI-TRAILER (1-1-3) [Heading amended O. Reg. 457/10, s. 29.]

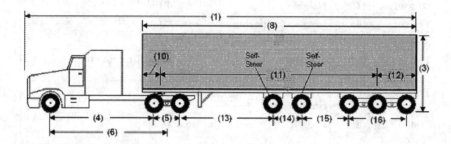

Configuration Description

Designated Tractor-Trailer Combination 5 is composed of a tractor and a single semi-trailer. The front axle of the tractor is a single axle with single tires. The drive axle of the tractor is a tandem axle. The semi-trailer has three axle units: two single self-steer axles in front and a tridem axle in the rear.

Qualifying Preconditions

Weight, see s. 14

Equipment and components, see ss. 5 to 9

Labelling, see s. 13

Alternatives

A combination that meets every requirement to be Designated Tractor-Trailer Combination 5 except that the front self-steer axle of the semi-trailer is not deployed is Designated Tractor-Trailer Combination 3. A combination that meets every requirement to be Designated Tractor-Trailer Combination 5 except that both self-steer axles of the semi-trailer are not deployed is Designated Tractor-Trailer Combination 1.

DIMENSIONAL LIMIT CHART

Vehicle	Ref.	Feature	Dimensional Limit
Overall	(1)	Overall Length	Max. 23.0m
Overall	(2)	Width	Max. 2.6m
Overall	(3)	Height	Max. 4.15m
Tractor	(4)	Inter-axle Spacing	Min. 3.0 m
Tractor	(5)	Tandem Axle Spread	1.3 to 1.85m
Tractor	(6)	Wheelbase	Max. 6.2m if tractor built after 2005
Tractor	(6)	Wheelbase — (long combination)	Max. 6.2m
Semi-Trailer	(8)	Length	Max. 16.2m
Semi-Trailer	(9)	End-Dump Semi-Trailer Bed Length	Max. 14.65m
Semi-Trailer	(10)	Swing Radius	Max. 2.0m
Semi-Trailer	(11)	Wheelbase	11.5 to 12.5m
Semi-Trailer	(12)	Effective Rear Overhang	Max. 35% of wheelbase
Semi-Trailer	(13)	Inter-vehicle-unit Distance	Min. 3.2m
Semi-Trailer	(14)	Inter-axle Spacing	1.5 to 2.8m
Semi-Trailer	(13) + (14)	Inter-vehicle unit Distance + Inter-axle Spacing	Min. 6.0m
Semi-Trailer	(15)	Inter-axle Spacing	>2.5 to 2.8m
Semi-Trailer	(16)	Tridem Spread	3.0 to 3.1m
Semi-Trailer	(19)	Track Width — tridem axle — trailer with single tires built before 2010	2.3 to 2.6m

DIMENSIONAL LIMIT CHART

Vehicle	Ref.	Feature	Dimensional Limit
Semi-Trailer	(19)	Track Width — tridem axle — trailer with single tires built after 2009	2.45 to 2.6m
Semi-Trailer	(19)	Track Width — tridem axle — all other trailers	2.5 to 2.6m

WEIGHT LIMIT CHART

Feature		Weight Limit	
Front Axle Maximum: (lowest of a, b and c)			
a) by manufacturer's axle rating or default	i. GAWR (if verified), or		
	ii. If GAWR not verified, the lower of:		
		1. 5,000 kg, and	
		2. the sum of the maximum tire load ratings	
b) by tire width	11 kg × combined tire widths in mm		
c) by axle unit description	Single		7,700 kg
Other Axle Maximums: (lowest of a, b and c)			
a) by manufacturer's axle rating or default	i. GAWR (if verified), or		
	ii. If GAWR not verified, the sum of the maximum tire load ratings		
b) by tire width	Self-steer axle	11 kg × combined tire widths in mm	
	Not self-steer axle	10 kg × combined tire widths in mm	
c) by axle unit description	Tractor Drive Axle — By tandem axle spread:		
	— 1.2 < 1.8m		18,000 kg
	— 1.8 to 1.85m (Single Tires)		18,000 kg
	— 1.8 to 1.85m (Dual Tires)		19,100 kg
	Trailer Axles:		

WEIGHT LIMIT CHART

Feature	Weight Limit			
	1. self-steer axle (load equalized)			7,500 kg
	2. self-steer axle (not load equalized)			6,600 kg
	3. tridem axle (load equalized)			22,500 kg
	4. tridem axle (not load equalized)			19,800 kg
Allowable Gross Vehicle Weight: (lower of i and ii)	i. actual weight on the front axle plus other axle maximums			
	ii. maximum weight based on base length and inter-vehicle-unit distance:			
	Base length	Inter-vehicle-unit Distance		
		3.2m<3.3m	3.3m<3.6m	3.6m or more
	< 17.75m	55,000 kg	56,000 kg	57,000 kg
	17.75m < 18.5m	57,500 kg	59,000 kg	59,500 kg
	18.50m < 19.25m	59,000 kg	60,500 kg	61,000 kg
	19.25m or more	60,000 kg	62,000 kg	63,500 kg

O. Reg. 435/08, s. 5; 457/10, s. 29; 16/14, s. 8

SCHEDULE 6 — DESIGNATED TRACTOR-TRAILER COMBINATION 6 — TRACTOR SELF-STEER 6-AXLE SEMI-TRAILER (1-4-1) [Heading amended O. Reg. 457/10, s. 29.]

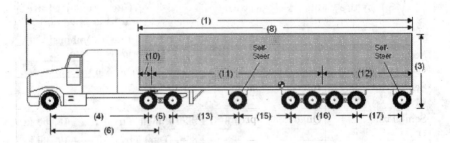

Configuration Description

Designated Tractor-Trailer Combination 6 is composed of a tractor and a single semi-trailer. The front axle of the tractor is a single axle with single tires. The drive axle of the tractor is a tandem axle. The semi-trailer has two axle units and one axle group: a single steer axle in front, a quadruple axle in the middle and a single self-steer axle in the rear.

Qualifying Preconditions

Weight, see s. 14

Equipment and components, see ss. 5 to 10

Labelling, see s. 13

DIMENSIONAL LIMIT CHART

Vehicle	Ref.	Feature	Dimensional Limit
Overall	(1)	Overall Length	Max. 23.0m
Overall	(2)	Width	Max. 2.6m
Overall	(3)	Height	Max. 4.15m
Tractor	(4)	Inter-axle Spacing	Min. 3.0m
Tractor	(5)	Tandem Axle Spread	1.3 to 1.85m
Tractor	(6)	Wheelbase	Max. 6.2m if tractor built after 2005
Tractor	(6)	Wheelbase — (long combination)	Max. 6.2m
Semi-Trailer	(8)	Length	Max. 16.2m
Semi-Trailer	(9)	End-Dump Semi-Trailer Bed Length	Max. 14.65m
Semi-Trailer	(10)	Swing Radius	Max. 2.0m
Semi-Trailer	(11)	Wheelbase	Min. 9.5m
Semi-Trailer	(12)	Effective Rear Overhang	Max. Lesser of 53% of wheelbase or 5.1m
Semi-Trailer	(13)	Inter-vehicle-unit Distance	Min. 3.8m
Semi-Trailer	(15)	Inter-axle Spacing	2.9 to 3.0m
Semi-Trailer	(16)	Quadruple Spread	3.9 to 4.0m
Semi-Trailer	(17)	Inter-axle Spacing	2.3 to 2.8m

DIMENSIONAL LIMIT CHART

Vehicle	Ref.	Feature	Dimensional Limit
Semi-Trailer	(19)	Track Width — quadruple axle — trailer with single tires built before 2010	2.3 to 2.6m
Semi-Trailer	(19)	Track Width — quadruple axle — trailer with single tires built after 2009	2.45 to 2.6m
Semi-Trailer	(19)	Track Width — quadruple axle — all other trailers	2.5 to 2.6m

WEIGHT LIMIT CHART

Feature		Weight Limit	
Front Axle Maximum: (lowest of a, b and c)			
a) by manufacturer's axle rating or default	i. GAWR (if verified), or		
	ii. If GAWR not verified, the lower of:		
	1. 5,000 kg, and		
	2. the sum of the maximum tire load ratings		
b) by tire width	11 kg × combined tire widths in mm		
c) by axle unit description	Single axle		7,700 kg
Other Axle Maximums: (lowest of a, b and c)			
a) by manufacturer's axle rating or default	i. GAWR (if verified), or		
	ii. If GAWR not verified, the sum of the maximum tire load ratings		
b) by tire width	Self-steer axle	11 kg × combined tire widths in mm	
	Not self-steer axle	10 kg × combined tire widths in mm	
c) by axle unit description	Tractor Drive axle — By tandem axle spread:		
	— 1.2 < 1.8m		18,000 kg

1228

WEIGHT LIMIT CHART

Feature	Weight Limit	
	— 1.8 to 1.85m (Single Tires)	**18,000 kg**
	— 1.8 to 1.85m (Dual Tires)	**19,100 kg**
	Trailer Axles:	
	1. self-steer axle (load equalized)	**6,500 kg**
	2. self-steer axle (not load equalized)	**5,750 kg**
	3. quadruple axle (load equalized)	**26,000 kg**
	4. quadruple axle (not load equalized)	**23,000 kg**
Allowable Gross Vehicle Weight: (lowest of i, ii and iii)	i. actual weight on the front axle plus other axle maximums	
	ii. maximum weight based on base length:	
	Base length	**Maximum**
	< 17.75m	**58,000 kg**
	17.75m < 18.25m	**59,000 kg**
	18.25m < 18.75m	**60,000 kg**
	18.75m < 19.25m	**61,500 kg**
	19.25m or more	**63,500 kg**
	iii. 62,500 kg, if the base length is 19.25m or more and front axle weight is less than 6,000 kg	

O. Reg. 435/08, s. 6; 457/10, s. 29; 16/14, s. 9

SCHEDULE 7 — DESIGNATED TRACTOR-TRAILER COMBINATION 7 — TRACTOR SELF-STEER 6-AXLE SEMI-TRAILER (1-1-4) [Heading amended O. Reg. 457/10, s. 29.]

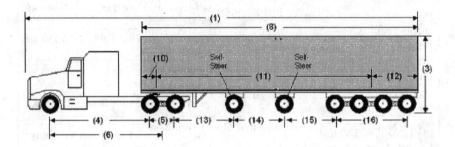

Configuration Description

Designated Tractor-Trailer Combination 7 is composed of a tractor and a single semi-trailer. The front axle of the tractor is a single axle with single tires. The drive axle of the tractor is a tandem axle. The semi-trailer has two axle units and one axle group: a single self-steer axle in front, another single self-steer axle in the middle and a quadruple axle in the rear.

Qualifying Preconditions

Weight, see s. 14

Equipment and components, see ss. 5 to 9

Labelling, see s. 13

DIMENSIONAL LIMIT CHART

Vehicle	Ref.	Feature	Dimensional Limit
Overall	(1)	Overall Length	Max. 23.0m
Overall	(2)	Width	Max. 2.6m
Overall	(3)	Height	Max. 4.15m
Tractor	(4)	Inter-axle Spacing	Min. 3.0m
Tractor	(5)	Tandem Axle Spread	1.3 to 1.85m
Tractor	(6)	Wheelbase	Max. 6.2m if tractor built after 2005

DIMENSIONAL LIMIT CHART

Vehicle	Ref.	Feature	Dimensional Limit
Tractor	(6)	Wheelbase — (long combination)	Max. 6.2m
Semi-Trailer	(8)	Length	Max. 16.2m
Semi-Trailer	(9)	End-Dump Semi-Trailer Bed Length	Max. 14.65m
Semi-Trailer	(10)	Swing Radius	Max. 2.0m
Semi-Trailer	(11)	Wheelbase	11.5 to 12.5m
Semi-Trailer	(12)	Effective Rear Over-hang	Max. 35% of wheelbase
Semi-Trailer	(13)	Inter-vehicle-unit Distance	Min. 3.0m
Semi-Trailer	(14)	Inter-axle Spacing	1.5 to 2.8m
Semi-Trailer	(15)	Inter-axle Spacing	2.7 to 2.8m
Semi-Trailer	(16)	Quadruple Spread	3.9 to 4.0m
Semi-Trailer	(19)	Track Width — quadruple axle — trailer with single tires built before 2010	2.3 to 2.6m
Semi-Trailer	(19)	Track Width — quadruple axle — trailer with single tires built after 2009	2.45 to 2.6m
Semi-Trailer	(19)	Track Width — quadruple axle — all other trailers	2.5 to 2.6m

WEIGHT LIMIT CHART

Feature	Weight Limit
Front Axle Maximum: (lowest of a, b and c)	
a) by manufacturer's axle rating or default	i. GAWR (if verified), or

WEIGHT LIMIT CHART

Feature	Weight Limit		
	ii. If GAWR not verified, the lower of:		
	1. 5,000 kg, and		
	2. the sum of the maximum tire load ratings		
b) by tire width	11 kg × combined tire widths in mm		
c) by axle unit type	Single Axle		7,700 kg
Other Axle Maximums: (lowest of a, b and c)			
a) by manufacturer's axle rating or default	i. GAWR (if verified), or		
	ii. If GAWR not verified, the sum of the maximum tire load ratings		
b) by tire width	Self-steer axle	11 kg × combined tire widths in mm	
	Not self-steer axle	10 kg × combined tire widths in mm	
c) by axle unit description	Tractor Drive Axle — By tandem axle spread:		
	—1.2 < 1.8m		18,000 kg
	—1.8 to 1.85m (Single Tires)		18,000 kg
	—1.8 to 1.85m (Dual Tires)		19,100 kg
	Trailer Axles:		
	1) self-steer axle (load equalized)		6,500 kg
	2) self-steer axle (not load equalized)		5,750 kg
	3) quadruple axle (load equalized)		26,000 kg
	4) quadruple axle (not load equalized)		23,000 kg
Allowable Gross Vehicle Weight: (lowest of i, ii and iii)	i. actual weight on the front axle plus other axle maximums		
	ii. maximum weight based on base length and inter-vehicle-unit distance:		
	Base length	Inter-vehicle-unit Distance	
		3.0m<3.3m	3.3m<3.6m	3.6m or more
	< 17.75m	55,000 kg	56,500 kg	57,000 kg

WEIGHT LIMIT CHART

Feature	Weight Limit			
	17.75m < 18.5m	57,500 kg	59,000 kg	59,500 kg
	18.50m < 19.25m	59,000 kg	60,500 kg	61,000 kg
	19.25m or more	60,500 kg	62,000 kg	63,500 kg
	iii. 62,500 kg, if the base length is 19.25m or more, the inter-vehicle-unit distance is 3.6m or more, and the front axle weight is less than 6,000 kg			

O. Reg. 435/08, s. 7; 457/10, s. 29; 16/14, s. 10

SCHEDULE 8 — DESIGNATED TRACTOR-TRAILER COMBINATION 8 — TRI-DRIVE TRACTOR FIXED AXLE SEMI-TRAILER [Heading amended O. Reg. 457/10, s. 29.]

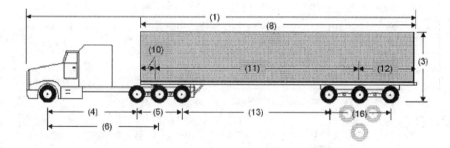

Configuration Description

Designated Tractor-Trailer Combination 8 is composed of a tractor and a single semi-trailer. The front axle of the tractor is a single axle with single tires. The drive axle of the tractor is a tri-drive. The semi-trailer has one axle unit that is either a single, tandem or tridem axle.

Qualifying Preconditions

Weight — The front axle weight must be at least 27 per cent of the tri-drive.

Equipment and components, see ss. 5, 6, 8, 11

DIMENSIONAL LIMIT CHART

Vehicle	Ref.	Feature	Dimensional Limit
Overall	(1)	Overall Length	Max. 23.5m
Overall	(2)	Width	Max. 2.6m
Overall	(3)	Height	Max. 4.15m
Tractor	(4)	Inter-axle Spacing	Not controlled
Tractor	(5)	Tridem Axle Spread	2.4 to 2.8m
Tractor	(6)	Wheelbase	6.6 to 6.8m
Tractor	(7)	Tridem Track Width — tractor with single tires built before 2010	2.3 to 2.6m
Tractor	(7)	Tridem Track Width — tractor with single tires built after 2009	2.45 to 2.6m
Tractor	(7)	Tridem Track Width — all other tractors	2.5 to 2.6m
Semi-Trailer	(8)	Length	Max. 16.2m
Semi-Trailer	(9)	End-Dump Semi-Trailer Bed Length	Max. 14.65m
Semi-Trailer	(10)	Swing Radius	Max. 2.0m
Semi-Trailer	(11)	Wheelbase	6.25 to 12.0m
Semi-Trailer	(12)	Effective Rear Over-hang	Max. 35% of wheelbase
Semi-Trailer	(13)	Inter-vehicle-unit Dis-tance — single to tridem	Min. 3.0m
Semi-Trailer	(13)	Inter-vehicle-unit Dis-tance — tandem to tridem	Min. 5.5m
Semi-Trailer	(13)	Inter-vehicle-unit Dis-tance — tridem to tridem	Min. 6.0m
Semi-Trailer	(16)	Tandem Spread	1.2 to 3.1m

DIMENSIONAL LIMIT CHART

Vehicle	Ref.	Feature	Dimensional Limit
Semi-Trailer	(16)	Tridem Spread	2.4 to 3.7m
Semi-Trailer	(19)	Track Width — trailer with single tires built before 2010	2.3 to 2.6m
Semi-Trailer	(19)	Track Width — trailer with single tires built after 2009	2.45 to 2.6m
Semi-Trailer	(19)	Track Width — all other trailers	2.5 to 2.6m

WEIGHT LIMIT CHART

Feature	Weight Limit	
Front Axle Maximum: (lowest of a, b and c)		
a) by manufacturer's axle rating or default	i. GAWR (if verified), or	
	ii. If GAWR not verified, the lower of:	
	1. 5,000 kg, and	
	2. the sum of the maximum tire load ratings	
b) by tire width	11 kg × combined tire widths in mm	
c) by axle unit description	Single Axle	7,700 kg
Other Axle Maximums: (lowest of a, b and c)		
a) by manufacturer's axle rating or default	i. GAWR (if verified), or	
	ii. If GAWR not verified, the sum of the maximum tire load ratings	
b) by tire width	10 kg × combined tire widths in mm	
c) by axle unit description	Tractor Drive Axle — by tridem axle spread:	
	— 2.4 < 2.7m	21,300 kg
	— 2.7 to 2.8m	22,000 kg
	Trailer Axles:	

WEIGHT LIMIT CHART

Feature	Weight Limit	
	Single Axle (Single Tires)	**9,000 kg**
	Single Axle (Dual Tires)	**10,000 kg**
	Tandem axle — by axle spread:	
	— 1.2 < 1.8m	**18,000 kg**
	— 1.8m or more (Single Tires)	**18,000 kg**
	— 1.8m or more (Dual Tires)	**19,100 kg**
	Tridem Axle — by axle spread:	
	— 2.4 < 3.0m	**21,300 kg**
	— 3.0 < 3.6m	**24,000 kg**
	— 3.6 to 3.7m	**26,000 kg**
Allowable Gross Vehicle Weight:	**actual weight on the front axle plus other axle maximums**	

O. Reg. 435/08, s. 8; 457/10, s. 29; 16/14, s. 11

SCHEDULE 9 — DESIGNATED TRACTOR-TRAILER COMBINATION 9 — TRI-DRIVE TRACTOR SELF-STEER TRIAXLE SEMI-TRAILER [Heading amended O. Reg. 457/10, s. 29.]

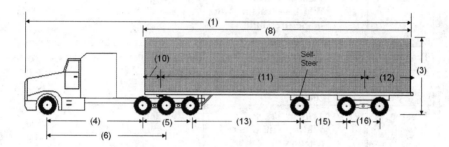

Configuration Description

Designated Tractor-Trailer Combination 9 is composed of a tractor and a single semi-trailer. The front axle of the tractor is a single axle with single tires. The drive axle of the tractor is a tri-drive. The semi-trailer has two axle units: a single self-steer axle in front and a tandem axle in the rear.

Qualifying Preconditions

Weight, see s. 14

The front axle weight must be at least 27 per cent of the tri-drive.

Equipment and components, see ss. 5, 6, 8 to 11

Labelling, see s. 13

Alternatives

A combination that meets every requirement to be Designated Tractor-Trailer Combination 9 except that the self-steer axle of the semi-trailer is not deployed is Designated Tractor-Trailer Combination 8.

DIMENSIONAL LIMIT CHART

Vehicle	Ref.	Feature	Dimensional Limit
Overall	(1)	Overall Length	Max. 23.5m
Overall	(2)	Width	Max. 2.6m
Overall	(3)	Height	Max. 4.15m

DIMENSIONAL LIMIT CHART

Vehicle	Ref.	Feature	Dimensional Limit
Tractor	(4)	Inter-axle Spacing	Not controlled
Tractor	(5)	Tridem Axle Spread	2.4 to 2.8m
Tractor	(6)	Wheelbase	6.6 to 6.8m
Tractor	(7)	Tridem Track Width — tractor with single tires built before 2010	2.3 to 2.6m
Tractor	(7)	Tridem Track Width — tractor with single tires built after 2009	2.45 to 2.6m
Tractor	(7)	Tridem Track Width — all other tractors	2.5 to 2.6m
Semi-Trailer	(8)	Length (long combination)	Max. 16.2m
Semi-Trailer	(9)	End-Dump Semi-Trailer Bed Length	Max. 14.65m
Semi-Trailer	(10)	Swing Radius	Max. 2.0m
Semi-Trailer	(11)	Wheelbase	6.25 to 12.0m
Semi-Trailer	(12)	Effective Rear Overhang	Max. 35% of wheelbase
Semi-Trailer	(13)	Inter-vehicle-unit Distance	Min. 3.7m
Semi-Trailer	(15)	Inter-axle Spacing	>2.5 to 3.0m
Semi-Trailer	(16)	Tandem Spread	1.2 to 2.8m
Semi-Trailer	(19)	Track Width — tandem — trailer with single tires built before 2010	2.3 to 2.6m
Semi-Trailer	(19)	Track Width — tandem — trailer with single tires built after 2009	2.45 to 2.6m

DIMENSIONAL LIMIT CHART

Vehicle	Ref.	Feature	Dimensional Limit
Semi-Trailer	(19)	Track Width — tandem — all other trailers	2.5 to 2.6m

WEIGHT LIMIT CHART

Feature	Weight Limit	
Front Axle Maximum: (lowest of a, b and c)		
a) by manufacturer's axle rating or default	i. GAWR (if verified), or	
	ii. If GAWR not verified, the lower of:	
	1. 5,000 kg, and	
	2. the sum of the maximum tire load ratings	
b) by tire width	11 kg × combined tire widths in mm	
c) by axle unit description	Single Axle	7,700 kg
Other Axle Maximums: (lowest of a, b and c)		
a) by manufacturer's axle rating or default	i. GAWR (if verified), or	
	ii. If GAWR not verified, the sum of the maximum tire load ratings	
b) by tire width	Self-steer axle	11 kg × combined tire widths in mm
	Not self-steer axle	10 kg × combined tire widths in mm
c) by axle unit description	Tractor Drive Axle — by tridem axle spread:	
	—2.4 < 2.7m	21,300 kg
	—2.7 to 2.8m	22,000 kg
	Trailer Axles:	
	i. If tandem axle spread is 1.2 < 1.8m or there are single tires on any wheel of trailer:	

WEIGHT LIMIT CHART

Feature	Weight Limit	
	1. self-steer axle (load equalized)	9,000 kg
	2. self-steer axle (not load equalized)	7,500 kg
	3. tandem axle (load equalized)	18,000 kg
	4. tandem axle (not load equalized)	15,000 kg
	ii. If tandem axle spread is 1.8 to 2.8m and there are no single tires on any wheel of trailer:	
	1. self-steer axle (load equalized)	9,550 kg
	2. self-steer axle (not load equalized)	8,000 kg
	3. tandem axle (load equalized)	19,100 kg
	4. tandem axle (not load equalized)	16,000 kg
Allowable Gross Vehicle Weight: (lower of i and ii)	i. actual weight on the front axle plus other axle maximums	
	ii. maximum weight based on base length:	
	Base length	Maximum
	< 16.0m	55,000 kg
	16.0m < 16.75m	56,500 kg
	16.75m or more	58,350 kg

O. Reg. 435/08, s. 9; 457/10, s. 29; 16/14, s. 12

SCHEDULE 10 — DESIGNATED TRACTOR-TRAILER COMBINATION 10 — TRI-DRIVE TRACTOR SELF-STEER QUAD SEMI-TRAILER [Heading amended O. Reg. 457/10, s. 29.]

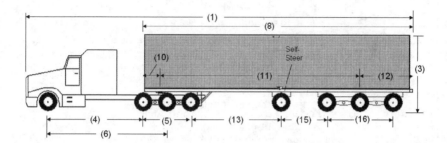

Configuration Description

Designated Tractor-Trailer Combination 10 is composed of a tractor and a single semi-trailer. The front axle of the tractor is a single axle with single tires. The drive axle of the tractor is a tri-drive. The semi-trailer has two axle units: a single self-steer axle in front and a tridem axle in the rear.

Qualifying Preconditions

Weight, see s. 14

The front axle weight must be at least 27 per cent of the tri-drive.

Equipment and components, see ss. 5, 6, 8, 9, 11

Labelling, see s. 13

Alternatives

A combination that meets every requirement to be Designated Tractor-Trailer Combination 10 except that the self-steer axle of the semi-trailer is not deployed is Designated Tractor-Trailer Combination 8.

DIMENSIONAL LIMIT CHART

Vehicle	Ref.	Feature	Dimensional Limit
Overall	(1)	Overall Length	Max. 23.5m
Overall	(2)	Width	Max. 2.6m
Overall	(3)	Height	Max. 4.15m

DIMENSIONAL LIMIT CHART

Vehicle	Ref.	Feature	Dimensional Limit
Tractor	(4)	Inter-axle Spacing	Not controlled
Tractor	(5)	Tridem Axle Spread	2.4 to 2.8m
Tractor	(6)	Wheelbase	6.6 to 6.8m
Tractor	(7)	Tridem Track Width — tractor with single tires built before 2010	2.3 to 2.6m
Tractor	(7)	Tridem Track Width — tractor with single tires built after 2009	2.45 to 2.6m
Tractor	(7)	Tridem Track Width — all other tractors	2.5 to 2.6m
Semi-Trailer	(8)	Length	Max. 16.2m
Semi-Trailer	(9)	End-Dump Semi-Trailer Bed Length	Max. 14.65m
Semi-Trailer	(10)	Swing Radius	Max. 2.0m
Semi-Trailer	(11)	Wheelbase	6.25 to 12.0m
Semi-Trailer	(12)	Effective Rear Over-hang	Max. 35% of wheelbase
Semi-Trailer	(13)	Inter-vehicle-unit Distance — if tridem spread is 3.0 < 3.6m	Min. 5.0m
Semi-Trailer	(13)	Inter-vehicle-unit Distance — if tridem spread is 3.6 to 3.7m	Min. 4.5m
Semi-Trailer	(15)	Inter-axle Spacing	>2.5 to 3.0m
Semi-Trailer	(16)	Tridem Spread	3.0 to 3.7m
Semi-Trailer	(19)	Track Width — tridem — trailer with single tires built before 2010	2.3 to 2.6m

DIMENSIONAL LIMIT CHART

Vehicle	Ref.	Feature	Dimensional Limit
Semi-Trailer	(19)	Track Width — tridem — trailer with single tires built after 2009	2.45 to 2.6m
Semi-Trailer	(19)	Track Width — tridem — all other trailers	2.5 to 2.6m

WEIGHT LIMIT CHART

Feature	Weight Limit	
Front Axle Maximum: (lowest of a, b and c)		
a) by manufacturer's axle rating or default	i. GAWR (if verified), or	
	ii. If GAWR not verified, the lower of:	
	1. 5,000 kg, and	
	2. the sum of the maximum tire load ratings	
b) by tire width	11 kg × combined tire widths in mm	
c) by axle unit description	Single Axle	7,700 kg
Other Axle Maximums: (lowest of a, b and c)		
a) by manufacturer's axle rating or default	i. GAWR (if verified), or	
	ii. If GAWR not verified, the sum of the maximum tire load ratings	
b) by tire width	Self-steer axle	11 kg × combined tire widths in mm
	Not self-steer axle	10 kg × combined tire widths in mm
c) by axle unit description	Tractor Drive Axle — by tridem axle spread:	
	— 2.4 < 2.7m	21,300 kg
	— 2.7 to 2.8m	22,000 kg
	Trailer Axles: — by tridem axle spread	

WEIGHT LIMIT CHART

Feature	Weight Limit	
	i. 3.0 < 3.6m	
	1. self-steer axle (load equalized)	8,000 kg
	2. self-steer axle (not load equalized)	6,900 kg
	3. tridem axle (load equalized)	24,000 kg
	4. tridem axle (not load equalized)	20,700 kg
	ii. 3.6 to 3.7m	
	1. self-steer axle (load equalized)	8,500 kg
	2. self-steer axle (not load equalized)	7,400 kg
	3. tridem axle (load equalized)	25,500 kg
	4. tridem axle (not load equalized)	22,200 kg
Allowable Gross Vehicle Weight: (lower of i and ii)	i. actual weight on the front axle plus other axle maximums	
	ii. 63,500 kg	

O. Reg. 435/08, s. 10; 457/10, s. 29; 16/14, s. 13

SCHEDULE 11 — DESIGNATED TRACTOR-TRAILER COMBINATION 11 — TRACTOR A-TRAIN DOUBLE TRAILERS [Heading amended O. Reg. 457/10, s. 29.]

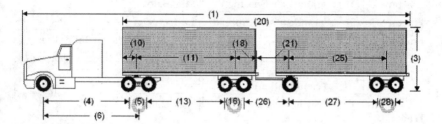

Configuration Description

Designated Tractor-Trailer Combination 11 is an A-train double. The front axle of the tractor is a single axle with single tires. The drive axle of the tractor is a single or tandem axle. The lead semi-trailer has one axle unit that is a single or tandem axle. If there is a trailer converter dolly, it has a single axle and the second semi-trailer has one axle unit that is a single or tandem axle. If there is no trailer converter dolly, the full trailer has two axle units: a single axle in front and a single or tandem axle in the rear.

Qualifying Preconditions

Weight

The sum of the weights of the converter dolly axle and the second trailer axles must not exceed the sum of the weights of the tractor drive axles and the lead semi-trailer axles.

If the inter-vehicle-unit distance between the trailers is less than 3 metres, the sum of the weight of the axles of the lead semi-trailer and the trailer converter dolly or forward axle of a full trailer must not exceed,

    (a) 17,000 kg, if there is a single axle on the lead semi-trailer; or

    (b) 23,000 kg, if there is a tandem axle unit on the lead semi-trailer.

Equipment and components, see ss. 5, 6, 8

DIMENSIONAL LIMIT CHART

Vehicle	Ref.	Feature	Dimensional Limit
Overall	(1)	Overall Length	Max. 25.0m
Overall	(2)	Width	Max. 2.6m
Overall	(3)	Height	Max. 4.15m
Tractor	(4)	Inter-axle Spacing	Min. 3.0m
Tractor	(5)	Tandem Axle Spread	1.2 to 1.85m
Tractor	(6)	Wheelbase	Max. 6.2m if tractor built after 2005
Tractor	(6)	Wheelbase — (long combination)	Max. 6.2m
Lead Semi-Trailer	(10)	Swing Radius	Max. 2.0m
Lead Semi-Trailer	(11)	Wheelbase	Min. 6.25m
Lead Semi-Trailer	(13)	Inter-vehicle-unit Distance — single to single or tandem	Min. 3.0m
Lead Semi-Trailer	(13)	Inter-vehicle-unit Distance — tandem to tandem	Min. 5.0m
Lead Semi-Trailer	(16)	Tandem Spread	1.2 to 1.85m
Lead Semi-Trailer	(18)	Hitch Offset	Max. 1.8m
Lead Semi-Trailer	(19)	Track Width — trailer with single tires built before 2010	2.3 to 2.6m
Lead Semi-Trailer	(19)	Track Width — trailer with single tires built after 2009	2.45 to 2.6m
Lead Semi-Trailer	(19)	Track Width — all other trailers	2.5 to 2.6m
Combination	(20)	Box Length	Max. 20.0m
Combination	(21)	Converter Dolly Drawbar Length	Not controlled

DIMENSIONAL LIMIT CHART

Vehicle	Ref.	Feature	Dimensional Limit
Combination	(22)	Converter Dolly Track Width — converter dolly with single tires built before 2010	2.3 to 2.6m
Combination	(22)	Converter Dolly Track Width — converter dolly with single tires built after 2009	2.45 to 2.6m
Combination	(22)	Converter Dolly Track Width — all other converter dollies	2.5 to 2.6m
Second Semi or Full Trailer	(25)	Wheelbase	Min. 6.25m
Second Semi or Full Trailer	(26)	Inter-vehicle-unit Distance	Not controlled
Second Semi or Full Trailer	(27)	Inter-axle Spacing	Min. 3.0m
Second Semi or Full Trailer	(28)	Tandem Spread	1.2 to 1.85m
Second Semi or Full Trailer	(29)	Track Width — trailer with single tires built before 2010	2.3 to 2.6m
Second Semi or Full Trailer	(29)	Track Width — trailer with single tires built after 2009	2.45 to 2.6m

DIMENSIONAL LIMIT CHART

Vehicle	Ref.	Feature	Dimensional Limit
Second Semi or Full Trailer	(29)	Track Width — all other trailers	2.5 to 2.6m

WEIGHT LIMIT CHART

Feature	Weight Limit	
Front Axle Maximum: (lowest of a, b and c)		
a) by manufacturer's axle rating or default	i. GAWR (if verified), or	
	ii. If GAWR not verified, the lower of:	
	1. 5,000 kg, and	
	2. the sum of the maximum tire load ratings	
b) by tire width	11 kg × combined tire widths in mm	
c) by axle unit description	Single Axle	7,700 kg
Other Axle Maximums: (lowest of a, b and c)		
a) by manufacturer's axle rating or default	i. GAWR (if verified), or	
	ii. If GAWR not verified, the sum of the maximum tire load ratings	
b) by tire width	10 kg × combined tire widths in mm	
c) by axle unit description	Other Tractor Axles and Trailer Axles:	
	Single Axle (Single Tires)	9,000 kg
	Single Axle (Dual Tires)	10,000 kg
	Tandem Axle — by axle spread:	
	—1.2 < 1.8m	18,000 kg
	—1.8 to 1.85m (Single Tires)	18,000 kg
	—1.8 to 1.85m (Dual Tires)	19,100 kg

WEIGHT LIMIT CHART

Feature	Weight Limit	
Allowable Gross Vehicle Weight: (lower of i and ii)	i. **actual weight on the front axle plus other axle maximums**	
	ii.	
	1. Until December 31, 2020,	
	A. if long combination or one of its trailers was built after 2005, maximum weight based on number of axles:	
	Number of axles	**Maximum**
	5	**41,900 kg**
	6	**49,800 kg**
	7 or 8	**53,500 kg**
	B. if not long combination and both trailers are built before 2006, AGVW is amount shown in appropriate Vehicle Weight Tables 3 to 29	
	2. After 2020, maximum weight based on number of axles:	
	Number of axles	**Maximum**
	5	**41,900 kg**
	6	**49,800 kg**
	7 or 8	**53,500 kg**

O. Reg. 435/08, s. 11; 457/10, s. 29; 16/14, s. 14

SCHEDULE 12 — DESIGNATED TRACTOR-TRAILER COMBINATION 12 — TRACTOR B-TRAIN DOUBLE TRAILERS [Heading amended O. Reg. 457/10, s. 29.]

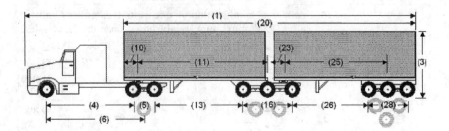

Configuration Description

Designated Tractor-Trailer Combination 12 is a B-train double. The front axle of the tractor is a single axle with single tires. The drive axle of the tractor is a single or tandem axle. The lead semi-trailer has one axle unit that is a tandem or tridem axle. The second semi-trailer has one axle unit that is a single, tandem or tridem axle.

Qualifying Preconditions

Equipment and components, see ss. 5, 6, 8

DIMENSIONAL LIMIT CHART

Vehicle	Ref.	Feature	Dimensional Limit
Overall	(1)	Overall Length	Max. 27.5m
Overall	(2)	Width	Max. 2.6m
Overall	(3)	Height	Max. 4.15m
Tractor	(4)	Inter-axle Spacing	Min. 3.0m
Tractor	(5)	Tandem Axle Spread	1.2 to 1.85m
Tractor	(6)	Wheelbase	Max. 6.8m if tractor built after 2005
Tractor	(6)	Wheelbase — (long combination)	Max. 6.8m

DIMENSIONAL LIMIT CHART

Vehicle	Ref.	Feature	Dimensional Limit
Lead Semi-Trailer	(10)	Swing Radius	Max. 2.0m
Lead Semi-Trailer	(11)	Wheelbase	Min. 6.25m
Lead Semi-Trailer	(13)	Inter-vehicle-unit Distance — single to tandem or tridem	Min. 3.0m
Lead Semi-Trailer	(13)	Inter-vehicle-unit Distance — tandem to tandem	Min. 5.0m
Lead Semi-Trailer	(13)	Inter-vehicle-unit Distance — tandem to tridem	Min. 5.5m
Lead Semi-Trailer	(16)	Tandem Spread	1.2 to 1.85m
Lead Semi-Trailer	(16)	Tridem Spread	2.4 to 3.1m
Lead Semi-Trailer	(19)	Track Width — trailer with single tires built before 2010	2.3 to 2.6m
Lead Semi-Trailer	(19)	Track Width — trailer with single tires built after 2009	2.45 to 2.6m
Lead Semi-Trailer	(19)	Track Width — all other trailers	2.5 to 2.6m
Combination	(20)	Box Length	Max. 20.0m
Combination	(11)+(25)	Sum of Trailer Wheelbases — if tractor wheelbase is 6.2m or less	Max. 17.0m
Combination	(11)+(25)	Sum of Trailer Wheelbases — if tractor wheelbase is >6.2m to 6.3m	Max. 16.53m
Combination	(11)+(25)	Sum of Trailer Wheelbases — if tractor wheelbase is >6.3m to 6.4m	Max. 16.44m

DIMENSIONAL LIMIT CHART

Vehicle	Ref.	Feature	Dimensional Limit
Combina-tion	(11)+(25)	Sum of Trailer Wheel-bases — if tractor wheelbase is >6.4m to 6.5m	Max. 16.36m
Combina-tion	(11)+(25)	Sum of Trailer Wheel-bases — if tractor wheelbase is >6.5m to 6.6m	Max. 16.27m
Combina-tion	(11)+(25)	Sum of Trailer Wheel-bases — if tractor wheelbase is >6.6m to 6.7m	Max. 16.19m
Combina-tion	(11)+(25)	Sum of Trailer Wheel-bases — if tractor wheelbase is >6.7m to 6.8m	Max. 16.10m
Second Trailer	(23)	Swing Radius	Max. 2.0m
Second Trailer	(24)	Kingpin behind rear-most axle of lead trail-er	Max. 0.3m
Second Trailer	(25)	Wheelbase	Min. 6.25m
Second Trailer	(26)	Inter-vehicle-unit Dis-tance — single to tan-dem or tridem	Min. 3.0m
Second Trailer	(26)	Inter-vehicle-unit Dis-tance — tandem to tandem	Min. 5.0m
Second Trailer	(26)	Inter-vehicle-unit Dis-tance — tandem to tridem	Min. 5.5m
Second Trailer	(26)	Inter-vehicle-unit Dis-tance — tridem to tridem	Min. 6.0m
Second Trailer	(28)	Tandem Spread	1.2 to 1.85m
Second Trailer	(28)	Tridem Spread	2.4 to 3.1m

DIMENSIONAL LIMIT CHART

Vehicle	Ref.	Feature	Dimensional Limit
Second Trailer	(29)	Track Width — trailer with single tires built before 2010	2.3 to 2.6m
Second Trailer	(29)	Track Width — trailer with single tires built after 2009	2.45 to 2.6m
Second Trailer	(29)	Track Width — all other trailers	2.5 to 2.6m

WEIGHT LIMIT CHART

Feature	Weight Limit	
Front Axle Maximum: (lowest of a, b and c)		
a) by manufacturer's axle rating or default	i. GAWR (if verified), or	
	ii. If GAWR not verified, the lower of:	
	1. 5,000 kg, and	
	2. the sum of the maximum tire load ratings	
b) by tire width	11 kg × combined tire widths in mm	
c) by axle unit description	Single Axle	7,700 kg
Other Axle Maximums: (lowest of a, b and c)		
a) by manufacturer's axle rating or default	i. GAWR (if verified), or	
	ii. If GAWR not verified, the sum of the maximum tire load ratings	
b) by tire width	10 kg × combined tire widths in mm	
c) by axle unit description	Other Tractor and Trailer Axles:	
	Single Axle (Single Tires)	9,000 kg
	Single Axle (Dual Tires)	10,000 kg
	Tandem Axle — by axle spread:	
	—1.2 < 1.8m	18,000 kg
	—1.8 to 1.85m (Single Tires)	18,000 kg
	—1.8 to 1.85m (Dual Tires)	19,100 kg

WEIGHT LIMIT CHART

Feature	Weight Limit	
	Tridem Axle — by axle spread	
	2.4 < 3.0m	**21,300 kg**
	3.0 to 3.1m	**24,000 kg**
Allowable Gross Vehicle Weight: (lower of i and ii)	i. actual weight on the front axle plus other axle maximums	
	ii. if a 7, 8 or 9-axle combination, maximum weight based on number of axles and base length:	
	If 7-axle combination:	
	Base length	**Maximum**
	< 17.0	**56,500 kg**
	17<18m	**57,000 kg**
	18<19m	**58,500 kg**
	19m or more	**60,300 kg**
	If 8 or 9-axle combination:	
	Base length	**Maximum**
	< 19.0	**61,000 kg**
	19.0<19.5m	**62,000 kg**
	19.5<20.5m	**63,000 kg**
	20.5m or more	**63,500 kg**

O. Reg. 435/08, s. 12; 457/10, s. 29; 16/14, s. 15; 8/16, s. 3

SCHEDULE 13 — DESIGNATED TRACTOR-TRAILER COMBINATION 13 — TRACTOR C-TRAIN DOUBLE TRAILERS [Heading amended O. Reg. 457/10, s. 29.]

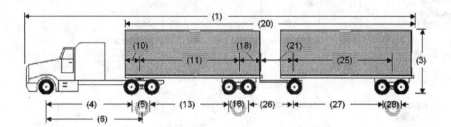

Configuration Description

Designated Tractor-Trailer Combination 13 is a C-train double. The front axle of the tractor is a single axle with single tires. The drive axle of the tractor is a single or tandem axle. The lead semi-trailer has one axle unit that is a single or tandem axle. The trailer converter dolly has one axle unit that is a single axle. The second semi-trailer has one axle unit that is a single or tandem axle.

Qualifying Preconditions

Weight

The sum of the weights of the converter dolly axle and the second trailer axles must not exceed the sum of the weights of the tractor drive axles and the lead semi-trailer axles.

If the inter-vehicle-unit distance between the trailers is less than 3 metres the sum of the weight of the axles of the lead semi-trailer and the trailer converter dolly must not exceed,

   (a) 17,000 kg, if there is a single axle on the lead semi-trailer; or

   (b) 23,000 kg, if there is a tandem axle unit on the lead semi-trailer.

Equipment and components, see ss. 5, 6, 8, 12

DIMENSIONAL LIMIT CHART

Vehicle	Ref.	Feature	Dimensional Limit
Overall	(1)	Overall Length	Max. 25.0m
Overall	(2)	Width	Max. 2.6m
Overall	(3)	Height	Max. 4.15m
Tractor	(4)	Inter-axle Spacing	Min. 3.0m
Tractor	(5)	Tandem Axle Spread	1.2 to 1.85m
Tractor	(6)	Wheelbase	Max. 6.2m if tractor built after 2005
Tractor	(6)	Wheelbase — (long combination)	Max. 6.2m
Lead Semi-Trailer	(10)	Swing Radius	Max. 2.0m
Lead Semi-Trailer	(11)	Wheelbase	Min. 6.25m
Lead Semi-Trailer	(13)	Inter-vehicle-unit Distance — single to single or tandem	Min. 3.0m
Lead Semi-Trailer	(13)	Inter-vehicle-unit Distance — tandem to tandem	Min. 5.0m
Lead Semi-Trailer	(16)	Tandem Spread	1.2 to 1.85m
Lead Semi-Trailer	(18)	Hitch Offset	Max. 1.8m
Lead Semi-Trailer	(19)	Track Width — trailer with single tires built before 2010	2.3 to 2.6m
Lead Semi-Trailer	(19)	Track Width — trailer with single tires built after 2009	2.45 to 2.6m
Lead Semi-Trailer	(19)	Track Width — all other trailers	2.5 to 2.6m
Combination	(20)	Box Length	Max. 20.0m
Combination	(21)	Converter Dolly Drawbar Length	Max. 2.0m

DIMENSIONAL LIMIT CHART

Vehicle	Ref.	Feature	Dimensional Limit
Combina-tion	(22)	Converter Dolly Track Width — converter dolly with single tires built before 2010	2.3 to 2.6m
Combina-tion	(22)	Converter Dolly Track Width — converter dolly with single tires built after 2009	2.45 to 2.6m
Combina-tion	(22)	Converter Dolly Track Width — all other converter dollies	2.5 to 2.6m
Second Trailer	(25)	Wheelbase	Min. 6.25m
Second Trailer	(26)	Inter-vehicle-unit Dis-tance	Not controlled
Second Trailer	(27)	Inter axle Spacing	Min. 3.0m
Second Trailer	(28)	Tandem Spread	1.2 to 1.85m
Second Trailer	(29)	Track Width — trailer with single tires built before 2010	2.3 to 2.6m
Second Trailer	(29)	Track Width — trailer with single tires built after 2009	2.45 to 2.6m
Second Trailer	(29)	Track Width — all other trailers	2.5 to 2.6m

WEIGHT LIMIT CHART

Feature	Weight Limit
Front Axle Maximum: (lowest of a, b and c)	
a) by manufacturer's axle rating or default	i. GAWR (if verified), or
	ii. If GAWR not verified, the lower of:
	1. 5,000 kg, and
	2. the sum of the maximum tire load ratings
b) by tire width	11 kg × combined tire widths in mm

WEIGHT LIMIT CHART

Feature	Weight Limit	
c) by axle unit description	Single Axle	7,700 kg
Other Axle Maximums: (lowest of a, b and c)		
a) by manufacturer's axle rating or default	i. GAWR (if verified), or	
	ii. If GAWR not verified, the sum of the maximum tire load ratings	
b) by tire width	10 kg × combined tire widths in mm	
c) by axle unit description	Other Tractor and Trailer Axles:	
	Single Axle (Single Tires)	9,000 kg
	Single Axle (Dual Tires)	10,000 kg
	Tandem Axle — by axle spread	
	— 1.2 < 1.8m	18,000 kg
	— 1.8 to 1.85m (Single Tires)	18,000 kg
	— 1.8 to 1.85m (Dual Tires)	19,100 kg
Allowable Gross Vehicle Weight: (lower of i and ii)	i. actual weight on the front axle plus other axle maximums	
	ii.	
	1. Until December 31, 2020,	
	A. if long combination or one of its trailers was built after 2005, maximum weight based on number of axles:	
	Number of axles	Maximum
	5	41,900 kg
	6	49,800 kg
	7	54,600 kg
	8	58,500 kg

WEIGHT LIMIT CHART

Feature	Weight Limit		
	B. if not long combination and both trailers are built before 2006, amount shown in appropriate Vehicle Weight Tables 3 to 29		
	2. After 2020, maximum weight based on number of axles:		
		Number of axles	**Maximum**
		5	41,900 kg
		6	49,800 kg
		7	54,600 kg
		8	58,500 kg

O. Reg. 435/08, s. 13; 457/10, s. 29; 16/14, s. 16

SCHEDULE 14 — DESIGNATED TRACTOR-TRAILER COMBINATION 14 — STINGER-STEER TRACTOR SEMI-TRAILER AUTO CARRIER [Heading added O. Reg. 457/10, s. 29.]

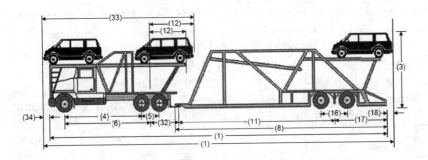

Configuration Description

Designated Tractor-Trailer Combination 14 is a stinger-steer combination composed of a tractor and semi-trailer. The fifth wheel assembly is mounted on a drop frame located behind and below the centre of the rearmost axle of the tractor. The front axle of the tractor is a single axle with single tires and the drive axle is single or tandem. The semi-trailer has a single or tandem axle.

Qualifying Preconditions

The width of the tractor or trailer rear load overhang, including extendable support plates, if any, does not exceed 2.3m.

Equipment and Components, see ss. 5, 6, 8

Exceptions

A non-enclosed auto carrier where only the loaded motor vehicles and support plates, if any, on which the motor vehicles rest extend beyond the Overall Length (1), Height (3) and Tractor Effective Rear Overhang (12) limits set out in the Dimensional Limit Chart below is exempt from those limits. The following limits apply to these exempted auto carriers:

Overall length (1) — 25 metres

Height (3) — 4.3 metres

Tractor Effective Rear Overhang (12) — 4.6 metres

DIMENSIONAL LIMIT CHART

Vehicle	Ref.	Feature	Dimensional Limit
Overall	(1)	Overall Length	Max. 23m
Overall	(2)	Width	Max. 2.6m
Overall	(3)	Height	Max. 4.15m
Tractor	(4)	Inter-axle Spacing	Min. 3.0m
Tractor	(5)	Tandem Axle Spread	1.2 to 1.85m
Tractor	(6)	Wheelbase	Not controlled
Tractor	(12)	Tractor Effective Rear Overhang	Max. 4.0m
Tractor	(32)	Hitch Offset	Max. 2.3m
Tractor	(33)	Length	Max. 12.5m
Tractor	(34)	Front Load Overhang	Max. 1.0 m
Semi-Trailer	(8)	Length	Max. 14.65m
Semi-Trailer	(11)	Wheelbase:	6.25 to 12.5m
Semi-Trailer	(16)	Tandem Axle Spread	1.2 to 3.10m

DIMENSIONAL LIMIT CHART

Vehicle	Ref.	Feature	Dimensional Limit
Semi-Trailer	(17)	Effective Rear Overhang (excluding rear load overhang)	Max. 4.0m or 42% of wheelbase (whichever is greater)
Semi-Trailer	(18)	Rear Load Overhang	Max. 1.2m
Semi-Trailer	(19)	Track Width — trailer with single tires built before 2010	2.3 to 2.6m
Semi-Trailer	(19)	Track Width — trailer with single tires built after 2009	2.45 to 2.6m
Semi-Trailer	(19)	Track Width — all other trailers	2.5 to 2.6m

WEIGHT LIMIT CHART

Feature	Weight Limit	
Front Axle Maximum: (lowest of a, b and c)		
a) by manufacturer's axle rating or default	i. GAWR (if verified), or	
	ii. If GAWR not verified, the lower of:	
	1. 5,000 kg, and	
	2. the sum of the maximum tire load ratings	
b) by tire width	11' kg × combined tire widths in mm	
c) by axle unit description	Single Axle	7,700 kg
Other Axles Maximums: (lowest of a, b and c)		
a) by manufacturer's axle rating or default	i. GAWR (if verified), or	
	ii. If GAWR not verified, the sum of the maximum tire load ratings	
b) by tire width	10 kg × combined tire widths in mm	
c) by axle unit description	Other Tractor Axles and Trailer Axles:	
	— Single Axle (Single Tires)	9,000 kg
	— Single Axle (Dual Tires)	10,000 kg
	Tandem Axle	18,000 kg

WEIGHT LIMIT CHART

Feature	Weight Limit
Allowable Gross Vehicle Weight:	actual weight on the front axle plus other axle maximums

O. Reg. 457/10, s. 29; 16/14, s. 17

SCHEDULE 15 — DESIGNATED TRACTOR-TRAILER COMBINATION 15 — TRACTOR HINGED SEMI-TRAILER [Heading added O. Reg. 457/10, s. 29.]

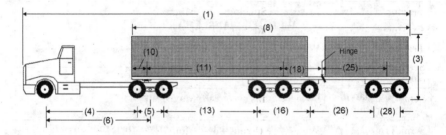

Configuration Description

Designated Tractor-Trailer Combination 15 is a combination composed of a tractor and a hinged single semi-trailer. The front axle of the tractor is a single axle with single tires. The drive axle of the tractor is a tandem axle. The semi-trailer consists of two portions permanently attached by a dual hinging system designed to prevent rotation (roll freedom) between the two portions of the semi-trailer. The front portion of the semi-trailer has a tridem axle and the rear portion of the trailer has a tandem axle.

The forward hinge of the dual hinging system allows at least 22 degrees horizontal articulation in either direction from the straight position. The rearward hinge allows the rear portion of the trailer to articulate downward, but does not allow upward articulation relative to the front portion of the trailer. The hinge position shown in the diagram refers to the articulation point of the forward horizontal hinge. The position of the rearward hinge is not controlled.

Qualifying Preconditions

Weight, see s. 14

Equipment and components, see ss. 5, 6, 7, 8

If equipped with a hinge locking device, the device must be disengaged when operating on a highway, other than when reversing.

Cargo must not span the hinge of the trailer if secured to both portions of the trailer.

Labelling, see s. 13

DIMENSIONAL LIMIT CHART

Vehicle	Ref.	Feature	Dimensional Limit
Overall	(1)	Overall Length	Max. 23.0m
Overall	(2)	Width	Max. 2.6m
Overall	(3)	Height	Max. 4.15m
Tractor	(4)	Inter-axle Spacing	Min. 3.0m
Tractor	(5)	Tandem Axle Spread	1.2 to 1.85m
Tractor	(6)	Wheelbase	Max. 6.2m
Semi-Trailer	(8)	Length	Max. 16.2m
Semi-Trailer	(10)	Swing Radius	Max. 2.0m
Semi-Trailer	(11)	Wheelbase (Front Portion)	Min. 7.9m
Semi-Trailer	(13)	Inter-vehicle-unit Distance	Min. 5.3m
Semi-Trailer	(16)	Tridem Spread	3.0 to 3.1m
Semi-Trailer	(18)	Hinge Offset	Max 2.0m
Semi-Trailer	(19)	Track Width of tandem axle and tridem axle — single tires	2.45 to 2.6m
Semi-Trailer	(19)	Track Width of tandem axle and tridem axle — dual tires	2.5 to 2.6m
Semi-Trailer	(25)	Wheelbase (Rear Portion)	Min. 4.0m
Semi-Trailer	(26)	Inter-axle Spacing	Min. 3.7m

DIMENSIONAL LIMIT CHART

Vehicle	Ref.	Feature	Dimensional Limit
Semi-Trailer	(28)	Tandem Spread	1.5 to 1.6m

WEIGHT LIMIT CHART

Feature	Weight Limit	
Front Axle (Maximum): (lowest of a, b and c)		
a) by manufacturer's axle rating or default	i. GAWR (if verified); or	
	ii. If GAWR not verified, the lower of:	
	1. 5,000 kg, and	
	2. the sum of the maximum tire load ratings	
b) by tire width	11 kg × combined tire widths in mm	
c) by axle unit description	Single Axle	7,700 kg
Other Axles (Maximum): (lowest of a, b and c)		
a) by manufacturer's axle rating or default	i. GAWR (if verified), or	
	ii. If GAWR not verified, the sum of the maximum tire load ratings	
b) by tire width	10 kg × combined tire widths in mm	
c) by axle unit description	Tractor Drive Axle — by tandem axle spread	
	— 1.2 < 1.8m	18,000 kg
	— 1.8 to 1.85m (single tires)	18, 000 kg
	— 1.8 to 1.85m (dual tires)	19,100 kg
	Trailer:	
	Tandem axle (load equalized)	16,000 kg
	Tandem axle (not load equalized)	14,000 kg
	Tridem axle (load equalized)	24,000 kg
	Tridem axle (not load equalized)	21,000 kg

WEIGHT LIMIT CHART

Feature	Weight Limit
Allowable Gross Vehicle Weight: (lower of i and ii)	i. actual weight on the front axle plus other axle maximums
	ii.
	— 62,000 kg if actual front axle weight is less than 6,000 kg
	— 63,000 kg if actual front axle weight is 6,000 kg to less than 7,000 kg
	— 63,500 kg if actual front axle weight is 7,000 kg or more

O. Reg. 457/10, s. 29; 16/14, s. 18

SCHEDULE 16 — DESIGNATED BUS OR RECREATIONAL VEHICLE 1 — STANDARD BUS OR COMPARABLE RECREATIONAL VEHICLE [Heading added O. Reg. 457/10, s. 29.]

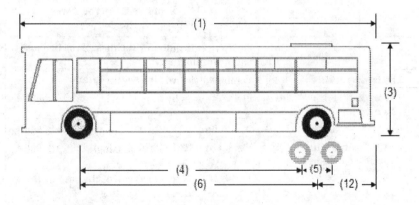

Vehicle Description

Designated Bus or Recreational Vehicle 1 is a bus or recreational vehicle. It is not an articulated bus. It may be a school bus, motor coach or double-decker bus. The front axle is a single axle with single tires. The drive axle is a single or tandem axle. If the drive axle is a single axle, it may form a two axle group with a tag axle to the rear. It is not equipped with a fifth wheel assembly.

1265

Qualifying Preconditions

Equipment and components, see s. 8

DIMENSIONAL LIMIT CHART

Vehicle	Ref.	Feature	Dimensional Limit
Bus or RV	(1)	Length	Max. 12.5m
Bus or RV	(2)	Width	Max. 2.6m
Bus or RV	(3)	Height	Max. 4.15m
Bus or RV	(4)	Inter-axle Spacing	Not controlled
Bus or RV	(5)	Rear Tandem or Two Axle Group	1.2 to 1.85m
Bus or RV	(6)	Wheelbase	Not controlled
Bus or RV	(12)	Effective Rear Over-hang	Not controlled

WEIGHT LIMIT CHART

Feature	Weight Limit	
Front Axle Maximum: (lowest of a, b and c)		
a) by manufacturer's axle rating or default	i. GAWR (if verified), or	
	ii. If GAWR not verified, the lower of:	
	1. 5,000 kg, and	
	2. the sum of the maximum tire load ratings	
b) by tire width	11 kg × combined tire widths in mm	
c) by axle unit description	Single Axle	9,000 kg
Other Axle Maximums: (lowest of a, b and c)		
a) by manufacturer's axle rating or default	i. GAWR (if verified), or	
	ii. If GAWR not verified, the sum of the maximum tire load ratings	
b) by tire width	Tag Axle — 10 kg × combined tire widths in mm	
	Tag Axle (vehicle manufactured before July 1, 2011) — 11 kg × combined tire widths in mm	
	Drive Axle — 10 kg × combined tire widths in mm	

WEIGHT LIMIT CHART

Feature	Weight Limit	
c) by axle unit description	Single Drive Axle (Single Tires)	9,000 kg
	Single Drive Axle (Dual Tires)	10,000 kg
	Single Drive Axle (Dual Tires) on Urban Transit Bus not equipped with a tag axle	11,400 kg
	Tag Axle (by Two Axle Group spacing)	
	— 1.2 < 1.3m	6,300 kg
	— 1.3 < 1.4m	6,700 kg
	— 1.4 < 1.5m	7,000 kg
	— 1.5 < 1.85m	7,400 kg
	Tandem Drive Axle	18,000 kg
Allowable Gross Vehicle Weight:	actual weight on the front axle plus other axle maximums	

O. Reg. 457/10, s. 29; 16/14, s. 19

SCHEDULE 17 — DESIGNATED BUS OR RECREATIONAL VEHICLE 2 — INTER-CITY BUS OR COMPARABLE RECREATIONAL VEHICLE [Heading added O. Reg. 457/10, s. 29.]

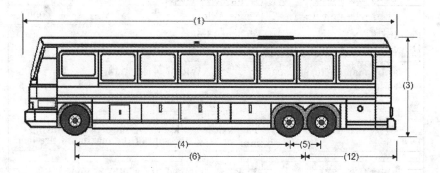

Vehicle Description

Designated Bus or Recreational Vehicle 2 is an inter-city bus or recreational vehicle that has two or three axles and exceeds 12.5 metres in length. It cannot be a school bus but can be a double-decker bus. The vehicle is not equipped with a fifth wheel assembly. If the vehicle is a recreational vehicle, it is equipped in the same manner as a motor coach with motive power mounted to the rear of the front axle and an air-ride or torsion-bar suspension.

Designated Bus or Recreational Vehicle 2 has two or three axles. The front axle unit is a single axle with single tires. The rear axles are a single or tandem drive axle or a two axle group. If the rear axles are a two axle group, they are composed of a single drive axle in front and a tag axle in the rear.

Qualifying Preconditions

Equipment and Components — see s. 8

DIMENSIONAL LIMIT CHART

Vehicle	Ref.	Feature	Dimensional Limit
Bus or RV	(1)	Length	Max. 14.0m
Bus or RV	(2)	Width	Max. 2.6m
Bus or RV	(3)	Height	Max. 4.15m
Bus or RV	(4)	Inter-axle Spacing	Not controlled
Bus or RV	(5)	Rear Tandem or Two Axle Group	1.2 to 1.85m
Bus or RV	(6)	Wheelbase	Not controlled
Bus or RV	(12)	Effective Rear Overhang	Max. 4.0m

WEIGHT LIMIT CHART

Feature	Weight Limit	
Front Axle: (lowest of a, b and c)		
a) by manufacturer's axle rating or default	i. GAWR (if verified), or	
	ii. If GAWR not verified, the lower of:	
	1. 5,000 kg, or	
	2. the sum of the maximum tire load ratings	
b) by tire width	11 kg × combined tire widths in mm	
c) by axle unit description	Single Axle	9,000 kg
Other Axle Maximums: (lowest of a, b and c)		

WEIGHT LIMIT CHART

Feature	Weight Limit	
a) by manufacturer's axle rating or default	i. GAWR (if verified), or	
	ii. If GAWR not verified, the sum of the maximum tire load ratings	
b) by tire width	Tag Axle	10 kg × combined tire widths in mm
	Tag Axle (Vehicle built before July 1, 2011)	11 kg × combined tire widths in mm
	Drive Axle	10 kg × combined tire widths in mm
c) by axle unit description	Single Drive Axle (Single Tires)	9,000 kg
	Single Drive Axle (Dual Tires)	10,000 kg
	Tag Axle (by Two Axle Group spacing)	
	— 1.2 < 1.3m	6,300 kg
	— 1.3 < 1.4m	6,700 kg
	— 1.4 < 1.5m	7,000 kg
	— 1.5 < 1.85m	7,400 kg
	Tandem Drive Axle	18,000 kg
Allowable Gross Vehicle Weight:	actual weight on the front axle plus other axle maximums	

O. Reg. 457/10, s. 29; 16/14, s. 20

SCHEDULE 18 — DESIGNATED BUS 3 — ARTICULATED BUS [Heading added O. Reg. 457/10, s. 29.]

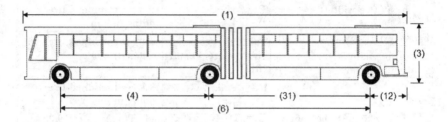

Vehicle Description

Designated Bus 3 is an articulated bus. It is not a recreational vehicle. An articulated bus has two portions with articulation between the portions, or has three portions with articulation between each portion.

It is equipped with a single axle at the rear of each portion of the bus. The front axle unit is a single axle with single tires.

DIMENSIONAL LIMIT CHART

Vehicle	Ref.	Feature	Dimensional Limit
Articulated Bus	(1)	Length	Max. 25m
Articulated Bus	(2)	Width	Max. 2.6m
Articulated Bus	(3)	Height	Max. 4.15m
Articulated Bus	(4)	Inter-axle Spacing	Not controlled
Articulated Bus	(6)	Wheelbase	Not controlled
Articulated Bus	(12)	Effective Rear Over-hang	Not controlled

DIMENSIONAL LIMIT CHART

Vehicle	Ref.	Feature	Dimensional Limit
Articulated Bus	(31)	Inter-axle Spacing	Not controlled

WEIGHT LIMIT CHART

Feature	Weight Limit	
Front Axle: (lowest of a, b and c)		
a) by manufacturer's axle rating or default	i. GAWR (if verified), or	
	ii. if GAWR not verified, the lower of:	
	1. 5,000 kg, or	
	2. the sum of the maximum tire load ratings	
b) by tire width	11 kg × combined tire widths in mm	
c) by axle unit description	Single Axle	9,000 kg
Other Axle Maximums: (lowest of a, b and c)		
a) by manufacturer's axle rating or default	i. GAWR (if verified), or	
	ii. If GAWR not verified, the sum of the maximum tire load ratings	
b) by sum of tire widths	10 kg × combined tire widths in mm	
c) by axle unit description	Single Axle (Single Tires)	9,000 kg
	Single Axle (Dual Tires)	10,000 kg
	Single Drive Axle (Dual Tires) on Urban Transit Bus	11,400 kg
Allowable Gross Vehicle Weight:	actual weight on the front axle plus other axle maximums	

O. Reg. 457/10, s. 29; 16/14, s. 21

SCHEDULE 19 — DESIGNATED TRUCK 1 — 2-AXLE
TRUCK [Heading added O. Reg. 457/10, s. 29.]

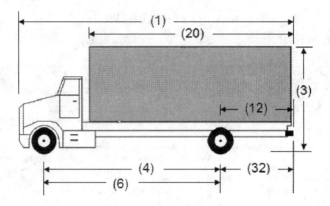

Vehicle Description

Designated Truck 1 is a 2-axle truck with a front single axle and rear single drive axle.

Qualifying Preconditions

Weight — The front axle weight must be at least 30 per cent of the gross vehicle weight at all times.

Equipment and components, see ss. 5, 8

Exceptions

Until December 31, 2025, the dimensional limit for Effective Rear Overhang (12) does not apply if the truck was built before July 1, 2011.

Until December 31, 2025, the dimensional limit for Hitch Offset (32) does not apply if either the truck or the trailer that it is drawing was built before July 1, 2011 or if both were built before July 1, 2011.

An overhanging boom of a rear-facing crane that extends 1.0 metre or less past the rearmost point of the truck is exempt from the dimensional limit for Effective Rear Overhang (12).

DIMENSIONAL LIMIT CHART

Vehicle	Ref.	Feature	Dimensional Limit
Truck	(1)	Length	Max. 12.5m
Truck	(2)	Width	Max. 2.6m

DIMENSIONAL LIMIT CHART

Vehicle	Ref.	Feature	Dimensional Limit
Truck	(3)	Height	Max. 4.15m
Truck	(4)	Inter-axle Spacing	Min. 3.0m
Truck	(6)	Wheelbase	Not controlled
Truck	(12)	Effective Rear Over-hang	Max. 4.0m
Truck	(20)	Box Length	Not controlled
Truck	(32)	Hitch Offset (if draw-ing trailer)	Max. 1.8m

WEIGHT LIMIT CHART

Feature	Weight Limit	
Front Axle Maximum: (lowest of a, b and c)		
a) by manufacturer's axle rating or default	i. GAWR (if verified), or	
	ii. If GAWR not verified, the lower of:	
	1. 5,000 kg, and	
	2. the sum of the maximum tire load ratings	
b) by tire width	11 kg × combined tire widths in mm	
c) by axle unit description	Single Axle	9,000 kg
Other Axle Maximums: (lowest of a, b and c)		
a) by manufacturer's axle rating or default	i. GAWR (if verified), or	
	ii. If GAWR not verified, the sum of the maximum tire load ratings	
b) by tire width	10 kg × combined tire widths in mm	
c) by axle unit description	Drive Axle	
	Single Axle (Single Tires)	9,000 kg
	Single Axle (Dual Tires)	10,000 kg
Allowable Gross Vehicle Weight:	actual weight on the front axle plus other axle maximums	

O. Reg. 457/10, s. 29; 16/14, s. 22; 8/16, s. 4

SCHEDULE 20 — DESIGNATED TRUCK 2 — TANDEM-AXLE TRUCK [Heading added O. Reg. 457/10, s. 29.]

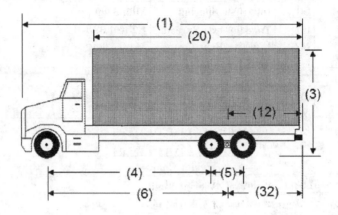

Vehicle Description

Designated Truck 2 is a 3-axle truck with a front single axle and rear tandem drive axle.

Qualifying Preconditions

Weight — The front axle weight must be at least 21 per cent of the gross vehicle weight at all times.

Equipment and components, see ss. 5, 8

Exceptions

Until December 31, 2025, the dimensional limit for Effective Rear Overhang (12) does not apply if the truck was built before July 1, 2011.

Until December 31, 2025, the dimensional limit for Hitch Offset (32) does not apply if either the truck or the trailer that it is drawing was built before July 1, 2011 or if both were built before July 1, 2011.

An overhanging boom of a rear-facing crane that extends 1.0 metre or less past the rearmost point of the truck is exempt from the dimensional limit for Effective Rear Overhang (12).

DIMENSIONAL LIMIT CHART

Vehicle	Ref.	Feature	Dimensional Limit
Truck	(1)	Length	Max. 12.5m
Truck	(2)	Width	Max. 2.6m

DIMENSIONAL LIMIT CHART

Vehicle	Ref.	Feature	Dimensional Limit
Truck	(3)	Height	Max. 4.15m
Truck	(4)	Inter-axle Spacing	Min. 3.0m
Truck	(5)	Tandem Axle Spread	1.2 to 1.88m
Truck	(6)	Wheelbase	Not controlled
Truck	(12)	Effective Rear Over-hang	Max. 4.0m
Truck	(20)	Box Length	Not controlled
Truck	(32)	Hitch Offset (if drawing trailer)	Max. 1.8m

WEIGHT LIMIT CHART

Feature	Weight Limit	
Front Axle Maximum: (lowest of a, b and c)		
a) by manufacturer's axle rating or default	i. GAWR (if verified), or	
	ii. If GAWR not verified, the lower of:	
	1. 5,000 kg, and	
	2. the sum of the maximum tire load ratings	
b) by tire width	11 kg × combined tire widths in mm	
c) by axle unit description	Single Axle	9,000 kg
Other Axle Maximums: (lowest of a, b and c)		
a) by manufacturer's axle rating or default	i. GAWR (if verified), or	
	ii. If GAWR not verified, the sum of the maximum tire load ratings	
b) by tire width	10 kg × combined tire widths in mm	
c) by axle unit description	Tandem Drive Axle by axle spread:	
	— 1.2 < 1.8m	18,000 kg
	— 1.8 to 1.88m (Single tires)	18,000 kg
	— 1.8 to 1.88m (Dual Tires)	19,100 kg
Allowable Gross Vehicle Weight: (lower of i and ii)	i. actual weight on the front axle plus other axle maximums	

WEIGHT LIMIT CHART

Feature	Weight Limit		
	ii. maximum weight based on base length:		
		Base length	Maximum
		< 4.5m	25,000 kg
		4.5m < 4.7m	26,000 kg
		4.7m < 4.9m	27,000 kg
		4.9m or more	28,100 kg

O. Reg. 457/10, s. 29; 16/14, s. 23; 8/16, s. 5

SCHEDULE 21 — DESIGNATED TRUCK 3 — 3-AXLE TRUCK PLUS AUXILIARY AXLE [Heading added O. Reg. 457/10, s. 29.]

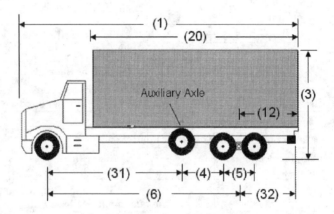

Vehicle Description

Designated Truck 3 is a 4-axle truck with a front single axle, a liftable auxiliary self-steer axle or an optionally liftable forced-steer auxiliary pusher axle, and a rear tandem drive axle.

Qualifying Preconditions

Weight, see s. 14

The front axle weight must be at least 19 per cent of the gross vehicle weight at all times. A liftable auxiliary self-steer axle must not be deployed if the resulting weight on the axle is less than 3,000 kilograms.

Equipment and components, see ss. 5, 8, 9

Labelling, see s. 13

Exceptions

Until December 31, 2025, the dimensional limits for Effective Rear Overhang (12) and Tandem Axle Track Width (35) do not apply if the truck was built before July 1, 2011.

Until December 31, 2025, the dimensional limit for Hitch Offset (32) does not apply if either the truck or the trailer that it is drawing was built before July 1, 2011 or if both were built before July 1, 2011.

An overhanging boom of a rear-facing crane that extends 1.0 metre or less past the rearmost point of the truck is exempt from the dimensional limit for Effective Rear Overhang (12)

Alternatives

A truck that meets every requirement to be Designated Truck 3 except that the liftable axle is not deployed is Designated Truck 2.

DIMENSIONAL LIMIT CHART

Vehicle	Ref.	Feature	Dimensional Limit
Truck	(1)	Length	Max. 12.5m
Truck	(2)	Width	Max. 2.6m
Truck	(3)	Height	Max. 4.15m
Truck	(4)	Inter-axle Spacing	2.3 to 2.8m
Truck	(5)	Tandem Axle Spread	1.3 to 1.6m
Truck	(6)	Wheelbase	Not controlled
Truck	(12)	Effective Rear Over-hang	Max. 4.0m
Truck	(20)	Box Length	Not controlled
Truck	(31)	Inter-Axle Spacing	Min. 3.0m
Truck	(32)	Hitch Offset (if drawing trailer)	Max. 1.8m
Truck	(35)	Tandem Axle Track Width	2.4 to 2.6m

WEIGHT LIMIT CHART

Feature	Weight Limit
Front Axle Maximum: (lowest of a, b and c)	
a) by manufacturer's axle rating or default	i. GAWR (if verified), or

WEIGHT LIMIT CHART

Feature	Weight Limit	
	ii. If GAWR not verified, the lower of:	
	1. 5,000 kg, and	
	2. the sum of the maximum tire load ratings	
b) by tire width	11 kg × combined tire widths in mm	
c) by axle unit description	Single Axle	9,000 kg
Other Axle Maximums: (lowest of a, b and c)		
a) by manufacturer's axle rating or default	i. GAWR (if verified), or	
	ii. If GAWR not verified, the sum of the maximum tire load ratings	
b) by tire width	Auxiliary axle	11 kg × combined tire widths in mm
	Not auxiliary axle	10 kg × combined tire widths in mm
c) by axle unit description	Auxiliary axle (load-equalized)	6,000 kg
	Auxiliary axle (not load-equalized)	4,500 kg
	Tandem drive axle (load-equalized)	18,000 kg
	Tandem drive axle (not load-equalized)	15,000 kg
Allowable Gross Vehicle Weight:	actual weight on the front axle plus other axle maximums	

O. Reg. 457/10, s. 29; 16/14, s. 24; 8/16, s. 6

SCHEDULE 22 — DESIGNATED TRUCK 4 — TWIN-STEER TANDEM-DRIVE TRUCK [Heading added O. Reg. 457/10, s. 29.]

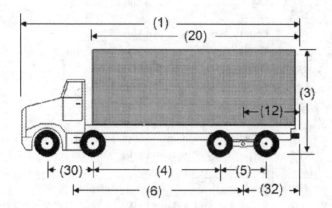

Vehicle Description

Designated Truck 4 is a 4-axle truck with a front tandem axle and a rear tandem drive axle.

Qualifying Preconditions

Weight — The front axle weight must be at least 38 per cent of the gross vehicle weight at all times.

Equipment and components, see ss. 5, 8

Exceptions

Until December 31, 2025, the dimensional limits for Effective Wheelbase (6), Effective Rear Overhang (12) and Rear Tandem Axle Track Width (35) do not apply if the truck, other than a concrete mixer fitted with a revolving drum, was built before July 1, 2011. In the case of a concrete mixer fitted with a revolving drum that was built before July 1, 2011, these dimensional limits do not apply on or before December 31, 2030.

In the case of a truck drawing a trailer, until December 31, 2025, the dimensional limit for Hitch Offset (32) does not apply on or before December 31, 2025, if either the truck or the trailer it is drawing was built before July 1, 2011 or if both were built before July 1, 2011.

An overhanging boom of a rear-facing crane that extends 1.0 metre or less past the rearmost point of the truck is exempt from the dimensional limit for Effective Rear Overhang (12).

DIMENSIONAL LIMIT CHART

Vehicle	Ref.	Feature	Dimensional Limit
Truck	(1)	Length	Max. 12.5m
Truck	(2)	Width	Max. 2.6m
Truck	(3)	Height	Max. 4.15m
Truck	(4)	Inter-axle Spacing	Not controlled
Truck	(5)	Rear Tandem Axle Spread	1.2 to 1.88m
Truck	(6)	Effective Wheelbase	Min. 5.3m
Truck	(12)	Effective Rear Over-hang	Max. 4.0m
Truck	(20)	Box Length	Not controlled
Truck	(30)	Front Tandem Axle Spread	1.2 to 2.7m
Truck	(32)	Hitch Offset (if draw-ing trailer)	Max. 1.8m
Truck	(35)	Rear Tandem Axle Track Width	2.4 to 2.6m

WEIGHT LIMIT CHART

Feature	Weight Limit	
Front Axle Maximum: (lowest of a, b and c)		
a) by manufacturer's axle rating or default	i. GAWR (if verified), or	
	ii. If GAWR not verified, the lower of:	
	1. 10,000 kg, and	
	2. the sum of the maximum tire load ratings	
b) by tire width	11 kg × combined tire widths in mm	
c) by axle unit description	Tandem Axle by axle spread:	
	— 1.2 < 1.6m	17,000 kg
	— 1.6 to 2.7m	18,000 kg
Other Axle Maximums: (lowest of a, b and c)		
a) by manufacturer's axle rating or default	i. GAWR (if verified), or	

WEIGHT LIMIT CHART

Feature	Weight Limit	
	ii. **If GAWR not verified, the sum of the maximum tire load ratings**	
b) by tire width	**10 kg × combined tire widths in mm**	
c) by axle unit description	**Tandem Axle by axle spread:**	
	— 1.2 < 1.8m	**18,000 kg**
	— 1.8 to 1.88m (Single Tires)	**18,000 kg**
	— 1.8 to 1.88m (Dual Tires)	**19,100 kg**
Allowable Gross Vehicle Weight: (lower of i and ii)	i. **actual weight on the front axle plus other axle maximums**	
	ii.	
	— 32,000 kg if the truck is drawing a trailer or has a wheelbase of 5.3 < 6.0m	
	— 37,100 kg if the truck has a wheelbase of 6.0m or greater and is not drawing a trailer	

O. Reg. 457/10, s. 29; 16/14, s. 25; 8/16, s. 7

SCHEDULE 23 — DESIGNATED TRUCK 5 — SELF-STEER TRIAXLE TRUCK [Heading added O. Reg. 457/10, s. 29.]

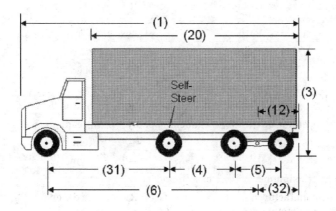

Vehicle Description

Designated Truck 5 is a 4-axle truck with a front single axle, a self-steer liftable pusher axle and a rear tandem drive axle.

Qualifying Preconditions

Weight, see s. 14

The front axle weight must be at least 23 per cent of the gross vehicle weight at all times. The liftable axle must not be deployed if the resulting weight on the axle is less than 4,000 kilograms.

Equipment and components, see ss. 5, 8, 9.

Labelling, see s. 13.

Exceptions

Until December 31, 2025, the dimensional limits for Effective Rear Overhang (12) and Tandem Axle Track Width (35) do not apply if the truck was built before July 1, 2011.

Until December 31, 2025, the dimensional limit for Hitch Offset (32) does not apply if either the truck or the trailer it is drawing was built before July 1, 2011 or if both were built before July 1, 2011.

An overhanging boom of a rear-facing crane that extends 1.0 metre or less past the rearmost point of the truck is exempt from the dimensional limit for Effective Rear Overhang (12).

Alternatives

A truck that meets every requirement to be Designated Truck 5 except that the liftable axle of the truck is not deployed is Designated Truck 2.

DIMENSIONAL LIMIT CHART

Vehicle	Ref.	Feature	Dimensional Limit
Truck	(1)	Length	Max. 12.5m
Truck	(2)	Width	Max. 2.6m
Truck	(3)	Height	Max. 4.15m
Truck	(31)	Inter-axle Spacing	Not controlled
Truck	(4)	Inter-axle Spacing	2.51 to 2.8m
Truck	(5)	Tandem Axle Spread	1.2 to 1.88m
Truck	(6)	Wheelbase	Min. 6.4m, if Tandem Axle Spread (5) is 1.2 < 1.8m
Truck	(6)	Wheelbase	Min. 6.85m, if Tandem Axle Spread (5) is 1.8 to 1.88m
Truck	(12)	Effective Rear Over-hang	Max. 4.0m

DIMENSIONAL LIMIT CHART

Vehicle	Ref.	Feature	Dimensional Limit
Truck	(20)	Box Length	Not controlled
Truck	(32)	Hitch Offset (if drawing trailer)	Max. 1.8m
Truck	(35)	Tandem Axle Track Width	2.4 to 2.6m

WEIGHT LIMIT CHART

Feature	Weight Limit	
Front Axle Maximum: (lowest of a, b and c)		
a) by manufacturer's axle rating or default	i. GAWR (if verified); or	
	ii. If GAWR not verified, the lower of:	
	1. 5,000 kg, and	
	2. the sum of the maximum tire load ratings	
b) by tire width	11 kg × combined tire widths in mm	
c) by axle unit description	Single Axle	9,000 kg
Other Axles Maximums: (lowest of a, b and c)		
a) by manufacturer's axle rating or default	i. GAWR (if verified), or	
	ii. If GAWR not verified, the sum of the maximum tire load ratings	
b) by tire width	Self-steer axle	11 kg × combined tire widths in mm
	Not self-steer axle	10 kg × combined tire widths in mm
c) by axle unit description	i. If tandem axle spread is 1.2 < 1.8m or there are single tires on any wheel:	
	1. self-steer axle (load equalized)	9,000 kg
	2. self-steer axle (not load equalized)	7,500 kg
	3. tandem drive axle (load equalized)	18,000 kg
	4. tandem drive axle (not load equalized)	15,000 kg

WEIGHT LIMIT CHART

Feature	Weight Limit	
	ii. If tandem axle spread is 1.8 to 1.88m and there are no single tires on any wheel:	
	1. self-steer axle (load equalized)	9,550 kg
	2. self-steer axle (not load equalized)	8,000 kg
	3. tandem drive axle (load equalized)	19,100 kg
	4. tandem drive axle (not load equalized)	16,000 kg
Allowable Gross Vehicle Weight:	actual weight on the front axle plus the other axle maximums	

O. Reg. 457/10, s. 29; 167/12, s. 5; 16/14, s. 26; 8/16, s. 8

SCHEDULE 24 — DESIGNATED TRUCK 6 — TRI-DRIVE 4-AXLE TRUCK [Heading added O. Reg. 457/10, s. 29.]

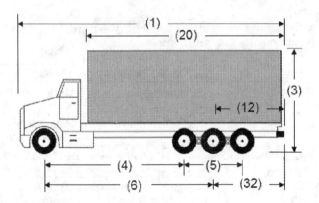

Vehicle Description

Designated Truck 6 is a 4-axle truck with a front single axle and a rear tri-drive axle.

Qualifying Preconditions

Weight — The front axle weight must be at least 23 per cent of the gross vehicle weight at all times.

Equipment and components, see ss. 5, 8, 11

Exceptions

Until December 31, 2025, the dimensional limits for Wheelbase (6), Effective Rear Overhang (12), Hitch Offset (32) and Rear Tandem Axle Track Width (35) do not apply if the truck was built before July 1, 2011.

An overhanging boom of a rear-facing crane that extends 1.0 metre or less past the rearmost point of the truck is exempt from the dimensional limit for Effective Rear Overhang (12).

DIMENSIONAL LIMIT CHART

Vehicle	Ref.	Feature	Dimensional Limit
Truck	(1)	Length	Max. 12.5m
Truck	(2)	Width	Max. 2.6m
Truck	(3)	Height	Max. 4.15m
Truck	(4)	Inter-axle Spacing	Not controlled
Truck	(5)	Tridem Axle Spread	2.4 to 2.8m
Truck	(6)	Wheelbase	Min. 6.6m
Truck	(12)	Effective Rear Over-hang	Max. 4.0m
Truck	(20)	Box Length	Not controlled
Truck	(32)	Hitch Offset (if draw-ing trailer)	Max. 2.5m
Truck	(35)	Tridem Track Width	2.5 to 2.6m

WEIGHT LIMIT CHART

Feature	Weight Limit	
Front Axle Maximum: (lowest of a, b and c)		
a) by manufacturer's axle rating or default	i. GAWR (if verified), or	
	ii. If GAWR not verified, the lower of:	
	1. 5,000 kg, and	
	2. the sum of the maximum tire load ratings	
b) by tire width	11 kg × combined tire widths in mm	

WEIGHT LIMIT CHART

Feature	Weight Limit	
c) by axle unit description	Single Axle	**9,000 kg**
Other Axles Maximums: (lowest of a, b and c)		
a) by manufacturer's axle rating or default	i. GAWR (if verified), or	
	ii. If GAWR not verified, the sum of the maximum tire load ratings	
b) by tire width	10 kg × combined tire widths in mm	
c) by axle unit description	Tridem Axle by axle spread:	
	— 2.4 < 2.7m	**21,300 kg**
	— 2.7 to 2.8m	**22,000 kg**
Allowable Gross Vehicle Weight:	actual weight on the front axle plus the other axle maximums	

O. Reg. 457/10, s. 29; 167/12, s. 6; 16/14, s. 27

SCHEDULE 25 — DESIGNATED TRUCK 7 — TWIN STEER TRI-DRIVE 5-AXLE TRUCK [Heading added O. Reg. 457/10, s. 29.]

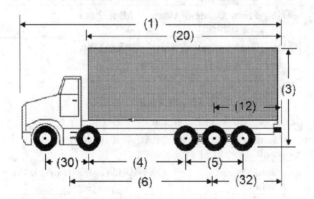

Vehicle Description

Designated Truck 7 is a 5-axle truck with a front tandem axle and a rear tri-drive axle.

Qualifying Preconditions

Weight — Front axle weight must be at least 23 per cent of the gross vehicle weight at all times.

Equipment and components, see ss. 5, 8, 11

Exceptions

Until December 31, 2025, the dimensional limits for Wheelbase (6), Effective Rear Overhang (12), Hitch Offset (32) and Rear Tandem Axle Track Width (35) do not apply if the truck was built before July 1, 2011.

An overhanging boom of a rear-facing crane that extends 1.0 metre or less past the rearmost point of the truck is exempt from the dimensional limit for Effective Rear Overhang (12).

DIMENSIONAL LIMIT CHART

Vehicle	Ref.	Feature	Dimensional Limit
Truck	(1)	Length	Max. 12.5m
Truck	(2)	Width	Max. 2.6m
Truck	(3)	Height	Max. 4.15m
Truck	(4)	Inter-axle Spacing	Not controlled
Truck	(5)	Tridem Axle Spread	2.4 to 2.8m
Truck	(6)	Effective wheelbase	Min. 6.0m
Truck	(12)	Effective Rear Overhang	Max. 4.0m
Truck	(20)	Box Length	Not controlled
Truck	(30)	Front Tandem Axle Spread	1.2 to 2.7m
Truck	(32)	Hitch Offset (if drawing trailer)	Max. 2.5m
Truck	(35)	Tridem Track Width	2.5 to 2.6m

WEIGHT LIMIT CHART

Feature	Weight Limit
Front Axle Maximum: (lowest of a, b and c)	
a) by manufacturer's axle rating or default	i. GAWR (if verified); or
	ii. If GAWR not verified, the lower of:
	1. 10,000 kg, and
	2. the sum of the maximum tire load ratings

WEIGHT LIMIT CHART

Feature	Weight Limit	
b) by tire width	11 kg × combined tire widths in mm	
c) by axle unit description	Tandem Axle by axle spread:	
	— 1.2 < 1.6m	**17,000 kg**
	— 1.6 to 2.7m	**18,000 kg**
Other Axles Maximums: (lowest of a, b and c)		
a) by manufacturer's axle rating or default	i. GAWR (if verified), or	
	ii. If GAWR not verified, the sum of the maximum tire load ratings	
b) by tire width	10 kg × combined tire widths in mm	
c) by axle unit description	Tridem Axle by axle spread	
	— 2.4 < 2.7m	**21,300 kg**
	— 2.7 to 2.8m	**22,000 kg**
Allowable Gross Vehicle Weight:	actual weight on the front axle plus the other axle maximums	

O. Reg. 457/10, s. 29; 167/12, s. 7; 16/14, s. 28

SCHEDULE 26 — DESIGNATED TRUCK-TRAILER COMBINATION 1 — TRUCK AND FIXED AXLE PONY TRAILER [Heading added O. Reg. 457/10, s. 29.]

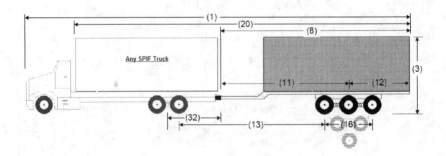

Configuration Description

Designated Truck-Trailer Combination 1 is composed of any designated truck and a pony trailer with one axle unit. The pony trailer's axle unit may be a single axle, tandem axle or tridem axle. The trailer has a single drawbar.

Qualifying Preconditions

Equipment and components for trailer, see ss. 5, 6, 8

Exceptions

If the trailer has a manufacturer's gross vehicle weight rating of less than 10,000 kilograms, the dimensional limits for Wheelbase (11), Inter-vehicle-unit Distance (13) and Track Width (19) do not apply.

Until December 31, 2025, the dimensional limit for Hitch Offset (32) does not apply if the truck was built before July 1, 2011.

Until December 31, 2025, the dimensional limits for Wheelbase (11), Effective Rear Overhang (12), Inter-vehicle-unit Distance (13), Track Width (19) and Box Length (20) do not apply if the trailer was built before July 1, 2011.

DIMENSIONAL LIMIT CHART

Vehicle	Ref.	Feature	Dimensional Limit
Overall	(1)	Overall Length	Max. 23m
Overall	(2)	Width	Max. 2.6m
Overall	(3)	Height	Max. 4.15m
Truck	na	Designated Trucks 1–7	Refer to Schedules 19–25
Pony Trailer	(8)	Length	Max. 12.5m
Pony Trailer	(11)	Wheelbase — single axle trailer	Min. 4.0m
Pony Trailer	(11)	Wheelbase — tandem and tridem trailer	Min. 6.25m
Pony Trailer	(12)	Effective Rear Overhang	Max. 4.0m
Pony Trailer	(13)	Inter-vehicle-unit Distance between single and single, tandem, or tridem	Min. 3.0m
Pony Trailer	(13)	Inter-vehicle-unit Distance between tandem and tandem	Min. 5.0m
Pony Trailer	(13)	Inter-vehicle-unit Distance between tandem and tridem	Min. 5.5m

DIMENSIONAL LIMIT CHART

Vehicle	Ref.	Feature	Dimensional Limit
Pony Trailer	(13)	Inter-vehicle-unit Distance between tridem and tridem	Min. 6.0m
Pony Trailer	(16)	Tandem Spread	1.2 to 1.85m
Pony Trailer	(16)	Tridem Spread	2.4 to 3.7m
Pony Trailer	(19)	Track Width — single tires	2.45 to 2.6m
Pony Trailer	(19)	Track Width — dual tires	2.5 to 2.6m
Pony Trailer	(20)	Box Length	Max. 20m
Pony Trailer	(32)	Hitch Offset — single or tandem drive truck	Max. 1.8m
Pony Trailer	(32)	Hitch Offset — tridem drive truck	Max. 2.5m

WEIGHT LIMIT CHART

Feature	Weight Limit	
Truck Weights — See Appropriate Weight Limit Chart (Schedules 19–25)		
Trailer Axle Maximum: (lowest of a, b and c)		
a) by manufacturer's axle rating or default	i. GAWR (if verified), or	
	ii. If GAWR not verified, the sum of the maximum tire load ratings	
b) by tire width	10 kg × combined tire widths in mm	
c) by axle unit description	Single Axle (Single Tires)	9,000 kg
	Single Axle (Dual Tires)	10,000 kg
	Tandem Axle by axle spread:	
	— 1.2 < 1.8m	18,000 kg
	— 1.8 to 1.85m (Single Tires)	18,000 kg
	— 1.8 to 1.85m (Dual Tires)	19,100 kg
	Tridem Axle by axle spread:	
	— 2.4 < 3.0m	21,300 kg

WEIGHT LIMIT CHART

Feature	Weight Limit	
	— 3.0 < 3.6m	24,000 kg
	— 3.6 to 3.7m	26,000 kg
Allowable Gross Vehicle Weight: (lower of i and ii)	**i. AGVW of Designated Truck plus trailer axle maximums**	
	ii.	
	Until December 31, 2025,	
	1. if trailer is built before July, 2011, the weight in Vehicle Weight Table 30	
	2. if trailer is built after June, 2011, has a tridem axle, a wheelbase less than 8.75m and is drawn by Designated Truck 1, 37,350 kg	
	3. if neither 1 nor 2 applies,	
	A. if trailer wheelbase is less than 8.75m, the weight in Vehicle Weight Table 31	
	B. if trailer wheelbase is 8.75m or greater, the weight in Vehicle Weight Table 30	
	After 2025,	
	1. if trailer has a tridem axle, a wheelbase less than 8.75m and is drawn by Designated Truck 1, 37,350 kg	
	2. if 1 does not apply,	
	A. if trailer wheelbase is less than 8.75m, the weight in Vehicle Weight Table 31	
	B. if trailer wheelbase is 8.75m or greater, the weight in Vehicle Weight Table 30	

O. Reg. 457/10, s. 29; 167/12, s. 8; 16/14, s. 29

SCHEDULE 27 — DESIGNATED TRUCK-TRAILER COMBINATION 2 — TRUCK AND SELF-STEER TRIAXLE PONY TRAILER [Heading added O. Reg. 457/10, s. 29.]

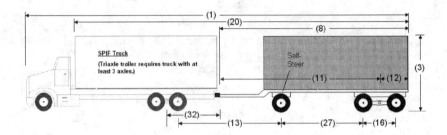

Configuration Description

Designated Truck-Trailer Combination 2 is composed of a designated truck, other than Designated Truck 1, and a self-steer triaxle pony trailer. The trailer has a single drawbar. The trailer has two axle units: an optionally liftable single self-steer axle in front and a tandem axle in the rear.

Qualifying Preconditions

Weight, see s. 14

Equipment and components, see ss. 5, 6, 8, 9

Labelling, see s. 13

Alternatives

A truck-trailer combination that meets every requirement to be Designated Truck-Trailer Combination 2, except that the liftable axle of the trailer is not deployed, shall be deemed to be Designated Truck-Trailer Combination 1.

Exceptions

Until December 31, 2025, the dimensional limit for Hitch Offset (32) does not apply if the truck was built before July 1, 2011.

Until December 31, 2025, the dimensional limits for Wheelbase (11), Effective Rear Overhang (12), Inter-vehicle-unit Distance (13), Track Width (19) and Box Length (20) do not apply if the trailer was built before July 1, 2011.

DIMENSIONAL LIMIT CHART

Vehicle	Ref.	Feature	Dimensional Limit
Overall	(1)	Overall Length	Max. 23m
Overall	(2)	Width	Max. 2.6m
Overall	(3)	Height	Max. 4.15m
Truck	na	Designated Trucks 2–7	Refer to Schedules 20–25
Self-Steer Trailer	(8)	Length	Max. 12.5m
Self-Steer Trailer	(11)	Wheelbase	Min. 7.0m
Self-Steer Trailer	(12)	Effective Rear Overhang	Max. 4.0m
Self-Steer Trailer	(13)	Inter-vehicle-unit Distance	Min. 3.0m
Self-Steer Trailer	(16)	Tandem Spread	1.2 to 1.85m
Self-Steer Trailer	(19)	Track Width of tandem axle — single tires	2.45 to 2.6m
Self-Steer Trailer	(19)	Track Width of tandem axle — dual tires	2.5 to 2.6m
Self-Steer Trailer	(20)	Box Length	Max. 20m
Self-Steer Trailer	(27)	Inter-Axle Spacing	< 2.5m
Self-Steer Trailer	(32)	Hitch Offset — tandem drive truck	Max. 1.8m
Self-Steer Trailer	(32)	Hitch Offset — tridem drive truck	Max. 2.5m

WEIGHT LIMIT CHART

Truck Weights — See Appropriate Weight Limit Chart (Schedules 20–25)	
Trailer Axle Maximum: (lowest of a, b and c)	
a) by manufacturer's axle rating or default	i. GAWR (if verified), or
	ii. If GAWR not verified the sum of the maximum tire load ratings,

WEIGHT LIMIT CHART

b) by tire width	Self-steer axle	11 kg × combined tire widths in mm	
	Not self-steer axle	10 kg × combined tire widths in mm	
c) by axle unit description	i. If tandem axle spread is 1.2 < 1.8m or there are single tires on any wheel:		
		1. self-steer axle (load equalized)	9,000 kg
		2. self-steer axle (not load equalized)	7,500 kg
		3. tandem axle (load equalized)	18,000 kg
		4. tandem axle (not load equalized)	15,000 kg
	ii. If tandem axle spread is 1.8 to 1.85m and there are no single tires on any wheel:		
		1. self-steer axle (load equalized)	9,550 kg
		2. self-steer axle (not load equalized)	8,000 kg
		3. tandem axle (load equalized)	19,100 kg
		4. tandem axle (not load equalized)	16,000 kg
Allowable Gross Vehicle Weight: (lower of i and ii)	i. AGVW of Designated Truck plus trailer axle maximums		
	ii. the maximum weight in Vehicle Weight Table 30		

O. Reg. 457/10, s. 29; 167/12, s. 9; 16/14, s. 30

SCHEDULE 28 — DESIGNATED TRUCK-TRAILER COMBINATION 3 — TRUCK AND FULL TRAILER [Heading added O. Reg. 457/10, s. 29.]

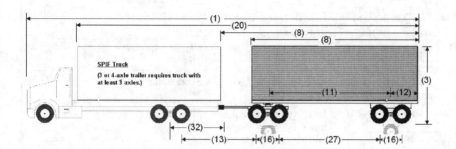

Configuration Description

Designated Truck-Trailer Combination 3 is composed of a Designated Truck 1 combined with a 2-axle full trailer or a Designated Truck 2, 3, 4, 5, 6, or 7 combined with a 2, 3 or 4-axle full trailer.

The trailer has a single drawbar connected to a front turntable or trailer converter dolly and has two axle units consisting of a single axle in front of a rear single axle, a single axle in front of a rear tandem axle or a tandem axle in front of a rear tandem axle.

Qualifying Preconditions

Equipment and components, see ss. 5, 6, 8

Exceptions

Until December 31, 2025, the dimensional limit for Hitch Offset (32) does not apply if the truck was built before July 1, 2011.

Until December 31, 2025, the dimensional limits for Wheelbase (11), Effective Rear Overhang (12), Inter-vehicle-unit Distance (13), Track Width (19), Box Length (20) and Inter-Axle Spacing (27) do not apply if the trailer was built before July 1, 2011.

DIMENSIONAL LIMIT CHART

Vehicle	Ref.	Feature	Dimensional Limit
Overall	(1)	Overall Length	Max. 23m
Overall	(2)	Width	Max. 2.6m

DIMENSIONAL LIMIT CHART

Vehicle	Ref.	Feature	Dimensional Limit
Overall	(3)	Height	Max. 4.15m
Truck	na	Designated Trucks 1–7	Refer to Schedules 19–25
Full Trailer	(8)	Length	Not controlled
Full Trailer	(8)	Length (excluding the drawbar)	Max. 12.5m
Full Trailer	(11)	Wheelbase	Min. 6.25m
Full Trailer	(12)	Effective Rear Overhang	Max. 4.0m
Full Trailer	(13)	Inter-vehicle-unit Distance between single and single, tandem, or tridem	Min. 3.0m
Full Trailer	(13)	Inter-vehicle-unit Distance between tandem and tandem	Min. 5.0m
Full Trailer	(13)	Inter-vehicle-unit Distance between tandem and tridem	Min. 5.5m
Full Trailer	(16)	Tandem Spread	1.2 to 1.85m
Full Trailer	(16)	Track Width — single tires	2.45 to 2.6m
Full Trailer	(16)	Track Width — dual tires	2.5 to 2.6m
Full Trailer	(20)	Box Length	Max. 20m
Full Trailer	(27)	Inter-Axle Spacing	Min. 5.0m
Full Trailer	(32)	Hitch Offset — single or tandem drive truck	Max. 1.8m

DIMENSIONAL LIMIT CHART

Vehicle	Ref.	Feature	Dimensional Limit
Full Trailer	(32)	Hitch Offset — tridem drive truck	Max. 2.5m

WEIGHT LIMIT CHART

Feature	Weight Limit	
Truck Weights	Refer to Appropriate Weight Limit Chart (Schedules 19–25)	
Trailer Axle Maximums: (lowest of a, b and c)		
a) by manufacturer's axle rating or default	i. GAWR, if verified	
	ii. If GAWR not verified, the sum of the maximum tire load ratings, as specified on the tire side walls.	
b) by tire width	10 kg × combined tire widths in mm	
c) by axle unit description	Single Axle (Single tires)	9,000 kg
	Single Axle (Dual tires)	9,100 kg
	Tandem Axle	18,000 kg
Allowable Gross Vehicle Weight: (lower of i and ii)	i. AGVW of Designated Truck plus trailer axle maximums	
	ii.	
	Until December 31, 2025,	
	1. if trailer is built before July 2011, the weight in Vehicle Weight Table 30	
	2. if trailer is built after June 2011 and	
	A. trailer wheelbase is less than 7.25m, the weight in Vehicle Weight Table 31	
	B. trailer wheelbase is 7.25m or greater, the weight in Vehicle Weight Table 30	
	After 2025,	
	1. if trailer wheelbase is less than 7.25m, the weight in Vehicle Weight Table 31	

WEIGHT LIMIT CHART

Feature	Weight Limit
	2. if trailer wheelbase is 7.25m or greater, the weight in Vehicle Weight Table 30

O. Reg. 457/10, s. 29; 167/12, s. 10; 16/14, s. 31

SCHEDULE 29 — DESIGNATED TRUCK-TRAILER COMBINATION 4 — TRUCK AND SELF-STEER TRIAXLE FULL TRAILER [Heading added O. Reg. 457/10, s. 29.]

Configuration Description

Designated Truck-Trailer Combination 4 is composed of Designated Truck 2, 3, 4, 5, 6 or 7 combined with a self-steer triaxle full trailer. A single drawbar is rigidly attached to the structure of the trailer horizontally, but hinges vertically so that the whole of the trailer weight is carried on its own axles. The trailer has two axle units composed of a single, non-liftable self-steer axle ahead of a tandem axle.

Qualifying Preconditions

Equipment and components, see ss. 5, 6, 8, 9

Labelling, see s. 13

Exceptions

Until December 31, 2025, the dimensional limit for Hitch Offset (32) does not apply if the truck was built before July 1, 2011.

Until December 31, 2025, the dimensional limits for Wheelbase (11), Effective Rear Overhang (12), Inter-vehicle-unit Distance (13), Track Width (19) and Box Length (20) do not apply if the trailer was built before July 1, 2011.

DIMENSIONAL LIMIT CHART

Vehicle	Ref.	Feature	Dimensional Limit
Overall	(1)	Overall Length	Max. 23m
Overall	(2)	Width	Max. 2.6m
Overall	(3)	Height	Max. 4.15m
Truck	na	Designated Trucks 2–7	Refer to Schedules 20–25
Self-Steer Trailer	(8)	Length	Max. 12.5m
Self-Steer Trailer	(11)	Wheelbase	Min 7.0m
Self-Steer Trailer	(12)	Effective Rear Over-hang	Max. 4.0m
Self-Steer Trailer	(13)	Inter-vehicle-unit Distance	Min. 3.0m
Self-Steer Trailer	(16)	Tandem Spread	1.2 to 1.85m
Self-Steer Trailer	(19)	Track Width of tandem axle — single tires	2.45 to 2.6m
Self-Steer Trailer	(19)	Track Width of tandem axle — dual tires	2.5 to 2.6m
Self-Steer Trailer	(20)	Box Length	Max. 20m
Self-Steer Trailer	(27)	Inter-Axle Spacing	Min. 3.0m
Self-Steer Trailer	(32)	Hitch Offset — tandem drive truck	Max. 1.8m
Self-Steer Trailer	(32)	Hitch Offset — tridem drive truck	Max. 2.5m

WEIGHT LIMIT CHART

Feature	Weight Limit
Truck Axle Weights	Refer to Schedules 20–25 for Designated Truck
Trailer Axle Maximums: (lowest of a, b and c)	

WEIGHT LIMIT CHART

Feature	Weight Limit		
a) by manufacturer's axle rating or default	i. GAWR (if verified)		
	ii. If GAWR not verified, the sum of the maximum tire load ratings		
b) by tire width	Self-steer axle	11 kg × combined tire widths in mm	
	Not self-steer axle	10 kg × combined tire widths in mm	
c) by axle unit description	Self-steer axle (single tires)		9,000 kg
	Self-steer axle (dual tires)		9,550 kg
	Tandem Axle — by axle spread:		
	— 1.2 < 1.8 m		18,000 kg
	— 1.8 to 1.85m (Single Tires)		18,000 kg
	— 1.8 to 1.85m (Dual Tires)		19,100 kg
Allowable Gross Vehicle Weight : (lower of i and ii)	i. AGVW of the Designated Truck plus trailer axle maximums		
	ii. the weight in Vehicle Weight Table 30.		

O. Reg. 457/10, s. 29; 167/12, s. 11; 16/14, s. 32

SCHEDULE 30 — DESIGNATED TRUCK-TRAILER COMBINATION 5 — TRUCK AND TRIDEM-AXLE FULL TRAILER [Heading added O. Reg. 457/10, s. 29.]

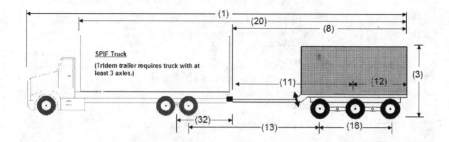

Configuration Description

Designated Truck-Trailer Combination 5 is composed of a Designated Truck 2, 3, 4, 5, 6 or 7 combined with a tridem-axle full trailer. A single drawbar is rigidly attached to the structure of the trailer horizontally, but hinges vertically so that the whole of the trailer weight is carried on its own axles.

Qualifying Preconditions

Equipment and components, see ss. 5, 6, 8

Exceptions

Until December 31, 2025, the dimensional limit for Hitch Offset (32) does not apply if the truck was built before 2011.

Until December 31, 2025, the dimensional limits for Wheelbase (11), Effective Rear Overhang (12), Inter-vehicle-unit Distance (13), Track Width (19), and Box Length (20) do not apply if the trailer was built before 2011.

DIMENSIONAL LIMIT CHART

Vehicle	Ref.	Feature	Dimensional Limit
Overall	(1)	Overall Length	Max. 23m
Overall	(2)	Width	Max. 2.6m
Overall	(3)	Height	Max. 4.15m
Truck	na	Designated Trucks 2–7	Refer to Schedules 20–25

DIMENSIONAL LIMIT CHART

Vehicle	Ref.	Feature	Dimensional Limit
Tridem Trailer	(8)	Length	Max. 12.5m
Tridem Trailer	(11)	Wheelbase	Min. 6.25m
Tridem Trailer	(12)	Effective Rear Overhang	Max. 4.0m
Tridem Trailer	(13)	Inter-vehicle-unit Distance between tandem and tridem	Min. 5.5m
Tridem Trailer	(13)	Inter-vehicle Distance between tridem and tandem	Min. 6.0m
Tridem Trailer	(16)	Tridem Spread	2.4 to 3.7m
Tridem Trailer	(19)	Track Width — single tires	2.45 to 2.6m
Tridem Trailer	(19)	Track Width — dual tires	2.5 to 2.6m
Tridem Trailer	(20)	Box Length	Max. 20m
Tridem Trailer	(32)	Hitch Offset — tandem drive truck	Max. 1.8m
Tridem Trailer	(32)	Hitch Offset — tridem drive truck	Max. 2.5m

WEIGHT LIMIT CHART

Feature	Weight Limit
Truck Weights	Refer to Appropriate Weight Limit Chart (Schedules 20–25)
Trailer Axle Maximum: (lowest of a, b and c)	
a) by manufacturer's axle rating or default	i. GAWR (if verified), or
	ii. If GAWR not verified, the sum of the maximum tire load ratings specified on tire side walls
b) by tire width	10 kg × combined tire widths in mm
c) by axle unit description	Tridem Axle by axle spread:

WEIGHT LIMIT CHART

Feature	Weight Limit	
	— 2.4 < 3.0m	21,300 kg
	— 3.0 < 3.6m	24,000 kg
	— 3.6 to 3.7m	26,000 kg
Allowable Gross Vehicle Weight: (lower of i and ii)	i. AGVW of Designated Truck plus the maximum allowable weights of all axles of trailer	
	ii.	
	Until December 31, 2025,	
	1. if trailer is drawn by Designated Truck 3, the weight in Vehicle Weight Table 31	
	2. if trailer is built before July 2011 and is drawn by a designated truck other than Designated Truck 3, the weight in Vehicle Weight Table 30	
	3. if neither 1 nor 2 applies,	
	A. if trailer wheelbase is less than 8.75m, the weight in Vehicle Weight Table 31	
	B. if trailer wheelbase is 8.75m or greater, the weight in Vehicle Weight Table 30	
	After 2025,	
	1. if trailer is drawn by Designated Truck 3 or has wheelbase less than 8.5m, the weight in Vehicle Weight Table 31	
	2. if trailer is not drawn by Designated Truck 3 and has wheelbase of 8.75m or greater, the weight in Vehicle Weight Table 30	

O. Reg. 457/10, s. 29; 167/12, s. 12; 16/14, s. 33

SCHEDULE 31 — DESIGNATED SADDLEMOUNT
COMBINATION [Heading added O. Reg. 457/10, s. 29.]

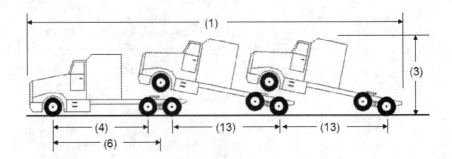

Configuration Description

A Designated Saddlemount Combination is composed of tractors, trucks or both. The second and any subsequent vehicle is connected to the vehicle ahead by means of a saddlemount device which performs as a fifth wheel assembly. The combination consists of two or three motor vehicles whose wheels are in contact with the highway. Only the rearmost such vehicle may carry an additional vehicle whose wheels do not contact the highway.

Qualifying Preconditions

Equipment and components, see ss. 5, 8

Exceptions

A Saddlemount Combination is exempt from the Overall Length (1) and Height (3) limits set out in the Dimension Limit Chart below if all vehicles in the combination (including any fully loaded vehicle) face forward. The following limits apply to exempted Saddlemount Combinations:

Overall Length (1) — 25m

Height (3) — 4.3m.

DIMENSIONAL LIMIT CHART

Vehicle	Ref.	Feature	Dimensional Limit
Overall	(1)	Overall Length	Max. 23m
Overall	(2)	Width	Max. 2.6m

DIMENSIONAL LIMIT CHART

Vehicle	Ref.	Feature	Dimensional Limit
Overall	(3)	Height	Max. 4.15m
Lead Tractor or Truck	(4)	Inter-axle Spacing	Min. 3.0m
Lead Tractor or Truck	(6)	Wheelbase	Not controlled
Drawn Tractors or Trucks	(13)	Inter-vehicle-unit Distance	Min. 3.0m

WEIGHT LIMIT CHART

Feature	Weight Limit	
Front Axle Maximum: (lowest of a, b and c)		
a) by manufacturer's axle rating or default	i. GAWR (if verified); or	
	ii. If GAWR not verified, the lower of:	
	1. 5,000 kg, and	
	2. the sum of the maximum tire load ratings	
b) by tire width	11 kg × combined tire widths in mm	
c) by axle unit description	Single Axle	7,700 kg
Other Axles Maximums: (lowest of a, b and c)		
a) by manufacturer's axle rating or default	i. GAWR (if verified), or	
	ii. If GAWR not verified, the sum of the maximum tire load ratings	
b) by tire width	Front axle (towed vehicle) 11 kg × combined tire widths in mm Not front axle (lead or towed vehicle) 10 kg × combined tire widths in mm	
c) by axle unit description	Lead Tractor or Truck and drawn Tractors or Trucks:	
	Single Axle (Single Tires)	9,000 kg
	Single Axle (Dual Tires)	10,000 kg
	Tandem Axle — by axle spread:	

WEIGHT LIMIT CHART

Feature	Weight Limit	
	— 1.2 < 1.8m	18,000 kg
	— 1.8 m or more (SingleTires)	18,000 kg
	— 1.8 m or more (Dual Tires)	19,100 kg
	Tridem Axle — by axle spread:	
	— 2.4 < 2.7m	21,300 kg
	— 2.7 m or more	22,000 kg
Allowable Gross Vehicle Weight: (lower of i and ii)	i. actual weight on the front axle plus other axle maximums	
	ii. 63,500 kg	

O. Reg. 457/10, s. 29; 16/14, s. 34

TABLES 1

VEHICLE WEIGHT TABLE 1
ALLOWABLE GROSS WEIGHT ON A VEHICLE WITH THREE AXLES (KILOGRAMS)
FRONT AXLE WEIGHT, (KILOGRAMS)

BASE LENGTH (METRES)	5 000 or Less	5 001 TO LESS THAN 5 500	5 500 TO LESS THAN 6 000	6 000 TO LESS THAN 6 500	6 500 TO LESS THAN 7 000	7 000 TO LESS THAN 7 500	7 500 TO LESS THAN 8 000	8 000 TO LESS THAN 8 500	8 500 TO LESS THAN 9 000	9 000 TO LESS THAN 9 500	9 500 TO AND INCL 10 000
LESS THAN 4.00	22,600	22,900	23,100	23,400	23,600	23,800	24,000	24,200	24,400	24,700	25,000
4.00 TO LESS THAN 4.10	22,900	23,200	23,400	23,700	23,900	24,100	24,300	24,500	24,700	25,000	25,300
4.10 TO LESS THAN 4.20	23,300	23,600	23,800	24,100	24,300	24,500	24,700	24,900	25,100	25,400	25,700
4.20 TO LESS THAN 4.30	23,600	23,900	24,100	24,400	24,600	24,800	25,000	25,200	25,400	25,700	26,000
4.30 TO LESS THAN 4.40	23,800	24,200	24,400	24,700	24,900	25,100	25,300	25,500	25,700	26,000	26,300
4.40 TO LESS THAN 4.50	23,800	24,300	24,800	25,100	25,300	25,500	25,700	25,900	26,100	26,400	26,700
4.50 TO LESS THAN 4.60	23,800	24,300	24,800	25,300	25,600	25,800	26,000	26,200	26,400	26,700	27,000
4.60 TO LESS THAN 4.70	23,800	24,300	24,800	25,300	25,800	26,100	26,300	26,500	26,700	27,000	27,300
4.70 TO LESS THAN 4.80	23,800	24,300	24,800	25,300	25,800	26,300	26,700	26,900	27,100	27,400	27,700
4.80 TO LESS THAN 4.90	23,800	24,300	24,800	25,300	25,800	26,300	26,800	27,200	27,400	27,700	28,000

VEHICLE WEIGHT TABLE 1
ALLOWABLE GROSS WEIGHT ON A VEHICLE WITH THREE AXLES (KILOGRAMS)
FRONT AXLE WEIGHT, (KILOGRAMS)

BASE LENGTH (METRES)	5 000 or Less	5 001 TO LESS THAN 5 500	5 500 TO LESS THAN 6 000	6 000 TO LESS THAN 6 500	6 500 TO LESS THAN 7 000	7 000 TO LESS THAN 7 500	7 500 TO LESS THAN 8 000	8 000 TO LESS THAN 8 500	8 500 TO LESS THAN 9 000	9 000 TO LESS THAN 9 500	9 500 TO AND INCL 10 000
4.90 TO LESS THAN 5.00	23,800	24,300	24,800	25,300	25,800	26,300	26,800	27,300	27,700	28,000	28,400
5.00 AND OVER	23,800	24,300	24,800	25,300	25,800	26,300	26,800	27,300	27,800	28,300	28,800

VEHICLE WEIGHT TABLE 2
ALLOWABLE GROSS WEIGHT ON A VEHICLE WITH FOUR AXLES (KILOGRAMS)
FRONT AXLE WEIGHT, (KILOGRAMS)

BASE LENGTH (METRES)	5 000 or Less	5 001 TO LESS THAN 5 500	5 500 TO LESS THAN 6 000	6 000 TO LESS THAN 6 500	6 500 TO LESS THAN 7 000	7 000 TO LESS THAN 7 500	7 500 TO LESS THAN 8 000	8 000 TO LESS THAN 8 500	8 500 TO LESS THAN 9 000	9 000 TO LESS THAN 9 500	9 500 TO AND INCL 10 000
LESS THAN 5.00	28,600	28,900	29,100	29,400	29,600	29,800	30,100	30,300	30,500	30,800	31,000
5.00 TO LESS THAN 5.25	29,100	29,400	29,600	29,900	30,200	30,400	30,700	30,900	31,100	31,400	31,600
5.25 TO LESS THAN 5.50	29,600	29,900	30,100	30,400	30,700	30,900	31,300	31,500	31,700	32,100	32,300
5.50 TO LESS THAN 5.75	30,000	30,400	30,600	31,000	31,300	31,500	31,900	32,100	32,400	32,700	33,000
5.75 TO LESS THAN 6.00	30,500	30,900	31,200	31,500	31,800	32,100	32,400	32,700	33,000	33,300	33,600
6.00 TO LESS THAN 6.25	31,000	31,400	31,700	32,000	32,400	32,700	33,000	33,300	33,600	34,000	34,300
6.25 TO LESS THAN 6.50	31,500	31,900	32,200	32,600	32,900	33,200	33,600	33,900	34,300	34,600	34,900
6.50 TO LESS THAN 6.75	32,000	32,400	32,700	33,100	33,500	33,800	34,200	34,500	34,900	35,200	35,500
6.75 TO LESS THAN 7.00	32,500	32,900	33,200	33,600	34,000	34,400	34,800	35,100	35,500	35,900	36,200
7.00 TO LESS THAN 7.25	33,000	33,400	33,700	34,100	34,600	35,000	35,400	35,700	36,100	36,500	36,900
7.25 TO LESS THAN 7.50	33,300	33,800	34,200	34,600	35,100	35,500	35,900	36,300	36,700	37,200	37,600
7.50 AND OVER	33,300	33,800	34,300	34,800	35,300	35,800	36,300	36,800	37,300	37,800	38,300

Tab. 1   Ont. Reg. 413/05 — Vehicle Weights and Dimensions

VEHICLE WEIGHT TABLE 3
ALLOWABLE GROSS WEIGHT ON A VEHICLE WITH FIVE AXLES (KILOGRAMS)
INTER-VEHICLE-UNIT DISTANCE, LESS THAN 2.4 METRES
(OR INTRA-VEHICLE-UNIT DISTANCE)
FRONT AXLE WEIGHT, (KILOGRAMS)

BASE LENGTH, (METRES)	5 000 or Less	5 001 TO LESS THAN 5 500	5 500 TO LESS THAN 6 000	6 000 TO LESS THAN 6 500	6 500 TO LESS THAN 7 000	7 000 TO LESS THAN 7 500	7 500 TO LESS THAN 8 000	8 000 TO LESS THAN 8 500	8 500 TO LESS THAN 9 000	9 000 TO LESS THAN 9 500	9 500 TO AND INCL 10 000
LESS THAN 7.00	30,200	30,600	31,000	31,300	31,700	32,100	32,500	32,900	33,300	33,700	34,100
7.00 TO LESS THAN 7.25	30,700	31,100	31,500	31,900	32,300	32,700	33,000	33,400	33,800	34,200	34,600
7.25 TO LESS THAN 7.50	31,200	31,600	32,000	32,400	32,800	33,200	33,600	34,000	34,400	34,800	35,200
7.50 TO LESS THAN 7.75	31,700	32,100	32,500	32,900	33,300	33,700	34,100	34,500	34,900	35,300	35,700
7.75 TO LESS THAN 8.00	32,200	32,600	33,000	33,400	33,800	34,200	34,600	35,000	35,400	35,800	36,200
8.00 TO LESS THAN 8.25	32,700	33,100	33,500	33,900	34,300	34,700	35,200	35,600	36,000	36,400	36,800
8.25 TO LESS THAN 8.50	33,200	33,600	34,000	34,400	34,900	35,300	35,700	36,100	36,500	36,900	37,300
8.50 TO LESS THAN 8.75	33,700	34,100	34,500	35,000	35,400	35,800	36,200	36,600	37,000	37,400	37,800
8.75 TO LESS THAN 9.00	34,200	34,600	35,100	35,500	35,900	36,300	36,700	37,100	37,600	38,000	38,400
9.00 TO LESS THAN 9.25	34,700	35,100	35,600	36,000	36,400	36,800	37,300	37,700	38,100	38,500	38,900
9.25 TO LESS THAN 9.50	35,200	35,700	36,100	36,500	36,900	37,400	37,800	38,200	38,600	39,100	39,500
9.50 TO LESS THAN 9.75	35,700	36,200	36,600	37,000	37,400	37,900	38,300	38,700	39,200	39,600	40,000
9.75 TO LESS THAN 10.00	36,200	36,700	37,100	37,500	38,000	38,400	38,800	39,300	39,700	40,100	40,500
10.00 TO LESS THAN 10.25	36,700	37,200	37,600	38,100	38,500	38,900	39,400	39,800	40,200	40,700	41,200
10.25 AND OVER	36,700	37,200	37,700	38,200	38,700	39,200	39,700	40,200	40,700	41,200	41,700

VEHICLE WEIGHT TABLE 4
ALLOWABLE GROSS WEIGHT ON A VEHICLE WITH FIVE AXLES (KILOGRAMS)
INTER-VEHICLE-UNIT DISTANCE, 2.4 METRES TO LESS THAN 2.7 METRES
(OR INTRA-VEHICLE-UNIT DISTANCE)
FRONT AXLE WEIGHT, (KILOGRAMS)

BASE LENGTH, (METRES)	5 000 or Less	5 001 TO LESS THAN 5 500	5 500 TO LESS THAN 6 000	6 000 TO LESS THAN 6 500	6 500 TO LESS THAN 7 000	7 000 TO LESS THAN 7 500	7 500 TO LESS THAN 8 000	8 000 TO LESS THAN 8 500	8 500 TO LESS THAN 9 000	9 000 TO LESS THAN 9 500	9 500 AND INCL 10 000
LESS THAN 7.25	31,700	32,100	32,500	32,900	33,200	33,600	34,000	34,400	34,700	35,100	35,500
7.25 TO LESS THAN 7.50	32,200	32,600	33,000	33,400	33,800	34,100	34,500	34,900	35,300	35,600	30,000
7.50 TO LESS THAN 7.75	32,700	33,100	33,500	33,900	34,300	34,700	35,100	35,400	35,800	36,200	36,000
7.75 TO LESS THAN 8.00	33,200	33,600	34,000	34,400	34,800	35,200	35,600	36,000	36,400	36,700	37,100
8.00 TO LESS THAN 8.25	33,700	34,100	34,500	34,900	35,300	35,700	36,100	36,500	36,900	37,300	37,700
8.25 TO LESS THAN 8.50	34,200	34,600	35,000	35,400	35,800	36,200	36,600	37,000	37,400	37,800	38,200
8.50 TO LESS THAN 8.75	34,800	35,200	35,600	36,000	36,400	36,800	37,200	37,600	38,000	38,400	38,800
8.75 TO LESS THAN 9.00	35,300	35,700	36,100	36,500	36,900	37,300	37,700	38,100	38,500	38,900	39,300
9.00 TO LESS THAN 9.25	35,800	36,200	36,600	37,000	37,400	37,800	38,200	38,700	39,100	39,500	39,900
9.25 TO LESS THAN 9.50	36,300	36,700	37,100	37,500	37,900	38,400	38,800	39,200	39,600	40,000	40,400
9.50 TO LESS THAN 9.75	36,800	37,200	37,600	38,000	38,500	38,900	39,300	39,700	40,200	40,600	41,000
9.75 TO LESS THAN 10.00	37,300	37,700	38,100	38,600	39,000	39,400	39,800	40,200	40,600	41,000	41,400
10.00 TO LESS THAN 10.25	37,800	38,200	38,700	39,100	39,500	39,900	40,300	40,700	41,100	41,400	41,800
10.25 TO LESS THAN 10.50	37,800	38,300	38,800	39,300	39,800	40,300	40,700	41,100	41,500	41,900	42,300
10.50 AND OVER	37,800	38,300	38,800	39,300	39,800	40,300	40,800	41,300	41,800	42,300	42,800

Tab. 1   Ont. Reg. 413/05 — Vehicle Weights and Dimensions

VEHICLE WEIGHT TABLE 5
ALLOWABLE GROSS WEIGHT ON A VEHICLE WITH FIVE AXLES (KILOGRAMS)
INTER-VEHICLE-UNIT DISTANCE, 2.7 METRES TO LESS THAN 3.0 METRES
(OR INTRA-VEHICLE-UNIT DISTANCE)
FRONT AXLE WEIGHT, (KILOGRAMS)

BASE LENGTH, (METRES)	5 000 or Less	5 001 TO LESS THAN 5 500	5 500 TO LESS THAN 6 000	6 000 TO LESS THAN 6 500	6 500 TO LESS THAN 7 000	7 000 TO LESS THAN 7 500	7 500 TO LESS THAN 8 000	8 000 TO LESS THAN 8 500	8 500 TO LESS THAN 9 000	9 000 TO LESS THAN 9 500	9 500 TO AND INCL 10 000
LESS THAN 7.50	33,600	33,900	34,300	34,600	35,000	35,300	35,700	36,000	36,400	36,700	37,100
7.50 TO LESS THAN 7.75	34,100	34,400	34,800	35,100	35,500	35,800	36,200	36,500	36,900	37,200	37,600
7.75 TO LESS THAN 8.00	34,500	34,900	35,300	35,600	36,000	36,300	36,700	37,100	37,400	37,800	38,200
8.00 TO LESS THAN 8.25	35,000	35,400	35,800	36,100	36,500	36,900	37,200	37,600	37,900	38,300	38,700
8.25 TO LESS THAN 8.50	35,500	35,900	36,300	36,600	37,000	37,400	37,700	38,100	38,500	38,800	39,200
8.50 TO LESS THAN 8.75	36,000	36,400	36,700	37,100	37,500	37,900	38,200	38,600	39,000	39,400	39,700
8.75 TO LESS THAN 9.00	36,400	36,800	37,200	37,600	38,000	38,400	38,800	39,100	39,500	39,900	40,300
9.00 TO LESS THAN 9.25	36,900	37,300	37,700	38,100	38,500	38,900	39,300	39,700	40,000	40,400	40,800
9.25 TO LESS THAN 9.50	37,400	37,800	38,200	38,600	39,000	39,400	39,800	40,200	40,600	41,000	41,400
9.50 TO LESS THAN 9.75	37,900	38,300	38,700	39,100	39,500	39,900	40,300	40,700	41,100	41,500	41,900
9.75 TO LESS THAN 10.00	38,400	38,800	39,200	39,600	40,000	40,400	40,800	41,200	41,600	42,000	42,400
10.00 TO LESS THAN 10.25	38,900	39,300	39,700	40,100	40,500	40,900	41,300	41,700	42,100	42,500	42,900
10.25 TO LESS THAN 10.50	39,100	39,600	40,100	40,600	41,000	41,400	41,800	42,300	42,700	43,100	43,600
10.50 AND OVER	39,100	39,600	40,100	40,600	41,100	41,600	42,100	42,600	43,100	43,600	44,100

VEHICLE WEIGHT TABLE 6
ALLOWABLE GROSS WEIGHT ON A VEHICLE WITH FIVE AXLES (KILOGRAMS)
INTER-VEHICLE-UNIT DISTANCE, 3.0 METRES TO LESS THAN 3.3 METRES
(OR INTRA-VEHICLE-UNIT DISTANCE)
FRONT AXLE WEIGHT, (KILOGRAMS)

BASE LENGTH, (METRES)	5 000 or Less	5 001 TO LESS THAN 5 500	5 500 TO LESS THAN 6 000	6 000 TO LESS THAN 6 500	6 500 TO LESS THAN 7 000	7 000 TO LESS THAN 7 500	7 500 TO LESS THAN 8 000	8 000 TO LESS THAN 8 500	8 500 TO LESS THAN 9 000	9 000 TO LESS THAN 9 500	9 500 TO AND INCL 10 000
LESS THAN 8.00	35,200	35,500	35,800	36,100	36,400	36,700	37,100	37,400	37,700	38,000	38,300
8.00 TO LESS THAN 8.25	35,700	36,000	36,300	36,600	37,000	37,300	37,600	37,900	38,200	38,600	38,900
8.25 TO LESS THAN 8.50	36,200	36,500	36,800	37,200	37,500	37,800	38,200	38,500	38,800	39,100	39,500
8.50 TO LESS THAN 8.75	36,700	37,000	37,300	37,700	38,000	38,400	38,700	39,000	39,400	39,700	40,000
8.75 TO LESS THAN 9.00	37,200	37,500	37,900	38,200	38,600	38,900	39,200	39,600	39,900	40,300	40,700
9.00 TO LESS THAN 9.25	37,700	38,000	38,400	38,700	39,100	39,400	39,800	40,100	40,500	40,900	41,200
9.25 TO LESS THAN 9.50	38,100	38,500	38,900	39,200	39,600	40,000	40,300	40,700	41,100	41,400	41,800
9.50 TO LESS THAN 9.75	38,600	39,000	39,400	39,800	40,100	40,500	40,900	41,300	41,600	42,000	42,400
9.75 TO LESS THAN 10.00	39,100	39,500	39,900	40,300	40,700	41,000	41,400	41,800	42,200	42,600	43,000
10.00 TO LESS THAN 10.25	39,600	40,000	40,400	40,800	41,200	41,600	42,000	42,300	42,700	43,100	43,500
10.25 TO LESS THAN 10.50	40,000	40,500	40,900	41,300	41,700	42,100	42,500	42,900	43,300	43,700	44,100
10.50 TO LESS THAN 10.75	40,300	40,800	41,300	41,800	42,200	42,600	43,000	43,400	43,800	44,200	44,600
10.75 AND OVER	40,300	40,800	41,300	41,800	42,300	42,800	43,300	43,800	44,300	44,800	45,300

Tab. 1   Ont. Reg. 413/05 — Vehicle Weights and Dimensions

VEHICLE WEIGHT TABLE 7
ALLOWABLE GROSS WEIGHT ON A VEHICLE WITH FIVE AXLES (KILOGRAMS)
INTER-VEHICLE-UNIT DISTANCE, 3.3 METRES TO LESS THAN 3.6 METRES
(OR INTRA-VEHICLE-UNIT DISTANCE)
FRONT AXLE WEIGHT, (KILOGRAMS)

BASE LENGTH, (METRES)	5 000 or Less	5 001 TO LESS THAN 5 500	5 500 TO LESS THAN 6 000	6 000 TO LESS THAN 6 500	6 500 TO LESS THAN 7 000	7 000 TO LESS THAN 7 500	7 500 TO LESS THAN 8 000	8 000 TO LESS THAN 8 500	8 500 TO LESS THAN 9 000	9 000 TO LESS THAN 9 500	9 500 AND INCL 10 000
LESS THAN 8.50	37,300	37,600	37,900	38,200	38,500	38,800	39,000	39,300	39,600	39,900	40,200
8.50 TO LESS THAN 8.75	37,700	38,000	38,300	38,600	38,900	39,200	39,500	39,800	40,100	40,400	40,700
8.75 TO LESS THAN 9.00	38,100	38,400	38,700	39,000	39,400	39,700	40,000	40,300	40,600	40,800	41,200
9.00 TO LESS THAN 9.25	38,500	38,800	39,200	39,500	39,800	40,100	40,400	40,800	41,100	41,400	41,700
9.25 TO LESS THAN 9.50	38,900	39,300	39,600	39,900	40,200	40,600	40,900	41,200	41,600	41,900	42,300
9.50 TO LESS THAN 9.75	39,300	39,700	40,000	40,300	40,700	41,000	41,400	41,700	42,100	42,400	42,800
9.75 TO LESS THAN 10.00	39,700	40,100	40,400	40,800	41,100	41,500	41,900	42,200	42,600	42,900	43,300
10.00 TO LESS THAN 10.25	40,100	40,500	40,800	41,200	41,600	42,000	42,300	42,700	43,100	43,500	43,800
10.25 TO LESS THAN 10.50	40,400	40,800	41,300	41,700	42,000	42,400	42,800	43,200	43,600	44,000	44,400
10.50 TO LESS THAN 10.75	40,800	41,200	41,700	42,100	42,500	42,900	43,300	43,700	44,100	44,600	45,000
10.75 AND OVER	40,900	41,400	41,900	42,400	42,900	43,400	43,800	44,200	44,700	45,100	45,500

VEHICLE WEIGHT TABLE 8
ALLOWABLE GROSS WEIGHT ON A VEHICLE WITH FIVE AXLES (KILOGRAMS)
INTER-VEHICLE-UNIT DISTANCE, 3.6 METRES OR MORE
(OR INTRA-VEHICLE-UNIT DISTANCE)
FRONT AXLE WEIGHT, (KILOGRAMS)

BASE LENGTH, (METRES)	5 000 or Less	5 001 TO LESS THAN 5 500	5 500 TO LESS THAN 6 000	6 000 TO LESS THAN 6 500	6 500 TO LESS THAN 7 000	7 000 TO LESS THAN 7 500	7 500 TO LESS THAN 8 000	8 000 TO LESS THAN 8 500	8 500 TO LESS THAN 9 000	9 000 TO LESS THAN 9 500	9 500 AND INCL 10 000
LESS THAN 8.50	38,200	38,400	38,700	38,900	39,200	39,400	39,700	39,900	40,200	40,400	40,700
8.50 TO LESS THAN 8.75	38,500	38,800	39,000	39,300	39,600	39,800	40,100	40,400	40,700	40,900	41,200

1312

VEHICLE WEIGHT TABLE 8
ALLOWABLE GROSS WEIGHT ON A VEHICLE WITH FIVE AXLES (KILOGRAMS)
INTER-VEHICLE-UNIT DISTANCE, 3.6 METRES OR MORE
(OR INTRA-VEHICLE-UNIT DISTANCE)
FRONT AXLE WEIGHT, (KILOGRAMS)

BASE LENGTH, (METRES)	5 000 or Less	5 001 TO LESS THAN 5 500	5 500 TO LESS THAN 6 000	6 000 TO LESS THAN 6 500	6 500 TO LESS THAN 7 000	7 000 TO LESS THAN 7 500	7 500 TO LESS THAN 8 000	8 000 TO LESS THAN 8 500	8 500 TO LESS THAN 9 000	9 000 TO LESS THAN 9 500	9 500 TO AND INCL 10 000
8.75 TO LESS THAN 9.00	38,800	39,100	39,400	39,700	40,000	40,300	40,600	40,900	41,200	41,400	41,700
9.00 TO LESS THAN 9.25	39,100	39,400	39,700	40,000	40,400	40,700	41,000	41,300	41,600	41,900	42,200
9.25 TO LESS THAN 9.50	39,400	39,800	40,100	40,400	40,800	41,100	41,500	41,800	42,100	42,400	42,700
9.50 TO LESS THAN 9.75	39,700	40,100	40,400	40,800	41,200	41,600	41,900	42,200	42,600	42,900	43,200
9.75 TO LESS THAN 10.00	40,000	40,400	40,800	41,200	41,600	42,000	42,400	42,700	43,100	43,400	43,800
10.00 TO LESS THAN 10.25	40,400	40,800	41,200	41,600	42,000	42,400	42,800	43,200	43,600	43,900	44,300
10.25 TO LESS THAN 10.50	40,700	41,100	41,500	42,000	42,400	42,800	43,200	43,600	44,000	44,400	44,800
10.50 TO LESS THAN 10.75	41,000	41,400	41,800	42,400	42,800	43,200	43,700	44,100	44,500	44,900	45,300
10.75 TO LESS THAN 11.00	41,400	41,800	42,200	42,700	43,200	43,700	44,100	44,600	45,000	45,500	45,900
11.00 TO LESS THAN 11.25	41,700	42,200	42,600	43,100	43,600	44,100	44,500	45,000	45,500	46,000	46,500
11.25 TO LESS THAN 11.50	42,000	42,500	43,000	43,500	44,000	44,500	45,000	45,500	46,000	46,500	47,000
11.50 TO LESS THAN 11.75	42,500	43,000	43,500	44,000	44,500	45,000	45,500	46,000	46,500	47,000	47,500
11.75 AND OVER	43,000	43,500	44,000	44,500	45,000	45,500	46,000	46,500	47,000	47,500	48,000

Tab. 1   Ont. Reg. 413/05 — Vehicle Weights and Dimensions

VEHICLE WEIGHT TABLE 9
ALLOWABLE GROSS WEIGHT ON A VEHICLE WITH SIX AXLES (KILOGRAMS)
INTER-VEHICLE-UNIT DISTANCE, LESS THAN 2.1 METRES
(OR INTRA-VEHICLE-UNIT DISTANCE)
FRONT AXLE WEIGHT, (KILOGRAMS)

BASE LENGTH, (METRES)	5 000 or Less	5 001 TO LESS THAN 5 500	5 500 TO LESS THAN 6 000	6 000 TO LESS THAN 6 500	6 500 TO LESS THAN 7 000	7 000 TO LESS THAN 7 500	7 500 TO LESS THAN 8 000	8 000 TO LESS THAN 8 500	8 500 TO LESS THAN 9 000	9 000 TO LESS THAN 9 500	9 500 TO AND INCL 10 000
LESS THAN 9.50	35,800	36,100	36,400	36,800	37,100	37,400	37,700	38,100	38,400	38,700	39,000
9.50 TO LESS THAN 9.75	36,400	36,700	37,000	37,300	37,600	38,000	38,300	38,600	38,900	39,300	39,600
9.75 TO LESS THAN 10.00	36,900	37,200	37,600	37,900	38,200	38,500	38,900	39,200	39,500	39,800	40,200
10.00 TO LESS THAN 10.25	37,500	37,800	38,100	38,400	38,800	39,100	39,400	39,700	40,100	40,400	40,800
10.25 TO LESS THAN 10.50	38,000	38,400	38,700	39,000	39,300	39,700	40,000	40,300	40,600	41,000	41,300
10.50 TO LESS THAN 10.75	38,600	38,900	39,200	39,600	39,900	40,200	40,500	40,900	41,200	41,500	41,800
10.75 TO LESS THAN 11.00	39,100	39,500	39,800	40,100	40,500	40,800	41,100	41,400	41,800	42,100	42,400
11.00 TO LESS THAN 11.25	39,700	40,000	40,400	40,700	41,000	41,300	41,700	42,000	42,300	42,700	43,000
11.25 TO LESS THAN 11.50	40,300	40,600	40,900	41,300	41,600	41,900	42,200	42,600	42,900	43,200	43,500
11.50 TO LESS THAN 11.75	40,800	41,200	41,500	41,800	42,100	42,500	42,800	43,100	43,500	43,800	44,100
11.75 TO LESS THAN 12.00	41,400	41,700	42,000	42,400	42,700	43,000	43,400	43,700	44,000	44,400	44,700
12.00 TO LESS THAN 12.25	41,900	42,300	42,600	42,900	43,300	43,600	43,900	44,300	44,600	44,900	45,300
12.25 TO LESS THAN 12.50	42,500	42,800	43,200	43,500	43,800	44,200	44,500	44,800	45,200	45,500	45,800
12.50 TO LESS THAN 12.75	43,100	43,400	43,700	44,100	44,400	44,700	45,100	45,400	45,700	46,000	46,400
12.75 TO LESS THAN 13.00	43,600	44,000	44,300	44,600	45,000	45,300	45,600	45,900	46,300	46,600	46,900
13.00 TO LESS THAN 13.25	44,200	44,500	44,800	45,200	45,500	45,800	46,200	46,500	46,800	47,200	47,500
13.25 TO LESS THAN 13.50	44,700	45,100	45,400	45,700	46,100	46,400	46,700	47,100	47,400	47,700	48,000
13.50 TO LESS THAN 13.75	45,300	45,600	46,000	46,300	46,600	47,000	47,300	47,600	48,000	48,300	48,600

1314

VEHICLE WEIGHT TABLE 9
ALLOWABLE GROSS WEIGHT ON A VEHICLE WITH SIX AXLES (KILOGRAMS)
INTER-VEHICLE-UNIT DISTANCE, LESS THAN 2.1 METRES
(OR INTRA-VEHICLE-UNIT DISTANCE)
FRONT AXLE WEIGHT, (KILOGRAMS)

BASE LENGTH, (METRES)	5 000 or Less	5 001 TO LESS THAN 5 500	5 500 TO LESS THAN 6 000	6 000 TO LESS THAN 6 500	6 500 TO LESS THAN 7 000	7 000 TO LESS THAN 7 500	7 500 TO LESS THAN 8 000	8 000 TO LESS THAN 8 500	8 500 TO LESS THAN 9 000	9 000 TO LESS THAN 9 500	9 500 TO AND INCL 10 000
13.75 TO LESS THAN 14.00	45,900	46,200	46,500	46,900	47,200	47,500	47,900	48,200	48,500	48,900	49,200
14.00 TO LESS THAN 14.25	46,400	46,800	47,100	47,400	47,800	48,100	48,400	48,800	49,100	49,400	49,700
14.25 TO LESS THAN 14.50	47,000	47,300	47,600	48,000	48,300	48,700	49,000	49,300	49,700	50,000	50,300
14.50 TO LESS THAN 14.75	47,500	47,900	48,200	48,500	48,900	49,200	49,600	49,900	50,200	50,600	50,900
14.75 TO LESS THAN 15.00	48,200	48,500	48,800	49,200	49,500	49,800	50,200	50,500	50,900	51,200	51,500
15.00 AND OVER	48,500	49,000	49,300	49,700	50,000	50,300	50,700	51,000	51,400	51,700	52,000

VEHICLE WEIGHT TABLE 10
ALLOWABLE GROSS WEIGHT ON A VEHICLE WITH SIX AXLES (KILOGRAMS)
INTER-VEHICLE-UNIT DISTANCE, 2.1 METRES TO LESS THAN 2.4 METRES
(OR INTRA-VEHICLE-UNIT DISTANCE)
FRONT AXLE WEIGHT, (KILOGRAMS)

BASE LENGTH, (METRES)	5 000 or Less	5 001 TO LESS THAN 5 500	5 500 TO LESS THAN 6 000	6 000 TO LESS THAN 6 500	6 500 TO LESS THAN 7 000	7 000 TO LESS THAN 7 500	7 500 TO LESS THAN 8 000	8 000 TO LESS THAN 8 500	8 500 TO LESS THAN 9 000	9 000 TO LESS THAN 9 500	9 500 TO AND INCL 10 000
LESS THAN 9.50	37,000	37,300	37,600	37,900	38,200	38,500	38,900	39,200	39,500	39,800	40,100
9.50 TO LESS THAN 9.75	37,500	37,800	38,100	38,500	38,800	39,100	39,400	39,700	40,000	40,400	40,700
9.75 TO LESS THAN 10.00	38,100	38,400	38,700	39,000	39,300	39,600	40,000	40,300	40,600	40,900	41,200
10.00 TO LESS THAN 10.25	38,600	38,900	39,200	39,600	39,900	40,200	40,500	40,800	41,200	41,500	41,800
10.25 TO LESS THAN 10.50	39,200	39,500	39,800	40,100	40,400	40,800	41,100	41,400	41,700	42,000	42,300
10.50 TO LESS THAN 10.75	39,700	40,000	40,400	40,700	41,000	41,300	41,600	41,900	42,300	42,600	42,900
10.75 TO LESS THAN 11.00	40,300	40,600	40,900	41,200	41,500	41,900	42,200	42,500	42,800	43,100	43,400

Tab. 1   Ont. Reg. 413/05 — Vehicle Weights and Dimensions

VEHICLE WEIGHT TABLE 10
ALLOWABLE GROSS WEIGHT ON A VEHICLE WITH SIX AXLES (KILOGRAMS)
INTER-VEHICLE-UNIT DISTANCE, 2.1 METRES TO LESS THAN 2.4 METRES
(OR INTRA-VEHICLE-UNIT DISTANCE)
FRONT AXLE WEIGHT, (KILOGRAMS)

BASE LENGTH, (METRES)	5 000 or Less	5 001 TO LESS THAN 5 500	5 500 TO LESS THAN 6 000	6 000 TO LESS THAN 6 500	6 500 TO LESS THAN 7 000	7 000 TO LESS THAN 7 500	7 500 TO LESS THAN 8 000	8 000 TO LESS THAN 8 500	8 500 TO LESS THAN 9 000	9 000 TO LESS THAN 9 500	9 500 AND INCL 10 000
11.00 TO LESS THAN 11.25	40,800	41,100	41,500	41,800	42,100	42,400	42,700	43,100	43,400	43,700	44,100
11.25 TO LESS THAN 11.50	41,400	41,700	42,000	42,300	42,600	43,000	43,300	43,600	43,900	44,300	44,600
11.50 TO LESS THAN 11.75	41,900	42,200	42,600	42,900	43,200	43,500	43,800	44,200	44,500	44,800	45,100
11.75 TO LESS THAN 12.00	42,500	42,800	43,100	43,400	43,800	44,100	44,400	44,700	45,000	45,400	45,700
12.00 TO LESS THAN 12.25	43,000	43,300	43,700	44,000	44,300	44,600	45,000	45,300	45,600	45,900	46,200
12.25 TO LESS THAN 12.50	43,600	43,900	44,200	44,500	44,900	45,200	45,500	45,800	46,200	46,500	46,800
12.50 TO LESS THAN 12.75	44,100	44,400	44,800	45,100	45,400	45,700	46,100	46,400	46,700	47,000	47,300
12.75 TO LESS THAN 13.00	44,700	45,000	45,300	45,600	46,000	46,300	46,600	46,900	47,300	47,600	47,900
13.00 TO LESS THAN 13.25	45,200	45,500	45,900	46,200	46,500	46,800	47,200	47,500	47,800	48,100	48,400
13.25 TO LESS THAN 13.50	45,800	46,100	46,400	46,700	47,100	47,400	47,700	48,100	48,400	48,700	49,000
13.50 TO LESS THAN 13.75	46,300	46,600	47,000	47,300	47,600	48,000	48,300	48,600	48,900	49,300	49,600
13.75 TO LESS THAN 14.00	46,900	47,200	47,500	47,900	48,200	48,500	48,800	49,200	49,500	49,800	50,200
14.00 TO LESS THAN 14.25	47,400	47,700	48,100	48,400	48,700	49,100	49,400	49,700	50,000	50,400	50,700
14.25 TO LESS THAN 14.50	48,000	48,300	48,600	49,000	49,300	49,600	49,900	50,300	50,600	50,900	51,300
14.50 TO LESS THAN 14.75	48,500	48,900	49,200	49,500	49,800	50,200	50,500	50,800	51,200	51,500	51,800
14.75 TO LESS THAN 15.00	49,100	49,400	49,700	50,100	50,400	50,700	51,100	51,400	51,700	52,000	52,400
15.00 AND OVER	49,400	49,900	50,300	50,700	51,000	51,300	51,600	52,000	52,300	52,600	53,000

VEHICLE WEIGHT TABLE 11
ALLOWABLE GROSS WEIGHT ON A VEHICLE WITH SIX AXLES (KILOGRAMS)
INTER-VEHICLE-UNIT DISTANCE, 2.4 METRES TO LESS THAN 2.7 METRES
(OR INTRA-VEHICLE-UNIT DISTANCE)
FRONT AXLE WEIGHT, (KILOGRAMS)

BASE LENGTH, (METRES)	5 000 or Less	5 001 TO LESS THAN 5 500	5 500 TO LESS THAN 6 000	6 000 TO LESS THAN 6 500	6 500 TO LESS THAN 7 000	7 000 TO LESS THAN 7 500	7 500 TO LESS THAN 8 000	8 000 TO LESS THAN 8 500	8 500 TO LESS THAN 9 000	9 000 TO LESS THAN 9 500	9 500 TO AND INCL 10 000
LESS THAN 9.50	37,900	38,200	38,500	38,700	39,000	39,300	39,600	39,900	40,200	40,500	40,700
9.50 TO LESS THAN 9.75	38,400	38,700	39,000	39,300	39,600	39,900	40,200	40,500	40,800	41,100	41,400
9.75 TO LESS THAN 10.00	39,000	39,300	39,600	39,900	40,100	40,400	40,700	41,000	41,300	41,600	41,900
10.00 TO LESS THAN 10.25	39,500	39,800	40,100	40,400	40,700	41,000	41,300	41,600	41,900	42,200	42,500
10.25 TO LESS THAN 10.50	40,100	40,400	40,700	41,000	41,300	41,600	41,900	42,200	42,500	42,800	43,100
10.50 TO LESS THAN 10.75	40,600	40,900	41,200	41,500	41,800	42,100	42,400	42,700	43,000	43,300	43,600
10.75 TO LESS THAN 11.00	41,200	41,500	41,800	42,100	42,400	42,700	43,000	43,300	43,600	43,900	44,200
11.00 TO LESS THAN 11.25	41,700	42,000	42,300	42,600	42,900	43,200	43,500	43,800	44,200	44,500	44,800
11.25 TO LESS THAN 11.50	42,200	42,600	42,900	43,200	43,500	43,800	44,100	44,400	44,700	45,000	45,300
11.50 TO LESS THAN 11.75	42,800	43,100	43,400	43,700	44,000	44,300	44,700	45,000	45,300	45,600	45,900
11.75 TO LESS THAN 12.00	43,300	43,700	44,000	44,300	44,600	44,900	45,200	45,500	45,800	46,200	46,500
12.00 TO LESS THAN 12.25	43,900	44,200	44,500	44,800	45,100	45,500	45,800	46,100	46,400	46,700	47,100
12.25 TO LESS THAN 12.50	44,400	44,800	45,100	45,400	45,700	46,000	46,300	46,600	47,000	47,300	47,600
12.50 TO LESS THAN 12.75	45,000	45,300	45,600	45,900	46,300	46,600	46,900	47,200	47,500	47,800	48,100
12.75 TO LESS THAN 13.00	45,500	45,800	46,200	46,500	46,800	47,100	47,500	47,800	48,100	48,400	48,700
13.00 TO LESS THAN 13.25	46,100	46,400	46,700	47,000	47,400	47,700	48,000	48,300	48,700	49,000	49,400
13.25 TO LESS THAN 13.50	46,600	46,900	47,300	47,600	47,900	48,200	48,600	48,900	49,200	49,500	49,800
13.50 TO LESS THAN 13.75	47,200	47,500	47,800	48,200	48,500	48,800	49,100	49,500	49,800	50,100	50,500

Tab. 1   Ont. Reg. 413/05 — Vehicle Weights and Dimensions

VEHICLE WEIGHT TABLE 11
ALLOWABLE GROSS WEIGHT ON A VEHICLE WITH SIX AXLES (KILOGRAMS)
INTER-VEHICLE-UNIT DISTANCE, 2.4 METRES TO LESS THAN 2.7 METRES
(OR INTRA-VEHICLE-UNIT DISTANCE)
FRONT AXLE WEIGHT, (KILOGRAMS)

BASE LENGTH, (METRES)	5 000 or Less	5 001 TO LESS THAN 5 500	5 500 TO LESS THAN 6 000	6 000 TO LESS THAN 6 500	6 500 TO LESS THAN 7 000	7 000 TO LESS THAN 7 500	7 500 TO LESS THAN 8 000	8 000 TO LESS THAN 8 500	8 500 TO LESS THAN 9 000	9 000 TO LESS THAN 9 500	9 500 TO AND INCL 10 000
13.75 TO LESS THAN 14.00	47,700	48,000	48,400	48,700	49,000	49,400	49,700	50,000	50,300	50,700	51,000
14.00 TO LESS THAN 14.25	48,300	48,600	48,900	49,300	49,600	49,900	50,200	50,600	50,900	51,200	51,600
14.25 TO LESS THAN 14.50	48,800	49,100	49,500	49,800	50,100	50,500	50,800	51,100	51,500	51,800	52,100
14.50 TO LESS THAN 14.75	49,400	49,700	50,000	50,400	50,700	51,000	51,400	51,700	52,000	52,400	52,700
14.75 TO LESS THAN 15.00	49,900	50,200	50,600	50,900	51,300	51,600	51,900	52,300	52,600	52,900	53,300
15.00 AND OVER	50,300	50,800	51,200	51,500	51,800	52,200	52,500	52,800	53,200	53,500	53,800

VEHICLE WEIGHT TABLE 12
ALLOWABLE GROSS WEIGHT ON A VEHICLE WITH SIX AXLES (KILOGRAMS)
INTER-VEHICLE-UNIT DISTANCE, 2.7 METRES TO LESS THAN 3.0 METRES
(OR INTRA-VEHICLE-UNIT DISTANCE)
FRONT AXLE WEIGHT, (KILOGRAMS)

BASE LENGTH, (METRES)	5 000 or Less	5 001 TO LESS THAN 5 500	5 500 TO LESS THAN 6 000	6 000 TO LESS THAN 6 500	6 500 TO LESS THAN 7 000	7 000 TO LESS THAN 7 500	7 500 TO LESS THAN 8 000	8 000 TO LESS THAN 8 500	8 500 TO LESS THAN 9 000	9 000 TO LESS THAN 9 500	9 500 TO AND INCL 10 000
LESS THAN 9.50	38,500	38,800	39,100	39,400	39,700	40,000	40,200	40,500	40,800	41,100	41,400
9.50 TO LESS THAN 9.75	39,100	39,400	39,700	39,900	40,200	40,500	40,800	41,100	41,400	41,700	41,900
9.75 TO LESS THAN 10.00	39,600	39,900	40,200	40,500	40,800	41,100	41,400	41,700	42,000	42,200	42,500
10.00 TO LESS THAN 10.25	40,200	40,500	40,800	41,100	41,400	41,600	41,900	42,200	42,500	42,800	43,100
10.25 TO LESS THAN 10.50	40,700	41,000	41,300	41,600	41,900	42,200	42,500	42,800	43,100	43,400	43,700
10.50 TO LESS THAN 10.75	41,300	41,600	41,900	42,200	42,500	42,800	43,100	43,400	43,700	43,900	44,200
10.75 TO LESS THAN 11.00	41,800	42,100	42,400	42,700	43,000	43,300	43,600	43,900	44,200	44,500	44,800

VEHICLE WEIGHT TABLE 12
ALLOWABLE GROSS WEIGHT ON A VEHICLE WITH SIX AXLES (KILOGRAMS)
INTER-VEHICLE-UNIT DISTANCE, 2.7 METRES TO LESS THAN 3.0 METRES
(OR INTRA-VEHICLE-UNIT DISTANCE)
FRONT AXLE WEIGHT, (KILOGRAMS)

BASE LENGTH, (METRES)	5 000 or Less	5 001 TO LESS THAN 5 500	5 500 TO LESS THAN 6 000	6 000 TO LESS THAN 6 500	6 500 TO LESS THAN 7 000	7 000 TO LESS THAN 7 500	7 500 TO LESS THAN 8 000	8 000 TO LESS THAN 8 500	8 500 TO LESS THAN 9 000	9 000 TO LESS THAN 9 500	9 500 TO AND INCL 10 000
11.00 TO LESS THAN 11.25	42,400	42,700	43,000	43,300	43,600	43,900	44,200	44,500	44,800	45,100	45,400
11.25 TO LESS THAN 11.50	43,000	43,300	43,600	43,900	44,200	44,500	44,800	45,100	45,400	45,700	46,000
11.50 TO LESS THAN 11.75	43,500	43,800	44,100	44,400	44,700	45,000	45,300	45,600	45,900	46,200	46,500
11.75 TO LESS THAN 12.00	44,100	44,400	44,700	45,000	45,300	45,600	45,900	46,200	46,500	46,800	47,100
12.00 TO LESS THAN 12.25	44,600	44,900	45,200	45,500	45,800	46,100	46,400	46,800	47,100	47,400	47,800
12.25 TO LESS THAN 12.50	45,200	45,500	45,800	46,100	46,400	46,700	47,000	47,300	47,600	47,900	48,200
12.50 TO LESS THAN 12.75	45,700	46,000	46,300	46,600	47,000	47,300	47,600	47,900	48,200	48,500	48,800
12.75 TO LESS THAN 13.00	46,300	46,600	46,900	47,200	47,500	47,800	48,100	48,400	48,800	49,100	49,400
13.00 TO LESS THAN 13.25	46,800	47,100	47,400	47,800	48,100	48,400	48,700	49,000	49,300	49,600	49,900
13.25 TO LESS THAN 13.50	47,400	47,700	48,000	48,300	48,600	48,900	49,300	49,600	49,900	50,200	50,500
13.50 TO LESS THAN 13.75	47,900	48,200	48,600	48,900	49,200	49,500	49,800	50,100	50,500	50,800	51,100
13.75 TO LESS THAN 14.00	48,500	48,800	49,100	49,400	49,700	50,100	50,400	50,700	51,000	51,400	51,700
14.00 TO LESS THAN 14.25	49,000	49,300	49,700	50,000	50,300	50,600	51,000	51,300	51,600	51,900	52,300
14.25 TO LESS THAN 14.50	49,600	49,900	50,200	50,500	50,900	51,200	51,500	51,800	52,200	52,500	52,800
14.50 TO LESS THAN 14.75	50,100	50,400	50,800	51,100	51,400	51,800	52,100	52,400	52,700	53,100	53,400
14.75 TO LESS THAN 15.00	50,700	51,000	51,300	51,700	52,000	52,300	52,600	53,000	53,300	53,600	54,000
15.00 AND OVER	51,200	51,500	51,800	52,200	52,500	52,800	53,200	53,500	53,900	54,200	54,500

Tab. 1   Ont. Reg. 413/05 — Vehicle Weights and Dimensions

VEHICLE WEIGHT TABLE 13
ALLOWABLE GROSS WEIGHT ON A VEHICLE WITH SIX AXLES (KILOGRAMS)
INTER-VEHICLE-UNIT DISTANCE, 3.0 METRES TO LESS THAN 3.3 METRES
(OR INTRA-VEHICLE-UNIT DISTANCE)
FRONT AXLE WEIGHT, (KILOGRAMS)

BASE LENGTH, (METRES)	5 000 or Less	5 001 TO LESS THAN 5 500	5 500 TO LESS THAN 6 000	6 000 TO LESS THAN 6 500	6 500 TO LESS THAN 7 000	7 000 TO LESS THAN 7 500	7 500 TO LESS THAN 8 000	8 000 TO LESS THAN 8 500	8 500 TO LESS THAN 9 000	9 000 TO LESS THAN 9 500	9 500 TO AND INCL 10 000
LESS THAN 9.50	39,200	39,500	39,700	40,000	40,300	40,600	40,900	41,200	41,500	41,800	42,100
9.50 TO LESS THAN 9.75	39,700	40,000	40,300	40,600	40,900	41,200	41,500	41,800	42,100	42,400	42,700
9.75 TO LESS THAN 10.00	40,300	40,600	40,800	41,100	41,400	41,700	42,000	42,300	42,600	42,900	43,200
10.00 TO LESS THAN 10.25	40,800	41,100	41,400	41,700	42,000	42,300	42,600	42,900	43,200	43,500	43,800
10.25 TO LESS THAN 10.50	41,400	41,700	41,900	42,200	42,500	42,800	43,200	43,500	43,800	44,100	44,400
10.50 TO LESS THAN 10.75	41,900	42,200	42,500	42,800	43,100	43,400	43,700	44,000	44,300	44,600	44,900
10.75 TO LESS THAN 11.00	42,400	42,800	43,000	43,300	43,700	44,000	44,300	44,600	44,900	45,200	45,500
11.00 TO LESS THAN 11.25	43,000	43,300	43,600	43,900	44,200	44,500	44,900	45,200	45,500	45,800	46,100
11.25 TO LESS THAN 11.50	43,500	43,900	44,200	44,500	44,800	45,100	45,400	45,700	46,000	46,300	46,600
11.50 TO LESS THAN 11.75	44,100	44,400	44,700	45,000	45,300	45,600	46,000	46,300	46,600	46,900	47,200
11.75 TO LESS THAN 12.00	44,600	45,000	45,300	45,600	45,900	46,200	46,600	46,900	47,200	47,500	47,800
12.00 TO LESS THAN 12.25	45,200	45,500	45,800	46,100	46,500	46,800	47,100	47,400	47,800	48,100	48,400
12.25 TO LESS THAN 12.50	45,700	46,100	46,400	46,700	47,000	47,300	47,700	48,000	48,300	48,600	48,900
12.50 TO LESS THAN 12.75	46,300	46,600	46,900	47,200	47,600	47,900	48,300	48,600	48,900	49,200	49,500
12.75 TO LESS THAN 13.00	46,800	47,200	47,500	47,800	48,100	48,400	48,800	49,100	49,500	49,800	50,100
13.00 TO LESS THAN 13.25	47,400	47,700	48,100	48,400	48,700	49,000	49,400	49,700	50,000	50,300	50,600
13.25 TO LESS THAN 13.50	47,900	48,300	48,600	48,900	49,300	49,600	50,000	50,300	50,600	50,900	51,200
13.50 TO LESS THAN 13.75	48,500	48,800	49,200	49,500	49,800	50,100	50,500	50,800	51,100	51,400	51,700

VEHICLE WEIGHT TABLE 13
ALLOWABLE GROSS WEIGHT ON A VEHICLE WITH SIX AXLES (KILOGRAMS)
INTER-VEHICLE-UNIT DISTANCE, 3.0 METRES TO LESS THAN 3.3 METRES
(OR INTRA-VEHICLE-UNIT DISTANCE)
FRONT AXLE WEIGHT, (KILOGRAMS)

BASE LENGTH, (METRES)	5 000 or Less	5 001 TO LESS THAN 5 500	5 500 TO LESS THAN 6 000	6 000 TO LESS THAN 6 500	6 500 TO LESS THAN 7 000	7 000 TO LESS THAN 7 500	7 500 TO LESS THAN 8 000	8 000 TO LESS THAN 8 500	8 500 TO LESS THAN 9 000	9 000 TO LESS THAN 9 500	9 500 TO AND INCL 10 000
13.75 TO LESS THAN 14.00	49,000	49,400	49,700	50,000	50,400	50,700	51,100	51,400	51,700	52,000	52,300
14.00 TO LESS THAN 14.25	49,600	49,900	50,300	50,600	50,900	51,200	51,700	52,000	52,300	52,600	52,900
14.25 TO LESS THAN 14.50	50,100	50,500	50,800	51,100	51,500	51,800	52,200	52,500	52,900	53,200	53,500
14.50 TO LESS THAN 14.75	50,700	51,000	51,400	51,700	52,100	52,400	52,800	53,100	53,500	53,800	54,100
14.75 TO LESS THAN 15.00	51,200	51,600	52,000	52,300	52,600	52,900	53,400	53,700	54,100	54,400	54,700
15.00 AND OVER	51,700	52,100	52,500	52,800	53,200	53,500	53,900	54,200	54,600	54,900	55,200

VEHICLE WEIGHT TABLE 14
ALLOWABLE GROSS WEIGHT ON A VEHICLE WITH SIX AXLES (KILOGRAMS)
INTER-VEHICLE-UNIT DISTANCE, 3.3 METRES TO LESS THAN 3.6 METRES
(OR INTRA-VEHICLE-UNIT DISTANCE)
FRONT AXLE WEIGHT, (KILOGRAMS)

BASE LENGTH, (METRES)	5 000 or Less	5 001 TO LESS THAN 5 500	5 500 TO LESS THAN 6 000	6 000 TO LESS THAN 6 500	6 500 TO LESS THAN 7 000	7 000 TO LESS THAN 7 500	7 500 TO LESS THAN 8 000	8 000 TO LESS THAN 8 500	8 500 TO LESS THAN 9 000	9 000 TO LESS THAN 9 500	9 500 TO AND INCL 10 000
LESS THAN 9.50	39,800	40,100	40,400	40,600	40,900	41,200	41,500	41,700	42,000	42,300	42,600
9.50 TO LESS THAN 9.75	40,400	40,600	40,900	41,200	41,500	41,800	42,000	42,300	42,600	42,900	43,200
9.75 TO LESS THAN 10.00	40,900	41,200	41,500	41,800	42,000	42,300	42,600	42,900	43,200	43,400	43,700
10.00 TO LESS THAN 10.25	41,500	41,800	42,000	42,300	42,600	42,900	43,200	43,500	43,700	44,000	44,300
10.25 TO LESS THAN 10.50	42,000	42,300	42,600	42,900	43,200	43,500	43,700	44,000	44,300	44,600	44,900
10.50 TO LESS THAN 10.75	42,600	42,900	43,100	43,400	43,700	44,000	44,300	44,600	44,900	45,200	45,500
10.75 TO LESS THAN 11.00	43,100	43,400	43,700	44,000	44,300	44,600	44,900	45,200	45,500	45,700	46,000

Tab. 1   Ont. Reg. 413/05 — Vehicle Weights and Dimensions

VEHICLE WEIGHT TABLE 14
ALLOWABLE GROSS WEIGHT ON A VEHICLE WITH SIX AXLES (KILOGRAMS)
INTER-VEHICLE-UNIT DISTANCE, 3.3 METRES TO LESS THAN 3.6 METRES
(OR INTRA-VEHICLE-UNIT DISTANCE)
FRONT AXLE WEIGHT, (KILOGRAMS)

BASE LENGTH, (METRES)	5 000 or Less	5 001 TO LESS THAN 5 500	5 500 TO LESS THAN 6 000	6 000 TO LESS THAN 6 500	6 500 TO LESS THAN 7 000	7 000 TO LESS THAN 7 500	7 500 TO LESS THAN 8 000	8 000 TO LESS THAN 8 500	8 500 TO LESS THAN 9 000	9 000 TO LESS THAN 9 500	9 500 AND INCL 10 000
11.00 TO LESS THAN 11.25	43,700	44,000	44,300	44,600	44,900	45,100	45,400	45,700	46,000	46,300	46,600
11.25 TO LESS THAN 11.50	44,200	44,500	44,800	45,100	45,400	45,700	46,000	46,300	46,600	46,900	47,200
11.50 TO LESS THAN 11.75	44,800	45,100	45,400	45,700	46,000	46,300	46,600	46,900	47,200	47,500	47,800
11.75 TO LESS THAN 12.00	45,300	45,600	45,900	46,200	46,500	46,800	47,100	47,400	47,700	48,000	48,300
12.00 TO LESS THAN 12.25	45,900	46,200	46,500	46,800	47,100	47,400	47,700	48,000	48,300	48,600	48,900
12.25 TO LESS THAN 12.50	46,400	46,700	47,100	47,400	47,700	48,000	48,300	48,600	48,900	49,200	49,500
12.50 TO LESS THAN 12.75	47,000	47,300	47,600	47,900	48,200	48,500	48,800	49,100	49,500	49,800	50,100
12.75 TO LESS THAN 13.00	47,500	47,900	48,200	48,500	48,800	49,100	49,400	49,700	50,000	50,300	50,600
13.00 TO LESS THAN 13.25	48,100	48,400	48,700	49,000	49,300	49,700	50,000	50,300	50,600	50,900	51,200
13.25 TO LESS THAN 13.50	48,700	49,000	49,300	49,600	49,900	50,200	50,500	50,900	51,200	51,500	51,900
13.50 TO LESS THAN 13.75	49,200	49,500	49,800	50,200	50,500	50,800	51,100	51,400	51,700	52,100	52,400
13.75 TO LESS THAN 14.00	49,800	50,100	50,400	50,700	51,000	51,400	51,700	52,000	52,300	52,600	52,900
14.00 TO LESS THAN 14.25	50,300	50,600	51,000	51,300	51,600	51,900	52,200	52,600	52,900	53,200	53,600
14.25 TO LESS THAN 14.50	50,900	51,200	51,500	51,800	52,200	52,500	52,800	53,100	53,500	53,800	54,200
14.50 TO LESS THAN 14.75	51,400	51,700	52,100	52,400	52,700	53,000	53,400	53,700	54,000	54,400	54,700
14.75 TO LESS THAN 15.00	52,000	52,300	52,600	53,000	53,300	53,600	53,900	54,300	54,600	54,900	55,300
15.00 AND OVER	52,000	52,500	53,000	53,300	53,600	54,000	54,300	54,600	55,000	55,300	55,600

VEHICLE WEIGHT TABLE 15
ALLOWABLE GROSS WEIGHT ON A VEHICLE WITH SIX AXLES (KILOGRAMS)
INTER-VEHICLE-UNIT DISTANCE, 3.6 METRES OR MORE
(OR INTRA-VEHICLE-UNIT DISTANCE)
FRONT AXLE WEIGHT, (KILOGRAMS)

BASE LENGTH, (METRES)	5 000 or Less	5 001 TO LESS THAN 5 500	5 500 TO LESS THAN 6 000	6 000 TO LESS THAN 6 500	6 500 TO LESS THAN 7 000	7 000 TO LESS THAN 7 500	7 500 TO LESS THAN 8 000	8 000 TO LESS THAN 8 500	8 500 TO LESS THAN 9 000	9 000 TO LESS THAN 9 500	9 500 TO AND INCL 10 000
LESS THAN 9.50	40,400	40,700	40,900	41,200	41,400	41,700	41,900	42,200	42,400	42,700	42,900
9.50 TO LESS THAN 9.75	41,000	41,200	41,500	41,700	42,000	42,300	42,500	42,800	43,000	43,300	43,500
9.75 TO LESS THAN 10.00	41,500	41,800	42,000	42,300	42,600	42,800	43,100	43,300	43,600	43,900	44,100
10.00 TO LESS THAN 10.25	42,100	42,300	42,600	42,900	43,100	43,400	43,700	43,900	44,200	44,400	44,700
10.25 TO LESS THAN 10.50	42,600	42,900	43,200	43,400	43,700	44,000	44,200	44,500	44,800	45,000	45,300
10.50 TO LESS THAN 10.75	43,200	43,400	43,700	44,000	44,300	44,500	44,800	45,100	45,300	45,600	45,900
10.75 TO LESS THAN 11.00	43,700	44,000	44,300	44,600	44,800	45,100	45,400	45,600	45,900	46,200	46,500
11.00 TO LESS THAN 11.25	44,300	44,600	44,800	45,100	45,400	45,700	45,900	46,200	46,500	46,800	47,100
11.25 TO LESS THAN 11.50	44,800	45,100	45,400	45,700	46,000	46,200	46,500	46,800	47,100	47,400	47,700
11.50 TO LESS THAN 11.75	45,400	45,700	46,000	46,200	46,500	46,800	47,100	47,400	47,700	47,900	48,200
11.75 TO LESS THAN 12.00	45,900	46,200	46,500	46,800	47,100	47,400	47,700	48,000	48,200	48,500	48,800
12.00 TO LESS THAN 12.25	46,500	46,800	47,100	47,400	47,700	47,900	48,200	48,500	48,800	49,100	49,400
12.25 TO LESS THAN 12.50	47,000	47,300	47,600	47,900	48,200	48,500	48,800	49,100	49,400	49,700	50,000
12.50 TO LESS THAN 12.75	47,600	47,900	48,200	48,500	48,800	49,100	49,400	49,700	50,000	50,300	50,600
12.75 TO LESS THAN 13.00	48,200	48,500	48,800	49,100	49,400	49,700	50,000	50,300	50,600	50,900	51,200
13.00 TO LESS THAN 13.25	48,700	49,000	49,300	49,600	49,900	50,200	50,500	50,800	51,100	51,400	51,700
13.25 TO LESS THAN 13.50	49,300	49,600	49,900	50,200	50,500	50,800	51,100	51,400	51,700	52,000	52,300
13.50 TO LESS THAN 13.75	49,800	50,100	50,400	50,700	51,100	51,400	51,700	52,000	52,300	52,600	52,900

Tab. 1   Ont. Reg. 413/05 — Vehicle Weights and Dimensions

VEHICLE WEIGHT TABLE 15
ALLOWABLE GROSS WEIGHT ON A VEHICLE WITH SIX AXLES (KILOGRAMS)
INTER-VEHICLE-UNIT DISTANCE, 3.6 METRES OR MORE
(OR INTRA-VEHICLE-UNIT DISTANCE)
FRONT AXLE WEIGHT, (KILOGRAMS)

BASE LENGTH, (METRES)	5 000 or Less	5 001 TO LESS THAN 5 500	5 500 TO LESS THAN 6 000	6 000 TO LESS THAN 6 500	6 500 TO LESS THAN 7 000	7 000 TO LESS THAN 7 500	7 500 TO LESS THAN 8 000	8 000 TO LESS THAN 8 500	8 500 TO LESS THAN 9 000	9 000 TO LESS THAN 9 500	9 500 TO AND INCL 10 000
13.75 TO LESS THAN 14.00	50,400	50,700	51,000	51,300	51,600	51,900	52,200	52,600	52,900	53,200	53,600
14.00 TO LESS THAN 14.25	50,900	51,200	51,500	51,900	52,200	52,500	52,800	53,100	53,500	53,800	54,100
14.25 TO LESS THAN 14.50	51,500	51,800	52,100	52,400	52,700	53,100	53,400	53,700	54,000	54,400	54,700
14.50 TO LESS THAN 14.75	52,000	52,300	52,700	53,000	53,300	53,600	54,000	54,300	54,600	54,900	55,300
14.75 TO LESS THAN 15.00	52,000	52,500	53,000	53,500	53,900	54,200	54,500	54,900	55,200	55,500	55,800
15.00 AND OVER	52,000	52,500	53,000	53,500	54,000	54,500	55,000	55,300	55,600	56,000	56,300

VEHICLE WEIGHT TABLE 16
ALLOWABLE GROSS WEIGHT ON A VEHICLE WITH SEVEN AXLES (KILOGRAMS)
INTER-VEHICLE-UNIT DISTANCE, LESS THAN 2.1 METRES
FRONT AXLE WEIGHT, (KILOGRAMS)

BASE LENGTH, (METRES)	5 000 or Less	5 001 TO LESS THAN 5 500	5 500 TO LESS THAN 6 000	6 000 TO LESS THAN 6 500	6 500 TO LESS THAN 7 000	7 000 TO LESS THAN 7 500	7 500 TO LESS THAN 8 000	8 000 TO LESS THAN 8 500	8 500 TO LESS THAN 9 000	9 000 TO LESS THAN 9 500	9 500 TO AND INCL 10 000
LESS THAN 13.50	45,500	46,000	46,500	47,000	47,500	48,000	48,400	48,900	49,400	49,900	50,400
13.50 TO LESS THAN 13.75	46,000	46,400	46,900	47,400	47,900	48,400	48,800	49,300	49,800	50,300	50,800
13.75 TO LESS THAN 14.00	46,400	46,900	47,300	47,800	48,300	48,800	49,200	49,700	50,200	50,700	51,200
14.00 TO LESS THAN 14.25	46,900	47,300	47,800	48,200	48,700	49,200	49,600	50,100	50,600	51,000	51,500
14.25 TO LESS THAN 14.50	47,400	47,800	48,200	48,600	49,100	49,600	50,000	50,500	51,000	51,400	51,900
14.50 TO LESS THAN 14.75	47,800	48,200	48,600	49,100	49,500	50,000	50,400	50,900	51,300	51,800	52,200
14.75 TO LESS THAN 15.00	48,300	48,600	49,000	49,500	49,900	50,400	50,800	51,300	51,700	52,200	52,600

VEHICLE WEIGHT TABLE 16
ALLOWABLE GROSS WEIGHT ON A VEHICLE WITH SEVEN AXLES (KILOGRAMS)
INTER-VEHICLE-UNIT DISTANCE, LESS THAN 2.1 METRES
FRONT AXLE WEIGHT, (KILOGRAMS)

BASE LENGTH, (METRES)	5 000 or Less	5 001 TO LESS THAN 5 500	5 500 TO LESS THAN 6 000	6 000 TO LESS THAN 6 500	6 500 TO LESS THAN 7 000	7 000 TO LESS THAN 7 500	7 500 TO LESS THAN 8 000	8 000 TO LESS THAN 8 500	8 500 TO LESS THAN 9 000	9 000 TO LESS THAN 9 500	9 500 TO AND INCL 10 000
15.00 TO LESS THAN 15.25	48,700	49,100	49,400	49,900	50,300	50,800	51,200	51,700	52,100	52,600	53,000
15.25 TO LESS THAN 15.50	49,200	49,500	49,900	50,300	50,700	51,200	51,600	52,100	52,500	52,900	53,300
15.50 TO LESS THAN 15.75	49,700	50,000	50,300	50,700	51,100	51,600	52,000	52,500	52,900	53,300	53,700
15.75 TO LESS THAN 16.00	50,100	50,400	50,700	51,100	51,600	52,000	52,400	52,800	53,300	53,700	54,100
16.00 TO LESS THAN 16.25	50,600	50,800	51,100	51,600	52,000	52,400	52,800	53,300	53,700	54,100	54,600
16.25 TO LESS THAN 16.50	51,000	51,300	51,600	52,000	52,400	52,800	53,200	53,700	54,100	54,500	55,000
16.50 TO LESS THAN 16.75	51,400	51,700	52,000	52,400	52,800	53,200	53,700	54,100	54,500	54,900	55,400
16.75 TO LESS THAN 17.00	51,800	52,100	52,400	52,800	53,200	53,700	54,100	54,500	54,900	55,300	55,800
17.00 TO LESS THAN 17.25	52,200	52,500	52,800	53,300	53,700	54,100	54,500	54,900	55,300	55,700	56,200
17.25 TO LESS THAN 17.50	52,700	53,000	53,300	53,700	54,100	54,500	54,900	55,300	55,700	56,200	56,600
17.50 TO LESS THAN 17.75	53,100	53,400	53,700	54,100	54,500	54,900	55,300	55,700	56,200	56,600	57,000
17.75 TO LESS THAN 18.00	53,500	53,800	54,100	54,500	54,900	55,300	55,700	56,200	56,600	57,000	57,400
18.00 TO LESS THAN 18.25	53,900	54,200	54,500	55,000	55,400	55,800	56,200	56,600	57,000	57,400	57,800
18.25 TO LESS THAN 18.50	54,300	54,700	55,000	55,400	55,800	56,200	56,600	57,000	57,400	57,800	58,200
18.50 TO LESS THAN 18.75	54,800	55,100	55,400	55,800	56,200	56,600	57,000	57,400	57,800	58,200	58,600
18.75 TO LESS THAN 19.00	55,200	55,500	55,900	56,200	56,600	57,000	57,400	57,800	58,200	58,600	59,000
19.00 TO LESS THAN 19.25	55,600	55,900	56,300	56,600	57,000	57,400	57,800	58,200	58,600	59,000	59,400
19.25 AND OVER	56,000	56,300	56,700	57,000	57,400	57,800	58,200	58,600	59,000	59,400	59,800

Tab. 1 Ont. Reg. 413/05 — Vehicle Weights and Dimensions

VEHICLE WEIGHT TABLE 17
ALLOWABLE GROSS WEIGHT ON A VEHICLE WITH SEVEN AXLES (KILOGRAMS)
INTER-VEHICLE-UNIT DISTANCE, 2.1 METRES TO LESS THAN 2.4 METRES
FRONT AXLE WEIGHT, (KILOGRAMS)

BASE LENGTH, (METRES)	5 000 or Less	5 001 TO LESS THAN 5 500	5 500 TO LESS THAN 6 000	6 000 TO LESS THAN 6 500	6 500 TO LESS THAN 7 000	7 000 TO LESS THAN 7 500	7 500 TO LESS THAN 8 000	8 000 TO LESS THAN 8 500	8 500 TO LESS THAN 9 000	9 000 TO LESS THAN 9 500	9 500 TO AND INCL 10 000
LESS THAN 13.50	46,500	47,000	47,500	47,900	48,400	48,800	49,200	49,600	50,100	50,500	50,900
13.50 TO LESS THAN 13.75	46,900	47,400	47,900	48,300	48,800	49,200	49,600	50,100	50,500	50,900	51,300
13.75 TO LESS THAN 14.00	47,300	47,800	48,300	48,700	49,200	49,600	50,000	50,500	50,900	51,300	51,700
14.00 TO LESS THAN 14.25	47,800	48,200	48,700	49,200	49,600	50,000	50,400	50,900	51,300	51,700	52,100
14.25 TO LESS THAN 14.50	48,200	48,700	49,100	49,600	50,000	50,400	50,900	51,300	51,700	52,100	52,500
14.50 TO LESS THAN 14.75	48,600	49,100	49,500	50,000	50,400	50,800	51,300	51,700	52,100	52,500	53,000
14.75 TO LESS THAN 15.00	49,100	49,500	50,000	50,400	50,800	51,200	51,700	52,100	52,500	53,000	53,400
15.00 TO LESS THAN 15.25	49,500	49,900	50,400	50,800	51,200	51,700	52,100	52,500	52,900	53,400	53,800
15.25 TO LESS THAN 15.50	49,900	50,400	50,800	51,200	51,600	52,100	52,500	52,900	53,400	53,800	54,200
15.50 TO LESS THAN 15.75	50,400	50,800	51,200	51,600	52,000	52,500	52,900	53,300	53,800	54,200	54,600
15.75 TO LESS THAN 16.00	50,800	51,200	51,600	52,000	52,500	52,900	53,300	53,700	54,200	54,600	55,000
16.00 TO LESS THAN 16.25	51,300	51,700	52,100	52,500	52,900	53,300	53,700	54,200	54,600	55,000	55,400
16.25 TO LESS THAN 16.50	51,700	52,100	52,500	52,900	53,300	53,800	54,200	54,600	55,000	55,400	55,900
16.50 TO LESS THAN 16.75	52,200	52,600	53,000	53,400	53,800	54,200	54,600	55,000	55,400	55,800	56,300
16.75 TO LESS THAN 17.00	52,600	53,000	53,400	53,800	54,200	54,600	55,000	55,400	55,800	56,200	56,700
17.00 TO LESS THAN 17.25	53,100	53,500	53,900	54,300	54,700	55,100	55,500	55,900	56,200	56,600	57,100
17.25 TO LESS THAN 17.50	53,600	53,900	54,300	54,700	55,100	55,500	55,900	56,300	56,700	57,100	57,500
17.50 TO LESS THAN 17.75	54,000	54,400	54,800	55,200	55,500	55,900	56,300	56,700	57,100	57,500	57,900

VEHICLE WEIGHT TABLE 17
ALLOWABLE GROSS WEIGHT ON A VEHICLE WITH SEVEN AXLES (KILOGRAMS)
INTER-VEHICLE-UNIT DISTANCE, 2.1 METRES TO LESS THAN 2.4 METRES
FRONT AXLE WEIGHT, (KILOGRAMS)

BASE LENGTH, (METRES)	5 000 or Less	5 001 TO LESS THAN 5 500	5 500 TO LESS THAN 6 000	6 000 TO LESS THAN 6 500	6 500 TO LESS THAN 7 000	7 000 TO LESS THAN 7 500	7 500 TO LESS THAN 8 000	8 000 TO LESS THAN 8 500	8 500 TO LESS THAN 9 000	9 000 TO LESS THAN 9 500	9 500 TO AND INCL 10 000
17.75 TO LESS THAN 18.00	54,500	54,900	55,200	55,600	56,000	56,400	56,700	57,100	57,500	57,900	58,300
18.00 TO LESS THAN 18.25	54,900	55,300	55,700	56,100	56,400	56,800	57,200	57,500	57,900	58,300	58,700
18.25 TO LESS THAN 18.50	55,400	55,800	56,100	56,500	56,900	57,200	57,600	58,000	58,300	58,700	59,100
18.50 TO LESS THAN 18.75	55,900	56,200	56,600	57,000	57,300	57,700	58,000	58,400	58,700	59,100	59,400
18.75 TO LESS THAN 19.00	56,400	56,700	57,000	57,400	57,700	58,100	58,400	58,800	59,100	59,500	59,900
19.00 TO LESS THAN 19.25	56,900	57,200	57,500	57,800	58,200	58,500	58,800	59,200	59,500	59,900	60,300
19.25 AND OVER	57,300	57,600	57,900	58,200	58,600	58,900	59,200	59,600	59,900	60,300	60,700

VEHICLE WEIGHT TABLE 18
ALLOWABLE GROSS WEIGHT ON A VEHICLE WITH SEVEN AXLES (KILOGRAMS)
INTER-VEHICLE-UNIT DISTANCE, 2.4 METRES TO LESS THAN 2.7 METRES
FRONT AXLE WEIGHT, (KILOGRAMS)

BASE LENGTH, (METRES)	5 000 or Less	5 001 TO LESS THAN 5 500	5 500 TO LESS THAN 6 000	6 000 TO LESS THAN 6 500	6 500 TO LESS THAN 7 000	7 000 TO LESS THAN 7 500	7 500 TO LESS THAN 8 000	8 000 TO LESS THAN 8 500	8 500 TO LESS THAN 9 000	9 000 TO LESS THAN 9 500	9 500 TO AND INCL 10 000
LESS THAN 13.50	47,300	47,800	48,300	48,800	49,200	49,700	50,100	50,600	51,000	51,500	51,900
13.50 TO LESS THAN 13.75	47,700	48,200	48,700	49,200	49,600	50,100	50,500	51,000	51,400	51,900	52,300
13.75 TO LESS THAN 14.00	48,200	48,600	49,100	49,600	50,000	50,500	50,900	51,400	51,800	52,300	52,700
14.00 TO LESS THAN 14.25	48,600	49,100	49,500	50,000	50,400	50,900	51,300	51,800	52,200	52,700	53,100
14.25 TO LESS THAN 14.50	49,000	49,500	49,900	50,400	50,800	51,300	51,700	52,200	52,600	53,100	53,500
14.50 TO LESS THAN 14.75	49,400	49,900	50,300	50,800	51,200	51,700	52,100	52,600	53,000	53,500	53,900
14.75 TO LESS THAN 15.00	49,900	50,300	50,800	51,200	51,700	52,100	52,600	53,000	53,500	53,900	54,300

Tab. 1   Ont. Reg. 413/05 — Vehicle Weights and Dimensions

VEHICLE WEIGHT TABLE 18
ALLOWABLE GROSS WEIGHT ON A VEHICLE WITH SEVEN AXLES (KILOGRAMS)
INTER-VEHICLE-UNIT DISTANCE, 2.4 METRES TO LESS THAN 2.7 METRES
FRONT AXLE WEIGHT, (KILOGRAMS)

BASE LENGTH, (METRES)	5 000 or Less	5 001 TO LESS THAN 5 500	5 500 TO LESS THAN 6 000	6 000 TO LESS THAN 6 500	6 500 TO LESS THAN 7 000	7 000 TO LESS THAN 7 500	7 500 TO LESS THAN 8 000	8 000 TO LESS THAN 8 500	8 500 TO LESS THAN 9 000	9 000 TO LESS THAN 9 500	9 500 AND INCL 10 000
15.00 TO LESS THAN 15.25	50,300	50,700	51,200	51,600	52,100	52,500	53,000	53,400	53,900	54,300	54,800
15.25 TO LESS THAN 15.50	50,700	51,100	51,600	52,000	52,500	52,900	53,400	53,800	54,300	54,700	55,200
15.50 TO LESS THAN 15.75	51,100	51,600	52,000	52,400	52,900	53,300	53,800	54,200	54,700	55,100	55,600
15.75 TO LESS THAN 16.00	51,600	52,000	52,400	52,800	53,300	53,700	54,200	54,600	55,100	55,500	56,000
16.00 TO LESS THAN 16.25	52,000	52,400	52,800	53,300	53,700	54,100	54,600	55,000	55,500	55,900	56,400
16.25 TO LESS THAN 16.50	52,500	52,900	53,300	53,700	54,100	54,600	55,000	55,400	55,900	56,300	56,700
16.50 TO LESS THAN 16.75	52,900	53,300	53,700	54,100	54,600	55,000	55,400	55,900	56,300	56,700	57,100
16.75 TO LESS THAN 17.00	53,400	53,700	54,100	54,500	55,000	55,400	55,800	56,300	56,700	57,100	57,500
17.00 TO LESS THAN 17.25	53,800	54,200	54,500	55,000	55,400	55,800	56,300	56,700	57,100	57,500	58,000
17.25 TO LESS THAN 17.50	54,300	54,600	55,000	55,400	55,800	56,200	56,700	57,100	57,500	58,000	58,400
17.50 TO LESS THAN 17.75	54,700	55,000	55,400	55,800	56,200	56,700	57,100	57,500	57,900	58,400	58,800
17.75 TO LESS THAN 18.00	55,200	55,500	55,800	56,200	56,700	57,100	57,500	57,900	58,400	58,800	59,300
18.00 TO LESS THAN 18.25	55,600	55,900	56,200	56,700	57,100	57,500	57,900	58,300	58,800	59,200	59,600
18.25 TO LESS THAN 18.50	56,100	56,400	56,700	57,100	57,500	57,900	58,300	58,800	59,200	59,600	60,000
18.50 TO LESS THAN 18.75	56,500	56,800	57,100	57,500	57,900	58,300	58,800	59,200	59,600	60,000	60,400
18.75 TO LESS THAN 19.00	57,000	57,300	57,500	57,900	58,300	58,800	59,200	59,600	60,000	60,400	60,800
19.00 TO LESS THAN 19.25	57,400	57,700	57,900	58,300	58,800	59,200	59,600	60,000	60,400	60,800	61,200
19.25 AND OVER	57,900	58,100	58,300	58,700	59,200	59,600	60,000	60,400	60,800	61,200	61,600

VEHICLE WEIGHT TABLE 19
ALLOWABLE GROSS WEIGHT ON A VEHICLE WITH SEVEN AXLES (KILOGRAMS)
INTER-VEHICLE-UNIT DISTANCE, 2.7 METRES TO LESS THAN 3.0 METRES
FRONT AXLE WEIGHT, (KILOGRAMS)

BASE LENGTH, (METRES)	5 000 or Less	5 001 TO LESS THAN 5 500	5 500 TO LESS THAN 6 000	6 000 TO LESS THAN 6 500	6 500 TO LESS THAN 7 000	7 000 TO LESS THAN 7 500	7 500 TO LESS THAN 8 000	8 000 TO LESS THAN 8 500	8 500 TO LESS THAN 9 000	9 000 TO LESS THAN 9 500	9 500 TO AND INCL 10 000
LESS THAN 14.00	48,700	49,200	49,600	50,000	50,500	50,900	51,300	51,700	52,200	52,600	53,000
14.00 TO LESS THAN 14.25	49,200	49,600	50,100	50,500	50,900	51,300	51,800	52,200	52,600	53,000	53,500
14.25 TO LESS THAN 14.50	49,700	50,100	50,500	50,900	51,400	51,800	52,200	52,600	53,100	53,500	53,900
14.50 TO LESS THAN 14.75	50,100	50,600	51,000	51,400	51,800	52,300	52,700	53,100	53,500	53,900	54,300
14.75 TO LESS THAN 15.00	50,600	51,000	51,400	51,900	52,300	52,700	53,100	53,600	54,000	54,400	54,800
15.00 TO LESS THAN 15.25	51,100	51,500	51,900	52,300	52,800	53,200	53,600	54,000	54,400	54,800	55,300
15.25 TO LESS THAN 15.50	51,500	52,000	52,400	52,800	53,200	53,600	54,000	54,500	54,900	55,300	55,700
15.50 TO LESS THAN 15.75	52,000	52,400	52,800	53,300	53,700	54,100	54,500	54,900	55,300	55,700	56,100
15.75 TO LESS THAN 16.00	52,500	52,900	53,300	53,700	54,100	54,500	55,000	55,400	55,800	56,200	56,600
16.00 TO LESS THAN 16.25	52,900	53,300	53,700	54,100	54,500	54,900	55,400	55,800	56,200	56,600	57,000
16.25 TO LESS THAN 16.50	53,300	53,700	54,100	54,500	54,900	55,300	55,800	56,200	56,600	57,000	57,400
16.50 TO LESS THAN 16.75	53,700	54,100	54,500	54,900	55,300	55,700	56,200	56,600	57,000	57,400	57,800
16.75 TO LESS THAN 17.00	54,100	54,500	54,900	55,300	55,700	56,100	56,600	57,000	57,400	57,800	58,200
17.00 TO LESS THAN 17.25	54,600	54,900	55,300	55,700	56,100	56,500	57,000	57,400	57,800	58,200	58,700
17.25 TO LESS THAN 17.50	55,000	55,300	55,600	56,100	56,500	56,900	57,400	57,800	58,200	58,700	59,100
17.50 TO LESS THAN 17.75	55,400	55,700	56,000	56,500	56,900	57,300	57,800	58,200	58,600	59,100	59,500
17.75 TO LESS THAN 18.00	55,800	56,100	56,400	56,900	57,300	57,700	58,200	58,600	59,000	59,500	59,900
18.00 TO LESS THAN 18.25	56,200	56,500	56,800	57,300	57,700	58,100	58,600	59,000	59,400	59,900	60,300

Tab. 1   Ont. Reg. 413/05 — Vehicle Weights and Dimensions

VEHICLE WEIGHT TABLE 19
ALLOWABLE GROSS WEIGHT ON A VEHICLE WITH SEVEN AXLES (KILOGRAMS)
INTER-VEHICLE-UNIT DISTANCE, 2.7 METRES TO LESS THAN 3.0 METRES
FRONT AXLE WEIGHT, (KILOGRAMS)

BASE LENGTH, (METRES)	5 000 or Less	5 001 TO LESS THAN 5 500	5 500 TO LESS THAN 6 000	6 000 TO LESS THAN 6 500	6 500 TO LESS THAN 7 000	7 000 TO LESS THAN 7 500	7 500 TO LESS THAN 8 000	8 000 TO LESS THAN 8 500	8 500 TO LESS THAN 9 000	9 000 TO LESS THAN 9 500	9 500 TO AND INCL 10 000
18.25 TO LESS THAN 18.50	56,600	56,900	57,200	57,600	58,100	58,500	59,000	59,400	59,900	60,300	60,700
18.50 TO LESS THAN 18.75	57,100	57,300	57,600	58,000	58,500	58,900	59,400	59,800	60,300	60,700	61,200
18.75 TO LESS THAN 19.00	57,500	57,700	58,000	58,400	58,900	59,300	59,800	60,200	60,700	61,100	61,600
19.00 TO LESS THAN 19.25	57,900	58,100	58,400	58,800	59,300	59,700	60,200	60,600	61,100	61,500	62,000
19.25 AND OVER	58,300	58,500	58,800	59,200	59,700	60,100	60,600	61,000	61,500	61,900	62,400

VEHICLE WEIGHT TABLE 20
ALLOWABLE GROSS WEIGHT ON A VEHICLE WITH SEVEN AXLES (KILOGRAMS)
INTER-VEHICLE-UNIT DISTANCE, 3.0 METRES TO LESS THAN 3.3 METRES
FRONT AXLE WEIGHT, (KILOGRAMS)

BASE LENGTH, (METRES)	5 000 or Less	5 001 TO LESS THAN 5 500	5 500 TO LESS THAN 6 000	6 000 TO LESS THAN 6 500	6 500 TO LESS THAN 7 000	7 000 TO LESS THAN 7 500	7 500 TO LESS THAN 8 000	8 000 TO LESS THAN 8 500	8 500 TO LESS THAN 9 000	9 000 TO LESS THAN 9 500	9 500 TO AND INCL 10 000
LESS THAN 14.00	49,300	49,700	50,200	50,700	51,100	51,600	52,000	52,500	52,900	53,400	53,800
14.00 TO LESS THAN 14.25	49,700	50,100	50,600	51,000	51,500	52,000	52,400	52,900	53,400	53,800	54,300
14.25 TO LESS THAN 14.50	50,100	50,500	51,000	51,400	51,900	52,400	52,800	53,300	53,800	54,200	54,700
14.50 TO LESS THAN 14.75	50,500	51,000	51,400	51,800	52,300	52,800	53,200	53,700	54,200	54,600	55,100
14.75 TO LESS THAN 15.00	51,000	51,400	51,700	52,200	52,700	53,200	53,600	54,100	54,600	55,000	55,600
15.00 TO LESS THAN 15.25	51,400	51,800	52,100	52,600	53,100	53,600	54,000	54,500	55,000	55,500	56,000
15.25 TO LESS THAN 15.50	51,800	52,200	52,500	53,000	53,500	54,000	54,400	54,900	55,400	55,900	56,400
15.50 TO LESS THAN 15.75	52,200	52,600	52,900	53,400	53,900	54,400	54,900	55,300	55,800	56,300	56,800
15.75 TO LESS THAN 16.00	52,700	53,000	53,300	53,800	54,300	54,800	55,200	55,700	56,200	56,700	57,200

VEHICLE WEIGHT TABLE 20
ALLOWABLE GROSS WEIGHT ON A VEHICLE WITH SEVEN AXLES (KILOGRAMS)
INTER-VEHICLE-UNIT DISTANCE, 3.0 METRES TO LESS THAN 3.3 METRES
FRONT AXLE WEIGHT, (KILOGRAMS)

BASE LENGTH, (METRES)	5 000 or Less	5 001 TO LESS THAN 5 500	5 500 TO LESS THAN 6 000	6 000 TO LESS THAN 6 500	6 500 TO LESS THAN 7 000	7 000 TO LESS THAN 7 500	7 500 TO LESS THAN 8 000	8 000 TO LESS THAN 8 500	8 500 TO LESS THAN 9 000	9 000 TO LESS THAN 9 500	9 500 TO AND INCL 10 000
16.00 TO LESS THAN 16.25	53,100	53,400	53,700	54,200	54,700	55,200	55,700	56,100	56,600	57,100	57,500
16.25 TO LESS THAN 16.50	53,500	53,800	54,100	54,600	55,100	55,600	56,100	56,600	57,000	57,500	57,900
16.50 TO LESS THAN 16.75	54,000	54,300	54,600	55,000	55,500	56,000	56,500	57,000	57,400	57,900	58,400
16.75 TO LESS THAN 17.00	54,400	54,700	55,000	55,500	55,900	56,400	56,900	57,400	57,900	58,300	58,800
17.00 TO LESS THAN 17.25	54,900	55,100	55,400	55,900	56,300	56,800	57,300	57,800	58,300	58,700	59,300
17.25 TO LESS THAN 17.50	55,300	55,600	55,800	56,300	56,800	57,200	57,700	58,200	58,700	59,200	59,700
17.50 TO LESS THAN 17.75	55,700	56,000	56,200	56,700	57,200	57,700	58,100	58,600	59,100	59,600	60,100
17.75 TO LESS THAN 18.00	56,200	56,400	56,600	57,100	57,600	58,100	58,500	59,000	59,500	60,000	60,500
18.00 TO LESS THAN 18.25	56,600	56,800	57,100	57,500	58,000	58,500	59,000	59,400	59,900	60,400	61,000
18.25 TO LESS THAN 18.50	57,100	57,300	57,500	58,000	58,400	58,900	59,400	59,800	60,300	60,800	61,200
18.50 TO LESS THAN 18.75	57,500	57,700	57,900	58,400	58,800	59,300	59,800	60,300	60,700	61,200	61,600
18.75 TO LESS THAN 19.00	58,100	58,300	58,500	58,800	59,200	59,600	60,100	60,600	61,000	61,500	61,900
19.00 TO LESS THAN 19.25	58,600	58,800	59,000	59,200	59,600	60,000	60,500	61,000	61,400	61,800	62,200
19.25 AND OVER	59,000	59,200	59,400	59,600	60,000	60,400	60,900	61,400	61,800	62,200	62,600

Tab. 1   Ont. Reg. 413/05 — Vehicle Weights and Dimensions

VEHICLE WEIGHT TABLE 21
ALLOWABLE GROSS WEIGHT ON A VEHICLE WITH SEVEN AXLES (KILOGRAMS)
INTER-VEHICLE-UNIT DISTANCE, 3.3 METRES TO LESS THAN 3.6 METRES
FRONT AXLE WEIGHT, (KILOGRAMS)

BASE LENGTH, (METRES)	5 000 or Less	5 001 TO LESS THAN 5 500	5 500 TO LESS THAN 6 000	6 000 TO LESS THAN 6 500	6 500 TO LESS THAN 7 000	7 000 TO LESS THAN 7 500	7 500 TO LESS THAN 8 000	8 000 TO LESS THAN 8 500	8 500 TO LESS THAN 9 000	9 000 TO LESS THAN 9 500	9 500 TO AND INCL 10 000
LESS THAN 15.00	51,600	52,000	52,400	52,800	53,300	53,700	54,200	54,600	55,100	55,500	56,000
15.00 TO LESS THAN 15.25	52,100	52,500	52,800	53,300	53,700	54,200	54,600	55,000	55,500	55,900	56,400
15.25 TO LESS THAN 15.50	52,500	52,900	53,200	53,700	54,100	54,600	55,000	55,500	55,900	56,300	56,800
15.50 TO LESS THAN 15.75	53,000	53,300	53,700	54,100	54,600	55,000	55,400	55,900	56,300	56,800	57,200
15.75 TO LESS THAN 16.00	53,400	53,800	54,100	54,500	55,000	55,400	55,900	56,300	56,800	57,200	57,600
16.00 TO LESS THAN 16.25	53,900	54,200	54,500	55,000	55,400	55,900	56,300	56,700	57,200	57,600	58,000
16.25 TO LESS THAN 16.50	54,300	54,600	54,900	55,400	55,800	56,300	56,700	57,200	57,600	58,000	58,500
16.50 TO LESS THAN 16.75	54,800	55,100	55,400	55,800	56,300	56,700	57,100	57,600	58,000	58,500	58,900
16.75 TO LESS THAN 17.00	55,200	55,500	55,800	56,200	56,700	57,100	57,600	58,000	58,500	58,900	59,400
17.00 TO LESS THAN 17.25	55,600	55,900	56,200	56,700	57,100	57,500	58,000	58,400	58,800	59,300	59,700
17.25 TO LESS THAN 17.50	56,100	56,400	56,700	57,100	57,500	57,900	58,400	58,800	59,200	59,700	60,100
17.50 TO LESS THAN 17.75	56,500	56,800	57,100	57,500	57,900	58,400	58,800	59,200	59,600	60,100	60,400
17.75 TO LESS THAN 18.00	57,000	57,300	57,500	57,900	58,400	58,800	59,200	59,600	60,000	60,400	60,800
18.00 TO LESS THAN 18.25	57,400	57,700	57,900	58,400	58,800	59,200	59,600	60,000	60,400	60,800	61,200
18.25 TO LESS THAN 18.50	57,900	58,100	58,400	58,800	59,200	59,600	60,000	60,400	60,800	61,200	61,600
18.50 TO LESS THAN 18.75	58,300	58,600	58,800	59,200	59,600	60,000	60,400	60,800	61,200	61,600	62,000
18.75 TO LESS THAN 19.00	58,700	59,000	59,300	59,600	60,000	60,400	60,800	61,200	61,600	62,000	62,400
19.00 TO LESS THAN 19.25	59,200	59,500	59,700	60,000	60,400	60,800	61,200	61,600	62,000	62,400	62,800

VEHICLE WEIGHT TABLE 21
ALLOWABLE GROSS WEIGHT ON A VEHICLE WITH SEVEN AXLES (KILOGRAMS)
INTER-VEHICLE-UNIT DISTANCE, 3.3 METRES TO LESS THAN 3.6 METRES
FRONT AXLE WEIGHT, (KILOGRAMS)

BASE LENGTH, (METRES)	5 000 or Less	5 001 TO LESS THAN 5 500	5 500 TO LESS THAN 6 000	6 000 TO LESS THAN 6 500	6 500 TO LESS THAN 7 000	7 000 TO LESS THAN 7 500	7 500 TO LESS THAN 8 000	8 000 TO LESS THAN 8 500	8 500 TO LESS THAN 9 000	9 000 TO LESS THAN 9 500	9 500 TO AND INCL 10 000
19.25 AND OVER	59,600	59,900	60,100	60,400	60,800	61,200	61,600	62,000	62,400	62,800	63,200

VEHICLE WEIGHT TABLE 22
ALLOWABLE GROSS WEIGHT ON A VEHICLE WITH SEVEN AXLES (KILOGRAMS)
INTER-VEHICLE-UNIT DISTANCE, 3.6 METRES OR MORE
FRONT AXLE WEIGHT, (KILOGRAMS)

BASE LENGTH, (METRES)	5 000 or Less	5 001 TO LESS THAN 5 500	5 500 TO LESS THAN 6 000	6 000 TO LESS THAN 6 500	6 500 TO LESS THAN 7 000	7 000 TO LESS THAN 7 500	7 500 TO LESS THAN 8 000	8 000 TO LESS THAN 8 500	8 500 TO LESS THAN 9 000	9 000 TO LESS THAN 9 500	9 500 TO AND INCL 10 000
LESS THAN 15.00	52,300	52,700	53,100	53,500	54,000	54,400	54,900	55,300	55,800	56,200	56,700
15.00 TO LESS THAN 15.25	52,800	53,100	53,500	54,000	54,400	54,800	55,300	55,700	56,200	56,600	57,100
15.25 TO LESS THAN 15.50	53,200	53,600	53,900	54,400	54,800	55,300	55,700	56,100	56,600	57,000	57,500
15.50 TO LESS THAN 15.75	53,700	54,000	54,400	54,800	55,200	55,700	56,100	56,500	57,000	57,400	57,900
15.75 TO LESS THAN 16.00	54,100	54,400	54,800	55,200	55,700	56,100	56,500	56,900	57,400	57,800	58,300
16.00 TO LESS THAN 16.25	54,500	54,900	55,200	55,600	56,100	56,500	56,900	57,300	57,800	58,200	58,600
16.25 TO LESS THAN 16.50	55,000	55,300	55,600	56,100	56,500	56,900	57,300	57,800	58,200	58,600	59,000
16.50 TO LESS THAN 16.75	55,400	55,700	56,100	56,500	56,900	57,300	57,700	58,200	58,600	59,000	59,400
16.75 TO LESS THAN 17.00	55,900	56,200	56,500	56,900	57,300	57,700	58,200	58,600	59,000	59,400	59,800
17.00 TO LESS THAN 17.25	56,300	56,600	56,900	57,300	57,700	58,100	58,500	59,000	59,400	59,800	60,300
17.25 TO LESS THAN 17.50	56,700	57,000	57,300	57,700	58,100	58,500	58,900	59,300	59,800	60,200	60,700
17.50 TO LESS THAN 17.75	57,100	57,400	57,700	58,100	58,500	58,900	59,300	59,700	60,100	60,600	61,000
17.75 TO LESS THAN 18.00	57,500	57,800	58,000	58,500	58,900	59,300	59,700	60,100	60,500	60,900	61,300

Tab. 1   Ont. Reg. 413/05 — Vehicle Weights and Dimensions

VEHICLE WEIGHT TABLE 22
ALLOWABLE GROSS WEIGHT ON A VEHICLE WITH SEVEN AXLES (KILOGRAMS)
INTER-VEHICLE-UNIT DISTANCE, 3.6 METRES OR MORE
FRONT AXLE WEIGHT, (KILOGRAMS)

BASE LENGTH, (METRES)	5 000 or Less	5 001 TO LESS THAN 5 500	5 500 TO LESS THAN 6 000	6 000 TO LESS THAN 6 500	6 500 TO LESS THAN 7 000	7 000 TO LESS THAN 7 500	7 500 TO LESS THAN 8 000	8 000 TO LESS THAN 8 500	8 500 TO LESS THAN 9 000	9 000 TO LESS THAN 9 500	9 500 TO AND INCL 10 000
18.00 TO LESS THAN 18.25	57,900	58,200	58,400	58,800	59,300	59,700	60,100	60,500	60,900	61,300	61,700
18.25 TO LESS THAN 18.50	58,400	58,600	58,800	59,200	59,600	60,100	60,500	60,900	61,300	61,700	62,100
18.50 TO LESS THAN 18.75	58,800	59,000	59,200	59,600	60,000	60,400	60,900	61,300	61,700	62,100	62,500
18.75 TO LESS THAN 19.00	59,300	59,500	59,700	60,000	60,400	60,900	61,300	61,700	62,100	62,500	62,900
19.00 TO LESS THAN 19.25	59,700	59,900	60,200	60,500	60,900	61,300	61,700	62,100	62,500	62,900	63,300
19.25 AND OVER	60,100	60,300	60,600	60,900	61,300	61,700	62,100	62,500	62,900	63,300	63,500

VEHICLE WEIGHT TABLE 23
ALLOWABLE GROSS WEIGHT ON A VEHICLE WITH EIGHT OR MORE AXLES (KILOGRAMS)
INTER-VEHICLE-UNIT DISTANCE, LESS THAN 2.1 METRES
FRONT AXLE WEIGHT, (KILOGRAMS)

BASE LENGTH, (METRES)	5 000 or Less	5 001 TO LESS THAN 5 500	5 500 TO LESS THAN 6 000	6 000 TO LESS THAN 6 500	6 500 TO LESS THAN 7 000	7 000 TO LESS THAN 7 500	7 500 TO LESS THAN 8 000	8 000 TO LESS THAN 8 500	8 500 TO LESS THAN 9 000	9 000 TO LESS THAN 9 500	9 500 TO AND INCL 10 000
LESS THAN 15.00	47,600	48,000	48,500	49,000	49,500	50,000	50,400	50,900	51,400	51,900	52,400
15.00 TO LESS THAN 15.25	48,100	48,600	49,000	49,500	50,000	50,500	51,000	51,400	51,900	52,400	52,900
15.25 TO LESS THAN 15.50	48,700	49,100	49,600	50,100	50,500	51,000	51,500	51,900	52,400	52,900	53,400
15.50 TO LESS THAN 15.75	49,200	49,700	50,100	50,600	51,100	51,500	52,000	52,400	52,900	53,400	53,800
15.75 TO LESS THAN 16.00	49,700	50,200	50,700	51,100	51,600	52,000	52,500	52,900	53,400	53,800	54,300
16.00 TO LESS THAN 16.25	50,300	50,700	51,200	51,700	52,100	52,500	53,000	53,400	53,900	54,300	54,800
16.25 TO LESS THAN 16.50	50,800	51,300	51,800	52,200	52,600	53,100	53,500	53,900	54,400	54,800	55,300
16.50 TO LESS THAN 16.75	51,300	51,800	52,300	52,700	53,200	53,600	54,000	54,400	54,900	55,300	55,700

VEHICLE WEIGHT TABLE 23
ALLOWABLE GROSS WEIGHT ON A VEHICLE WITH EIGHT OR MORE AXLES (KILOGRAMS)
INTER-VEHICLE-UNIT DISTANCE, LESS THAN 2.1 METRES
FRONT AXLE WEIGHT, (KILOGRAMS)

BASE LENGTH, (METRES)	5 000 or Less THAN 5 500	5 001 TO LESS THAN 6 000	5 500 TO LESS THAN 6 500	6 000 TO LESS THAN 7 000	6 500 TO LESS THAN 7 500	7 000 TO LESS THAN 8 000	7 500 TO LESS THAN 8 500	8 000 TO LESS THAN 9 000	8 500 TO LESS THAN 9 500	9 000 TO LESS THAN 10 000	9 500 TO AND INCL 10 000
16.75 TO LESS THAN 17.00	51,800	52,300	52,800	53,200	53,600	54,000	54,500	54,900	55,300	55,700	56,100
17.00 TO LESS THAN 17.25	52,300	52,800	53,200	53,700	54,100	54,500	54,900	55,300	55,700	56,100	56,500
17.25 TO LESS THAN 17.50	52,800	53,300	53,700	54,100	54,500	54,900	55,400	55,800	56,200	56,600	57,000
17.50 TO LESS THAN 17.75	53,300	53,800	54,200	54,600	55,000	55,400	55,800	56,200	56,600	57,000	57,400
17.75 TO LESS THAN 18.00	53,800	54,300	54,700	55,100	55,500	55,900	56,200	56,600	57,000	57,400	57,800
18.00 TO LESS THAN 18.25	54,300	54,700	55,100	55,500	55,900	56,300	56,700	57,100	57,500	57,800	58,300
18.25 TO LESS THAN 18.50	54,800	55,200	55,600	56,000	56,400	56,800	57,100	57,500	57,900	58,300	58,800
18.50 TO LESS THAN 18.75	55,300	55,700	56,100	56,500	56,800	57,200	57,600	58,000	58,300	58,700	59,300
18.75 TO LESS THAN 19.00	55,900	56,300	56,700	57,000	57,400	57,700	58,000	58,400	58,800	59,200	59,700
19.00 TO LESS THAN 19.25	56,400	56,800	57,200	57,400	57,800	58,100	58,400	58,800	59,200	59,600	60,100
19.25 AND OVER	56,800	57,200	57,600	57,800	58,200	58,500	58,800	59,200	59,600	60,000	60,500

VEHICLE WEIGHT TABLE 24
ALLOWABLE GROSS WEIGHT ON A VEHICLE WITH EIGHT OR MORE AXLES (KILOGRAMS)
INTER-VEHICLE-UNIT DISTANCE, 2.1 METRES TO LESS THAN 2.4 METRES
FRONT AXLE WEIGHT, (KILOGRAMS)

BASE LENGTH, (METRES)	5 000 or Less THAN 5 500	5 001 TO LESS THAN 6 000	5 500 TO LESS THAN 6 500	6 000 TO LESS THAN 7 000	6 500 TO LESS THAN 7 500	7 000 TO LESS THAN 8 000	7 500 TO LESS THAN 8 500	8 000 TO LESS THAN 9 000	8 500 TO LESS THAN 9 500	9 000 TO LESS THAN 10 000	9 500 TO AND INCL 10 000
LESS THAN 15.00	48,600	49,000	49,500	50,000	50,400	50,900	51,400	51,900	52,300	52,800	53,300
15.00 TO LESS THAN 15.25	49,100	49,500	50,000	50,500	50,900	51,400	51,900	52,300	52,800	53,300	53,700
15.25 TO LESS THAN 15.50	49,600	50,100	50,500	51,000	51,400	51,900	52,300	52,800	53,300	53,700	54,200

Tab. 1   Ont. Reg. 413/05 — Vehicle Weights and Dimensions

VEHICLE WEIGHT TABLE 24
ALLOWABLE GROSS WEIGHT ON A VEHICLE WITH EIGHT OR MORE AXLES (KILOGRAMS)
INTER-VEHICLE-UNIT DISTANCE, 2.1 METRES TO LESS THAN 2.4 METRES
FRONT AXLE WEIGHT, (KILOGRAMS)

BASE LENGTH, (METRES)	5 000 or Less	5 001 TO LESS THAN 5 500	5 500 TO LESS THAN 6 000	6 000 TO LESS THAN 6 500	6 500 TO LESS THAN 7 000	7 000 TO LESS THAN 7 500	7 500 TO LESS THAN 8 000	8 000 TO LESS THAN 8 500	8 500 TO LESS THAN 9 000	9 000 TO LESS THAN 9 500	9 500 TO AND INCL 10 000
15.50 TO LESS THAN 15.75	50,100	50,600	51,000	51,500	51,900	52,400	52,800	53,300	53,700	54,200	54,500
15.75 TO LESS THAN 16.00	50,600	51,100	51,600	52,000	52,400	52,900	53,300	53,800	54,200	54,600	55,100
16.00 TO LESS THAN 16.25	51,100	51,600	52,100	52,500	52,900	53,400	53,800	54,200	54,700	55,100	55,500
16.25 TO LESS THAN 16.50	51,700	52,100	52,600	53,000	53,400	53,900	54,300	54,700	55,100	55,500	55,900
16.50 TO LESS THAN 16.75	52,200	52,600	53,100	53,500	53,900	54,300	54,800	55,200	55,600	56,000	56,400
16.75 TO LESS THAN 17.00	52,700	53,200	53,600	54,000	54,400	54,800	55,200	55,600	56,000	56,400	56,800
17.00 TO LESS THAN 17.25	53,200	53,700	54,100	54,500	54,900	55,300	55,700	56,100	56,500	56,900	57,200
17.25 TO LESS THAN 17.50	53,700	54,200	54,600	55,000	55,400	55,800	56,200	56,600	57,000	57,300	57,700
17.50 TO LESS THAN 17.75	54,300	54,700	55,100	55,500	55,900	56,300	56,700	57,000	57,400	57,800	58,200
17.75 TO LESS THAN 18.00	54,800	55,200	55,700	56,000	56,400	56,800	57,100	57,500	57,900	58,200	58,600
18.00 TO LESS THAN 18.25	55,300	55,700	56,200	56,500	56,900	57,300	57,600	58,000	58,300	58,700	59,000
18.25 TO LESS THAN 18.50	55,800	56,300	56,700	57,000	57,400	57,700	58,100	58,400	58,800	59,100	59,500
18.50 TO LESS THAN 18.75	56,400	56,800	57,200	57,500	57,900	58,200	58,600	58,900	59,300	59,600	60,000
18.75 TO LESS THAN 19.00	56,900	57,400	57,800	58,100	58,500	58,800	59,200	59,500	59,900	60,200	60,500
19.00 TO LESS THAN 19.25	57,500	57,900	58,300	58,600	59,000	59,300	59,700	60,000	60,400	60,700	61,000
19.25 AND OVER	57,900	58,300	58,700	59,000	59,400	59,700	60,100	60,400	60,800	61,100	61,400

VEHICLE WEIGHT TABLE 25
ALLOWABLE GROSS WEIGHT ON A VEHICLE WITH EIGHT OR MORE AXLES (KILOGRAMS)
INTER-VEHICLE-UNIT DISTANCE, 2.4 METRES TO LESS THAN 2.7 METRES
FRONT AXLE WEIGHT, (KILOGRAMS)

BASE LENGTH, (METRES)	5 000 or Less	5 001 TO LESS THAN 5 500	5 500 TO LESS THAN 6 000	6 000 TO LESS THAN 6 500	6 500 TO LESS THAN 7 000	7 000 TO LESS THAN 7 500	7 500 TO LESS THAN 8 000	8 000 TO LESS THAN 8 500	8 500 TO LESS THAN 9 000	9 000 TO LESS THAN 9 500	9 500 TO AND INCL 10 000
LESS THAN 15.00	49,700	50,100	50,600	51,000	51,500	51,900	52,400	52,800	53,300	53,700	54,200
15.00 TO LESS THAN 15.25	50,200	50,600	51,100	51,500	52,000	52,400	52,800	53,300	53,700	54,200	54,600
15.25 TO LESS THAN 15.50	50,700	51,100	51,600	52,000	52,400	52,900	53,300	53,700	54,200	54,600	55,100
15.50 TO LESS THAN 15.75	51,200	51,600	52,100	52,500	52,900	53,300	53,800	54,200	54,600	55,100	55,500
15.75 TO LESS THAN 16.00	51,600	52,100	52,500	53,000	53,400	53,800	54,200	54,700	55,100	55,500	56,000
16.00 TO LESS THAN 16.25	52,100	52,600	53,000	53,500	53,900	54,300	54,700	55,100	55,600	56,000	56,400
16.25 TO LESS THAN 16.50	52,600	53,100	53,500	53,900	54,400	54,800	55,200	55,600	56,000	56,400	56,900
16.50 TO LESS THAN 16.75	53,100	53,500	54,000	54,400	54,800	55,200	55,700	56,100	56,500	56,900	57,300
16.75 TO LESS THAN 17.00	53,600	54,000	54,500	54,900	55,300	55,700	56,100	56,500	56,900	57,300	57,700
17.00 TO LESS THAN 17.25	54,100	54,500	54,900	55,300	55,700	56,200	56,600	57,000	57,400	57,800	58,200
17.25 TO LESS THAN 17.50	54,500	55,000	55,400	55,800	56,200	56,600	57,000	57,400	57,800	58,200	58,600
17.50 TO LESS THAN 17.75	55,000	55,400	55,800	56,300	56,700	57,100	57,500	57,900	58,300	58,700	59,100
17.75 TO LESS THAN 18.00	55,500	55,900	56,300	56,700	57,100	57,500	57,900	58,300	58,700	59,100	59,500
18.00 TO LESS THAN 18.25	56,000	56,400	56,800	57,200	57,600	58,000	58,400	58,800	59,200	59,600	60,000
18.25 TO LESS THAN 18.50	56,500	56,800	57,200	57,600	58,000	58,400	58,800	59,200	59,600	60,000	60,400
18.50 TO LESS THAN 18.75	56,900	57,300	57,700	58,100	58,500	58,900	59,300	59,700	60,100	60,500	60,900
18.75 TO LESS THAN 19.00	57,500	57,700	58,100	58,500	58,900	59,300	59,700	60,100	60,500	60,900	61,300
19.00 TO LESS THAN 19.25	57,900	58,100	58,500	58,900	59,300	59,700	60,100	60,500	60,900	61,300	61,700

Tab. 1   Ont. Reg. 413/05 — Vehicle Weights and Dimensions

VEHICLE WEIGHT TABLE 25
ALLOWABLE GROSS WEIGHT ON A VEHICLE WITH EIGHT OR MORE AXLES (KILOGRAMS)
INTER-VEHICLE-UNIT DISTANCE, 2.4 METRES TO LESS THAN 2.7 METRES
FRONT AXLE WEIGHT, (KILOGRAMS)

BASE LENGTH, (METRES)	5 000 or Less	5 001 TO LESS THAN 5 500	5 500 TO LESS THAN 6 000	6 000 TO LESS THAN 6 500	6 500 TO LESS THAN 7 000	7 000 TO LESS THAN 7 500	7 500 TO LESS THAN 8 000	8 000 TO LESS THAN 8 500	8 500 TO LESS THAN 9 000	9 000 TO LESS THAN 9 500	9 500 TO AND INCL 10 000
19.25 AND OVER	58,300	58,500	58,900	59,300	59,700	60,100	60,500	60,900	61,300	61,700	62,100

VEHICLE WEIGHT TABLE 26
ALLOWABLE GROSS WEIGHT ON A VEHICLE WITH EIGHT OR MORE AXLES (KILOGRAMS)
INTER-VEHICLE-UNIT DISTANCE, 2.7 METRES TO LESS THAN 3.0 METRES
FRONT AXLE WEIGHT, (KILOGRAMS)

BASE LENGTH, (METRES)	5 000 or Less	5 001 TO LESS THAN 5 500	5 500 TO LESS THAN 6 000	6 000 TO LESS THAN 6 500	6 500 TO LESS THAN 7 000	7 000 TO LESS THAN 7 500	7 500 TO LESS THAN 8 000	8 000 TO LESS THAN 8 500	8 500 TO LESS THAN 9 000	9 000 TO LESS THAN 9 500	9 500 TO AND INCL 10 000
LESS THAN 15.50	51,600	52,000	52,400	52,900	53,300	53,800	54,200	54,700	55,100	55,600	56,000
15.50 TO LESS THAN 15.75	52,000	52,400	52,900	53,300	53,800	54,200	54,700	55,100	55,600	56,000	56,500
15.75 TO LESS THAN 16.00	52,500	52,900	53,300	53,800	54,200	54,700	55,100	55,600	56,000	56,500	56,900
16.00 TO LESS THAN 16.25	52,900	53,400	53,800	54,200	54,700	55,100	55,600	56,000	56,500	56,900	57,400
16.25 TO LESS THAN 16.50	53,400	53,800	54,300	54,700	55,200	55,600	56,100	56,500	57,000	57,400	57,800
16.50 TO LESS THAN 16.75	53,900	54,300	54,700	55,200	55,600	56,100	56,500	57,000	57,400	57,800	58,300
16.75 TO LESS THAN 17.00	54,300	54,800	55,200	55,600	56,100	56,500	57,000	57,400	57,900	58,300	58,700
17.00 TO LESS THAN 17.25	54,800	55,200	55,700	56,100	56,500	57,000	57,400	57,900	58,300	58,700	59,200
17.25 TO LESS THAN 17.50	55,200	55,700	56,100	56,600	57,000	57,400	57,900	58,300	58,700	59,200	59,600
17.50 TO LESS THAN 17.75	55,700	56,100	56,600	57,000	57,400	57,900	58,300	58,800	59,200	59,600	60,000
17.75 TO LESS THAN 18.00	56,200	56,600	57,000	57,500	57,900	58,300	58,800	59,200	59,600	60,100	60,500
18.00 TO LESS THAN 18.25	56,600	57,100	57,500	57,900	58,400	58,800	59,200	59,600	60,100	60,500	61,000
18.25 TO LESS THAN 18.50	57,100	57,500	57,900	58,400	58,800	59,200	59,700	60,100	60,500	61,000	61,400

VEHICLE WEIGHT TABLE 26
ALLOWABLE GROSS WEIGHT ON A VEHICLE WITH EIGHT OR MORE AXLES (KILOGRAMS)
INTER-VEHICLE-UNIT DISTANCE, 2.7 METRES TO LESS THAN 3.0 METRES
FRONT AXLE WEIGHT, (KILOGRAMS)

BASE LENGTH, (METRES)	5 000 or Less	5 001 TO LESS THAN 5 500	5 500 TO LESS THAN 6 000	6 000 TO LESS THAN 6 500	6 500 TO LESS THAN 7 000	7 000 TO LESS THAN 7 500	7 500 TO LESS THAN 8 000	8 000 TO LESS THAN 8 500	8 500 TO LESS THAN 9 000	9 000 TO LESS THAN 9 500	9 500 AND INCL 10 000
18.50 TO LESS THAN 18.75	57,500	58,000	58,400	58,800	59,300	59,700	60,100	60,500	61,000	61,400	61,900
18.75 TO LESS THAN 19.00	58,000	58,400	58,800	59,200	59,700	60,100	60,600	60,900	61,400	61,800	62,300
19.00 TO LESS THAN 19.25	58,400	58,800	59,200	59,600	60,100	60,500	61,000	61,300	61,800	62,200	62,700
19.25 AND OVER	58,800	59,200	59,600	60,000	60,500	60,900	61,400	61,700	62,200	62,600	63,100

VEHICLE WEIGHT TABLE 27
ALLOWABLE GROSS WEIGHT ON A VEHICLE WITH EIGHT OR MORE AXLES (KILOGRAMS)
INTER-VEHICLE-UNIT DISTANCE, 3.0 METRES TO LESS THAN 3.3 METRES
FRONT AXLE WEIGHT, (KILOGRAMS)

BASE LENGTH, (METRES)	5 000 or Less	5 001 TO LESS THAN 5 500	5 500 TO LESS THAN 6 000	6 000 TO LESS THAN 6 500	6 500 TO LESS THAN 7 000	7 000 TO LESS THAN 7 500	7 500 TO LESS THAN 8 000	8 000 TO LESS THAN 8 500	8 500 TO LESS THAN 9 000	9 000 TO LESS THAN 9 500	9 500 AND INCL 10 000
LESS THAN 16.00	53,100	53,400	53,800	54,300	54,700	55,200	55,700	56,200	56,600	57,100	57,600
16.00 TO LESS THAN 16.25	53,500	53,900	54,300	54,700	55,200	55,700	56,100	56,600	57,100	57,600	58,000
16.25 TO LESS THAN 16.50	54,000	54,400	54,700	55,200	55,700	56,100	56,600	57,100	57,500	58,000	58,500
16.50 TO LESS THAN 16.75	54,400	54,800	55,200	55,700	56,100	56,600	57,100	57,500	58,000	58,500	58,900
16.75 TO LESS THAN 17.00	54,900	55,300	55,600	56,100	56,600	57,100	57,500	58,000	58,500	58,900	59,400
17.00 TO LESS THAN 17.25	55,300	55,700	56,100	56,600	57,000	57,500	58,000	58,500	58,900	59,400	59,900
17.25 TO LESS THAN 17.50	55,800	56,200	56,500	57,000	57,500	58,000	58,500	59,000	59,400	59,900	60,500
17.50 TO LESS THAN 17.75	56,300	56,600	57,000	57,500	58,000	58,500	59,000	59,500	60,000	60,500	61,000
17.75 TO LESS THAN 18.00	56,700	57,100	57,500	58,000	58,500	59,000	59,500	60,000	60,500	61,000	61,500
18.00 TO LESS THAN 18.25	57,200	57,500	57,900	58,400	58,900	59,500	60,000	60,500	61,000	61,500	62,000

Tab. 1   Ont. Reg. 413/05 — Vehicle Weights and Dimensions

VEHICLE WEIGHT TABLE 27
ALLOWABLE GROSS WEIGHT ON A VEHICLE WITH EIGHT OR MORE AXLES (KILOGRAMS)
INTER-VEHICLE-UNIT DISTANCE, 3.0 METRES TO LESS THAN 3.3 METRES
FRONT AXLE WEIGHT, (KILOGRAMS)

BASE LENGTH, (METRES)	5 000 or Less	5 001 TO LESS THAN 5 500	5 500 TO LESS THAN 6 000	6 000 TO LESS THAN 6 500	6 500 TO LESS THAN 7 000	7 000 TO LESS THAN 7 500	7 500 TO LESS THAN 8 000	8 000 TO LESS THAN 8 500	8 500 TO LESS THAN 9 000	9 000 TO LESS THAN 9 500	9 500 AND INCL 10 000
18.25 TO LESS THAN 18.50	57,600	58,000	58,400	58,900	59,400	59,900	60,500	61,000	61,500	62,100	62,500
18.50 TO LESS THAN 18.75	58,100	58,400	58,800	59,300	59,900	60,400	61,000	61,500	62,100	62,600	63,000
18.75 TO LESS THAN 19.00	58,600	58,800	59,400	59,700	60,300	60,800	61,400	61,900	62,500	63,000	63,500
19.00 TO LESS THAN 19.25	59,000	59,200	59,800	60,100	60,700	61,200	61,800	62,300	62,900	63,400	63,500
19.25 AND OVER	59,400	59,600	60,200	60,500	61,100	61,600	62,200	62,700	63,300	63,500	63,500

VEHICLE WEIGHT TABLE 28
ALLOWABLE GROSS WEIGHT ON A VEHICLE WITH EIGHT OR MORE AXLES (KILOGRAMS)
INTER-VEHICLE-UNIT DISTANCE, 3.3 METRES TO LESS THAN 3.6 METRES
FRONT AXLE WEIGHT, (KILOGRAMS)

BASE LENGTH, (METRES)	5 000 or Less	5 001 TO LESS THAN 5 500	5 500 TO LESS THAN 6 000	6 000 TO LESS THAN 6 500	6 500 TO LESS THAN 7 000	7 000 TO LESS THAN 7 500	7 500 TO LESS THAN 8 000	8 000 TO LESS THAN 8 500	8 500 TO LESS THAN 9 000	9 000 TO LESS THAN 9 500	9 500 AND INCL 10 000
LESS THAN 16.00	54,300	54,700	55,100	55,500	55,900	56,300	56,800	57,200	57,600	58,000	58,400
16.00 TO LESS THAN 16.25	54,700	55,200	55,600	56,000	56,400	56,800	57,200	57,700	58,100	58,500	59,000
16.25 TO LESS THAN 16.50	55,200	55,700	56,100	56,500	56,900	57,300	57,700	58,100	58,600	59,000	59,500
16.50 TO LESS THAN 16.75	55,700	56,100	56,600	57,000	57,400	57,800	58,200	58,600	59,000	59,400	59,900
16.75 TO LESS THAN 17.00	56,200	56,600	57,100	57,500	57,900	58,300	58,700	59,100	59,500	59,900	60,400
17.00 TO LESS THAN 17.25	56,600	57,100	57,600	58,000	58,400	58,800	59,200	59,600	60,000	60,400	60,900
17.25 TO LESS THAN 17.50	57,100	57,600	58,100	58,500	58,900	59,300	59,700	60,100	60,500	60,900	61,400
17.50 TO LESS THAN 17.75	57,600	58,100	58,600	59,000	59,400	59,800	60,200	60,600	61,000	61,400	61,900
17.75 TO LESS THAN 18.00	58,100	58,600	59,100	59,500	59,900	60,300	60,700	61,100	61,500	61,900	62,500

VEHICLE WEIGHT TABLE 28
ALLOWABLE GROSS WEIGHT ON A VEHICLE WITH EIGHT OR MORE AXLES (KILOGRAMS)
INTER-VEHICLE-UNIT DISTANCE, 3.3 METRES TO LESS THAN 3.6 METRES
FRONT AXLE WEIGHT, (KILOGRAMS)

BASE LENGTH, (METRES)	5 000 or Less	5 001 TO LESS THAN 5 500	5 500 TO LESS THAN 6 000	6 000 TO LESS THAN 6 500	6 500 TO LESS THAN 7 000	7 000 TO LESS THAN 7 500	7 500 TO LESS THAN 8 000	8 000 TO LESS THAN 8 500	8 500 TO LESS THAN 9 000	9 000 TO LESS THAN 9 500	9 500 AND INCL 10 000
18.00 TO LESS THAN 18.25	58,600	59,100	59,600	60,000	60,400	60,800	61,200	61,600	62,100	62,500	63,000
18.25 TO LESS THAN 18.50	59,100	59,600	60,100	60,500	60,900	61,300	61,700	62,200	62,600	63,000	63,500
18.50 TO LESS THAN 18.75	59,600	60,100	60,600	61,000	61,400	61,800	62,300	62,700	63,100	63,500	63,500
18.75 TO LESS THAN 19.00	60,100	60,500	61,000	61,400	61,800	62,200	62,700	63,100	63,500	63,500	63,500
19.00 TO LESS THAN 19.25	60,600	60,900	61,400	61,800	62,200	62,600	63,100	63,500	63,500	63,500	63,500
19.25 AND OVER	61,000	61,300	61,800	62,200	62,600	63,000	63,500	63,500	63,500	63,500	63,500

VEHICLE WEIGHT TABLE 29
ALLOWABLE GROSS WEIGHT ON A VEHICLE WITH EIGHT OR MORE AXLES (KILOGRAMS)
INTER-VEHICLE-UNIT DISTANCE, 3.6 METRES OR MORE
FRONT AXLE WEIGHT, (KILOGRAMS)

BASE LENGTH, (METRES)	5 000 or Less	5 001 TO LESS THAN 5 500	5 500 TO LESS THAN 6 000	6 000 TO LESS THAN 6 500	6 500 TO LESS THAN 7 000	7 000 TO LESS THAN 7 500	7 500 TO LESS THAN 8 000	8 000 TO LESS THAN 8 500	8 500 TO LESS THAN 9 000	9 000 TO LESS THAN 9 500	9 500 AND INCL 10 000
LESS THAN 16.00	54,800	55,200	55,600	56,000	56,400	56,800	57,300	57,700	58,100	58,500	59,000
16.00 TO LESS THAN 16.25	55,200	55,700	56,100	56,500	56,900	57,300	57,700	58,200	58,600	59,000	59,500
16.25 TO LESS THAN 16.50	55,700	56,200	56,600	57,000	57,400	57,800	58,200	58,600	59,100	59,500	59,900
16.50 TO LESS THAN 16.75	56,200	56,600	57,100	57,500	57,900	58,300	58,700	59,100	59,500	59,900	60,300
16.75 TO LESS THAN 17.00	56,700	57,100	57,600	58,000	58,400	58,800	59,200	59,600	60,000	60,400	60,800
17.00 TO LESS THAN 17.25	57,100	57,600	58,100	58,500	58,900	59,300	59,700	60,100	60,500	60,900	61,300
17.25 TO LESS THAN 17.50	57,600	58,100	58,600	59,000	59,400	59,800	60,200	60,600	61,000	61,400	61,800
17.50 TO LESS THAN 17.75	58,100	58,600	59,100	59,500	59,900	60,300	60,700	61,100	61,500	61,900	62,300

Tab. 1   Ont. Reg. 413/05 — Vehicle Weights and Dimensions

VEHICLE WEIGHT TABLE 29
ALLOWABLE GROSS WEIGHT ON A VEHICLE WITH EIGHT OR MORE AXLES (KILOGRAMS)
INTER-VEHICLE-UNIT DISTANCE, 3.6 METRES OR MORE
FRONT AXLE WEIGHT, (KILOGRAMS)

BASE LENGTH, (METRES)	5 000 or Less	5 001 TO LESS THAN 5 500	5 500 TO LESS THAN 6 000	6 000 TO LESS THAN 6 500	6 500 TO LESS THAN 7 000	7 000 TO LESS THAN 7 500	7 500 TO LESS THAN 8 000	8 000 TO LESS THAN 8 500	8 500 TO LESS THAN 9 000	9 000 TO LESS THAN 9 500	9 500 AND INCL 10 000
17.75 TO LESS THAN 18.00	58,600	59,100	59,600	60,000	60,400	60,800	61,200	61,600	62,000	62,400	62,900
18.00 TO LESS THAN 18.25	59,100	59,600	60,100	60,500	60,900	61,300	61,700	62,100	62,600	63,000	63,500
18.25 TO LESS THAN 18.50	59,600	60,100	60,600	61,000	61,400	61,800	62,200	62,700	63,100	63,500	63,500
18.50 TO LESS THAN 18.75	60,100	60,600	61,100	61,500	61,900	62,300	62,700	63,200	63,500	63,500	63,500
18.75 TO LESS THAN 19.00	60,600	61,000	61,500	61,900	62,300	62,700	63,100	63,500	63,500	63,500	63,500
19.00 TO LESS THAN 19.25	61,100	61,400	61,900	62,300	62,700	63,100	63,500	63,500	63,500	63,500	63,500
19.25 AND OVER	61,500	61,800	62,300	62,700	63,100	63,500	63,500	63,500	63,500	63,500	63,500

VEHICLE WEIGHT TABLE 30
ALLOWABLE GROSS WEIGHT ON DESIGNATED TRUCK-TRAILER COMBINATIONS (KILOGRAMS)

Base Length (metres)	Inter-Vehicle-Unit Distance (metres)	Number of Axles					
		3	4	5	6	7	8+
any base length	less than 3.6	25,450	33,000	35,000	39,000	49,000	53,000
less than 11m	3.6 and over	25,450	35,000	41,000	42,500	52,000	55,000
11.0 to less than 12.0	3.6 and over	25,450	35,000	42,500	45,000	52,000	55,000
12.0 to less than 13.0	3.6 and over	25,450	35,000	44,500	47,000	52,000	55,000
13.0 to less than14.0	3.6 and over	25,450	35,000	44,500	49,500	52,000	55,000
14.0 to less than 15.0	3.6 and over	25,450	35,000	44,500	51,500	53,000	55,000
15.0 to less than 16.0	3.6 and over	25,450	37,000	44,500	53,500	53,500	55,000
16.0 to less than 17.5	3.6 and over	25,450	37,000	46,000	53,500	55,000	55,500

VEHICLE WEIGHT TABLE 30
ALLOWABLE GROSS WEIGHT ON DESIGNATED TRUCK-TRAILER COMBINATIONS (KILOGRAMS)

Base Length (metres)	Inter-Vehicle-Unit Distance (metres)	Number of Axles					
		3	4	5	6	7	8+
17.5 to less than 18.5	3.6 and over	25,450	37,000	46,000	55,000	58,000	59,000
18.5 to less than 19.5	3.6 and over	25,450	37,000	46,000	55,000	60,500	61,500
19.5 and over (front axle less than 8,000 kg)	3.6 and over	25,450	37,000	46,000	55,000	61,500	62,500
19.5 and over (front axle 8,000 kg or more)	3.6 and over	25,450	37,000	46,000	56,000	63,000	63,500

VEHICLE WEIGHT TABLE 31
ALLOWABLE GROSS WEIGHT ON DESIGNATED TRUCK-TRAILER COMBINATIONS (KILOGRAMS)

Base Length (metres)	Inter-Vehicle-Unit Distance (metres)	Number of Axles					
		3	4	5	6	7	8+
Any base length	less than 3.6m	24,000	30,000	32,000	34,500	44,500	48,000
less than 11	3.6m and over	24,000	32,000	38,000	38,000	47,500	50,000
11.0 to less than 12.0	3.6m and over	24,000	32,000	39,000	40,500	47,500	50,000
12.0 to less than 13.0	3.6m and over	24,000	32,000	41,000	42,500	47,500	50,000
13.0 to less than 14.0	3.6m and over	24,000	32,000	41,000	45,000	47,500	50,000
14.0 to less than 15.0	3.6m and over	25,450	32,000	41,000	47,000	48,500	50,000
15.0 to less than 16.0	3.6m and over	25,450	32,000	41,000	47,000	49,000	50,000
16.0 to less than 17.5	3.6m and over	25,450	32,000	41,000	47,000	50,000	50,500
17.5 to less than 18.5	3.6m and over	25,450	33,500	41,250	48,000	52,000	53,000

Tab. 1   Ont. Reg. 413/05 — Vehicle Weights and Dimensions

VEHICLE WEIGHT TABLE 31
ALLOWABLE GROSS WEIGHT ON DESIGNATED TRUCK-TRAILER COMBINATIONS (KILOGRAMS)

Base Length (metres)	Inter-Vehicle-Unit Distance (metres)	3	4	5	6	7	8+
18.5 to less than 19.5	3.6m and over	25,450	33,500	41,250	48,000	53,000	54,000
19.5 and over	3.6m and over	25,450	33,500	41,250	48,000	53,500	54,000

VEHICLE WEIGHT TABLE 32
ALLOWABLE GROSS WEIGHT ON NON-DESIGNATED VEHICLES AND COMBINATIONS (OTHER THAN B-TRAIN COMBINATIONS) THAT ARE GOVERNED BY SECTION 21

Base Length (metres)	2	3	4	5	6	7	8+
Less than 8	15,000	21,500	27,000	28,000	32,000	36,000	36,000
8 to less than 10	15,000	21,500	28,000	31,000	33,000	36,000	36,000
10 to less than 12	15,000	21,500	28,000	34,000	37,000	39,000	39,000
12 to less than 14	15,000	21,500	29,000	36,500	42,000	43,000	43,000
14 to less than 15	15,000	21,500	29,000	36,500	45,000	46,000	46,000
15 to less than 16	15,000	21,500	29,000	36,500	46,000	47,000	48,000
16 to less than 18	15,000	21,500	29,000	36,500	46,000	48,000	50,000
18 and over	15,000	21,500	29,000	36,500	46,000	50,000	52,000

VEHICLE WEIGHT TABLE 33
ALLOWABLE GROSS WEIGHT ON NON-DESIGNATED B-TRAIN COMBINATIONS THAT ARE GOVERNED BY SECTION 21

Base Length (metres)	4	5	6	7	8+
less than 15	27,000	28,000	32,000	36,000	36,000
15 to less than 16	29,000	36,500	45,000	48,000	49,000
16 to less than 18	29,000	36,500	46,000	50,000	51,000
18 to less than 19	29,000	36,500	46,000	53,000	54,000
19 and over	30,000	37,000	47,000	54,000	57,000

O. Reg. 457/10, s. 30; 167/12, ss. 13–15; 16/14, s. 35

ONT. REG. 630 — VEHICLES ON CONTROLLED-ACCESS HIGHWAYS

made under the *Highway Traffic Act*

R.R.O. 1990, Reg. 630, as am. O. Reg. 446/92; 24/93; 805/93; 468/96; 102/97; 433/97; 465/00; 598/05; 45/08; 314/08; 265/09; 368/09; 416/10; 476/10; 454/11; 28/12; 193/12; 233/12; 240/12; 360/12; 229/13; 367/15; 26/16.

1. (1) Subject to subsection (2), no person shall operate,

(a) a bicycle;

(b) a motorcycle having a cylinder swept volume of 50 cubic centimetres or less;

(c) a motorcycle driven by electricity stored in the vehicle;

(c.1) a limited-speed motorcycle, as defined in Ontario Regulation 340/94 (Drivers' Licences) made under the Act;

(c.2) a power-assisted bicycle;

(d) a motor assisted bicycle; or

(e) a wheelchair,

on those controlled-access highways and parts of controlled-access highways described in the schedules.

(2) Subsection (1) does not apply to a person who resides on lands adjoining the controlled-access highway to which lands there is no other means of access by highway while such person is engaged in gaining access or egress from such lands, and provided that in gaining such access or egress the person proceeds by the shortest route over such controlled-access highway to the lands.

O. Reg. 598/05, s. 1; 368/09, s. 1

2. Where a highway is referred to in a Schedule by a number or name, the reference is to that part of the King's Highway or to the private toll highway that is known thereby.

O. Reg. 367/15, s. 1

. . . . .

ONT. REG. 631 — YIELD RIGHT-OF-WAY SIGNS IN TERRITORY WITHOUT MUNICIPAL ORGANIZATION

made under the *Highway Traffic Act*

R.R.O. 1990, Reg. 631, as am. O. Reg. 432/91; 279/93; 28/94; 228/94; 295/94; 566/94; 125/95; 307/95; 387/95; 494/95; 150/96; 151/96; 368/96; 412/96; 210/97; 363/97; 376/97; 435/99; 441/00; 295/02; 12/03; 307/06; 6/07; 420/09; 416/11; 185/12; 225/12; 124/13; 106/15.

(Schedules omitted.)

1. The intersections on highways in territory without municipal organization that are described in paragraph 1 of each Schedule are designated as intersections at which yield right-of-way signs shall be erected to face traffic travelling in the direction referred to in paragraph 2 of each Schedule.

2. Where a highway is referred to in a Schedule by a number or name, the reference is to that part of the highway in a territory without municipal organization that is known thereby.

COMPULSORY AUTOMOBILE INSURANCE ACT

R.S.O. 1990, c. C.25, as am. S.O. 1993, c. 10, s. 52; 1994, c. 11, s. 383; 1996, c. 21, s. 50; 1997, c. 19, s. 2; 1997, c. 28, ss. 29–33; 2002, c. 22, ss. 33–36; 2005, c. 31, Sched. 4; 2012, c. 8, Sched. 8; 2014, c. 7, Sched. 6.

1. (1) Definitions — In this Act,

"agent" means an agent or broker within the meaning of the *Insurance Act* who is authorized to solicit automobile insurance;

"Association" means the Facility Association referred to in subsection 7(1);

"automobile insurance" means insurance against liability arising out of bodily injury to or the death of a person or loss of or damage to property caused by a motor vehicle or the use or operation thereof, and which,

    (a) insures at least to the limit required by section 251 of the *Insurance Act*,

    (b) provides the statutory accident benefits set out in the *Statutory Accident Benefits Schedule* under the *Insurance Act*, and

    (c) provides the benefits prescribed under section 265 of the *Insurance Act*;

"Commissioner" [Repealed 1997, c. 28, s. 30(1).]

"driver's licence" has the same meaning as in the *Highway Traffic Act*;

"highway" has the same meaning as in the *Highway Traffic Act*;

"insurance card" means,

    (a) a Motor Vehicle Liability Insurance Card in the form approved by the Superintendent;

    (b) a policy of automobile insurance or a certificate of a policy in the form approved by the Superintendent, or

    (c) a document in a form approved by the Superintendent;

"insurer" means an insurer licensed under the *Insurance Act* and carrying on the business of automobile insurance, but does not include an insurer whose licence is limited to contracts of reinsurance;

"justice" means a justice under the *Provincial Offences Act*;

"lessee" means, in respect of a motor vehicle, a person who is leasing or renting the motor vehicle for a period of 30 days or more;

"motor vehicle" has the same meaning as in the *Highway Traffic Act* and includes trailers and accessories and equipment of a motor vehicle;

"Plan" means the Plan of Operation referred to in subsection 7(3);

"police officer" means a chief of police or other police officer or a person appointed under section 223 of the *Highway Traffic Act* for the purpose of carrying out the provisions of that Act;

"Registrar" means the Registrar of Motor Vehicles;

"regulations" means the regulations made under this Act;

"Superintendent" means the Superintendent of Financial Services appointed under the *Financial Services Commission of Ontario Act, 1997.*

(2) Streetcars — An electric streetcar that runs on rails principally on a highway shall be deemed to be a motor vehicle for the purposes of this Act.

(3) Exception re: excluded driver — Even if a motor vehicle is insured under a contract of automobile insurance, it shall be deemed to be an uninsured motor vehicle for the purposes of this Act while it is being operated by an excluded driver as defined in the *Insurance Act* with respect to that contract unless the excluded driver is a named insured under another contract of automobile insurance.
1993, c. 10, s. 52(1); 1996, c. 21, s. 50(1), (2); 1997, c. 19, s. 2(1); 1997, c. 28, ss. 29, 30; 2005, c. 31, Sched. 4, s. 1

Case Law

General

R. v. Blackburn (1980), 57 C.C.C. (2d) 7, 1980 CarswellBC 353, 25 B.C.L.R. 218, 9 M.V.R. 146 (B.C.C.A.) — Driving or operating a motor vehicle without insurance is an offence of strict liability.

R. v. Carter, 1985 CarswellNfld 3, 53 Nfld. & P.E.I.R. 145, 34 M.V.R. 294, 156 A.P.R. 145, [1985] N.J. No. 135 (Nfld. Dist. Ct.) — The purpose of the provisions respecting insurance was to ensure that persons injured in automobile accidents would be able to recover damages through insurance coverage on the vehicle at fault. The burden is on the driver to confirm prior to driving the vehicle that appropriate insurance is in effect.

R. v. Hufsky (1988), 40 C.C.C. (3d) 398, 1988 CarswellOnt 54, 1988 CarswellOnt 956, EYB 1988-67448, [1988] 1 S.C.R. 621, 63 C.R. (3d) 14, 4 M.V.R. (2d) 170, 32 C.R.R. 193, 84 N.R. 365, 27 O.A.C. 103, [1988] S.C.J. No. 30 (S.C.C.), [1988] 1 S.C.R. 621 (S.C.C.) — The surrender of an insurance card does not violate s. 8.

R. v. Zwicker, 1994 CarswellOnt 1, 17 O.R. (3d) 171, 21 C.C.L.I. (2d) 171, 1 M.V.R. (3d) 1, [1994] I.L.R. 1-3032, 69 O.A.C. 169, [1994] O.J. No. 197 (Ont. C.A.) — "Owner" in the Act is not restricted to "registered owner".

R. v. Zwicker, 1994 CarswellOnt 1, 17 O.R. (3d) 171, 21 C.C.L.I. (2d) 171, 1 M.V.R. (3d) 1, [1994] I.L.R. 1-3032, 69 O.A.C. 169, [1994] O.J. No. 197 (Ont. C.A.) — "Owner" in the Act is not restricted to "registered owner".

The purposes of the legislation include the protection of the public from loss due to the negligence of an insured motorist by setting up a motor vehicle accident claims fund with a contributory fee.

Laurentian Casual Company of Canada v. State Farm Mutual Automobile Insurance Company (1999), 4 O.R. (3d) 690 (Ont. C.A.) — One of the purposes of then s. 6(2) was to prevent the liability insurance card from showing a coverage date earlier than the date when the contact of insurance was in fact made. The card must reflect the true coverage period.

R. v. Edwards, 2007 CarswellOnt 7845, 56 C.R. (6th) 192, 60 M.V.R. (5th) 59, [2007] O.J. No. 4729, 2007 ONCJ 581 (Ont. C.J.) — Section 13.1(1)(a) created a full *mens rea* offence so that knowledge or willful blindness about a false or invalid nature of the insurance card must be proved.

R. v. Sirriani, 2010 CarswellOnt 10635, 12 M.V.R. (6th) 306, [2010] O.J. No. 5981, 2010 ONCJ 725 (Ont. C.J.) — Sections 7(5)(c), 11(2) and 12(1)(f) of the *Highway Traffic Act* and s. 2(1)(a) of the *Compulsory Automobile Insurance Act* are strict liability offences.

R. v. Ikponmwosa, 2011 CarswellOnt 2067, 2011 ONCJ 149, 13 M.V.R. (6th) 301, [2011] O.J. No. 1367 (Ont. C.J.) — Section 2(1)(b) is a strict liability offence.

Motor Vehicle

Regele v. Slusarczyk (1997), 147 D.L.R. (4th) 294, 1997 CarswellOnt 1354, 33 O.R. (3d) 556, 43 C.C.L.I. (2d) 90, 100 O.A.C. 39, [1997] O.J. No. 1849 (Ont. C.A.) — A farm tractor is not a "motor vehicle" under the *Highway Traffic Act* and therefore not a "motor vehicle" under the *Compulsory Automobile Insurance Act*. Therefore it is not an automobile under the *Insurance Act*.

Copely v. Kerr Farms Ltd. (2002), 212 D.L.R. (4th) 700, 2002 CarswellOnt 1421, 59 O.R. (3d) 346, 36 C.C.L.I. (3d) 161, 27 M.V.R. (4th) 189, 159 O.A.C. 66, [2002] O.J. No. 1644 (Ont. C.A.) — A trailer unattached to a truck was not a trailer for purposes of the Act. A tomato wagon without an engine was not a vehicle under the Act.

Adams v. Pineland Amusements Ltd (2007), 289 D.L.R. (4th) 744, 2007 CarswellOnt 7800, 88 O.R. (3d) 321, 55 C.C.L.I. (4th) 1, 54 M.V.R. (5th) 25, [2008] I.L.R. I-4660, 231 O.A.C. 177, [2007] O.J. No. 4724, 2007 ONCA 844 (Ont. C.A.) — The test was whether the go-cart required motor vehicle insurance at the time and circumstance of the accident. It did not as it was being driving on a private track.

Sentence

R. v. Raymond, 1996 CarswellAlta 1102, 199 A.R. 324, 51 Alta. L.R. (3d) 86, 27 M.V.R. (3d) 257, [1997] 7 W.W.R. 484 (Alta. Prov. Ct.) — A declaration was denied that the then minimum fine of $2,500 represented cruel and unusual punishment, considering that payment schedules and work options were available.

R. v. Fagbemi, 2000 CarswellOnt 2411, 4 M.V.R. (4th) 221, [2000] O.J. No. 2550 (Ont. C.J.); applying *R. v. Turcotte* (2000), 144 C.C.C. (3d) 139, 2000 CarswellOnt 1251, 48 O.R. (3d) 97, 32 C.R. (5th) 296, 131 O.A.C. 311, [2000] O.J. No. 1316 (Ont. C.A.) — Unless an error in principle is disclosed or the sentence is demonstrably unfit, relief from a *Provincial Offences Act* sentence should not be granted. The fact that a minimum fine is beyond the offender's present means does not qualify as an exceptional circumstance.

R. v. Hitchon, 2000 CarswellOnt 5167, 25 C.C.L.I. (3d) 147, 10 M.V.R. (4th) 35, [2000] O.J. No. 5260 (Ont. C.J.) — The minimum fines had to be tempered by s. 59 of the *Provincial Offences Act*.

R. v. Fong, 2004 CarswellOnt 4063, 2004 ONCJ 222, 11 M.V.R. (5th) 29, [2004] O.J. No. 4117 (Ont. C.J.) — The issue of financial hardship in relation to the minimum fine of $5,000 was considered.

R. v. Nerian, 2010 CarswellOnt 881, 92 M.V.R. (5th) 157, 2010 ONCJ 46 (Ont. C.J.) —
The minimum fine was reduced to $1,000 in view of the appellant's severe injuries flow-
ing from the accident and limited employment opportunities.

2. (1) Compulsory automobile insurance — Subject to the regulations, no
owner or lessee of a motor vehicle shall,

    (a) operate the motor vehicle; or

    (b) cause or permit the motor vehicle to be operated,

on a highway unless the motor vehicle is insured under a contract of automobile
insurance.

(2) Definition — For the purposes of subsection (1), where a permit for a motor
vehicle has been issued under subsection 7(7) of the *Highway Traffic Act*, "contract
of automobile insurance" with respect to that motor vehicle means a contract of
automobile insurance made with an insurer. ("contrat d'assurance automobile")

(3) Offence — Every owner or lessee of a motor vehicle who,

    (a) contravenes subsection (1) of this section or subsection 13(11); or

    (b) surrenders an insurance card for inspection to a police officer, when re-
    quested to do so, purporting to show that the motor vehicle is insured under a
    contract of automobile insurance when the motor vehicle is not so insured,

is guilty of an offence and is liable on a first conviction to a fine of not less than
$5,000 and not more than $25,000 and on a subsequent conviction to a fine of not
less than $10,000 and not more than $50,000 and, in addition, his or her driver's
licence may be suspended for a period of not more than one year.

(4) Justice to secure possession of driver's licence — Where a justice
makes a conviction under subsection (3) and the driver's licence of the person convicted is suspended by the justice, the justice shall take the driver's licence and forward it to the Registrar.

(5) Police officer may secure possession — Where a driver's licence is suspended under this section and the person to whom the suspension applies refuses or
fails to surrender his or her licence to the justice forthwith, any police officer may,
and upon the direction of the Registrar shall, take possession of the licence and forward it to the Registrar.

(6) Offence — Every person who fails or refuses to surrender his or her driver's
licence when required by a police officer under subsection (5) is guilty of an offence
and on conviction is liable to a fine of not more than $200.

(7) Impounding motor vehicle — In the event of a conviction under subsection
(3), the justice may order that the motor vehicle,

    (a) that was operated in contravention of subsection (1);

    (b) for which a false statement in respect of insurance was made in contraven-
    tion of subsection 13(11); or

    (c) for which an insurance card was produced in contravention of clause (3)(b), shall be seized, impounded and taken into the custody of the law for a period of not more than three months.

(8) Cost of storage — All costs and charges for the care and storage of the motor vehicle are a lien upon the motor vehicle that may be enforced in the manner provided by the *Repair and Storage Liens Act.*

(9) Release of vehicle on security given by owner — If the person convicted under subsection (3) gives security to the satisfaction of the convicting justice, by bond, recognizance or otherwise, that the motor vehicle will not be operated upon a highway during the period specified by the justice in making an order under subsection (7), the motor vehicle may be released to the person convicted, and if the motor vehicle is operated upon a highway during such period it shall be deemed to have been operated without a permit, as defined in subsection 6(1) of the *Highway Traffic Act.*

(10) Three year limitation period — Proceedings may be commenced at any time within three years after the date on which an offence was, or is alleged to have been, committed under subsection (1) or clause (3)(b) or subsection 13(11).

1994, c. 11, s. 383; 1996, c. 21, s. 50(3)–(6); 2002, c. 22, s. 33

3. (1) Operator to carry insurance card — An operator of a motor vehicle on a highway shall have in the motor vehicle at all times,

(a) an insurance card for the motor vehicle; or

(b) an insurance card evidencing that the operator is insured under a contract of automobile insurance,

and the operator shall surrender the insurance card for reasonable inspection upon the demand of a police officer.

(2) Excluded driver to carry insurance card — Despite subsection (1), an operator of a motor vehicle who is named as an excluded driver under the contract of automobile insurance under which the vehicle is insured shall have in the vehicle at all times an insurance card evidencing that the operator is a named insured under another contract of automobile insurance, and the operator shall surrender the insurance card for reasonable inspection upon the demand of a police officer.

(3) Offence — A person who contravenes this section is guilty of an offence and on conviction is liable to a fine of not more than $400.

1996, c. 21, s. 50(7)

4. (1) Particulars to be disclosed — An operator of a motor vehicle on a highway who is directly or indirectly involved in an accident shall, on the request of any person directly or indirectly involved in the accident, disclose to the person the particulars of the contract of automobile insurance insuring the motor vehicle.

(2) Definition — For the purposes of subsection (1), "particulars of the contract of automobile insurance" means,

(a) the name and adddress of the insured;

(b) the make, model and serial number of the insured vehicle;

(c) the effective date and expiry date of the contract;

(d) the name of the insurer;

(e) the name of the insurer's agent, if any; and

(f) the policy number of the contract.

(3) **Offence** — A person who contravenes subsection (1) is guilty of an offence and on conviction is liable to a fine of not more than $400.

1993, c. 10, s. 52(2); 1996, c. 21, s. 50(8)

5. Obligations of agents — An agent shall,

(a) provide to an owner or lessee of a motor vehicle who is a resident of Ontario an application for automobile insurance; and

(b) submit to an insurer a completed application for automobile insurance,

when requested to do so by the owner or lessee of a motor vehicle.

1996, c. 21, s. 50(9)

6. (1) Insurance card to be issued — An insurer shall issue, or cause its agent to issue, an insurance card to a person with whom a contract of automobile insurance is made or whose contract of automobile insurance is renewed.

(2) **Misrepresentations** — No insurer or its agent shall, on an insurance card, specify an effective date earlier than the date on which the contract of automobile insurance was actually made or misrepresent in any other way the particulars of the automobile insurance.

7. (1) Facility Association continued — The unincorporated non-profit association of insurers known as the Facility Association is continued under the name Facility Association in English and under the name Association des assureurs in French.

(2) **Membership** — Every insurer is a member of the Association.

(3) **The Plan** — The Association shall, in its articles of association, establish a plan, to be known as the Plan of Operation, for providing a contract of automobile insurance to owners, lessees and licensed drivers of motor vehicles who, but for the Plan, would be unable to obtain such insurance.

(3.1) **Compliance with Plan, etc.** — Every member of the Association shall comply with the Plan and the articles of association, by-laws, rules and resolutions of the Association.

(4) **Duty of Association** — The Association shall ensure, through its members, that a contract of automobile insurance is provided with respect to every application for automobile insurance submitted under the Plan to an insurer under clause 5(b).

(5) **Agents bound by articles of association, etc.** — Where an agent submits an application under the Plan to an insurer, the agent shall be bound by the applicable articles of association and by-laws of the Association.

(6) Risk sharing — The Plan may include provisions with respect to the establishment and operation of a risk sharing pool for members of the Association.

(6.1) Catastrophic claims — The Plan may include provisions with respect to the establishment and operation of a catastrophic claims fund for members of the Association.

(7) Actions by and against Association — The Association may, in its name,

(a) [Repealed 1993, c. 10, s. 52(6).]

(b) sue and be sued.

1993, c. 10, s. 52(3)–(6); 1996, c. 21, s. 50(10)

8. (1) Board of directors — The affairs of the Association shall be administered by a board of directors established in accordance with its articles of association.

(2) Information to be provided to Superintendent — The Association shall notify the Superintendent of the names and residence addresses of the persons elected or appointed as officers and directors of the Association forthwith after such election or appointment, and such names and addresses may be made available to the public by the Superintendent.

(3) Service on Association — Service on the directors or officers of the Association, or any of them, is good and sufficient service on the Association, and such service may be by personal service or by registered mail.

(4) Idem — Where service on the Association is made by registered mail on a director or officer of the Association under subsection (3), the service shall be deemed to have been made on the fifth day after the day of mailing unless the notice is not delivered or the director or officer to whom notice is given establishes that he or she did not, acting in good faith, through absence, accident, illness or other cause beyond his or her control, receive the notice until a later date.

1997, c. 28, s. 29

9. (1) By-laws — The Association may pass by-laws relating to its affairs and not inconsistent with this Act or the regulations,

(a) providing for the execution of documents by the Association;

(b) respecting banking and finance;

(c) fixing the financial year of the Association and providing for the audit of the accounts and transactions of the Association;

(d) providing for the appointment and remuneration of officers and employees of the Association;

(e) respecting the calling, holding and conducting of meetings of the Association and the duties of members of the Association;

(f) delegating to an operating committee such powers and duties of the board of directors as are set out in the by-law, other than the power to make, amend or revoke by-laws;

(g) prescribing forms and providing for their use;

(h) respecting management of the property of the Association;

(i) respecting the application of the funds of the Association and the investment and reinvestment of any of its funds not immediately required and for the safe-keeping of its securities;

(j) imposing assessments on members of the Association for the purpose of meeting the operating costs of the Association and the Plan and providing for the collection of such assessments;

(k) prescribing rules and procedures related to the operation of the Plan; and

(l) respecting all of the things that are considered necessary for the operation of the Plan, the attainment of the objects of the Association and the efficient conduct of its affairs.

(2) **Articles of association** — Any power of the Association that may be exercised by by-law under subsection (1) may be provided for in the articles of association of the Association.

10. (1) **Filing of by-laws and amendments** — The Association shall file with the Superintendent every by-law and every amendment, revision or consolidation of the Plan or of the articles of association, by-laws, rules or resolutions of the Association at least thirty days before the effective date of the by-law or of the amendment, revision or consolidation.

(2) **Approval of Superintendent** — No by-law and no amendment, revision or consolidation of the Plan or of the articles of association, by-laws, rules or resolutions of the Association shall come into effect unless it is approved by the Superintendent.

(3) **Rates** — The Association may prepare rates in respect of contracts provided under the Plan.

(4) **Idem** — Rates prepared under subsection (3) do not come into effect until approved under the *Insurance Act*.

1993, c. 10, s. 52(7); 1997, c. 28, ss. 29, 31

11. Investigatory powers — The Superintendent has the same powers in respect of the Association that the Superintendent has in respect of an insurer under sections 442.1, 442.2, 442.3, 443 and 444 of the *Insurance Act*.

1993, c. 10, s. 52(8); 1997, c. 28, s. 29; 2014, c. 7, Sched. 6, s. 1

11.1 Annual report — The Superintendent shall make an annual report to the Minister of Finance on the affairs of the Association and the Minister shall then lay the report before the Assembly if it is in session or, if not, at the next session.

1993, c. 10, s. 52(8); 1997, c. 28, s. 29

12. (1) Termination of contracts of insurance — Where a contract of automobile insurance has been in effect for more than sixty days, the insurer may only terminate the contract for one or more of the following reasons:

    1. Non-payment of, or any part of, the premium due under the contract or of any charge under any agreement ancillary to the contract.

    2. The insured has given false particulars of the described automobile to the prejudice of the insurer.

    3. The insured has knowingly misrepresented or failed to disclose in an application for insurance any fact required to be stated therein.

    4. For a material change of risk within the meaning of the statutory conditions referred to in section 234 of the *Insurance Act*.

(2) Exception — Subsection (1) does not apply to,

    (a) an insurer running off its business, where the insurer has specific approval of the Superintendent to cancel a contract; or

    (b) a contract in respect of a motor vehicle used in the course of carrying on a business, trade or profession.

1993, c. 10, s. 52(9), (10); 1997, c. 28, s. 29

13. (1) Validation or transfer of permits — No person shall apply for the issuance, validation or transfer of a permit for a motor vehicle unless the motor vehicle is insured under a contract of automobile insurance.

(2) Ministry to be satisfied of insurance — The Ministry of Transportation shall not issue, validate or transfer a permit for a motor vehicle unless it is satisfied that, at the time that the application for the issuance, validation or transfer is made, the motor vehicle is insured under a contract of automobile insurance.

(3) Minister may require information — The following persons shall, upon the request of the Minister of Transportation, give the Registrar such information as may be prescribed, including personal information, for any purpose related to this Act or any provision of the *Highway Traffic Act* concerning automobile insurance, subject to such conditions as may be prescribed:

    1. A particular insurer.

    2. Every insurer in a prescribed class of insurers.

    3. A particular person.

    4. Every person in a prescribed class of persons.

(4) Collection of information on Minister's behalf — The Minister of Transportation may enter into agreements authorizing one or more persons to collect and keep information provided under subsection (3) on behalf of the Registrar, and require those persons to provide the information to the Registrar.

(5) Format of information — The Minister of Transportation may require that information provided or kept under subsection (3) or (4) be in any format that the Minister considers appropriate, and be provided by any means that the Minister considers appropriate.

(6) **Verifying accuracy** — The Minister of Transportation may verify the accuracy of information provided or kept under subsection (3) or (4) by comparing the information with information that is collected under the authority of the *Highway Traffic Act*.

(7) **Use of information for other purposes** — Nothing in this section limits or controls the collection, use or disclosure of, or access to, any information provided to a person authorized under subsection (4), for any purpose other than one set out in this section.

(8) **Proof of insurance** — Despite anything in this Act or the *Highway Traffic Act*, the Ministry of Transportation may require a person who applies for the issuance, validation or transfer of a permit for a motor vehicle to do any or all of the following:

　　1. Certify in a form approved by the Superintendent that the motor vehicle is insured under a contract of automobile insurance.

　　2. Produce for inspection an insurance card for the motor vehicle.

　　3. Produce for inspection any other evidence that is satisfactory to the Ministry of Transportation that the motor vehicle is insured under a contract of automobile insurance.

(9) **Ministry of Transportation may rely on information** — The Ministry of Transportation, for the purpose of determining that it is satisfied under subsection (2), may rely on information obtained pursuant to this section.

(10) **No liability** — Where the Ministry of Transportation has relied on information obtained pursuant to this section, the Crown, the Minister of Transportation, the Ministry, the Registrar and the employees, officers and agents of the Minister or the Ministry are not liable in any action relating to the issuance, validation or transfer of a permit for a motor vehicle that arises out of that reliance or any failure or refusal to issue, validate or transfer a permit that arises out of that reliance.

(11) **Offence for false statement** — No person shall, in certifying under paragraph 1 of subsection (8) that a motor vehicle is insured under a contract of automobile insurance, make a statement that he or she knows or ought to know is false.

(12) **Definition** — In this section,

"contract of automobile insurance" means a contract of automobile insurance made with an insurer.

2002, c. 22, s. 34

13.1 (1) Possession, use, sale, etc., of false or invalid insurance card — No person shall,

　　(a) have a false or invalid insurance card in his or her possession that he or she knows or ought to know is false or invalid;

　　(b) use a false or invalid insurance card that he or she knows or ought to know is false or invalid;

(c) sell, give, deliver or distribute a false or invalid insurance card that he or she knows or ought to know is false or invalid; or

(d) produce for inspection any other evidence, that he or she knows or ought to know is false or invalid, that the motor vehicle is insured under a contract of automobile insurance.

(2) **Offence** — A person who contravenes this section is guilty of an offence and is liable on a first conviction to a fine of not less than $10,000 and not more than $50,000 and on a subsequent conviction to a fine of not less than $20,000 and not more than $100,000.

(3) **Definition** — In this section,

"contract of automobile insurance" means a contract of automobile insurance made with an insurer.

1996, c. 21, s. 50(11); 2002, c. 22, s. 34

13.2 (1) **Evidence in certain prosecutions** — This section applies with respect to prosecutions for offences under sections 2, 13 and 13.1.

(2) **Statutory declaration** — A statutory declaration by a person who is identified in the declaration as an officer or employee of an insurer is admissible in evidence as proof, in the absence of evidence to the contrary, that the motor vehicle identified in the declaration was or was not insured by the insurer on the date or dates specified in the declaration.

2002, c. 22, s. 34

14. (1) **Definition** — In this section, "person" includes the Association.

(2) **General penalty** — Every person who contravenes any provision of this Act or the regulations is guilty of an offence and, except where otherwise provided, on conviction is liable on a first conviction to a fine of not more than $250,000 and on each subsequent conviction to a fine of not more than $500,000.

(3) **Insurers, Association** — If an insurer or the Association is convicted of an offence under subsection (2), the fine shall not be less than $5,000.

(4) **Directors, officers, etc.** — Every director, officer or chief agent of an insurer or the Association is guilty of an offence who,

(a) caused, authorized, permitted or participated in the insurer or Association committing an offence to which subsection (2) applies; or

(b) failed to take reasonable care to prevent the insurer or Association from committing an offence to which subsection (2) applies.

(5) **Penalty** — On conviction for an offence under subsection (4), the person convicted is liable on a first conviction to a fine of not more than $100,000 and on a subsequent conviction to a fine of not more than $200,000.

(6) **Application** — Subsection (4) applies whether or not the insurer or Association has been prosecuted for or convicted of an offence to which subsection (2) applies.

(7) Restitution — A court that convicts a person of an offence to which this section applies may, in addition to any other penalty, order the person to make compensation or restitution in relation to the offence.

1993, c. 10, s. 52(11); 2012, c. 8, Sched. 8, s. 1

14.1 (1) Suspension or cancellation of licence — In addition to any penalty under this Act, if an insurer contravenes this Act, the Superintendent may suspend or cancel the insurer's licence issued under the *Insurance Act*.

(2) Hearing — If the Superintendent intends to suspend or cancel the licence of an insurer, the procedure set out in section 58 of the *Insurance Act* applies to the suspension or cancellation, as the case may be.

1993, c. 10, s. 52(11); 1997, c. 28, s. 32

14.2 Definitions — In sections 14.3 to 14.7 and subsection 15(3),

"person" includes the Association;

"requirement established under this Act" means,

(a) a requirement imposed by a provision of this Act that is prescribed for the purpose of section 14.4 or 14.5 or by a provision of a regulation that is prescribed for the purpose of either of those sections,

(b) a requirement imposed by order, or

(c) an obligation assumed by way of undertaking.

2012, c. 8, Sched. 8, s. 2

14.3 (1) Administrative penalties — An administrative penalty may be imposed under section 14.4 or 14.5 for either of the following purposes:

1. To promote compliance with the requirements established under this Act.

2. To prevent a person from deriving, directly or indirectly, any economic benefit as a result of contravening or failing to comply with a requirement established under this Act.

(2) Same — An administrative penalty may be imposed alone or in conjunction with any other regulatory measure provided by this Act, including an order under section 14.1 for the suspension or cancellation of an insurer's licence.

2012, c. 8, Sched. 8, s. 2

14.4 (1) General administrative penalties — If the Superintendent is satisfied that a person is contravening or not complying with or has contravened or failed to comply with any of the following, the Superintendent may, by order, impose an administrative penalty on the person in accordance with this section and the regulations:

1. A provision of this Act or the regulations as may be prescribed.

2. A requirement or obligation described in clause (b) or (c) of the definition of "requirement established under this Act" in section 14.2.

(2) Procedure — If the Superintendent proposes to impose an administrative penalty under subsection (1), the procedure set out in section 441.3 of the *Insurance Act* applies, with necessary modifications.

2012, c. 8, Sched. 8, s. 2

14.5 (1) Summary administrative penalties — If the Superintendent is satisfied that a person is contravening or not complying with or has contravened or failed to comply with a provision of this Act or the regulations as may be prescribed, the Superintendent may, by order, impose an administrative penalty on the person in accordance with this section and the regulations.

(2) Procedure — The procedure set out in section 441.4 of the *Insurance Act* applies, with necessary modifications, to the imposition of an administrative penalty under subsection (1).

2012, c. 8, Sched. 8, s. 2

14.6 (1) Maximum administrative penalties — An administrative penalty imposed under section 14.4 shall not exceed the following amounts:

1. For a contravention or failure to comply by a person, other than an individual, $200,000 or such lesser amount as may be prescribed for a prescribed requirement established under this Act.

2. For a contravention or failure to comply by an individual, $100,000 or such lesser amount as may be prescribed for a prescribed requirement established under this Act.

(2) Same — An administrative penalty imposed under section 14.5 shall not exceed $25,000 or such lesser amount as may be prescribed for a prescribed requirement established under this Act.

2012, c. 8, Sched. 8, s. 2

14.7 Enforcement of administrative penalties — Section 441.6 of the *Insurance Act* applies, with necessary modifications, with respect to the payment and enforcement of administrative penalties imposed under this Act.

2012, c. 8, Sched. 8, s. 2

15. (1) Regulations — The Lieutenant Governor in Council may make regulations,

(a) exempting any person or class of persons or vehicle or class of vehicles from this Act or any provision of this Act, subject to such conditions as are set out in the regulations;

(b) prescribing identifying markers for all automobiles licensed in Ontario and providing for their use;

(c) [Repealed 1997, c. 19, s. 2(2).]

(c.1) making amendments to the Plan and to the articles of association, by-laws, rules and resolutions of the Association;

(c.2) prescribing persons, classes of persons, insurers, classes of insurers, information and conditions for the purposes of subsection 13(3).

(d) [Repealed 1997, c. 19, s. 2(3).]

(2) **Regulation under cl. (1)(c.1)** — A regulation shall not be made under clause (1)(c.1) unless the Superintendent has consulted with the Association on the subject matter of the regulation and has submitted a report on the consultation to the Minister of Finance.

(3) **Regulations, administrative penalties** — The Lieutenant Governor in Council may make regulations governing the administrative penalties that may be imposed under sections 14.4 and 14.5 and, without limiting the generality of the foregoing, may make regulations,

(a) prescribing provisions of this Act or the regulations for the purposes of sections 14.4 and 14.5;

(b) prescribing criteria the Superintendent is required or permitted to consider when imposing a penalty under section 14.4 or 14.5;

(c) prescribing the amount of a penalty, or the method for calculating the amount of a penalty, and prescribing different penalties or ranges of penalties for different types of contraventions or failures to comply and for different classes of persons;

(d) authorizing the Superintendent to determine the amount of a penalty, if the amount of the penalty or the method for calculating the amount of the penalty is not prescribed, and prescribing criteria the Superintendent is required or permitted to consider when determining this;

(e) authorizing a penalty to be imposed for each day or part of a day on which a contravention or failure to comply continues;

(f) authorizing higher penalties (not to exceed the maximum penalty established under section 14.6 or prescribed under clause (j)) for a second or subsequent contravention or failure to comply by a person;

(g) governing the manner of paying the penalties;

(h) requiring that a penalty be paid before a specified deadline or before a deadline specified by the Superintendent;

(i) authorizing the imposition of late payment fees respecting penalties that are not paid before the deadline, including graduated late payment fees;

(j) prescribing lesser maximum administrative penalties and the requirements established under this Act to which the lesser maximum penalties apply for the purpose of subsection 14.6(1) or (2).

1993, c. 10, s. 52(13); 1996, c. 21, s. 50; 1997, c. 19, s. 2; 1997, c. 28, s. 29; 2002, c. 22, s. 35; 2012, c. 8, Sched. 8, s. 3

16. (1) Forms — The Superintendent may approve forms for the purposes of this Act and the forms may provide for such information to be furnished as the Superintendent may require.

(2) **Electronic forms** — The Superintendent may approve an electronic version of a form.

1997, c. 19, s. 2(4); 1997, c. 28, s. 33(2)

ONT. REG. 409/12 — ADMINISTRATIVE PENALTIES

made under the *Compulsory Automobile Insurance Act*

O. Reg. 409/12

GENERAL ADMINISTRATIVE PENALTIES IMPOSED UNDER SECTION 14.4 OF THE ACT

1. Prescribed provisions — The provisions of the Act that are listed in Schedule 1 are prescribed for the purpose of imposing a general administrative penalty under section 14.4 of the Act.

2. Maximum penalty — The maximum penalty that may be imposed under section 14.4 of the Act for a contravention of or failure to comply with a requirement imposed by a provision listed in Schedule 1 is,

    (a) $100,000 for a person other than an individual;

    (b) $50,000 for an individual.

3. Determination of amount of penalty — (1) The Superintendent is authorized to determine the amount of a penalty imposed under section 14.4 of the Act, subject to the limits set out in section 2.

(2) The Superintendent shall consider only the following criteria when determining the amount of an administrative penalty to be imposed under section 14.4 of the Act for a purpose set out in section 14.3 of the Act:

    1. The degree to which the contravention or failure was intentional, reckless or negligent.

    2. The extent of the harm or potential harm to others resulting from the contravention or failure.

    3. The extent to which the person tried to mitigate any loss or to take other remedial action.

    4. The extent to which the person derived or reasonably might have expected to derive, directly or indirectly, any economic benefit from the contravention or failure.

    5. Any other contraventions of or failures to comply with a requirement established under the Act or with any other financial services legislation of Ontario or of any jurisdiction during the preceding five years by the person.

4. Deadline for paying penalty — (1) A person on whom a penalty has been imposed under section 14.4 of the Act shall pay the penalty no later than 30 days after the person is given notice of the order imposing the penalty or such longer time as may be specified in the order.

(2) If a person requests a hearing on the notice of a proposal to impose a penalty pursuant to subsection 14.4(2) of the Act and in accordance with subsection 441.3(5) of the *Insurance Act*, the person shall pay the penalty no later than 30 days after the matter is finally determined or such longer time as may be specified in the order.

SUMMARY ADMINISTRATIVE PENALTIES IMPOSED UNDER SECTION 14.5 OF THE ACT

5. Prescribed provisions — The provisions of the Act that are set out in Column 1 of Schedule 2 are prescribed for the purpose of imposing a summary administrative penalty under section 14.5 of the Act.

6. Amount of penalty — The amount that is set out in Column 2 of Schedule 2 opposite a provision set out in Column 1 of Schedule 2 is the penalty that may be imposed under section 14.5 of the Act for a contravention of or failure to comply with a requirement imposed by that provision.

7. Deadline for paying penalty — (1) A person on whom a penalty has been imposed under section 14.5 of the Act shall pay the penalty no later than 30 days after the person is given notice of the order imposing the penalty or such longer time as may be specified in the order.

(2) If a person appeals the Superintendent's order pursuant to subsection 14.5(2) of the Act and in accordance with subsection 441.4(4) of the *Insurance Act*, the person shall pay the penalty no later than 30 days after the matter is finally determined or such longer time as may be specified in the varied or confirmed order.

COMMENCEMENT

8. Commencement — This Regulation comes into force on the later of the day section 1 of Schedule 8 to the *Strong Action for Ontario Act (Budget Measures), 2012* comes into force and the day this Regulation is filed.

SCHEDULE 1 — GENERAL ADMINISTRATIVE PENALTIES IMPOSED UNDER SECTION 14.4 OF THE ACT — LESSER MAXIMUM PENALTIES PRESCRIBED

Item	Provision
1.	subsection 6(1)
2.	subsection 6(2)
3.	subsection 7(3.1)
4.	subsection 7(4)

Item	Provision
5.	subsection 12(1)

Schedule 2 — Summary Administrative Penalties Imposed under Section 14.5 of the Act — Prescribed Penalty

Item	Column 1 — Provision	Column 2 — Penalty
1.	section 5	$3,000
2.	subsection 8(2)	$1,000
3.	subsection 10(1)	$1,000

ONT. REG. 239/10 — AUTOMOBILE INSURANCE REPORTING INFORMATION

made under the *Compulsory Automobile Insurance Act*

O. Reg. 239/10

1. Definitions — In this Regulation,

"automobile insurance reporting information" means the information prescribed by subsection 2(2);

"Minister" means the Minister of Transportation.

2. Prescribed persons and information — (1) Every person who is an insurer within the meaning of subsection 1(1) of the Act is prescribed for the purposes of subsection 13(3) of the Act.

(2) The following information concerning automobile insurance with respect to a motor vehicle is prescribed for the purposes of subsection 13(3) of the Act:

1. The vehicle identification number of the motor vehicle.

2. Whether the motor vehicle is insured under a contract of automobile insurance.

3. The effective date of the contract of automobile insurance with respect to the motor vehicle.

4. The expiry date of the contract of automobile insurance.

5. Information on any renewal and new expiry date of the contract of automobile insurance with respect to the motor vehicle.

6. Information on any cancellation, expiration or termination of the contract of automobile insurance with respect to the motor vehicle.

7. Information on any deletion or change in coverage which results in the motor vehicle ceasing to be insured for any mandatory coverage required under a contract of automobile insurance.

8. Information on the addition of a motor vehicle to a contract of automobile insurance or the deletion of a motor vehicle from a contract of automobile insurance.

9. Any change to any automobile insurance reporting information described in paragraphs 1 to 8 that has been previously provided with respect to the motor vehicle or the contract of insurance.

10. The name of the insurer submitting the automobile insurance reporting information.

3. Compliance time limits — (1) Every insurer shall provide automobile insurance reporting information in accordance with the following requirements with respect to every motor vehicle in a class of motor vehicles specified in the Minister's request that is insured under a contract of automobile insurance issued by the insurer:

1. Automobile insurance reporting information described in paragraphs 1, 3 and 4 of subsection 2(2) must be provided,

i. on or before the day specified in the request with respect to motor vehicles insured under contracts of insurance in effect on the day of the request,

ii. as soon as practicable after the effective date of any new contract of automobile insurance issued before December 1, 2011, and

iii. no later than 14 days after the effective date of any new contract of automobile insurance issued after November 30, 2011.

2. Automobile insurance reporting information described in paragraphs 5, 6, 7 and 9 of subsection 2(2) that includes the vehicle identification number of the motor vehicle must be provided as soon as practicable after the effective date of any of the following, if the effective date is before December 1, 2011, and no later than 14 days after the effective date of any of the following, if the effective date is after November 30, 2011:

i. Any renewal, cancellation, expiry or termination of the contract of insurance with respect to the motor vehicle.

ii. Any deletion or change in coverage described in paragraph 7 of subsection 2(2) with respect to the motor vehicle.

iii. Any other change to the automobile insurance reporting information previously provided with respect to the motor vehicle.

3. Automobile insurance reporting information described in paragraph 8 of subsection 2(2) that includes the vehicle identification number of the motor vehicle must be provided,

i. as soon as practicable after the date the insurer is notified of the addition or deletion described in that paragraph, if the insurer is notified before December 1, 2011, and

ii. no later than 14 days after the insurer is notified of the addition or deletion described in that paragraph if the insurer is notified after November 30, 2011.

(2) Despite subparagraph 1 i of subsection (1), an insurer that, before receiving the request from the Minister, has already provided automobile insurance reporting information to the Registrar, or to a person authorized under subsection 13(4) of the Act to collect and keep the information, with respect to a motor vehicle in a class of motor vehicles specified in the Minister's request,

(a) is not required to provide the same information again after receiving the request; and

(b) is required to provide, on or before the day specified in the request, any applicable automobile insurance reporting information required under para-

graph 1, 2 or 3 of subsection (1) that has not been provided with respect to the motor vehicle.

4. Commencement — This Regulation comes into force on the latest of,

(a) the day section 34 of the *Keeping the Promise for a Strong Economy Act (Budget Measures), 2002* comes into force;

(b) the day subsection 35(2) of the *Keeping the Promise for a Strong Economy Act (Budget Measures), 2002* comes into force; and

(c) the day this Regulation is filed.

ONT. REG. 95 — EXEMPTIONS

made under the *Compulsory Automobile Insurance Act*

R.R.O. 1990, Reg. 95, as am. O. Reg. 51/05.

1. The Act does not apply to,

(a) the Governor General;

(b) a department of the Government of Canada;

(c) the operator of a motor vehicle owned by or leased to the Governor General or a department of the Government of Canada.

2. (1) Subject to the conditions set out in subsection (2), the Act does not apply to,

(a) a member in good standing of the Conservative Mennonite Churches of Ontario who is a member of the Conservative Mennonite Automobile Brotherhood Assistance Plan; or

(b) the operator of a motor vehicle owned by or leased to a person referred to in clause (a).

(2) The following conditions apply to the exemption granted by subsection (1):

1. The Conservative Mennonite Churches of Ontario shall establish a plan to provide for financial responsibility, resulting from motor vehicle accidents, for its members.

2. The Plan referred to in paragraph 1 shall be known as the Conservative Mennonite Automobile Brotherhood Assistance Plan.

3. Where a new Plan Administrator is appointed, the new Plan Administrator shall forthwith advise the Superintendent of their name and address.

4. Any Mennonite who is a member in good standing of one of the Conservative Mennonite Churches of Ontario may, by written application to his or her pastor, apply for membership in the Plan.

5. If the pastor approves the application, the pastor shall submit the application to the Plan Administrator who shall keep a record of all approved applications.

6. The Plan Administrator shall issue to each member of the Plan a completed identification card in a form approved by the Superintendent.

7. The Plan Administrator may cancel any membership by giving thirty days written notice of the cancellation to the member by registered mail.

8. Where the death of or personal injury to or loss of or damage to property of any person is occasioned in Ontario by a member of the Plan or a person operating a motor vehicle of a member of the Plan, the Plan shall pay claims to persons who are not members of the Plan to the same extent as if the Plan were an insurer and as if the motor vehicle of the member was insured under a contract of automobile insurance but the liability of the Plan shall be limited to the minimum liability provided for in subsection 251(1) of the *Insurance Act*, in respect of any one accident.

9. The Plan Administrator shall, at the request of the Superintendent, provide the Superintendent with proof that the Plan has established an irrevocable line of credit in the amount of at least $100,000 with chartered banks operating in Ontario.

10. For the purposes of completing the Certificate of Insurance required by the Act, a member of the Plan shall mark on the certificate "Exempt — C.M.A.B.A. Plan" and shall sign the Certificate.

10.1 At the time of submitting the Certificate of Insurance, the member shall submit for inspection the identification card issued to the member under paragraph 6.

11. A member of the Plan or the operator of a motor vehicle owned by a member of the Plan, as the case may be, shall have the identification card issued under paragraph 6 in the motor vehicle at all times while operating the motor vehicle on a highway and shall surrender the identification card for reasonable inspection upon the demand of a police officer.

O. Reg. 51/05, s. 1

3. The TTC Insurance Company Limited is exempt from the requirements of section 7 of the Act.

O. Reg. 51/05, s. 2

Form 1 [Revoked O. Reg. 51/05, s. 3.]

[Revoked O. Reg. 51/05, s. 3.]

CIVIL REMEDIES ACT, 2001

S.O. 2001, c. 28, as am. S.O. 2002, c. 2, s. 19(3); 2005, c. 33, ss. 20–30; 2007, c. 13, ss. 25–41; 2015, c. 38, Sched. 4, s. 26 [To come into force December 10, 2016.].

[Note: The title of this Act was changed from "Remedies for Organized Crime and Other Unlawful Activities Act, 2001" to "Civil Remedies Act, 2001" by 2007, c. 13, s. 25.]

Her Majesty, by and with the advice and consent of the Legislative Assembly of the Province of Ontario, enacts as follows:

. . . . .

PART III.1 — UNLAWFUL ACTIVITIES RELATED TO ROAD SAFETY

[Heading added 2007, c. 13, s. 32.]

11.1 Definitions — In this Part,

"approved ignition interlock device" has the same meaning as in section 41.2 of the *Highway Traffic Act*;

"Director" means the Director of Asset Management — Civil appointed under section 15.1;

"owner", with respect to a vehicle, means,

(a) each person whose name appears on the vehicle portion and the plate portion of the permit, or

(b) if the vehicle is registered in a jurisdiction outside Ontario, each person whose name appears on the certificate of title or registration in that jurisdiction;

"responsible vehicle owner" means an owner of a vehicle, or other person who has an interest in a vehicle, who has done all that can reasonably be done to prevent the vehicle from being used to engage in vehicular unlawful activity, including,

(a) promptly notifying appropriate law enforcement agencies whenever the person knows or ought to know that the vehicle has been, is being or is likely to be used to engage in vehicular unlawful activity,

(b) refusing or withdrawing any permission that the person has authority to give if the person knows or ought to know that such permission has facilitated, is facilitating or is likely to facilitate the vehicle being used to engage in vehicular unlawful activity, and

(c) denying access to the vehicle or to the keys to the vehicle if the person knows or ought to know that the other person is using, has used or is likely to use the vehicle to engage in vehicular unlawful activity,

and does not include an owner of the vehicle or other person who has an interest in the vehicle who has given permission to another person to operate the vehicle if the owner or other person with an interest knows or ought to know that,

(d) the other person's driver's licence is suspended as a result of vehicular unlawful activity, or

(e) the vehicle is likely to be used to engage in vehicular unlawful activity;

"vehicle" means,

(a) a vehicle within the meaning of the *Highway Traffic Act*, or

(b) a motorized snow vehicle within the meaning of the *Motorized Snow Vehicles Act*;

"vehicular unlawful activity" means an act or omission that,

(a) is an offence under section 253, 254 or 255 of the *Criminal Code* (Canada) or another provision of the *Criminal Code* (Canada) that is prescribed by the regulations made under this Act,

(b) is an offence under subsection 53(1.1) of the *Highway Traffic Act* or another provision of the *Highway Traffic Act* that is prescribed by the regulations made under this Act, subject to the conditions or in the circumstances prescribed by the regulation, or

(c) is an offence under an Act of a jurisdiction outside Ontario, if a similar act or omission would be an offence described in clause (a) or (b) if it were committed in Ontario,

whether the act or omission occurred before or after this Part came into force.

2007, c. 13, s. 32

11.2 (1) Forfeiture order — In a proceeding commenced by the Attorney General, the Superior Court of Justice shall, subject to subsection (4) and except where it would clearly not be in the interests of justice, make an order forfeiting a vehicle to the Crown in right of Ontario if the court finds that the vehicle,

(a) was or is likely to be used to engage in vehicular unlawful activity; and

(b) is owned by or is in the care, control or possession of a person whose driver's licence has been suspended under the *Highway Traffic Act* for vehicular unlawful activity two or more times in the preceding 10 years.

(2) Action or application — The proceeding may be by action or application.

(3) Vehicle sold, disposed of — Where a vehicle that is the subject of a proceeding under this section is sold or otherwise disposed of after the proceeding has been commenced but before an order is made under subsection (1), the proceeding shall be continued in respect of any other vehicle or vehicles owned or in the care, control or possession of a person who, before the sale or other disposition of the original vehicle, owned or had the care, control or possession of the original vehicle and, if the original vehicle would have been found to be subject to an order under subsection (1), the court shall make an order against the other vehicle or vehicles under subsection (1).

(4) **Responsible vehicle owners** — If the court would make an order against a vehicle under subsection (1) and a party to the proceeding proves that he, she or it is a responsible vehicle owner of the vehicle, the court, except where it would clearly not be in the interests of justice, shall make such order as it considers necessary to protect the responsible vehicle owner's interest in the vehicle.

(5) **Same** — Without limiting the generality of subsection (4), an order made under subsection (4) may,

(a) sever any interest in the vehicle or require any interest in the vehicle to be sold or otherwise disposed of, to protect a responsible vehicle owner's interest in the vehicle; or

(b) provide that the Crown in right of Ontario takes the vehicle subject to the interest of a responsible vehicle owner.

(6) **No limitation period** — There is no limitation period for a proceeding under this section.

2007, c. 13, s. 32

11.3 (1) **Interlocutory order for preservation, impounding, modification or disposition of vehicle** — On motion by the Attorney General in a proceeding or intended proceeding under section 11.2, the Superior Court of Justice may make any or all of the following interlocutory orders for the preservation, impounding, modification or disposition of any vehicle that is the subject of the proceeding:

1. An order restraining the disposition or encumbrance of the vehicle or its use as collateral under the *Personal Property Security Act* or otherwise.

2. An order for the vehicle to be impounded by the Director and for the vehicle to be released only on a further order of the court.

3. An order for the possession, delivery or safekeeping of the vehicle.

4. An order requiring that the vehicle be equipped with an approved ignition interlock device.

5. An order for the sale or other disposition of the vehicle.

6. An order that any proceeds of sale or other disposition of the vehicle be paid into court pending the conclusion of the proceeding under section 11.2.

7. An order to sever any interest in the vehicle or to require any interest in the vehicle to be sold or otherwise disposed of.

8. An order giving the Crown in right of Ontario a lien for an amount fixed by the court on the vehicle to secure performance of an obligation imposed by another order made under this subsection.

9. An order requiring the owner or owners to agree, as a condition of the vehicle not being impounded or as a condition of the release of the vehicle from impoundment, that the vehicle shall not be operated by a person whose driver's licence is suspended as a result of vehicular unlawful activity or has

been suspended two or more times in the preceding 10 years as a result of vehicular unlawful activity.

10. An order for the vehicle to be impounded by the Director if an owner of the vehicle fails to comply with an order made under paragraph 4, 5, 6 or 9 or an order made under paragraph 11 relating to the operation of the vehicle, and for the vehicle to be released only on a further order of the court.

11. Any other order relating to the vehicle that the court considers just.

(2) **Same** — The court shall make an order under subsection (1) if the court is satisfied that there are reasonable grounds to believe that the vehicle is owned by or is in the care, control or possession of a person whose driver's licence has been suspended under the *Highway Traffic Act* for vehicular unlawful activity two or more times in the preceding 10 years and that the vehicle,

(a) is impounded under the *Highway Traffic Act* as a result of vehicular unlawful activity; or

(b) was or is likely to be used to engage in vehicular unlawful activity.

(3) **Vehicle sold, disposed of** — Where a vehicle that is the subject of a proceeding or intended proceeding under section 11.2 is sold or otherwise disposed of, a motion under this section may be continued or brought in respect of any other vehicle or vehicles owned or in the care, control or possession of a person who owned or had care, control or possession of the original vehicle and, if the court would have made an order under subsection (1) in respect of the original vehicle, the court shall make an order under subsection (1) in respect of such other vehicle or vehicles.

(4) **Release of impounded vehicle** — A vehicle ordered released under subsection (1) shall not be released,

(a) if it is still subject to impoundment under the *Highway Traffic Act*;

(b) if all of the costs incurred by the Crown relating to a proceeding or intended proceeding under this Part with respect to the preservation, impounding, modification or storage of the vehicle have not been paid; or

(c) if the impound costs have not been paid to the operator of the impound facility.

(5) **Motion made without notice** — An order under subsection (1) may be made on motion without notice for a period not exceeding 30 days.

(6) **Extension** — If an order under subsection (1) is made on a motion without notice, a motion to extend the order may be made only on notice to every party affected by the order unless the court is satisfied that because a party has been evading service or because there are other exceptional circumstances, the order ought to be extended without notice to the party.

(7) **Same** — An extension may be granted on a motion without notice for a further period not exceeding 30 days.

(8) Liens on vehicles — If an order under paragraph 8 of subsection (1) gives the Crown a lien on a vehicle,

(a) the *Personal Property Security Act* applies with necessary modifications to the lien, despite clause 4(1)(a) of that Act;

(b) the lien shall be deemed to be a security interest that has attached for the purposes of the *Personal Property Security Act*; and

(c) the Attorney General may perfect the security interest referred to in clause (b) for the purposes of the *Personal Property Security Act* by the registration of a financing statement under that Act.

(9) Costs — The costs associated with the forfeiture, preservation, impounding, modification, storage or disposition of a vehicle under this Part, including the costs of equipping the vehicle with an approved ignition interlock device, incurred by the Crown or any person are a debt due by the owner of the vehicle at the time the order was made to the Crown or person who incurred the costs, and the debt may be recovered in any court of competent jurisdiction.

(10) Assignment of duties to Director — When the Attorney General requests it, the court making an order under subsection (1) shall assign any duties in respect of the vehicle to the Director.

2007, c. 13, s. 32

11.4 (1) Special purpose account — If a vehicle forfeited to the Crown in right of Ontario under this Part is converted to money, the money shall be deposited in a separate, interest bearing account in the Consolidated Revenue Fund.

(2) Same — For the purpose of the *Financial Administration Act*, money deposited under subsection (1) shall be deemed to be money paid to Ontario for a special purpose.

(3) Payments out of account for Crown's costs — If money is deposited in an account under subsection (1), the Minister of Finance shall make payments out of the account, at the request of the Director and in the amounts determined by the Director under subsection (8), to compensate the Crown in right of Ontario for its costs incurred,

(a) in conducting the proceeding under this Part;

(b) in determining whether the proceeding under this Part should be commenced;

(c) in preserving, impounding, modifying, storing, forfeiting or disposing of the vehicle under this Part; and

(d) in enforcing or complying with orders made under this Part in respect of the vehicle.

(4) Other payments out of account — Subject to the regulations made under this Act and after making the payments, if any, out of the account under subsection

(3), the Minister of Finance may make payments out of the account described in subsection (1) for the following purposes:

1. To compensate persons who suffered pecuniary or non-pecuniary losses, including losses recoverable under Part V of the *Family Law Act*, as a result of the vehicular unlawful activity that gave rise to the forfeiture.

2. To assist victims of vehicular unlawful activities or to prevent vehicular unlawful activities that result in victimization.

3. To compensate the Crown in right of Ontario for costs incurred in respect of any proceeding under this Part other than the costs described in subsection (3), and for pecuniary losses suffered as a result of the vehicular unlawful activity that gave rise to the forfeiture, including costs incurred in remedying the effects of that vehicular unlawful activity.

4. To compensate a municipal corporation or a public body that belongs to a class prescribed by the regulations made under this Act for pecuniary losses that were suffered as a result of the vehicular unlawful activity that gave rise to the forfeiture and that are costs incurred in remedying the effects of that vehicular unlawful activity.

5. If, according to the criteria prescribed by the regulations made under this Act, the amount of money in the account is more than is required for the purposes referred to in paragraphs 1 to 4, such other purposes as are prescribed by the regulations.

(5) **Director's election to give priority to persons who suffered loss —** The Director may elect not to request payment out of the account under subsection (3) if, in his or her opinion, all or substantially all of the money in the account is needed to compensate the persons who are entitled to compensation under paragraph 1 of subsection (4).

(6) **Payment for Crown's costs after payment to persons who suffered loss —** If the Director elects not to request payment under subsection (3), the Minister of Finance shall, at the request of the Director and in the amounts determined by the Director under subsection (8), make payments to compensate the Crown in right of Ontario for its costs incurred as described in subsection (3) out of the account, after the payments are made to compensate the persons who are entitled to compensation under paragraph 1 of subsection (4).

(7) **Payment for Crown's costs out of other accounts —** If the amount of money in the account is insufficient to satisfy the Crown's costs pursuant to a request made by the Director under subsection (3) or (6), the Minister of Finance shall make payments to compensate the Crown in right of Ontario for its unsatisfied costs out of another account into which money is deposited under subsection (1) as a result of another proceeding, after payments have been made out of that account to compensate the persons who are entitled to compensation out of that account under paragraph 1 of subsection (4) and to compensate the Crown for its costs incurred in respect of that account.

(8) **Determination of Crown's costs —** The amount of the Crown's costs under subsection (3) or (6) shall be determined by the Director on any basis, or

combination of them, that he or she considers appropriate in the circumstances, including,

    (a) a flat rate for every forfeiture;

    (b) a flat rate for every step taken;

    (c) an hourly rate;

    (d) the actual costs; or

    (e) a percentage of the value of the vehicle forfeited.

(9) Related vehicles — If money is required to be deposited under subsection (1) in respect of two or more vehicles and the Minister of Finance is of the opinion that the vehicles are related, the money may be deposited into a single account and, for the purpose of payments out of the account, a reference in subsection (3), (4) or (8) to "the vehicle" shall be deemed to be a reference to any of the vehicles.

2007, c. 13, s. 32

. . . . .

PHOTO CARD ACT, 2008

An Act to permit the issuance of photo cards to residents of Ontario and to make complementary amendments to the *Highway Traffic Act*

S.O. 2008, c. 17, as am. S.O. 2008, c. 17, ss. 24–27.

Her Majesty, by and with the advice and consent of the Legislative Assembly of the Province of Ontario, enacts as follows:

INTERPRETATION

1. Definitions — In this Act,

"basic photo card" means a card issued under this Act that has on it the holder's name and photograph and additional information about the holder that may be prescribed;

"combined photo card" means a card issued under this Act that constitutes an enhanced photo card and driver's licence;

"driver's licence" has the same meaning as in the *Highway Traffic Act*;

"enhanced photo card" means a card issued under this Act that has on it the holder's name and photograph and additional information about the holder that may be prescribed, that bears a mark, symbol or other notation that indicates that the holder is a Canadian citizen and that has security and other features that may allow it to be used for travel;

"Minister" means the Minister of Transportation or any other member of the Executive Council to whom responsibility for the administration of this Act is assigned or transferred under the *Executive Council Act*;

"Ministry" means the ministry of the Minister;

"phasing-in period" [Repealed 2008, c. 17, s. 24.]

"photo card" means a basic photo card, enhanced photo card or combined photo card;

"prescribed" means prescribed by regulations made under this Act;

"regulation" means a regulation made under this Act;

"valid driver's licence" means a driver's licence that is not suspended, cancelled or expired.

2008, c. 17, s. 24

2. Information on or embedded in a photo card — A reference in this Act or a regulation to a photograph or information on a photo card includes a photograph or information embedded in a photo card.

ISSUANCE AND USE OF PHOTO CARDS

3. Issuance of photo cards to non-drivers — (1) **Basic photo cards** — The Minister may issue a basic photo card to an individual who,

 (a) submits an application for the photo card in accordance with the regulations;

 (b) is a resident of Ontario;

 (c) does not hold a valid driver's licence; and

 (d) meets any other requirements that may be prescribed.

(2) **Enhanced photo cards** — The Minister may issue an enhanced photo card to an individual who,

 (a) submits an application for the photo card in accordance with the regulations;

 (b) is a resident of Ontario;

 (c) does not hold a valid driver's licence;

 (d) satisfies the Minister that he or she is a Canadian citizen; and

 (e) meets any other requirements that may be prescribed.

2008, c. 17, s. 25

4. (1) Issuance of combined photo card to drivers — The Minister may issue a combined photo card to an individual who,

 (a) submits an application for the photo card in accordance with the regulations;

 (b) is a resident of Ontario;

 (c) holds a valid driver's licence;

 (d) satisfies the Minister that he or she is a Canadian citizen; and

 (e) meets any other requirements that may be prescribed.

(2) **Surrender of driver's licence** — A combined photo card shall not be issued to an applicant until he or she surrenders his or her driver's licence.

(3) **Combined photo card is also driver's licence** — A combined photo card issued under subsection (1) is also the holder's driver's licence for all purposes and the holder shall be issued one combined photo card that constitutes his or her enhanced photo card and driver's licence.

(4) **Combined photo card ceases to be valid if driver's licence ceases to be valid** — If a combined photo card holder's driver's licence ceases to be valid for any reason, the combined photo card issued to him or her also ceases to be valid and is cancelled.

(5) Same, combined photo card does not regain validity — A combined photo card does not become valid again upon reinstatement of the holder's driver's licence; the driver's licence holder must apply for a new photo card if he or she wishes to be issued one.

2008, c. 17, s. 26

5. Photograph requirement — The Minister may require an applicant for the issuance or renewal of a photo card to submit to being photographed by equipment provided by the Ministry.

6. Photo card, distinguishing physical feature — The Minister shall ensure that each photo card contains a distinguishing physical feature such that an individual, particularly a visually impaired individual, can readily locate the card and distinguish it from other cards that the individual may be carrying.

7. (1) Photo-comparison technology — The Minister may use photo-comparison technology to compare the photographs taken of any applicants for or holders of a photo card or driver's licence.

(2) Not admissible — The photo-comparison technology used by the Minister, the methodology used to compare photographs and the measurements and results used for comparison are not admissible in evidence for any purpose and cannot be required for production in a civil proceeding before a court or tribunal.

(3) Definition — In this section,

"photo-comparison technology" means a software application that measures the characteristics of a person's face in a photograph and compares the results of that measurement with those of other photographs.

8. Fees — The Minister,

 (a) may require that applicants for and holders of photo cards pay a fee to the Minister or to a person who provides any service for the Minister for anything done or provided by or on behalf of the Minister under this Act; and

 (b) may require different fees for different classes of applicants and holders, for basic photo cards, enhanced photo cards and combined photo cards and for different circumstances.

9. (1) Voluntary use of photo card — The holder of a photo card may, in his or her discretion, present it in any transaction or circumstance, including any transaction or circumstance where the holder wishes to identify himself or herself.

(2) No requirement to have or use photo card — However, a photo card is issued solely for the convenience of the holder of the photo card and there is no requirement under this or any other Act that an individual obtain or carry a photo card or that a photo card be presented or accepted.

(3) Exception, combined photo card — Despite subsections (1) and (2), a provision of the *Highway Traffic Act* or any other Act imposing a duty on the holders of drivers' licences, including a requirement to carry, present, surrender or return a driver's licence, applies to the holder of a combined photo card as if the combined photo card were a driver's licence.

10. (1) Cancellation of photo card — The Minister may cancel a photo card if,

(a) the Minister is satisfied that the photo card was used in the commission of an offence under section 13 or 15;

(b) the Minister is satisfied that the holder of the photo card committed an offence under section 13, 14 or 15;

(c) the Minister is satisfied that any information provided by the holder of a photo card under this Act is false;

(d) the Minister is satisfied that any information appearing on the photo card is incorrect; or

(e) the payment of a fee in respect of the photo card is dishonoured.

(2) Same — The Minister may also cancel a photo card if the Minister is of the opinion that it is necessary to do so to ensure that the photo card is not used improperly, and in any circumstance that may be prescribed.

11. (1) Return of photo card — The Minister may require the return of a photo card that was cancelled under subsection 4(4) or section 10 from the holder of the photo card or other person in possession of the photo card.

(2) Same — A person who is required by the Minister to return a photo card shall return the photo card as specified by the Minister.

COLLECTION AND DISCLOSURE OF INFORMATION

12. Collection and disclosure of information — **(1) Collection by Minister** — The Minister may request and collect information from any public body or related government, as he or she considers appropriate, if the Minister considers it necessary for a purpose set out in subsection (5).

(2) Disclosure by Minister — The Minister may disclose information to any public body or related government, as he or she considers appropriate, if the Minister considers it necessary for a purpose set out in subsection (5).

(3) Disclosure to Minister — Upon receipt of a request for information from the Minister under subsection (1), a public body shall disclose to the Minister any information from their records that may assist the Minister with a purpose set out in subsection (5).

(4) Exception — The Minister may not disclose under subsection (2) the measurements used for comparison of photographs as described in section 7.

(5) Purposes for collection and disclosure of information — The only purposes for which information may be collected or disclosed under this section are the following:

1. To verify the accuracy of any information provided under this Act by an applicant for or holder of a photo card.

2. To verify the authenticity of any document provided under this Act by an applicant for or holder of a photo card.

3. To detect a false statement in any document provided under this Act by any person.

4. To detect or prevent the improper use of a photo card.

5. To detect or prevent the improper issuance or renewal of a photo card, including by conducting an audit or review of any issuance, renewal or cancellation of a photo card or the conduct of any person or entity involved in issuing, renewing or cancelling a photo card.

6. To provide the Canada Border Services Agency or the Department of Citizenship and Immigration, or the successor to either of them, with information and records regarding the issuance, renewal or cancellation of an enhanced photo card or a combined photo card.

7. To provide a public body or related government with the information that the Minister believes is necessary to assist it with a purpose similar to a purpose set out in paragraph 1, 2, 3 or 4 if the holder of a photo card has presented his or her photo card in order to obtain a benefit or service under a legislatively authorized program or service administered or provided by that public body or related government.

(6) Deemed compliance with privacy legislation — Any disclosure of information under this section is deemed to be in compliance with clause 42(1)(e) of the *Freedom of Information and Protection of Privacy Act* and clause 32(e) of the *Municipal Freedom of Information and Protection of Privacy Act*.

(7) Notice under privacy legislation — Any collection by a public body of personal information, as defined in the *Freedom of Information and Protection of Privacy Act* and the *Municipal Freedom of Information and Protection of Privacy Act*, disclosed to the public body under this section is exempt from the application of subsection 39(2) of the *Freedom of Information and Protection of Privacy Act* and subsection 29(2) of the *Municipal Freedom of Information and Protection of Privacy Act*.

(8) Otherwise authorized collection or disclosure — The authority to collect and disclose information under this section is in addition to any other authority under this or any other Act for the Ministry to collect and disclose information.

(9) Definitions — In this section,

"public body" means,

(a) any ministry, agency, board, commission, official or other body of the Government of Ontario,

(b) any municipality in Ontario,

(c) a local board, as defined in the *Municipal Affairs Act*, and any authority, board, commission, corporation, office or organization of persons some or all of whose members, directors or officers are appointed or chosen by or under the authority of the council of a municipality in Ontario, or

(d) a prescribed person or entity;

"related government" means,

(a) the Government of Canada and the Crown in right of Canada, and any ministry, agency, board, commission or official of either of them, or

(b) the government of any other province or territory of Canada and the Crown in right of any other province of Canada, and any ministry, agency, board, commission or official of any of them.

OFFENCES

13. (1) Offences re possession and use of photo card — No person shall,

(a) have in his or her possession a fictitious, imitation, altered or fraudulently obtained photo card;

(b) lend his or her photo card to another person to be used contrary to clause (c) or permit such use of the photo card by another person;

(c) represent as his or her own a photo card not issued to him or her; or

(d) apply for, secure or retain in his or her possession more than one photo card.

(2) Same, while holding a driver's licence — No person who holds a valid driver's licence shall apply for, secure or retain in his or her possession a photo card other than a combined photo card.

(3) Seizure of photo card — Where a police officer has reason to believe that a person has a photo card in his or her possession or is using a photo card in contravention of clause (1)(a), (b), (c) or (d) or subsection (2), the police officer may take possession of the photo card and, where the officer does so, he or she shall forward the photo card to the Minister upon disposition of the case.

(4) Penalty — Every person who contravenes clause (1)(a), (b), (c) or (d) or subsection (2) is guilty of an offence and on conviction is liable to a fine of not less than $100 and not more than $20,000.

14. (1) Offence re false statement, inaccurate information — Every person who submits a false or inaccurate document, makes a false statement or includes inaccurate information in or with a written or electronic application, declaration, affidavit or other document required by the Ministry or under this Act is guilty of an offence and on conviction, in addition to any other penalty or punishment to which the person may be liable, is liable to a fine of not less than $400 and not more than $20,000 or to imprisonment for a term of not more than six months, or to both.

(2) Defence — A person is not guilty of an offence under subsection (1) if the person exercised all reasonable care to avoid submitting a false or inaccurate document or making a false statement or including inaccurate information.

(3) Limitation — No proceeding for an offence under this section shall be instituted more than six years after the facts on which the proceeding is based are alleged to have occurred.

15. Other offences — Every person who contravenes or fails to comply with subsection 11(2) or a regulation is guilty of an offence and on conviction is liable to a fine of not less than $100 and not more than $20,000.

ADMINISTRATIVE MATTERS

16. Powers and duties of Ministry — Where by this Act powers are conferred or duties are imposed upon the Ministry, the powers may be exercised by the Minister and the duties discharged by the Minister.

17. (1) Delegation of powers — The Minister may authorize the deputy minister of the Ministry, one or more employees in the Ministry or in any other ministry or any other person or persons to exercise any or all of the powers and duties of the Minister under this Act, and where a power or duty is delegated to more than one person, any one of them may exercise that power or duty.

(2) Delegate may retain portion of fee — Despite section 2 of the *Financial Administration Act*, any person who issues or renews photo cards or provides any service for the Minister or his or her delegate relating to photo cards pursuant to an agreement with the Minister or delegate, as the case may be, may retain, from the fee paid, the amount that is approved by the Minister from time to time.

18. Forms — The Minister may require that forms approved by the Minister be used for any purpose under this Act.

19. (1) Power to do things electronically — Anything that the Minister or Registrar of Motor Vehicles is required or authorized to do or to provide under this Act may be done or provided by electronic means or in an electronic format.

(2) Same — Anything that any person is required or authorized to do or to provide to the Minister or the Ministry under this Act may be done or provided by electronic means or in an electronic format, in the circumstances and in the manner specified by the Ministry.

20. (1) Records — The Minister shall keep a record of every photo card that is issued, renewed or cancelled, and of every application made for a photo card, and shall keep a record of the particulars of each issuance, renewal, cancellation and application.

(2) Same — The Minister may keep any other records that he or she considers necessary for the administration of this Act.

21. Evidence — (1) **Certified copy, document admissible** — A copy of any document filed in the Ministry under this Act, or any statement containing information from the records required or authorized to be kept under this Act, that purports to be certified by the Registrar of Motor Vehicles under the seal of the Ministry as being a true copy of the original shall be received in evidence in all courts without proof of the seal, the Registrar of Motor Vehicles' signature or the manner of preparing the copy or statement, and is proof, in the absence of evidence to the contrary, of the facts contained in the copy or statement.

(2) **Registrar's signature** — The Registrar of Motor Vehicles' signature on a copy or statement described in subsection (1) may be an original signature or an engraved, lithographed, printed or otherwise mechanically or electronically reproduced signature or facsimile signature.

(3) **Ministry seal** — The seal of the Ministry on a copy or statement described in subsection (1) may be affixed by impression or may be an engraved, lithographed, printed or otherwise mechanically or electronically reproduced seal or facsimile of a seal.

(4) **Signature and seal only required on first page** — The Registrar of Motor Vehicles' signature on a copy or statement described in subsection (1) need only be on the first page of the copy or statement.

(5) **Same** — The seal of the Ministry on a copy or statement described in subsection (1) need only be on the first page of the copy or statement if the following pages are sequentially numbered, by hand or otherwise; if the pages following the first page are not sequentially numbered, the seal must be on each page.

(6) **Electronic filing in court** — A copy or statement described in subsection (1) may be filed in a court by direct electronic transmission in accordance with the regulations.

(7) **Definition** — In this section,

"document" includes a photograph.

22. (1) **Protection from liability** — No action or other proceeding for damages shall be instituted against the Minister, the Registrar of Motor Vehicles, a public servant, a delegate or agent of the Minister or any other person authorized or required to do anything under this Act for anything done in good faith in the performance or intended performance of a duty under this Act or in the exercise or intended exercise of a power under this Act or any neglect or default in the performance or exercise in good faith of such duty or power.

(2) **Same** — No action or other proceeding for damages shall be instituted against the Crown in right of Ontario, the Minister, the Registrar of Motor Vehicles, a public servant, a delegate or agent of the Minister or any other person authorized or required to do anything under this Act arising from,

  (a) the use by any person of a photo card;

  (b) the use by any person of any photograph or information on a photo card; or

(c) the use by any person of any photograph or information in a record provided by the Ministry under this Act.

(3) Crown liability — Despite subsections 5(2) and (4) of the *Proceedings Against the Crown Act*, subsection (1) does not relieve the Crown of liability in respect of a tort committed by a person mentioned in subsection (1) to which it would otherwise be subject.

23. Regulations — The Lieutenant Governor in Council may make regulations,

(a) [Repealed 2008, c. 17, s. 27.]

(b) prescribing additional information about the holder that may be included on a basic photo card, enhanced photo card or combined photo card;

(c) defining "resident of Ontario";

(d) prescribing other requirements for the issuance of a photo card, including prescribing a minimum age for an individual to be issued a photo card and requiring notice to and consent from an applicant's parents or guardian if the applicant for a photo card is under 16 years old;

(e) governing the application and reapplication for and renewal of photo cards;

(f) prescribing circumstances in which a photo card shall not be issued or renewed;

(g) governing the term of validity of photo cards;

(h) requiring a holder of a photo card to notify the Ministry of a change in his or her name or address or other specified information, and prescribing the time and manner of such notification;

(i) prescribing circumstances under which the Minister may cancel a photo card under subsection 10(2) and prescribing and governing procedures for cancelling a photo card;

(j) governing the return of photo cards under subsection 11(2);

(k) prescribing a person or entity, or any class of person or entity, as a public body for the purposes of section 12;

(l) requiring and governing the submission of reports and information and documents to the Ministry by holders of photo cards;

(m) respecting the filing of copies and statements in court by direct electronic transmission and the manner in which the signature of the Registrar of Motor Vehicles and the seal of the Ministry may be represented when such a copy or statement is printed for the purpose of subsection 21(6);

(n) providing that any provision or requirement of this Act or of a regulation does not apply to a specified class of photo cards, or photo cards held by a specified class of persons or in specified circumstances, and prescribing conditions and circumstances for such non-applications;

(o) exempting any person or class of persons from any provision or requirement of this Act or of a regulation, and prescribing conditions and circumstances for such exemptions.

2008, c. 17, s. 27

AMENDMENTS TO THIS ACT

24. The definition of "phasing-in period" in section 1 of this Act is repealed.

25. (1) Subsection 3(1) of this Act is amended by striking out "After the phasing-in period" at the beginning.

(2) Subsection 3(2) of this Act is amended by striking out "After the phasing-in period" at the beginning.

26. Subsection 4(1) of this Act is amended by striking out "During and after the phasing-in period" at the beginning.

27. Clause 23(a) of this Act is repealed.

. . . . .

COMMENCEMENT AND SHORT TITLE

49. Commencement — This Act comes into force on a day to be named by proclamation of the Lieutenant Governor.

50. Short title — The short title of this Act is the *Photo Card Act, 2008*.

ONT. REG. 176/09 — GENERAL

made under the *Photo Card Act, 2008*

O. Reg. 176/09, as am. O. Reg. 225/11.

INTERPRETATION

1. Resident of Ontario — (1) For the purposes of clause 3(1)(b) the Act,

"resident of Ontario" means an individual who lives primarily in Ontario, whether or not the individual has a permanent residence in Ontario.

(2) For the purposes of clauses 3(2)(b) and 4(1)(b) of the Act,

"resident of Ontario" means an individual whose primary residence is an actual physical location in Ontario where an individual may be personally served with a document and, for greater certainty, an individual whose only address in Ontario is a post office box is not a resident of Ontario.

2. Renewal — A provision of this Regulation that governs the issuance of a photo card also governs an application for its renewal.

O. Reg. 225/11, s. 1

ALL PHOTO CARDS

[Heading added O. Reg. 225/11, s. 1.]

3. Specified time, form and manner — Where an individual is required to submit information or documents to the Minister or Ministry, or to do any other thing in connection with the issuance, renewal or cancellation of a photo card, the information or document shall be submitted or the thing done, as the case may be, in the form and manner and within the time specified by the Minister, unless otherwise specified in this Regulation.

O. Reg. 225/11, s. 1

[Heading repealed O. Reg. 225/11, s. 1.]

4. Minister may require information, documents — (1) The Minister may require that an applicant for or the holder of a photo card submit such information and documents as may be required to satisfy the Minister that a photo card may be issued or retained, and that the information shown on an application or on the card is correct.

(2) The Minister may notify a holder of a photo card of a requirement under subsection (1) by any means, including by mailing a notice to the latest address for the

person appearing on the records of the Ministry, in which case the notice is deemed to have been received on the seventh day after it was mailed.

(3) A person who is notified under subsection (2) shall submit the information and documents within the time specified by the Minister in the notice.

(4) The Minister may retain any documents submitted by an applicant for or a holder of a photo card for as long as may be required to make a decision in respect of the photo card.

(5) The Minister may retain a record of all information and copies of all documents submitted by an applicant for or a holder of a photo card.

O. Reg. 225/11, s. 1

5. Refusal to issue or renew photo card — The Minister shall not issue or renew a photo card if the applicant for issuance or renewal does not meet the requirements of the Act or of this Regulation.

O. Reg. 225/11, s. 1

[Heading repealed O. Reg. 225/11, s. 1.]

6. Requirements — (1) An applicant for a photo card shall be at least 16 years of age.

(2) An applicant for a photo card shall pay the required fee.

(3) An applicant for a photo card shall not be the holder of any of the following issued by another province or a territory of Canada, by a state of the United States of America or by any other jurisdiction:

  1. A driver's licence.

  2. A photo card.

  3. An identification card that is similar to a photo card.

(4) [Repealed O. Reg. 225/11, s. 1.]

(5) [Repealed O. Reg. 225/11, s. 1.]

(6) [Repealed O. Reg. 225/11, s. 1.]

O. Reg. 225/11, s. 1

7. Cancellation — (1) The Minister may cancel a photo card upon the request of the holder.

(2) Where a photo card appears to contain a defect, error or inaccuracy, the Minister may cancel the photo card and issue a replacement card to the holder without requiring any application by the holder.

(3) The Minister shall cancel a photo card if the holder ceases to meet the requirements of the Act or of this Regulation.

(4) Notice of cancellation of a photo card may be mailed to the holder of the photo card at his or her latest address appearing on the records of the Ministry and is deemed to have been received on the seventh day after it was mailed.

O. Reg. 225/11, s. 1

8. Period of validity of photo card — A photo card shall remain valid only for the period covered by the fee that is required to be paid in respect of the photo card.

O. Reg. 225/11, s. 1

[Heading repealed O. Reg. 225/11, s. 1.]

9. Change of information — The holder of a photo card shall notify the Ministry within six days after any change to his or her name or address or to any other information that appears on the photo card.

O. Reg. 225/11, s. 1

10. Additional information displayed on card — A photo card may display the holder's address, date of birth, signature, sex and height.

O. Reg. 225/11, s. 1

ENHANCED AND COMBINED PHOTO CARDS

[Heading added O. Reg. 225/11, s. 1.]

11. Requirements — **(1)** An applicant for or the holder of an enhanced photo card or a combined photo card must satisfy the Minister that he or she is not under any legal restriction that prevents him or her from travelling outside Canada.

(2) The Minister may require an applicant for or the holder of an enhanced photo card or a combined photo card to attend at an interview with an official of the Ministry or other specified person to satisfy the Minister that he or she meets all the requirements for the issuance or renewal of the photo card.

O. Reg. 225/11, s. 1

12. Card lost or stolen, etc. — **(1)** A holder of an enhanced photo card or a combined photo card shall notify the Ministry forthwith upon discovering that his or her photo card has been lost, stolen, destroyed or damaged.

(2) Where the Minister is satisfied that the holder's photo card has been lost, stolen, destroyed or damaged and that the holder continues to meet the requirements for an enhanced photo card or a combined photo card, the Minister may issue a replacement card to the holder.

(3) [Repealed O. Reg. 225/11, s. 1.]

(4) [Repealed O. Reg. 225/11, s. 1.]

(5) [Repealed O. Reg. 225/11, s. 1.]

O. Reg. 225/11, s. 1

13. Loss of citizenship or right to travel — (1) A holder of an enhanced photo card or a combined photo card shall notify the Ministry within six days after he or she ceases to be a Canadian citizen or comes under a legal restriction that prevents him or her from travelling outside Canada.

(2) The notice must be given by mail or by the holder attending in person at an office that is designated by the Ministry as a place where such notice may be given.

(3) The holder shall return his or her photo card to the Ministry together with the notice.

(4) Upon being satisfied that the holder will cease to be or has ceased to be a Canadian citizen or will come or has come under a legal restriction that prevents him or her from travelling outside Canada, the Minister shall cancel the holder's enhanced photo card or combined photo card.

(5) [Repealed O. Reg. 225/11, s. 1.]

O. Reg. 225/11, s. 1

[Heading repealed O. Reg. 225/11, s. 1.]

14. Return of photo card — The holder of an enhanced photo card or a combined photo card that has been cancelled shall, unless subsection 13(3) applies, return his or her photo card to the Ministry by mail or by attending in person at an office that is designated by the Ministry as a place where photo cards may be returned, within seven days after the date of receipt or deemed receipt, as the case may be, of the notice of cancellation.

O. Reg. 225/11, s. 1

ONT. REG. 132/14 — CERTIFIED EVIDENCE

made under the *Provincial Offences Act*

O. Reg. 132/14

1. Specified offences — (1) Every offence for which there is a set fine, other than an offence referred to in subsection (2), is specified for the purposes of clause 48.1(1)(b) of the Act.

(2) The following offences for which there is a set fine are not specified for the purposes of clause 48.1(1)(b) of the Act:

1. Every offence under a provision of an Act, regulation or municipal by-law that, on the offence date indicated in the offence notice, is set out in the Table to Ontario Regulation 339/94 (*Demerit Point System*) made under the *Highway Traffic Act*.

2. An offence under section 128 of the *Highway Traffic Act*.

2. Other types of certified evidence — The following types of certified evidence are specified for the purposes of paragraph 3 of subsection 48.1(2) of the Act:

1. A certified copy of a photograph taken by a provincial offences officer.

2. In respect of a document, a certified statement by a provincial offences officer that he or she served the document on the person charged, with the date and method of service indicated.

3. A certified statement by a provincial offences officer respecting the configuration, weight, dimensions or other characteristics of a vehicle inspected by the provincial offences officer.

3. Commencement — This Regulation comes into force on the later of the day subsection 1(40) of Schedule 4 to the *Good Government Act, 2009* comes into force and the day this Regulation is filed.

SMOKE-FREE ONTARIO ACT

S.O. 1994, c. 10, as am. S.O. 1997, c. 10, s. 26; 2002, c. 8, Sched. P, s. 6; 2005, c. 18, ss. 1–15; 2006, c. 4, s. 54; 2007, c. 8, s. 227; 2007, c. 10, Sched. J, s. 4; 2008, c. 12; 2008, c. 26; 2009, c. 33, Sched. 18, s. 31, Sched. 19; 2010, c. 1, Sched. 27; 2014, c. 11, Sched. 6, s. 8; 2015, c. 7, Sched. 2 [s. 6 not in force at date of publication.].

[Note: The title of this Act was changed from "Tobacco Control Act, 1994" to "Smoke-Free Ontario Act" by 2005, c. 18, s. 1.]

· · · · ·

CONTROLS RELATING TO SMOKING TOBACCO

· · · · ·

9.2 (1) Protection for people under 16 years old in motor vehicles — No person shall smoke tobacco or have lighted tobacco in a motor vehicle while another person who is less than 16 years old is present in the vehicle.

(2) Proof of age — In a prosecution under this section, a court may find evidence that the person enforcing this section honestly and reasonably believed another person to be less than 16 years old to be sufficient proof of the other person's age.

(3) Enforcement — Despite section 14, this section shall be enforced by police officers.

(4) Definition — In this section,

"motor vehicle" means, subject to the regulations, a motor vehicle as defined in subsection 1(1) of the *Highway Traffic Act*.

2008, c. 12, s. 1

· · · · ·

OFFENCES

15. (1) Offences — A person who contravenes section 3, 3.1 or 3.2, subsection 4(1), section 5, 6.1 or 9 or subsection 13(4), 14(16), 16(4), 17(6), 18(4) or (5) is guilty of an offence and on conviction is liable to a fine determined in accordance with subsection (3).

(2) Same — A person who contravenes section 6 or 10 or subsection 18(1) is guilty of an offence and on conviction is liable, for each day or part of a day on which the offence occurs or continues, to a fine determined in accordance with subsection (3).

(3) **Determining maximum fine** — The fine, or daily fine, as the case may be, shall not exceed an amount determined as follows:

1. Establish the number of times the defendant has been convicted of the same offence during the five years preceding the current conviction.

2. If the defendant is an individual, the amount is set out in Column 3 of the Table of this section, opposite the number of previous convictions in Column 2 and the section or subsection number of the provision contravened in Column 1.

3. If the defendant is a corporation, the amount is set out in Column 4 of the Table to this section, opposite the number of previous convictions in Column 2 and the section or subsection number of the provision contravened in Column 1.

(4) **Sequence of convictions** — In establishing the number of times the defendant has been convicted of the same offence for the purposes of subsection (3), the only question to be considered is the sequence of convictions, and no consideration shall be given to the sequence of commission of offences or to whether an offence occurred before or after a conviction.

(5) **Continuing offence, vending machine** — A person who contravenes subsection 7(1) is guilty of an offence and on conviction is liable, for each day or part of a day on which the offence occurs or continues, to a fine of not more than $2,000.

(6) **Offence, failure to submit report** — A person who contravenes section 8 or a regulation made under clause 19(1)(f) is guilty of an offence and on conviction is liable to a fine of not more than $100,000.

(6.1) **Offence, smoking in motor vehicle** — A person who contravenes section 9.2 is guilty of an offence and on conviction is liable to a fine of not more than $250.

(7) **Duty of directors and officers** — A director or officer of a corporation that engages in the manufacture, sale or distribution of tobacco has a duty to take all reasonable care to prevent the corporation from contravening this Act.

(8) [Repealed 2005, c. 18, s. 13(2).]

(9) **Offence** — A person who has the duty imposed by subsection (7) and fails to carry it out is guilty of an offence and on conviction is liable to a fine of not more than $100,000.

(10) Same — A person may be prosecuted and convicted under subsection (9) even if the corporation has not been prosecuted or convicted.

TABLE

Column 1 Provision Contravened	Column 2 Number of Earlier Convictions	Column 3 Maximum Fine — Individual (amount in dollars)	Column 4 Maximum Fine — Corporation (amount in dollars)
3(1), 3(2), 3.1, 3.2	0	8,000	20,000
3(1), 3(2), 3.1, 3.2	1	20,000	40,000
3(1), 3(2), 3.1, 3.2	2	40,000	100,000
3(1), 3(2), 3.1, 3.2	3 or more	200,000	300,000
3(6), 4(1), 6, 10, 14(16), 16(4), 17(6), 18(1), 18(4), 18(5)	0	2,000	5,000
3(6), 4(1), 6, 10, 14(16), 16(4), 17(6), 18(1), 18(4), 18(5)	1	5,000	10,000
3(6), 4(1), 6, 10, 14(16), 16(4), 17(6), 18(1), 18(4), 18(5)	2	10,000	25,000
3(6), 4(1), 6, 10, 14(16), 16(4), 17(6), 18(1), 18(4), 18(5)	3 or more	50,000	75,000
5, 6.1	0	4,000	200,000
5, 6.1	1	10,000	600,000
5, 6.1	2	20,000	600,000
5, 6.1	3 or more	100,000	600,000
9(1), 9(2)	0	1,000	
9(1), 9(2)	1 or more	5,000	
9(3), 9(6)	0	1,000	100,000
9(3), 9(6)	1 or more	5,000	300,000
9(4)	any	4,000	10,000
13(4)	any	4,000	10,000

1997, c. 10, s. 26; 2005, c. 18, s. 13; 2007, c. 10, Sched. J, s. 4; 2008, c. 12, s. 2; 2008, c. 26, s. 4; 2015, c. 7, Sched. 2, s. 5

. . . . .

ONTARIO-QUÉBEC AGREEMENT

Ontario-Québec Agreement

Effective April 1, 1989 Ontario and Québec entered into a reciprocal agreement covering licence suspensions following Criminal Code convictions for Québec drivers committed in Ontario and vice versa. The agreement also applies to serious highway traffic offences and failure to pay the fines relating thereto.

The text of the news release, dated November 8, 1988, is as follows:

Québec and Ontario sign
the first reciprocal agreement
on traffic violations in Canada

MONTREAL — Ontario Minister of Transportation Ed Fulton and Québec Transport Minister Marc-Yvan Côté have taken advantage of the occasion of the Canadian Symposium on Road Safety in Montreal to sign the first reciprocal agreement between two Canadian provinces to monitor road infractions.

The agreement stems from a project presented by representatives from Ontario and Québec at the 1986 annual conference of the Canadian Council of Motor Transportation Administrators (CCMTA). That initiative paved the way for the exchange of driver licensing and vehicle registration information between the two provinces.

Under the terms of the new agreement, which comes into effect April 1, 1989, infractions committed under the Traffic Act of the neighbouring province will result in demerit points being recorded on the driver's record — just as if those infractions were committed in the home province.

The agreement also provides for the suspension of the right to drive in the neighbouring province when any fine for a traffic violation has not been paid. Furthermore, it will facilitate exchange of driver's licences for Québecers and Ontarians moving to the other province.

In 1987, Ontario drivers were responsible for 17,913 infractions under the Québec Highway Safety Code. Those infractions represented 65 per cent of the total number of offences committed in Québec by non-resident drivers.

During the same period, there were 18,631 offences committed by Québecers under the Ontario Highway Traffic Act.

In both Québec and Ontario, offences such as exceeding the speed limit and failing to obey a red light or a stop sign represent 94 per cent of all demerit point infractions committed by drivers from the neighbouring province.

During 1987, approximately 500 infractions under the Criminal Code were committed by Ontarians in Québec and 304 were committed by Québecers in Ontario.

While this agreement is the first to be signed between two Canadian provinces, Québec has had a similar pact with the state of New York since the beginning of 1988.

Côté and Fulton said they hope the signing will mark the first step toward a series of similar agreements which will eventually bind all the Canadian provinces and North American states.

What does the reciprocal agreement mean for drivers in Ontario and Québec?

The reciprocal agreement signed by Québec and Ontario, which comes into effect April 1, 1989, affects all the drivers of both jurisdictions who travel through the other province. The main points of the agreement are described below:

Criminal Code Offences

The following criminal offences are included in the agreement:

- Driving or having care and control of a motor vehicle while ability impaired by alcohol or drugs (the legal blood alcohol concentration limit is equal to or greater than 0.08 percent)
- Criminal negligence causing bodily harm or death
- Dangerous driving
- Failing to remain at the scene of an accident

When these infractions are committed by a Québec driver in Ontario or by an Ontario driver in Québec, they will result in the suspension of the driver's licence, or the revocation of the right to obtain one, for a minimum one-year period.

Highway Traffic Act Offences

The following infractions resulting in demerit points being recorded on the driver's record are included in the agreement:

- Exceeding prescribed speed limit
- Failing to obey a traffic signal or stop sign
- Failing to stop for a school bus with red lights flashing
- Dangerous or careless driving
- Failing to report an accident to a police officer
- Failing to remain at the scene of an accident
- Driving a vehicle for a bet, a stake or a race

The above infractions committed by a Québec driver in Ontario or by an Ontario driver in Québec will result in demerit points being recorded on the driver's record.

Suspension of the right to drive

Québecers who do not pay the fine corresponding to the offence committed in the province of Ontario, as well as Ontarians who do not pay the applicable Québec fine for any of the infractions listed above, will have their right to drive suspended in the neighbouring province.

Driver's licence exchange

When a Québecer settles in Ontario or an Ontarian settles in Québec, the driver's former home province transfers the driver's record to the new place of residence. The information in the record concerns driving experience and conditions related to the permit, including any suspensions and revocations imposed on the driver.

The text and schedules of the Reciprocal Agreement, signed November 8, 1988 and in force April 1, 1989, is as follows:

Reciprocal Agreement Between the Province of Ontario and Québec Concerning Drivers' Licences and Traffic Offences

WHEREAS the Province of Ontario and Québec wish to:

1. Promote compliance with traffic laws and iprove highway safety within their own borders;

2. Facilitate, for their respective residents who hold a valid driver's licence, the issuance of a licence from the other jurisdiction to which they are moving;

3. Further highway safety by treating offences for which their residents have been declared guilty in the other jurisdiction, as if they had been committed in the home jurisdiction for the purposes of updating and maintaining driver's licence records;

4. Strengthen cooperation between the two jurisdictions so that residents satisfy fines imposed as a result of offences committed within the other jurisdiction and for which they have been found guilty;

5. Allow motorists to accept traffic citations for certain offences and proceed on their way without delay.

THEREFORE, the Province of Ontario and Québec agree to the measures set forth in this Agreement.

Article 1 — Definitions

For the purposes of this Agreement:

1.1 **"Jurisdiction"** refers to the Province of Ontario or to Québec.

1.2 **"Home jurisdiction"** means:

the jurisdiction that issues a driver's licence and has the authority to suspend or revoke it.

1.3 **"Jurisdiction of origin"** means:

the jurisdiction which has issued the driver's licence that the holder wants to exchange for a licence of the jurisdiction where he has moved.

1.4 **"Declaration of guilt"** means:

an admission of guilt entered by or on behalf of the driver or a finding of guilt after trial in a competent court or payment of a fine for an offence mentioned under article 3.1 committed in one jurisdiction by a resident of the other jurisdiction.

1.5 **"Class G driver's licence"** means:

a licence issued by the Ministry of Transportation of the Province of Ontario authorizing its holder to drive any motor vehicle, including a motor assisted bicycle, not exceeding 11,000 kg gross weight or registered gross weight, and any combination of a motor vehicle not exceeding a total gross weight or registered gross weight of 11,000 kg and towed vehicles where the towed vehicles do not exceed a total gross weight of 4,600 kg, but not:

    a) a motorcycle;

    b) a bus carrying passengers; or

    c) an ambulance in the course of providing ambulance service.

1.6 **"Class 42 driver's licence"** means:

a licence issued by the Régie de l'assurance automobile du Québec authorizing its holder to drive a motor vehicle or a combination of road vehicles whose gross vehicle weight is under 11,000 kg, except a commercial vehicle carrying goods for which a permit from the Commission des transports du Québec is required, as well as a farm tractor and a moped.

1.7 **"Valid driver's licence"** means:

a driver's licence that at the time of exchange has not expired and is not revoked or suspended in accordance with the laws of the issuing jurisdiction.

Article 2 — Driver's Licence Exchange

2.1 A resident of Ontario holder of a valid class "G" driver's licence may, when moving to Québec, exchange such licence without examination, other than a vision test, for a class 42 driver's licence, on payment of the fees prescribed by regulation and of the amount fixed by Section 151 of the *Automobile Insurance Act* (R.S.Q., chapter A-25).

2.2 A resident of Québec holder of a valid class 42 driver's licence may, when moving to the Province of Ontario, exchange such licence without an examination, other than a vision test, for a class "G" driver's licence, on payment of the fees prescribed by regulation under the *Highway Traffic Act* (R.S.O., chapter 198).

2.3 The exchanged licence shall be returned to the jurisdiction of origin.

2.4 The jurisdiction of origin will verify the validity of the licence by disclosing to the home jurisdiction the following information, if available:

* the holder's name, address and date of birth;
* the holder's height and sex;
* the holder's driving record of convictions, collision involvement and date first licensed;
* the driver's licence number;
* the expiry date of the licence;
* any restrictions to which the holder is subject;
* any suspensions or revocations of record, including;
* the reason for such suspension or revocation;
* the expired suspensions or revocations;
* the date of disclosure.

2.5 Information obtained by the new jurisdiction of residence pursuant to article 2.4 becomes part of the driver's record.

2.6 A driver's licence issued pursuant to articles 2.1 or 2.2 may be subsequently suspended, revoked, cancelled or restricted, or additional examination may be required based upon information received pursuant to article 2.4.

Article 3 — Reports and Effects of Conviction

3.1 Declarations of guilt concerning the following offences shall be reported to the home jurisdiction by the jurisdiction in which the offence was committed:

3.1.1 *Criminal offences*

- Offences relating to the operation of a motor vehicle while under the influence of alcohol or drugs, under Sections 237, 238 and 239 of the *Criminal Code* (R.S.C., chapter C-34);
- Offences relating to criminal negligence or manslaughter resulting from the operation of a motor vehicle, under Sections 203, 204 and 219 of the *Criminal Code*;
- Offences relating to dangerous driving, under Section 233 of the *Criminal Code*;
- Offences relating to the failure to stop at the scene of a fatal accident or personal injury accident or leaving without reporting, under section 236(1)(a) of the *Criminal Code*;

3.1.2 *Traffic offences*

- Offences relating to driving over a prescribed or posted speed limit under Section 109 of the *Highway Traffic Act* of the Province of Ontario and under Sections 328 and 329 of the Québec *Highway Safety Code* (R.S.Q., chapter C-24.2);
- Offences relating to the failure to obey a red light or a stop sign, under Sections 116 and 124 of the *Highway Traffic Act* and under Sections 359, 360 and 368 of the *Highway Safety Code*;
- Offences relating to the failure to stop at the approach of a school bus with its flashing lights in operation, under Section 151 of the *Highway Traffic Act* and under Section 460 of the *Highway Safety Code*;
- Offences relating to dangerous or careless driving under Section 111 of the *Highway Traffic Act* and under Section 327 of the *Highway Safety Code*;
- Offences relating to the failure to report an accident to a police or peace officer under Section 173 of the *Highway Traffic Act* and under Sections 169, 170 and 171 of the *Highway Safety Code*;
- Offences relating to the failure to remain at the scene of an accident under Section 174 of the *Highway Traffic Act* and under Section 168 of the *Highway Safety Code*;
- Offences relating to driving a road vehicle in a race or a bet or wager under Section 148 of the *Highway Traffic Act* and under Section 422 of the *Highway Safety Code*.

3.1.3 *Other offences*

- Offences under municipal by-laws or ordinances, an Act of Canada or a regulation thereunder which correspond to those offences listed in paragraph 3.1.2.

3.2 Information reported under article 3.1 shall be transmitted in a manner mutually agreeable to both parties.

3.3 For the purposes of driver licensing records, each jurisdiction shall recognize a declaration of guilt in the other jurisdiction concerning one of its residents as if the violation had been committed in the home jurisdiction. Demerit points shall be assessed or suspensions or revocations issued in accordance with the Appendix to this Agreement.

Article 4 — Issuance of Citation

4.1 Except as provided under article 4.2, a police officer issuing a citation to a resident of the other jurisdiction, shall not require the posting of collateral or take the resident into custody unless the officer has reasonable grounds to believe that the resident will not comply with the terms of the citation.

4.2 A police officer may, for an offence mentioned under paragraph 3.1.1, require the posting of collateral or take the resident of the other jurisdiction into custody.

Article 5 — Compliance with Traffic Citations

5.1 Whenever a resident of the other jurisdiction has failed following a declaration of guilt, to pay a fine imposed as a result thereof, within 30 days, for an offence mentioned under paragraph 3.1.2 or 3.1.3 of article 3, the jurisdiction in which the ticket was issued may, as soon thereafter as possible, notify the home jurisdiction of such failure.

5.2 Upon receipt of the notification prescribed in article 5.1, the home jurisdiction shall inform the driver that his driving privileges are suspended in the other jurisdiction pending compliance with the terms of the citation and other legal requirements that may apply.

5.3 No report shall be transmitted under article 5.1 if the date of transmission is more than six (6) months from the date of sentencing.

Article 6 — Administration of the Agreement

6.1 The Régie de l'assurance automobile du Québec and the Registrar of Motor Vehicles of the Ministry of Transportation of the Province of Ontario shall be the administrators of this Agreement and shall be empowered to develop the forms and procedures necessary to administer this Agreement.

6.2 The administrator in each party jurisdiction shall furnish to the other any information or documents necessary to facilitate administration of this Agreement. Such information shall include notification of any changes in provincial laws or regulations which materially affect the terms of this Agreement.

6.3 Notwithstanding article 6.2, the provisions of this Agreement shall remain in force, mutatis mutandis, when any amendment to the laws or regulations of either jurisdiction do not substantially affect these provisions.

6.4 The parties shall conform to any statutory provisions applicable to the access to documents held by governmental institutions and to the protection of personal information.

Article 7 — Validity of Other Laws

This Agreement does not invalidate any provision of a law or a regulation relating to driver licences in effect in either jurisdiction, nor does it affect other reciprocal agreements.

Article 8 — Effective Dates and Withdrawal

The provisions of this Agreement will be effective the first (1st) day of April 1989. Either jurisdiction may withdraw from this Agreement by written notice to the other jurisdiction, but no such withdrawal shall take effect until 90 days after receipt of such notice.

Article 9 — Severability

The provisions of this Agreement are severable.

Signed at Montréal, Québec this 8th day of November 1988.

In duplicate in the English and French languages each text being equally authentic.

PROVINCE OF ONTARIO   QUÉBEC

E. Fulton	M.Y. Côté
Minister of Transportation	Ministre des Transports

Appendix — Reciprocal Agreement Between the Province of Ontario and Québec Concerning Drivers' Licences and Traffic Offences

Article I — Penalties Applied by Québec

In accordance with article 3 of the Agreement, Québec will apply the following penalties to its residents convicted of offences in the Province of Ontario.

OFFENCES PURSUANT TO THE LEGISLATION OF THE PROVINCE OF ONTARIO	APPLICABLE PENALTY QUÉBEC

I — CRIMINAL OFFENCES

1.1	Section 237, 238 or 239 of the *Criminal code*	1.1	Licence revocation or suspension of the right to obtain a licence: at least one year
1.2	Section 203, 204 or 219 of the *Criminal code*	1.2	Licence revocation or suspension of the right to obtain a licence: at least one year
1.3	Section 233 of the *Criminal code*	1.3	Licence revocation or suspension of the right to obtain a licence: at least one year
1.4	Section 236(1)(a) of the *Criminal code*	1.4	Licence revocation or suspension of the right to obtain a licence: at least one year

II — TRAFFIC AND OTHER OFFENCES

OFFENCES PURSUANT TO THE LEGISLATION OF THE PROVINCE OF ONTARIO	APPLICABLE PENALTY QUÉBEC
2.1 Section 109 of *Highway Traffic Act* or like section of a municipal traffic by-law, an Act of Canada or regulation thereunder	2.1 Assessment of at least one (1) demerit point on the driver's record
2.2 Section 116 and 124 of *Highway Traffic Act* or like section of a municipal traffic by-law, an Act of Canada or regulation thereunder	2.2 Assessment of at least two (2) demerit points on the driver's record
2.3 Section 151 of *Highway Traffic Act* or like section of a municipal traffic by-law, an Act of Canada or regulation thereunder	2.3 Assessment of at least nine (9) demerit points on the driver's record
2.4 Section 111 of *Highway Traffic Act* or like section of a municipal traffic by-law, an Act of Canada or regulation thereunder	2.4 Assessment of at least four (4) demerit points on the driver's record
2.5 Section 173 of *Highway Traffic Act* or like section of a municipal traffic by-law, an Act of Canada or regulation thereunder	2.5 Assessment of at least nine (9) demerit points on the driver's record
2.6 Section 174 of *Highway Traffic Act* or like section of a municipal traffic by-law, an Act of Canada or regulation thereunder	2.6 Assessment of at least nine (9) demerit points on the driver's record
2.7 Section 148 of *Highway Traffic Act* or like section of a municipal traffic by-law, an Act of Canada or regulation thereunder	2.7 Assessment of at least six (6) demerit points on the driver's record

Article II — Penalties Applied by the Province of Ontario

In accordance with article 3 of the Agreement, the Province of Ontario will apply the following penalties to its residents convicted of offences in Québec.

OFFENCES PURSUANT TO QUÉBEC LEGISLATION	APPLICABLE PENALTY IN ONTARIO
I — CRIMINAL OFFENCES	
1.1 Section 237, 238 or 239 of the *Criminal code*	1.1 Licence revocation or suspension of the right to obtain a licence: at least one year
1.2 Section 203, 204 or 219 of the *Criminal code*	1.2 Licence revocation or suspension of the right to obtain a licence: at least one year

OFFENCES PURSUANT TO QUÉBEC LEGISLATION	APPLICABLE PENALTY IN ONTARIO
1.3 Section 233 of the *Criminal code*	1.3 Licence revocation or suspension of the right to obtain a licence: at least one year
1.4 Section 236(1)(a) of the *Criminal code*	1.4 Licence revocation or suspension of the right to obtain a licence: at least one year

II — TRAFFIC AND OTHER OFFENCES

2.1 Section 238 and 329 of the *Highway Safety Code* or like section of a municipal traffic by-law, an Act of Canada or regulation thereunder	2.1 Assessment of at least three (3) demerit point on the driver's record if the speed limit was exceeded by more than 15 km/h.
2.2 Section 359, 360 and 368 of the *Highway Safety Code* or like section of a municipal traffic by-law, an Act of Canada or regulation thereunder	2.2 Assessment of at least three (3) demerit points on the driver's record
2.3 Section 460 of the *Highway Safety Code* or like section of a municipal traffic by-law, an Act of Canada or regulation thereunder	2.3 Assessment of at least six (6) demerit points on the driver's record
2.4 Section 327 of the *Highway Safety Code* or like section of a municipal traffic by-law, an Act of Canada or regulation thereunder	2.4 Assessment of at least six (6) demerit points on the driver's record
2.5 Section 169, 170 or 171 of the *Highway Safety Code* or like section of a municipal traffic by-law, an Act of Canada or regulation thereunder	2.5 Assessment of at least three (3) demerit points on the driver's record
2.6 Section 168 of the *Highway Safety Code* or like section of a municipal traffic by-law, an Act of Canada or regulation thereunder	2.6 Assessment of at least seven (7) demerit points on the driver's record
2.7 Section 422 of the *Highway Safety Code* or like section of a municipal traffic by-law, an Act of Canada or regulation thereunder	2.7 Assessment of at least six (6) demerit points on the driver's record

CANADIAN DRIVER LICENCE COMPACT

Canadian Driver Licence Compact

[Amended June 2003.]

The Canadian Driver Licence Compact, an agreement among most provinces and the territories to exchange traffic offence information, was signed in 1990 by Ontario.

Under the compact's terms specified infractions committed under the highway traffic acts of each participating province will result in the application of demerit points to the driver's home province record.

As of June 1, 1991, Ontario began exchanging traffic offence conviction information with Manitoba, Alberta and Newfoundland.

As well as the safety-related features of the Compact, it provides for easy transfer of driver licence information for people relocating to other provinces.

Ontario has a separate agreement with Quebec, *supra*.

In June 2001, the Canadian Council of Motor Transport Administrators approved changes to the Canadian Driver Licence Compact designed to increase road safety and move further towards the one driver licence-one driver record concept. Under the changes, the jurisdiction where the offence has taken place is now obligated to notify the home jurisdiction, which will then take action as if the offence had remained unpaid in the home jurisdiction. In addition, the changes also allow the home jurisdiction a number of options to either withhold or suspend the person's driving privileges or deny vehicle registration. In the original agreement, Article 5 was written in permissive language which allowed jurisdictions the option of not taking action for unpaid fines.

The Compact was further amended in June 2003, with the addition of several definitions (including "Board", "Driver Control Record", "Member jurisdiction" and "Withdrawal") to Article 1, and revisions throughout to reflect the new terminology. In addition, the offence under s. 249.1 of the *Criminal Code* was added to the list of offences reportable under Article 4.

The following is the Canadian Driver Licence Compact between the provinces and territories, as amended:

Council of Ministers Responsible for Transportation and Highway Safety

ENTERED INTO this 27th day of September, A.D. 1990 by and between:

The Government of Ontario herein represented by the Minister of Transportation and;

The Government of Québec herein represented by le Ministre des Transports and;

The Government of Nova Scotia herein represented by the Minister of Transportation and Communications and;

The Government of New Brunswick herein represented by the Minister of Transportation and;

The Government of British Columbia herein represented by the Solicitor General and;

The Government of Manitoba herein represented by the Minister of Highways and Transportation and;

The Government of Prince Edward Island herein represented by the Minister of Transportation and Public Works and;

The Government of Saskatchewan herein represented by the Minister Responsible for Saskatchewan Government Insurance and;

The Government of Alberta herein represented by the Solicitor General and;

The Government of Newfoundland and Labrador herein represented by the Minister of Works, Services and Transportation and;

The Government of Yukon herein represented by the Minister of Community and Transportation Services and;

The Government of Northwest Territories herein represented by the Minister of Transportation.

WHEREAS the jurisdictions which are signatories wish to:

1. Promote compliance with traffic laws and improve highway safety within their respective borders;

2. Facilitate, for their respective residents who hold valid drivers' licences, the issuance of a licence by a party jurisdiction to which they are moving;

3. Pursue compatibility by the implementation of the one driver licence and one driver record concept;

4. Further highway safety by treating offences for which their residents have been convicted in the jurisdiction of any other party as if they had been committed in the home jurisdiction for the purposes of updating and maintaining driver's licence records and imposing sanctions;

5. Strengthen cooperation among the member jurisdictions so that persons are required to satisfy penalties imposed as a result of convictions for certain traffic offences committed outside their jurisdiction of record.

WHEREAS greater uniformity is required among all member jurisdictions concerning the exchange of information on licences, records, convictions, withdrawals and other data related to the driver licensing process;

WHEREAS member jurisdictions agree to act in the best interest of the safety of the citizens of their respective jurisdictions and to work, in the spirit of mutual cooperation, in the monitoring of compliance with the agreement and in the resolution of disputes at the lowest possible level of decision through negotiations and cooperative efforts;

THEREFORE, acting by and through their respective ministers, pursuant to and in conformity with their respective laws, as amended from time to time, they hereby undertake to pursue the courses of action provided for herein.

Article 1 — Definitions

For the purposes of this Compact:

"Administrator" means:

> the official of a member jurisdiction charged with administering the provisions of the Compact.

"Board" means:

> the Canadian Council of Motor Transport Administrators' Board of Directors who is the governing body responsible for the administration of the Compact.

"CCMTA" means:

> the Canadian Council of Motor Transport Administrators.

"Conviction" includes:

> an admission, finding or determination of guilt or the voluntary payment of a fine for an offence mentioned under Article 4 committed in a member jurisdiction a person of any other member jurisdiction, and "convicted" has a like meaning.

"Driver Control Record" means:

> the record maintained by the jurisdiction of record in accordance with the Compact.

"Jurisdiction" means:

> a Canadian province or territory.

"Jurisdiction of Record" means:

> the jurisdiction that has issued the last licence to a person or if a person has not been issued a licence, the jurisdiction of the person's address indicated on the charge, offence notice, ticket or report.

"Licence" means:

> a licence to drive a motor vehicle on a highway, issued under the laws of a member jurisdiction that is recognized by all member jurisdictions.

"Member jurisdiction" means:

> a jurisdiction signatory to this Compact.

"Withdrawal" means:

> the suspension, revocation, cancellation or denial of a licence or of the privilege to operate a motor vehicle or to obtain a licence.

Article 2 — Application for Driver's Licence

2.1 Upon receiving an application for a driver's licence, a member jurisdiction shall, determine whether the applicant has ever held, or is the holder of, a driver's licence issued by any other member jurisdiction.

2.2 A member jurisdiction should not issue a driver's licence to the applicant if:

- The applicant's right to obtain or to hold a licence is withdrawn in any member jurisdiction, as evidenced by the driver control record for convictions specified in Article 4, as well as for non-payment of fines; or

- The applicant is the holder of a valid driver's licence issued in another jurisdiction unless the applicant surrenders such licence.

Article 3 — Driver's Licence Exchange

3.1 A person who holds a valid driver's licence issued by a member jurisdiction, upon application in another member jurisdiction may exchange such licence without examination for an equivalent licence.

Notwithstanding the preceding provisions, the person may, for cause, be required to successfully complete a medical examination, a vision screening and/or a written and road test, when exchanging the licence.

3.2 The exchanged licence or a report of the surrender thereof shall be forwarded to the former jurisdiction of record which will confirm the validity of that licence and supply to the new jurisdiction the following information, to the extent available:

- personal identification data: address, birth date, client number, licence number, name, alias name, height, sex, weight;
- licence verification data: conditions, jurisdiction of record, licence effective date, licence expiry date, licence home class, licence standard class, licence status, re-licence, total demerits;
- conviction data: a record of each offence committed including date, location, section/act of the *Highway Traffic Act*, conviction equivalency code and textual description, etc.;
- accident data: a record for each accident including date, location, severity (fatal, property damage), damage amount;
- medical data: a record containing information s to dates when medical examinations are required and examination frequency requirements;
- appeals data: a record for each appeal against a conviction or suspension including the date of appeal and status or result;
- driver improvement data: a record for each occurrence when a driver was interviewed by the Registrar for purposes of improvement. Each record contains data as to the type of interview, action taken and reinstatement requirements;
- merit course data: a record for each course taken that may reduce the amount of demerit points against a driver.

3.3 A licence issued pursuant to paragraph 3.1 may be subsequently withdrawn or restricted, or additional actions may be required based upon information received pursuant to paragraph 3.2.

Article 4 — Reports and Effects of Conviction

4.1 Where a person licenced in one member jurisdiction is convicted of one of the following offences in another member jurisdiction, the latter shall report the conviction to the jurisdiction of record or if a person has not been issued a licence, the jurisdiction of the person's address indicated on the offence notice, charge, ticket or report.

4.1.1 *Criminal Code offences*

- Offences relating to the operation of a motor vehicle while under the influence of alcohol or drugs, under sections 253, 254 and 255 of the *Criminal Code of Canada* (R.S.C. (1985), C-46) hereinafter referred to as the "Criminal Code";
- Offences relating to criminal negligence or manslaughter resulting from the operation of a motor vehicle under sections 220, 221, and 236 of the *Criminal Code*;
- Offences relating to dangerous driving, under section 249 of the *Criminal Code*;
- Offences relating to the failure to stop at the scene of an accident or leaving without reporting, under section 252 of the *Criminal Code*;
- Offences relating to driving while prohibited, under section 259 of the *Criminal Code*.
- Offences relating to failure to stop at the direction of police under section 249.1 of the *Criminal Code*.

4.1.2 *Traffic offences*

- Offences relating to driving over a prescribed or posted speed limit;
- Offences relating to the failure to obey a red light or a stop sign;
- Offences relating to the failure to stop at the approach of a school bus with its flashing lights in operation;
- Offences relating to dangerous or careless driving;
- Offences relating to the failure to report an accident to a police or peace officer;
- Offences relating to the failure to remain at the scene of an accident;
- Offences relating to driving a motor vehicle in a race or on a bet or wager;
- Offences relating to passing where prohibited.

4.1.3 *Municipal offences*

- Offences under municipal by-laws or regulations, similar to those offences listed in sub-paragraph 4.1.2.

4.2 Criminal Code offences relating to the operation of motor vehicles and traffic offences not referred to in paragraph 4.1 should also wherever possible be reported by the convicting jurisdiction to the jurisdiction of record.

4.3 Information reported under paragraphs 4.1 and 4.2 shall be transmitted in a manner mutually agreeable to the member jurisdictions.

4.4 For the purposes of the driver control record, each member jurisdiction shall recognize a conviction referred to in paragraph 4.1 of a person in any other member jurisdiction as if the offence had been committed in the jurisdiction of record and take appropriate sanctions.

Article 5 — Non Payment of Fines

5.1 Where a person licensed by or resident in a jurisdiction is convicted in another jurisdiction of an offence as reported in accordance with Article 4, and the person fails to pay any fine imposed as a result of such conviction, the jurisdiction in which the offence was committed shall notify the home jurisdiction of such unpaid fine.

5.2 Upon receipt of the notification referred to in paragraph 5.1, the jurisdiction of record shall take such action to withdraw the person's driving privileges or such other action as would be taken if the offence for which the person was convicted had occurred in the jurisdiction of record and the fine had remained unpaid.

5.3 Action taken by the jurisdiction of record in accordance with the provisions in paragraph 5.2 may include denial of vehicle registration.

Article 6 — Administration of the Agreement

6.1 Where a jurisdiction is prepared to implement the course of action provided for herein, it shall give written notice to the Board.

Such notice shall include the designation of the jurisdiction's proposed:

- Administrator;
- effective date of implementation;
- list of exceptions, if any; and
- additions to be made to the Conviction Equivalency Table

6.2 Upon acceptance of such notice, the Board shall set an effective date for the implementation of the Compact for that jurisdiction.

6.3 The Board shall administer this Compact in compliance with Appendix 1, and may prescribe and amend the necessary forms and procedures.

6.4 CCMTA shall be the official repository of this Compact. The Board shall be responsible for the required duties attendant to the administration of this Compact.

6.5 Each member jurisdiction shall provide to CCMTA any information or document necessary to facilitate the administration of this Compact. Such information shall include notification of any changes in the laws or regulations which materially affect the terms of this Compact.

6.6 The provisions of this Compact shall remain in force, with necessary modifications, when any amendments to the laws or regulations of any member jurisdiction do not substantially affect the terms of this Compact.

Article 7 — Amendments and Exceptions

7.1 This Compact may be amended, with the approval of at least two-thirds of the member jurisdictions which have implemented the provisions of this Compact pursuant to article 6. All proposed amendments shall be placed in writing and shall be presented to each jurisdiction for approval or rejection.

7.2 Provisions of this Compact amended by less than a unanimous vote may be retained, subject to approval by the Board, as exceptions at the request of the dissenting member jurisdictions.

1412

7.3 Member jurisdictions not rejecting proposed amendments in writing within a period of ninety (90) days of presentation shall be deemed in favour thereof and an affirmative vote shall be recorded on their behalf.

7.4 Amendments to this Compact shall become effective within ninety (90) days of approval or as otherwise required by the laws of the member jurisdictions.

7.5 Exceptions to the provisions of this Compact, which may be required as a condition of implementation by a member jurisdiction, and which have been approved by all the Board, will form part of this Compact by appendix listing.

Article 8 — General Provisions

8.1 This Compact shall supersede any Agreement between member jurisdictions covering in whole or in part matters covered by this Compact.

8.2 This Compact is subject to all provisions of law in effect within the member jurisdictions.

8.3 Member jurisdictions shall conform to any statutory provisions applicable to the access to records held by government institutions and to the protection of personal information, and personal information with respect to drivers received by one member jurisdiction from another member jurisdiction shall be used only for purposes which are consistent with the uses for which it was held by the member jurisdiction which supplies the information.

8.4 Any member jurisdiction may withdraw from this Compact by written notice to the CCMTA and to each member jurisdiction, but no such withdrawal shall take effect until ninety (90) days after receipt of such notice.

THEREFORE, we the undersigned do mutually agree to adopt the Canadian Driver Licence Compact

SIGNED THIS 27th DAY OF September, 1990
[by the various representatives from the provinces and territories]

Appendix 1 — Administration, Rules and Procedures of the Agreement

Article 1 — Committee

1.1 The Administrators shall form a Committee, the purposes of which are:

- to administer the provisions of the Compact;
- to serve as the governing body for the administration and resolution of all matters relating to the operation of this Compact;
- to recommend revisions to the Compact that will enhance its objectives, goals and benefits;
- to provide and promote a reasonable and uniform reporting system among the party jurisdictions;
- to promote closer contacts between party jurisdictions for exchange of information and solution of mutual problems;
- to assist non-participating jurisdictions with matters relating to the Compact, including implementation of the provisions therein.

1.2 Each Administrator shall have one vote in the Committee.

1.3 The Committee shall meet with a quorum of more than two-thirds of its members present to consider and recommend proposed amendments and to consider other changes and interpretations which may be offered pursuant to this Compact.

1.4 Recommendations and decisions regarding interpretations of any questions at issue shall be reached by a majority vote of at least two-thirds of the Committee and shall be placed in writing and retained by CCMTA as part of the permanent record.

Article 2 — Secretariat

2.1 The Committee shall have its secretariat and administrative functions performed by CCMTA, which, as authorized by the Committee, shall:

- conduct routine business;
- collect and analyze data;
- prepare and distribute materials and information;
- publish and maintain an Administrative Guide, which shall contain the jurisdictions' procedures, equivalency tables, technical definitions and such other information as may be required to efficiently administer this Compact;
- perform other duties as may be assigned by the Administrators.

Appendix 2 — Exceptions by Province

[Sections of the Canadian Driver Licence Compact that the individual provinces and territories choose not to follow through with, shall be listed here]

INDEX

All references are to the Ontario Highway Traffic Act unless otherwise noted. [Compulsory Automobile Insurance Act (CAIA), Canada Driver Licence Compact (CDLC), Civil Remedies Act, 2001 (CRA), Ontario-Québec Agreement (OQA), Photo Card Act, 2008 (PCA), Provincial Offences Act (POA), Smoke-free Ontario Act (SFOA).]

A

Abandoned Vehicles, 221

Accessible Parking Permits, *see* Parking Permits, Persons with Disabilities

Accessories, 101

Accessible Vehicles
- defined, Reg. 611, s. 1, Reg. 629, s. 1
- evidence of inspection, Reg. 611, s. 10
- regulation re, Reg. 629
- • definitions, Reg. 629, s. 1
- • equipment, specific, Reg. 629, ss. 3, 5-7, 9, 10
- • lifts and ramps, Reg. 629, ss. 5, 9, 10
- • occupant restraint assemblies, Reg. 629, ss. 7, 11
- • securement devices, Reg. 629, s. 6, 11
- • signage, Reg. 629, s. 4
- • standards generally, Reg. 629, ss. 2, 8, 10-12
- • urban transit buses, Reg. 629, s. 11
- school buses, *see* SCHOOL BUS

Accident
- duties of Registrar, 205
- duty of person in charge of vehicle, 200
- duty to remain at scene of, 200
- duty to report, 199

- • fatal, 202

Administrative Cancellation, *see also* Administrative Penalty
- of licence or permit
- • liability, protection from, 5.4
- • where false information provided, 5.2
- • where incorrect information provided, 5.3
- • where monetary penalty unpaid, Reg. 273/07, ss. 3, 5

Administrative Driver's Licence Suspension, *see also* Administrative Penalty
- appeal, availability of
- • novice driver, 48.1(8.1)
- • over .05, 48(9)
- • over .08, 50.1
- • racing, stunts, etc. 172(13)
- • young driver, 48.2.1(16)
- approved instrument test, 48(3)
- concurrent
- • novice driver, 48.1(5.3)
- • over .05, 48(5)
- • young driver, 48.2.1(13)
- criteria
- • novice driver, 48.1(3),(4)
- • over .05, 48(2), (3)
- • over .08, 48.3(1), (3)

Number Plates *(cont'd)*
- historic vehicles, for, 7(1)(b)(ii), (1)(c)(ii), (7.2)
- improper, 14
- issuance of, 7(7)
- kept clean, 13(2)
- • penalty, 13(3)
- no other numbers to be exposed, 13
- numbers to be plainly visible, 13
- obstruction prohibited, 13
- regulations, Reg. 628, ss. 9, 10
- removal, 85(3)
- seizure, 20(2), 82(13), 82.1(6)
- • court application for possession, 20(5)
- • • security posted, 20(6)
- • • • return of, 20(7)
- • • lien for costs, 20(4)
- suspension
- • grounds for, 47(1)
- • • restriction, 47(2)
- temporary use of, 11(3), (4)
- to be clearly identifiable, 13(1)
- use of, 7(8)
- violations as to, 12

O

Obstructed View
- driving with, 73

Odometers, 66

Off Road Vehicles
- defined, 191.8(5)
- definitions, 191.8(5), Reg. 316/03, s. 1
- municipal by-laws concerning, 191.8(3)-(4)
- operation permitted in accordance with by-laws/regulations, 191.8(1)
- regulations concerning, 191.8(2), Reg. 316/03

Offences, *see also* Penalties
- accessible parking permits, 27
- approach motor vehicle on roadway, 177(2)-(4)
- approach stopped emergency vehicle, 159(6)-(8)
- attempt to stop motor vehicle on roadway, 177(2)-(4)
- commercial motor vehicle, 190(8)-(9)
- contest, 172, Reg. 455/07
- direction to novice driver, re, 48.2(9)
- disabled parking permit, 27
- drive without insurance, CAIA 2(1)
- driver's licences, re, 32; CAIA 2(6)
- false statements, 9; CAIA 13(11), 13.2
- inspection and maintenance, 107(15)–(16)
- insurance
- • liability for, 23(4)-(5)
- International Registration Plan
- • failure to comply with direction or requirement of inspector, 7.2(12)(a), (13)
- • failure to keep records re cab cards, 7.2(2)
- • false statements on documents, 7.10
- • misleading inspector, 7.2(12), (13)
- irreparable vehicles, 199.1(6), (7), (9), (17), (21), (25)
- nitrous oxide fuel systems, 172.1
- photo cards, re
- • contravention of regulation, PCA 15
- • failure to return, 35(1)(e.1), 214; PCA 11(2), 15
- • possession and use, of, 35(1)(e.1), 214; PCA 13
- pre-empting traffic control signal devices, 79.1(5)
- procedure for prosecution of provincial, 208
- racing on highway, 172, Reg. 455/07

Index

R

Racing

- defined, 172(20)(c), Reg. 455/07, ss. 2, 4
- demerit points, Reg. 339, Table
- detention of vehicle, 172(5)
- forfeiture of vehicle, *see* Forfeiture
- generally, 172, Reg. 455/07
- horse, 173
- impoundment of vehicle, 172(7)-(9), (11)-(16), (18)
- in community safety zone, 214.1(7)
- penalties, 172(2),(5)-(7), 214.1(7)
- regulations, 172(20), Reg. 455/07
- subsequent convictions, 172(3),(4)
- surrender of licence, 172(5)
- suspension of licence, 172(6),(10), (13), (18)

Radar Warning Device

- definition, 79(1)
- forfeiture of device, 79(4)
- generally, 79
- penalty, 79(5)
- police search powers, 79(3)
- prohibition, 79(2)
- • exception, 79(6)

Railway Crossing

- driving around/under crossing gate
- • demerit points, Reg. 339, Table
- • generally, 164
- duty of public vehicles, 174
- vehicles required to stop, 163

Rate of Speed, *see also* Speed Limits

- demerit points, Reg. 339, Table
- generally, 128, 128.1
- miles/kilometres conversion, 129
- penalty, 128

- regulations, 128(1.1), (7), Reg. 619-621, 8/03
- slow driving, 132
- speed limit signs, Reg. 615, ss. 1-7
- suspension, 128

Rear View Mirror, 66

Rebuilt Vehicles

- application of legislation, 199.1(2), (3), (20), Reg. 376/02, s. 8
- classification
- • powers of registrar, 199.1(22), (23)
- definitions, 199.1(1), Reg. 376/02, ss. 1, 7
- permit
- • replacement, 199.1(18), (24)
- • requirements, prescribed, Reg. 628, ss. 2(1), 2.1
- • return
- • • duty, 199.1(16), (24), Reg. 376/02, s. 6
- structural inspection certificate
- • condition for issuance of permit, as, Reg. 628, ss. 2(1), 2.1
- • documentation requirements, Reg. 601, s. 10.1(1)-(3.1), (6), Sched.

Reciprocal Agreements

- agreements with other jurisdictions, 40
- Canadian Driver Licence Compact, text, p. 1245
- Ontario-Québec Agreement, p. 1235
- records to be kept, 7.2
- seizure of out-of-province permits, 47

Reciprocal Suspension of Driver's Licence, O. Reg. 37/93

Records

- accident, 205
- copies, 225(3)-(4)
- electronic format, 205, 210
- inspection, 7.3, 225(1)-(2)

1453

Vehicle Inspection Sticker *(cont'd)*
- replacement sticker, Reg. 611, s. 13
- seizure, 82(13), 82.1(6)
- to be supplied by Ministry, 86
- when not to be issued, Reg. 611, ss. 2.2-5.2

Vehicle Ownership
- out of province evidence Re, 210.1

View
- signs, objects obstructing, 73
- windows to afford clear, 74

Visual Acuity
- measurement, Reg. 340/94, s. 15(1)(e)
- requirements
- - corrective lenses and, Reg. 340/94, ss. 1(1), 17(1)(j), 18(1)(a), 18(2)(a), 21.1(b)(i)
- - generally, Reg. 340/94, ss. 15(1)(e), 15(1.1), 17(1)(j), 18(1)(a), 18(2)(a)
- - *Human Rights Code* and, Reg. 340/94, s. 19(1)
- - waiver, Reg. 340/94, ss. 21.1, 21.2

Visual Field, Horizontal
- measurement, Reg. 340/94, s. 15(1)(e), 15(5)(e)
- requirements
- - corrective lenses and, Reg. 340/94, ss. 1(1), 15(5)
- - generally, Reg. 340/94, ss. 15(1)(e), 15(1.1), 17(1)(k), 18(1)(b), 18(2)(b)
- - *Human Rights Code* and, Reg. 340/94, s. 19(1)
- - waiver, Reg. 340/94, ss. 21.1, 21.2

W

Warrant, Arrest Without, 217

Weight
- aggregate vehicles, 116-118

- allowable gross vehicle weights, 118, Regs. 103/97, 594, s. 2, 413/05, ss. 20–22, 36.1
- application of regulations, Reg. 413/05, s. 1
- application of vehicle weight tables, Reg. 413/05, s. 38
- axle group weights, 117
- axle weight limits, 116, Reg. 413/05, s. 34.1
- bridges, permitted on, 123, Reg. 103/97, 598
- - standards to determine allowable gross, Reg. 103/97
- class B highways, 120
- definitions, 114, Reg. 413/05, ss. 2, 37
- designated combinations, Reg. 413/05, ss. 3-4 Scheds
- gross vehicle weights, 118, Regs. 103/97, 598, 413/05
- operating within weight permitted by permit, 121
- penalties
- - additional fines applicable, 125(2)-(4)
- - general, 125(1)
- - overloading by consignor, 126
- - special permits, breach of conditions, 110.2(3), 125(2)-(4)
- permits, Reg. 413/05, s. 34
- power to have load weighed/removed, 124
- pre-conditions to designation, Reg. 413/05, s. 5-14
- raw forest products allowance, 119
- reduced load periods, 122
- regulations, generally, 127
- restriction as to weight on tires, 115
- vehicle and axle weights, 116, 117, 118, Reg. 413/05

Wheels-Flanges, Clamps, 69